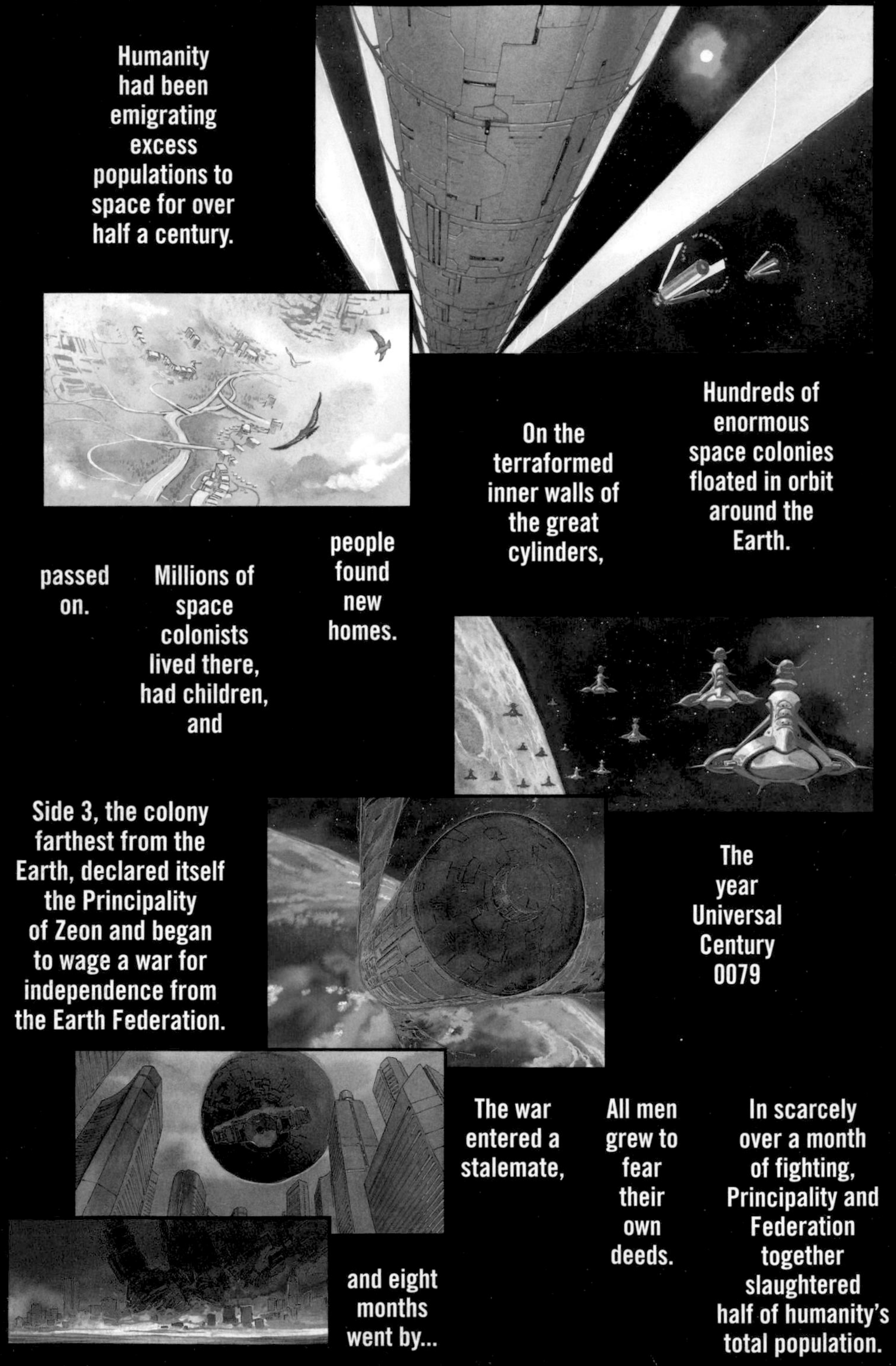

Humanity had been emigrating excess populations to space for over half a century.
Hundreds of enormous space colonies floated in orbit around the Earth.
On the terraformed inner walls of the great cylinders,
people found new homes.
Millions of space colonists lived there, had children, and
passed on.
The year Universal Century 0079
Side 3, the colony farthest from the Earth, declared itself the Principality of Zeon and began to wage a war for independence from the Earth Federation.
In scarcely over a month of fighting, Principality and Federation together slaughtered half of humanity's total population.
All men grew to fear their own deeds.
The war entered a stalemate,
and eight months went by...

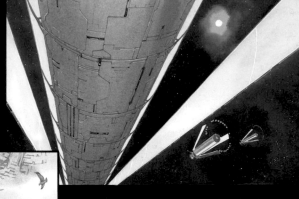

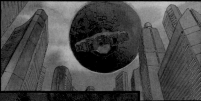

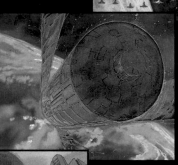

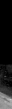

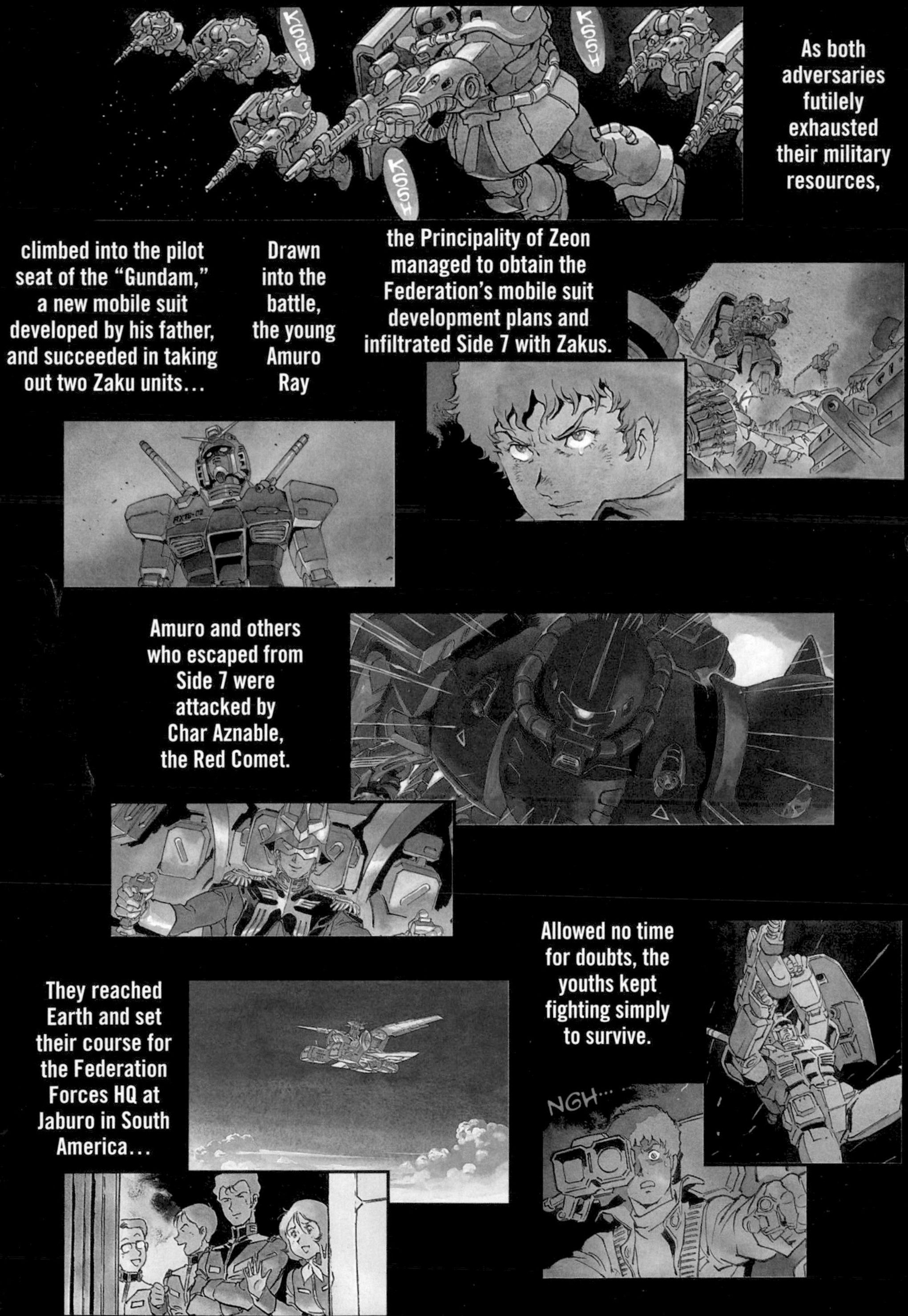
As both adversaries futilely exhausted their military resources,
KSSH
KSSH
KSSH
the Principality of Zeon managed to obtain the Federation's mobile suit development plans and infiltrated Side 7 with Zakus.
Drawn into the battle, the young Amuro Ray
climbed into the pilot seat of the "Gundam," a new mobile suit developed by his father, and succeeded in taking out two Zaku units...
Amuro and others who escaped from Side 7 were attacked by Char Aznable, the Red Comet.
Allowed no time for doubts, the youths kept fighting simply to survive.
NGH...
They reached Earth and set their course for the Federation Forces HQ at Jaburo in South America...

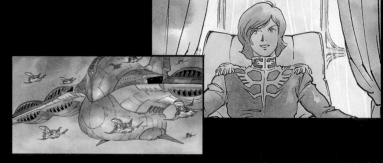

But Garma Zabi, the youngest son of House Zabi, lay in wait for them with the Zeon North American Forces at his command.

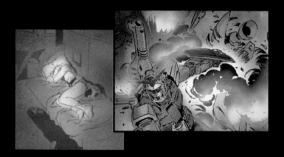

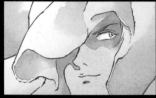

Serving under Garma, Char began to put his own ambitions in motion.

Meanwhile, Amuro was coming to accept his role as a soldier even as he struggled to overcome the terror of battle.

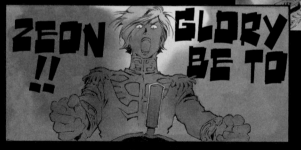

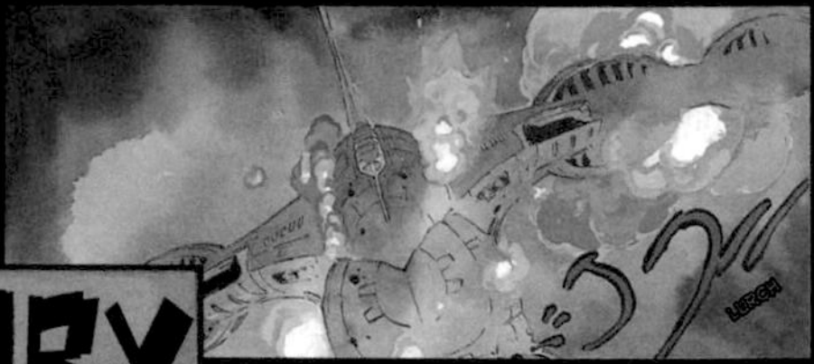

In his zeal to destroy *White Base*, Garma fell into Char's trap and met a fiery end.

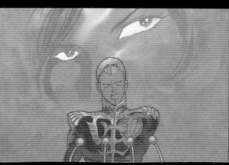

His death, however, only served to rally Zeon, and the war began to escalate.

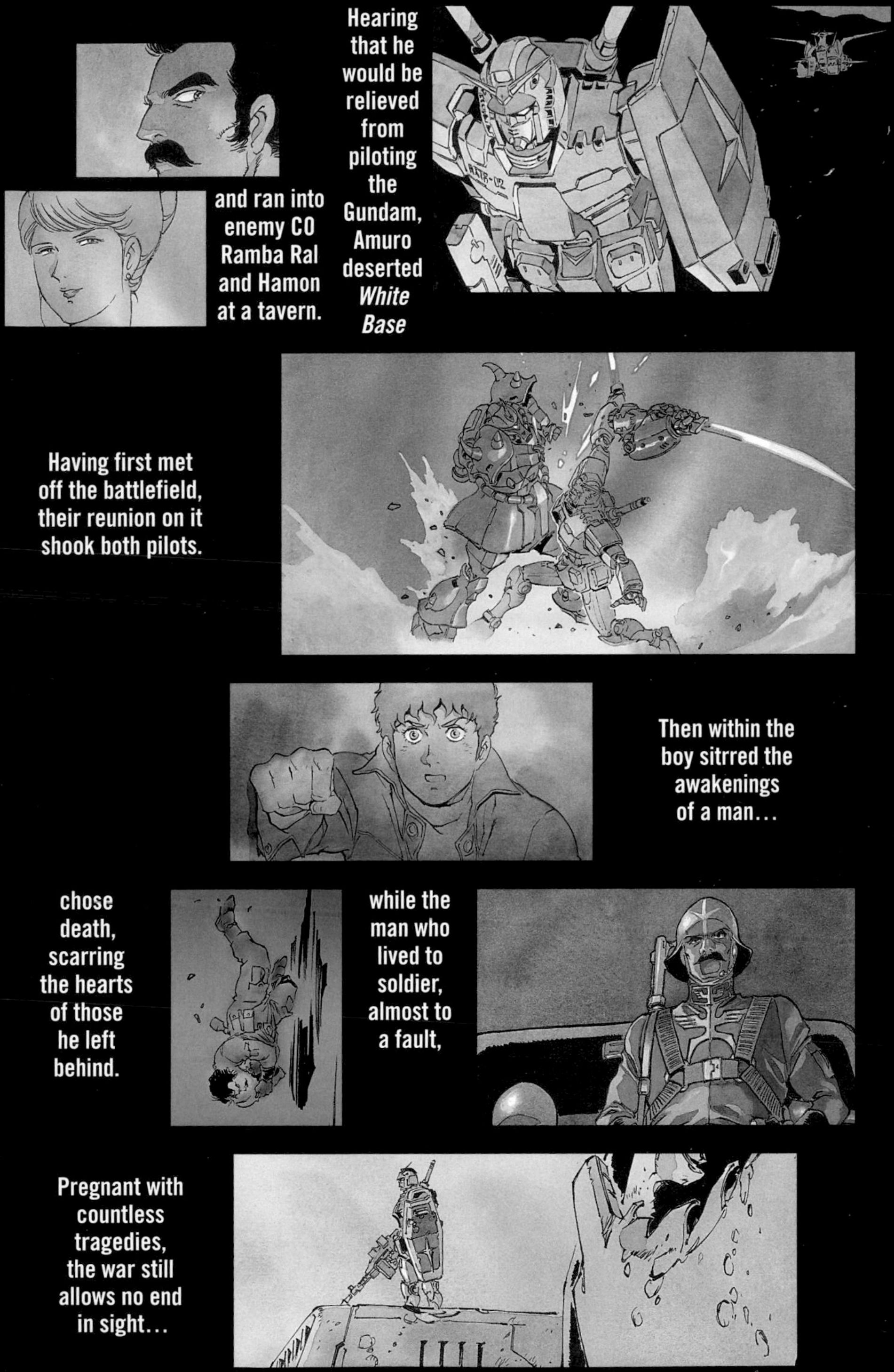
Hearing that he would be relieved from piloting the Gundam, Amuro deserted *White Base*
and ran into enemy CO Ramba Ral and Hamon at a tavern.
Having first met off the battlefield, their reunion on it shook both pilots.
Then within the boy sitrred the awakenings of a man…
while the man who lived to soldier, almost to a fault,
chose death, scarring the hearts of those he left behind.
Pregnant with countless tragedies, the war still allows no end in sight…

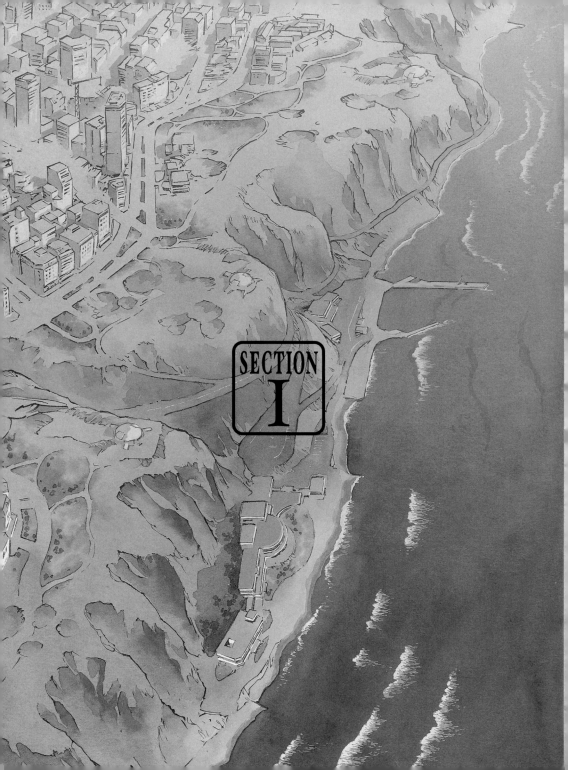

SECTION
I

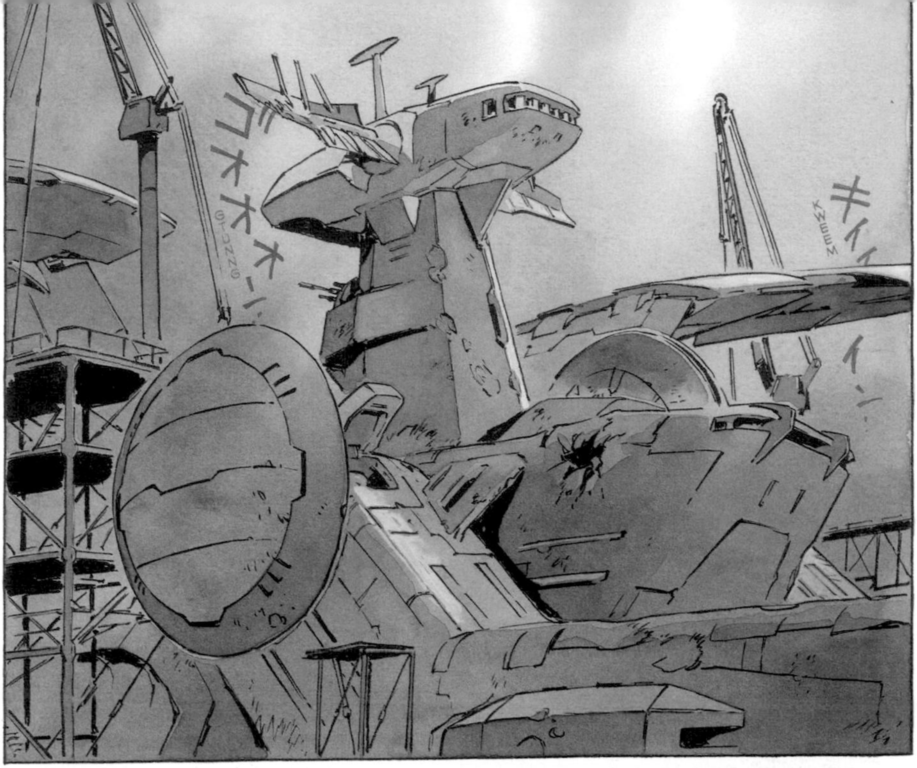
キイイイーン
KWEEM
ゴオオオーン
GTUNNG
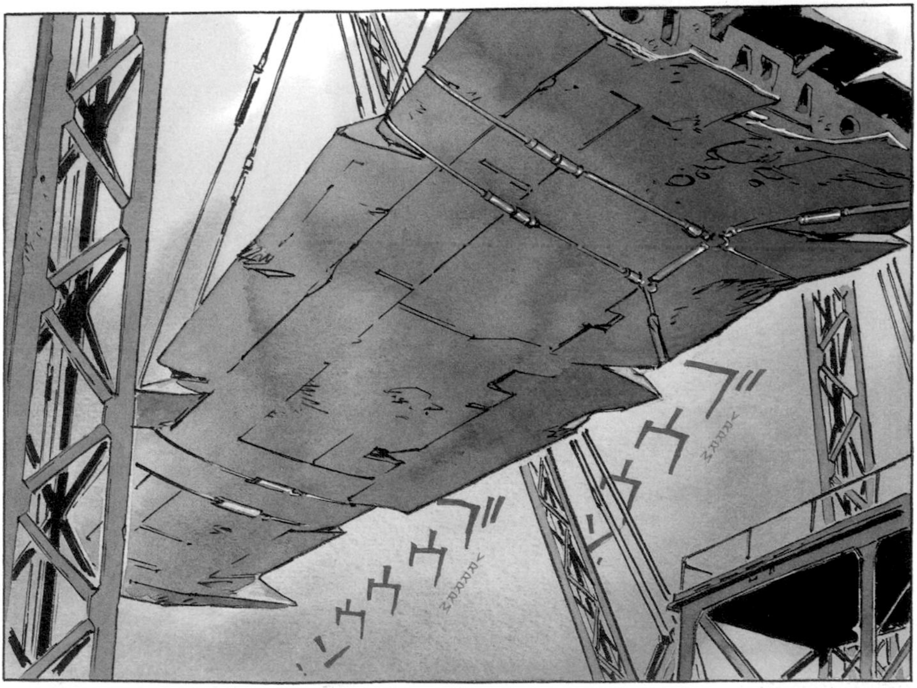
ブウウン
ブウウウン

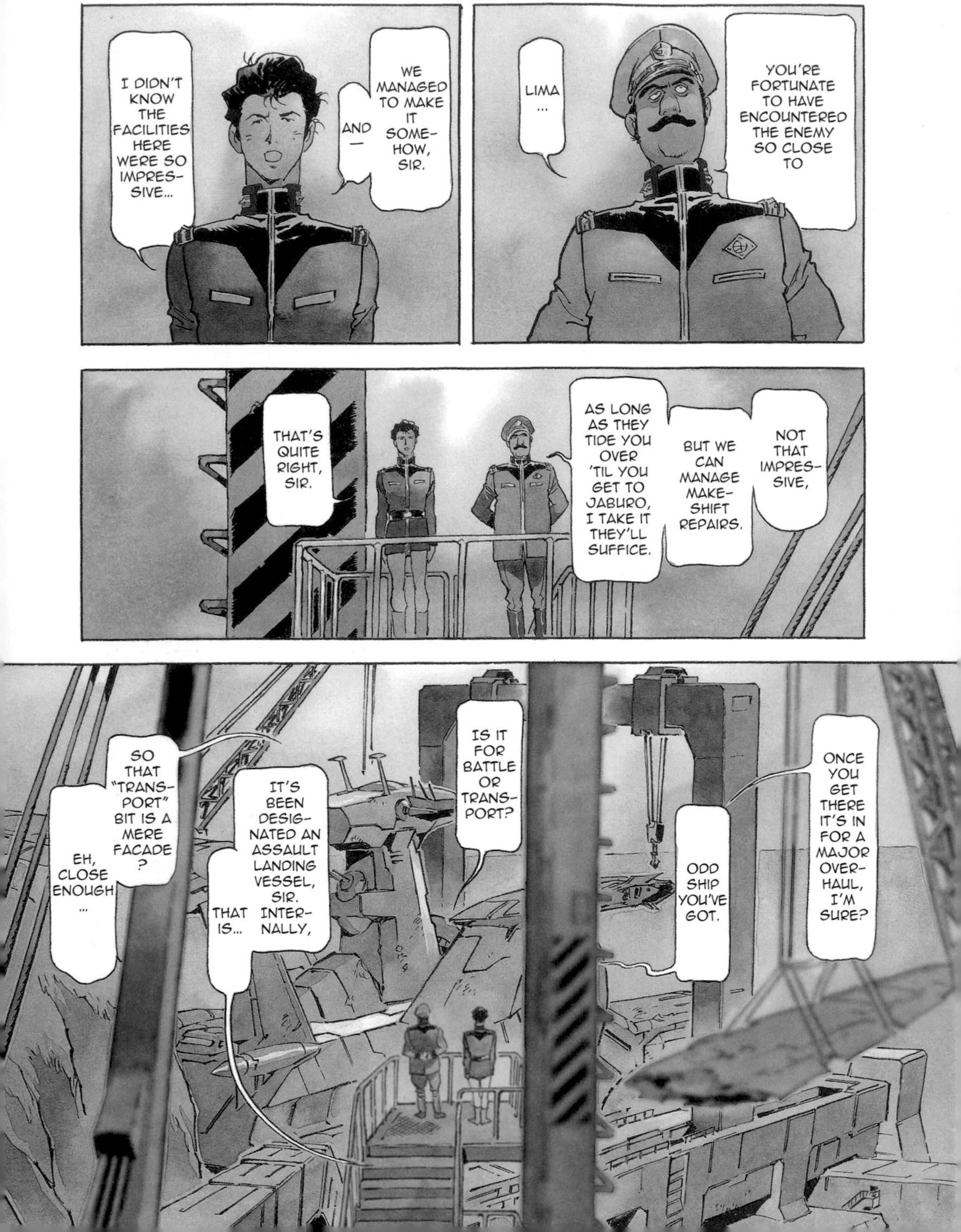
YOU'RE FORTUNATE TO HAVE ENCOUNTERED THE ENEMY SO CLOSE TO
LIMA ...
WE MANAGED TO MAKE IT SOMEHOW, SIR.
AND —
I DIDN'T KNOW THE FACILITIES HERE WERE SO IMPRESSIVE...
NOT THAT IMPRESSIVE,
BUT WE CAN MANAGE MAKESHIFT REPAIRS.
AS LONG AS THEY TIDE YOU OVER 'TIL YOU GET TO JABURO, I TAKE IT THEY'LL SUFFICE.
THAT'S QUITE RIGHT, SIR.
ONCE YOU GET THERE IT'S IN FOR A MAJOR OVERHAUL, I'M SURE?
ODD SHIP YOU'VE GOT.
IS IT FOR BATTLE OR TRANSPORT?
IT'S BEEN DESIGNATED AN ASSAULT LANDING VESSEL, SIR.
INTERNALLY,
THAT IS...
SO THAT "TRANSPORT" BIT IS A MERE FACADE?
EH, CLOSE ENOUGH...

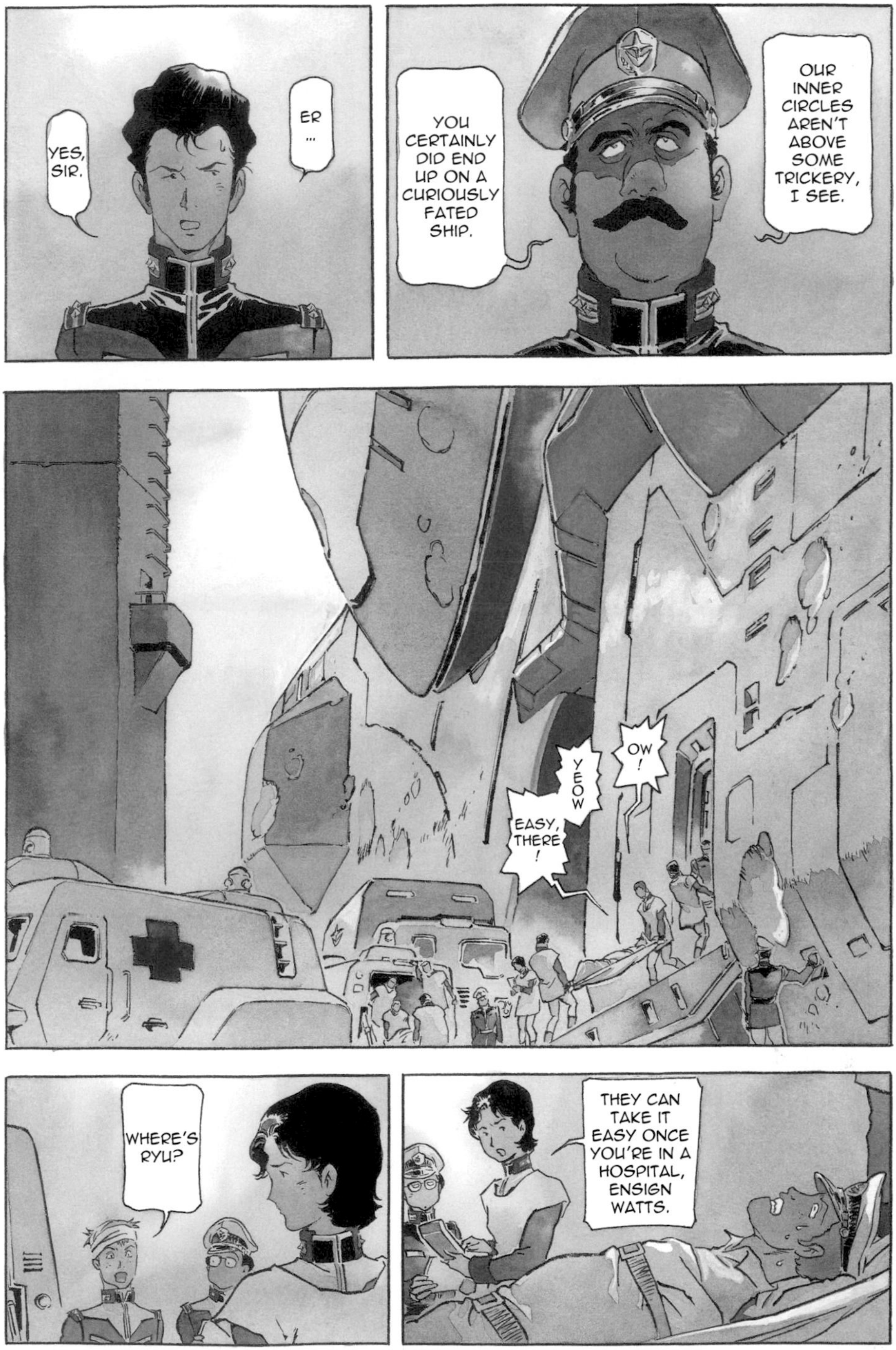
OUR INNER CIRCLES AREN'T ABOVE SOME TRICKERY, I SEE.
YOU CERTAINLY DID END UP ON A CURIOUSLY FATED SHIP.
ER ...
YES, SIR.
OW!
YEOW
EASY, THERE!
THEY CAN TAKE IT EASY ONCE YOU'RE IN A HOSPITAL, ENSIGN WATTS.
WHERE'S RYU?

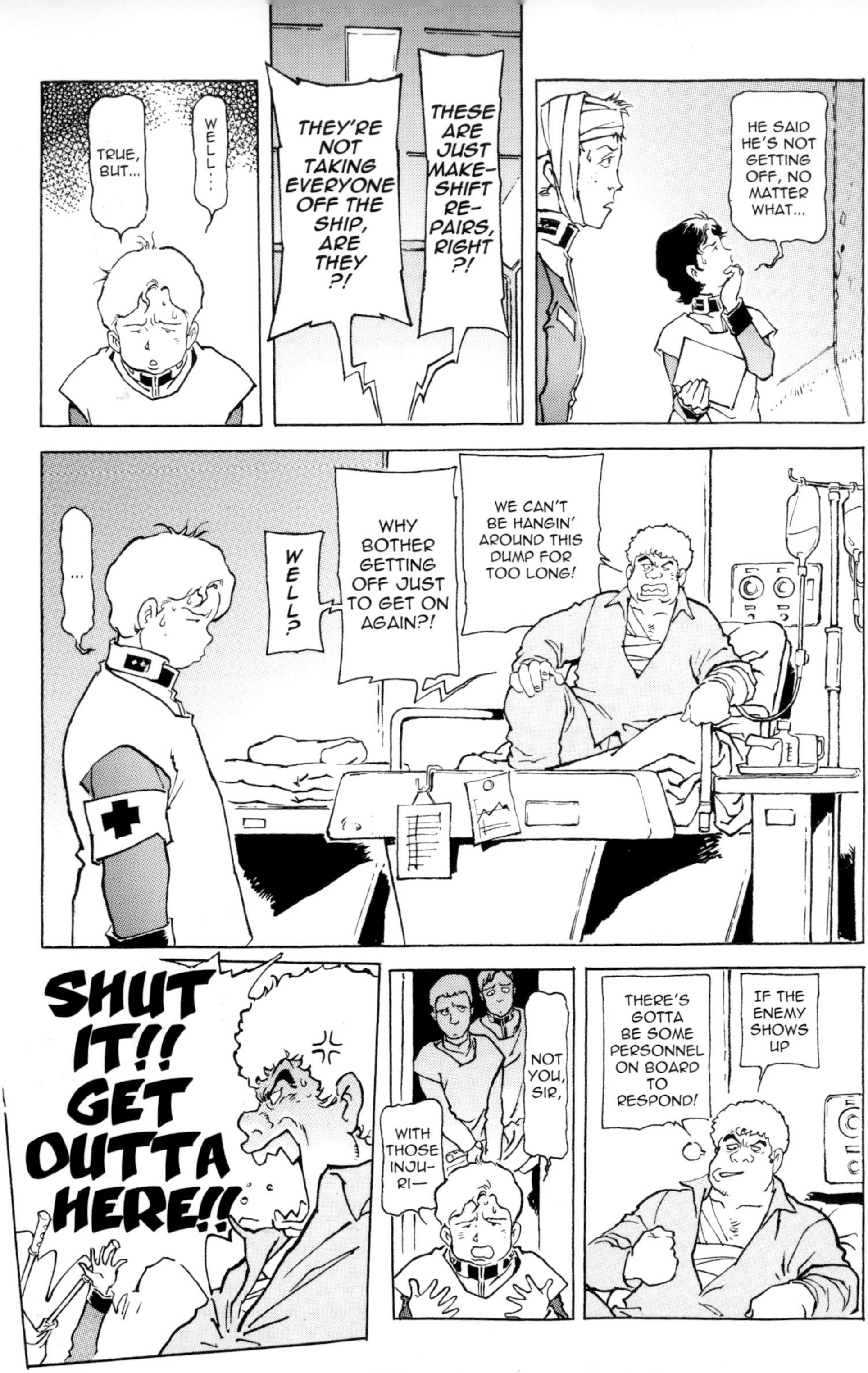
HE SAID HE'S NOT GETTING OFF, NO MATTER WHAT...
THESE ARE JUST MAKESHIFT REPAIRS, RIGHT?!
THEY'RE NOT TAKING EVERYONE OFF THE SHIP, ARE THEY?!
WELL...
TRUE, BUT...
WE CAN'T BE HANGIN' AROUND THIS DUMP FOR TOO LONG!
WHY BOTHER GETTING OFF JUST TO GET ON AGAIN?!
WELL?
...
IF THE ENEMY SHOWS UP
THERE'S GOTTA BE SOME PERSONNEL ON BOARD TO RESPOND!
NOT YOU, SIR,
WITH THOSE INJURI—
SHUT IT!! GET OUTTA HERE!!

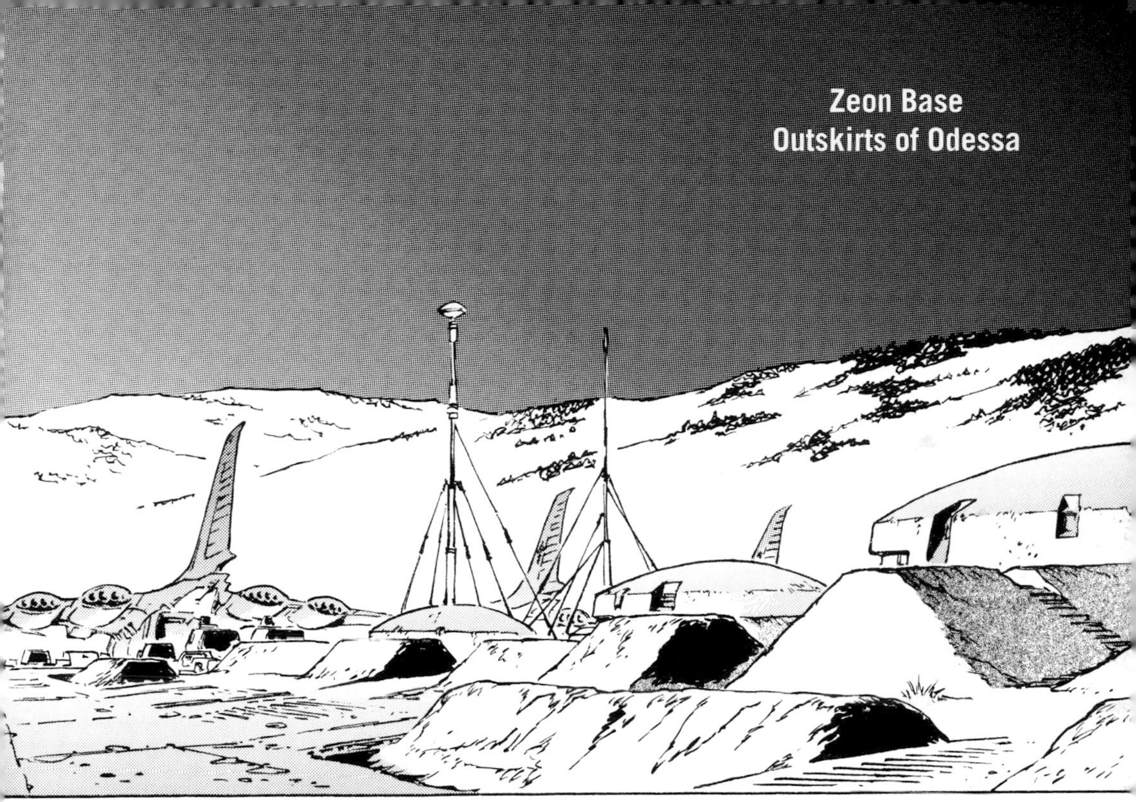
Zeon Base
Outskirts of Odessa

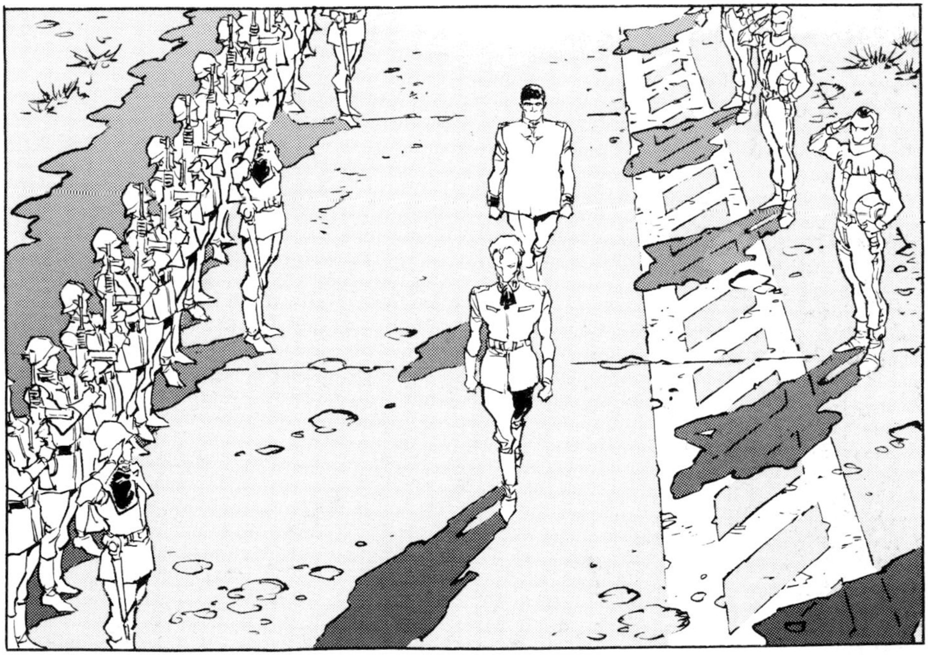

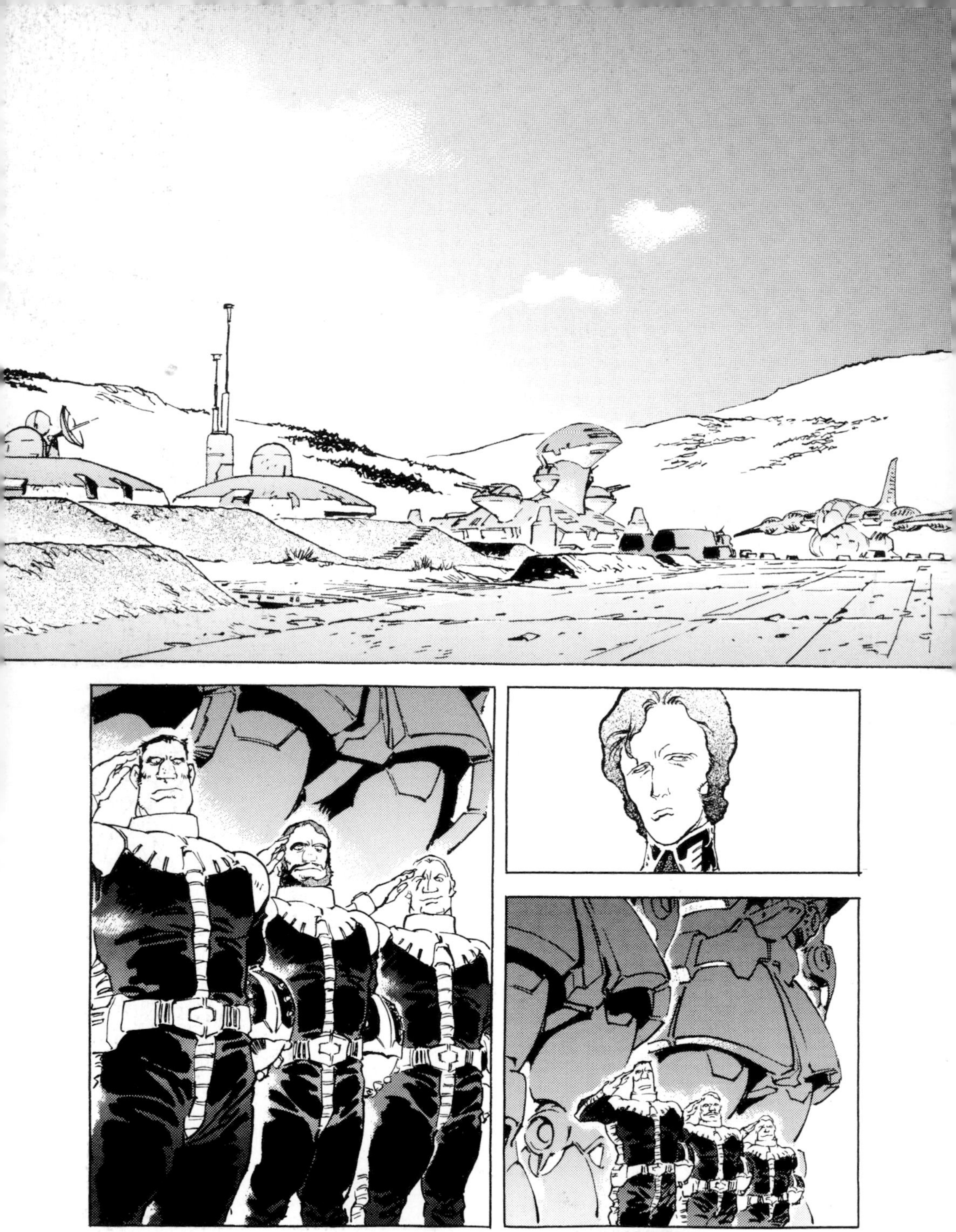

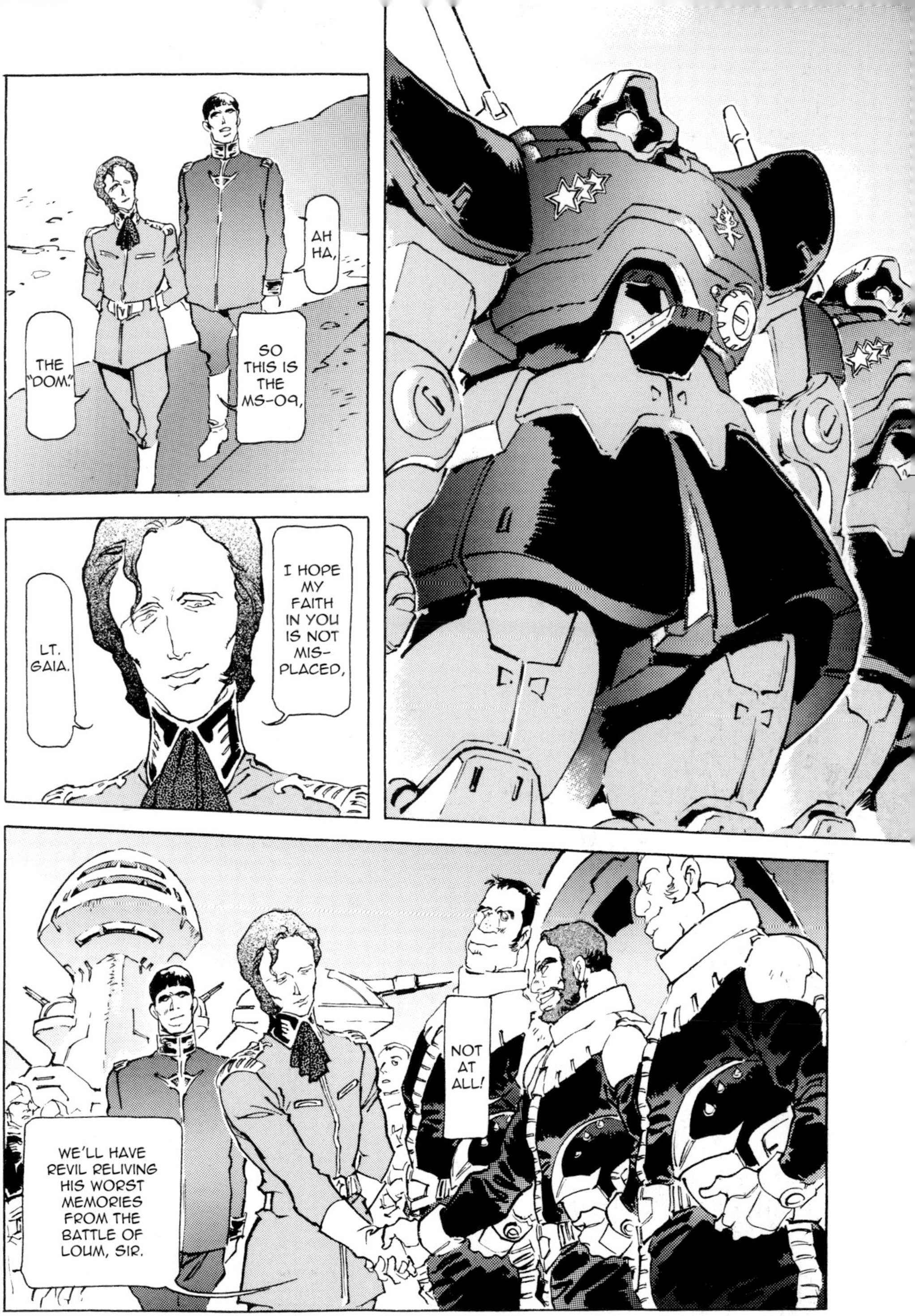
AH HA,
SO THIS IS THE MS-09,
THE "DOM."
I HOPE MY FAITH IN YOU IS NOT MIS-PLACED,
LT. GAIA.
NOT AT ALL!
WE'LL HAVE REVIL RELIVING HIS WORST MEMORIES FROM THE BATTLE OF LOUM, SIR.

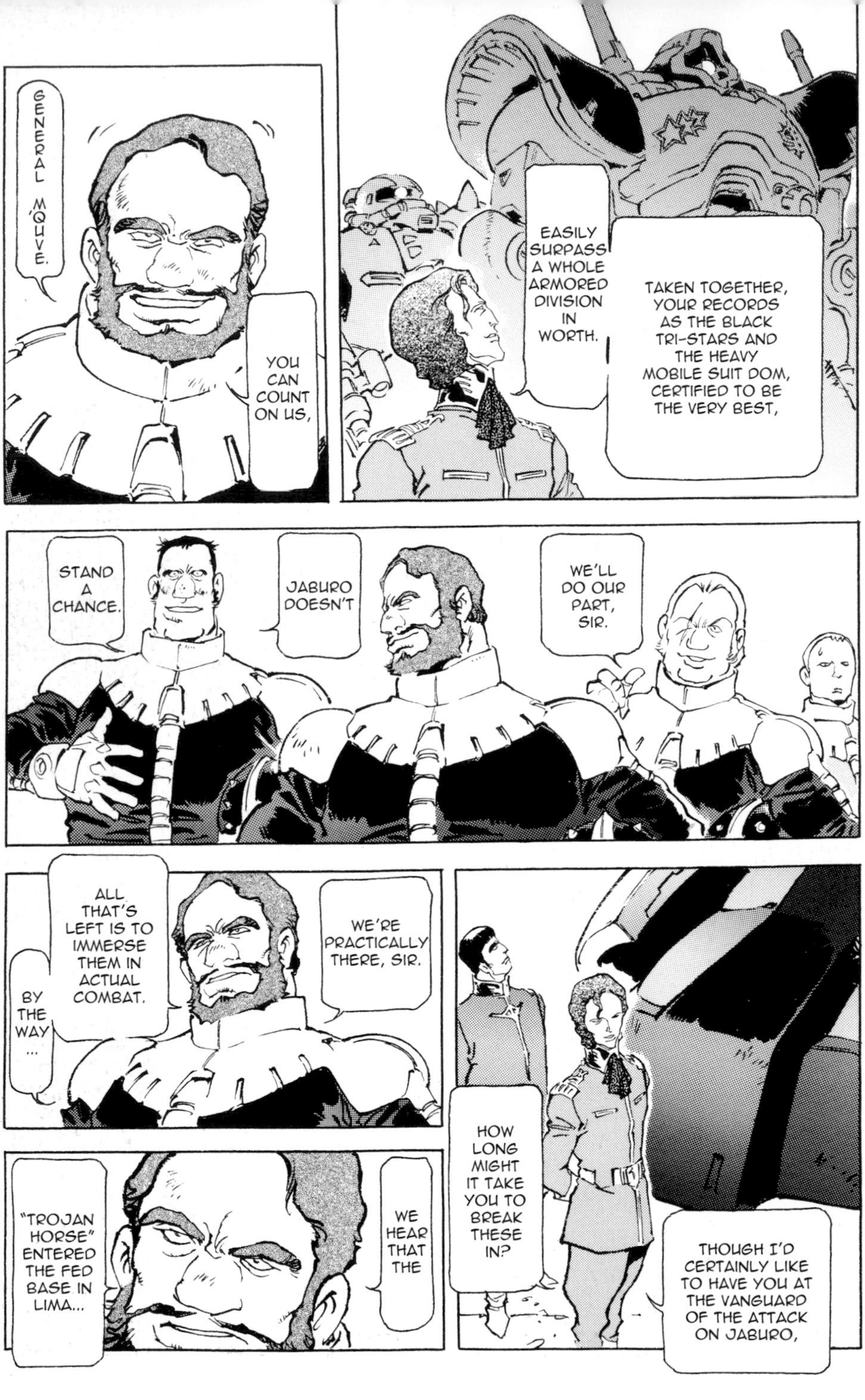
TAKEN TOGETHER, YOUR RECORDS AS THE BLACK TRI-STARS AND THE HEAVY MOBILE SUIT DOM, CERTIFIED TO BE THE VERY BEST,
EASILY SURPASS A WHOLE ARMORED DIVISION IN WORTH.
YOU CAN COUNT ON US,
GENERAL M'QUVE.
WE'LL DO OUR PART, SIR.
JABURO DOESN'T
STAND A CHANCE.
THOUGH I'D CERTAINLY LIKE TO HAVE YOU AT THE VANGUARD OF THE ATTACK ON JABURO,
HOW LONG MIGHT IT TAKE YOU TO BREAK THESE IN?
WE'RE PRACTICALLY THERE, SIR.
ALL THAT'S LEFT IS TO IMMERSE THEM IN ACTUAL COMBAT.
BY THE WAY ...
WE HEAR THAT THE
"TROJAN HORSE" ENTERED THE FED BASE IN LIMA...

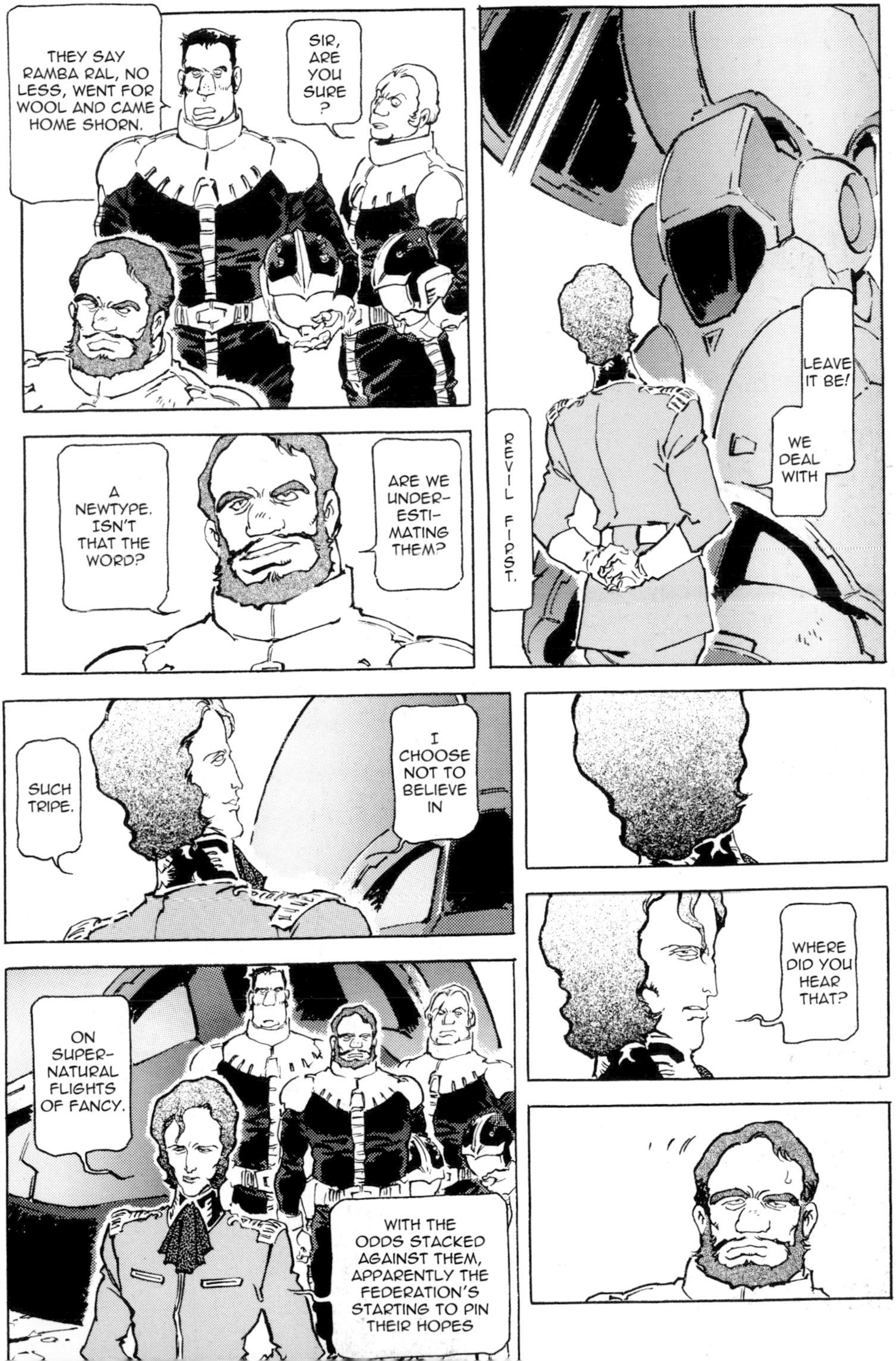
LEAVE IT BE!
WE DEAL WITH
REVIL FIRST.
SIR, ARE YOU SURE?
THEY SAY RAMBA RAL, NO LESS, WENT FOR WOOL AND CAME HOME SHORN.
ARE WE UNDER-ESTI-MATING THEM?
A NEWTYPE. ISN'T THAT THE WORD?
WHERE DID YOU HEAR THAT?
I CHOOSE NOT TO BELIEVE IN
SUCH TRIPE.
WITH THE ODDS STACKED AGAINST THEM, APPARENTLY THE FEDERATION'S STARTING TO PIN THEIR HOPES
ON SUPER-NATURAL FLIGHTS OF FANCY.

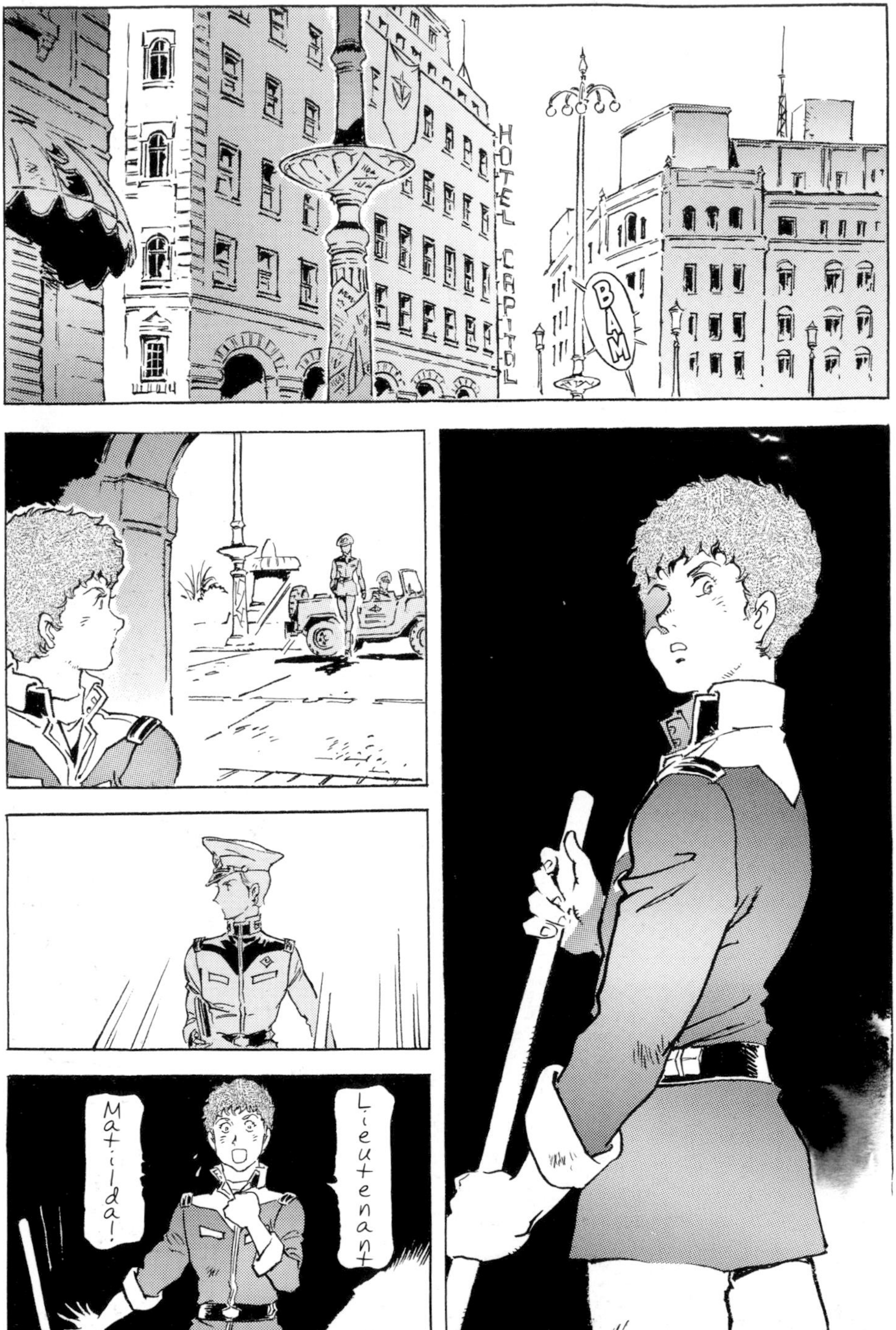
HOTEL CAPITOL
BAM
Lieutenant Matilda!

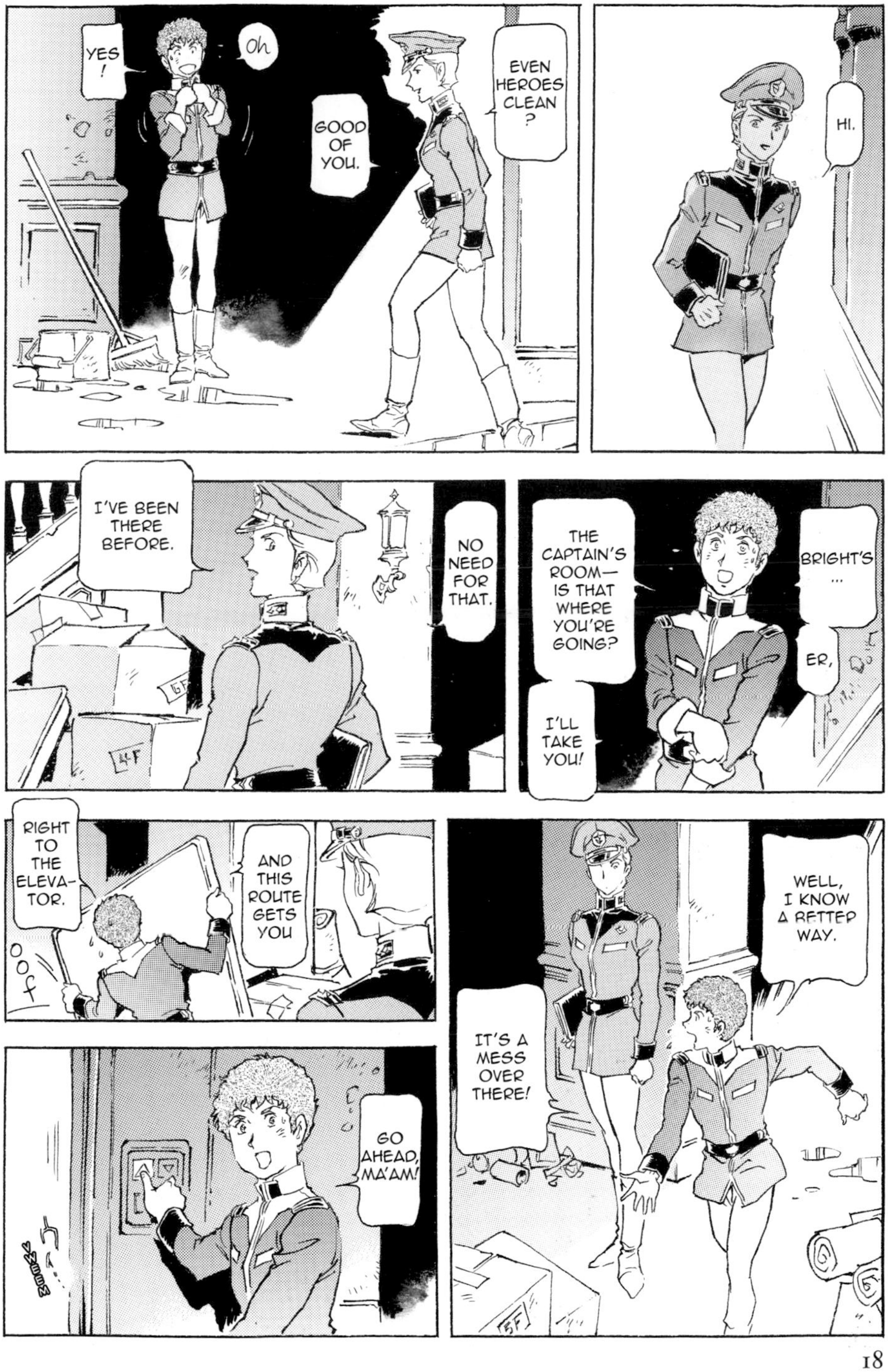
HI.
EVEN HEROES CLEAN?
Oh
YES!
GOOD OF YOU.
BRIGHT'S...
ER,
THE CAPTAIN'S ROOM—IS THAT WHERE YOU'RE GOING?
I'LL TAKE YOU!
NO NEED FOR THAT.
I'VE BEEN THERE BEFORE.
WELL, I KNOW A BETTER WAY.
IT'S A MESS OVER THERE!
AND THIS ROUTE GETS YOU
RIGHT TO THE ELEVA-TOR.
oof
GO AHEAD, MA'AM!
VWEEM

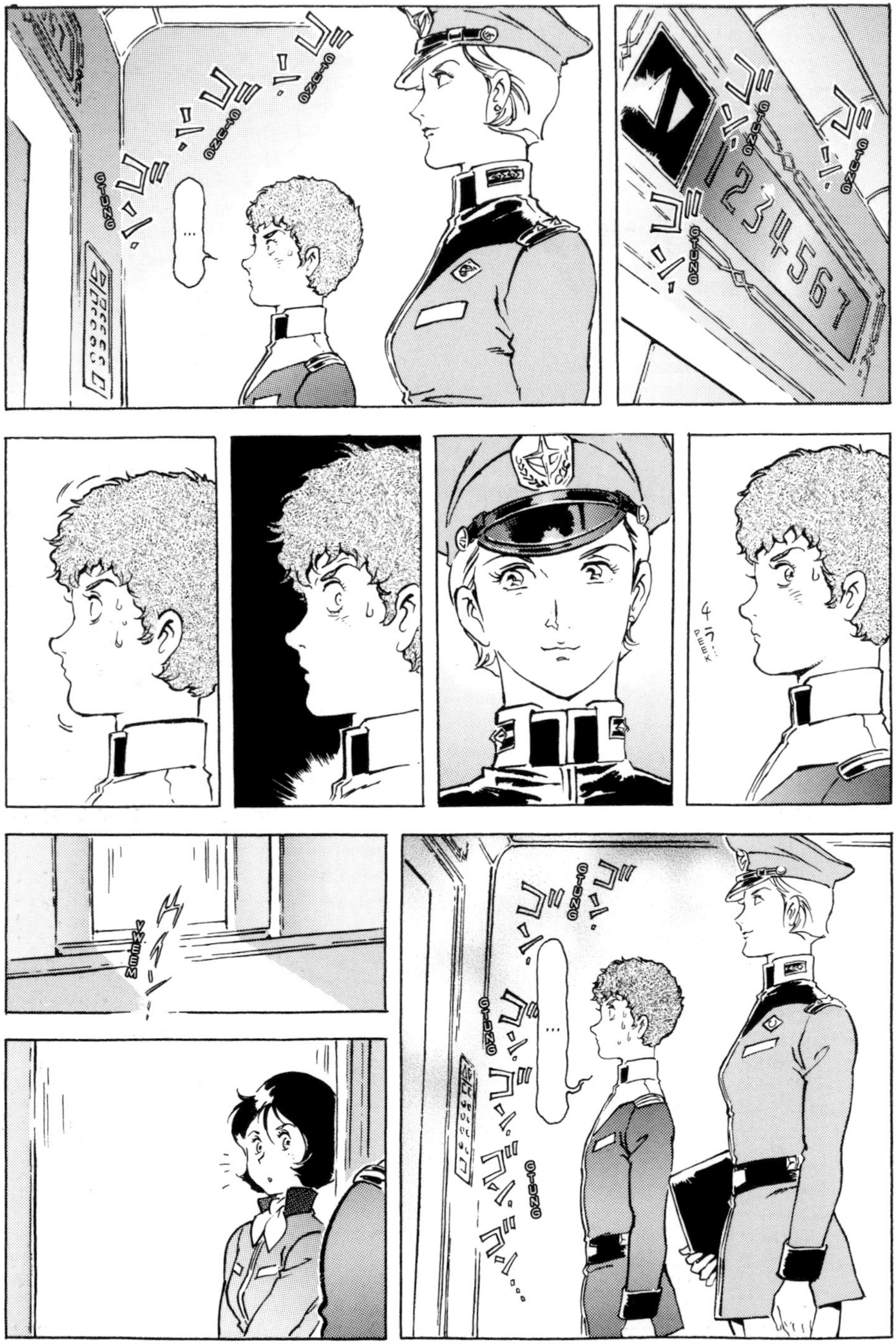

GTUNG
GTUNG
GTUNG
GTUNG
...
PEEK
GTUNG
GTUNG
...
GTUNG
VWEEM

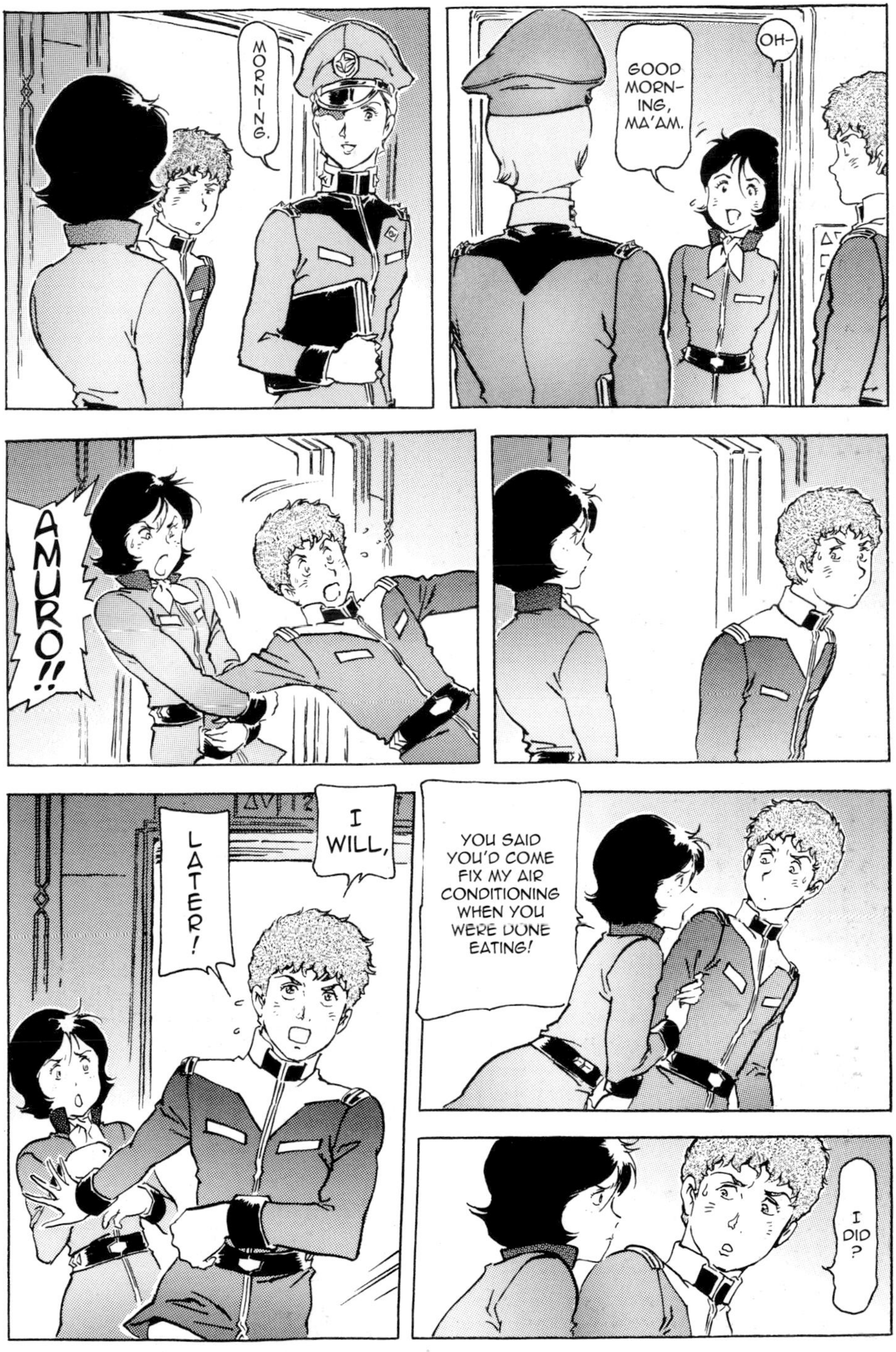
OH-
GOOD MORNING, MA'AM.
MORNING.
AMURO!!
YOU SAID YOU'D COME FIX MY AIR CONDITIONING WHEN YOU WERE DONE EATING!
I DID?
I WILL,
LATER!

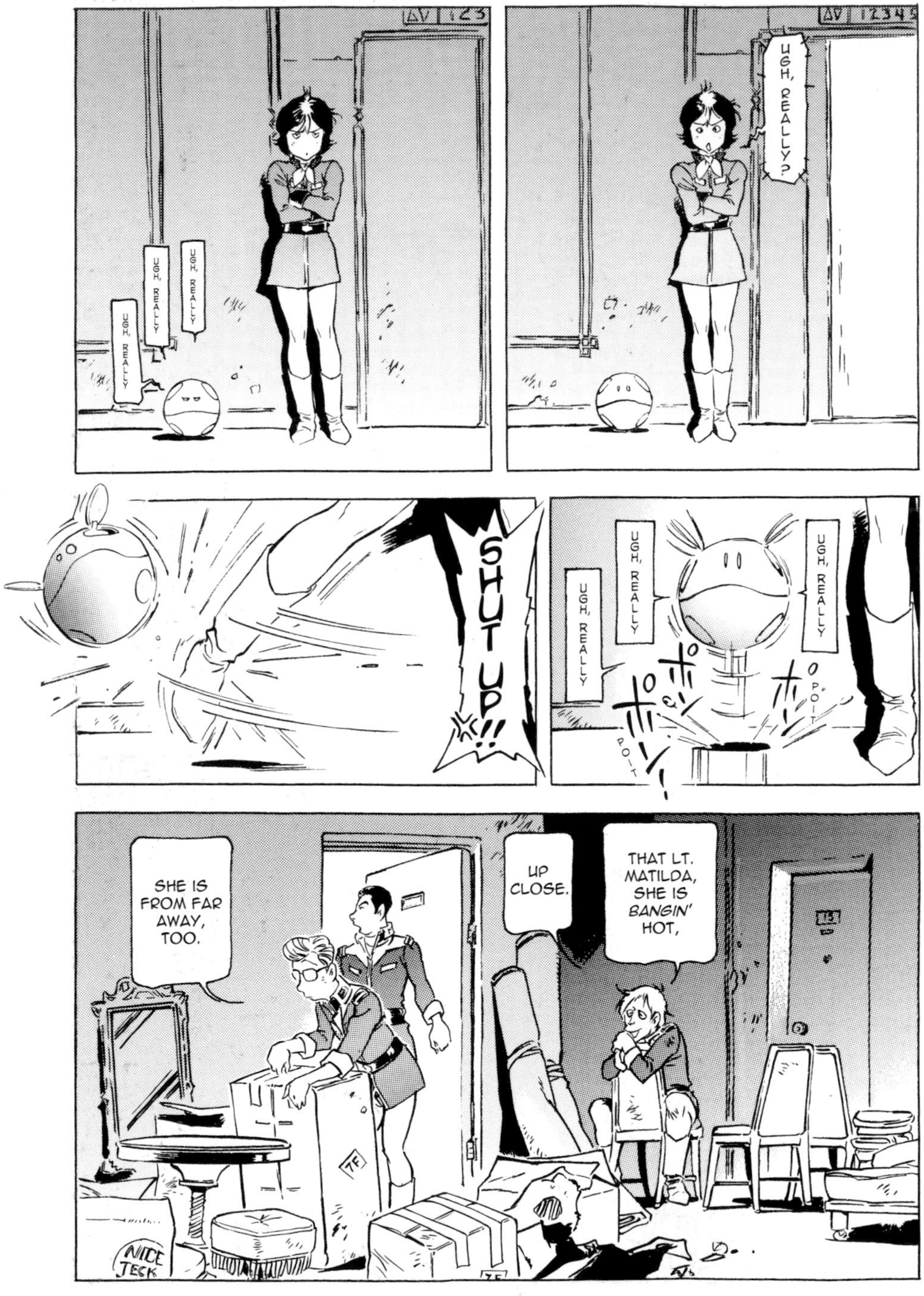
UGH, REALLY?
UGH, REALLY
UGH, REALLY
UGH, REALLY
UGH, REALLY
UGH, REALLY
UGH, REALLY
POIT
POIT
SHUT UP!!
THAT LT. MATILDA, SHE IS BANGIN' HOT,
UP CLOSE.
SHE IS FROM FAR AWAY, TOO.

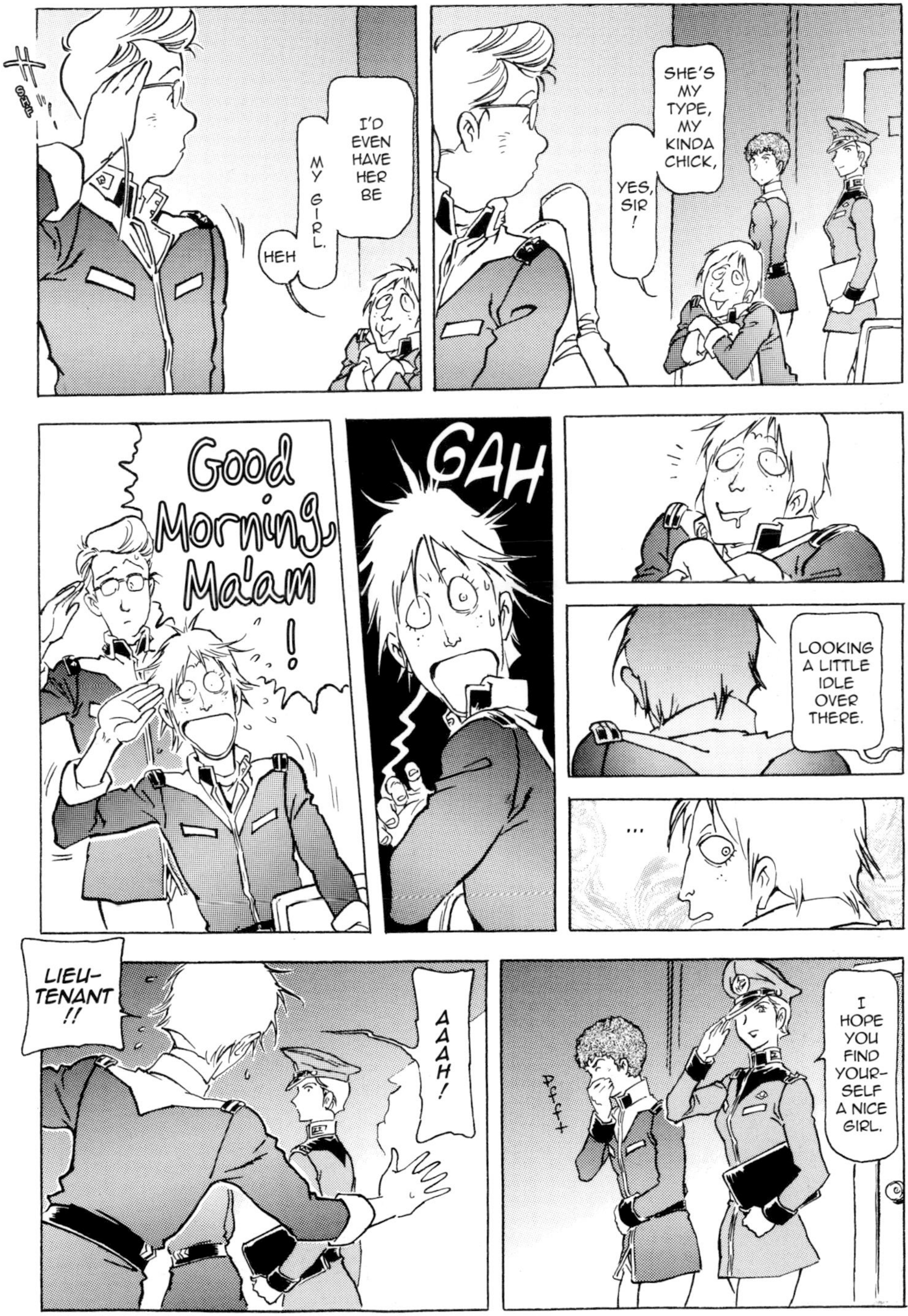
SHE'S MY TYPE, MY KINDA CHICK,
YES, SIR!
I'D EVEN HAVE HER BE MY GIRL.
HEH
LOOKING A LITTLE IDLE OVER THERE.
...
GAH
Good Morning Ma'am!
I HOPE YOU FIND YOURSELF A NICE GIRL.
LIEU-TENANT!!
AAAH!

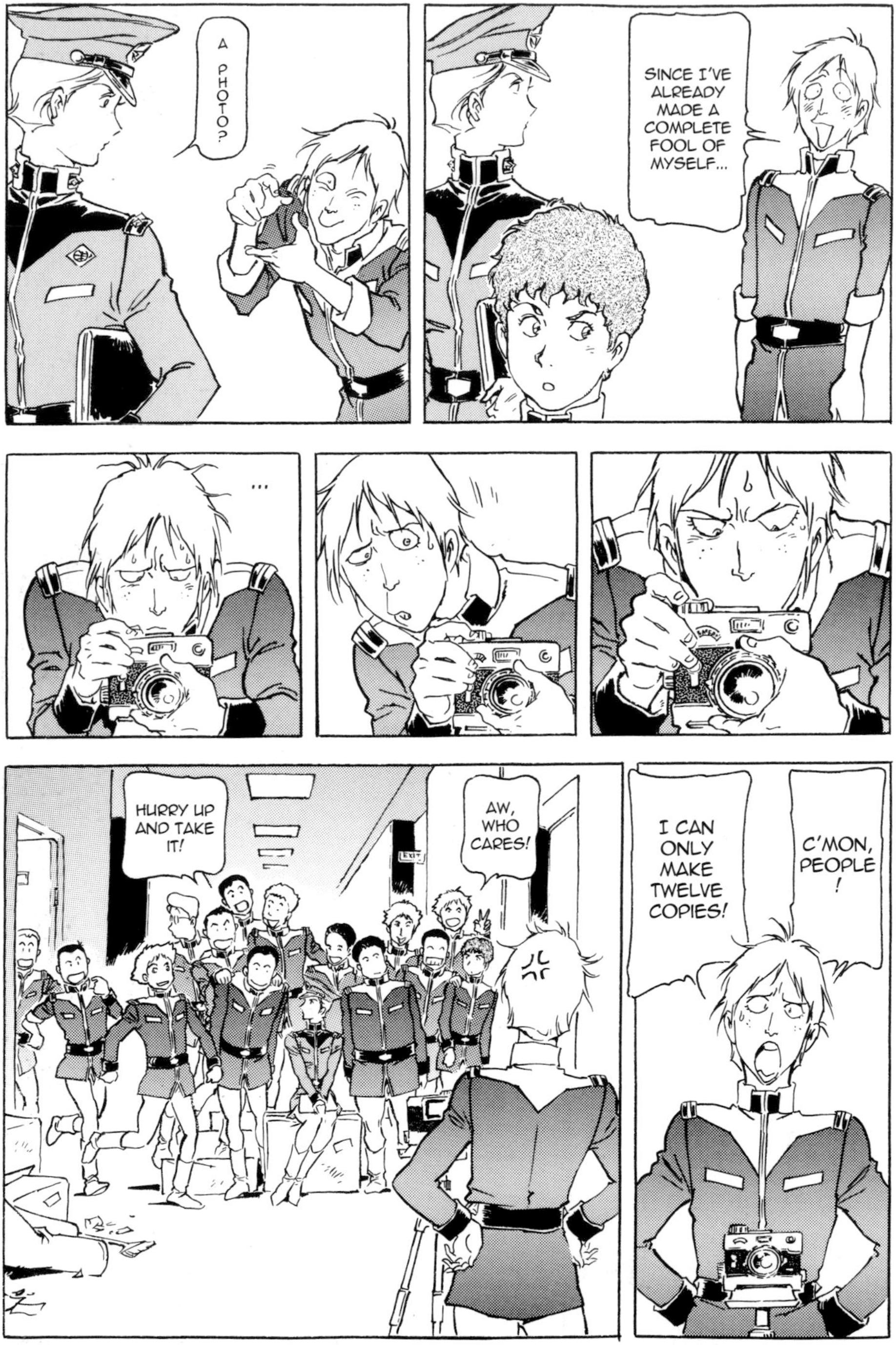
SINCE I'VE ALREADY MADE A COMPLETE FOOL OF MYSELF...
A PHOTO?
...
C'MON, PEOPLE!
I CAN ONLY MAKE TWELVE COPIES!
AW, WHO CARES!
HURRY UP AND TAKE IT!

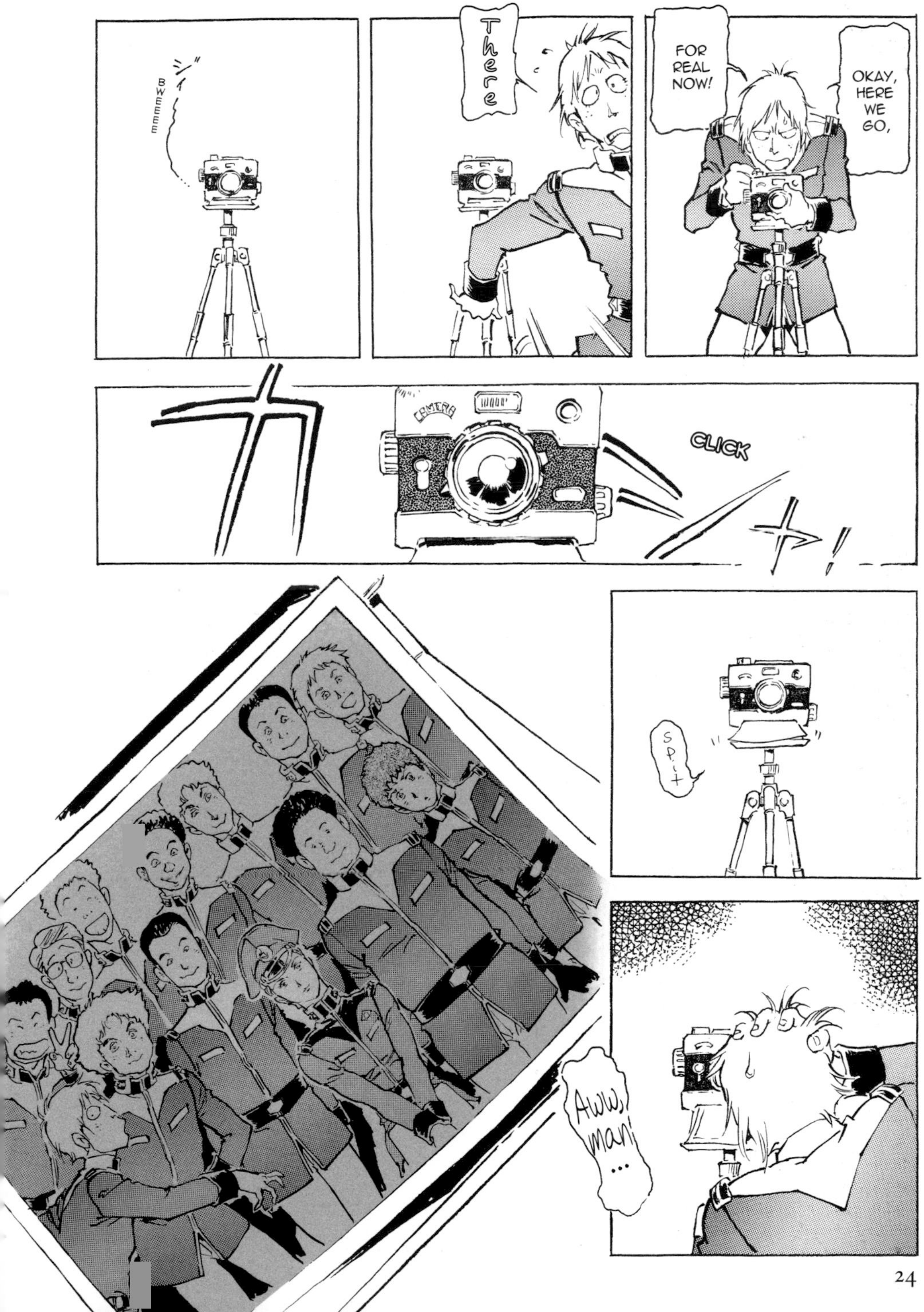

OKAY, HERE WE GO,
FOR REAL NOW!
There
BWEEEEE
CLICK
SPit
Aww, man! ...

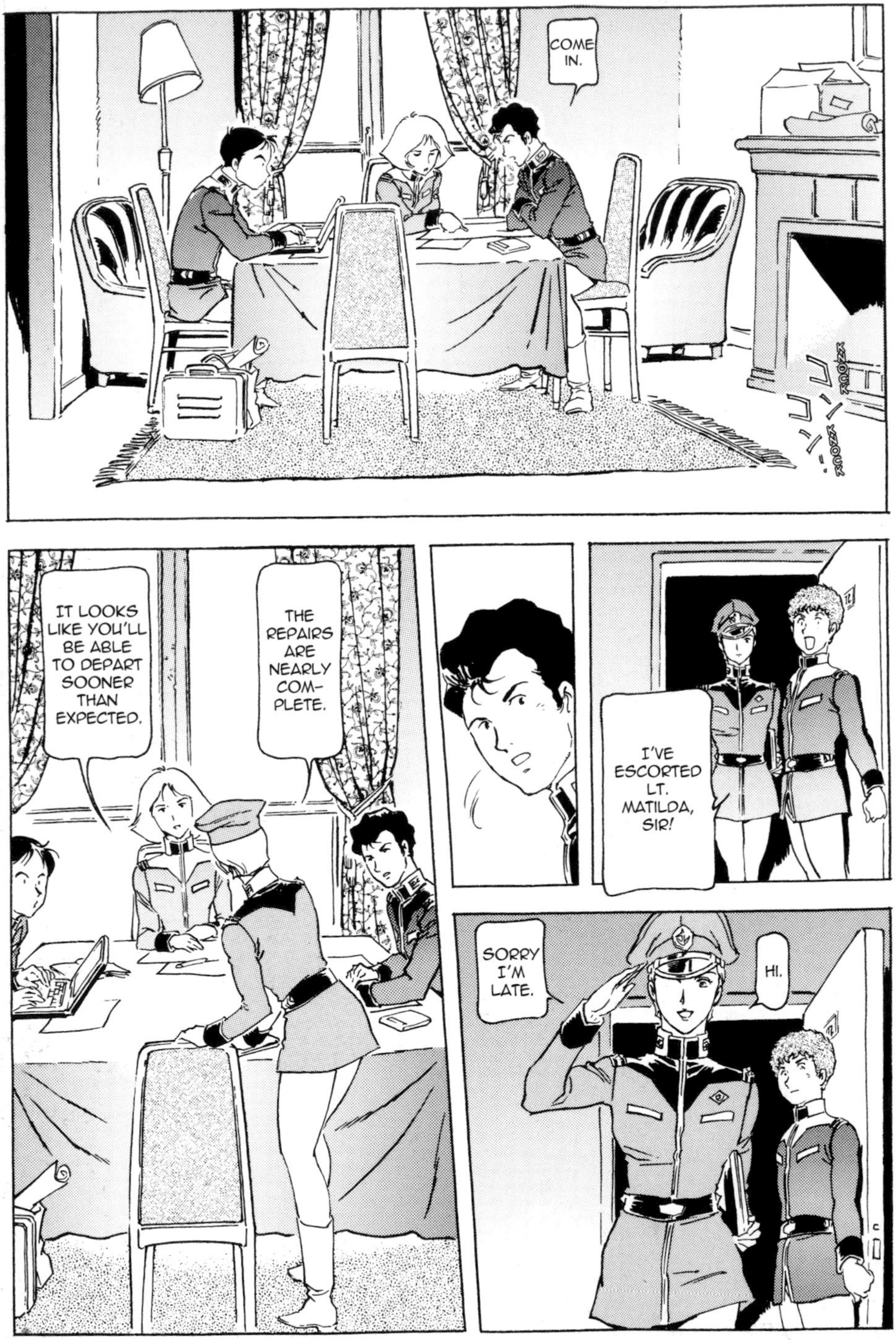
COME IN.
KNOCK
KNOCK
I'VE ESCORTED LT. MATILDA, SIR!
HI.
SORRY I'M LATE.
THE REPAIRS ARE NEARLY COMPLETE.
IT LOOKS LIKE YOU'LL BE ABLE TO DEPART SOONER THAN EXPECTED.

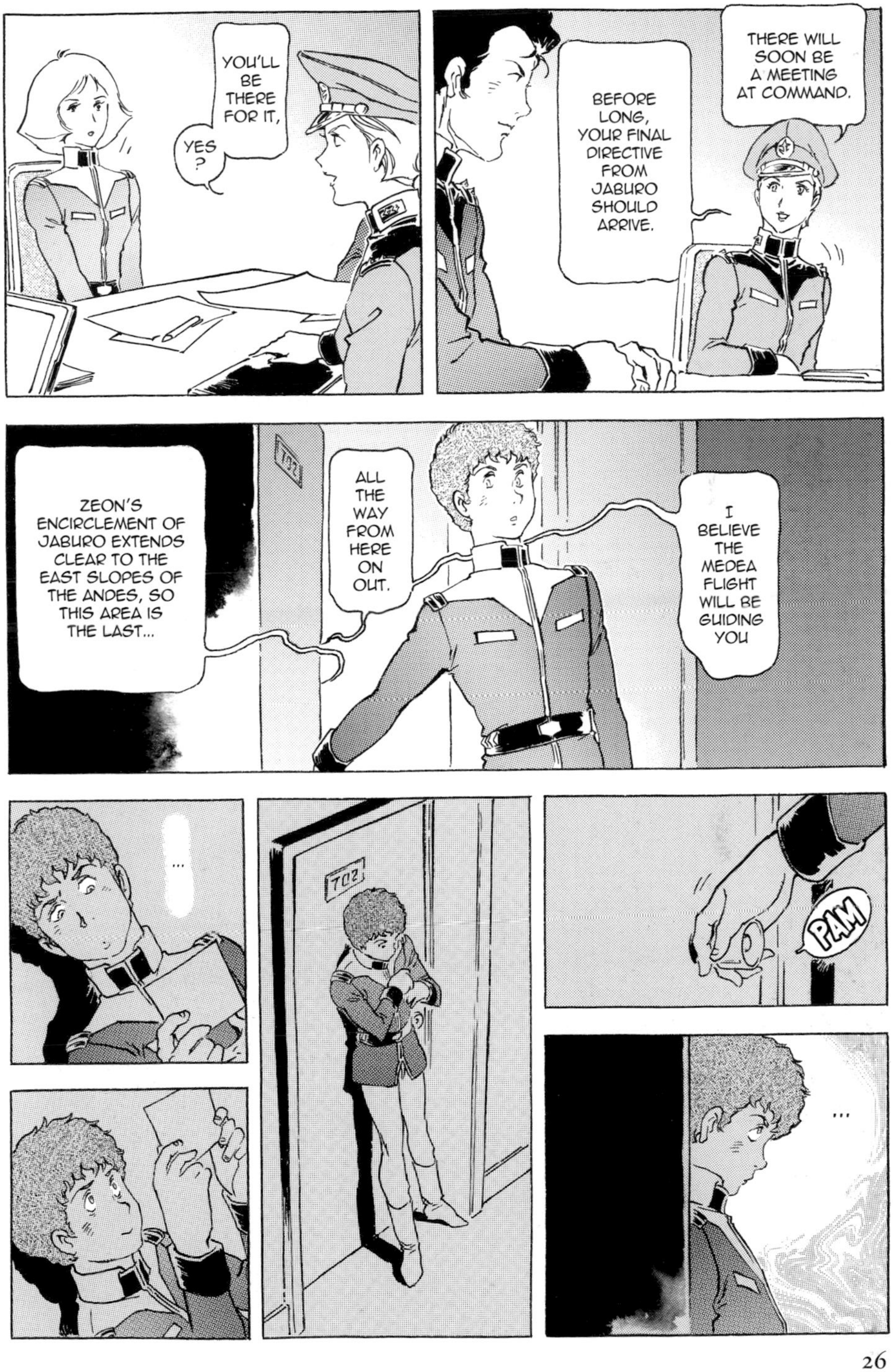
THERE WILL SOON BE A MEETING AT COMMAND.
BEFORE LONG, YOUR FINAL DIRECTIVE FROM JABURO SHOULD ARRIVE.
YOU'LL BE THERE FOR IT,
YES?
I BELIEVE THE MEDEA FLIGHT WILL BE GUIDING YOU
ALL THE WAY FROM HERE ON OUT.
ZEON'S ENCIRCLEMENT OF JABURO EXTENDS CLEAR TO THE EAST SLOPES OF THE ANDES, SO THIS AREA IS THE LAST...
PAM
...
...

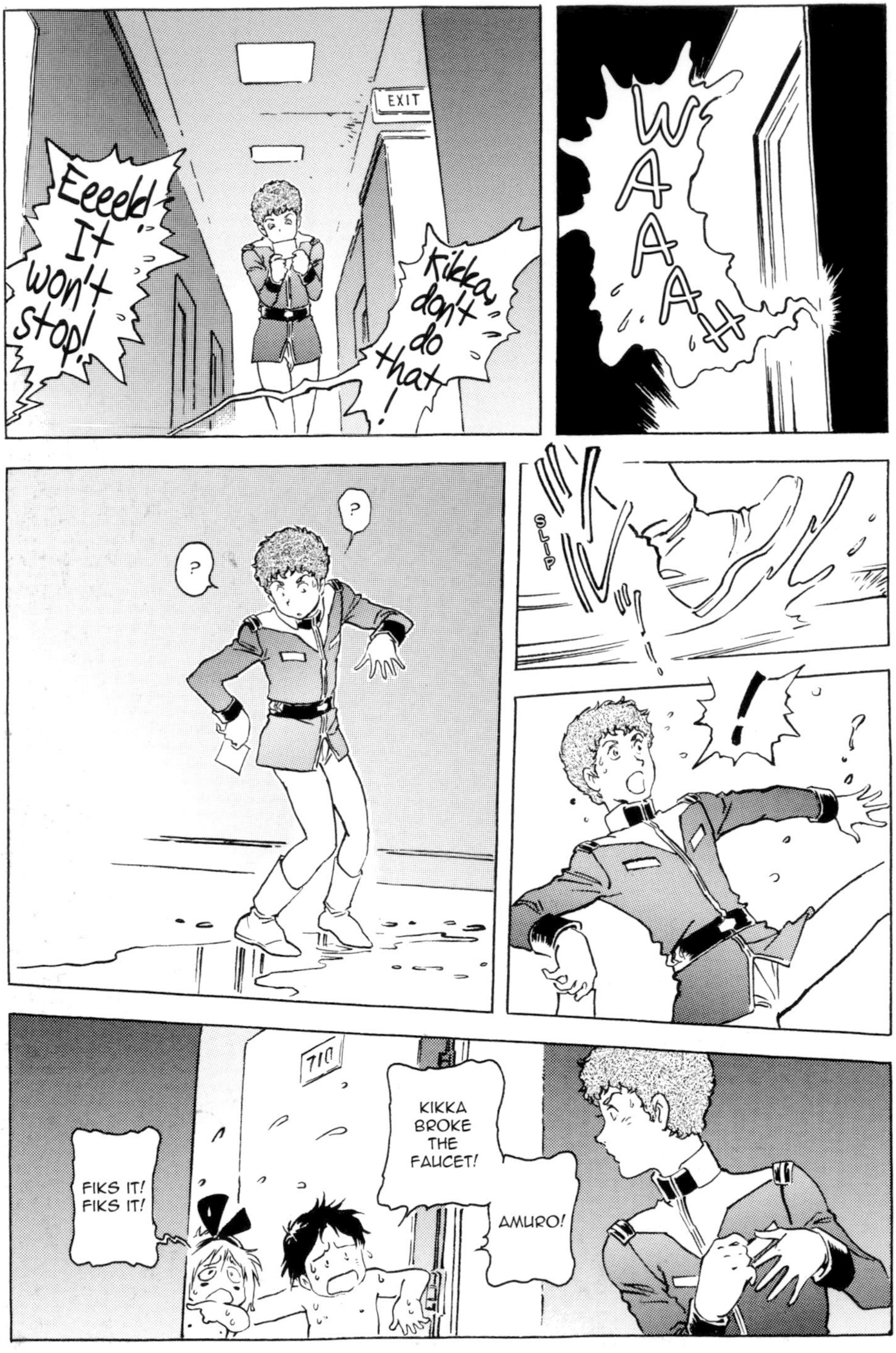
WAAAAH
EXIT
Kikka, don't do that!
Eeeek! It won't stop!
SLIP
!
?
?
?
?
710
KIKKA BROKE THE FAUCET!
AMURO!
FIKS IT! FIKS IT!

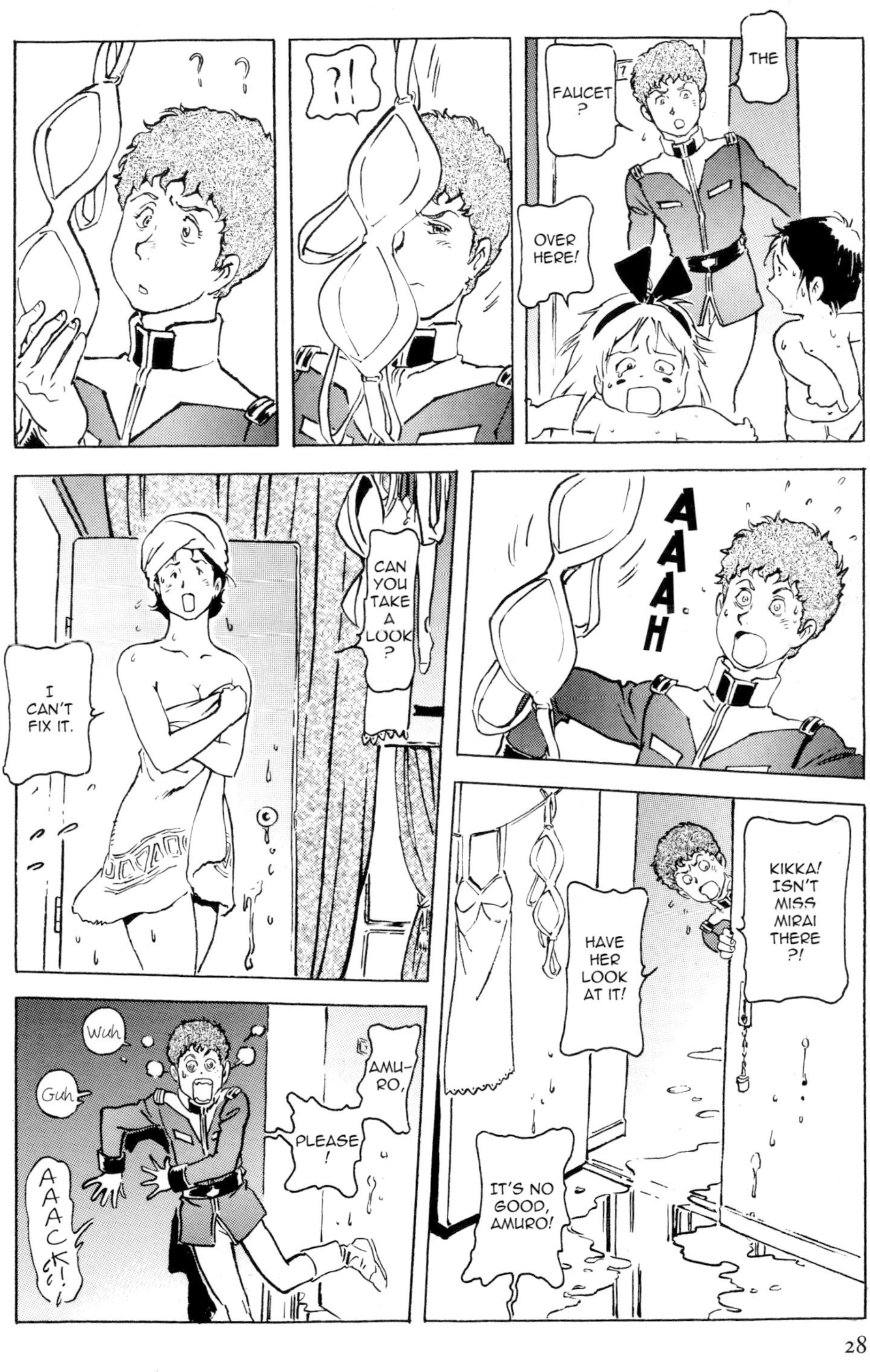
THE
FAUCET ?
OVER HERE!
?!
? ?
AAAAH
CAN YOU TAKE A LOOK ?
I CAN'T FIX IT.
KIKKA! ISN'T MISS MIRAI THERE ?!
HAVE HER LOOK AT IT!
IT'S NO GOOD, AMURO!
AMU-RO,
PLEASE !
Wuh
Guh
AAACK!!

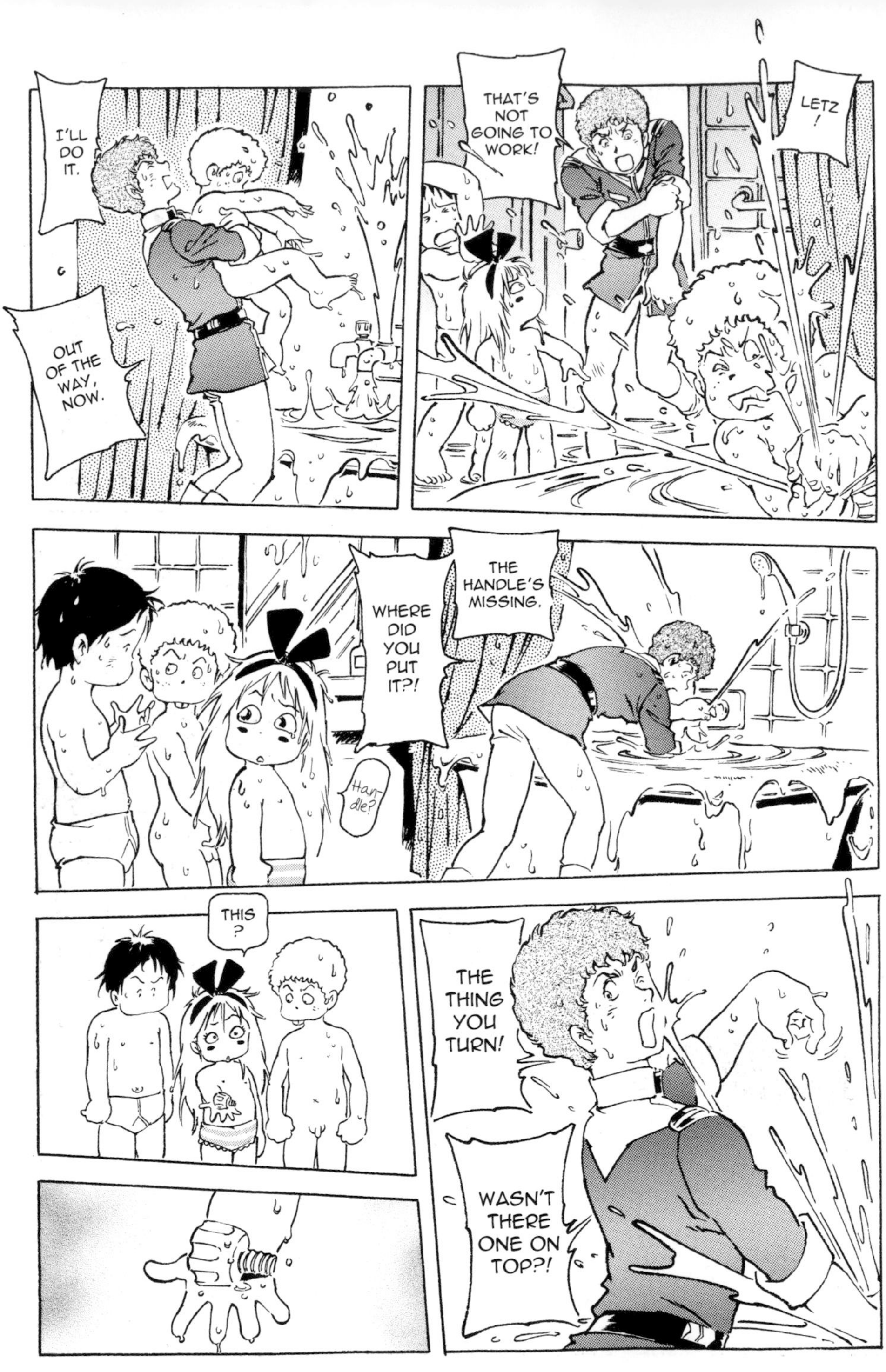
LETZ!
THAT'S NOT GOING TO WORK!
I'LL DO IT.
OUT OF THE WAY, NOW.
THE HANDLE'S MISSING.
WHERE DID YOU PUT IT?!
Han-dle?
THE THING YOU TURN!
WASN'T THERE ONE ON TOP?!
THIS?

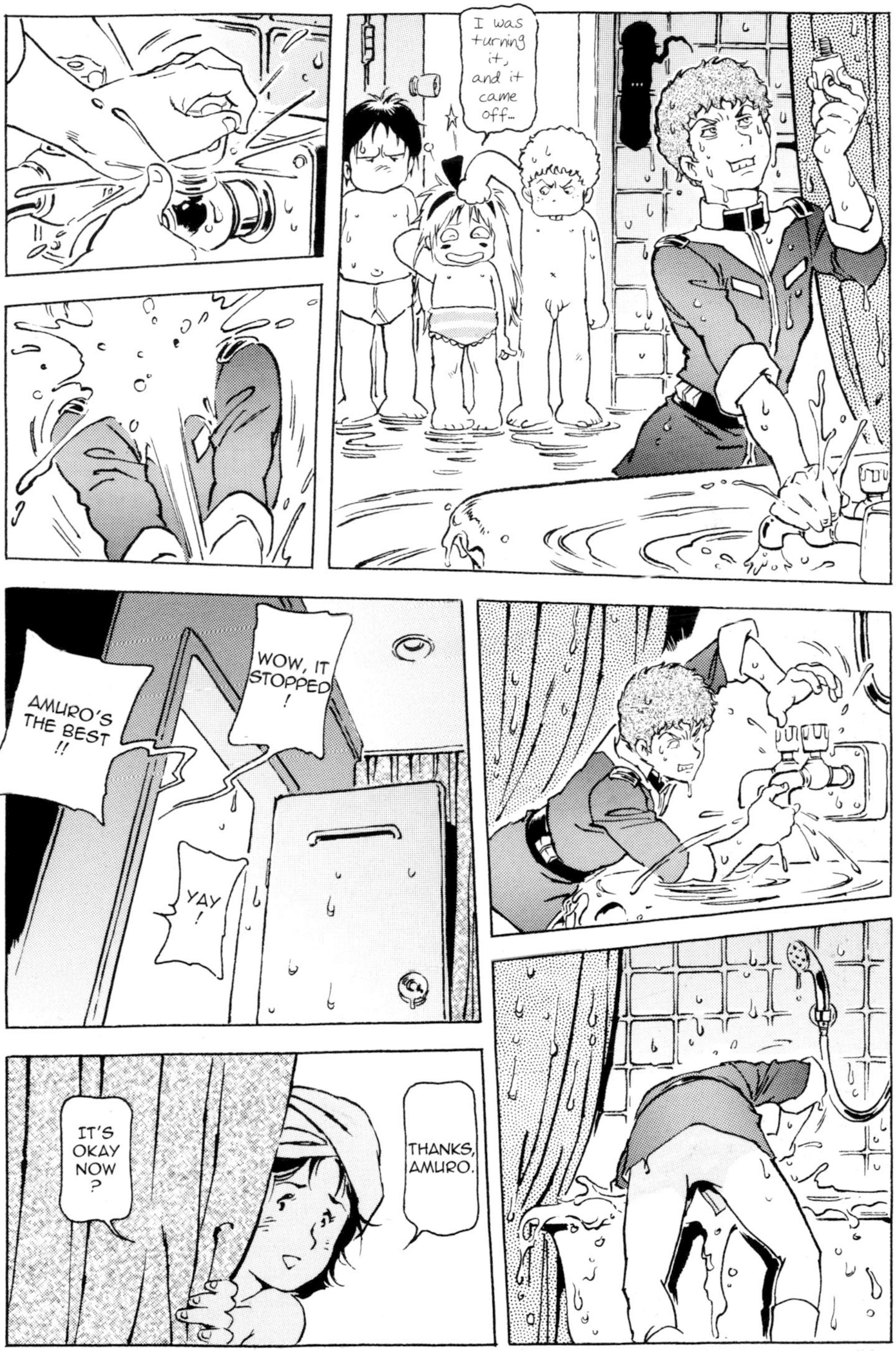
I was turning it, and it came off...
...
WOW, IT STOPPED!
AMURO'S THE BEST!!
YAY!
THANKS, AMURO.
IT'S OKAY NOW?

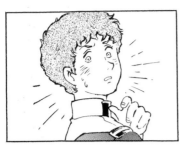

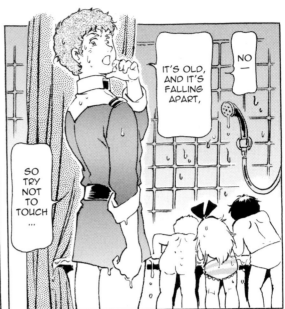

NO —

IT'S OLD, AND IT'S FALLING APART,

SO TRY NOT TO TOUCH ...

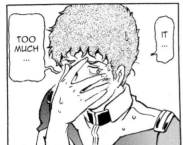

TOO MUCH ...

IT ...

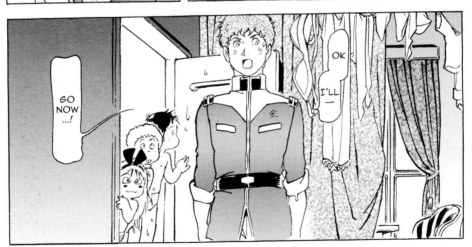

GO NOW ...!

OK

I'LL —

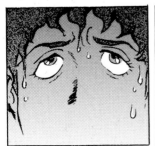

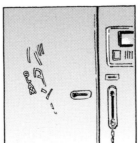

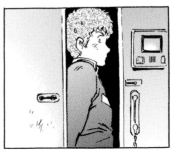

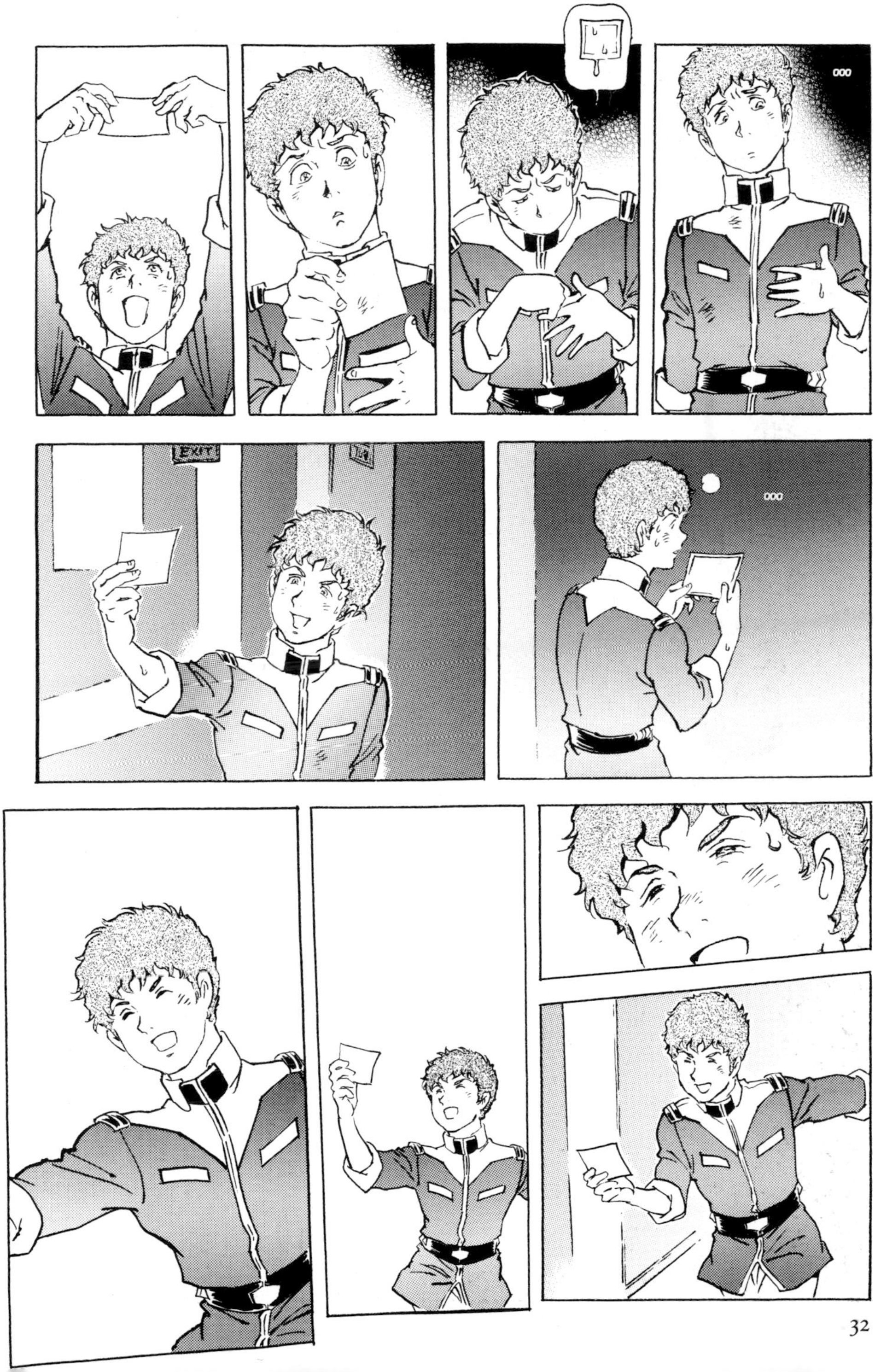
EXIT

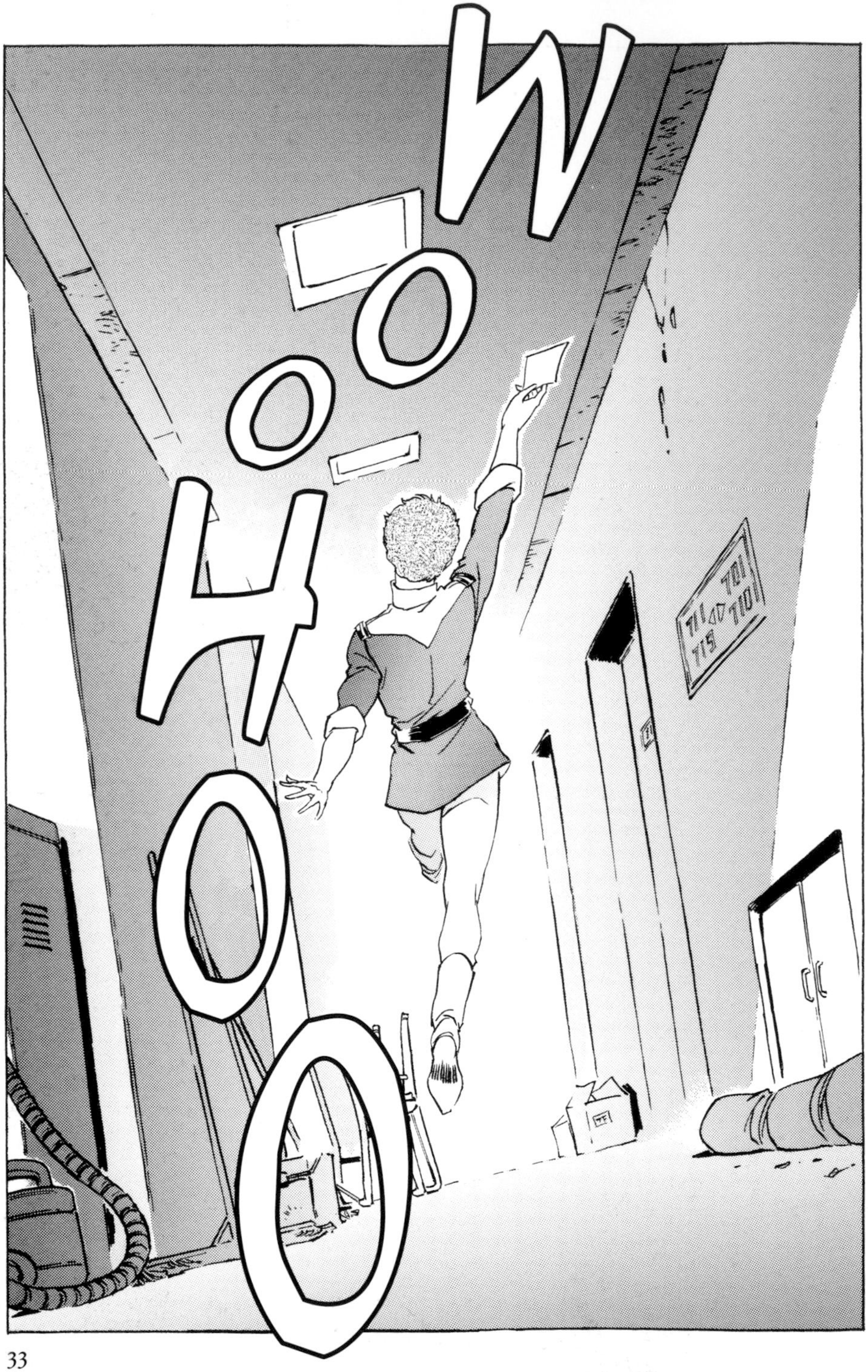
WOOHOO

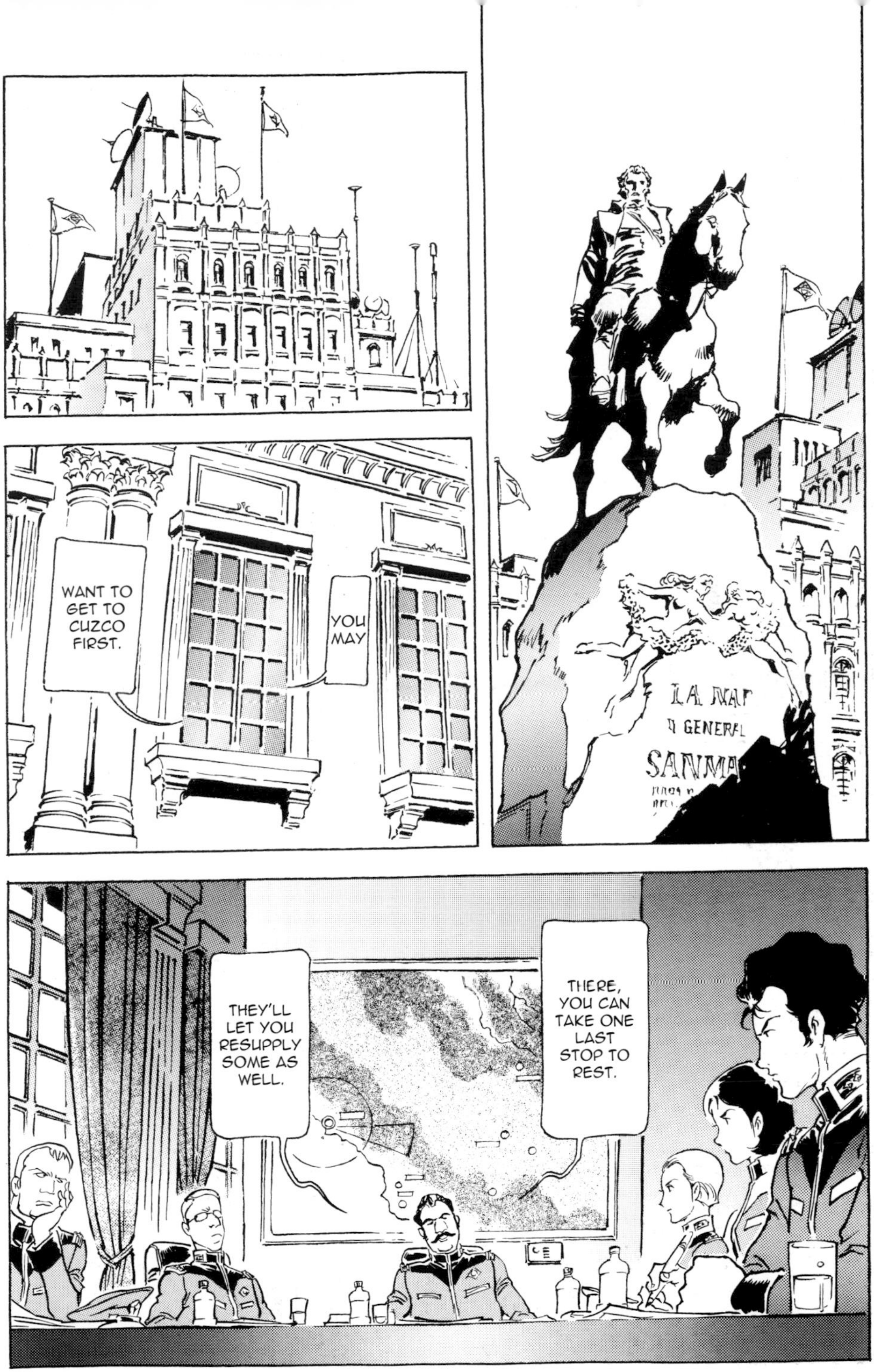
YOU MAY
WANT TO GET TO CUZCO FIRST.
THERE, YOU CAN TAKE ONE LAST STOP TO REST.
THEY'LL LET YOU RESUPPLY SOME AS WELL.

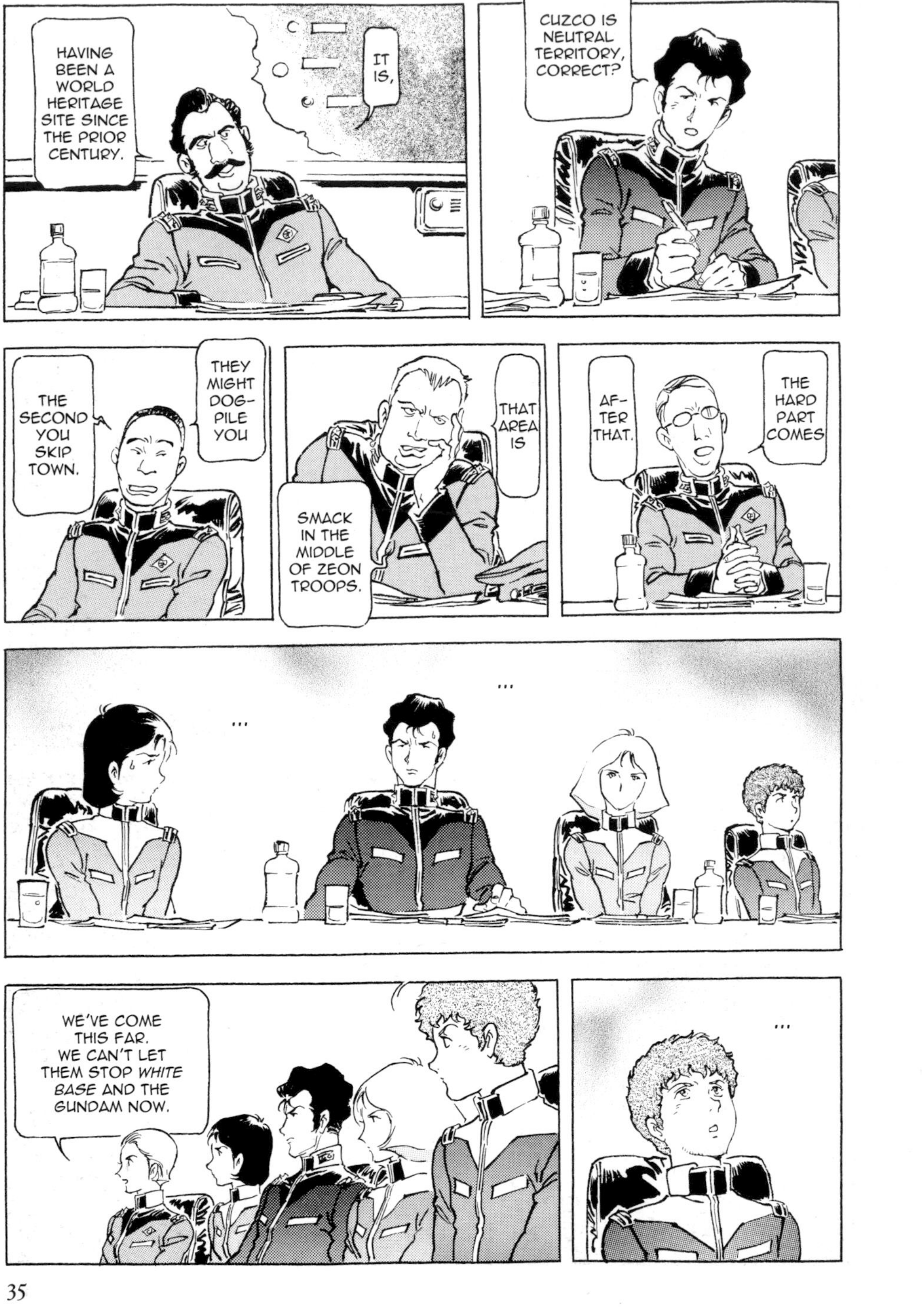
CUZCO IS NEUTRAL TERRITORY, CORRECT?
IT IS,
HAVING BEEN A WORLD HERITAGE SITE SINCE THE PRIOR CENTURY.
THE HARD PART COMES
AFTER THAT.
THAT AREA IS
SMACK IN THE MIDDLE OF ZEON TROOPS.
THEY MIGHT DOG-PILE YOU
THE SECOND YOU SKIP TOWN.
...
...
...
WE'VE COME THIS FAR. WE CAN'T LET THEM STOP *WHITE BASE* AND THE GUNDAM NOW.

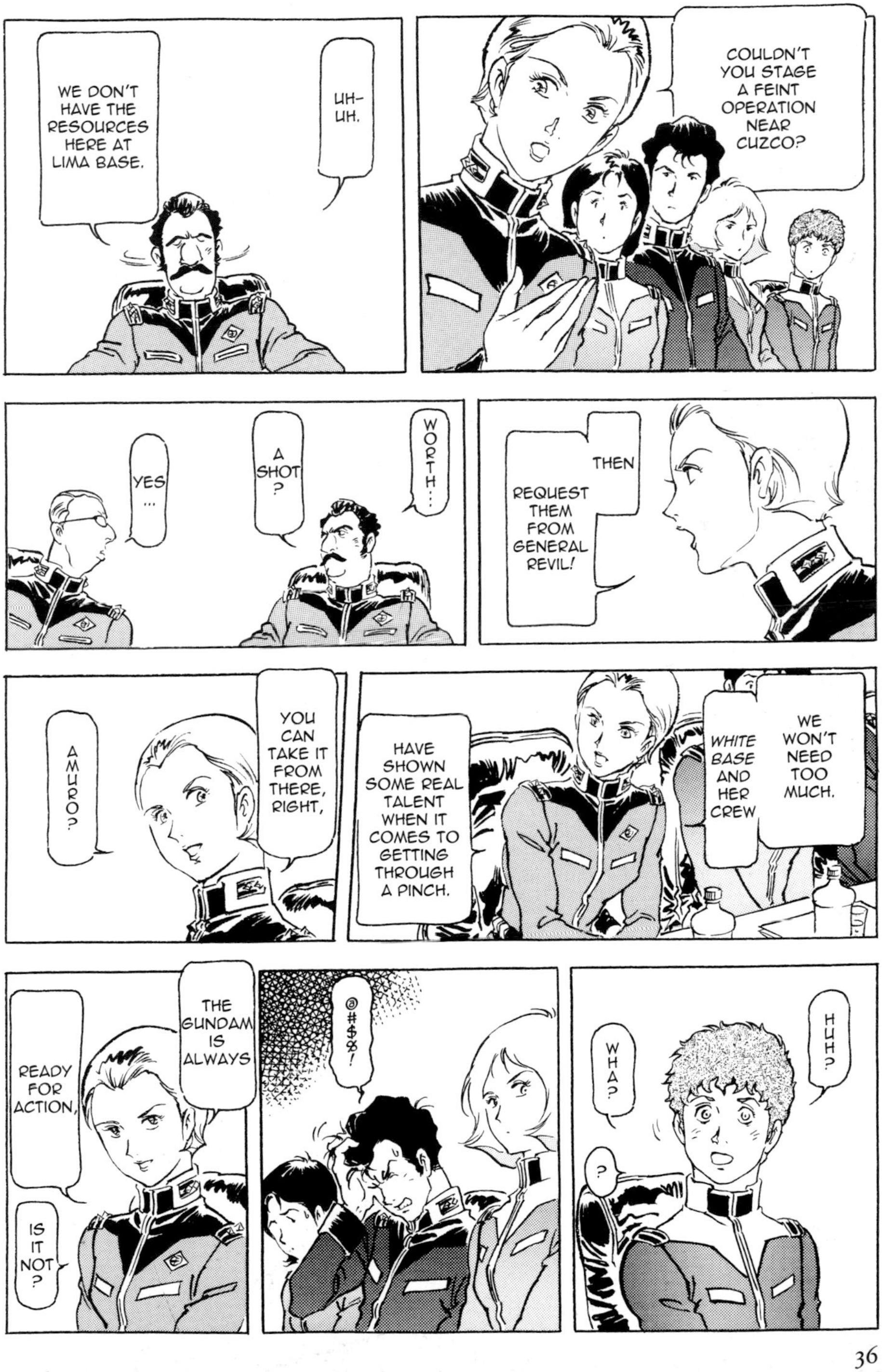
COULDN'T YOU STAGE A FEINT OPERATION NEAR CUZCO?
UH-UH.
WE DON'T HAVE THE RESOURCES HERE AT LIMA BASE.
THEN
REQUEST THEM FROM GENERAL REVIL!
WORTH...
A SHOT?
YES...
WE WON'T NEED TOO MUCH.
WHITE BASE AND HER CREW
HAVE SHOWN SOME REAL TALENT WHEN IT COMES TO GETTING THROUGH A PINCH.
YOU CAN TAKE IT FROM THERE, RIGHT,
AMURO?
HUH?
WHA?
?
@#$%!
THE GUNDAM IS ALWAYS
READY FOR ACTION,
IS IT NOT?

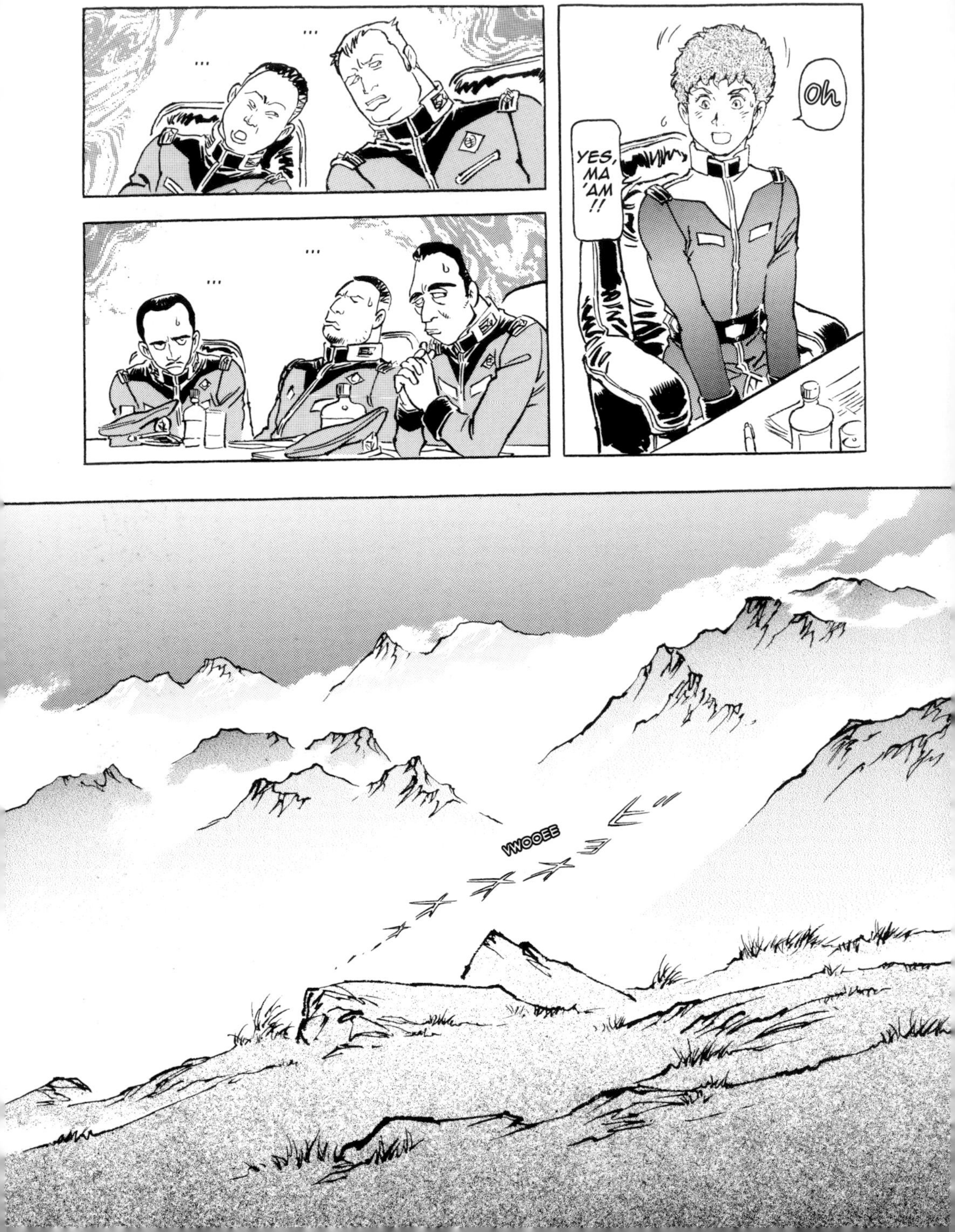
Oh
YES, MA'AM!!
...
...
...
...
VWOOEE

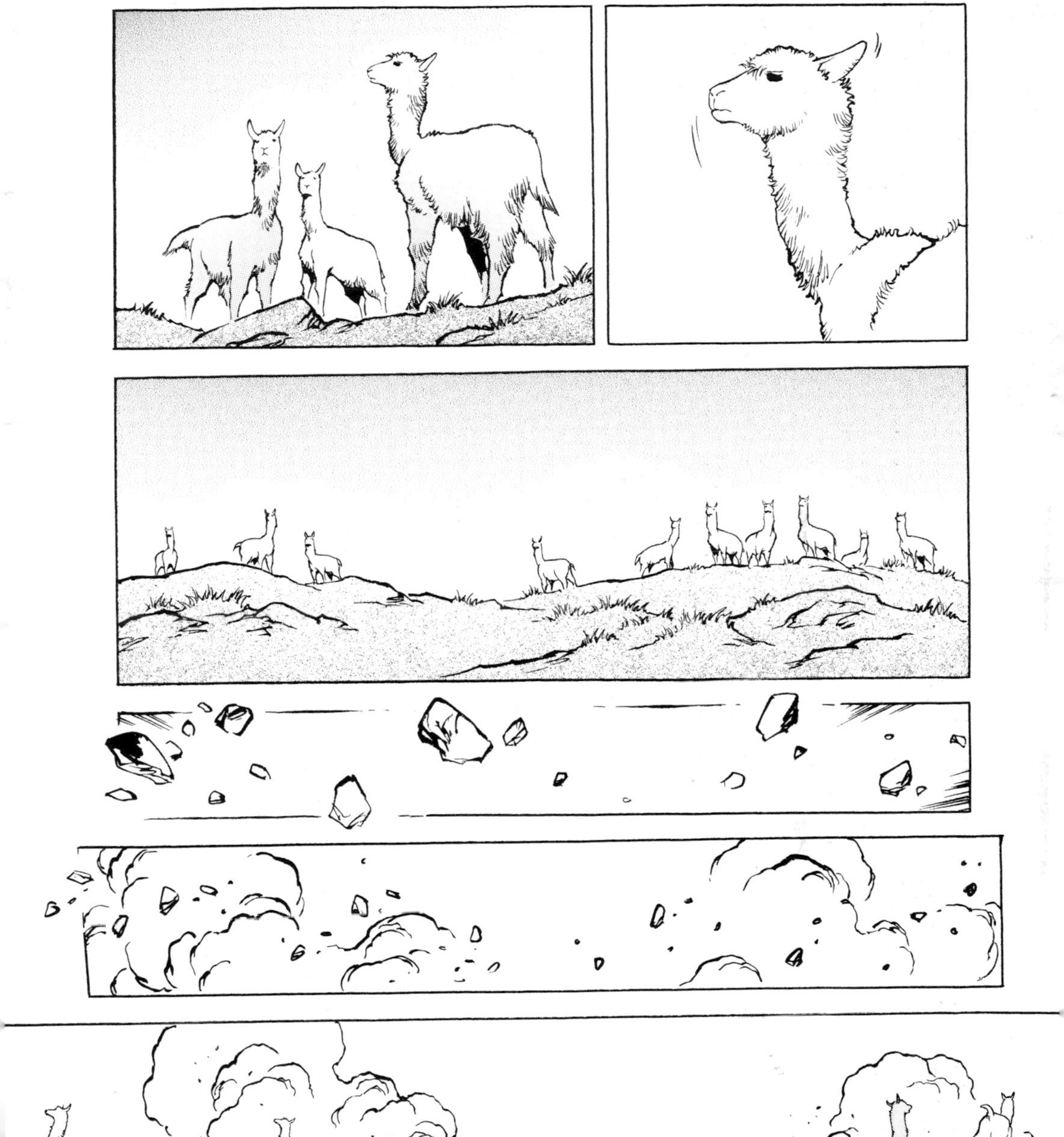

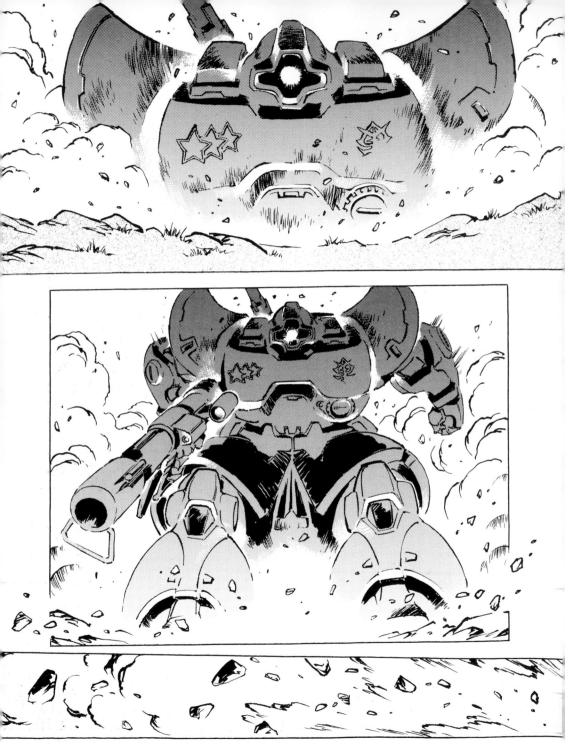

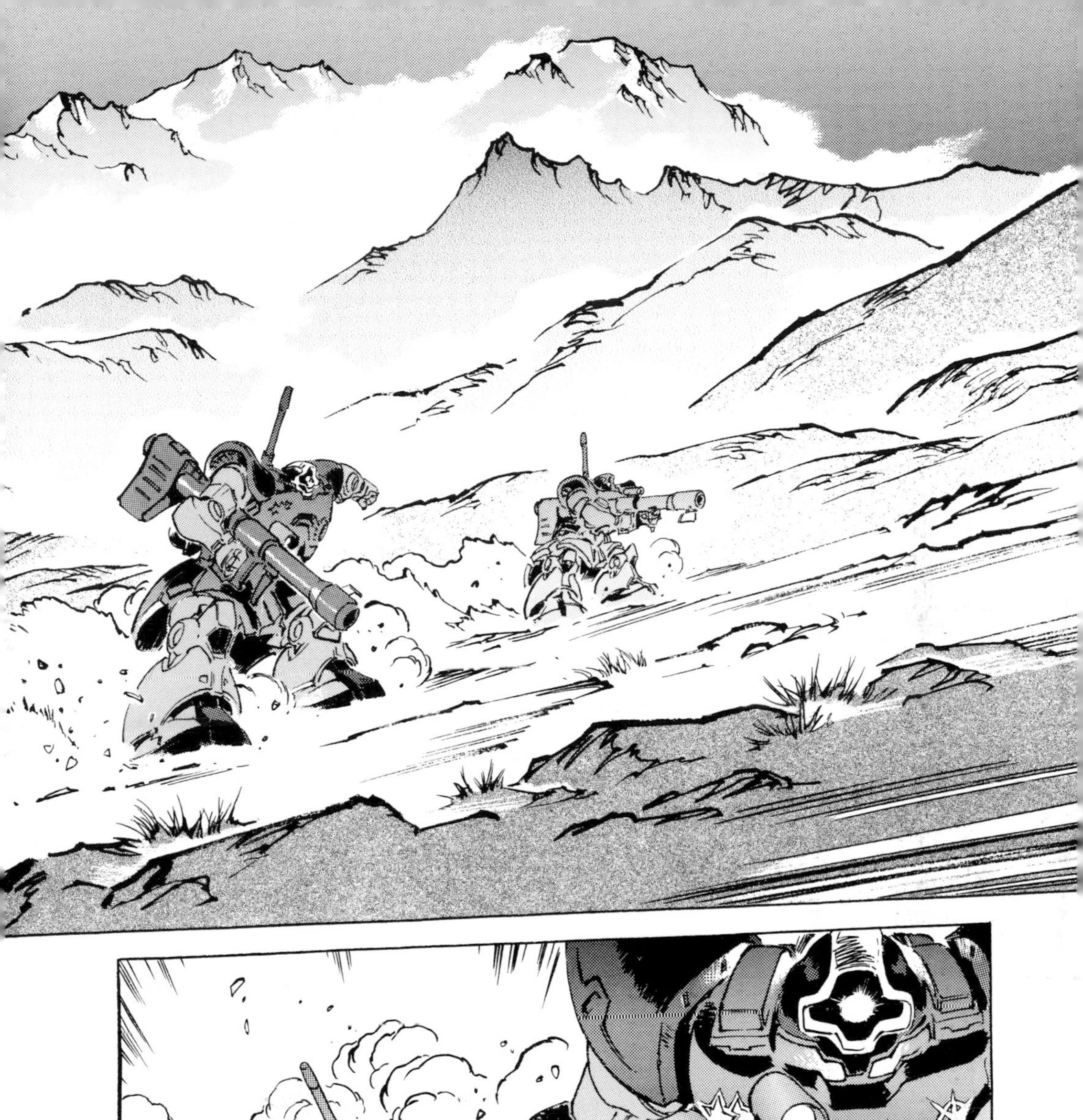

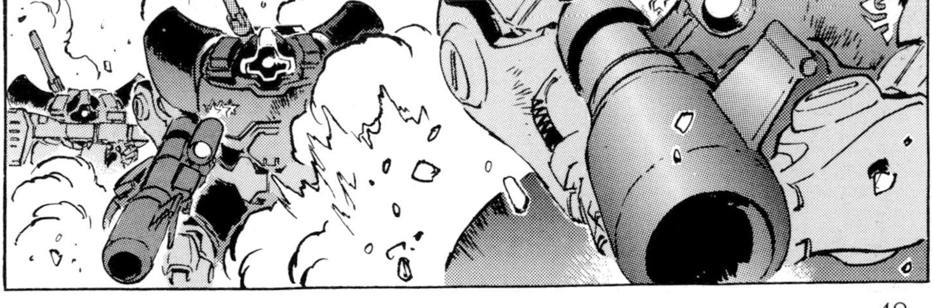

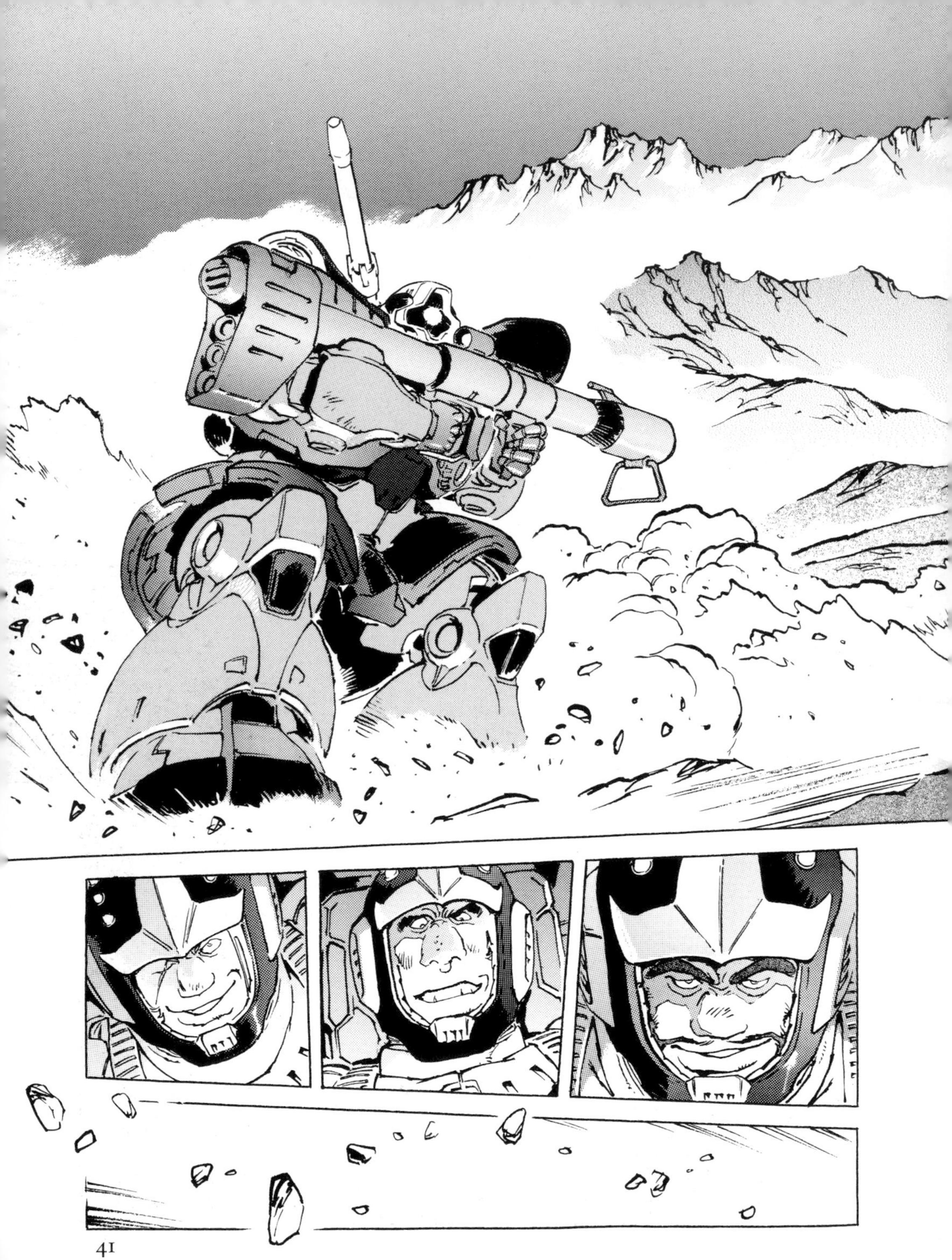

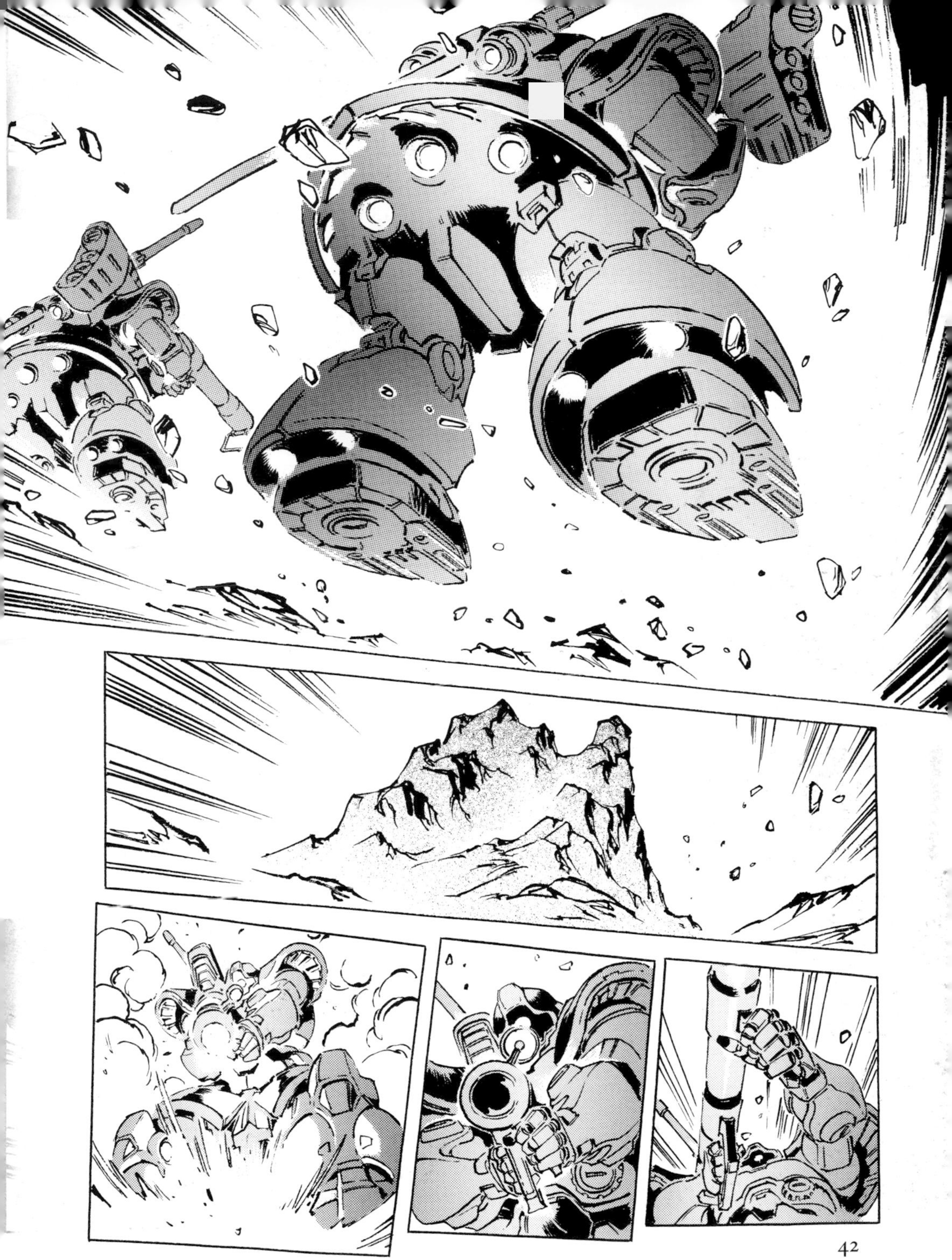

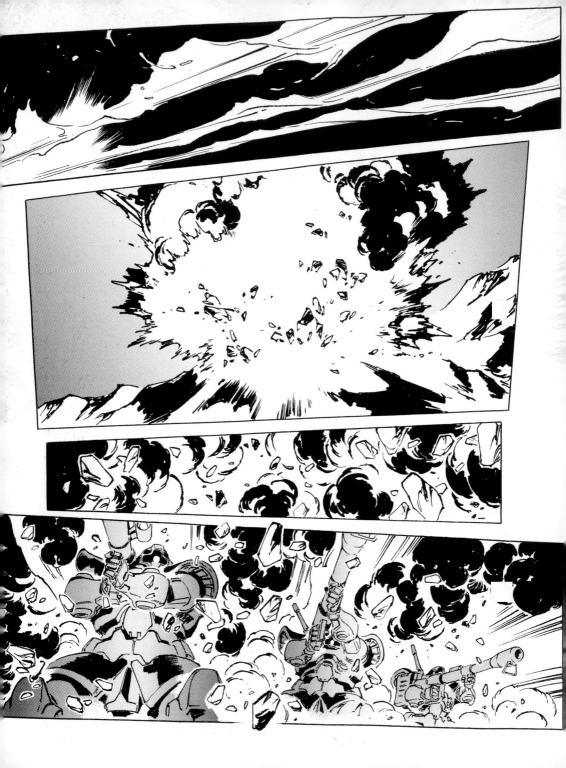

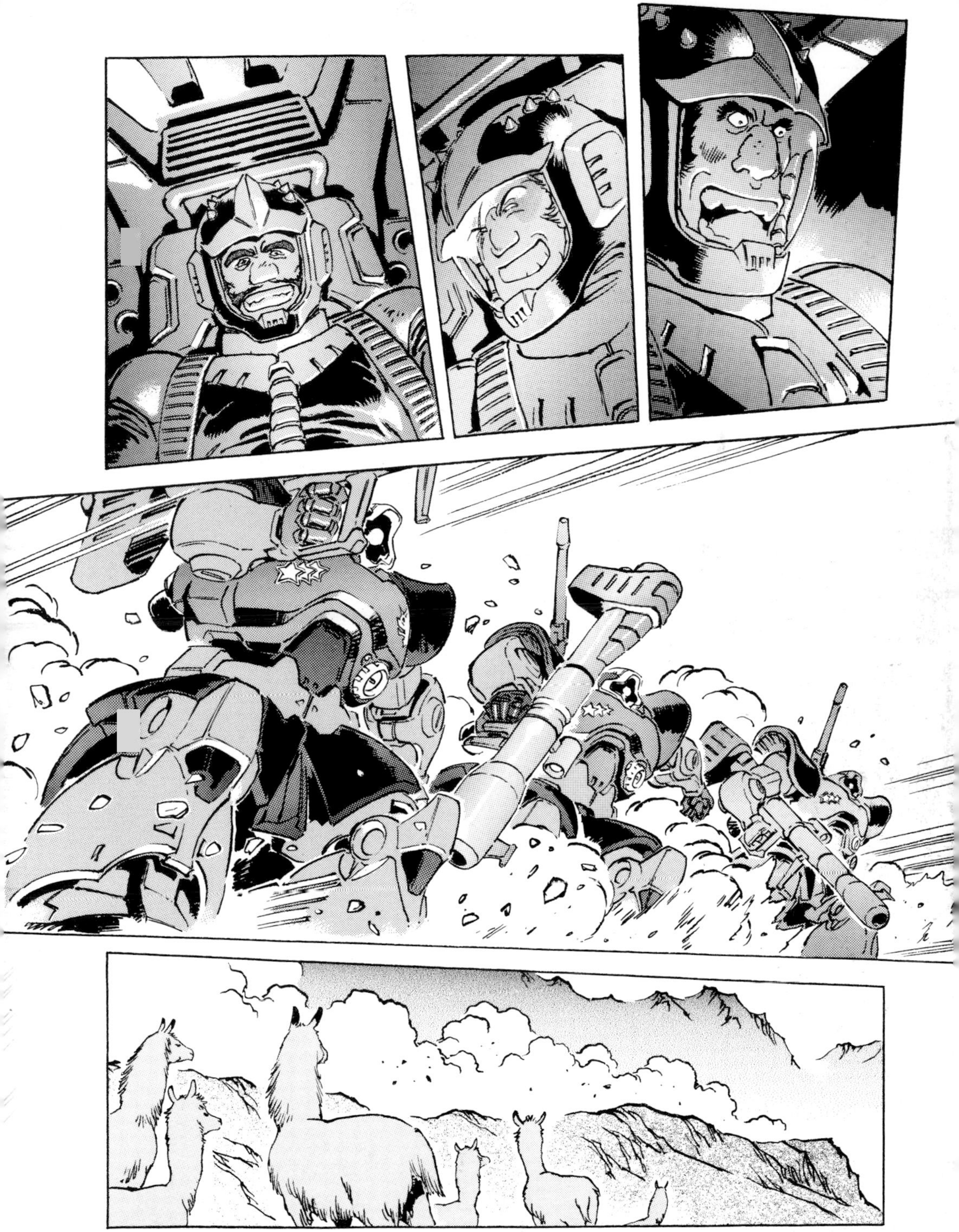

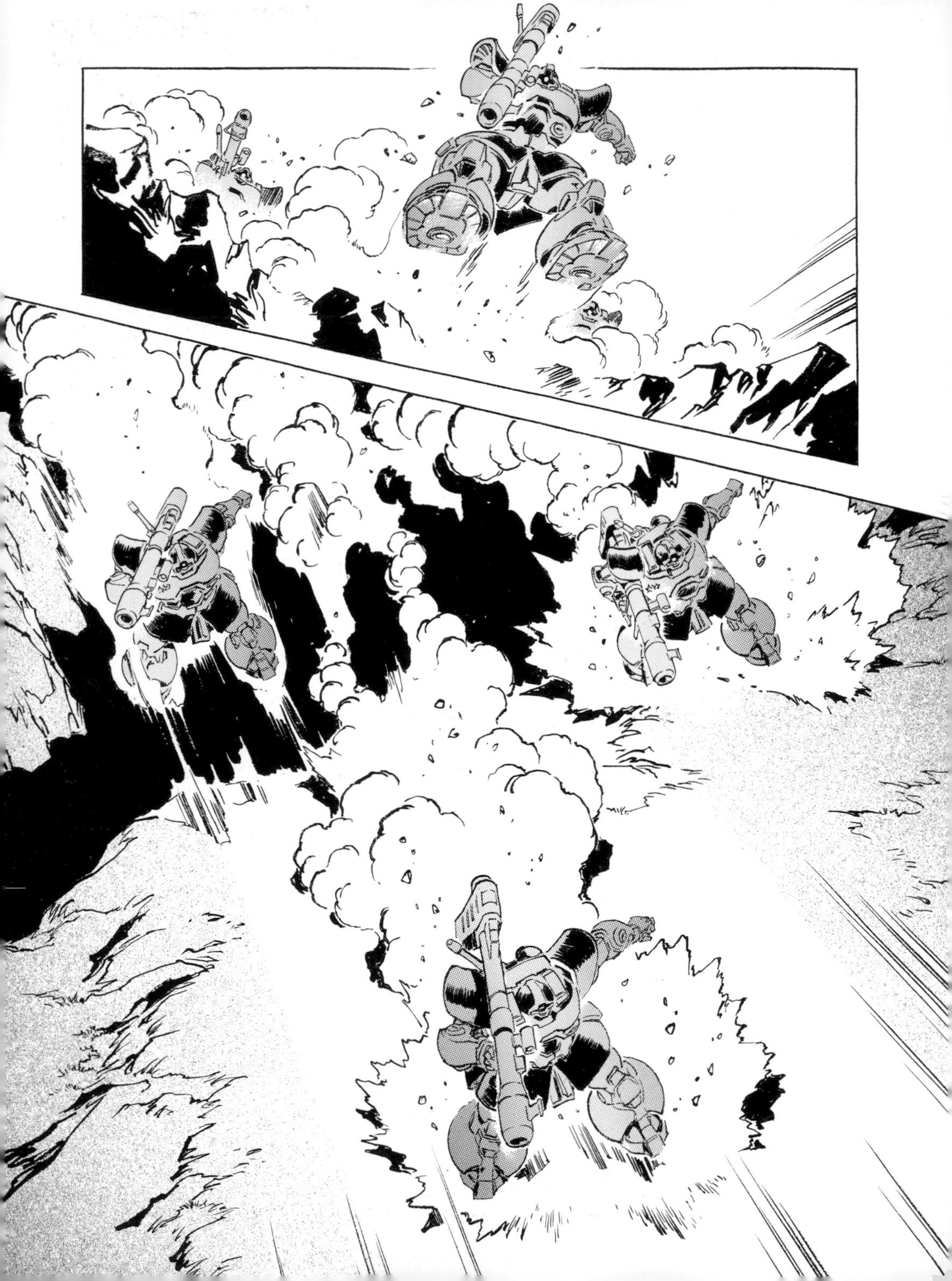

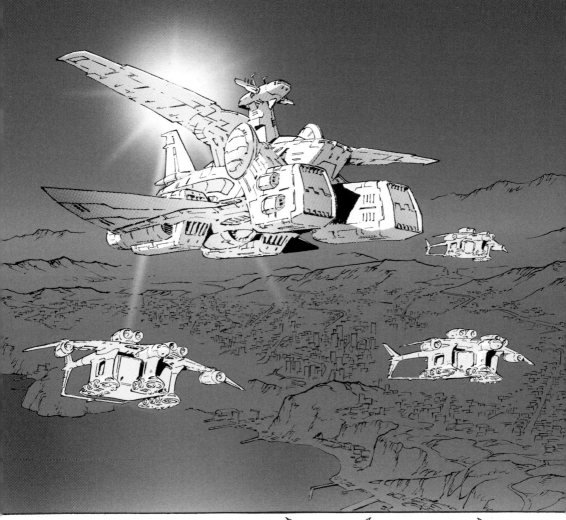

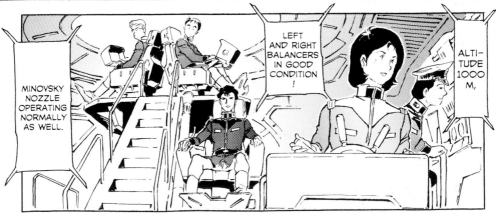

MINOVSKY NOZZLE OPERATING NORMALLY AS WELL.

LEFT AND RIGHT BALANCERS IN GOOD CONDITION !

ALTI-TUDE 1000 M,

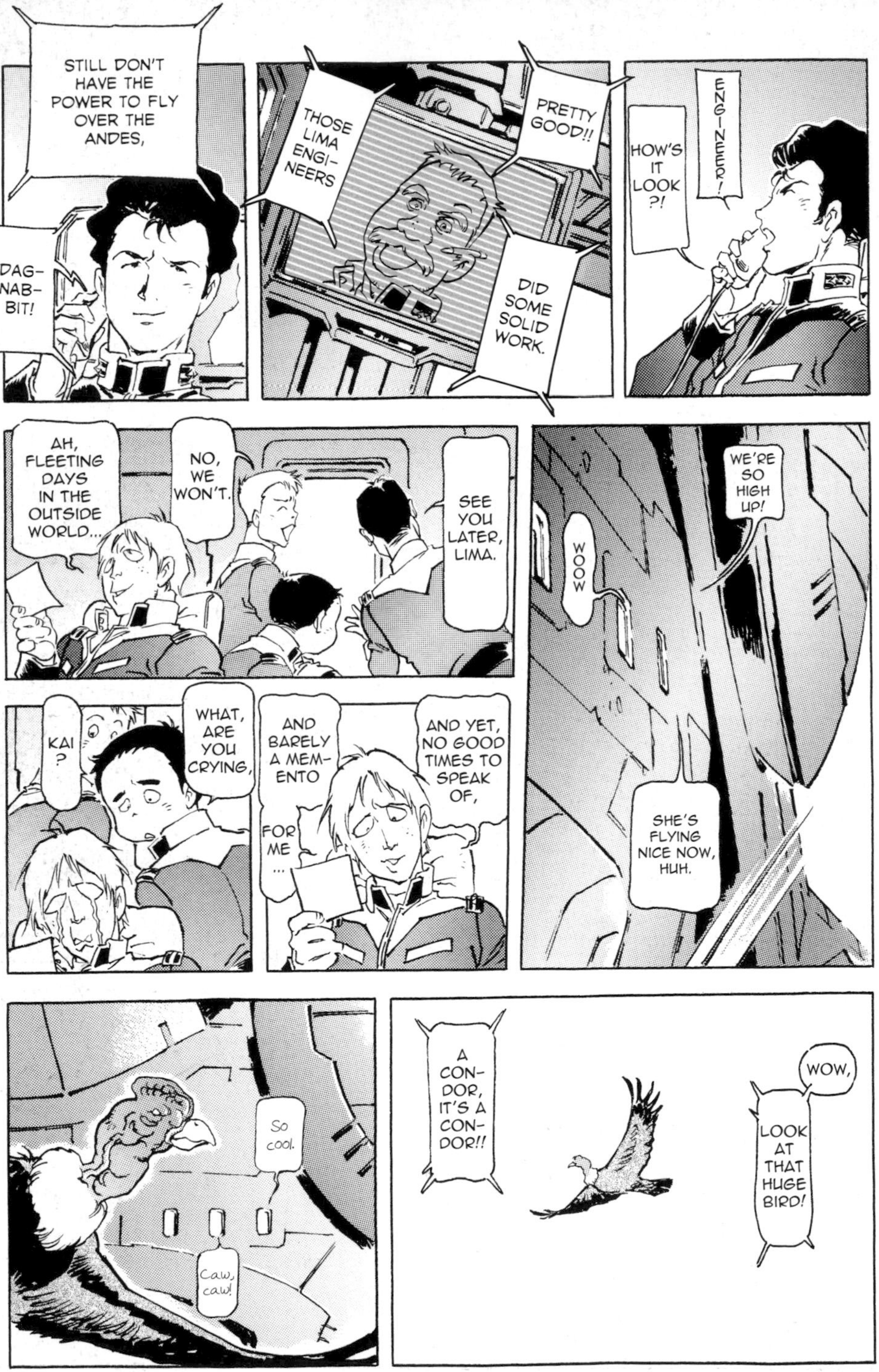
ENGINEER!
HOW'S IT LOOK?!
PRETTY GOOD!!
THOSE LIMA ENGINEERS
DID SOME SOLID WORK.
STILL DON'T HAVE THE POWER TO FLY OVER THE ANDES,
DAG-NAB-BIT!
WE'RE SO HIGH UP!
WOOW
SHE'S FLYING NICE NOW, HUH.
SEE YOU LATER, LIMA.
NO, WE WON'T.
AH, FLEETING DAYS IN THE OUTSIDE WORLD...
AND YET, NO GOOD TIMES TO SPEAK OF,
AND BARELY A MEMENTO
FOR ME ...
WHAT, ARE YOU CRYING,
KAI?
WOW,
LOOK AT THAT HUGE BIRD!
A CONDOR, IT'S A CONDOR!!
So cool.
Caw, caw!

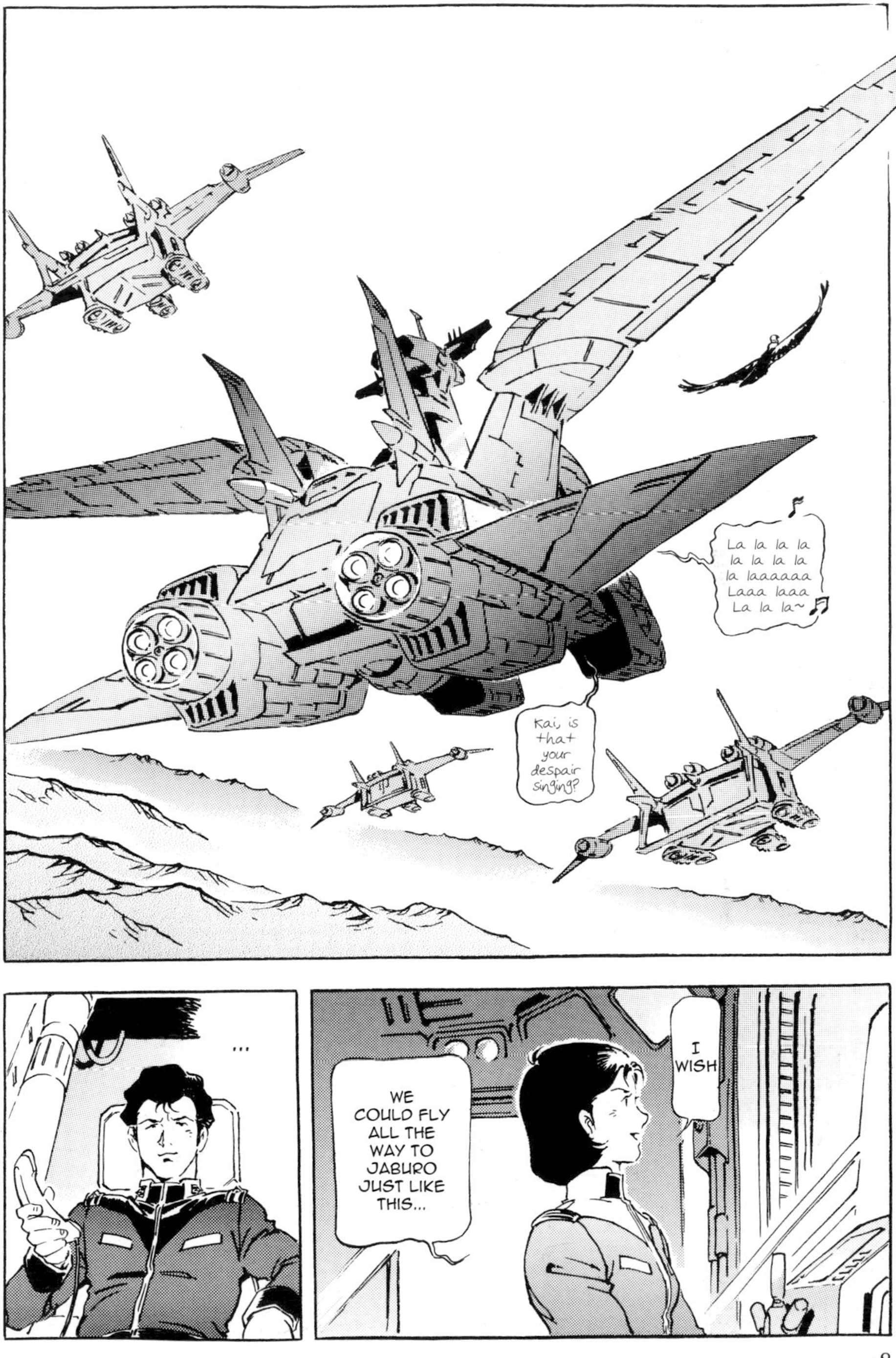
La la la la la la la la la laaaaaa Laaa laaa La la la~
Kai, is that your despair singing?
I WISH
WE COULD FLY ALL THE WAY TO JABURO JUST LIKE THIS...
...

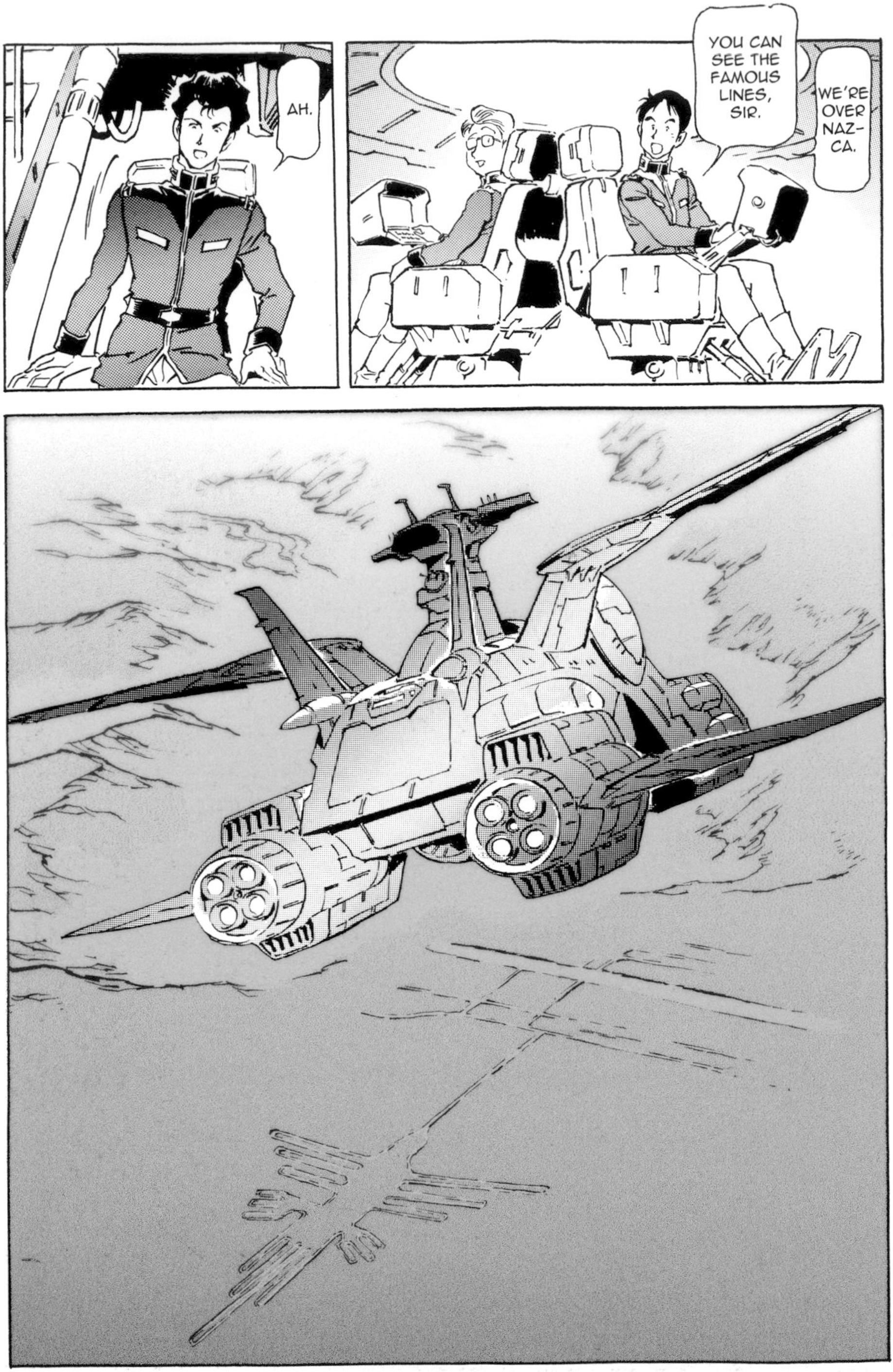
WE'RE OVER NAZ- CA.
YOU CAN SEE THE FAMOUS LINES, SIR.
AH.

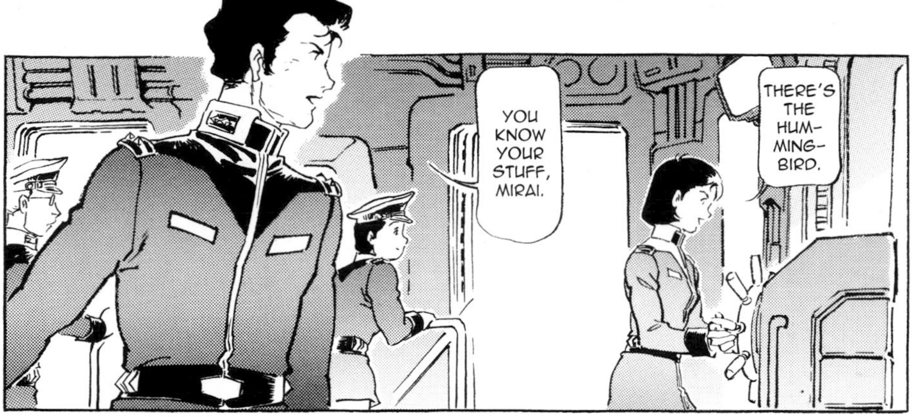
THERE'S THE HUMMING-BIRD.
YOU KNOW YOUR STUFF, MIRAI.

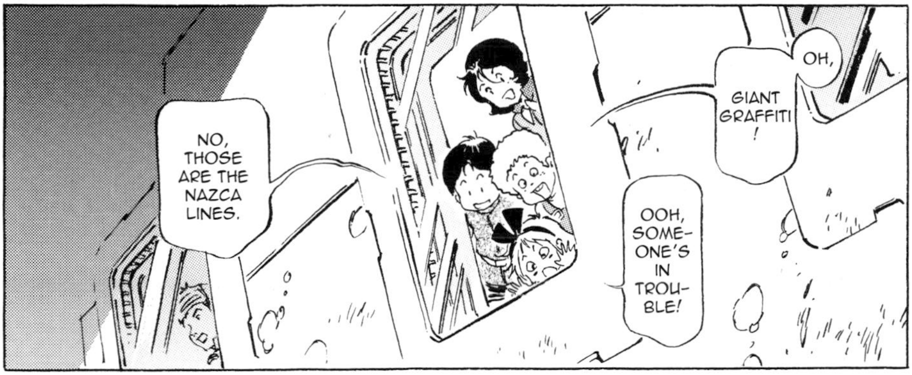
OH,
GIANT GRAFFITI!
OOH, SOMEONE'S IN TROUBLE!
NO, THOSE ARE THE NAZCA LINES.

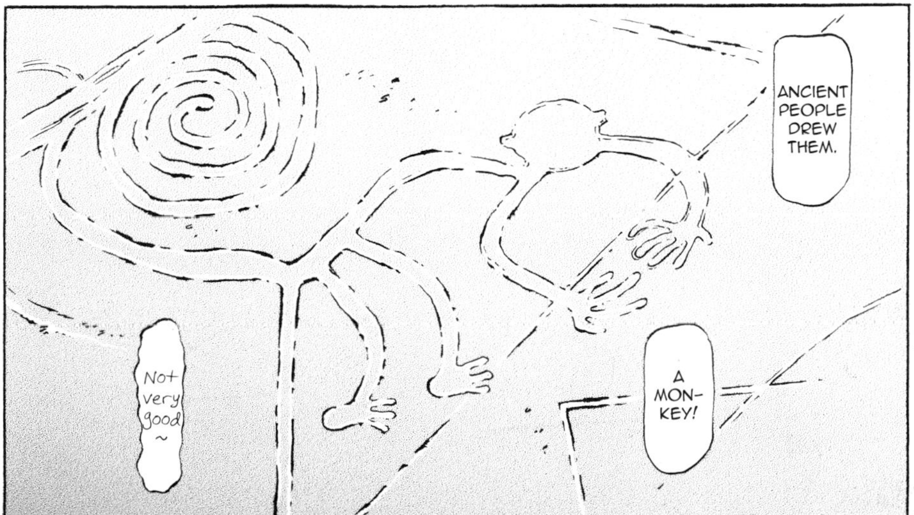
ANCIENT PEOPLE DREW THEM.
A MONKEY!
Not very good ~

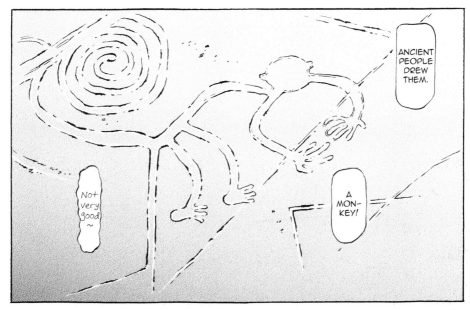

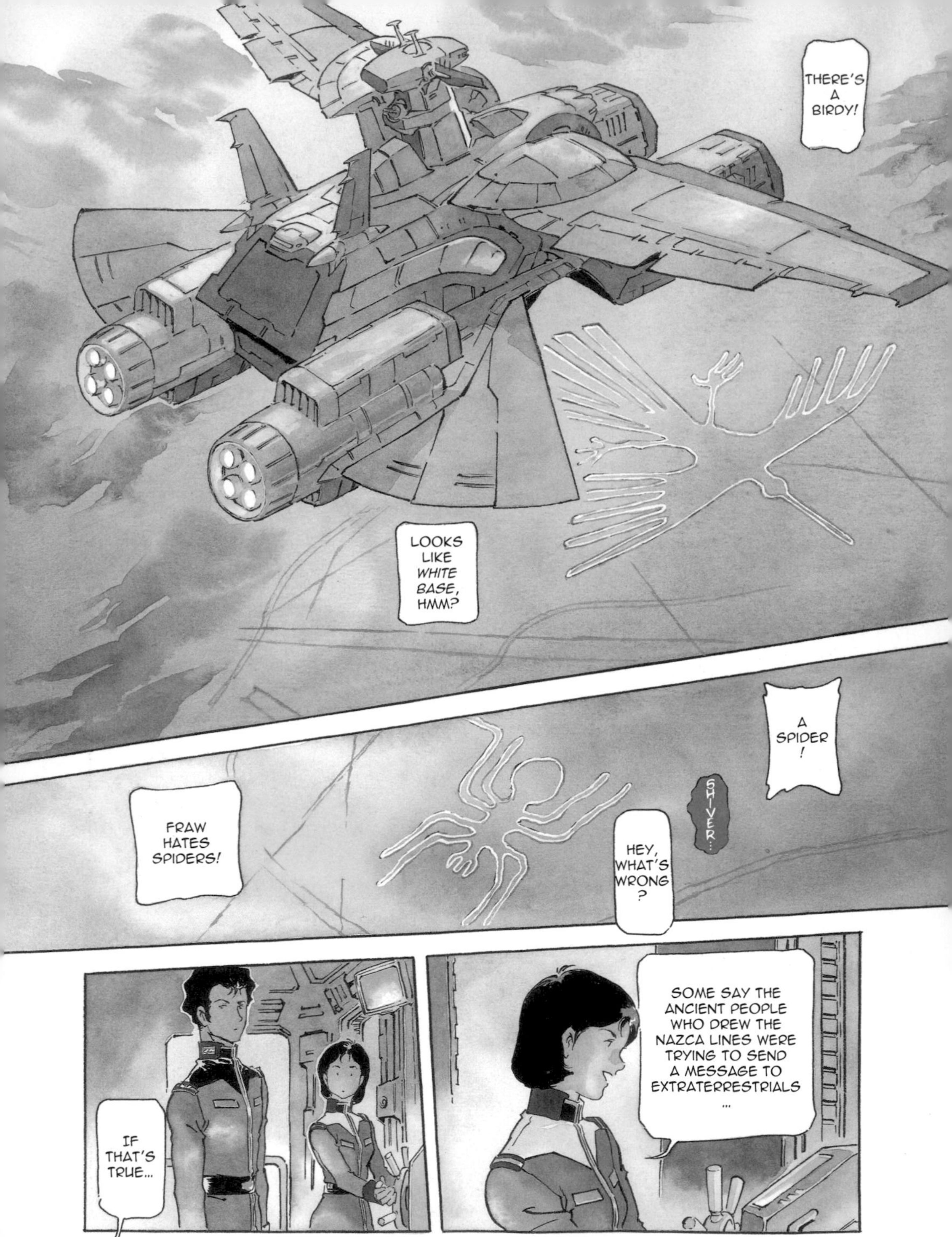
THERE'S A BIRDY!
LOOKS LIKE *WHITE BASE,* HMM?
A SPIDER!
SHIVER...
HEY, WHAT'S WRONG?
FRAW HATES SPIDERS!
SOME SAY THE ANCIENT PEOPLE WHO DREW THE NAZCA LINES WERE TRYING TO SEND A MESSAGE TO EXTRATERRESTRIALS...
IF THAT'S TRUE...

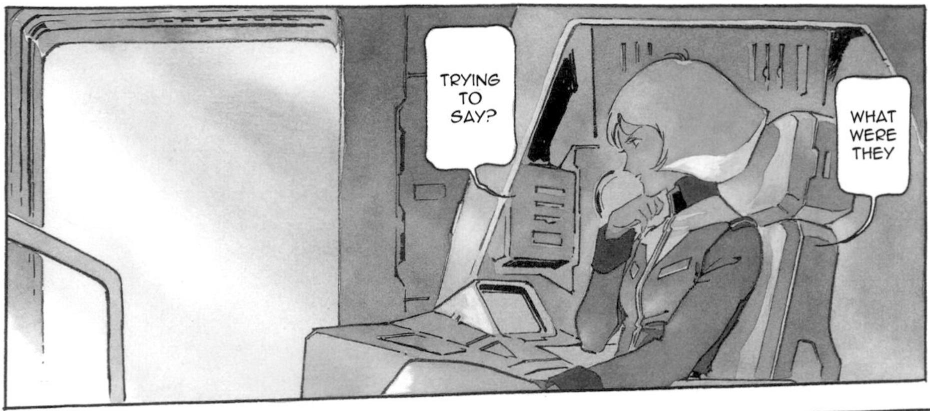
WHAT WERE THEY
TRYING TO SAY?

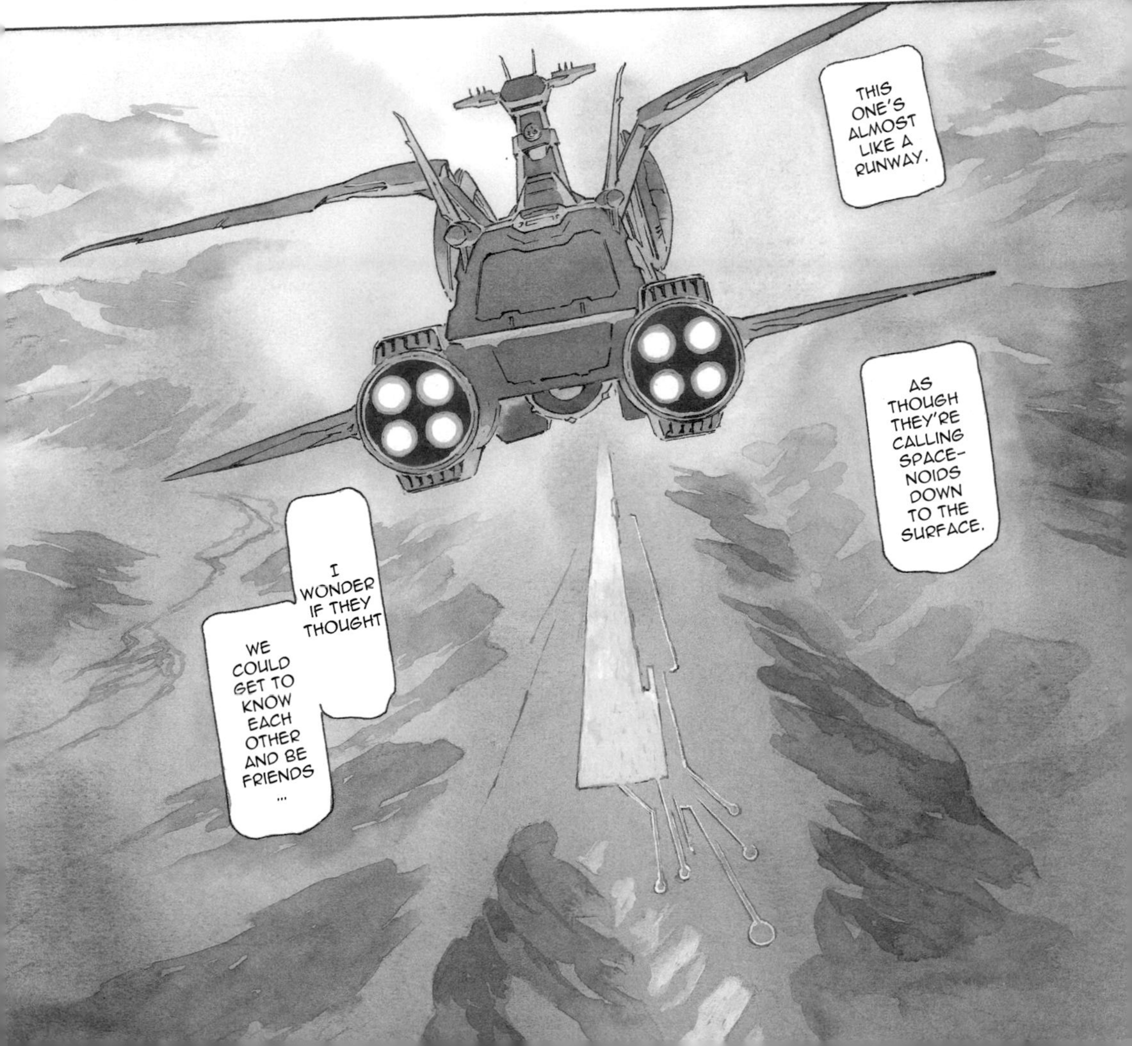
THIS ONE'S ALMOST LIKE A RUNWAY.
AS THOUGH THEY'RE CALLING SPACE-NOIDS DOWN TO THE SURFACE.
I WONDER IF THEY THOUGHT
WE COULD GET TO KNOW EACH OTHER AND BE FRIENDS ...

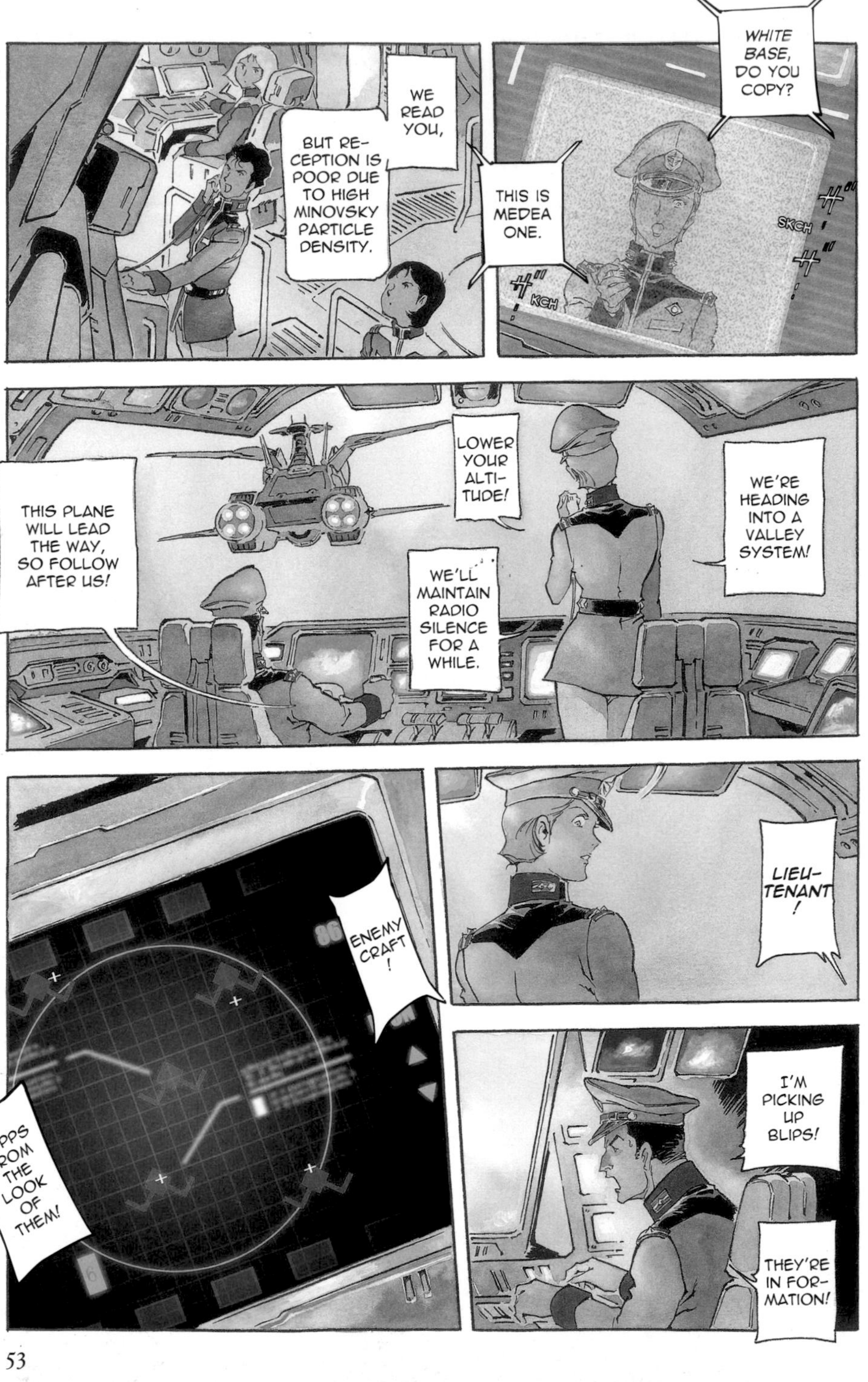
WHITE BASE, DO YOU COPY?
THIS IS MEDEA ONE.
SKCH
KCH
WE READ YOU,
BUT RECEPTION IS POOR DUE TO HIGH MINOVSKY PARTICLE DENSITY.
WE'RE HEADING INTO A VALLEY SYSTEM!
LOWER YOUR ALTITUDE!
WE'LL MAINTAIN RADIO SILENCE FOR A WHILE.
THIS PLANE WILL LEAD THE WAY, SO FOLLOW AFTER US!
LIEUTENANT!
I'M PICKING UP BLIPS!
THEY'RE IN FORMATION!
ENEMY CRAFT!
DOPPS FROM THE LOOK OF THEM!

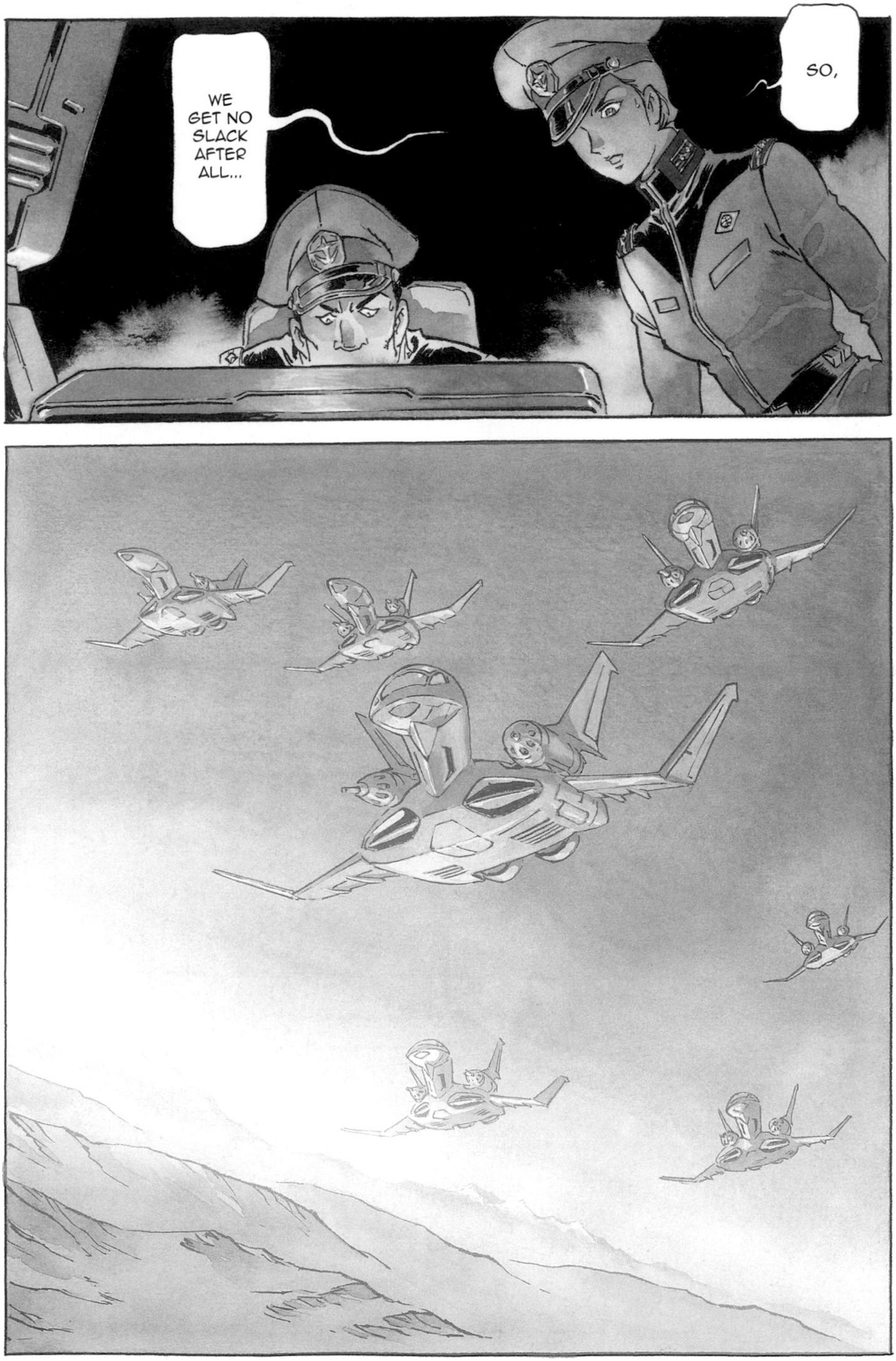
SO,
WE GET NO SLACK AFTER ALL...

SECTION II

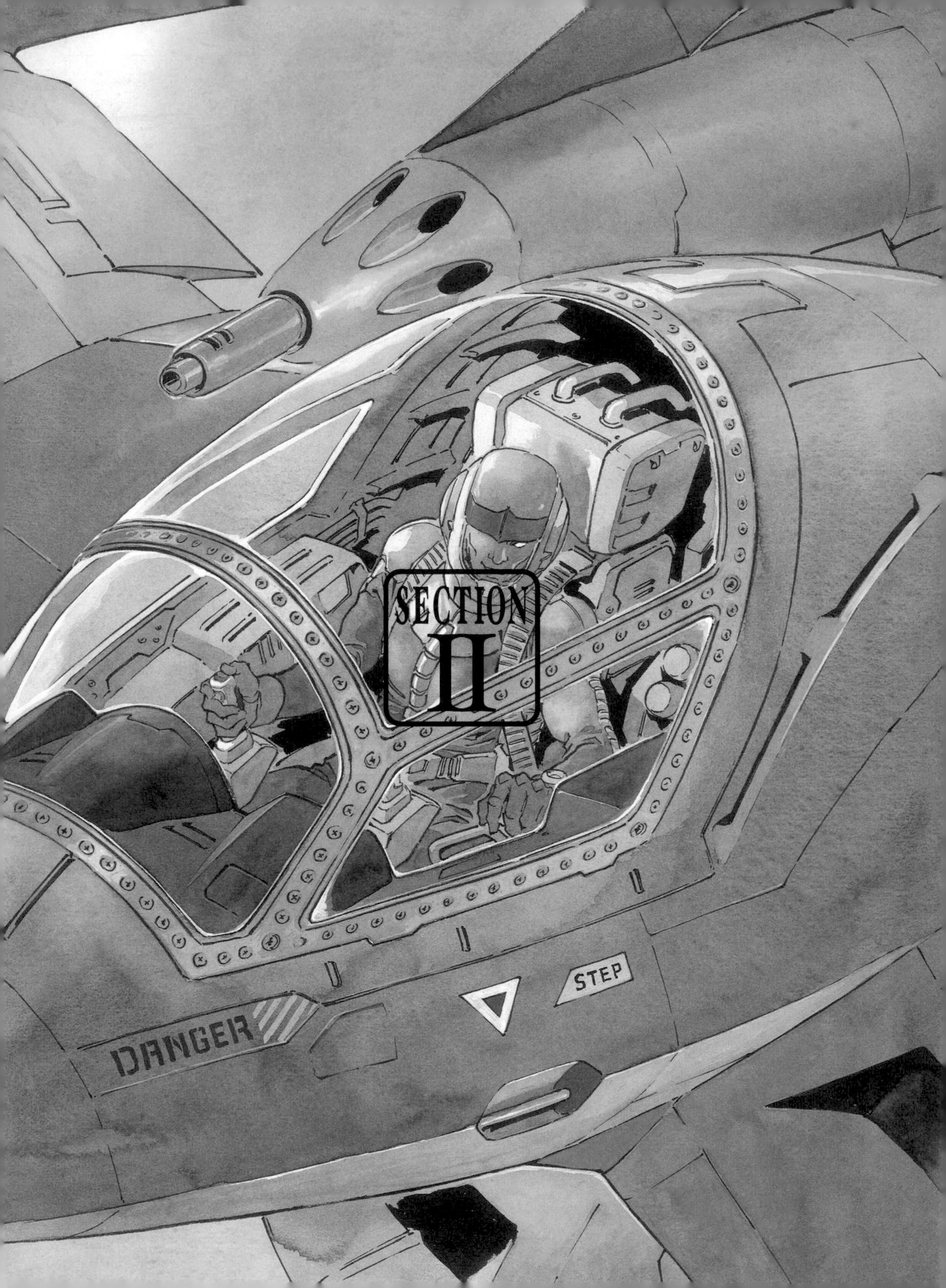

STEP
DANGER

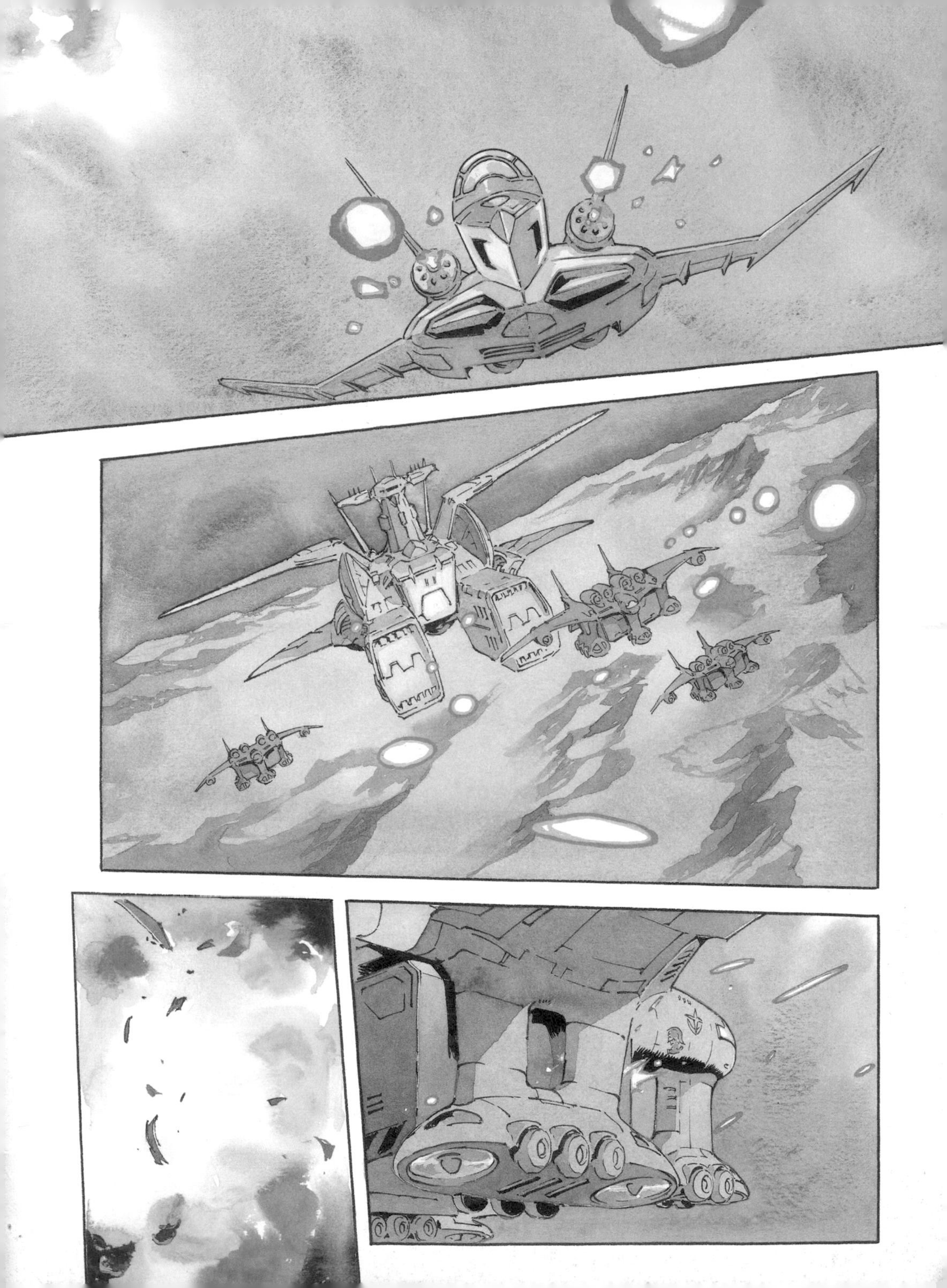

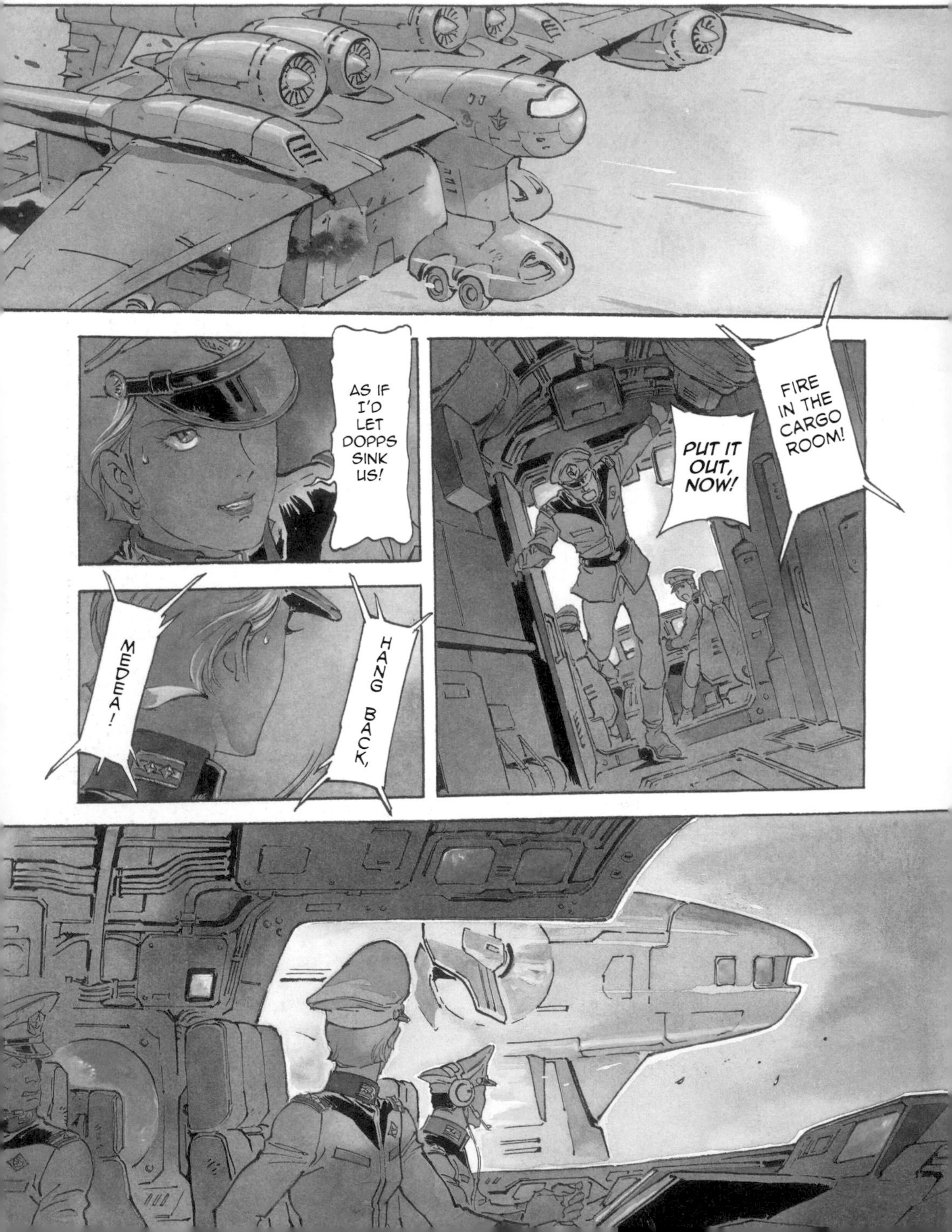
FIRE IN THE CARGO ROOM!
PUT IT OUT, NOW!
AS IF I'D LET DOPPS SINK US!
HANG BACK, MEDEA!

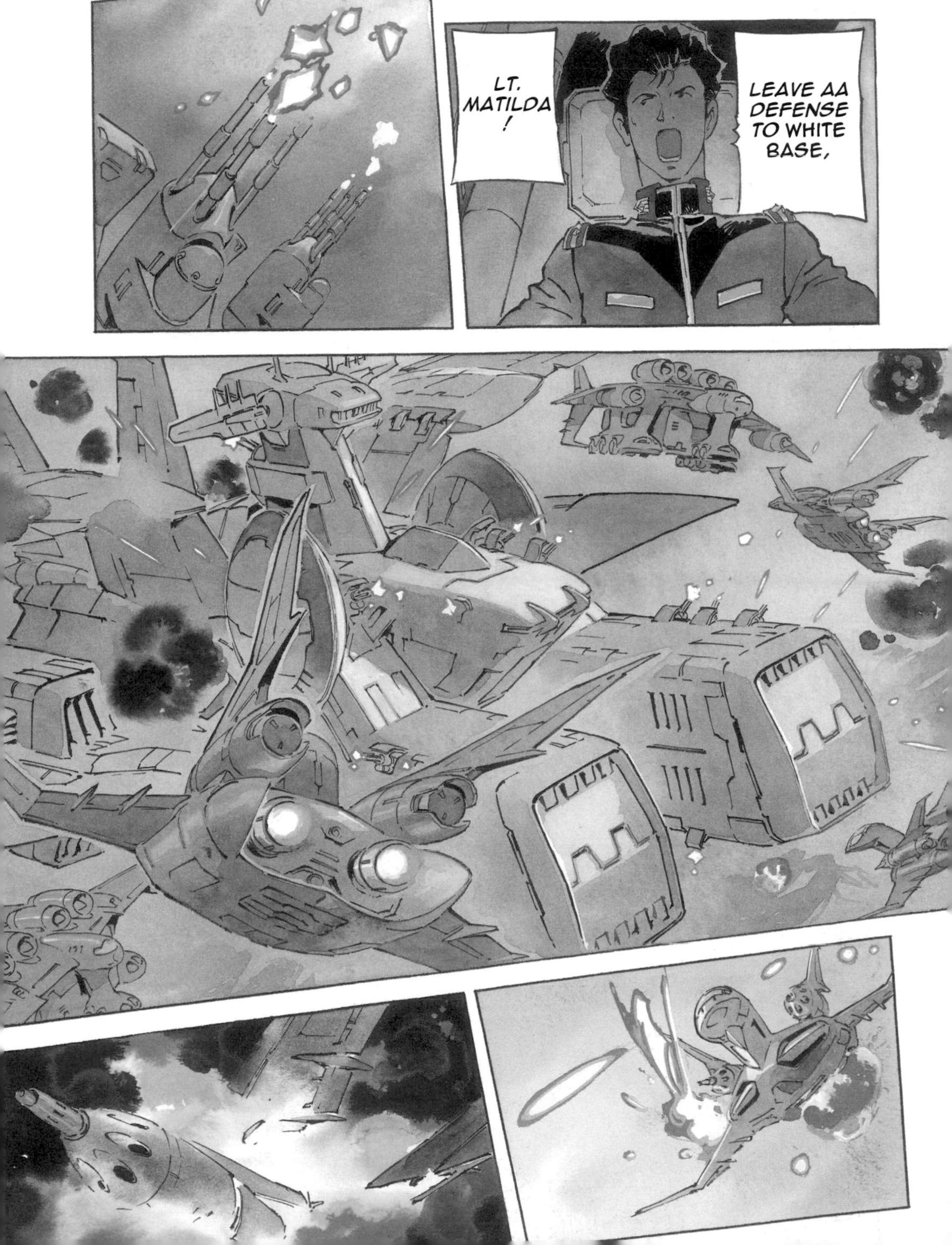
LEAVE AA DEFENSE TO WHITE BASE,
LT. MATILDA!

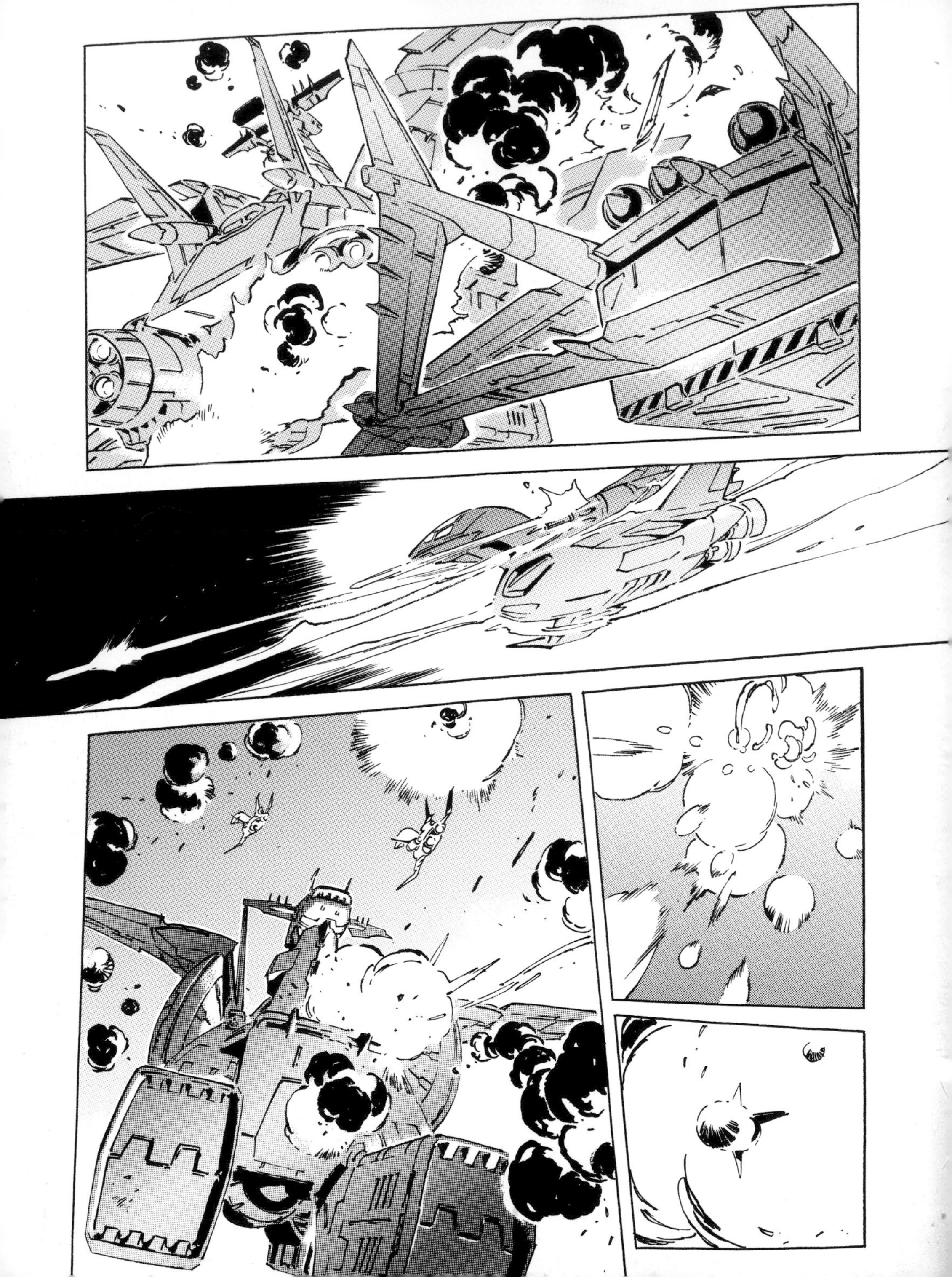

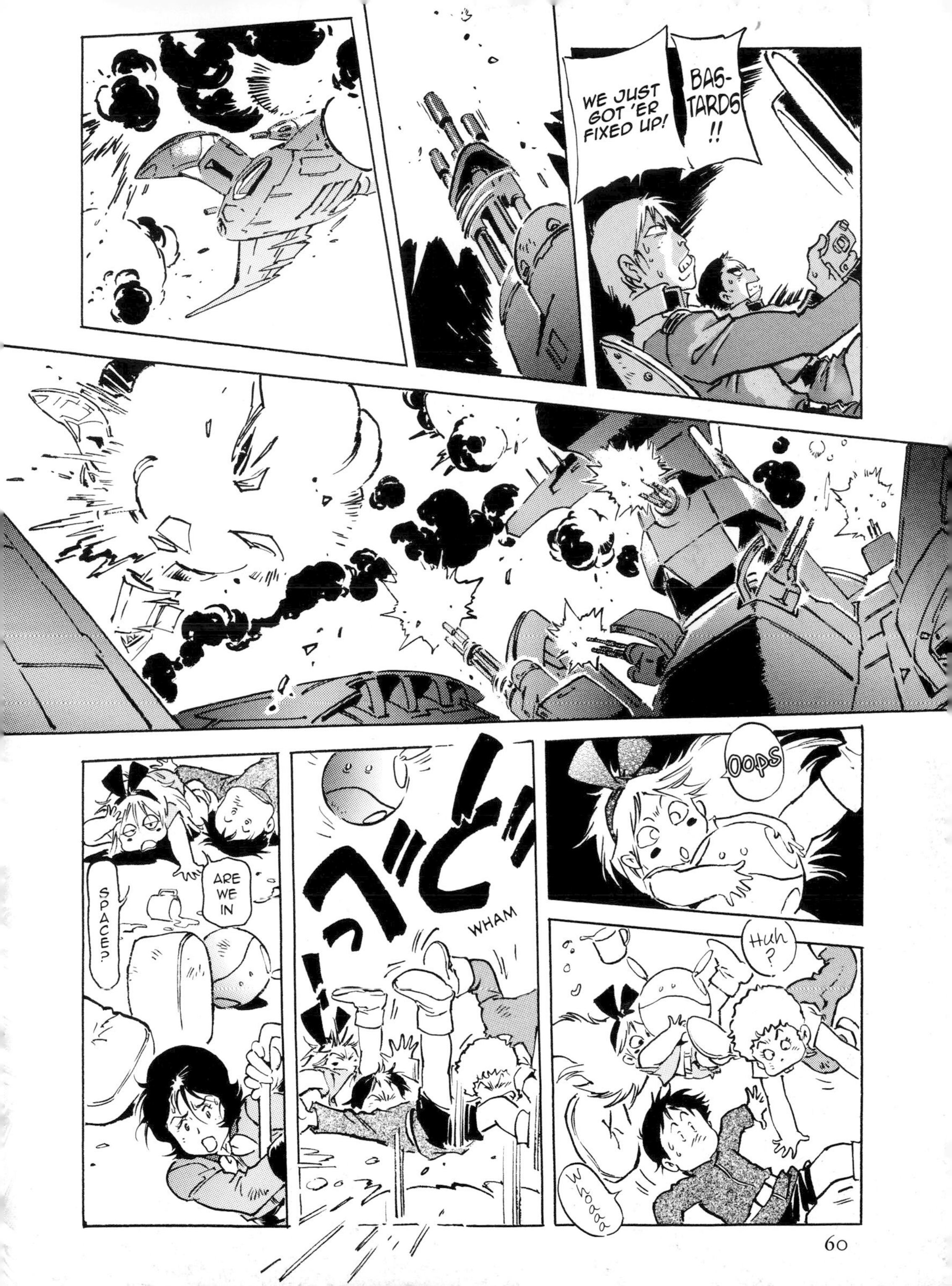
BAS-TARDS !!
WE JUST GOT 'ER FIXED UP!
OOPS
Huh ?
Whoooa
WHAM
ARE WE IN
SPACE?

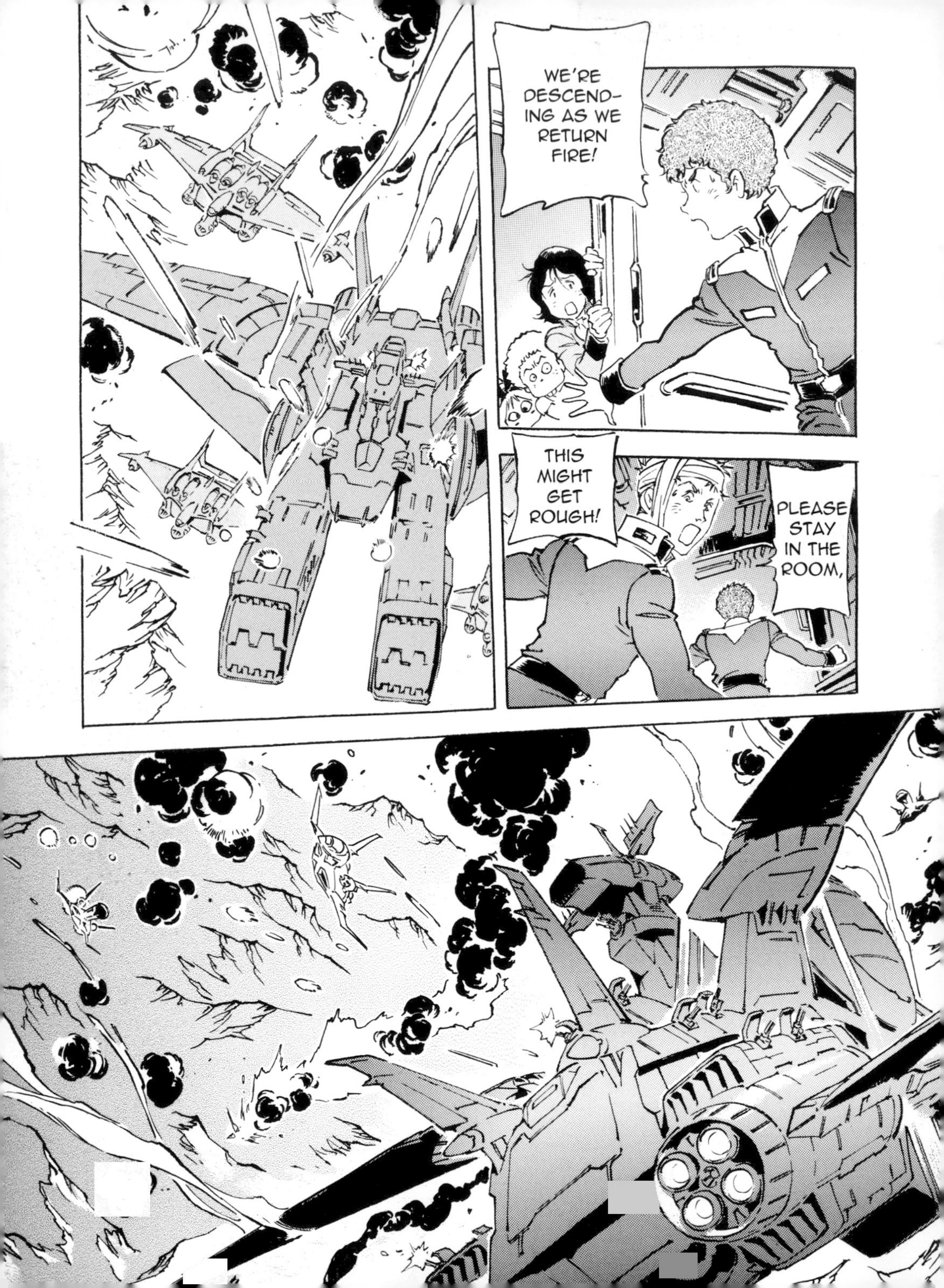
WE'RE DESCEND-ING AS WE RETURN FIRE!
PLEASE STAY IN THE ROOM,
THIS MIGHT GET ROUGH!

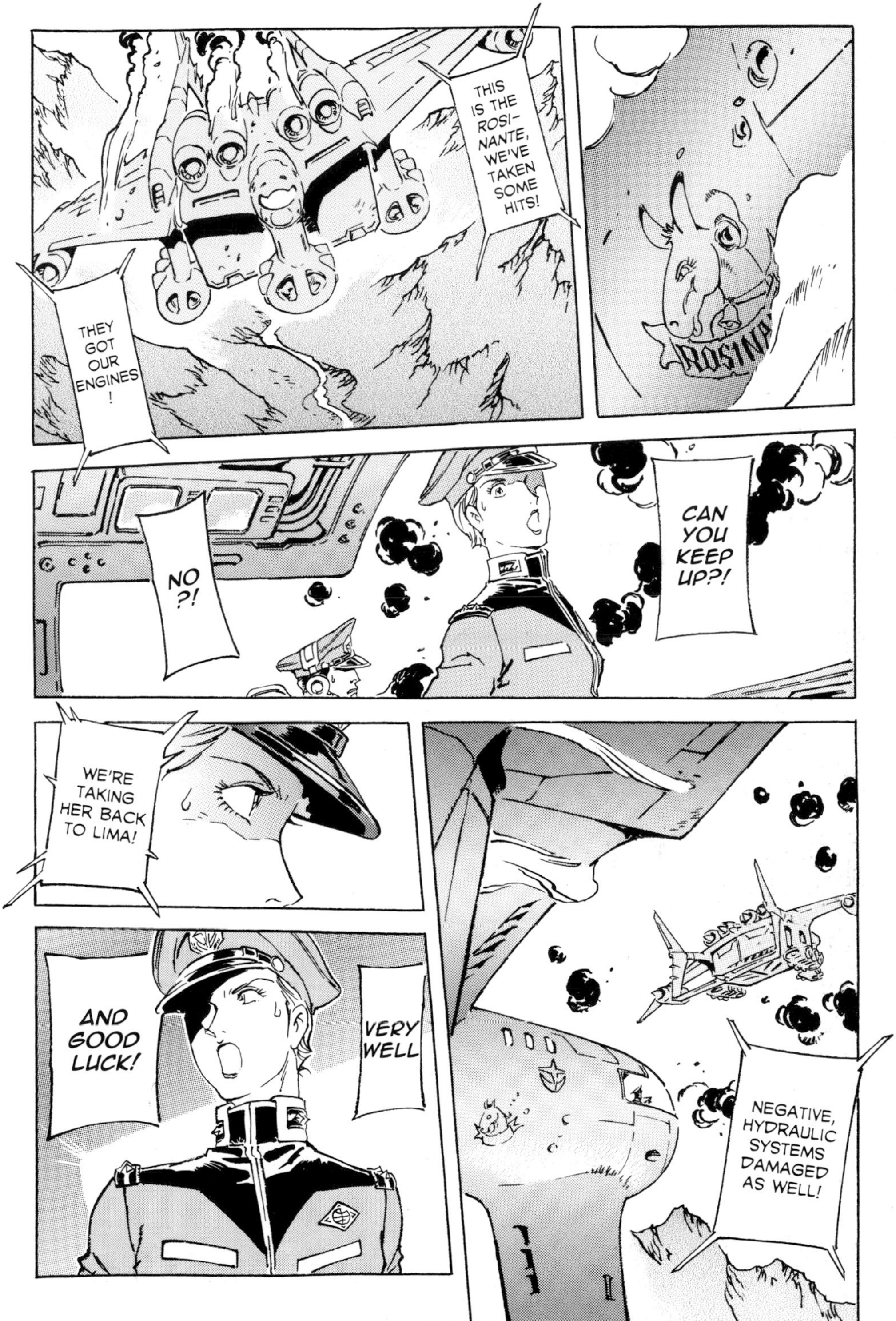
ROSINA
THIS IS THE ROSI-NANTE, WE'VE TAKEN SOME HITS!
THEY GOT OUR ENGINES!
CAN YOU KEEP UP?!
NO ?!
NEGATIVE, HYDRAULIC SYSTEMS DAMAGED AS WELL!
WE'RE TAKING HER BACK TO LIMA!
VERY WELL
AND GOOD LUCK!

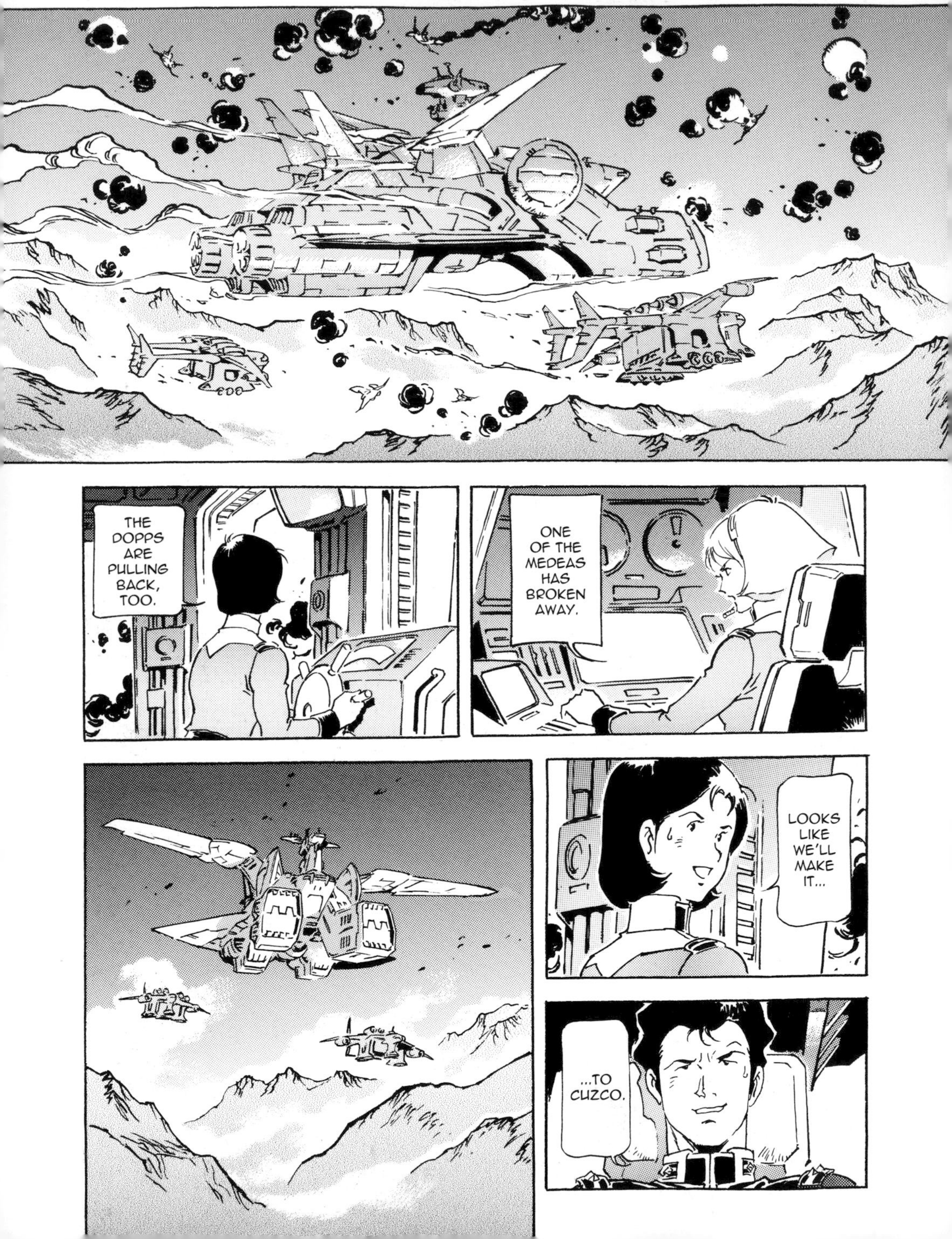
ONE OF THE MEDEAS HAS BROKEN AWAY.
THE DOPPS ARE PULLING BACK, TOO.
LOOKS LIKE WE'LL MAKE IT...
...TO CUZCO.

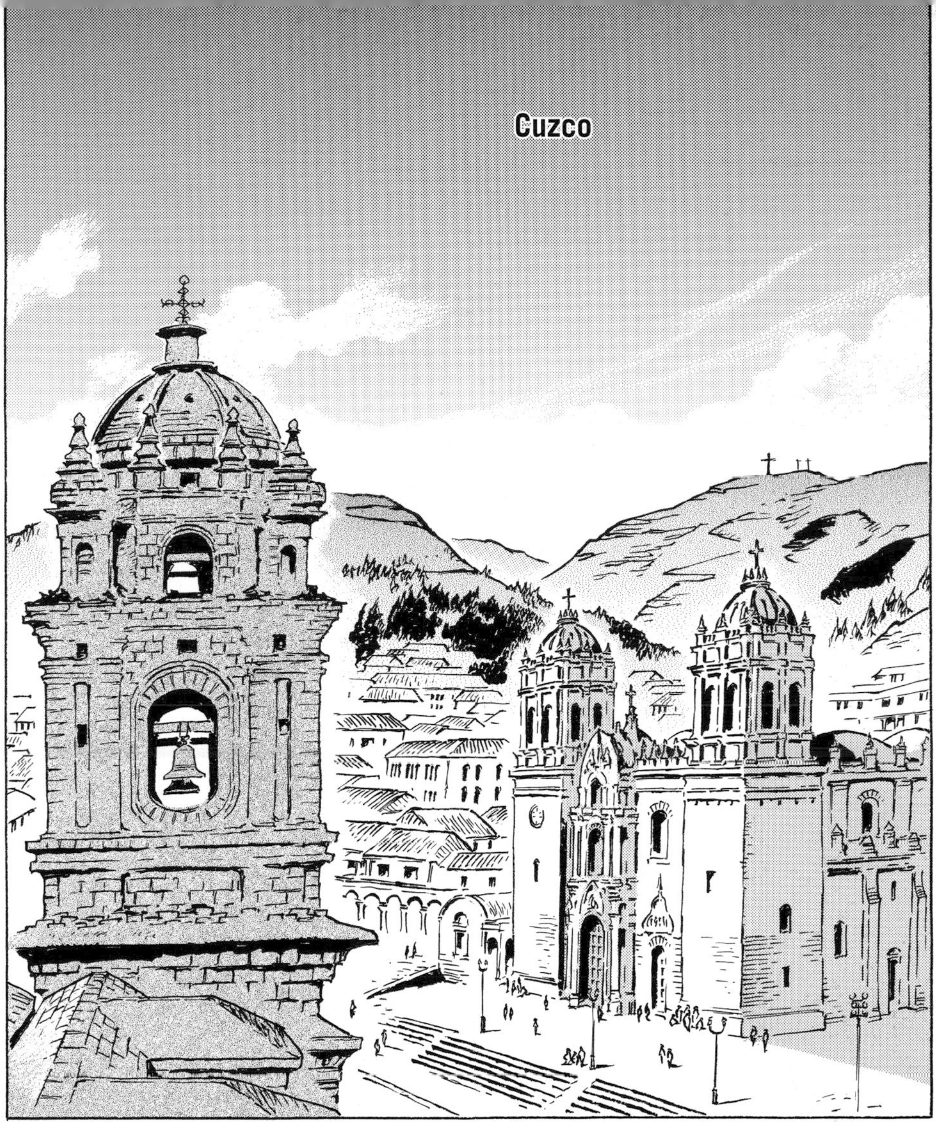
Cuzco
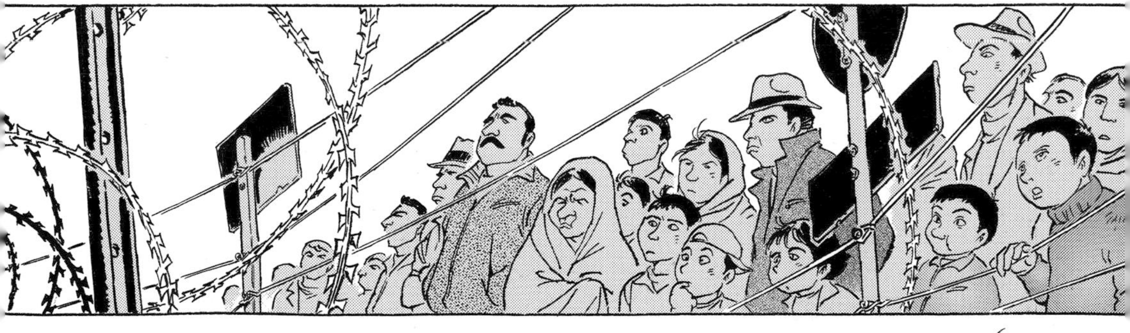

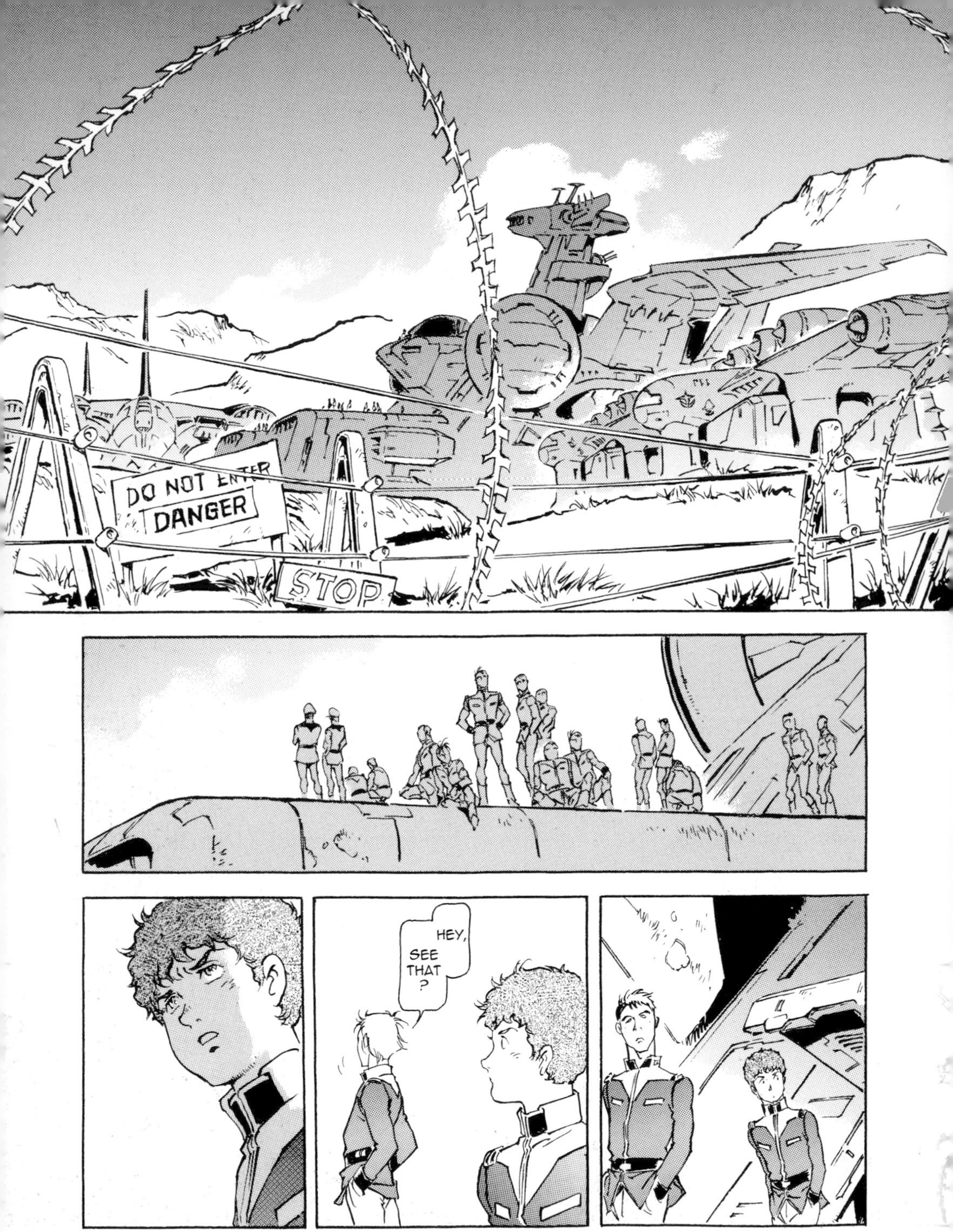
DO NOT ENTER
DANGER
STOP
HEY, SEE THAT?

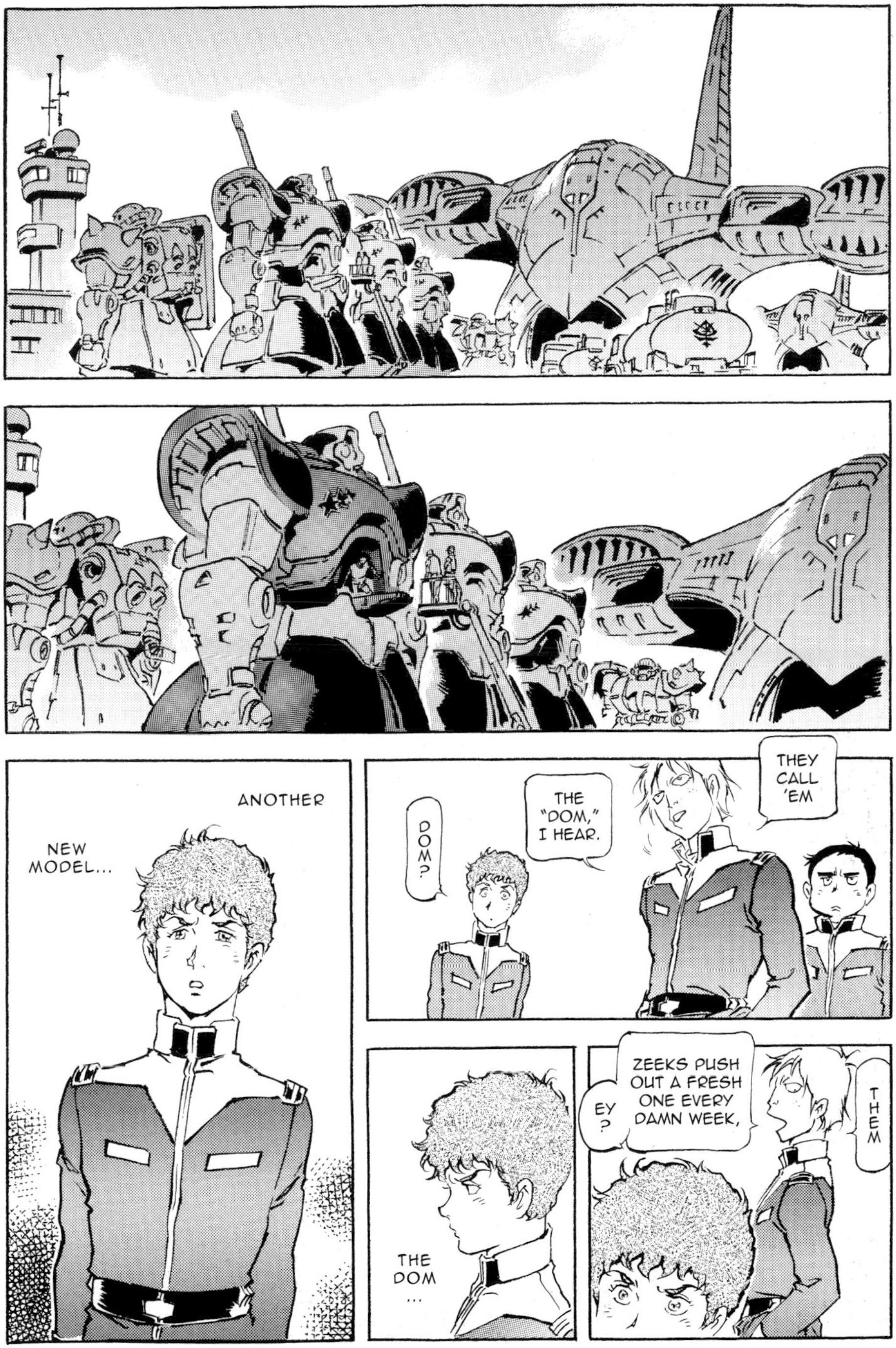
THEY CALL 'EM
THE "DOM," I HEAR.
DOM?
THEM
ZEEKS PUSH OUT A FRESH ONE EVERY DAMN WEEK,
EY?
THE DOM ...
ANOTHER
NEW MODEL...

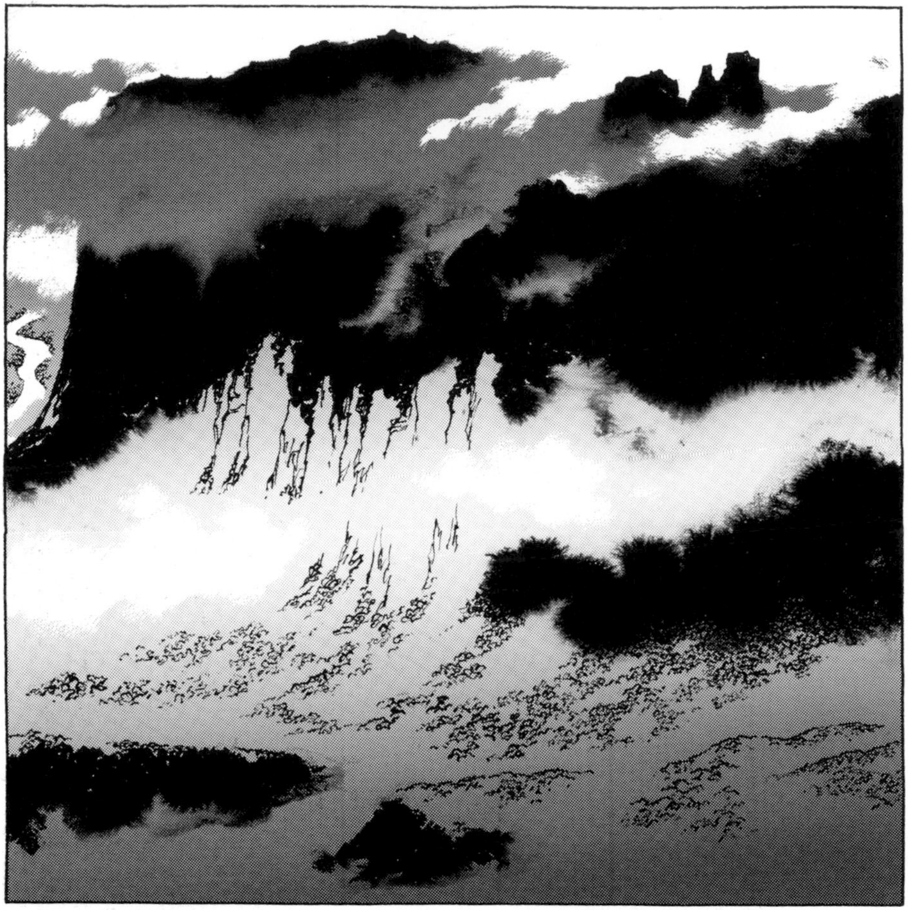
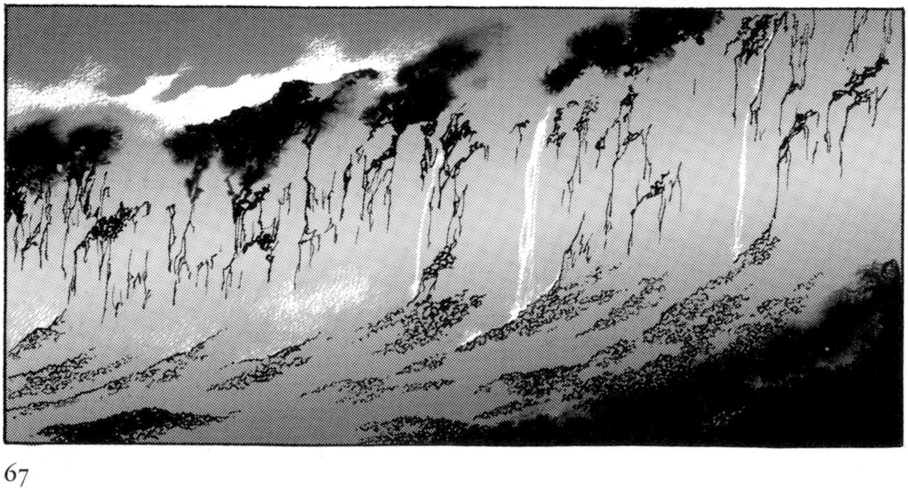

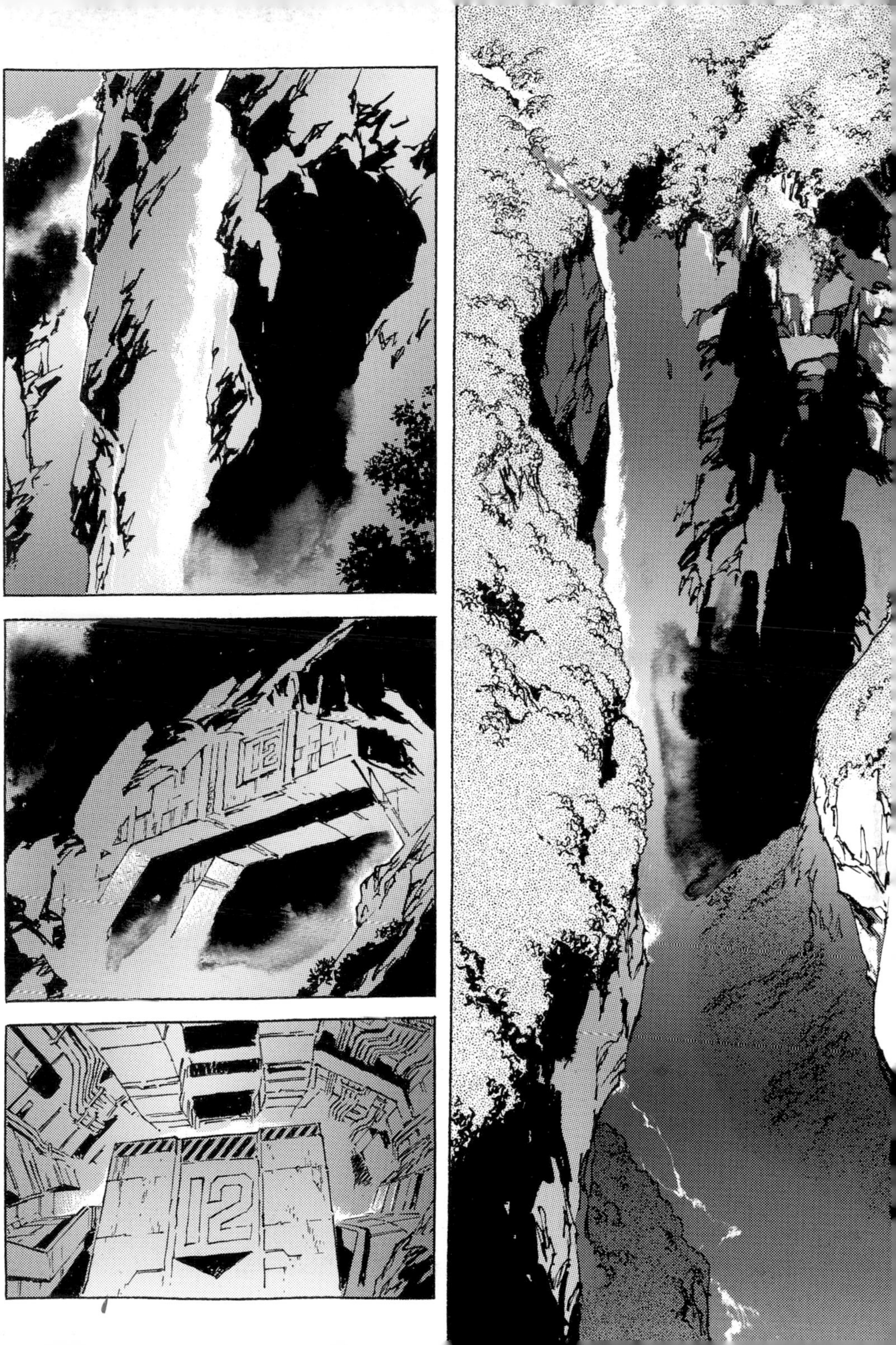
12
12

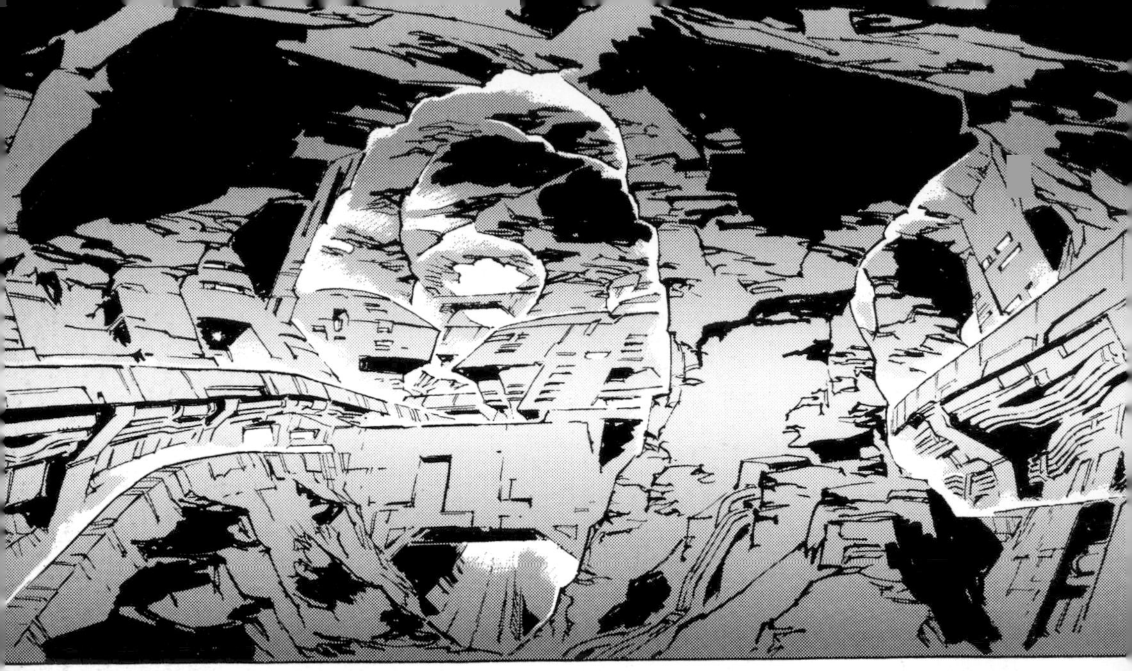

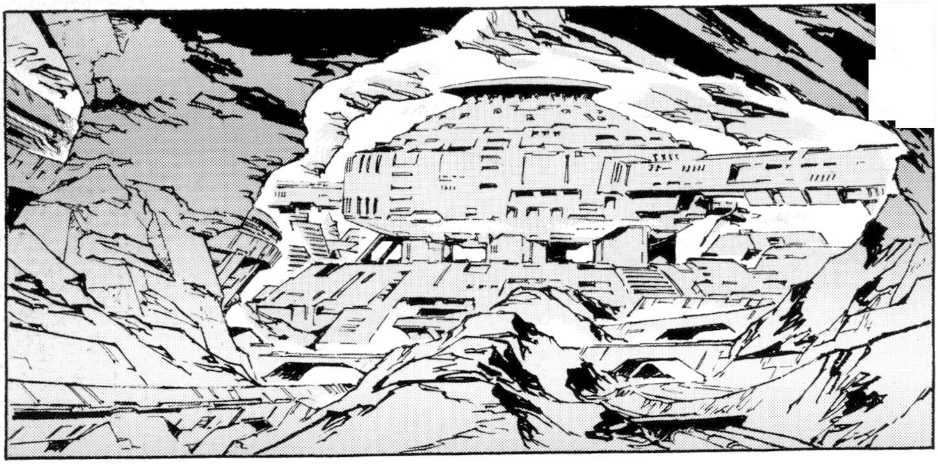

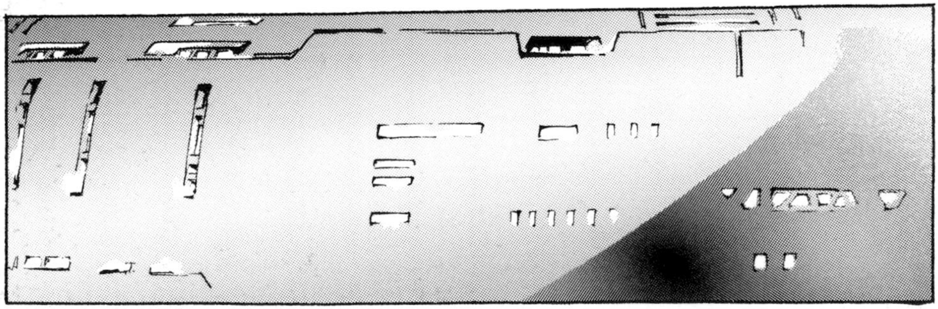

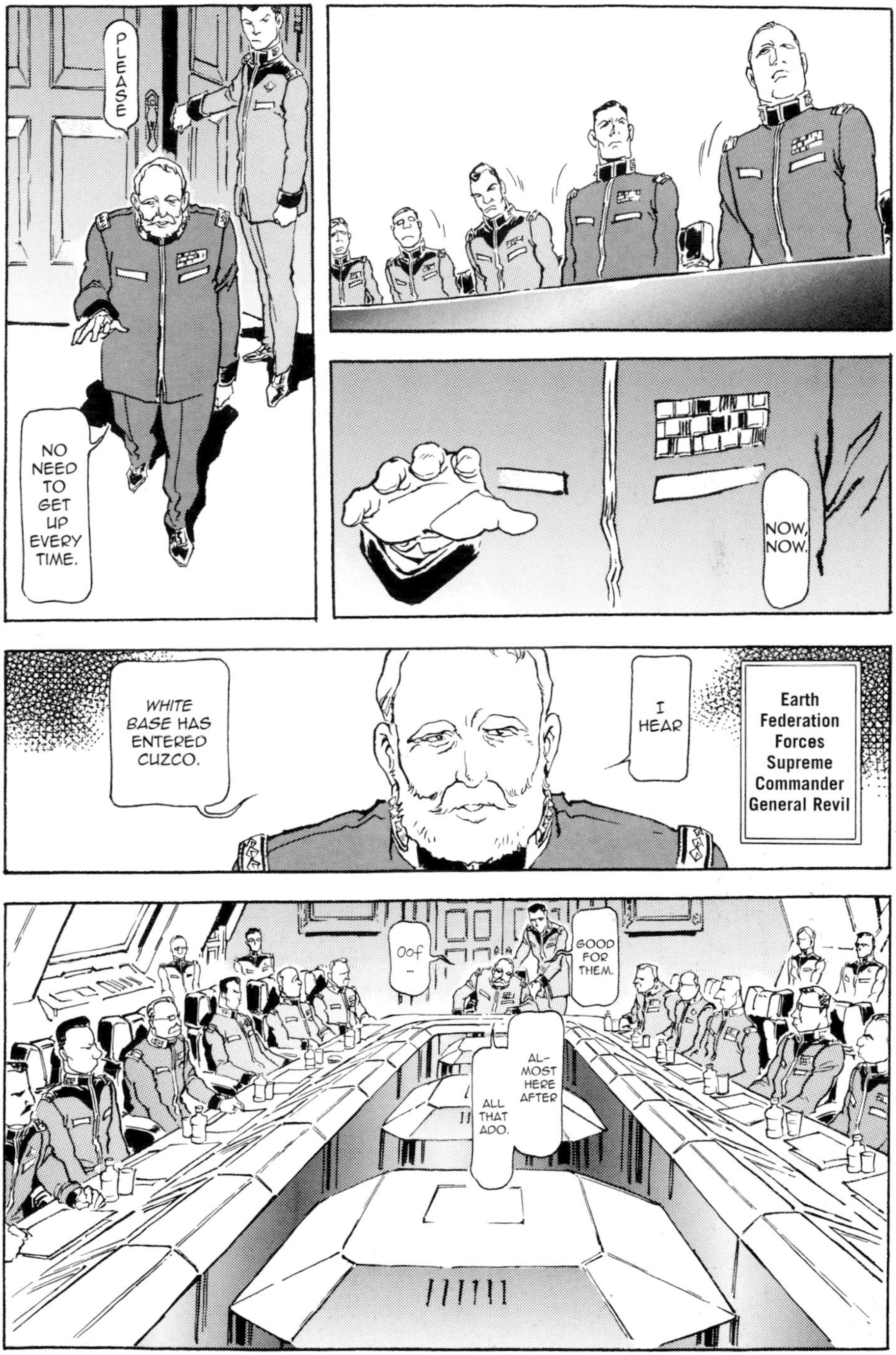
NOW, NOW.
PLEASE
NO NEED TO GET UP EVERY TIME.
Earth Federation Forces Supreme Commander General Revil
I HEAR
WHITE BASE HAS ENTERED CUZCO.
GOOD FOR THEM.
Oof ...
ALMOST HERE AFTER ALL THAT ADO.

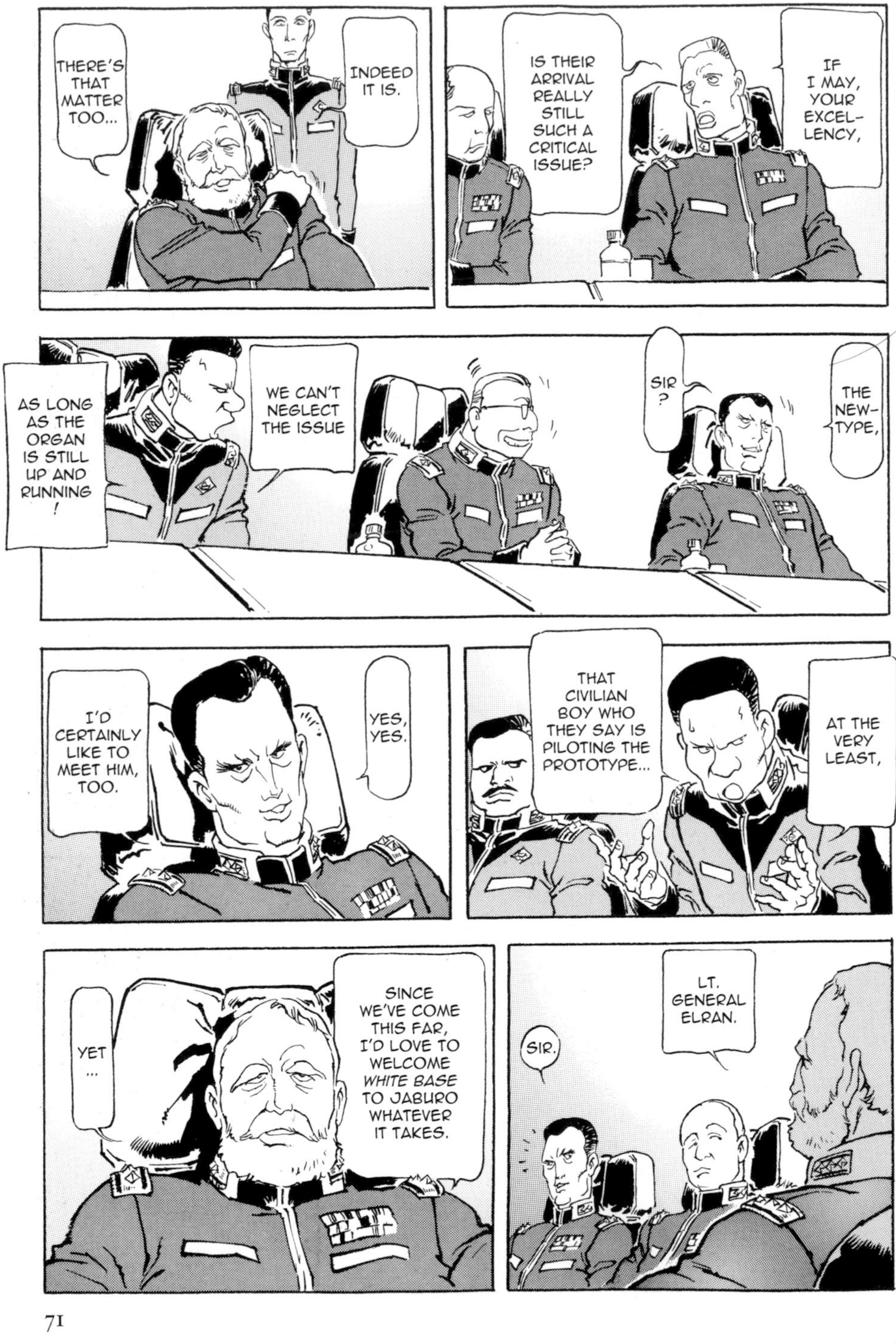
IF I MAY, YOUR EXCELLENCY,
IS THEIR ARRIVAL REALLY STILL SUCH A CRITICAL ISSUE?
INDEED IT IS.
THERE'S THAT MATTER TOO...
THE NEW-TYPE,
SIR?
WE CAN'T NEGLECT THE ISSUE
AS LONG AS THE ORGAN IS STILL UP AND RUNNING!
AT THE VERY LEAST,
THAT CIVILIAN BOY WHO THEY SAY IS PILOTING THE PROTOTYPE...
YES, YES.
I'D CERTAINLY LIKE TO MEET HIM, TOO.
LT. GENERAL ELRAN.
SIR.
SINCE WE'VE COME THIS FAR, I'D LOVE TO WELCOME *WHITE BASE* TO JABURO WHATEVER IT TAKES.
YET...

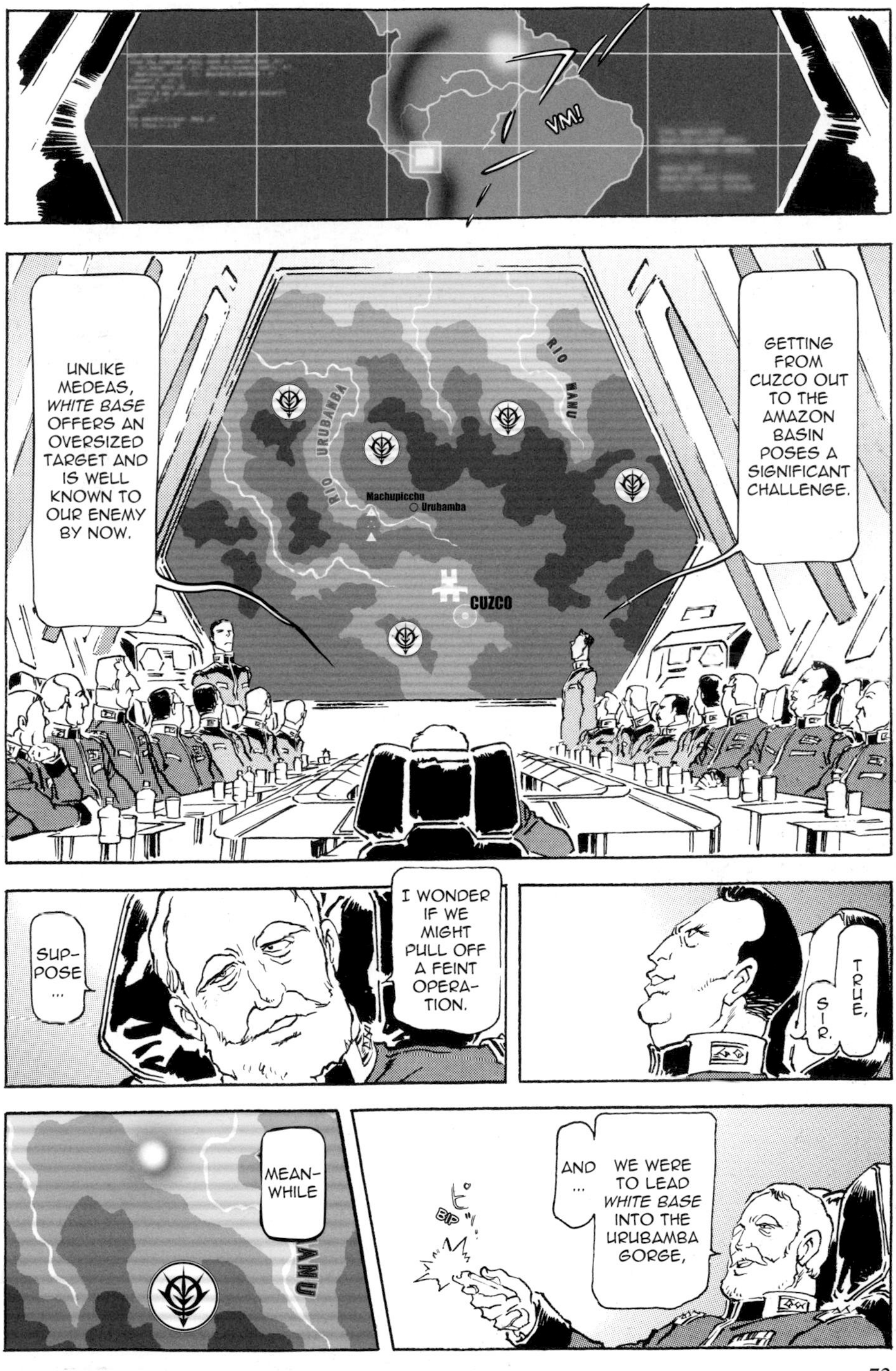
VM!
GETTING FROM CUZCO OUT TO THE AMAZON BASIN POSES A SIGNIFICANT CHALLENGE.
RIO MANU
RIO URUBAMBA
Machupicchu
Urubamba
CUZCO
UNLIKE MEDEAS, *WHITE BASE* OFFERS AN OVERSIZED TARGET AND IS WELL KNOWN TO OUR ENEMY BY NOW.
TRUE, SIR.
I WONDER IF WE MIGHT PULL OFF A FEINT OPERATION.
SUP-POSE ...
AND ...
WE WERE TO LEAD *WHITE BASE* INTO THE URUBAMBA GORGE,
ピ
BIP
MEAN-WHILE
ANU

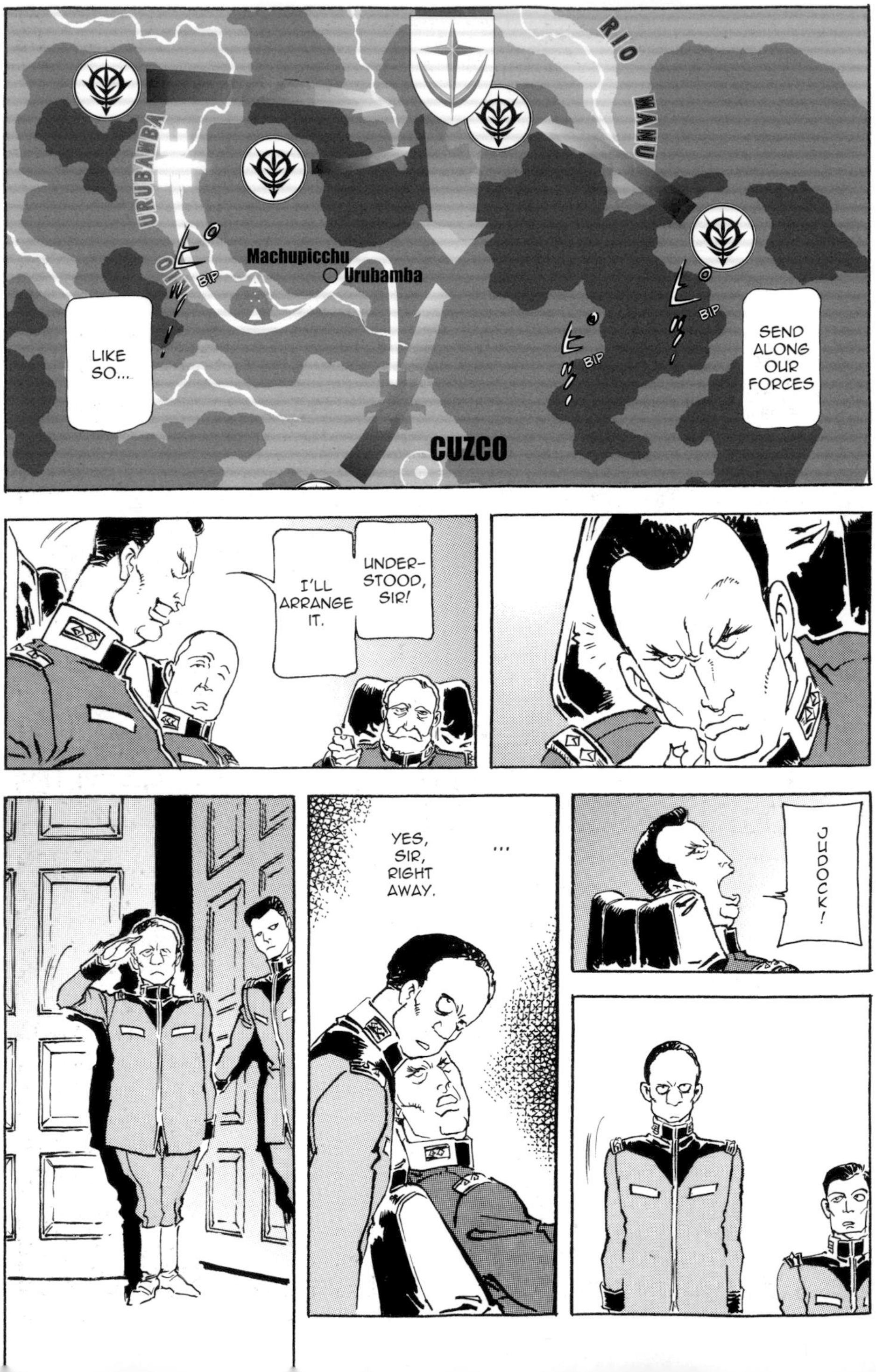
RIO MANU
BIP
BIP
SEND ALONG OUR FORCES
Machupicchu
Urubamba
RIO URUBAMBA
BIP
LIKE SO...
CUZCO
UNDER-STOOD, SIR!
I'LL ARRANGE IT.
JUDOCK!
...
YES, SIR, RIGHT AWAY.

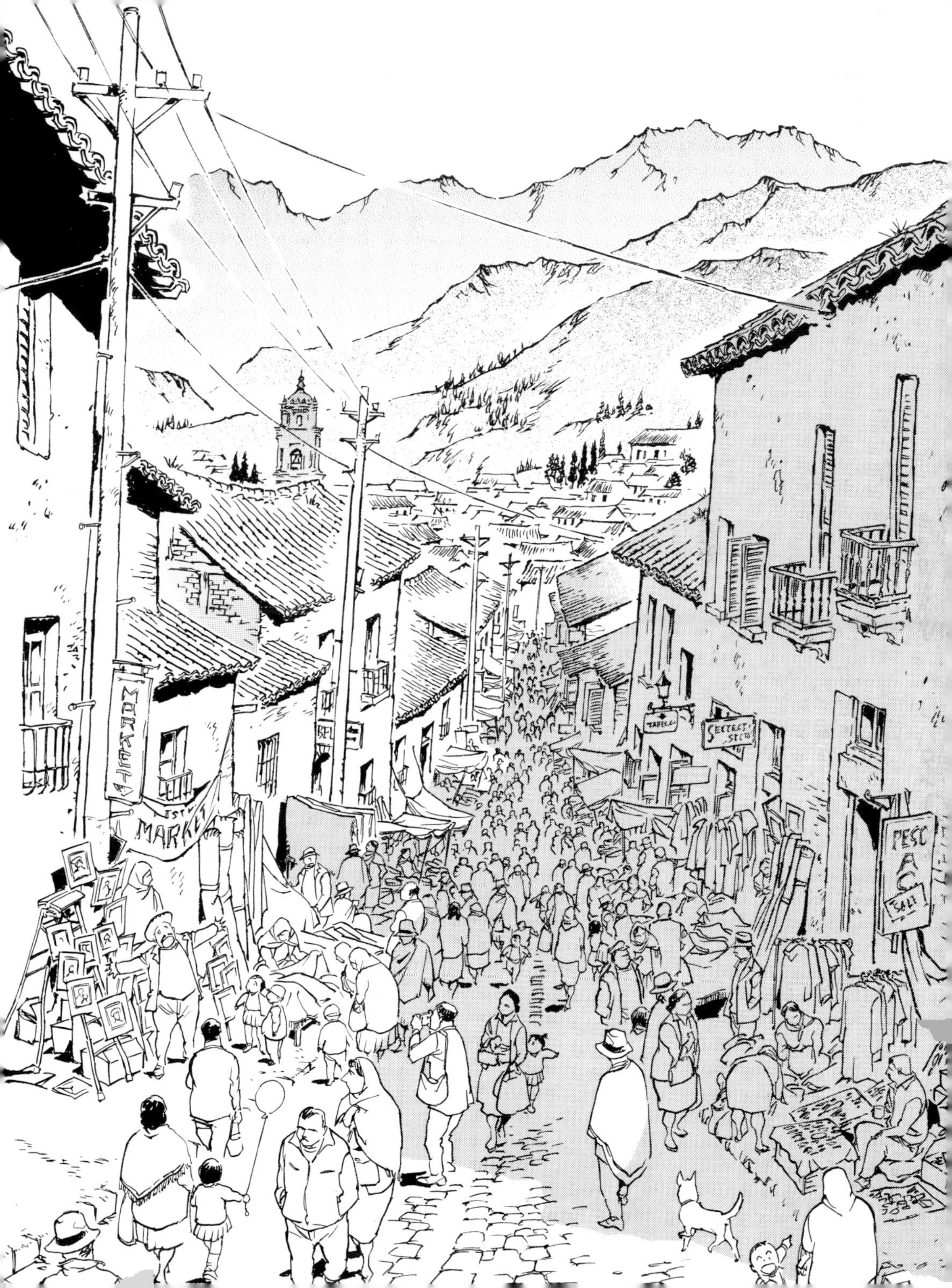
MARKET
MARKET
SALE

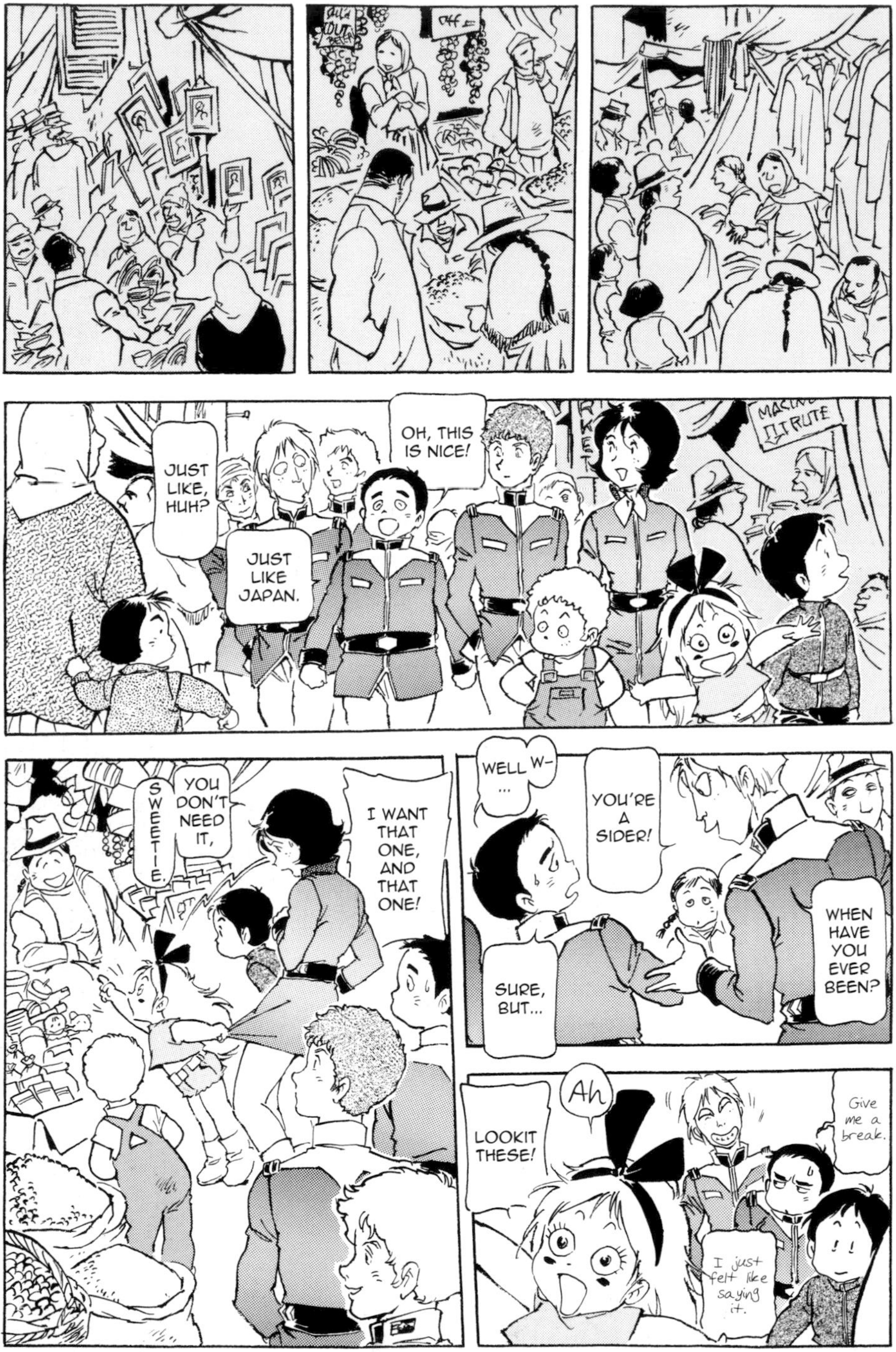
OH, THIS IS NICE!
JUST LIKE, HUH?
JUST LIKE JAPAN.
YOU'RE A SIDER!
WELL W- ...
WHEN HAVE YOU EVER BEEN?
SURE, BUT...
Give me a break.
Ah
LOOKIT THESE!
I just felt like saying it.
I WANT THAT ONE, AND THAT ONE!
YOU DON'T NEED IT,
SWEETIE.

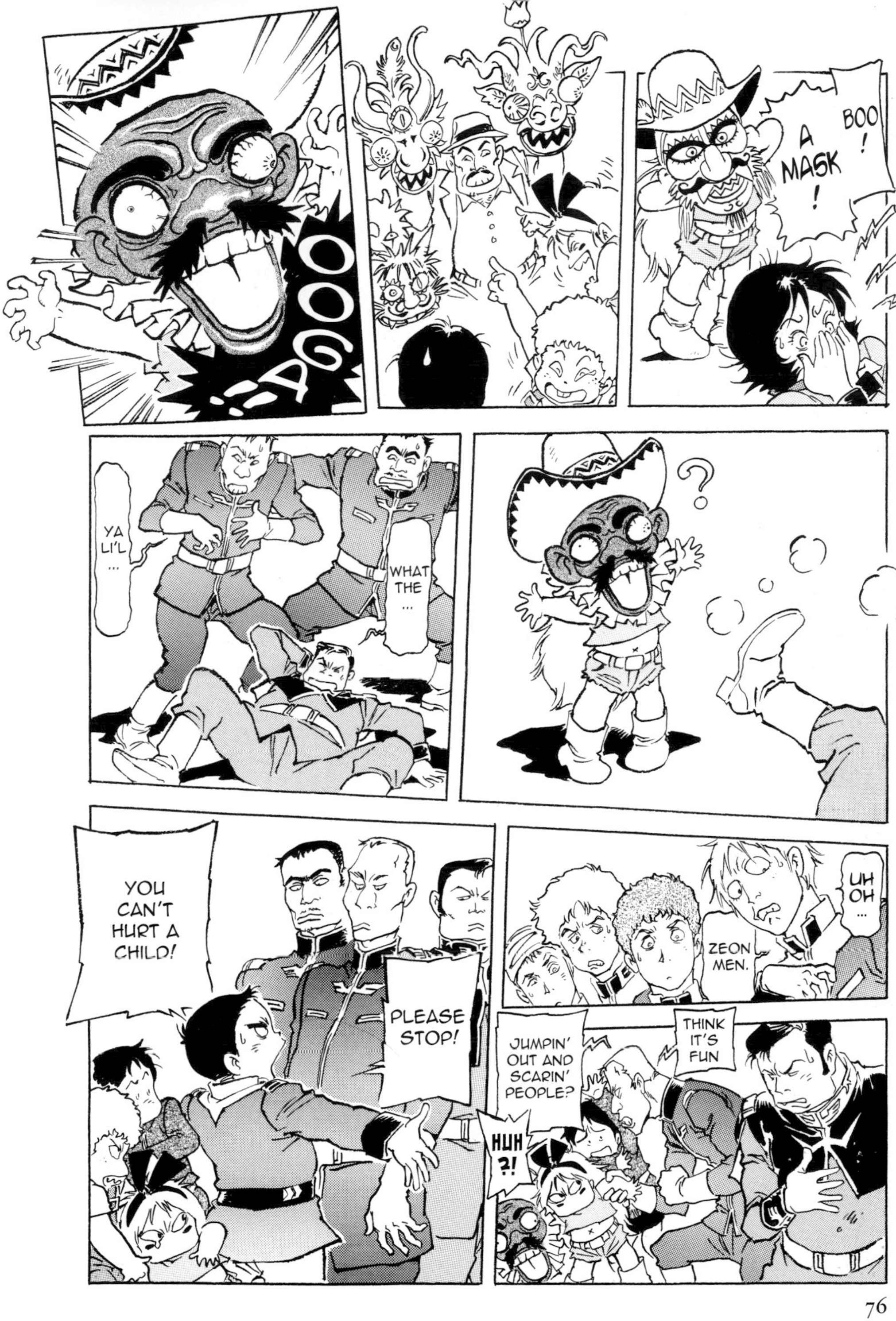
BOO!
A MASK!
OOGA!!
?
WHAT THE ...
YA LI'L ...
UH OH ...
ZEON MEN.
THINK IT'S FUN
JUMPIN' OUT AND SCARIN' PEOPLE?
HUH?!
YOU CAN'T HURT A CHILD!
PLEASE STOP!

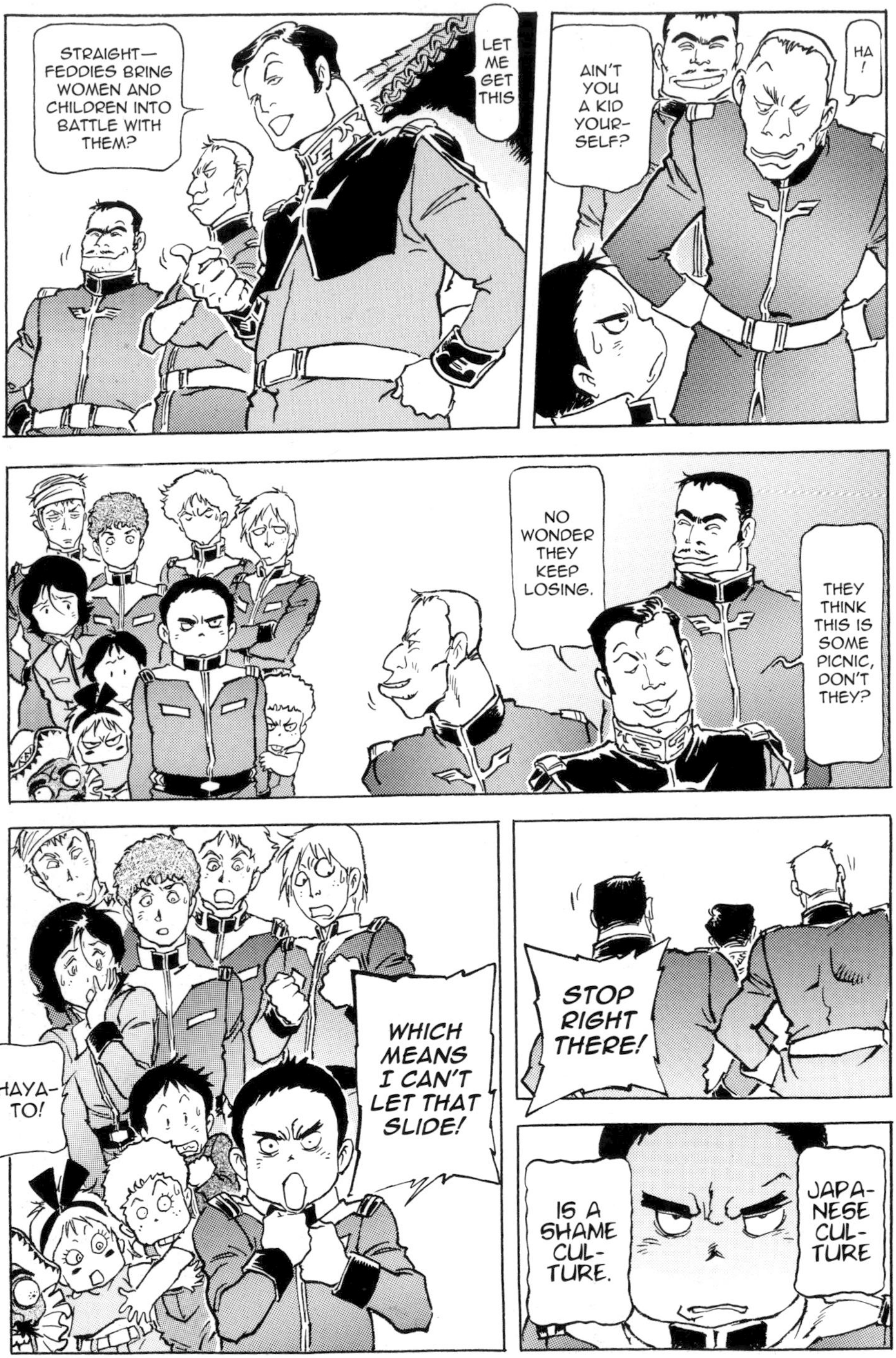
HA!
AIN'T YOU A KID YOURSELF?
LET ME GET THIS
STRAIGHT—FEDDIES BRING WOMEN AND CHILDREN INTO BATTLE WITH THEM?
THEY THINK THIS IS SOME PICNIC, DON'T THEY?
NO WONDER THEY KEEP LOSING.
STOP RIGHT THERE!
JAPANESE CULTURE
IS A SHAME CULTURE.
WHICH MEANS I CAN'T LET THAT SLIDE!
HAYATO!

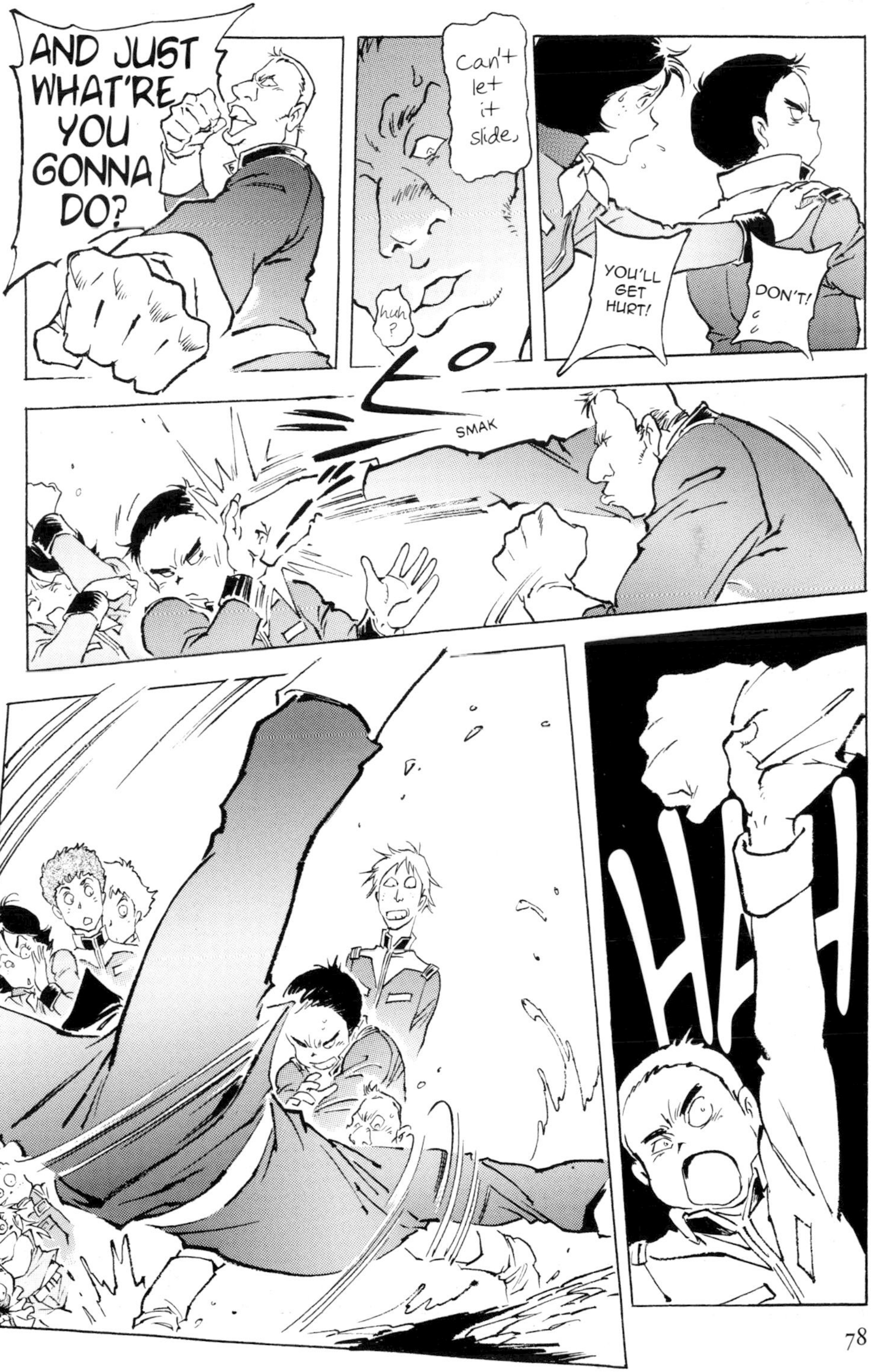
DON'T!
YOU'LL GET HURT!
Can't let it slide,
huh?
AND JUST WHAT'RE YOU GONNA DO?
SMAK
HAH

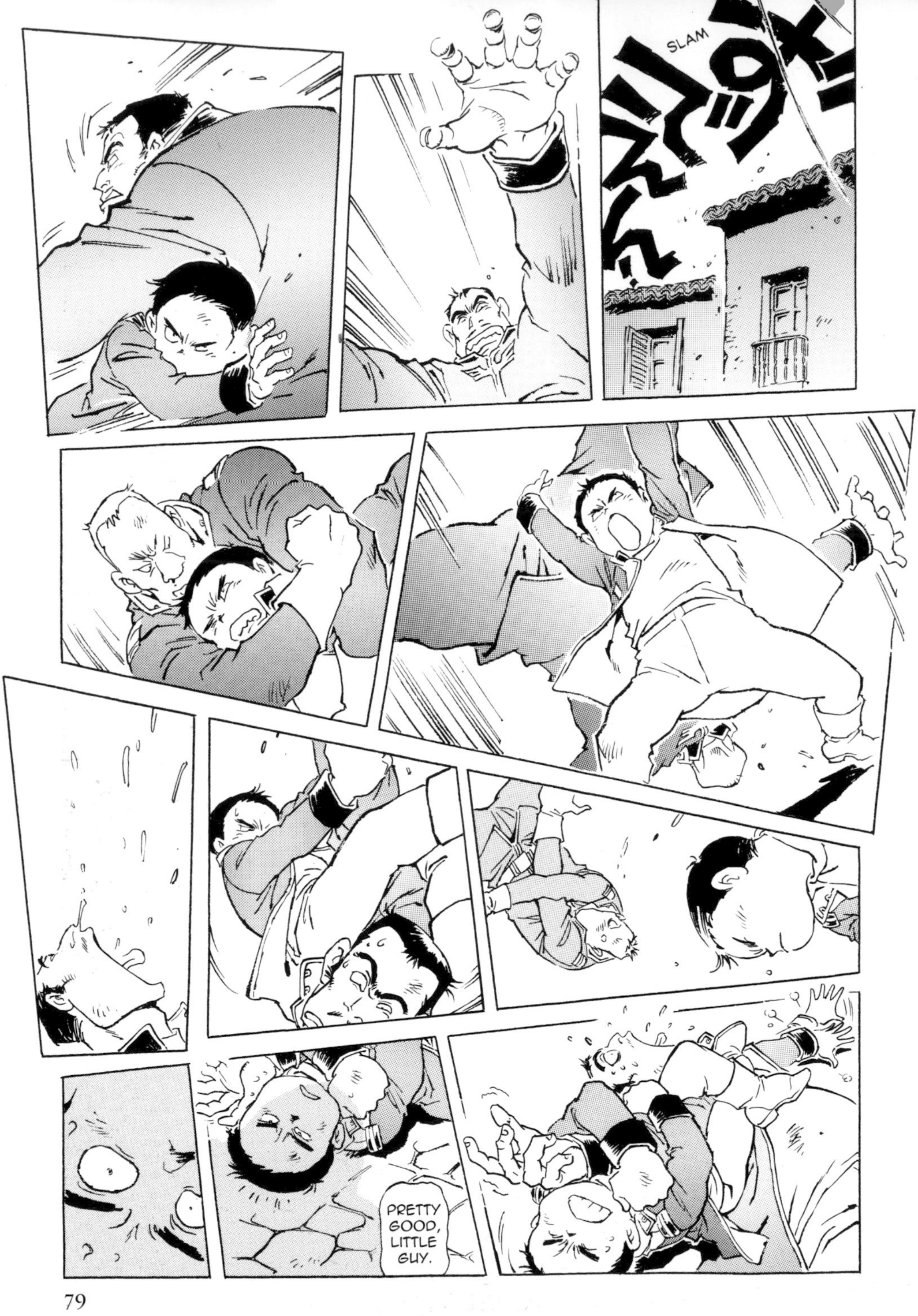
SLAM
PRETTY GOOD, LITTLE GUY.

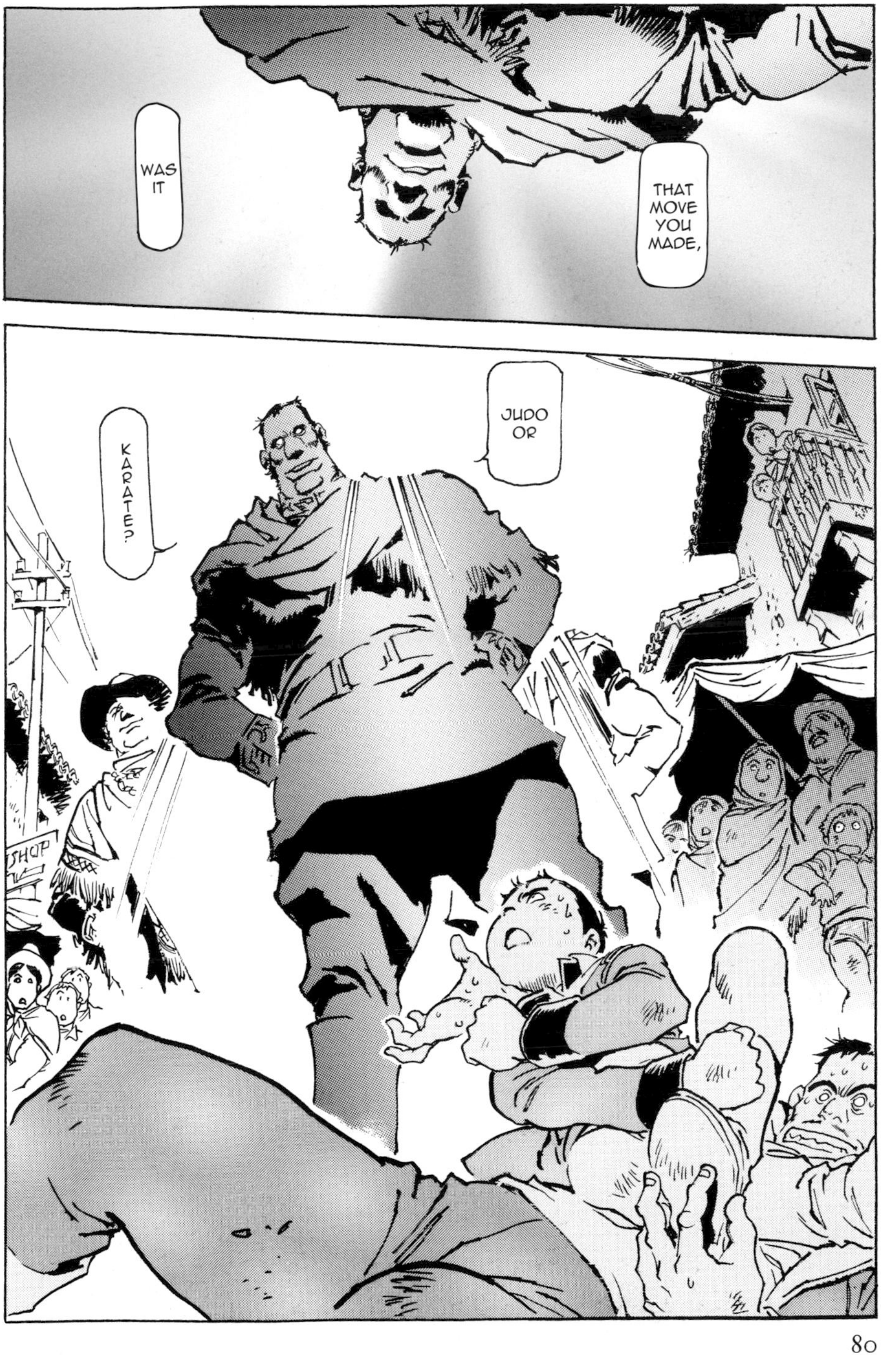
THAT MOVE YOU MADE,
WAS IT
JUDO OR
KARATE?
SHOP

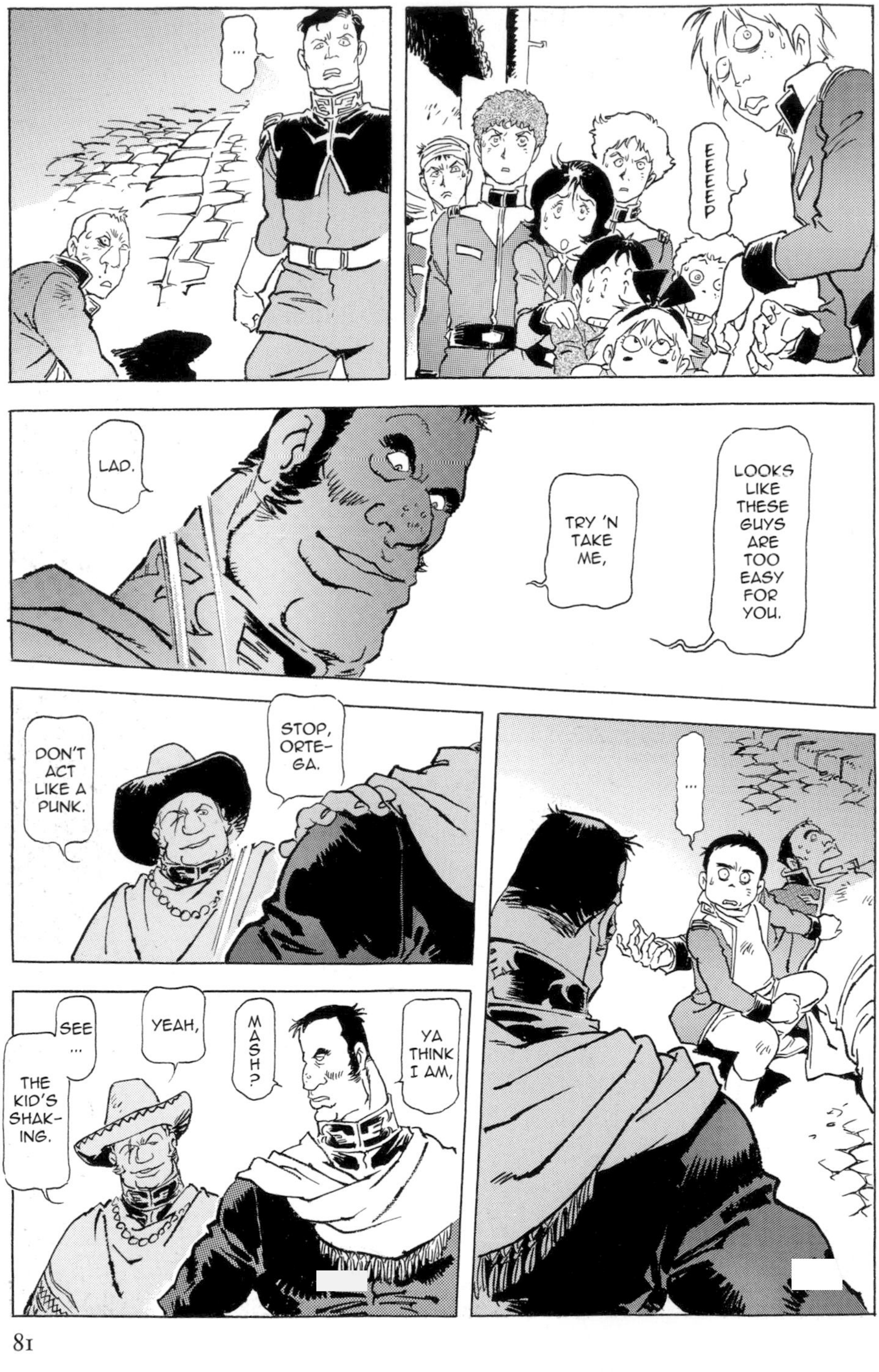
EEEEEP
...
LOOKS LIKE THESE GUYS ARE TOO EASY FOR YOU.
TRY 'N TAKE ME,
LAD.
...
STOP, ORTEGA.
DON'T ACT LIKE A PUNK.
YA THINK I AM,
MASH?
YEAH,
SEE ... THE KID'S SHAKING.

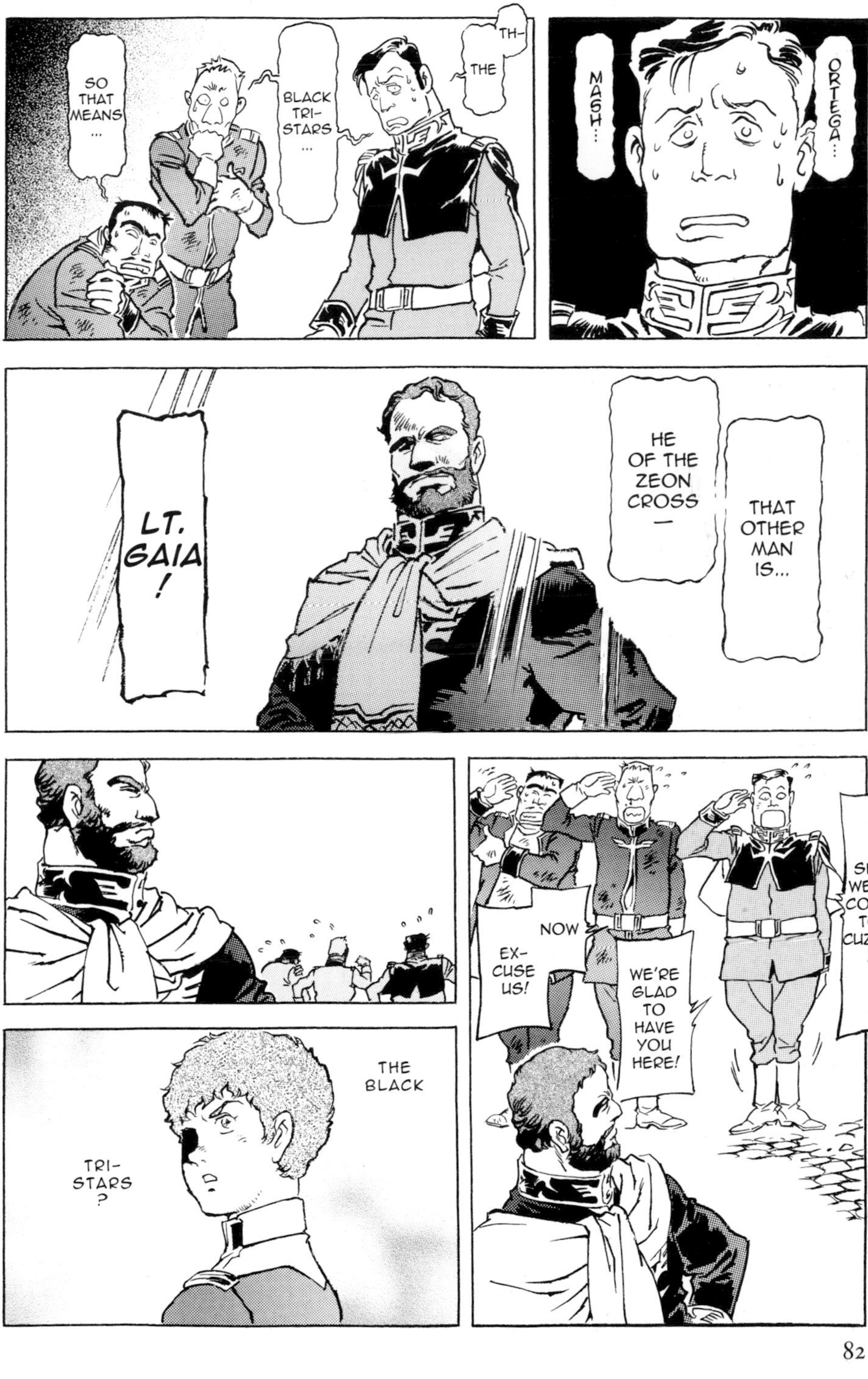
ORTEGA...
MASH...
TH-
THE
BLACK TRI-STARS...
SO THAT MEANS...
HE OF THE ZEON CROSS —
THAT OTHER MAN IS...
LT. GAIA!
SIR, WELCOME TO CUZCO!
WE'RE GLAD TO HAVE YOU HERE!
NOW EXCUSE US!
THE BLACK
TRI-STARS?

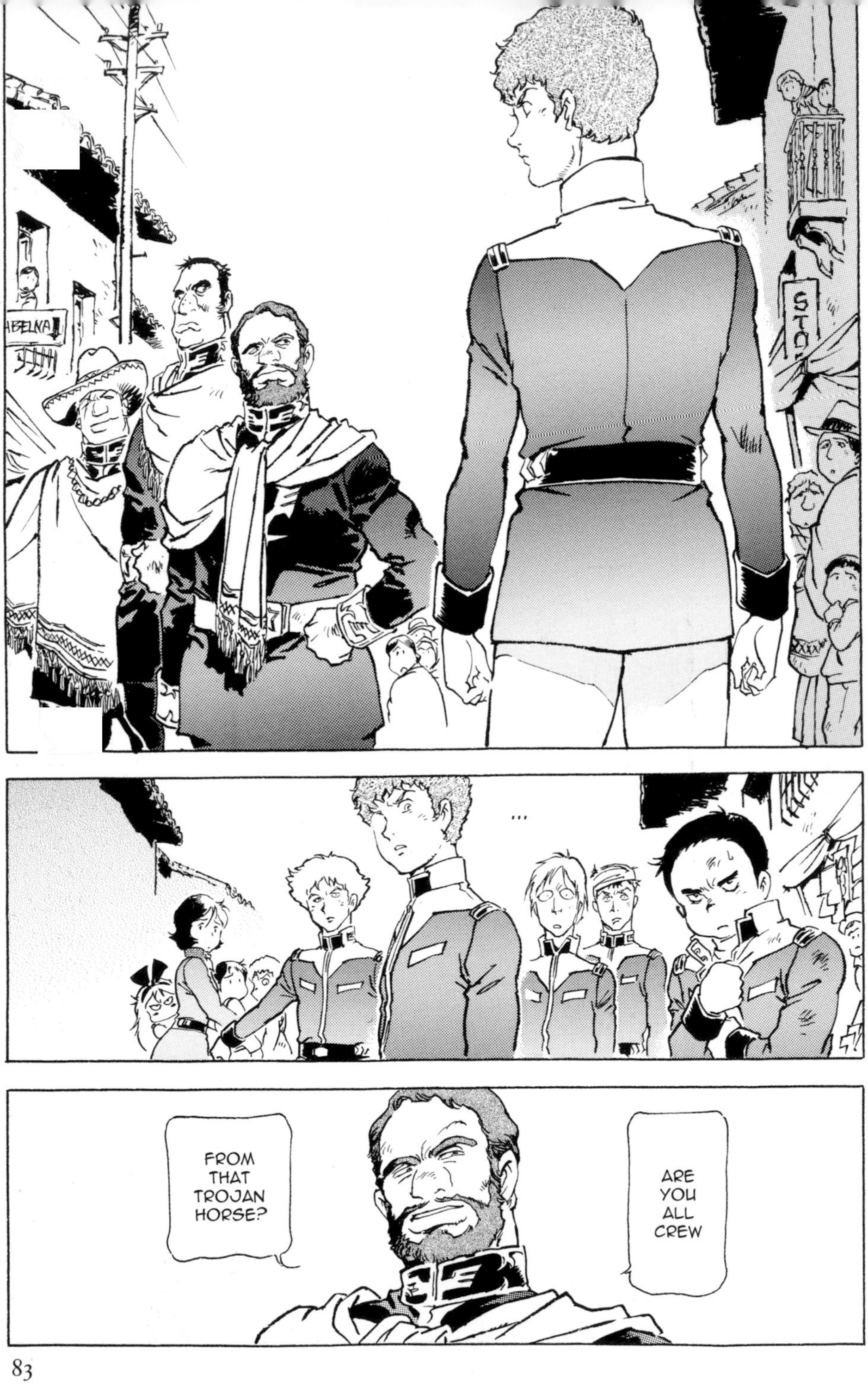
...
ARE YOU ALL CREW
FROM THAT TROJAN HORSE?

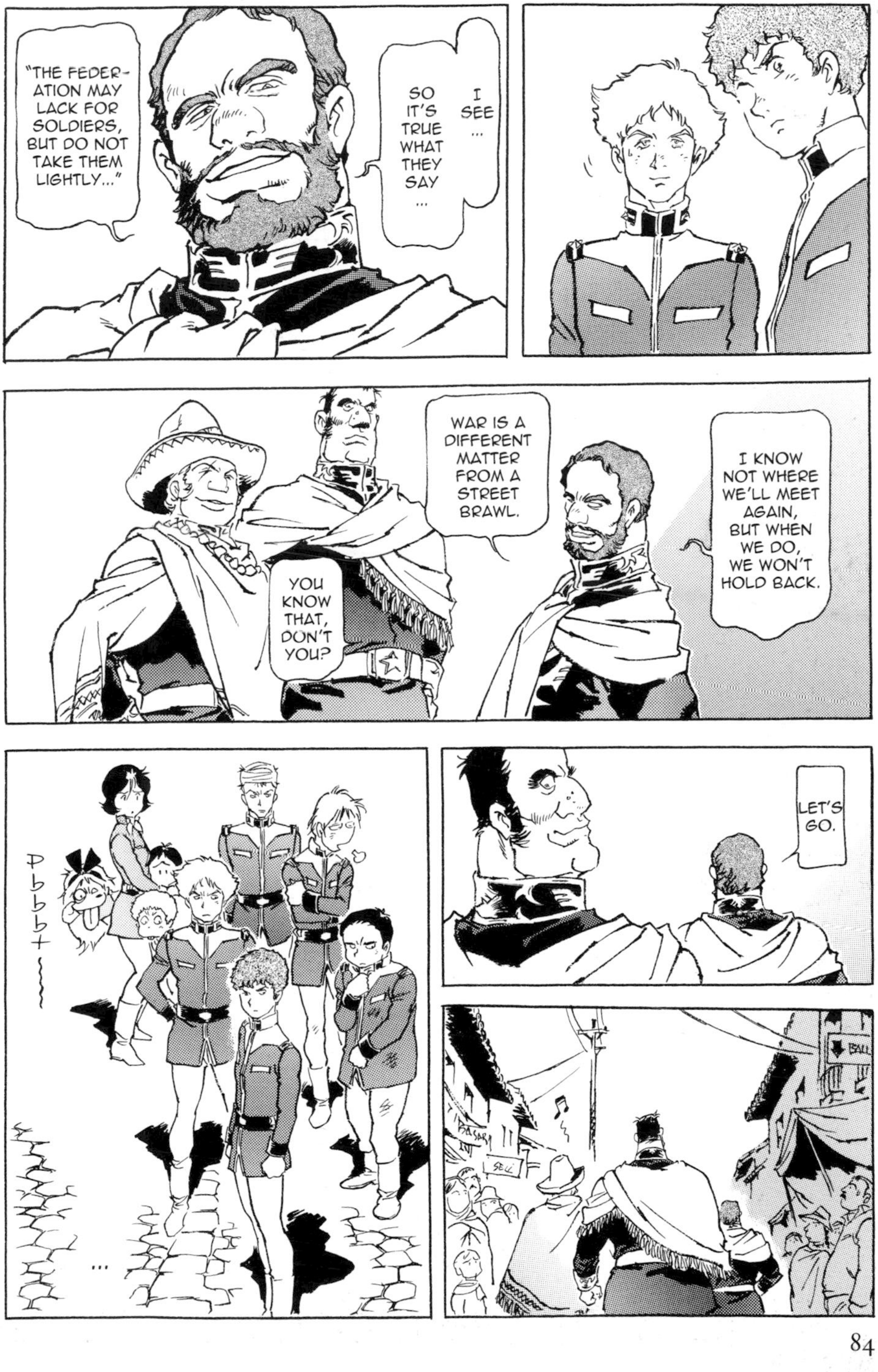
I SEE ...
SO IT'S TRUE WHAT THEY SAY ...
"THE FEDERATION MAY LACK FOR SOLDIERS, BUT DO NOT TAKE THEM LIGHTLY..."
I KNOW NOT WHERE WE'LL MEET AGAIN, BUT WHEN WE DO, WE WON'T HOLD BACK.
WAR IS A DIFFERENT MATTER FROM A STREET BRAWL.
YOU KNOW THAT, DON'T YOU?
LET'S GO.
Pbbbt ~~~
...

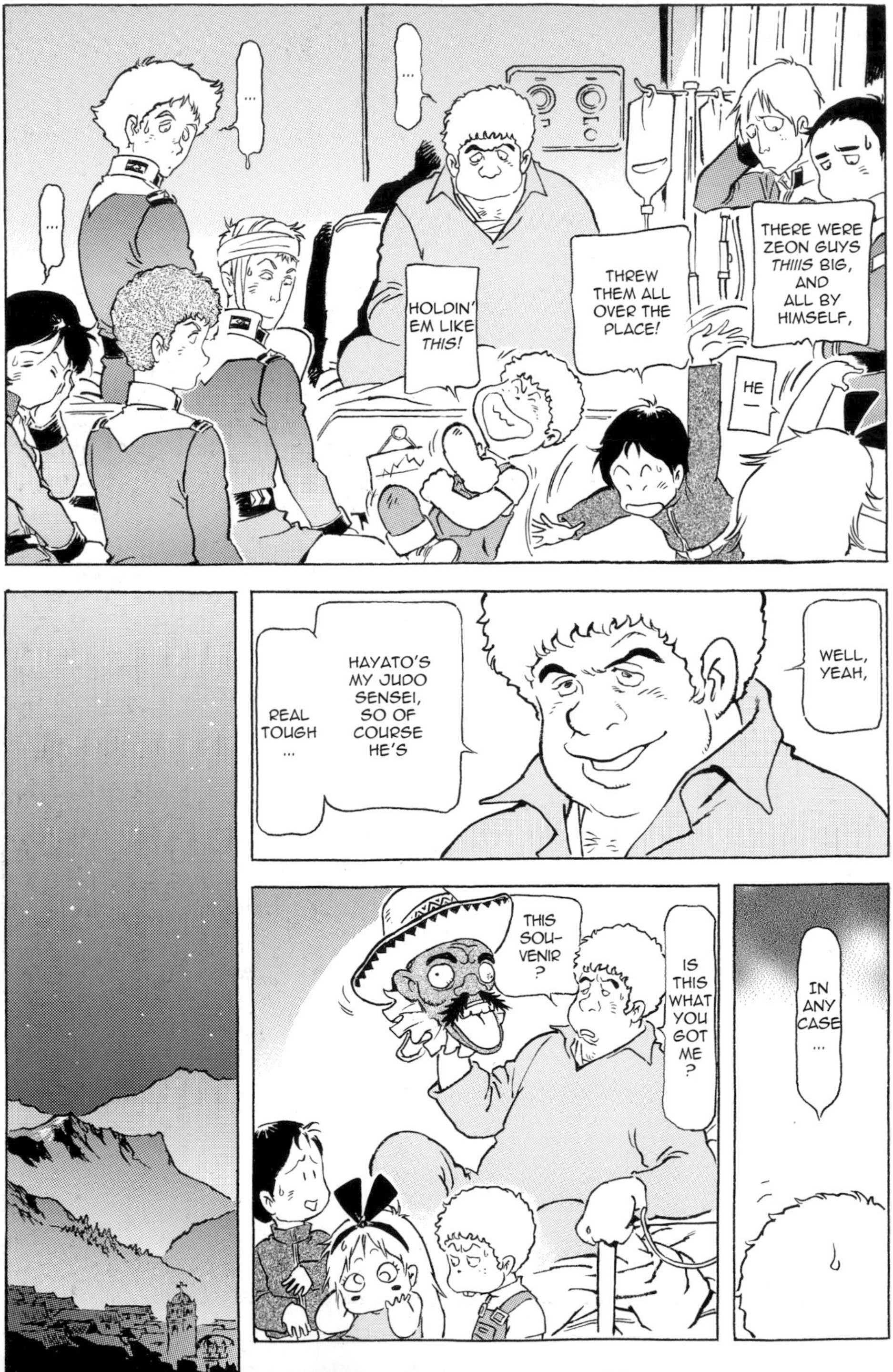
THERE WERE ZEON GUYS *THIIIS* BIG, AND ALL BY HIMSELF,
HE —
THREW THEM ALL OVER THE PLACE!
HOLDIN' EM LIKE *THIS!*
...
...
...
WELL, YEAH,
HAYATO'S MY JUDO SENSEI, SO OF COURSE HE'S
REAL TOUGH ...
IN ANY CASE ...
IS THIS WHAT YOU GOT ME?
THIS SOU-VENIR?

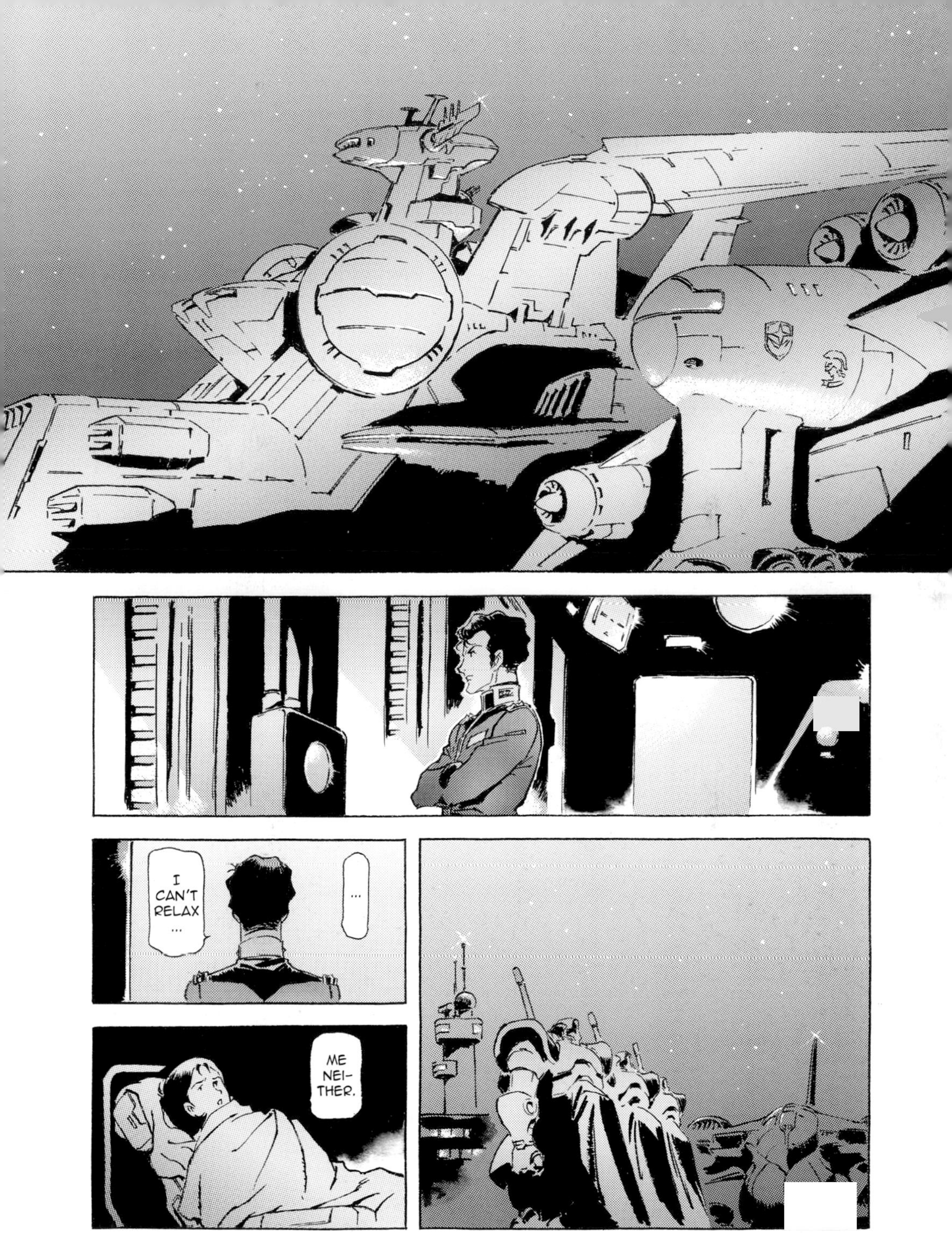
...
I CAN'T RELAX ...
ME NEI-THER.

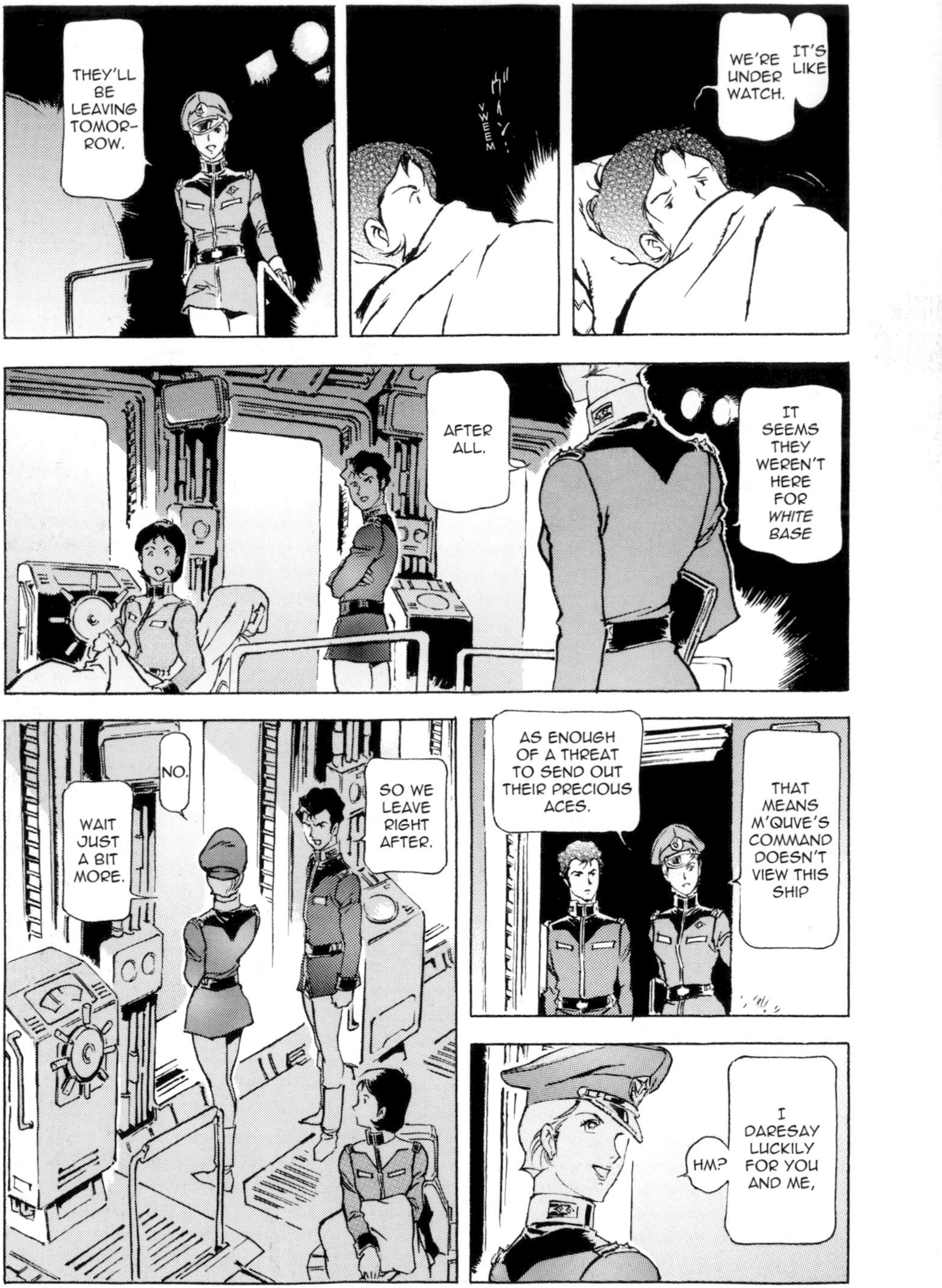
IT'S LIKE
WE'RE UNDER WATCH.
VWEEM
THEY'LL BE LEAVING TOMOR-ROW.
IT SEEMS THEY WEREN'T HERE FOR *WHITE BASE*
AFTER ALL.
THAT MEANS M'QUVE'S COMMAND DOESN'T VIEW THIS SHIP
AS ENOUGH OF A THREAT TO SEND OUT THEIR PRECIOUS ACES.
I DARESAY LUCKILY FOR YOU AND ME,
HM?
SO WE LEAVE RIGHT AFTER.
NO.
WAIT JUST A BIT MORE.

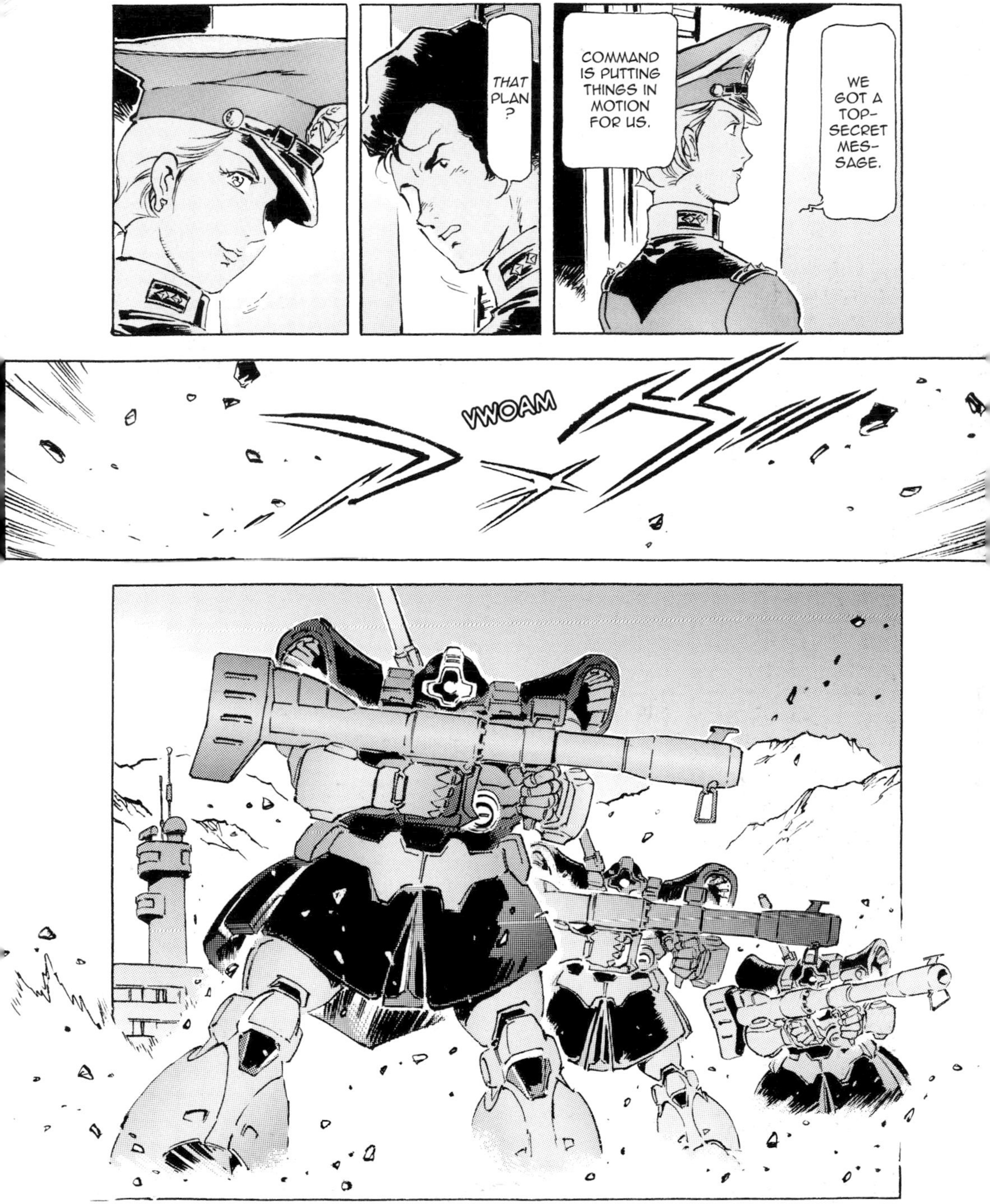
WE GOT A TOP-SECRET MESSAGE.
COMMAND IS PUTTING THINGS IN MOTION FOR US.
THAT PLAN?
VWOAM

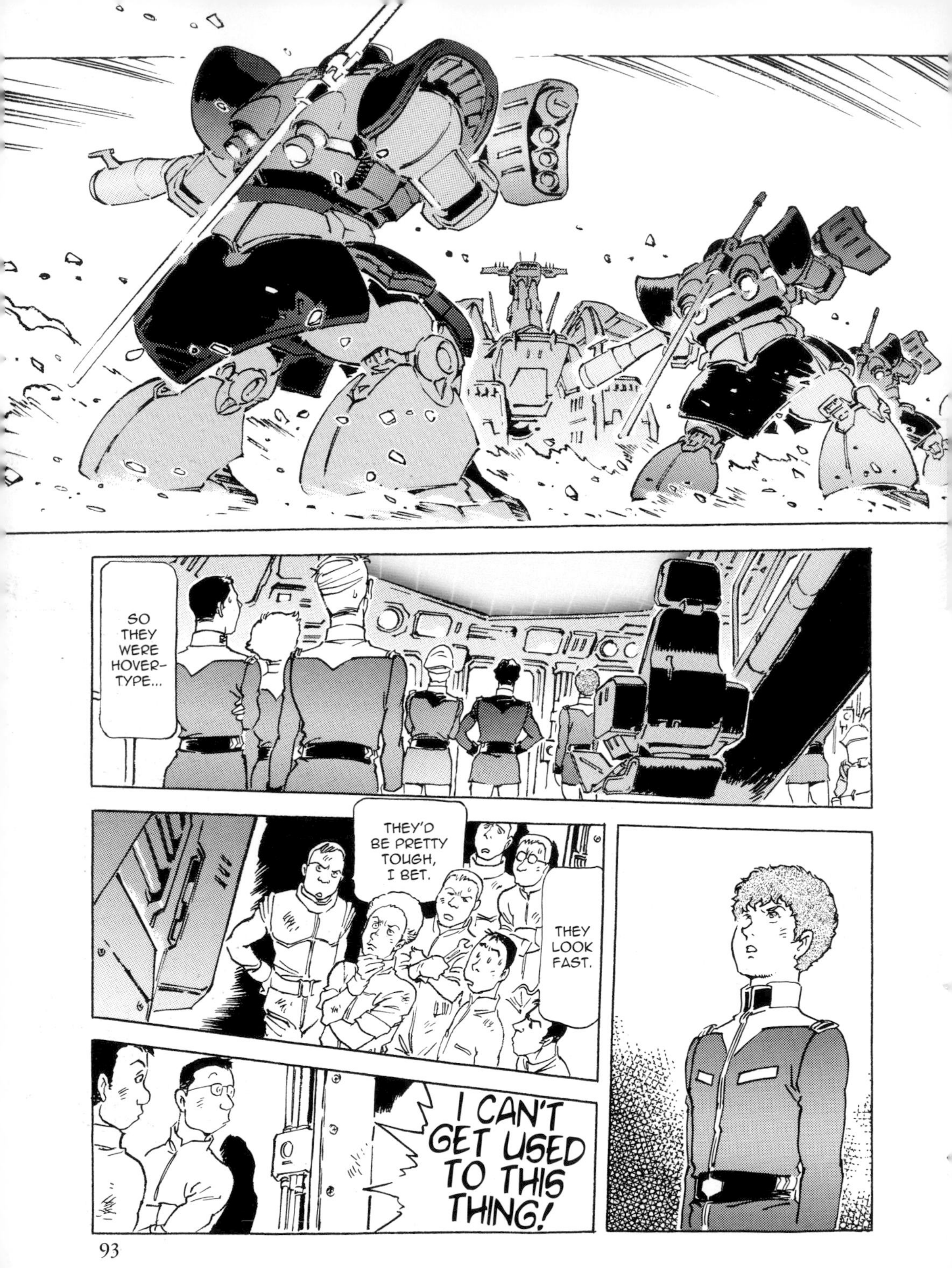
SO THEY WERE HOVER-TYPE...
THEY LOOK FAST.
THEY'D BE PRETTY TOUGH, I BET.
I CAN'T GET USED TO THIS THING!

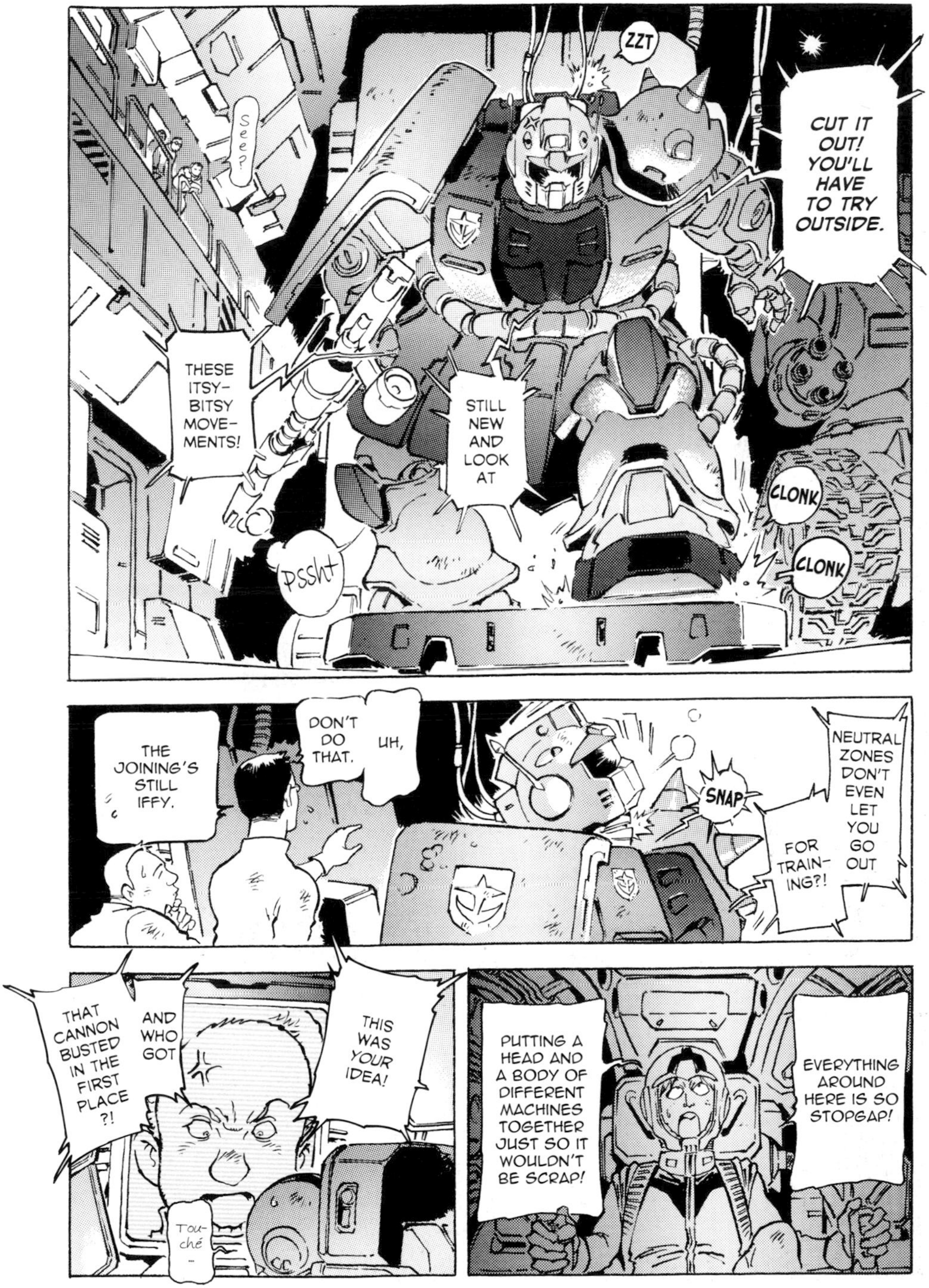
ZZT
CUT IT OUT! YOU'LL HAVE TO TRY OUTSIDE.
See?
CLONK
CLONK
STILL NEW AND LOOK AT
THESE ITSY-BITSY MOVEMENTS!
Psssht
NEUTRAL ZONES DON'T EVEN LET YOU GO OUT
FOR TRAINING?!
SNAP
UH,
DON'T DO THAT.
THE JOINING'S STILL IFFY.
EVERYTHING AROUND HERE IS SO STOPGAP!
PUTTING A HEAD AND A BODY OF DIFFERENT MACHINES TOGETHER JUST SO IT WOULDN'T BE SCRAP!
THIS WAS YOUR IDEA!
AND WHO GOT
THAT CANNON BUSTED IN THE FIRST PLACE?!
Touché...

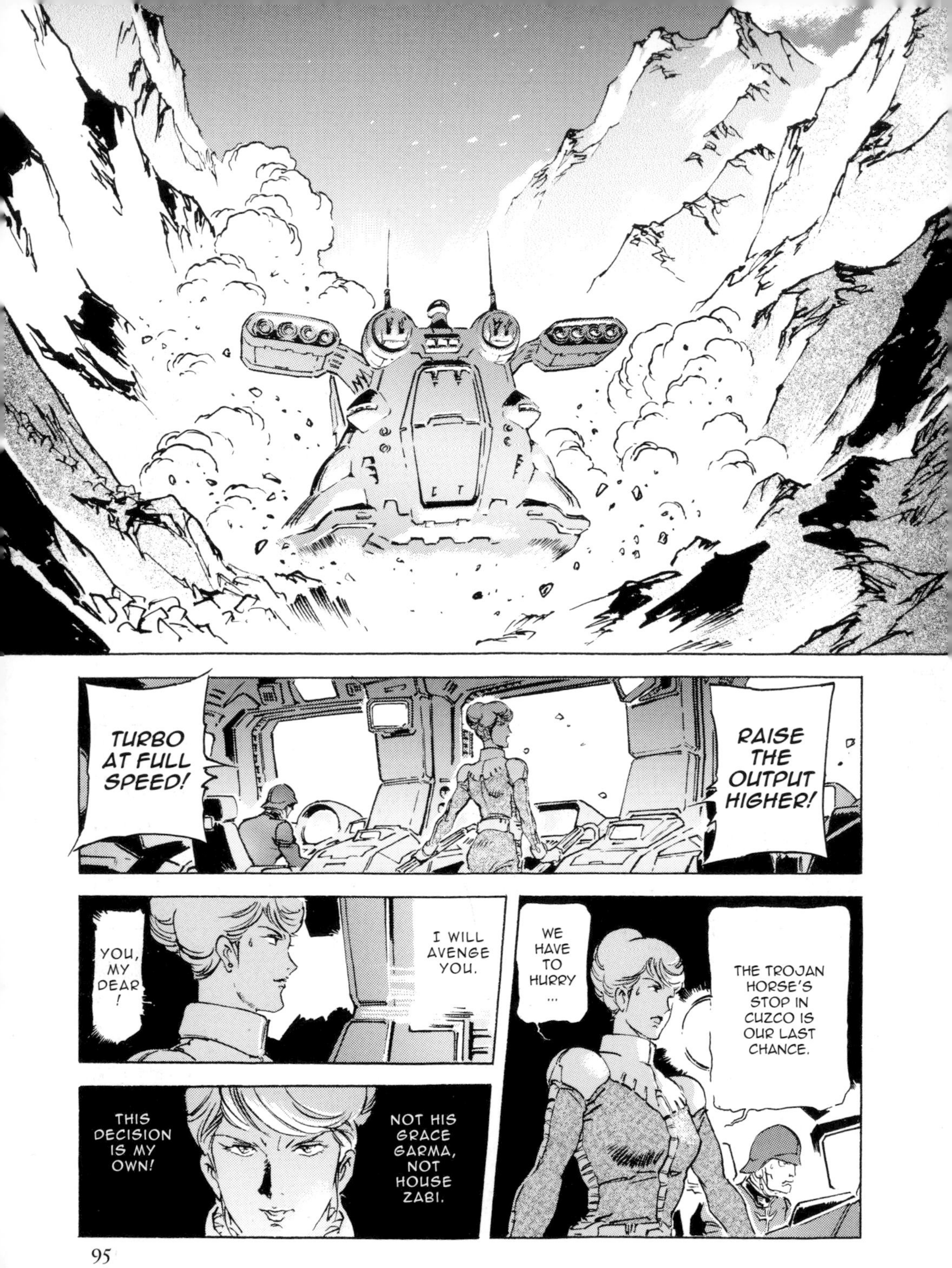
RAISE THE OUTPUT HIGHER!
TURBO AT FULL SPEED!
THE TROJAN HORSE'S STOP IN CUZCO IS OUR LAST CHANCE.
WE HAVE TO HURRY...
I WILL AVENGE YOU.
YOU, MY DEAR!
NOT HIS GRACE GARMA, NOT HOUSE ZABI.
THIS DECISION IS MY OWN!

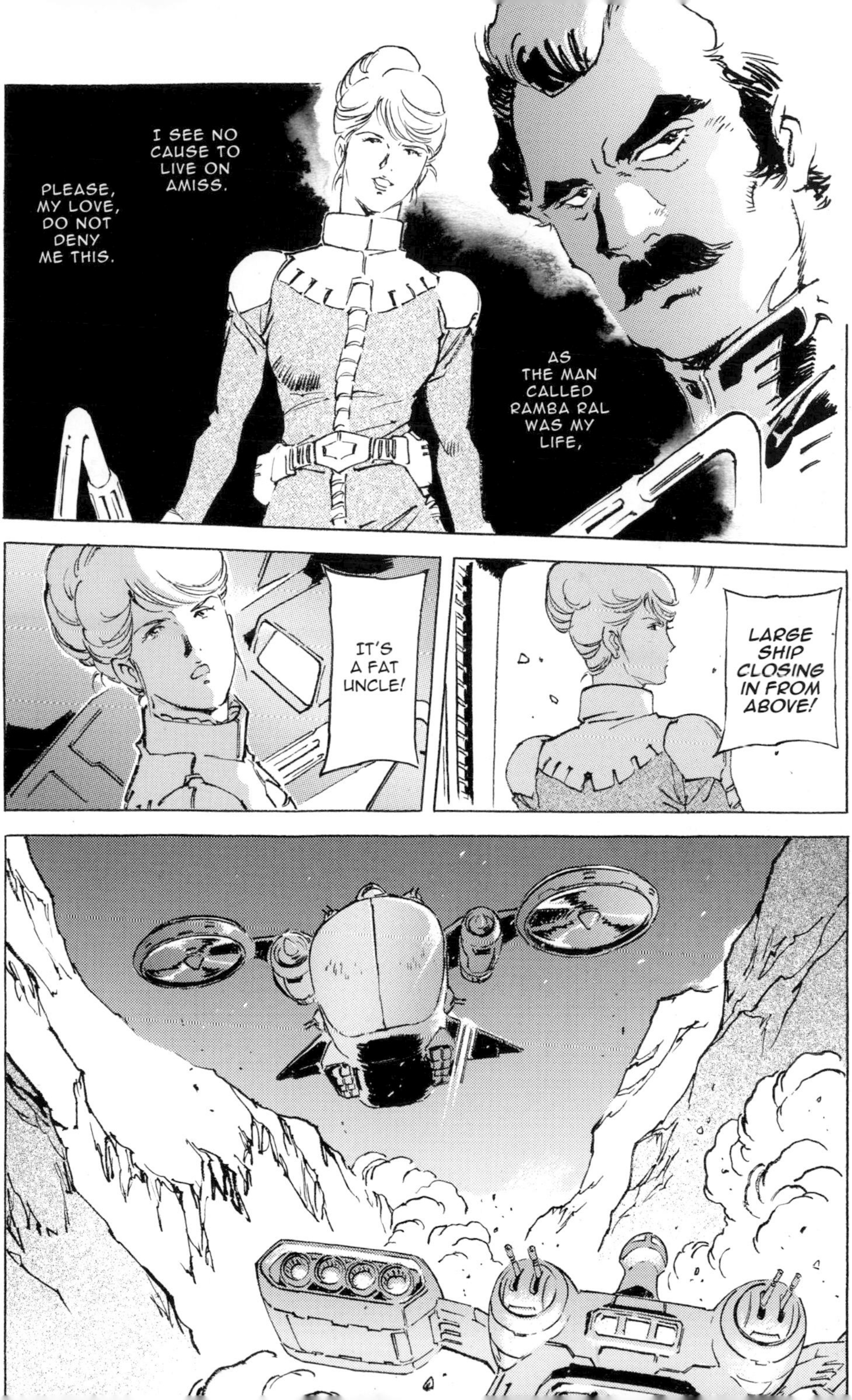
AS THE MAN CALLED RAMBA RAL WAS MY LIFE,
I SEE NO CAUSE TO LIVE ON AMISS.
PLEASE, MY LOVE, DO NOT DENY ME THIS.
LARGE SHIP CLOSING IN FROM ABOVE!
IT'S A FAT UNCLE!

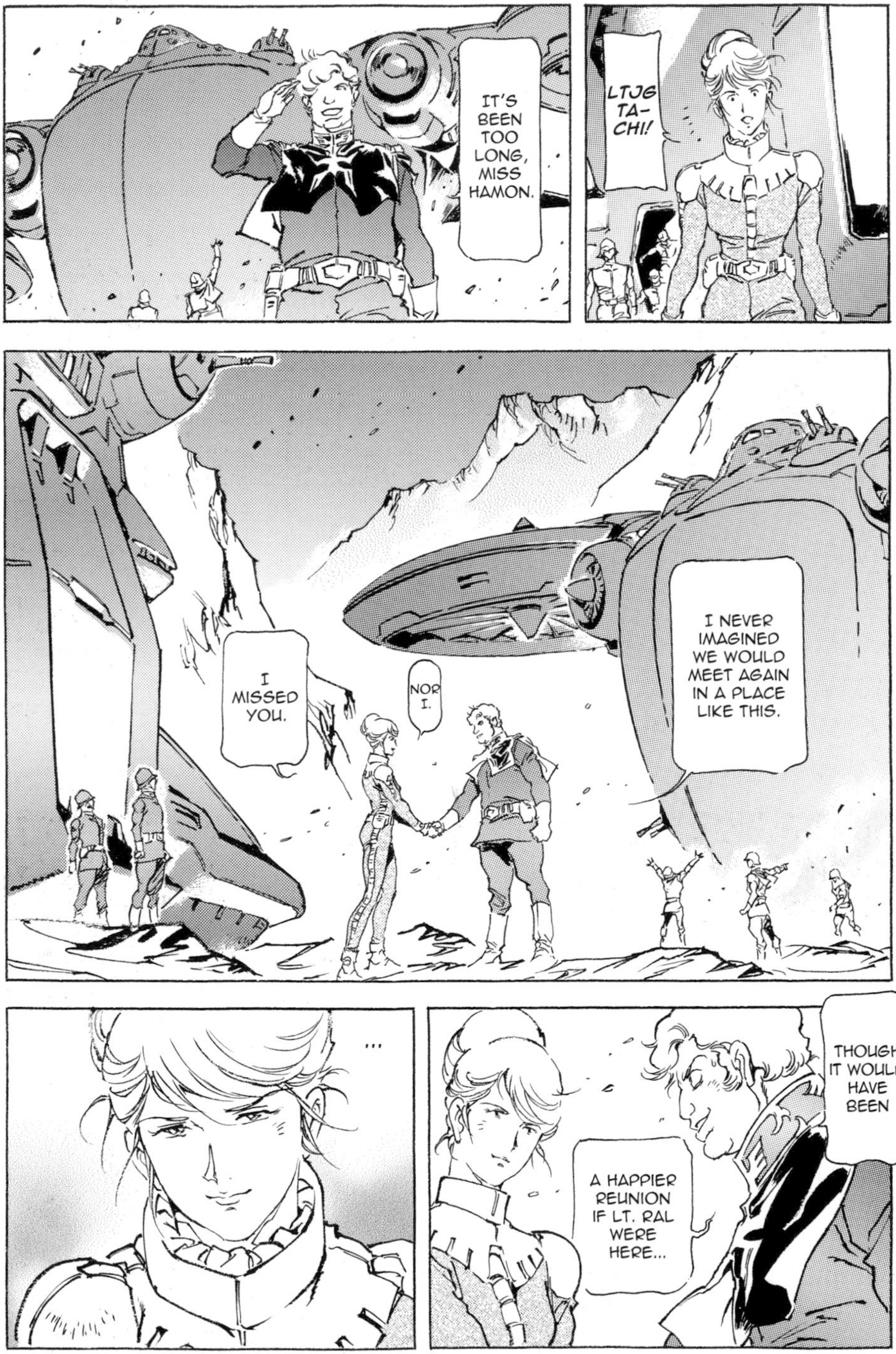
LTJG TA-CHI!
IT'S BEEN TOO LONG, MISS HAMON.
I NEVER IMAGINED WE WOULD MEET AGAIN IN A PLACE LIKE THIS.
NOR I.
I MISSED YOU.
THOUGH IT WOULD HAVE BEEN
A HAPPIER REUNION IF LT. RAL WERE HERE...
...

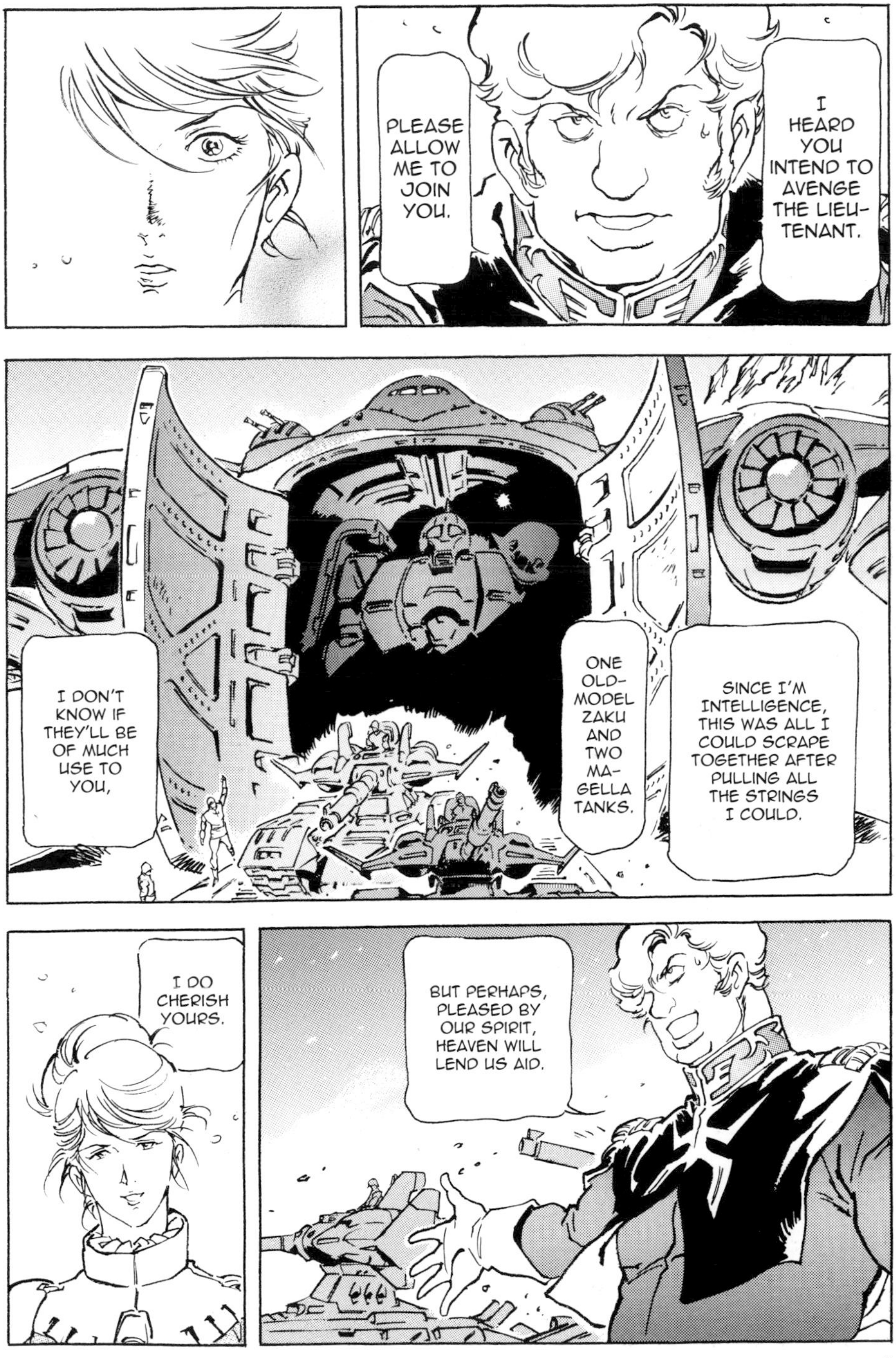
I HEARD YOU INTEND TO AVENGE THE LIEU-TENANT.
PLEASE ALLOW ME TO JOIN YOU.
SINCE I'M INTELLIGENCE, THIS WAS ALL I COULD SCRAPE TOGETHER AFTER PULLING ALL THE STRINGS I COULD.
ONE OLD-MODEL ZAKU AND TWO MA-GELLA TANKS.
I DON'T KNOW IF THEY'LL BE OF MUCH USE TO YOU,
BUT PERHAPS, PLEASED BY OUR SPIRIT, HEAVEN WILL LEND US AID.
I DO CHERISH YOURS.

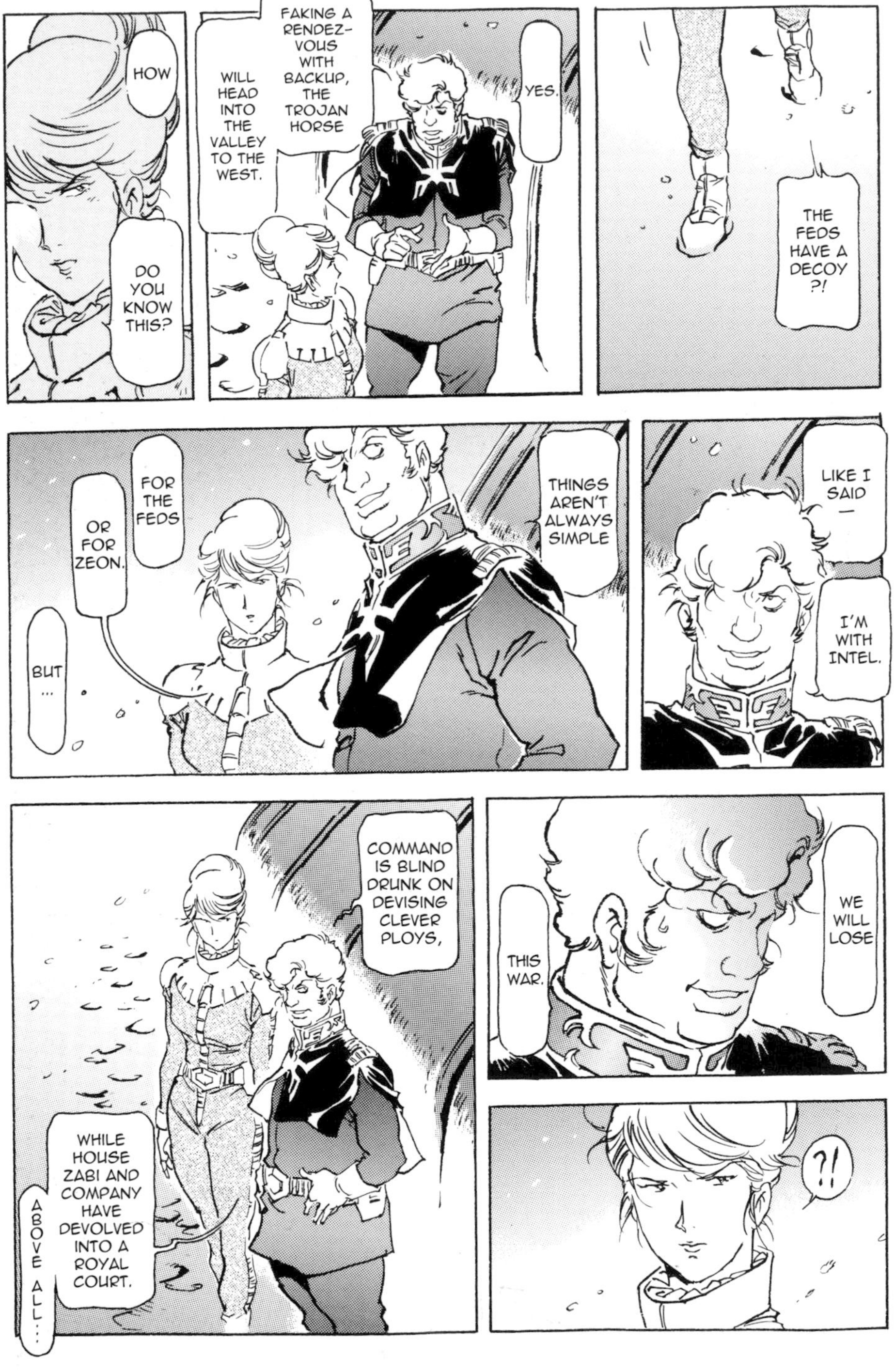

THE FEDS HAVE A DECOY ?!
YES.
FAKING A RENDEZVOUS WITH BACKUP, THE TROJAN HORSE
WILL HEAD INTO THE VALLEY TO THE WEST.
HOW
DO YOU KNOW THIS?
LIKE I SAID —
I'M WITH INTEL.
THINGS AREN'T ALWAYS SIMPLE
FOR THE FEDS
OR FOR ZEON.
BUT ...
WE WILL LOSE
THIS WAR.
?!
COMMAND IS BLIND DRUNK ON DEVISING CLEVER PLOYS,
WHILE HOUSE ZABI AND COMPANY HAVE DEVOLVED INTO A ROYAL COURT.
ABOVE ALL...

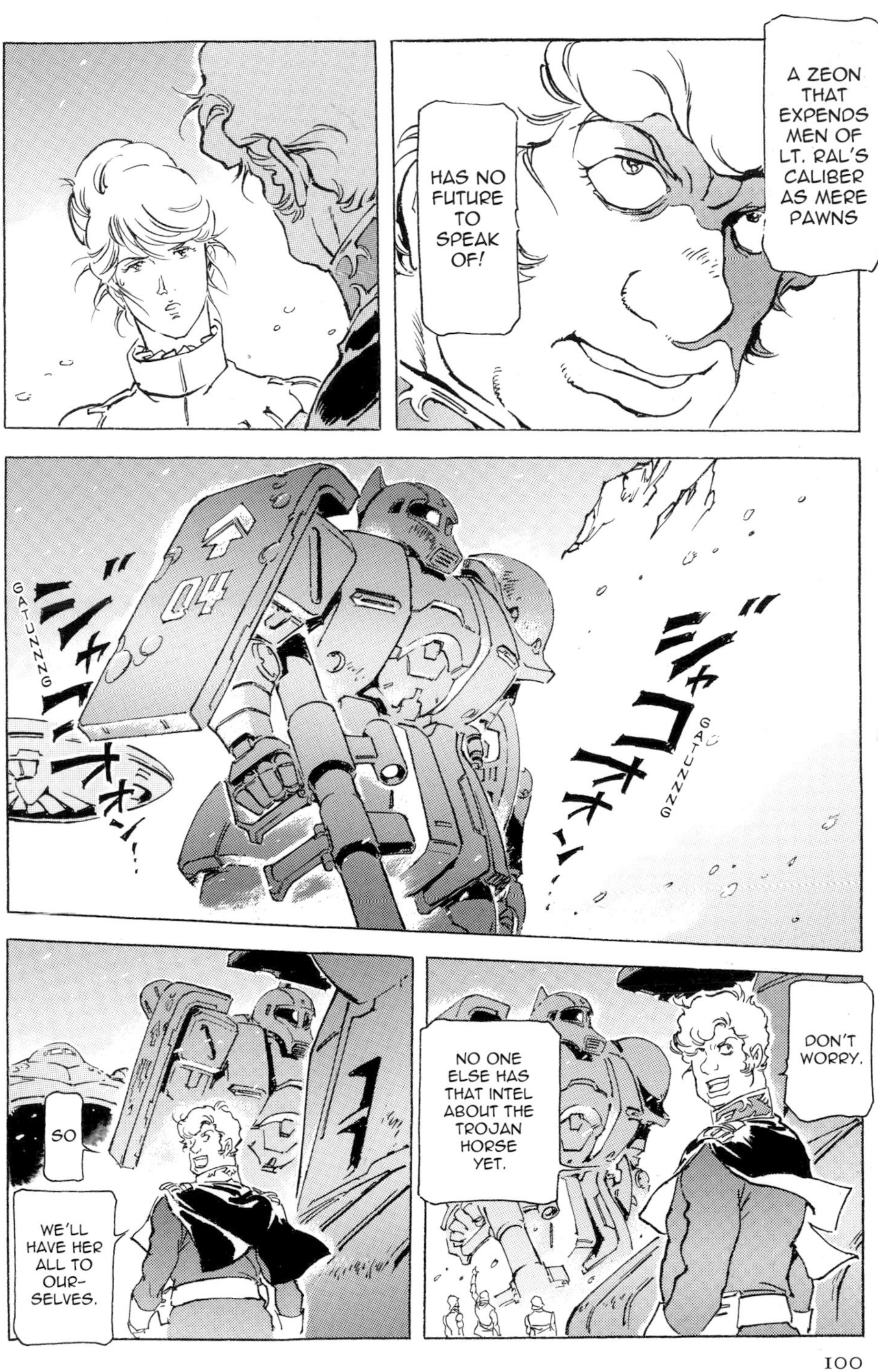
A ZEON THAT EXPENDS MEN OF LT. RAL'S CALIBER AS MERE PAWNS
HAS NO FUTURE TO SPEAK OF!
ジャコオォン
GATUNNG
GATUNNG
DON'T WORRY.
NO ONE ELSE HAS THAT INTEL ABOUT THE TROJAN HORSE YET.
SO
WE'LL HAVE HER ALL TO OUR-SELVES.

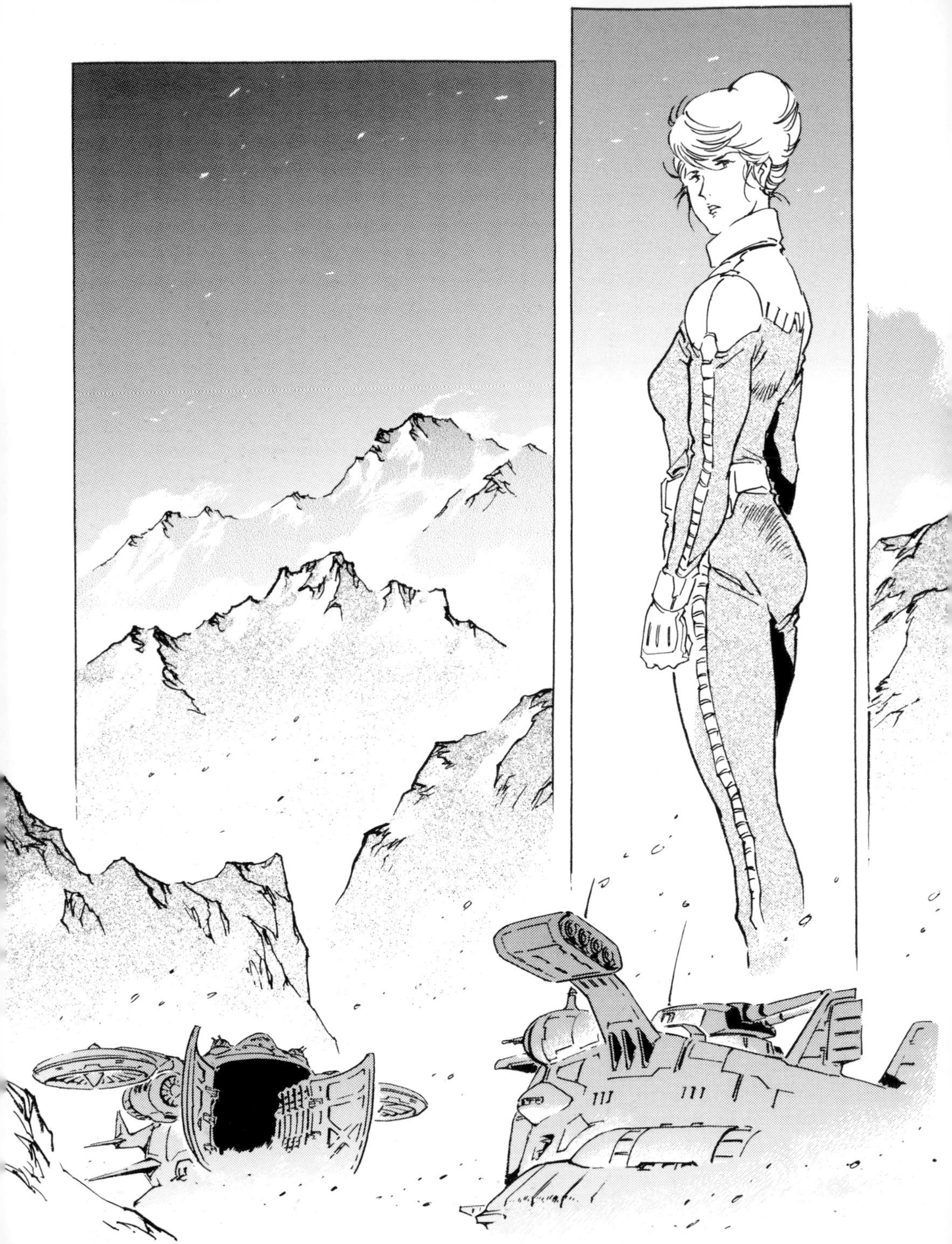

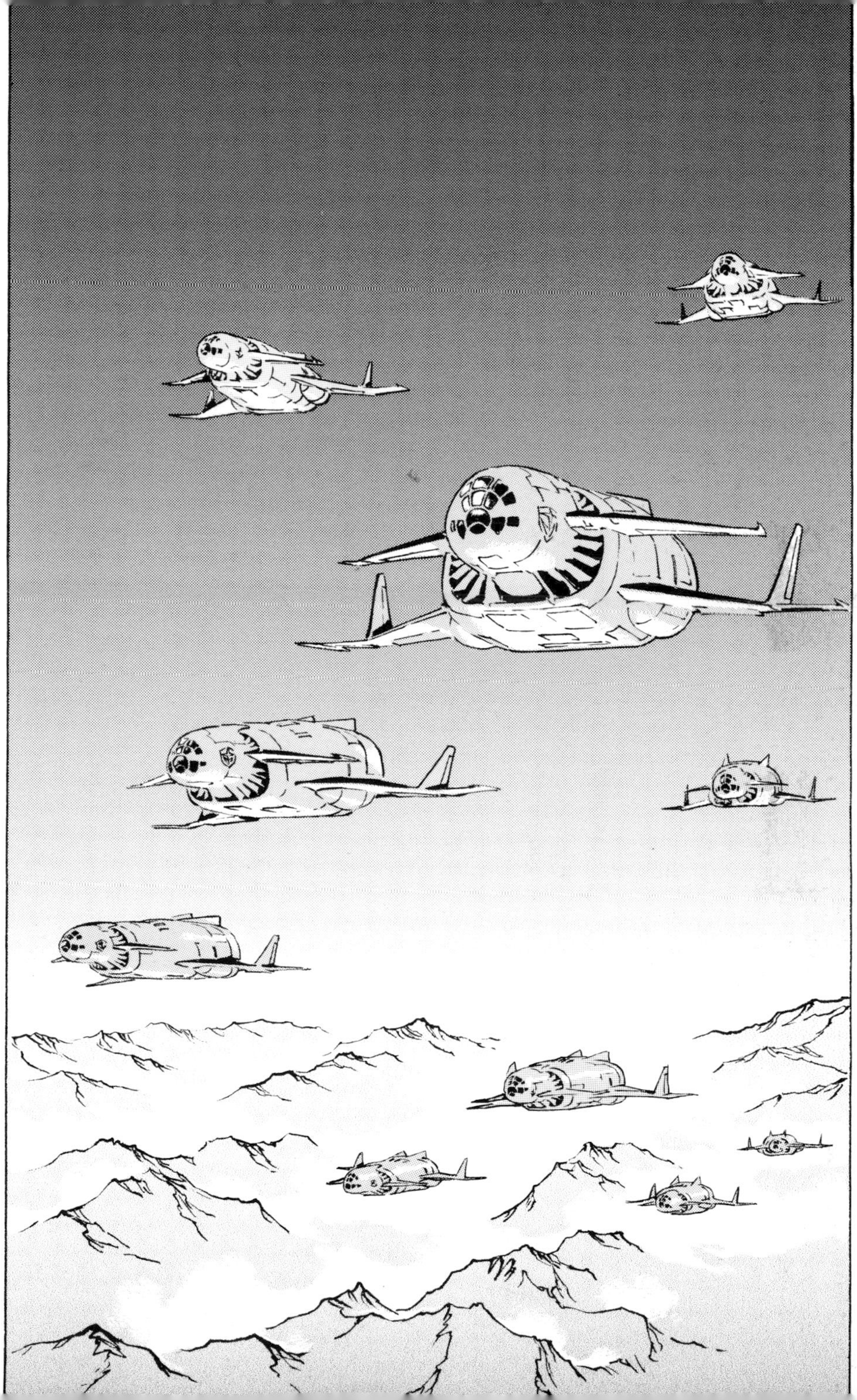

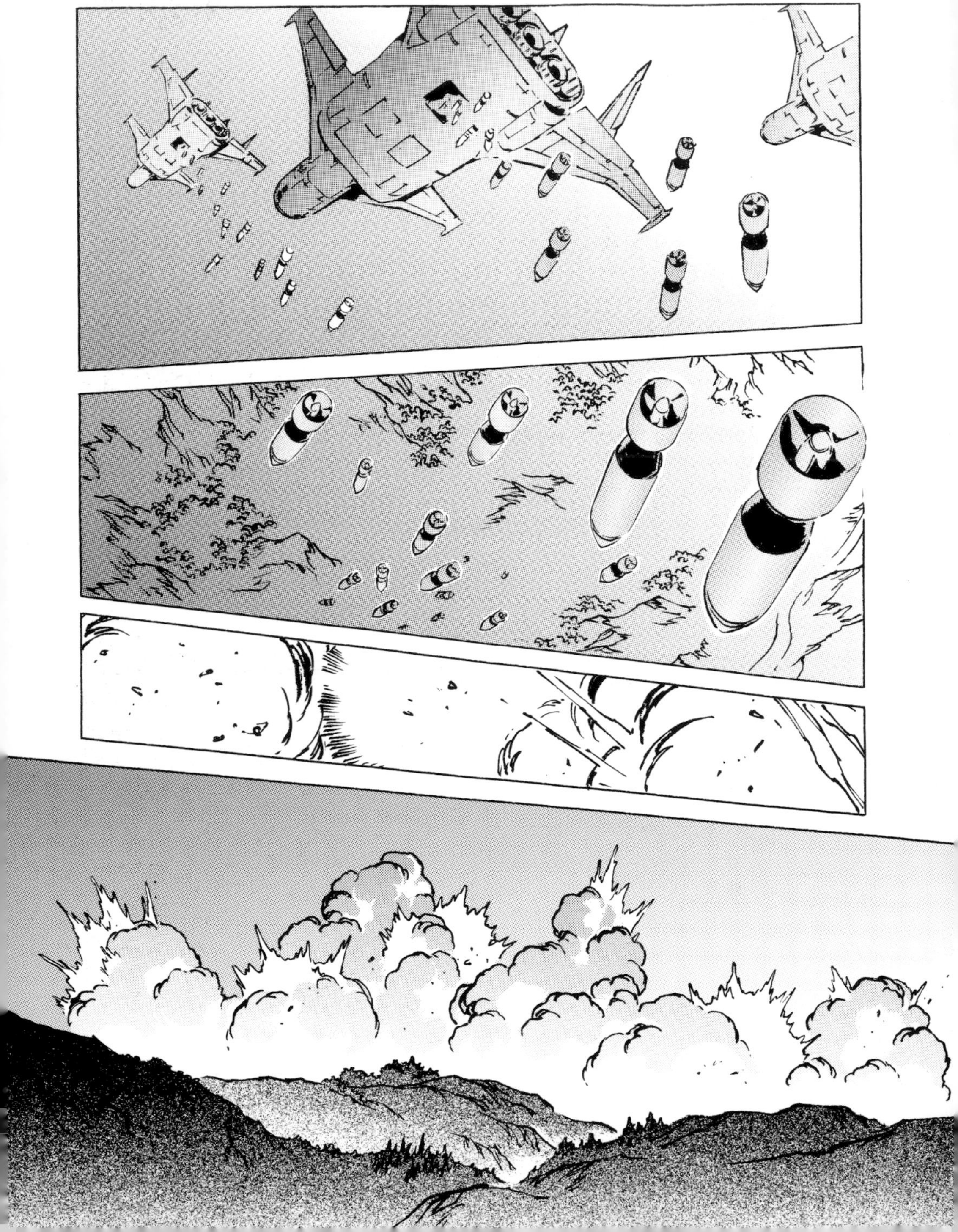

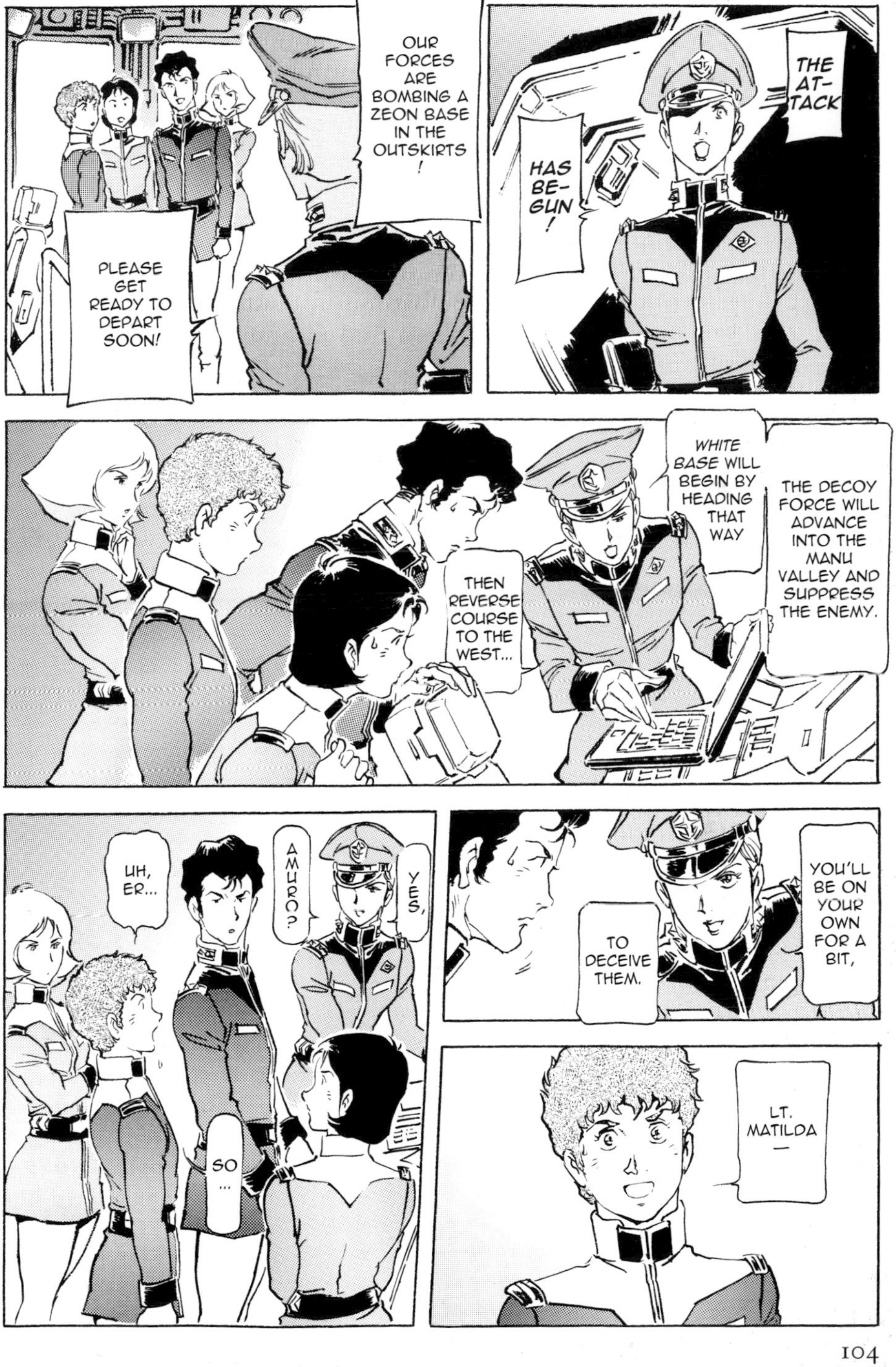
THE AT-TACK
HAS BE-GUN!
OUR FORCES ARE BOMBING A ZEON BASE IN THE OUTSKIRTS!
PLEASE GET READY TO DEPART SOON!
THE DECOY FORCE WILL ADVANCE INTO THE MANU VALLEY AND SUPPRESS THE ENEMY.
WHITE BASE WILL BEGIN BY HEADING THAT WAY
THEN REVERSE COURSE TO THE WEST...
YOU'LL BE ON YOUR OWN FOR A BIT,
TO DECEIVE THEM.
LT. MATILDA—
YES,
AMURO?
UH, ER...
SO...

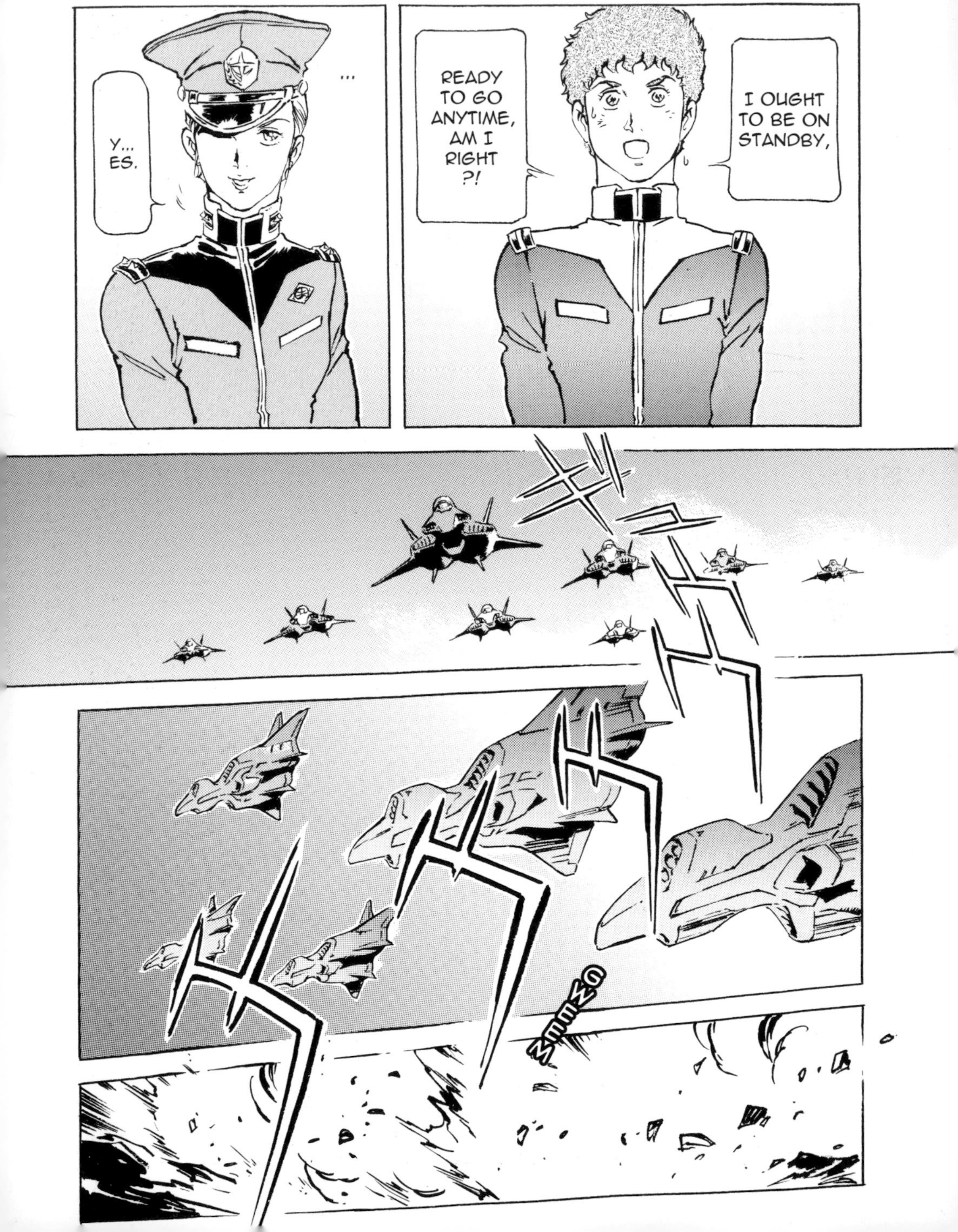
I OUGHT TO BE ON STANDBY,
READY TO GO ANYTIME, AM I RIGHT ?!
...
Y... ES.

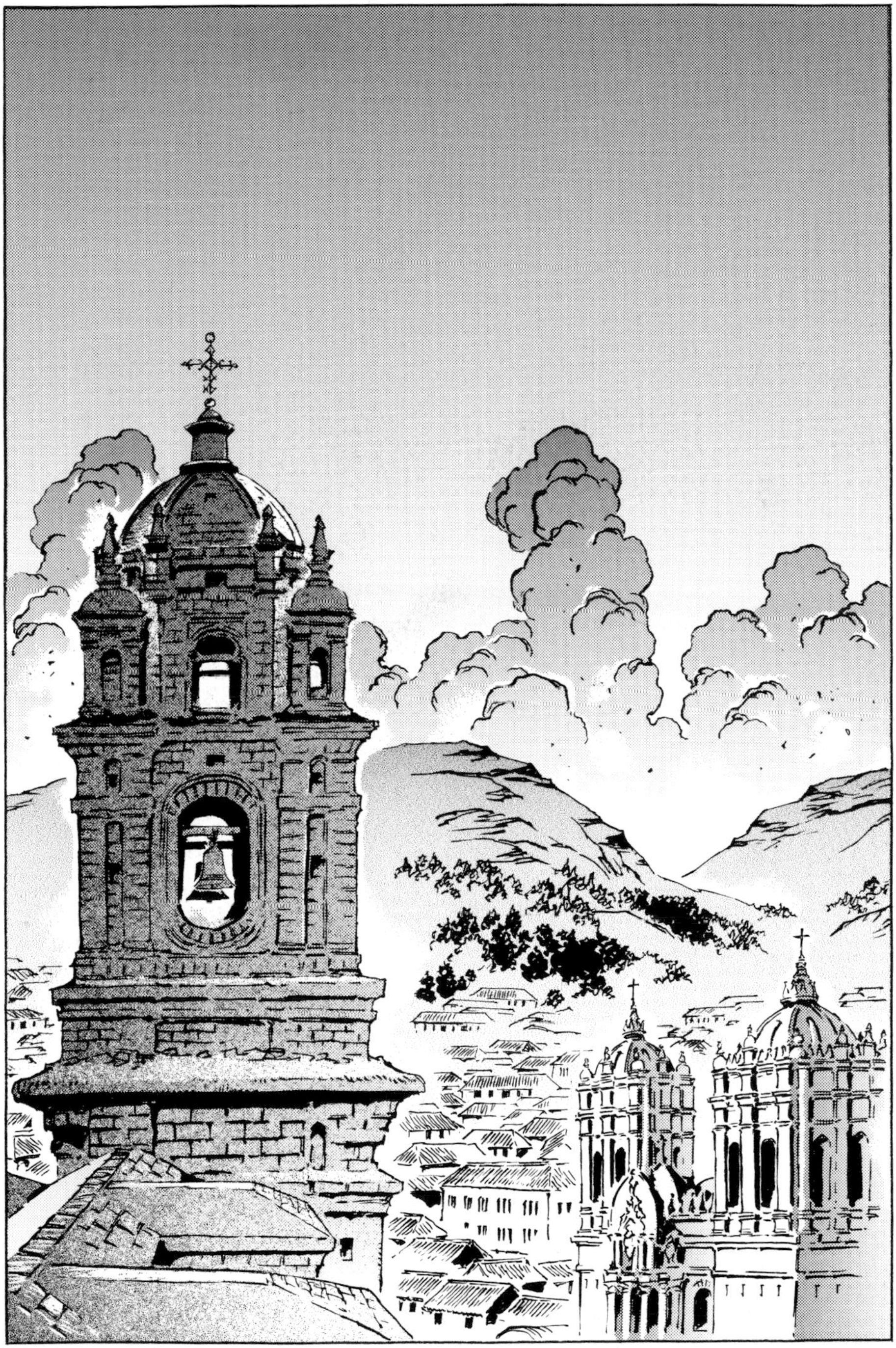

SECTION III

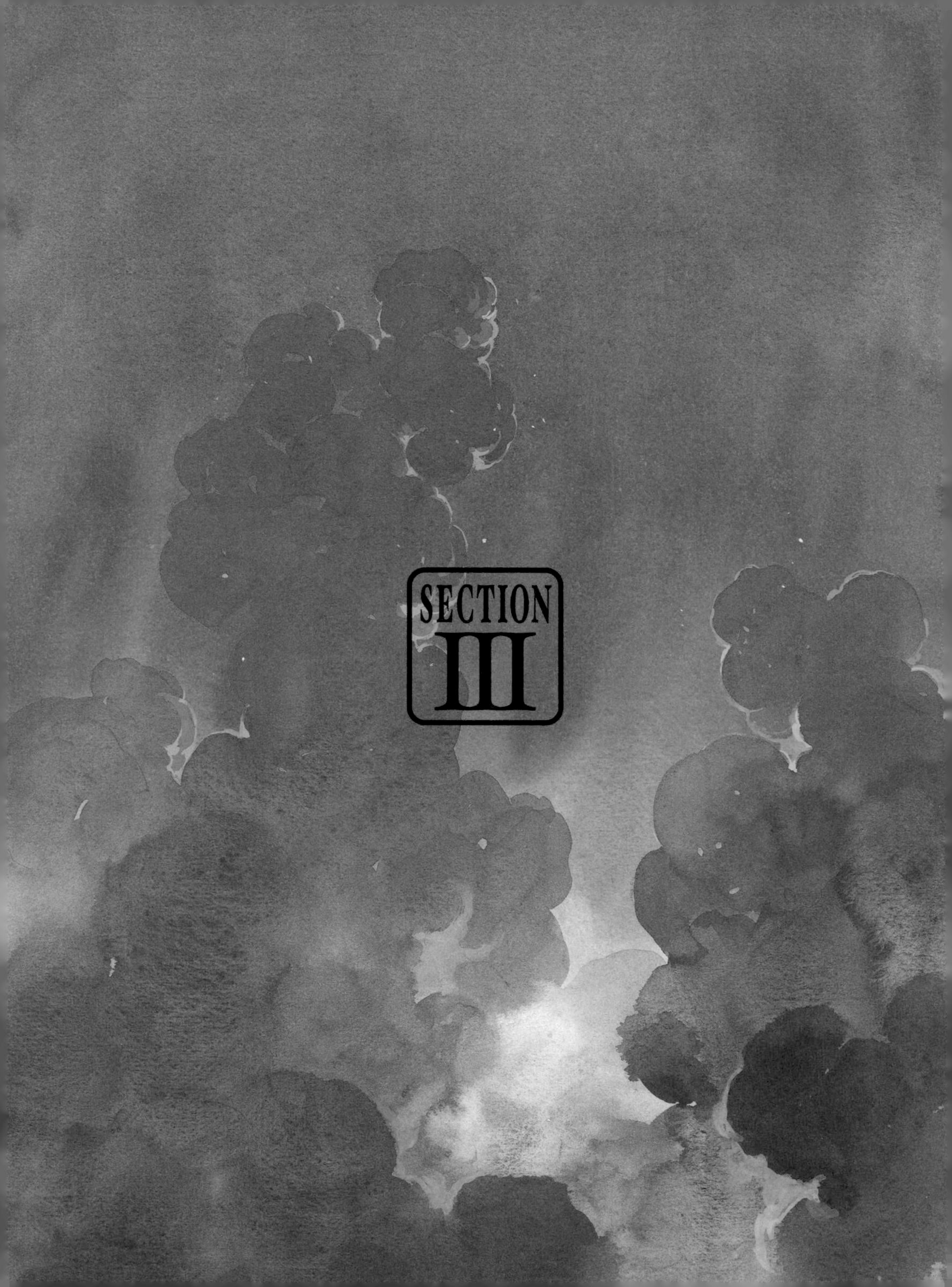

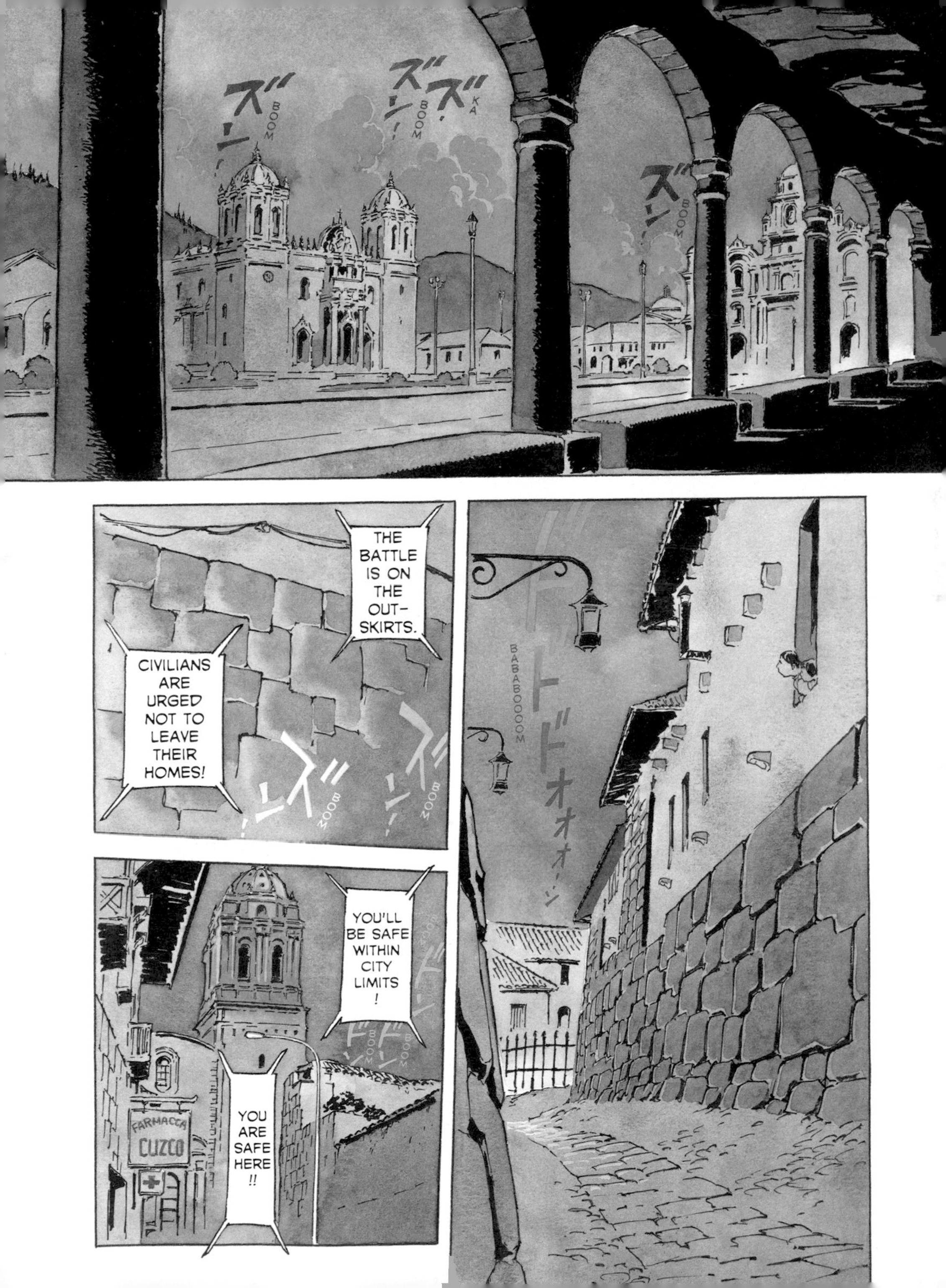
ズン BOOM
ズ KA
ズン! BOOM
ズン! BOOM
ドドドオオオーッ
BABABOOOOOM
THE BATTLE IS ON THE OUT-SKIRTS.
CIVILIANS ARE URGED NOT TO LEAVE THEIR HOMES!
ズン! BOOM
ズン! BOOM
YOU'LL BE SAFE WITHIN CITY LIMITS!
ドン BOOM
ドン BOOM
FARMACCA CUZCO
YOU ARE SAFE HERE!!

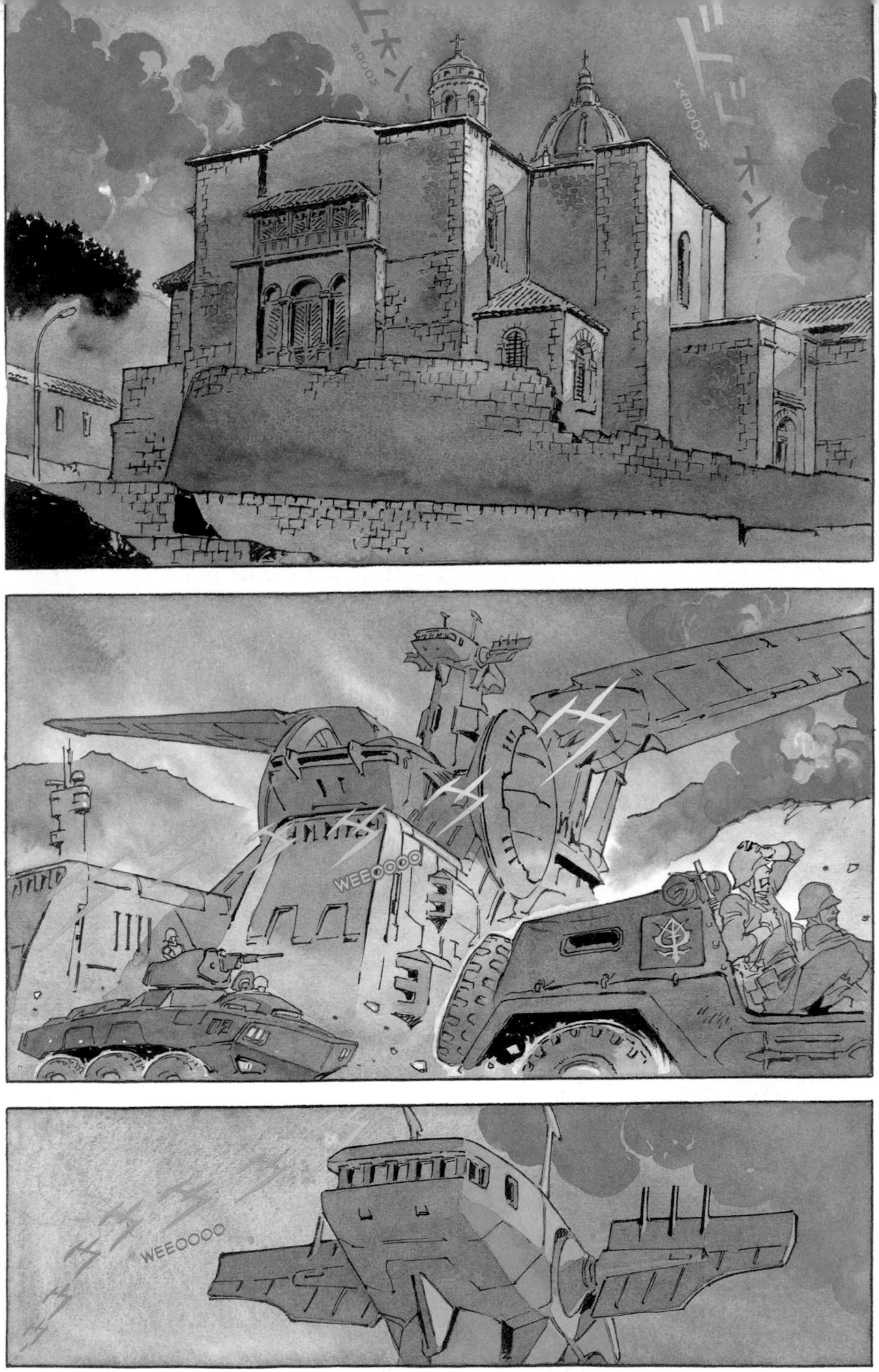
KABOOOM
BOOOOM
WEEOOOO
WEEOOOO

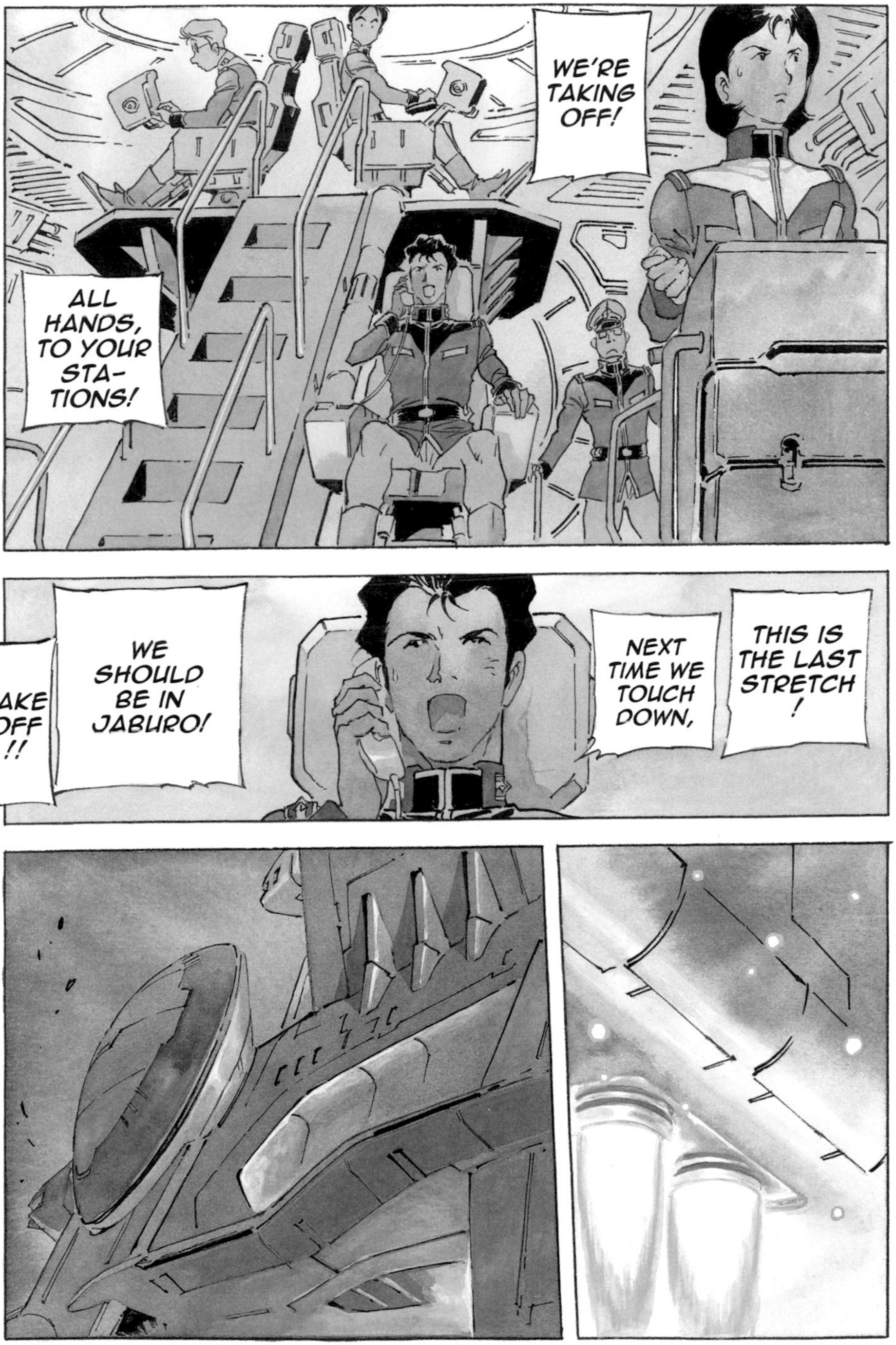
WE'RE TAKING OFF!
ALL HANDS, TO YOUR STATIONS!
THIS IS THE LAST STRETCH!
NEXT TIME WE TOUCH DOWN,
WE SHOULD BE IN JABURO!
TAKE OFF!!

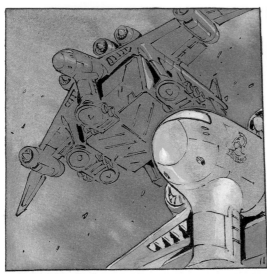

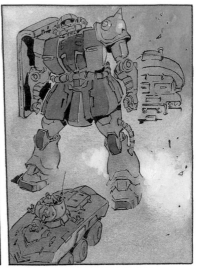

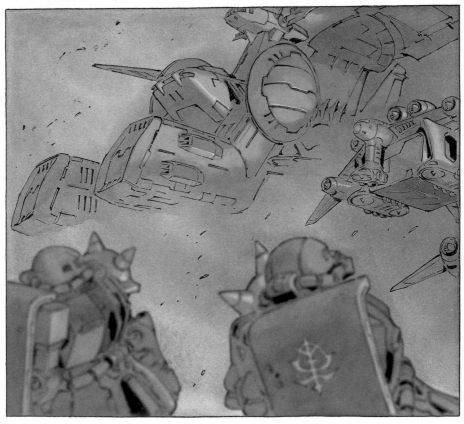

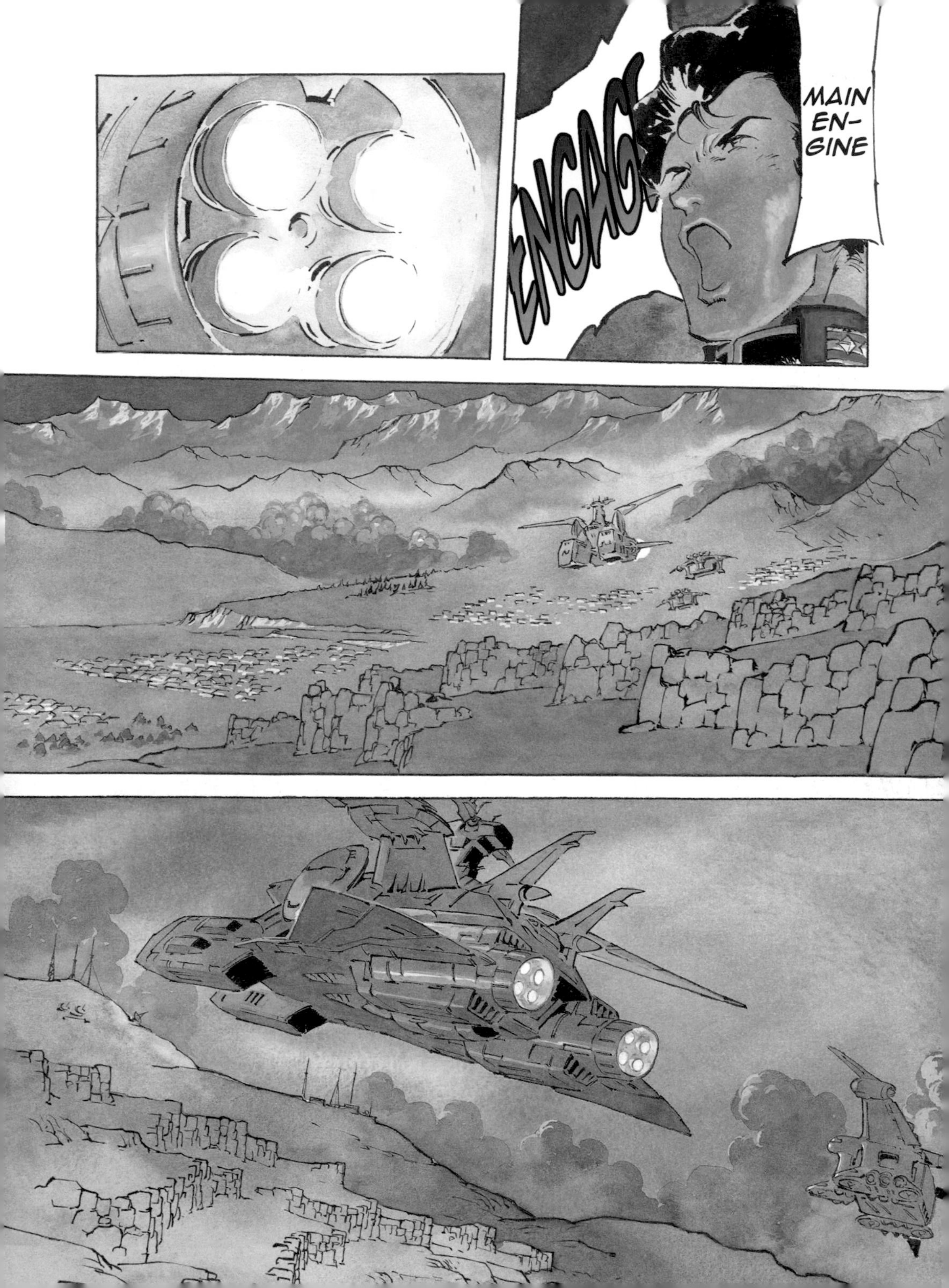
MAIN EN-GINE
ENGAG

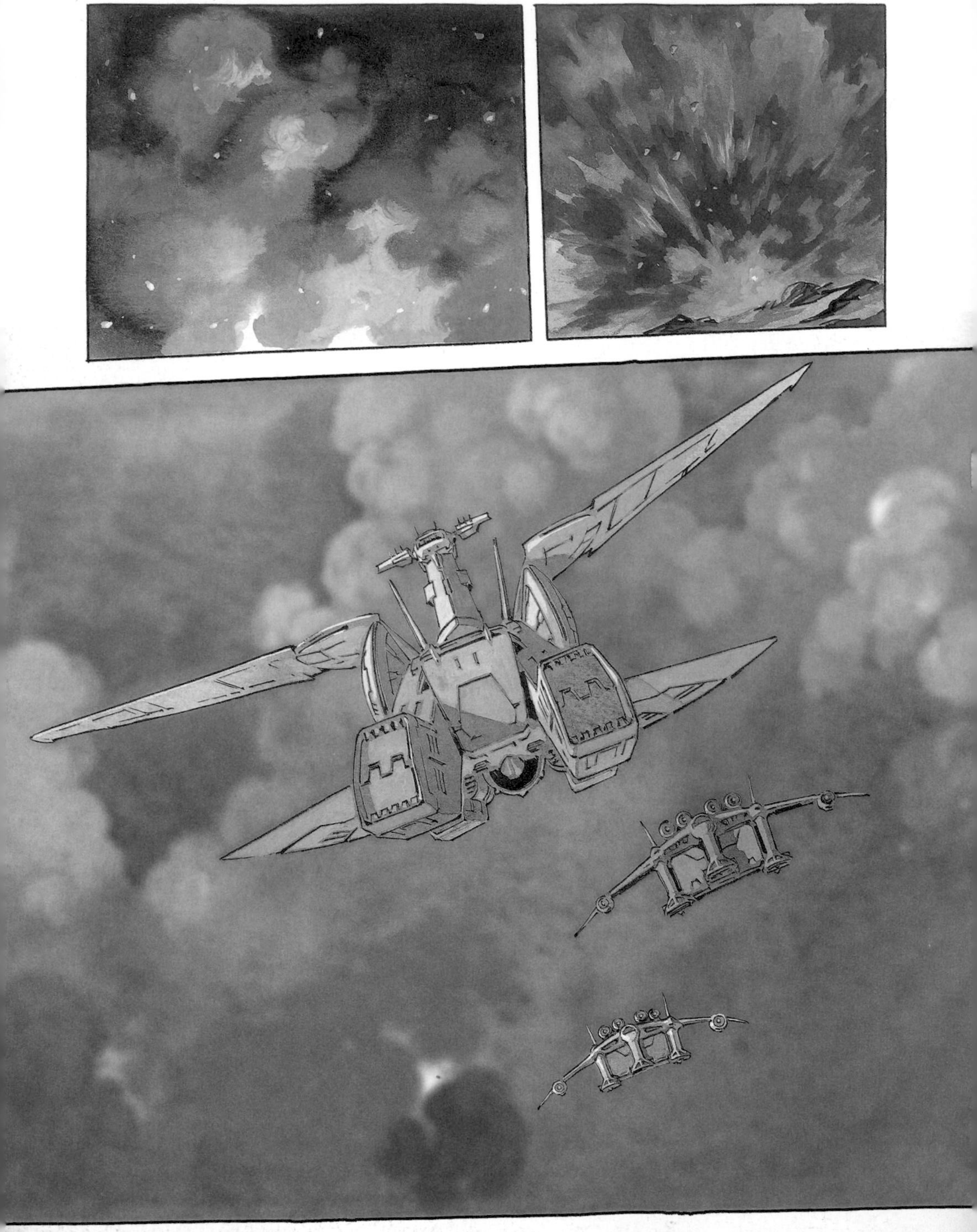

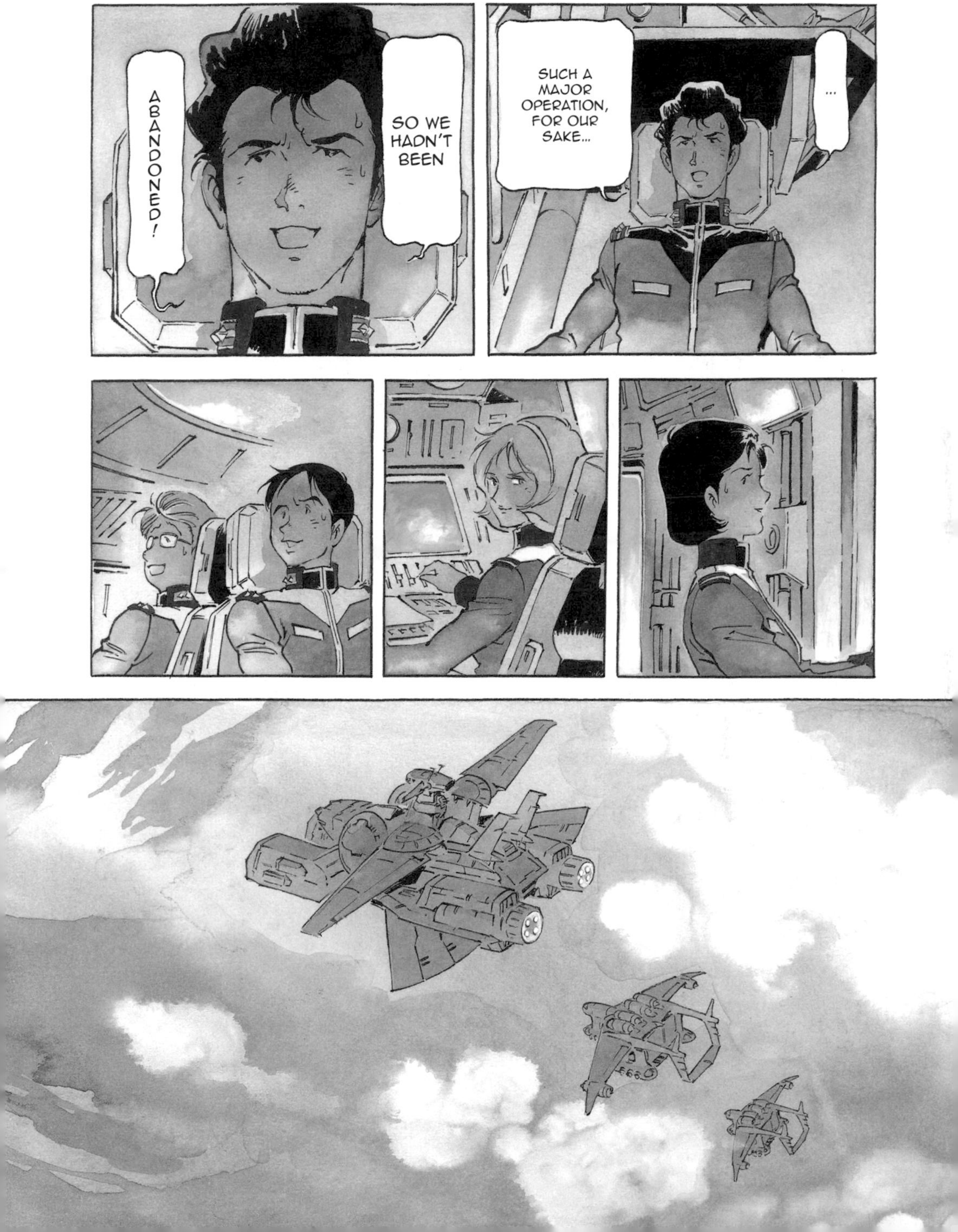
...
SUCH A MAJOR OPERATION, FOR OUR SAKE...
SO WE HADN'T BEEN
ABANDONED!

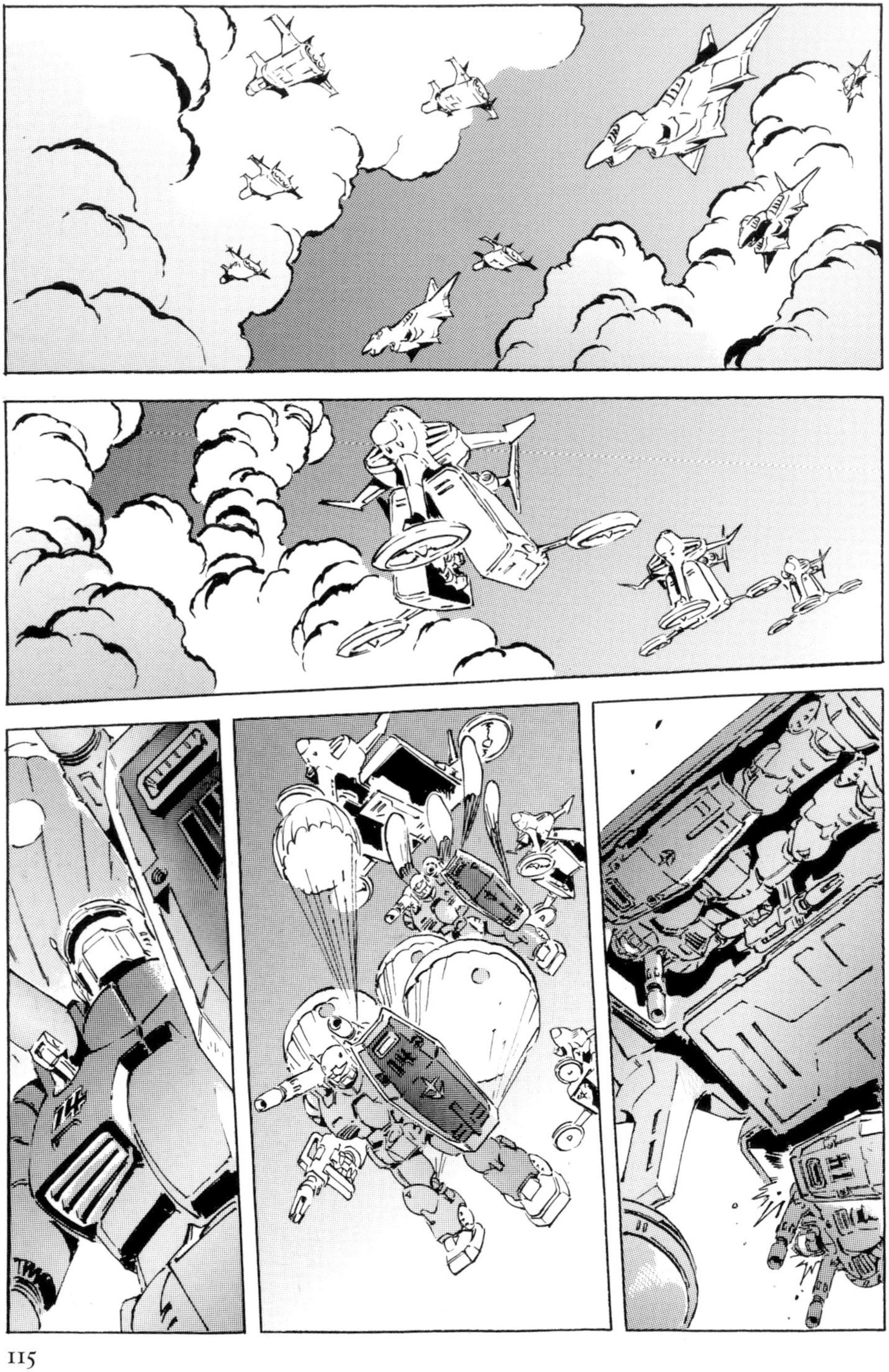

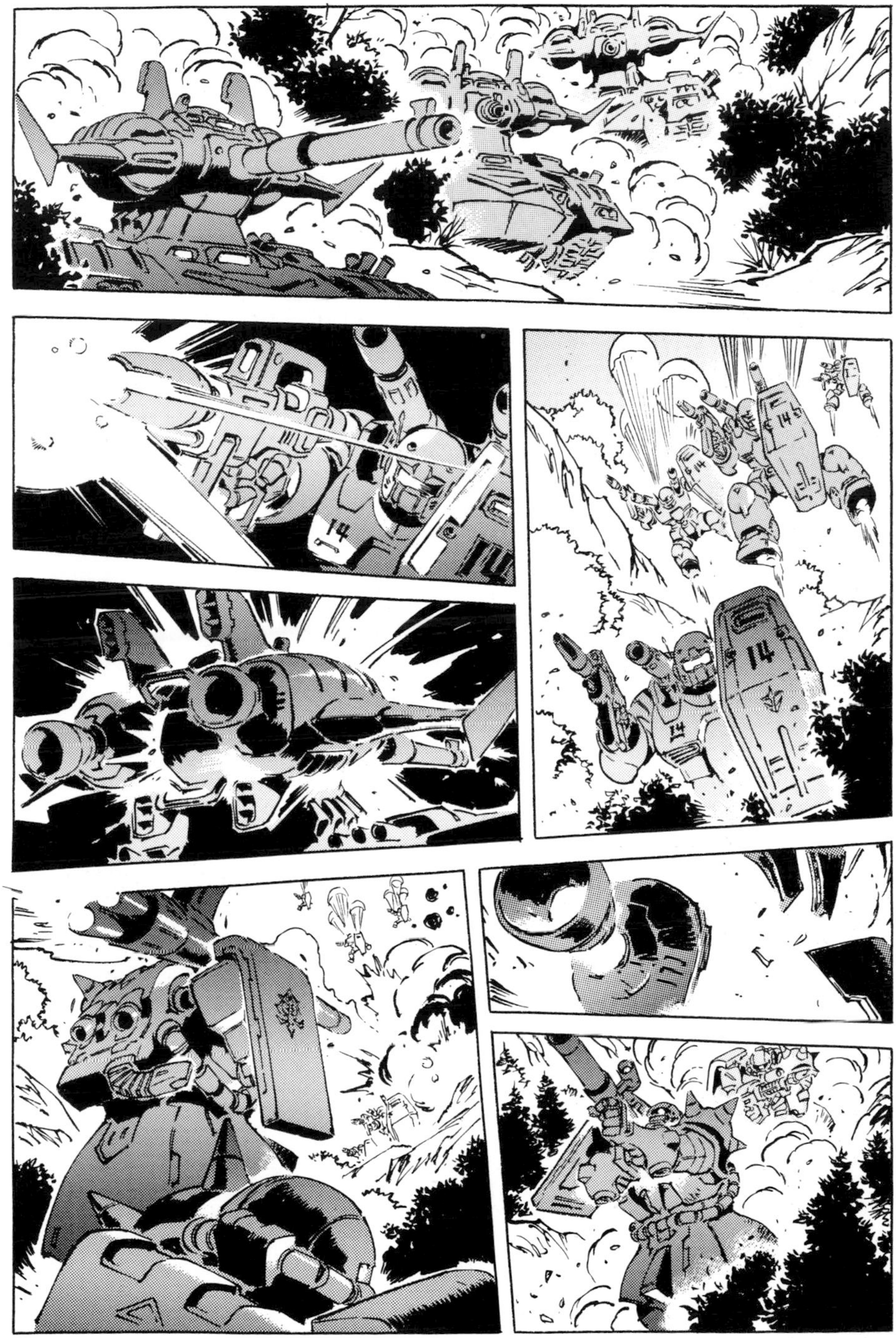

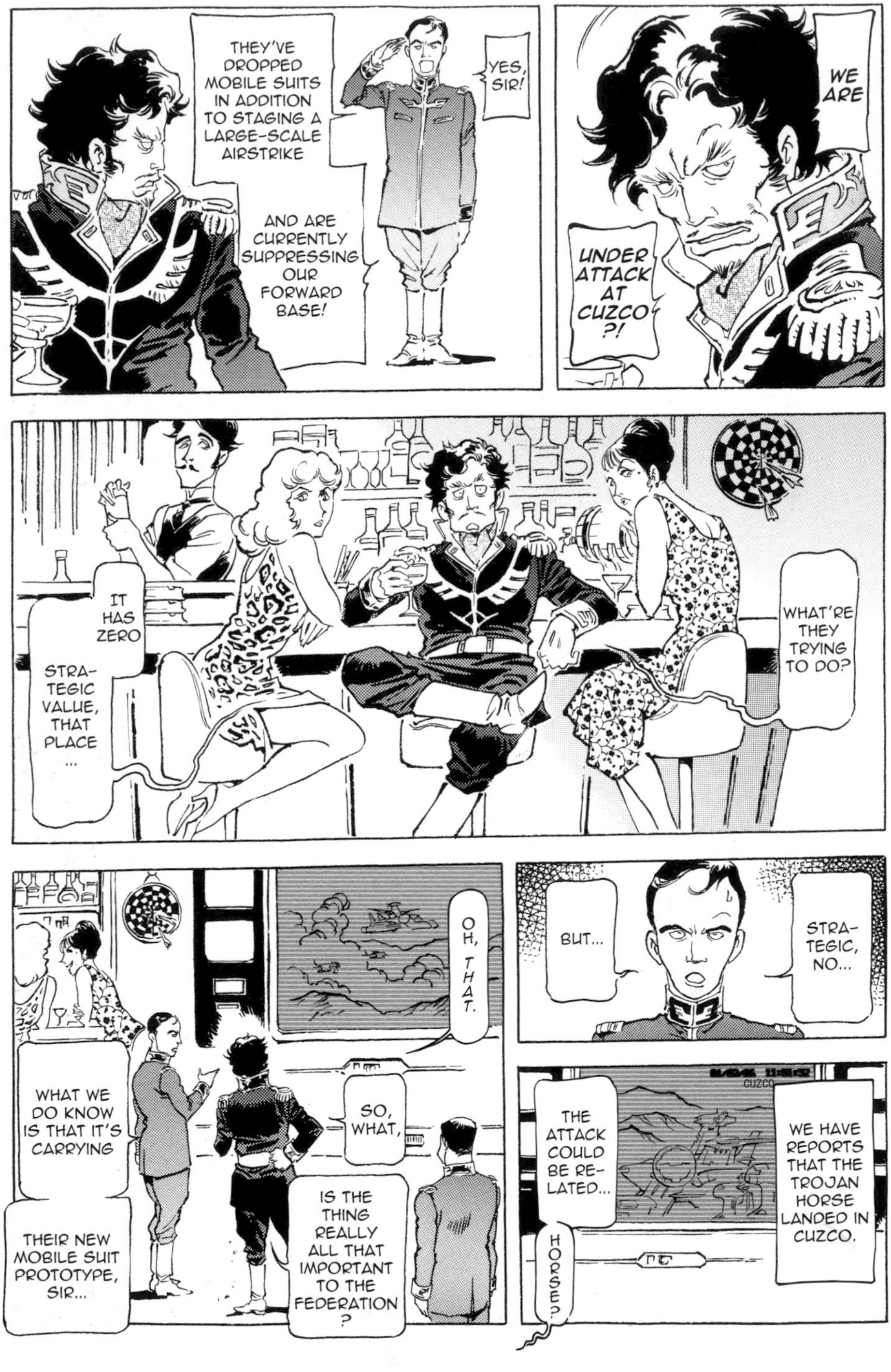
WE ARE
UNDER ATTACK AT CUZCO ?!
YES, SIR!
THEY'VE DROPPED MOBILE SUITS IN ADDITION TO STAGING A LARGE-SCALE AIRSTRIKE
AND ARE CURRENTLY SUPPRESSING OUR FORWARD BASE!
WHAT'RE THEY TRYING TO DO?
IT HAS ZERO
STRA-TEGIC VALUE, THAT PLACE ...
STRA-TEGIC, NO...
BUT...
WE HAVE REPORTS THAT THE TROJAN HORSE LANDED IN CUZCO.
CUZCO
THE ATTACK COULD BE RE-LATED...
HORSE?
OH, THAT.
SO, WHAT,
IS THE THING REALLY ALL THAT IMPORTANT TO THE FEDERATION ?
WHAT WE DO KNOW IS THAT IT'S CARRYING
THEIR NEW MOBILE SUIT PROTOTYPE, SIR...

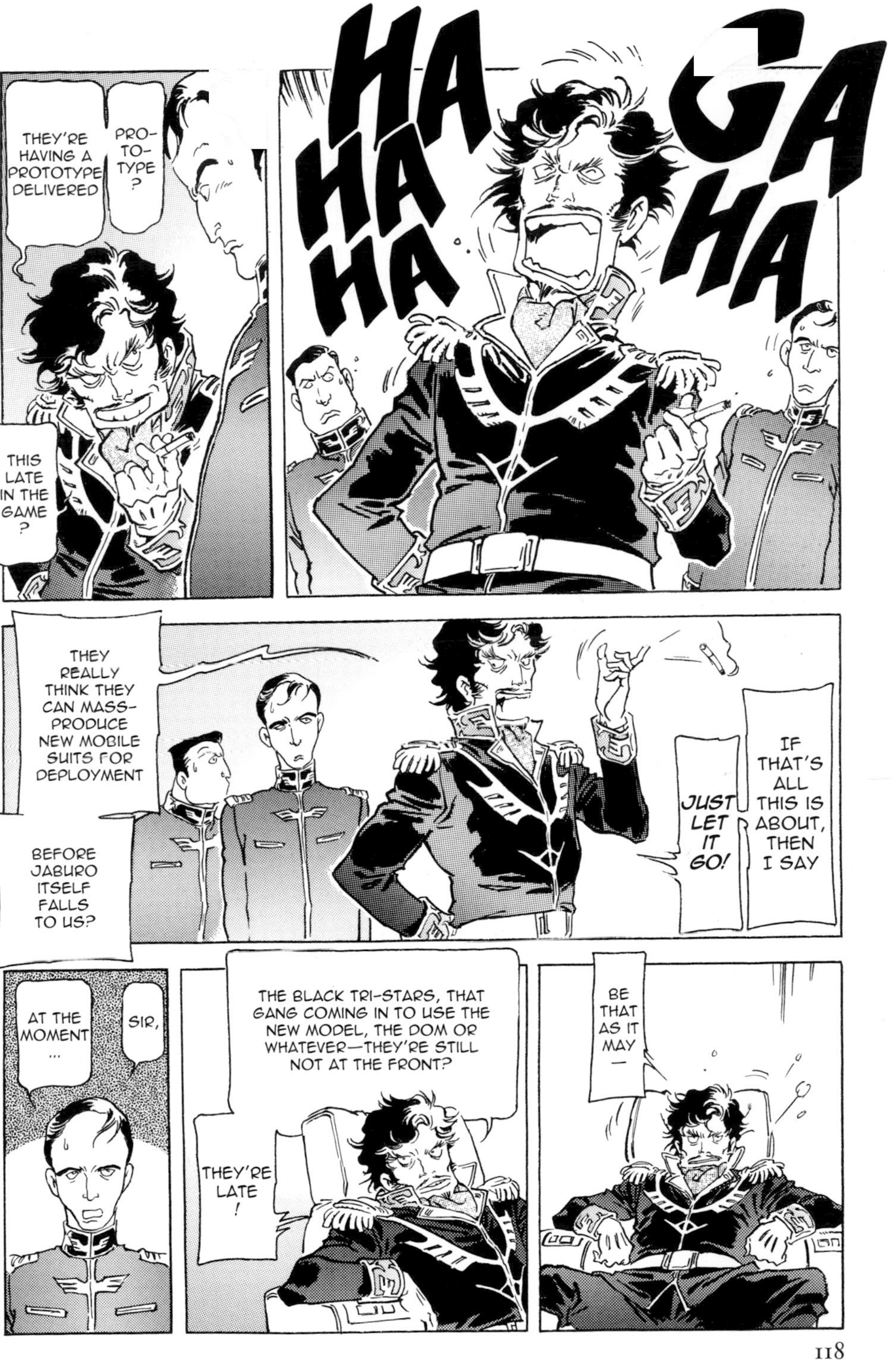
GA HA HA
HA HA HA HA HA
PROTO-TYPE?
THEY'RE HAVING A PROTOTYPE DELIVERED
THIS LATE IN THE GAME?
IF THAT'S ALL THIS IS ABOUT, THEN I SAY
JUST LET IT GO!
THEY REALLY THINK THEY CAN MASS-PRODUCE NEW MOBILE SUITS FOR DEPLOYMENT
BEFORE JABURO ITSELF FALLS TO US?
BE THAT AS IT MAY—
THE BLACK TRI-STARS, THAT GANG COMING IN TO USE THE NEW MODEL, THE DOM OR WHATEVER—THEY'RE STILL NOT AT THE FRONT?
THEY'RE LATE!
SIR,
AT THE MOMENT...

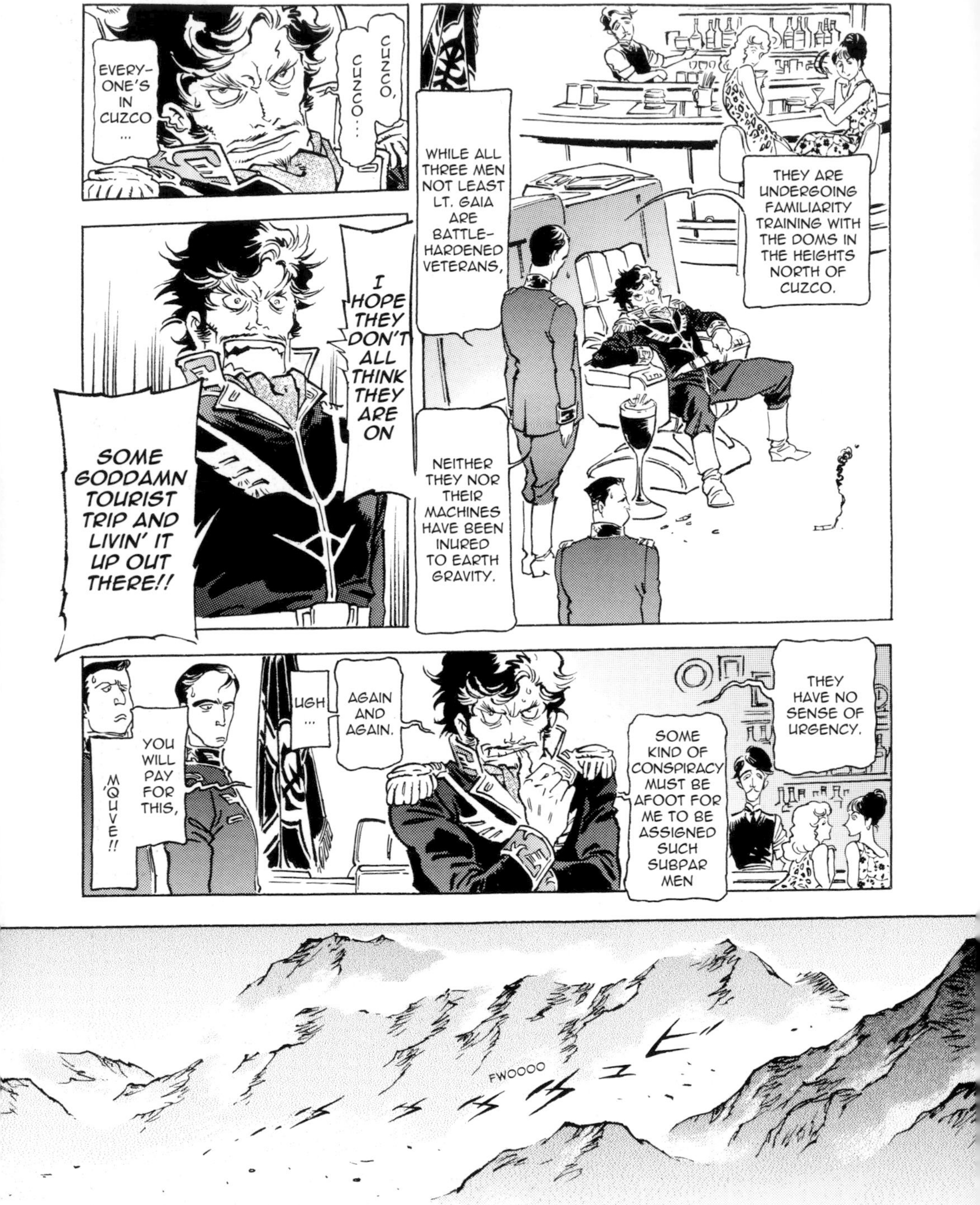
THEY ARE UNDERGOING FAMILIARITY TRAINING WITH THE DOMS IN THE HEIGHTS NORTH OF CUZCO.
WHILE ALL THREE MEN NOT LEAST LT. GAIA ARE BATTLE-HARDENED VETERANS,
NEITHER THEY NOR THEIR MACHINES HAVE BEEN INURED TO EARTH GRAVITY.
CUZCO, CUZCO...
EVERYONE'S IN CUZCO...
I HOPE THEY DON'T ALL THINK THEY ARE ON
SOME GODDAMN TOURIST TRIP AND LIVIN' IT UP OUT THERE!!
THEY HAVE NO SENSE OF URGENCY.
SOME KIND OF CONSPIRACY MUST BE AFOOT FOR ME TO BE ASSIGNED SUCH SUBPAR MEN
AGAIN AND AGAIN.
UGH...
YOU WILL PAY FOR THIS,
M'QUVE!!
FWOOOO

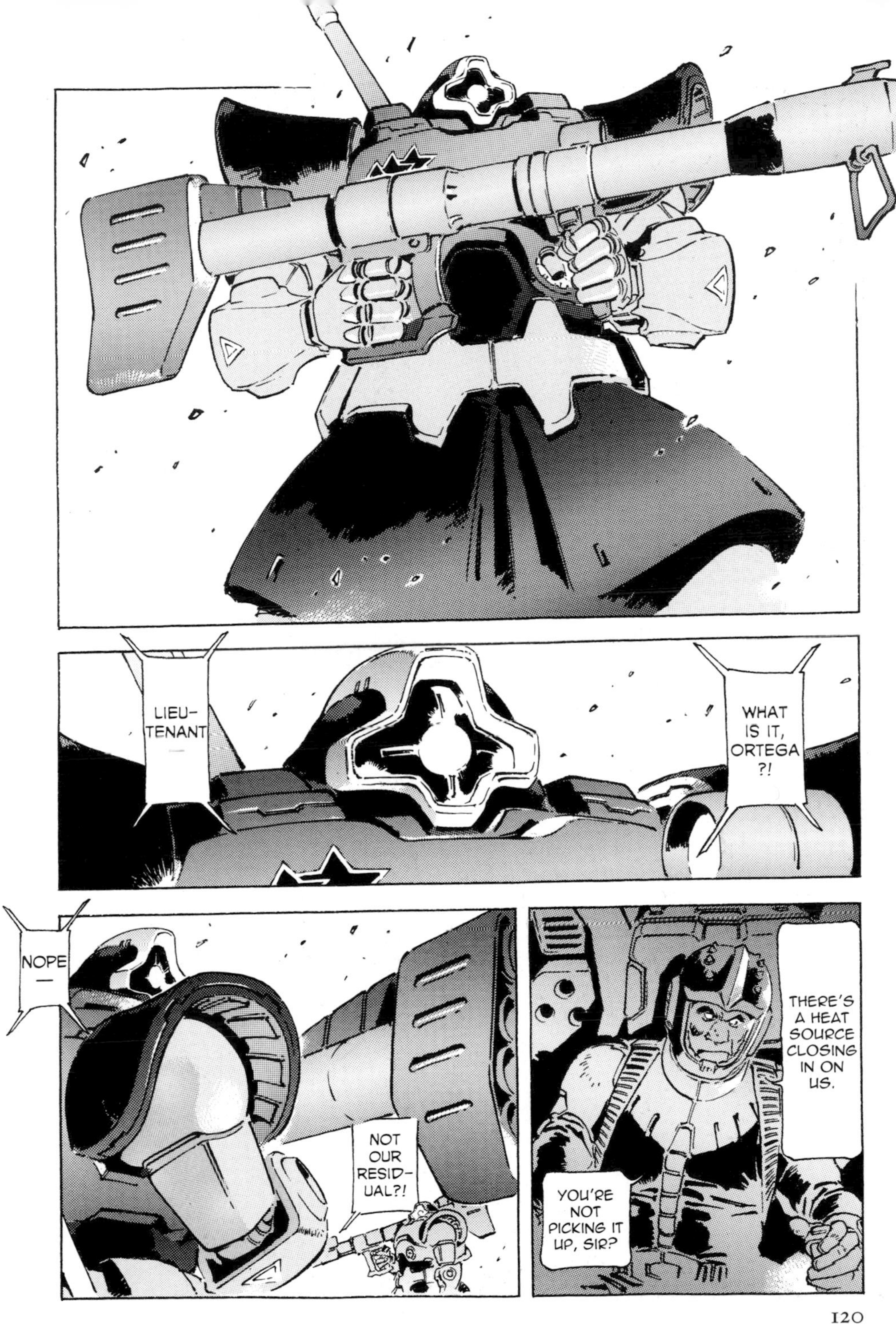
LIEU-TENANT—
WHAT IS IT, ORTEGA?!
THERE'S A HEAT SOURCE CLOSING IN ON US.
YOU'RE NOT PICKING IT UP, SIR?
NOPE—
NOT OUR RESID-UAL?!

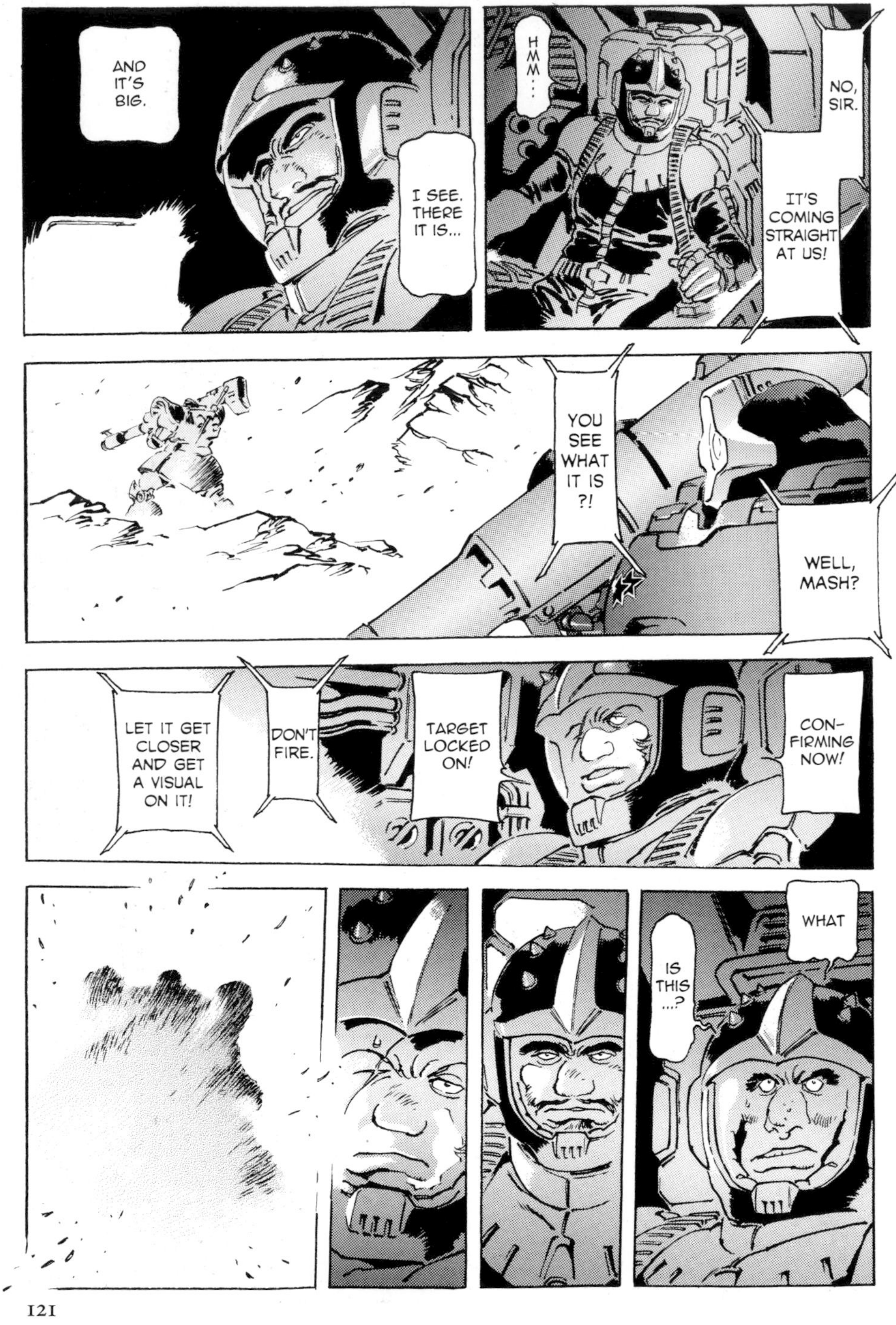
NO, SIR.
HMM...
IT'S COMING STRAIGHT AT US!
I SEE. THERE IT IS...
AND IT'S BIG.
WELL, MASH?
YOU SEE WHAT IT IS ?!
CON-FIRMING NOW!
TARGET LOCKED ON!
DON'T FIRE.
LET IT GET CLOSER AND GET A VISUAL ON IT!
WHAT
IS THIS ...?

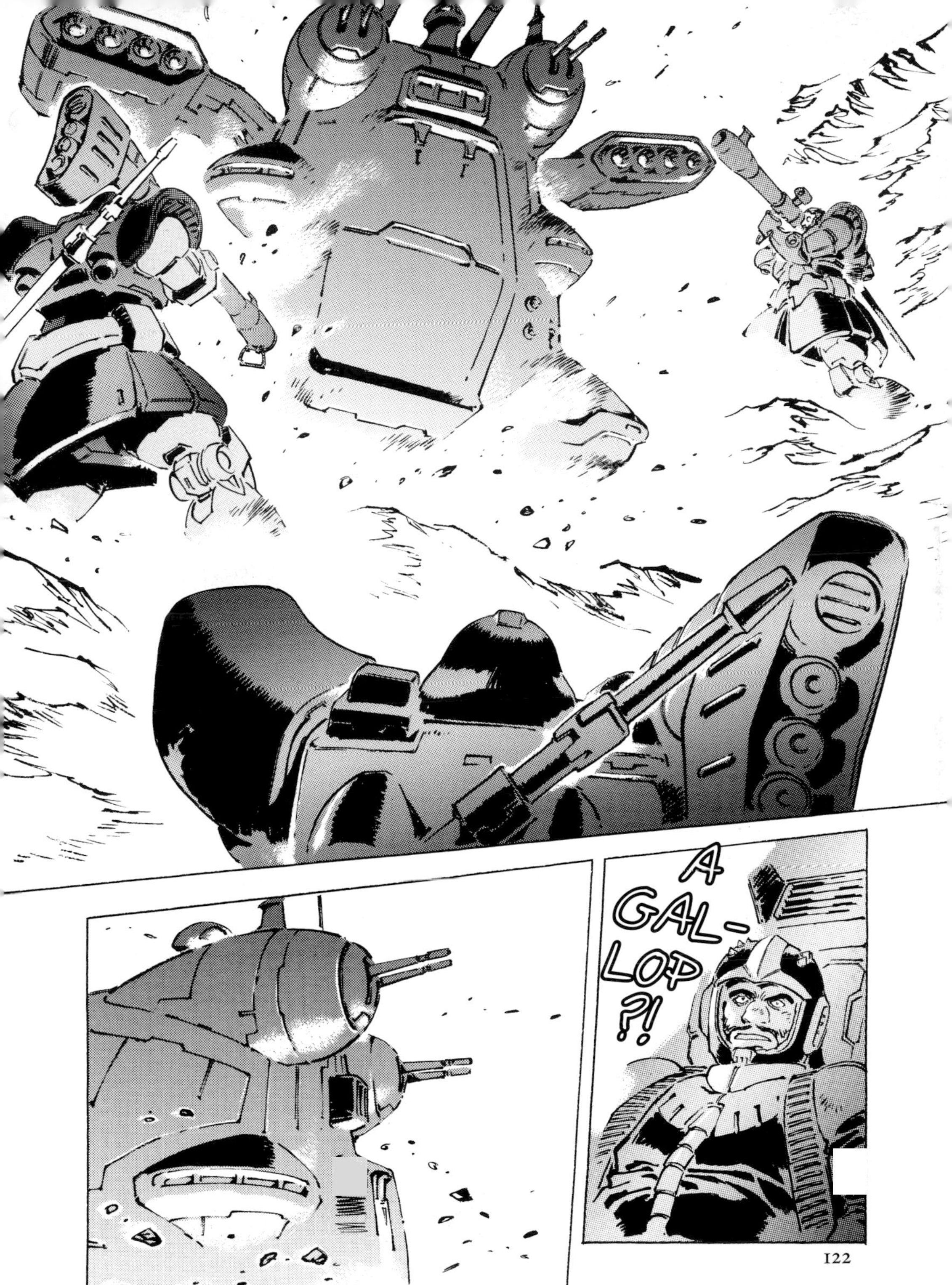
A GAL-LOP?!

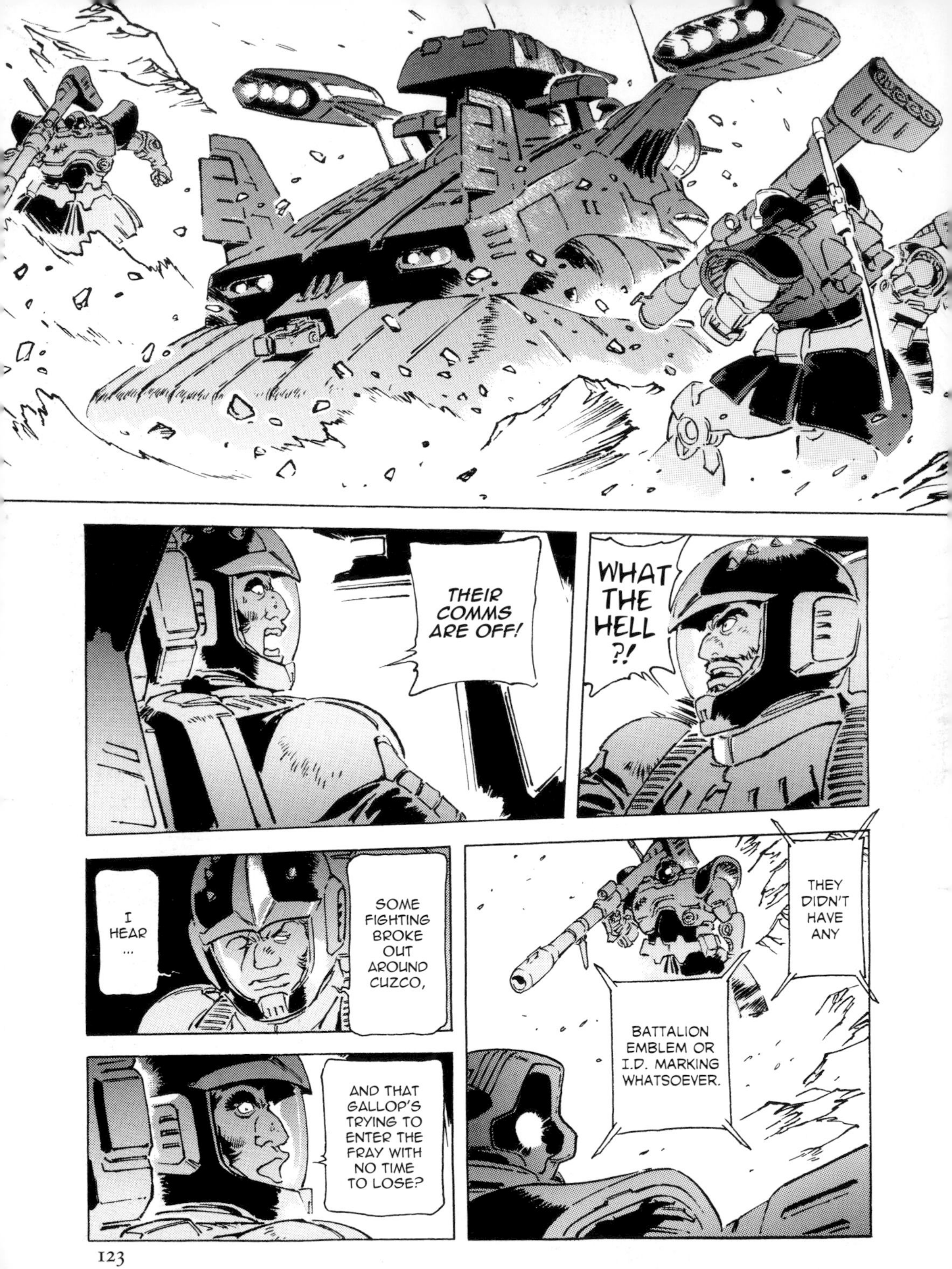
WHAT THE HELL ?!
THEIR COMMS ARE OFF!
THEY DIDN'T HAVE ANY
BATTALION EMBLEM OR I.D. MARKING WHATSOEVER.
SOME FIGHTING BROKE OUT AROUND CUZCO,
I HEAR ...
AND THAT GALLOP'S TRYING TO ENTER THE FRAY WITH NO TIME TO LOSE?

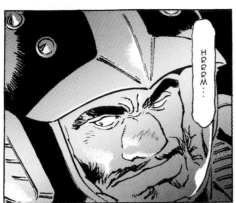

HRRRM...

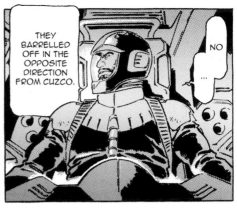

THEY BARRELLED OFF IN THE OPPOSITE DIRECTION FROM CUZCO.

NO
...

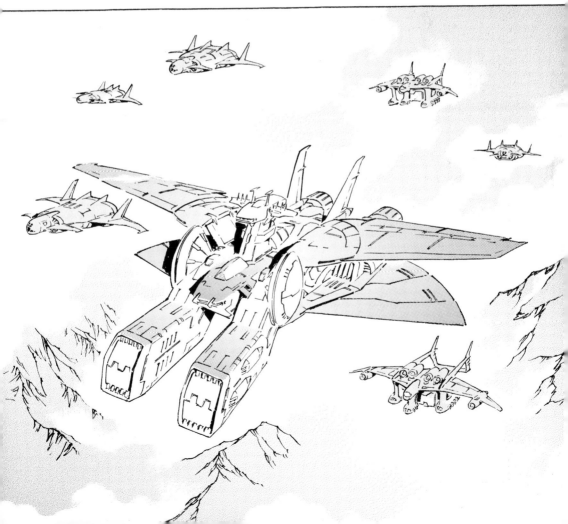

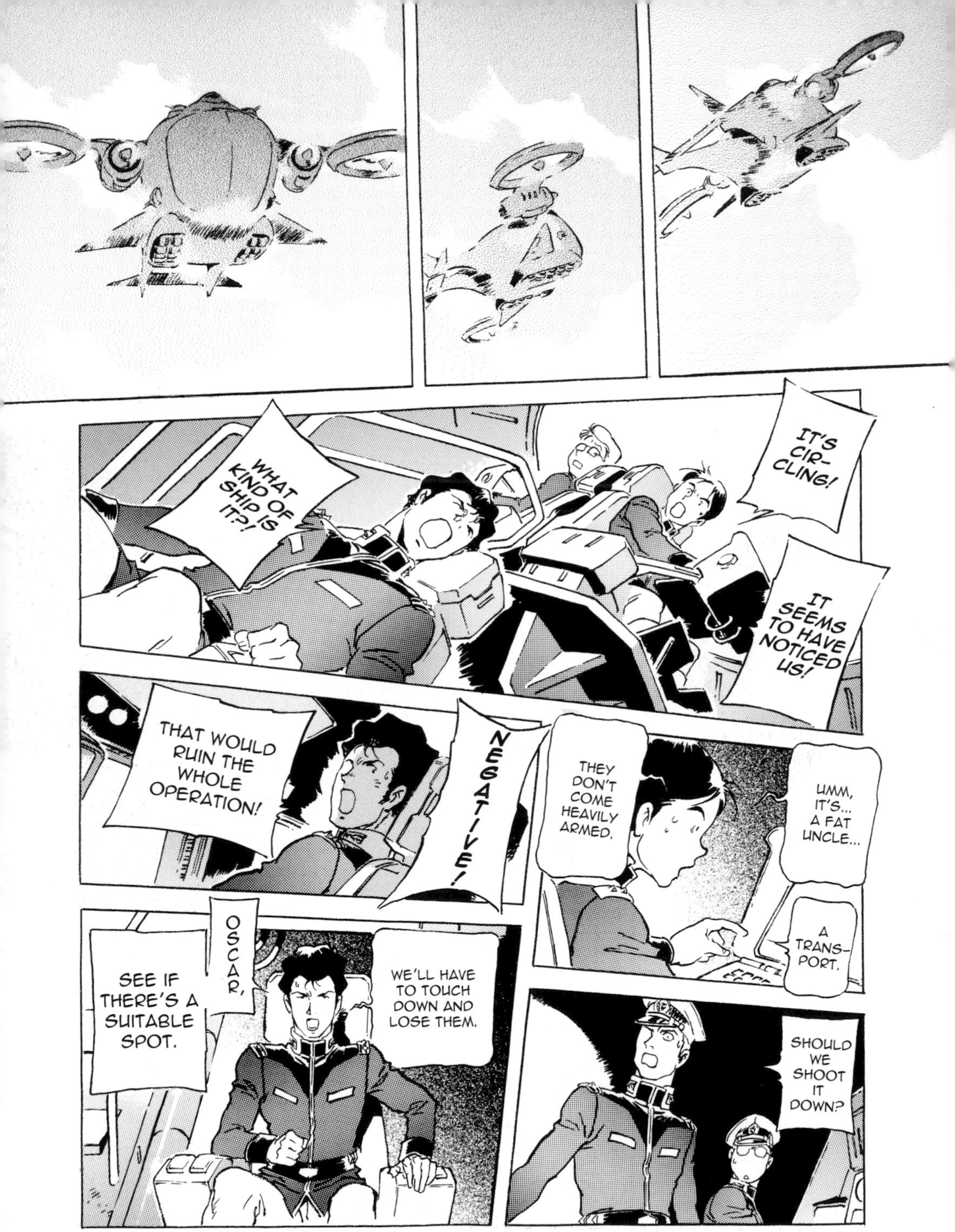

IT'S CIR-CLING!
IT SEEMS TO HAVE NOTICED US!
WHAT KIND OF SHIP IS IT?!
UMM, IT'S... A FAT UNCLE...
THEY DON'T COME HEAVILY ARMED.
A TRANS-PORT.
SHOULD WE SHOOT IT DOWN?
NEGATIVE!
THAT WOULD RUIN THE WHOLE OPERATION!
WE'LL HAVE TO TOUCH DOWN AND LOSE THEM.
OSCAR,
SEE IF THERE'S A SUITABLE SPOT.

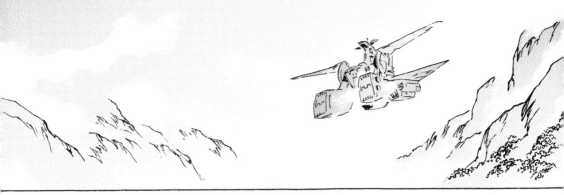

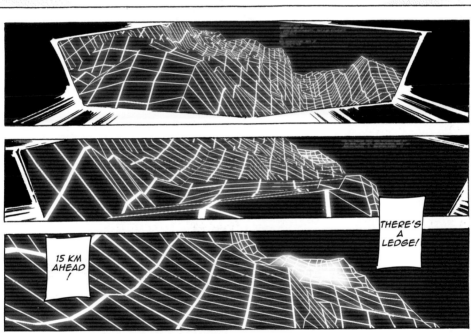

THERE'S A LEDGE!

15 KM AHEAD !

IT WILL DO!

FINE,

IT'S NARROW, THOUGH, AND DIPS HARD TOWARD THE RIVER...

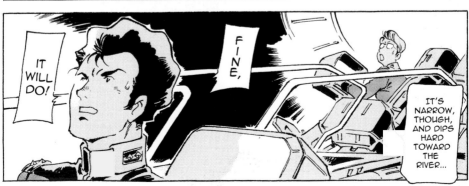

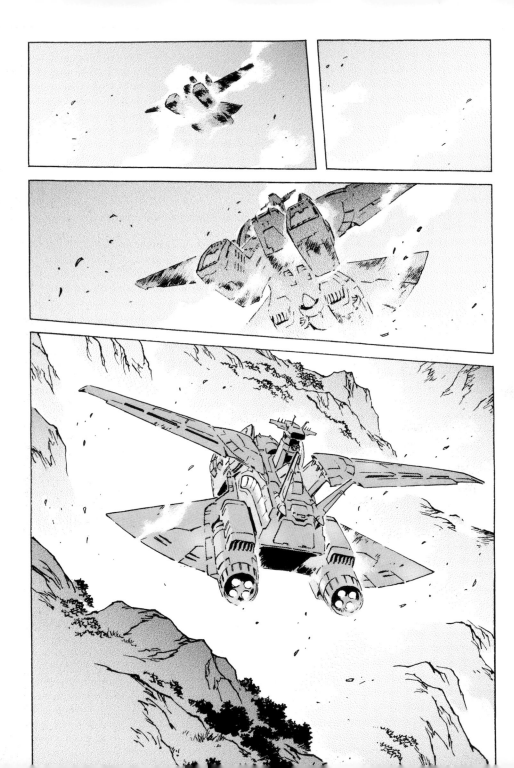

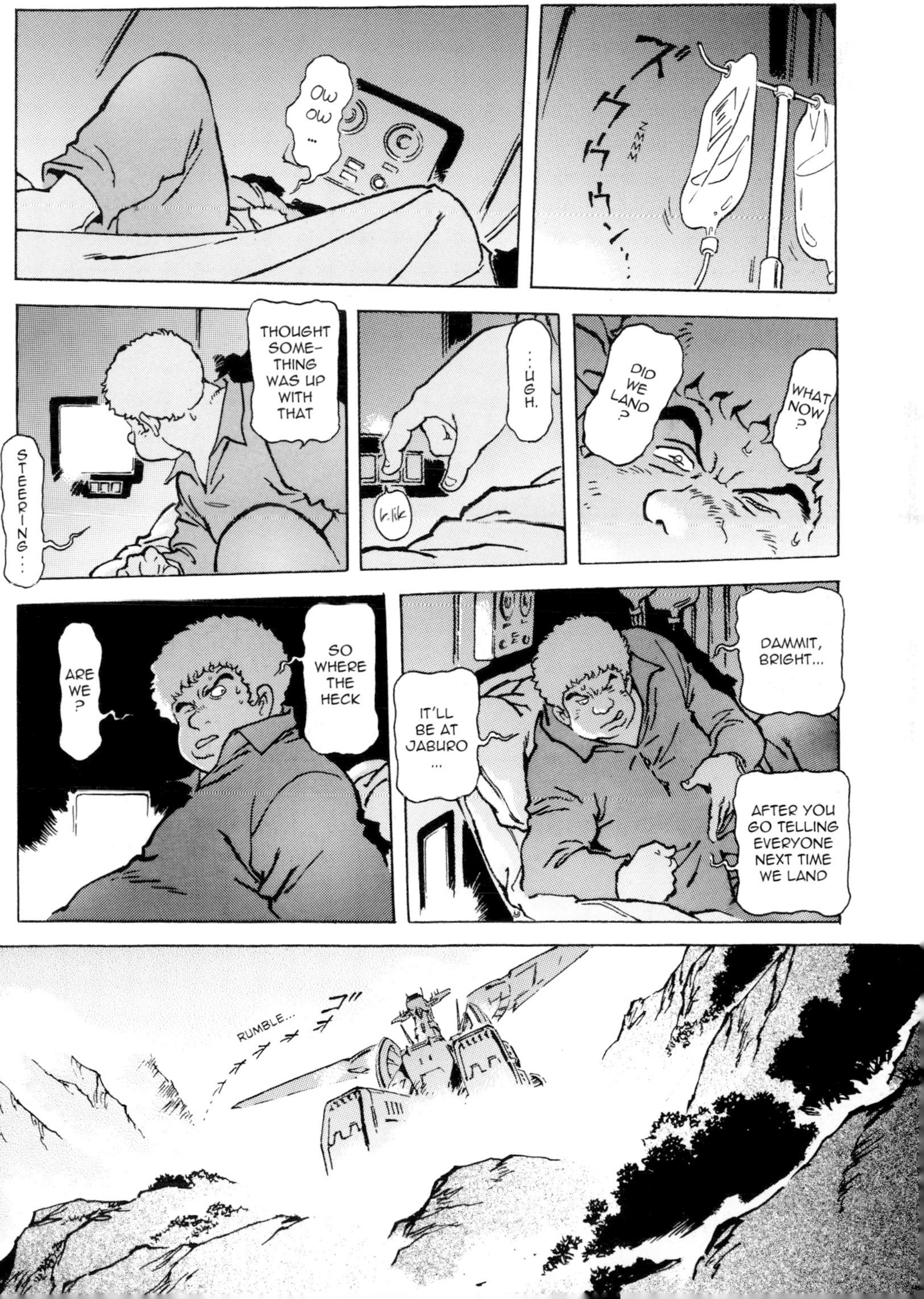

ズウウウン…
ZMMM
OW OW …
WHAT NOW?
DID WE LAND?
…UGH.
k-lik
THOUGHT SOME-THING WAS UP WITH THAT
STEERING…
DAMMIT, BRIGHT…
AFTER YOU GO TELLING EVERYONE NEXT TIME WE LAND
IT'LL BE AT JABURO …
SO WHERE THE HECK
ARE WE?
ゴォォォォォ…
RUMBLE…

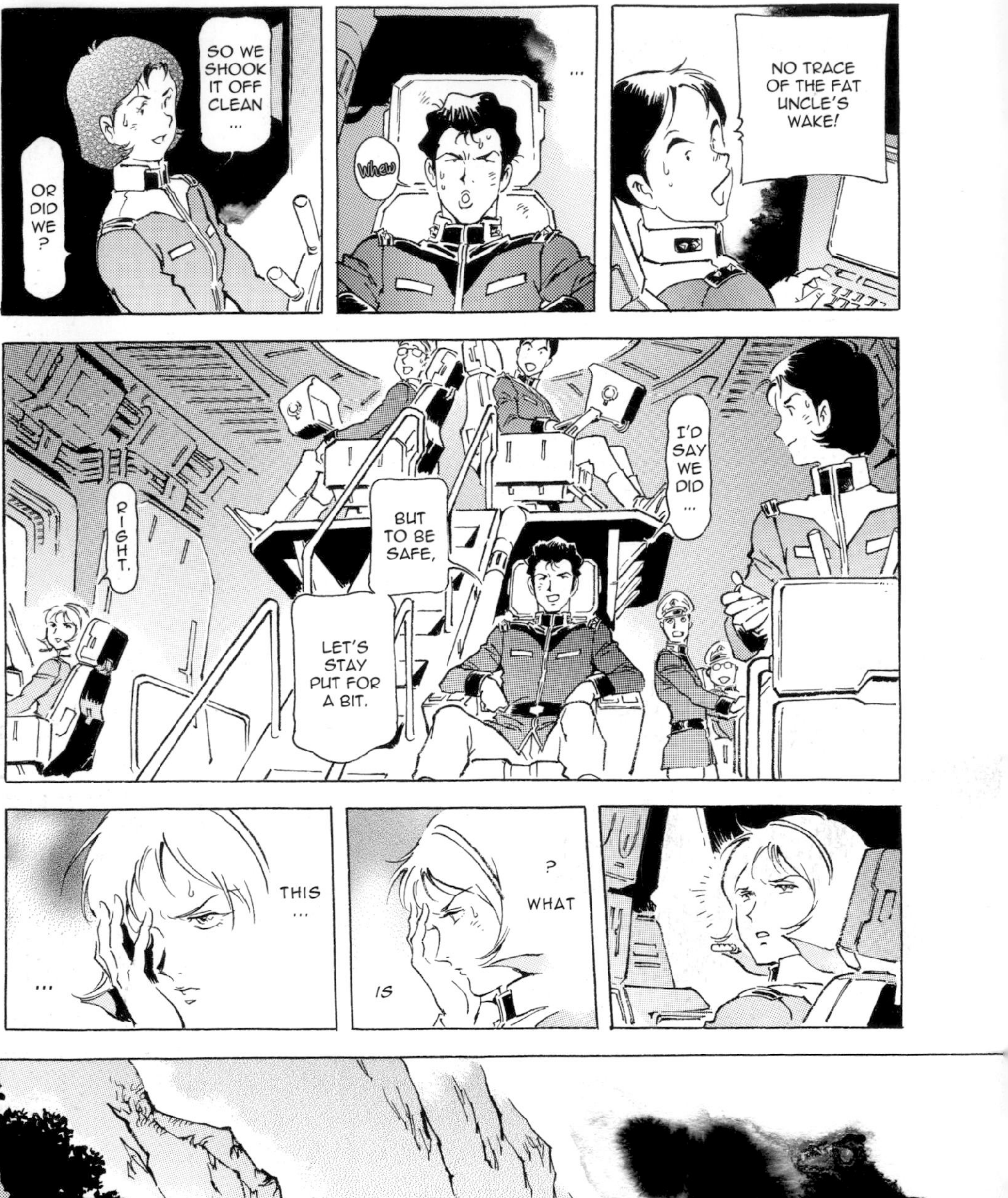
NO TRACE OF THE FAT UNCLE'S WAKE!
...
Whew
SO WE SHOOK IT OFF CLEAN ...
OR DID WE ?
I'D SAY WE DID ...
BUT TO BE SAFE,
LET'S STAY PUT FOR A BIT.
RIGHT.
? WHAT
IS
THIS ...
...
RUMBLE

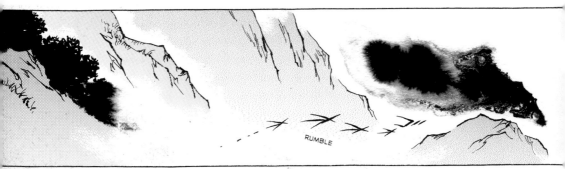

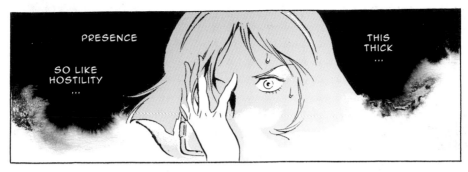

PRESENCE
SO LIKE
HOSTILITY
...

THIS
THICK
...

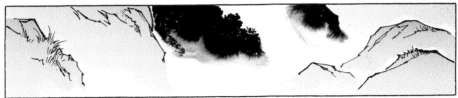

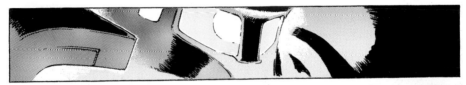

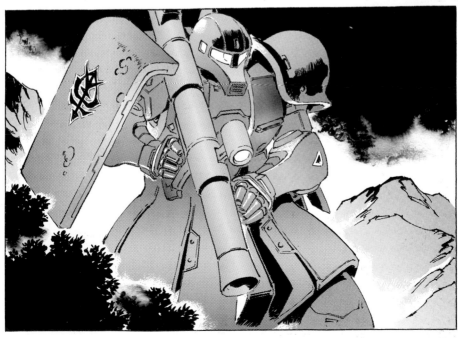

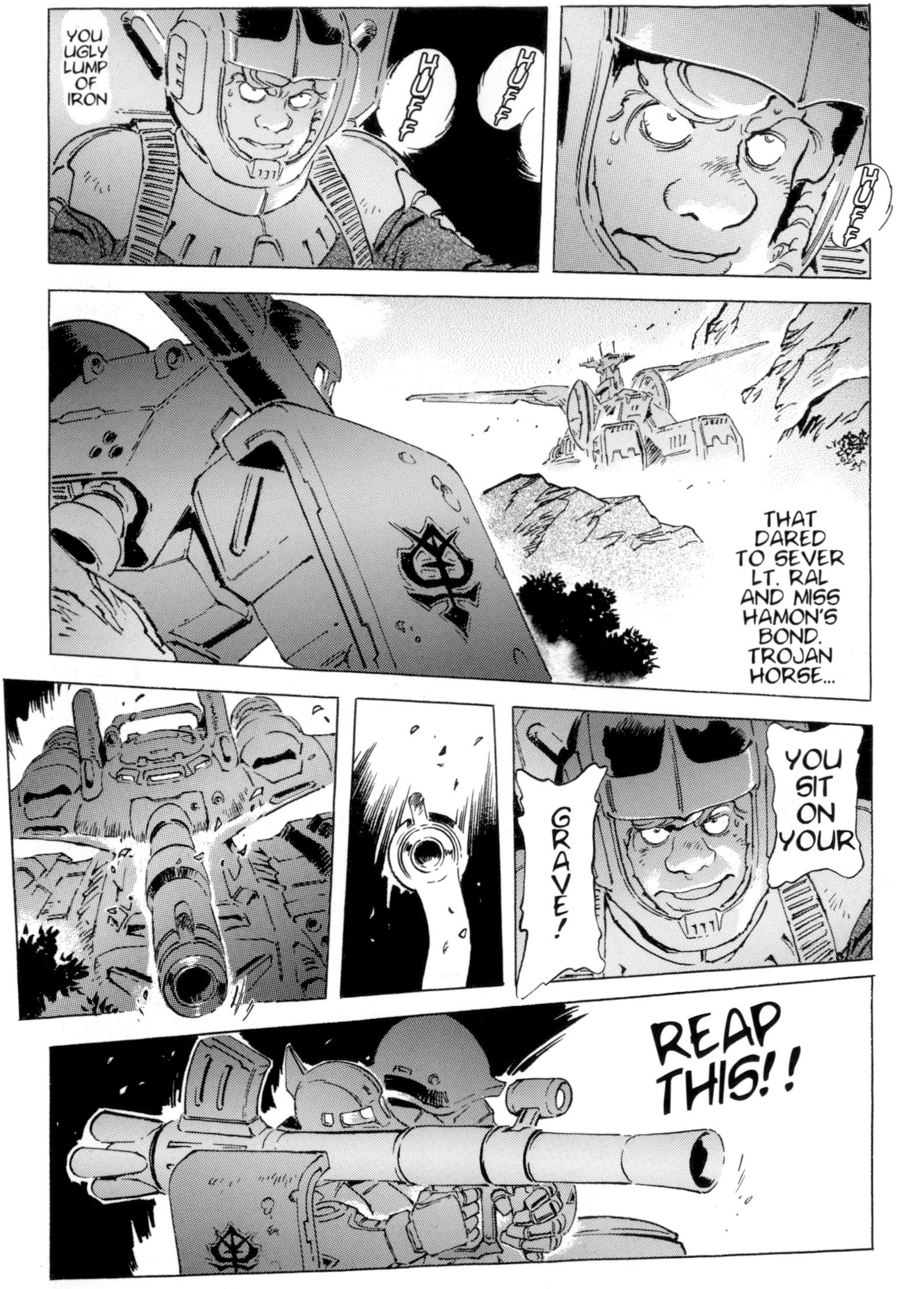
HUFF
HUFF
HUFF
YOU UGLY LUMP OF IRON
THAT DARED TO SEVER LT. RAL AND MISS HAMON'S BOND. TROJAN HORSE...
YOU SIT ON YOUR
GRAVE!
REAP THIS!!

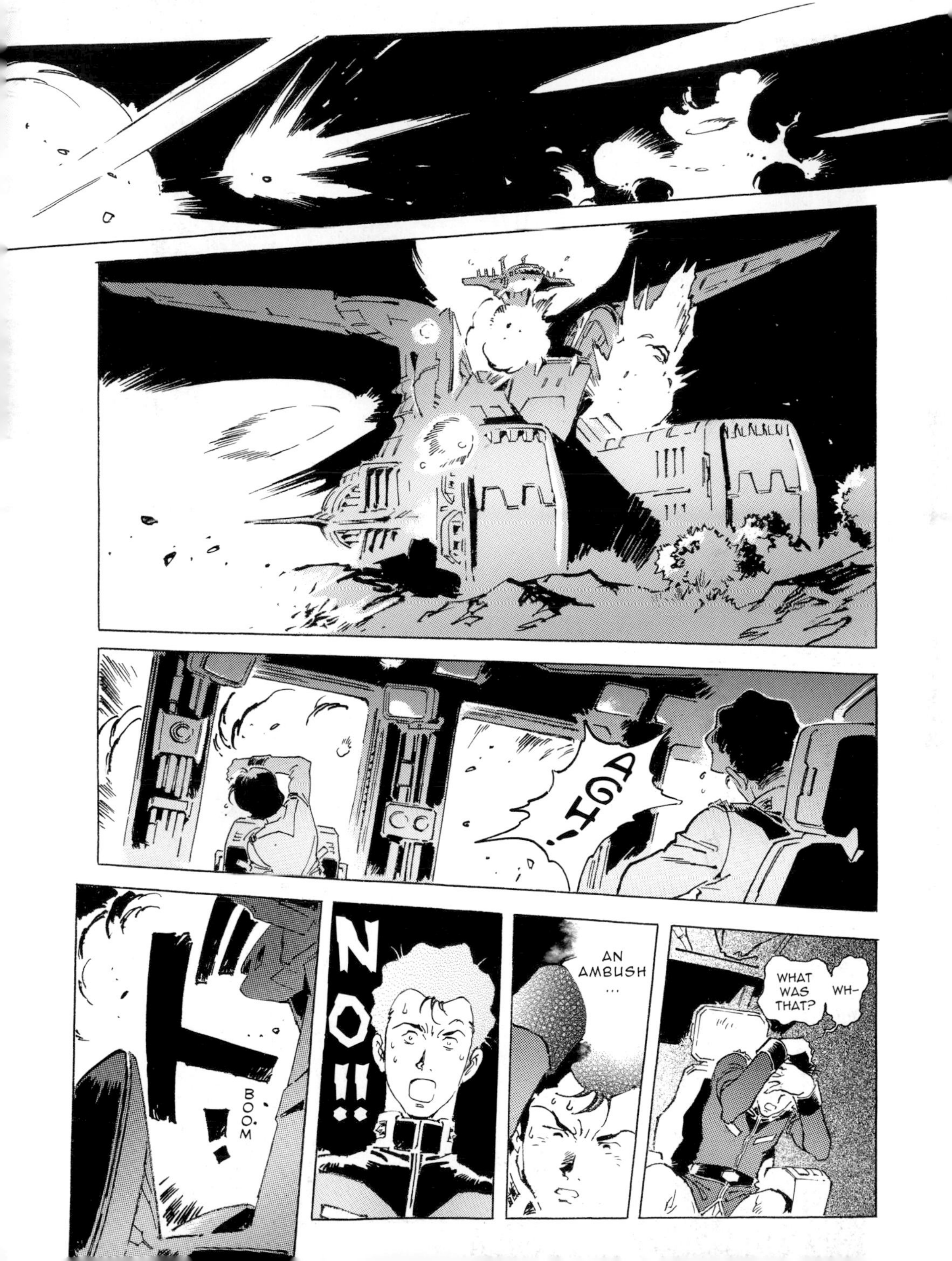
GOH!!
WH-
WHAT WAS THAT?
AN AMBUSH ...
NO!!
BOOM

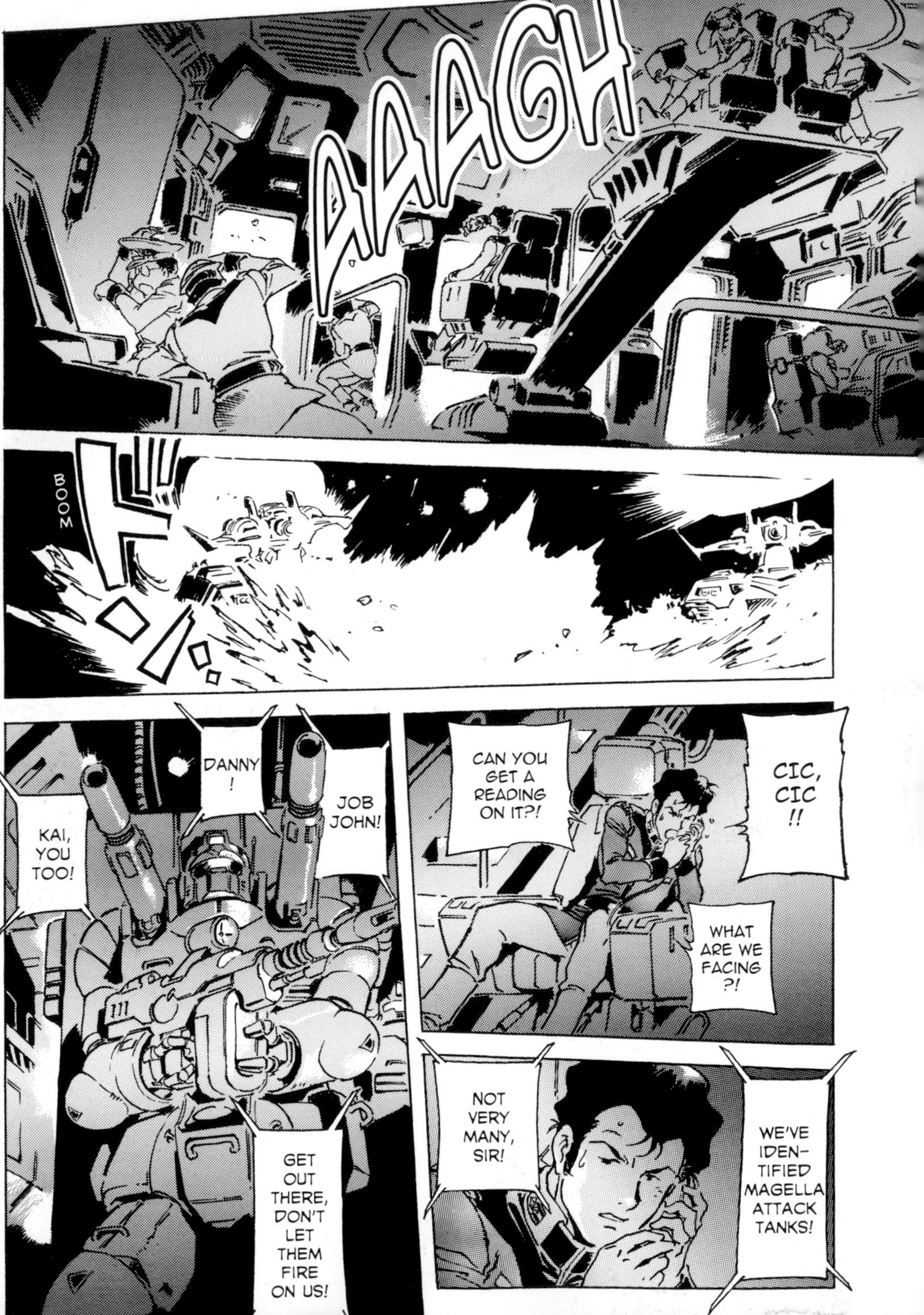
AAAGH
BOOM
CIC, CIC!!
CAN YOU GET A READING ON IT?!
WHAT ARE WE FACING?!
WE'VE IDEN-TIFIED MAGELLA ATTACK TANKS!
NOT VERY MANY, SIR!
DANNY!
JOB JOHN!
KAI, YOU TOO!
GET OUT THERE, DON'T LET THEM FIRE ON US!

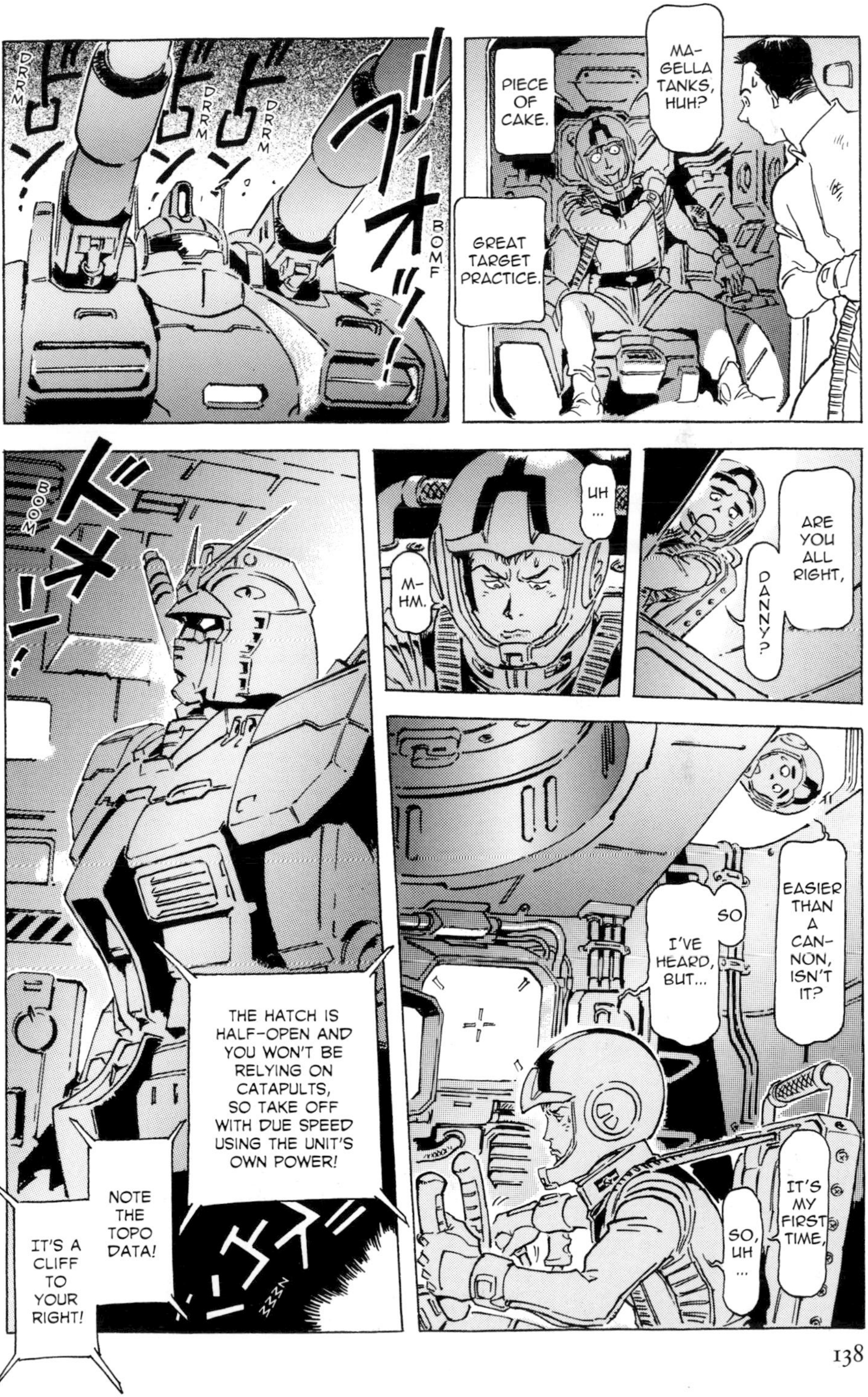
MA-GELLA TANKS, HUH?
PIECE OF CAKE.
GREAT TARGET PRACTICE.
DRRM
DRRM
DRRM
BOMF
ARE YOU ALL RIGHT, DANNY?
UH ...
M-HM.
EASIER THAN A CAN-NON, ISN'T IT?
SO I'VE HEARD, BUT...
IT'S MY FIRST TIME,
SO, UH ...
BOOM
THE HATCH IS HALF-OPEN AND YOU WON'T BE RELYING ON CATAPULTS, SO TAKE OFF WITH DUE SPEED USING THE UNIT'S OWN POWER!
NOTE THE TOPO DATA!
IT'S A CLIFF TO YOUR RIGHT!
ZZZN

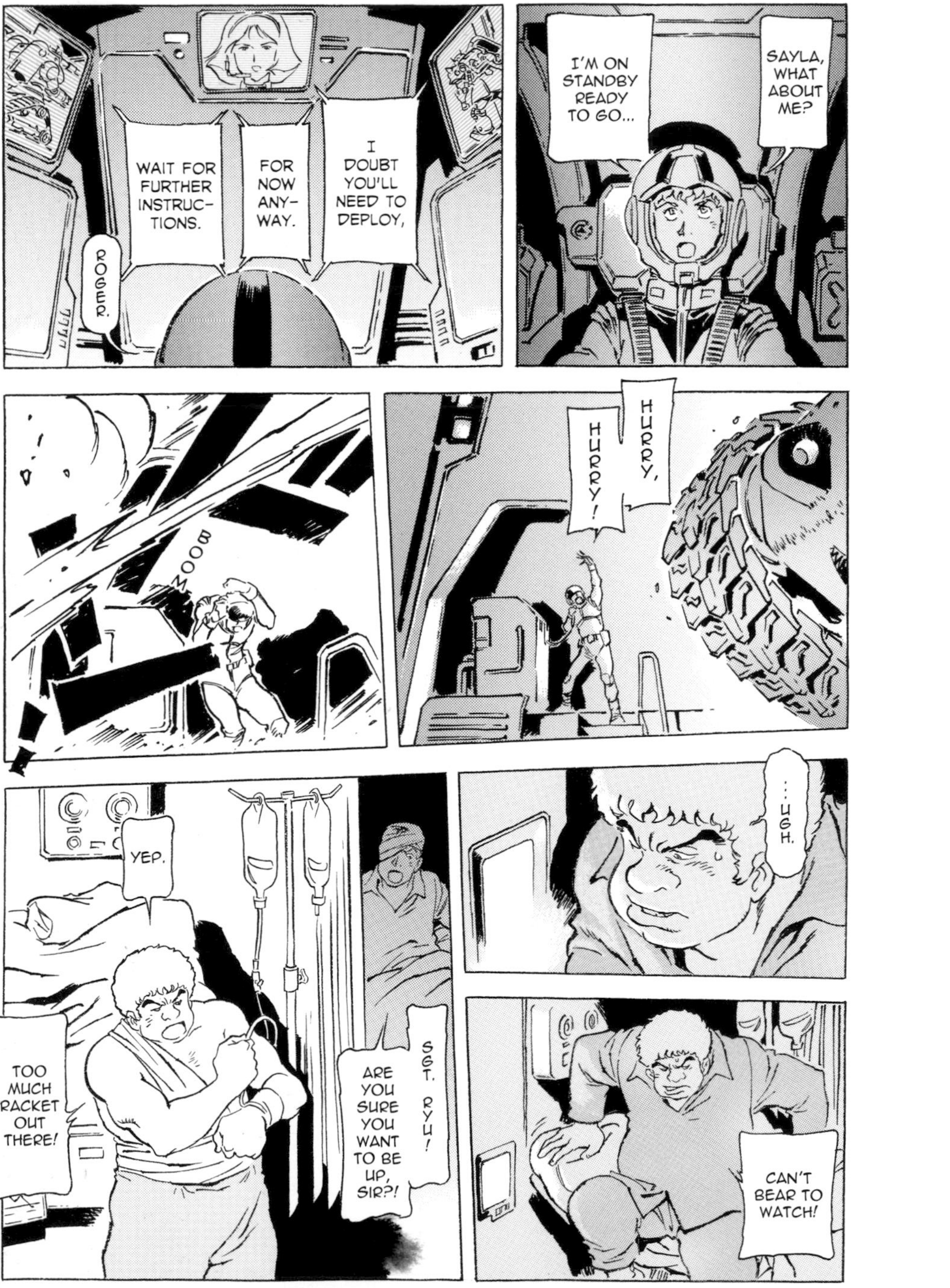
SAYLA, WHAT ABOUT ME?
I'M ON STANDBY READY TO GO...
I DOUBT YOU'LL NEED TO DEPLOY,
FOR NOW ANYWAY.
WAIT FOR FURTHER INSTRUCTIONS.
ROGER.
HURRY, HURRY!
BOOM
...UGH.
CAN'T BEAR TO WATCH!
SGT. RYU!
ARE YOU SURE YOU WANT TO BE UP, SIR?!
YEP.
TOO MUCH RACKET OUT THERE!

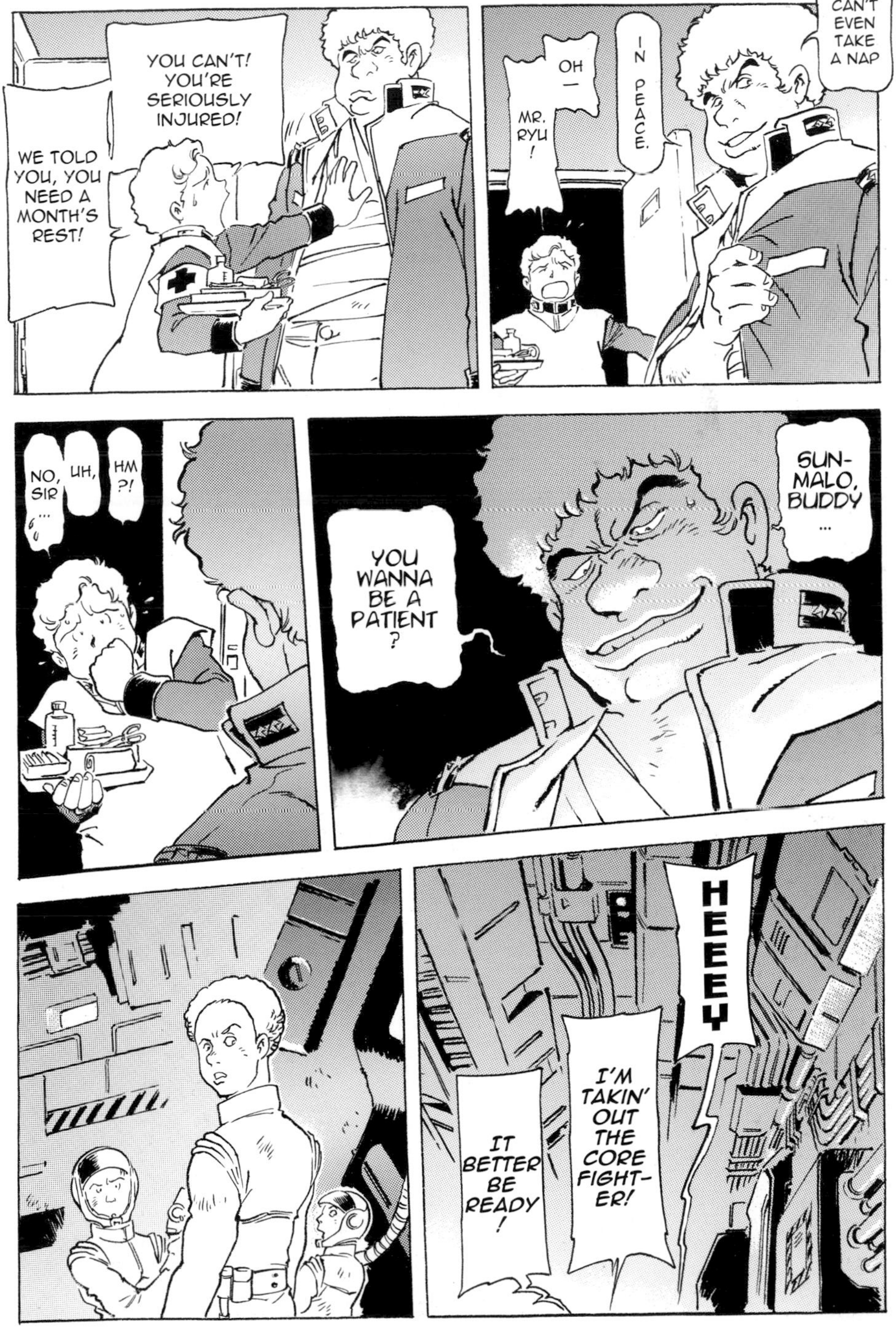
CAN'T EVEN TAKE A NAP
IN PEACE.
OH — MR. RYU!
YOU CAN'T! YOU'RE SERIOUSLY INJURED!
WE TOLD YOU, YOU NEED A MONTH'S REST!
SUN-MALO, BUDDY ...
YOU WANNA BE A PATIENT?
HM?!
UH,
NO, SIR ...
HEEEY
I'M TAKIN' OUT THE CORE FIGHTER!
IT BETTER BE READY!

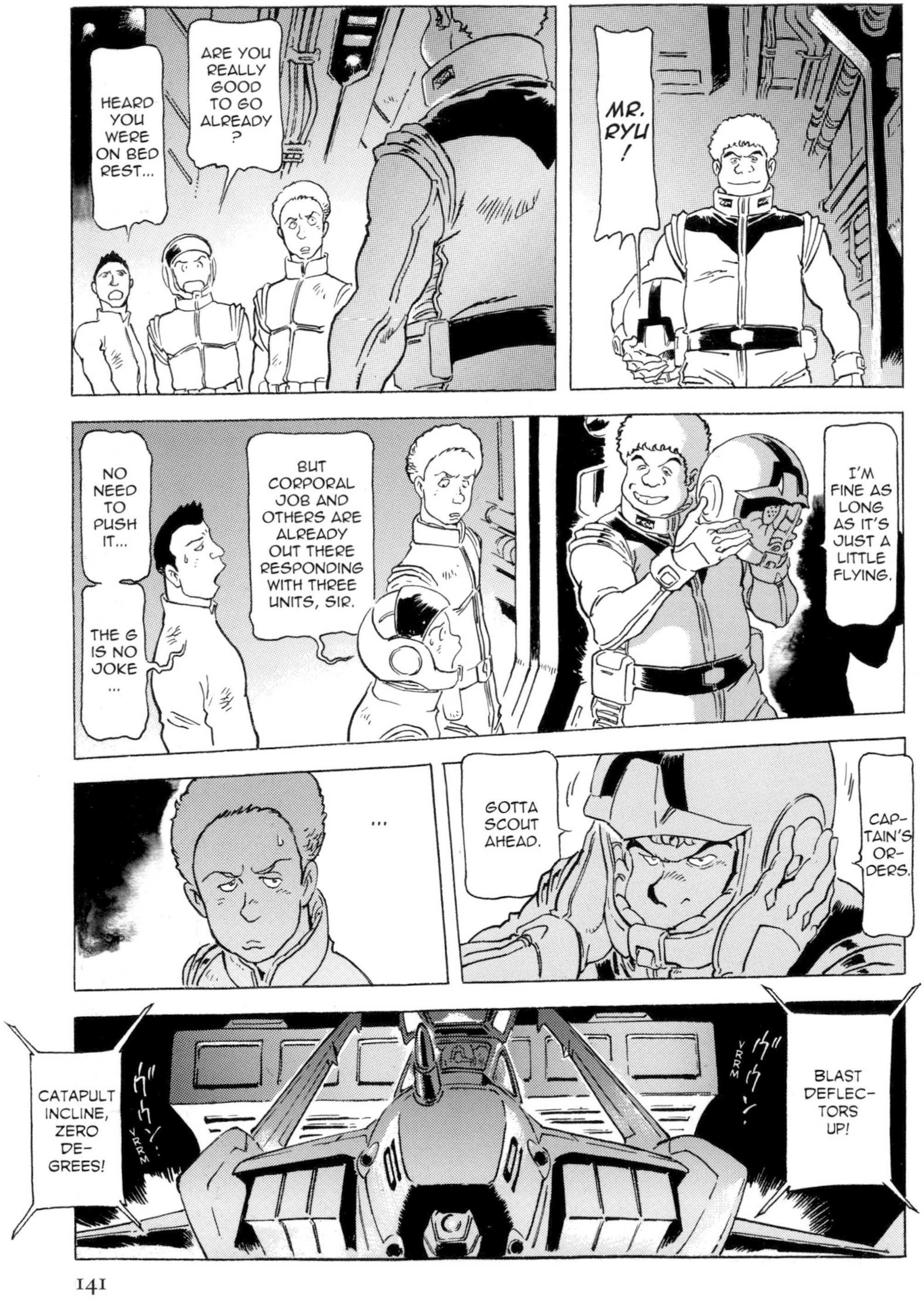
MR. RYU!
ARE YOU REALLY GOOD TO GO ALREADY?
HEARD YOU WERE ON BED REST...
I'M FINE AS LONG AS IT'S JUST A LITTLE FLYING.
BUT CORPORAL JOB AND OTHERS ARE ALREADY OUT THERE RESPONDING WITH THREE UNITS, SIR.
NO NEED TO PUSH IT...
THE G IS NO JOKE...
CAP-TAIN'S OR-DERS.
GOTTA SCOUT AHEAD.
...
BLAST DEFLEC-TORS UP!
VRRM
CATAPULT INCLINE, ZERO DE-GREES!
VRRM

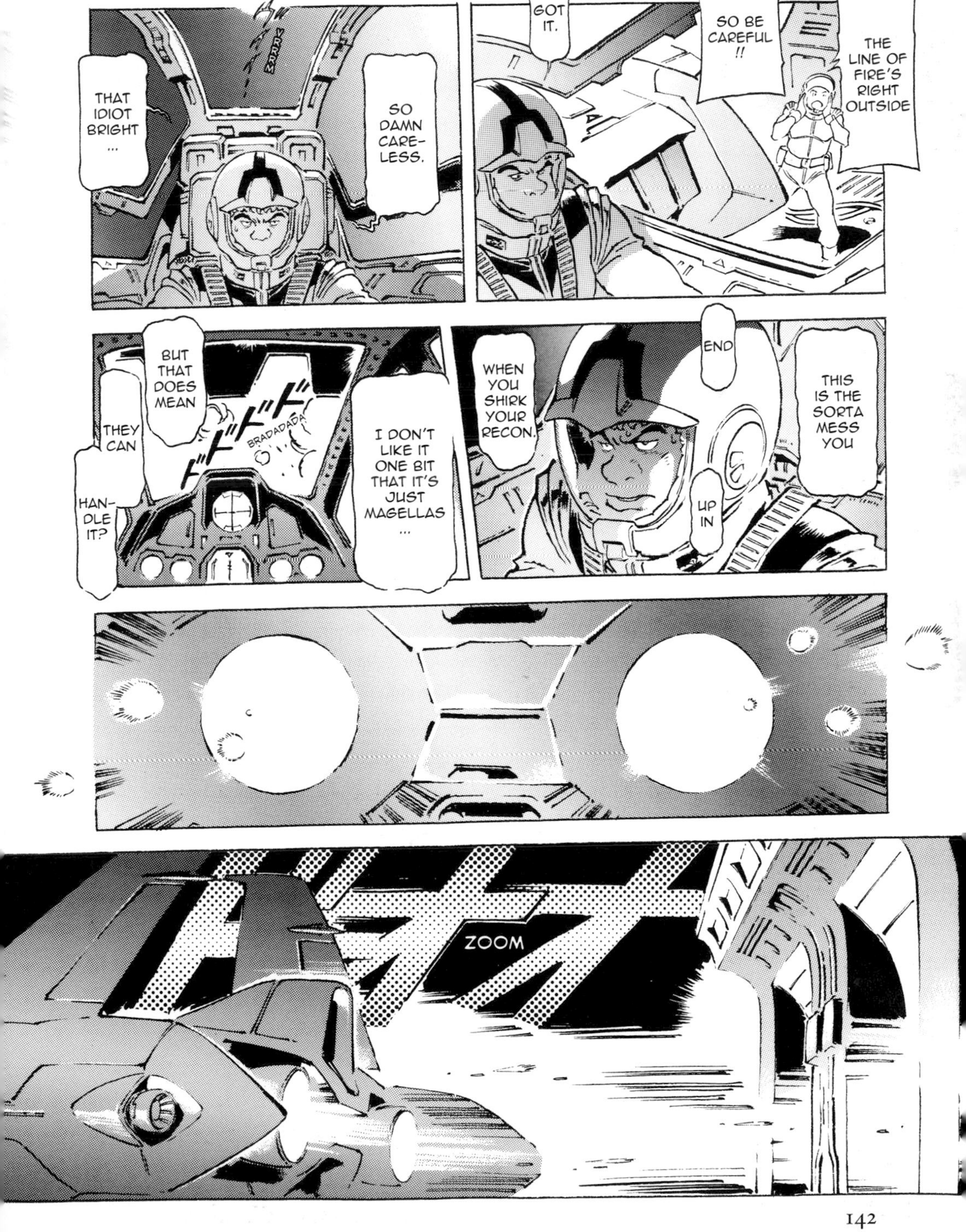
THE LINE OF FIRE'S RIGHT OUTSIDE
SO BE CAREFUL !!
GOT IT.
VRRRM
SO DAMN CARE-LESS.
THAT IDIOT BRIGHT ...
THIS IS THE SORTA MESS YOU
END
UP IN
WHEN YOU SHIRK YOUR RECON.
I DON'T LIKE IT ONE BIT THAT IT'S JUST MAGELLAS ...
BUT THAT DOES MEAN
BRADADADA
THEY CAN
HAN-DLE IT?
ZOOM

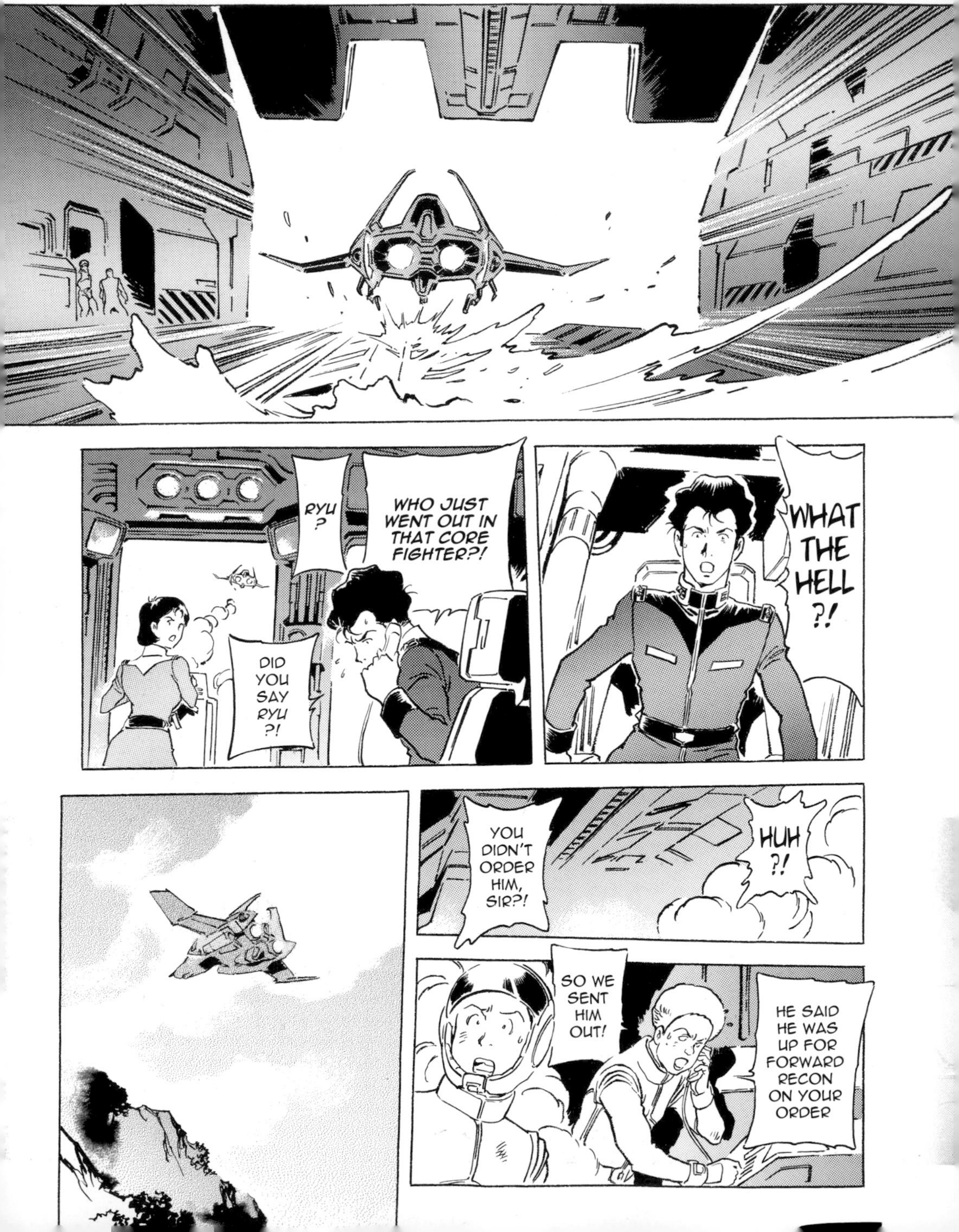
WHAT THE HELL ?!
WHO JUST WENT OUT IN THAT CORE FIGHTER?!
RYU ?
DID YOU SAY RYU ?!
HUH ?!
YOU DIDN'T ORDER HIM, SIR?!
HE SAID HE WAS UP FOR FORWARD RECON ON YOUR ORDER
SO WE SENT HIM OUT!

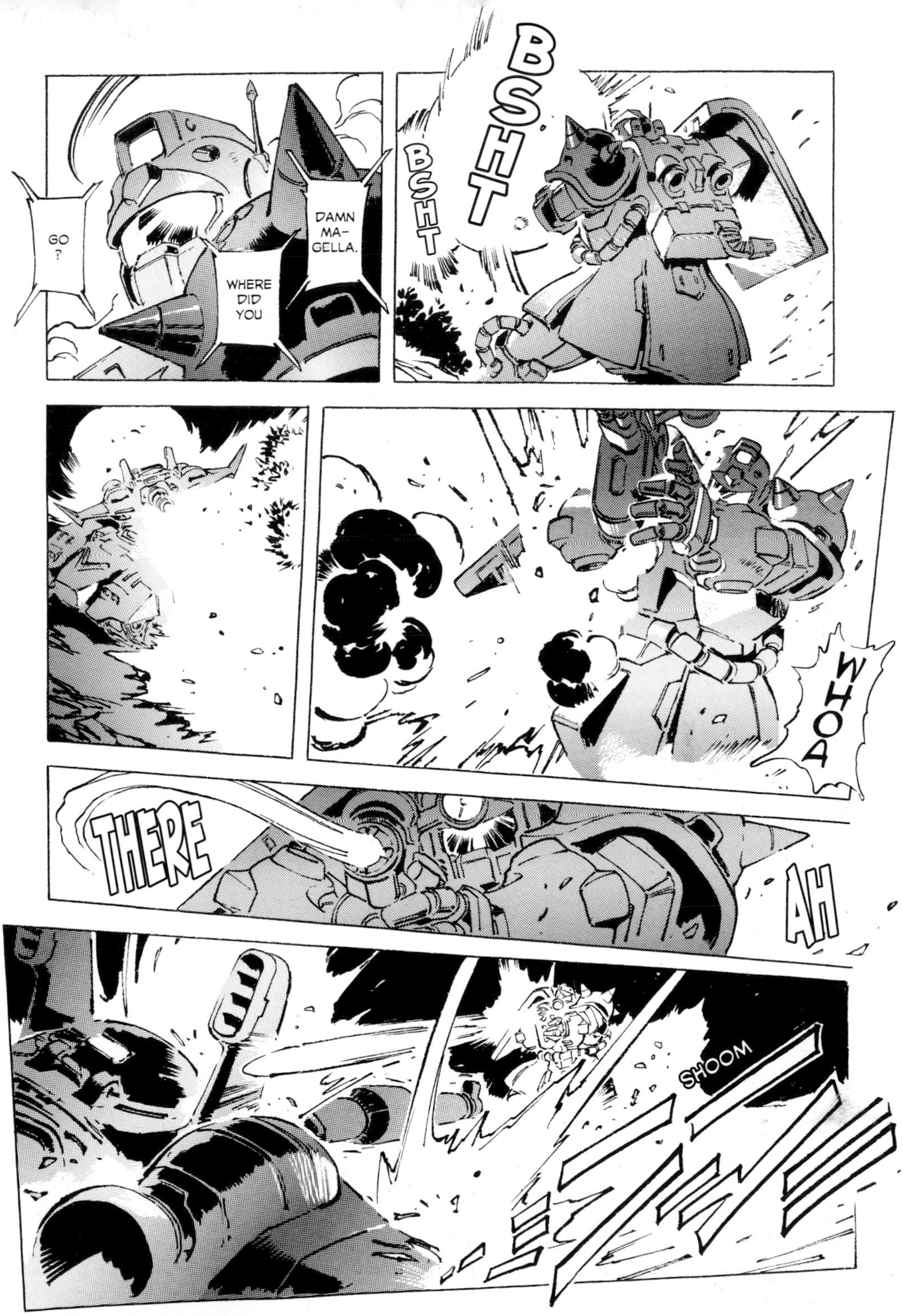
BSHT
BSHT
DAMN MA-GELLA.
WHERE DID YOU
GO ?
WHOA
THERE
AH
SHOOM

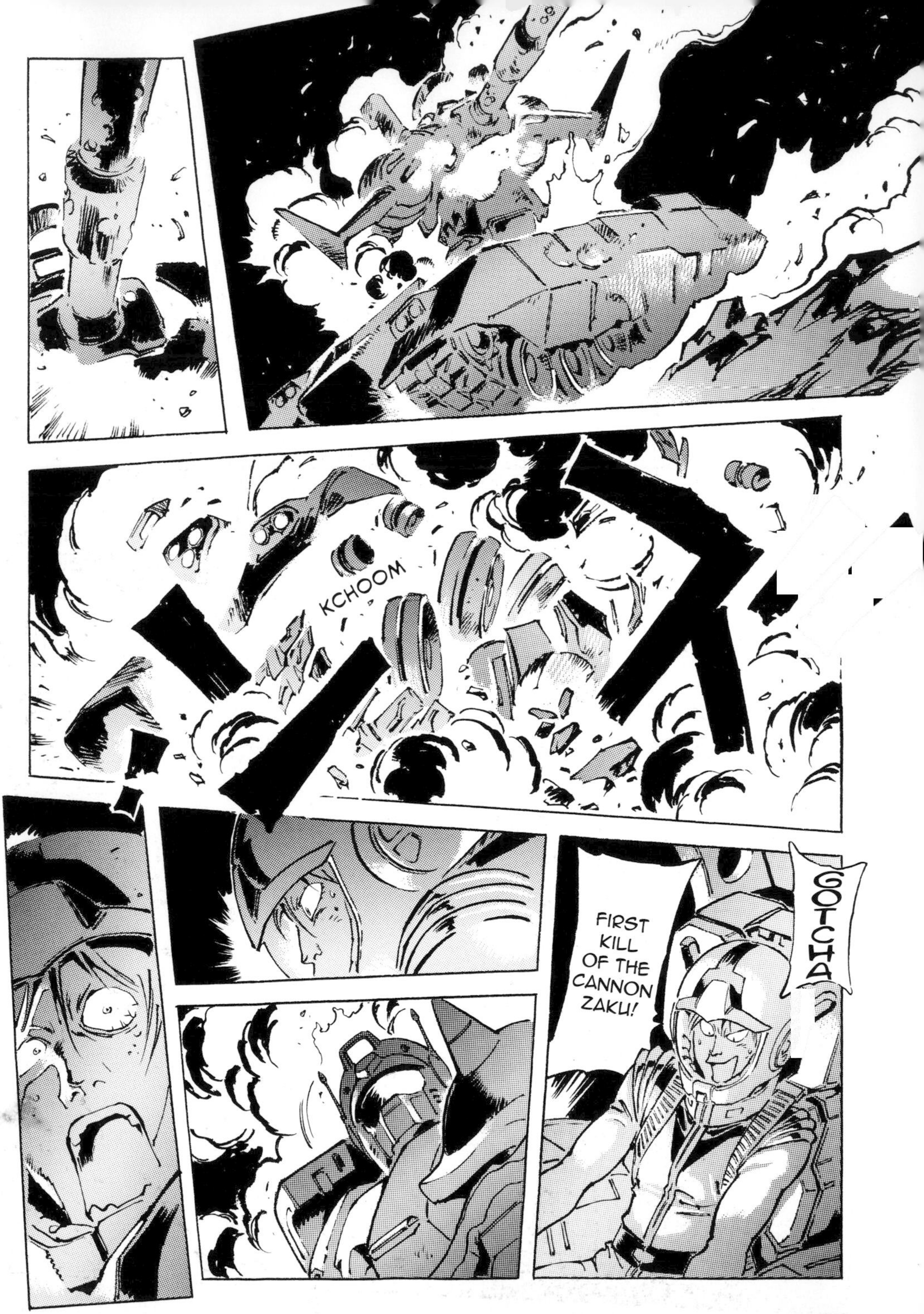
KCHOOM
GOTCHA
FIRST KILL OF THE CANNON ZAKU!

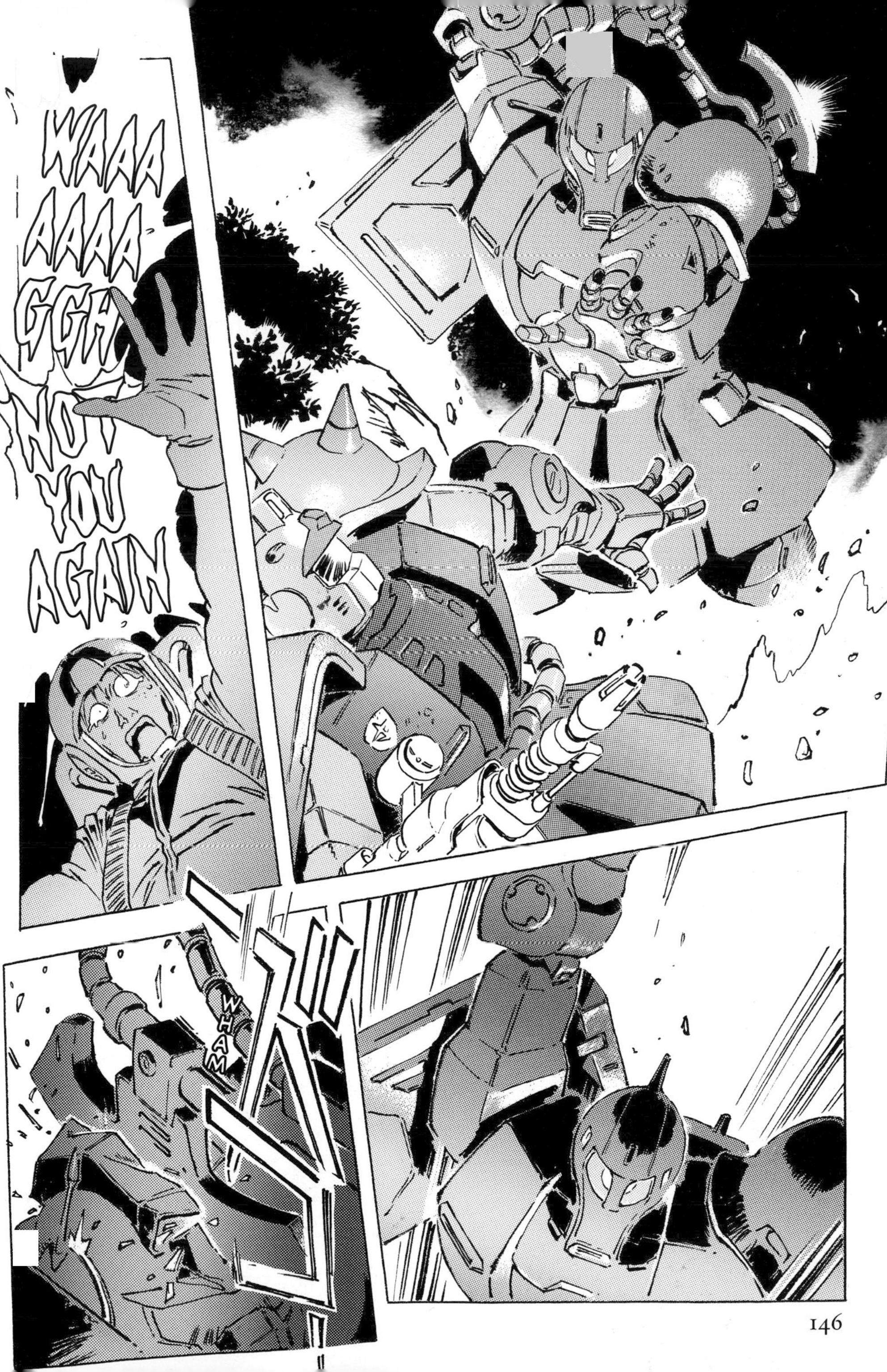
WAAAAAAAGGH NOT YOU AGAIN
WHAM

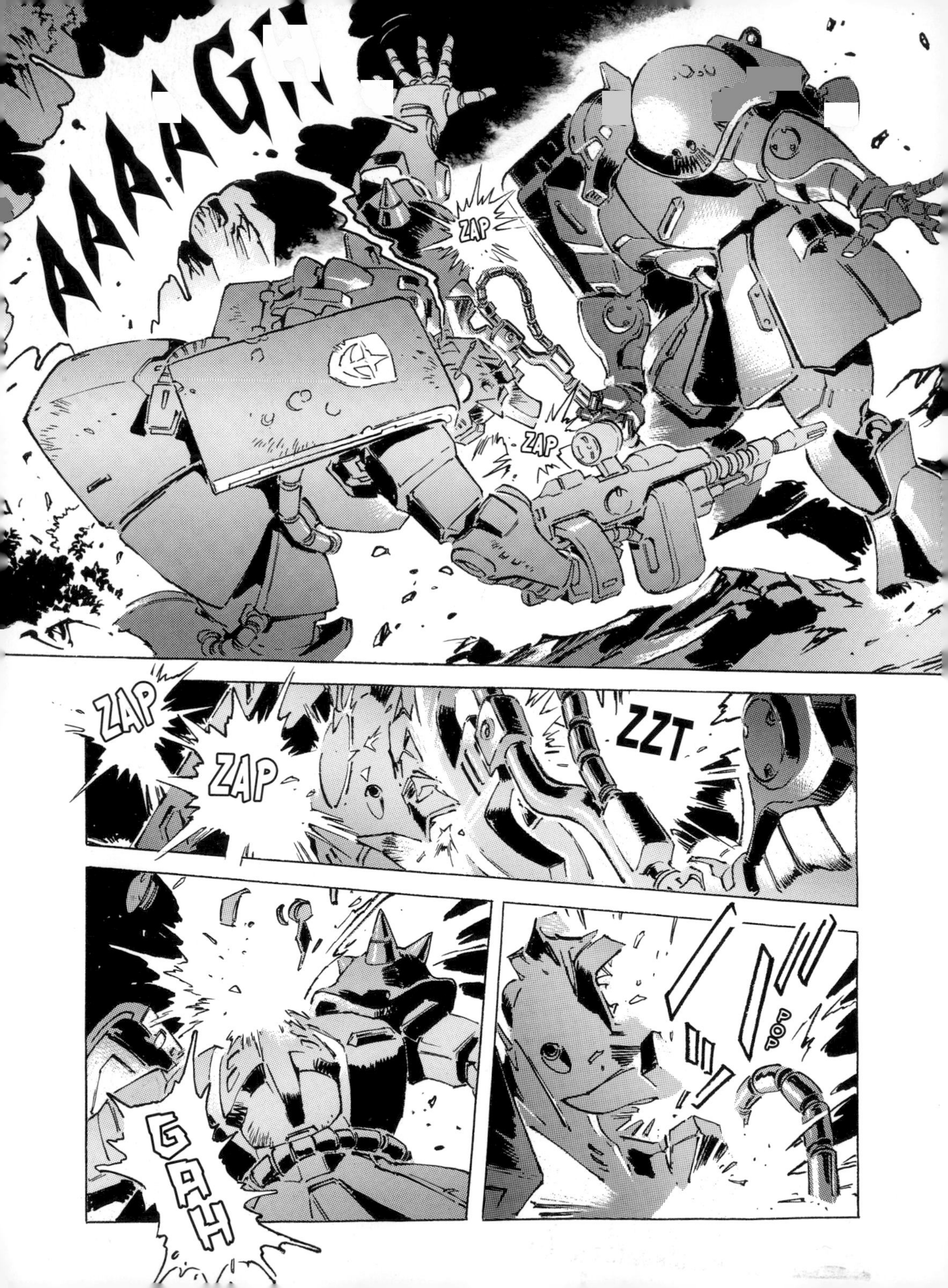
AAAAGH
ZAP
ZAP
ZZT
ZAP
ZAP
POP
GAH

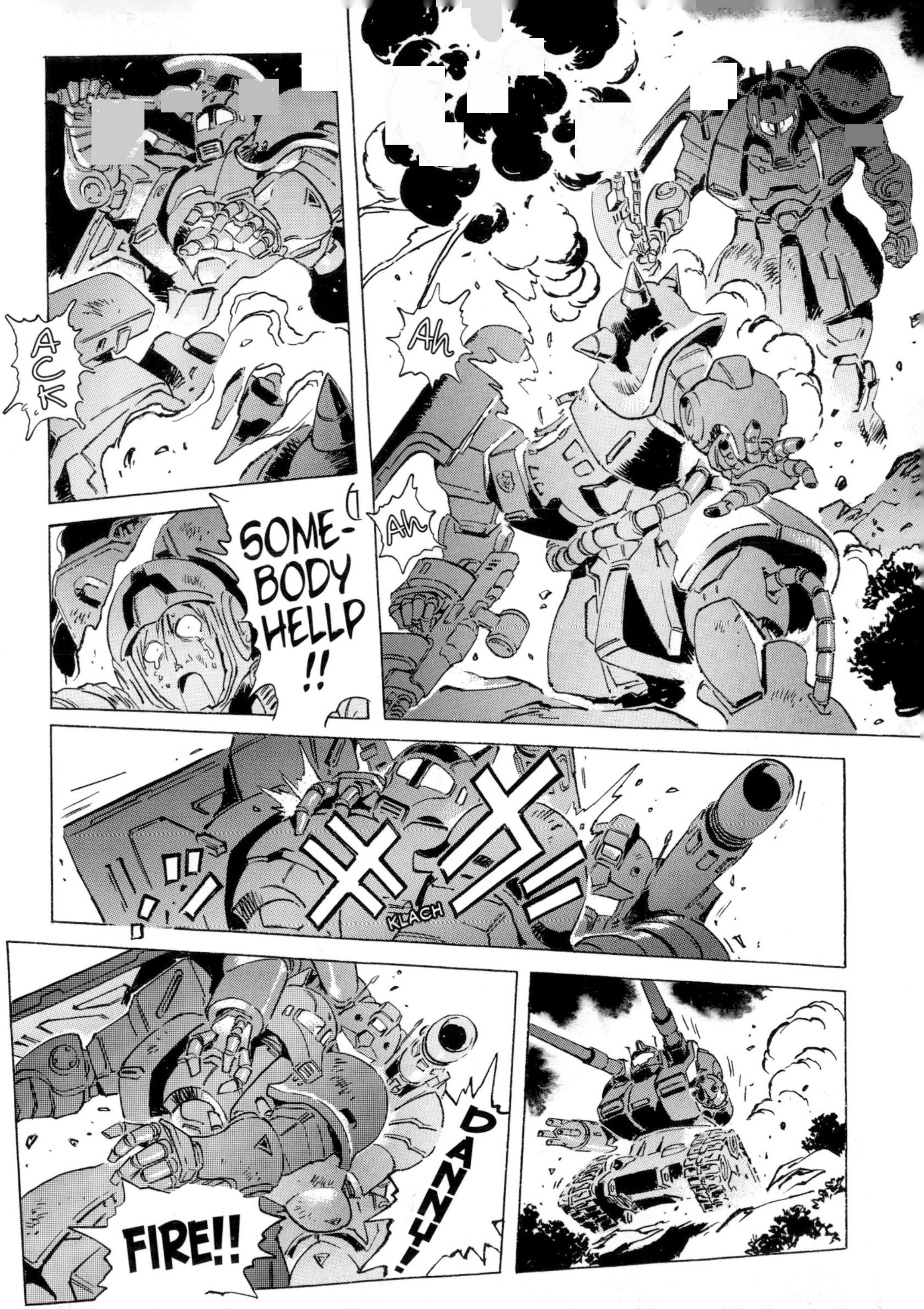
Ah
Ah
ACK
SOME-BODY HELLP !!
KLACH
DANNY!!
FIRE!!

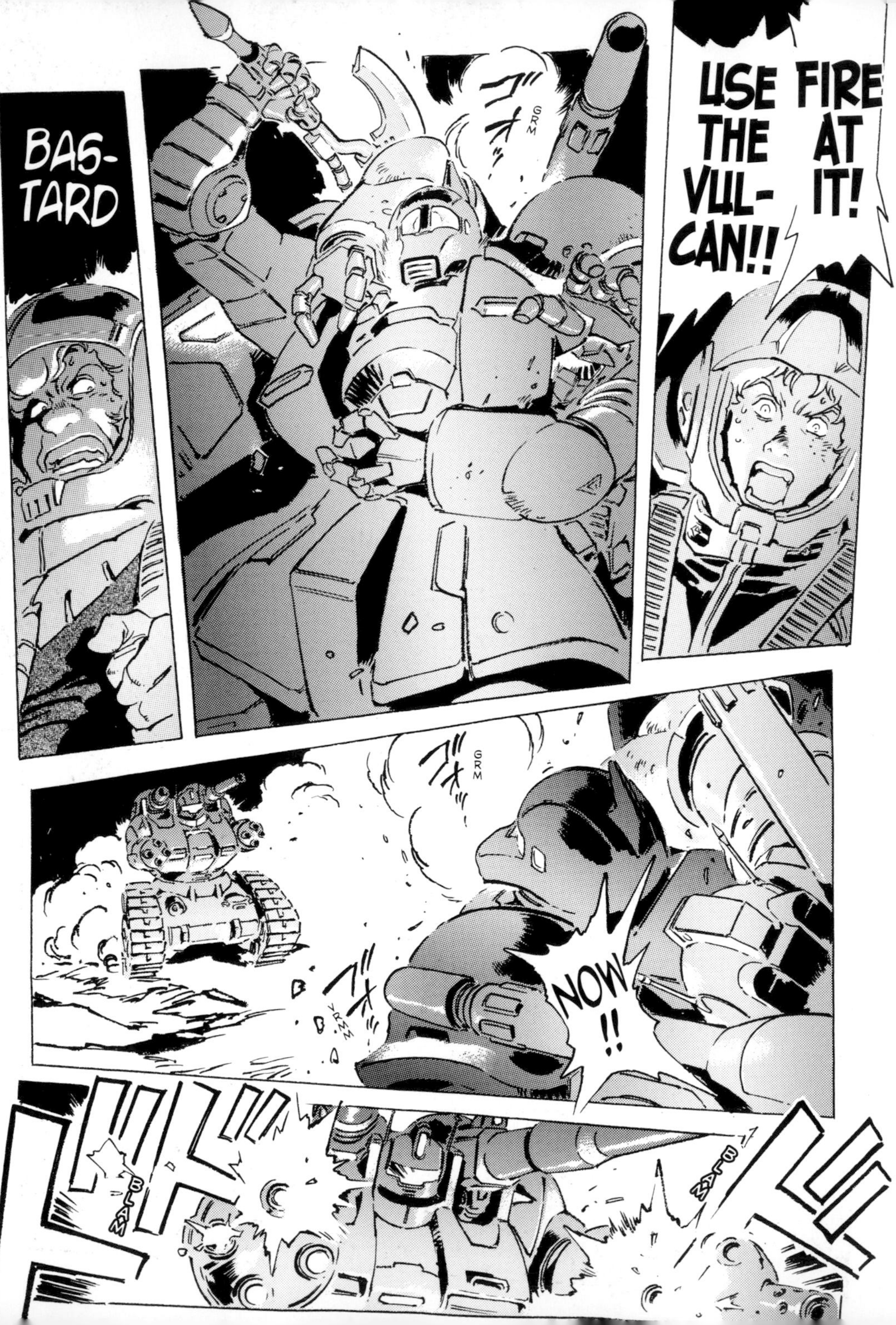

USE THE VUL-CAN!!
FIRE AT IT!
GRM
BAS-TARD
GRM
NOW!!
VRMM
BLAM
BLAM

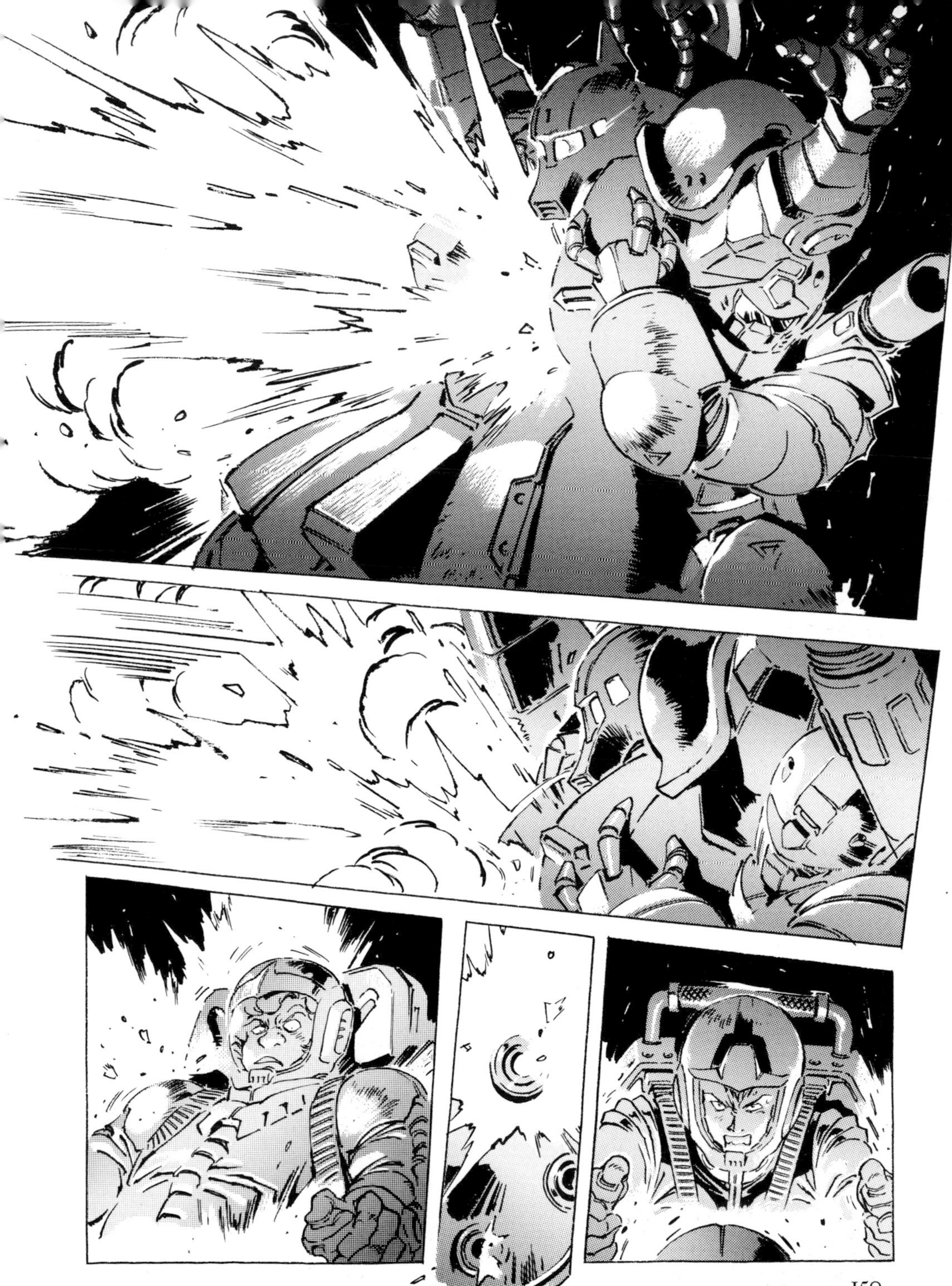

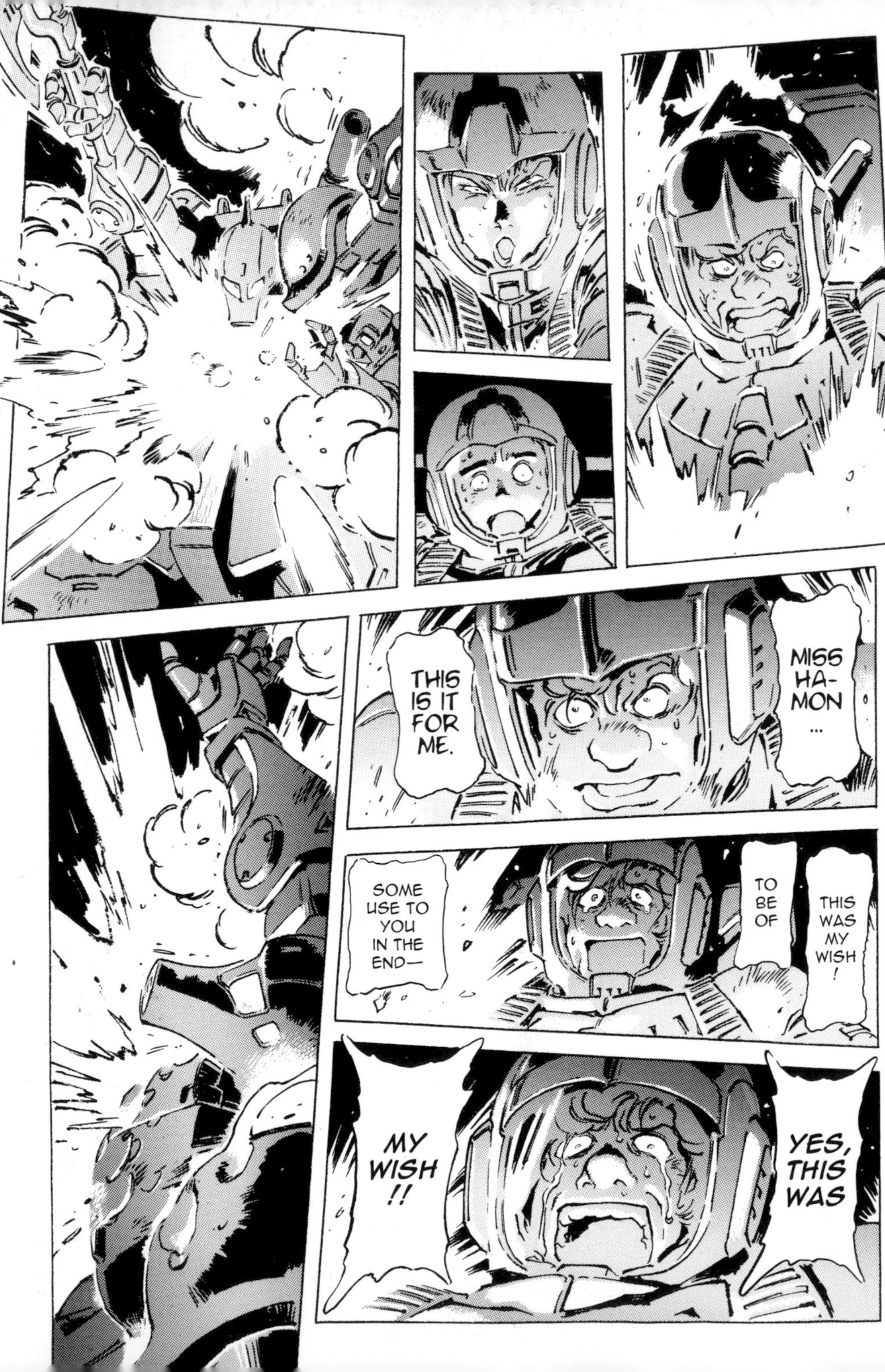
MISS HA-MON ...
THIS IS IT FOR ME.
THIS WAS MY WISH!
TO BE OF
SOME USE TO YOU IN THE END—
YES, THIS WAS
MY WISH!!

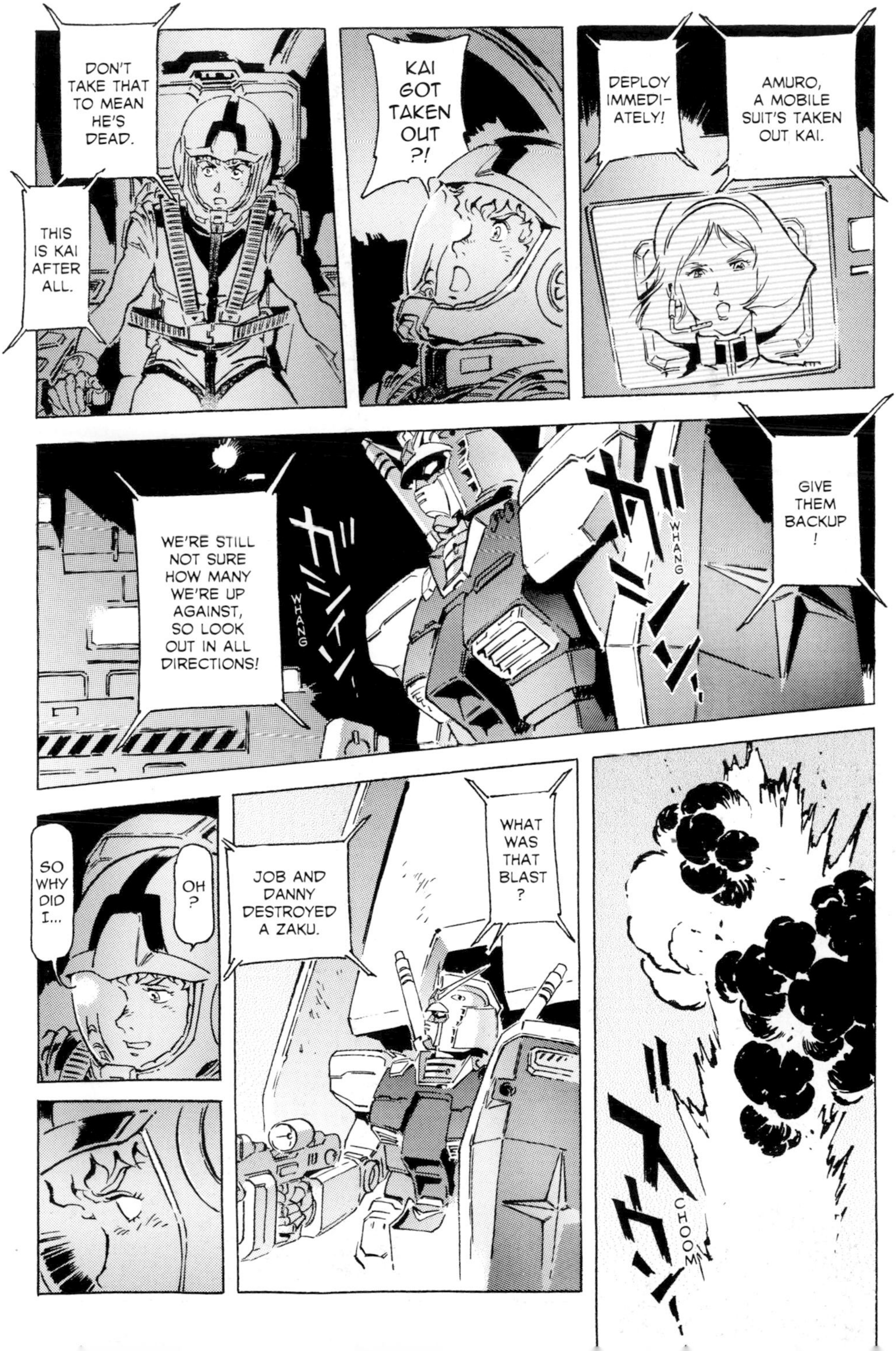
AMURO, A MOBILE SUIT'S TAKEN OUT KAI.
DEPLOY IMMEDI-ATELY!
KAI GOT TAKEN OUT ?!
DON'T TAKE THAT TO MEAN HE'S DEAD.
THIS IS KAI AFTER ALL.
GIVE THEM BACKUP !
WHANG
WE'RE STILL NOT SURE HOW MANY WE'RE UP AGAINST, SO LOOK OUT IN ALL DIRECTIONS!
WHANG
CHOOM
WHAT WAS THAT BLAST ?
JOB AND DANNY DESTROYED A ZAKU.
OH ?
SO WHY DID I...

...
HUFF
ROAR
...
HUFF!!
BWMM

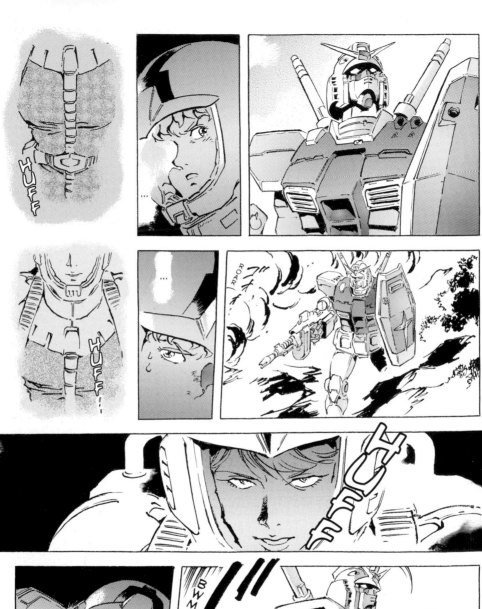

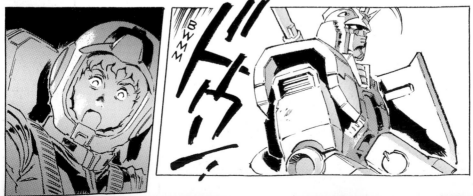

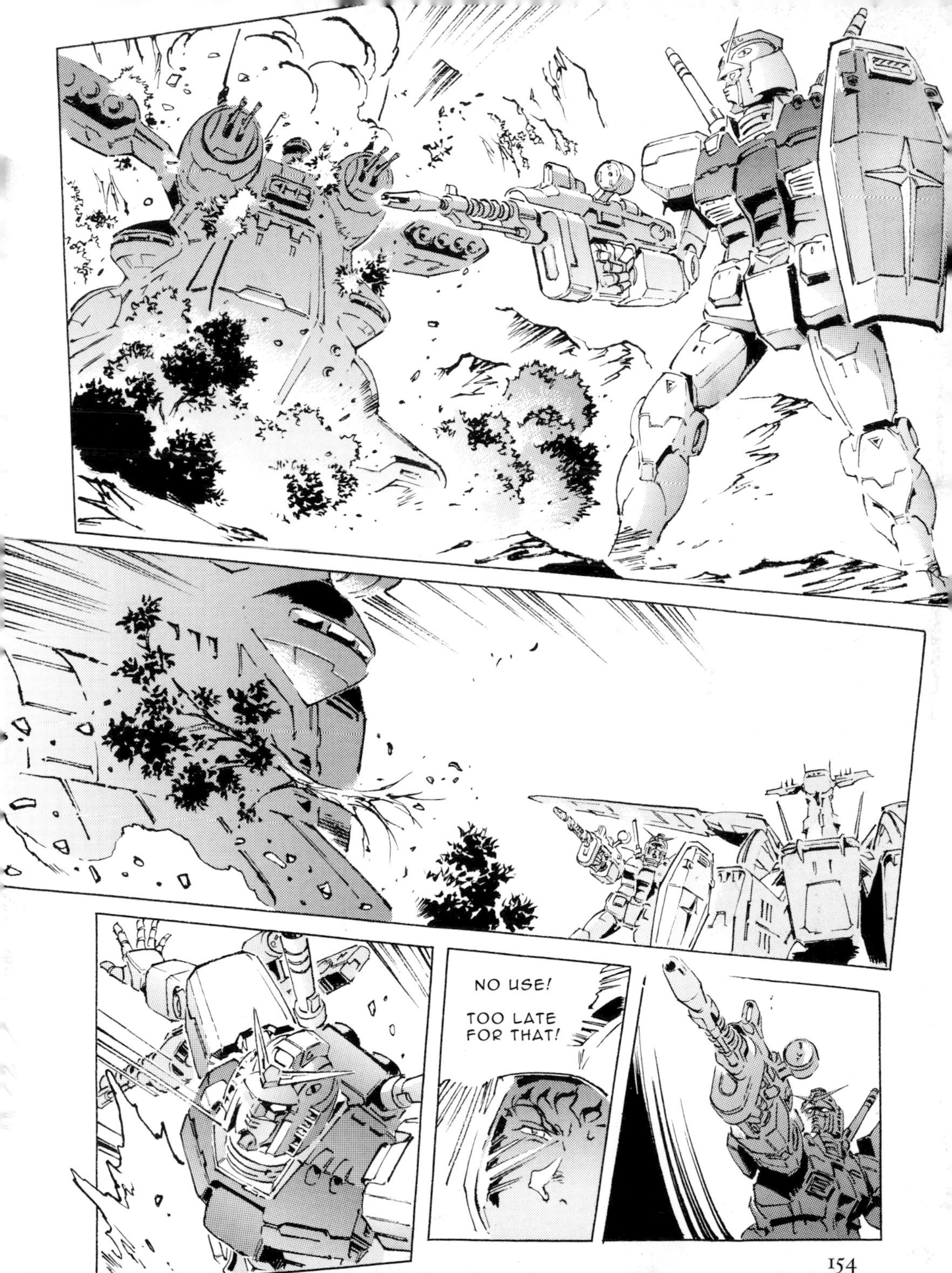
NO USE!
TOO LATE FOR THAT!

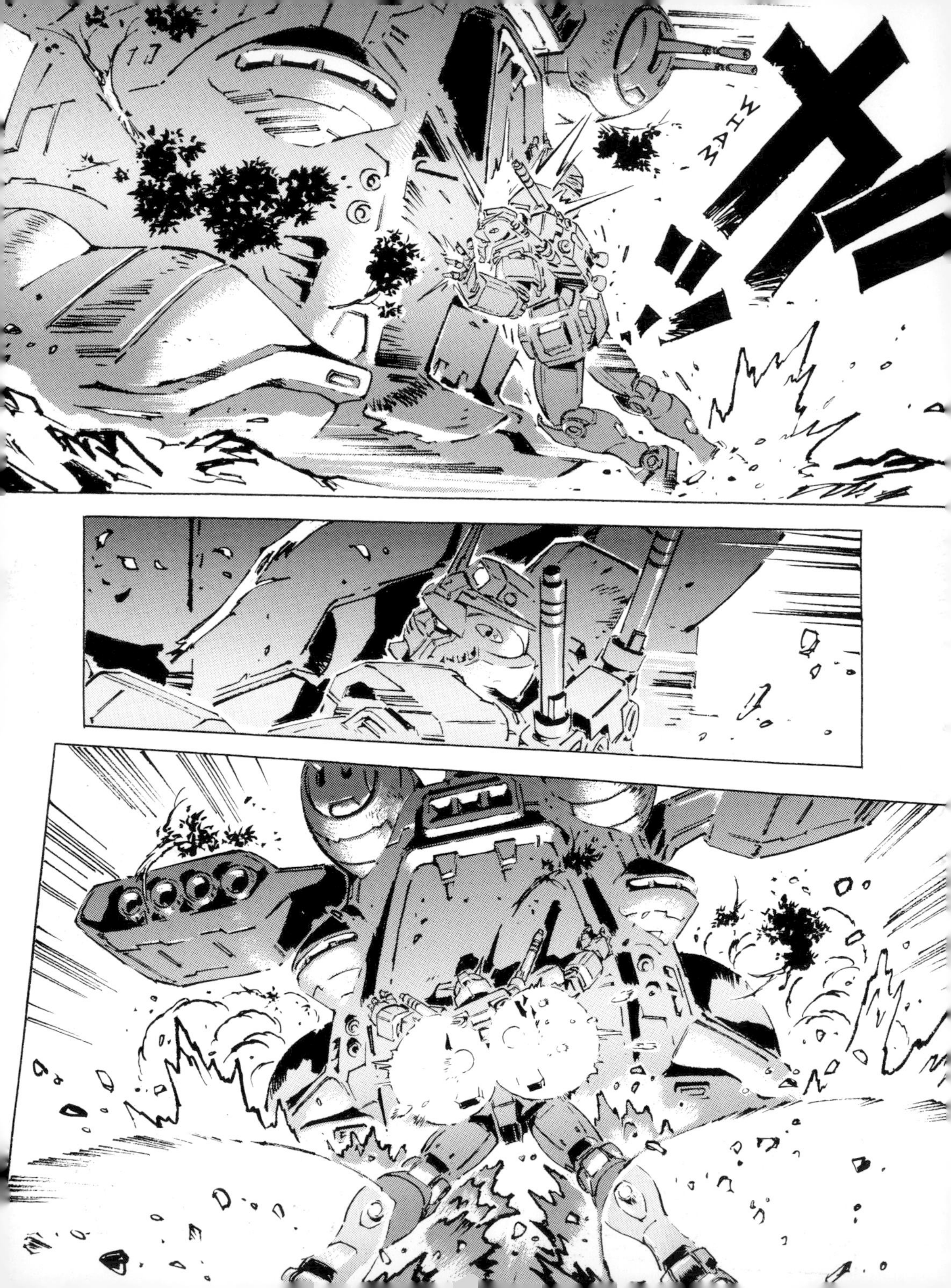

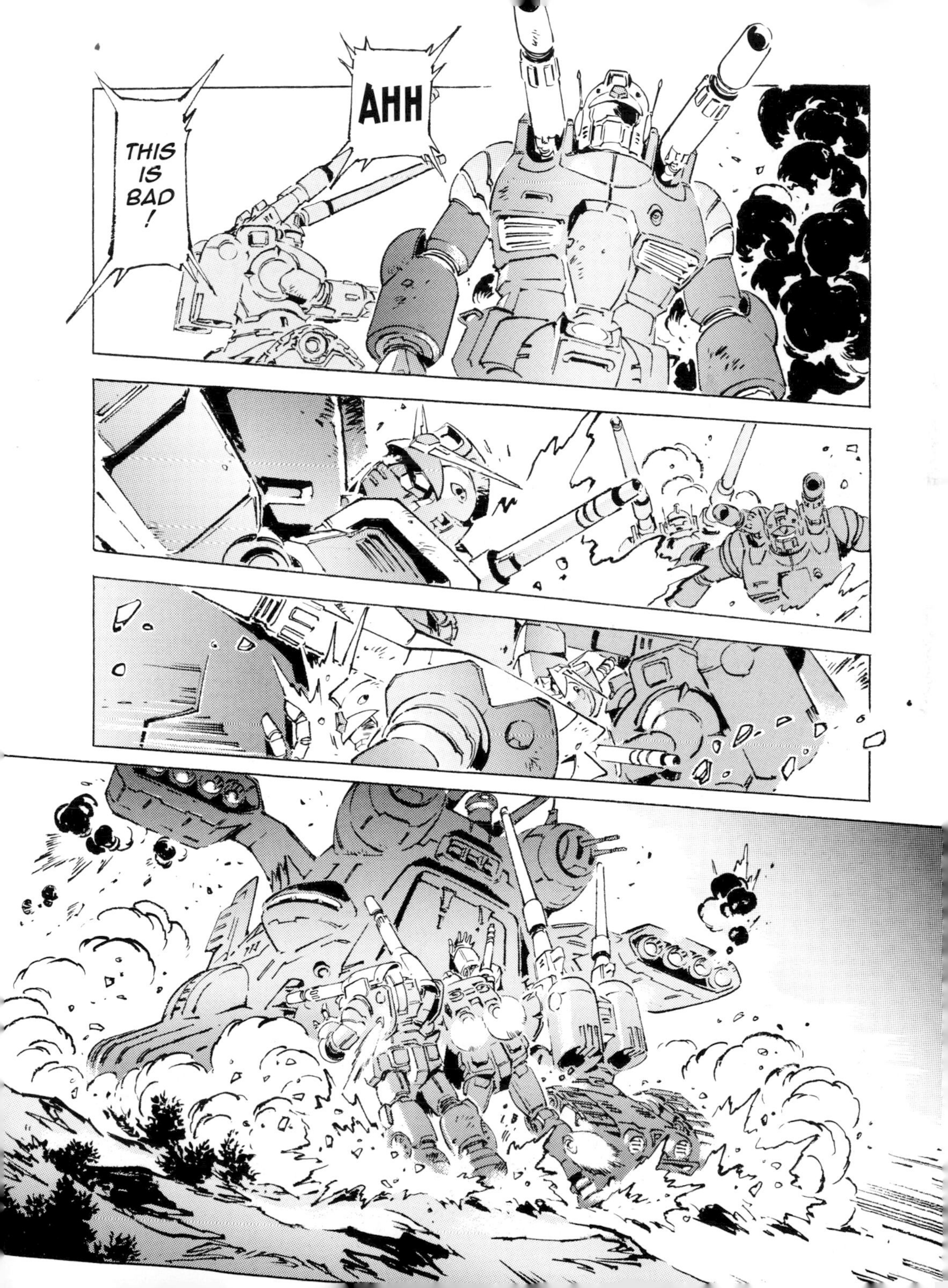
AHH
THIS IS BAD!

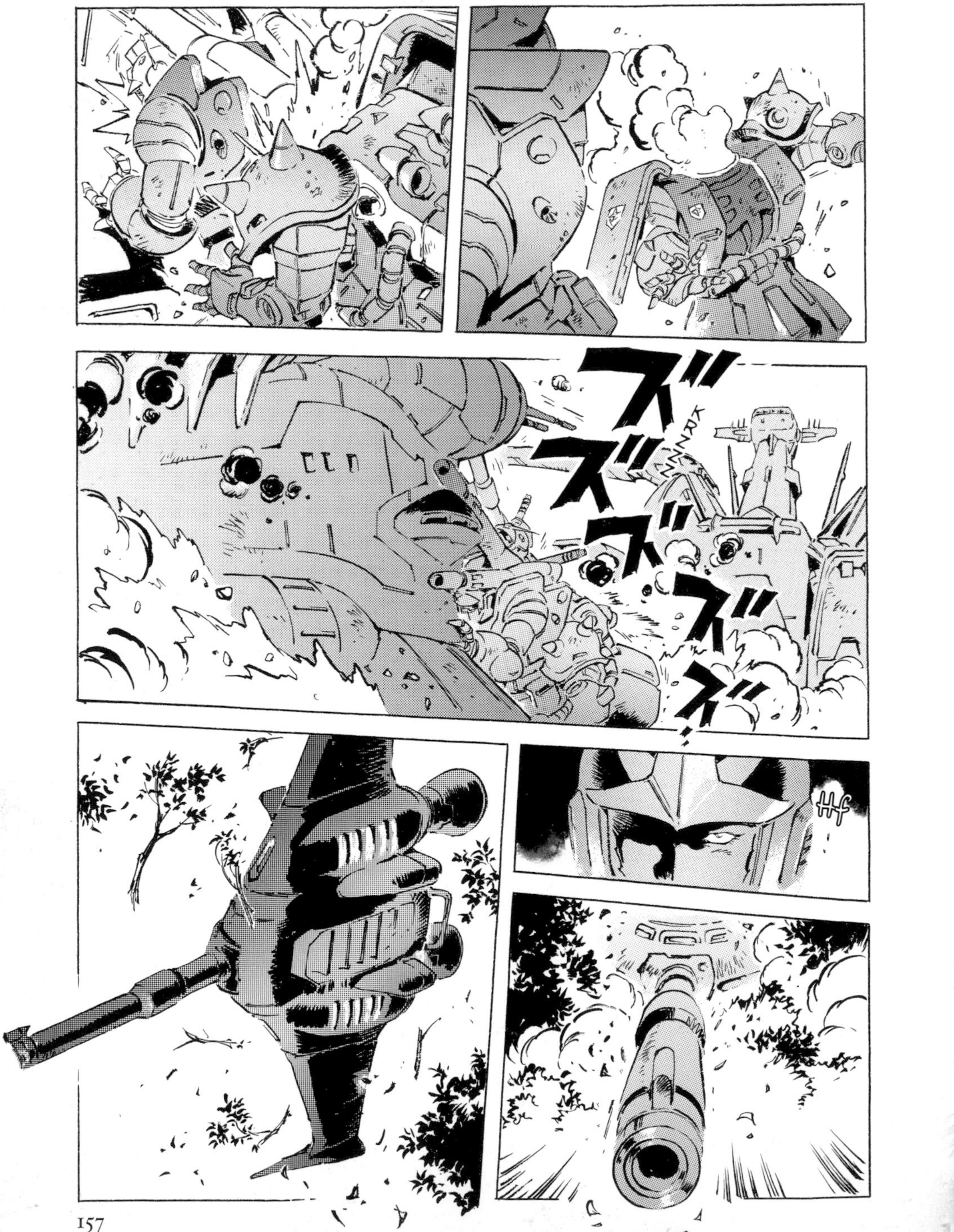
ズズズズズ
KRNNNN
Hf

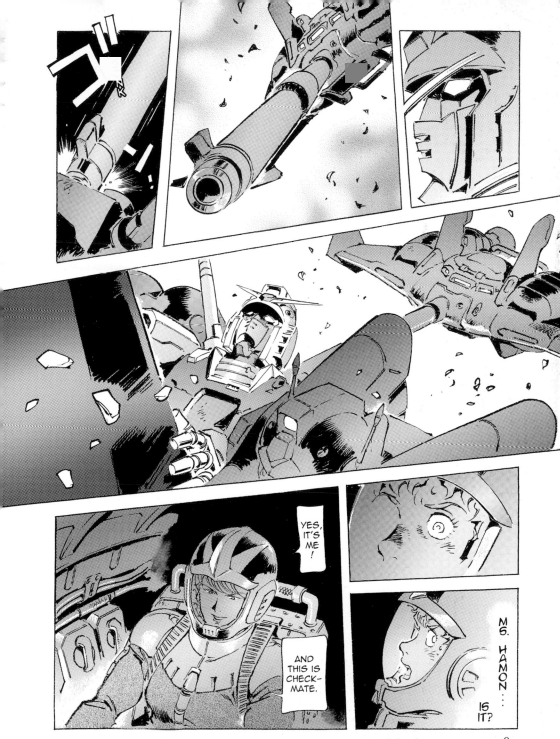

YES, IT'S ME!

AND THIS IS CHECKMATE.

MS. HAMON...

IS IT?

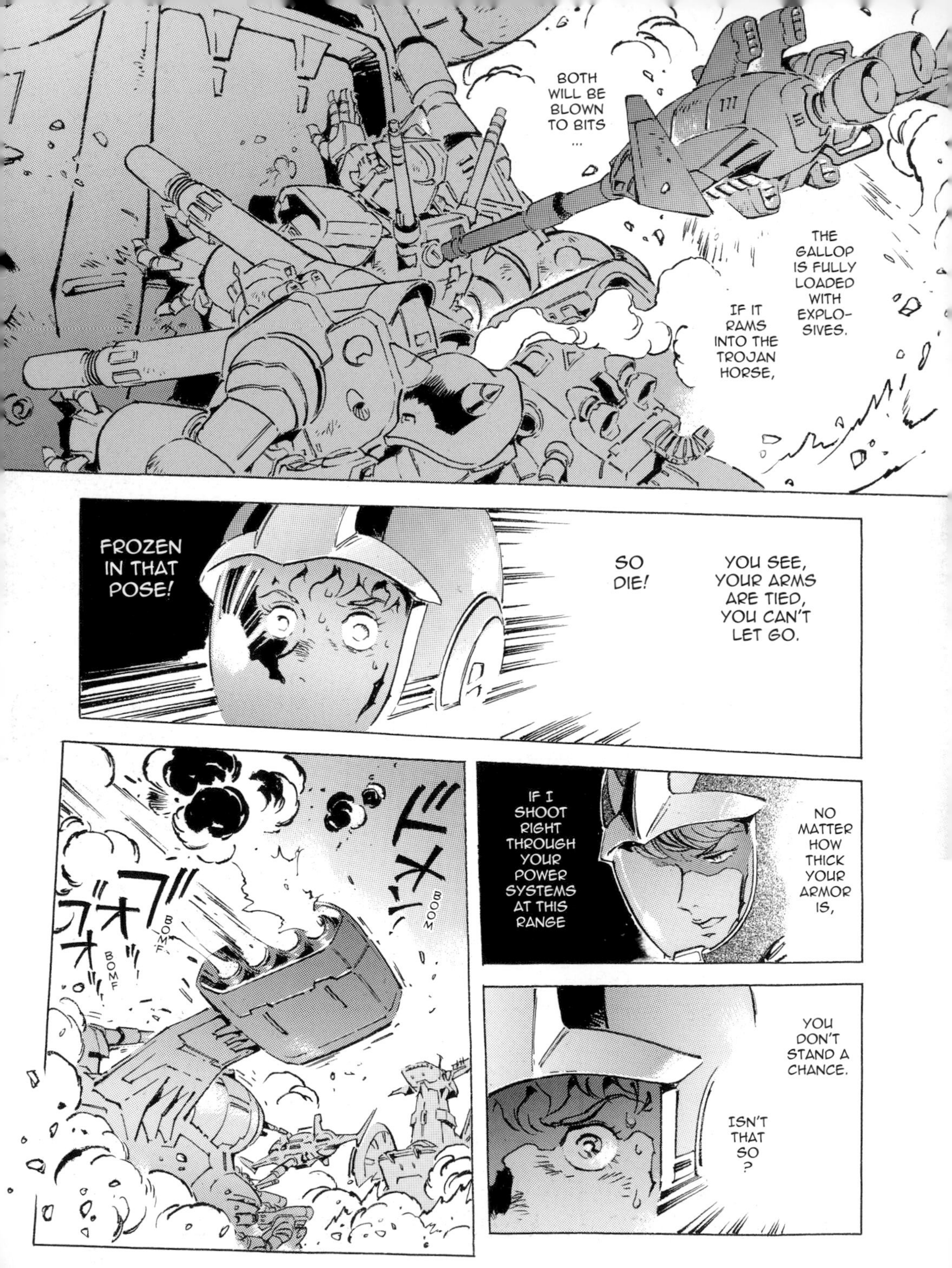
THE GALLOP IS FULLY LOADED WITH EXPLOSIVES.
IF IT RAMS INTO THE TROJAN HORSE,
BOTH WILL BE BLOWN TO BITS ...
YOU SEE, YOUR ARMS ARE TIED, YOU CAN'T LET GO.
SO DIE!
FROZEN IN THAT POSE!
NO MATTER HOW THICK YOUR ARMOR IS,
IF I SHOOT RIGHT THROUGH YOUR POWER SYSTEMS AT THIS RANGE
YOU DON'T STAND A CHANCE.
ISN'T THAT SO?
BOOM
BOMF
BOMF

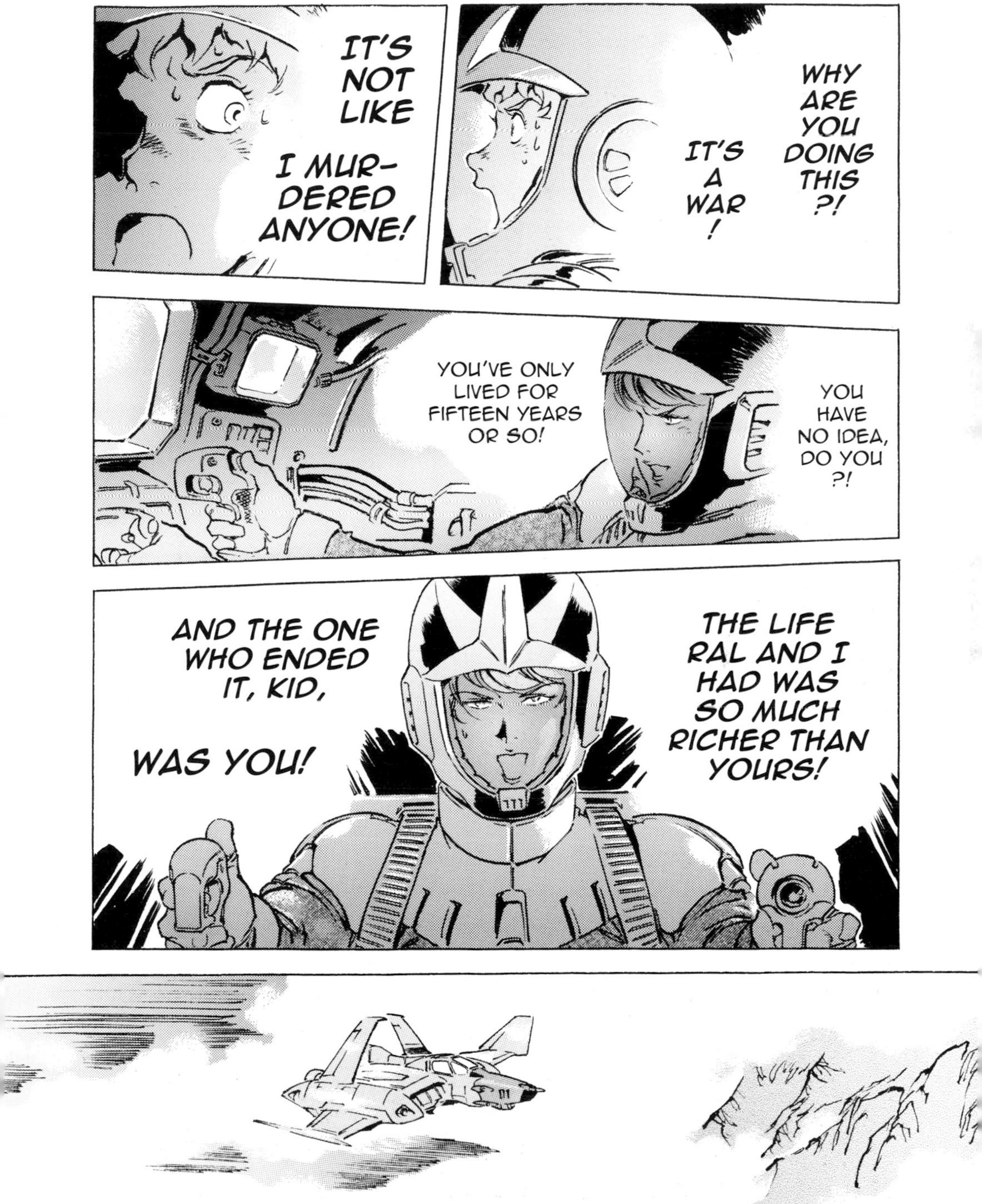
WHY ARE YOU DOING THIS?!
IT'S A WAR!
IT'S NOT LIKE I MURDERED ANYONE!
YOU HAVE NO IDEA, DO YOU?!
YOU'VE ONLY LIVED FOR FIFTEEN YEARS OR SO!
THE LIFE RAL AND I HAD WAS SO MUCH RICHER THAN YOURS!
AND THE ONE WHO ENDED IT, KID,
WAS YOU!

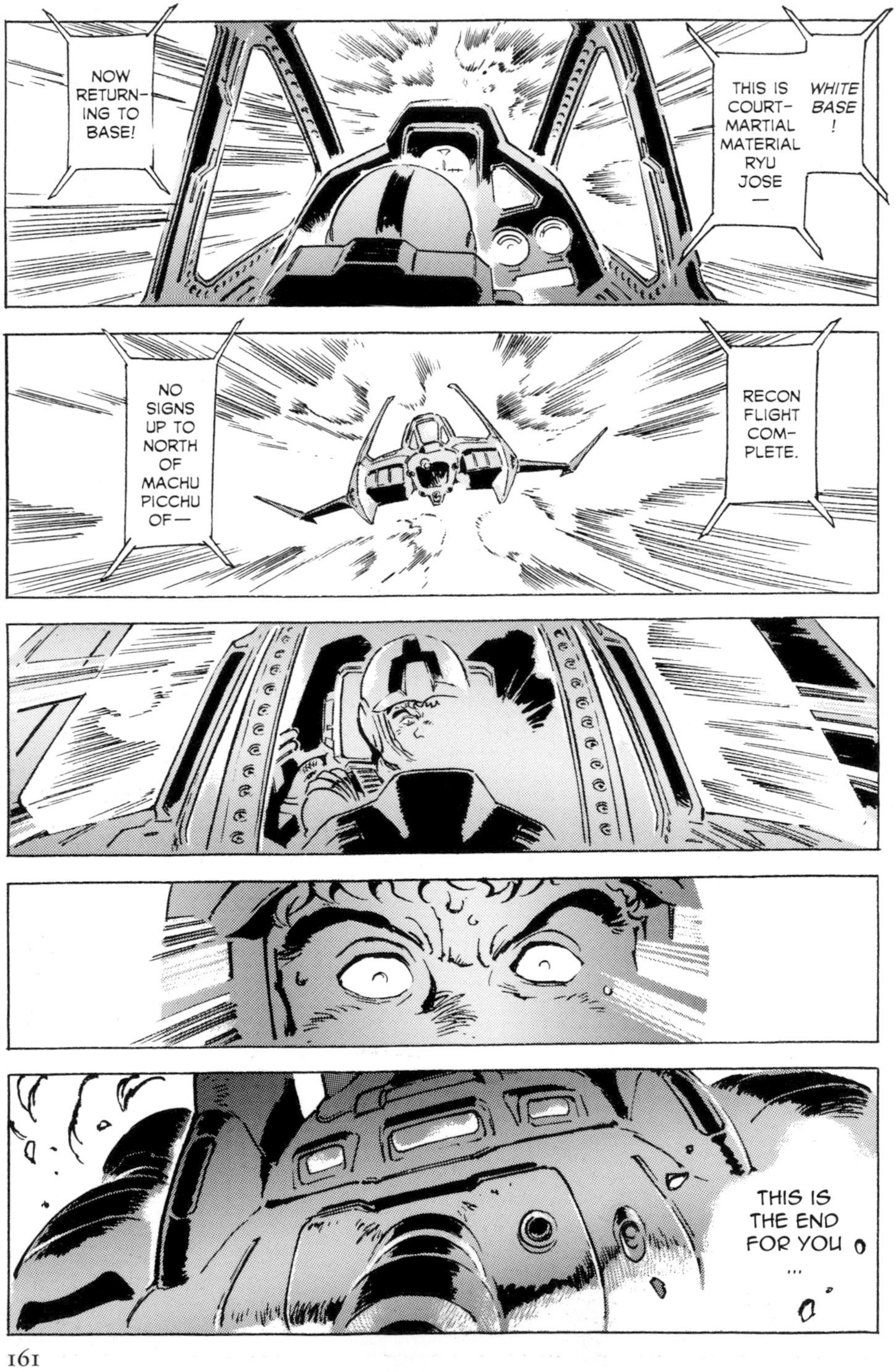
WHITE BASE!
THIS IS COURT-MARTIAL MATERIAL RYU JOSE—
NOW RETURNING TO BASE!
RECON FLIGHT COMPLETE.
NO SIGNS UP TO NORTH OF MACHU PICCHU OF—
THIS IS THE END FOR YOU ...

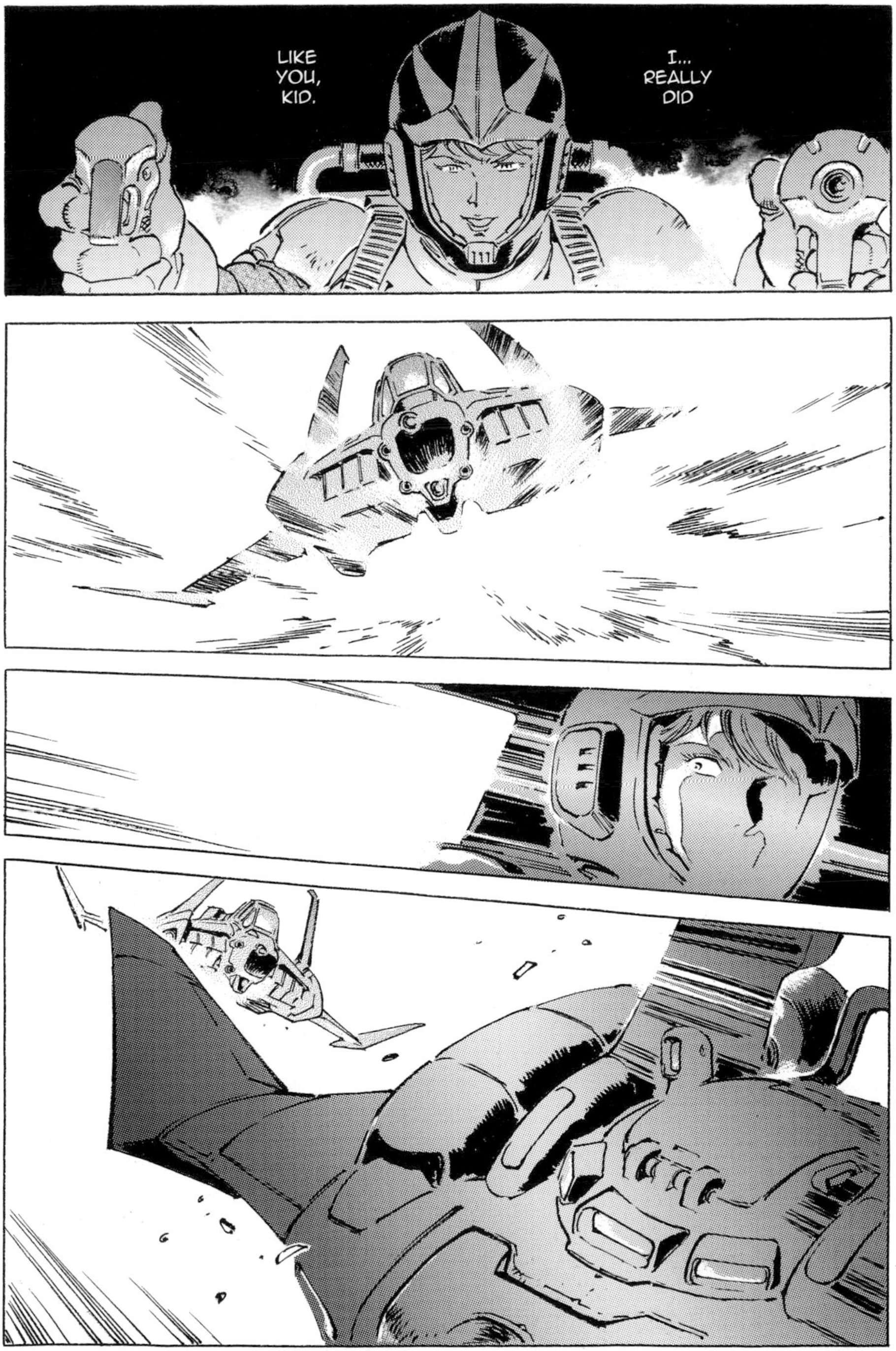
I... REALLY DID
LIKE YOU, KID.

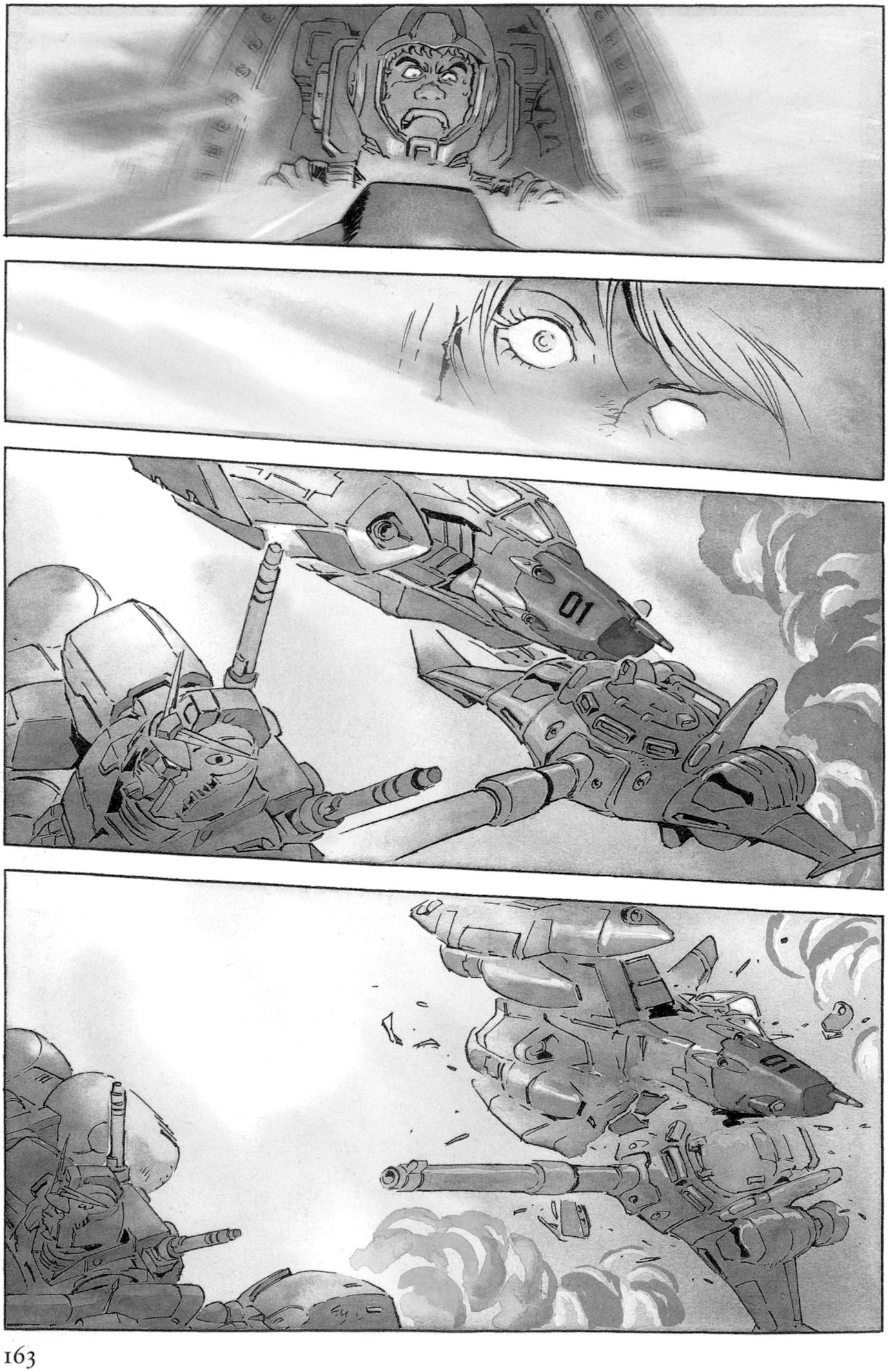
01

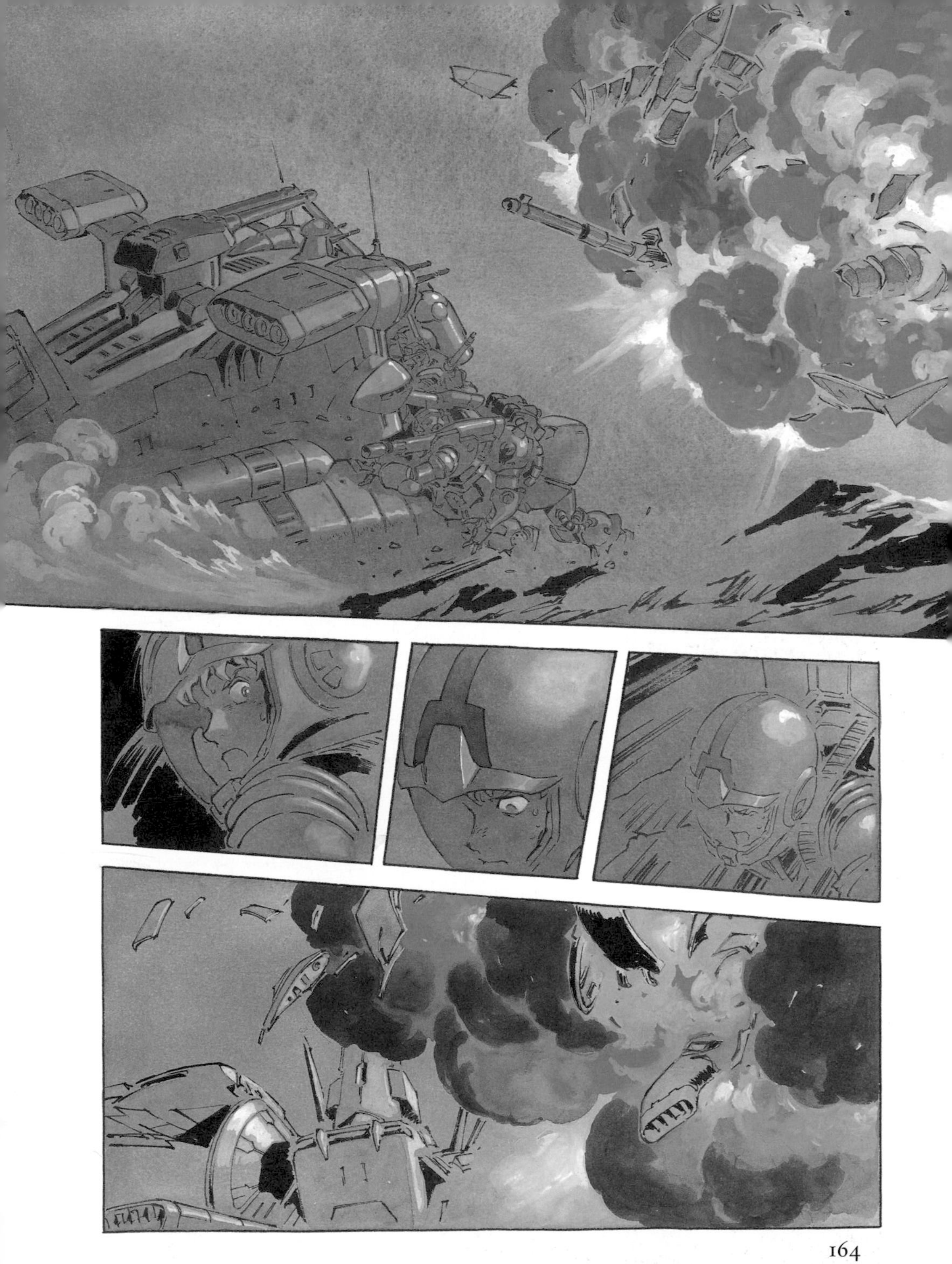

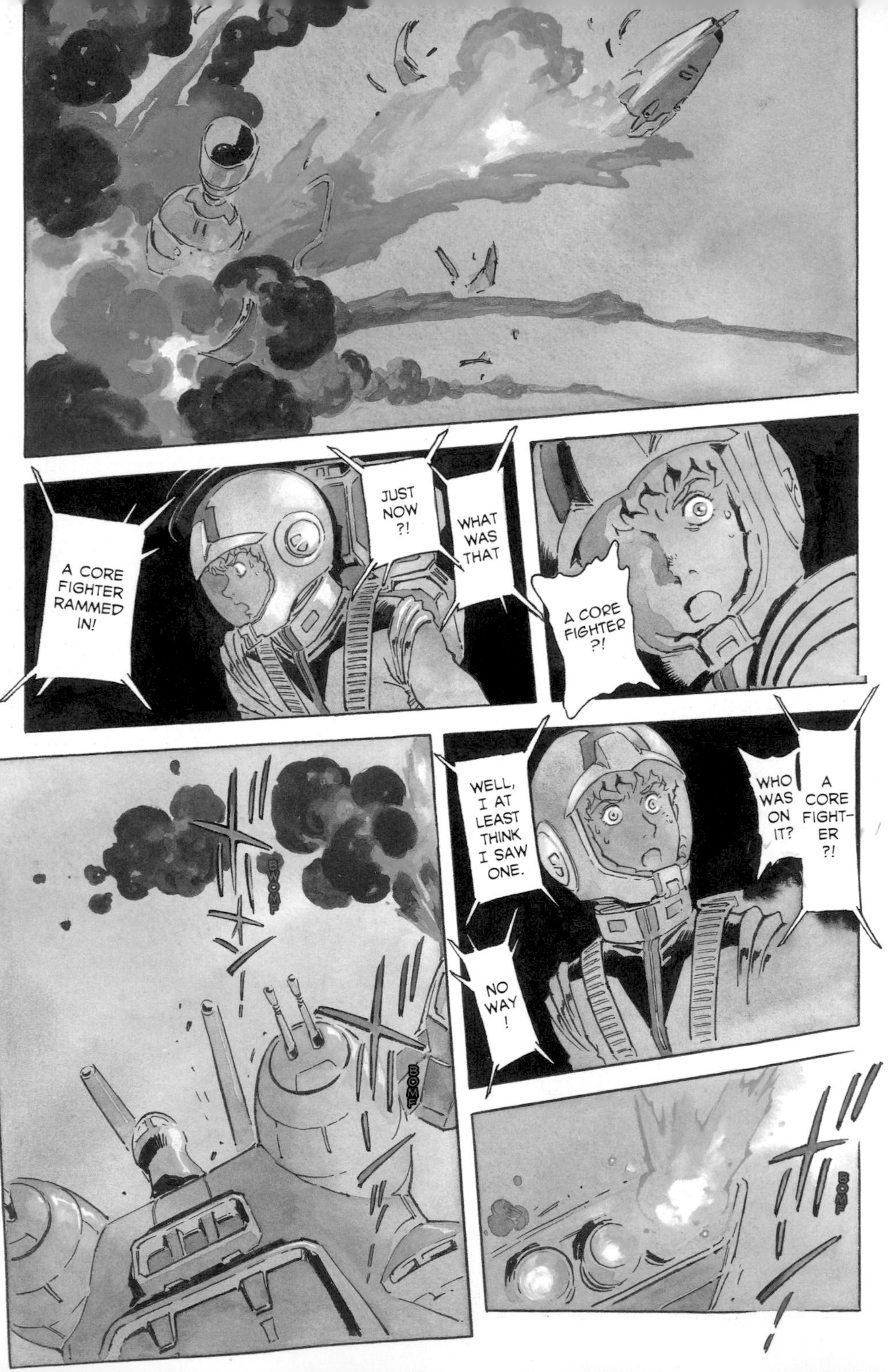
A CORE FIGHTER ?!
WHAT WAS THAT
JUST NOW ?!
A CORE FIGHTER RAMMED IN!
A CORE FIGHTER ?!
WHO WAS ON IT?
WELL, I AT LEAST THINK I SAW ONE.
NO WAY !
BOMF
BWOMF
BOMF

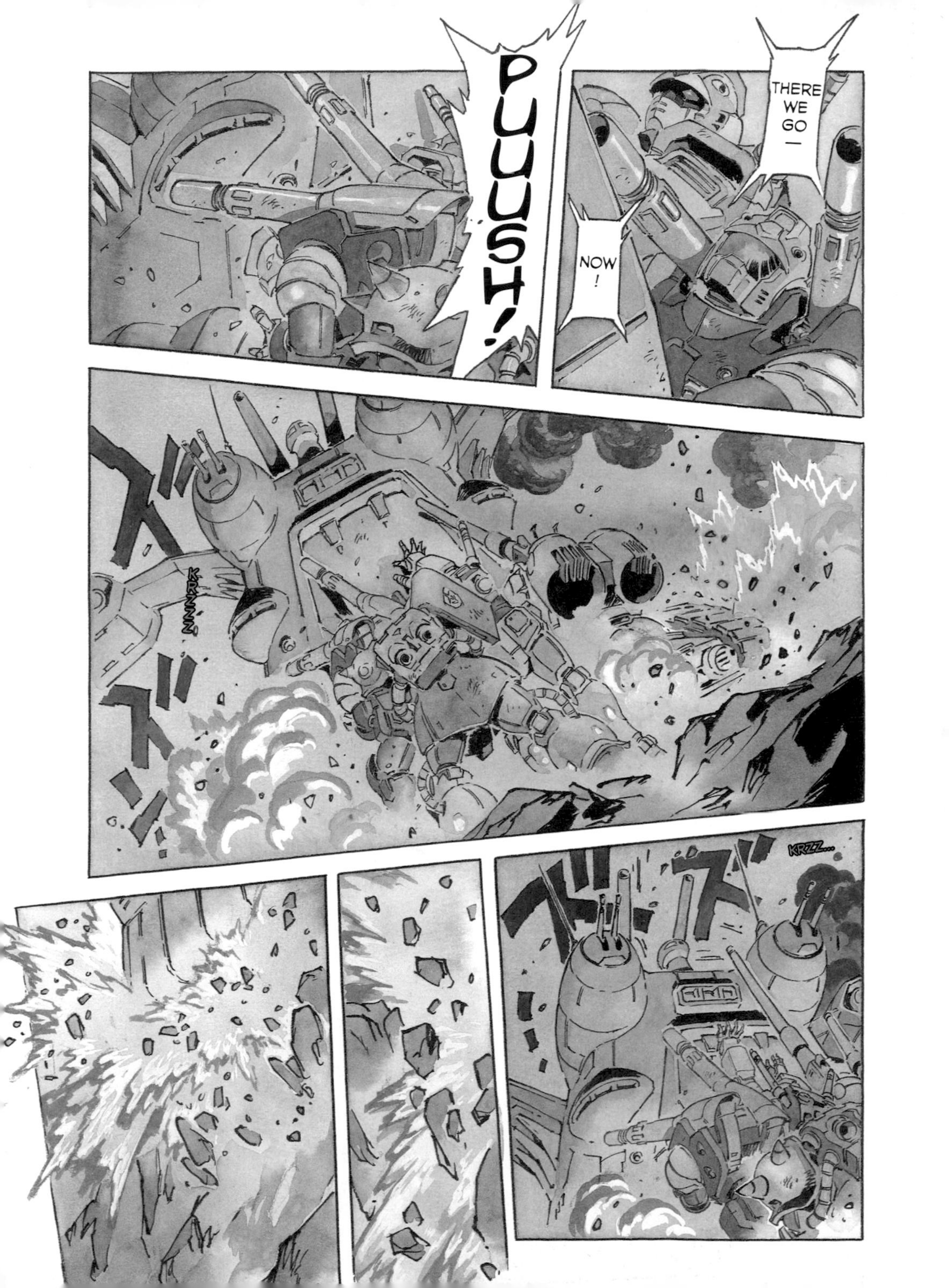
THERE WE GO —
NOW!
PUUUSH!
KRZZZZ
KRZZ...

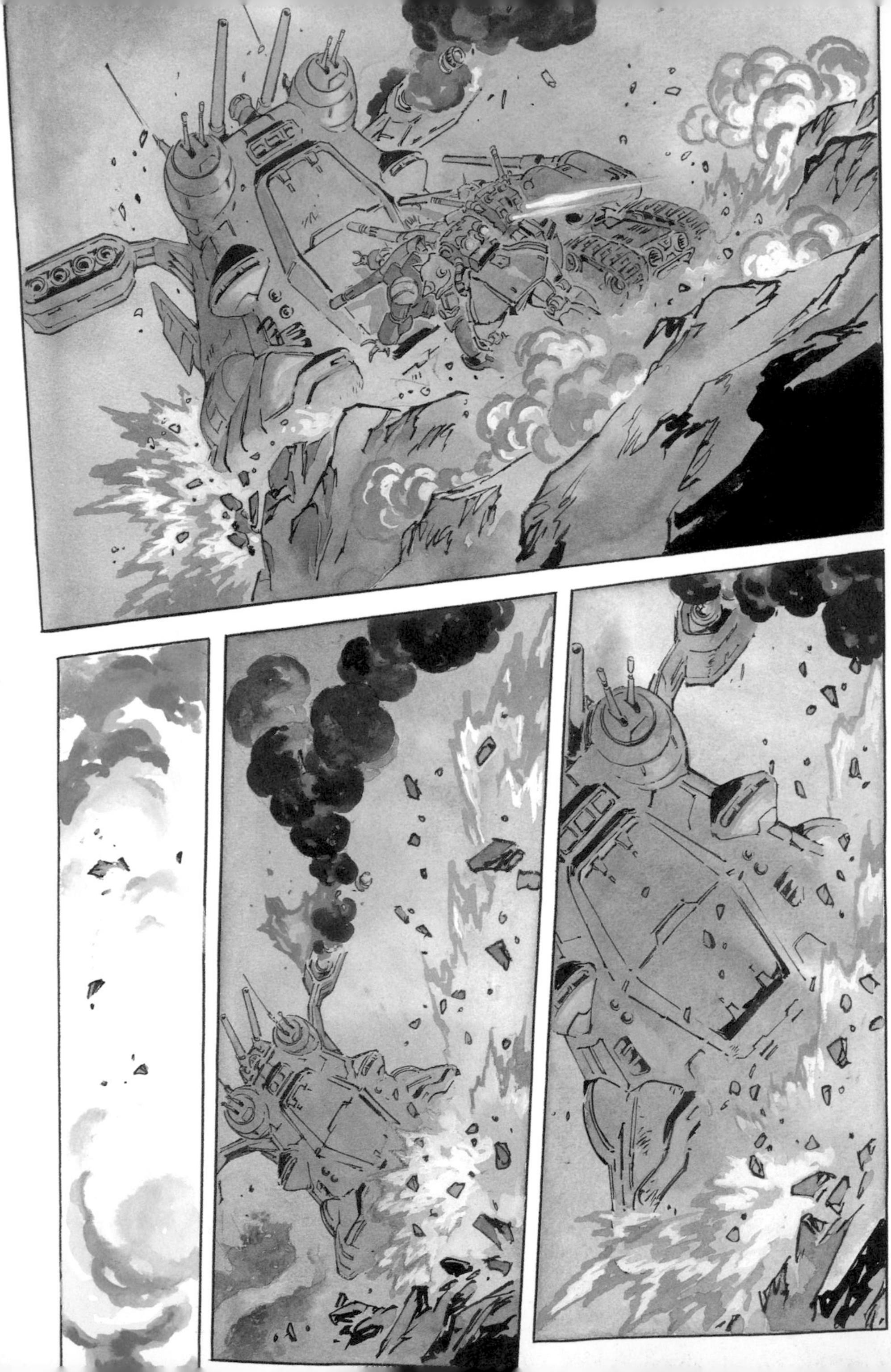

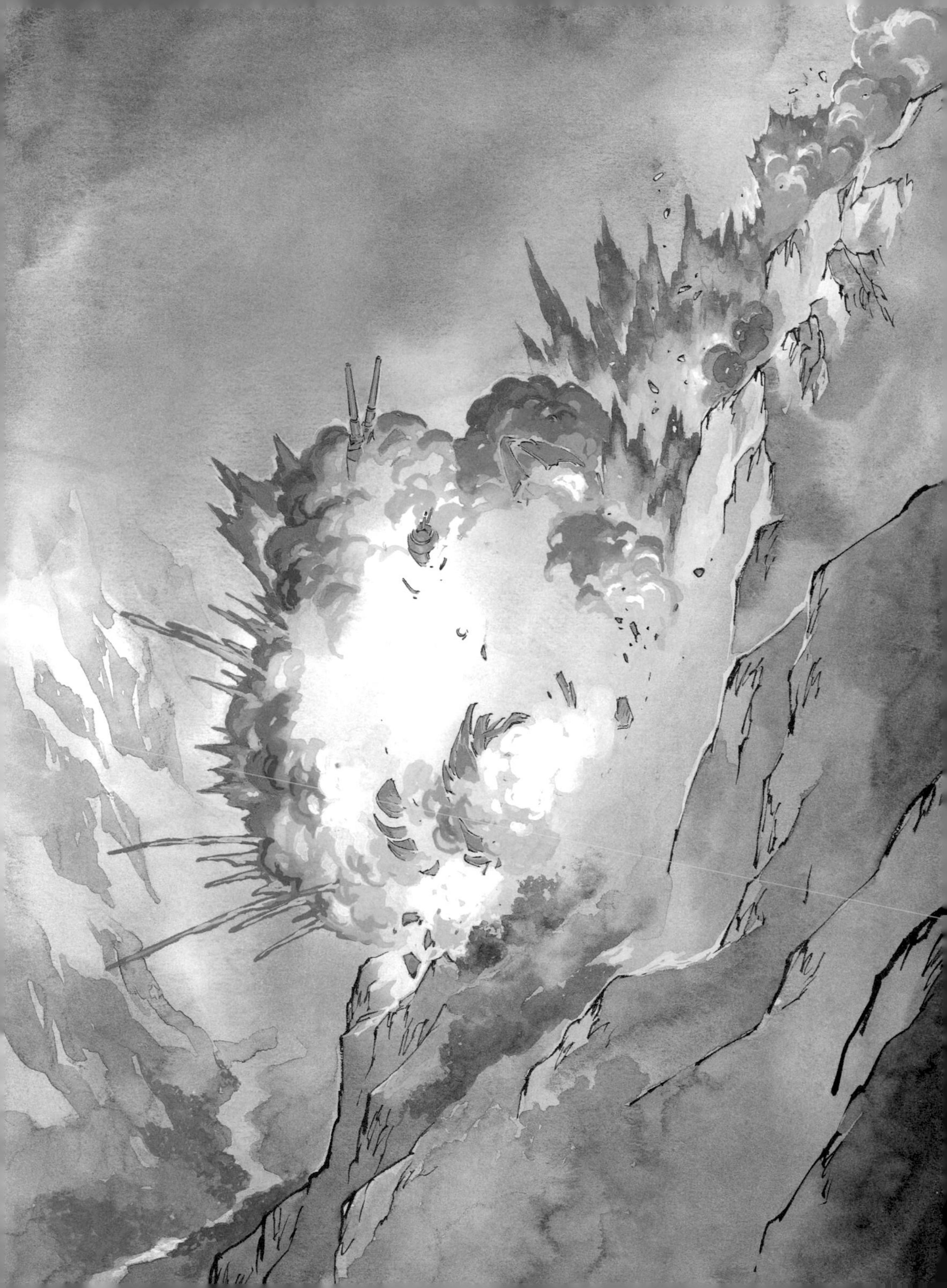

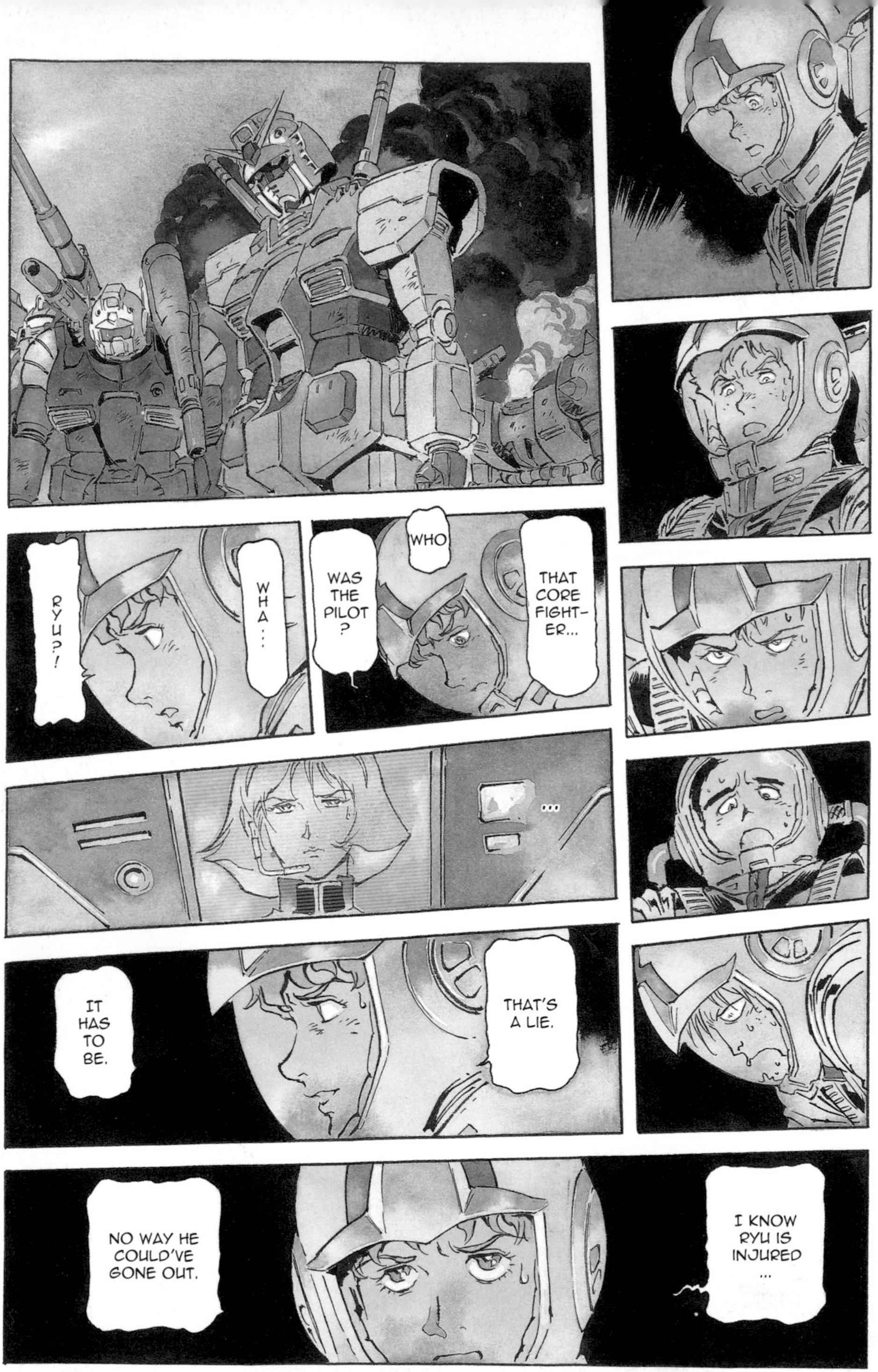
THAT CORE FIGHTER-ER...
WHO
WAS THE PILOT?
WHA...
RYU?!
...
THAT'S A LIE.
IT HAS TO BE.
I KNOW RYU IS INJURED...
NO WAY HE COULD'VE GONE OUT.

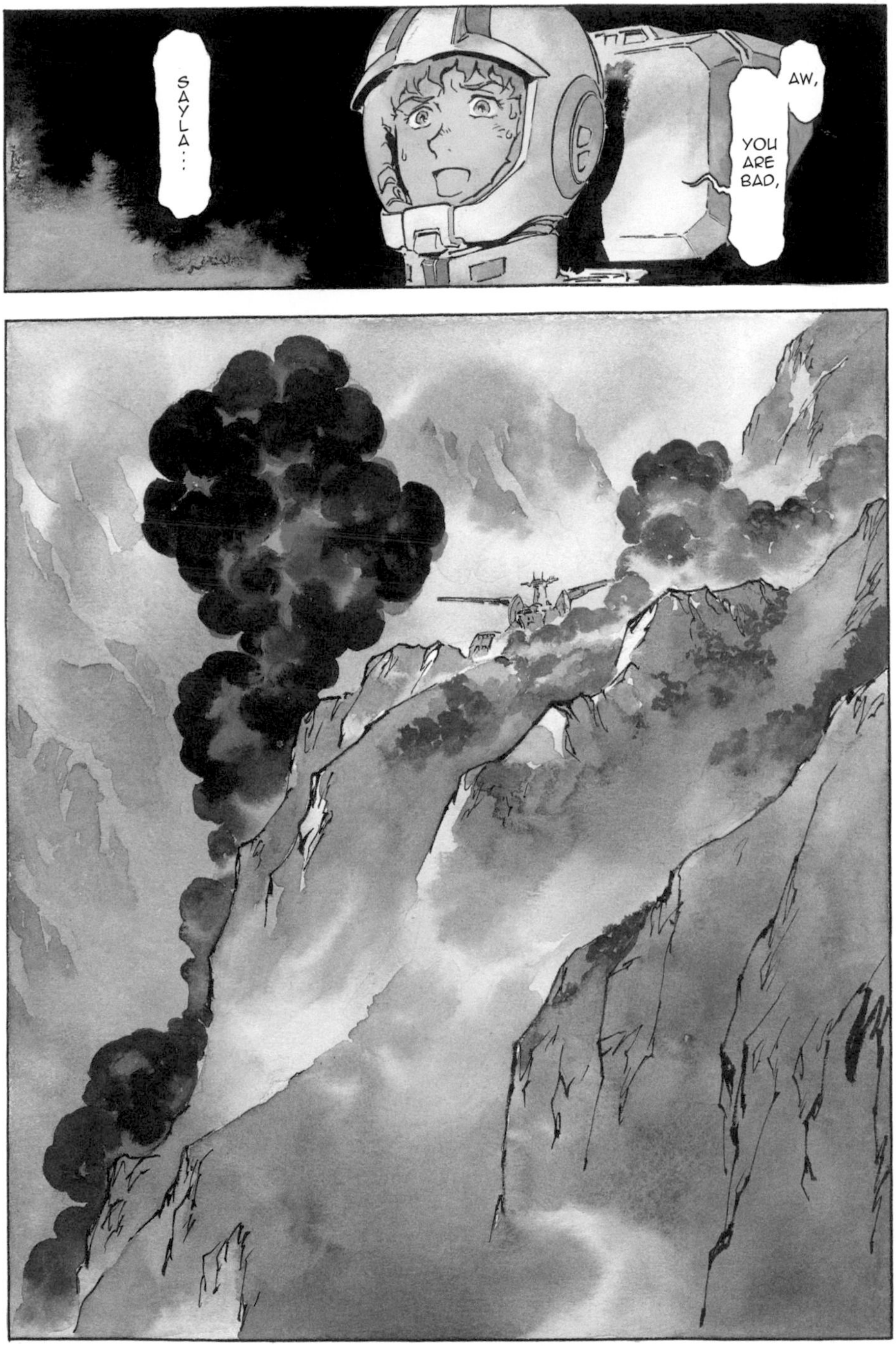
AW,
YOU ARE BAD,
SAYLA...

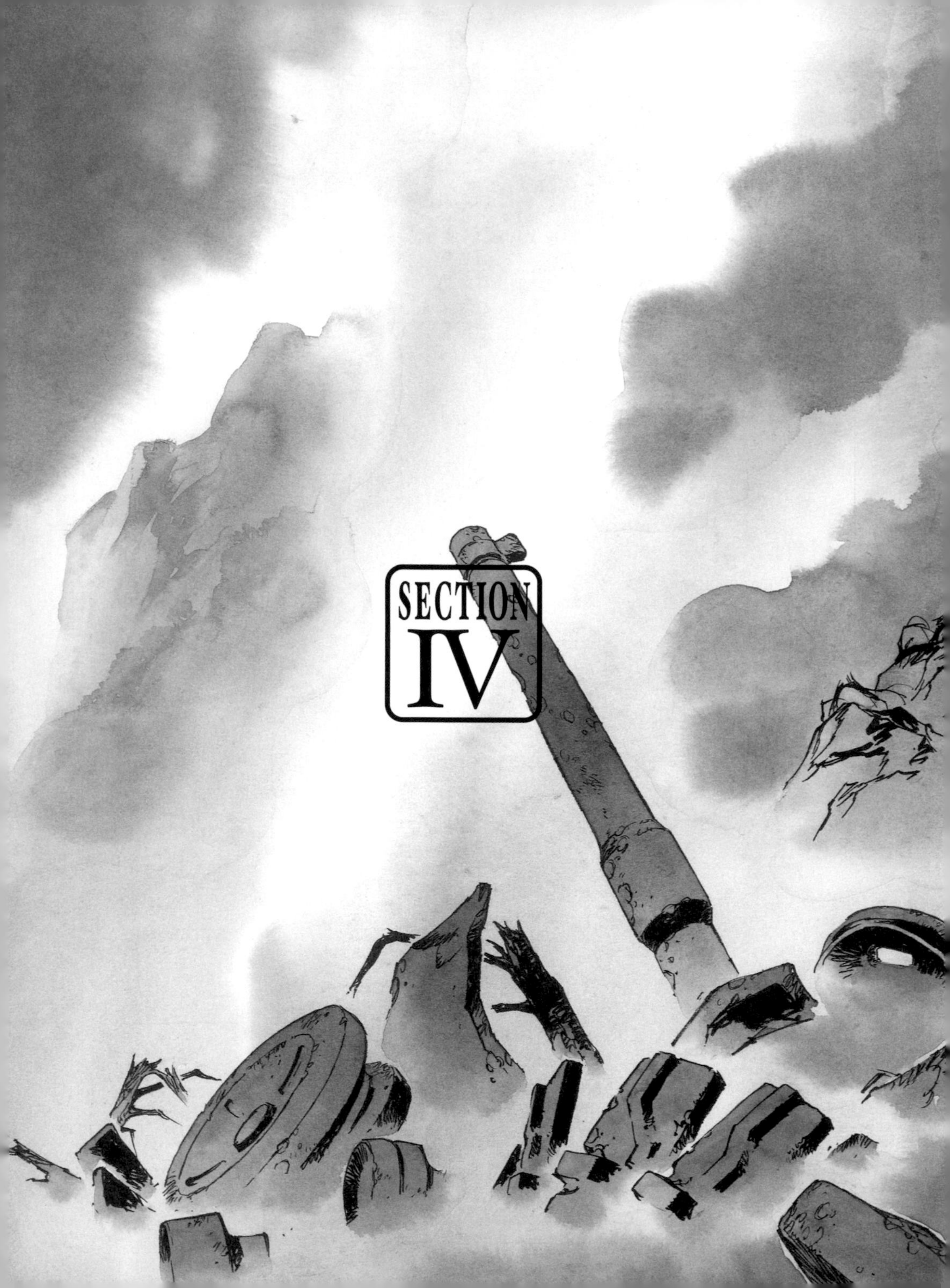
SECTION
IV

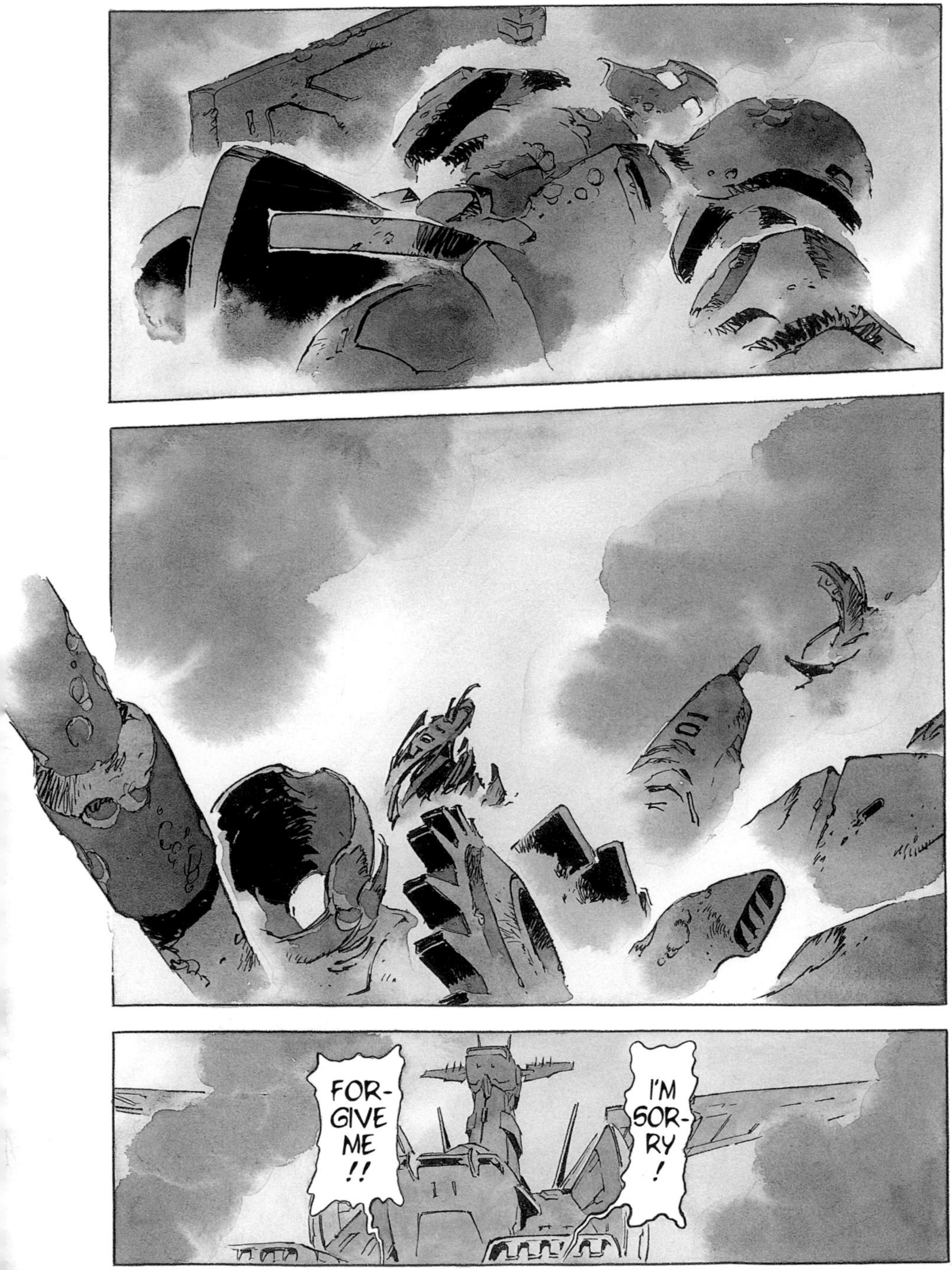
I'M SOR-RY!
FOR-GIVE ME!!

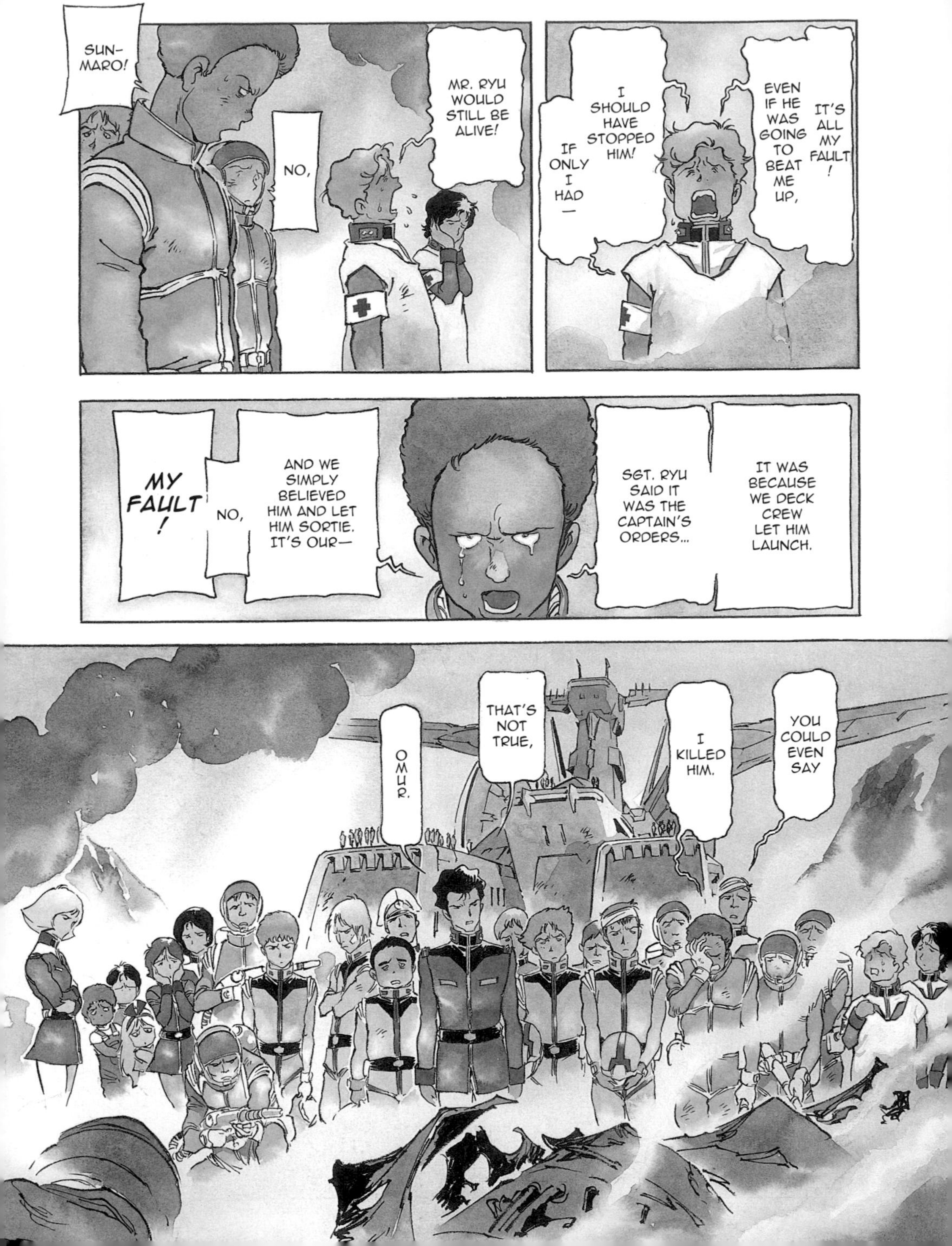
IT'S ALL MY FAULT!
EVEN IF HE WAS GOING TO BEAT ME UP,
I SHOULD HAVE STOPPED HIM!
IF ONLY I HAD—
MR. RYU WOULD STILL BE ALIVE!
NO,
SUN-MARO!
IT WAS BECAUSE WE DECK CREW LET HIM LAUNCH.
SGT. RYU SAID IT WAS THE CAPTAIN'S ORDERS...
AND WE SIMPLY BELIEVED HIM AND LET HIM SORTIE. IT'S OUR—
NO,
MY FAULT!
YOU COULD EVEN SAY
I KILLED HIM.
THAT'S NOT TRUE,
OMUR.

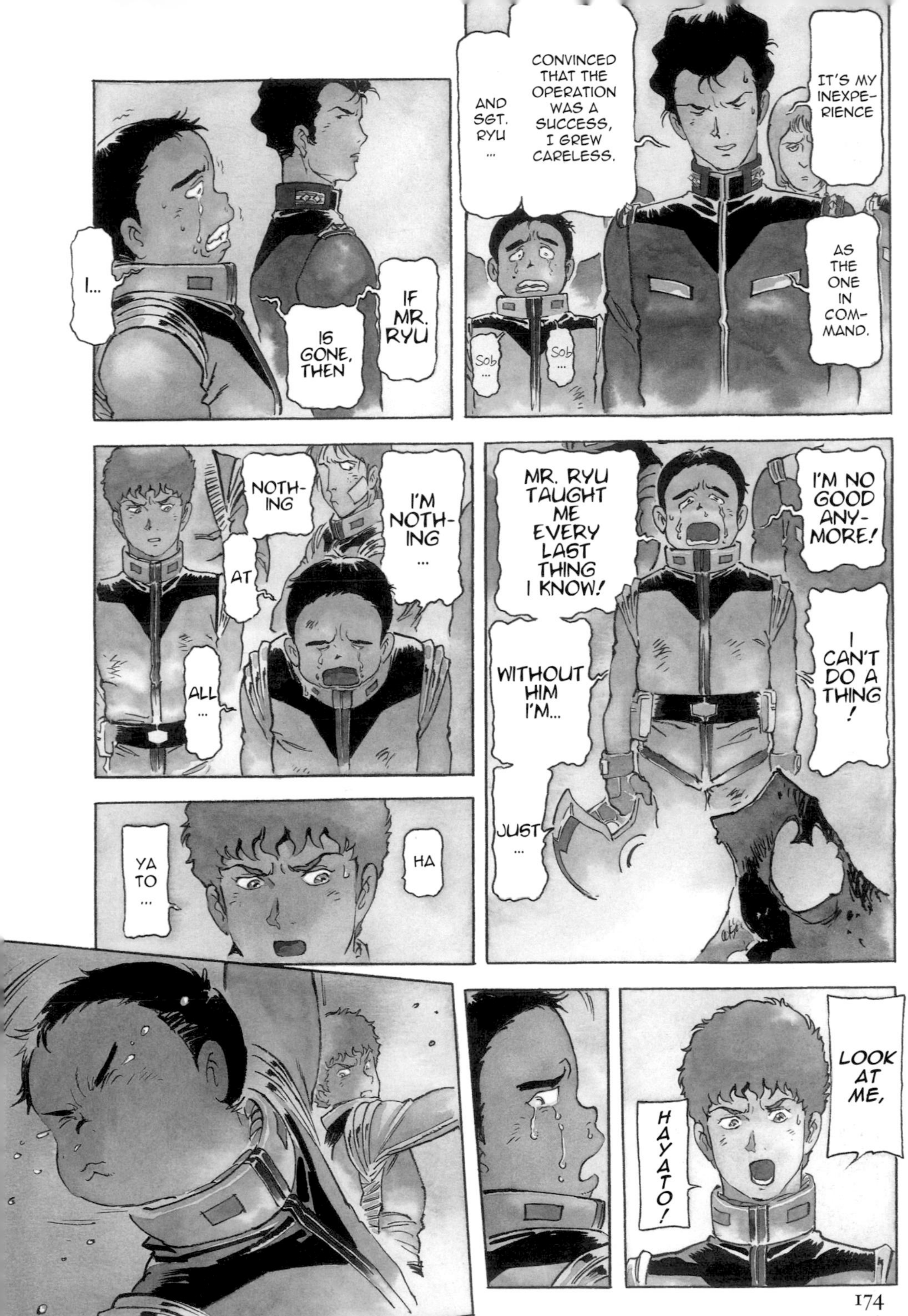
IT'S MY INEXPERIENCE
AS THE ONE IN COMMAND.
CONVINCED THAT THE OPERATION WAS A SUCCESS, I GREW CARELESS.
AND SGT. RYU ...
Sob ...
Sob ...
IF MR. RYU
IS GONE, THEN
I...
I'M NO GOOD ANYMORE!
I CAN'T DO A THING!
MR. RYU TAUGHT ME EVERY LAST THING I KNOW!
WITHOUT HIM I'M...
JUST ...
I'M NOTHING ...
NOTHING
AT
ALL ...
HA
YA TO ...
LOOK AT ME,
HAYATO!

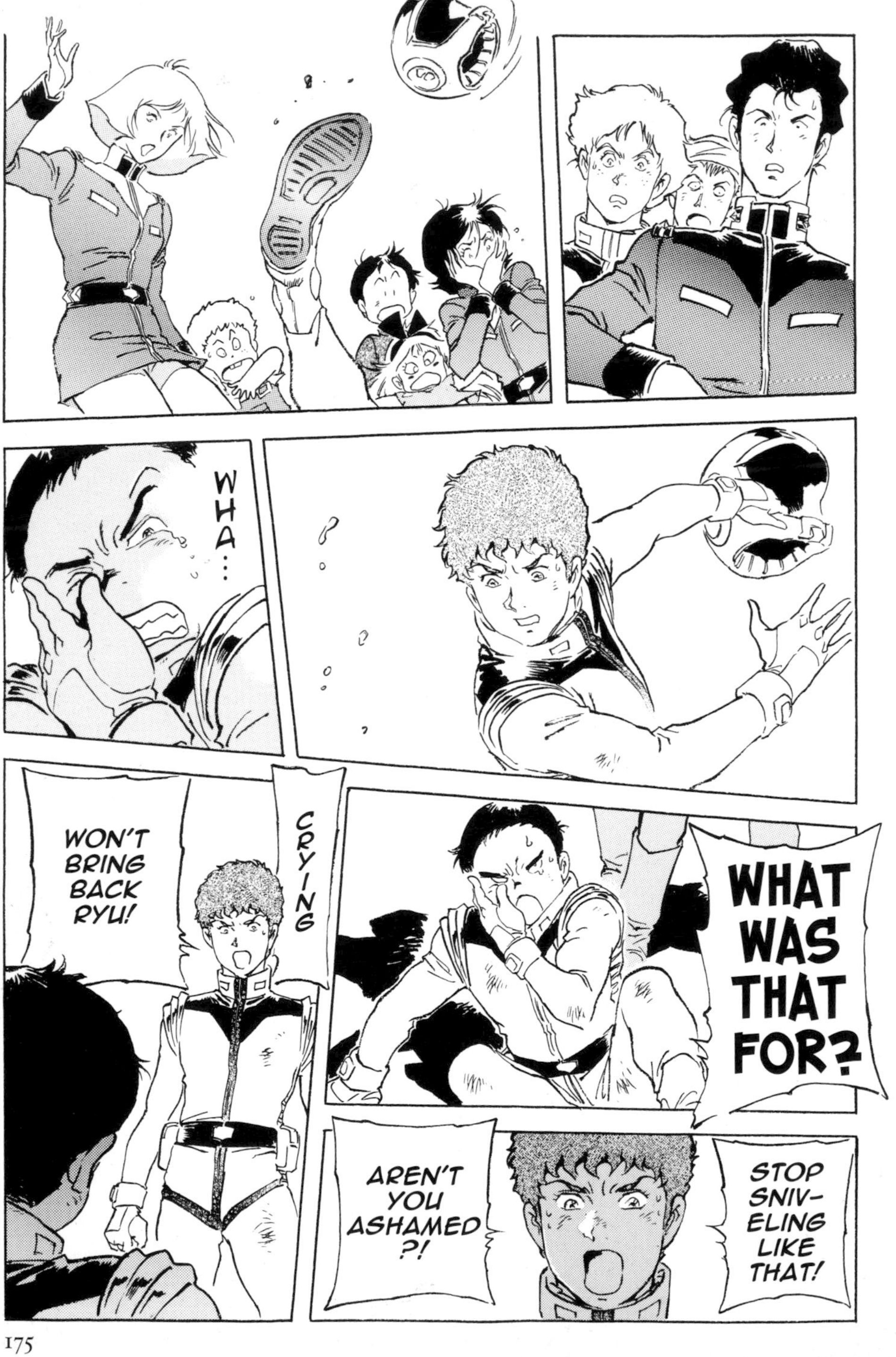
WHA...
WHAT WAS THAT FOR?
STOP SNIVELING LIKE THAT!
AREN'T YOU ASHAMED?!
CRYING
WON'T BRING BACK RYU!

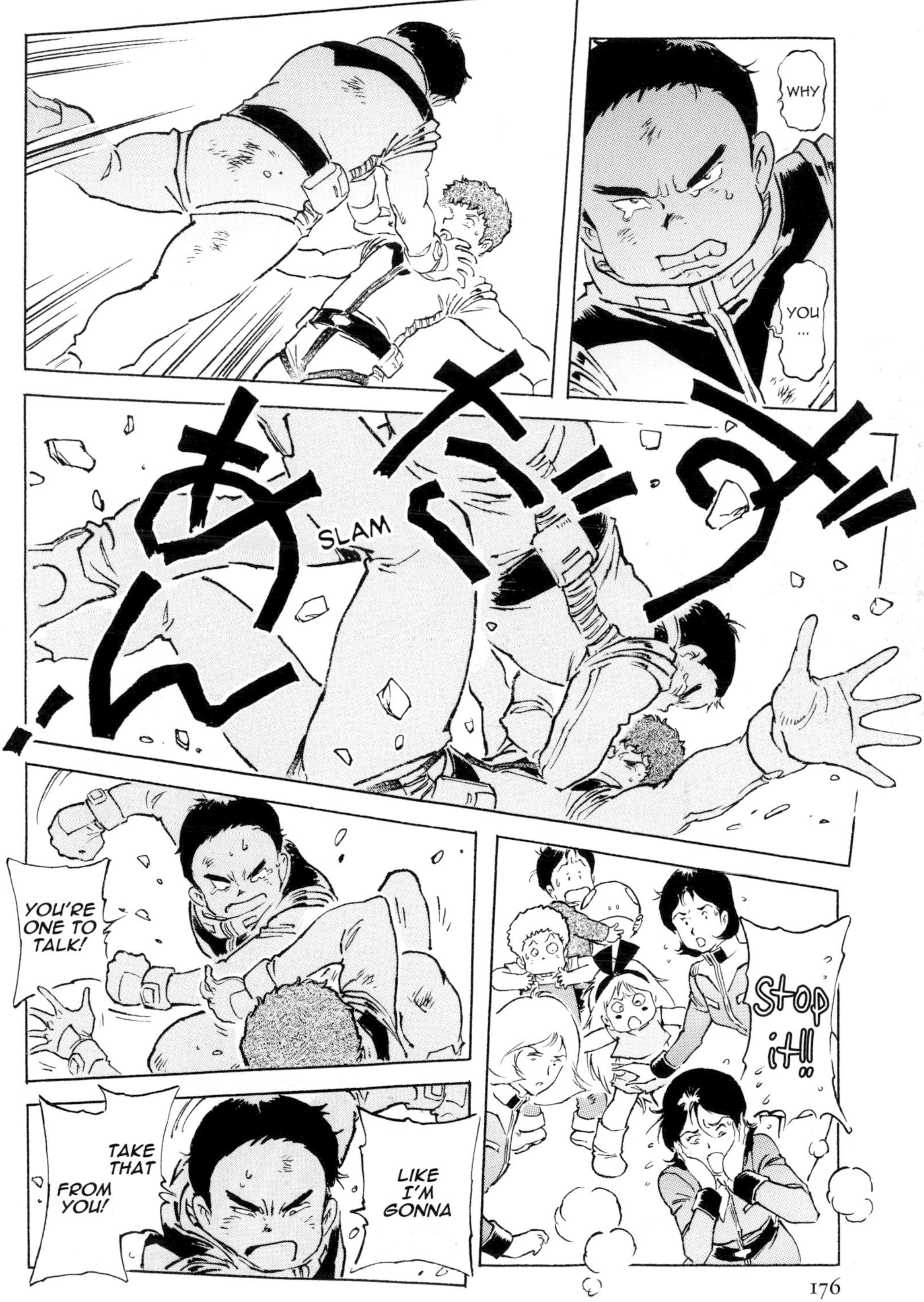
WHY
YOU ...
SLAM
Stop it!!
YOU'RE ONE TO TALK!
LIKE I'M GONNA
TAKE THAT FROM YOU!

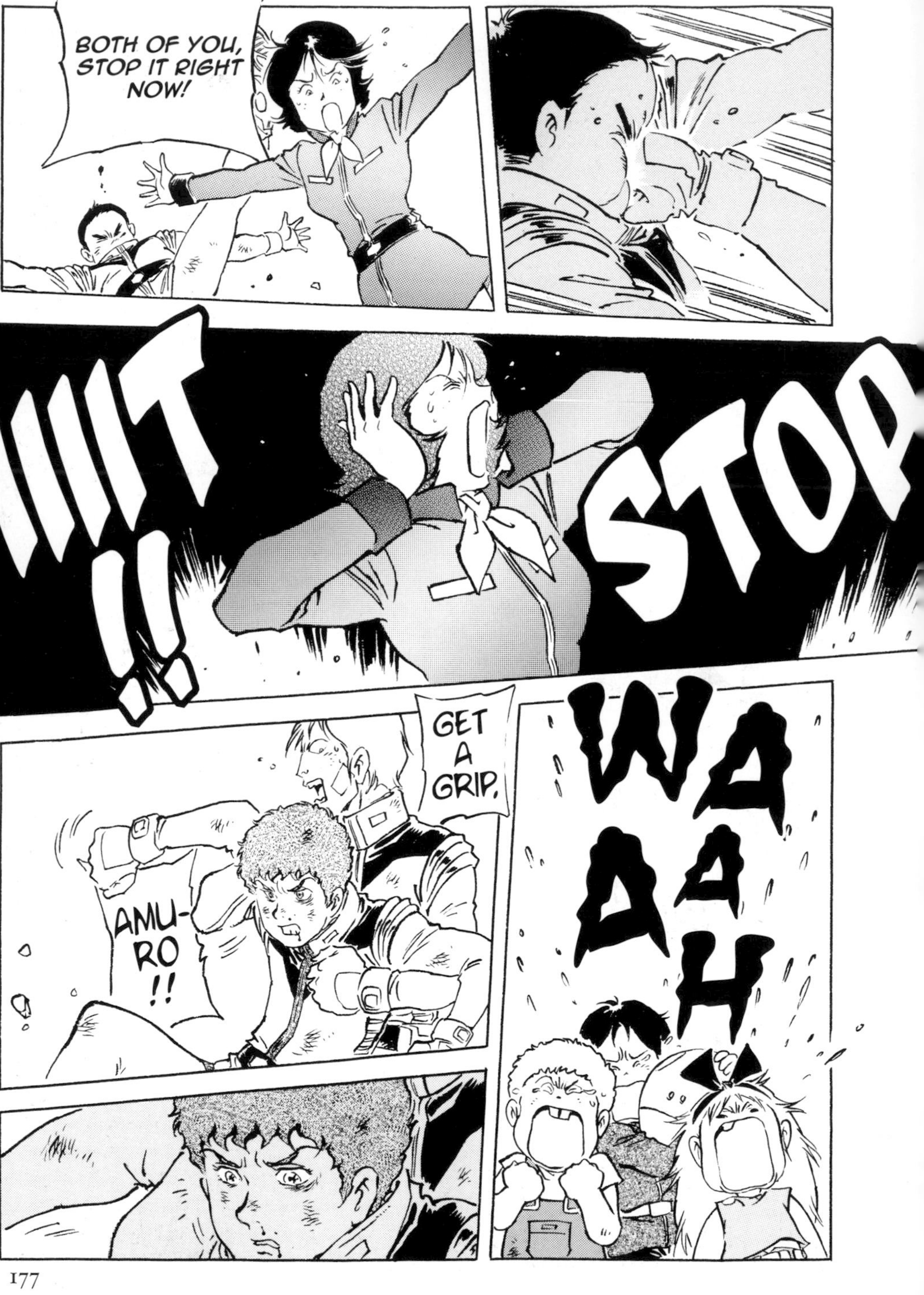
BOTH OF YOU, STOP IT RIGHT NOW!
STOP
IIIIIT!!
WAAAH
GET A GRIP,
AMURO!!

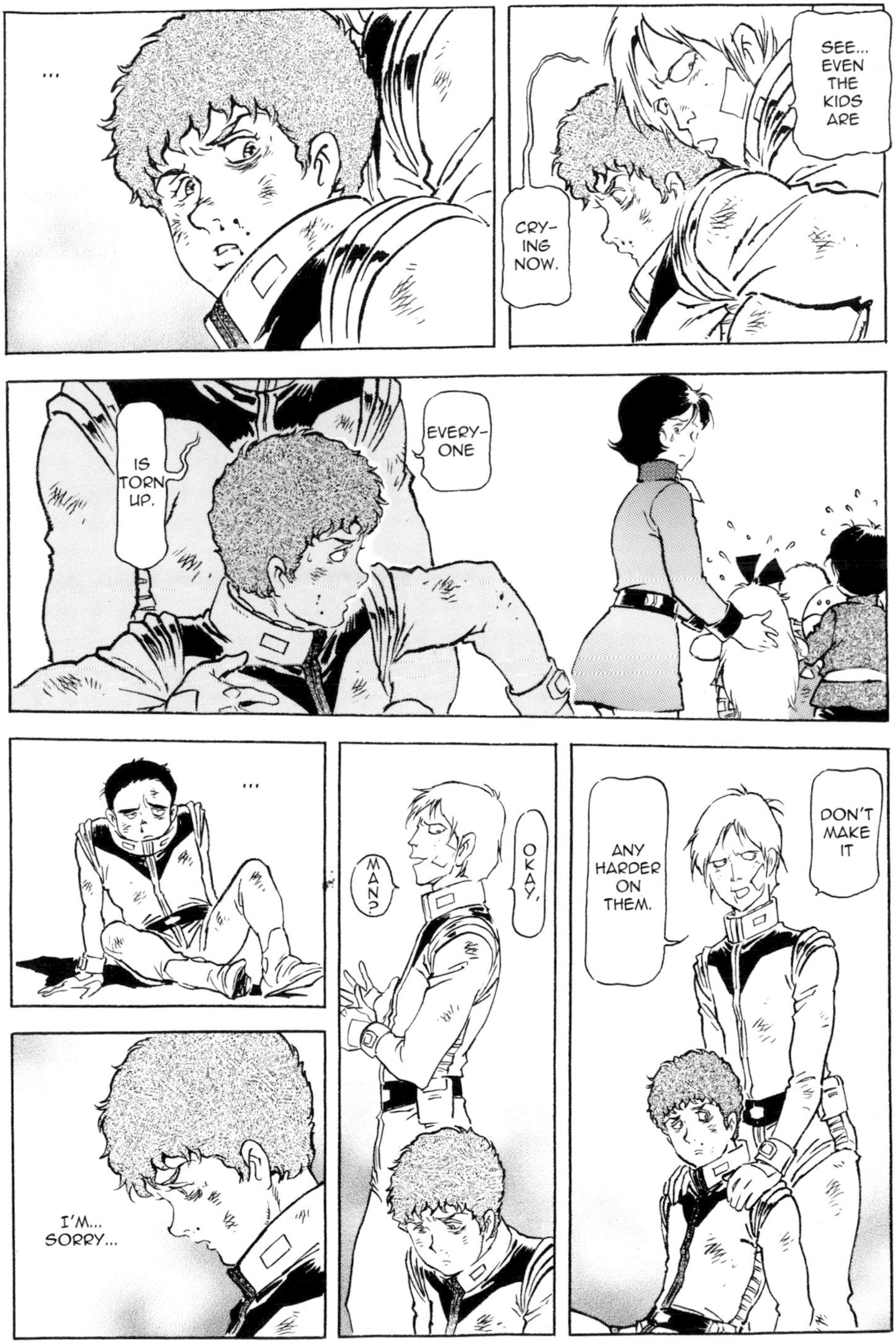
SEE... EVEN THE KIDS ARE
CRY-ING NOW.
...
EVERY-ONE
IS TORN UP.
DON'T MAKE IT
ANY HARDER ON THEM.
OKAY,
MAN?
...
I'M... SORRY...

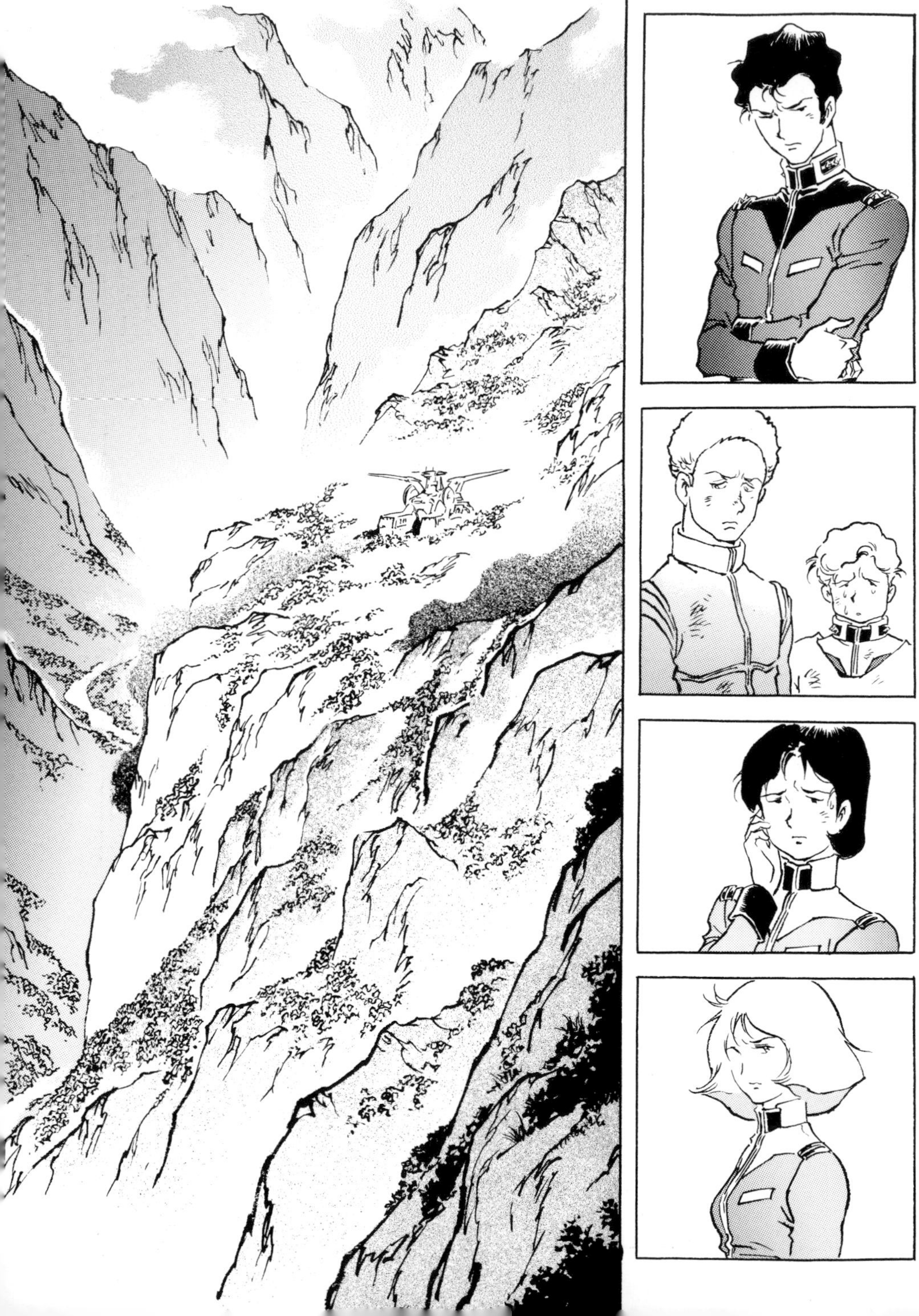

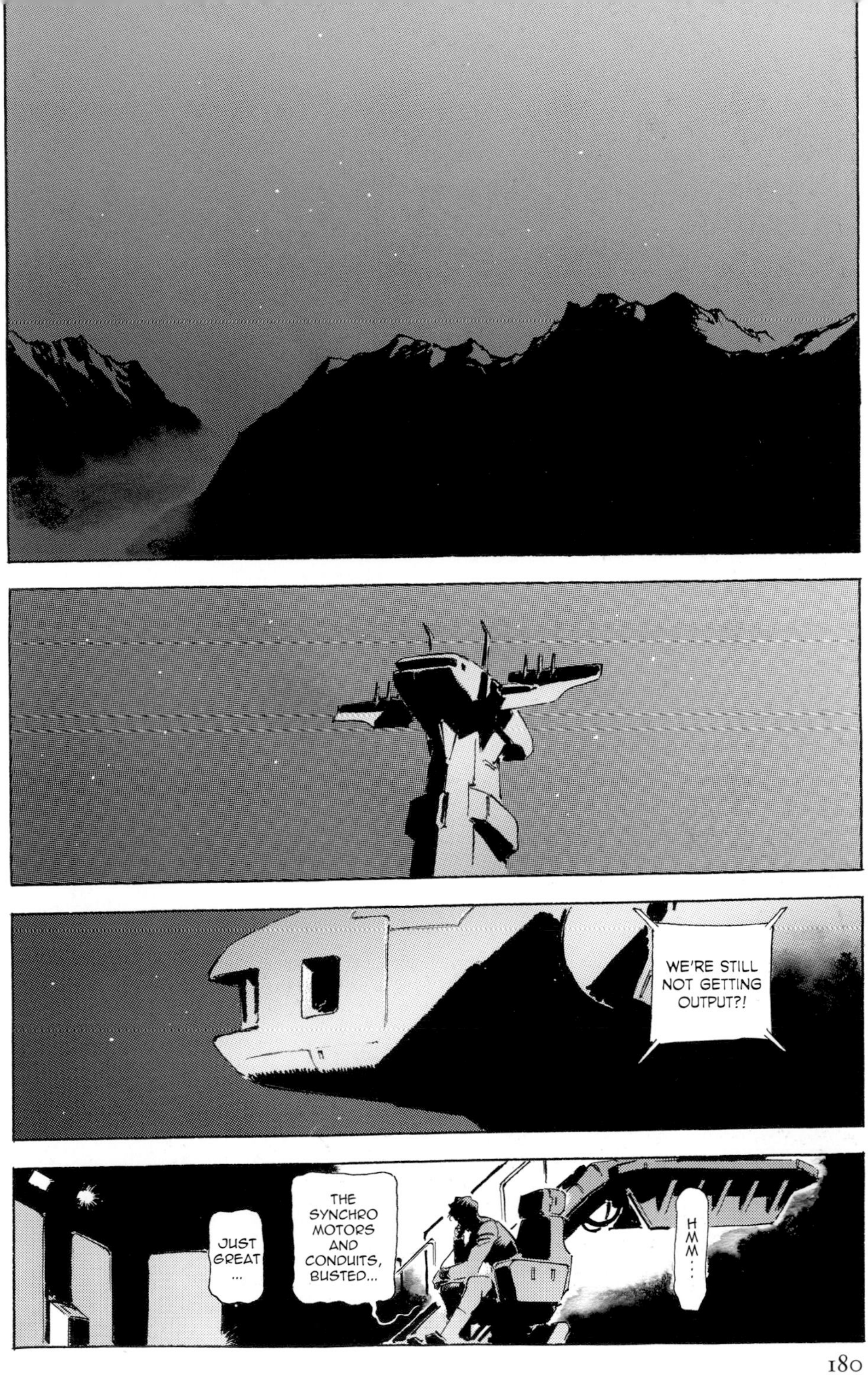
WE'RE STILL NOT GETTING OUTPUT?!
HMM...
THE SYNCHRO MOTORS AND CONDUITS, BUSTED...
JUST GREAT...

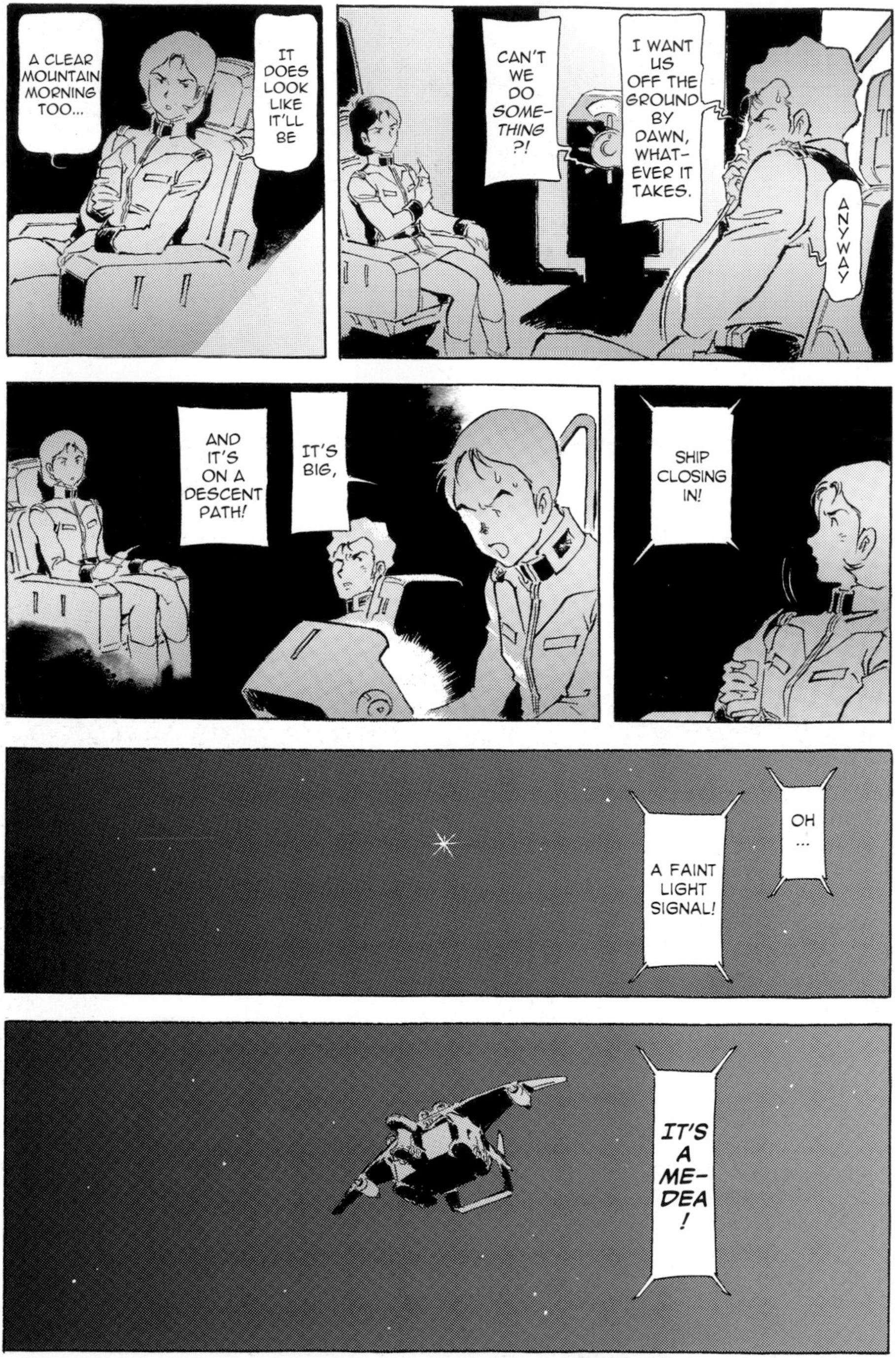
ANYWAY
I WANT US OFF THE GROUND BY DAWN, WHATEVER IT TAKES.
CAN'T WE DO SOME-THING ?!
IT DOES LOOK LIKE IT'LL BE
A CLEAR MOUNTAIN MORNING TOO...
SHIP CLOSING IN!
IT'S BIG,
AND IT'S ON A DESCENT PATH!
OH ...
A FAINT LIGHT SIGNAL!
IT'S A ME-DEA !

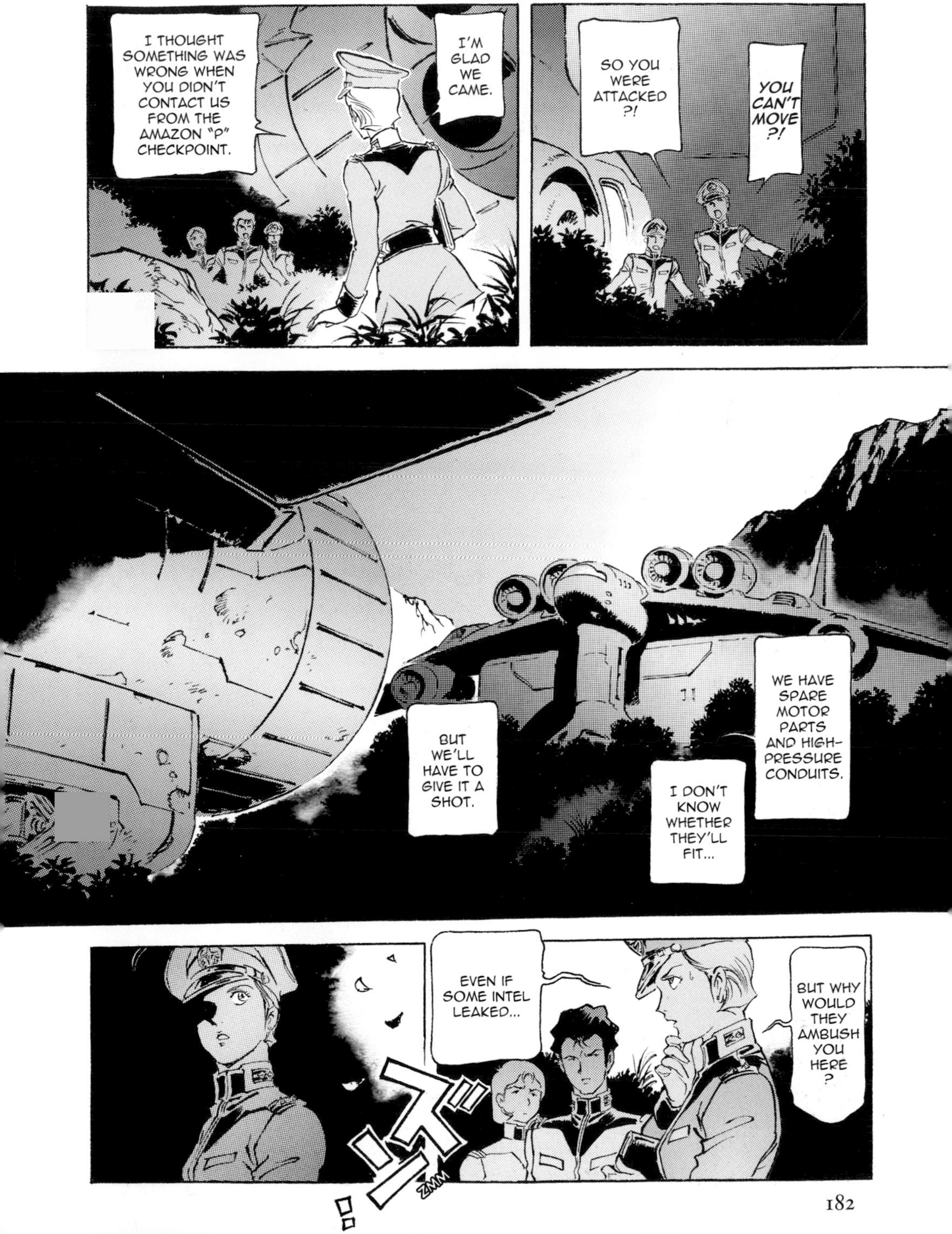
YOU CAN'T MOVE ?!
SO YOU WERE ATTACKED ?!
I'M GLAD WE CAME.
I THOUGHT SOMETHING WAS WRONG WHEN YOU DIDN'T CONTACT US FROM THE AMAZON "P" CHECKPOINT.
WE HAVE SPARE MOTOR PARTS AND HIGH-PRESSURE CONDUITS.
I DON'T KNOW WHETHER THEY'LL FIT...
BUT WE'LL HAVE TO GIVE IT A SHOT.
BUT WHY WOULD THEY AMBUSH YOU HERE ?
EVEN IF SOME INTEL LEAKED...
ZMM

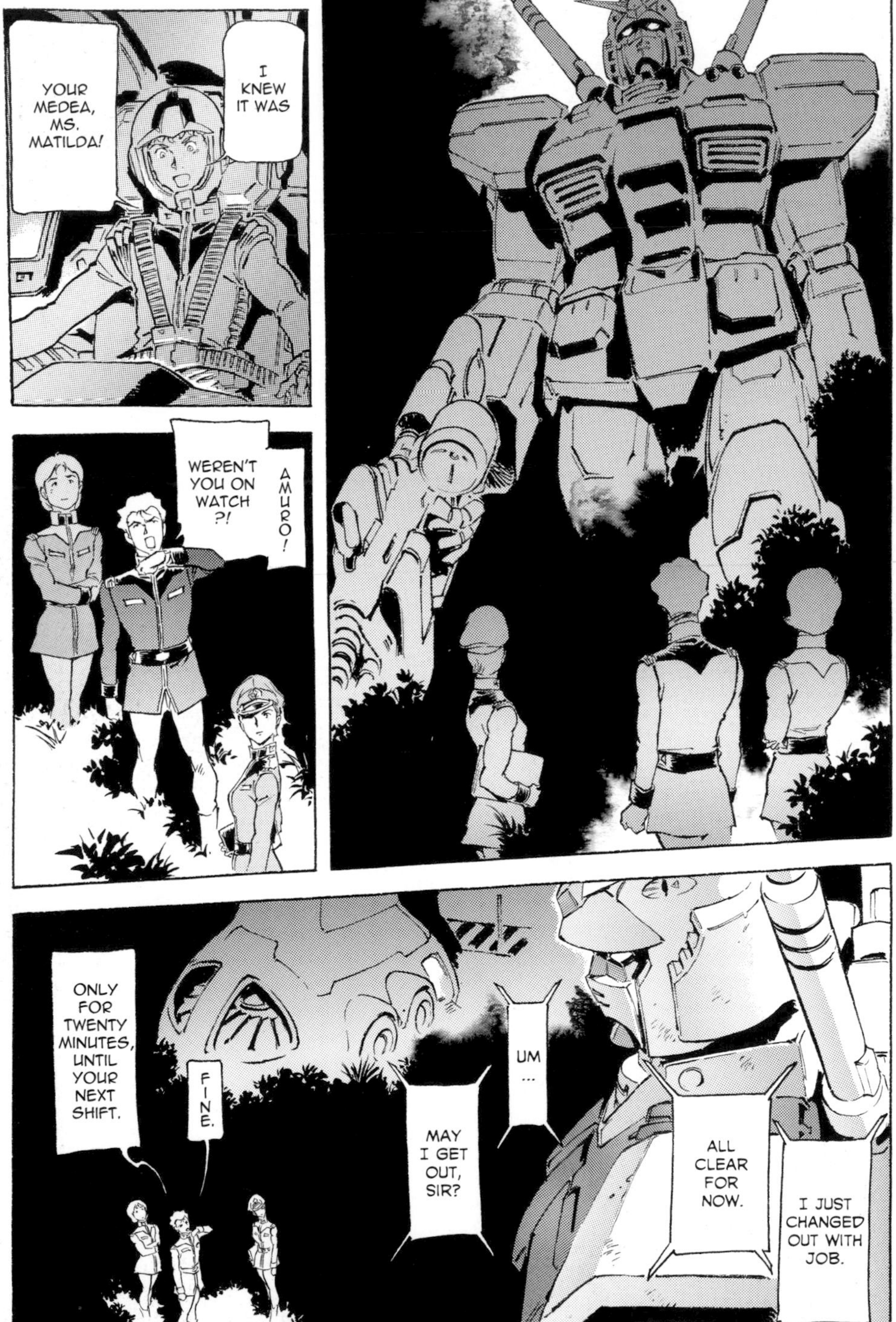

I KNEW IT WAS
YOUR MEDEA, MS. MATILDA!
AMURO!
WEREN'T YOU ON WATCH ?!
I JUST CHANGED OUT WITH JOB.
ALL CLEAR FOR NOW.
UM ...
MAY I GET OUT, SIR?
FINE.
ONLY FOR TWENTY MINUTES, UNTIL YOUR NEXT SHIFT.

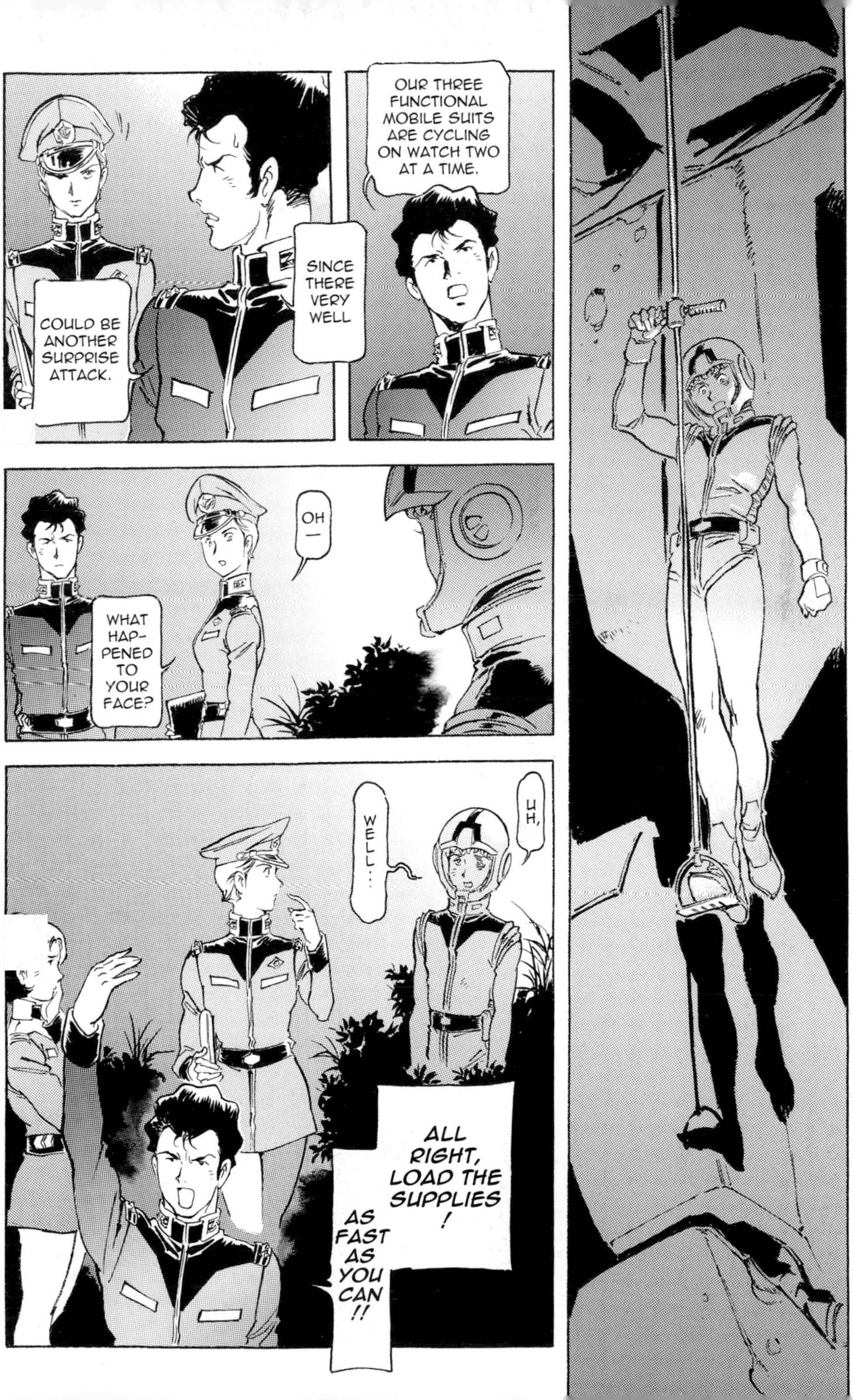
OUR THREE FUNCTIONAL MOBILE SUITS ARE CYCLING ON WATCH TWO AT A TIME.
SINCE THERE VERY WELL
COULD BE ANOTHER SURPRISE ATTACK.
OH—
WHAT HAPPENED TO YOUR FACE?
UH,
WELL...
ALL RIGHT, LOAD THE SUPPLIES!
AS FAST AS YOU CAN!!

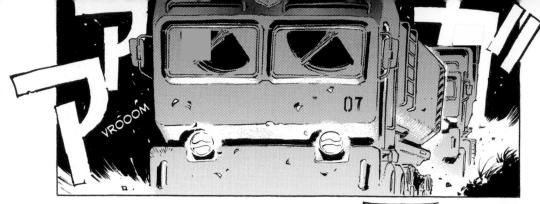

VROOOM

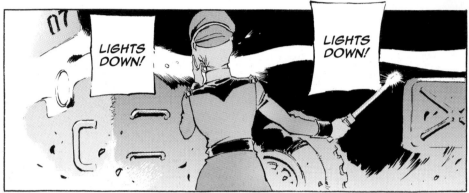

LIGHTS DOWN!

LIGHTS DOWN!

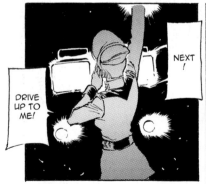

NEXT!

DRIVE UP TO ME!

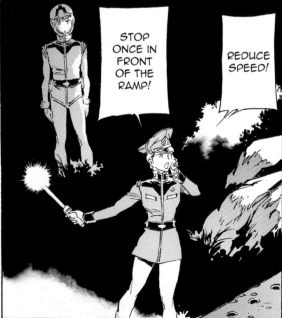

STOP ONCE IN FRONT OF THE RAMP!

REDUCE SPEED!

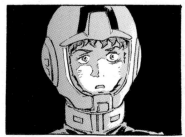

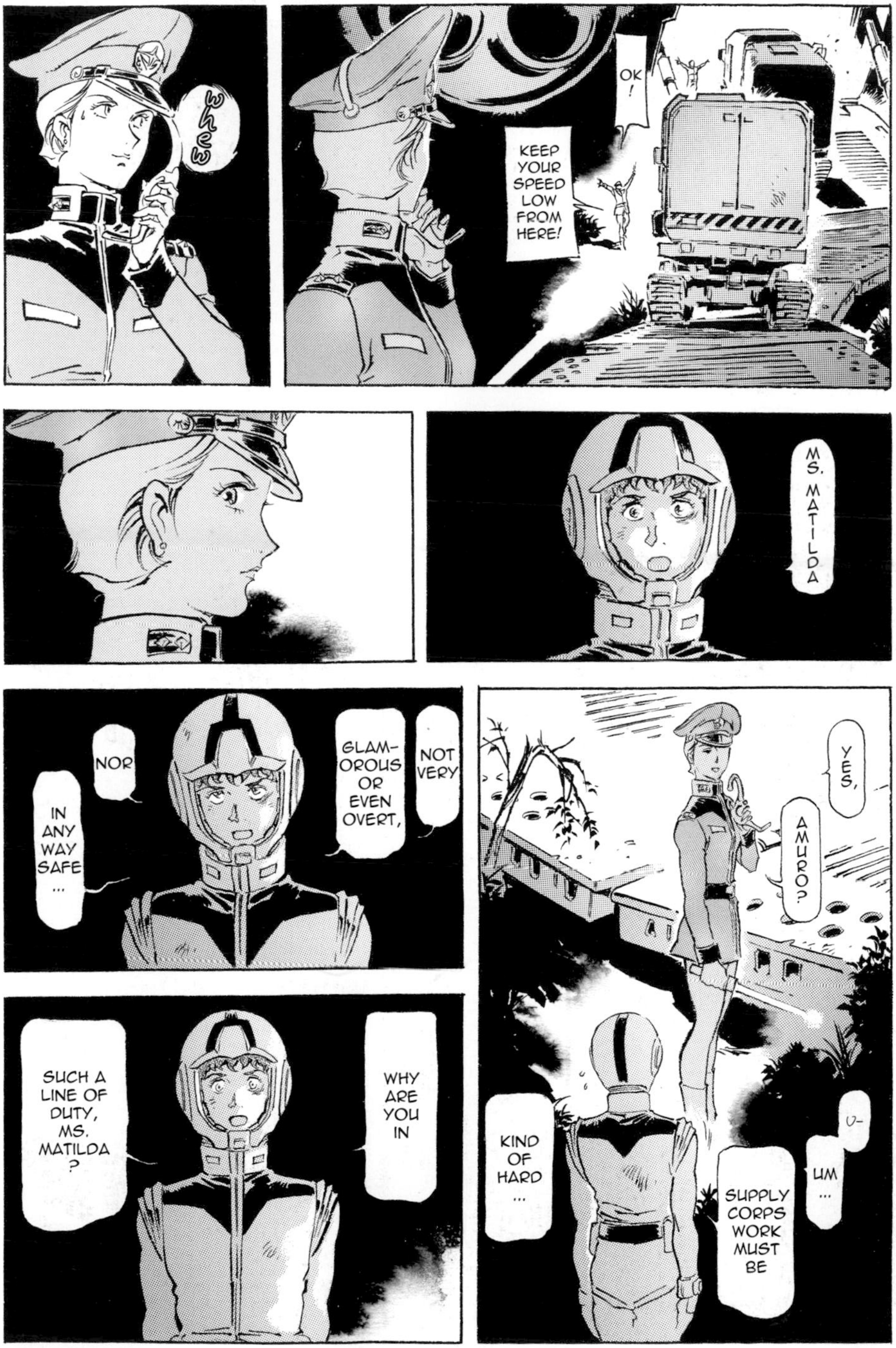
OK!
KEEP YOUR SPEED LOW FROM HERE!
whew
MS. MATILDA
YES,
AMURO?
U-
UM...
SUPPLY CORPS WORK MUST BE
KIND OF HARD...
NOT VERY
GLAM-OROUS OR EVEN OVERT,
NOR
IN ANY WAY SAFE...
WHY ARE YOU IN
SUCH A LINE OF DUTY, MS. MATILDA?

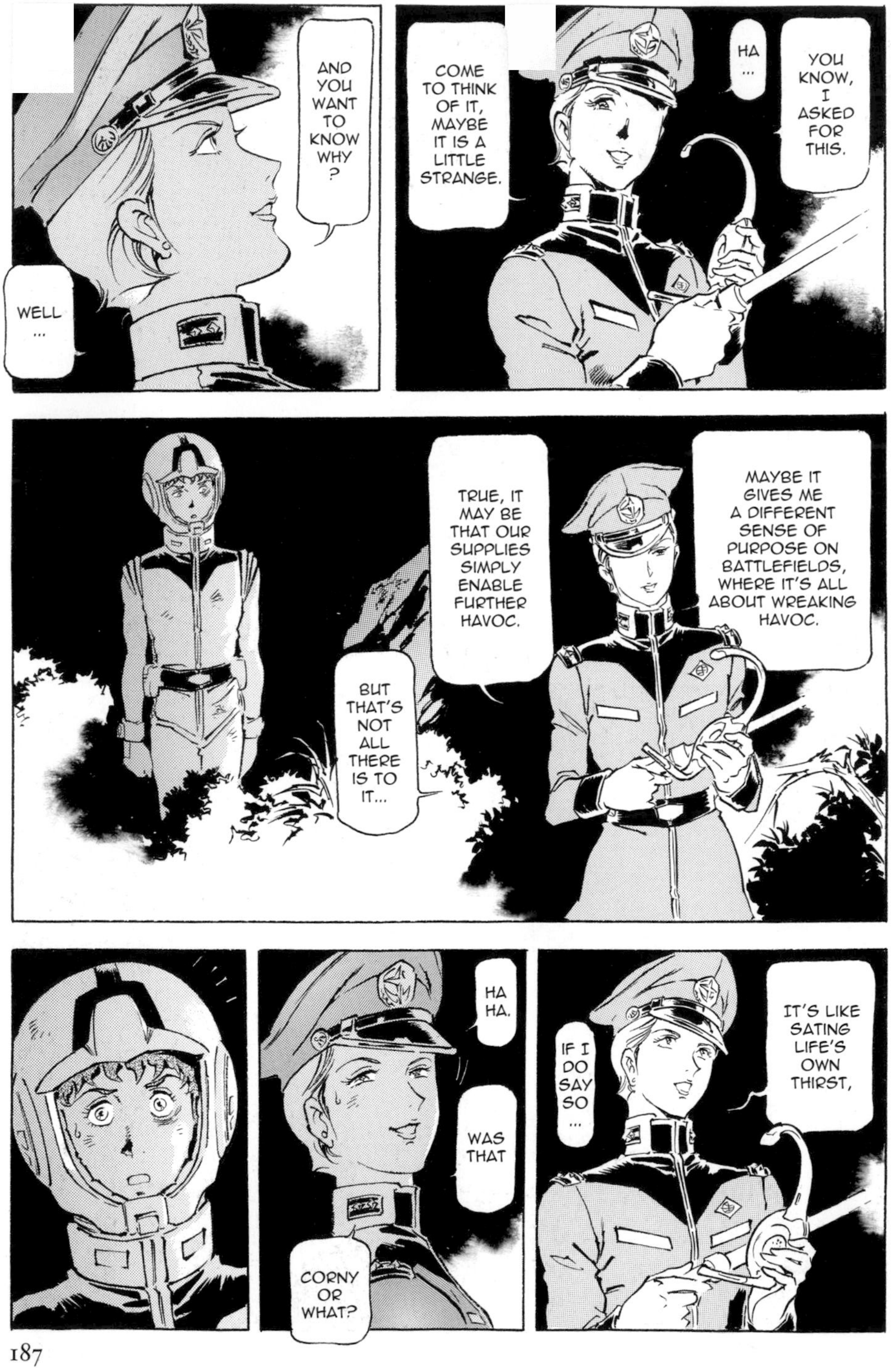
YOU KNOW, I ASKED FOR THIS.
HA ...
COME TO THINK OF IT, MAYBE IT IS A LITTLE STRANGE.
AND YOU WANT TO KNOW WHY?
WELL ...
MAYBE IT GIVES ME A DIFFERENT SENSE OF PURPOSE ON BATTLEFIELDS, WHERE IT'S ALL ABOUT WREAKING HAVOC.
TRUE, IT MAY BE THAT OUR SUPPLIES SIMPLY ENABLE FURTHER HAVOC.
BUT THAT'S NOT ALL THERE IS TO IT...
IT'S LIKE SATING LIFE'S OWN THIRST,
IF I DO SAY SO ...
HA HA.
WAS THAT
CORNY OR WHAT?

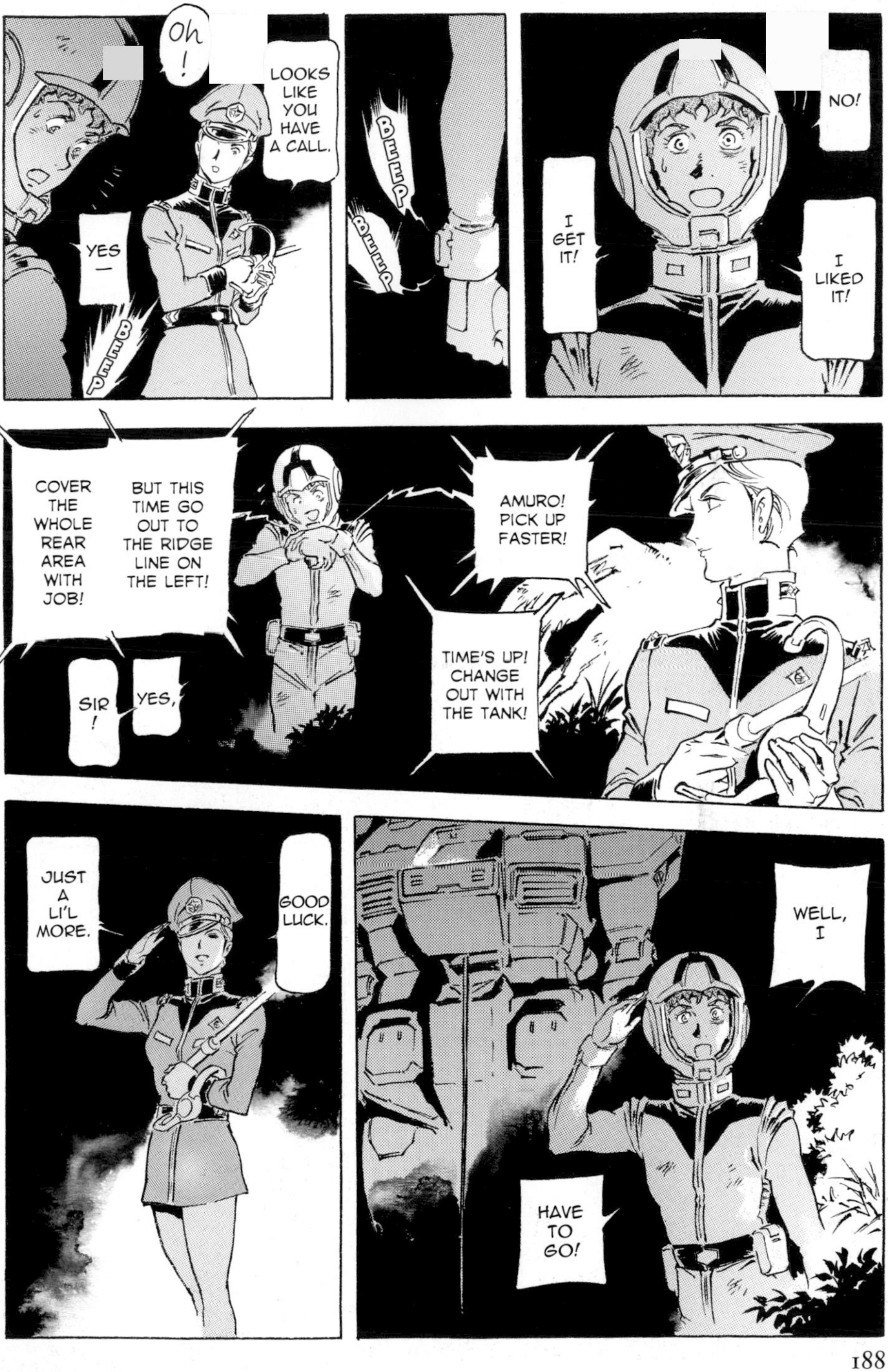
NO!
I LIKED IT!
I GET IT!
BEEP
BEEP
BEEP
Oh!
LOOKS LIKE YOU HAVE A CALL.
YES —
BEEP
AMURO! PICK UP FASTER!
TIME'S UP! CHANGE OUT WITH THE TANK!
BUT THIS TIME GO OUT TO THE RIDGE LINE ON THE LEFT!
COVER THE WHOLE REAR AREA WITH JOB!
YES,
SIR!
WELL, I
HAVE TO GO!
GOOD LUCK.
JUST A LI'L MORE.

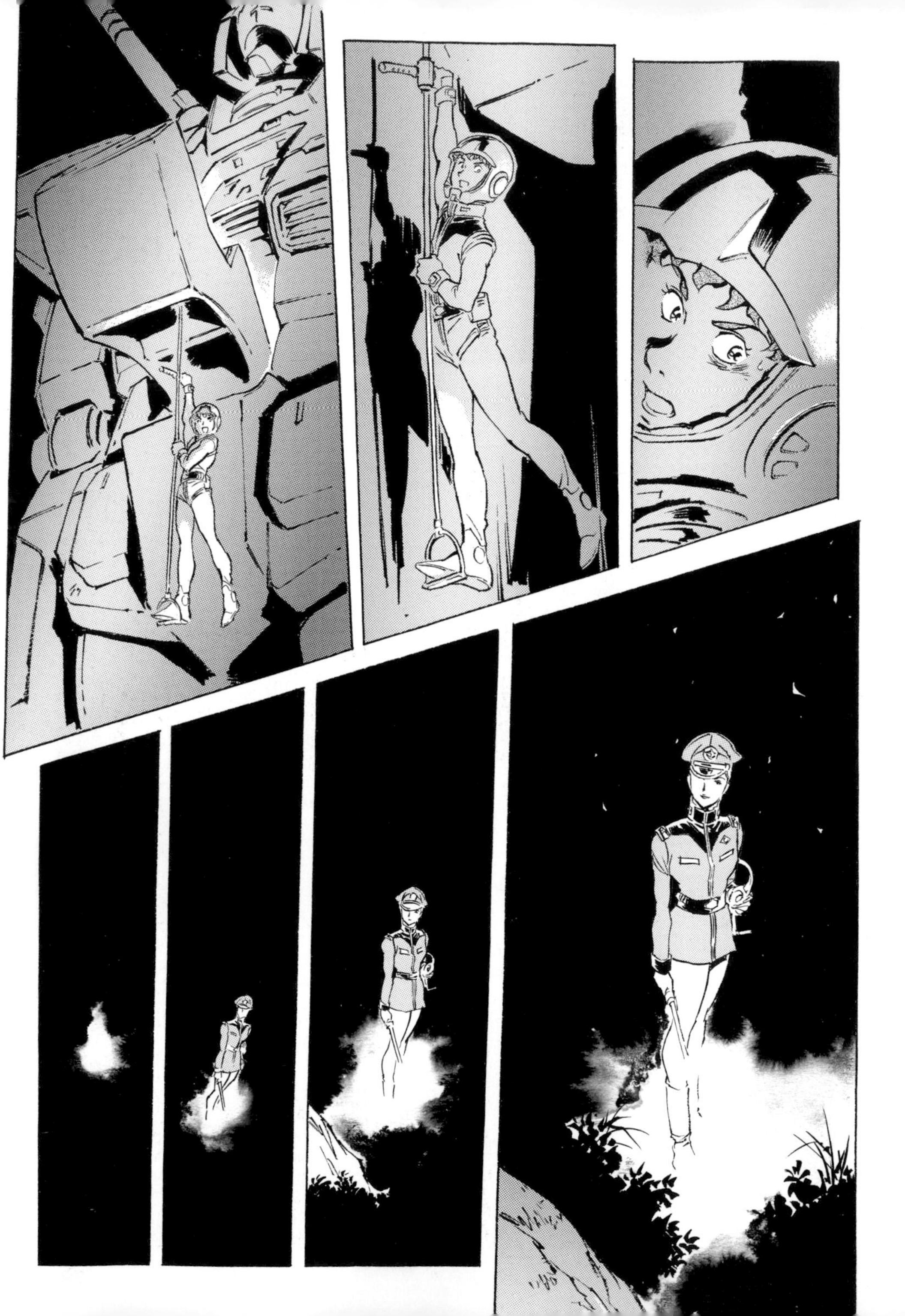

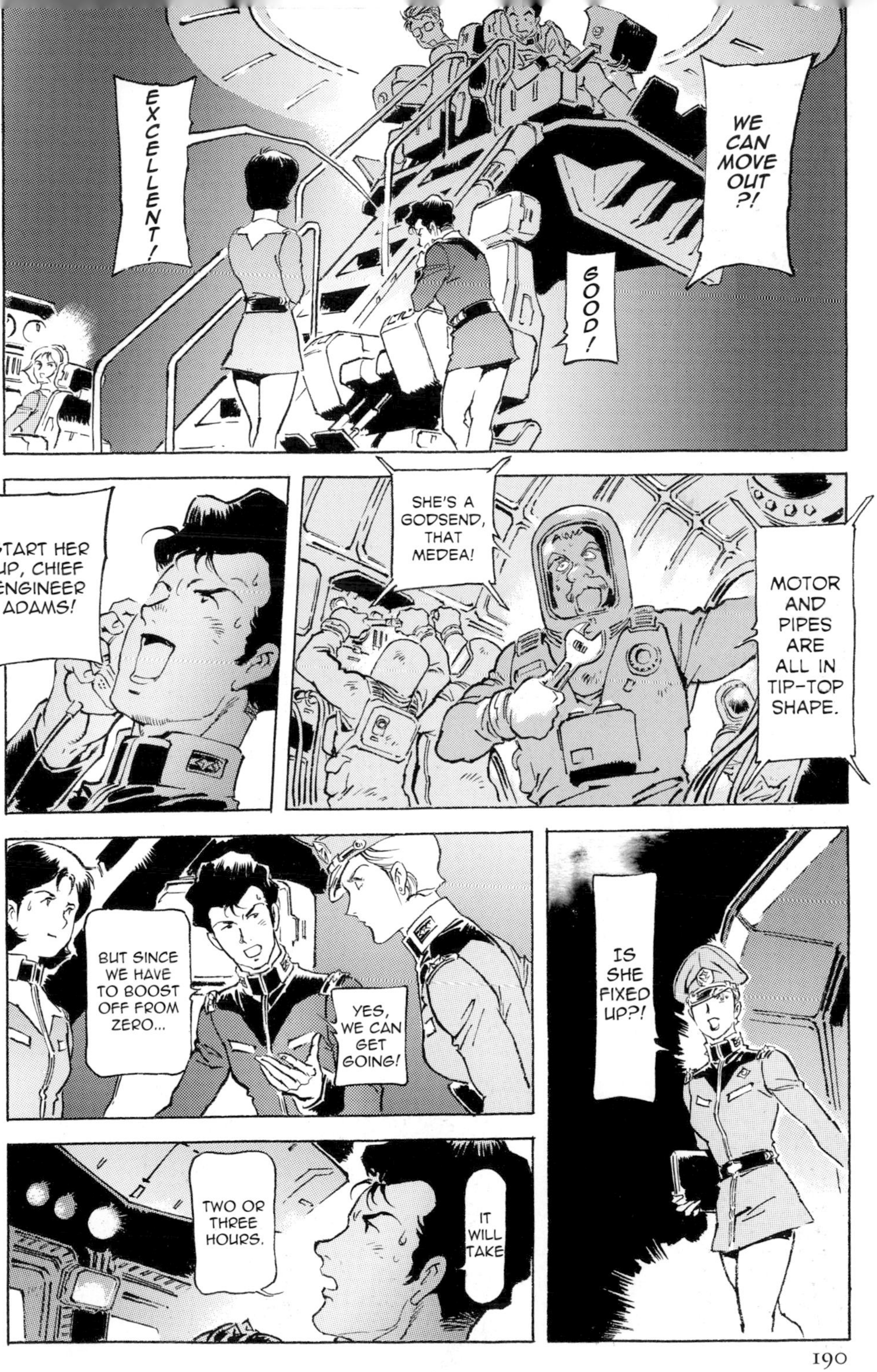
WE CAN MOVE OUT?!
GOOD!
EXCELLENT!
MOTOR AND PIPES ARE ALL IN TIP-TOP SHAPE.
SHE'S A GODSEND, THAT MEDEA!
START HER UP, CHIEF ENGINEER ADAMS!
IS SHE FIXED UP?!
YES, WE CAN GET GOING!
BUT SINCE WE HAVE TO BOOST OFF FROM ZERO...
IT WILL TAKE
TWO OR THREE HOURS.

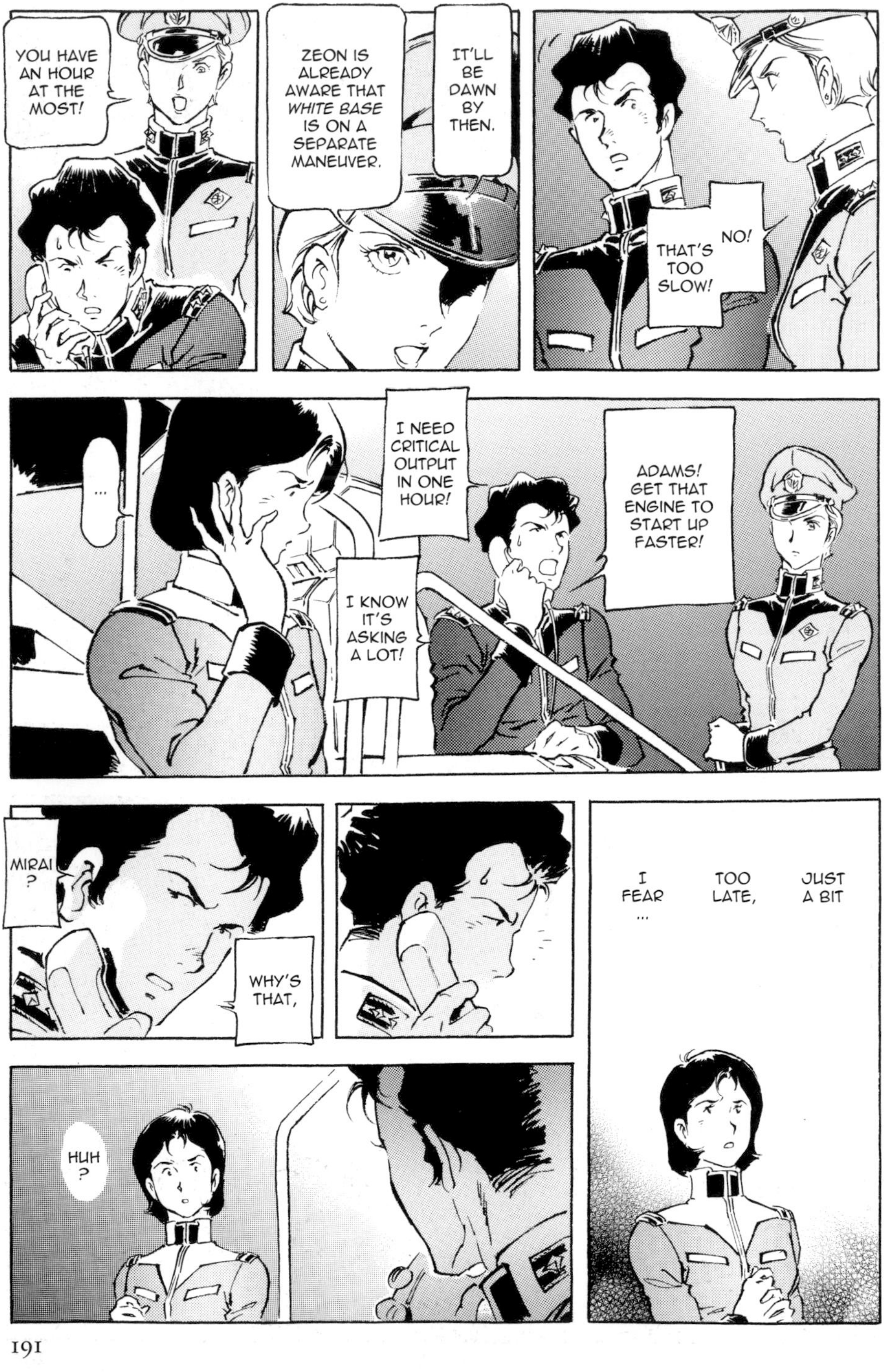
NO! THAT'S TOO SLOW!
IT'LL BE DAWN BY THEN.
ZEON IS ALREADY AWARE THAT *WHITE BASE* IS ON A SEPARATE MANEUVER.
YOU HAVE AN HOUR AT THE MOST!
ADAMS! GET THAT ENGINE TO START UP FASTER!
I NEED CRITICAL OUTPUT IN ONE HOUR!
I KNOW IT'S ASKING A LOT!
...
JUST A BIT
TOO LATE,
I FEAR ...
WHY'S THAT,
MIRAI?
HUH?

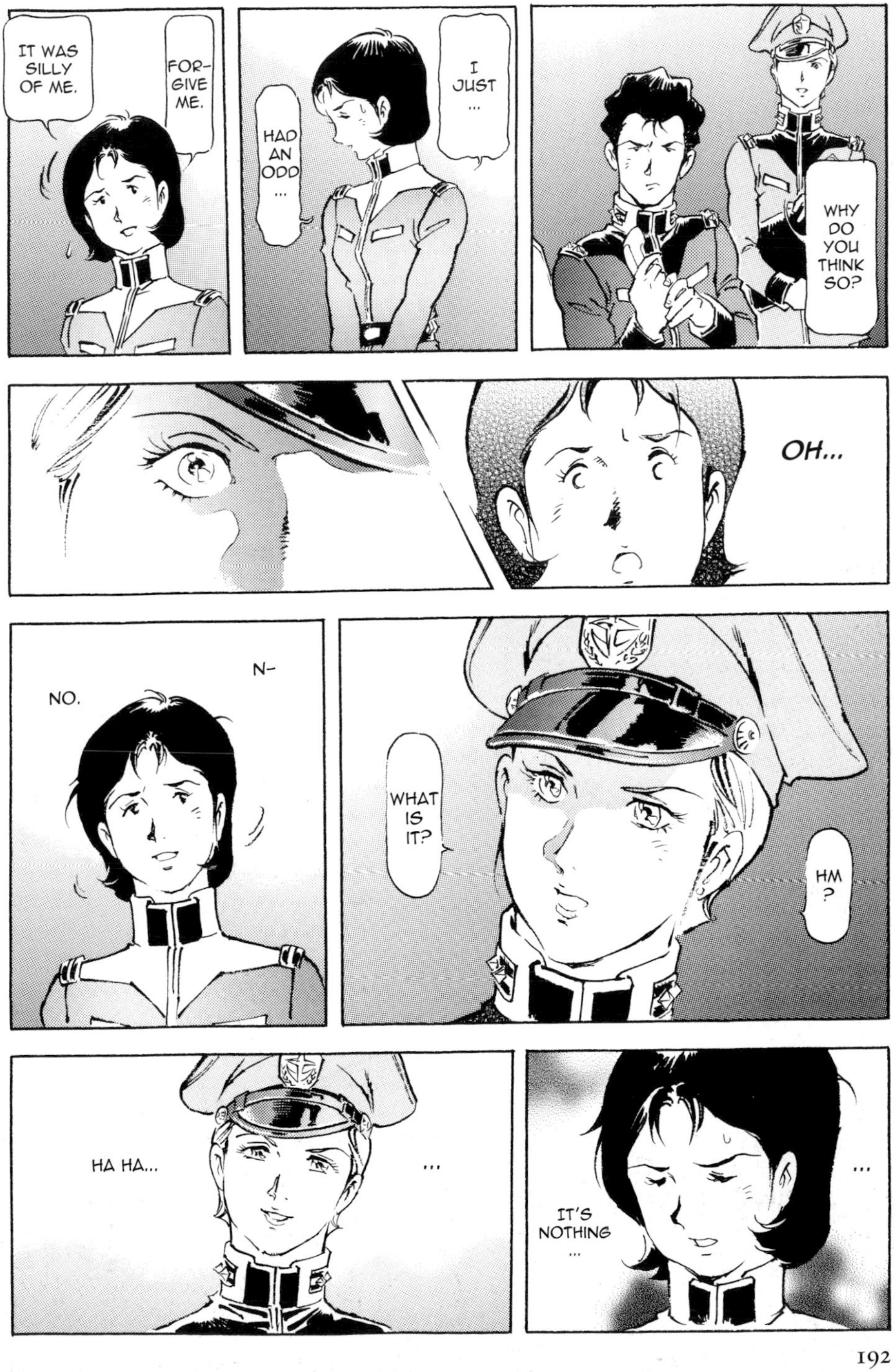
WHY DO YOU THINK SO?
I JUST ...
HAD AN ODD ...
FORGIVE ME.
IT WAS SILLY OF ME.
OH...
HM?
WHAT IS IT?
N-
NO.
...
IT'S NOTHING ...
...
HA HA...

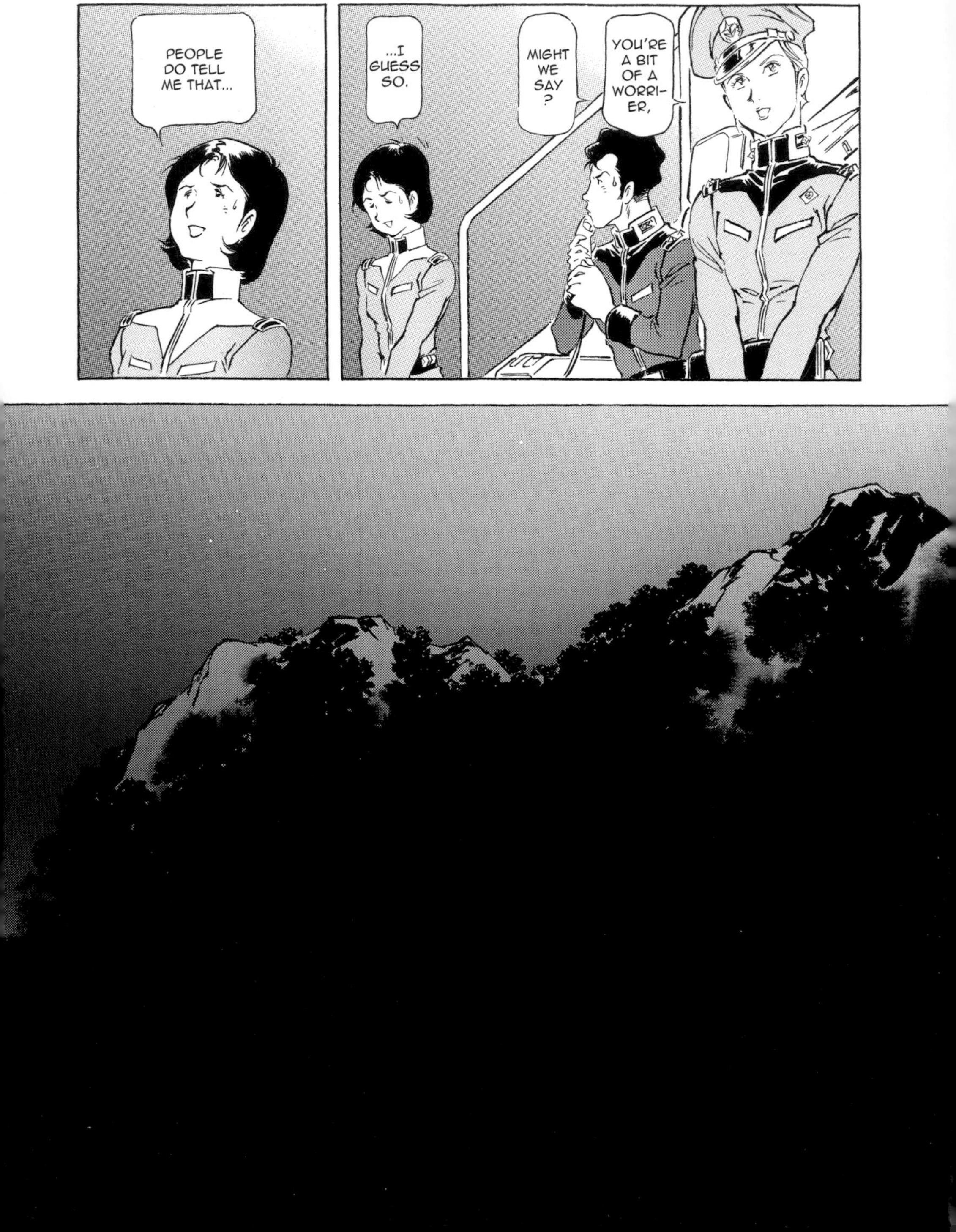
YOU'RE A BIT OF A WORRI-ER,
MIGHT WE SAY?
...I GUESS SO.
PEOPLE DO TELL ME THAT...

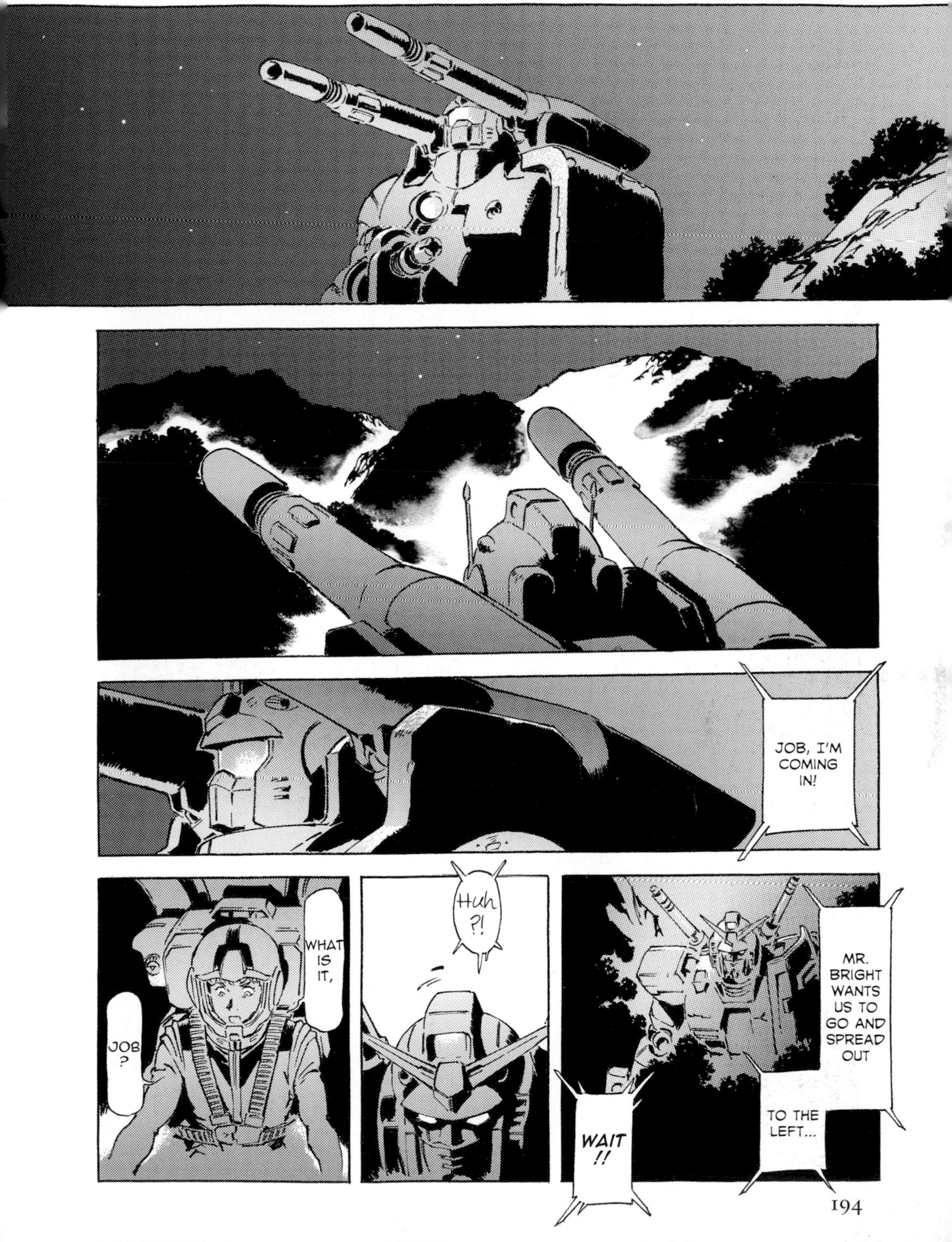
JOB, I'M COMING IN!
MR. BRIGHT WANTS US TO GO AND SPREAD OUT
TO THE LEFT...
WAIT!!
Huh ?!
WHAT IS IT,
JOB ?

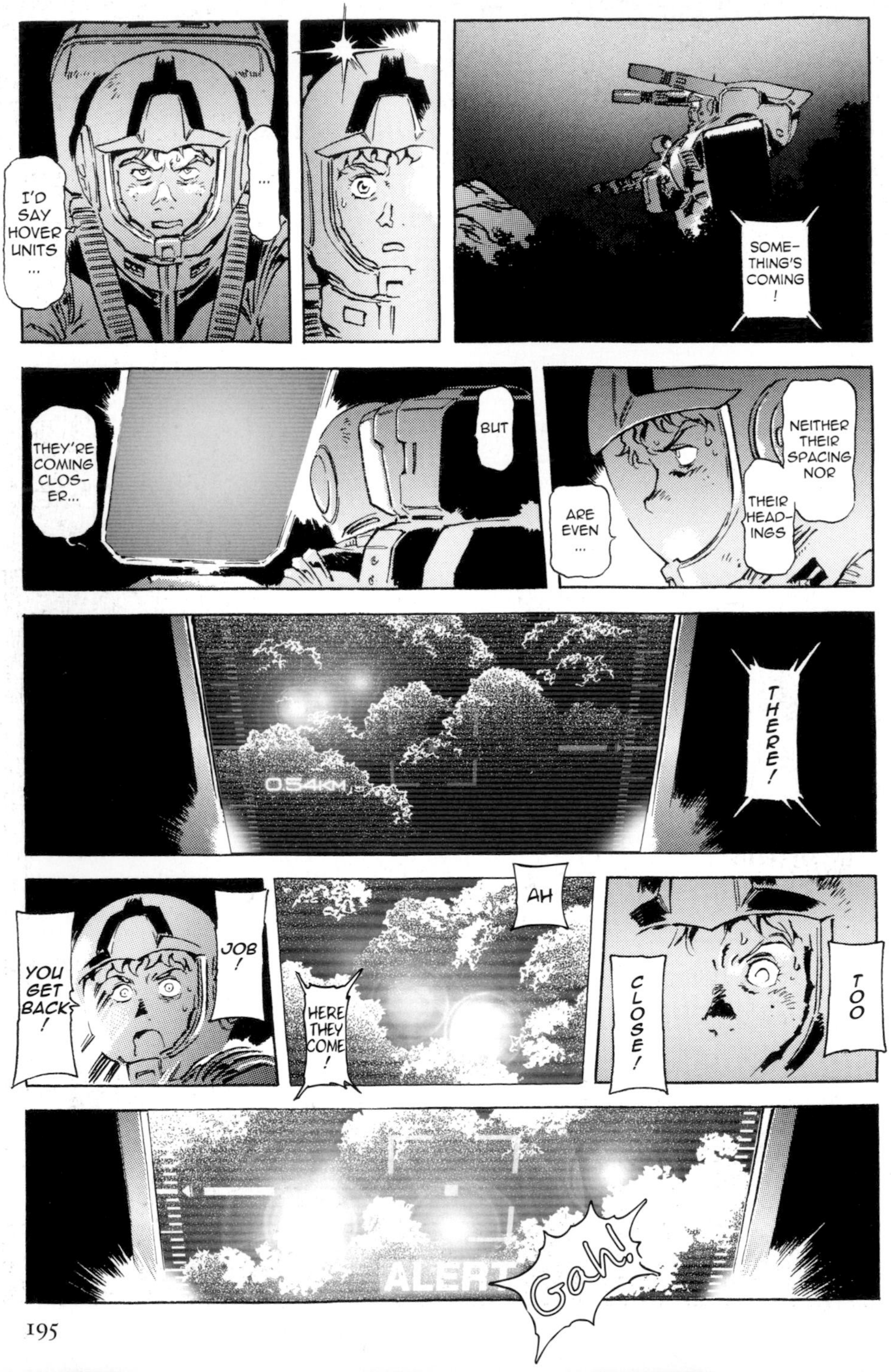
SOME-THING'S COMING!
...
I'D SAY HOVER UNITS...
NEITHER THEIR SPACING NOR
THEIR HEADINGS
ARE EVEN...
BUT
THEY'RE COMING CLOS-ER...
THERE!
0.54KM
TOO
CLOSE!
AH
HERE THEY COME!
JOB!
YOU GET BACK!
ALERT
Gah!

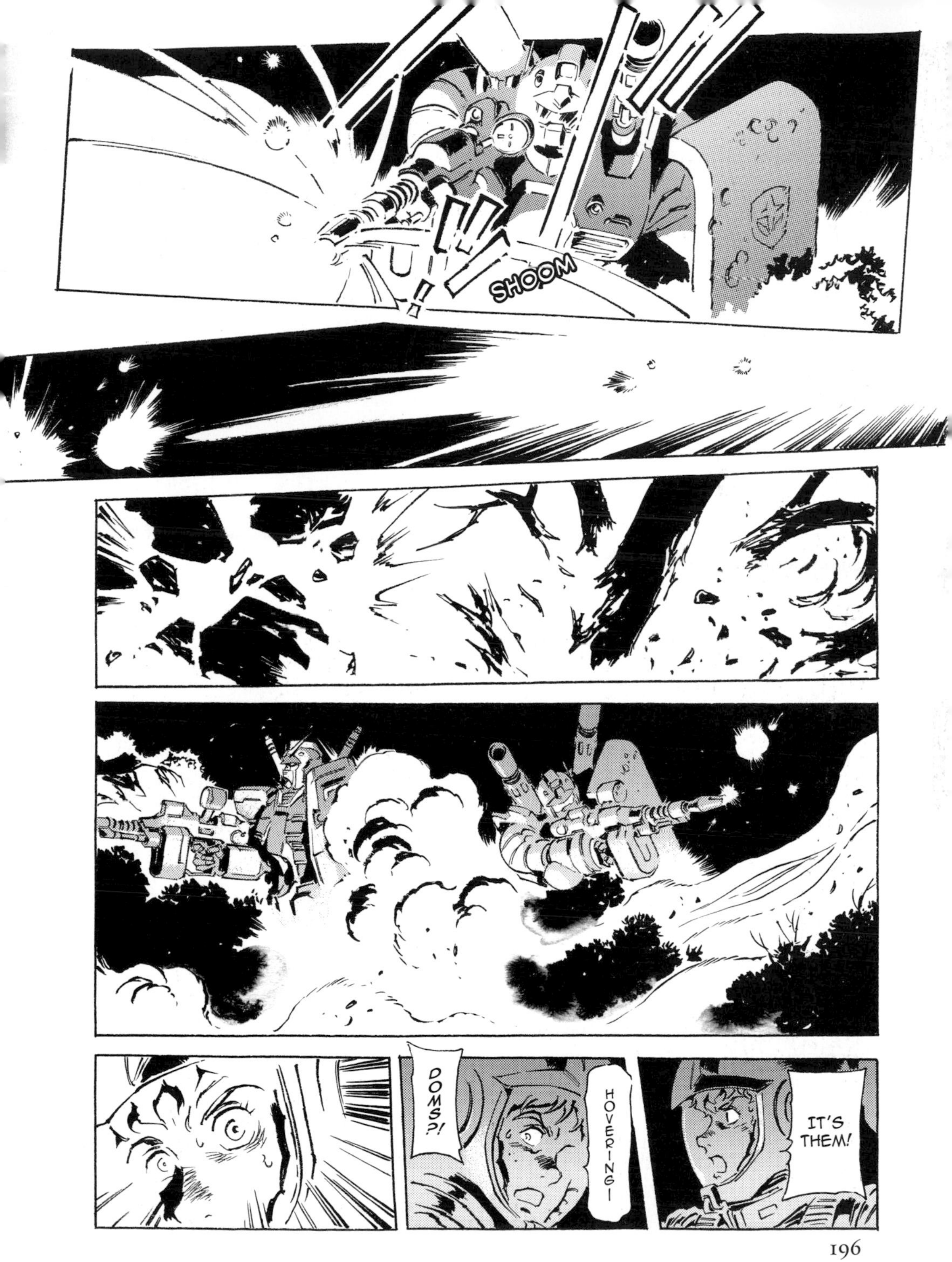
SHOOM
IT'S THEM!
HOVERING!
DOMS?!

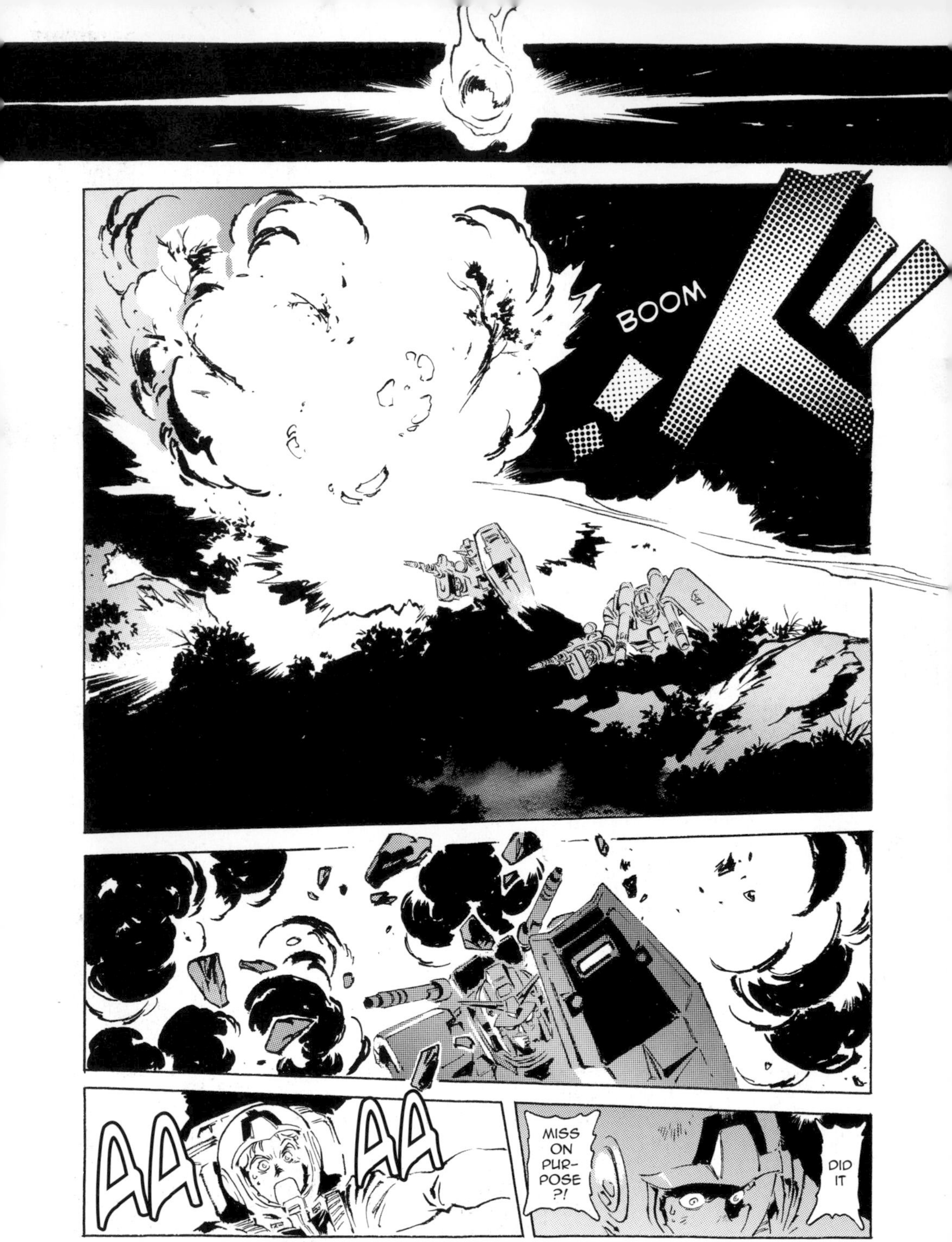

BOOM
DID IT
MISS ON PUR-POSE ?!
AA
AA

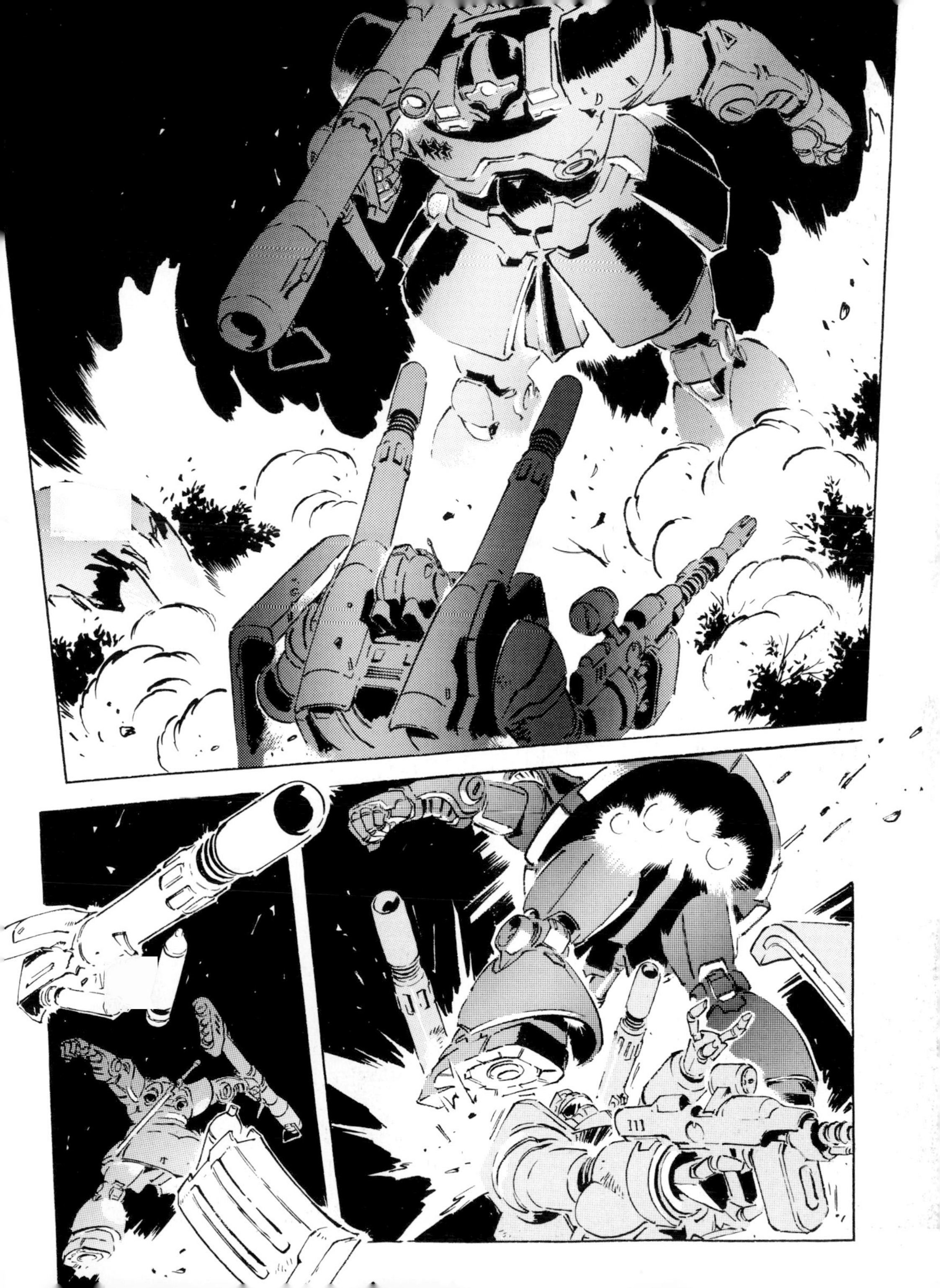

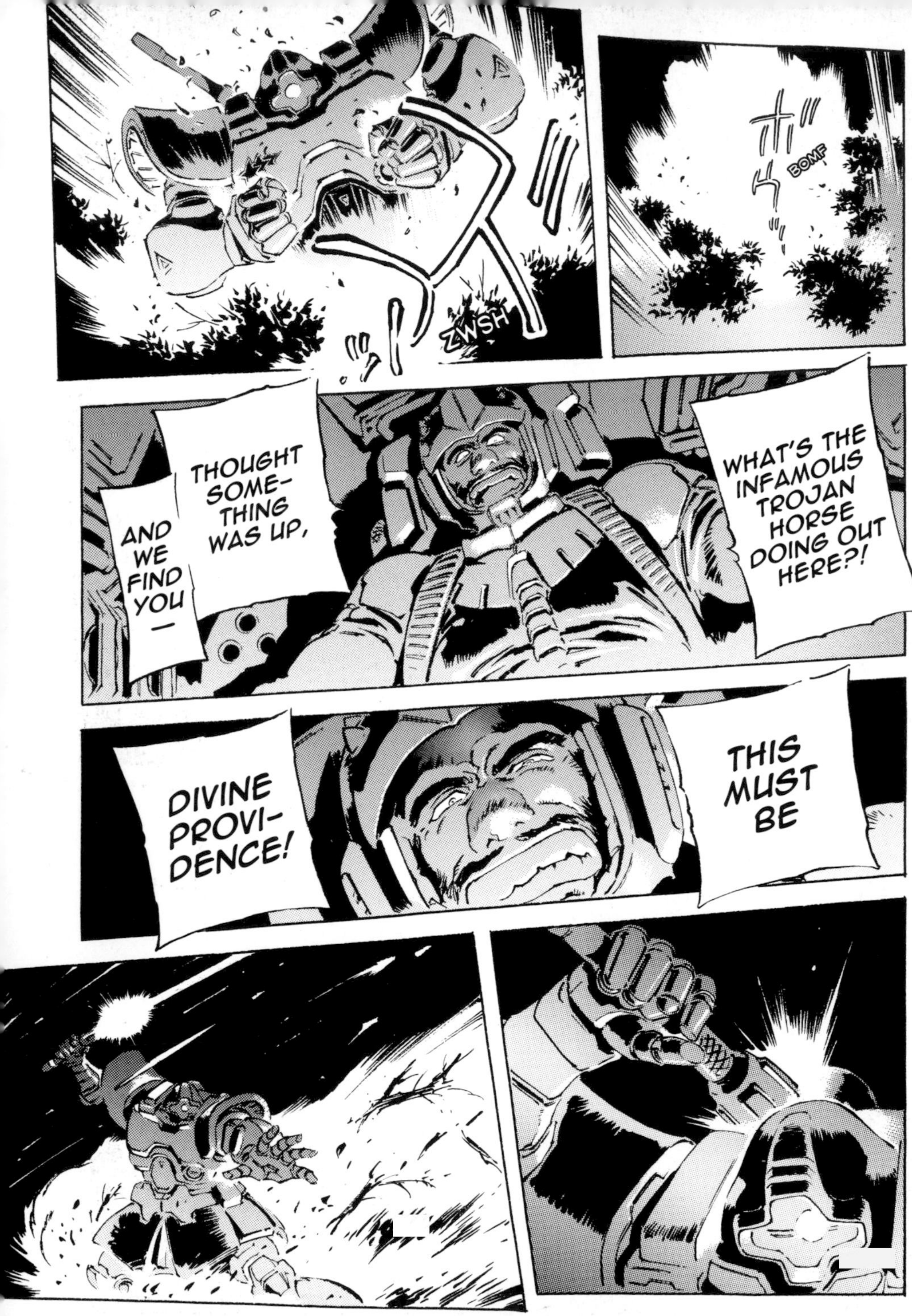
BOMF
ZWSH
WHAT'S THE INFAMOUS TROJAN HORSE DOING OUT HERE?!
THOUGHT SOME-THING WAS UP,
AND WE FIND YOU—
THIS MUST BE
DIVINE PROVI-DENCE!

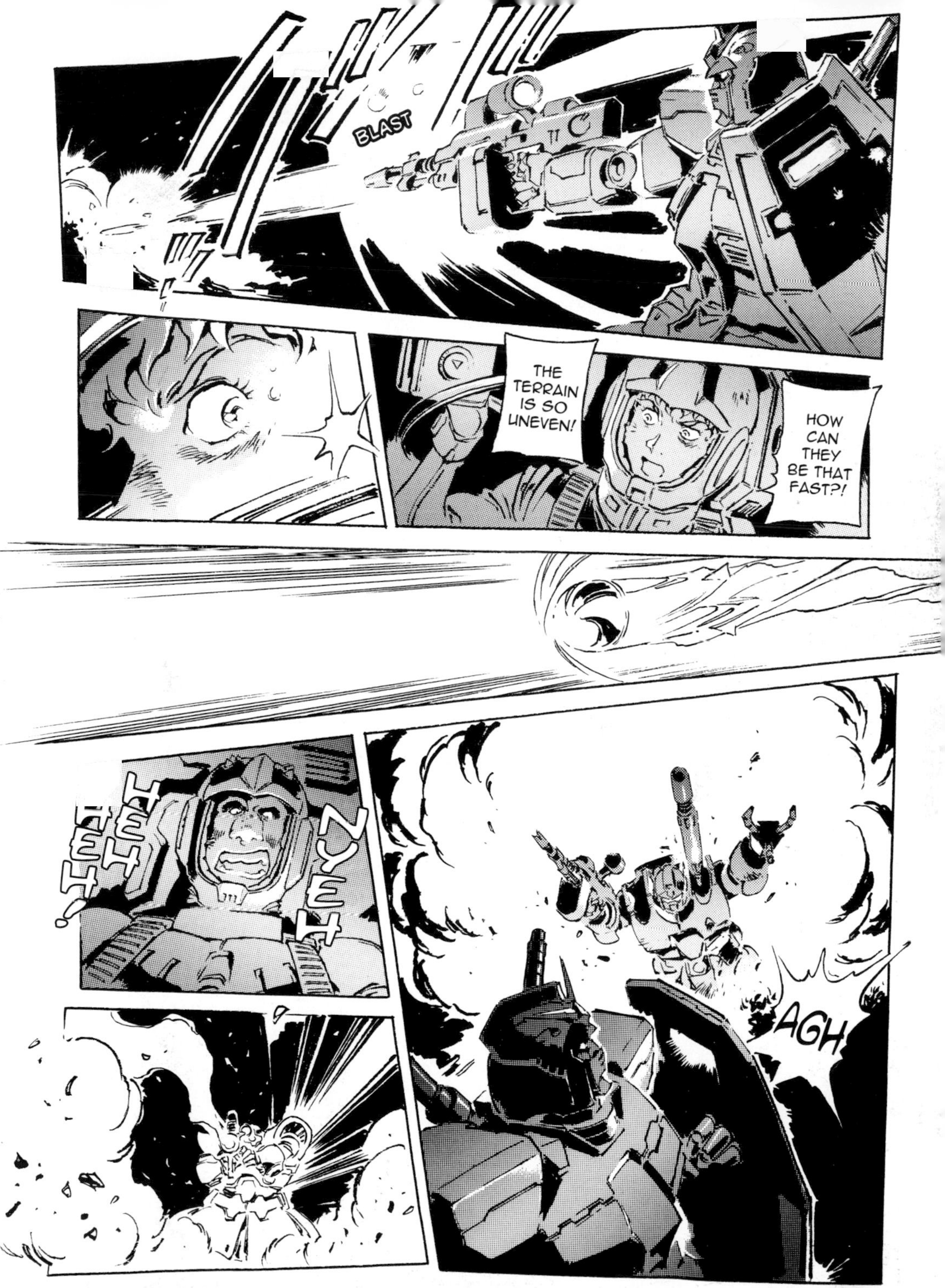

BLAST
THE TERRAIN IS SO UNEVEN!
HOW CAN THEY BE THAT FAST?!
AGH
NYEH
HEH HEH!

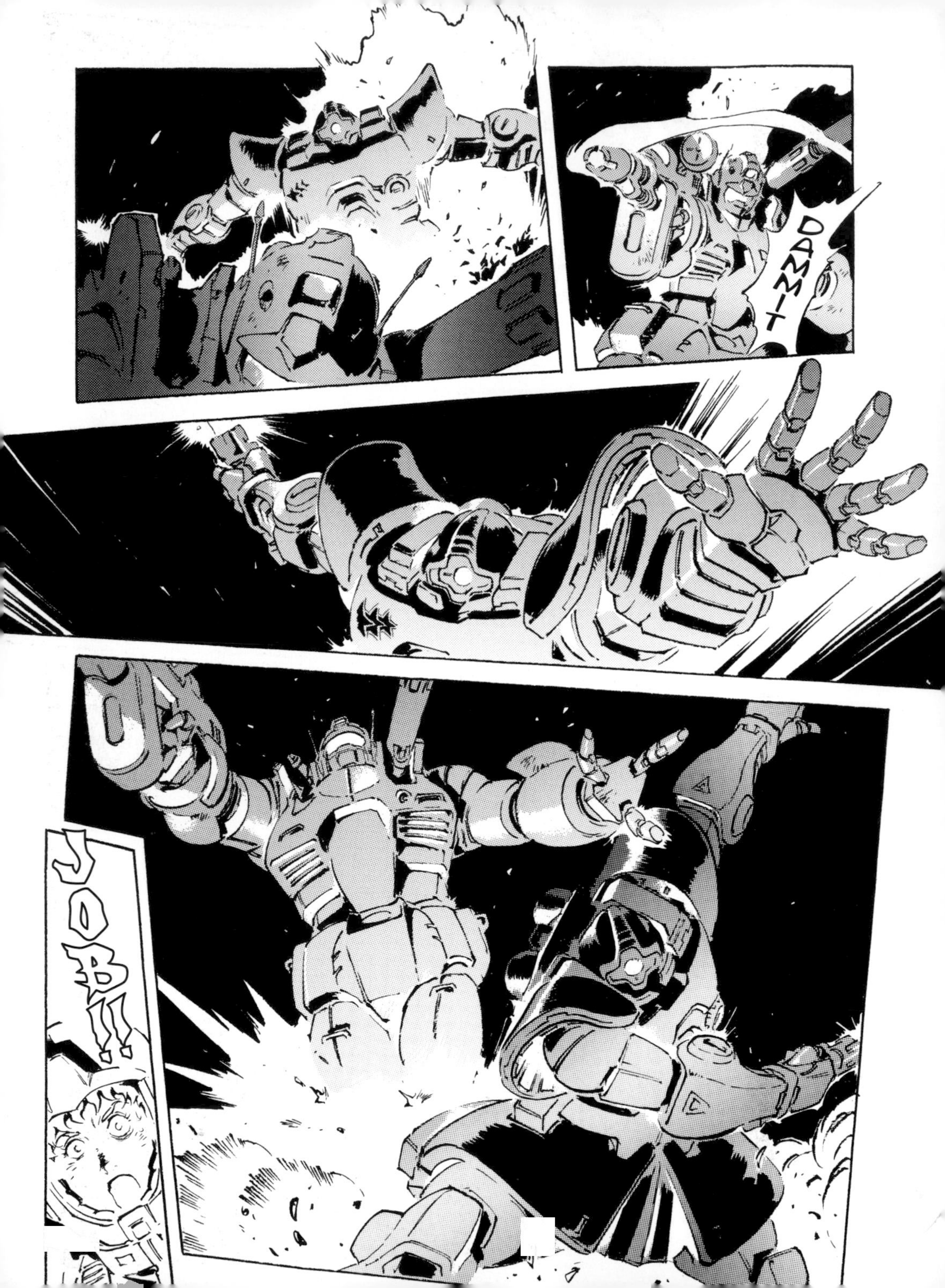
DAMMIT
JOB!!

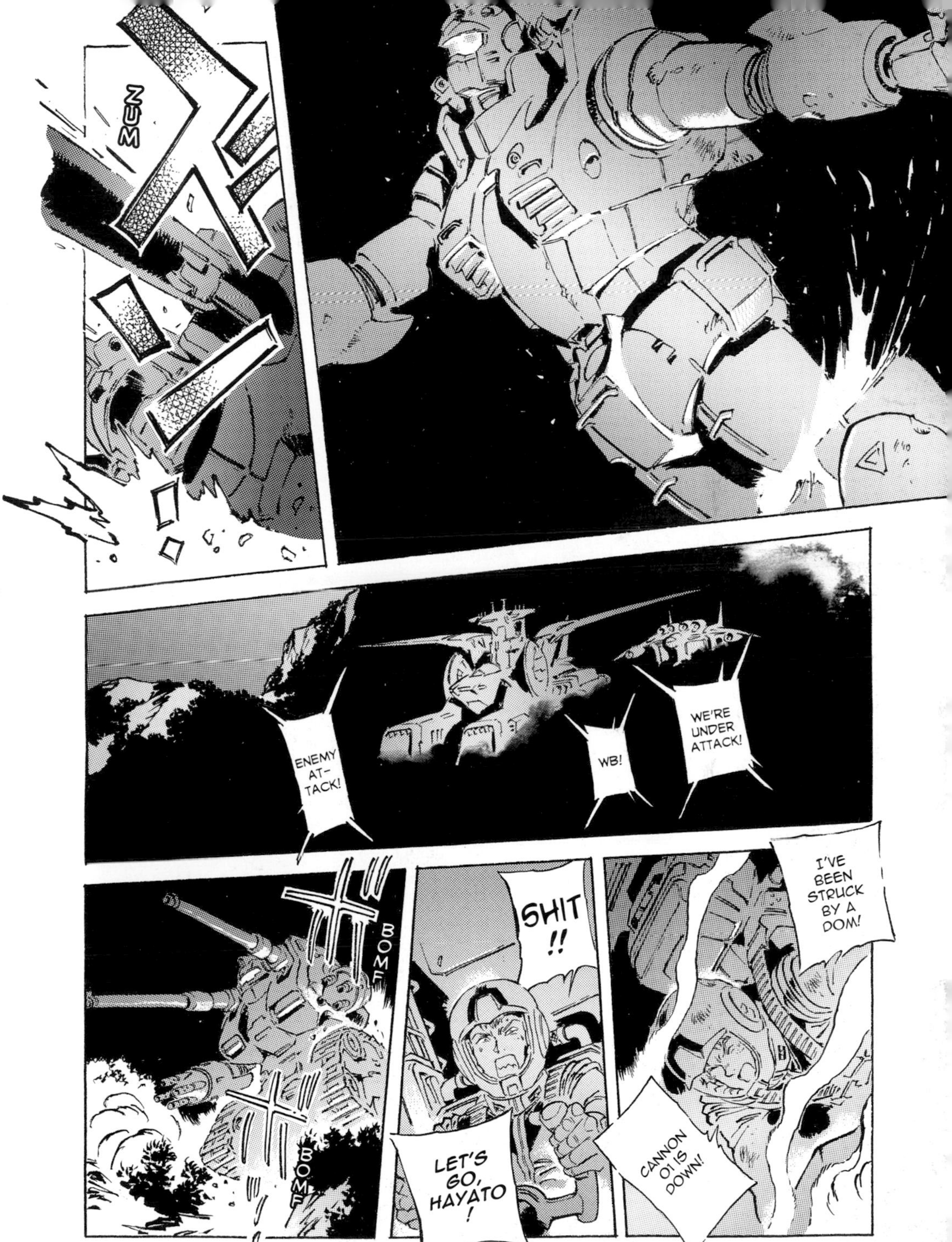
ZUN
WE'RE UNDER ATTACK!
WB!
ENEMY AT-TACK!
I'VE BEEN STRUCK BY A DOM!
CANNON 01 IS DOWN!
SHIT !!
LET'S GO, HAYATO !
BOMF
BOMF

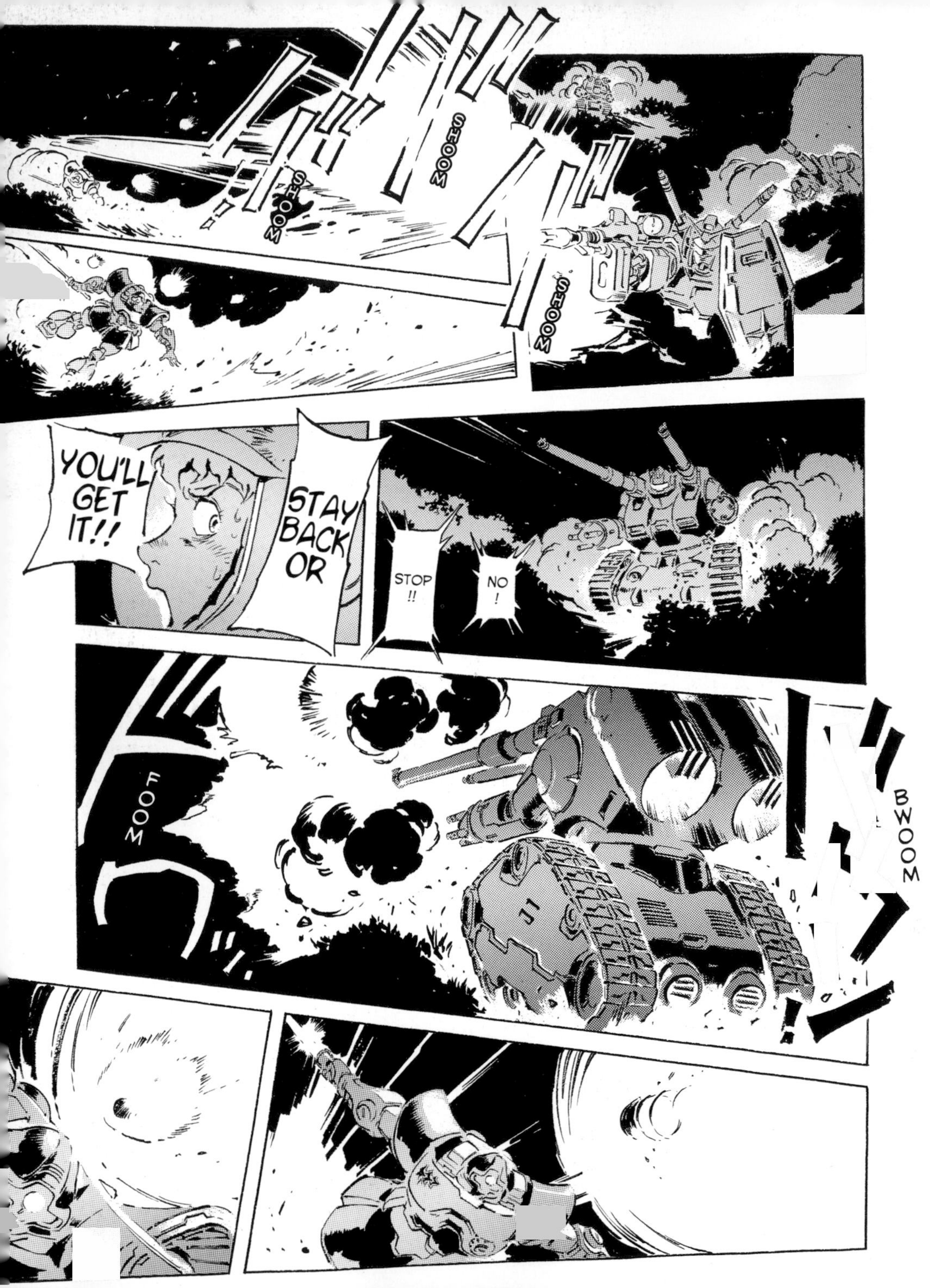
SHOOM
SHOOM
SHOOM
NO!
STOP!!
STAY BACK OR
YOU'LL GET IT!!
BWOOM
FOOM

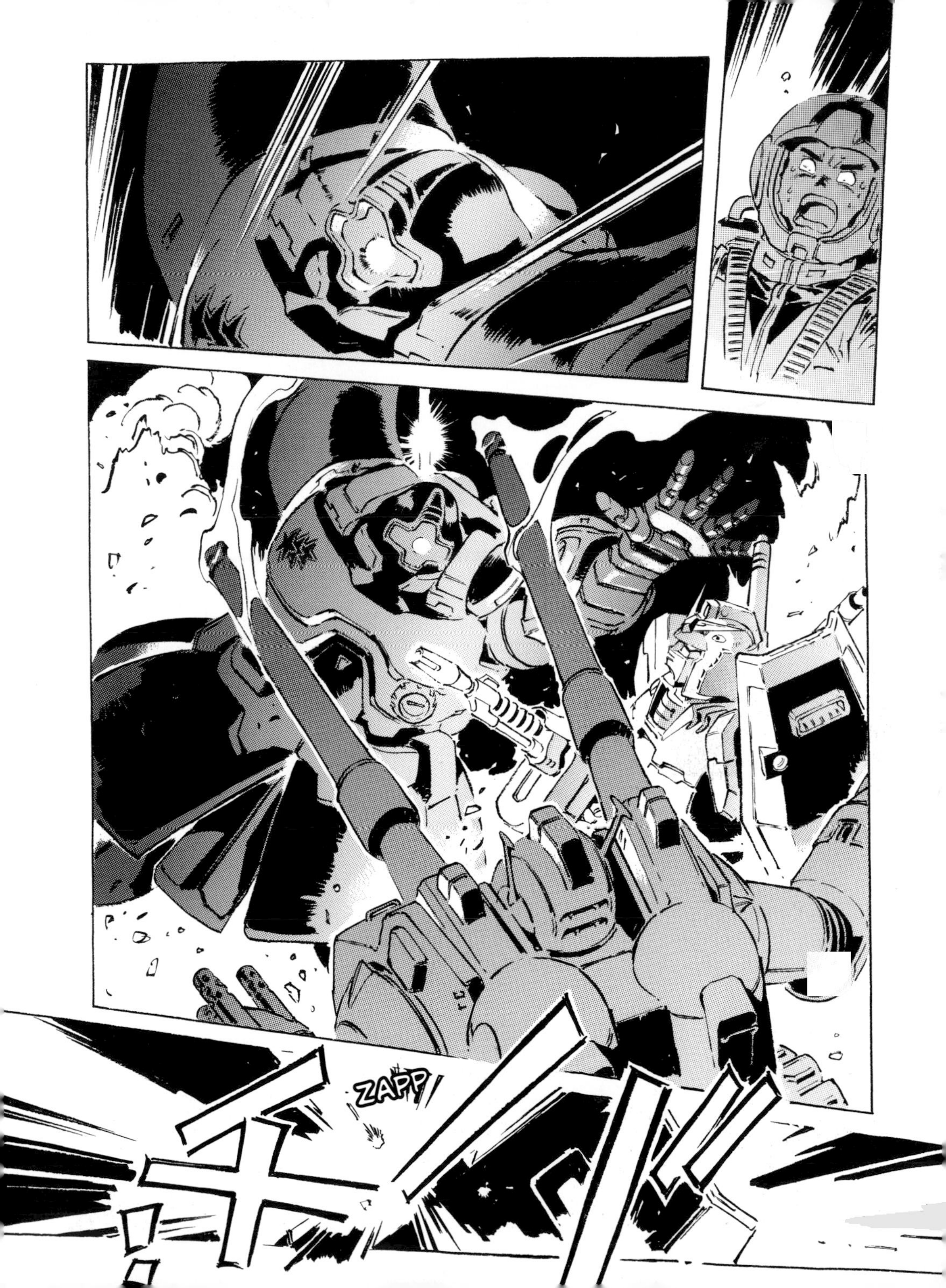
ZAPP

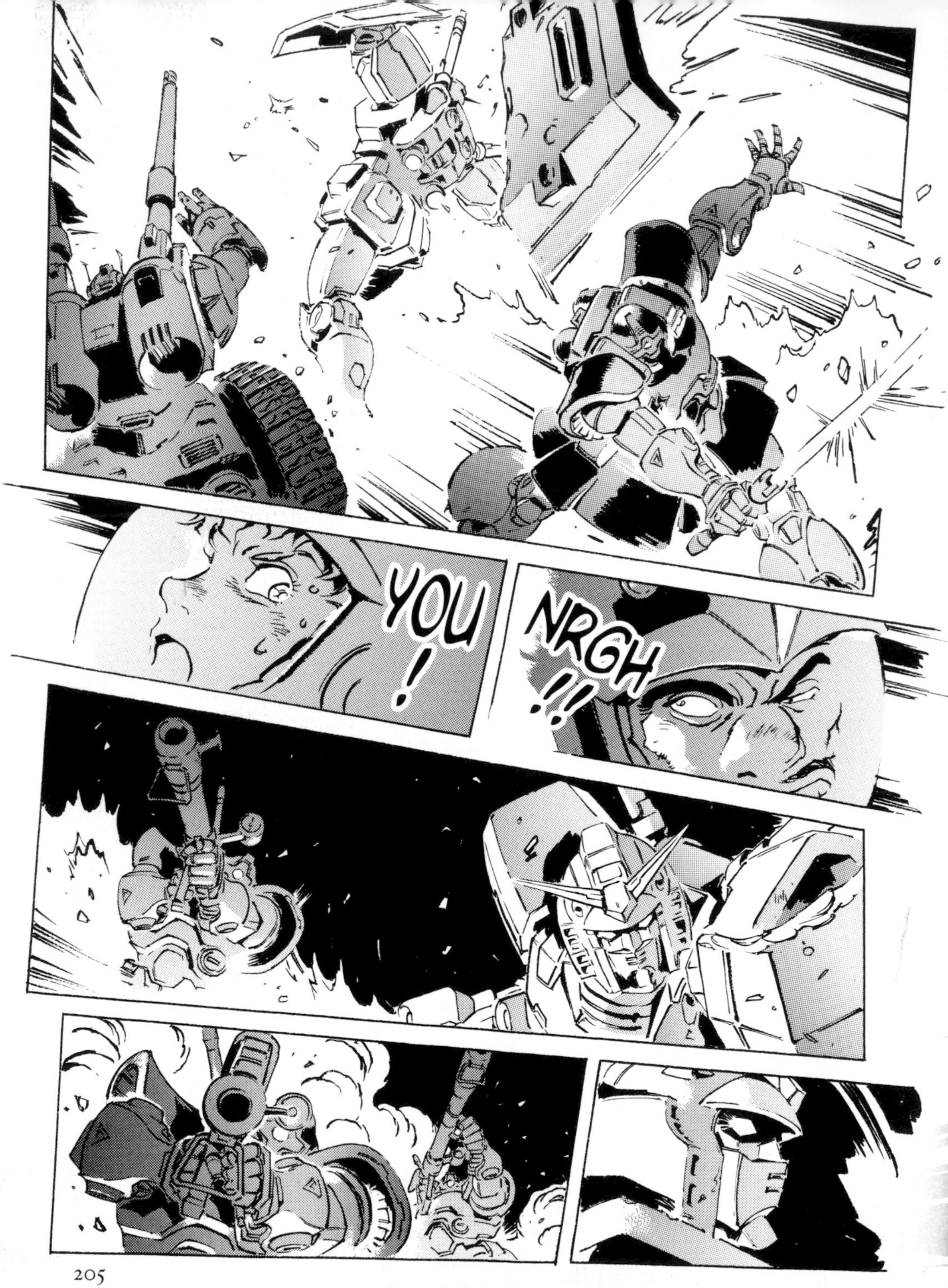
NRGH!!
YOU!

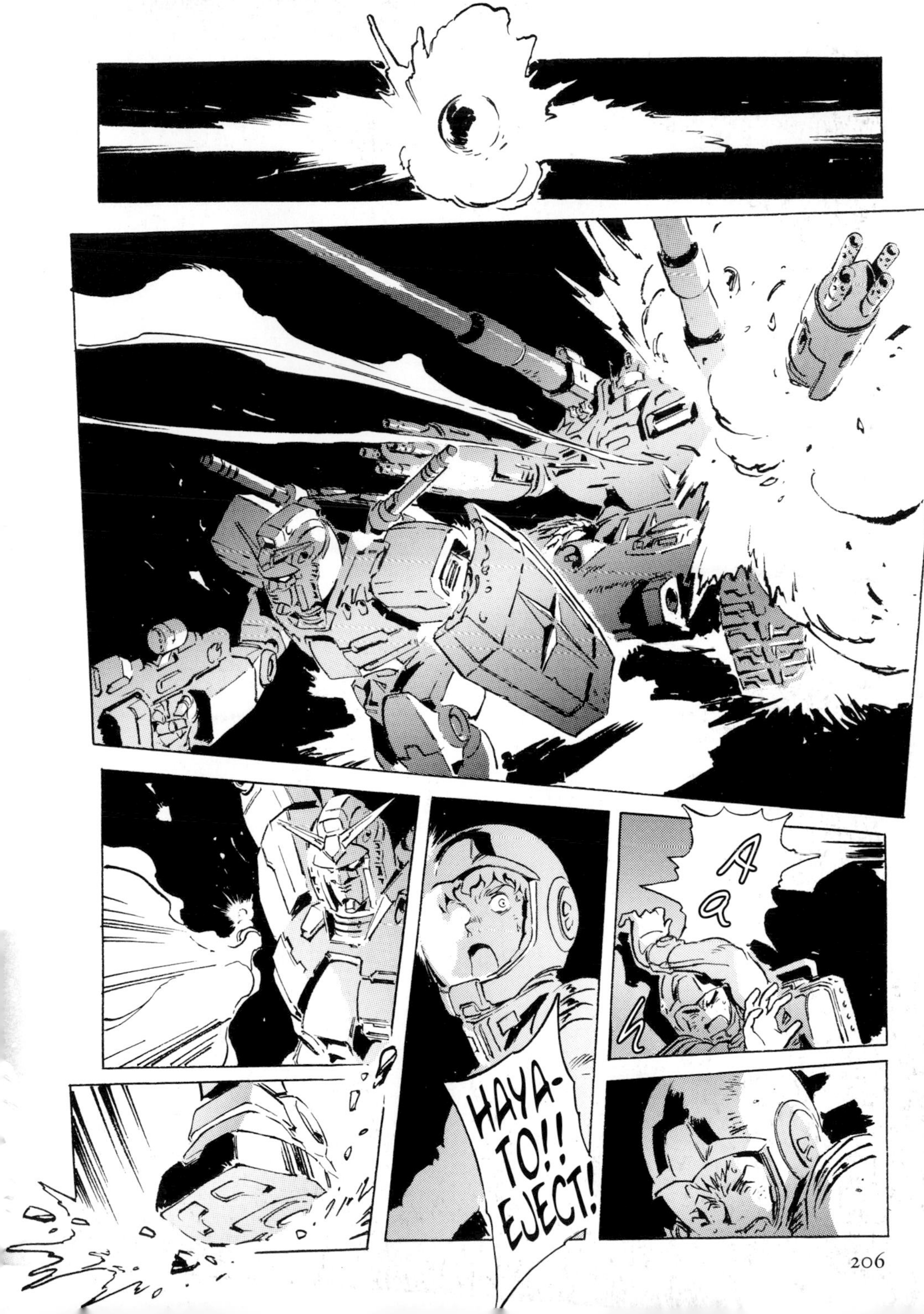
Aah
HAYA-TO!! EJECT!

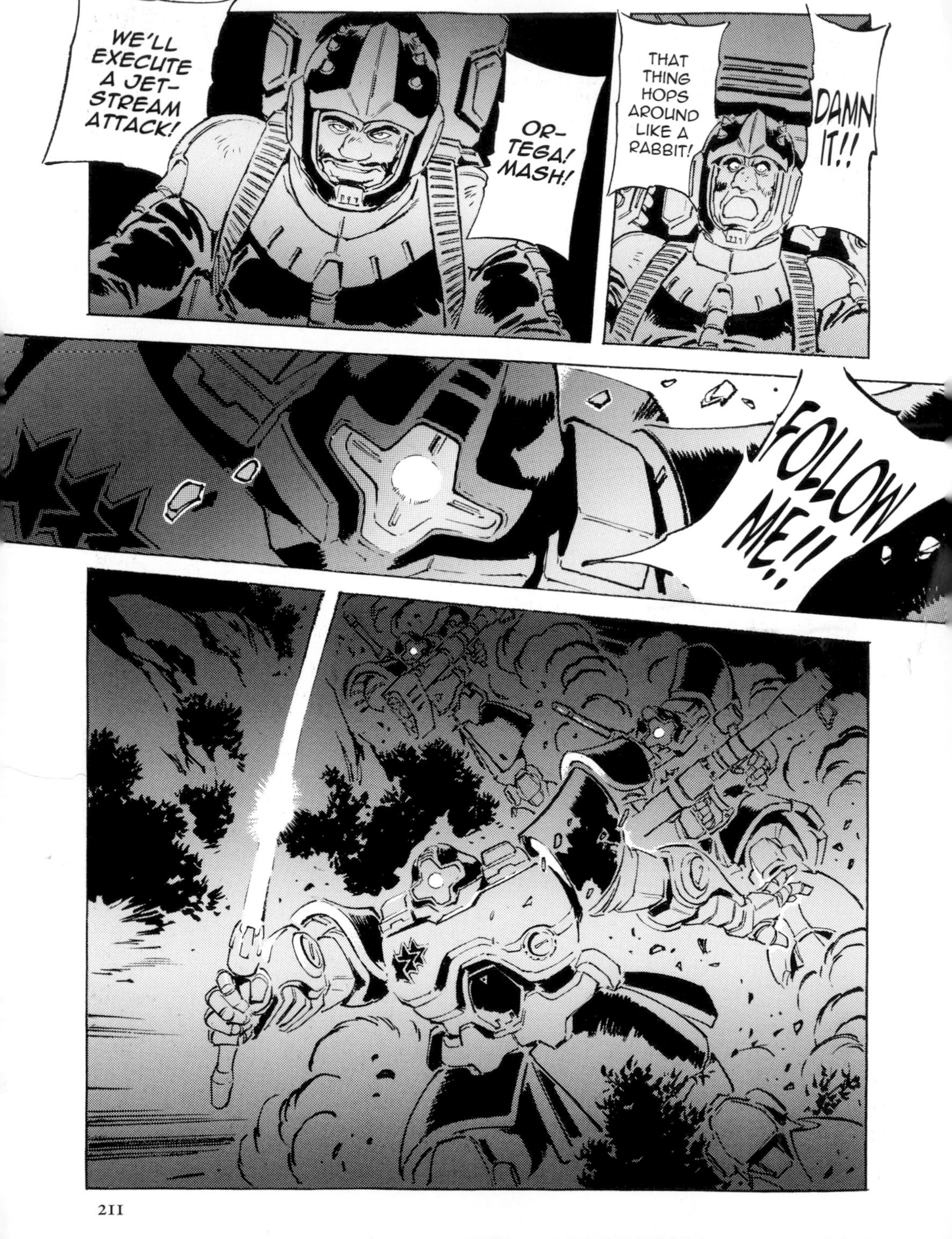
DAMN IT!!
THAT THING HOPS AROUND LIKE A RABBIT!
OR-TEGA! MASH!
WE'LL EXECUTE A JET-STREAM ATTACK!
FOLLOW ME!!

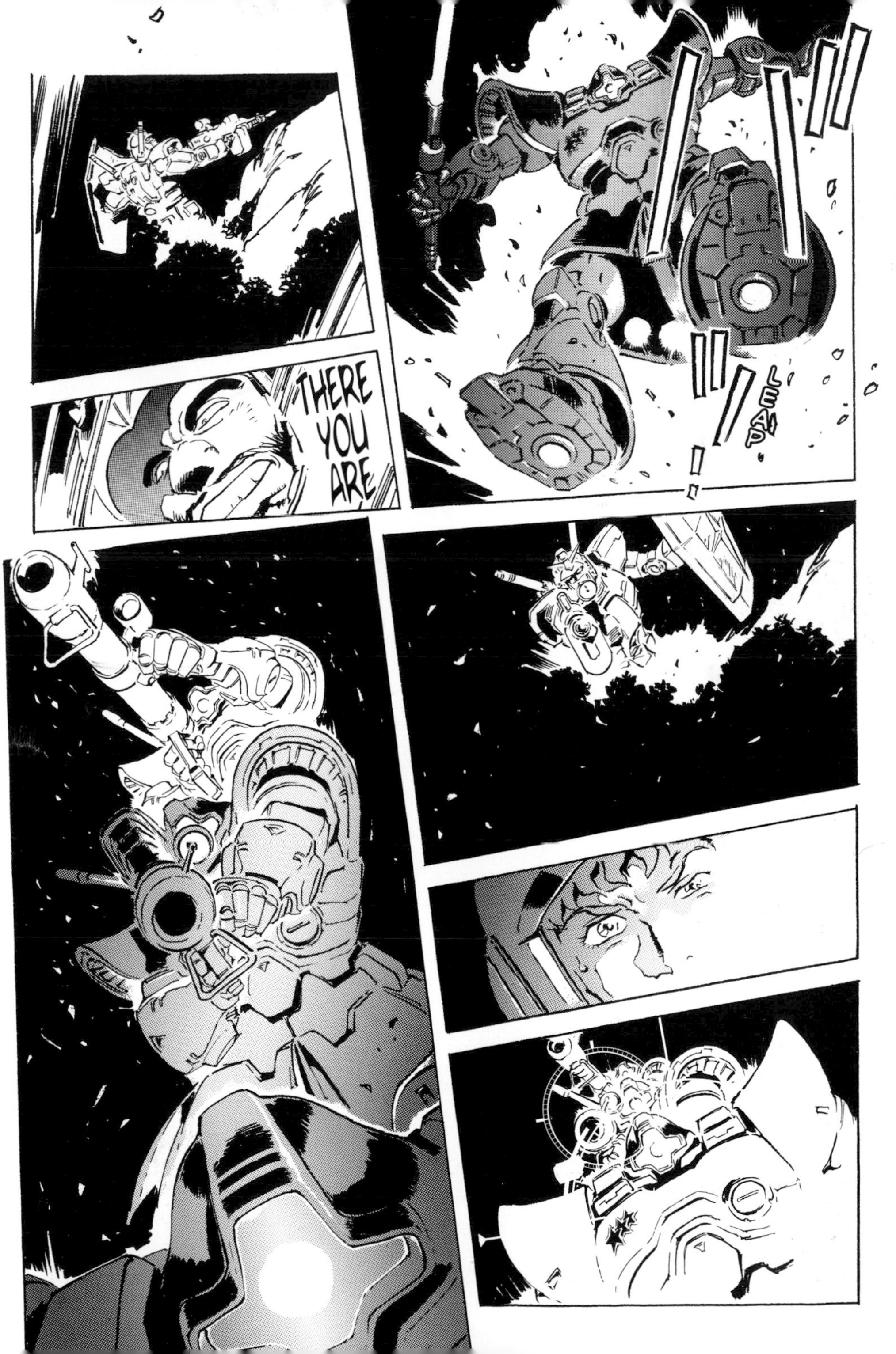
LEAP
THERE YOU ARE

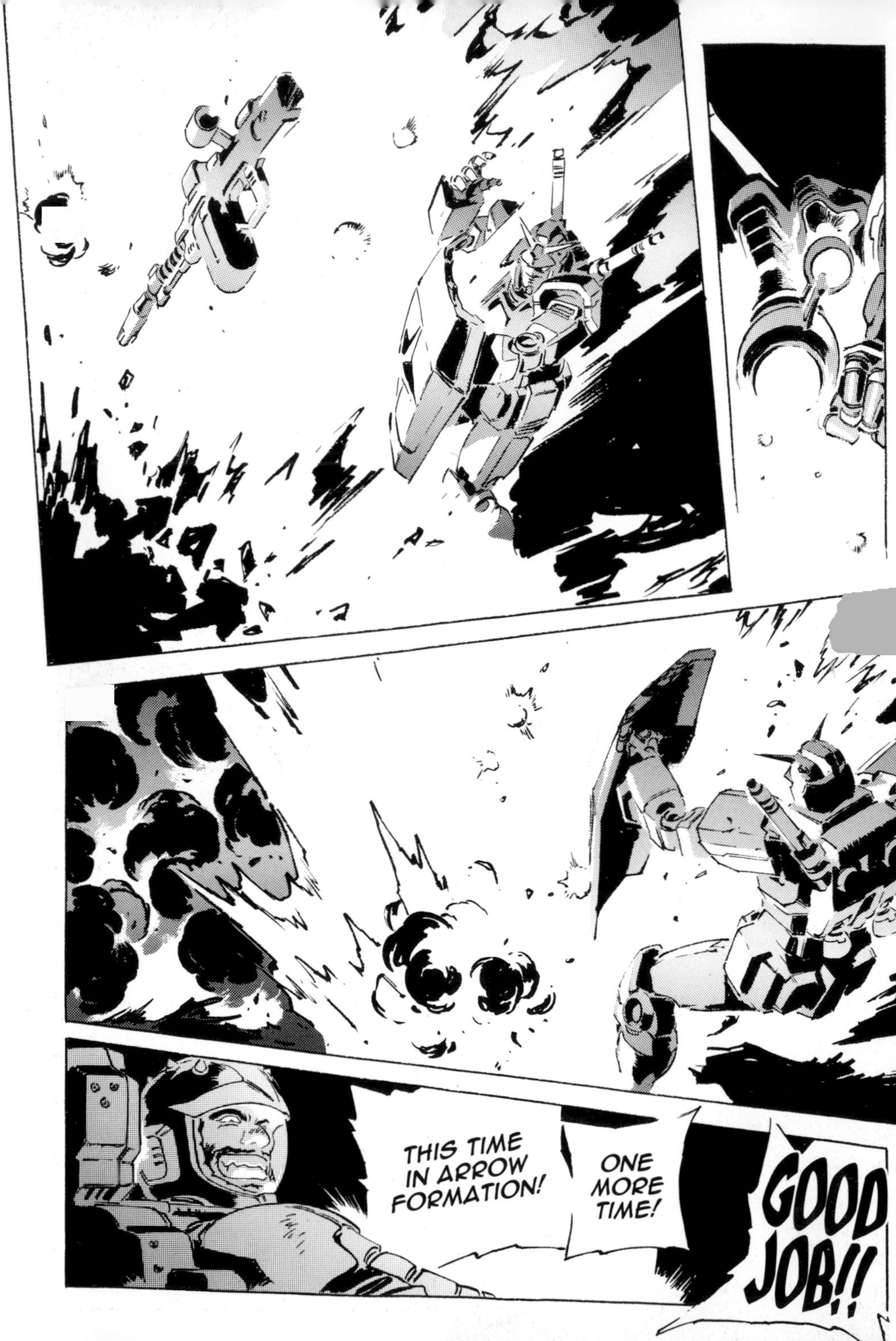
GOOD JOB!!
ONE MORE TIME!
THIS TIME IN ARROW FORMATION!

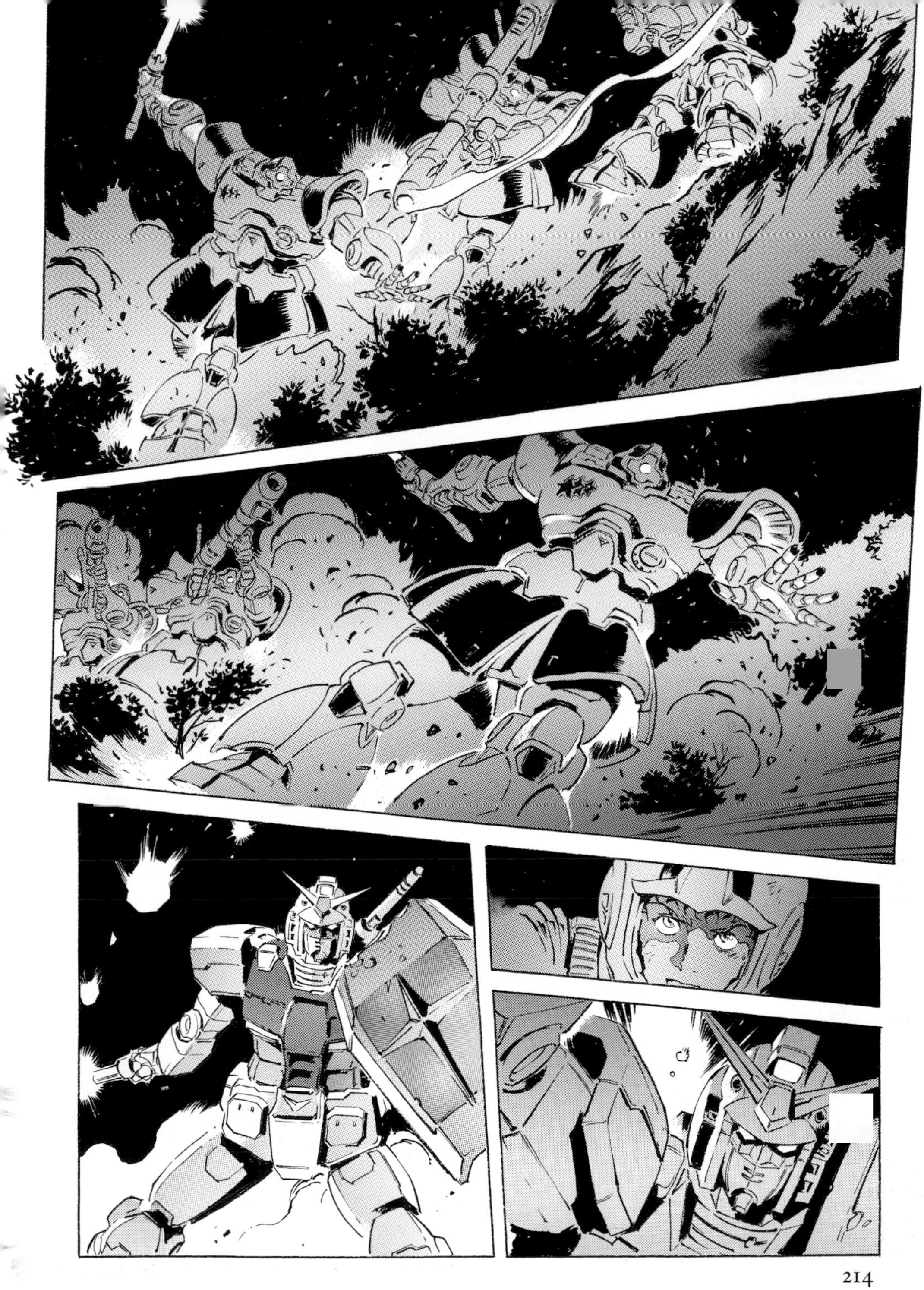

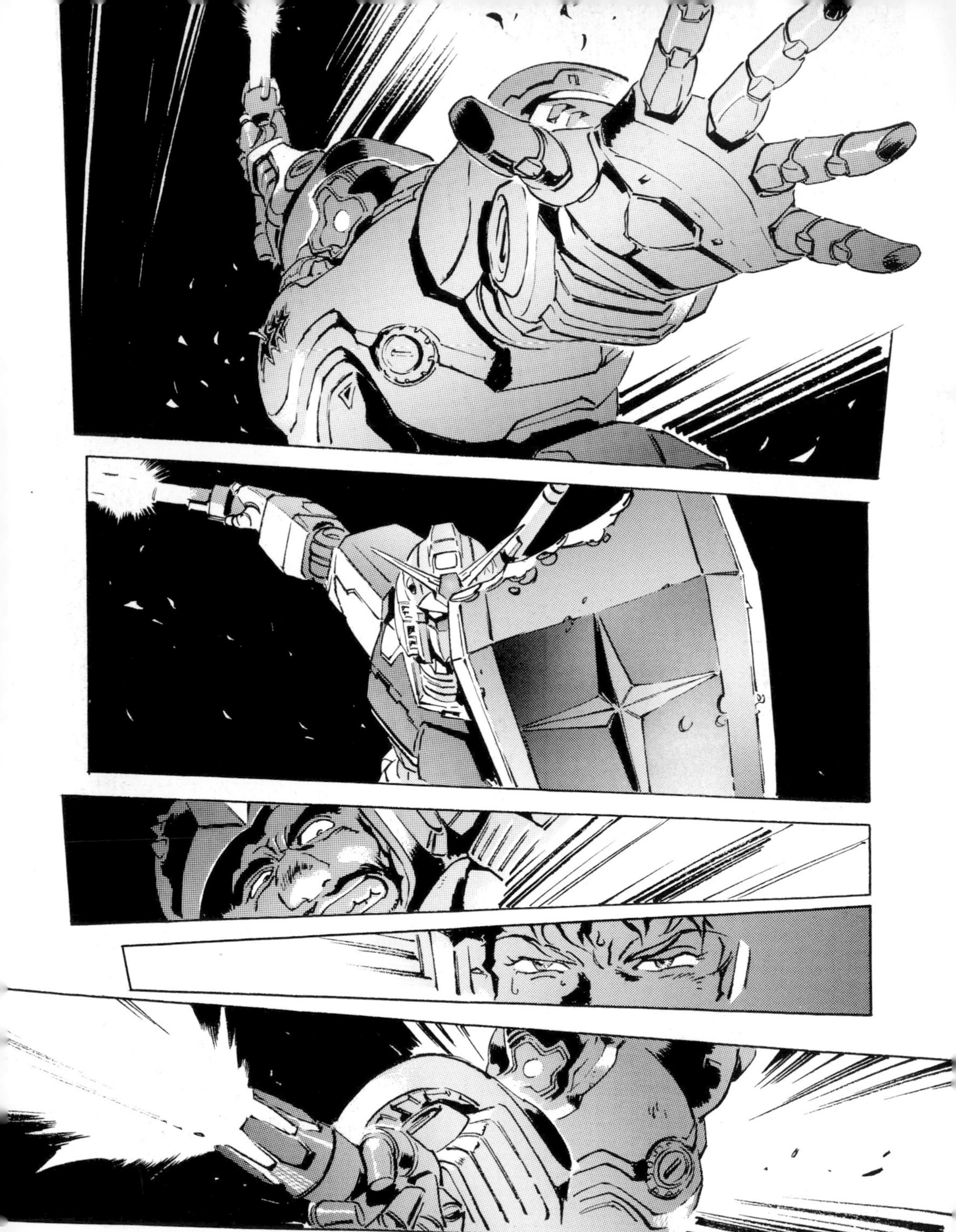

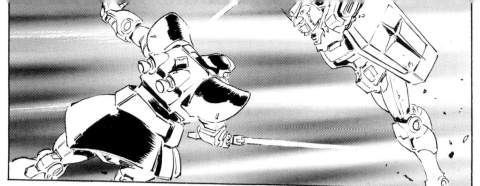

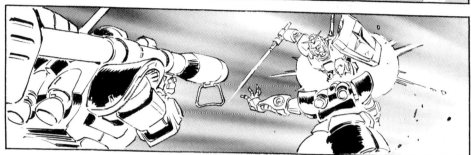

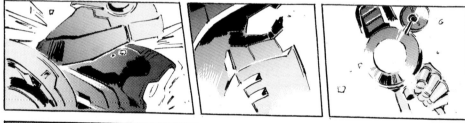

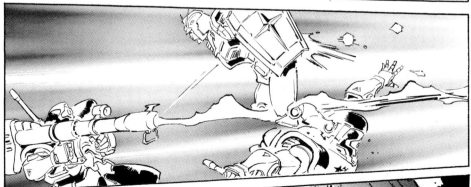

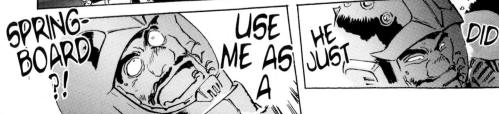

SPRING-BOARD?!

USE ME AS A

HE JUST

DID

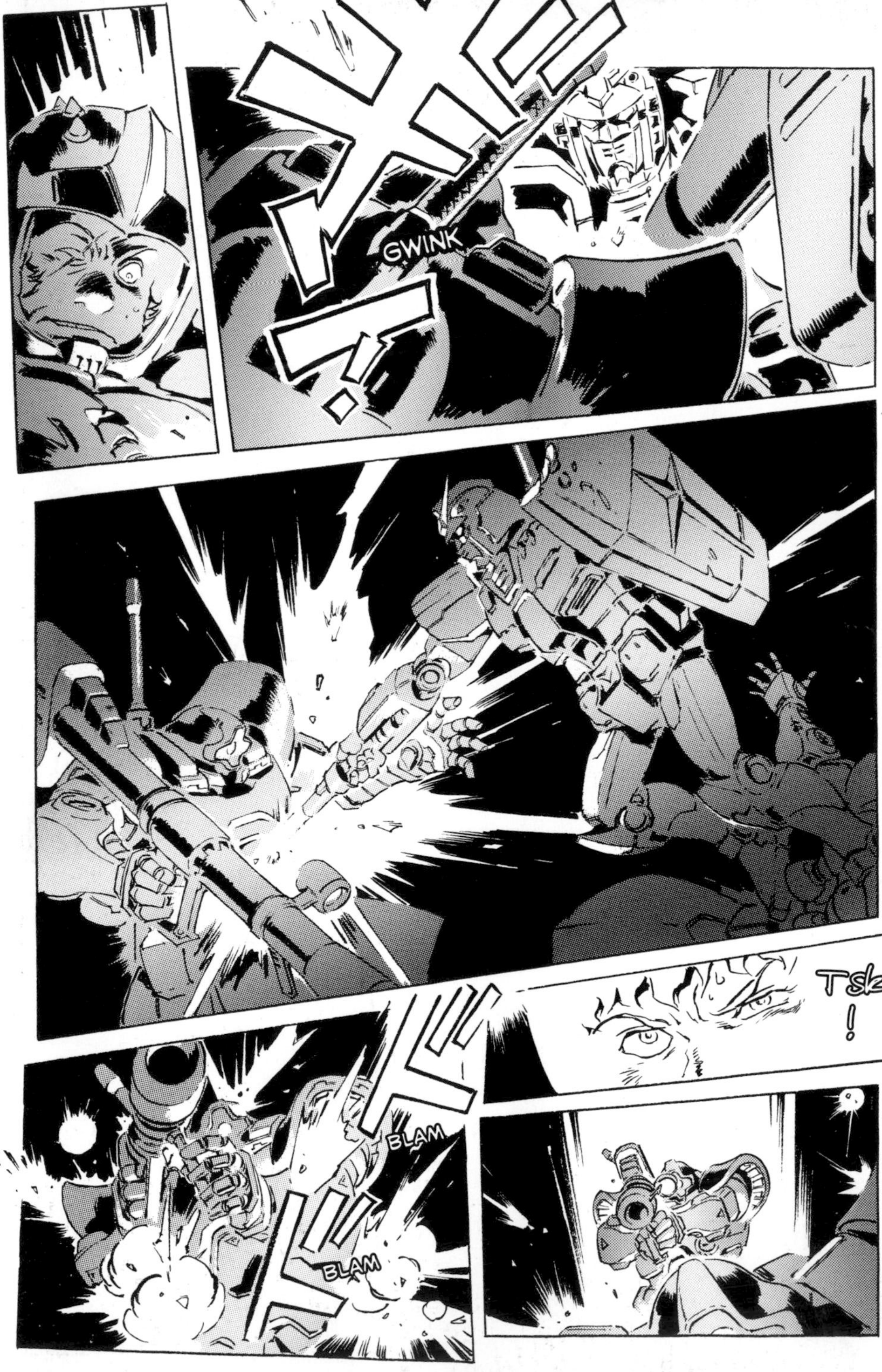
GWINK
Tsk!
BLAM
BLAM

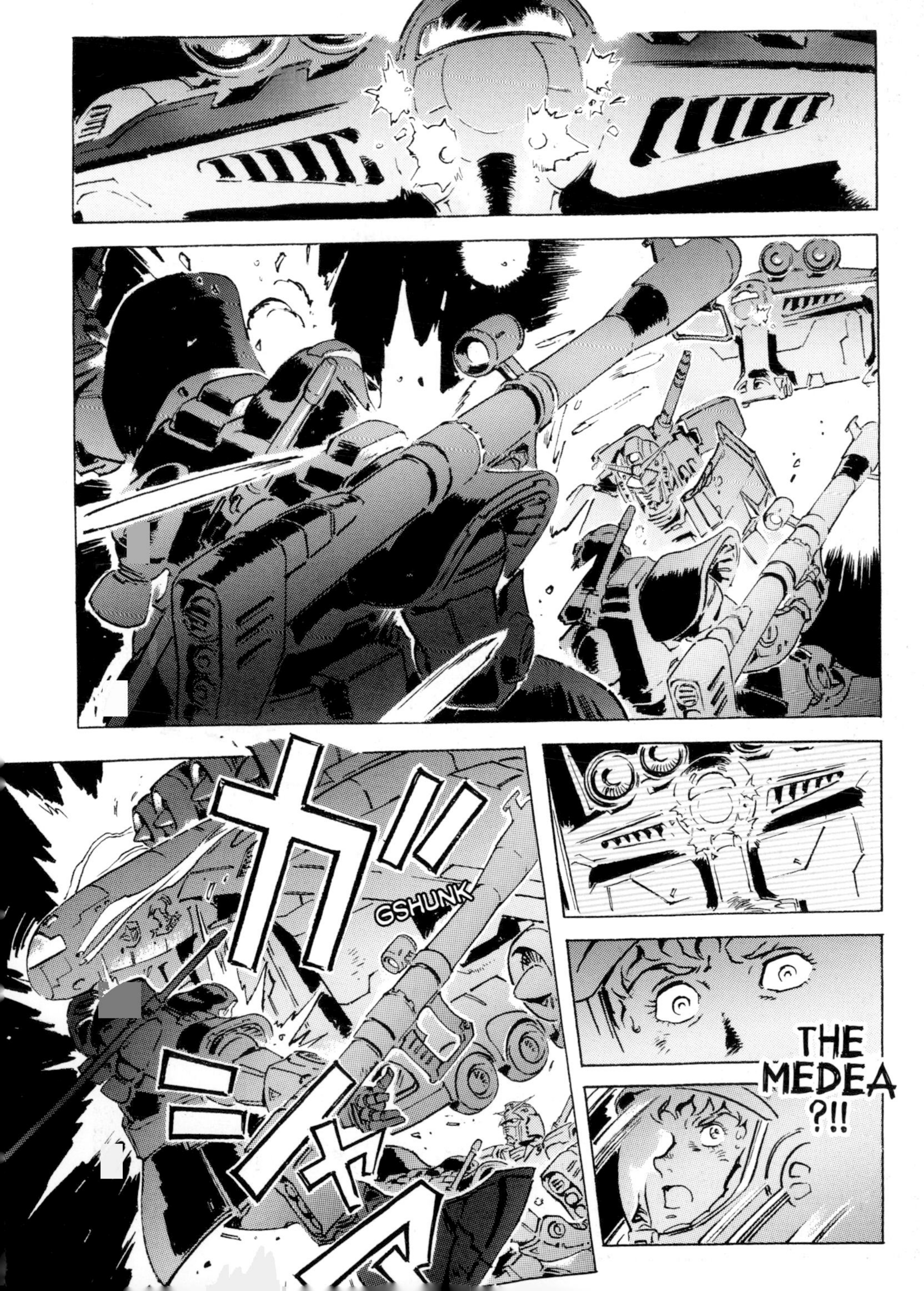
THE MEDEA ?!!
GSHUNK

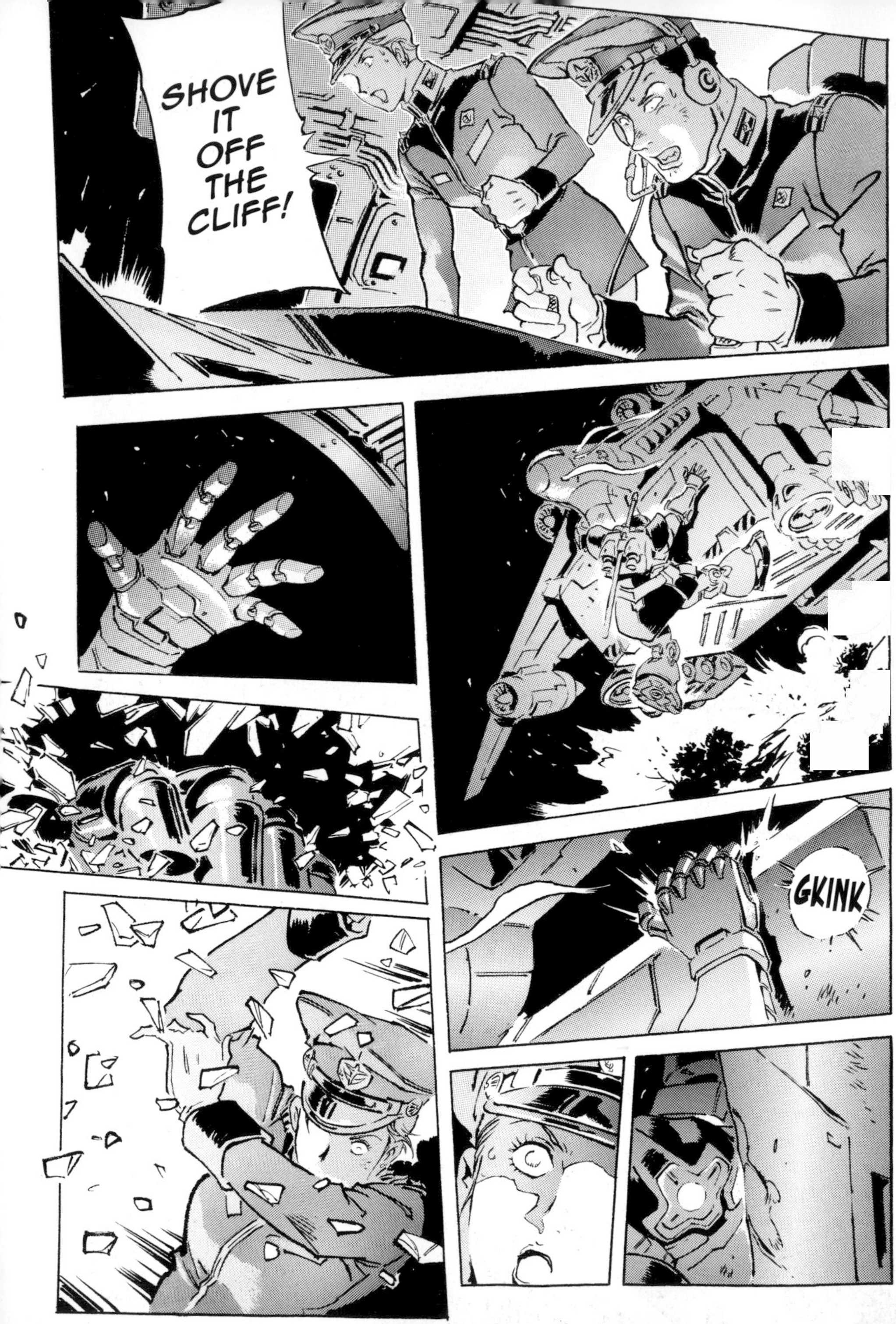
SHOVE IT OFF THE CLIFF!
GKINK

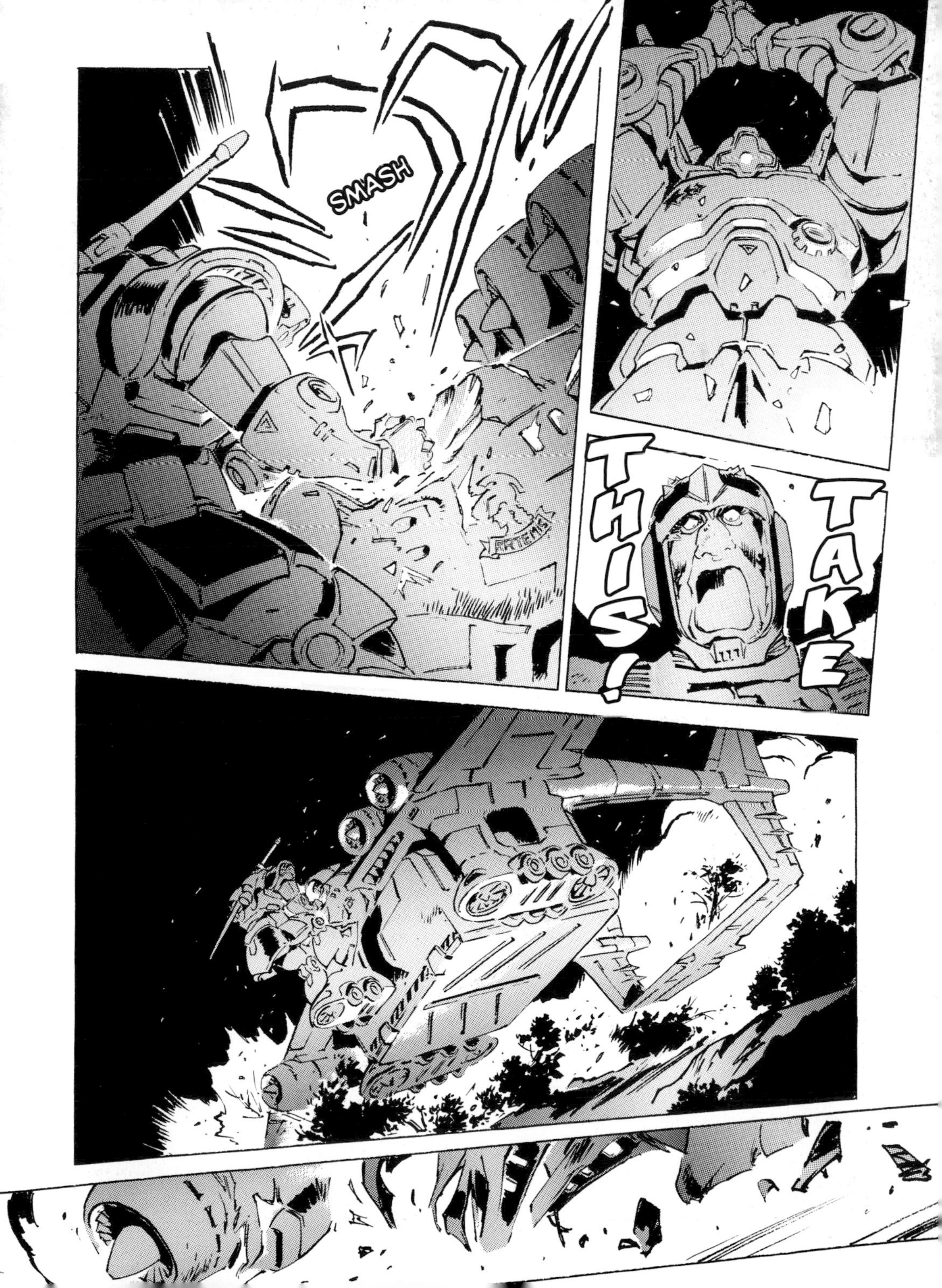
TAKE THIS!
SMASH

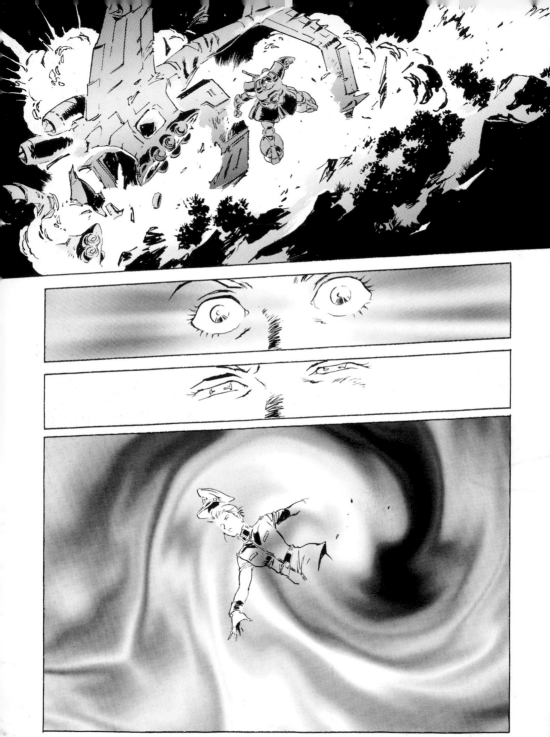

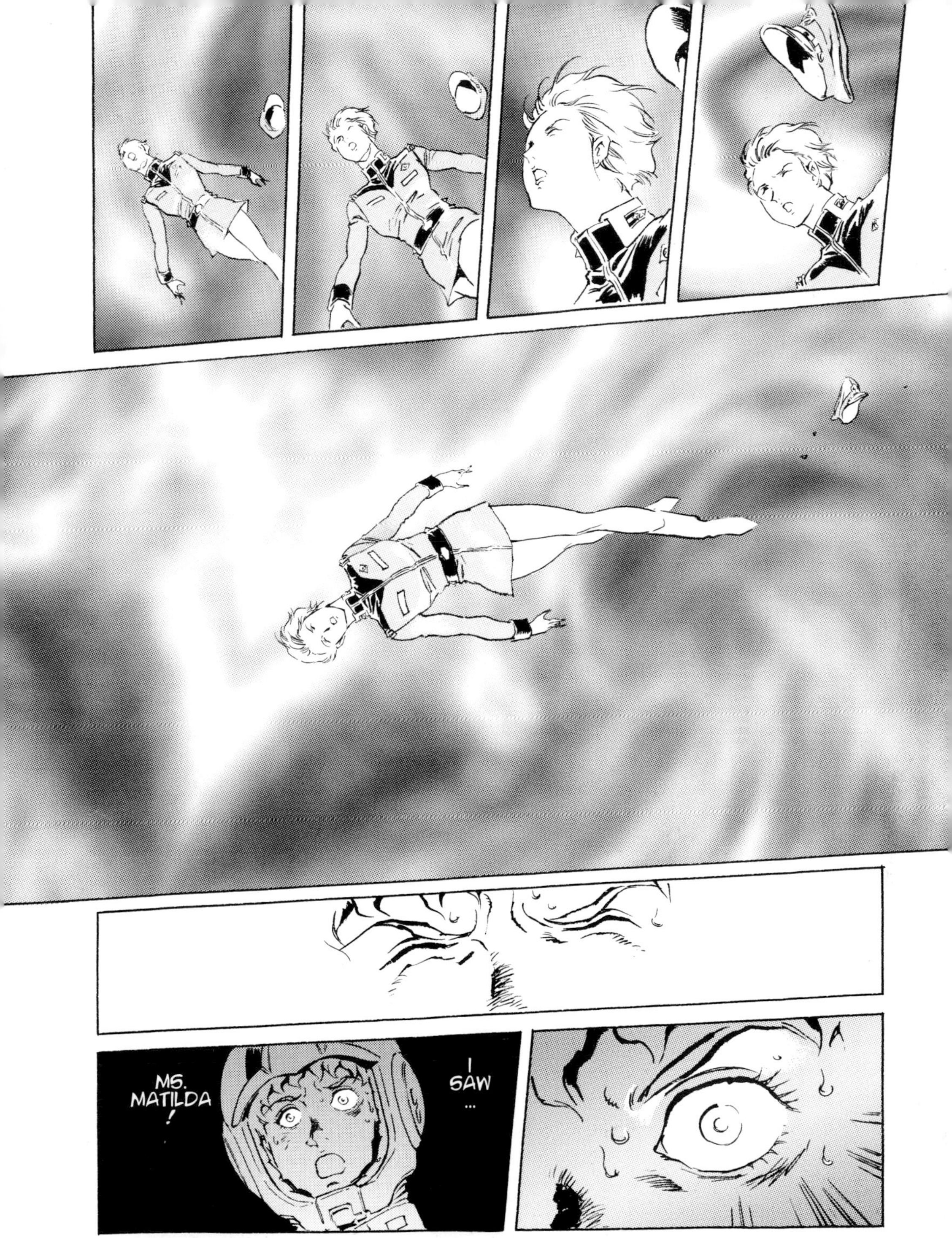
I SAW ...
MS. MATILDA !

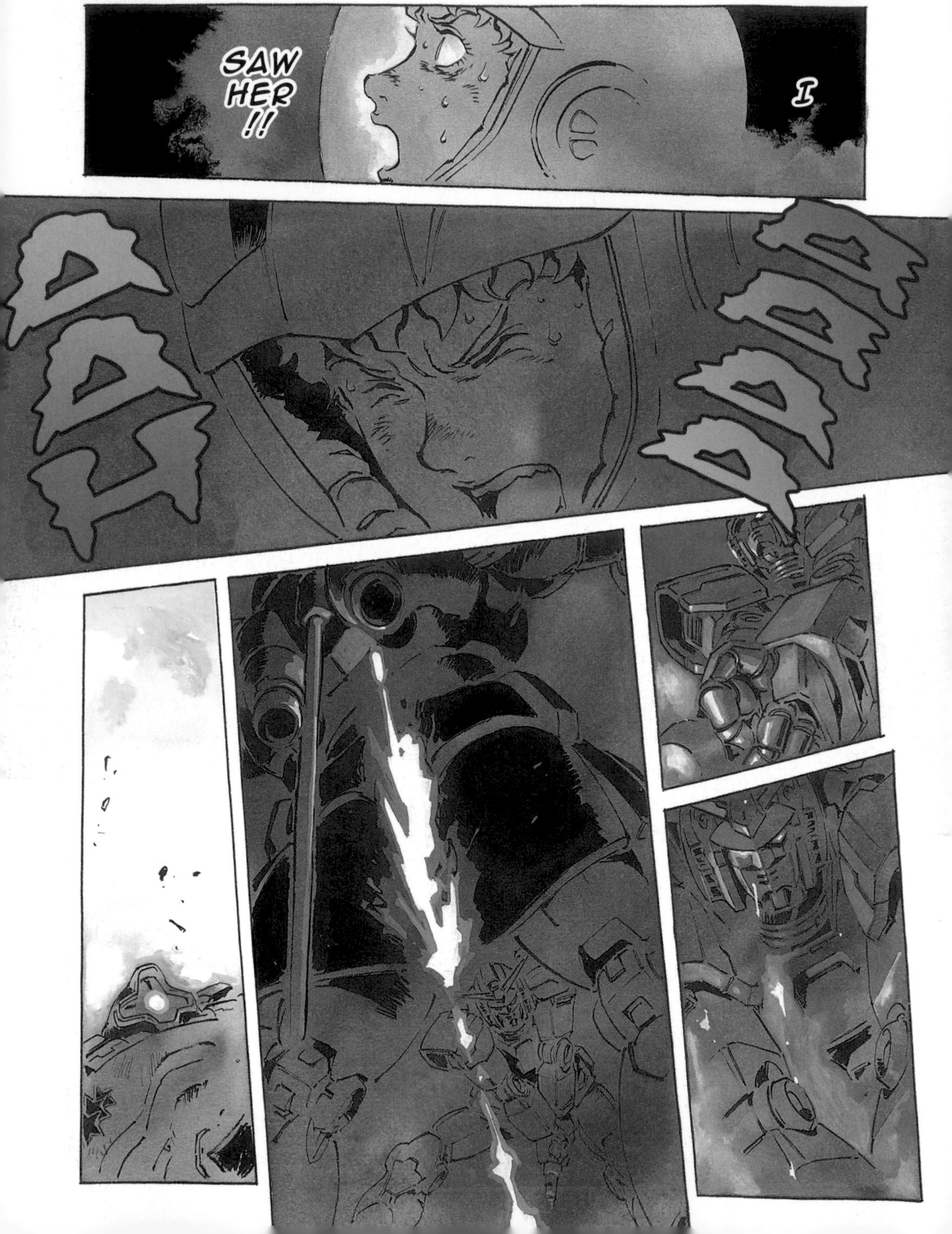
I
SAW HER !!

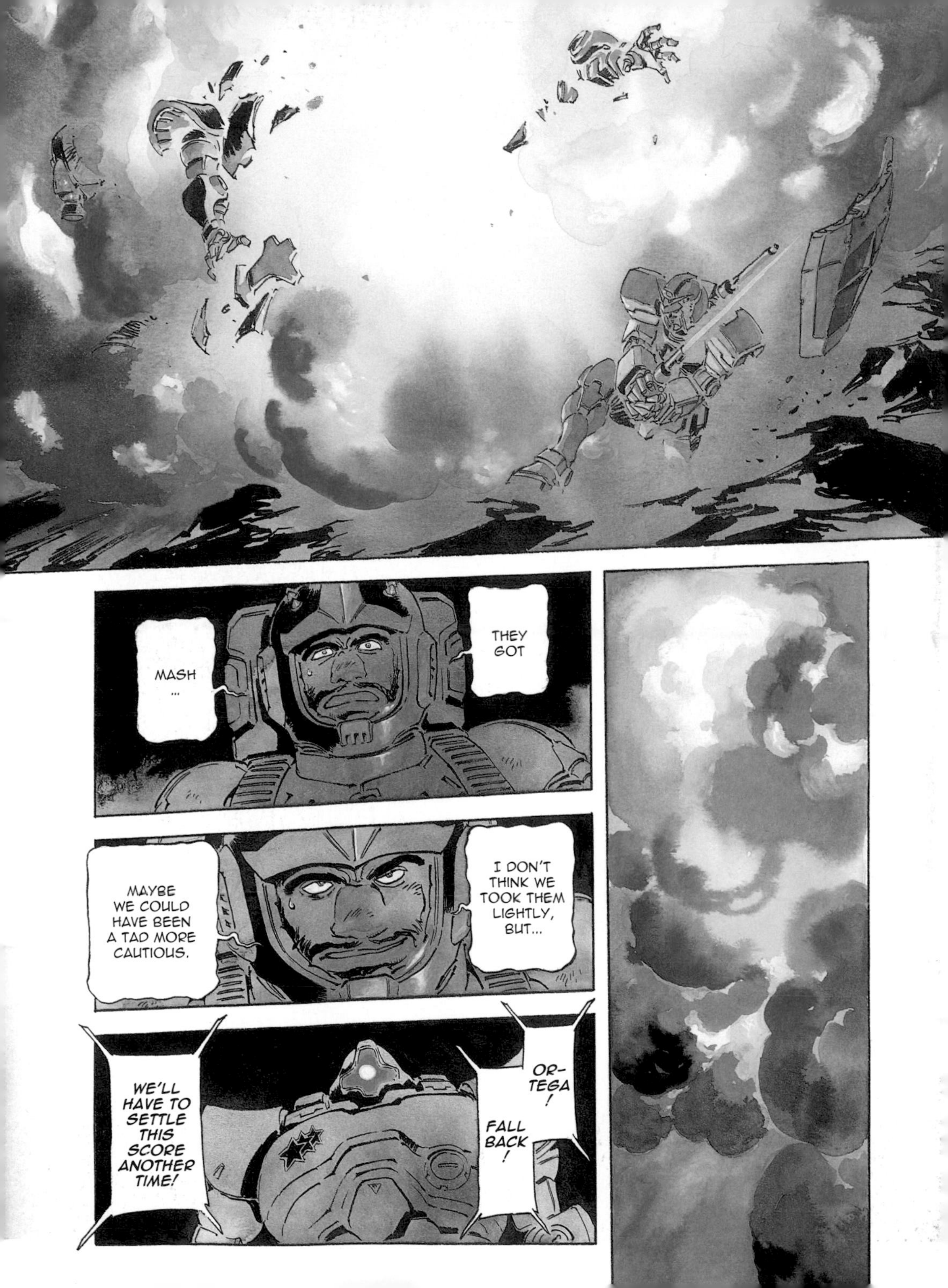
THEY GOT
MASH ...
I DON'T THINK WE TOOK THEM LIGHTLY, BUT...
MAYBE WE COULD HAVE BEEN A TAD MORE CAUTIOUS.
OR-TEGA!
FALL BACK!
WE'LL HAVE TO SETTLE THIS SCORE ANOTHER TIME!

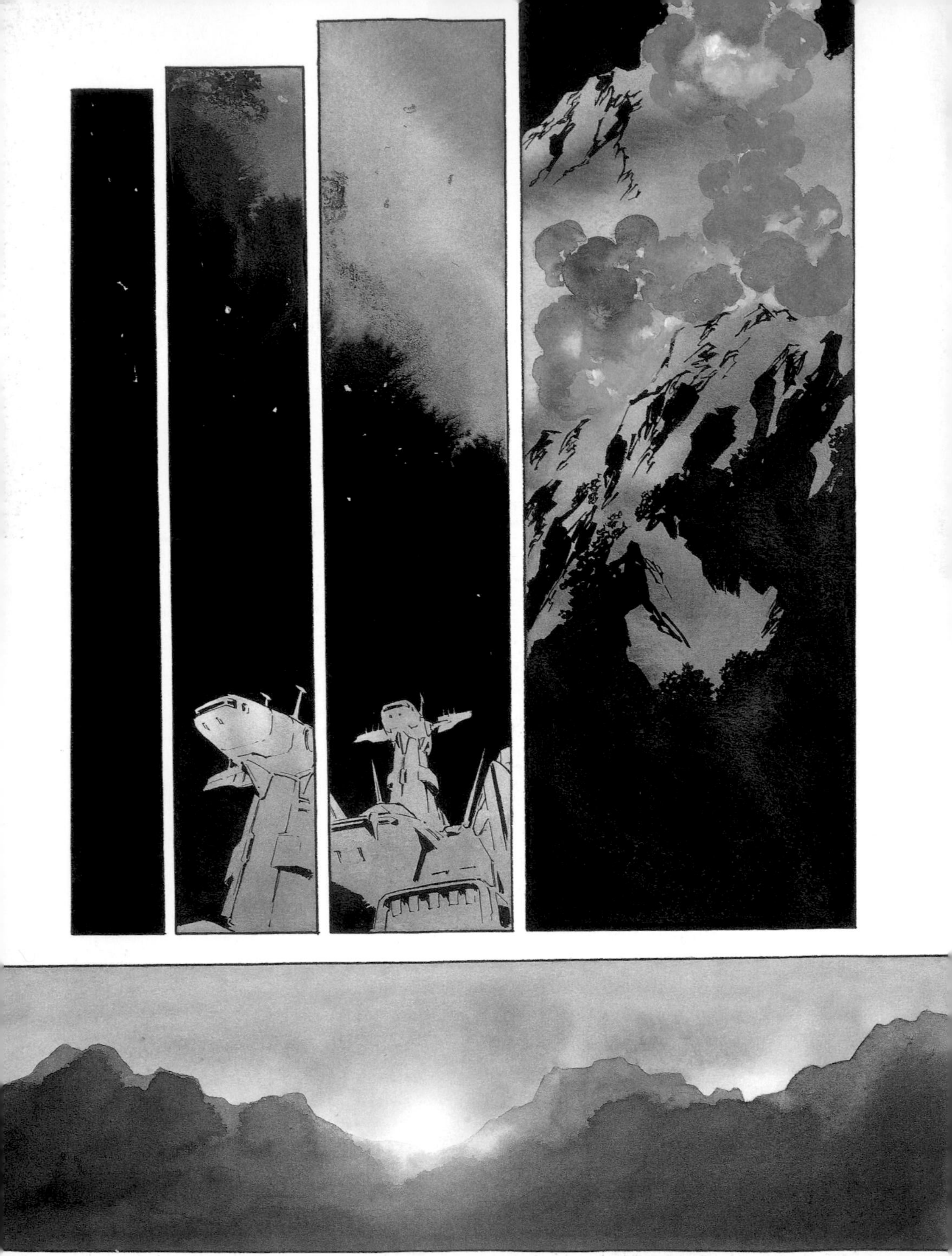

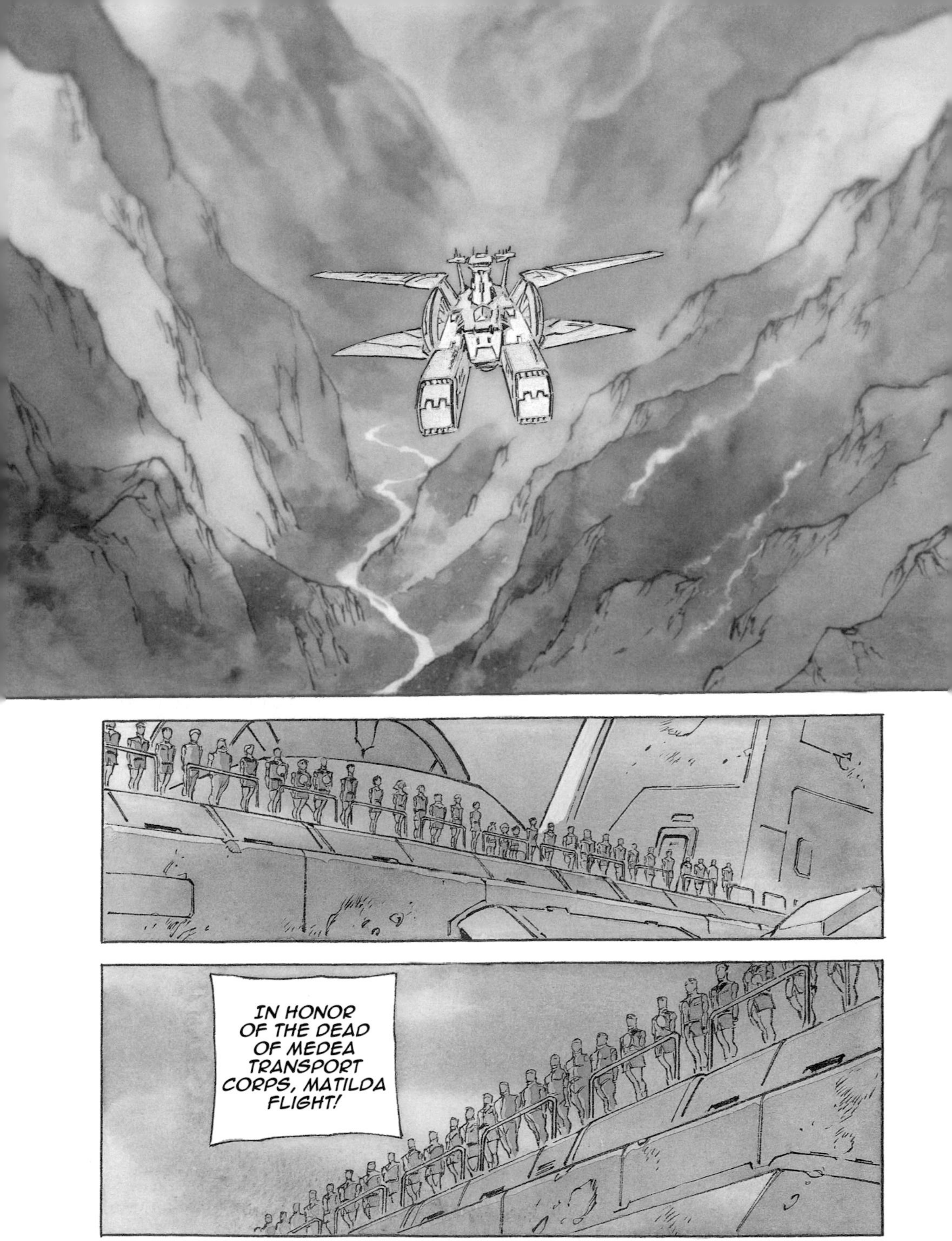
IN HONOR OF THE DEAD OF MEDEA TRANSPORT CORPS, MATILDA FLIGHT!

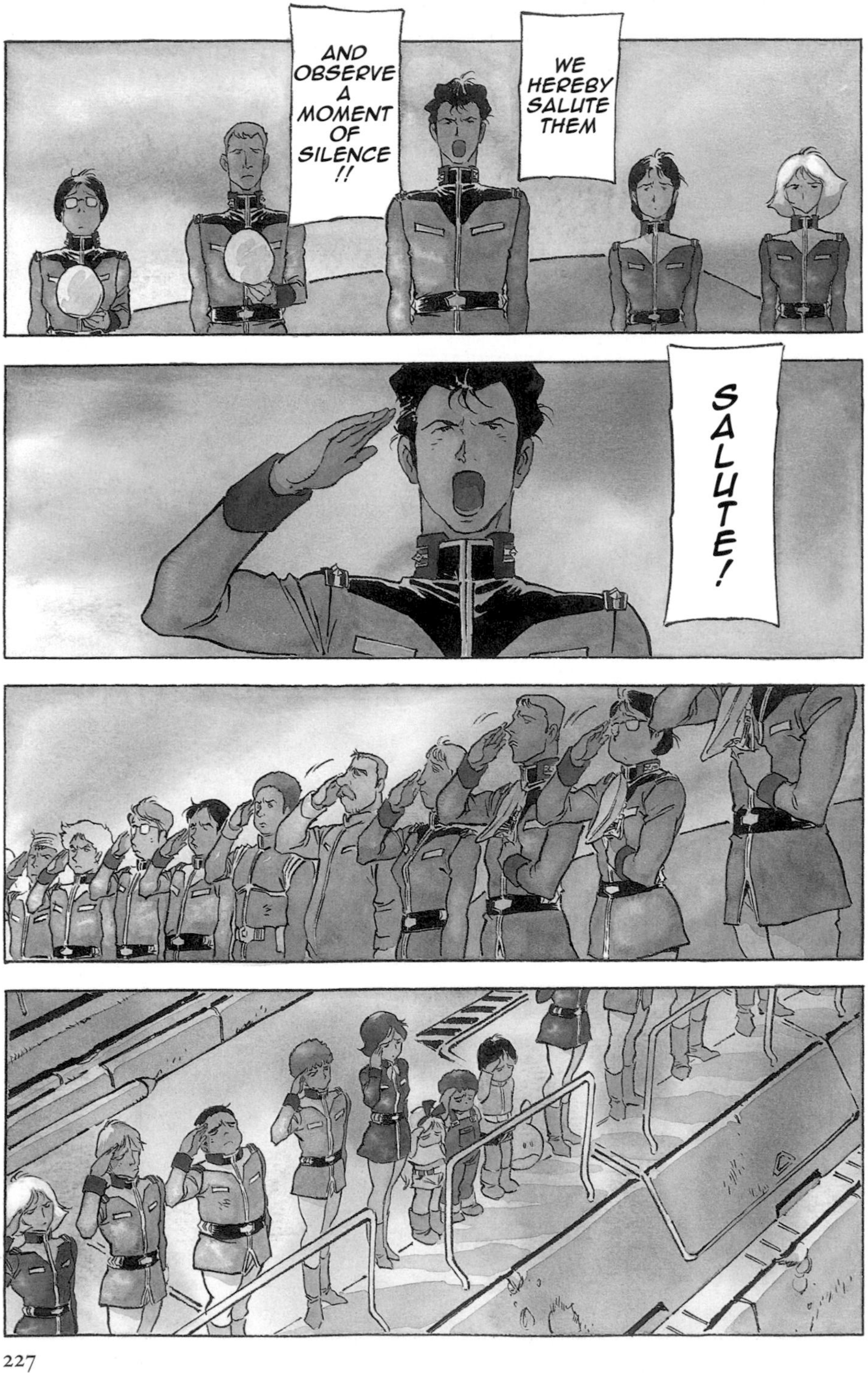
WE HEREBY SALUTE THEM
AND OBSERVE A MOMENT OF SILENCE!!
SALUTE!

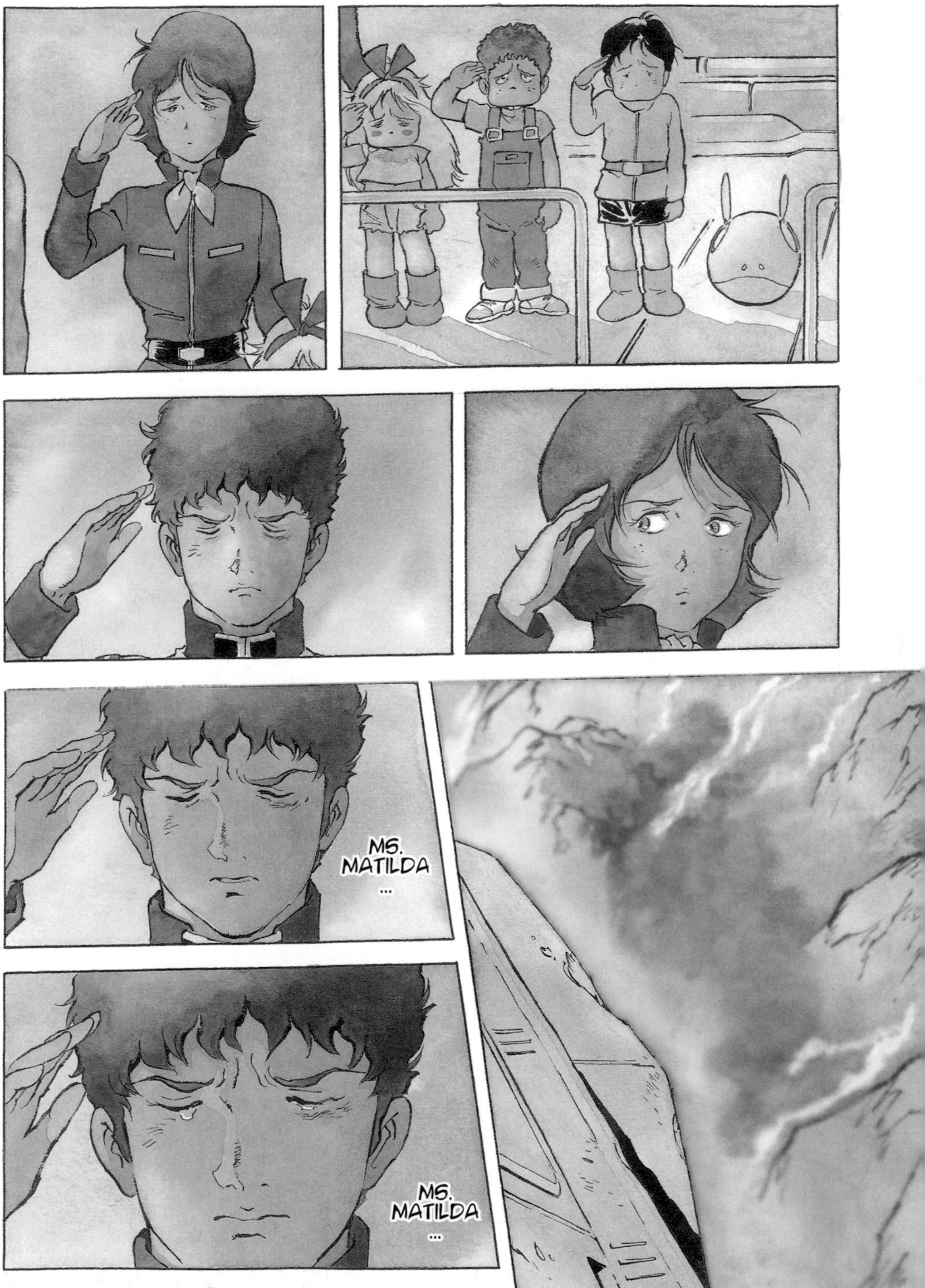
MS. MATILDA ...
MS. MATILDA ...

SECTION V

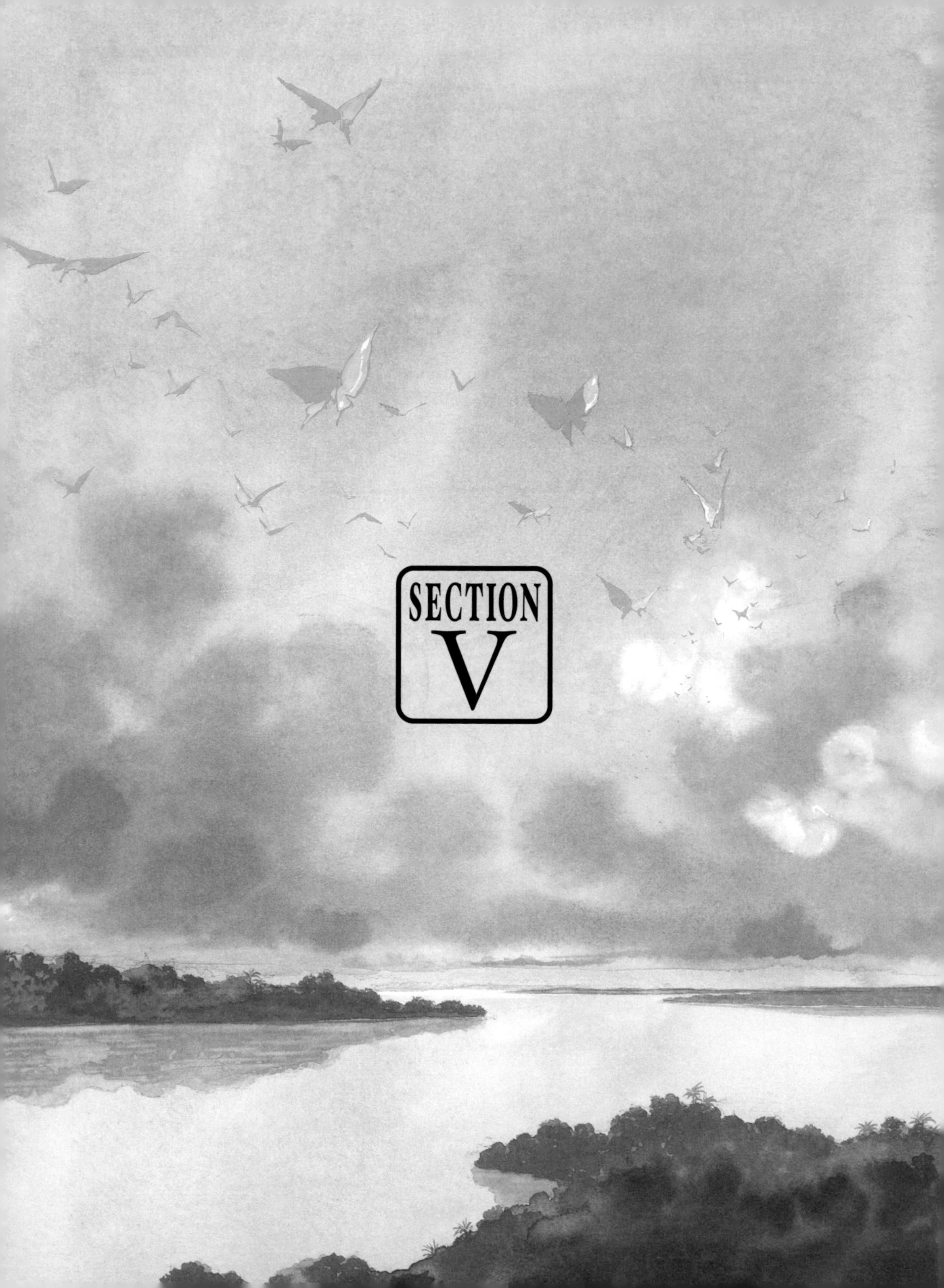

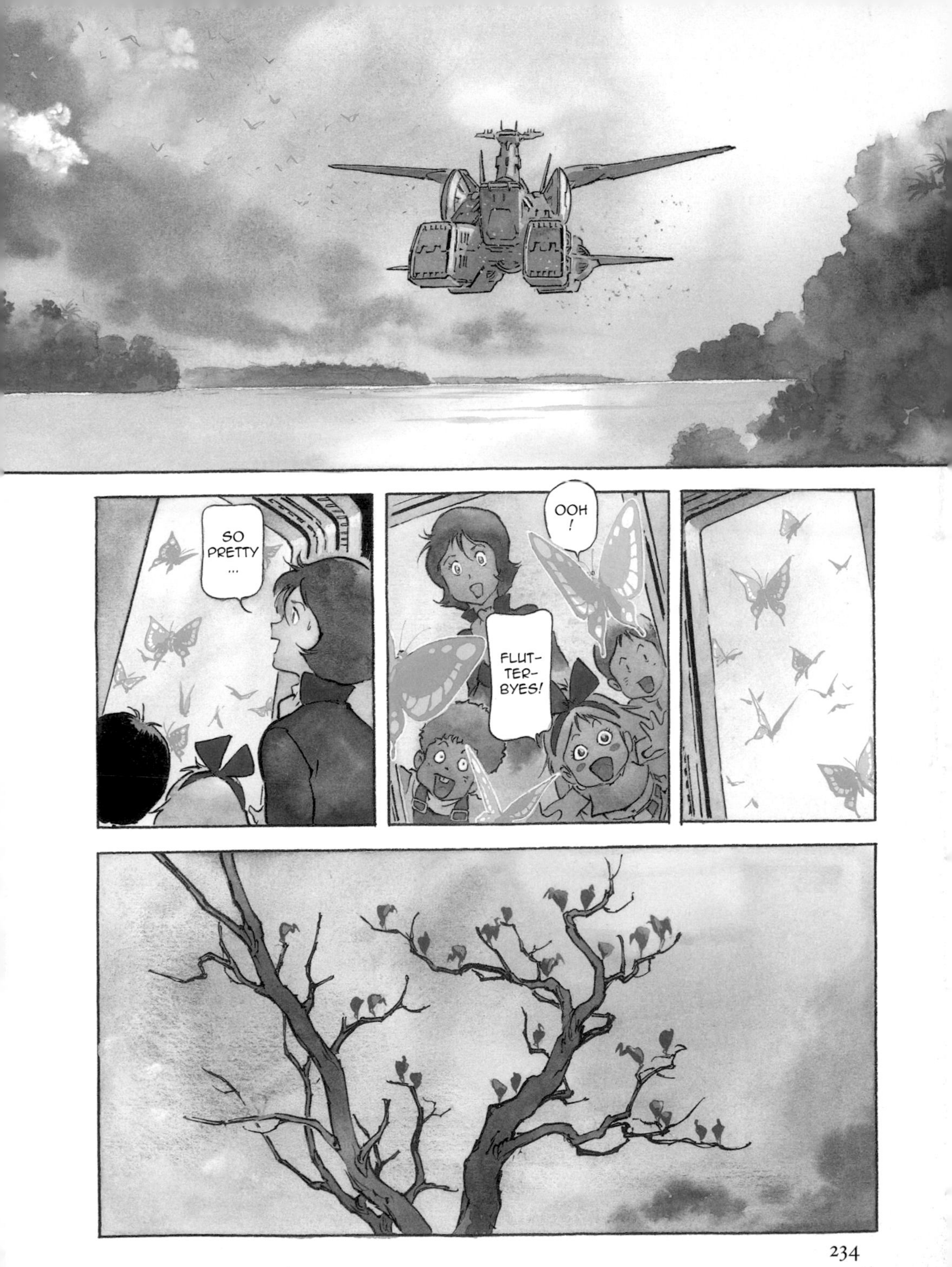
OOH!
FLUT-TER-BYES!
SO PRETTY...

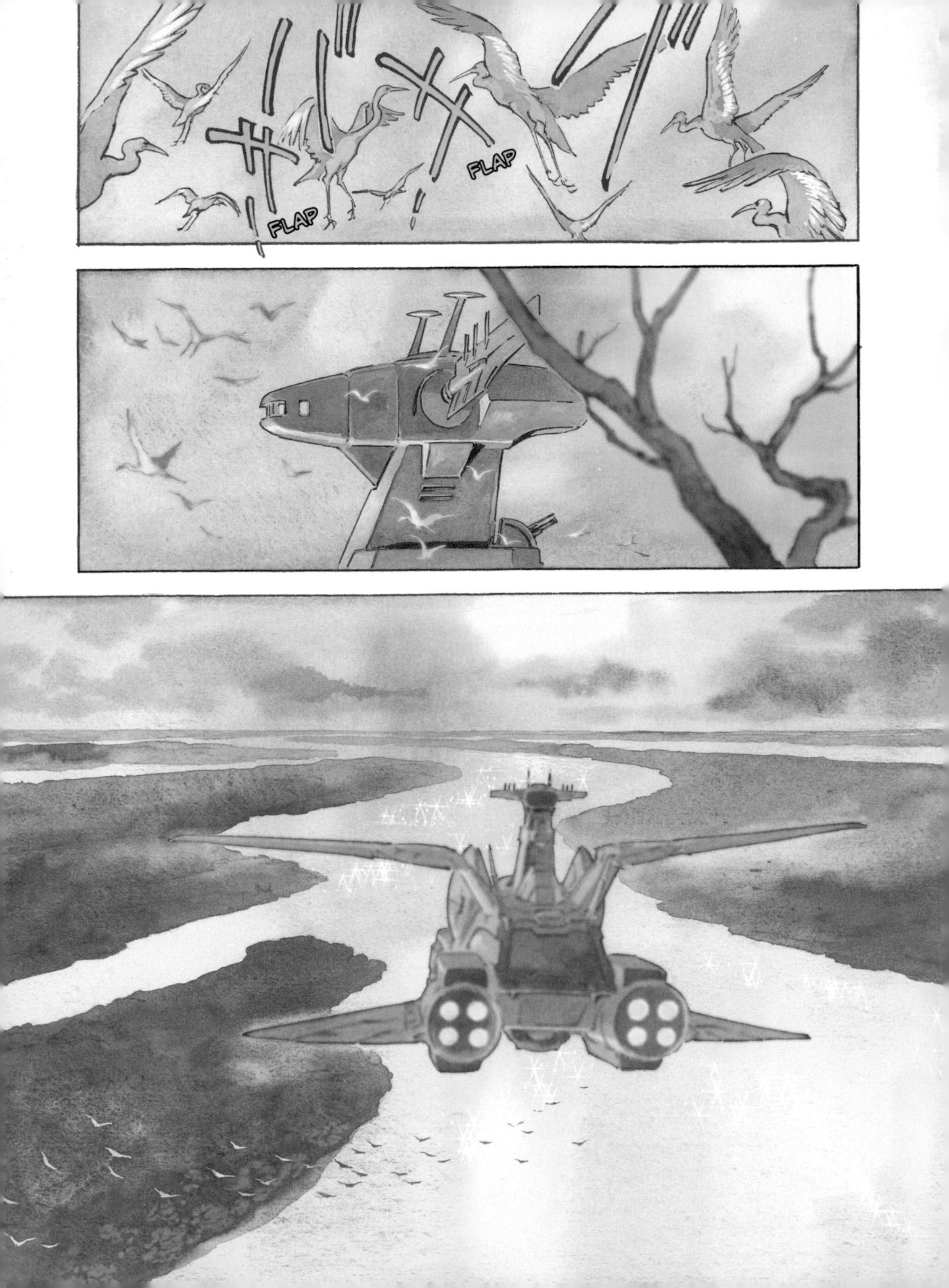
FLAP
FLAP

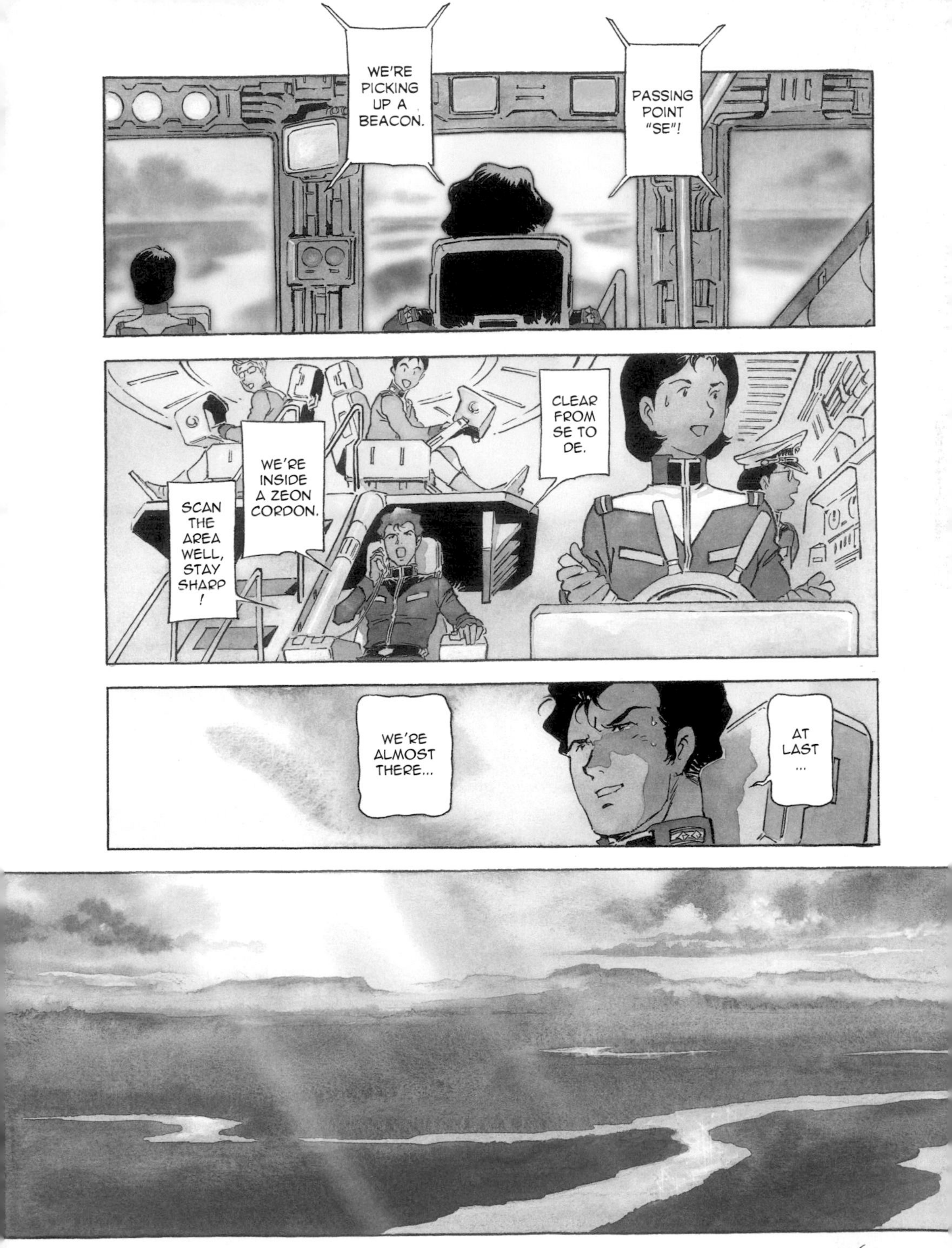
PASSING POINT "SE"!
WE'RE PICKING UP A BEACON.
CLEAR FROM SE TO DE.
WE'RE INSIDE A ZEON CORDON.
SCAN THE AREA WELL, STAY SHARP!
AT LAST...
WE'RE ALMOST THERE...

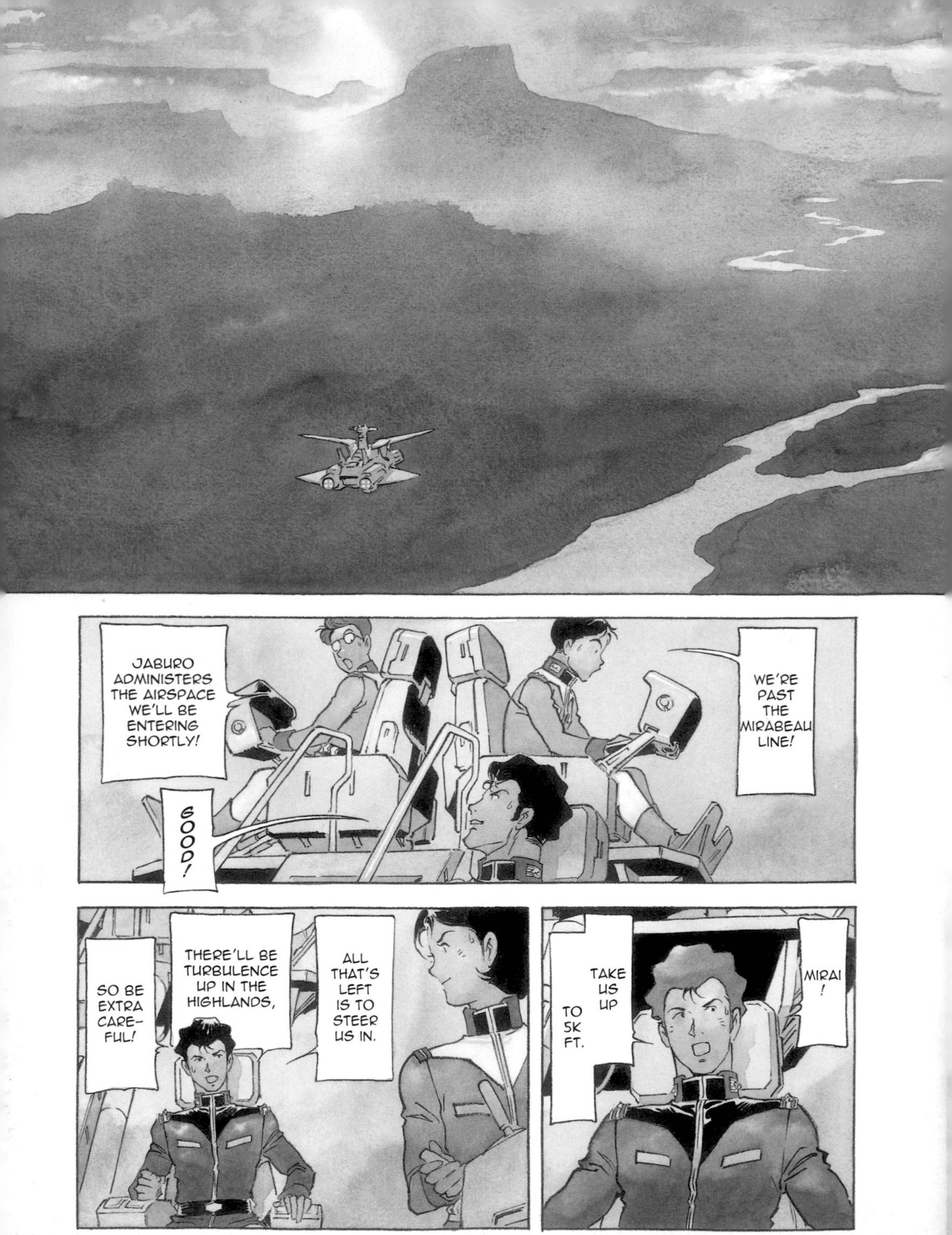
WE'RE PAST THE MIRABEAU LINE!
JABURO ADMINISTERS THE AIRSPACE WE'LL BE ENTERING SHORTLY!
GOOD!
MIRAI!
TAKE US UP
TO 5K FT.
ALL THAT'S LEFT IS TO STEER US IN.
THERE'LL BE TURBULENCE UP IN THE HIGHLANDS,
SO BE EXTRA CARE-FUL!

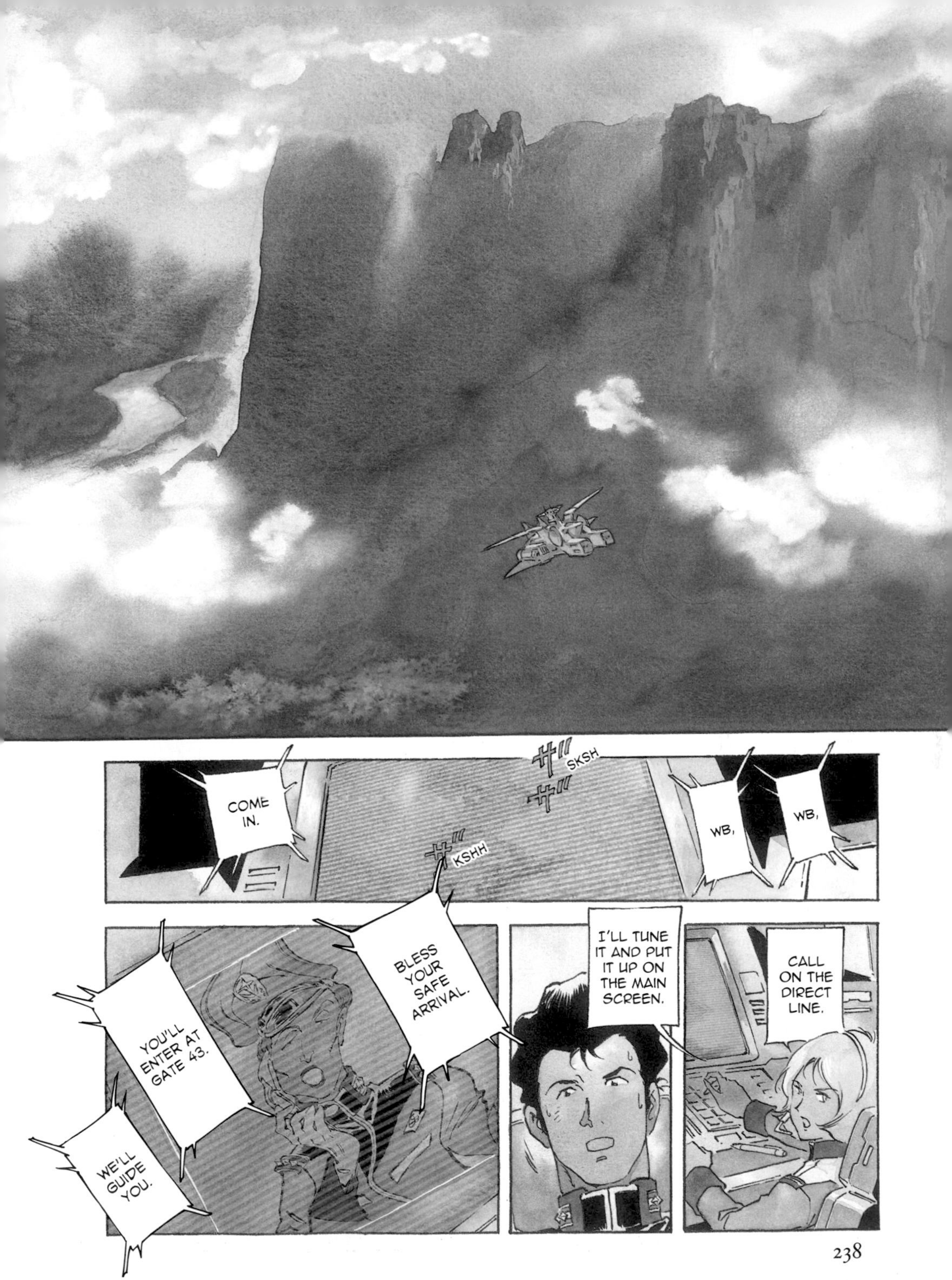
WB,
WB,
SKSH
COME IN.
KSHH
CALL ON THE DIRECT LINE.
I'LL TUNE IT AND PUT IT UP ON THE MAIN SCREEN.
BLESS YOUR SAFE ARRIVAL.
YOU'LL ENTER AT GATE 43.
WE'LL GUIDE YOU.

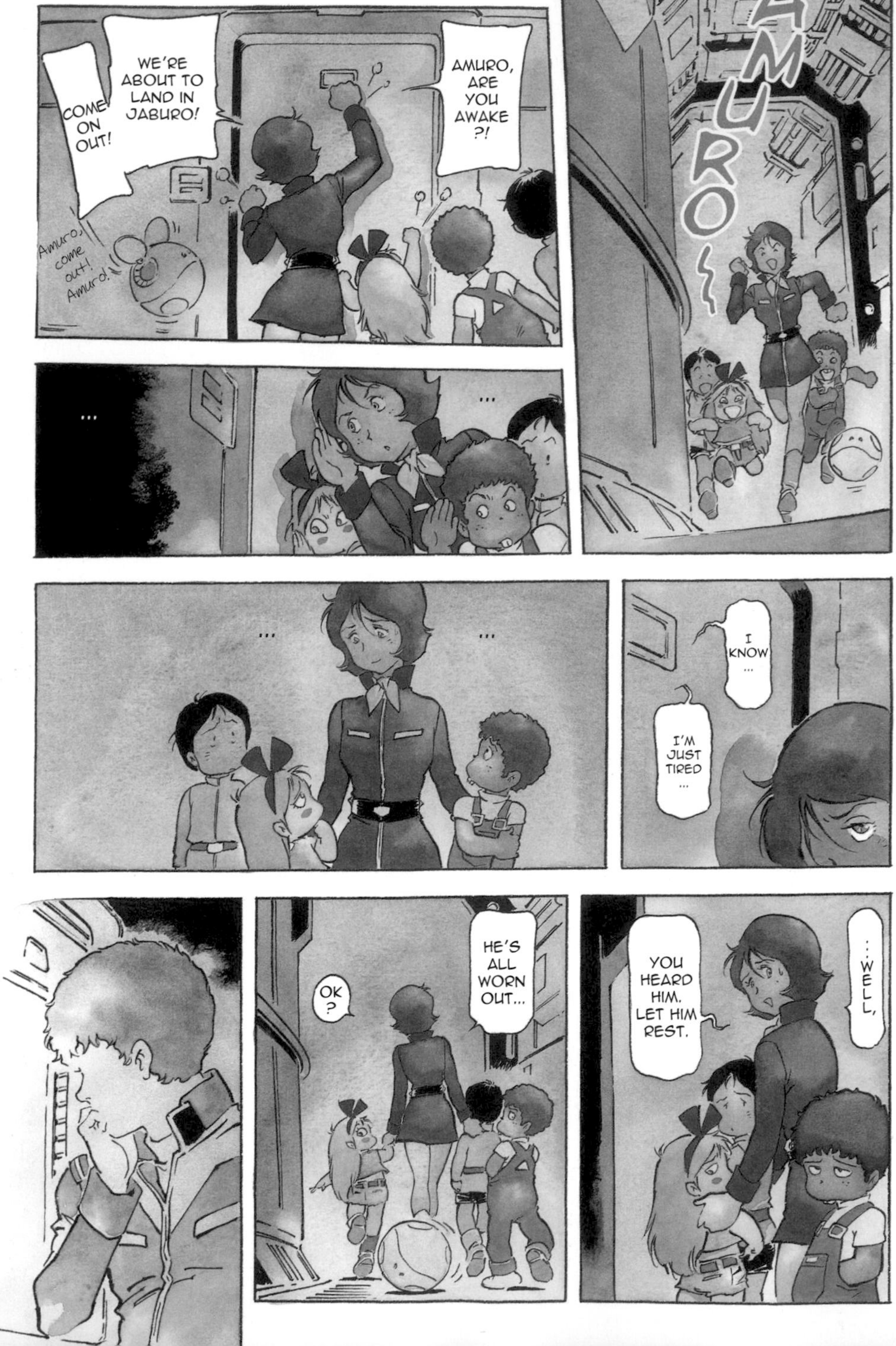
AMURO~
AMURO, ARE YOU AWAKE?!
WE'RE ABOUT TO LAND IN JABURO!
COME ON OUT!
Amuro, come out! Amuro!
...
...
I KNOW...
I'M JUST TIRED...
...
...
...WELL,
YOU HEARD HIM. LET HIM REST.
HE'S ALL WORN OUT...
OK?

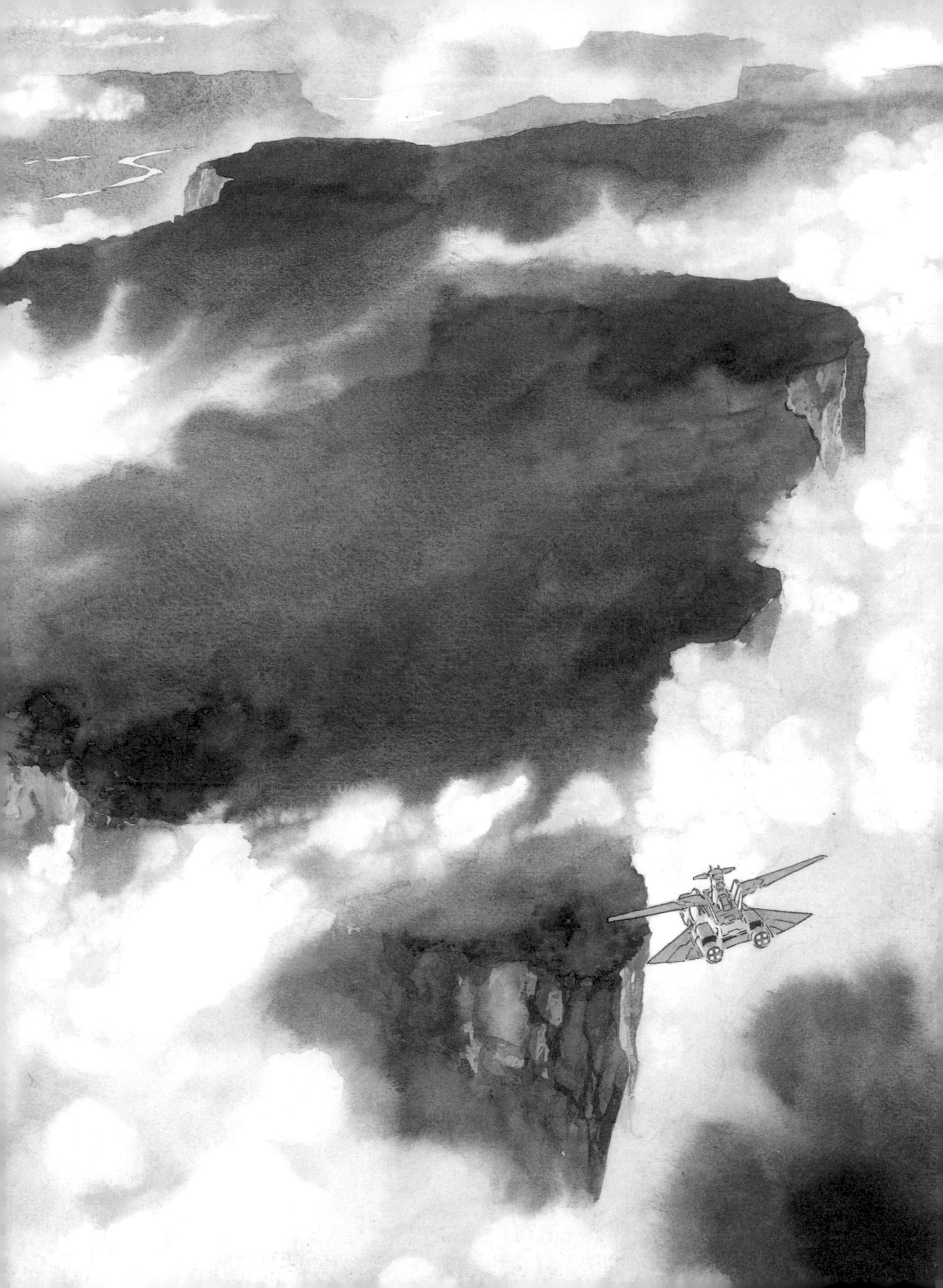

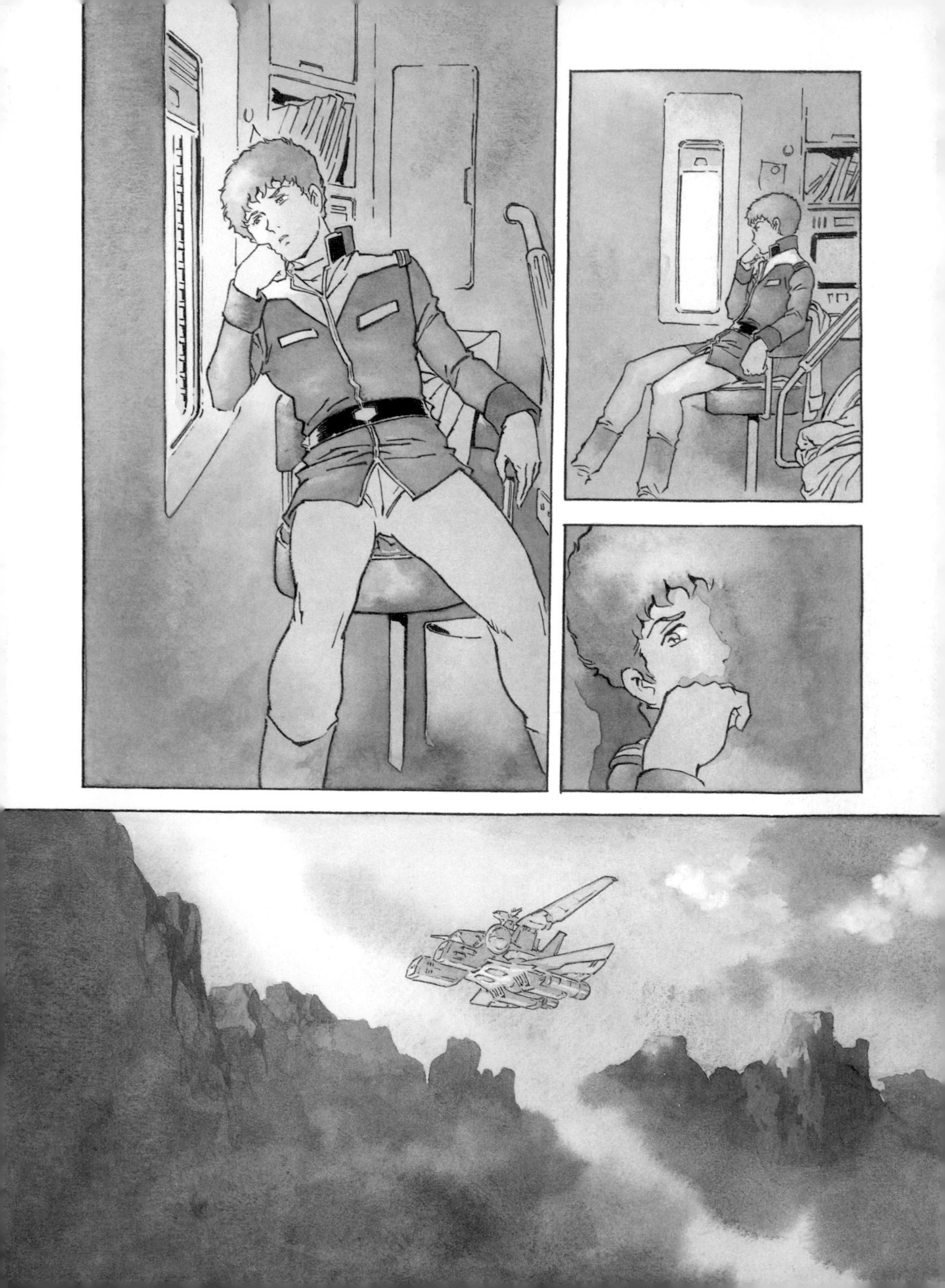

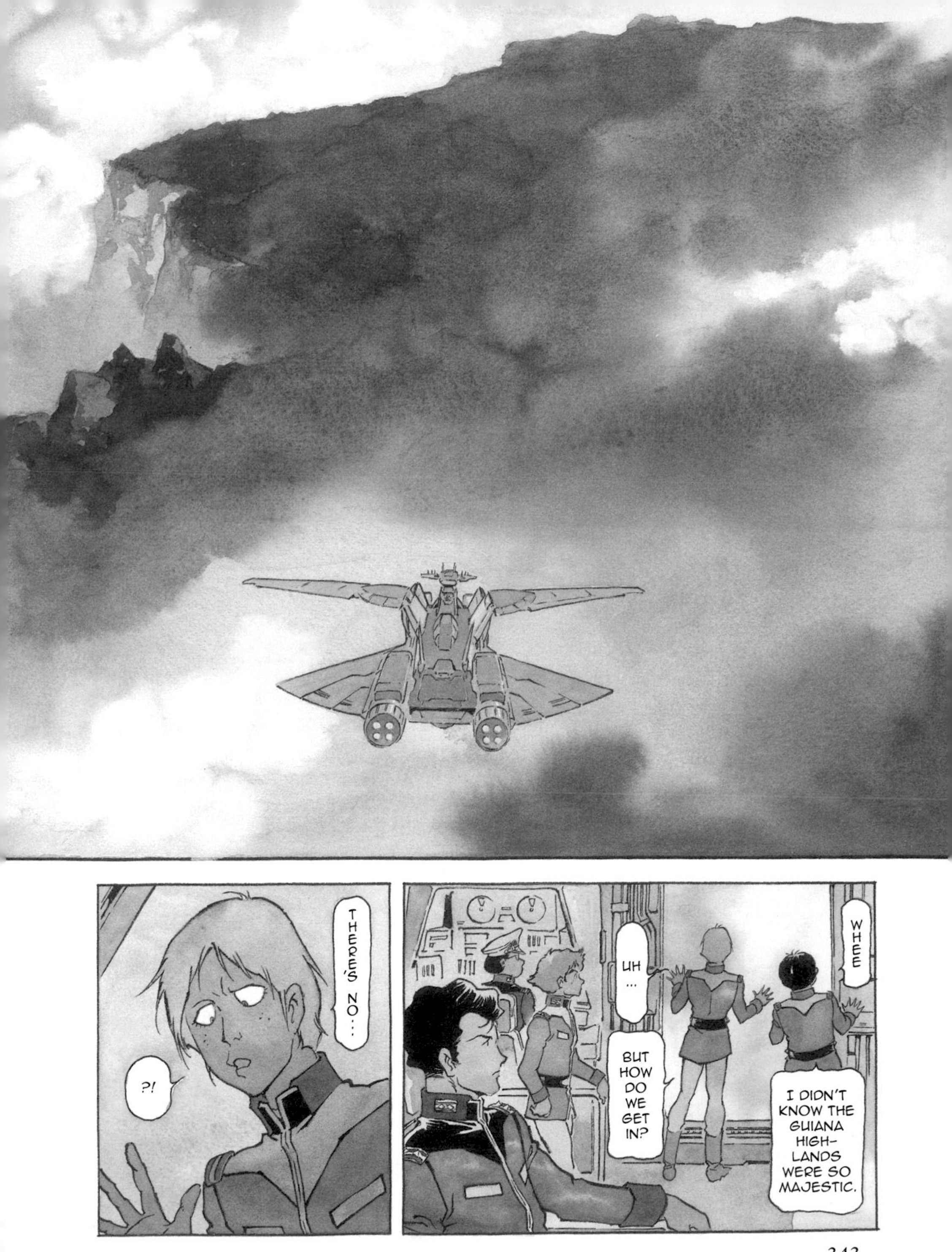
WHEE
I DIDN'T KNOW THE GUIANA HIGHLANDS WERE SO MAJESTIC.
UH...
BUT HOW DO WE GET IN?
THERE'S NO...
?!

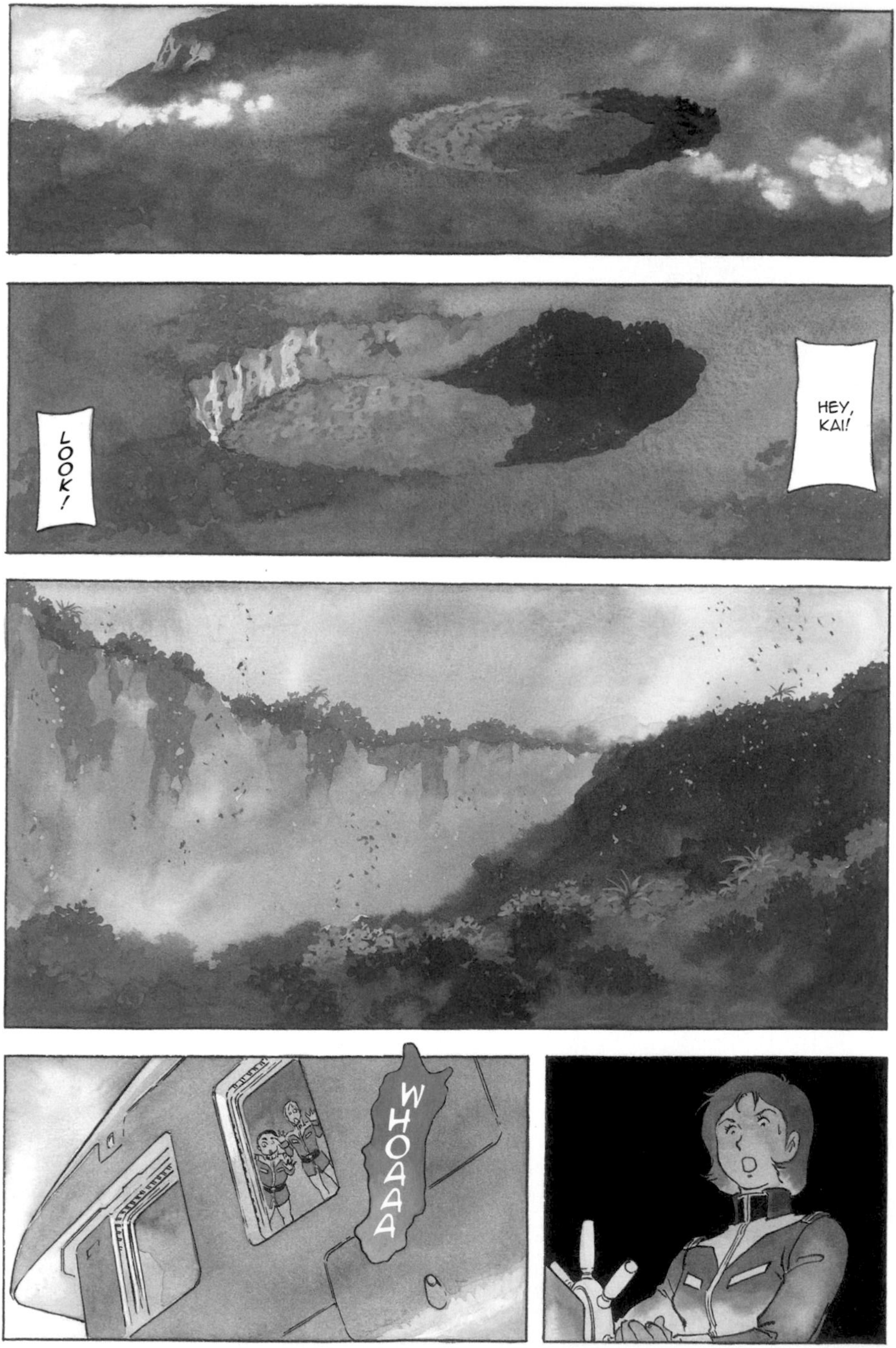
HEY, KAI!
LOOK!
WHOAAA

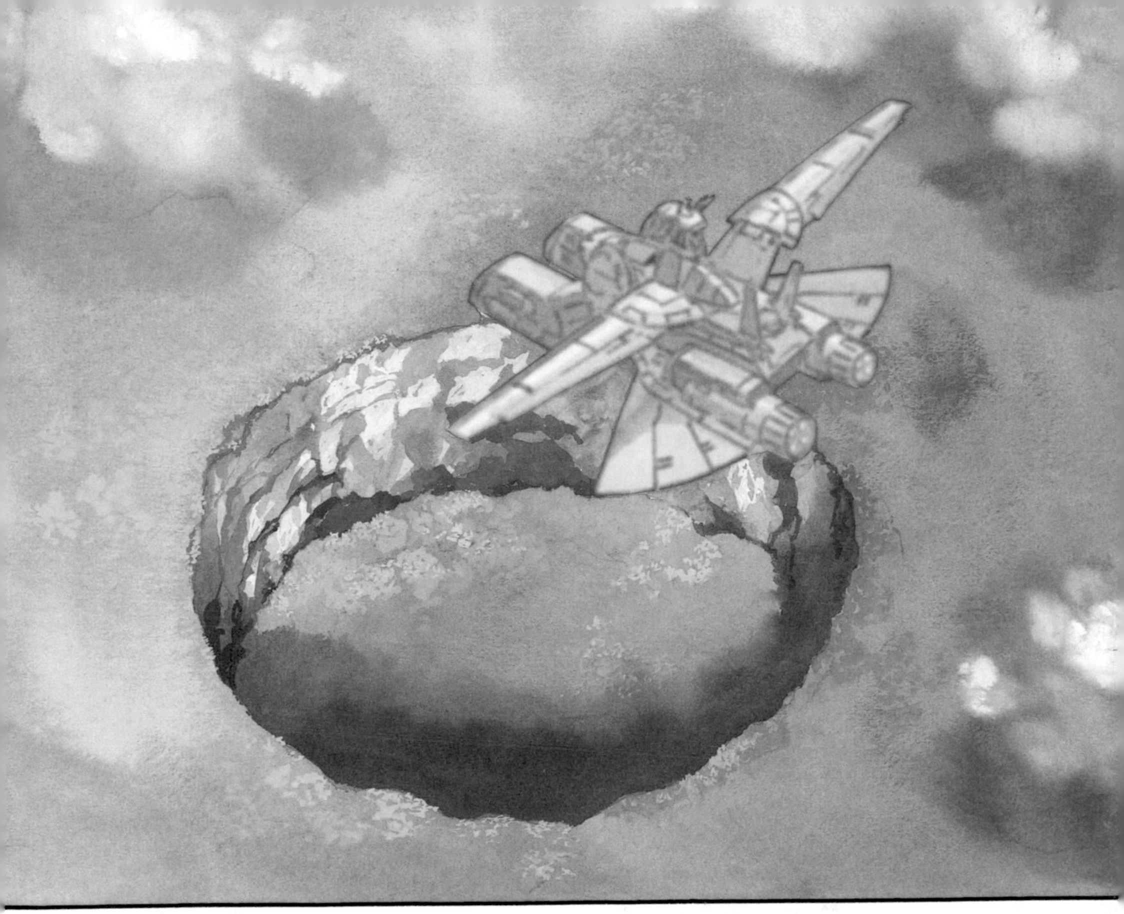
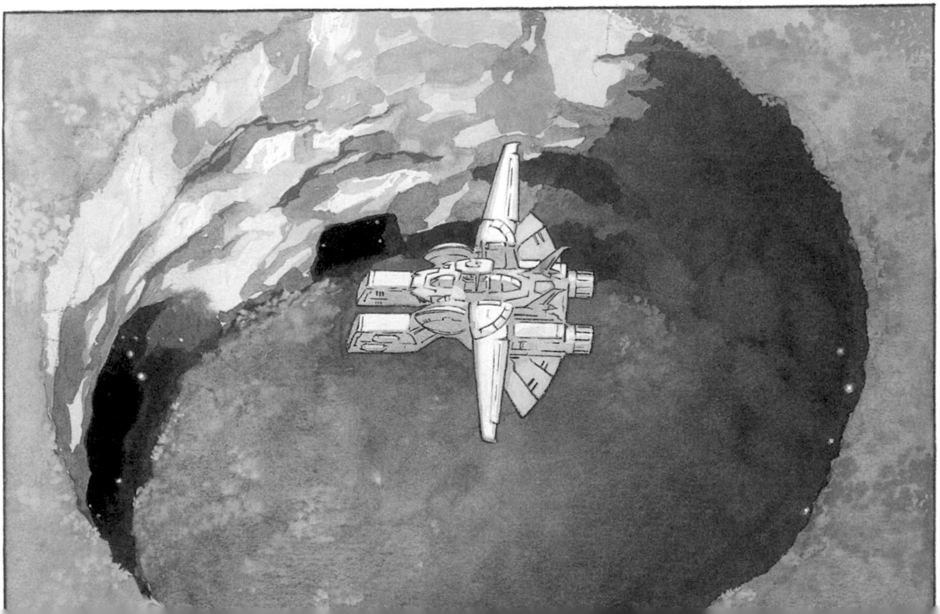

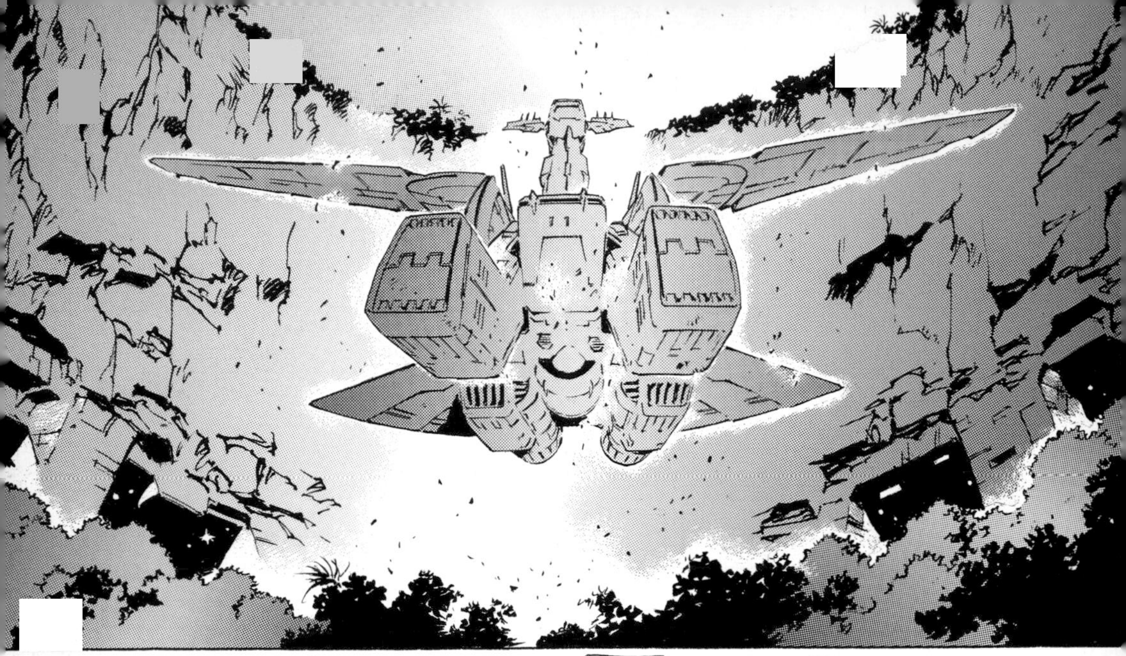

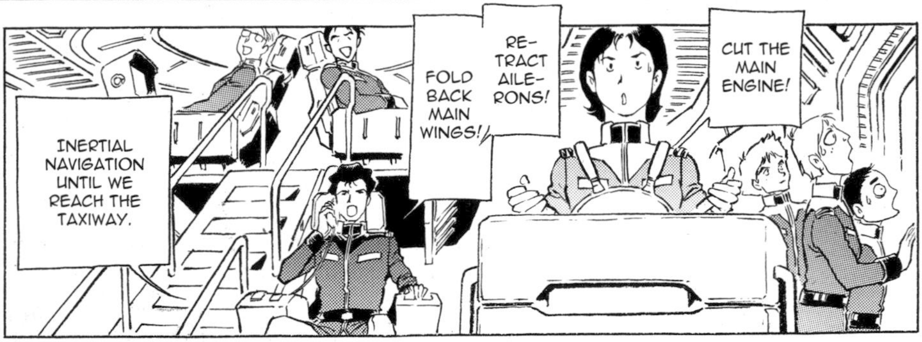
CUT THE MAIN ENGINE!
RE-TRACT AILE-RONS!
FOLD BACK MAIN WINGS!
INERTIAL NAVIGATION UNTIL WE REACH THE TAXIWAY.

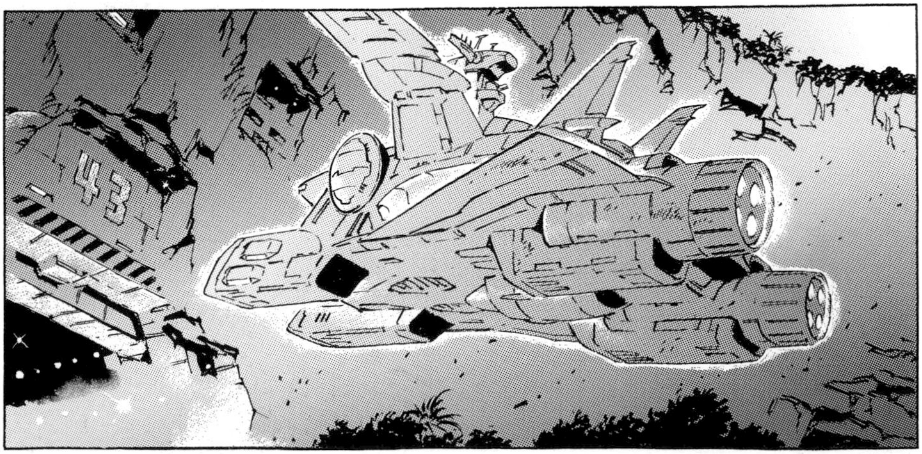

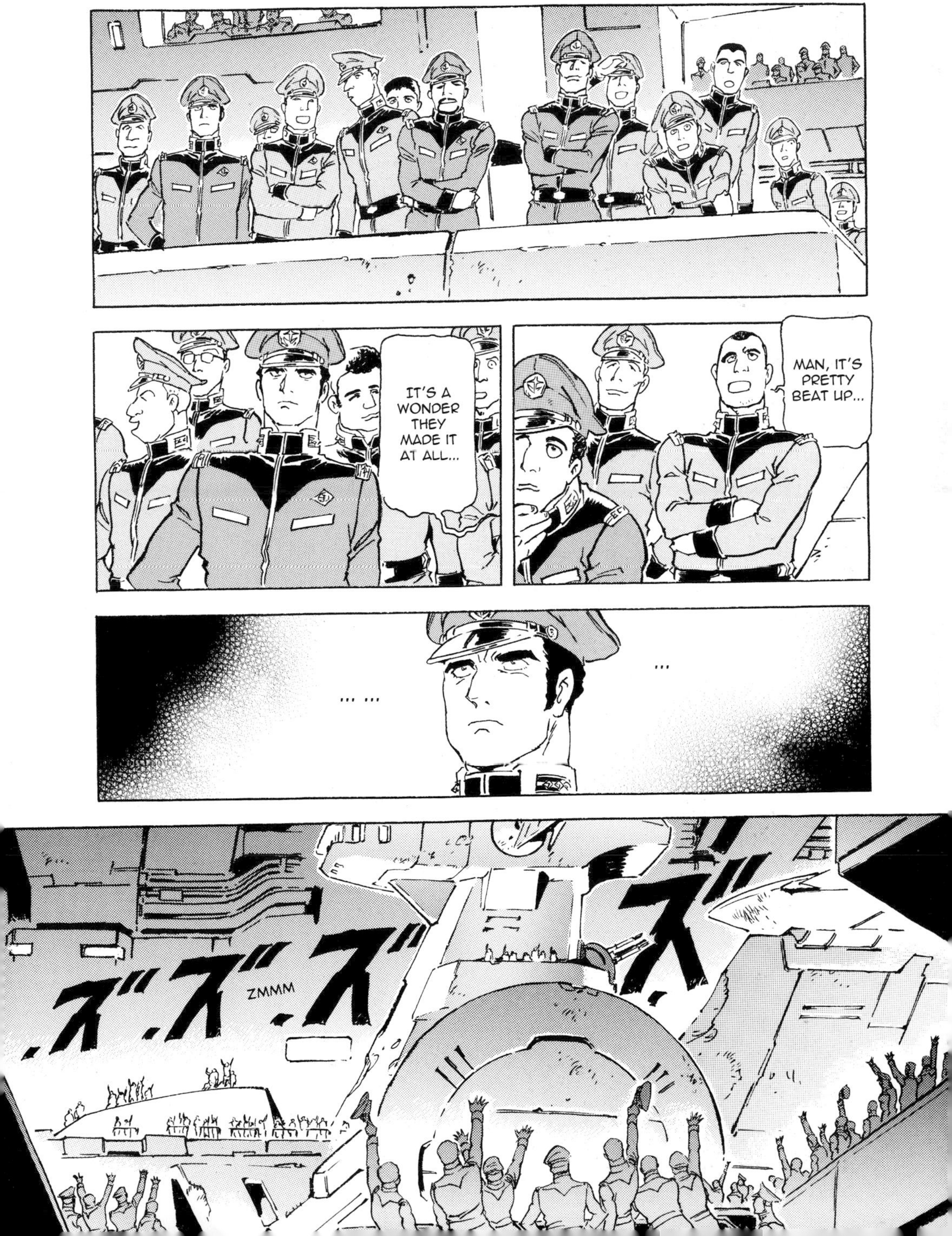
MAN, IT'S PRETTY BEAT UP...
IT'S A WONDER THEY MADE IT AT ALL...
...
... ...
ZMMM

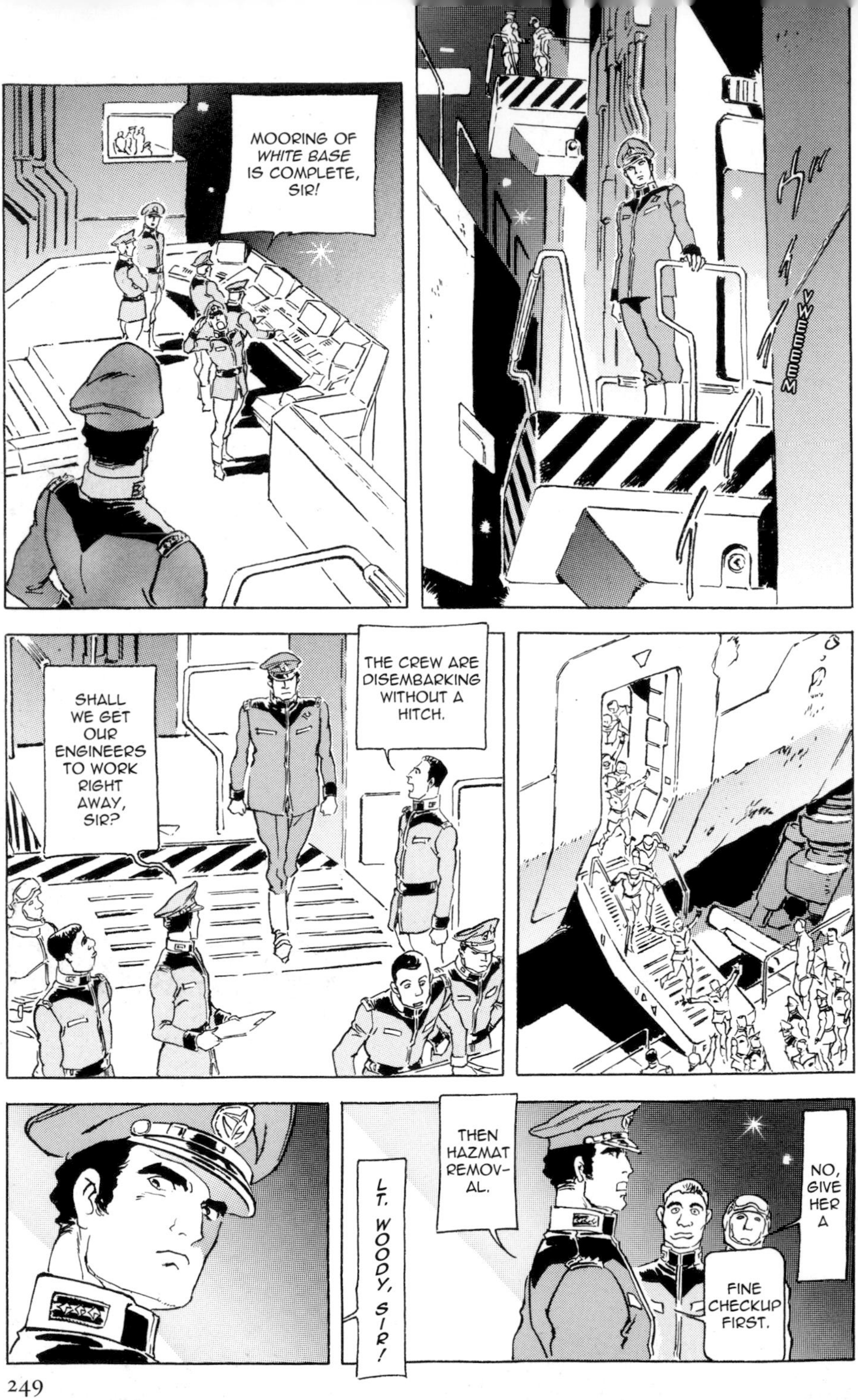
VWEEEEMM
MOORING OF WHITE BASE IS COMPLETE, SIR!
THE CREW ARE DISEMBARKING WITHOUT A HITCH.
SHALL WE GET OUR ENGINEERS TO WORK RIGHT AWAY, SIR?
NO, GIVE HER A
FINE CHECKUP FIRST.
THEN HAZMAT REMOV-AL.
LT. WOODY, SIR!

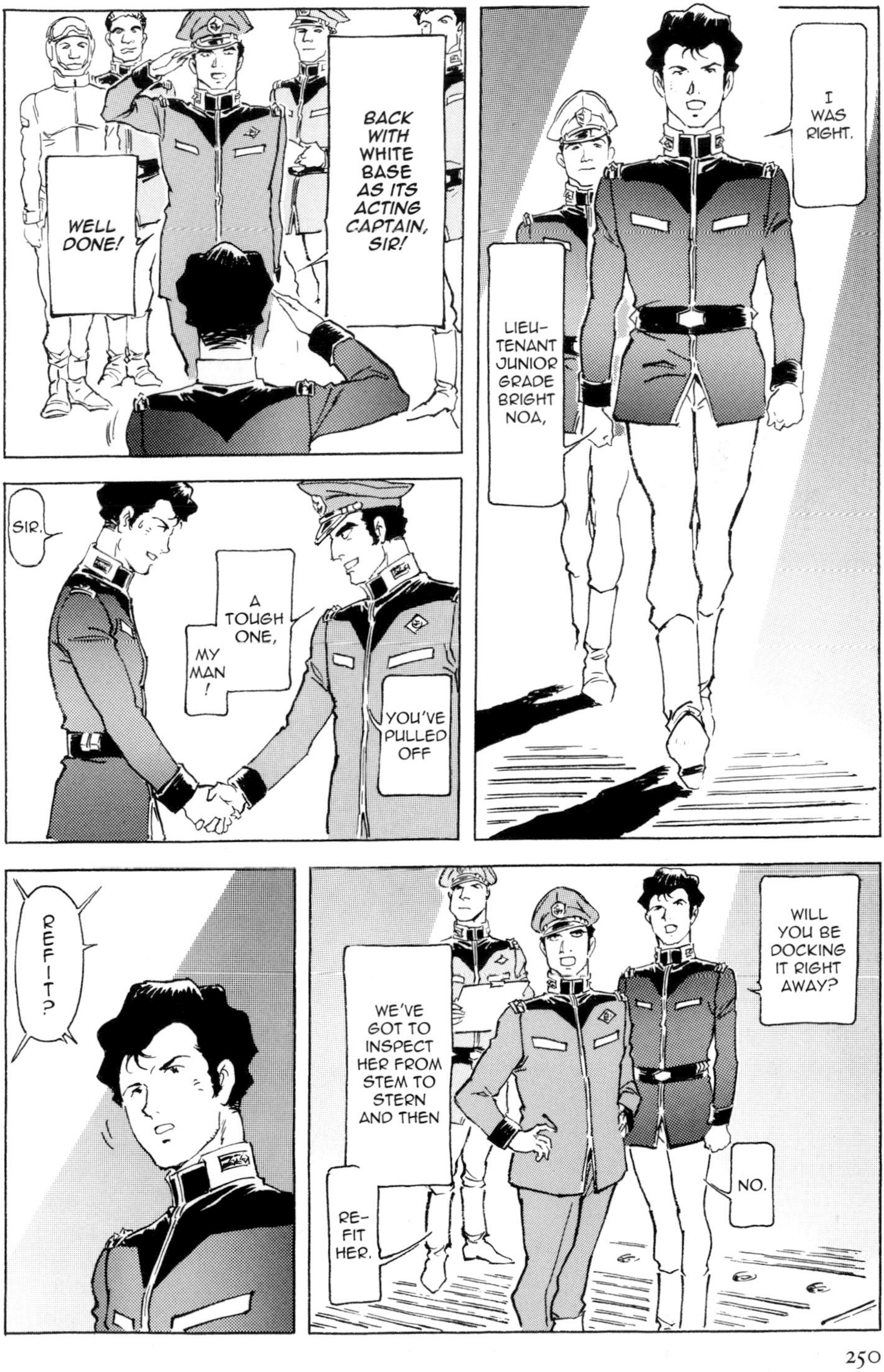
I WAS RIGHT.
LIEU-TENANT JUNIOR GRADE BRIGHT NOA,
BACK WITH WHITE BASE AS ITS ACTING CAPTAIN, SIR!
WELL DONE!
YOU'VE PULLED OFF
A TOUGH ONE,
MY MAN!
SIR.
WILL YOU BE DOCKING IT RIGHT AWAY?
NO.
WE'VE GOT TO INSPECT HER FROM STEM TO STERN AND THEN
RE-FIT HER.
REFIT?

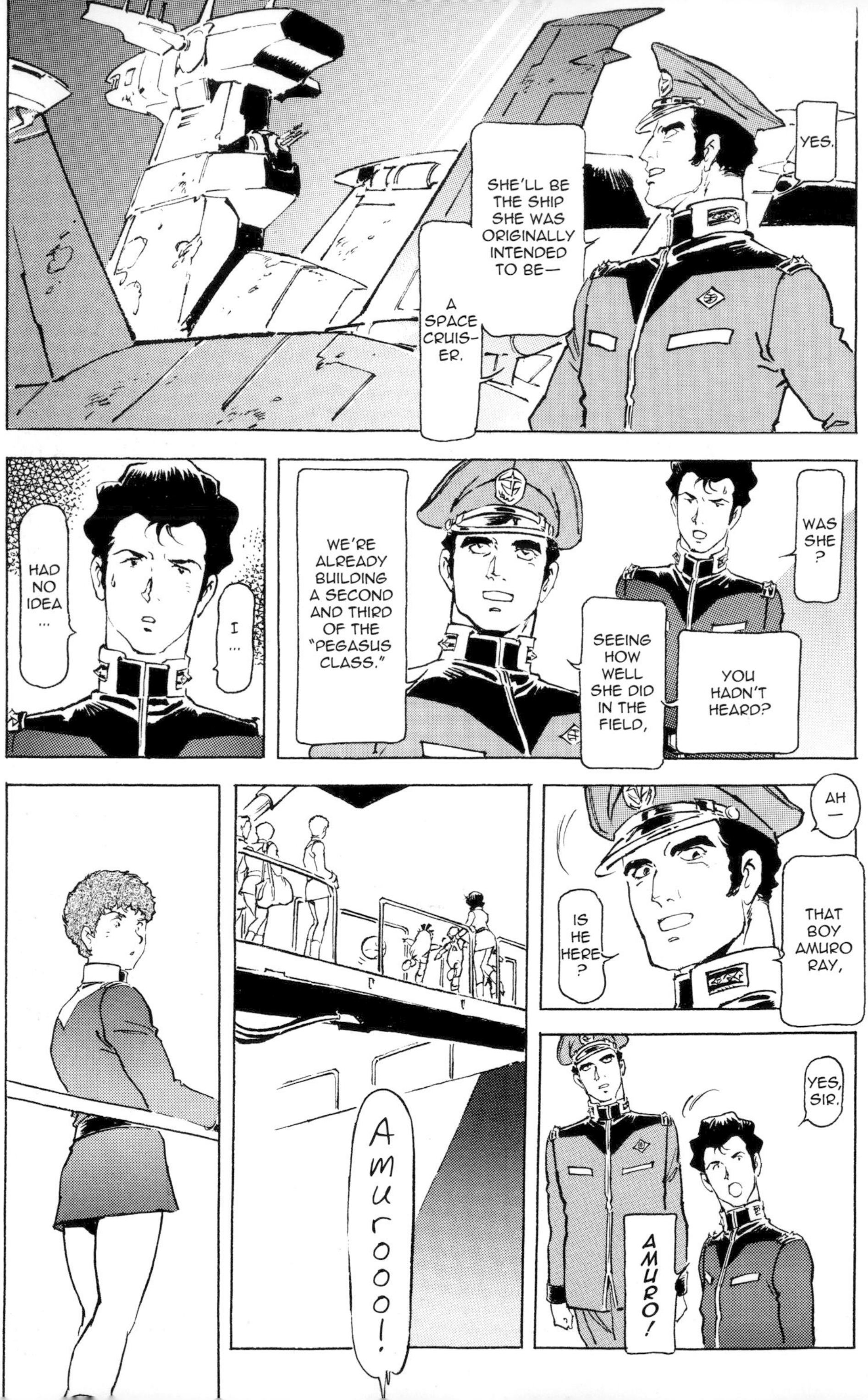
YES.
SHE'LL BE THE SHIP SHE WAS ORIGINALLY INTENDED TO BE—
A SPACE CRUIS-ER.
WAS SHE?
YOU HADN'T HEARD?
SEEING HOW WELL SHE DID IN THE FIELD,
WE'RE ALREADY BUILDING A SECOND AND THIRD OF THE "PEGASUS CLASS."
I ...
HAD NO IDEA ...
AH—
THAT BOY AMURO RAY,
IS HE HERE?
YES, SIR.
AMURO!
AMUROOO!

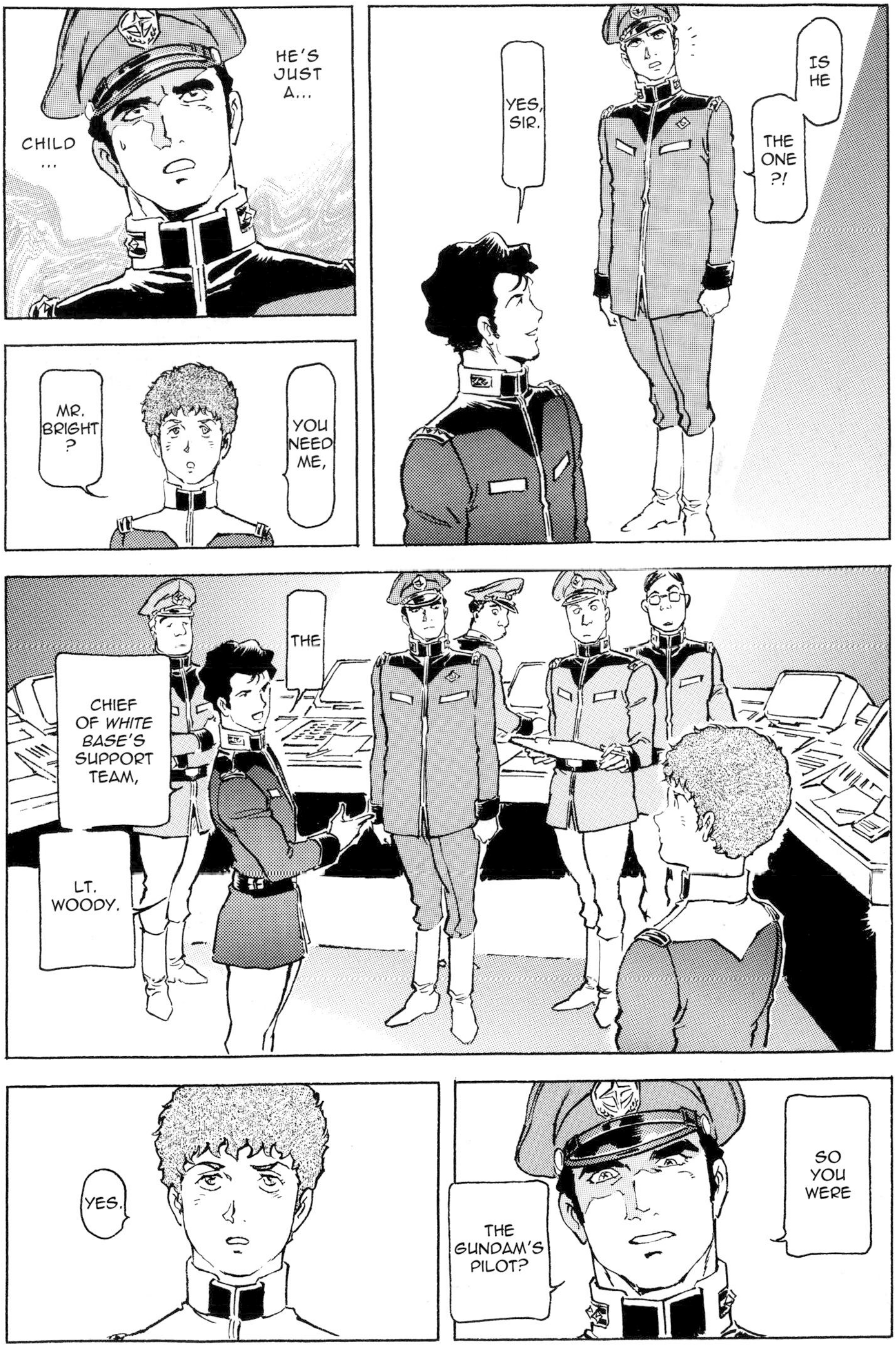
IS HE THE ONE ?!
YES, SIR.
HE'S JUST A...
CHILD ...
YOU NEED ME,
MR. BRIGHT ?
THE
CHIEF OF WHITE BASE'S SUPPORT TEAM,
LT. WOODY.
SO YOU WERE
THE GUNDAM'S PILOT?
YES.

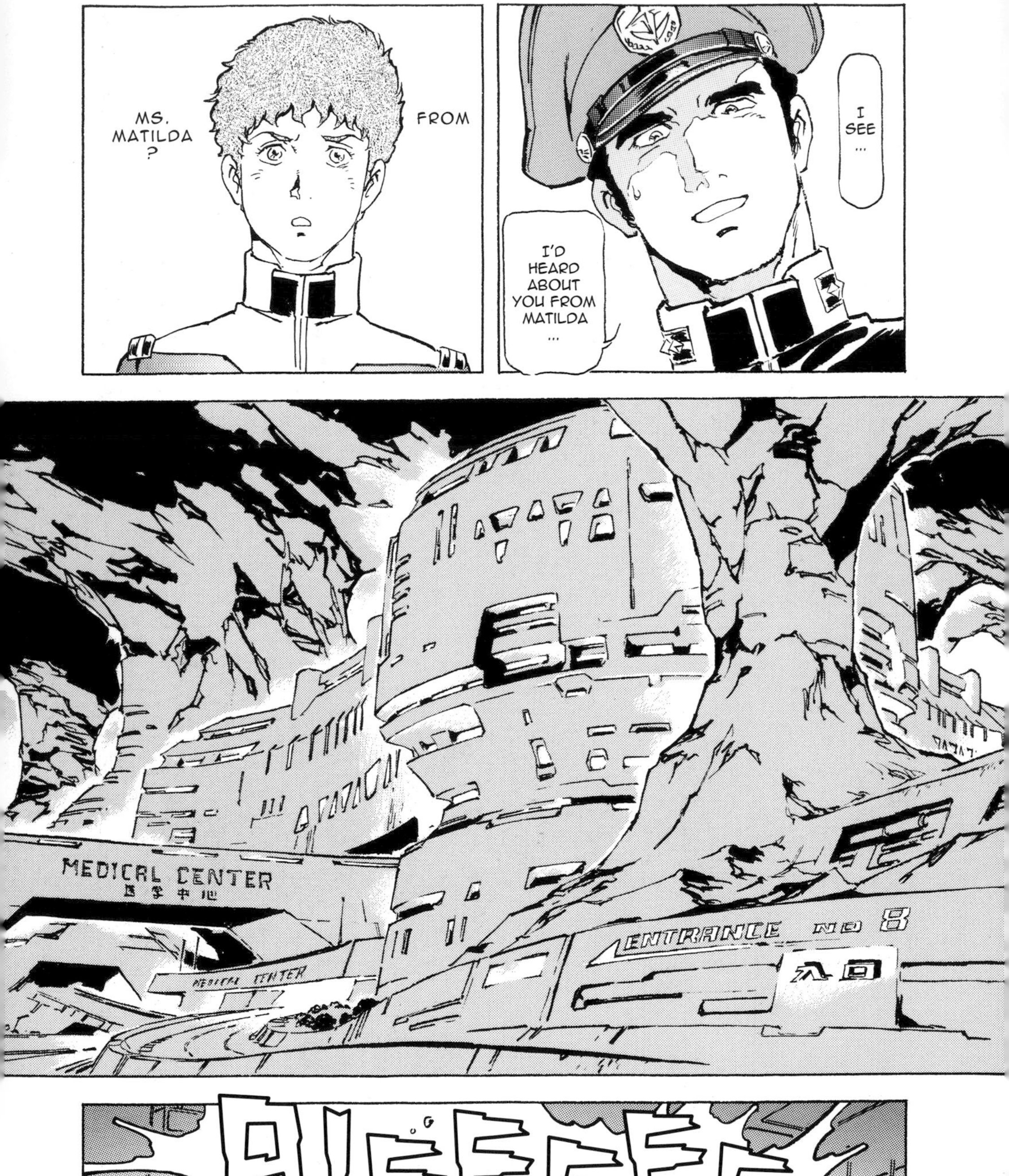
I SEE ...
I'D HEARD ABOUT YOU FROM MATILDA ...
FROM
MS. MATILDA ?
MEDICAL CENTER
医学中心
MEDICAL CENTER
ENTRANCE NO 8
入口
AIEEEEE

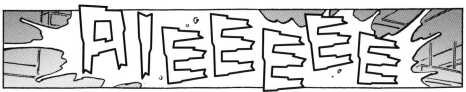

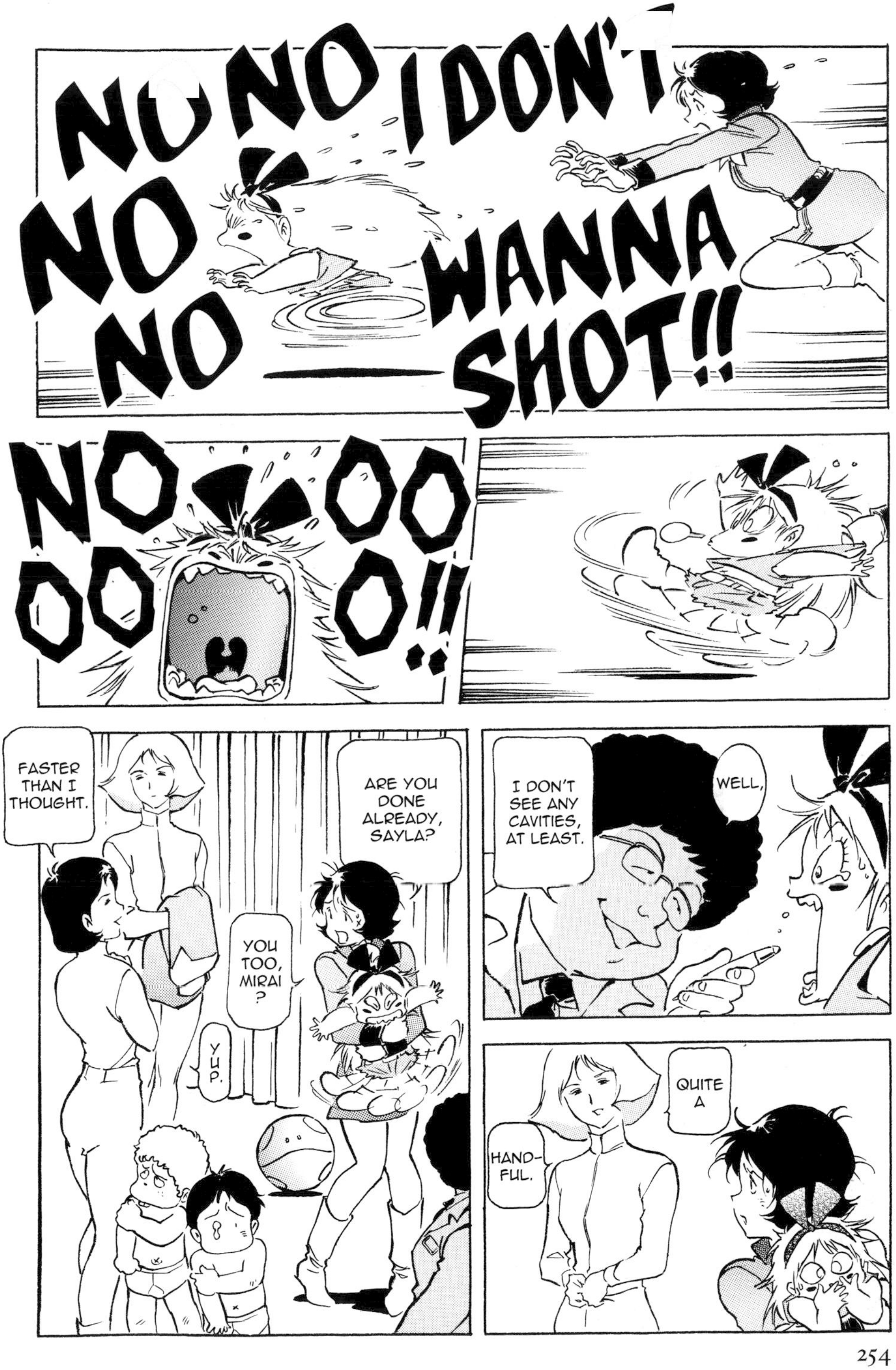
NO NO I DON'T
NO
NO WANNA SHOT!!
NOOOOOOOOO!!
WELL,
I DON'T SEE ANY CAVITIES, AT LEAST.
QUITE A
HAND-FUL.
ARE YOU DONE ALREADY, SAYLA?
FASTER THAN I THOUGHT.
YOU TOO, MIRAI?
YUP.

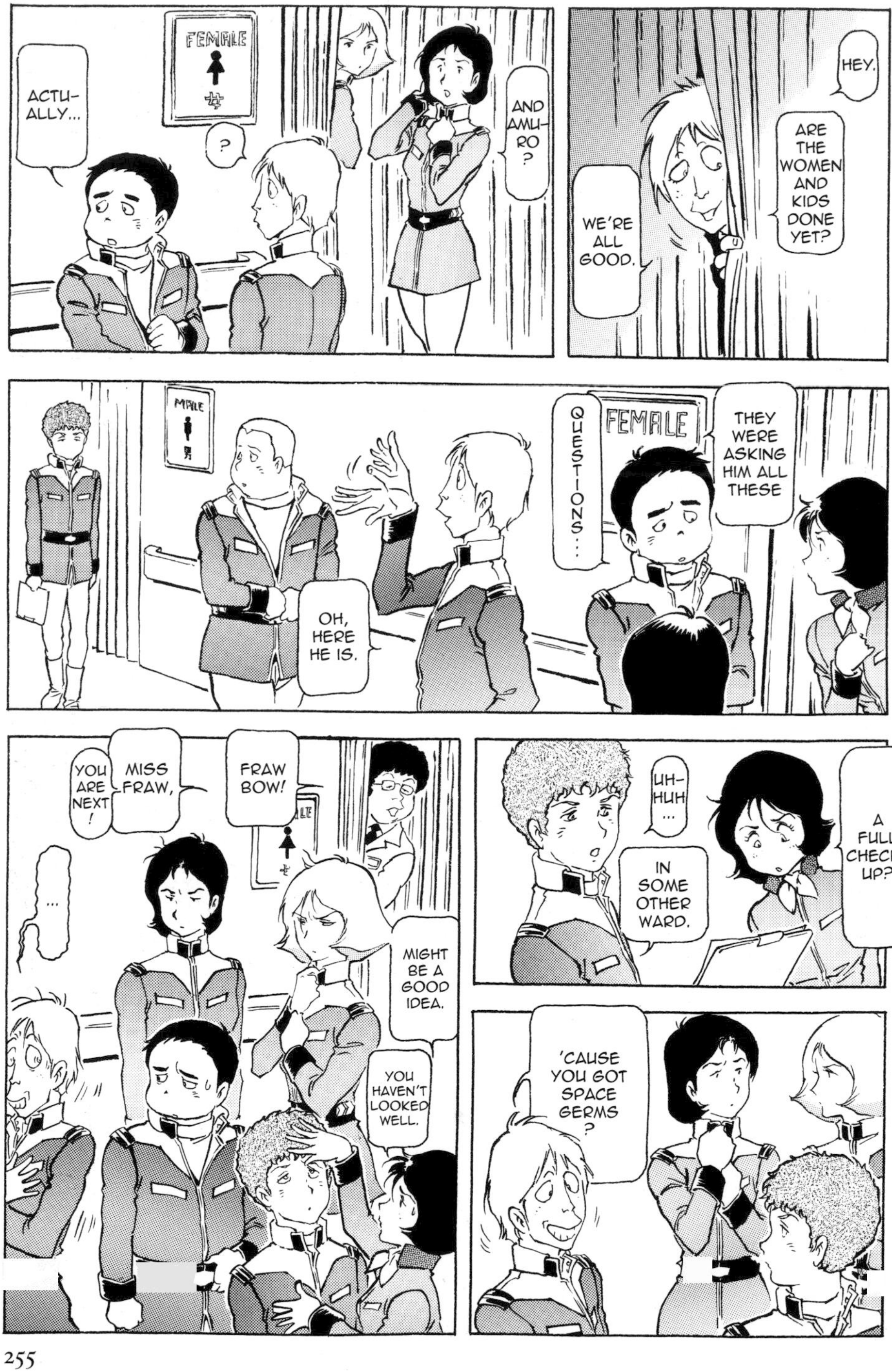
HEY.
ARE THE WOMEN AND KIDS DONE YET?
WE'RE ALL GOOD.
FEMALE
AND AMURO?
?
ACTU-ALLY...
FEMALE
THEY WERE ASKING HIM ALL THESE
QUESTIONS...
MALE
OH, HERE HE IS.
A FULL CHECK-UP?
UH-HUH...
IN SOME OTHER WARD.
'CAUSE YOU GOT SPACE GERMS?
FRAW BOW!
MISS FRAW,
YOU ARE NEXT!
MIGHT BE A GOOD IDEA.
...
YOU HAVEN'T LOOKED WELL.

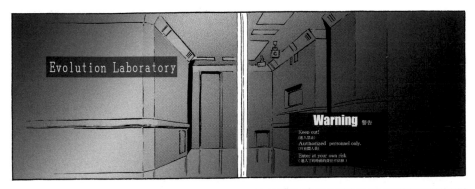

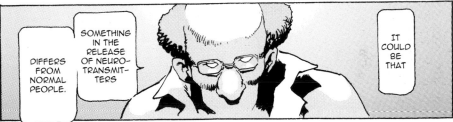

Warning 警告
Keep out!
Authorized personnel only.
Enter at your own risk
Evolution Laboratory
IT COULD BE THAT
SOMETHING IN THE RELEASE OF NEURO-TRANSMITTERS
DIFFERS FROM NORMAL PEOPLE.
LIKE ACE-TYL-CHO-LINE AND
DOPAMINE?
ANY DIFFERENCE IN THE SPEED OF THE ACTION POTENTIAL?
THAT OUGHT TO BE STEADY
THOUGH WE WON'T KNOW UNTIL WE LOOK...
WELL, THE BEST WAY TO FIND OUT WOULD BE TO USE
A BRAIN-MACHINE INTERFACE TO CONVERT HIS THOUGHTS INTO ACTUAL MOTION.
YEAH, RIGHT.
THAT'LL GO OVER WELL.
TAKING THE HERO OF *WHITE BASE* AND PUTTING A CHIP IN HIS HEAD!

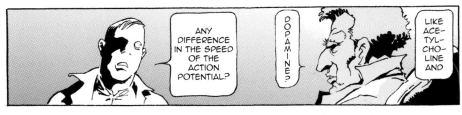

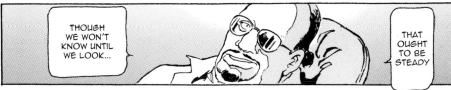

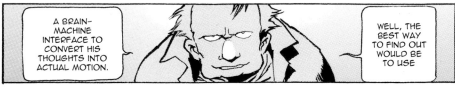

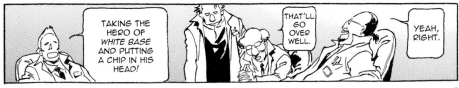

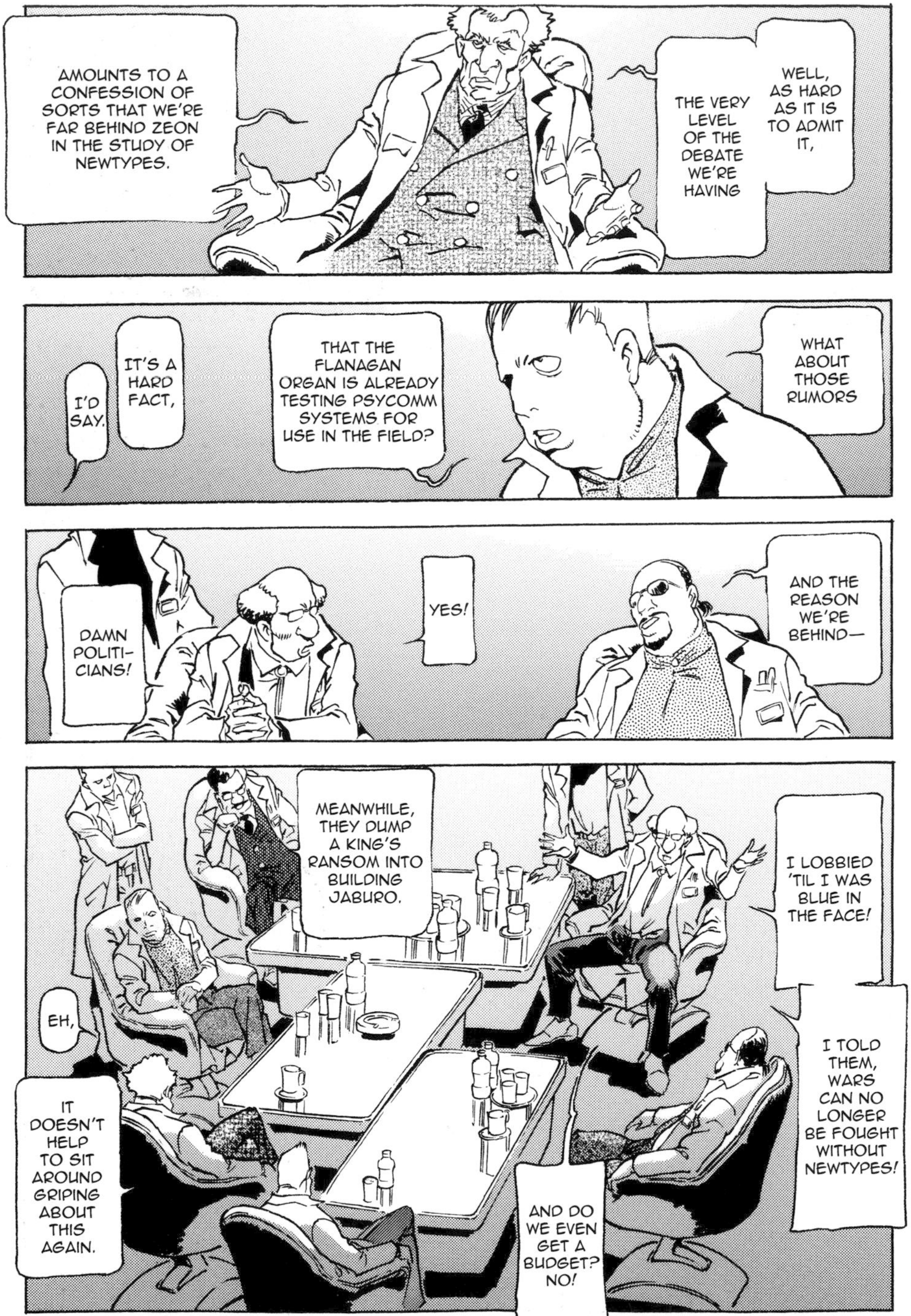
WELL, AS HARD AS IT IS TO ADMIT IT,
THE VERY LEVEL OF THE DEBATE WE'RE HAVING
AMOUNTS TO A CONFESSION OF SORTS THAT WE'RE FAR BEHIND ZEON IN THE STUDY OF NEWTYPES.
WHAT ABOUT THOSE RUMORS
THAT THE FLANAGAN ORGAN IS ALREADY TESTING PSYCOMM SYSTEMS FOR USE IN THE FIELD?
IT'S A HARD FACT,
I'D SAY.
AND THE REASON WE'RE BEHIND—
YES!
DAMN POLITICIANS!
I LOBBIED 'TIL I WAS BLUE IN THE FACE!
MEANWHILE, THEY DUMP A KING'S RANSOM INTO BUILDING JABURO.
I TOLD THEM, WARS CAN NO LONGER BE FOUGHT WITHOUT NEWTYPES!
AND DO WE EVEN GET A BUDGET? NO!
EH,
IT DOESN'T HELP TO SIT AROUND GRIPING ABOUT THIS AGAIN.

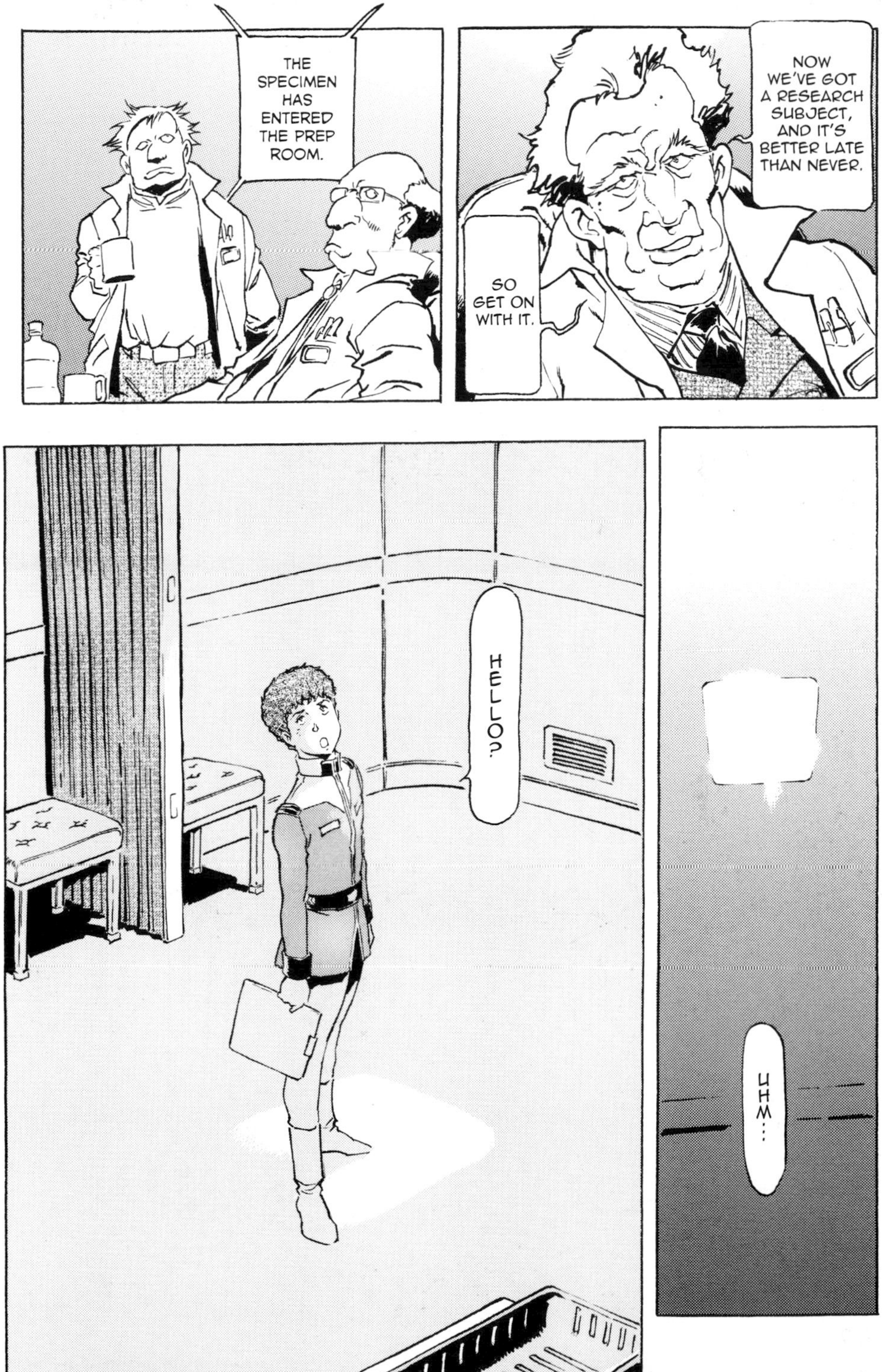
NOW WE'VE GOT A RESEARCH SUBJECT, AND IT'S BETTER LATE THAN NEVER.
SO GET ON WITH IT.
THE SPECIMEN HAS ENTERED THE PREP ROOM.
UHM...
HELLO?

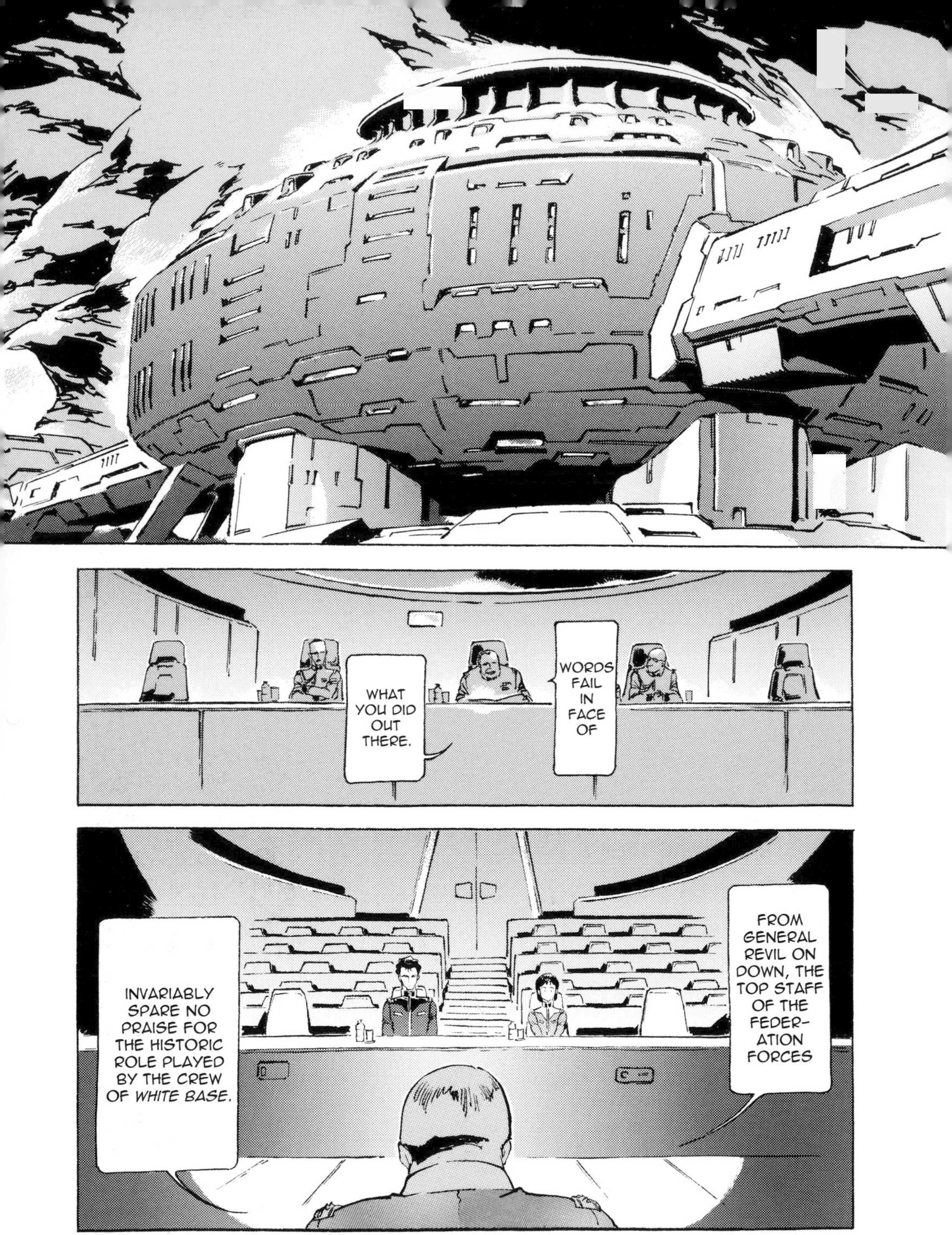
WORDS FAIL IN FACE OF
WHAT YOU DID OUT THERE.
FROM GENERAL REVIL ON DOWN, THE TOP STAFF OF THE FEDER-ATION FORCES
INVARIABLY SPARE NO PRAISE FOR THE HISTORIC ROLE PLAYED BY THE CREW OF *WHITE BASE*.

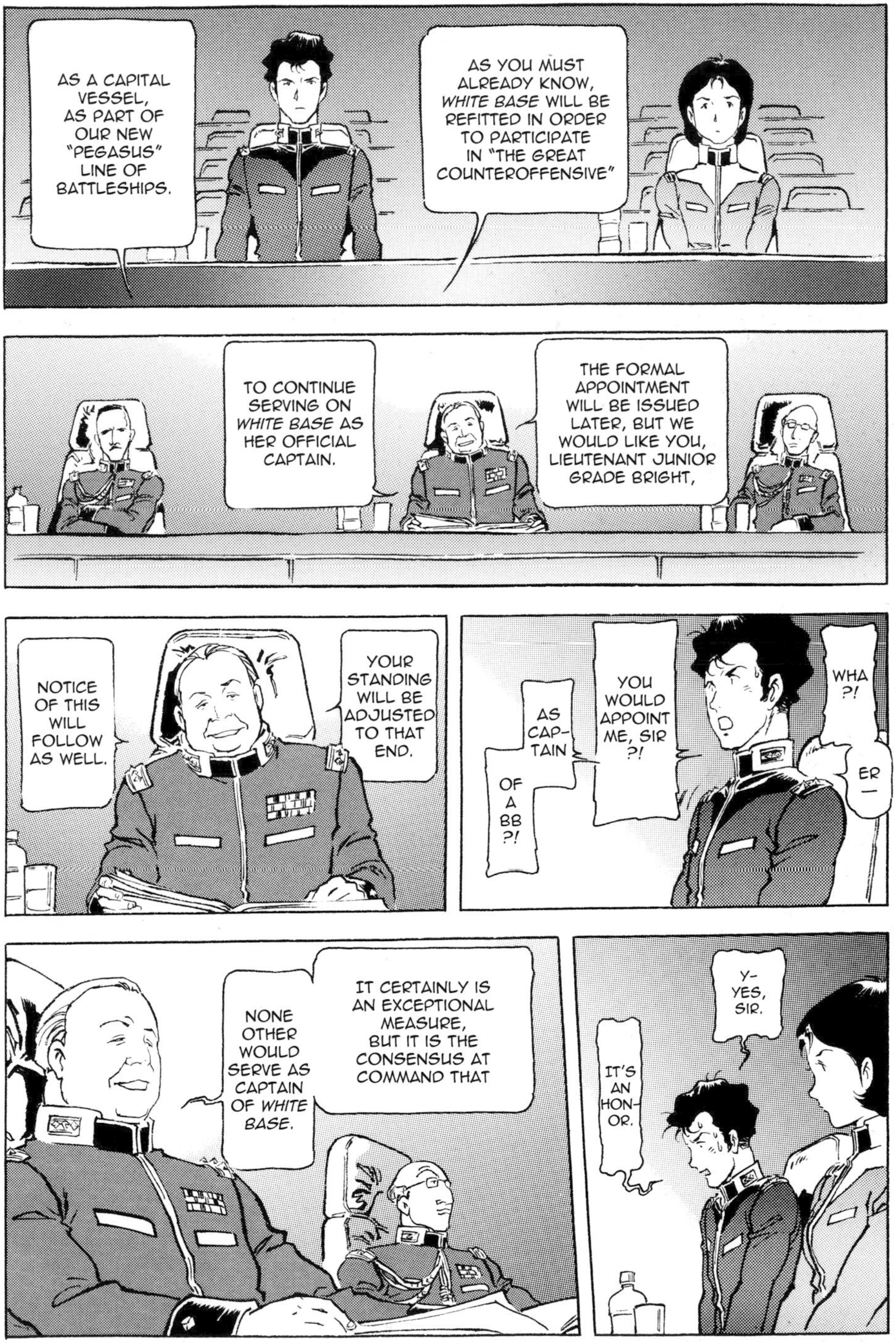
AS YOU MUST ALREADY KNOW, *WHITE BASE* WILL BE REFITTED IN ORDER TO PARTICIPATE IN "THE GREAT COUNTEROFFENSIVE"
AS A CAPITAL VESSEL, AS PART OF OUR NEW "PEGASUS" LINE OF BATTLESHIPS.
THE FORMAL APPOINTMENT WILL BE ISSUED LATER, BUT WE WOULD LIKE YOU, LIEUTENANT JUNIOR GRADE BRIGHT,
TO CONTINUE SERVING ON *WHITE BASE* AS HER OFFICIAL CAPTAIN.
WHA ?!
ER —
YOU WOULD APPOINT ME, SIR ?!
AS CAPTAIN
OF A BB ?!
YOUR STANDING WILL BE ADJUSTED TO THAT END.
NOTICE OF THIS WILL FOLLOW AS WELL.
Y- YES, SIR.
IT'S AN HONOR.
IT CERTAINLY IS AN EXCEPTIONAL MEASURE, BUT IT IS THE CONSENSUS AT COMMAND THAT
NONE OTHER WOULD SERVE AS CAPTAIN OF *WHITE BASE*.

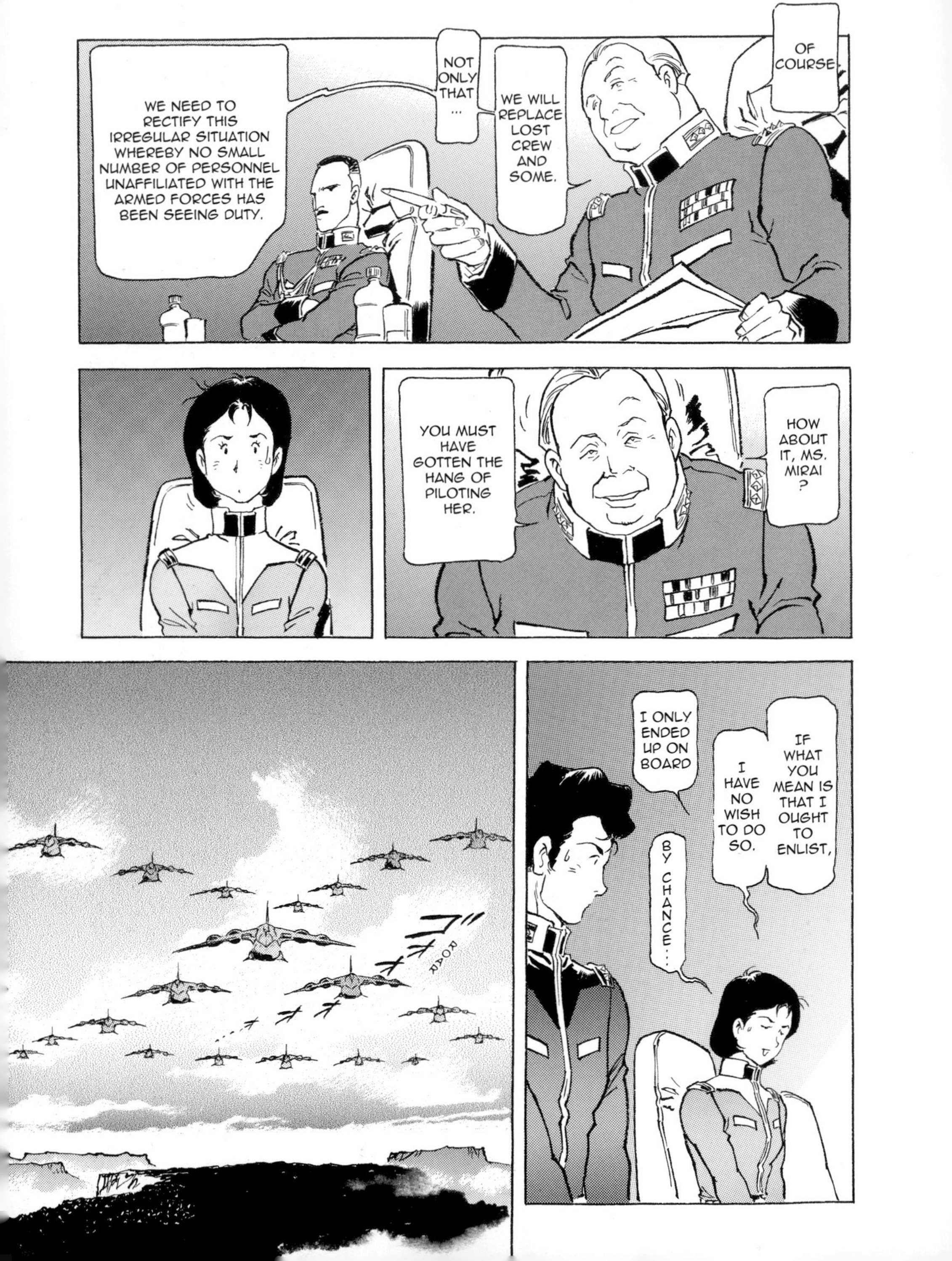
OF COURSE
WE WILL REPLACE LOST CREW AND SOME.
NOT ONLY THAT ...
WE NEED TO RECTIFY THIS IRREGULAR SITUATION WHEREBY NO SMALL NUMBER OF PERSONNEL UNAFFILIATED WITH THE ARMED FORCES HAS BEEN SEEING DUTY.
HOW ABOUT IT, MS. MIRAI ?
YOU MUST HAVE GOTTEN THE HANG OF PILOTING HER.
IF WHAT YOU MEAN IS THAT I OUGHT TO ENLIST,
I HAVE NO WISH TO DO SO.
I ONLY ENDED UP ON BOARD
BY CHANCE...
ROAR

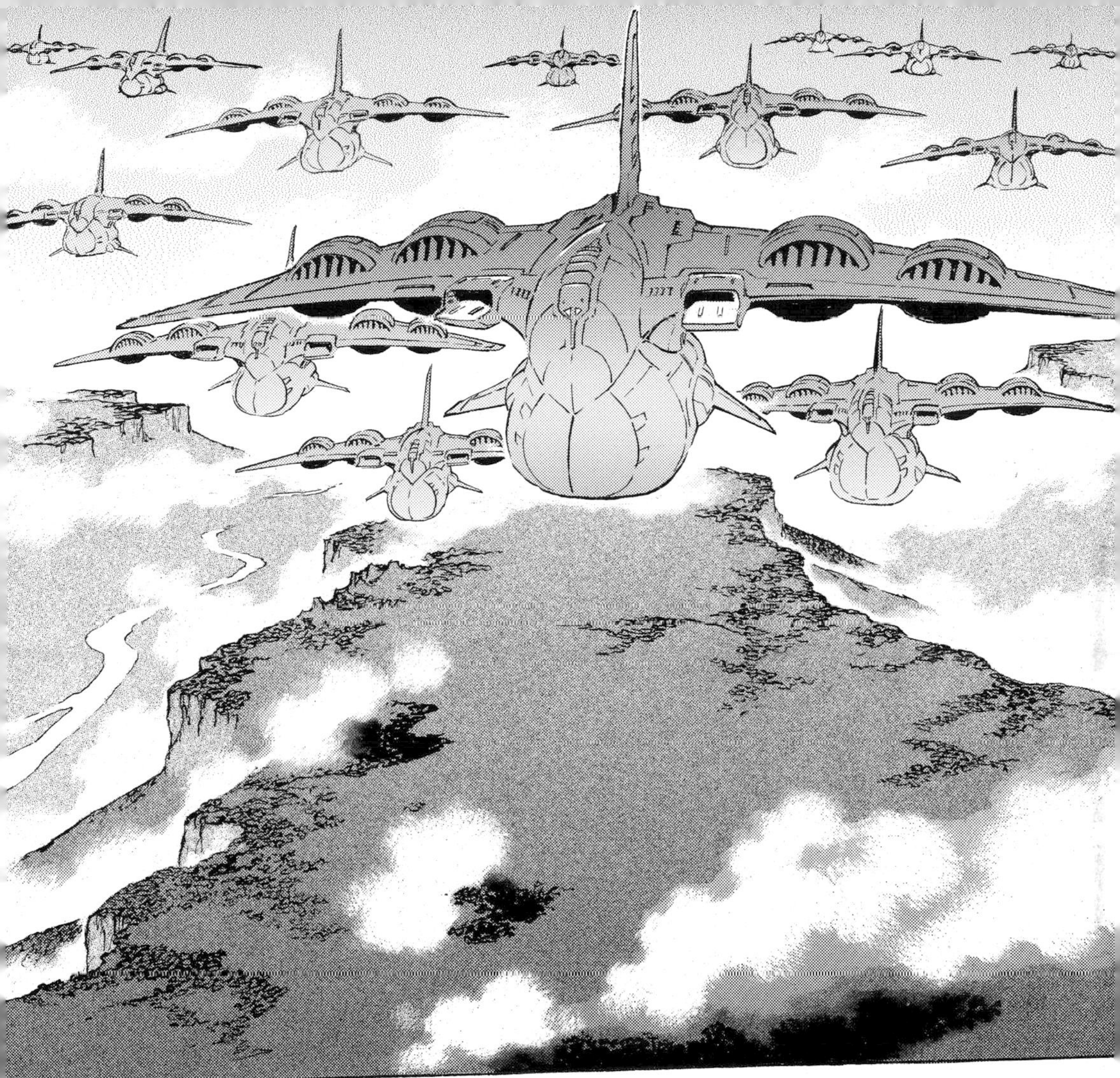

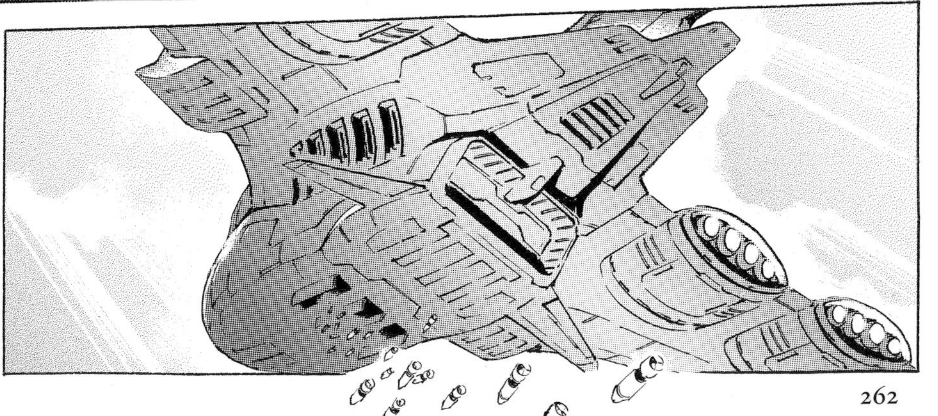

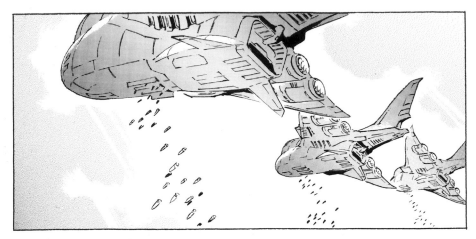

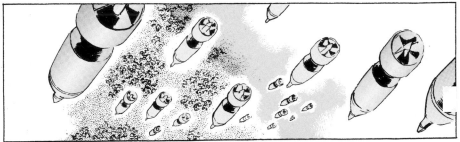

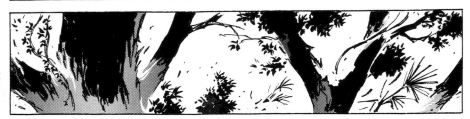

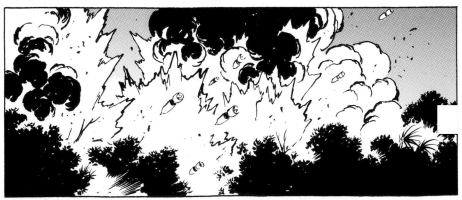

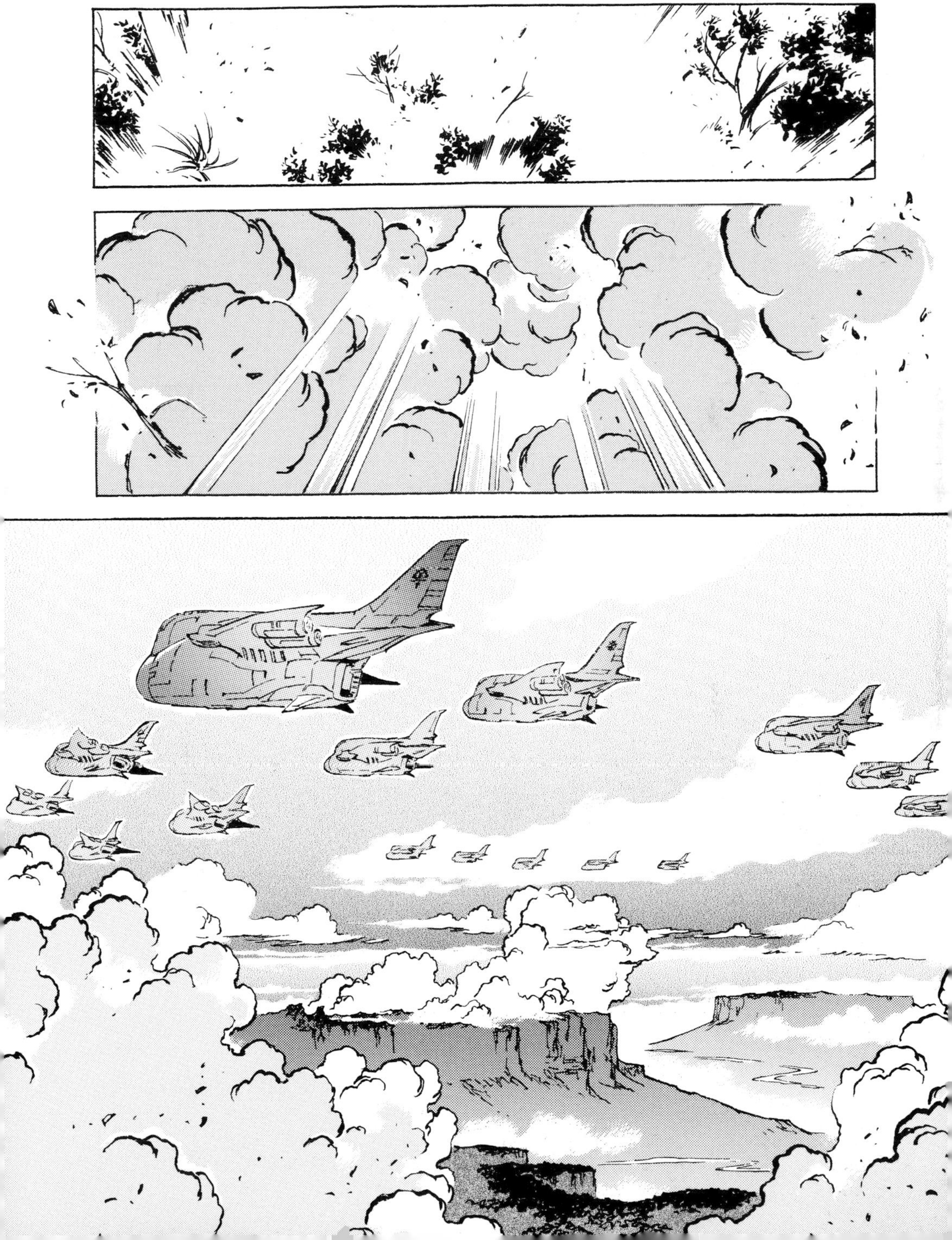

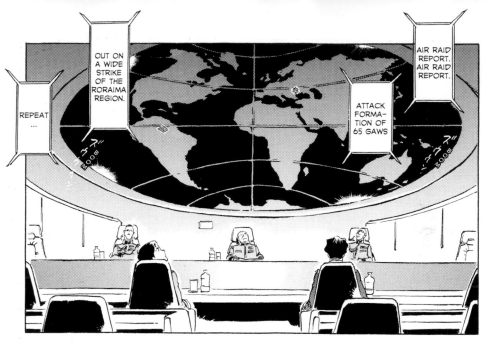

AIR RAID REPORT. AIR RAID REPORT.
ATTACK FORMATION OF 65 GAWS
BOOM
OUT ON A WIDE STRIKE OF THE RORAIMA REGION.
REPEAT...
BOOM
TODAY'S REGULAR FLIGHT IS RATHER... AMPLE.
BOOOOM
WELL...
MS. MIRAI,
IF I MAY...
YOUR LATE FATHER WOULD,
I'M SURE—
COULD WE
PLEASE LEAVE MY FATHER OUT OF THIS?

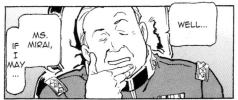

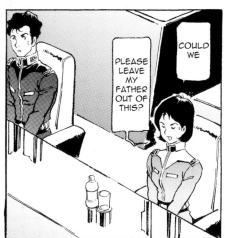

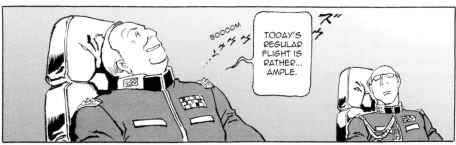

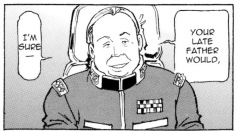

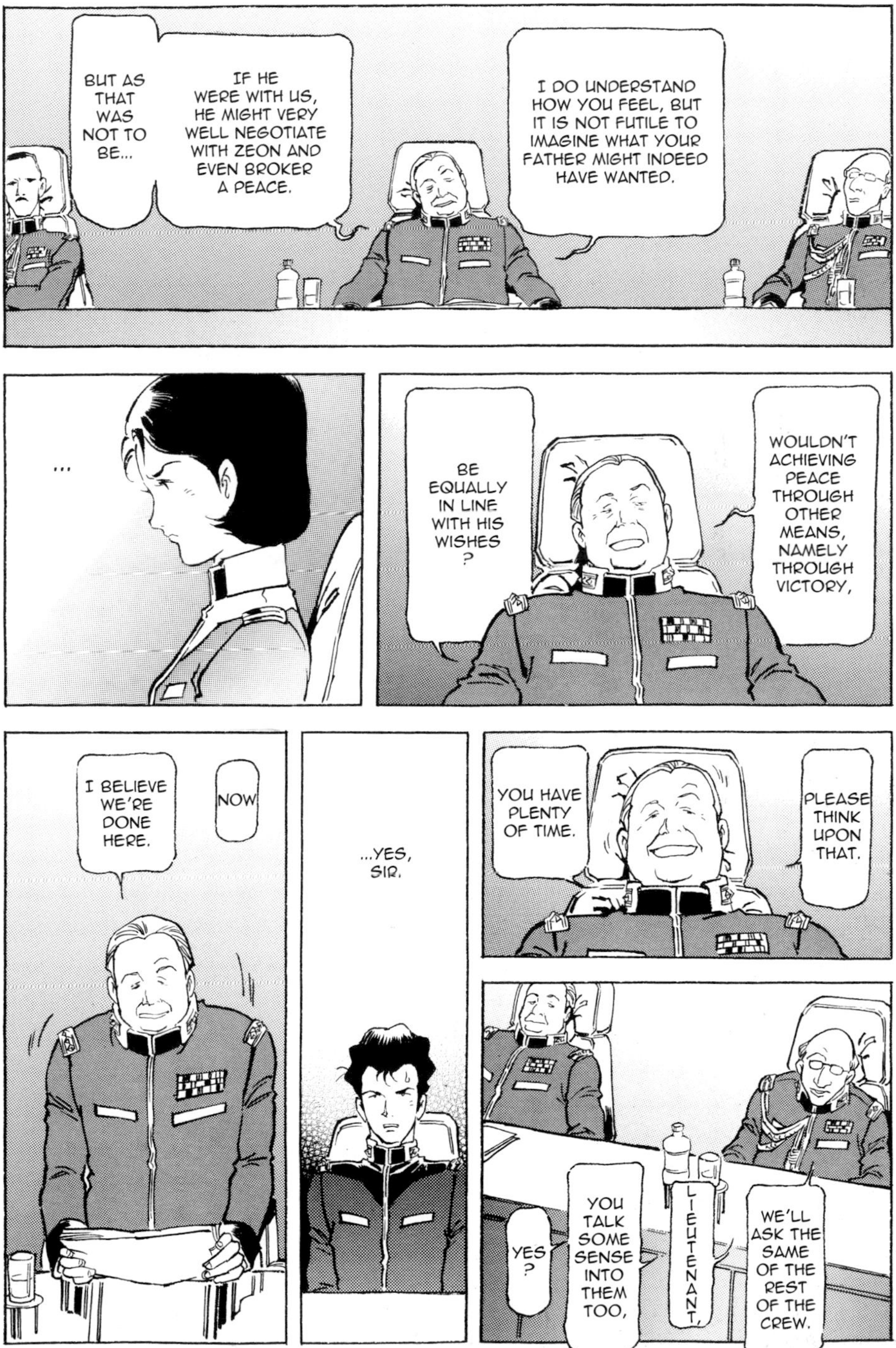

I DO UNDERSTAND HOW YOU FEEL, BUT IT IS NOT FUTILE TO IMAGINE WHAT YOUR FATHER MIGHT INDEED HAVE WANTED.
IF HE WERE WITH US, HE MIGHT VERY WELL NEGOTIATE WITH ZEON AND EVEN BROKER A PEACE.
BUT AS THAT WAS NOT TO BE...
WOULDN'T ACHIEVING PEACE THROUGH OTHER MEANS, NAMELY THROUGH VICTORY,
BE EQUALLY IN LINE WITH HIS WISHES?
...
PLEASE THINK UPON THAT.
YOU HAVE PLENTY OF TIME.
WE'LL ASK THE SAME OF THE REST OF THE CREW.
LIEUTENANT,
YOU TALK SOME SENSE INTO THEM TOO,
YES?
...YES, SIR.
NOW
I BELIEVE WE'RE DONE HERE.

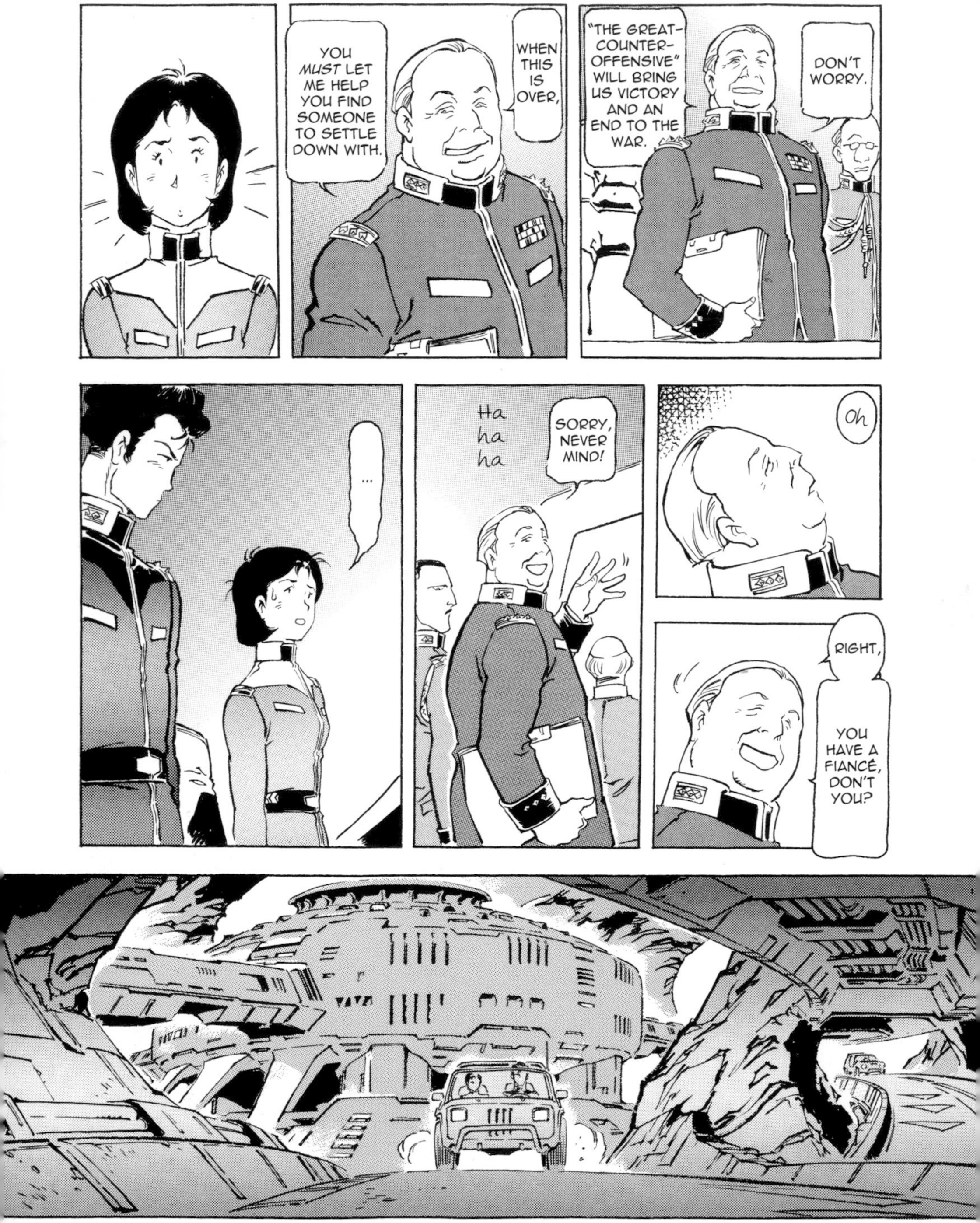
DON'T WORRY.
"THE GREAT-COUNTER-OFFENSIVE" WILL BRING US VICTORY AND AN END TO THE WAR.
WHEN THIS IS OVER,
YOU *MUST* LET ME HELP YOU FIND SOMEONE TO SETTLE DOWN WITH.
Oh
RIGHT,
YOU HAVE A FIANCÉ, DON'T YOU?
SORRY, NEVER MIND!
Ha ha ha
...

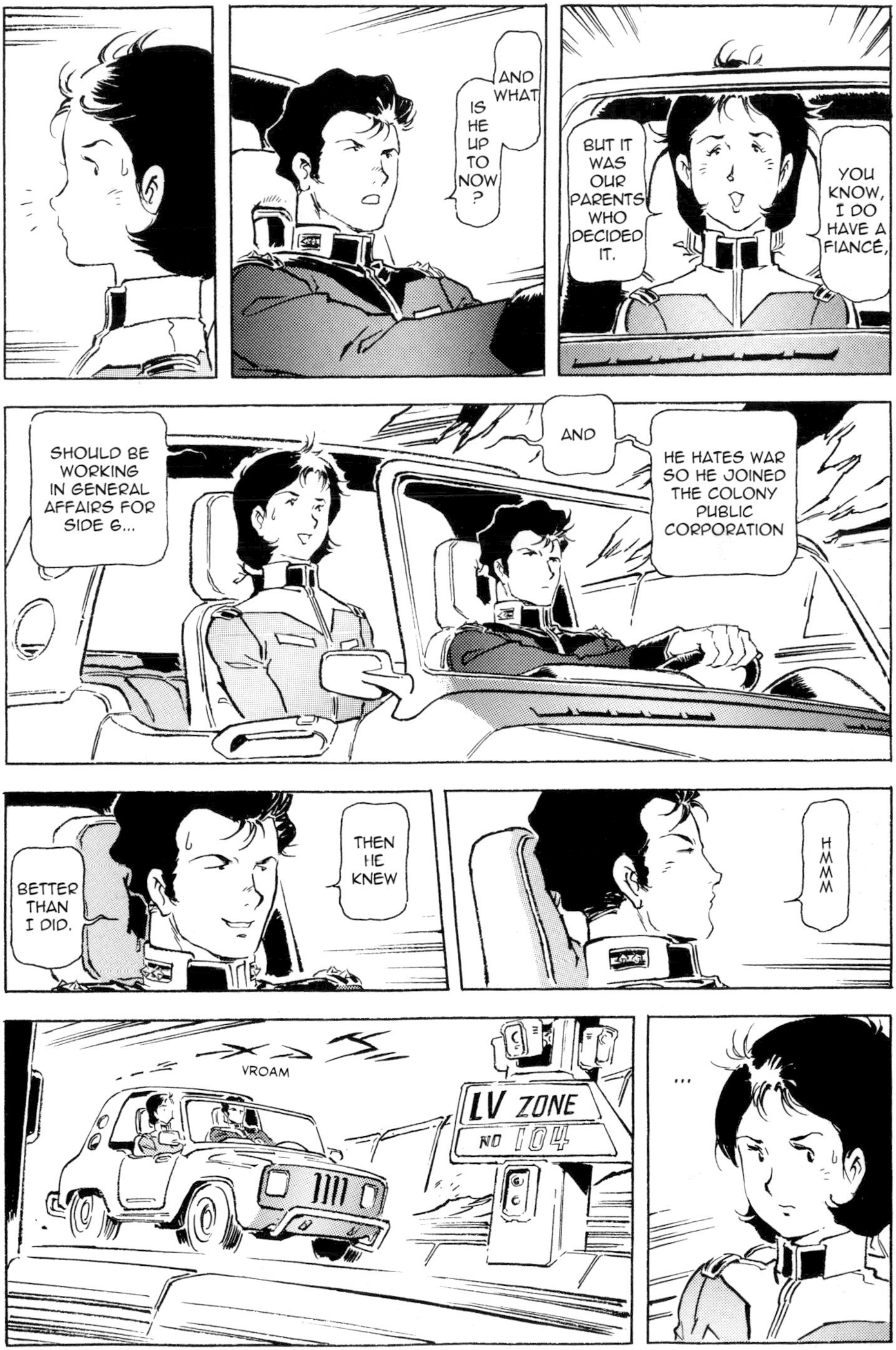
YOU KNOW, I DO HAVE A FIANCÉ,
BUT IT WAS OUR PARENTS WHO DECIDED IT.
AND WHAT IS HE UP TO NOW?
HE HATES WAR SO HE JOINED THE COLONY PUBLIC CORPORATION
AND
SHOULD BE WORKING IN GENERAL AFFAIRS FOR SIDE 6...
HMMM
THEN HE KNEW
BETTER THAN I DID.
...
VROAM
LV ZONE
NO 104

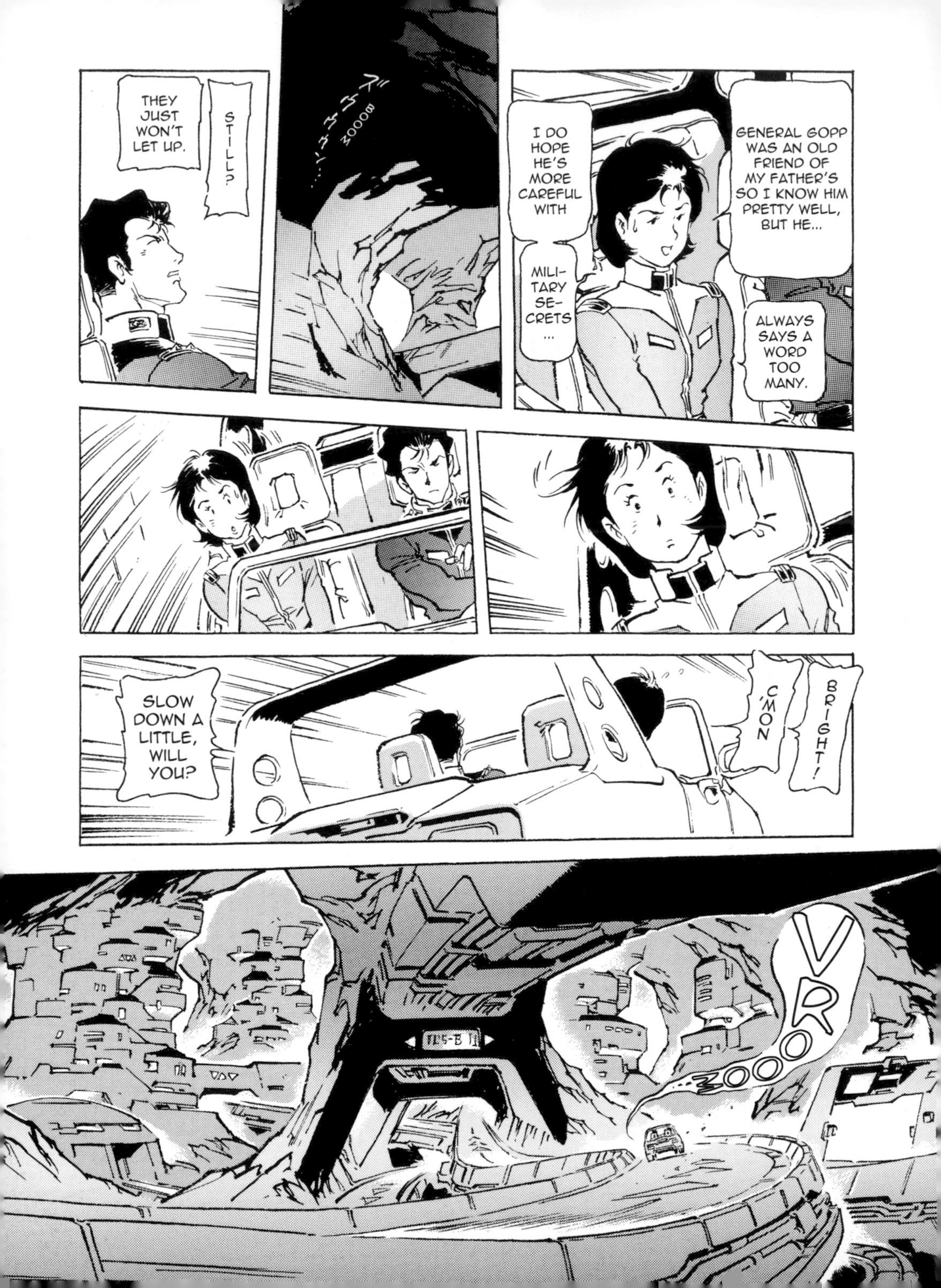
GENERAL GOPP WAS AN OLD FRIEND OF MY FATHER'S SO I KNOW HIM PRETTY WELL, BUT HE...
ALWAYS SAYS A WORD TOO MANY.
I DO HOPE HE'S MORE CAREFUL WITH
MILITARY SECRETS...
BOOOM
STILL?
THEY JUST WON'T LET UP.
BRIGHT!
C'MON
SLOW DOWN A LITTLE, WILL YOU?
VROOOOM

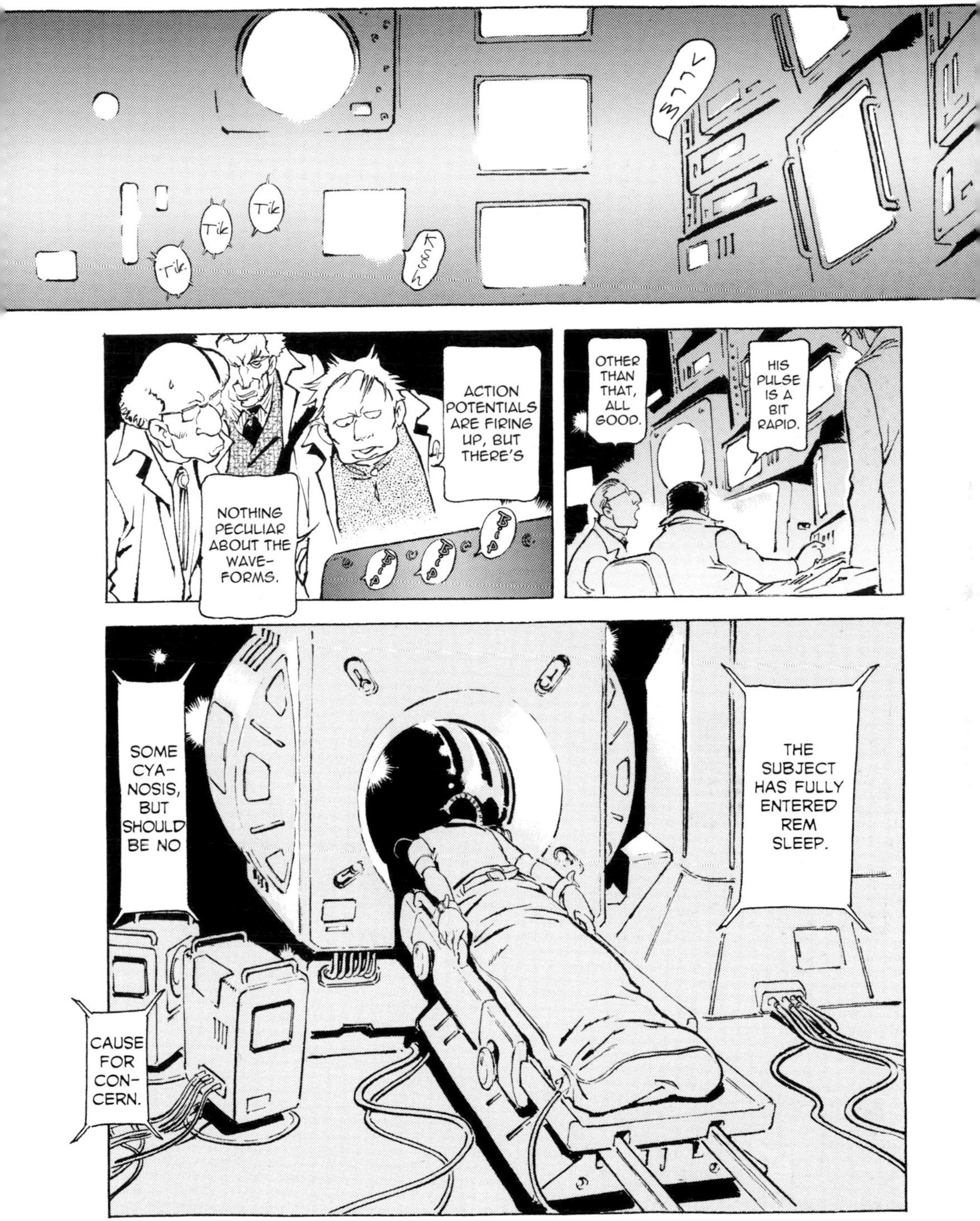
Kssh
Tik
Tik
Tik
HIS PULSE IS A BIT RAPID.
OTHER THAN THAT, ALL GOOD.
ACTION POTENTIALS ARE FIRING UP, BUT THERE'S
Beep
Beep
Beep
NOTHING PECULIAR ABOUT THE WAVE-FORMS.
THE SUBJECT HAS FULLY ENTERED REM SLEEP.
SOME CYA-NOSIS, BUT SHOULD BE NO
CAUSE FOR CON-CERN.

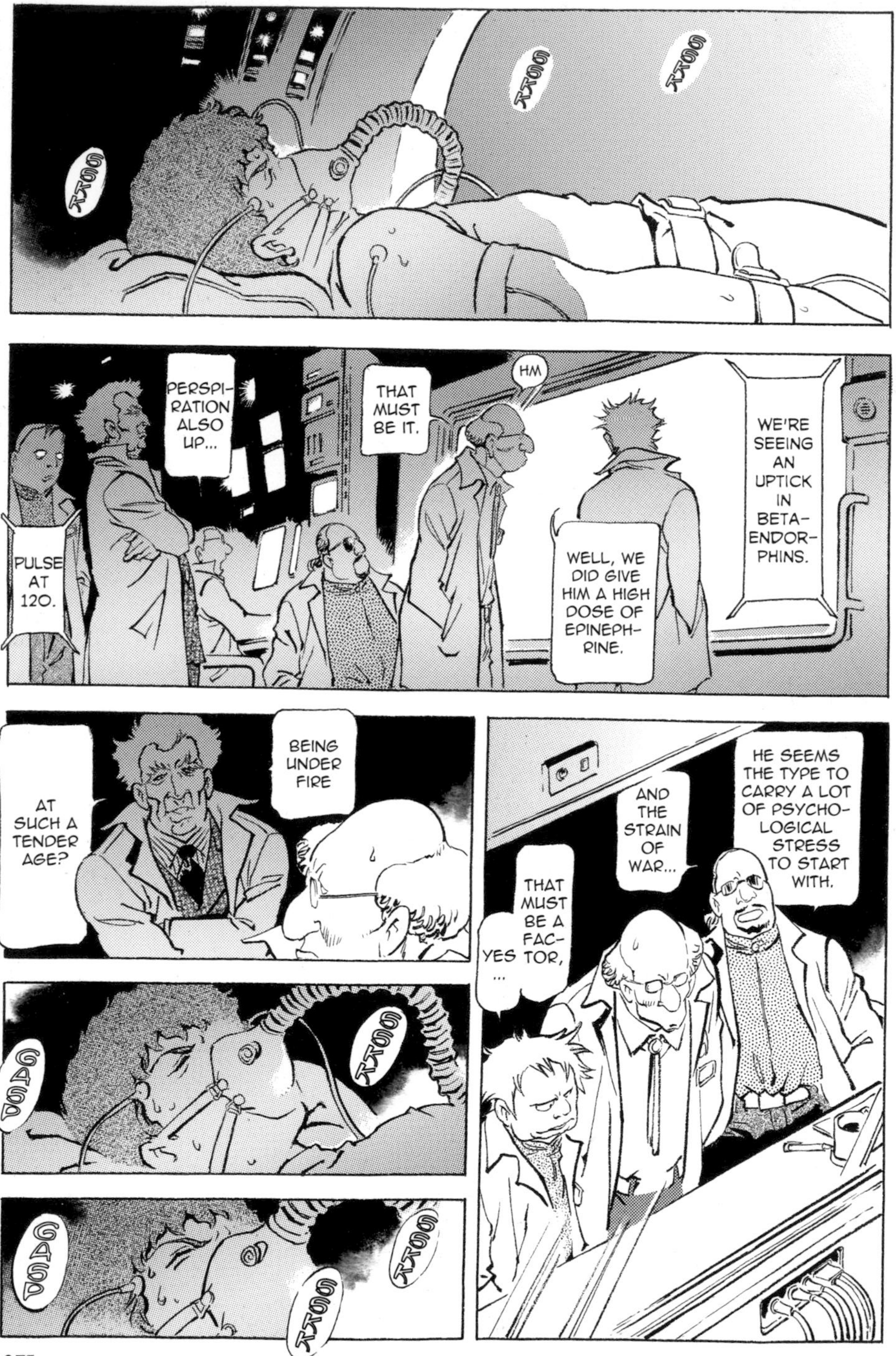
WE'RE SEEING AN UPTICK IN BETA-ENDORPHINS.
HM
WELL, WE DID GIVE HIM A HIGH DOSE OF EPINEPHRINE.
THAT MUST BE IT.
PERSPIRATION ALSO UP...
PULSE AT 120.
HE SEEMS THE TYPE TO CARRY A LOT OF PSYCHOLOGICAL STRESS TO START WITH.
AND THE STRAIN OF WAR...
THAT MUST BE A FACTOR,
YES...
BEING UNDER FIRE
AT SUCH A TENDER AGE?
GASP
GASP

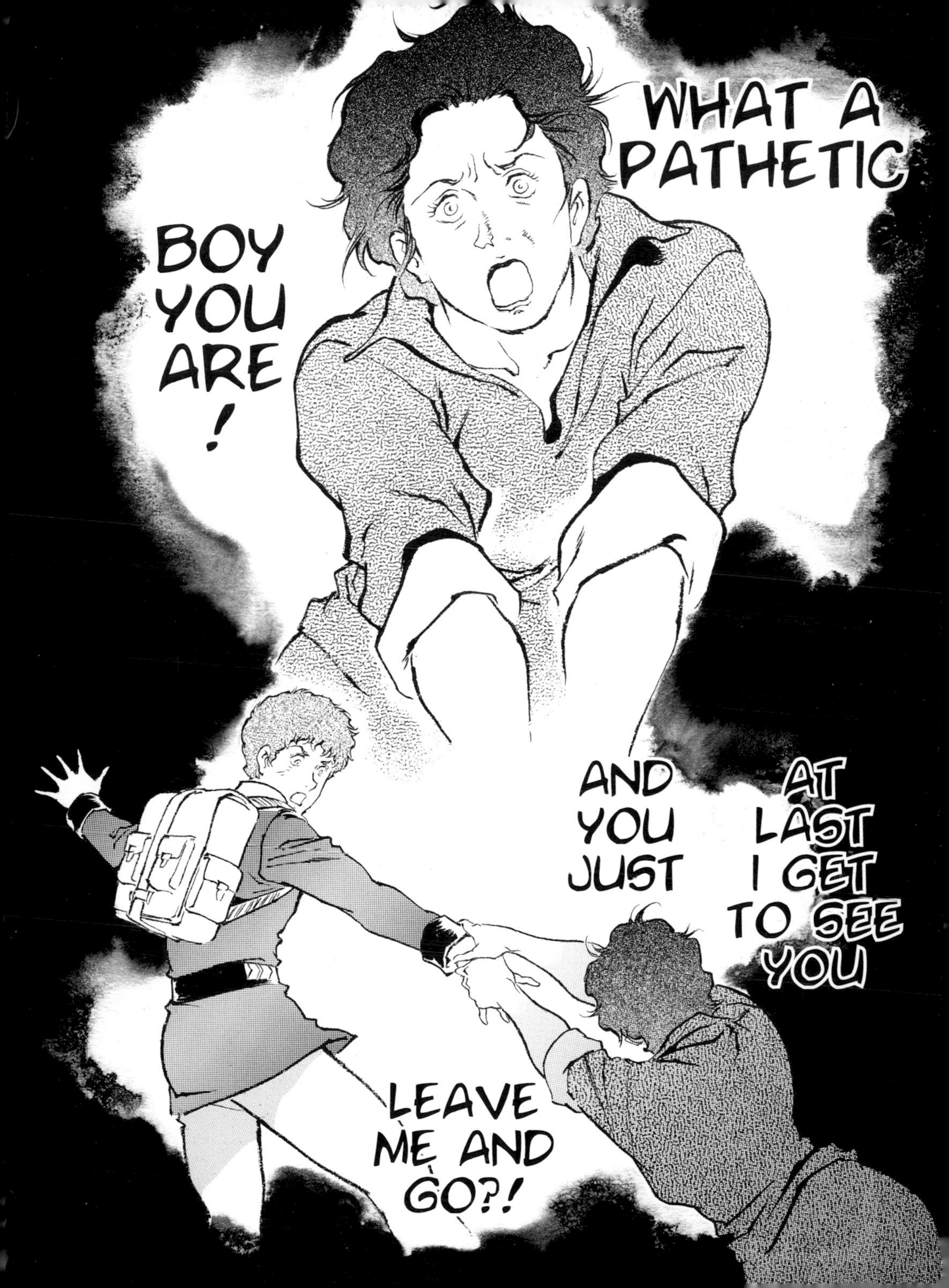
WHAT A PATHETIC
BOY YOU ARE!
AT LAST I GET TO SEE YOU
AND YOU JUST
LEAVE ME AND GO?!

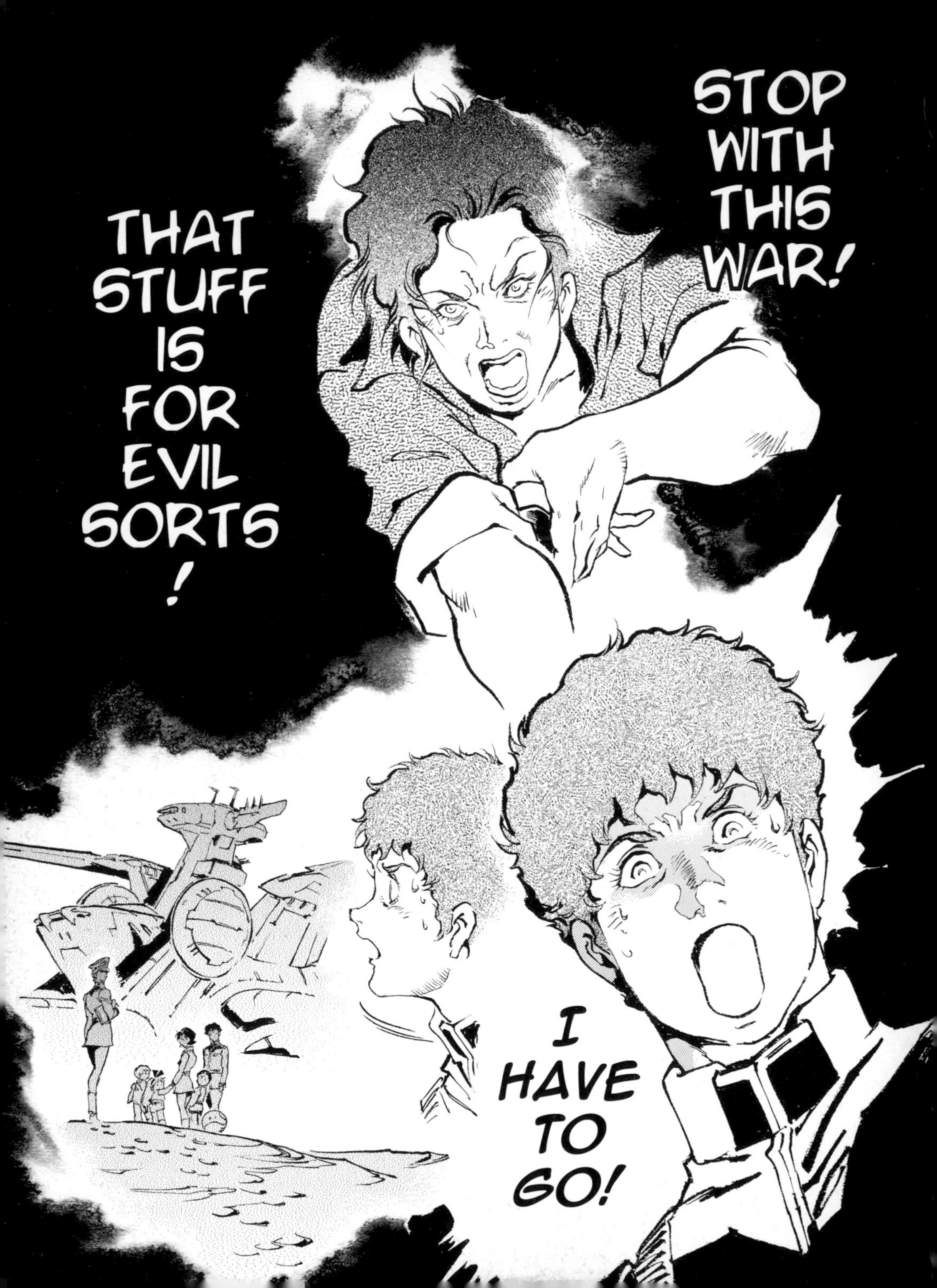
STOP WITH THIS WAR!
THAT STUFF IS FOR EVIL SORTS!
I HAVE TO GO!

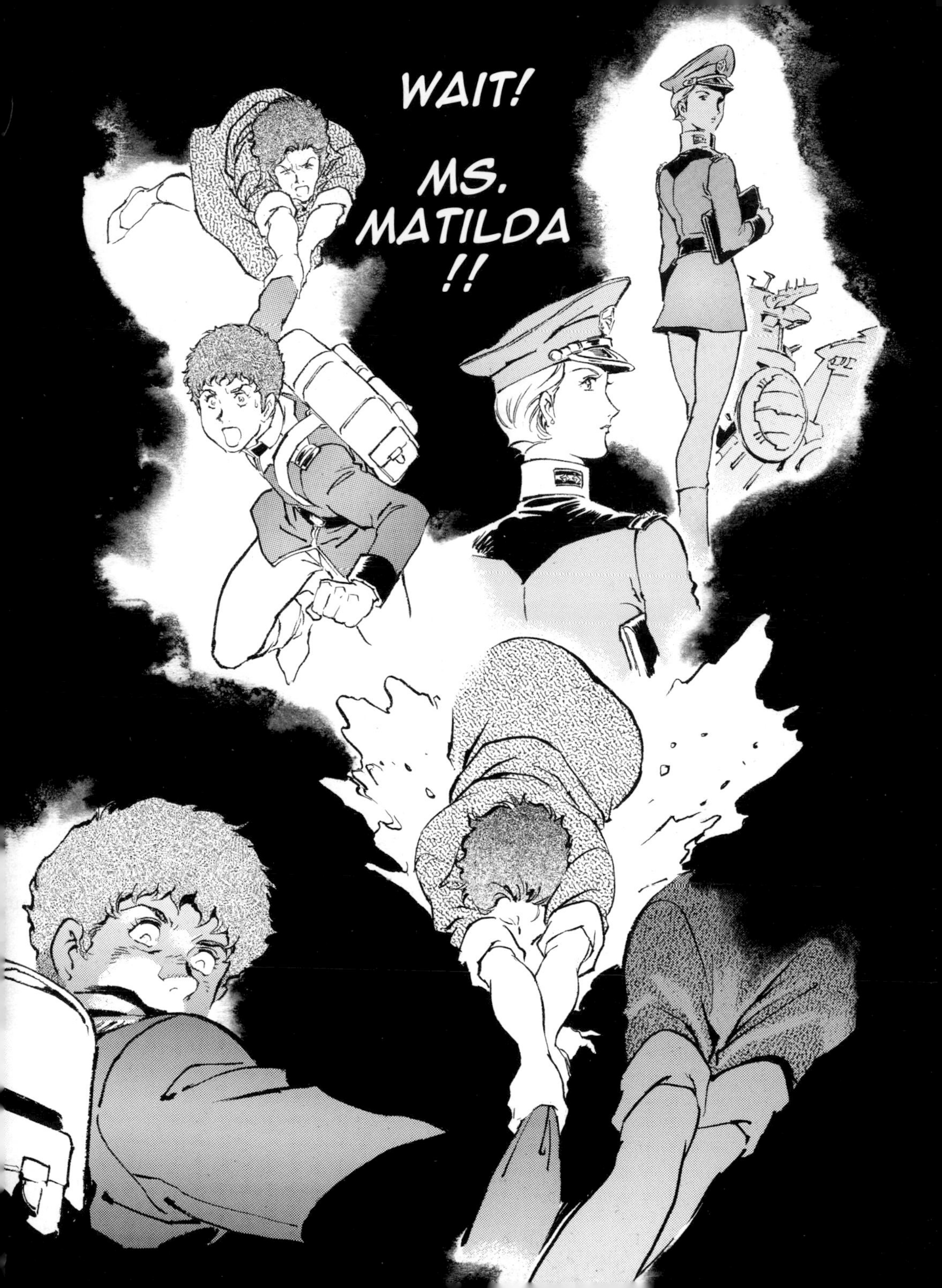
WAIT!
MS. MATILDA !!

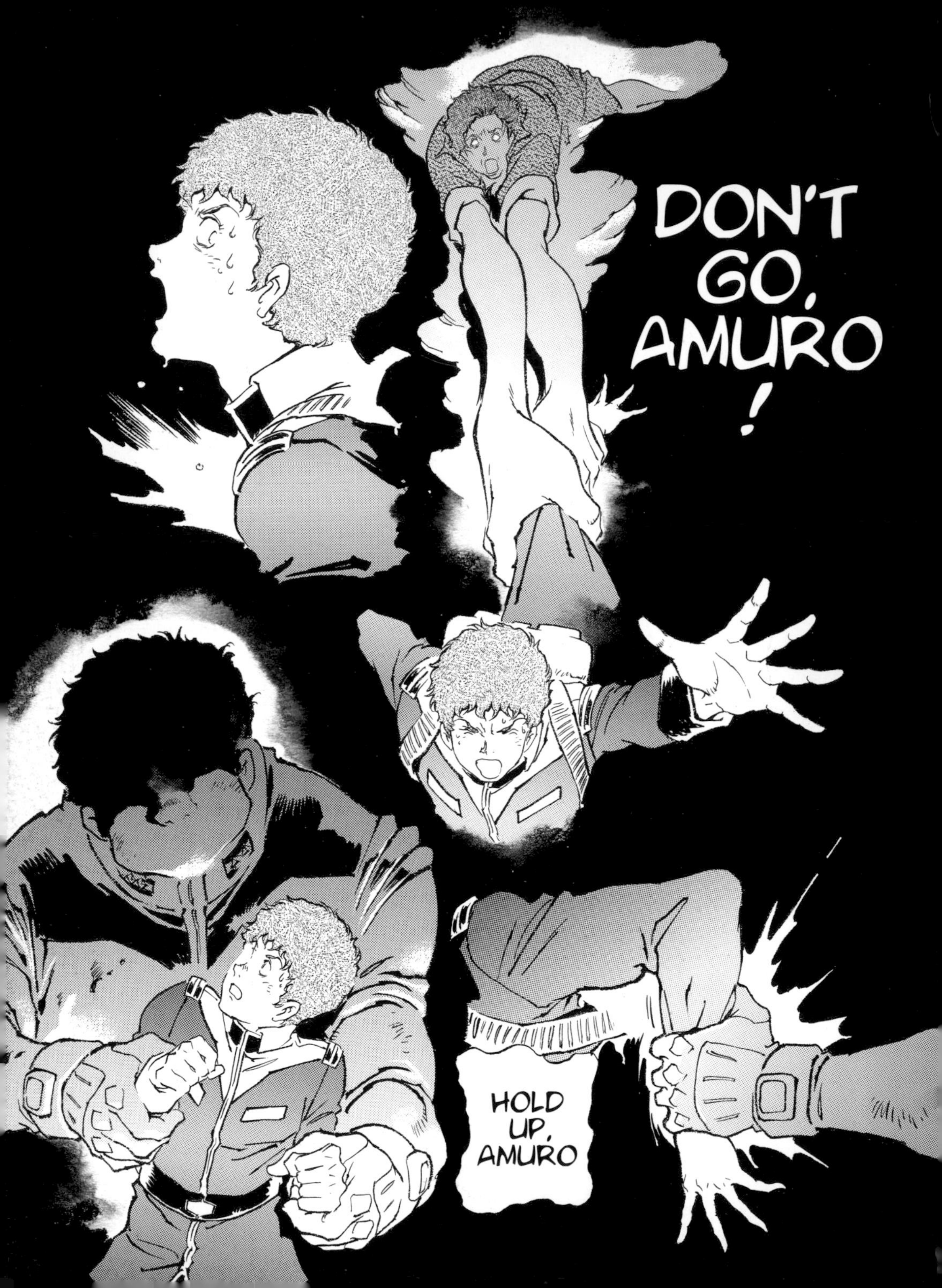
DON'T GO, AMURO!
HOLD UP, AMURO

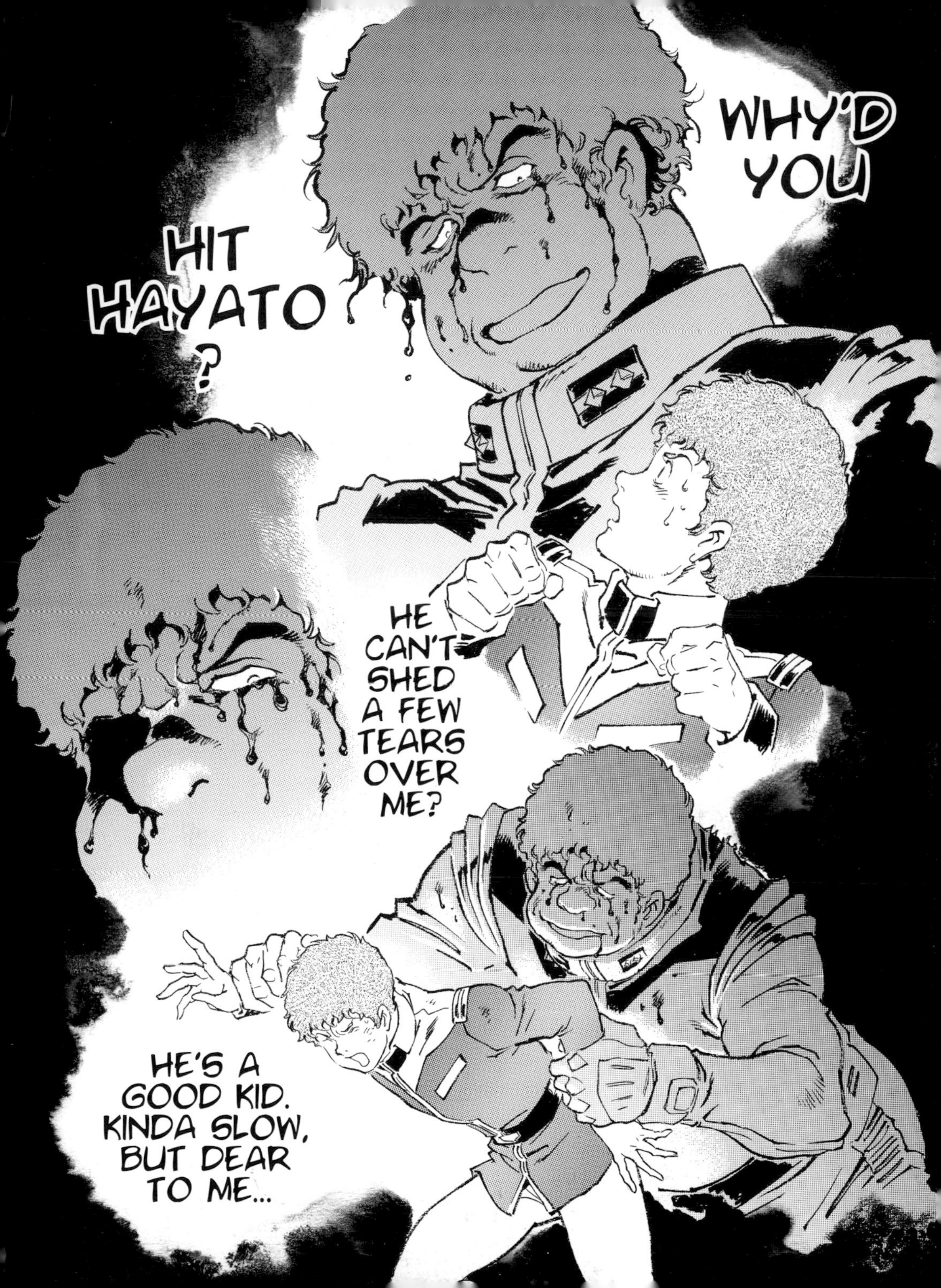
WHY'D YOU
HIT HAYATO?
HE CAN'T SHED A FEW TEARS OVER ME?
HE'S A GOOD KID. KINDA SLOW, BUT DEAR TO ME...

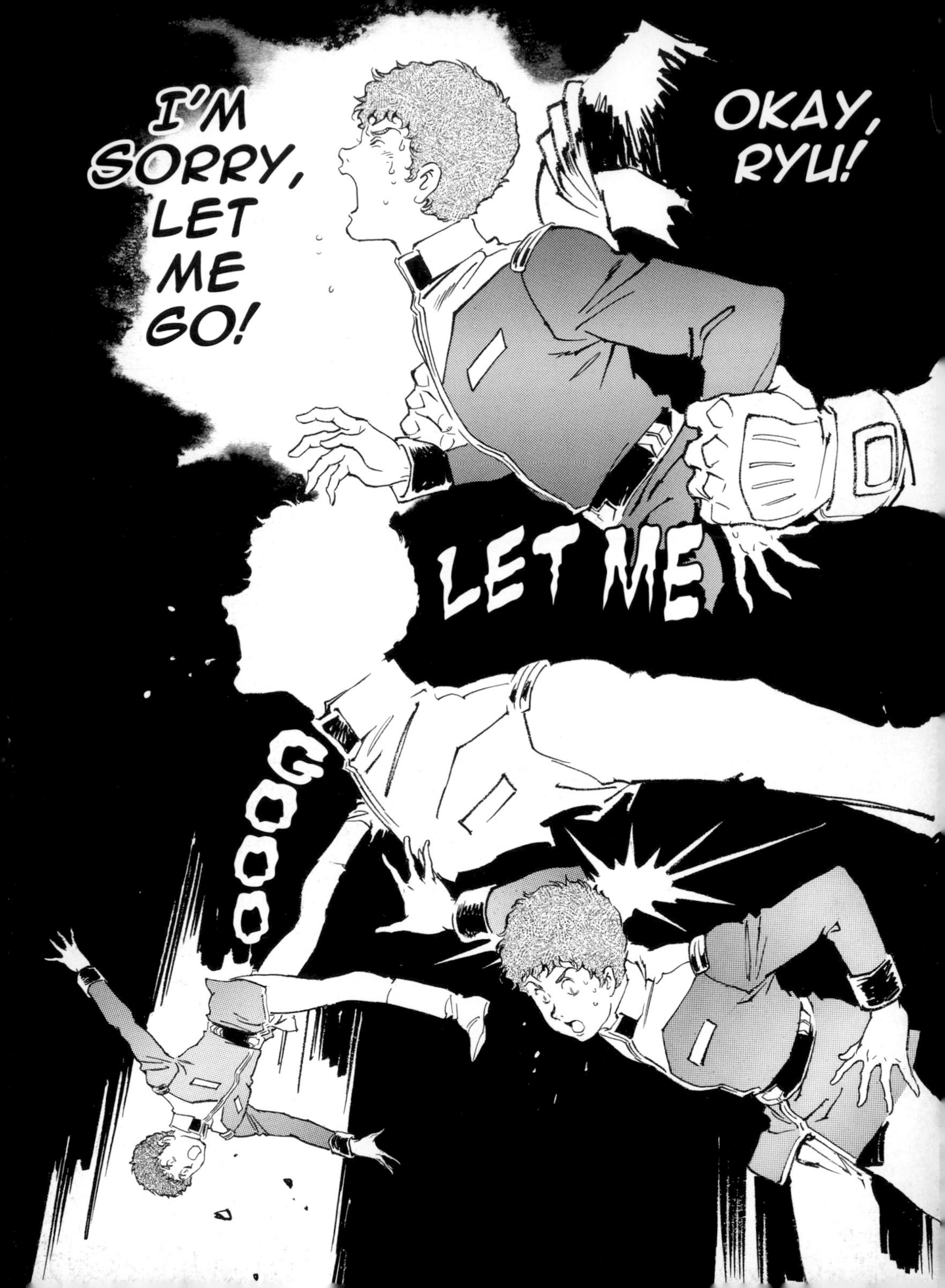
OKAY, RYU!
I'M SORRY, LET ME GO!
LET ME GOOOO

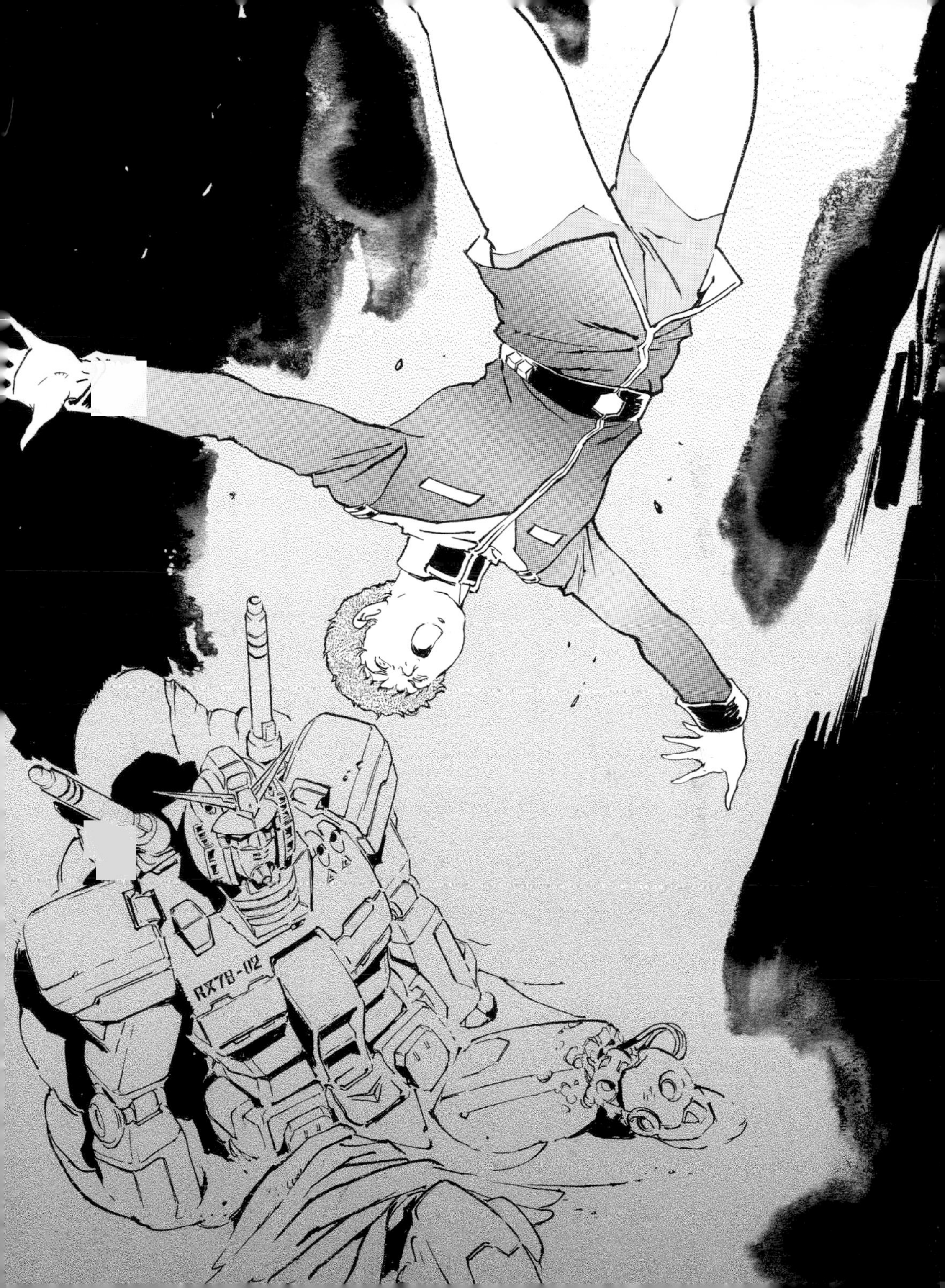
RX78-02

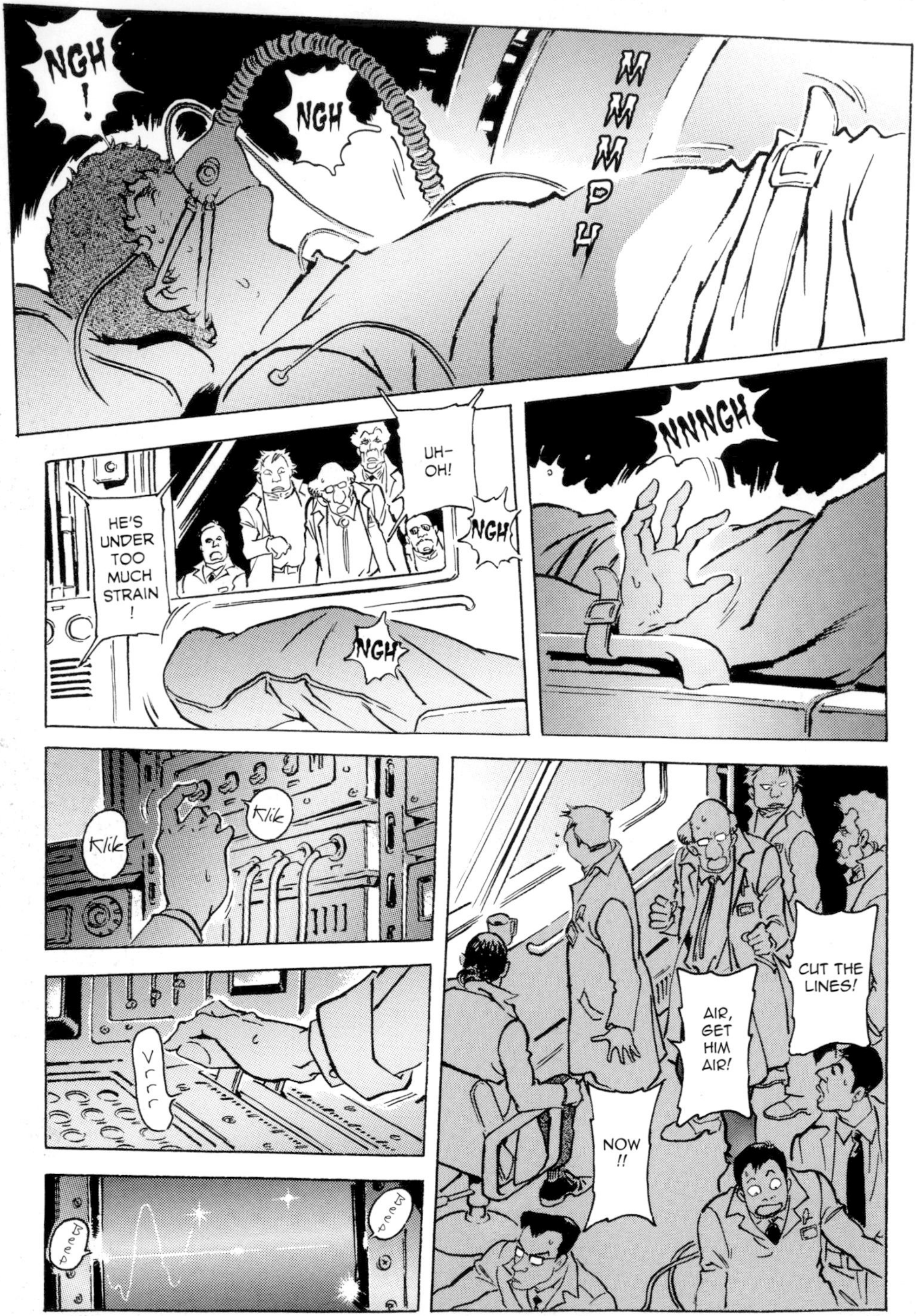
MMMPH
NGH
NGH!
NNNGH
UH-OH!
NGH
HE'S UNDER TOO MUCH STRAIN!
NGH
CUT THE LINES!
AIR, GET HIM AIR!
NOW!!
Klik
Klik
Vrrr
Beep
Beep

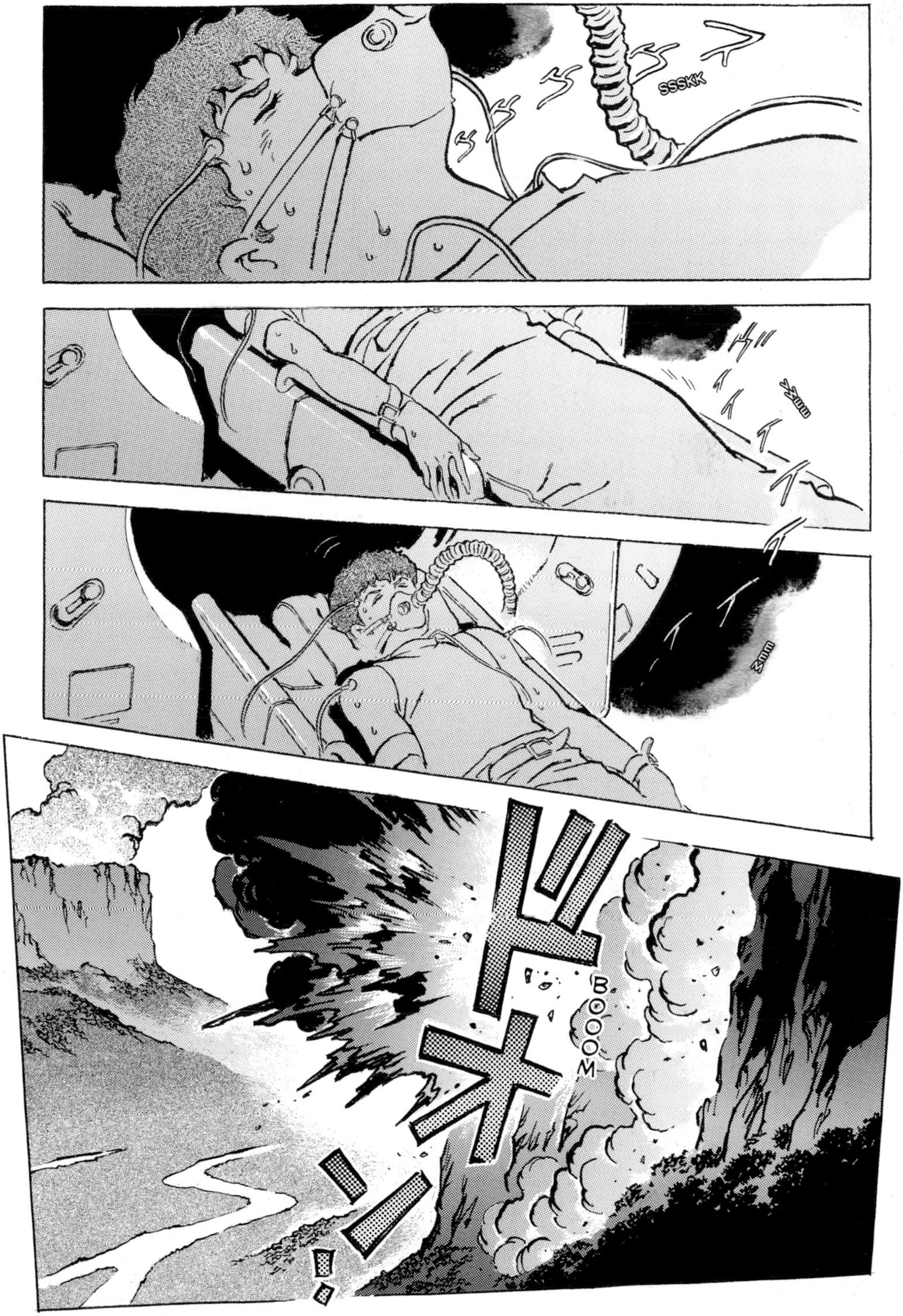
SSSKK
BOOOM

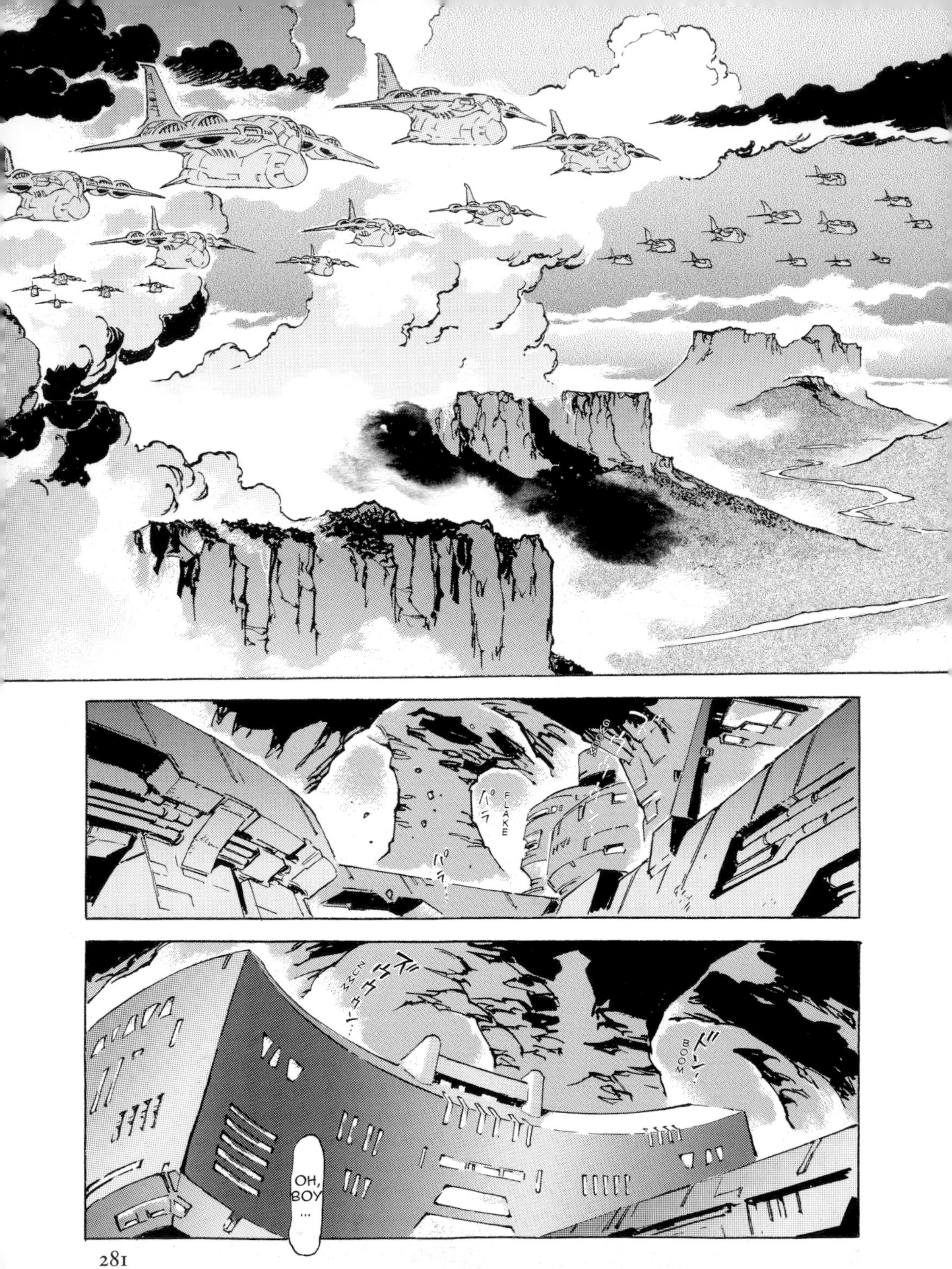
GWOOM
FLAKE
パラ
パラ…
ドーン
BOOM
ズウウウーン…
ZUMMM
OH, BOY ...

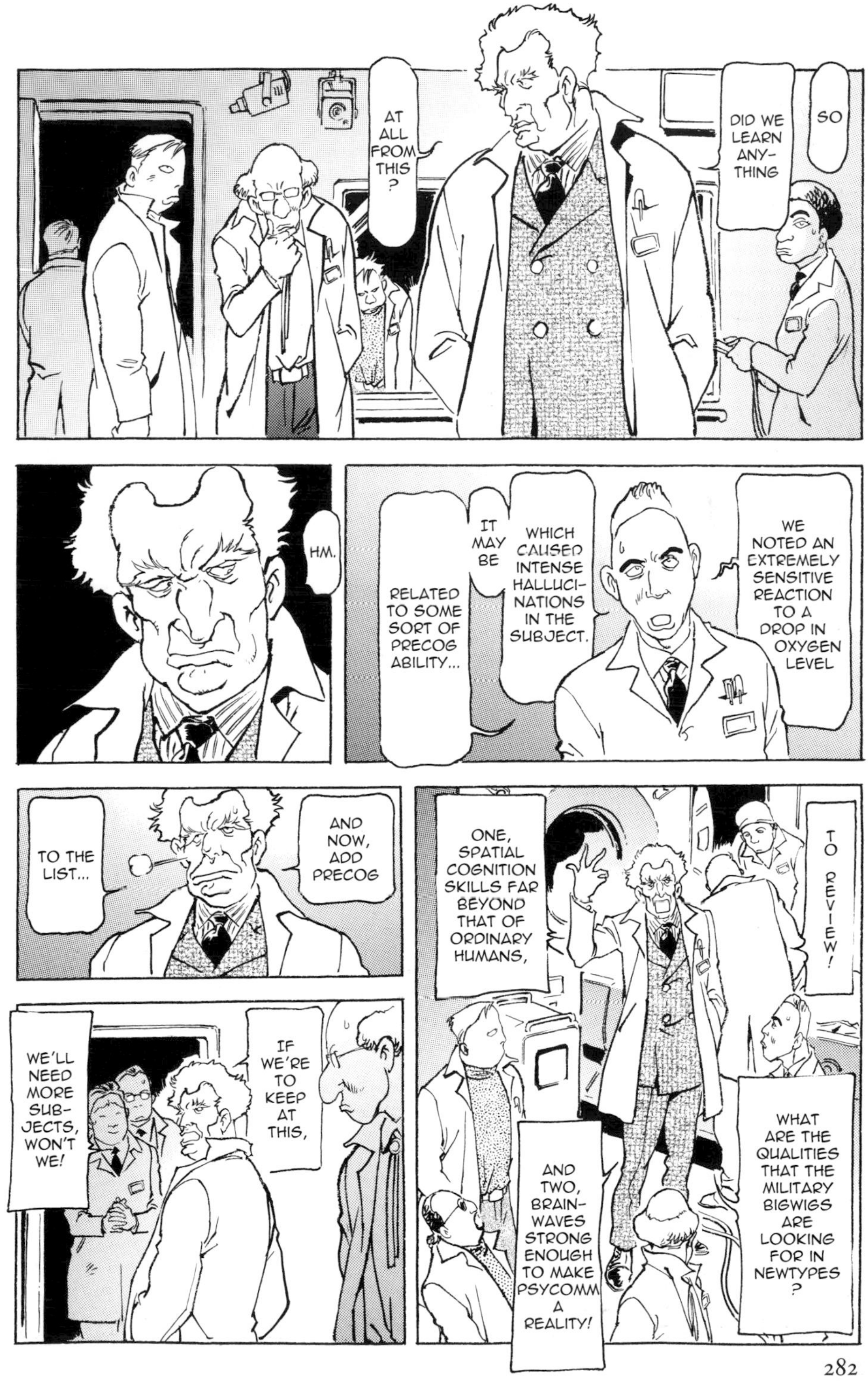
SO
DID WE LEARN ANYTHING
AT ALL FROM THIS?
WE NOTED AN EXTREMELY SENSITIVE REACTION TO A DROP IN OXYGEN LEVEL
WHICH CAUSED INTENSE HALLUCINATIONS IN THE SUBJECT.
IT MAY BE
RELATED TO SOME SORT OF PRECOG ABILITY...
HM.
TO REVIEW!
WHAT ARE THE QUALITIES THAT THE MILITARY BIGWIGS ARE LOOKING FOR IN NEWTYPES?
ONE, SPATIAL COGNITION SKILLS FAR BEYOND THAT OF ORDINARY HUMANS,
AND TWO, BRAIN-WAVES STRONG ENOUGH TO MAKE PSYCOMM A REALITY!
AND NOW, ADD PRECOG
TO THE LIST...
IF WE'RE TO KEEP AT THIS,
WE'LL NEED MORE SUB-JECTS, WON'T WE!

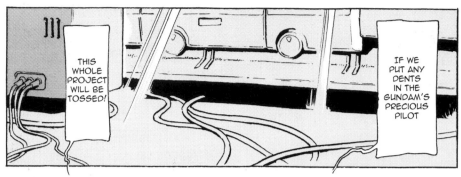

IF WE PUT ANY DENTS IN THE GUNDAM'S PRECIOUS PILOT
THIS WHOLE PROJECT WILL BE TOSSED!
ズウウウウウ
ZUMMM
HUFFF...
HUFF
HUFF
HUFF
HUFF

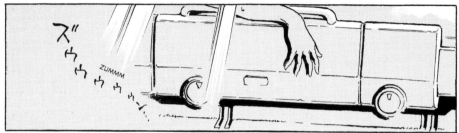

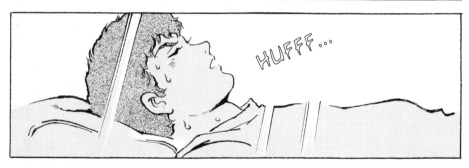

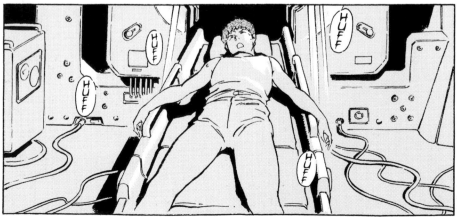

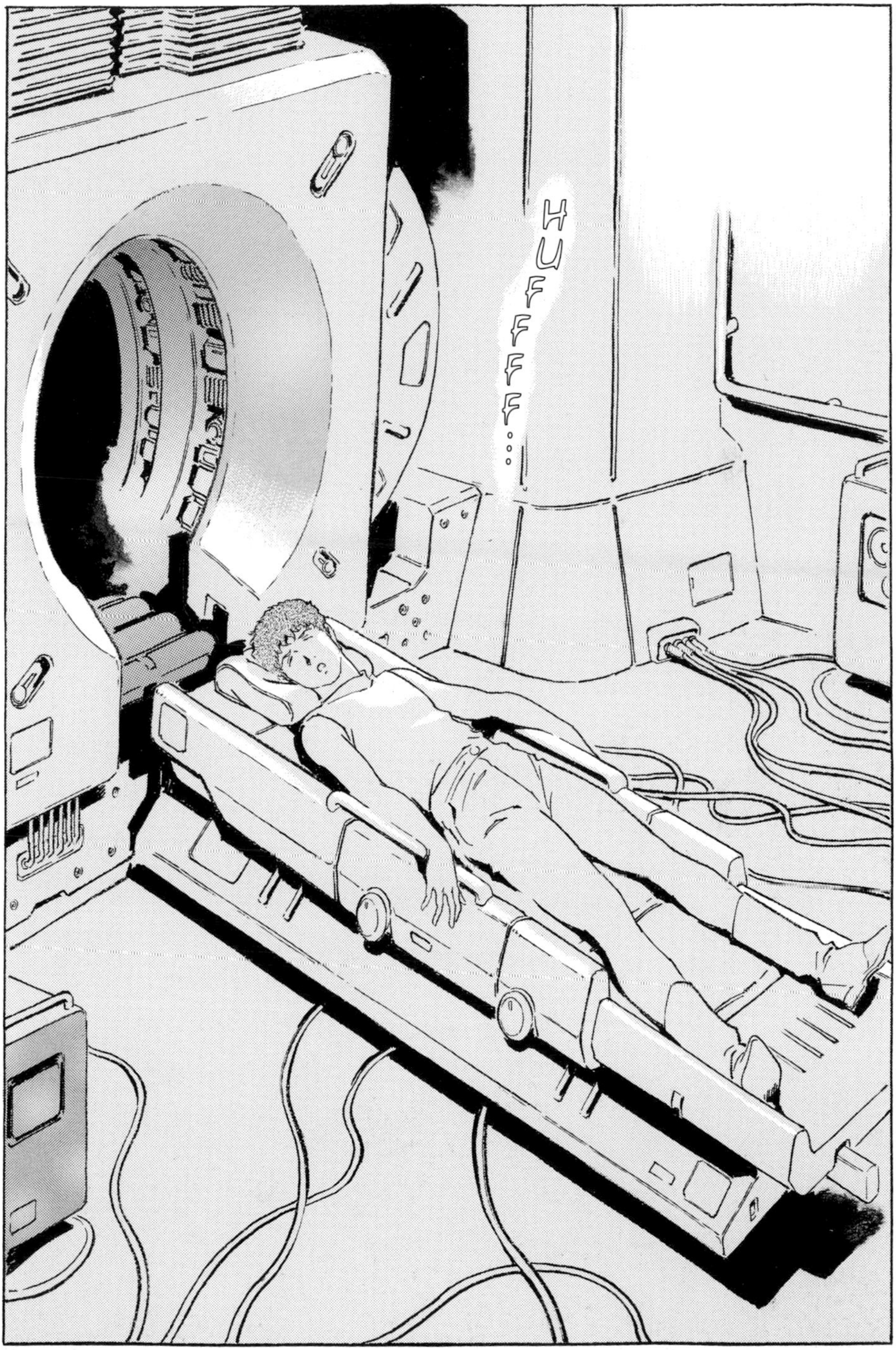
HUFFFFF...

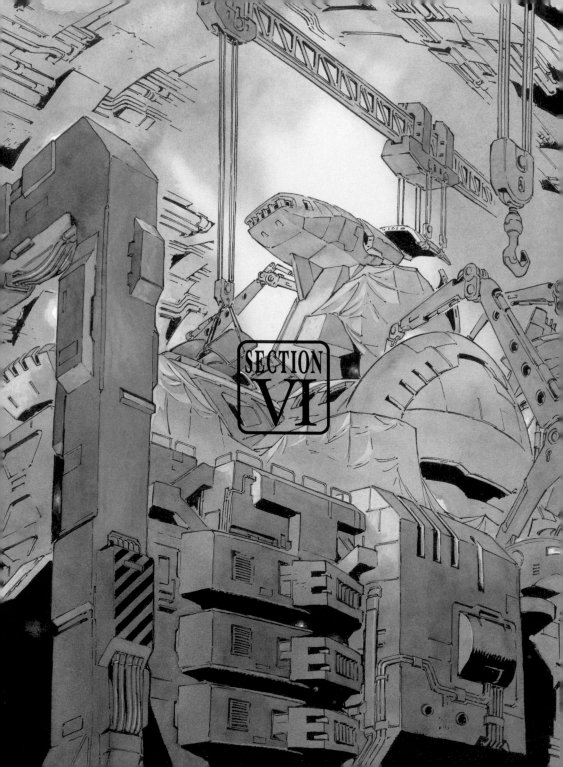

SECTION
VI

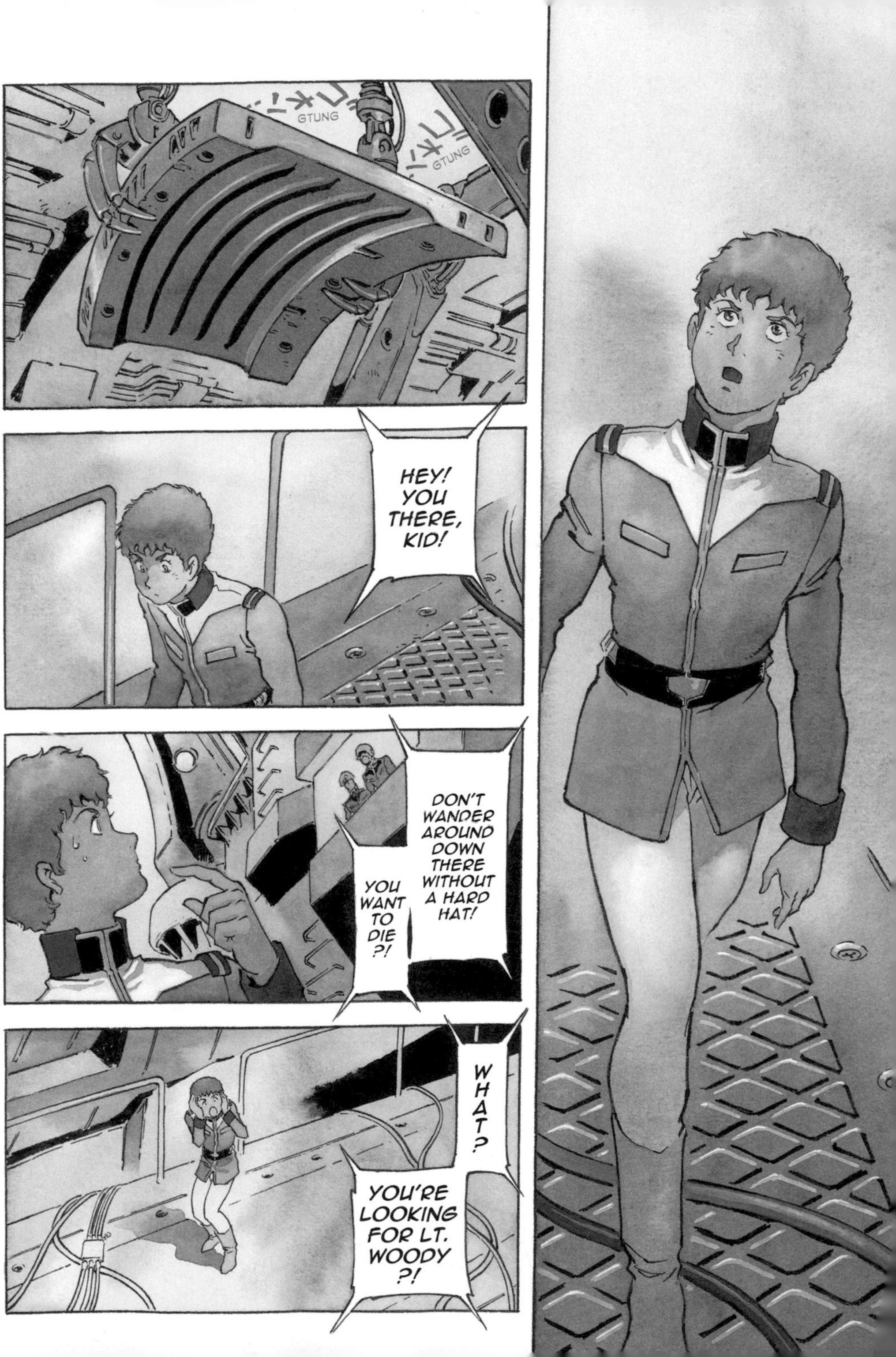
GTUNG
GTUNG
HEY! YOU THERE, KID!
DON'T WANDER AROUND DOWN THERE WITHOUT A HARD HAT!
YOU WANT TO DIE?!
WHAT?
YOU'RE LOOKING FOR LT. WOODY?!

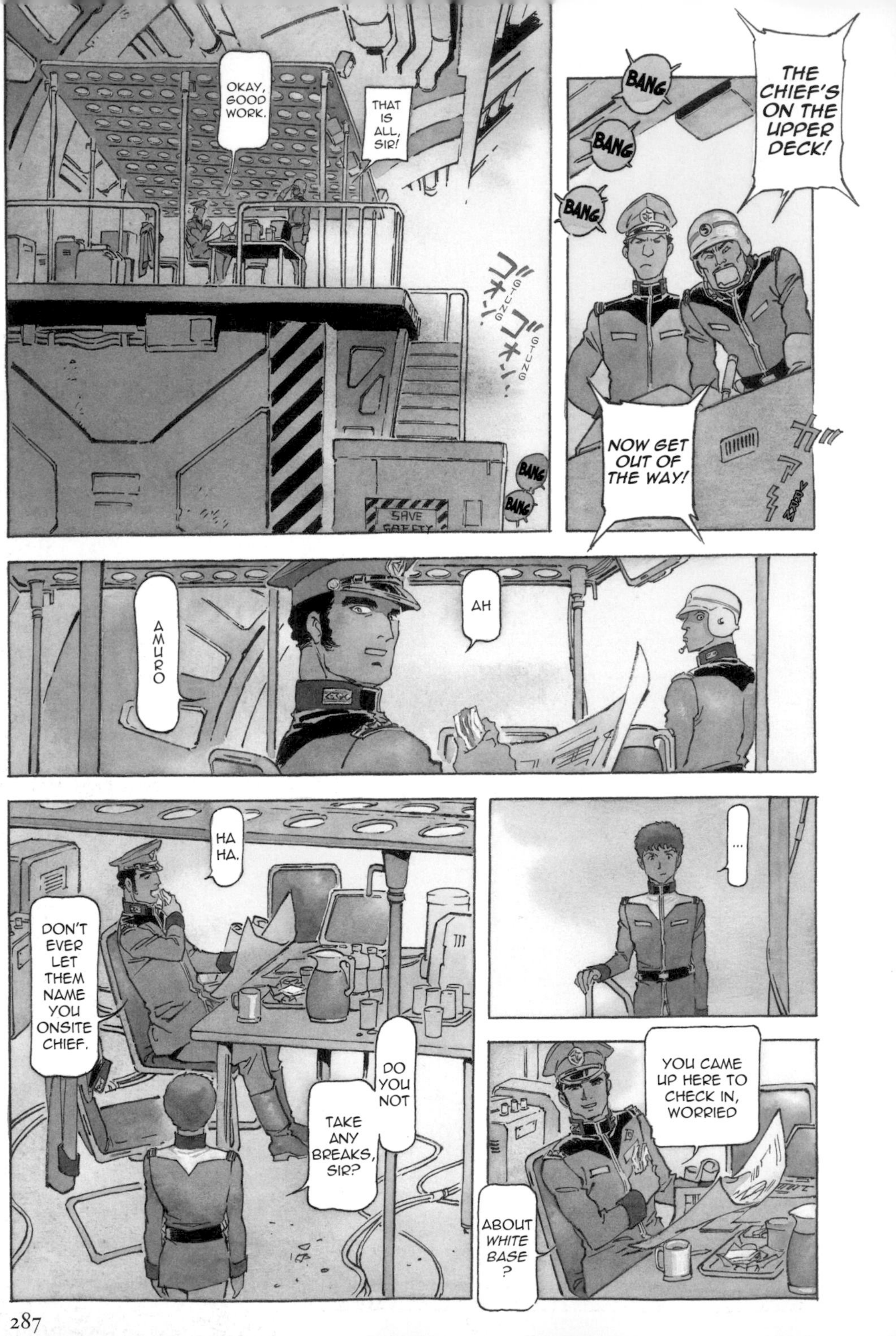
BANG
BANG
BANG
THE CHIEF'S ON THE UPPER DECK!
NOW GET OUT OF THE WAY!
THAT IS ALL, SIR!
OKAY, GOOD WORK.
ゴォン！ GTUNG
ゴォン！ GTUNG
BANG
BANG
AH
AMURO
...
YOU CAME UP HERE TO CHECK IN, WORRIED
ABOUT WHITE BASE?
HA HA.
DON'T EVER LET THEM NAME YOU ONSITE CHIEF.
DO YOU NOT
TAKE ANY BREAKS, SIR?

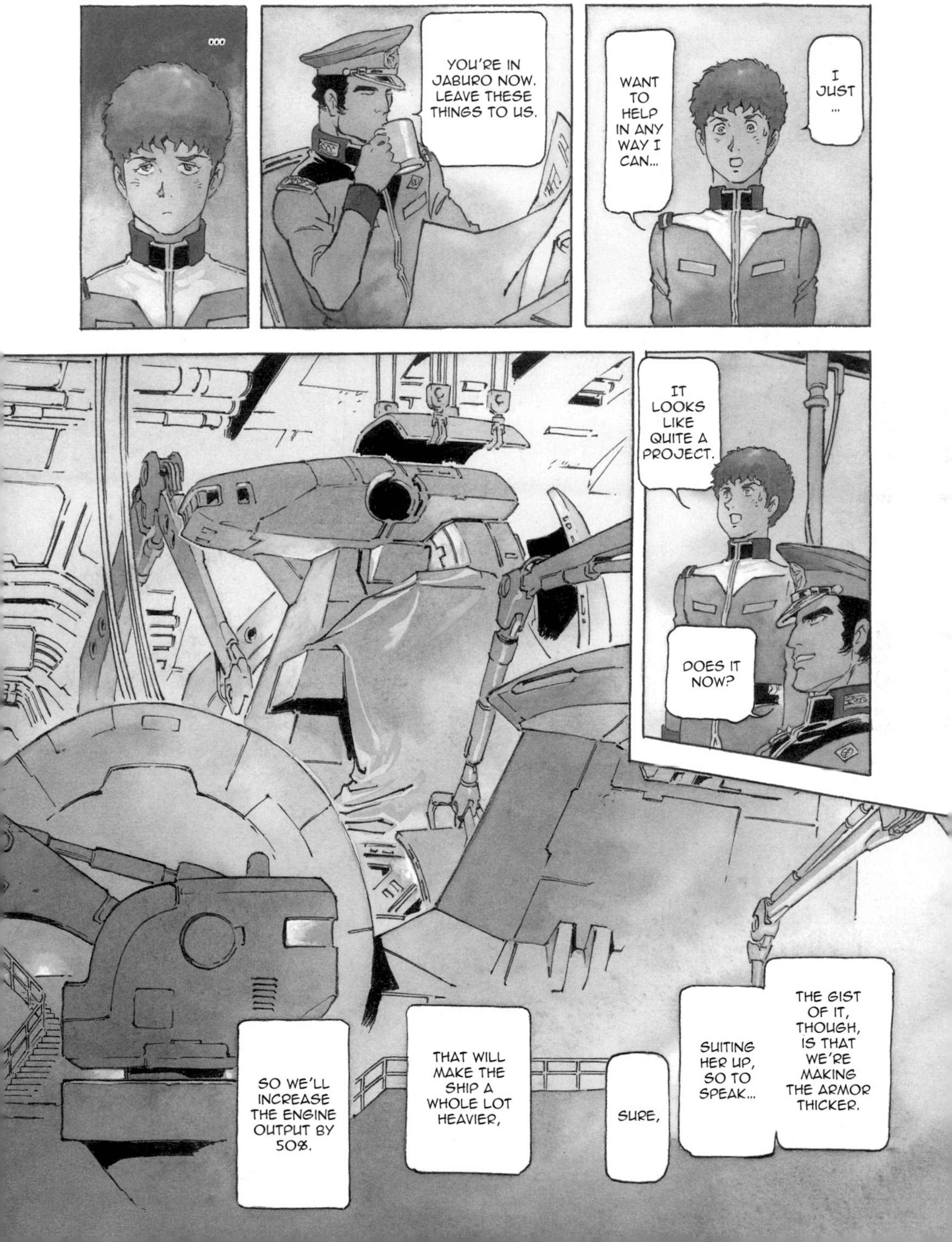
I JUST ...
WANT TO HELP IN ANY WAY I CAN...
YOU'RE IN JABURO NOW. LEAVE THESE THINGS TO US.
...
IT LOOKS LIKE QUITE A PROJECT.
DOES IT NOW?
THE GIST OF IT, THOUGH, IS THAT WE'RE MAKING THE ARMOR THICKER.
SUITING HER UP, SO TO SPEAK...
SURE,
THAT WILL MAKE THE SHIP A WHOLE LOT HEAVIER,
SO WE'LL INCREASE THE ENGINE OUTPUT BY 50%.

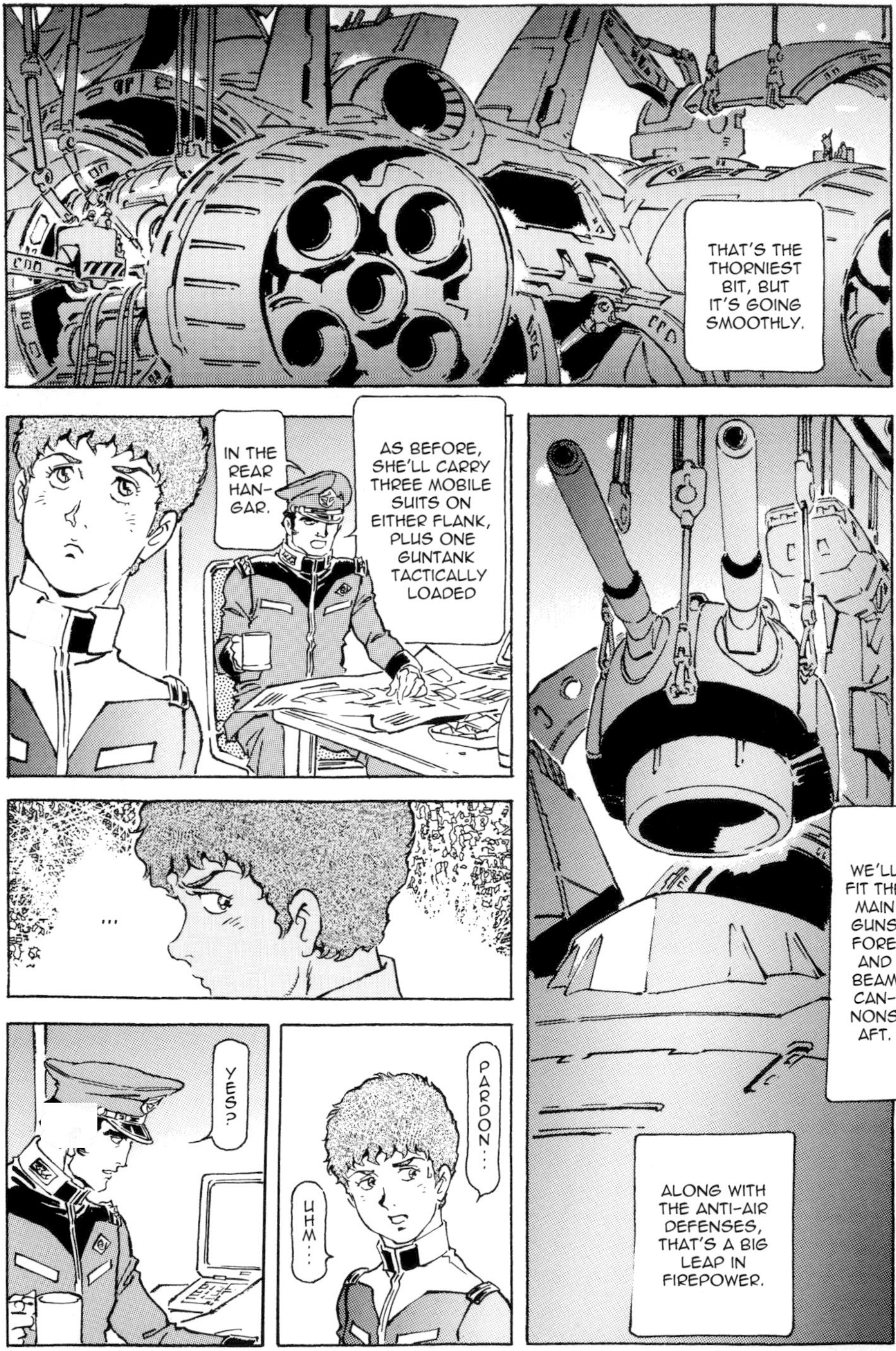
THAT'S THE THORNIEST BIT, BUT IT'S GOING SMOOTHLY.
WE'LL FIT THE MAIN GUNS FORE, AND BEAM CAN-NONS AFT.
ALONG WITH THE ANTI-AIR DEFENSES, THAT'S A BIG LEAP IN FIREPOWER.
AS BEFORE, SHE'LL CARRY THREE MOBILE SUITS ON EITHER FLANK, PLUS ONE GUNTANK TACTICALLY LOADED
IN THE REAR HAN-GAR.
...
PARDON...
UHM...
YES?

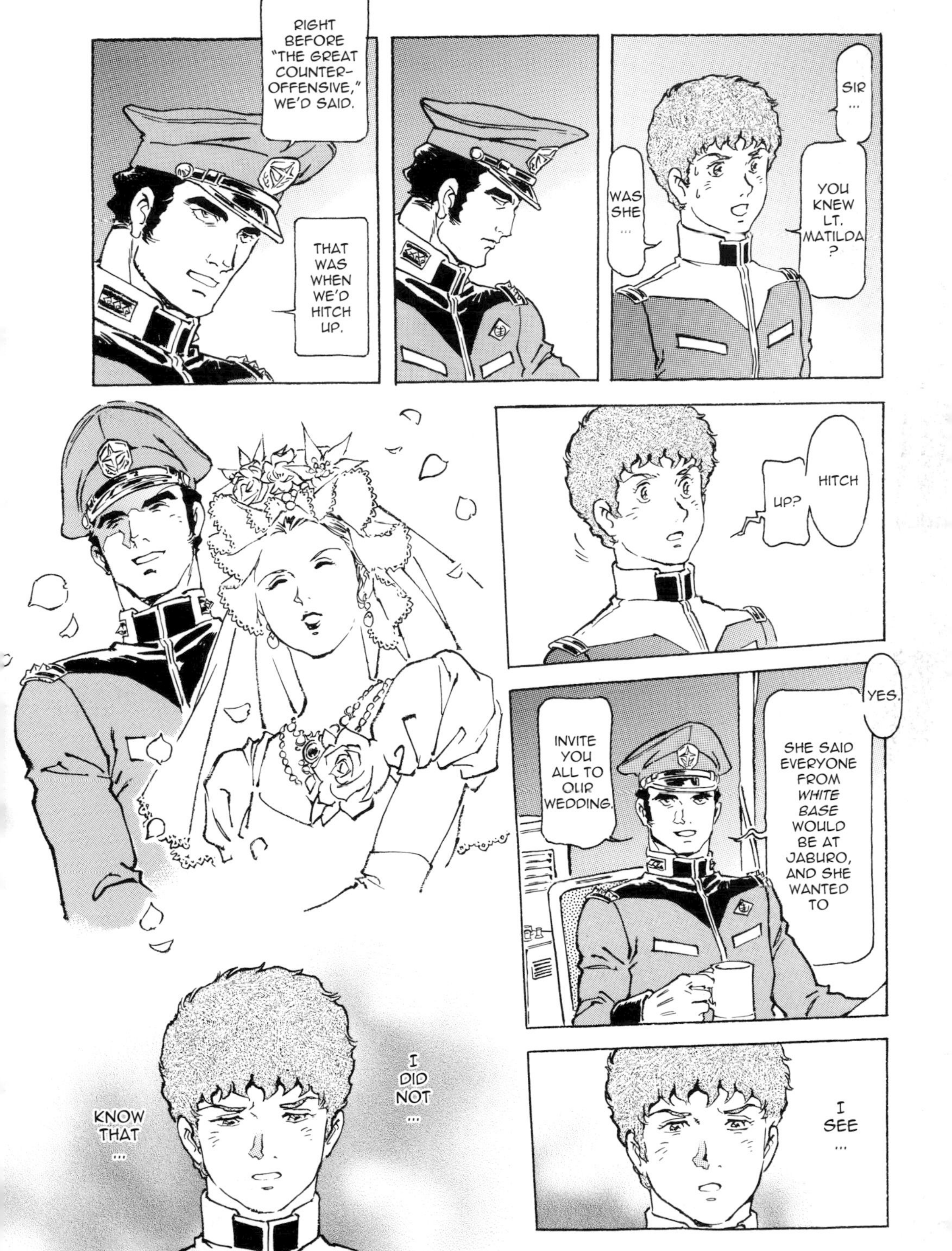
SIR ...
YOU KNEW LT. MATILDA?
WAS SHE ...
RIGHT BEFORE "THE GREAT COUNTER-OFFENSIVE," WE'D SAID.
THAT WAS WHEN WE'D HITCH UP.
HITCH
UP?
YES.
SHE SAID EVERYONE FROM *WHITE BASE* WOULD BE AT JABURO, AND SHE WANTED TO
INVITE YOU ALL TO OUR WEDDING.
I SEE ...
I DID NOT ...
KNOW THAT ...

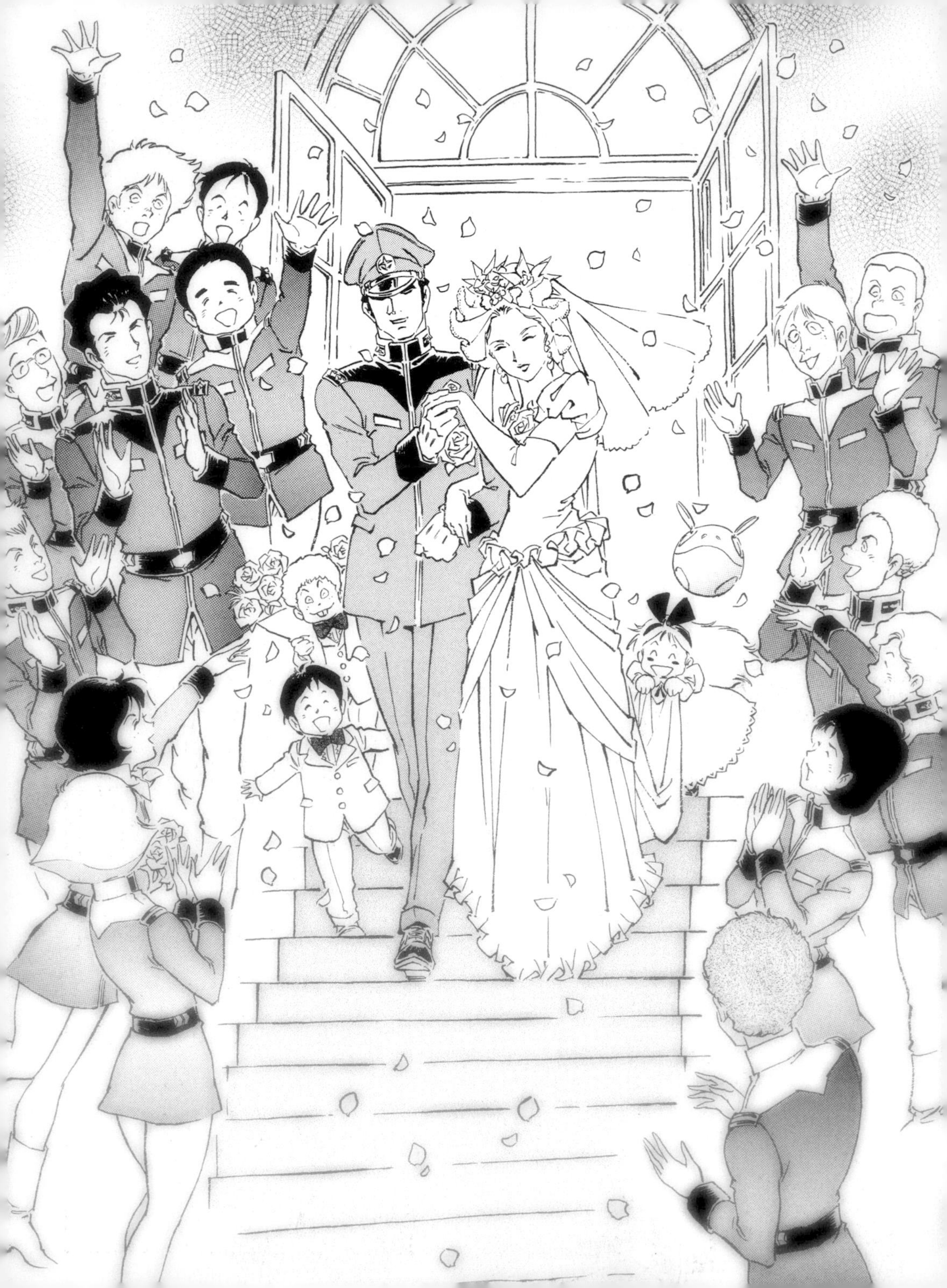

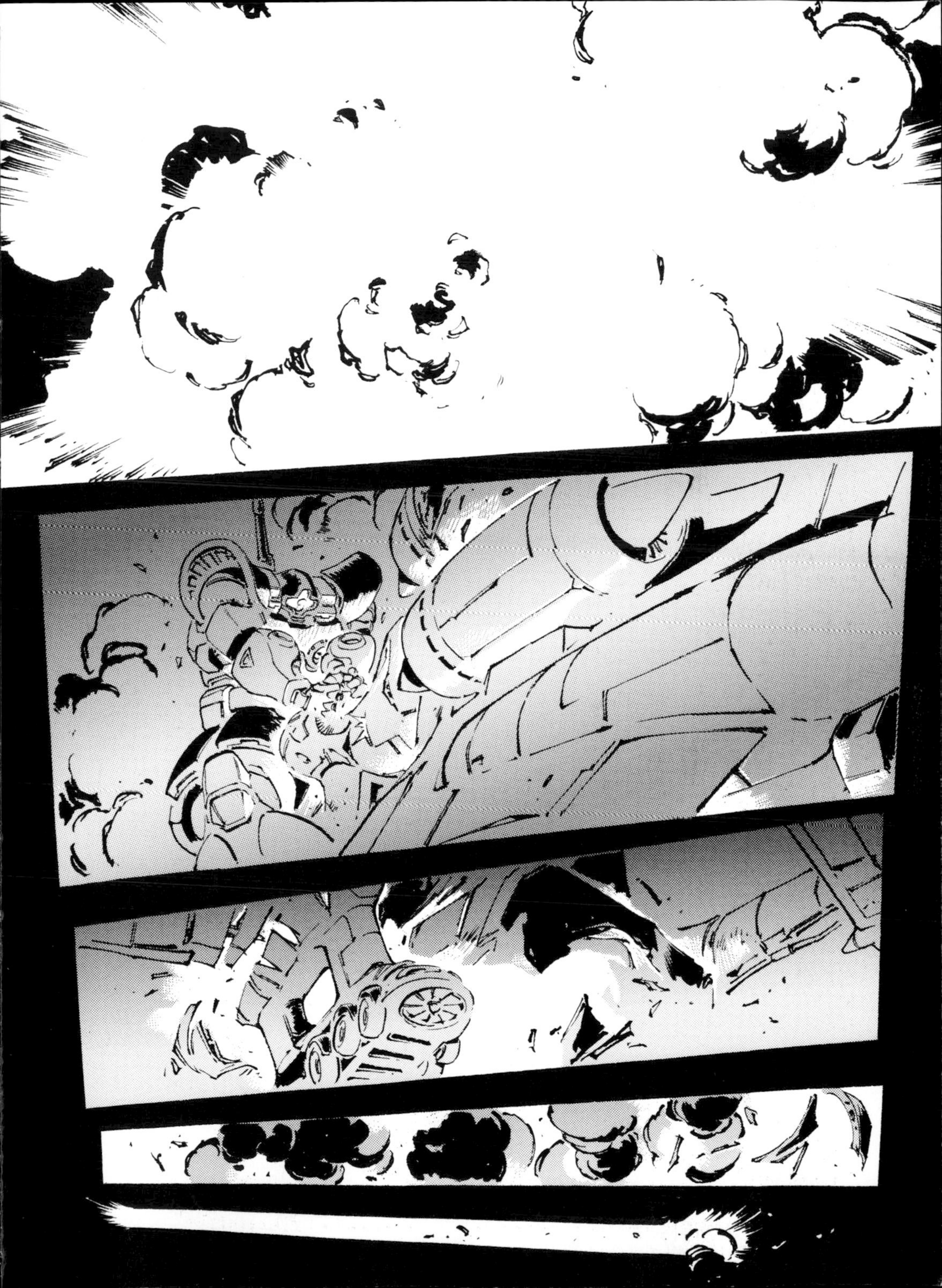

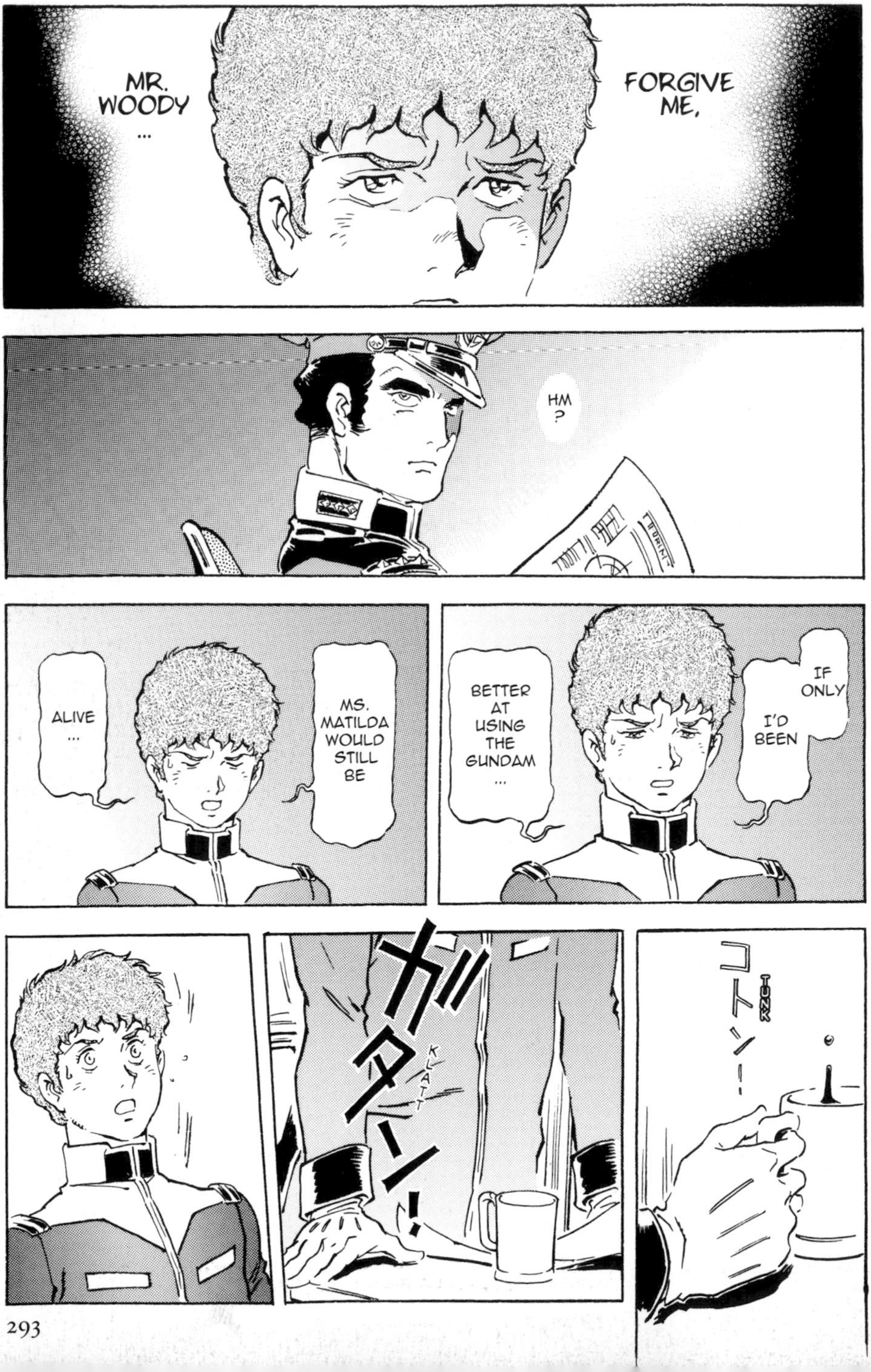
FORGIVE ME,
MR. WOODY ...
HM ?
IF ONLY I'D BEEN
BETTER AT USING THE GUNDAM ...
MS. MATILDA WOULD STILL BE
ALIVE ...
コトン！！
TONK
ガタン！！
KLATT

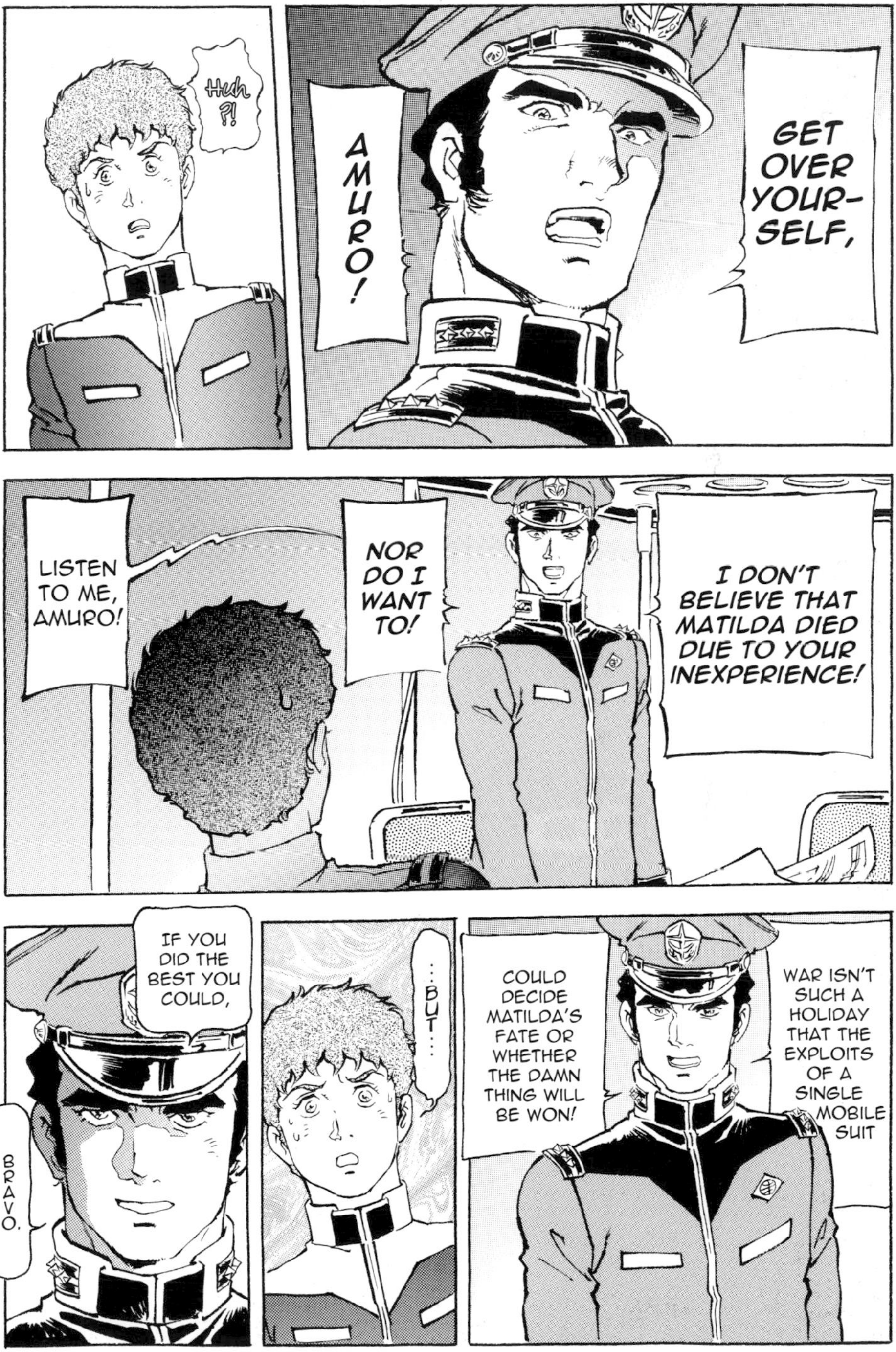
GET OVER YOURSELF,
AMURO!
Huh ?!
I DON'T BELIEVE THAT MATILDA DIED DUE TO YOUR INEXPERIENCE!
NOR DO I WANT TO!
LISTEN TO ME, AMURO!
WAR ISN'T SUCH A HOLIDAY THAT THE EXPLOITS OF A SINGLE MOBILE SUIT
COULD DECIDE MATILDA'S FATE OR WHETHER THE DAMN THING WILL BE WON!
...BUT...
IF YOU DID THE BEST YOU COULD,
BRAVO.

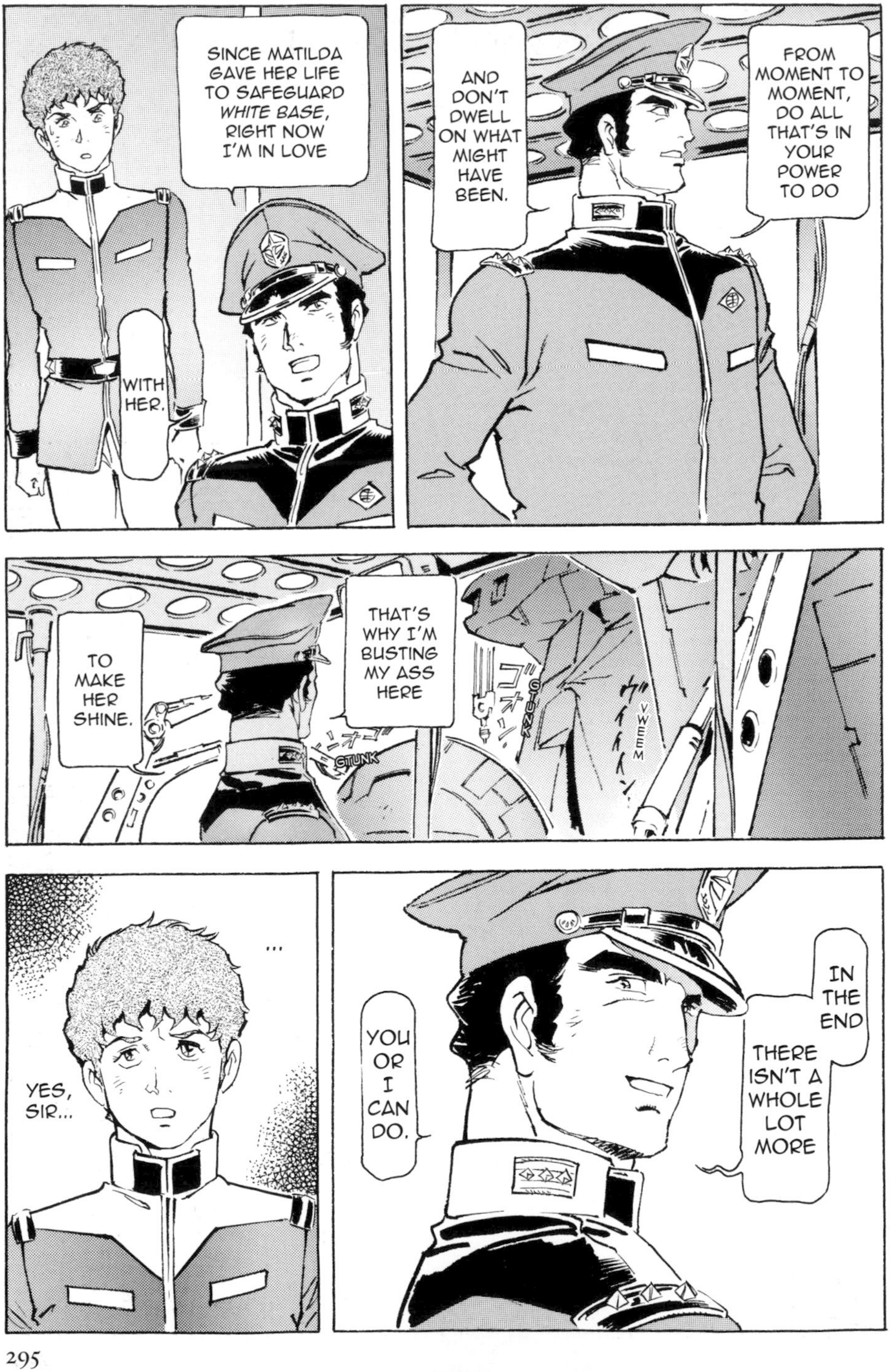
FROM MOMENT TO MOMENT, DO ALL THAT'S IN YOUR POWER TO DO
AND DON'T DWELL ON WHAT MIGHT HAVE BEEN.
SINCE MATILDA GAVE HER LIFE TO SAFEGUARD *WHITE BASE*, RIGHT NOW I'M IN LOVE
WITH HER.
VWEEM
GIUNK
THAT'S WHY I'M BUSTING MY ASS HERE
GTUNK
TO MAKE HER SHINE.
IN THE END
THERE ISN'T A WHOLE LOT MORE
YOU OR I CAN DO.
...
YES, SIR...

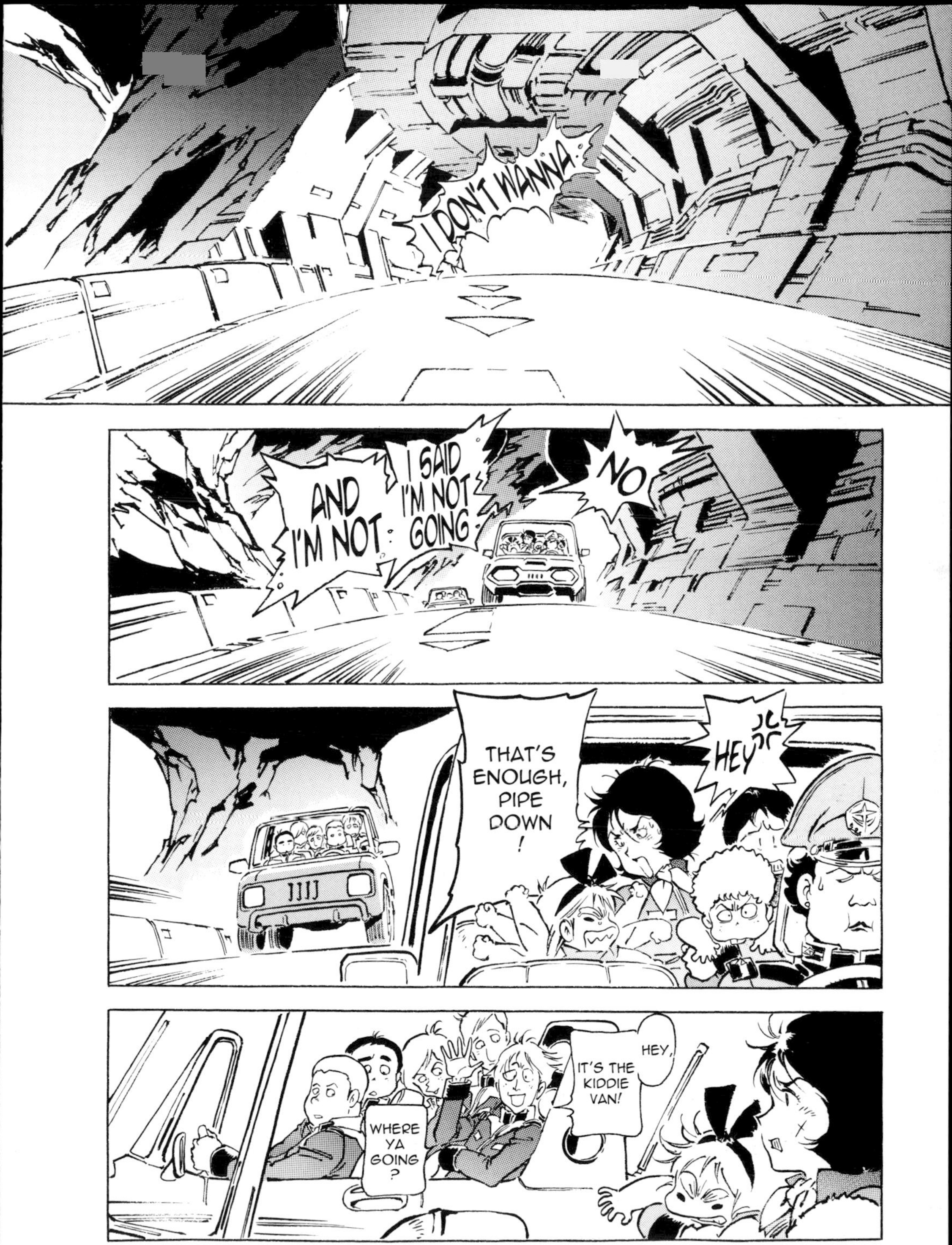
I DON'T WANNA
NO
I SAID I'M NOT GOING
AND I'M NOT
HEY
THAT'S ENOUGH, PIPE DOWN!
HEY, IT'S THE KIDDIE VAN!
WHERE YA GOING?

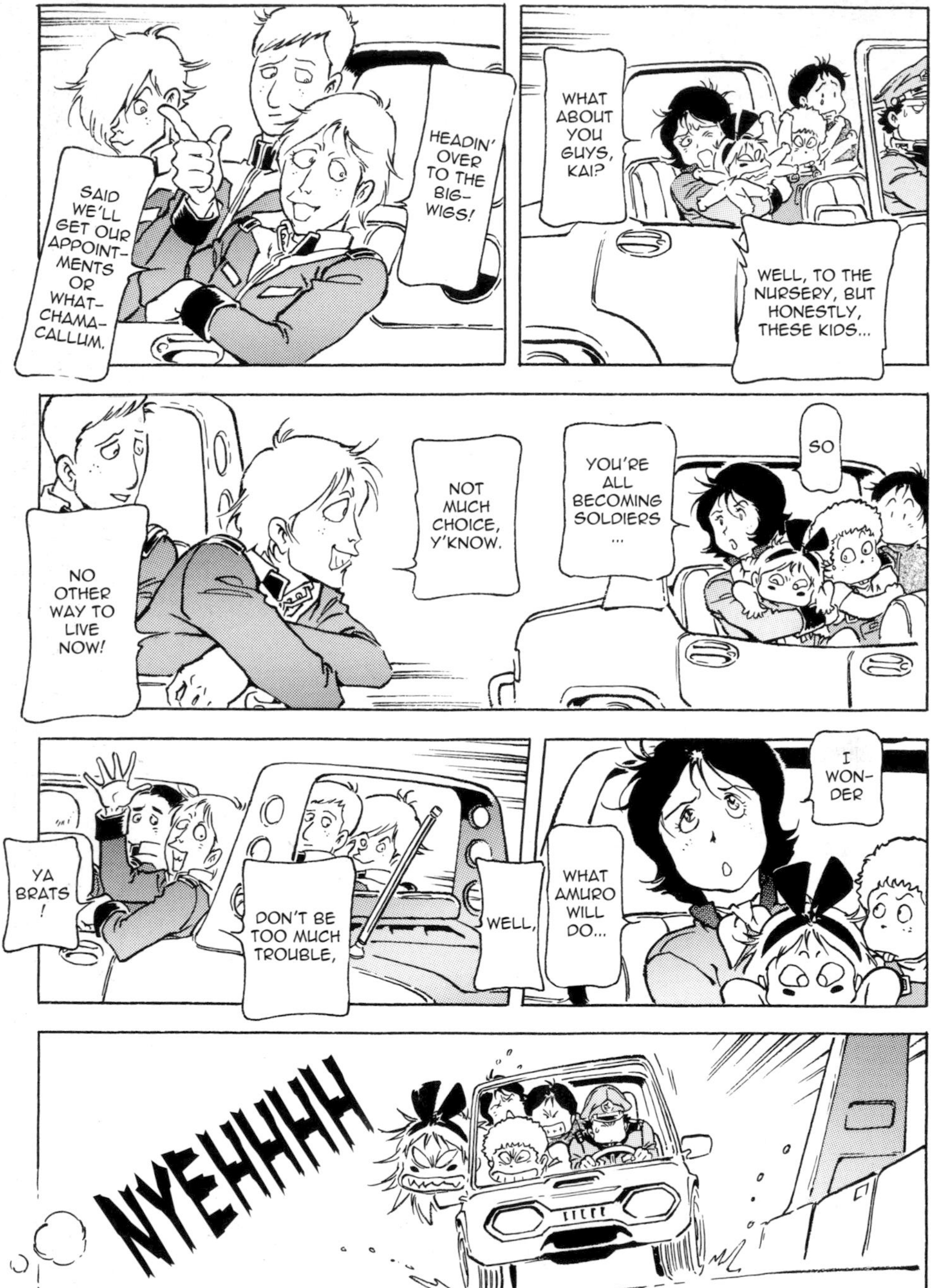
WHAT ABOUT YOU GUYS, KAI?
WELL, TO THE NURSERY, BUT HONESTLY, THESE KIDS...
HEADIN' OVER TO THE BIG-WIGS!
SAID WE'LL GET OUR APPOINT-MENTS OR WHAT-CHAMA-CALLUM.
SO
YOU'RE ALL BECOMING SOLDIERS ...
NOT MUCH CHOICE, Y'KNOW.
NO OTHER WAY TO LIVE NOW!
I WON-DER
WHAT AMURO WILL DO...
WELL,
DON'T BE TOO MUCH TROUBLE,
YA BRATS !
NYEHHHH

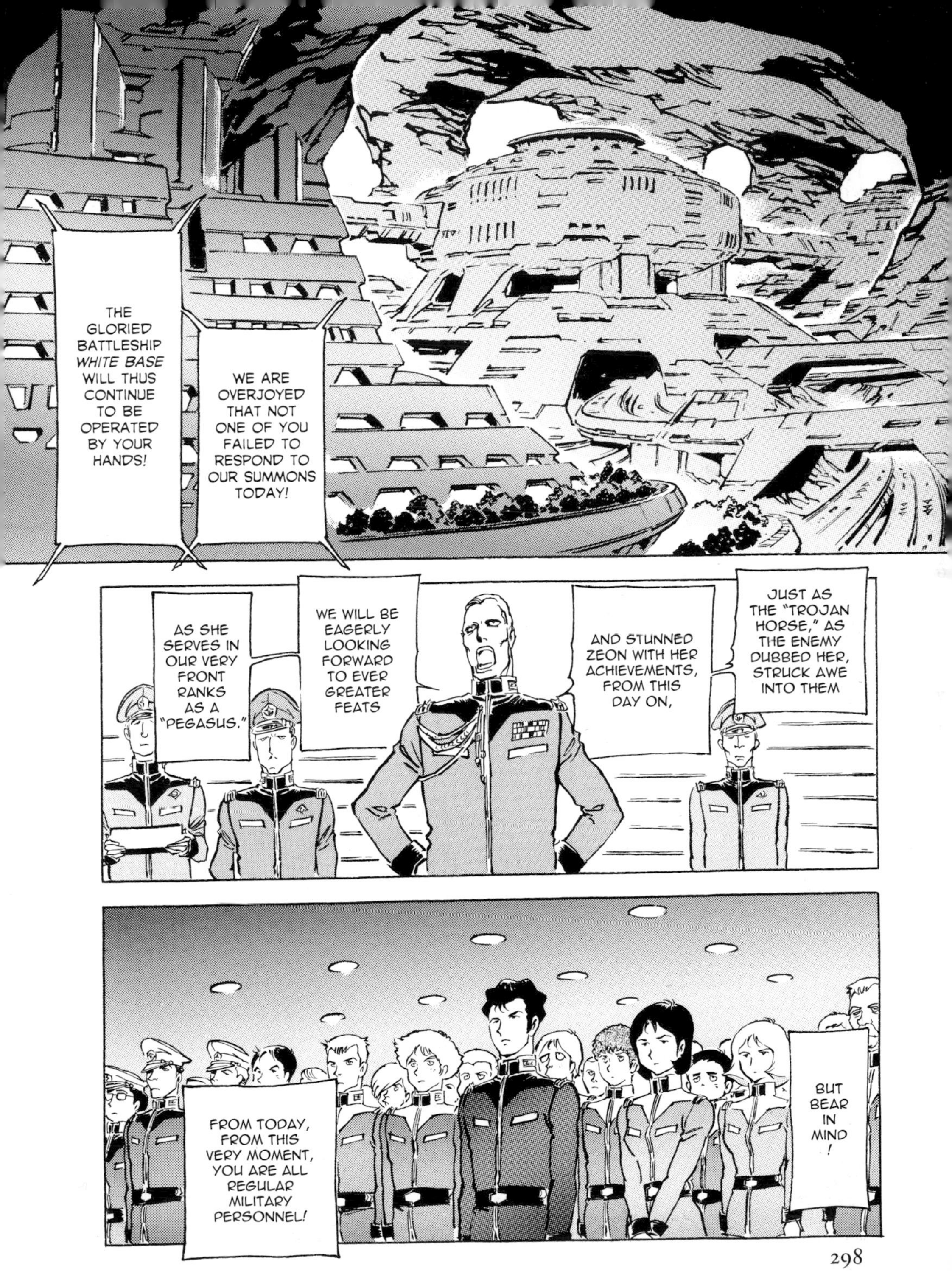
WE ARE OVERJOYED THAT NOT ONE OF YOU FAILED TO RESPOND TO OUR SUMMONS TODAY!
THE GLORIED BATTLESHIP *WHITE BASE* WILL THUS CONTINUE TO BE OPERATED BY YOUR HANDS!
JUST AS THE "TROJAN HORSE," AS THE ENEMY DUBBED HER, STRUCK AWE INTO THEM
AND STUNNED ZEON WITH HER ACHIEVEMENTS, FROM THIS DAY ON,
WE WILL BE EAGERLY LOOKING FORWARD TO EVER GREATER FEATS
AS SHE SERVES IN OUR VERY FRONT RANKS AS A "PEGASUS."
BUT BEAR IN MIND!
FROM TODAY, FROM THIS VERY MOMENT, YOU ARE ALL REGULAR MILITARY PERSONNEL!

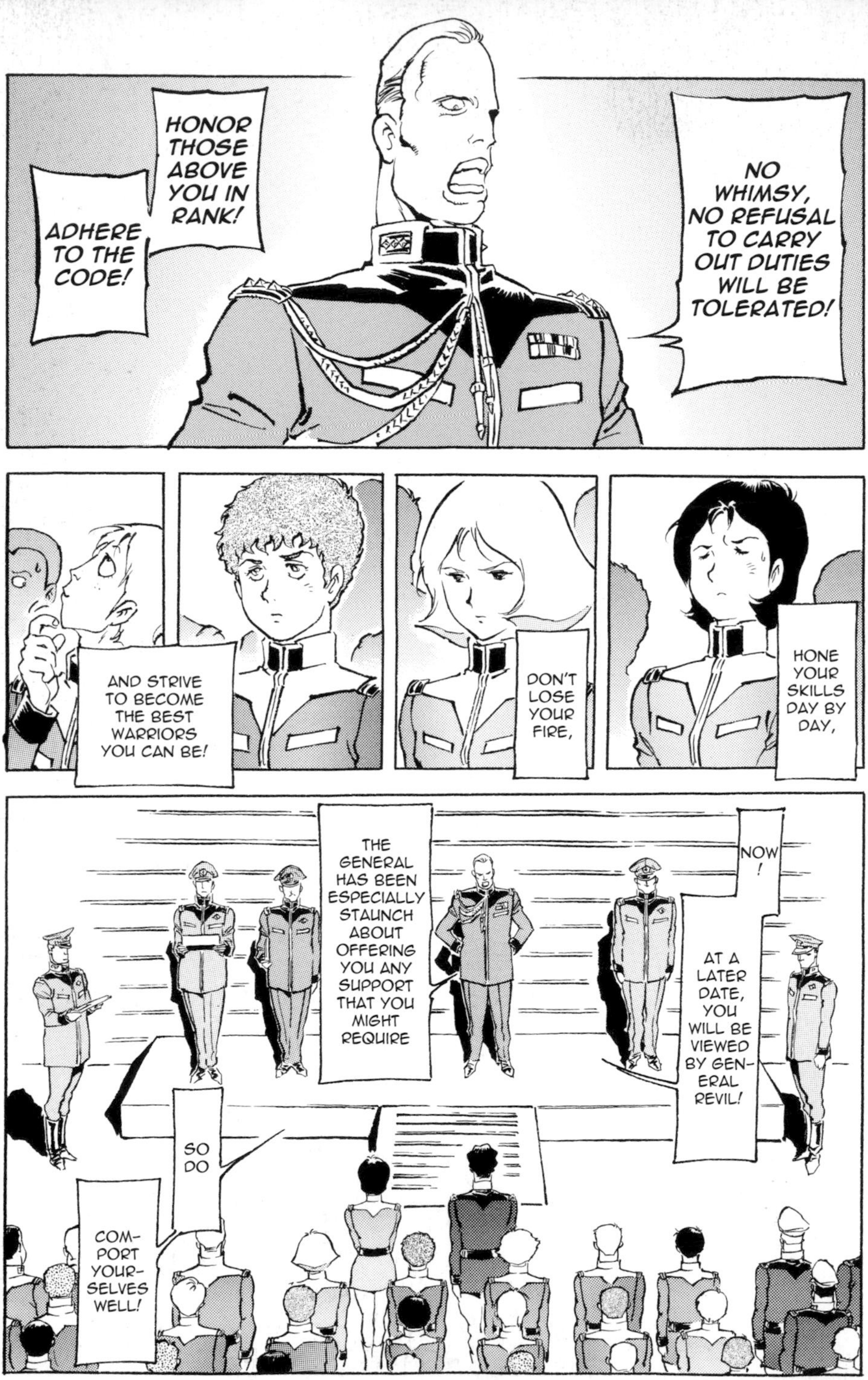
NO WHIMSY, NO REFUSAL TO CARRY OUT DUTIES WILL BE TOLERATED!
HONOR THOSE ABOVE YOU IN RANK!
ADHERE TO THE CODE!
HONE YOUR SKILLS DAY BY DAY,
DON'T LOSE YOUR FIRE,
AND STRIVE TO BECOME THE BEST WARRIORS YOU CAN BE!
NOW!
AT A LATER DATE, YOU WILL BE VIEWED BY GEN-ERAL REVIL!
THE GENERAL HAS BEEN ESPECIALLY STAUNCH ABOUT OFFERING YOU ANY SUPPORT THAT YOU MIGHT REQUIRE
SO DO
COM-PORT YOUR-SELVES WELL!

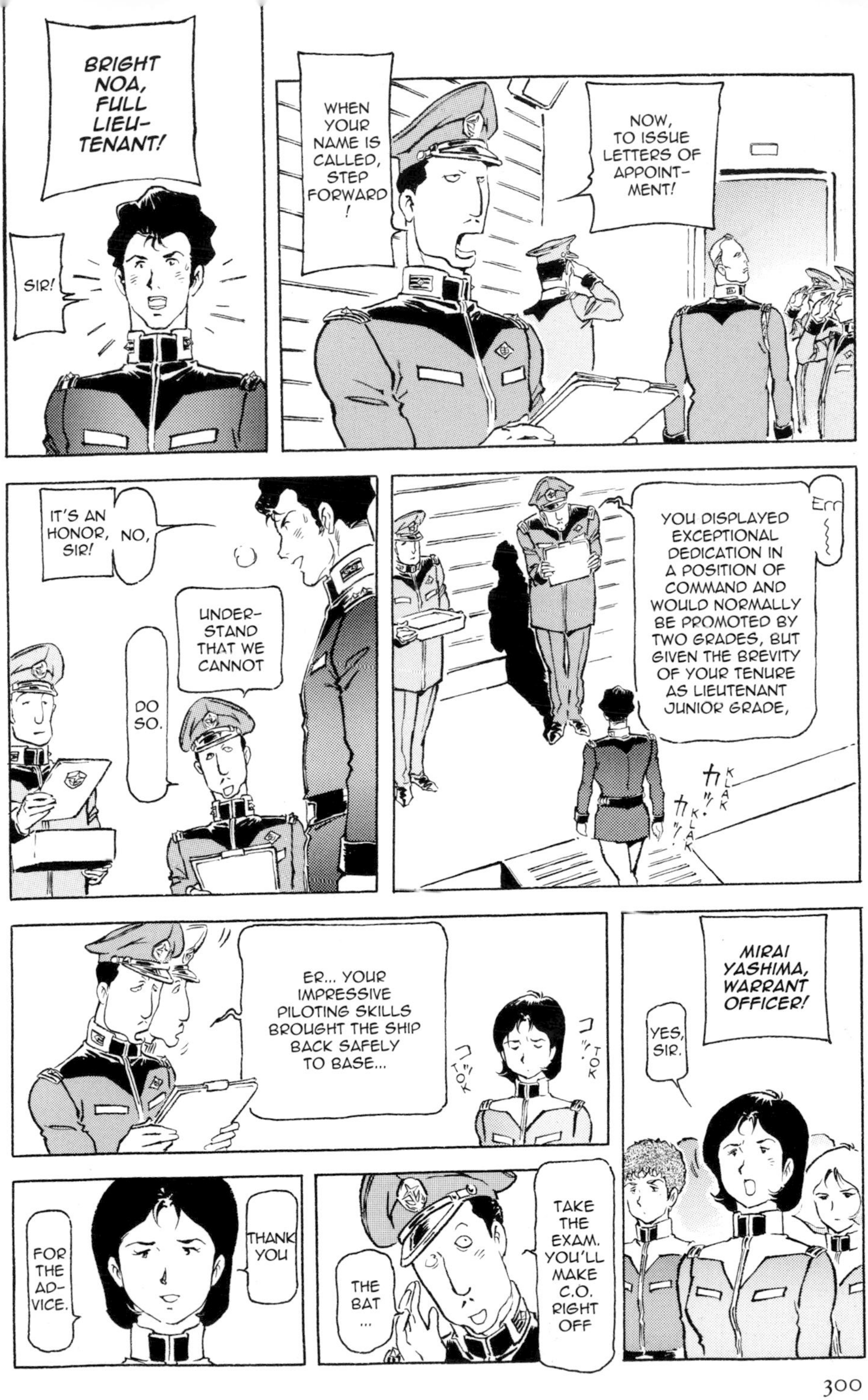
NOW, TO ISSUE LETTERS OF APPOINTMENT!
WHEN YOUR NAME IS CALLED, STEP FORWARD!
BRIGHT NOA, FULL LIEUTENANT!
SIR!
Err
YOU DISPLAYED EXCEPTIONAL DEDICATION IN A POSITION OF COMMAND AND WOULD NORMALLY BE PROMOTED BY TWO GRADES, BUT GIVEN THE BREVITY OF YOUR TENURE AS LIEUTENANT JUNIOR GRADE,
KLAK
KLAK
UNDERSTAND THAT WE CANNOT
DO SO.
NO,
IT'S AN HONOR, SIR!
MIRAI YASHIMA, WARRANT OFFICER!
YES, SIR.
TOK
ER... YOUR IMPRESSIVE PILOTING SKILLS BROUGHT THE SHIP BACK SAFELY TO BASE...
TOK
TAKE THE EXAM. YOU'LL MAKE C.O. RIGHT OFF
THE BAT...
THANK YOU
FOR THE ADVICE.

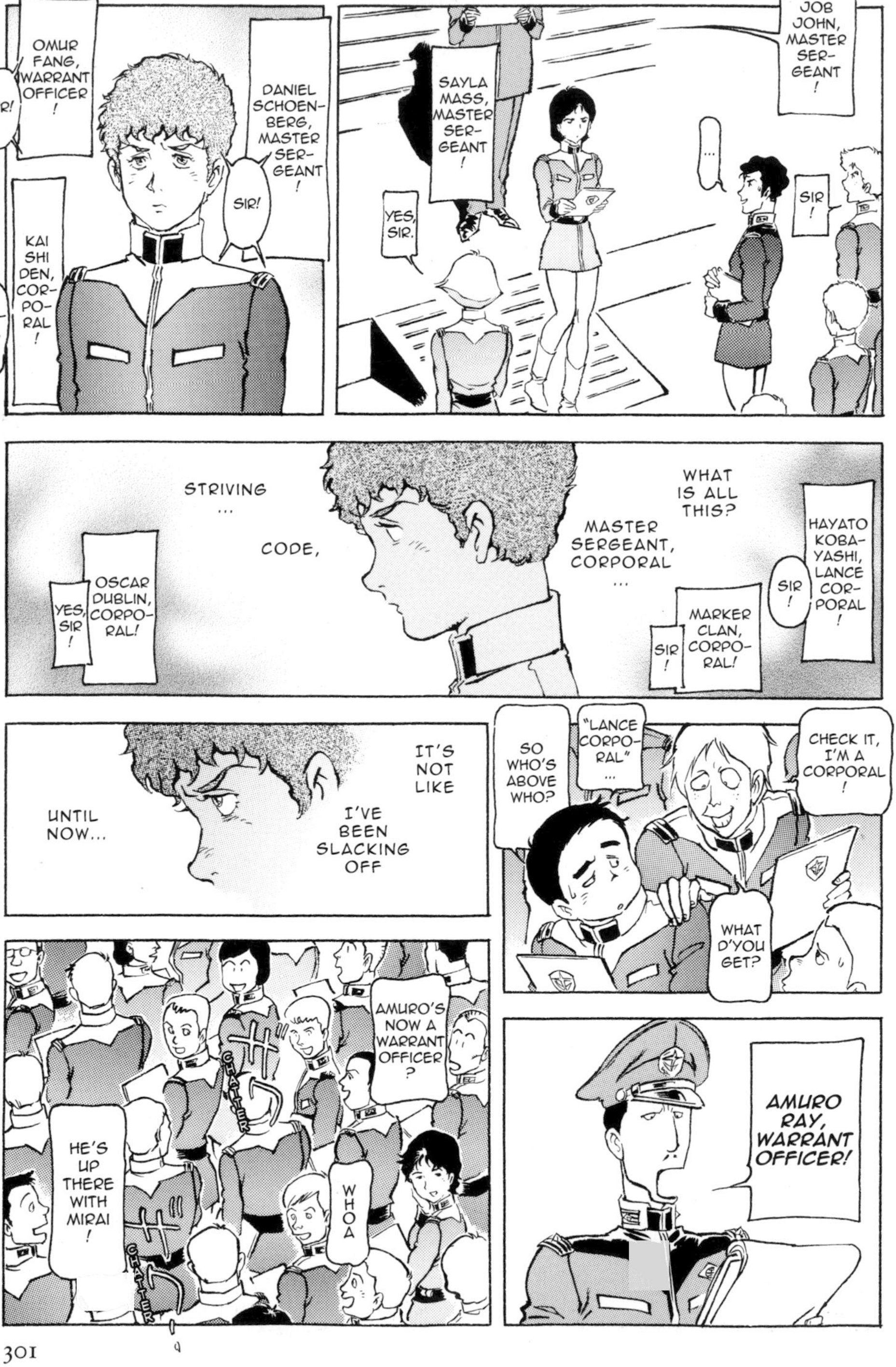
JOB JOHN, MASTER SER-GEANT!
SIR!
...
SAYLA MASS, MASTER SER-GEANT!
YES, SIR.
DANIEL SCHOEN-BERG, MASTER SER-GEANT!
SIR!
OMUR FANG, WARRANT OFFICER!
SIR!
KAI SHI DEN, COR-PO-RAL!
YES-SIR.
HAYATO KOBA-YASHI, LANCE COR-PORAL!
SIR!
WHAT IS ALL THIS?
MARKER CLAN, CORPO-RAL!
SIR!
MASTER SERGEANT, CORPORAL...
CODE,
STRIVING...
OSCAR DUBLIN, CORPO-RAL!
YES, SIR!
CHECK IT, I'M A CORPORAL!
"LANCE CORPO-RAL"...
SO WHO'S ABOVE WHO?
WHAT D'YOU GET?
IT'S NOT LIKE
I'VE BEEN SLACKING OFF
UNTIL NOW...
AMURO RAY, WARRANT OFFICER!
AMURO'S NOW A WARRANT OFFICER?
CHATTER
WHOA
HE'S UP THERE WITH MIRAI!
CHATTER

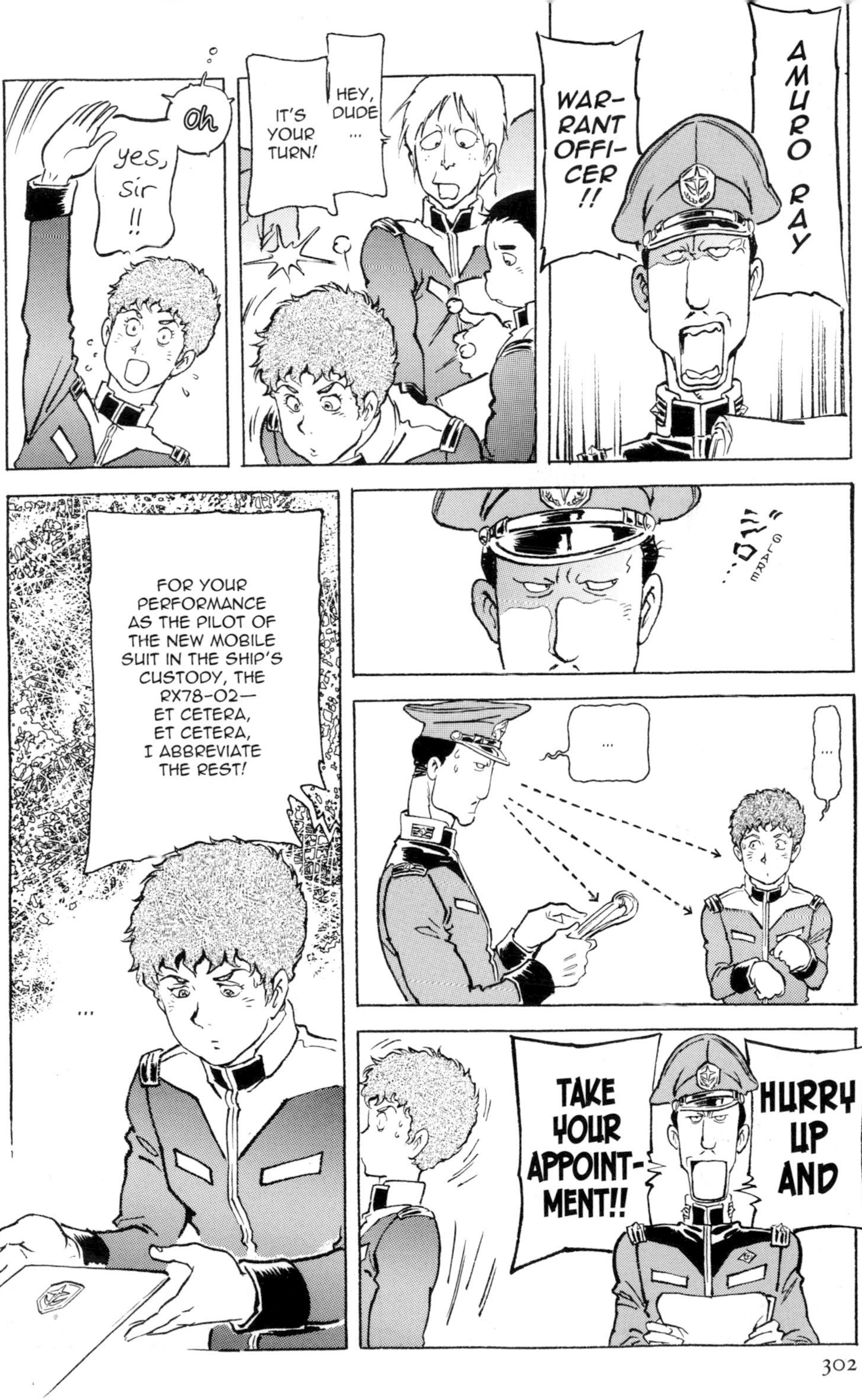
AMURO RAY
WARRANT OFFICER!!
HEY, DUDE ...
IT'S YOUR TURN!
Oh
yes, sir!!
GLARE
...
...
HURRY UP AND
TAKE YOUR APPOINTMENT!!
FOR YOUR PERFORMANCE AS THE PILOT OF THE NEW MOBILE SUIT IN THE SHIP'S CUSTODY, THE RX78-02— ET CETERA, ET CETERA, I ABBREVIATE THE REST!
...

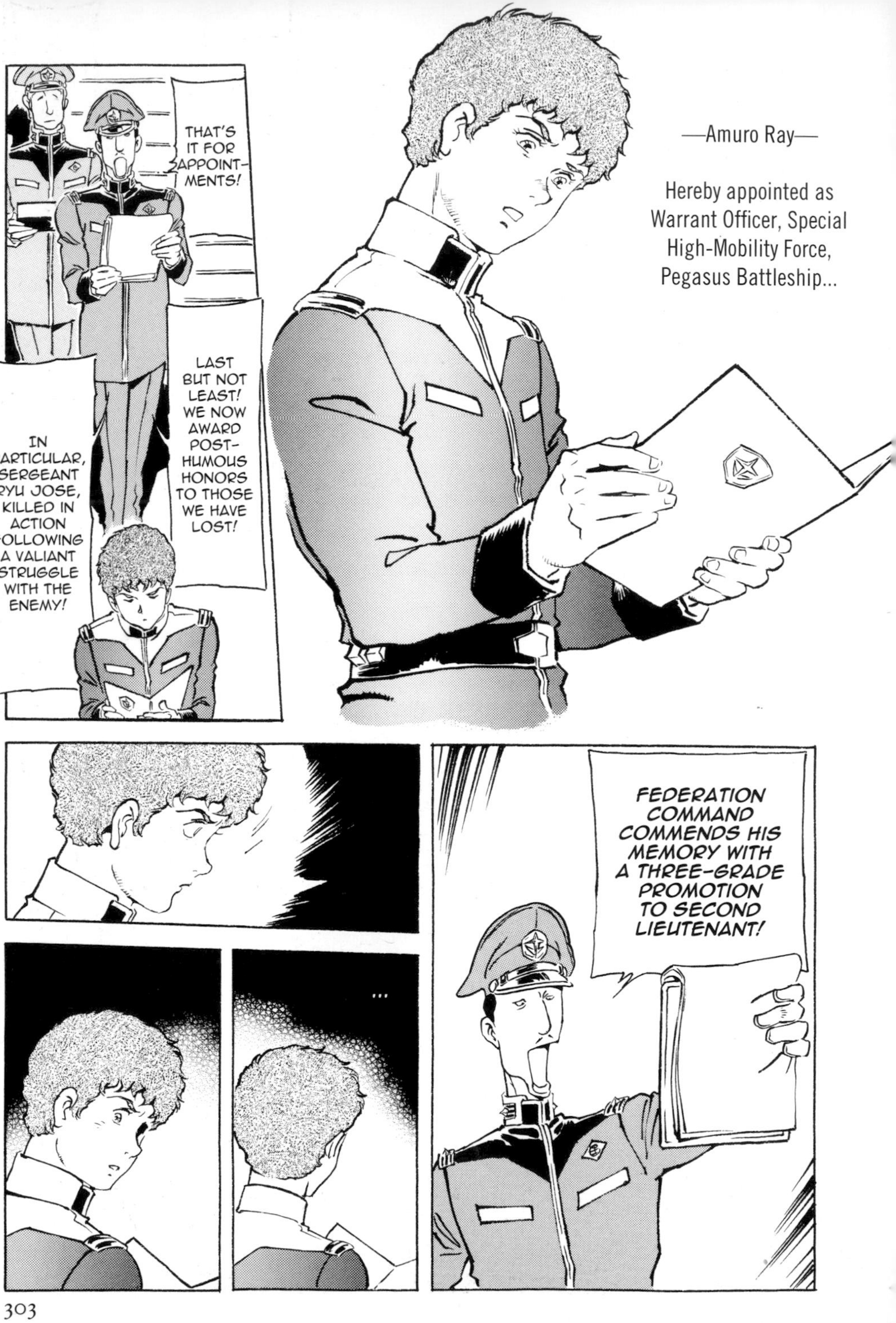
—Amuro Ray—
Hereby appointed as Warrant Officer, Special High-Mobility Force, Pegasus Battleship...
THAT'S IT FOR APPOINTMENTS!
LAST BUT NOT LEAST! WE NOW AWARD POSTHUMOUS HONORS TO THOSE WE HAVE LOST!
IN PARTICULAR, SERGEANT RYU JOSE, KILLED IN ACTION FOLLOWING A VALIANT STRUGGLE WITH THE ENEMY!
FEDERATION COMMAND COMMENDS HIS MEMORY WITH A THREE-GRADE PROMOTION TO SECOND LIEUTENANT!
...

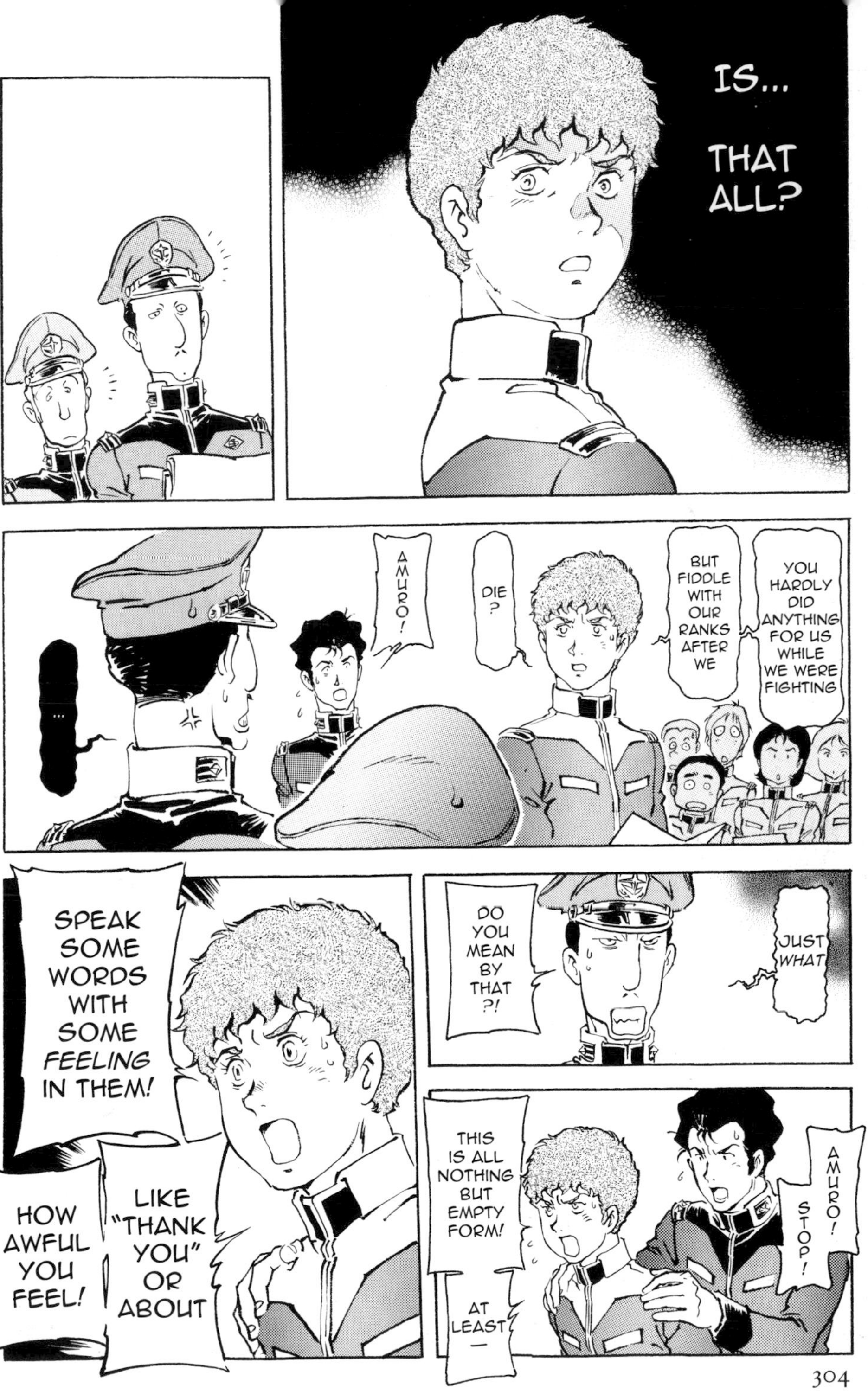
IS...
THAT ALL?
YOU HARDLY DID ANYTHING FOR US WHILE WE WERE FIGHTING
BUT FIDDLE WITH OUR RANKS AFTER WE
DIE?
AMURO!
...
JUST WHAT
DO YOU MEAN BY THAT?!
AMURO! STOP!
THIS IS ALL NOTHING BUT EMPTY FORM!
AT LEAST—
SPEAK SOME WORDS WITH SOME FEELING IN THEM!
LIKE "THANK YOU" OR ABOUT
HOW AWFUL YOU FEEL!

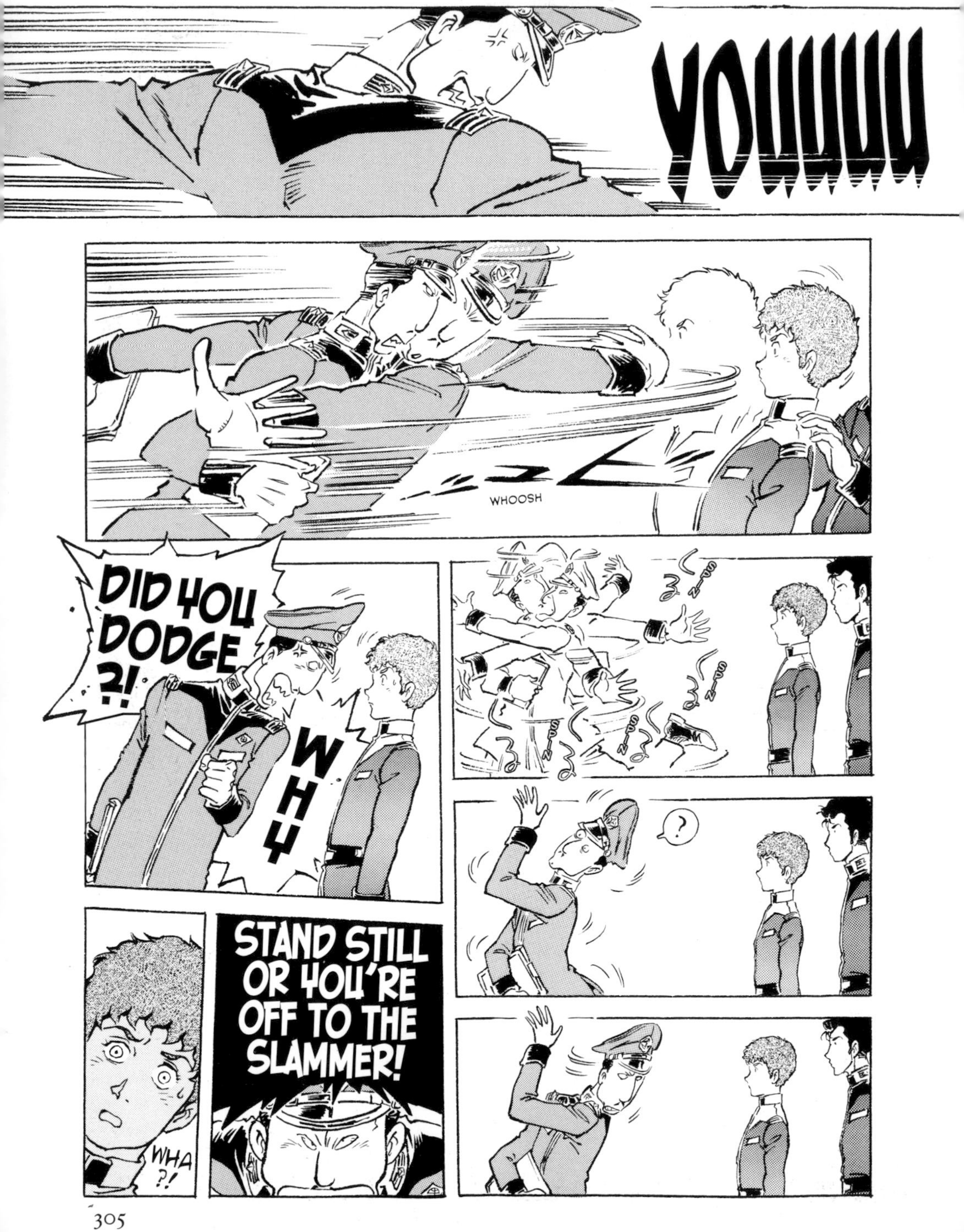
YOUUUU
WHOOSH
?
DID YOU DODGE?!
WHY
STAND STILL OR YOU'RE OFF TO THE SLAMMER!
WHA?!

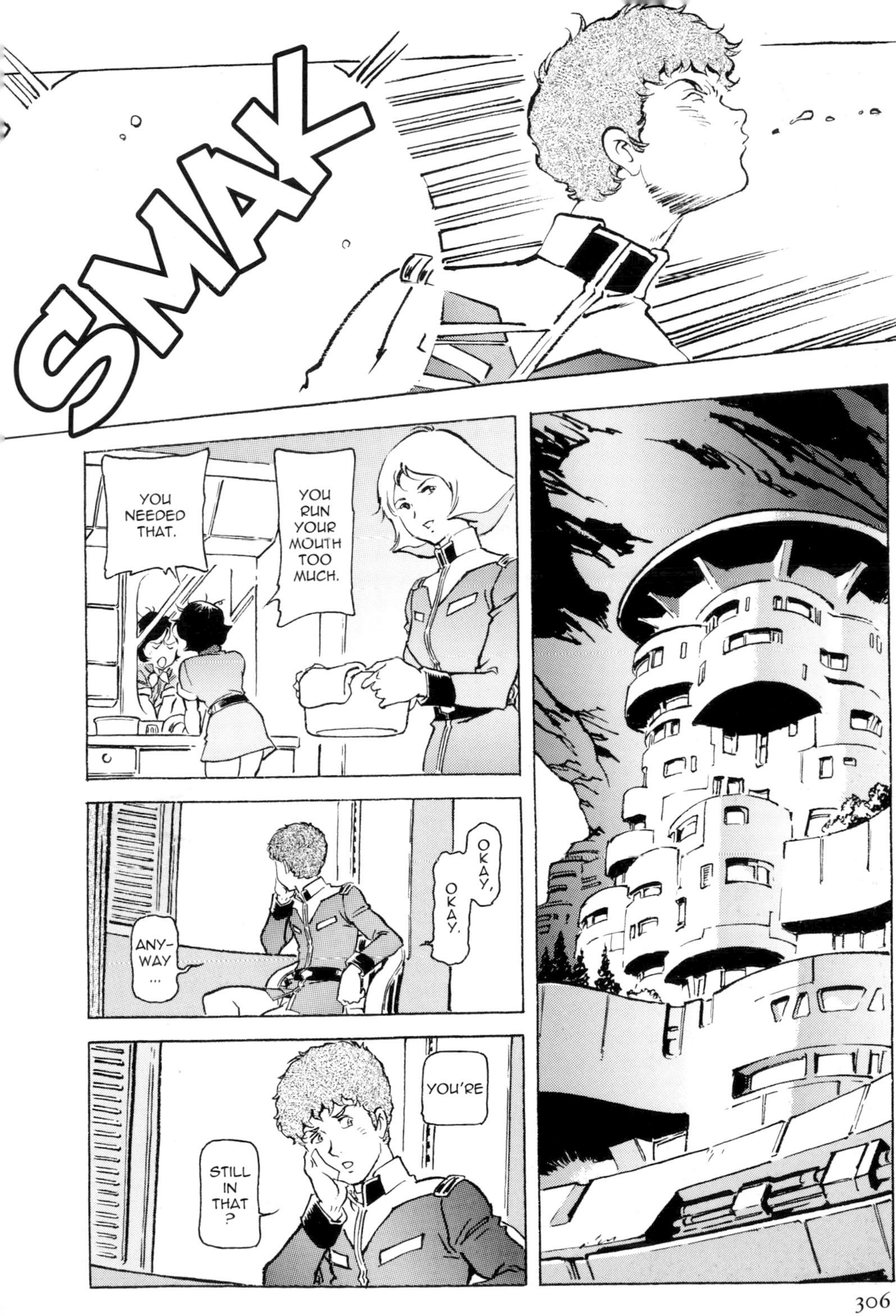
SMAK
YOU RUN YOUR MOUTH TOO MUCH.
YOU NEEDED THAT.
OKAY, OKAY.
ANY-WAY ...
YOU'RE
STILL IN THAT ?

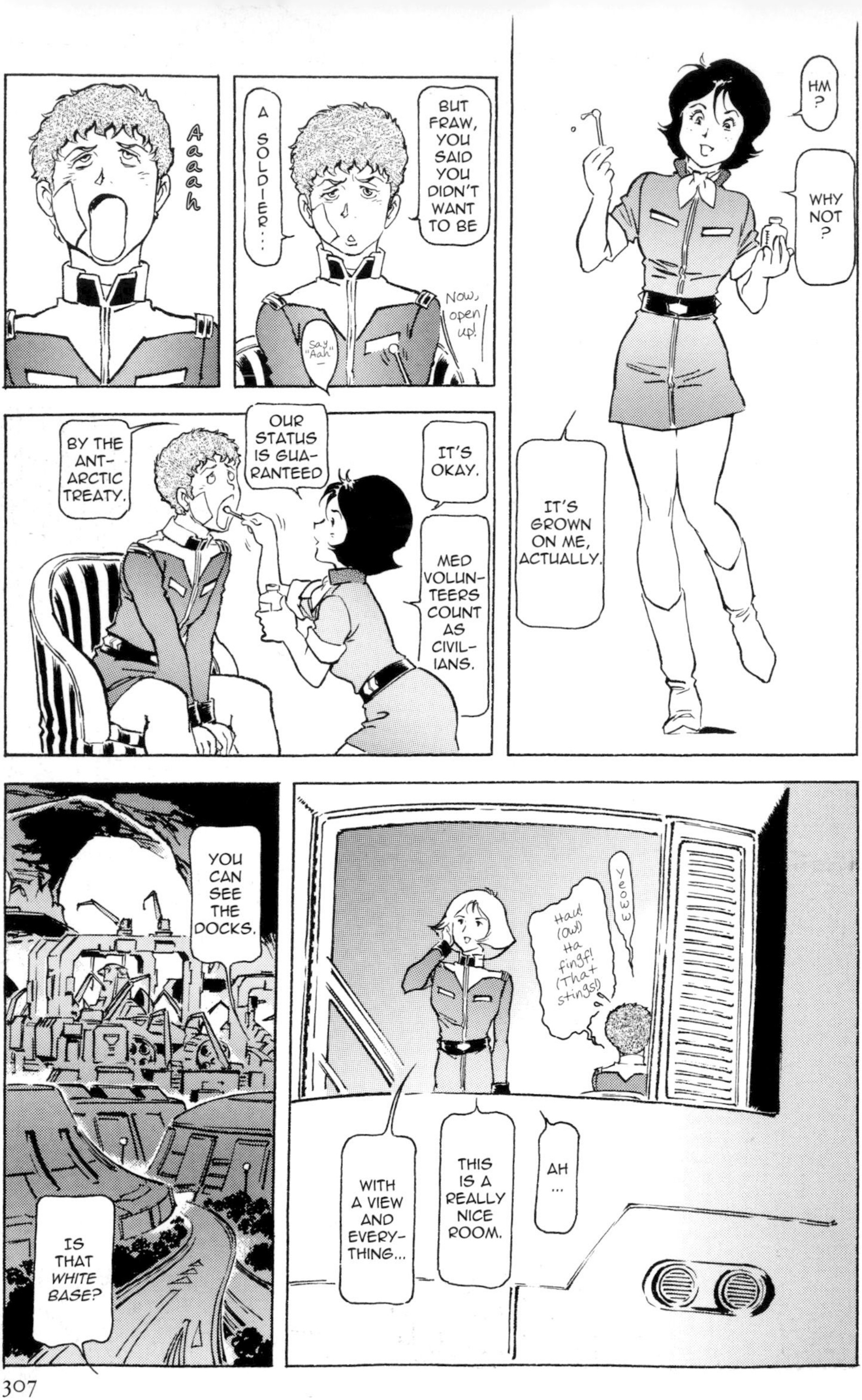
HM?
WHY NOT?
IT'S GROWN ON ME, ACTUALLY.
BUT FRAW, YOU SAID YOU DIDN'T WANT TO BE
A SOLDIER...
Now, open up!
Say "Aah"
Aaaah
IT'S OKAY.
MED VOLUNTEERS COUNT AS CIVILIANS.
OUR STATUS IS GUARANTEED
BY THE ANTARCTIC TREATY.
Yeoww
Hau! (Ow!) Ha fingf! (That stings!)
AH...
THIS IS A REALLY NICE ROOM.
WITH A VIEW AND EVERYTHING...
YOU CAN SEE THE DOCKS.
IS THAT WHITE BASE?

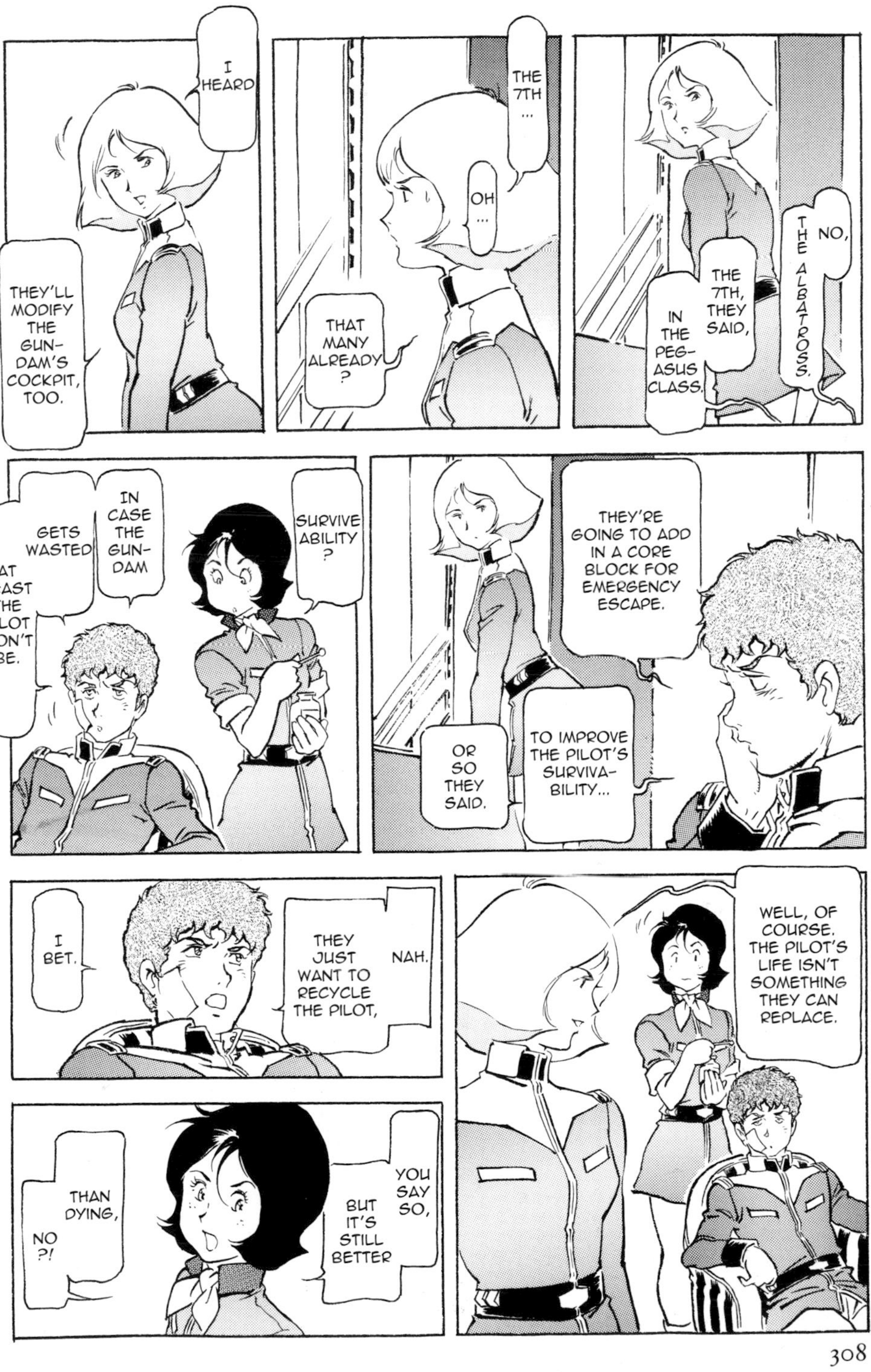
NO,
THE ALBATROSS.
THE 7TH, THEY SAID,
IN THE PEGASUS CLASS.
THE 7TH ...
OH ...
THAT MANY ALREADY ?
I HEARD
THEY'LL MODIFY THE GUNDAM'S COCKPIT, TOO.
THEY'RE GOING TO ADD IN A CORE BLOCK FOR EMERGENCY ESCAPE.
TO IMPROVE THE PILOT'S SURVIVABILITY...
OR SO THEY SAID.
SURVIVE ABILITY ?
IN CASE THE GUNDAM
GETS WASTED
AT LEAST THE PILOT WON'T BE.
WELL, OF COURSE. THE PILOT'S LIFE ISN'T SOMETHING THEY CAN REPLACE.
NAH.
THEY JUST WANT TO RECYCLE THE PILOT,
I BET.
YOU SAY SO,
BUT IT'S STILL BETTER
THAN DYING,
NO ?!

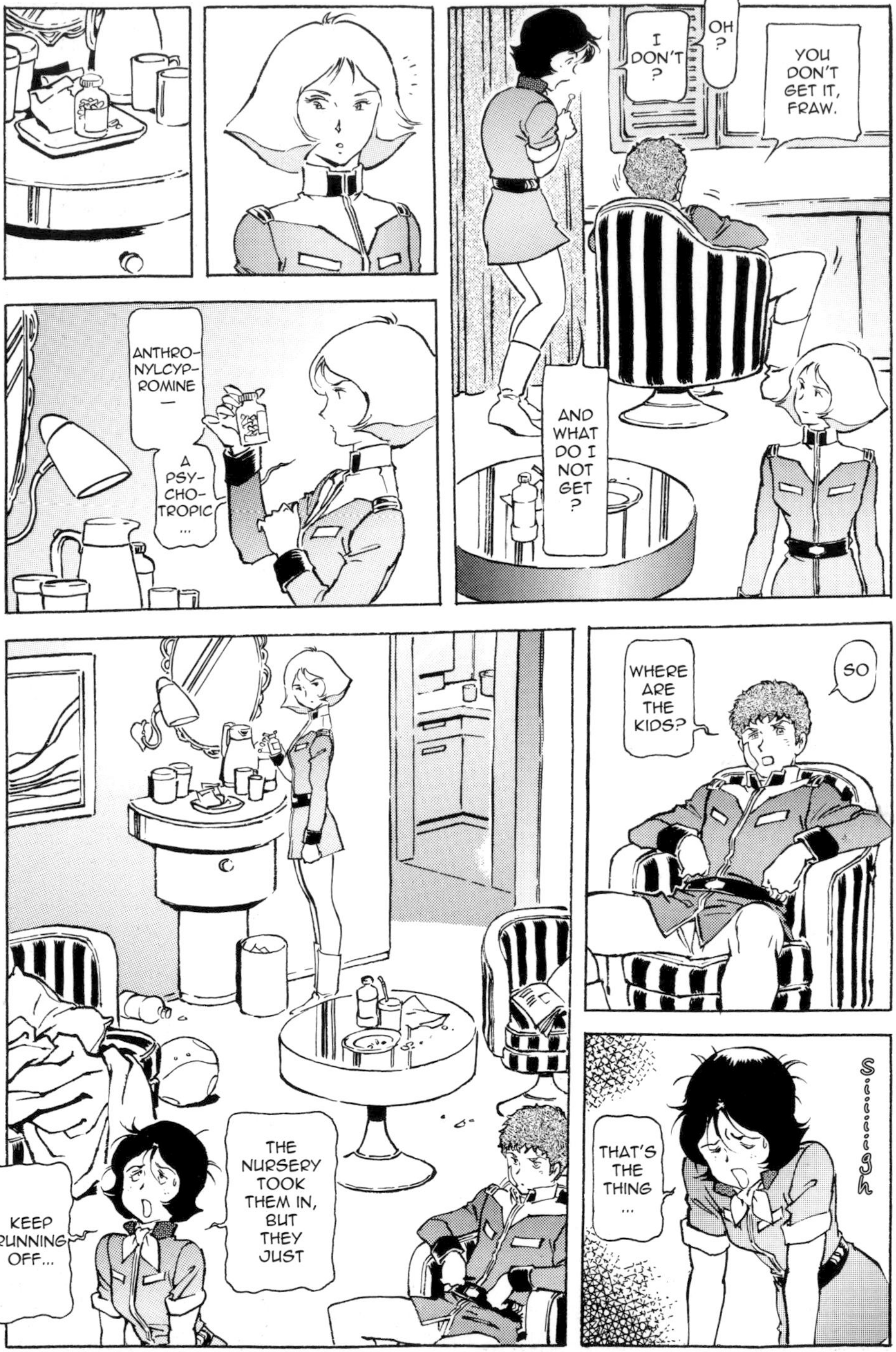
YOU DON'T GET IT, FRAW.
OH?
I DON'T?
AND WHAT DO I NOT GET?
ANTHRONYLCYPROMINE —
A PSYCHOTROPIC ...
SO
WHERE ARE THE KIDS?
Siiiigh
THAT'S THE THING ...
THE NURSERY TOOK THEM IN, BUT THEY JUST
KEEP RUNNING OFF...

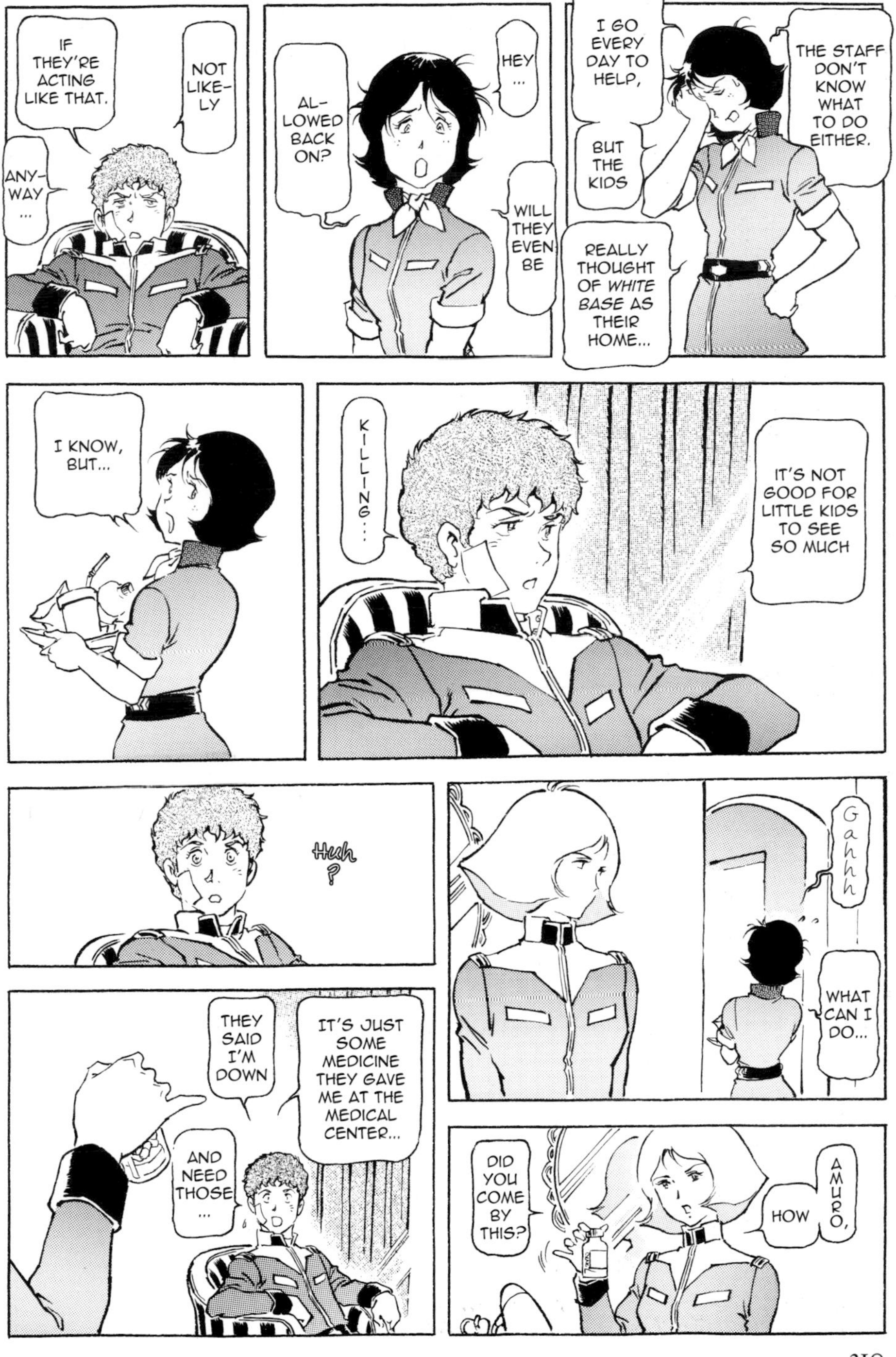
THE STAFF DON'T KNOW WHAT TO DO EITHER.
I GO EVERY DAY TO HELP,
BUT THE KIDS
REALLY THOUGHT OF *WHITE BASE* AS THEIR HOME...
HEY ...
WILL THEY EVEN BE
AL-LOWED BACK ON?
NOT LIKE-LY
IF THEY'RE ACTING LIKE THAT.
ANY-WAY ...
IT'S NOT GOOD FOR LITTLE KIDS TO SEE SO MUCH
KILLING...
I KNOW, BUT...
Gahhh
WHAT CAN I DO...
Huh?
AMURO,
HOW
DID YOU COME BY THIS?
IT'S JUST SOME MEDICINE THEY GAVE ME AT THE MEDICAL CENTER...
THEY SAID I'M DOWN
AND NEED THOSE ...

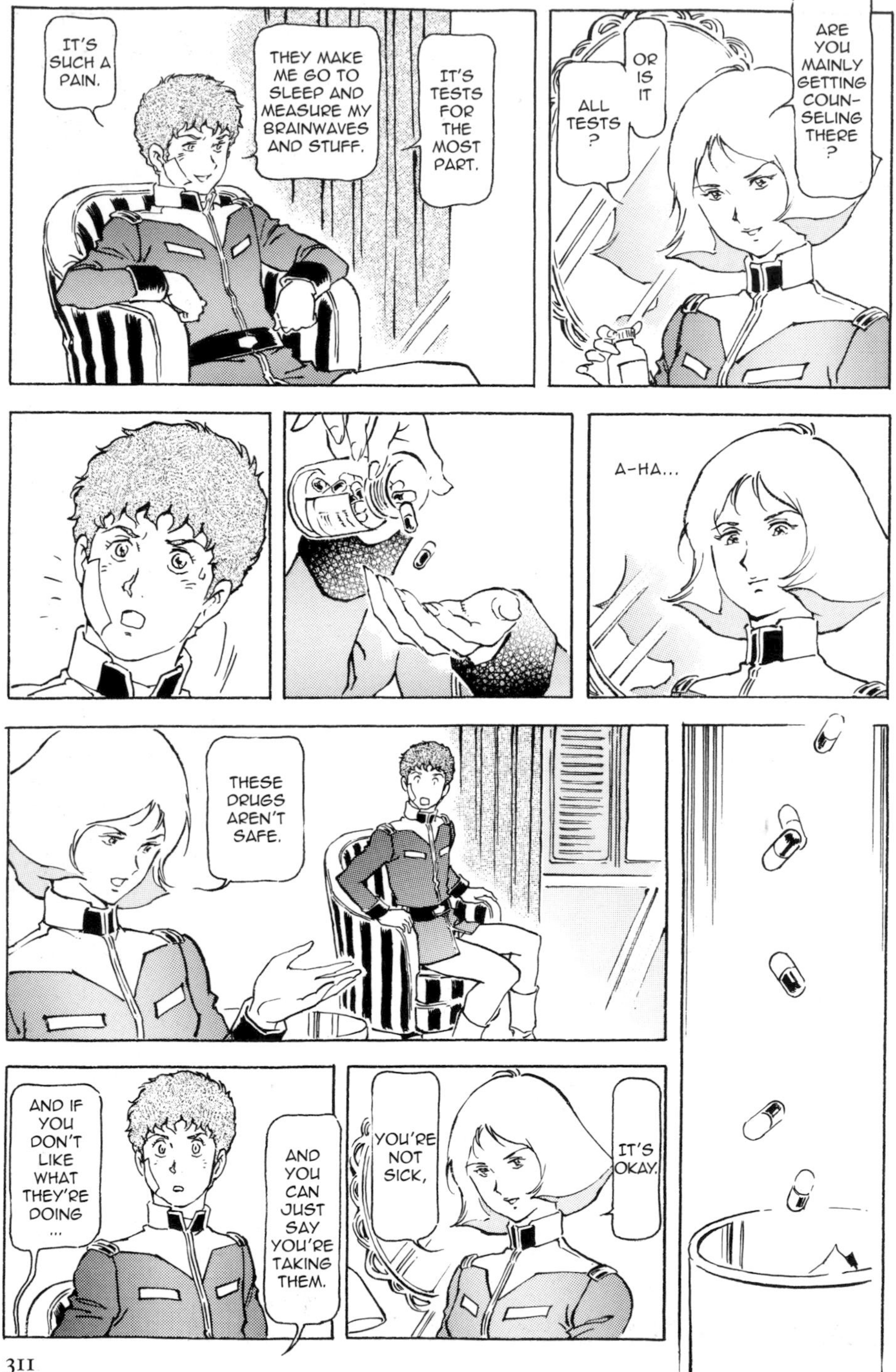
ARE YOU MAINLY GETTING COUN-SELING THERE?
OR IS IT
ALL TESTS?
IT'S TESTS FOR THE MOST PART.
THEY MAKE ME GO TO SLEEP AND MEASURE MY BRAINWAVES AND STUFF.
IT'S SUCH A PAIN.
A-HA...
THESE DRUGS AREN'T SAFE.
IT'S OKAY.
YOU'RE NOT SICK,
AND IF YOU DON'T LIKE WHAT THEY'RE DOING...
AND YOU CAN JUST SAY YOU'RE TAKING THEM.

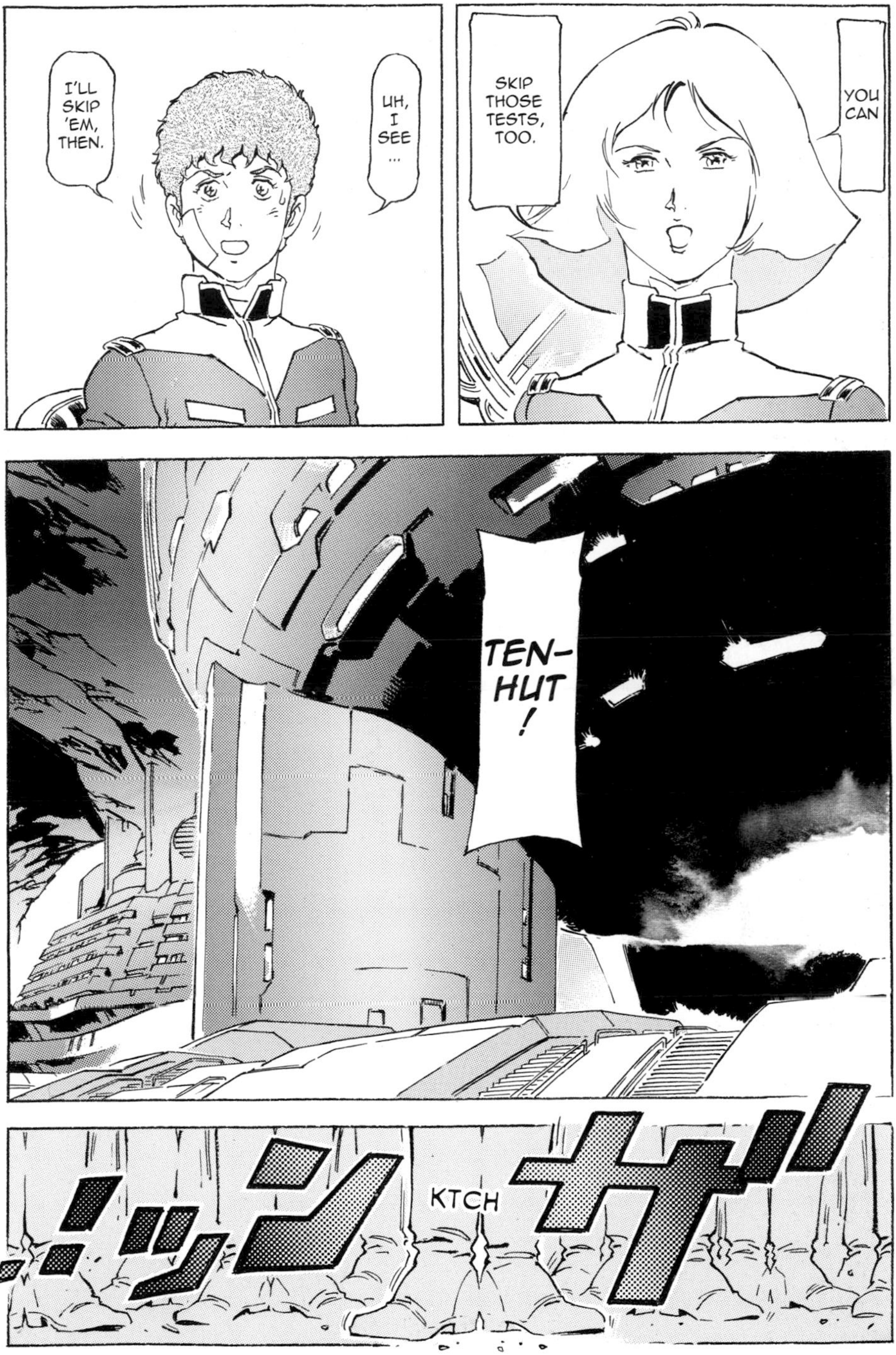
YOU CAN
SKIP THOSE TESTS, TOO.
UH, I SEE ...
I'LL SKIP 'EM, THEN.
TEN-HUT!
KTCH

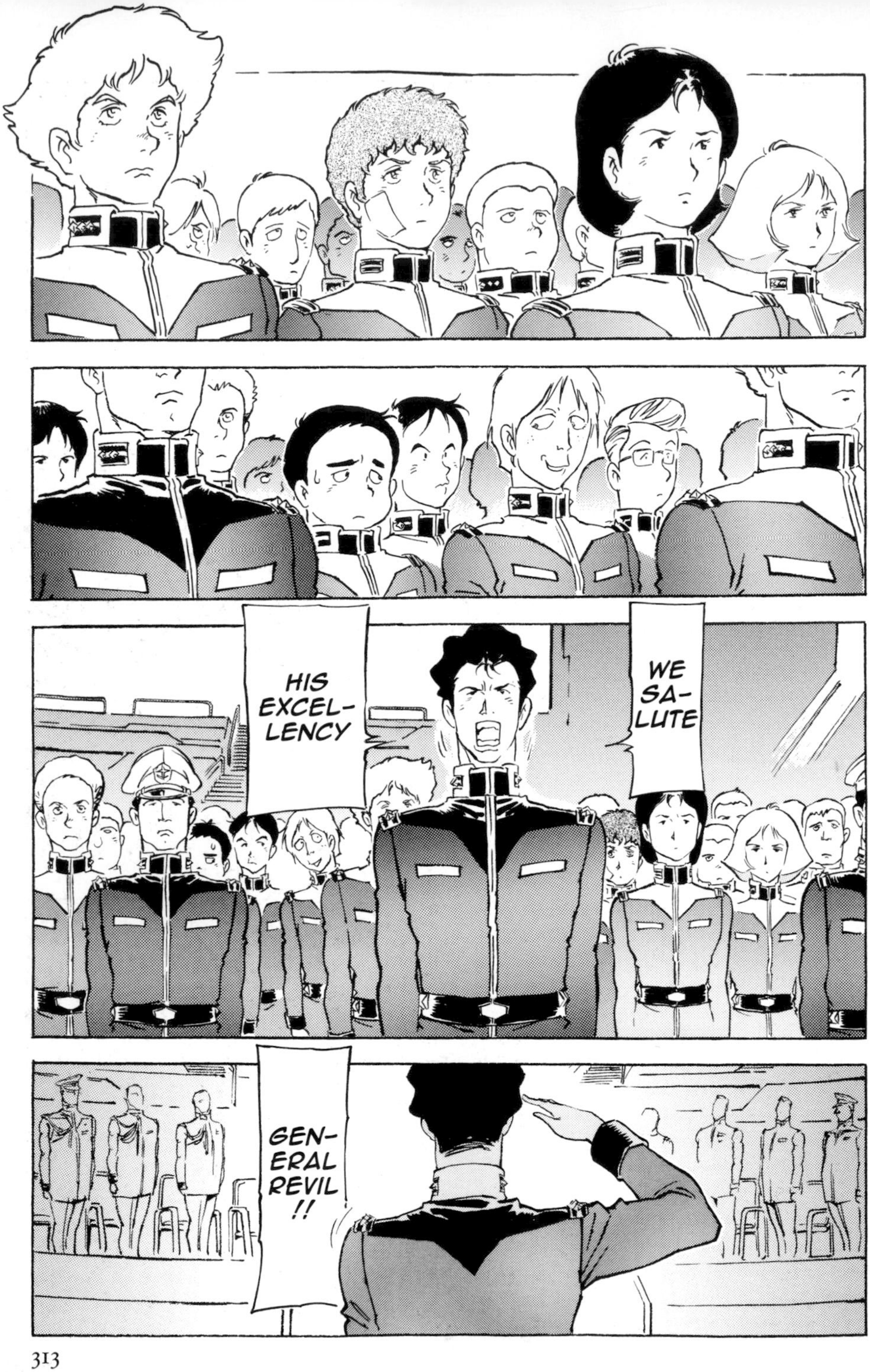
WE SA- LUTE
HIS EXCEL- LENCY
GEN- ERAL REVIL !!

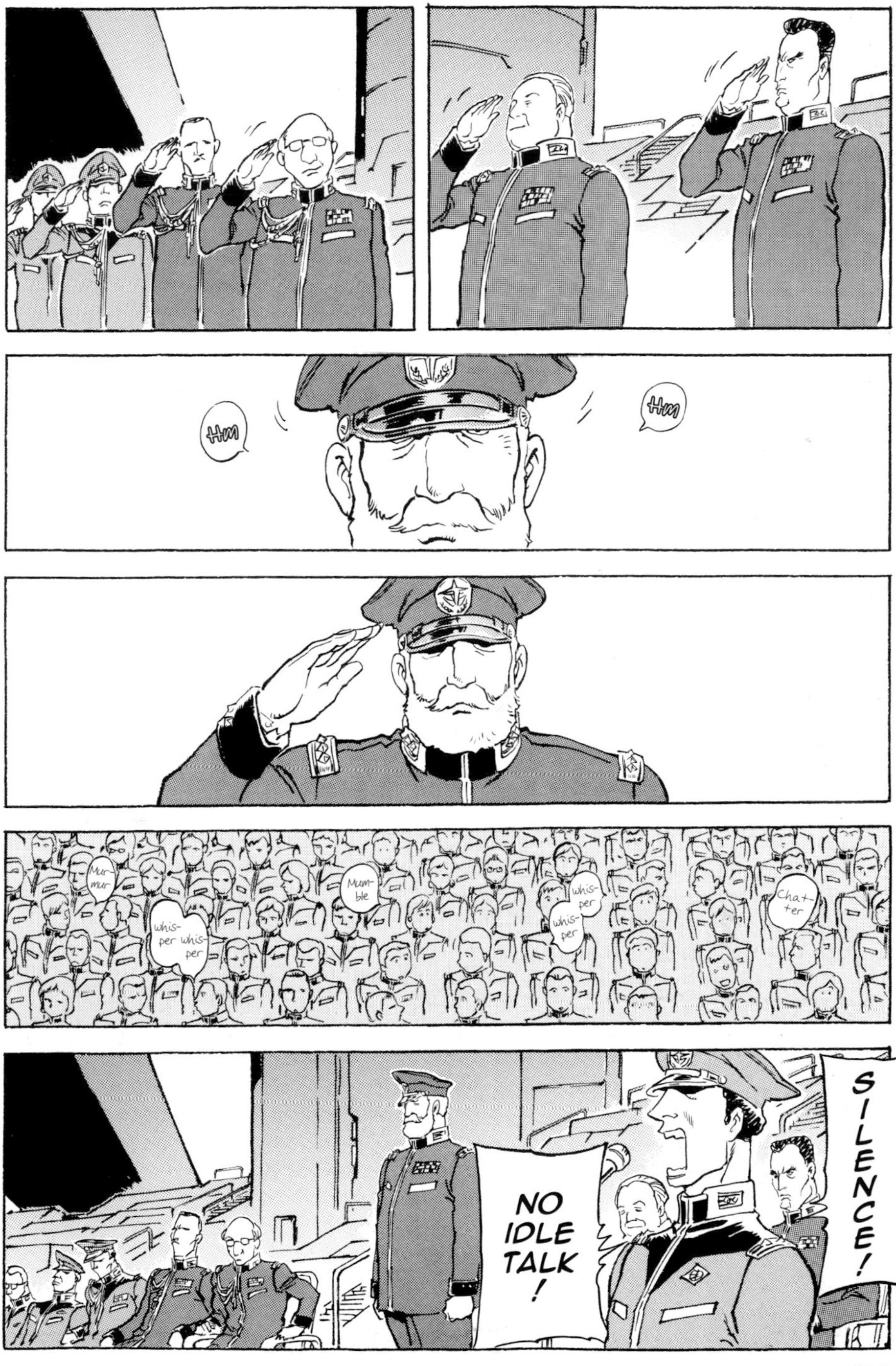
Hm
Hm
Chatter
whisper
whisper
Mumble
Murmur
whisper whisper
SILENCE!
NO IDLE TALK!

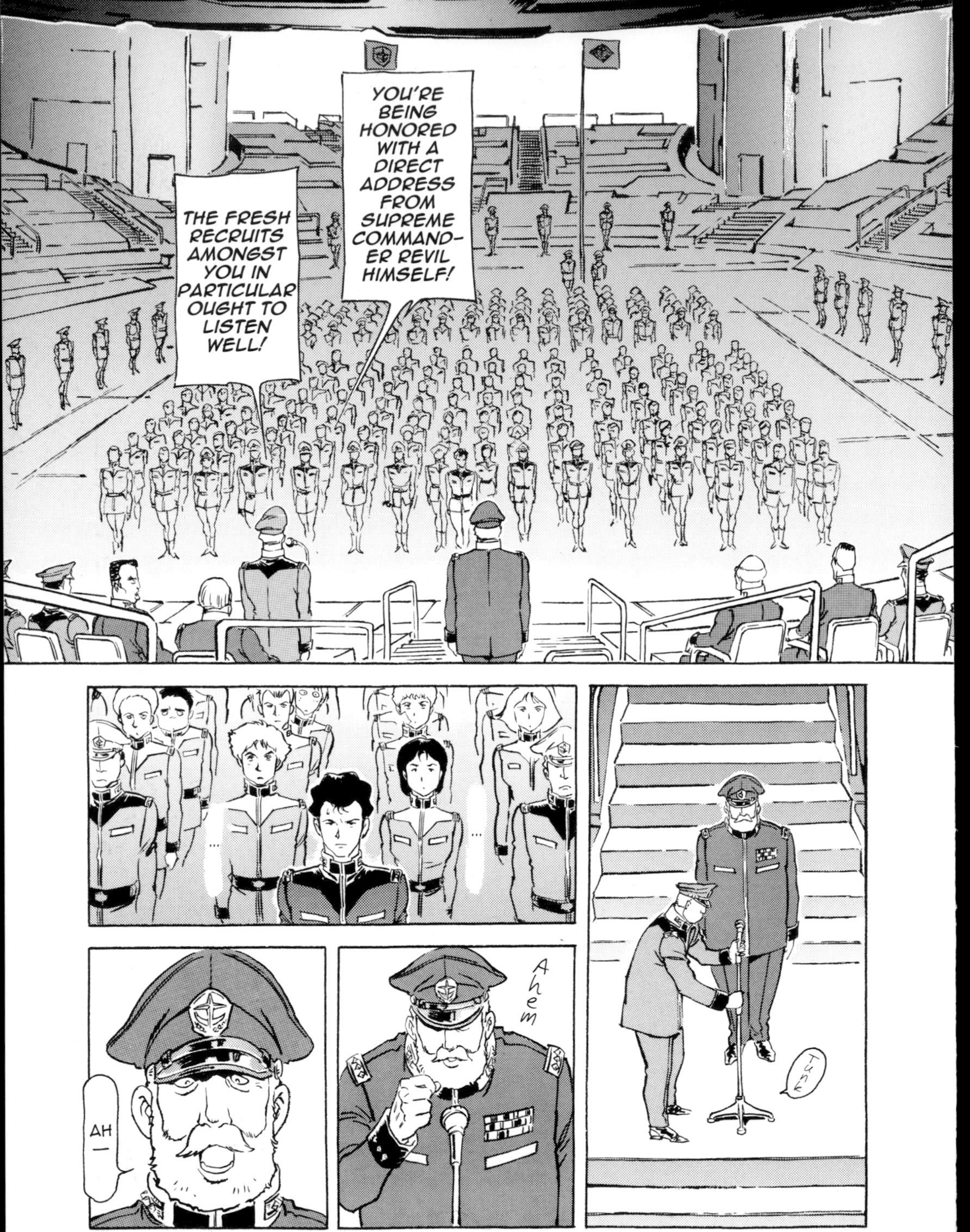

YOU'RE BEING HONORED WITH A DIRECT ADDRESS FROM SUPREME COMMANDER REVIL HIMSELF!
THE FRESH RECRUITS AMONGST YOU IN PARTICULAR OUGHT TO LISTEN WELL!
Tunk
...
...
Ahem
AH—

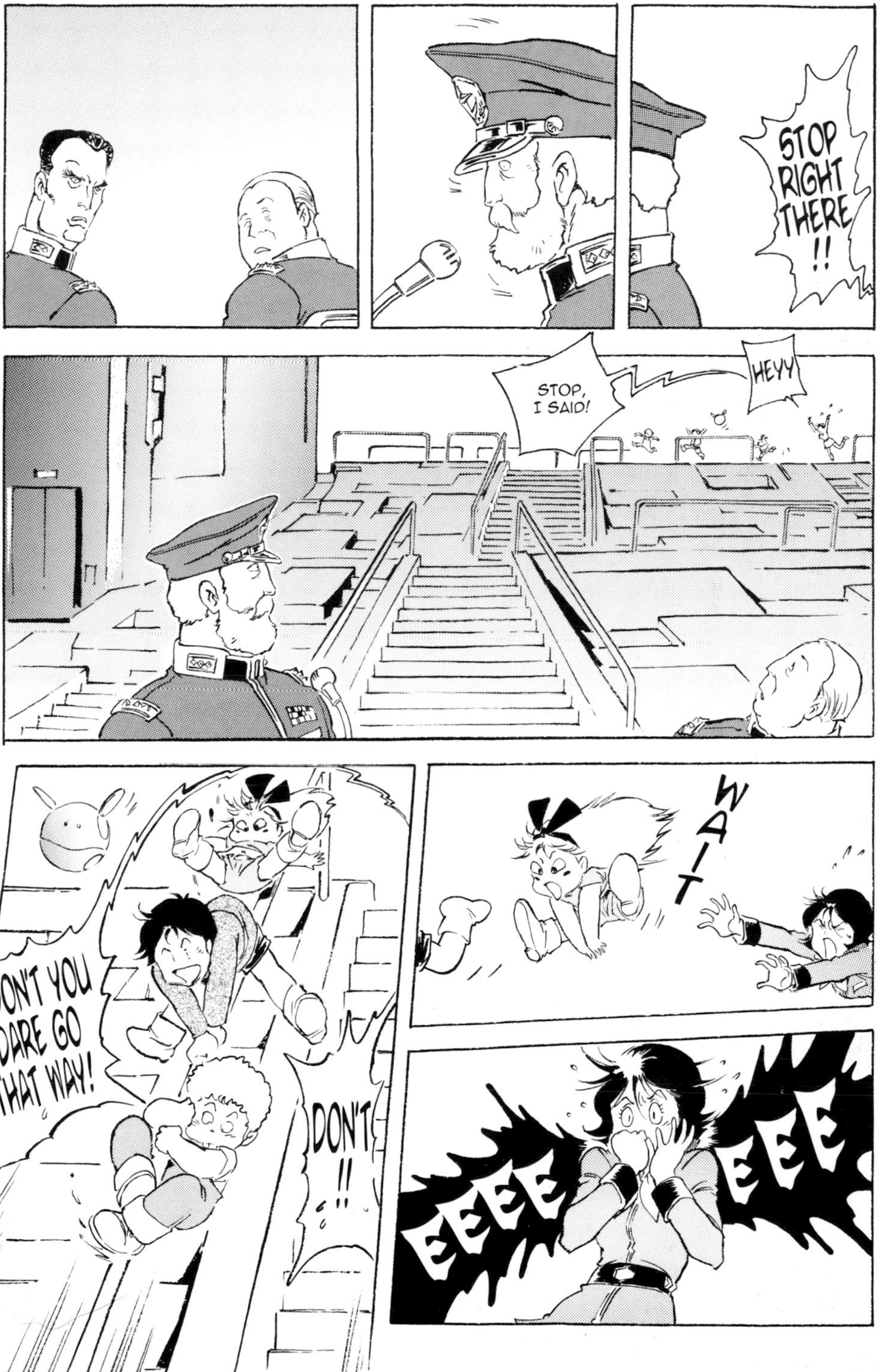
STOP RIGHT THERE!!
HEYY
STOP, I SAID!
WAIT
EEEE EEE
DON'T YOU DARE GO THAT WAY!
DON'T!!

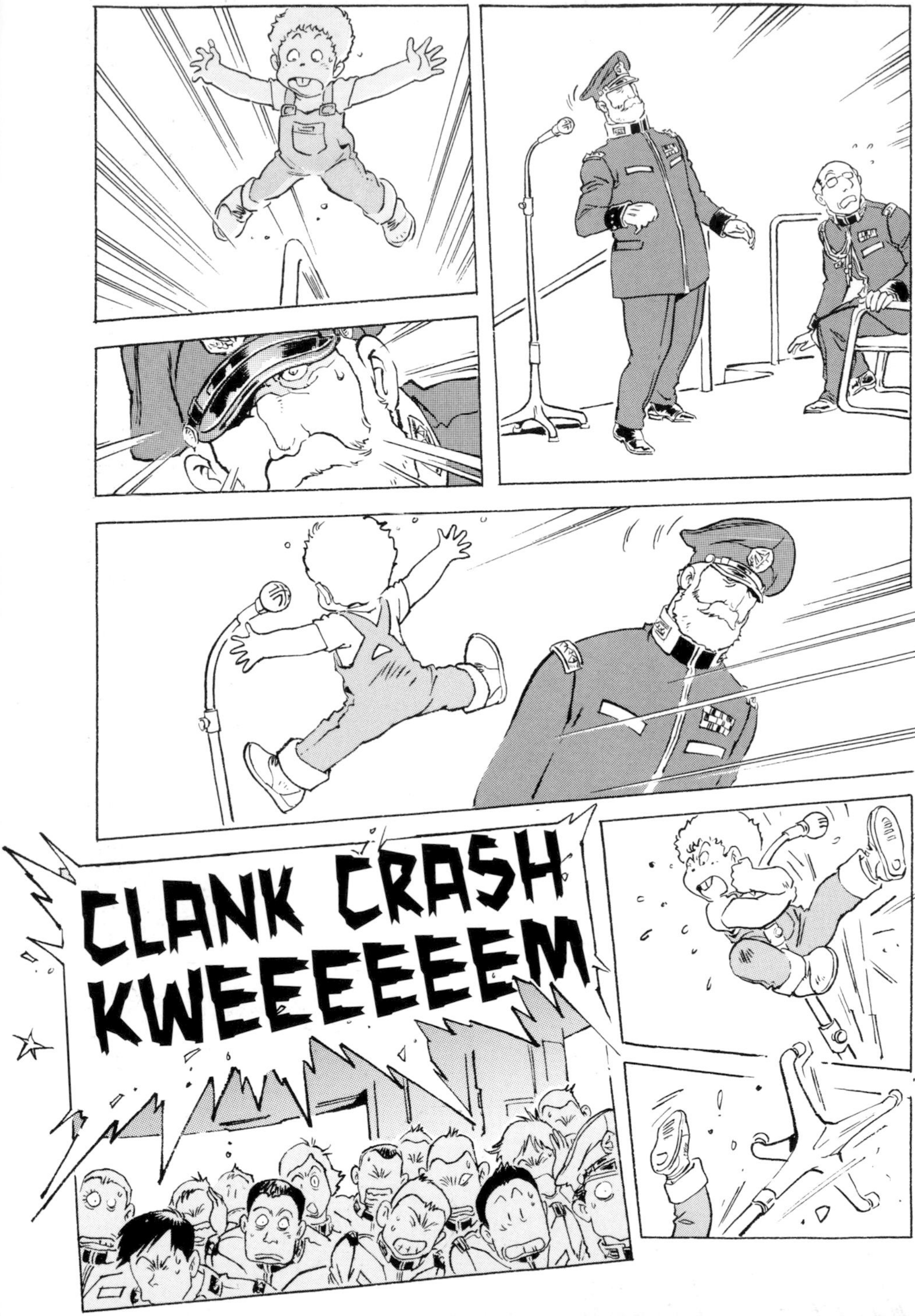
CLANK CRASH
KWEEEEEEM

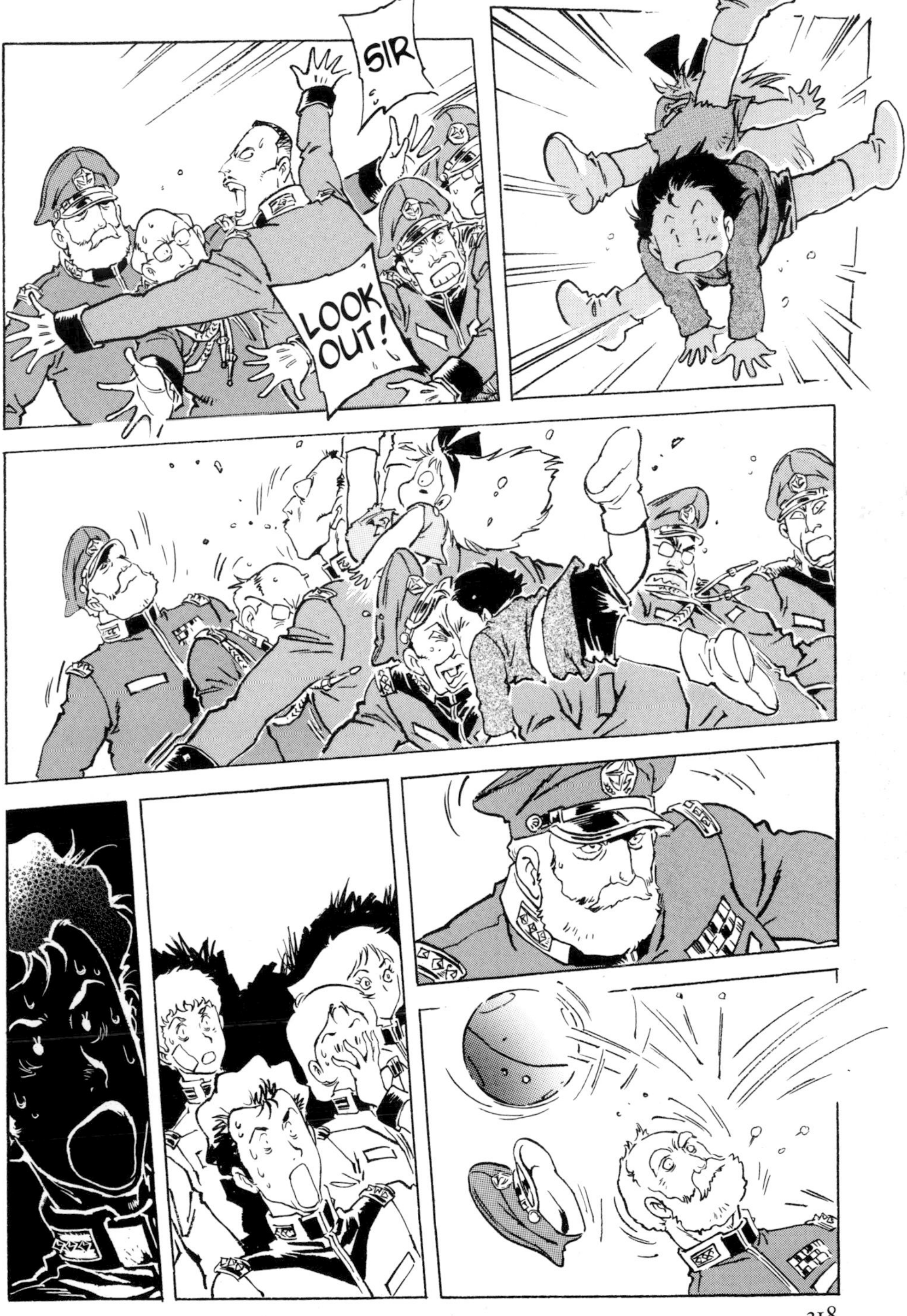
SIR
LOOK OUT!

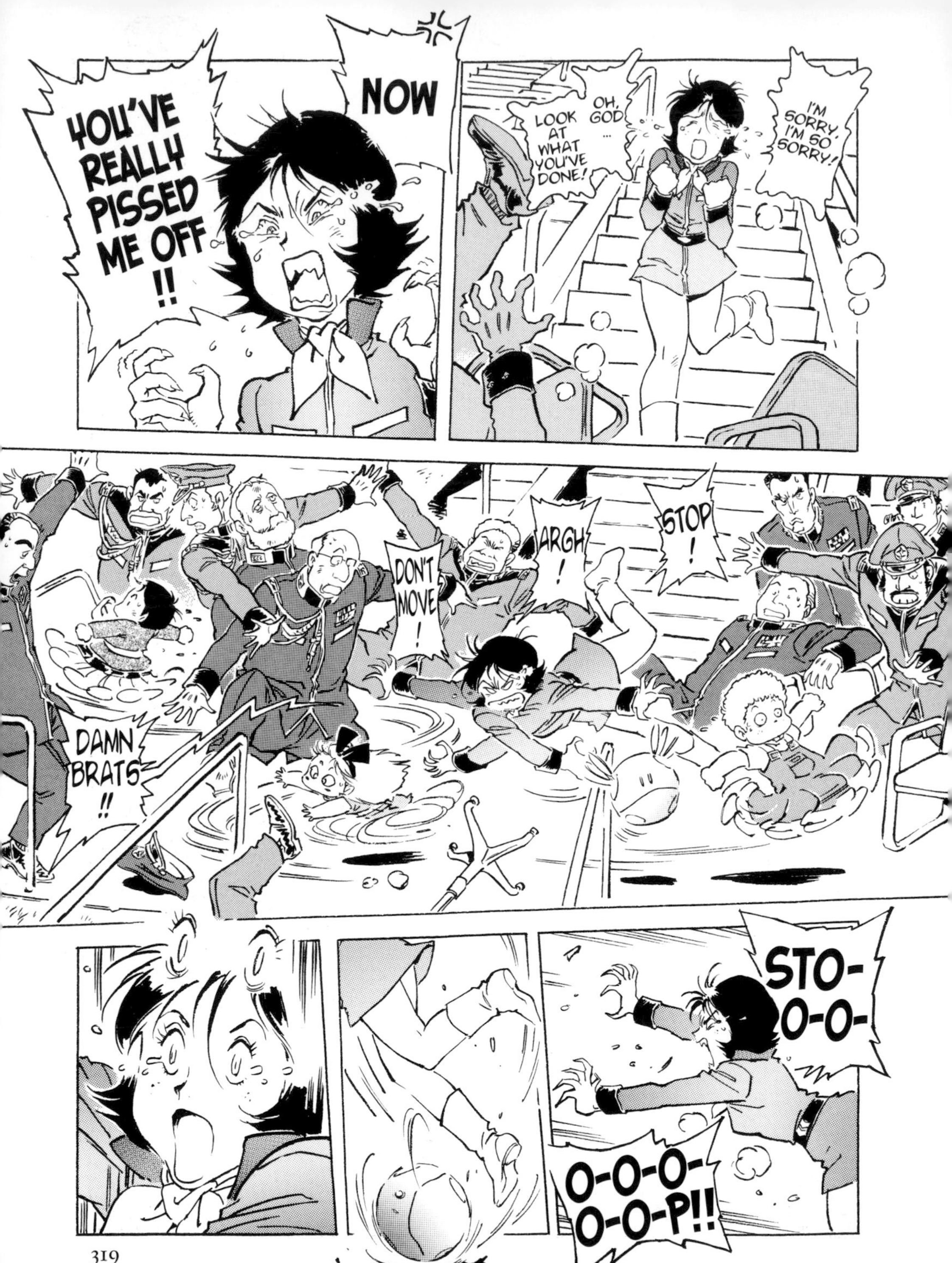
I'M SORRY, I'M SO SORRY!
OH, GOD ...
LOOK AT WHAT YOU'VE DONE!
NOW
YOU'VE REALLY PISSED ME OFF !!
STOP !
ARGH !
DON'T MOVE !
DAMN BRATS !!
STO-O-O-
O-O-O-O-O-P!!

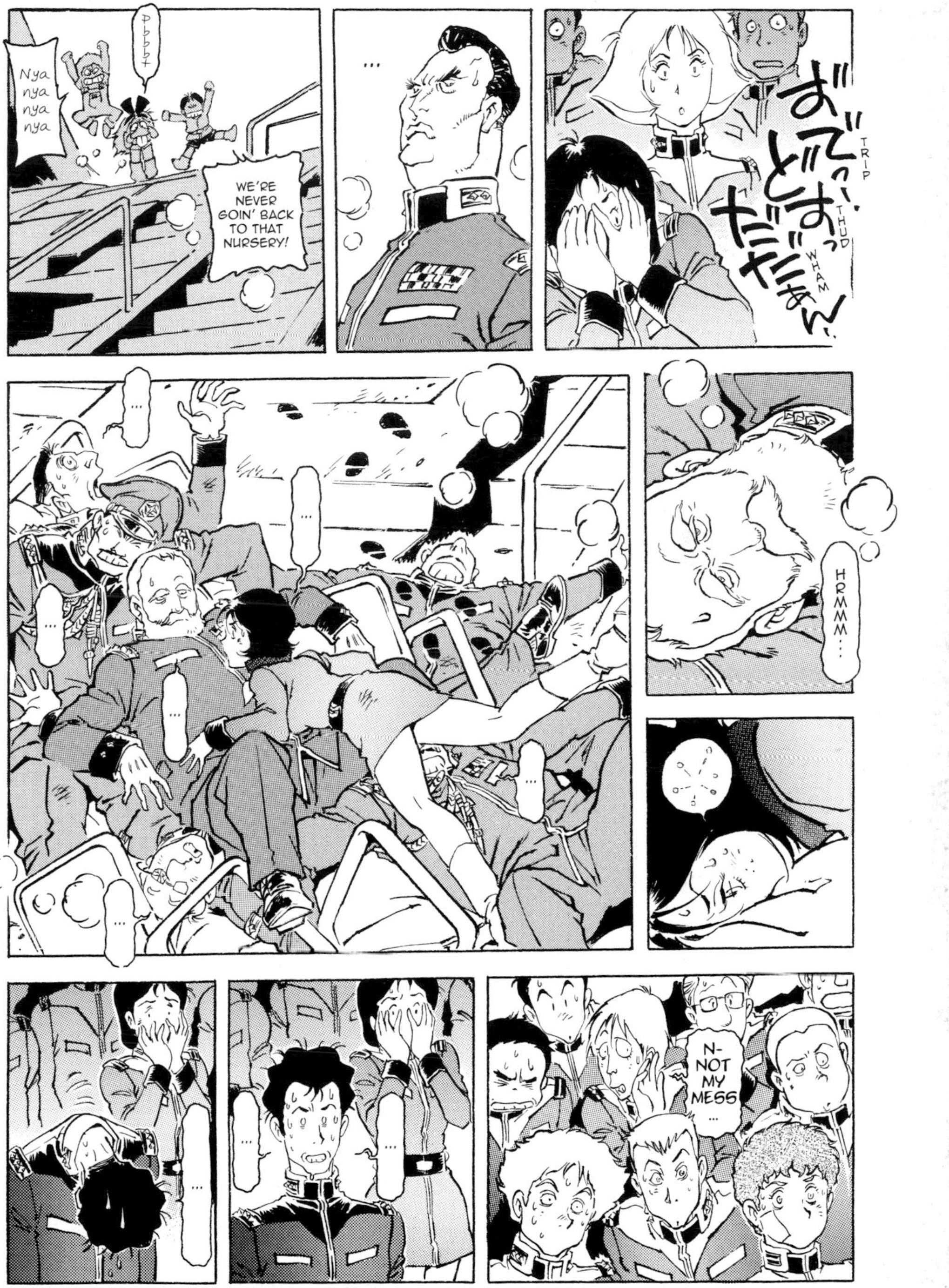
ずでっ
TRIP
どすっ
THUD
だだだあん
WHAM
...
Pbbbbt
Nya nya nya nya
WE'RE NEVER GOIN' BACK TO THAT NURSERY!
HRMMM...
...
...
...
...
...
...
N-NOT MY MESS ...
...
...
...

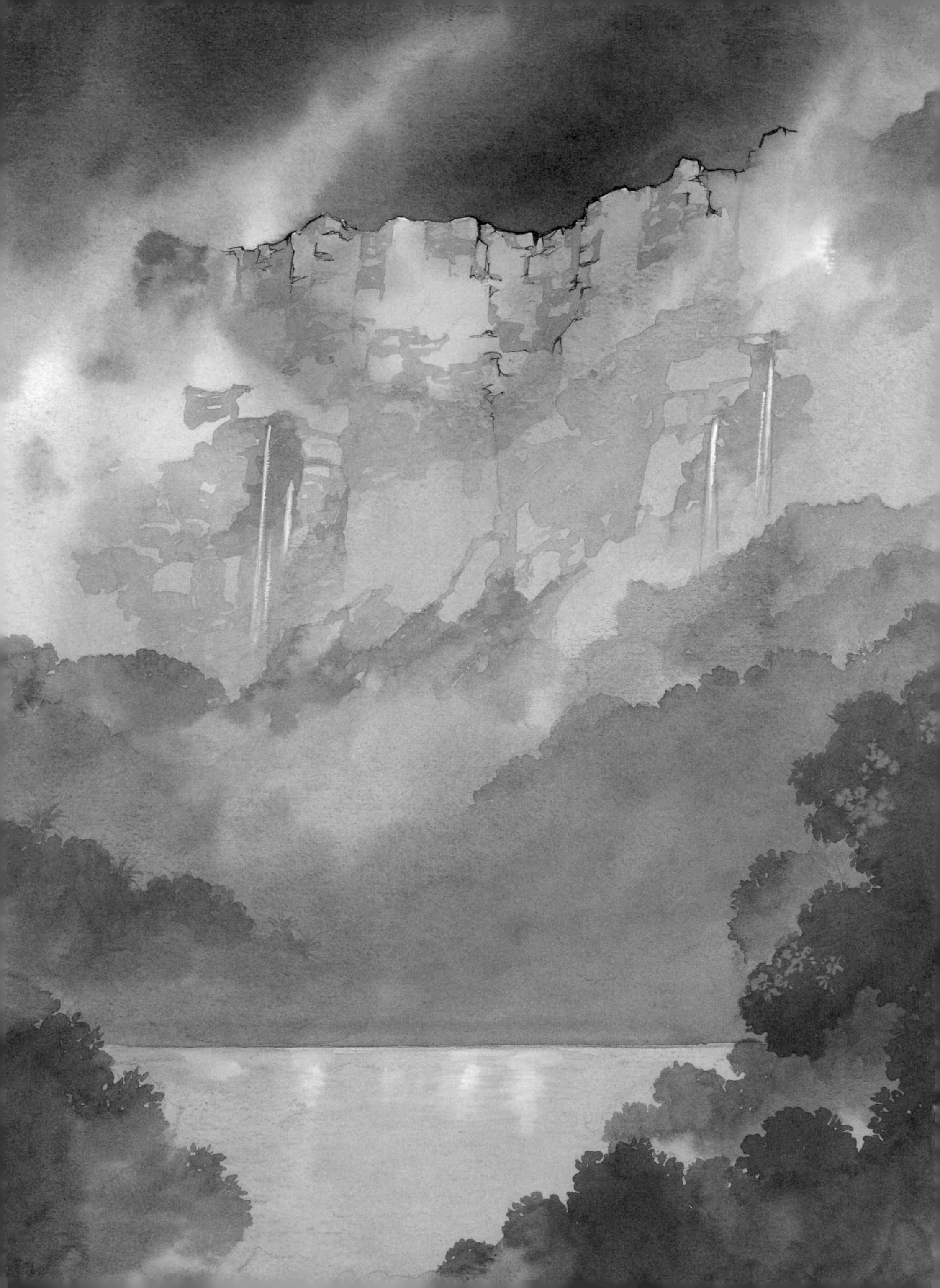

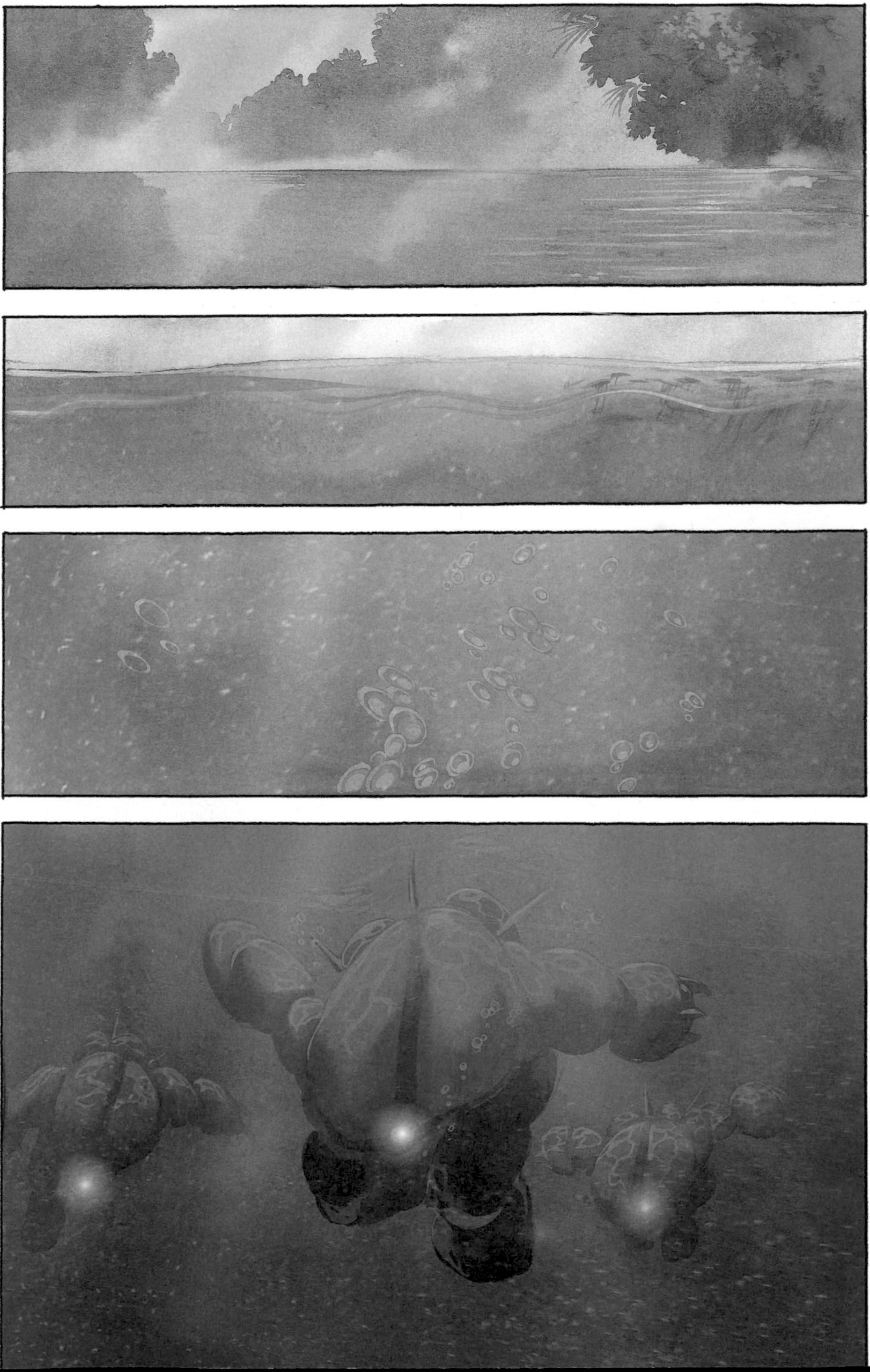

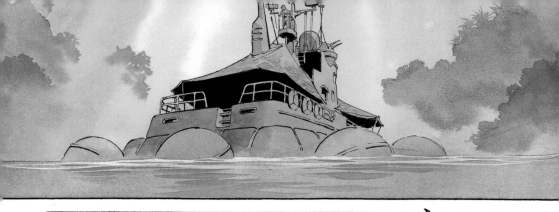

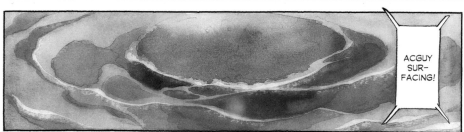

ACGUY SUR-FACING!

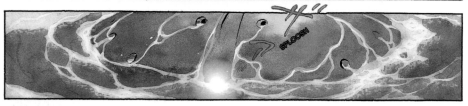

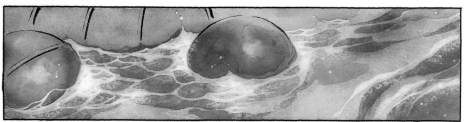

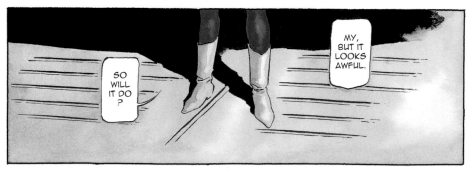

MY, BUT IT LOOKS AWFUL.

SO WILL IT DO ?

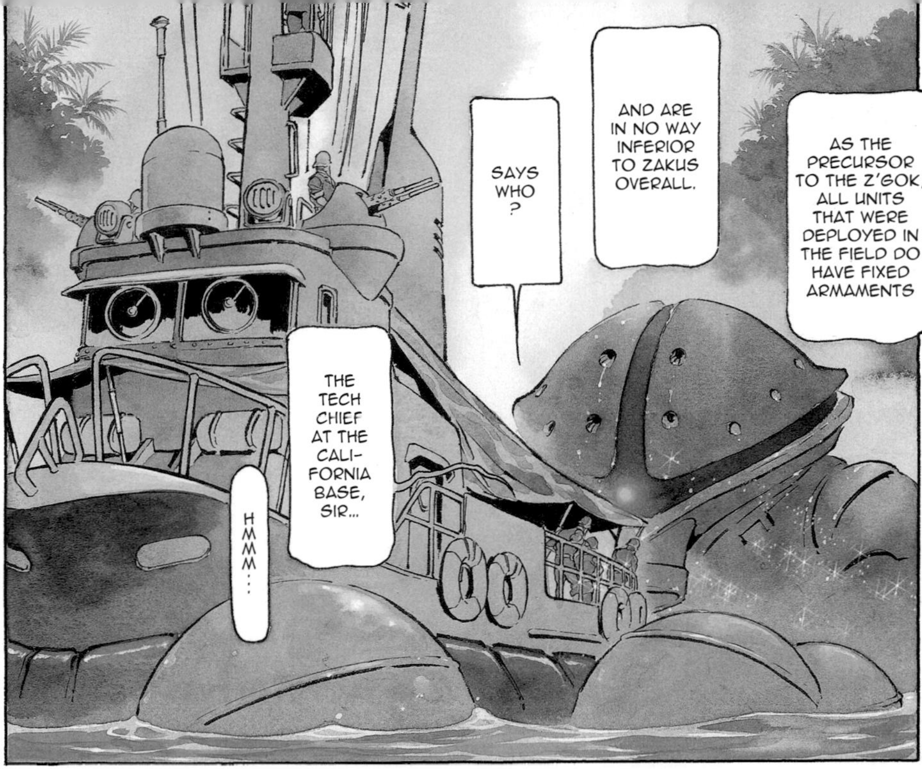
AS THE PRECURSOR TO THE Z'GOK, ALL UNITS THAT WERE DEPLOYED IN THE FIELD DO HAVE FIXED ARMAMENTS
AND ARE IN NO WAY INFERIOR TO ZAKUS OVERALL.
SAYS WHO?
THE TECH CHIEF AT THE CALIFORNIA BASE, SIR...
HMMM...
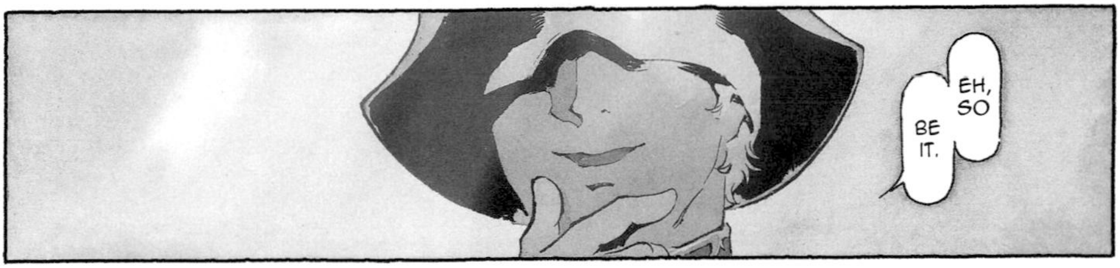
EH, SO BE IT.
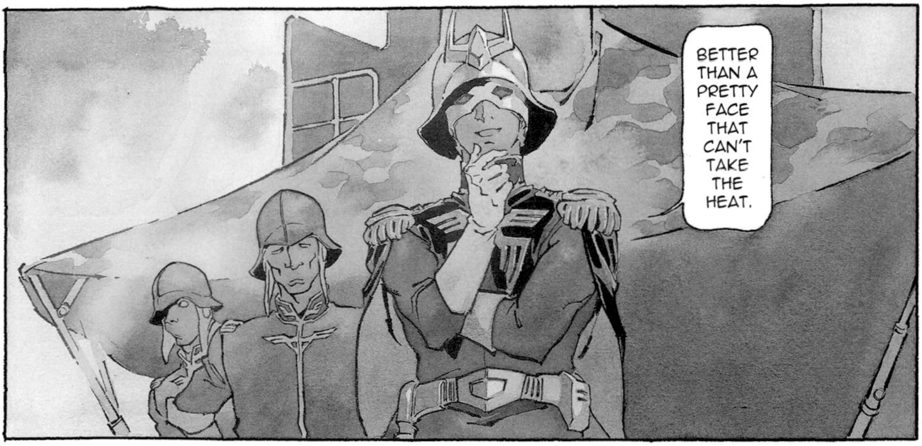
BETTER THAN A PRETTY FACE THAT CAN'T TAKE THE HEAT.

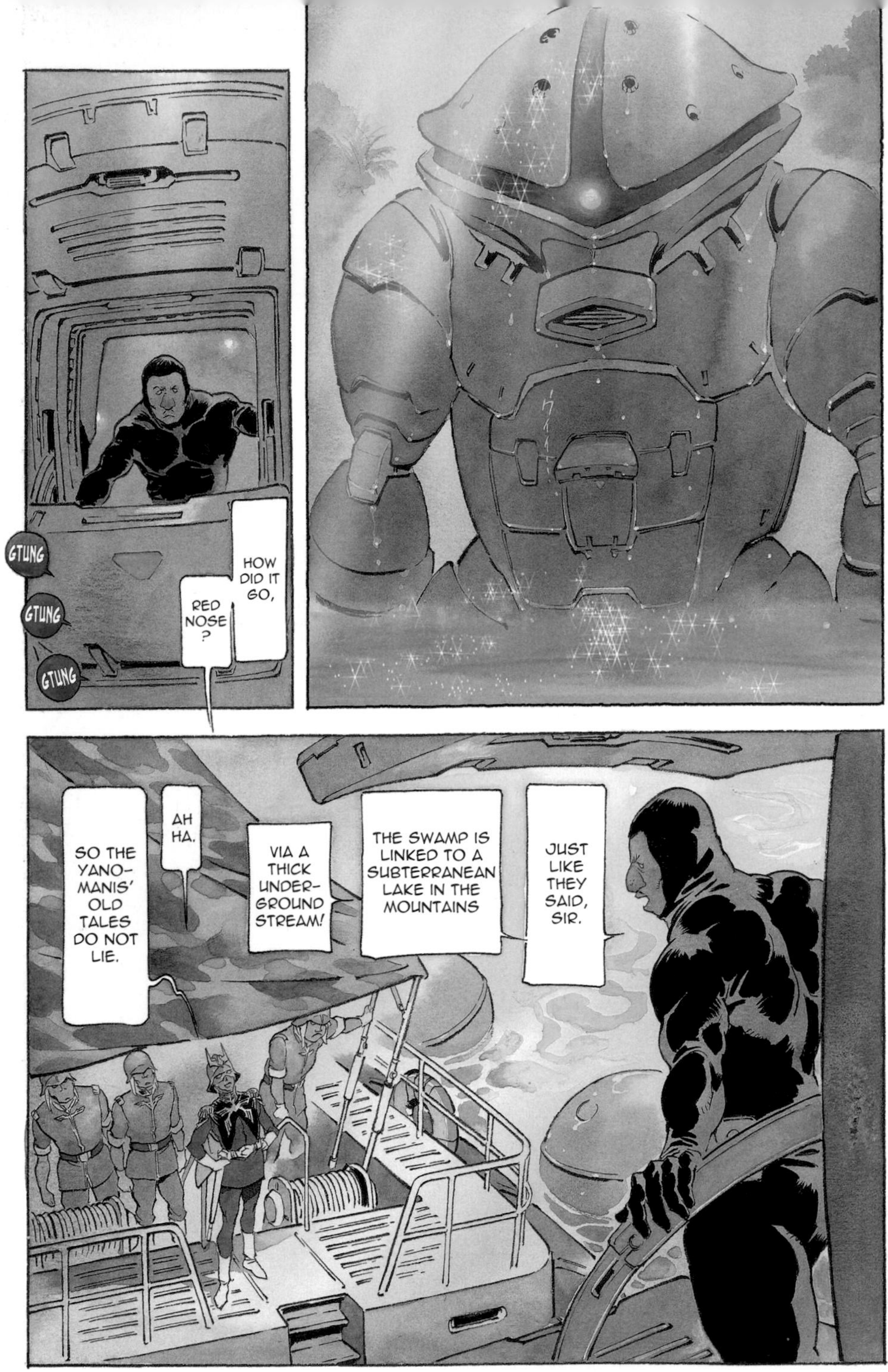
GTUNG
GTUNG
GTUNG
HOW DID IT GO,
RED NOSE?
JUST LIKE THEY SAID, SIR.
THE SWAMP IS LINKED TO A SUBTERRANEAN LAKE IN THE MOUNTAINS
VIA A THICK UNDERGROUND STREAM!
AH HA.
SO THE YANOMANIS' OLD TALES DO NOT LIE.

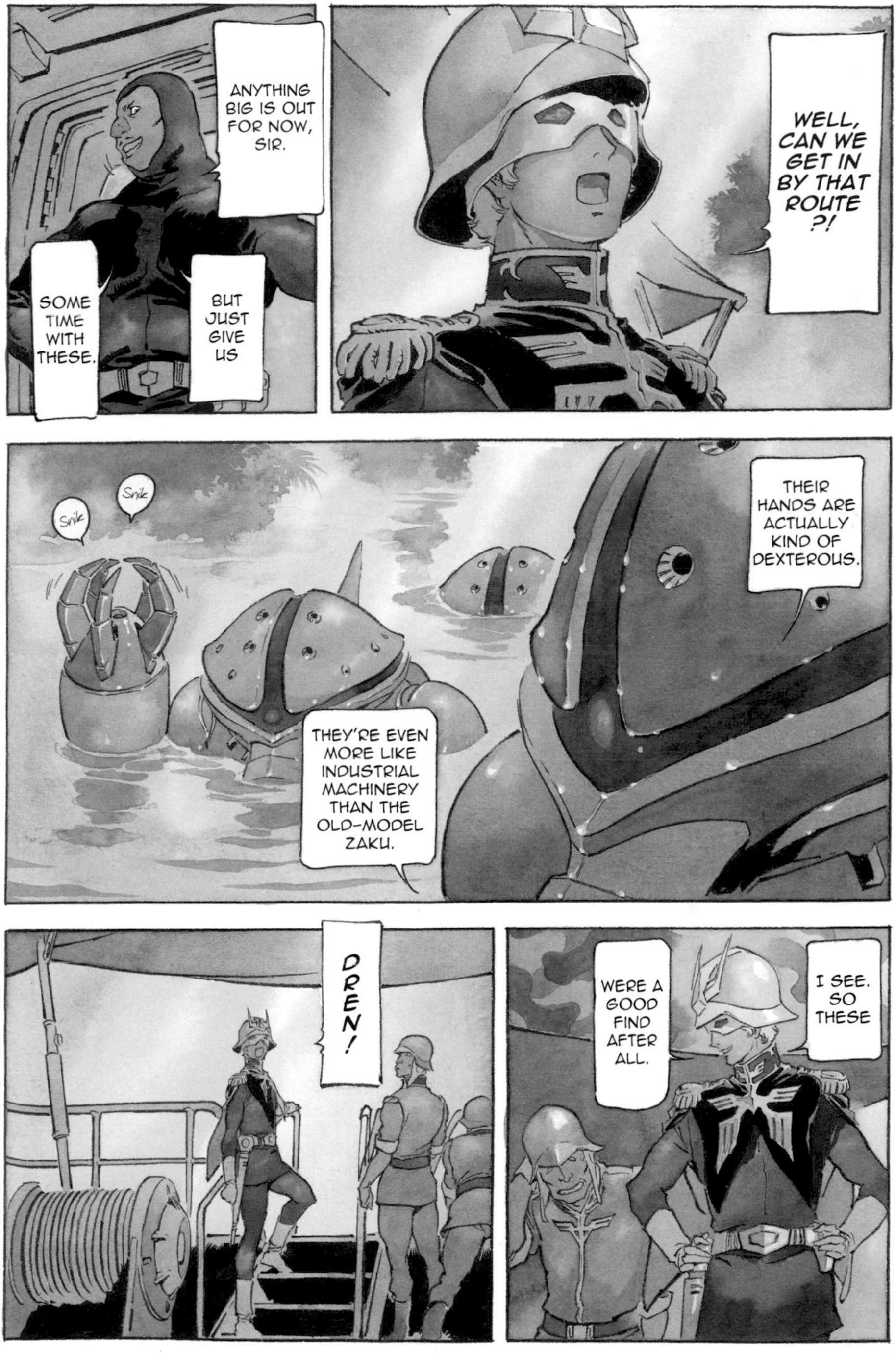
WELL, CAN WE GET IN BY THAT ROUTE?!
ANYTHING BIG IS OUT FOR NOW, SIR.
BUT JUST GIVE US
SOME TIME WITH THESE.
THEIR HANDS ARE ACTUALLY KIND OF DEXTEROUS.
Snik
Snik
THEY'RE EVEN MORE LIKE INDUSTRIAL MACHINERY THAN THE OLD-MODEL ZAKU.
I SEE. SO THESE
WERE A GOOD FIND AFTER ALL.
DREN!

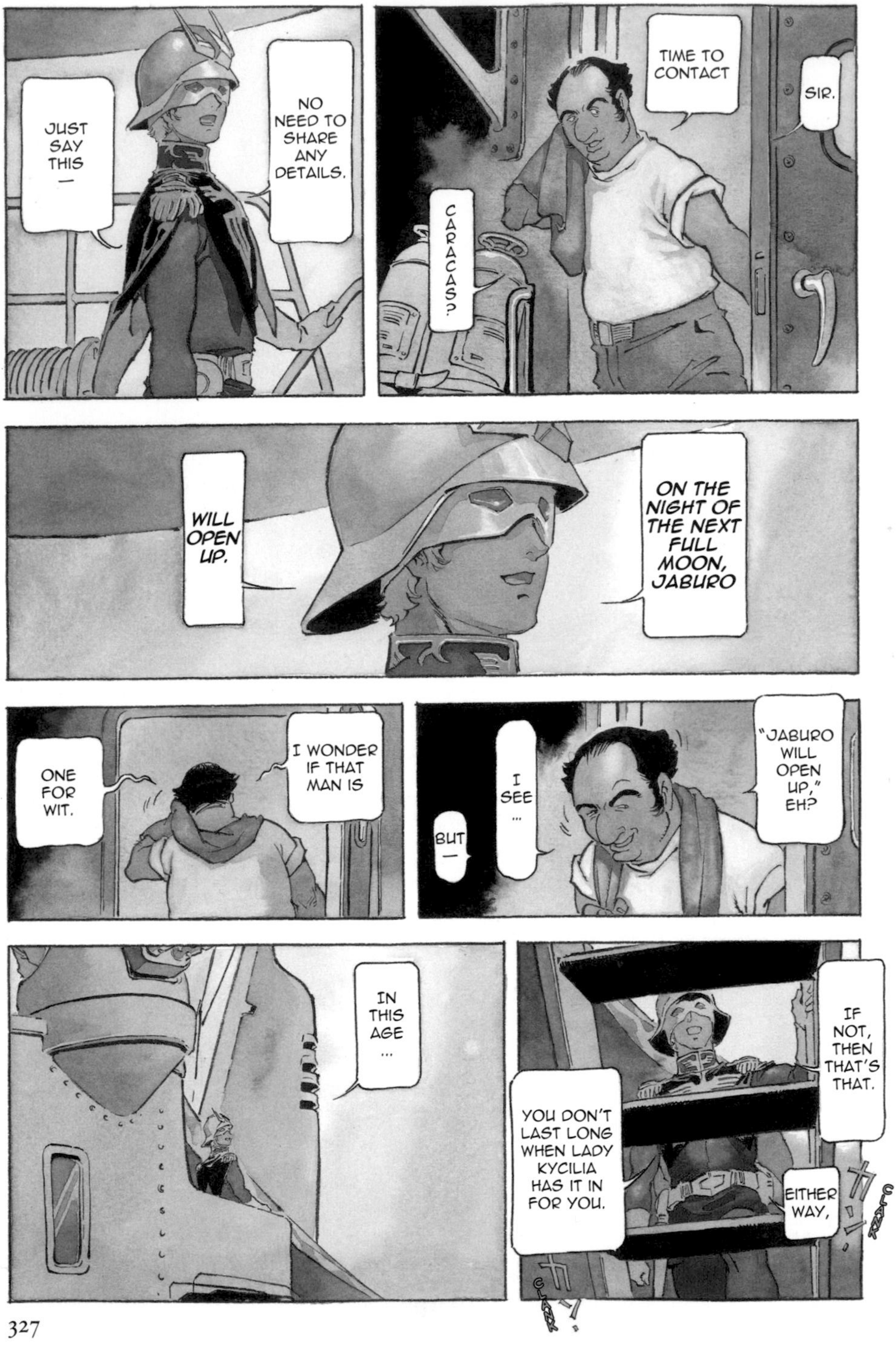
TIME TO CONTACT
SIR.
CARACAS?
NO NEED TO SHARE ANY DETAILS.
JUST SAY THIS —
ON THE NIGHT OF THE NEXT FULL MOON, JABURO
WILL OPEN UP.
"JABURO WILL OPEN UP," EH?
I SEE ...
BUT —
I WONDER IF THAT MAN IS
ONE FOR WIT.
IF NOT, THEN THAT'S THAT.
EITHER WAY,
CLANK
YOU DON'T LAST LONG WHEN LADY KYCILIA HAS IT IN FOR YOU.
CLANK
IN THIS AGE ...

...OF RECKONING, THE ONLY ONES WHO SURVIVE
IN THE END
ARE THE CHOSEN FEW...

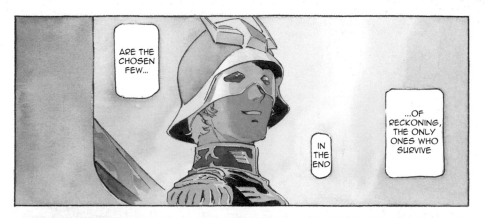

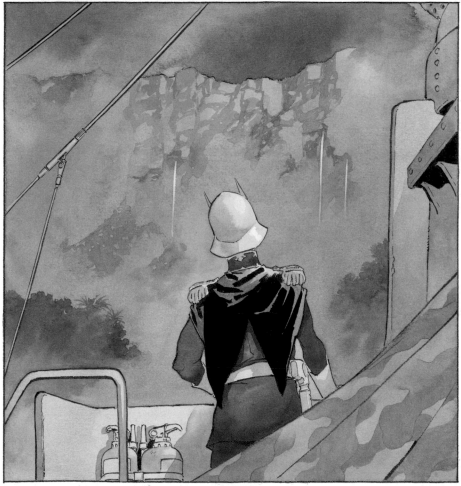

SECTION VII

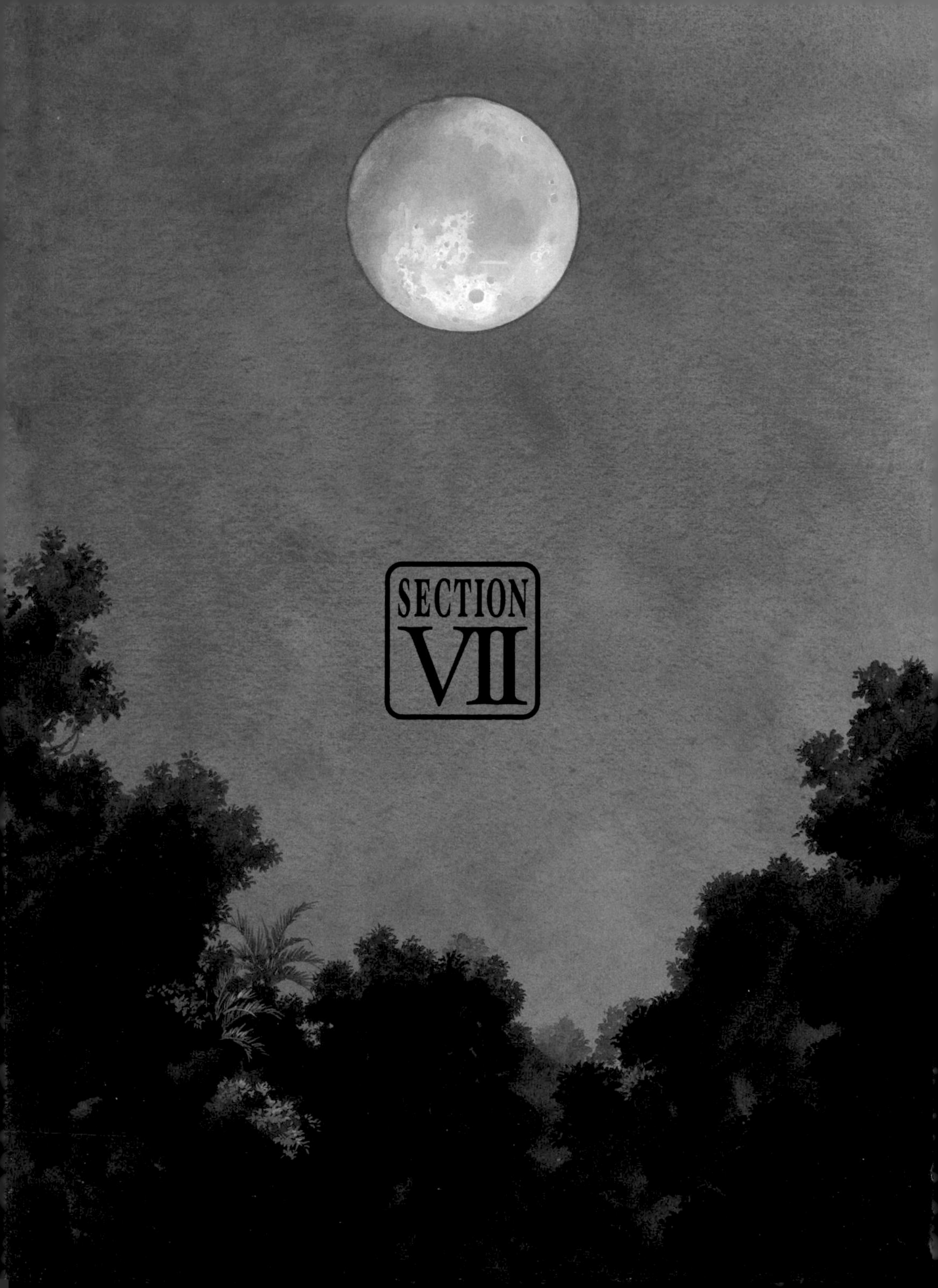

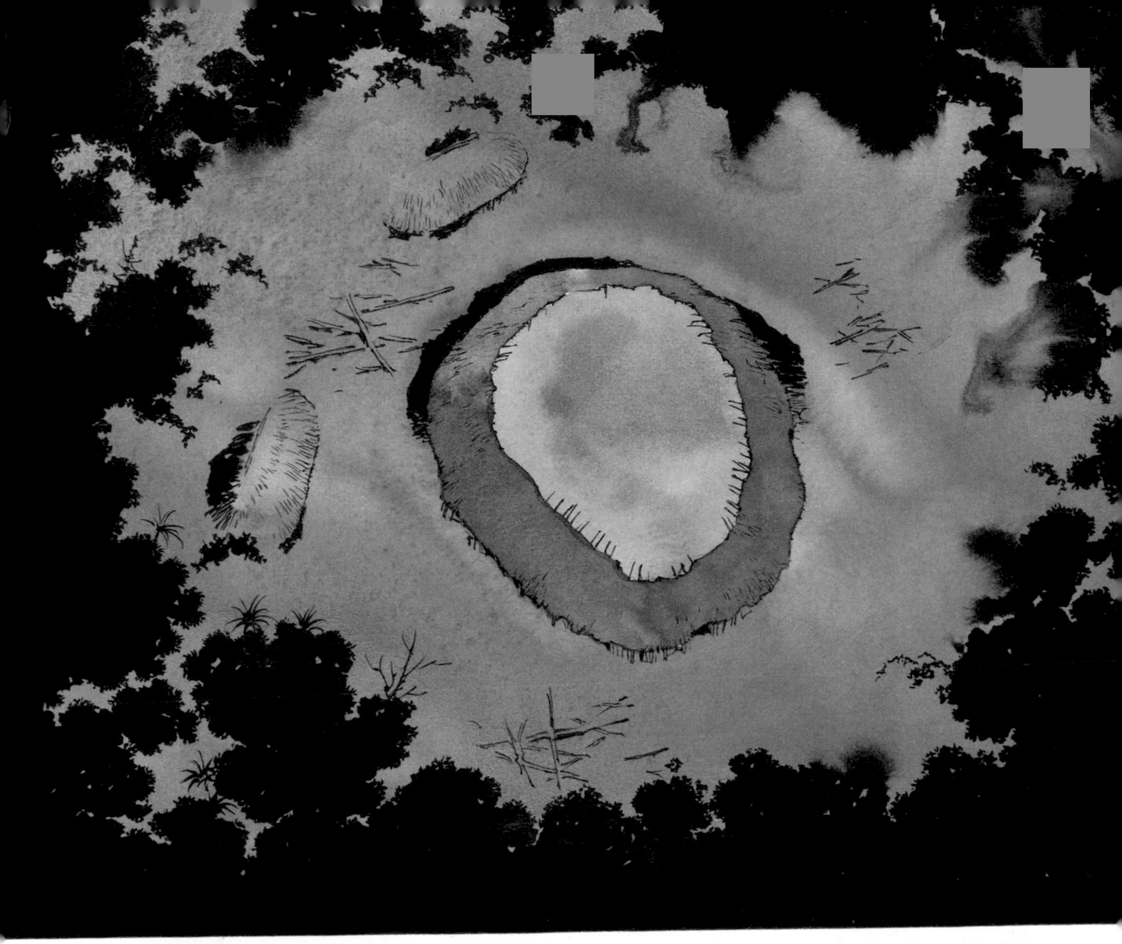
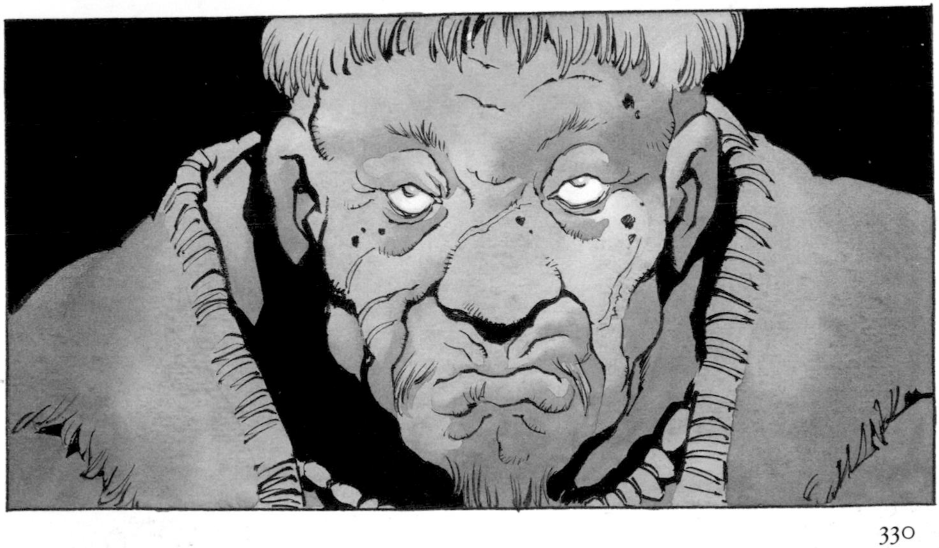

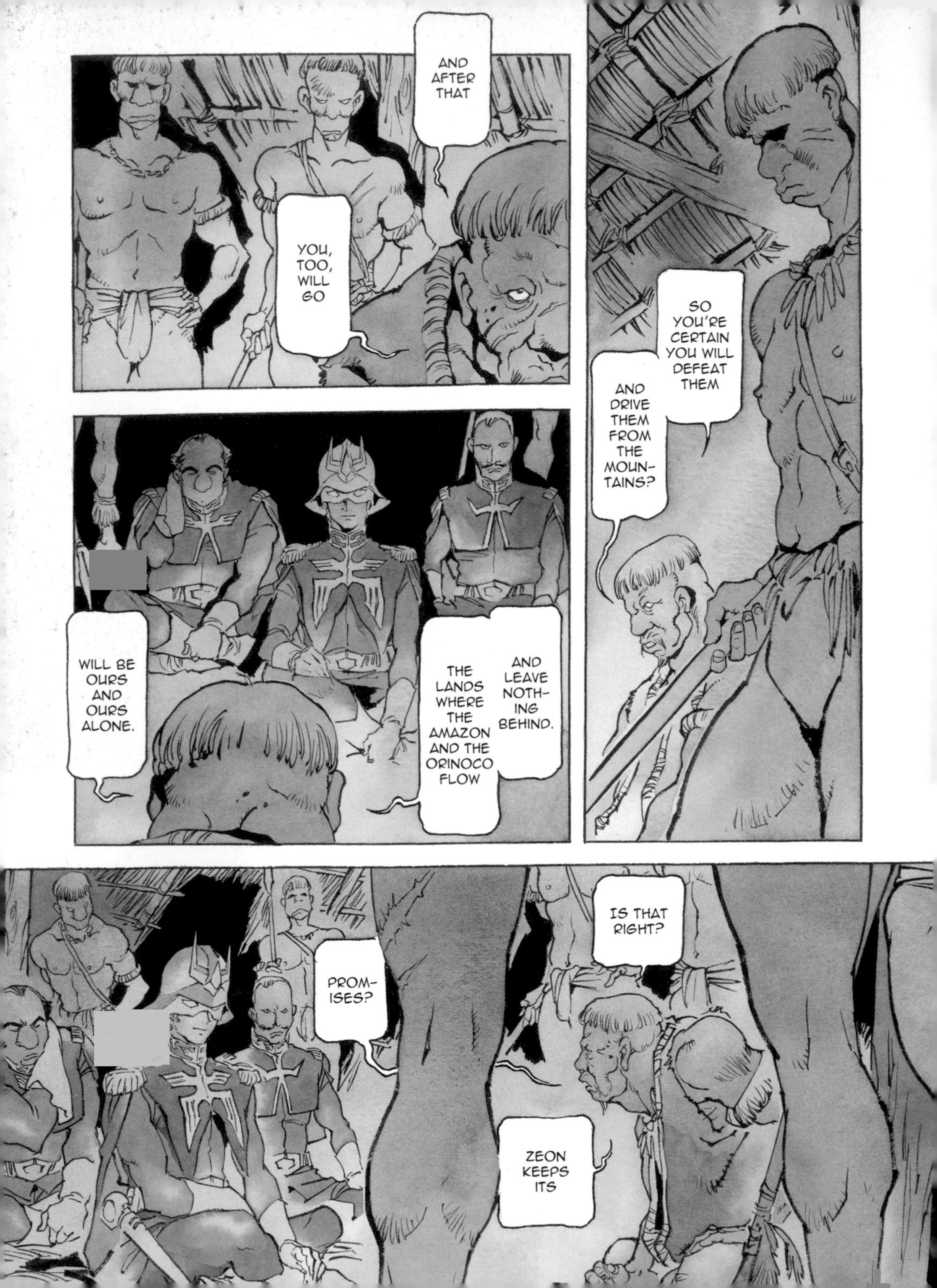
SO YOU'RE CERTAIN YOU WILL DEFEAT THEM
AND DRIVE THEM FROM THE MOUNTAINS?
AND AFTER THAT
YOU, TOO, WILL GO
AND LEAVE NOTHING BEHIND.
THE LANDS WHERE THE AMAZON AND THE ORINOCO FLOW
WILL BE OURS AND OURS ALONE.
IS THAT RIGHT?
ZEON KEEPS ITS
PROMISES?

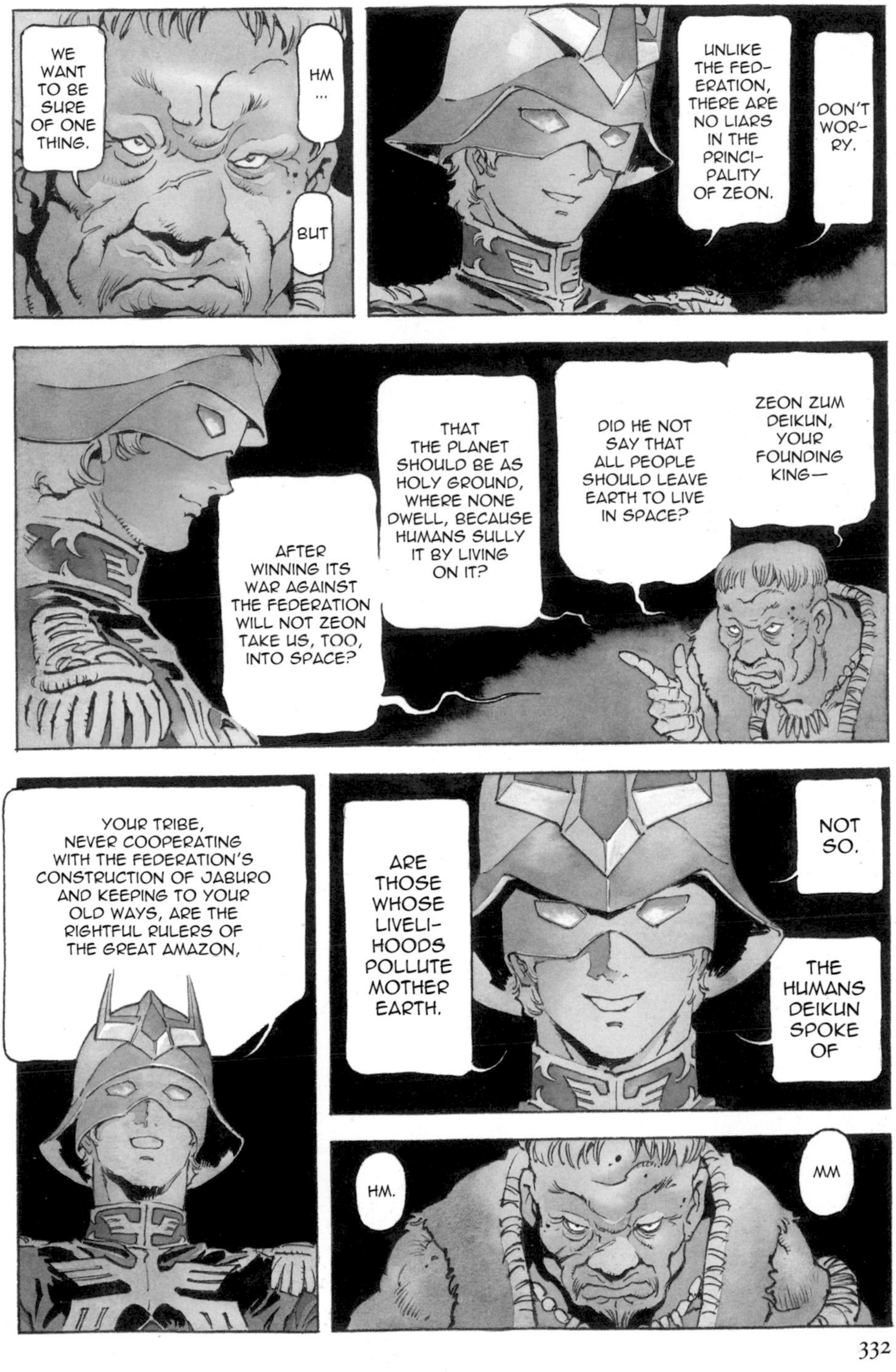
DON'T WOR-RY.
UNLIKE THE FED-ERATION, THERE ARE NO LIARS IN THE PRINCI-PALITY OF ZEON.
HM ...
BUT
WE WANT TO BE SURE OF ONE THING.
ZEON ZUM DEIKUN, YOUR FOUNDING KING—
DID HE NOT SAY THAT ALL PEOPLE SHOULD LEAVE EARTH TO LIVE IN SPACE?
THAT THE PLANET SHOULD BE AS HOLY GROUND, WHERE NONE DWELL, BECAUSE HUMANS SULLY IT BY LIVING ON IT?
AFTER WINNING ITS WAR AGAINST THE FEDERATION WILL NOT ZEON TAKE US, TOO, INTO SPACE?
NOT SO.
THE HUMANS DEIKUN SPOKE OF
ARE THOSE WHOSE LIVELI-HOODS POLLUTE MOTHER EARTH.
MM
HM.
YOUR TRIBE, NEVER COOPERATING WITH THE FEDERATION'S CONSTRUCTION OF JABURO AND KEEPING TO YOUR OLD WAYS, ARE THE RIGHTFUL RULERS OF THE GREAT AMAZON,

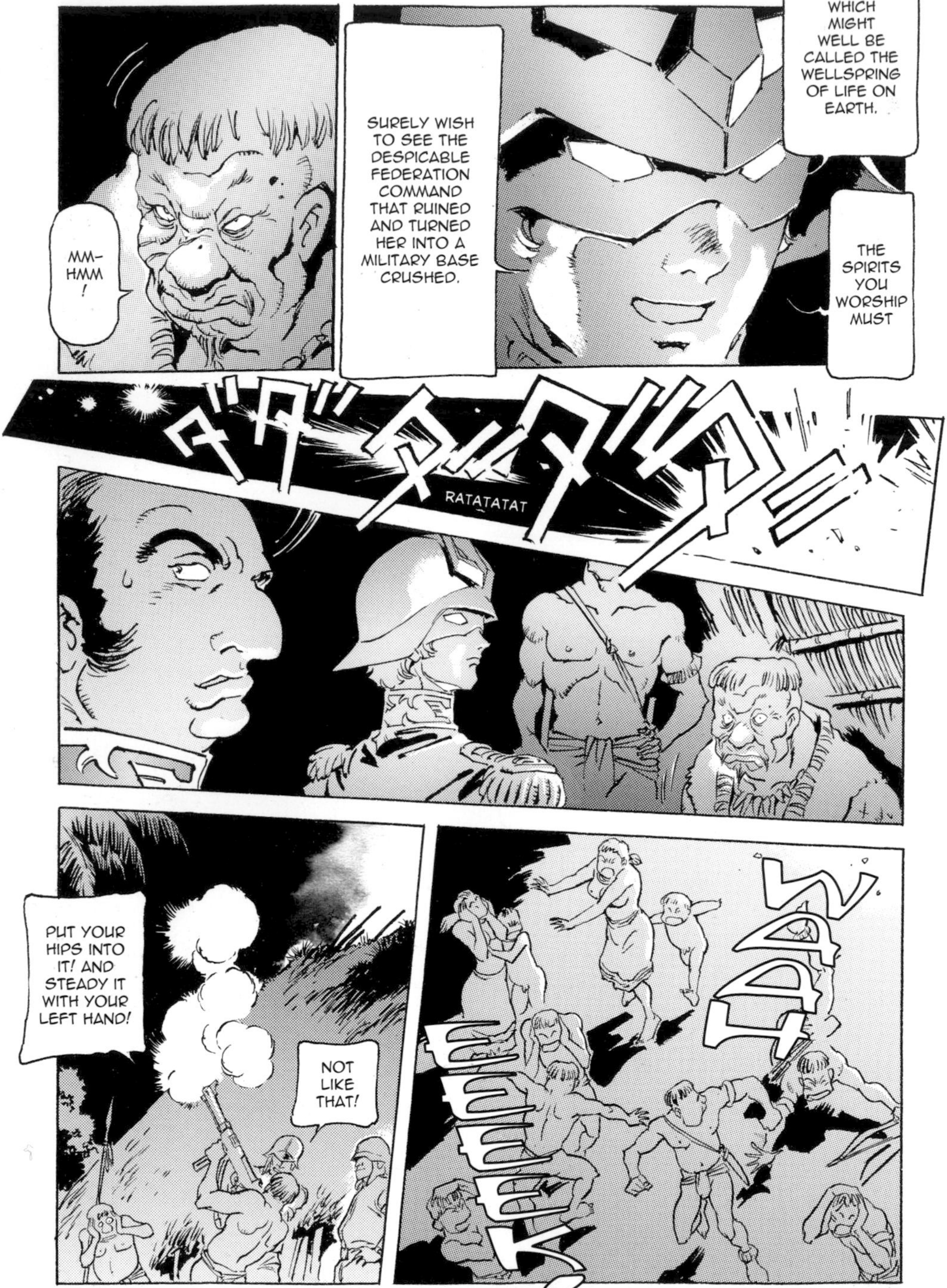
WHICH MIGHT WELL BE CALLED THE WELLSPRING OF LIFE ON EARTH.
THE SPIRITS YOU WORSHIP MUST
SURELY WISH TO SEE THE DESPICABLE FEDERATION COMMAND THAT RUINED AND TURNED HER INTO A MILITARY BASE CRUSHED.
MM-HMM!
RATATATAT
EEEEK
PUT YOUR HIPS INTO IT! AND STEADY IT WITH YOUR LEFT HAND!
NOT LIKE THAT!

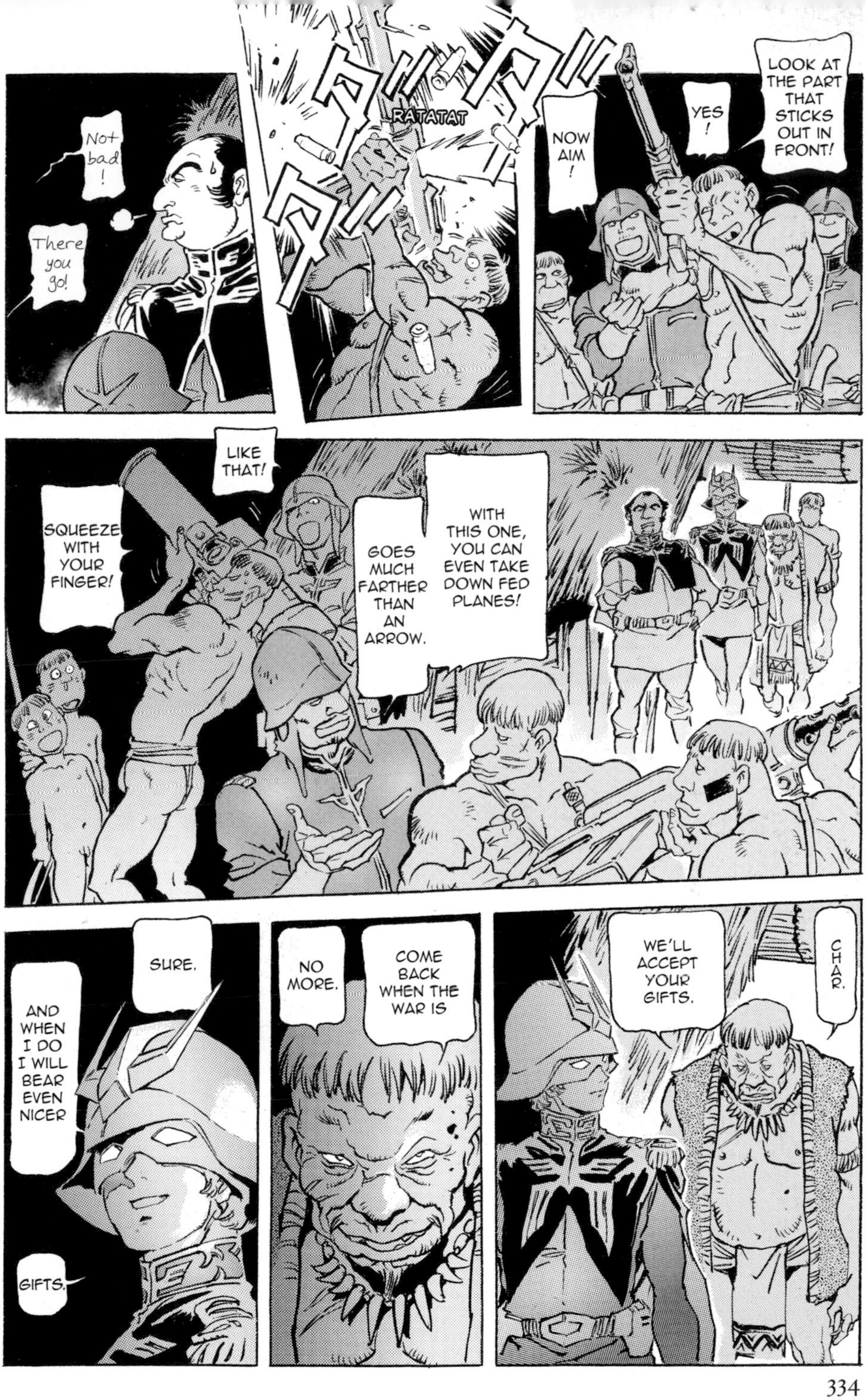
LOOK AT THE PART THAT STICKS OUT IN FRONT!
YES!
NOW AIM!
RATATAT
Not bad!
There you go!
WITH THIS ONE, YOU CAN EVEN TAKE DOWN FED PLANES!
GOES MUCH FARTHER THAN AN ARROW.
LIKE THAT!
SQUEEZE WITH YOUR FINGER!
CHAR.
WE'LL ACCEPT YOUR GIFTS.
COME BACK WHEN THE WAR IS
NO MORE.
SURE.
AND WHEN I DO I WILL BEAR EVEN NICER
GIFTS.

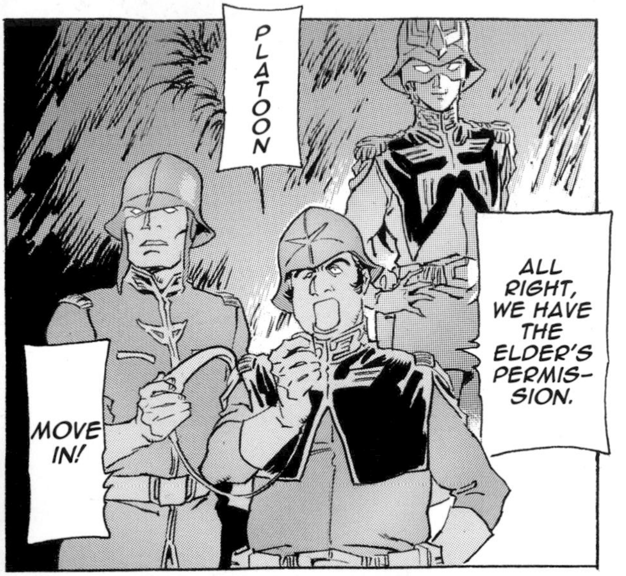
ALL RIGHT, WE HAVE THE ELDER'S PERMIS-SION.
PLATOON
MOVE IN!
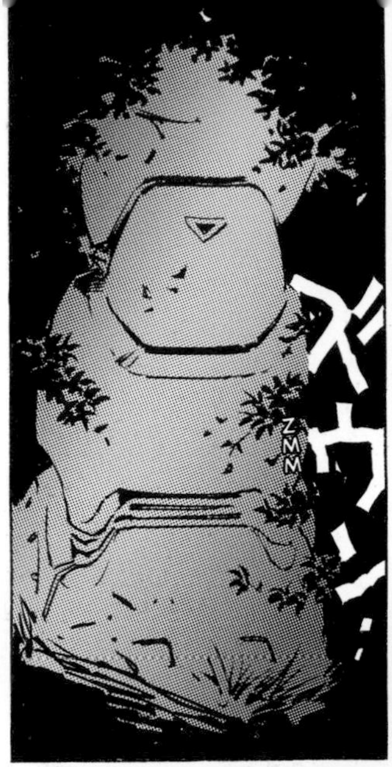
ZMM
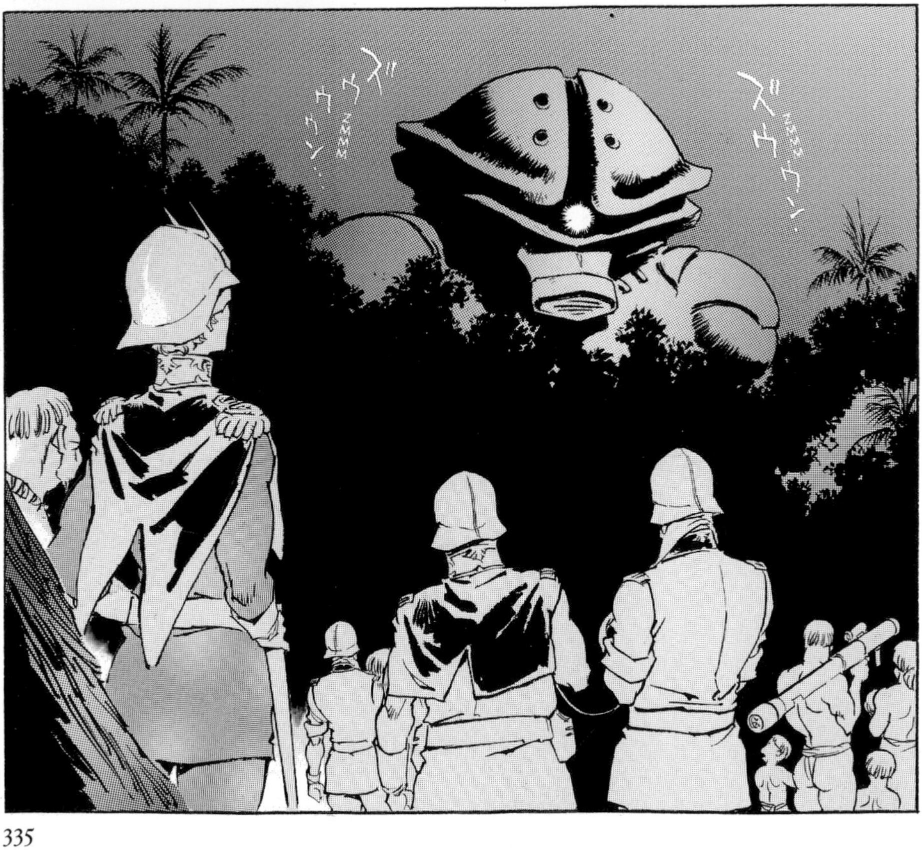

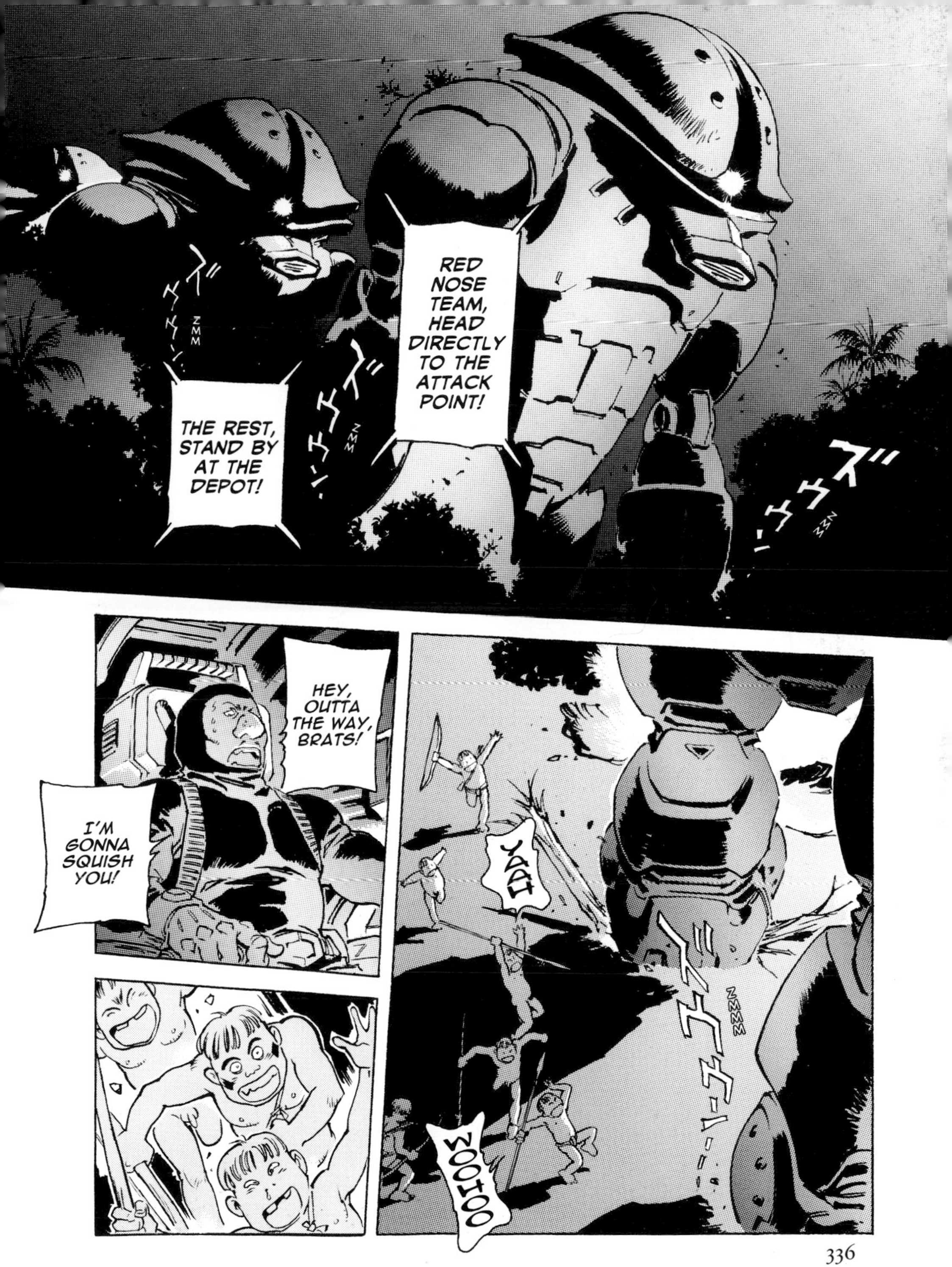
RED NOSE TEAM, HEAD DIRECTLY TO THE ATTACK POINT!
ZMM
ZMM
THE REST, STAND BY AT THE DEPOT!
ZMM
ZMMM
YAAY
WOOHOO
HEY, OUTTA THE WAY, BRATS!
I'M GONNA SQUISH YOU!

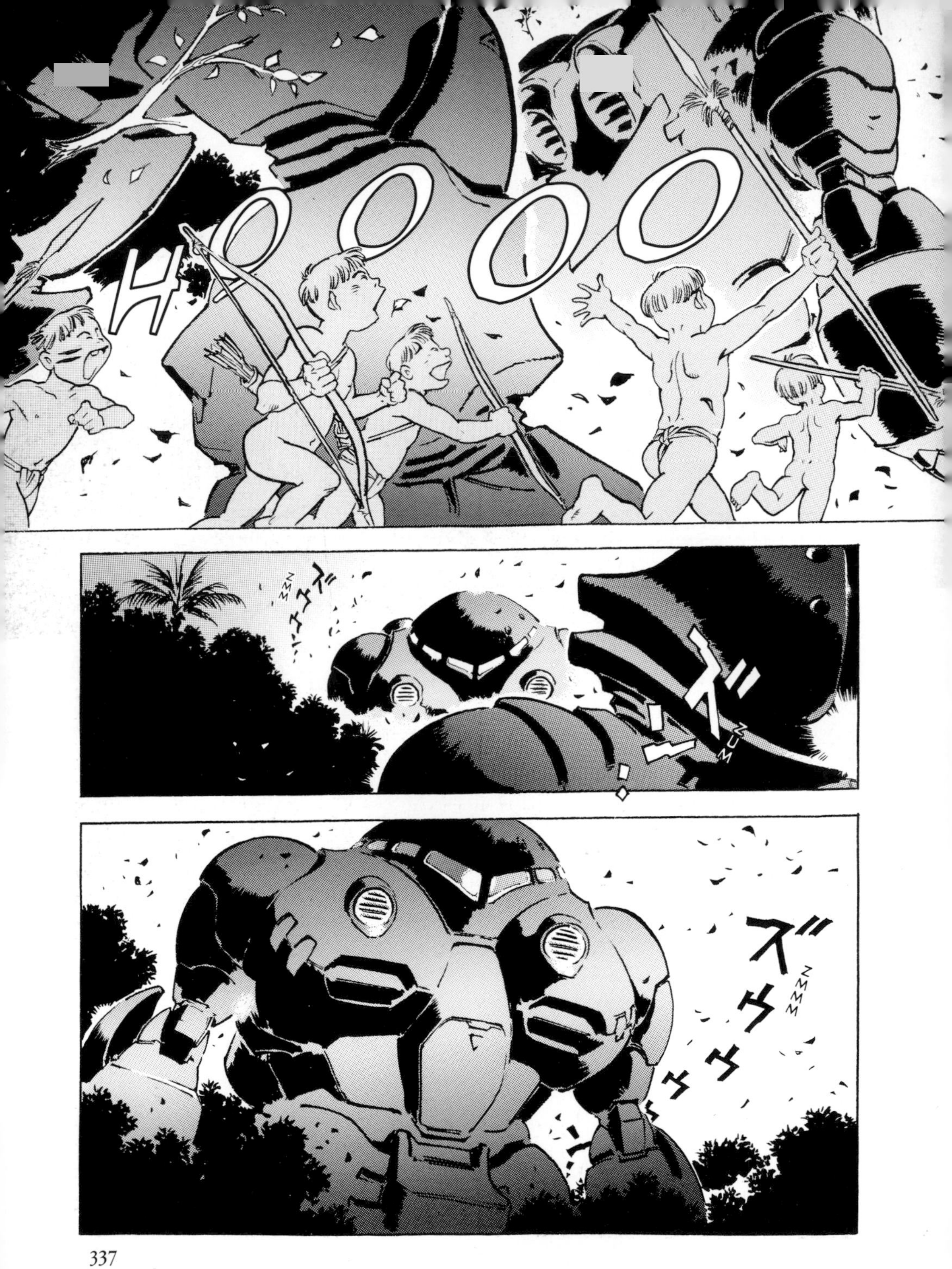
HOOOOO
ZMMM
ZUM
ズウウウ
ZMMM

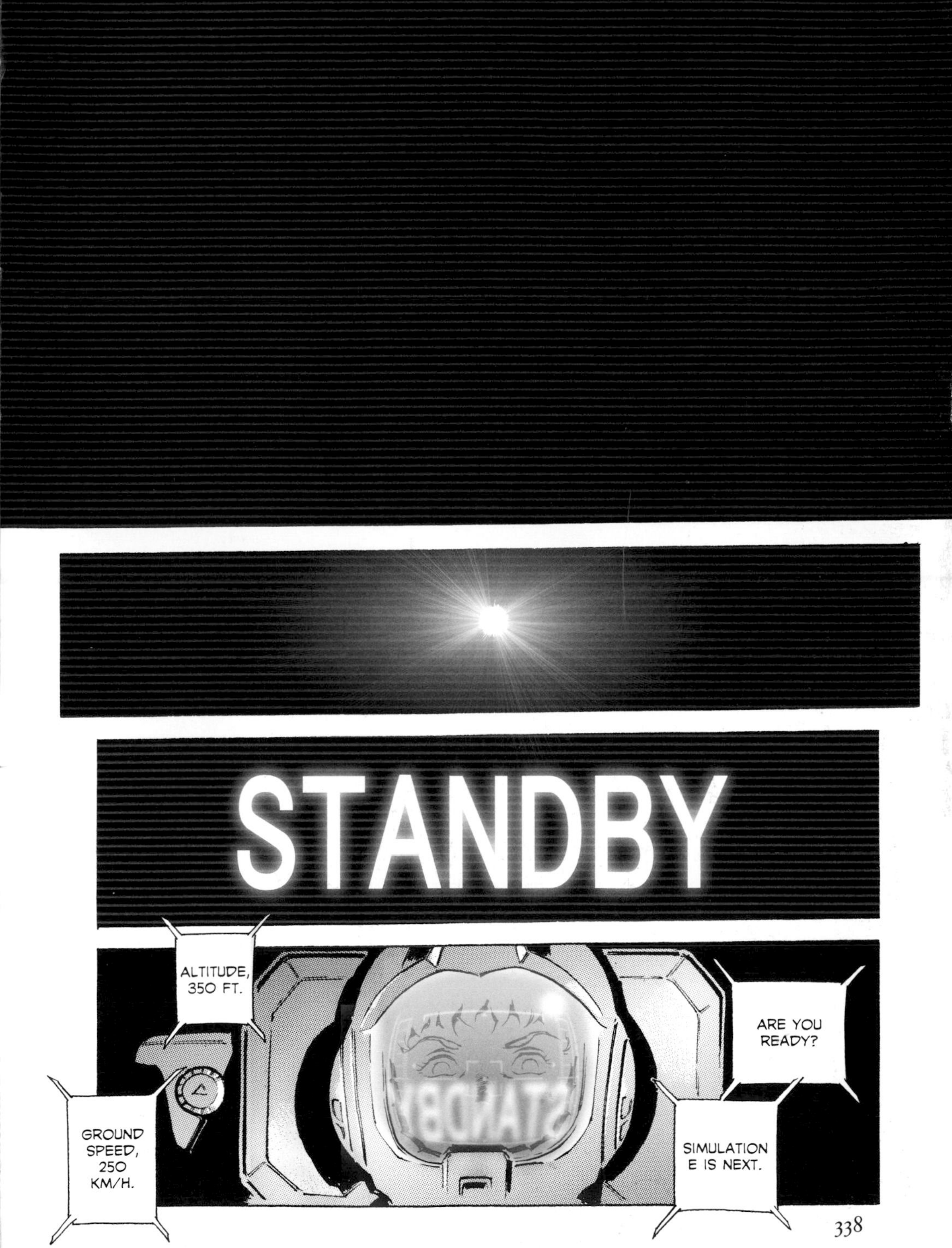
STANDBY
ARE YOU READY?
SIMULATION E IS NEXT.
ALTITUDE, 350 FT.
GROUND SPEED, 250 KM/H.

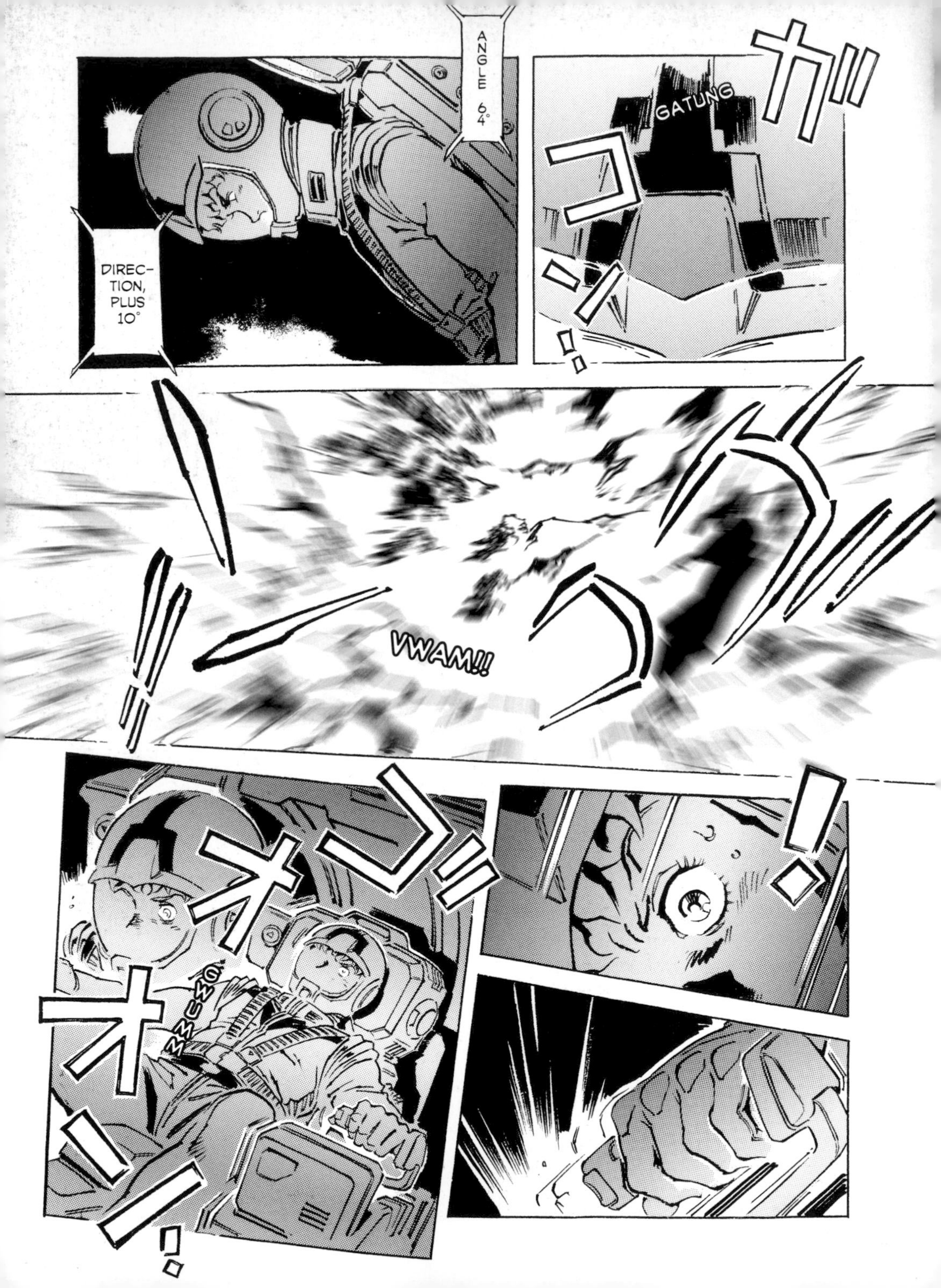
GATUNG
ANGLE 64°
DIRECTION, PLUS 10°
VWAM!!!
GWUMMM

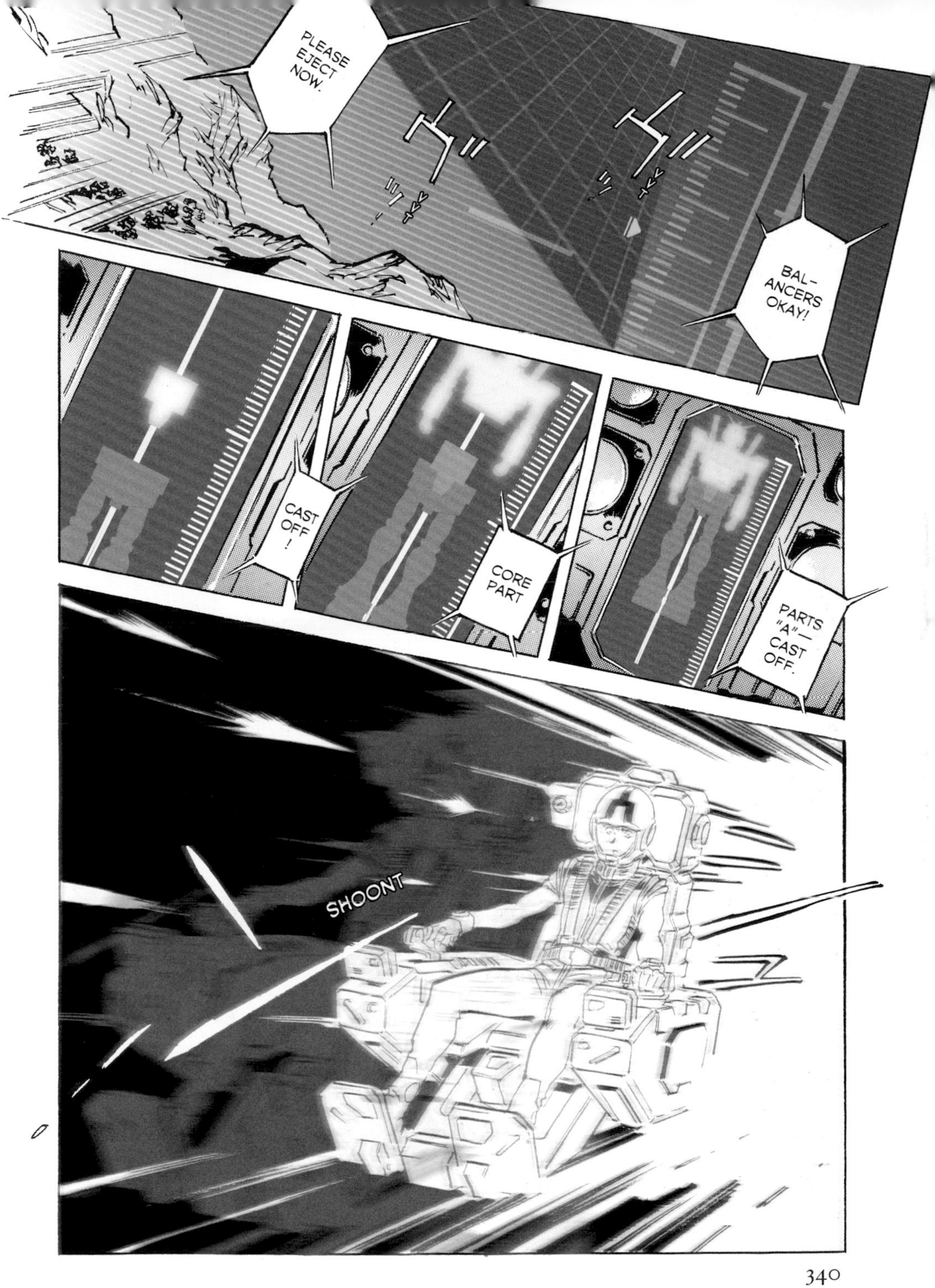
BAL-
ANCERS
OKAY!
PLEASE
EJECT
NOW.
PARTS
"A"—
CAST
OFF.
CORE
PART
CAST
OFF
!
SHOONT

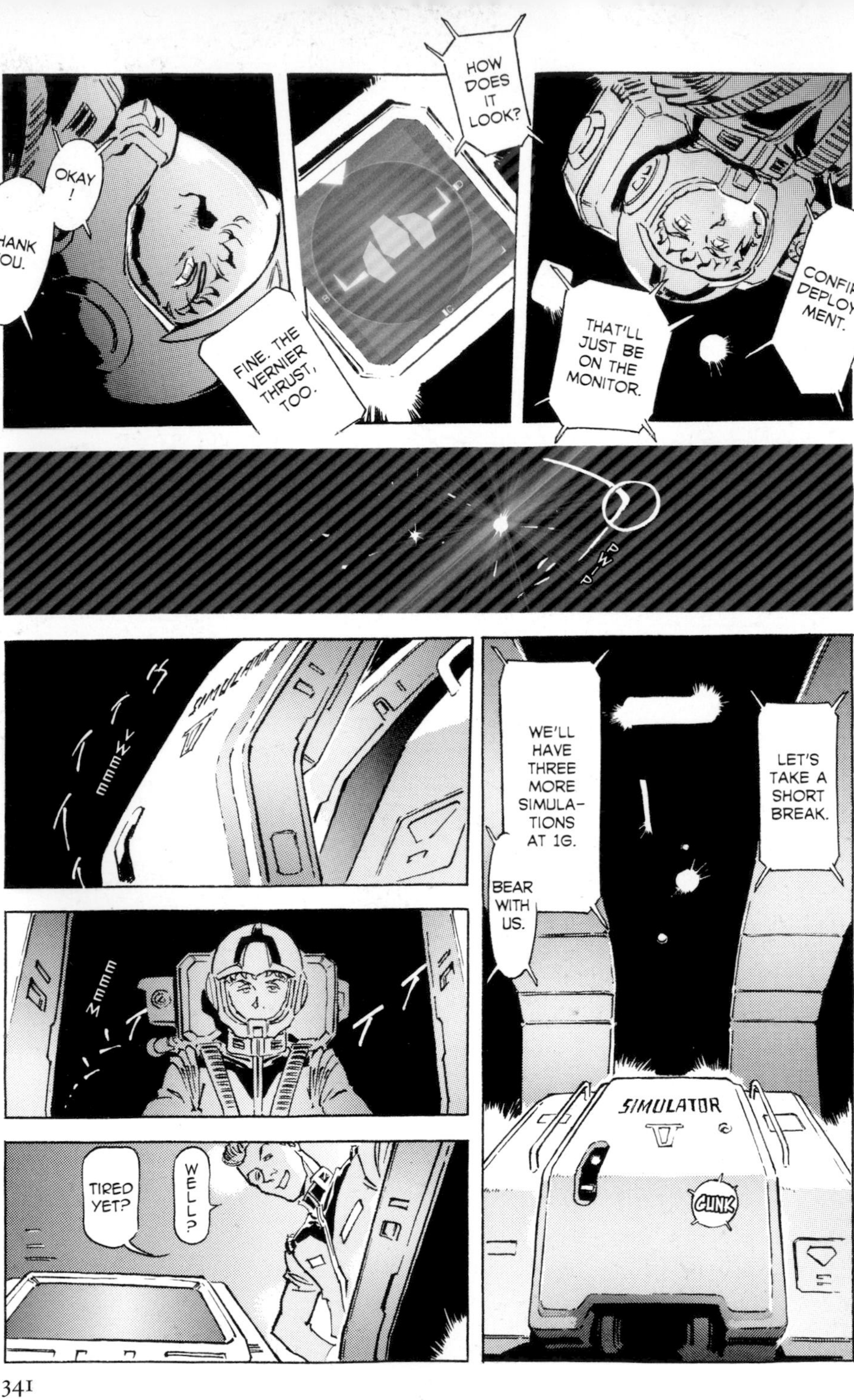
CONFIRM DEPLOYMENT.
THAT'LL JUST BE ON THE MONITOR.
HOW DOES IT LOOK?
FINE. THE VERNIER THRUST, TOO.
OKAY!
THANK YOU.
PW-IP
LET'S TAKE A SHORT BREAK.
WE'LL HAVE THREE MORE SIMULATIONS AT 1G.
BEAR WITH US.
SIMULATOR
GUNK
SIMULATOR
WELL?
TIRED YET?

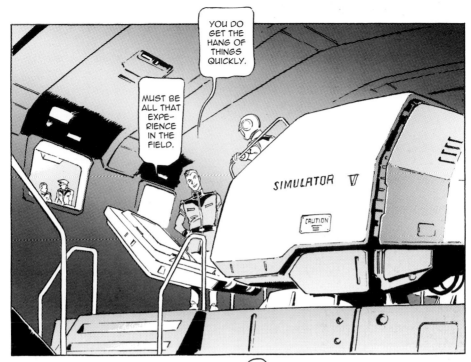

YOU DO GET THE HANG OF THINGS QUICKLY.
MUST BE ALL THAT EXPERIENCE IN THE FIELD.
SIMULATOR V
CAUTION
UH,
I'M NOT SURE THAT
HAS
MUCH TO DO WITH IT.
Vweem
BUT I
DON'T SEE THE POINT OF USING
CORE PARTS UNDER ONE G...
OH?
AND WHY'S THAT,
UM,
W.O. AMURO?
AT LOW ALTITUDE, IT'S BETTER FOR THE WHOLE SUIT TO MAKE A SOFT LANDING.
I THINK THE BASIC DATA INPUT FOR THAT SIM IS OFF.

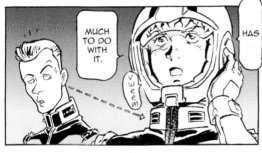

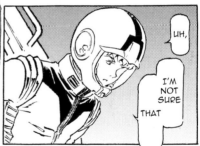

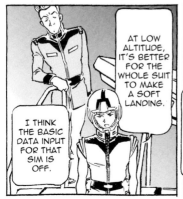

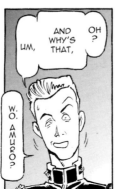

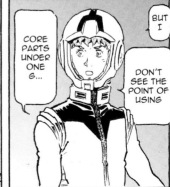

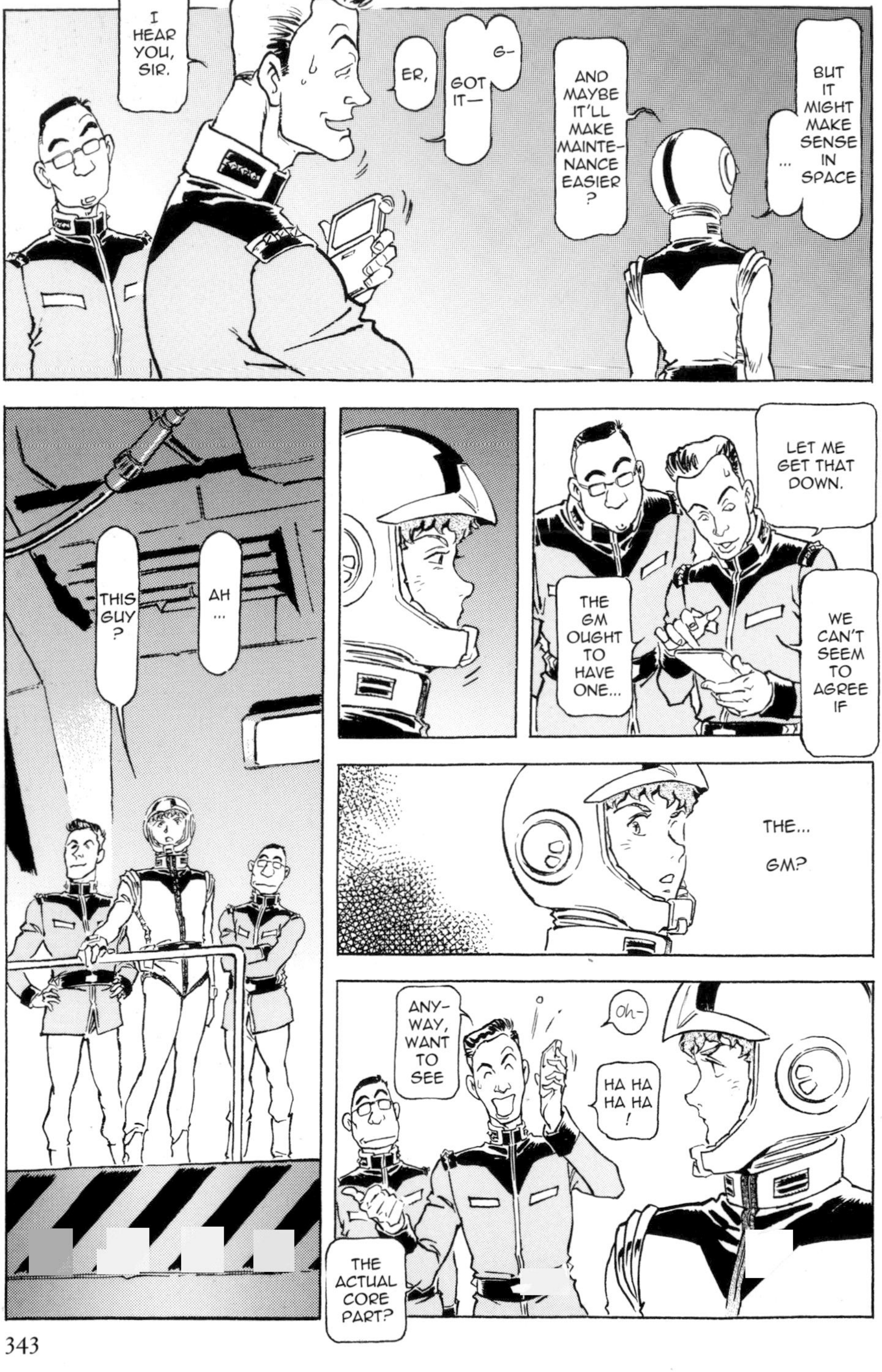
... BUT IT MIGHT MAKE SENSE IN SPACE
AND MAYBE IT'LL MAKE MAINTENANCE EASIER?
G- GOT IT—
ER,
I HEAR YOU, SIR.
LET ME GET THAT DOWN.
WE CAN'T SEEM TO AGREE IF
THE GM OUGHT TO HAVE ONE...
THE... GM?
Oh-
HA HA HA HA!
ANYWAY, WANT TO SEE
THE ACTUAL CORE PART?
AH...
THIS GUY?

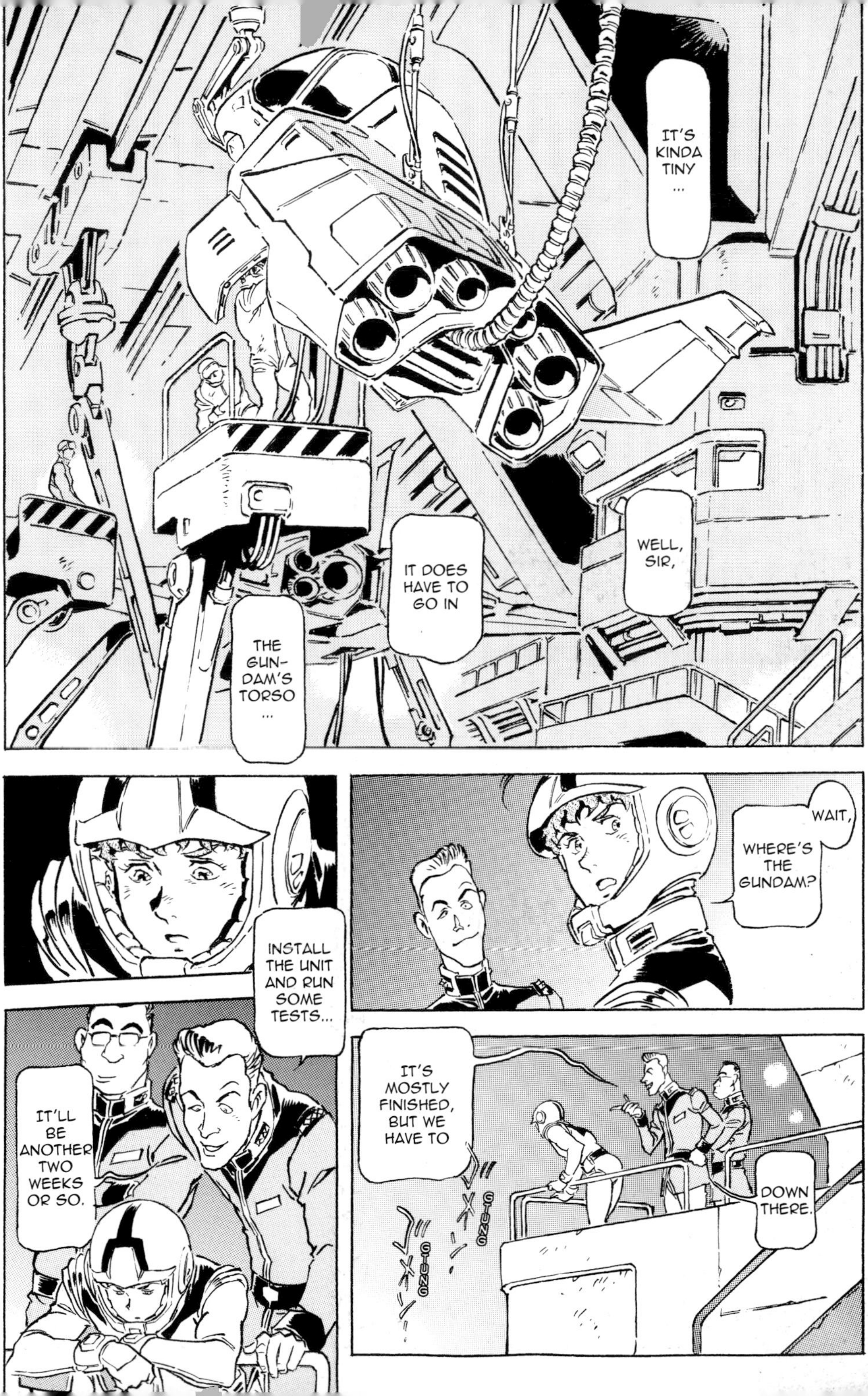
IT'S KINDA TINY...
WELL, SIR,
IT DOES HAVE TO GO IN
THE GUNDAM'S TORSO...
WAIT, WHERE'S THE GUNDAM?
DOWN THERE.
IT'S MOSTLY FINISHED, BUT WE HAVE TO
GIUNG
GIUNG
INSTALL THE UNIT AND RUN SOME TESTS...
IT'LL BE ANOTHER TWO WEEKS OR SO.

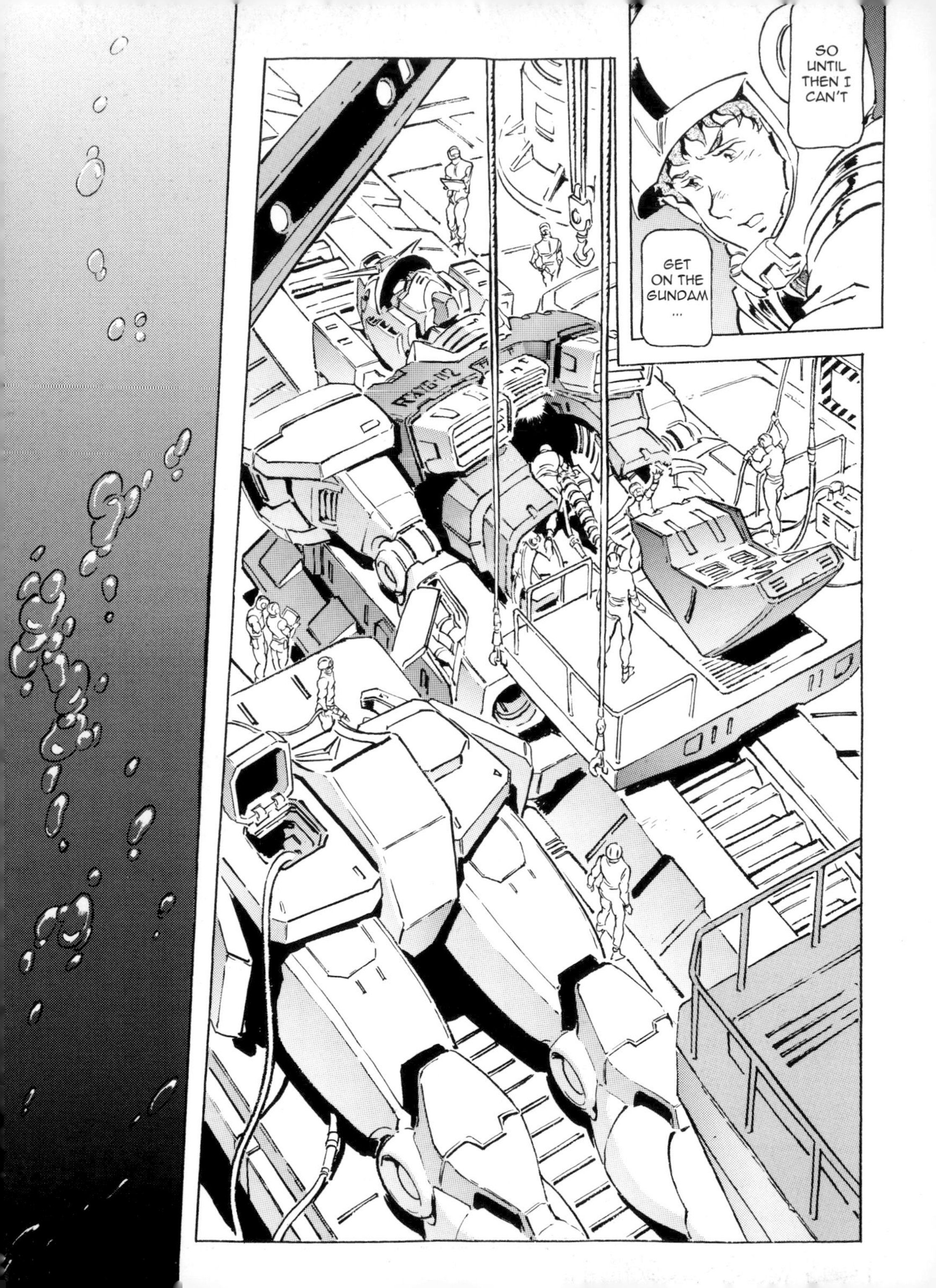
SO UNTIL THEN I CAN'T
GET ON THE GUNDAM ...

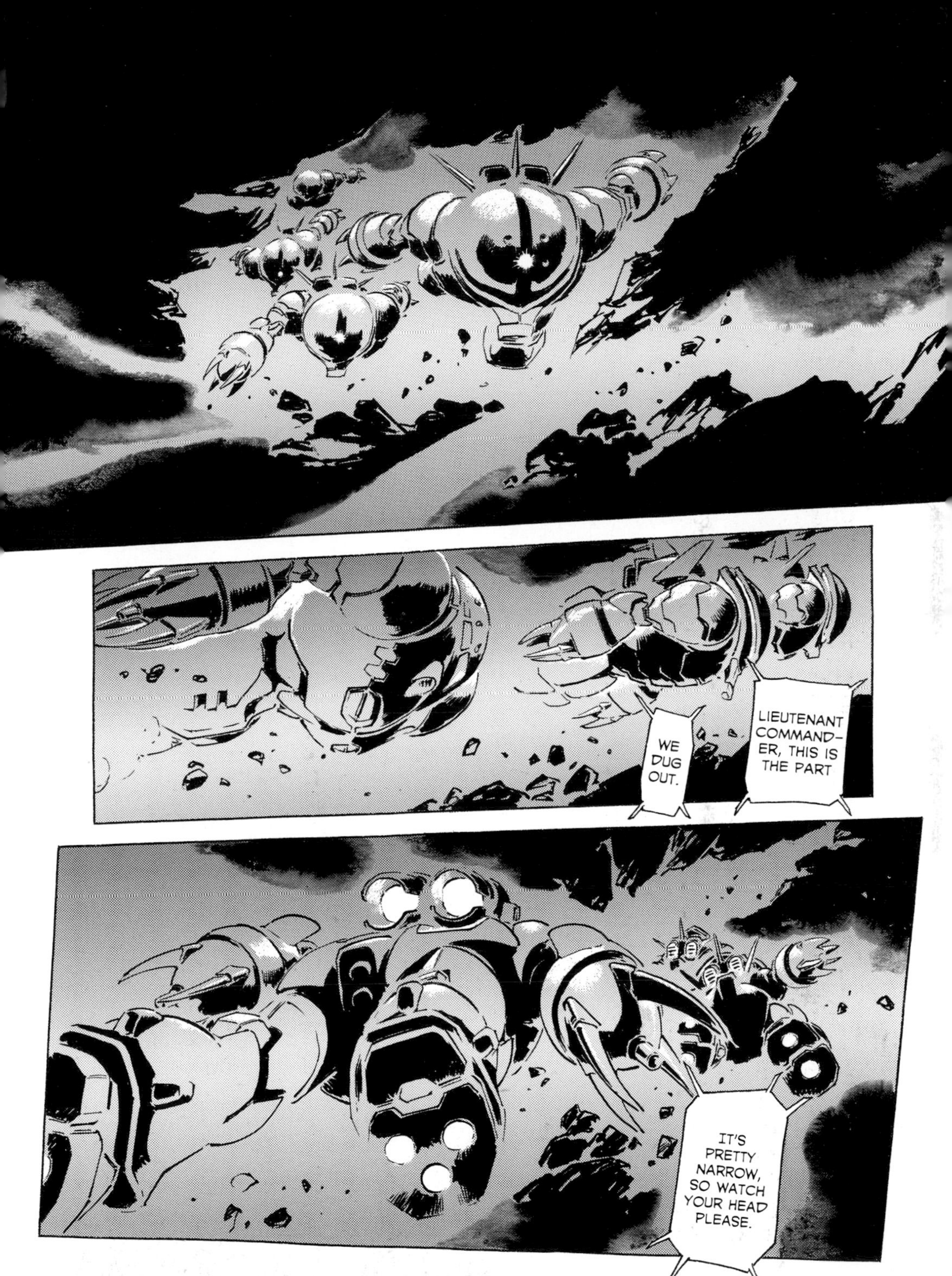
LIEUTENANT COMMANDER, THIS IS THE PART
WE DUG OUT.
IT'S PRETTY NARROW, SO WATCH YOUR HEAD PLEASE.

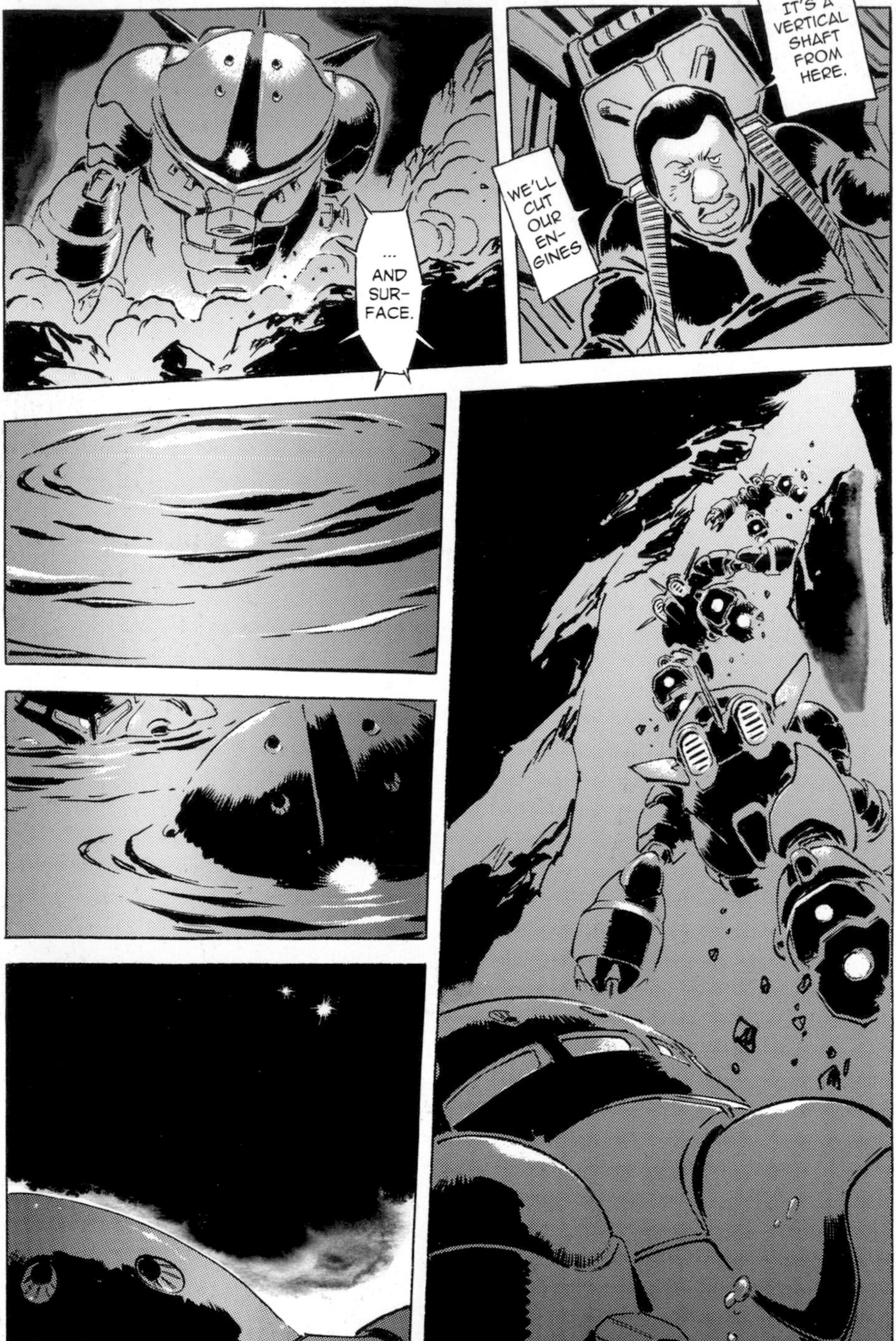
IT'S A VERTICAL SHAFT FROM HERE.
WE'LL CUT OUR EN-GINES
... AND SUR-FACE.

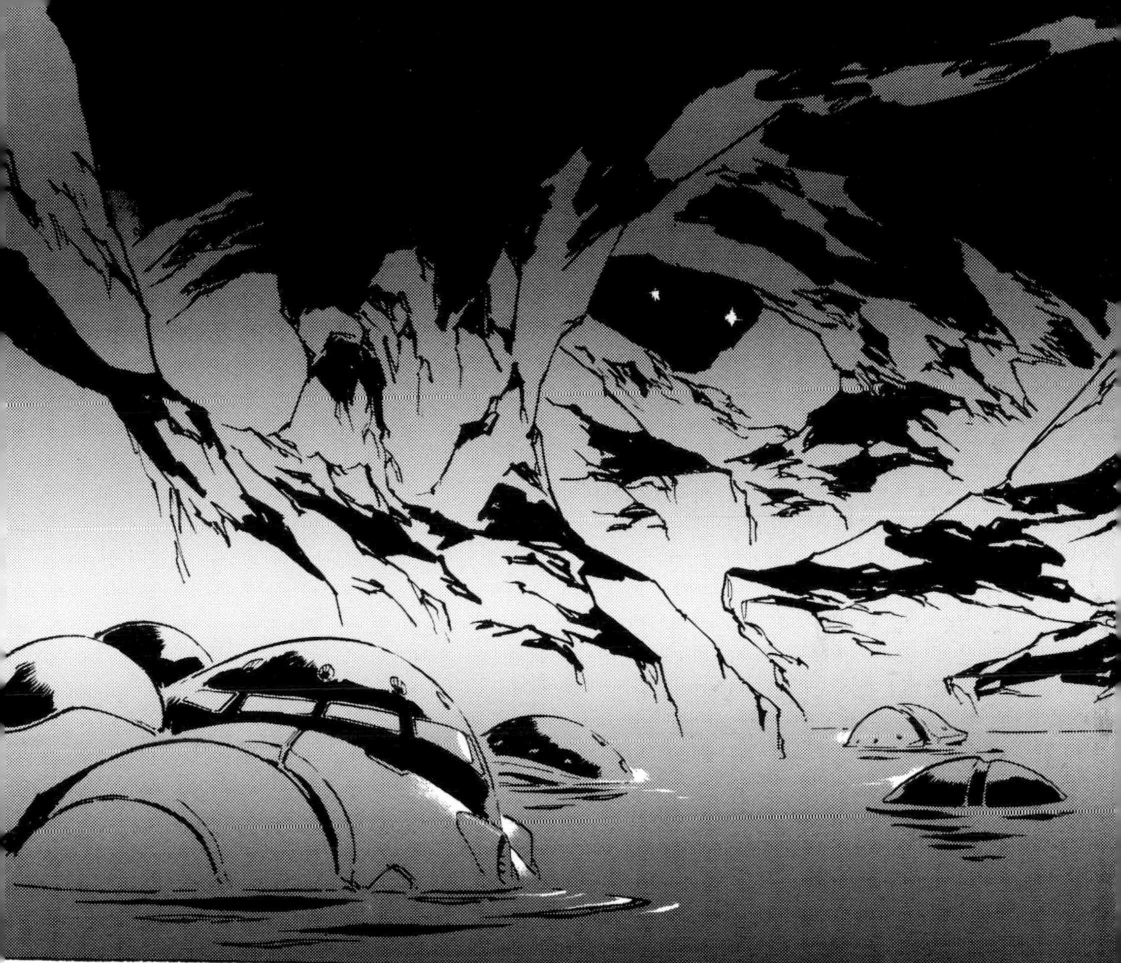

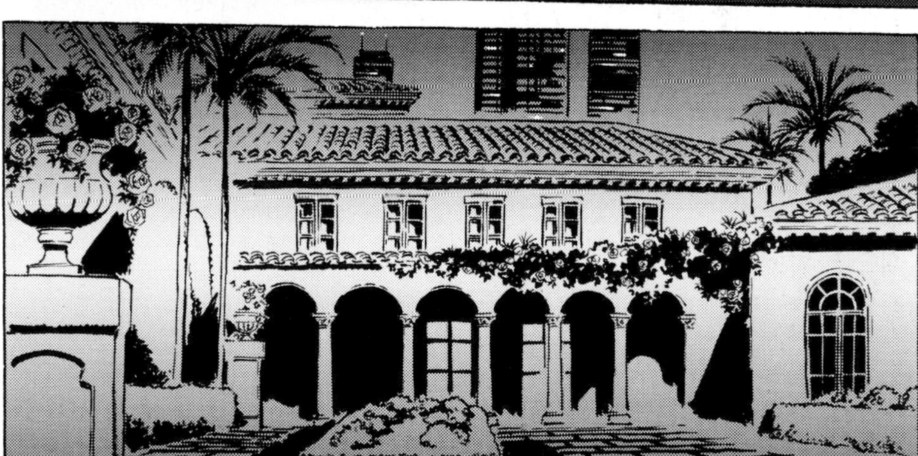

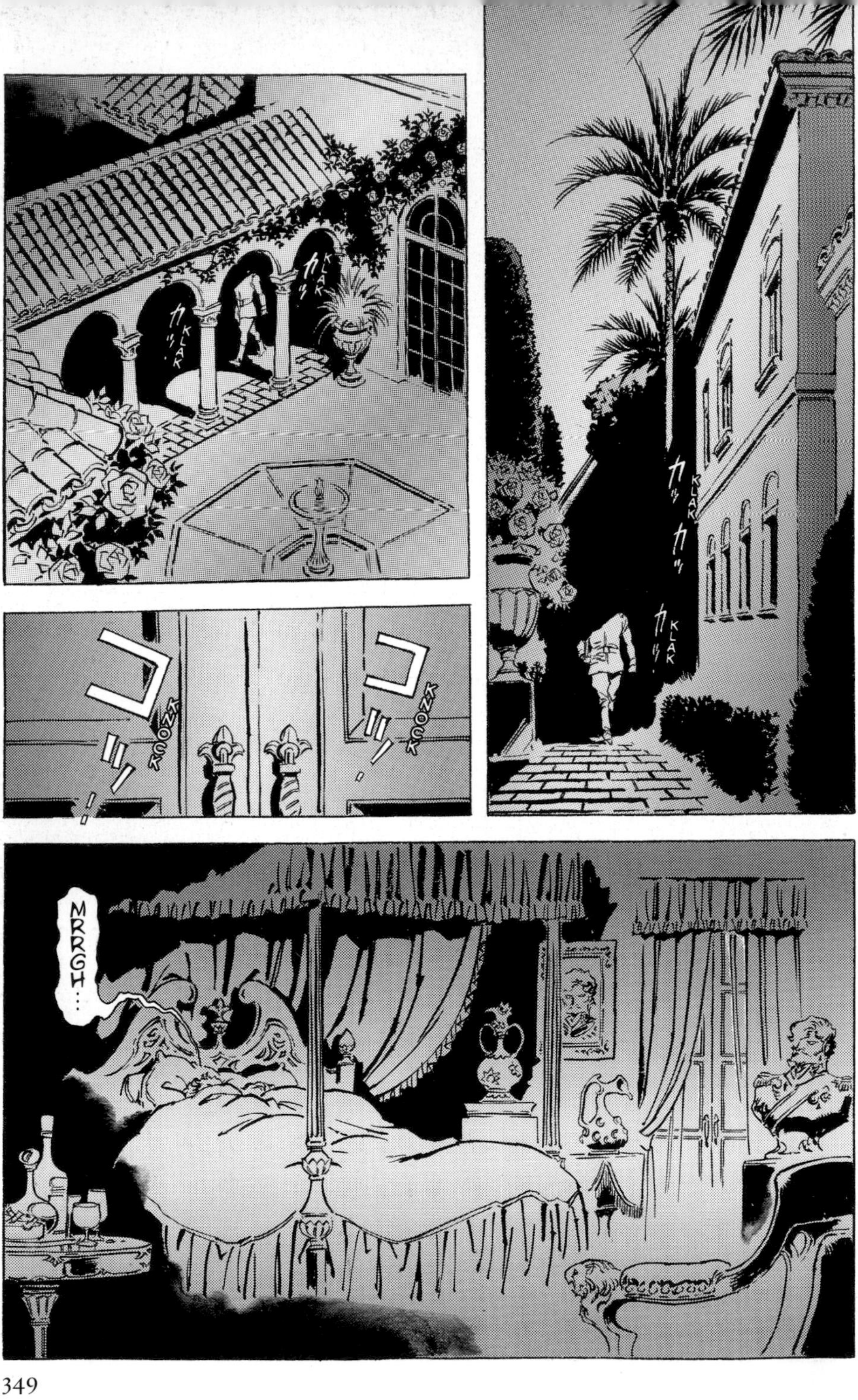
KLAK
KLAK
KLAK
KLAK
KLAK
KNOCK
KNOCK
MRRGH...

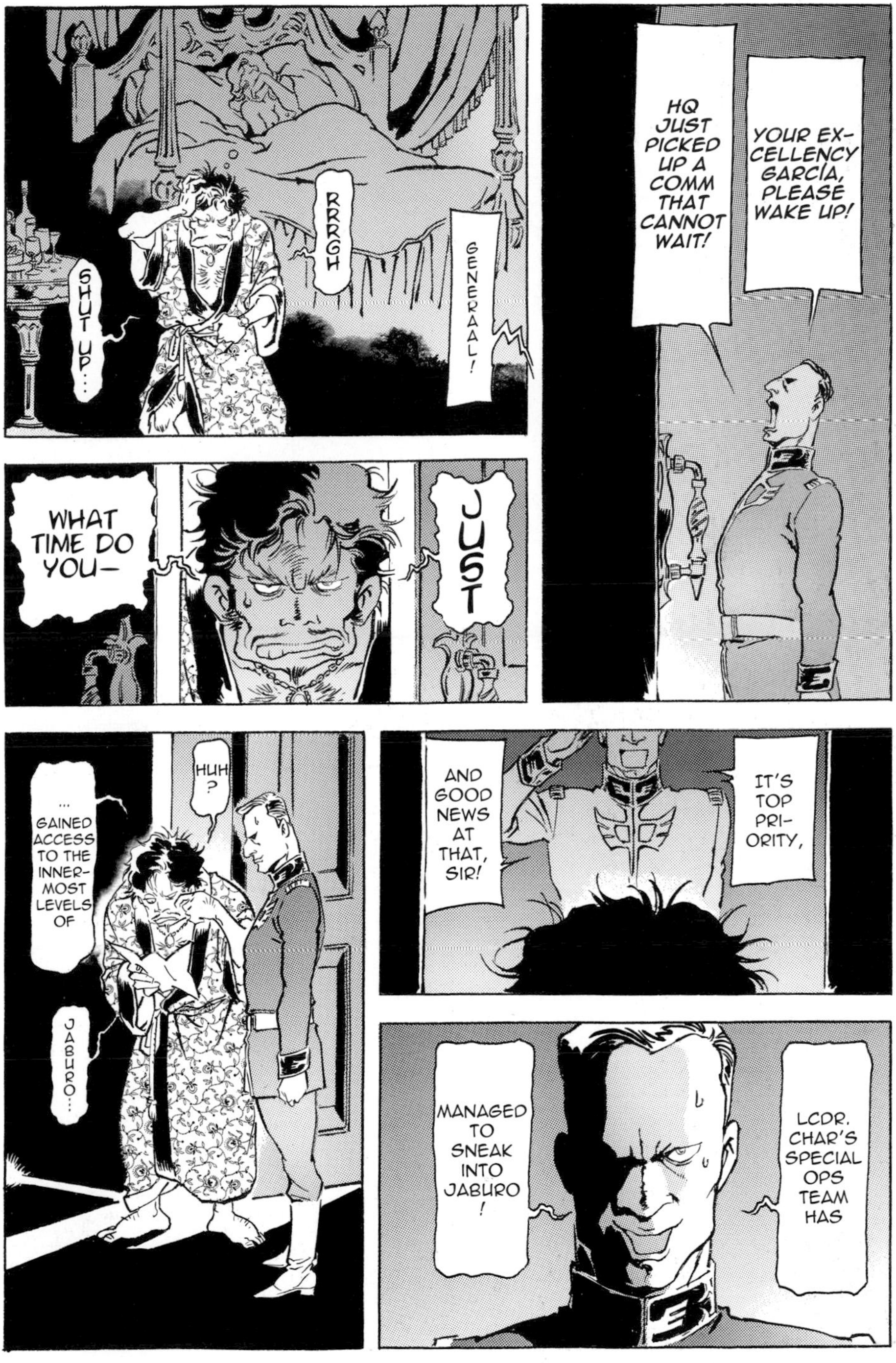
YOUR EX-CELLENCY GARCÍA, PLEASE WAKE UP!
HQ JUST PICKED UP A COMM THAT CANNOT WAIT!
GENERAAL!
RRRGH
SHUT UP...
JUST
WHAT TIME DO YOU—
IT'S TOP PRI-ORITY,
AND GOOD NEWS AT THAT, SIR!
LCDR. CHAR'S SPECIAL OPS TEAM HAS
MANAGED TO SNEAK INTO JABURO!
HUH?
...GAINED ACCESS TO THE INNER-MOST LEVELS OF
JABURO...

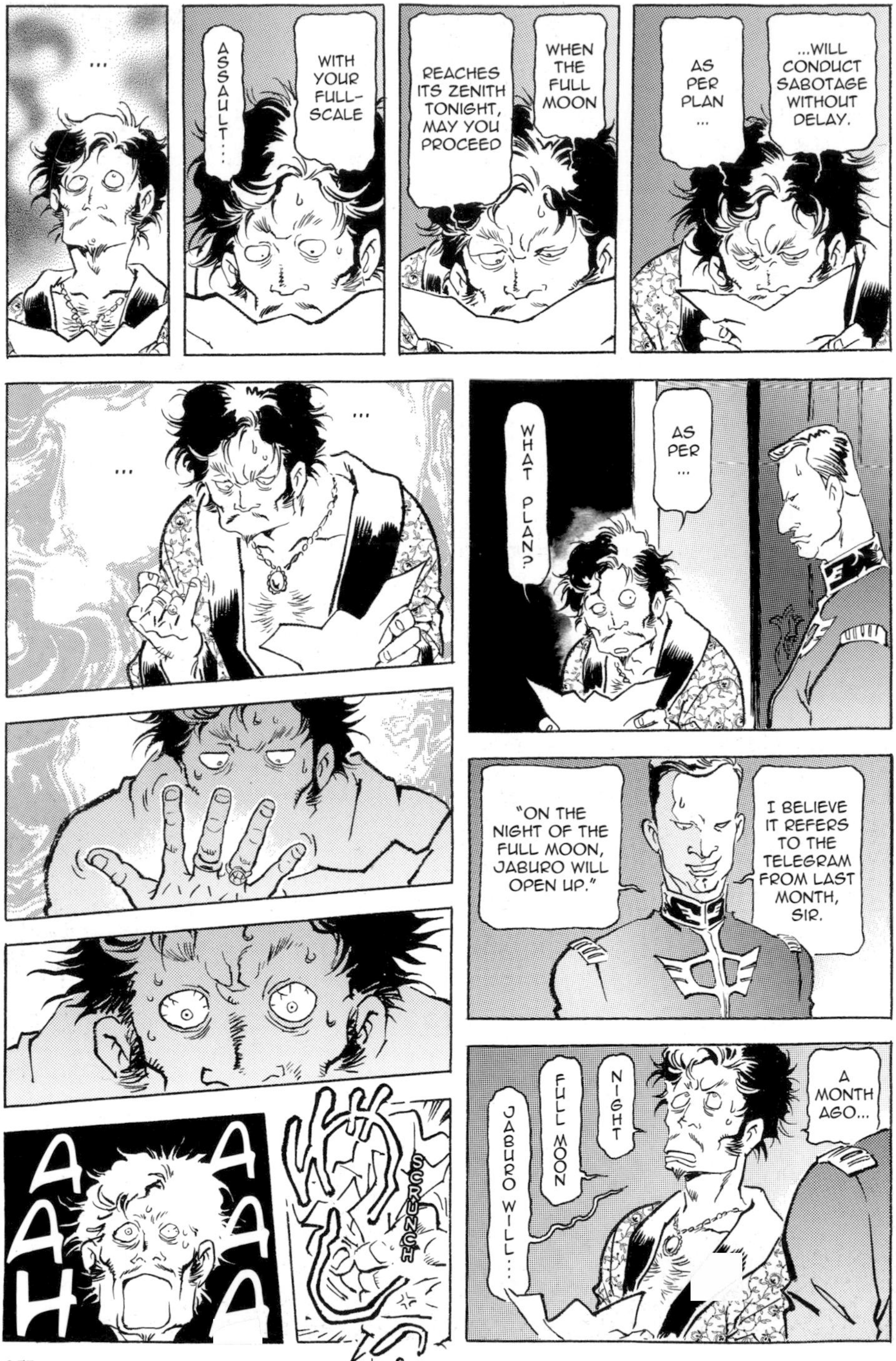
...WILL CONDUCT SABOTAGE WITHOUT DELAY.
AS PER PLAN ...
WHEN THE FULL MOON
REACHES ITS ZENITH TONIGHT, MAY YOU PROCEED
WITH YOUR FULL-SCALE
ASSAULT...
...
AS PER ...
WHAT PLAN?
I BELIEVE IT REFERS TO THE TELEGRAM FROM LAST MONTH, SIR.
"ON THE NIGHT OF THE FULL MOON, JABURO WILL OPEN UP."
A MONTH AGO...
NIGHT
FULL MOON
JABURO WILL...
...
...
SCRUNCH
AAAAAH

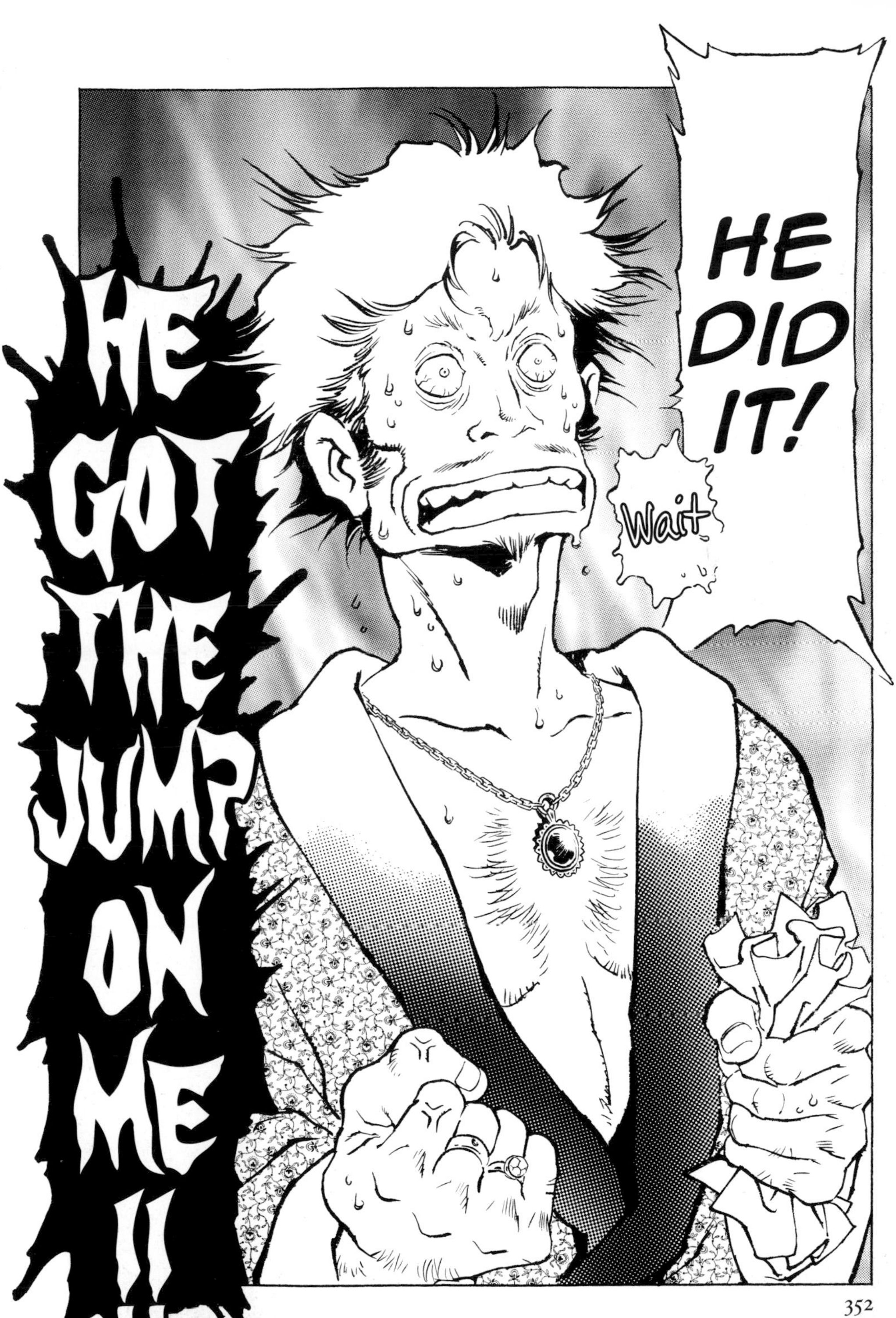
HE DID IT!
Wait
HE GOT THE JUMP ON ME!!

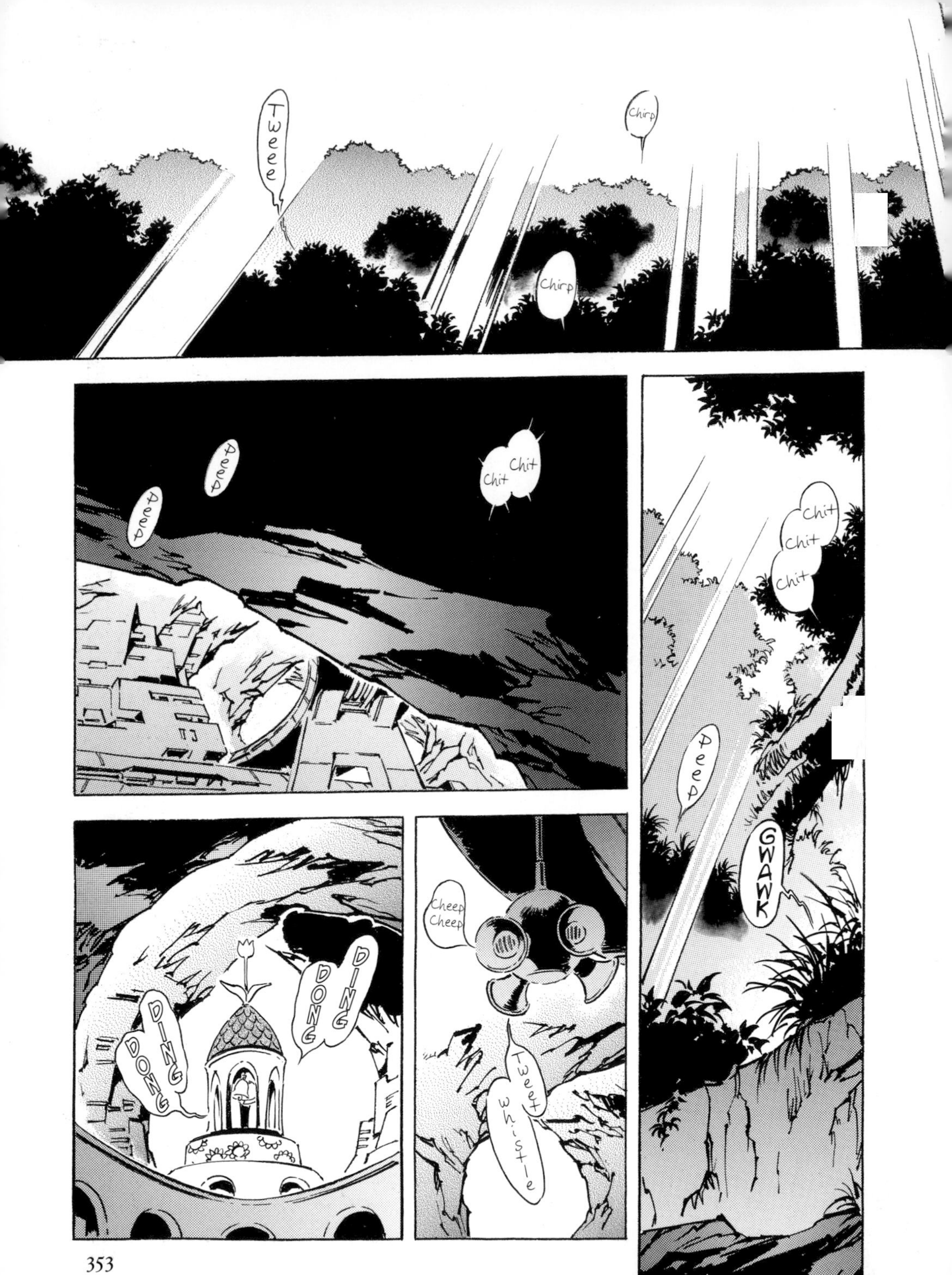
Chirp
Tweee
Chirp
Chit
Chit
Chit
Peep
GWAWK
Chit
Chit
Peep
Peep
Cheep
Cheep
Tweet
whistle
DING
DONG
DING
DONG

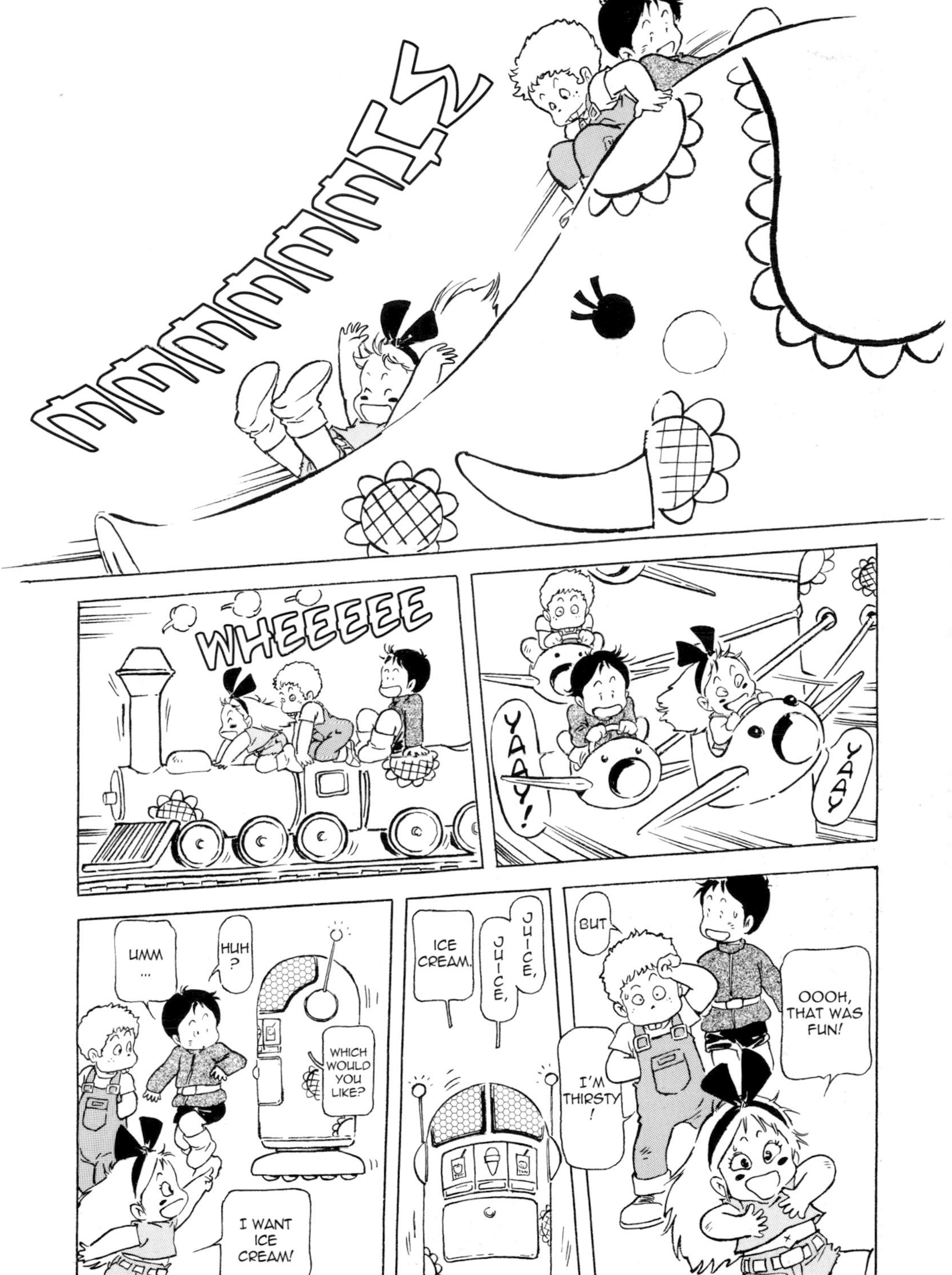
YAAY!
YAAY
WHEEEEEE
OOOH, THAT WAS FUN!
BUT
I'M THIRSTY!
JUICE, JUICE,
ICE CREAM.
WHICH WOULD YOU LIKE?
HUH?
UMM ...
I WANT ICE CREAM!

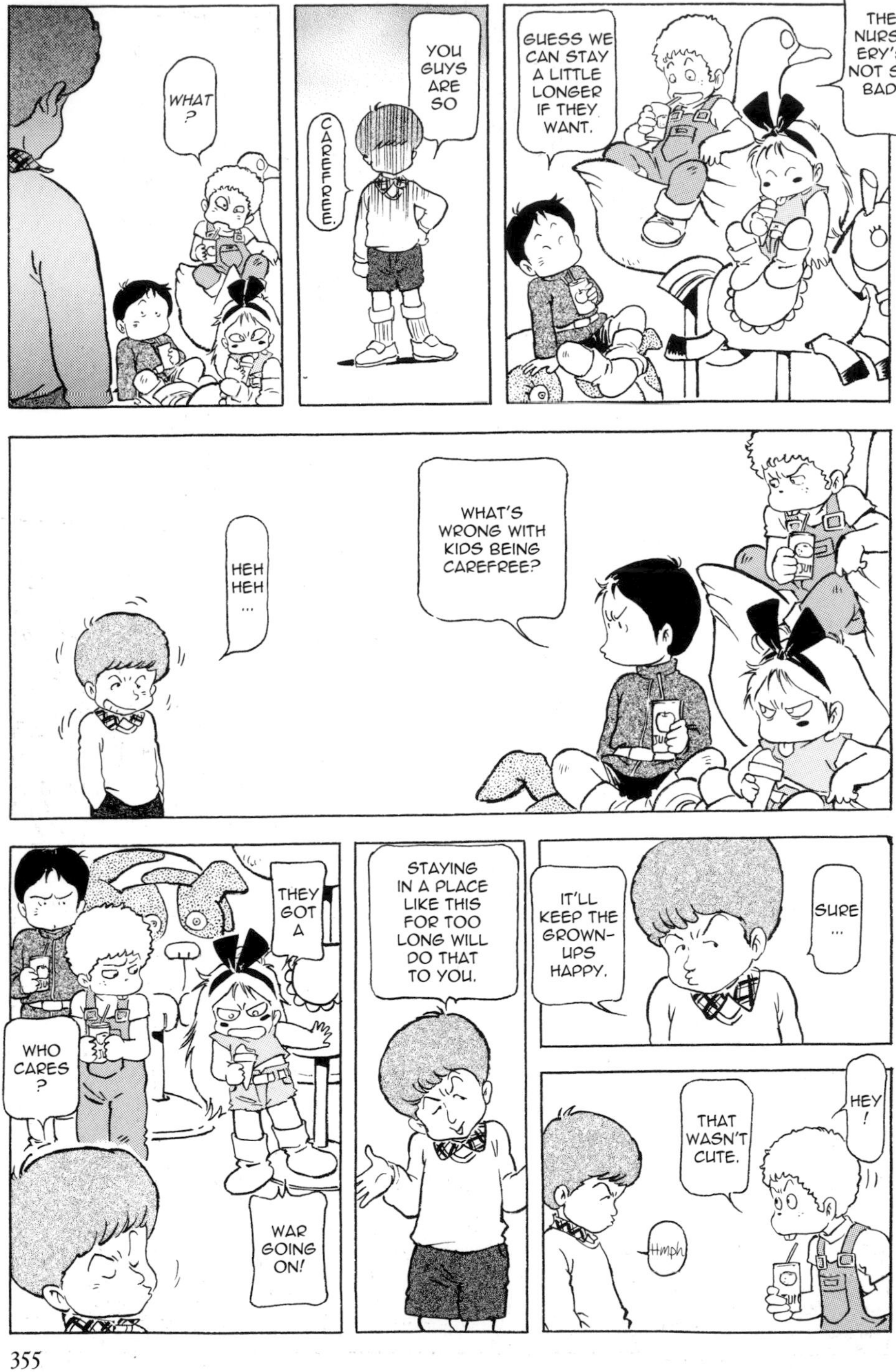
THE NURSERY'S NOT SO BAD.
GUESS WE CAN STAY A LITTLE LONGER IF THEY WANT.
YOU GUYS ARE SO
CAREFREE.
WHAT?
WHAT'S WRONG WITH KIDS BEING CAREFREE?
HEH HEH ...
SURE ...
IT'LL KEEP THE GROWN-UPS HAPPY.
HEY!
THAT WASN'T CUTE.
Hmph
STAYING IN A PLACE LIKE THIS FOR TOO LONG WILL DO THAT TO YOU.
THEY GOT A
WAR GOING ON!
WHO CARES?

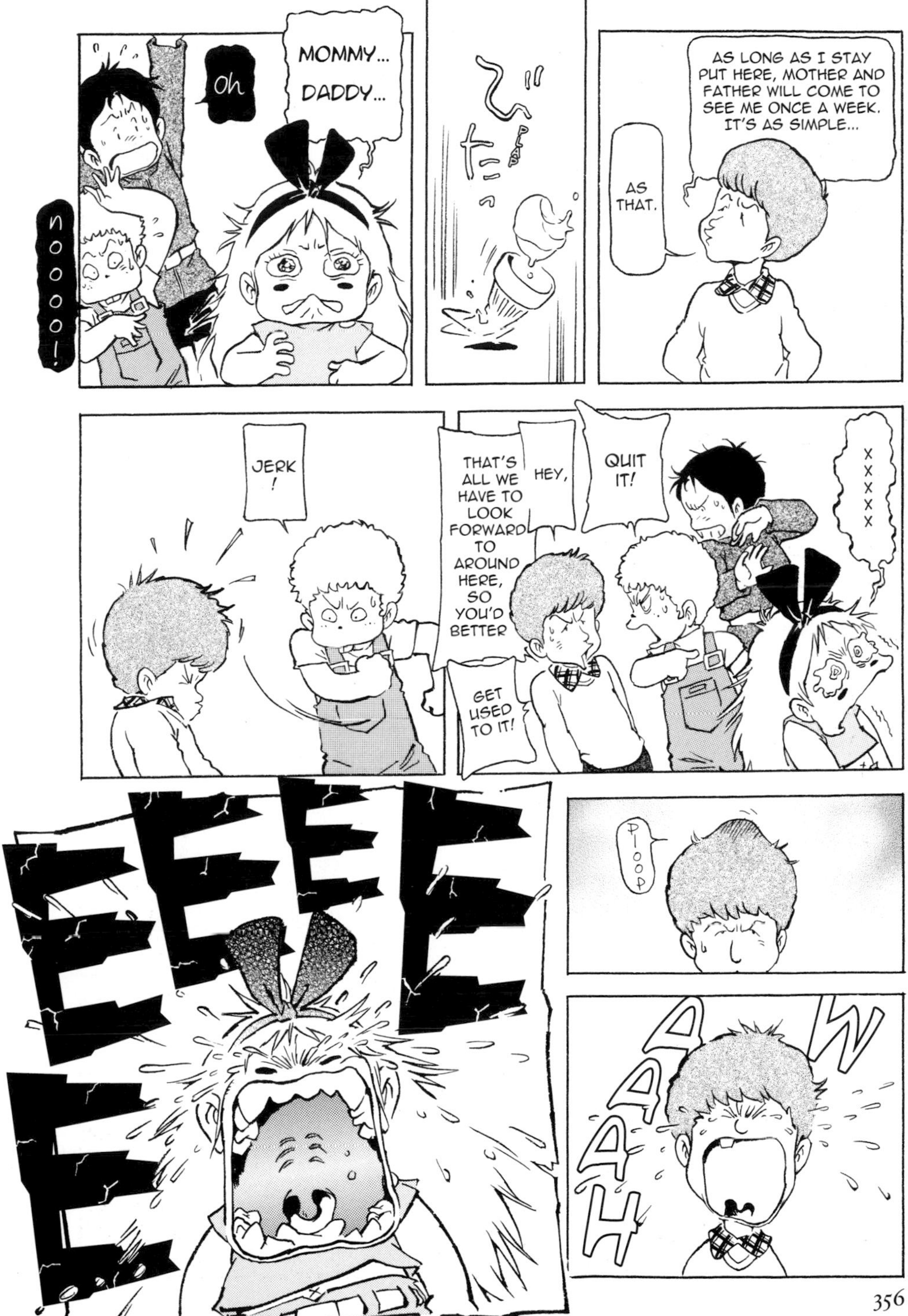

AS LONG AS I STAY PUT HERE, MOTHER AND FATHER WILL COME TO SEE ME ONCE A WEEK. IT'S AS SIMPLE...
AS THAT.
PLAP
MOMMY... DADDY...
Oh
noooo!
XXXXX
QUIT IT!
HEY,
THAT'S ALL WE HAVE TO LOOK FORWARD TO AROUND HERE, SO YOU'D BETTER
GET USED TO IT!
JERK!
PLOOP
WAAAH
EEEEEE...

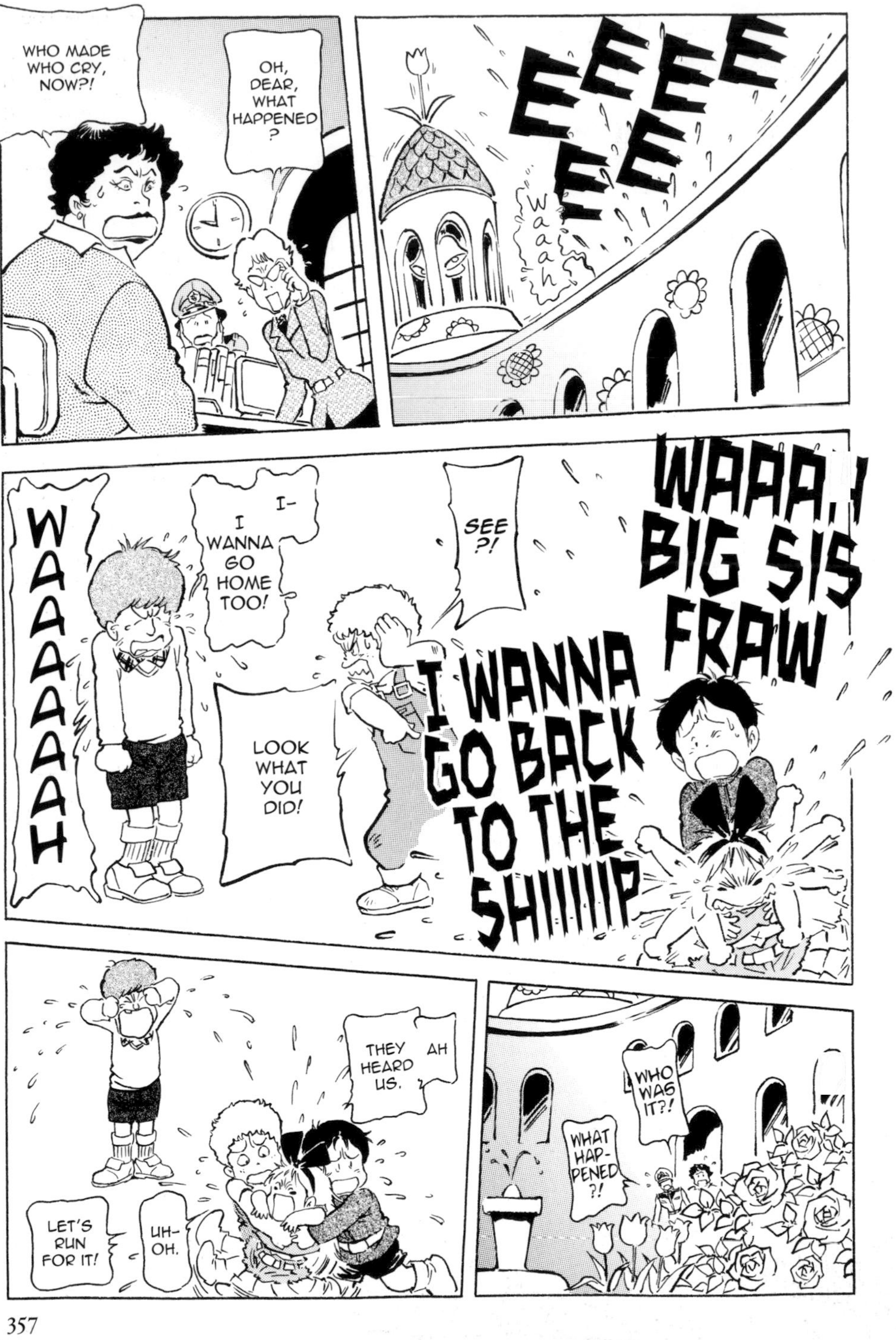
EEEEEEEEE
Waaah
OH, DEAR, WHAT HAPPENED?
WHO MADE WHO CRY, NOW?!
WAAAAH BIG SIS FRAW
I WANNA GO BACK TO THE SHIIIIIP
SEE?!
LOOK WHAT YOU DID!
I- I WANNA GO HOME TOO!
WAAAAAAAH
WHO WAS IT?!
WHAT HAPPENED?!
AH
THEY HEARD US.
UH-OH.
LET'S RUN FOR IT!

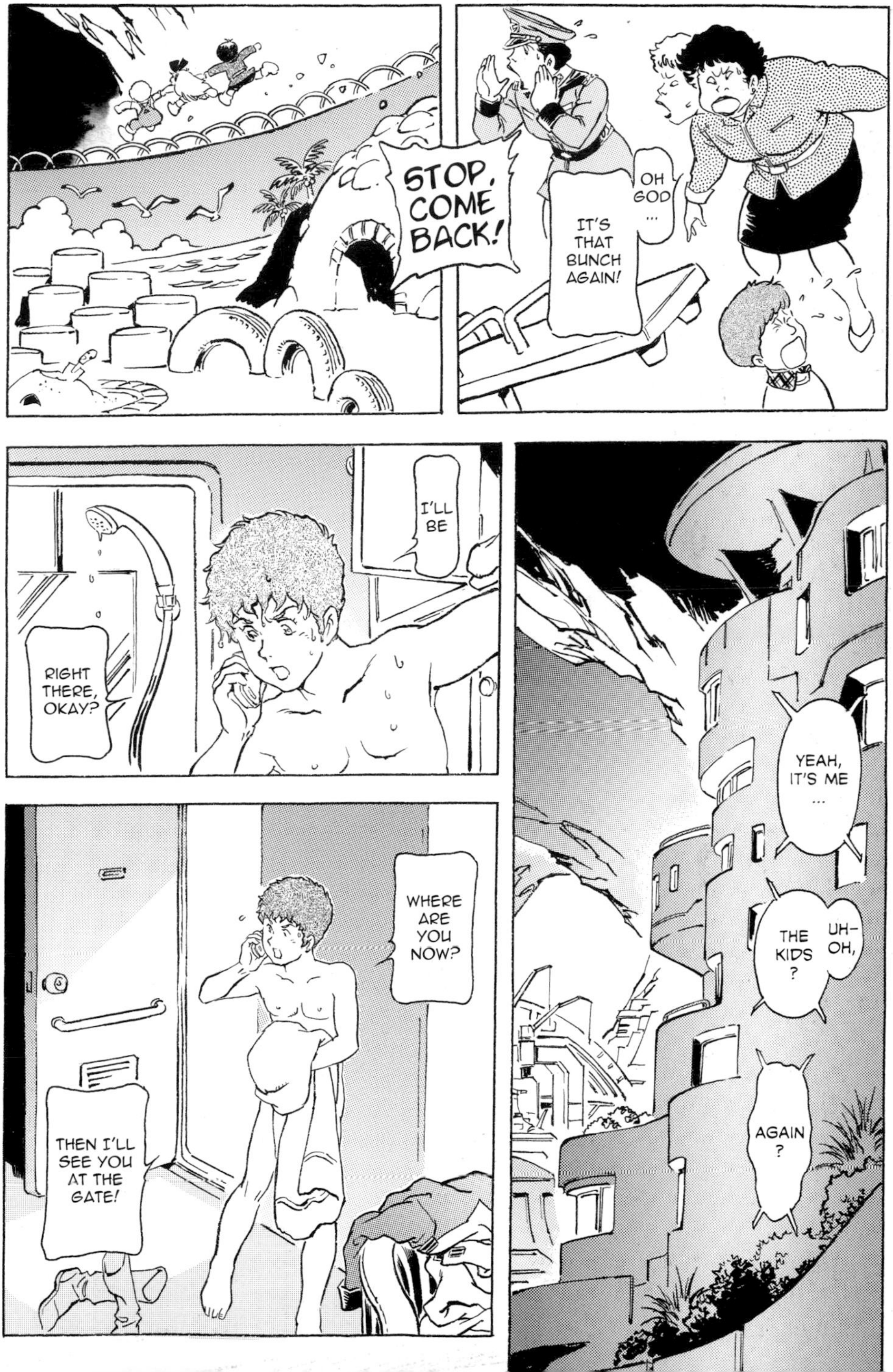
OH GOD ...
IT'S THAT BUNCH AGAIN!
STOP, COME BACK!
YEAH, IT'S ME ...
UH-OH, THE KIDS?
AGAIN?
I'LL BE
RIGHT THERE, OKAY?
WHERE ARE YOU NOW?
THEN I'LL SEE YOU AT THE GATE!

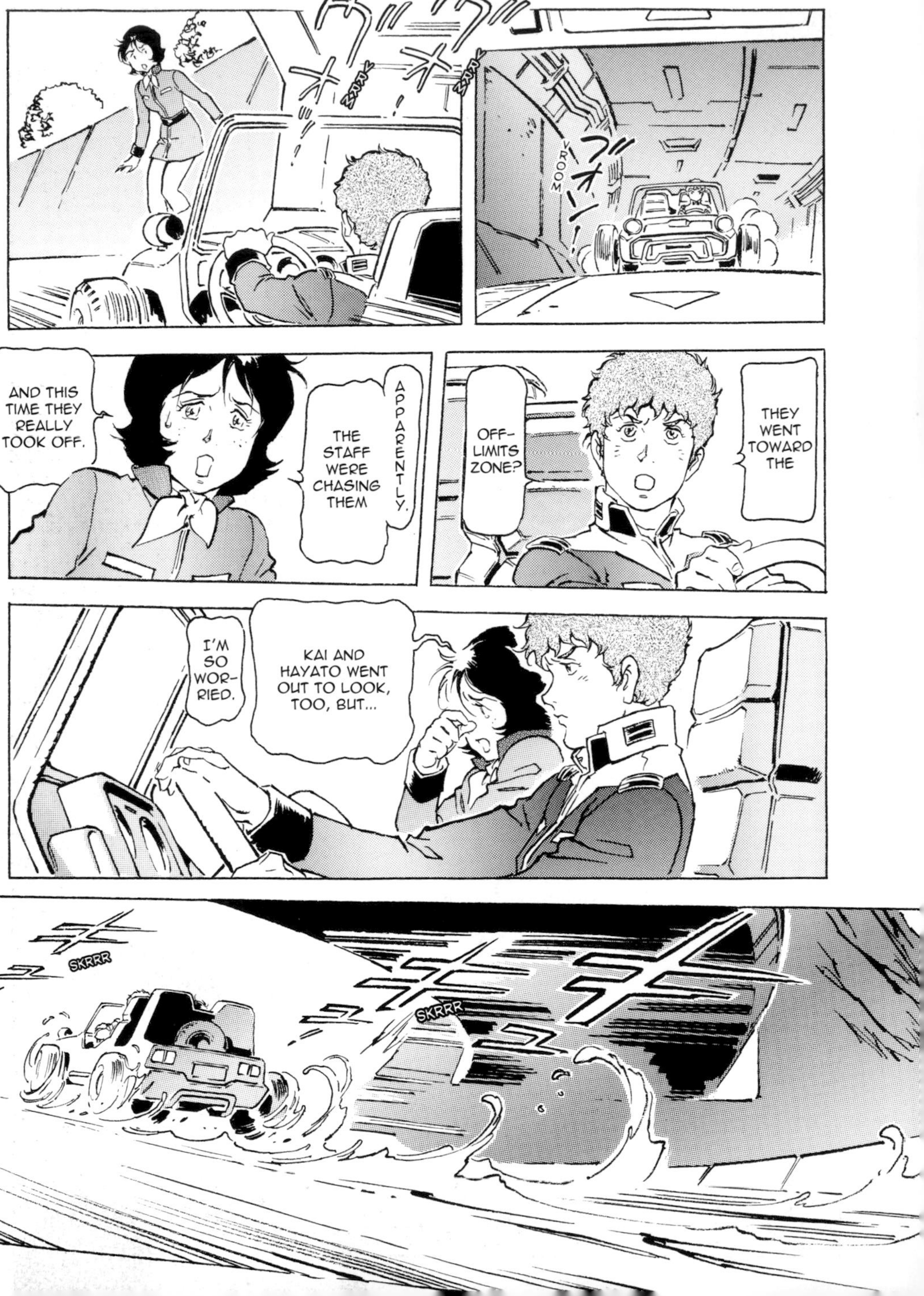
VROOM
THEY WENT TOWARD THE
OFF-LIMITS ZONE?
APPARENTLY.
THE STAFF WERE CHASING THEM
AND THIS TIME THEY REALLY TOOK OFF.
KAI AND HAYATO WENT OUT TO LOOK, TOO, BUT...
I'M SO WORRIED.
SKRRR
SKRRR

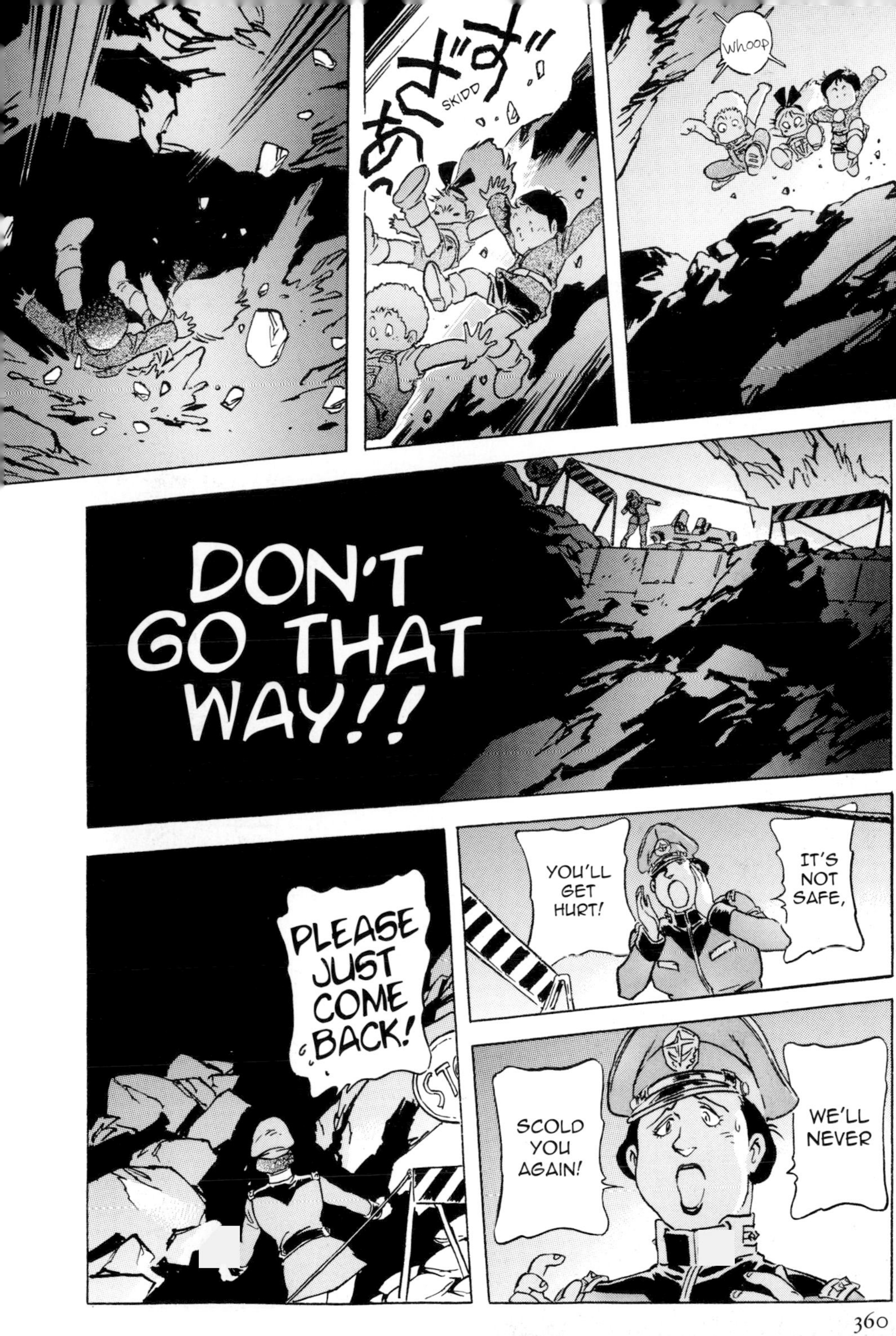
Whoop
ずざあっ
SKIDD
DON'T GO THAT WAY!!
IT'S NOT SAFE,
YOU'LL GET HURT!
WE'LL NEVER
SCOLD YOU AGAIN!
PLEASE JUST COME BACK!

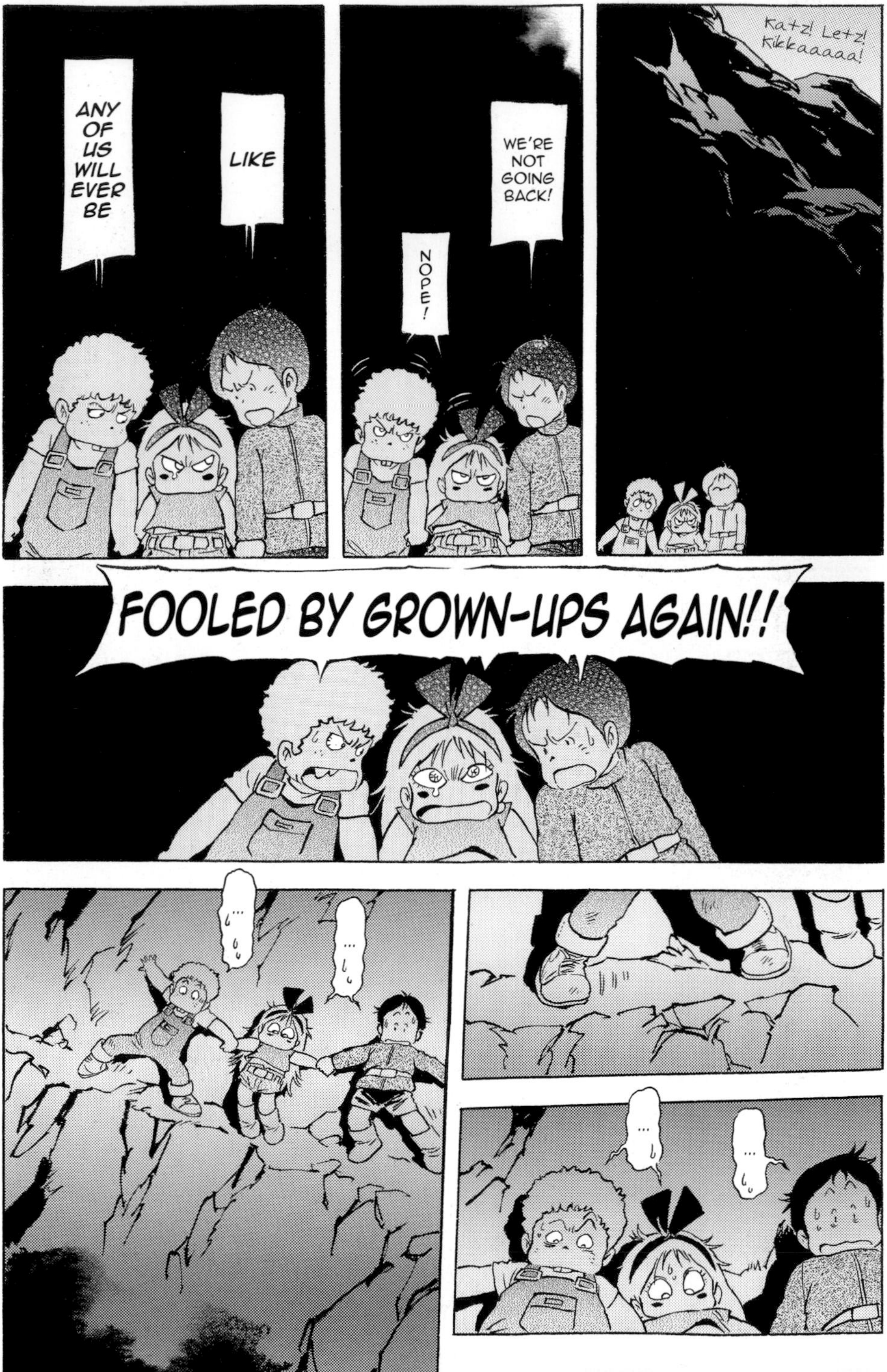
Katz! Letz! Kikkaaaaa!
WE'RE NOT GOING BACK!
NOPE!
LIKE
ANY OF US WILL EVER BE
FOOLED BY GROWN-UPS AGAIN!!
...
...
...
...

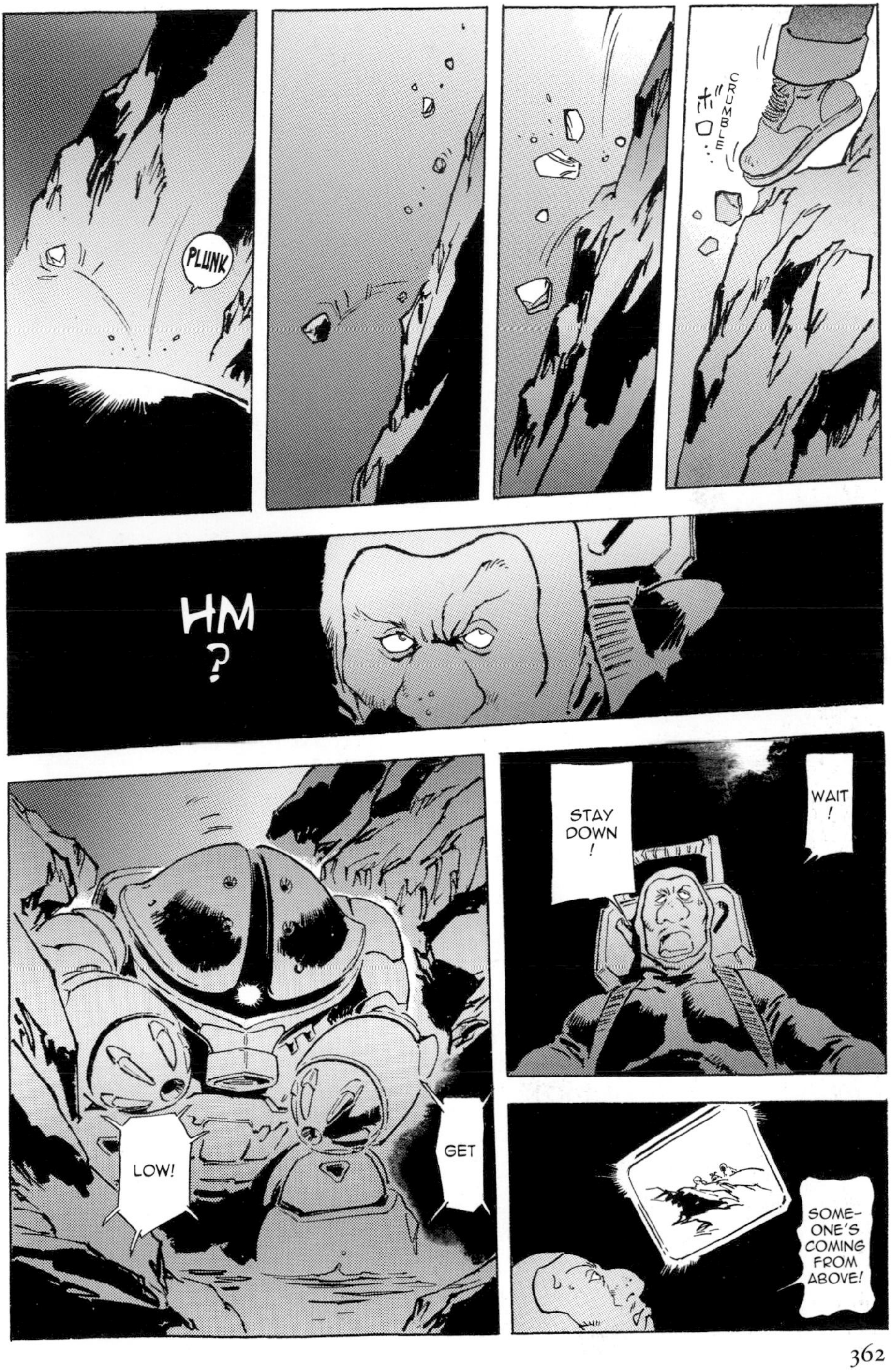
ボロ…
CRUMBLE
PLUNK
HM ?
WAIT!
STAY DOWN!
SOME-ONE'S COMING FROM ABOVE!
GET
LOW!

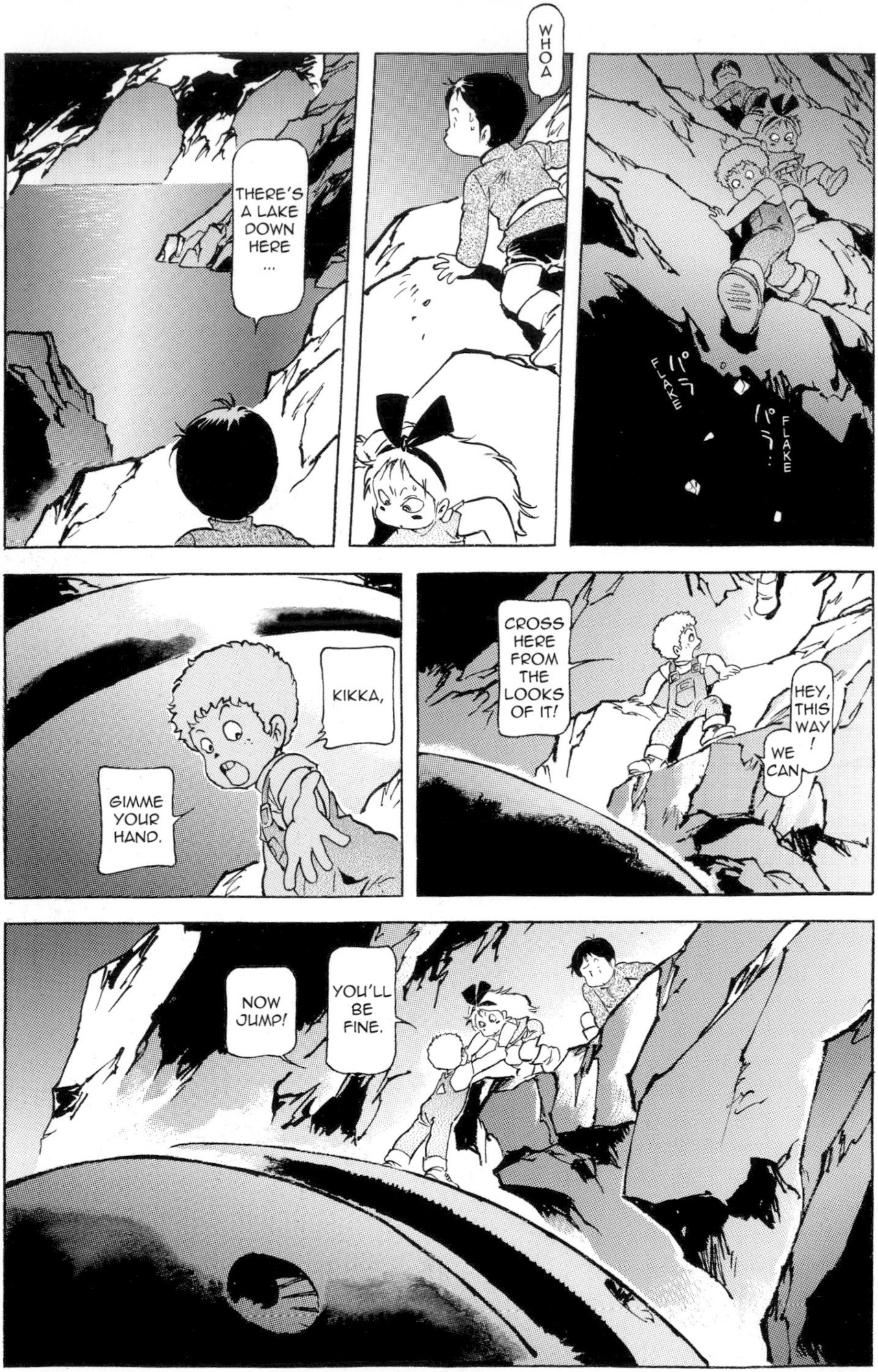

パラ…
FLAKE
パラ
FLAKE
WHOA
THERE'S A LAKE DOWN HERE ...
HEY, THIS WAY!
WE CAN
CROSS HERE FROM THE LOOKS OF IT!
KIKKA,
GIMME YOUR HAND.
YOU'LL BE FINE.
NOW JUMP!

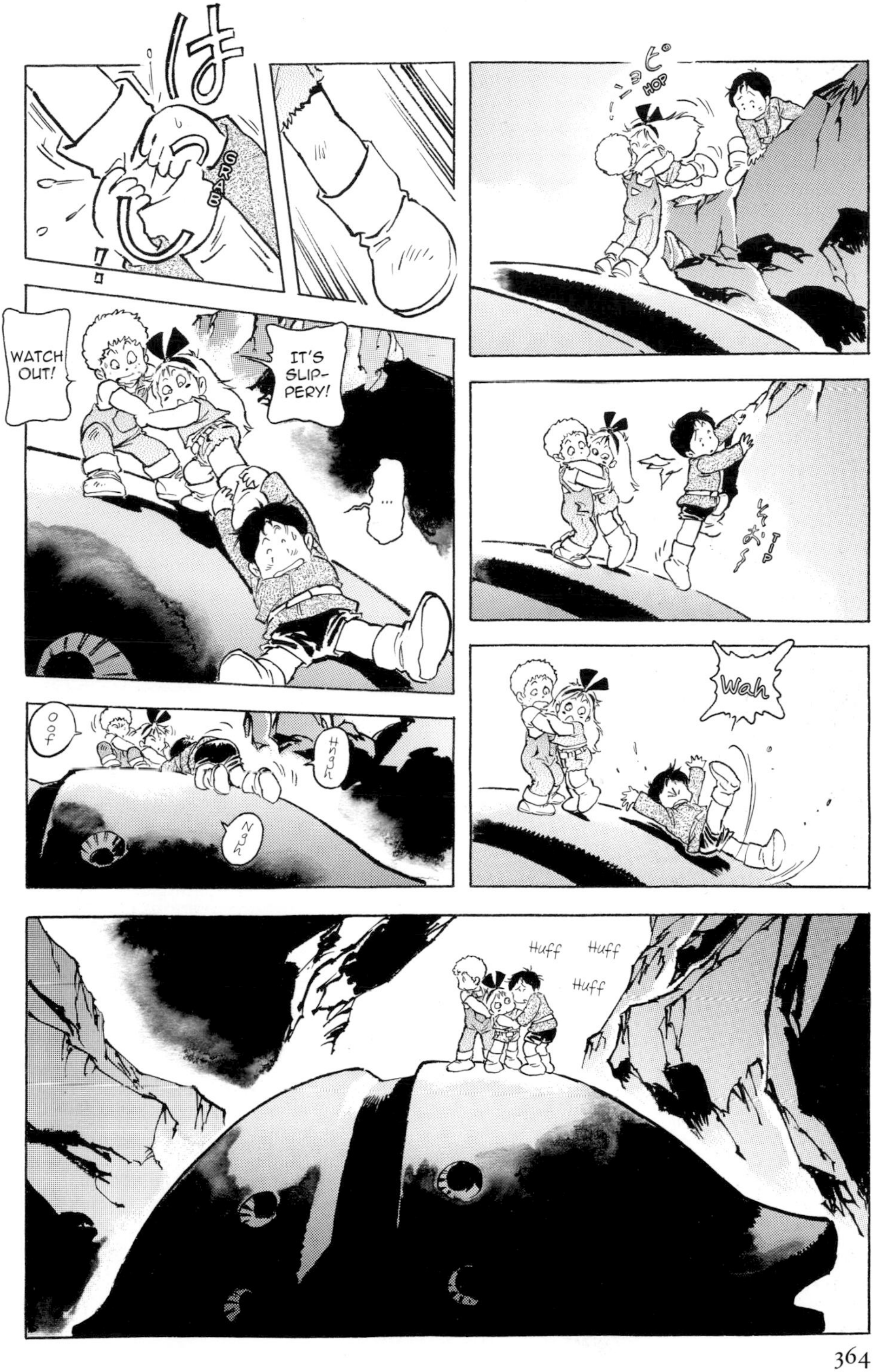
HOP
はっし
GRAB
!!
TIP
WATCH OUT!
IT'S SLIPPERY!
...
Wah
Oof
Hngh
Ngh
Huff
Huff
Huff

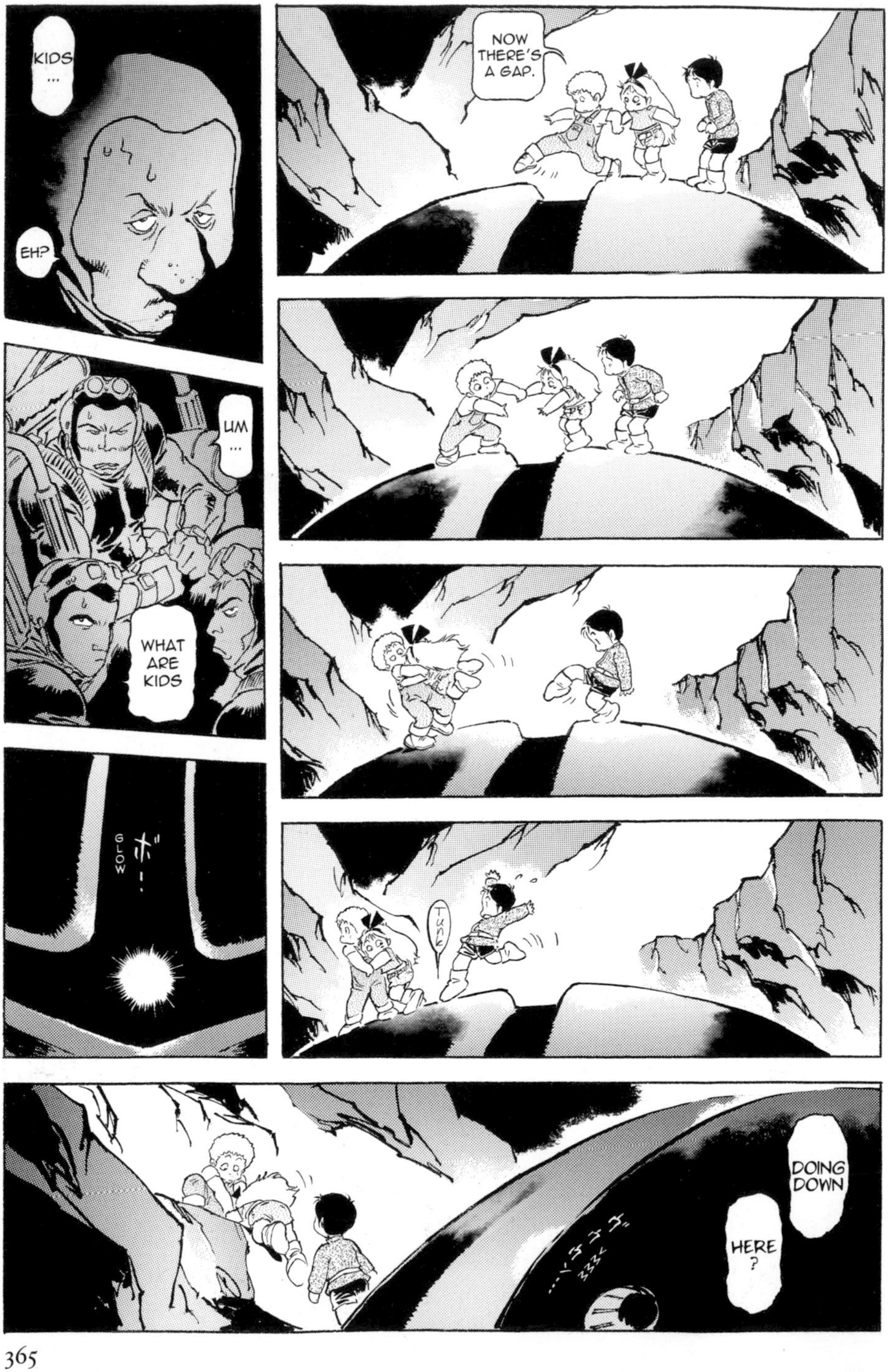
NOW THERE'S A GAP.
TUNK
KIDS ...
EH?
UM ...
WHAT ARE KIDS
GLOW
DOING DOWN
HERE ?

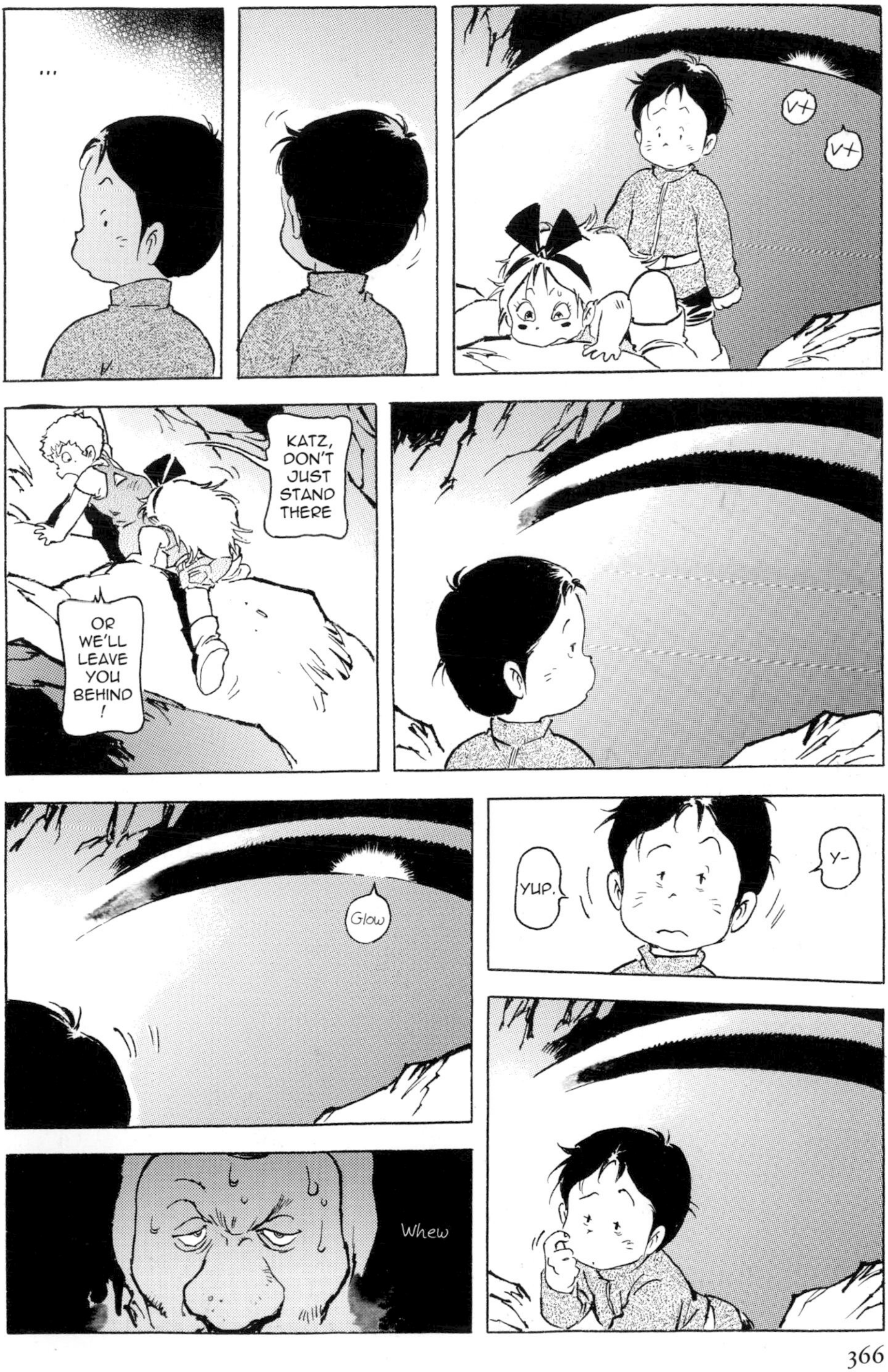
V+
V+
...
KATZ, DON'T JUST STAND THERE
OR WE'LL LEAVE YOU BEHIND!
Y-
YUP.
Glow
Whew

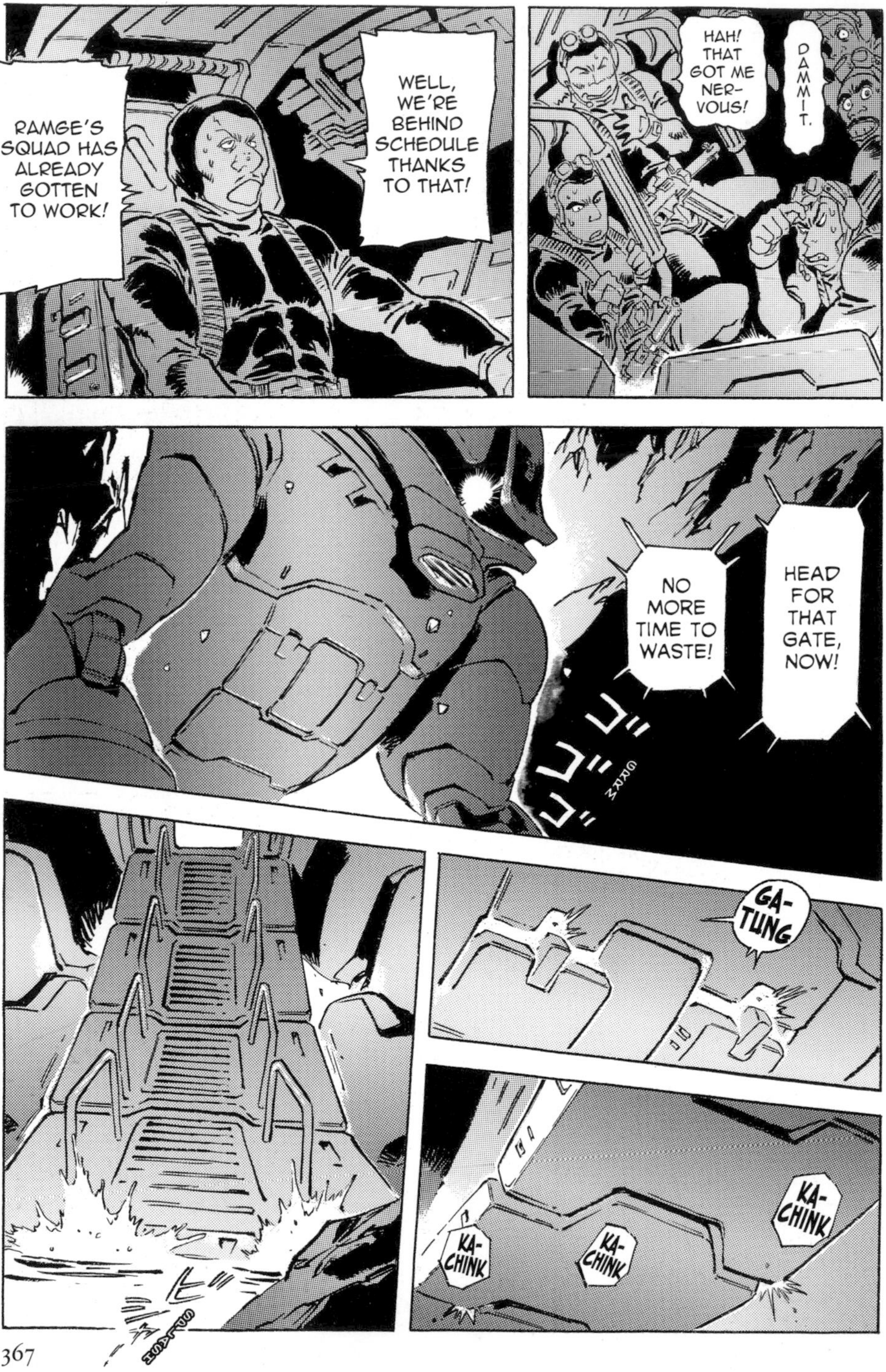
DAMMIT.
HAH! THAT GOT ME NER-VOUS!
WELL, WE'RE BEHIND SCHEDULE THANKS TO THAT!
RAMGE'S SQUAD HAS ALREADY GOTTEN TO WORK!
HEAD FOR THAT GATE, NOW!
NO MORE TIME TO WASTE!
GA-TUNG
KA-CHINK
KA-CHINK
KA-CHINK

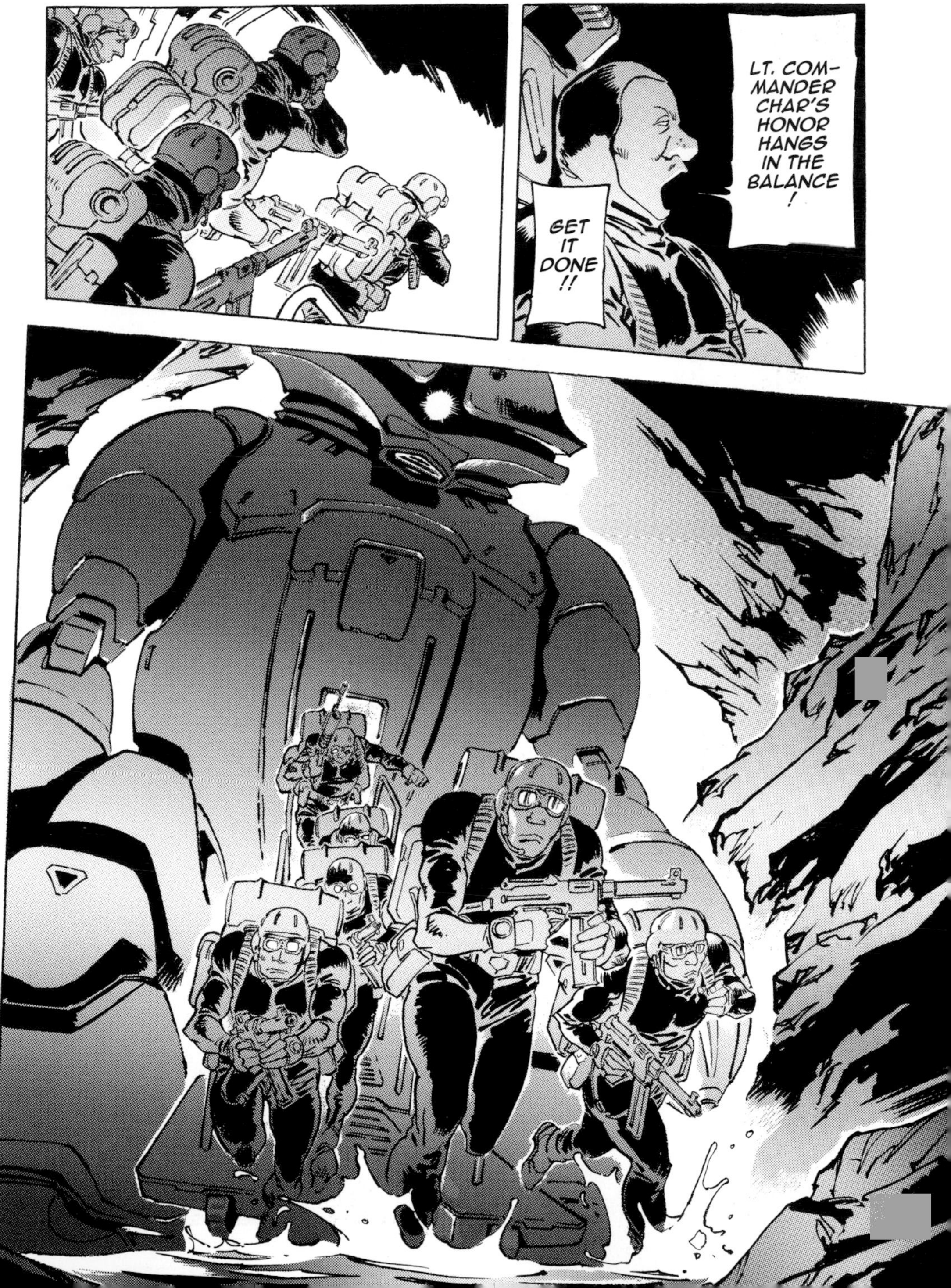
LT. COMMANDER CHAR'S HONOR HANGS IN THE BALANCE!
GET IT DONE!!

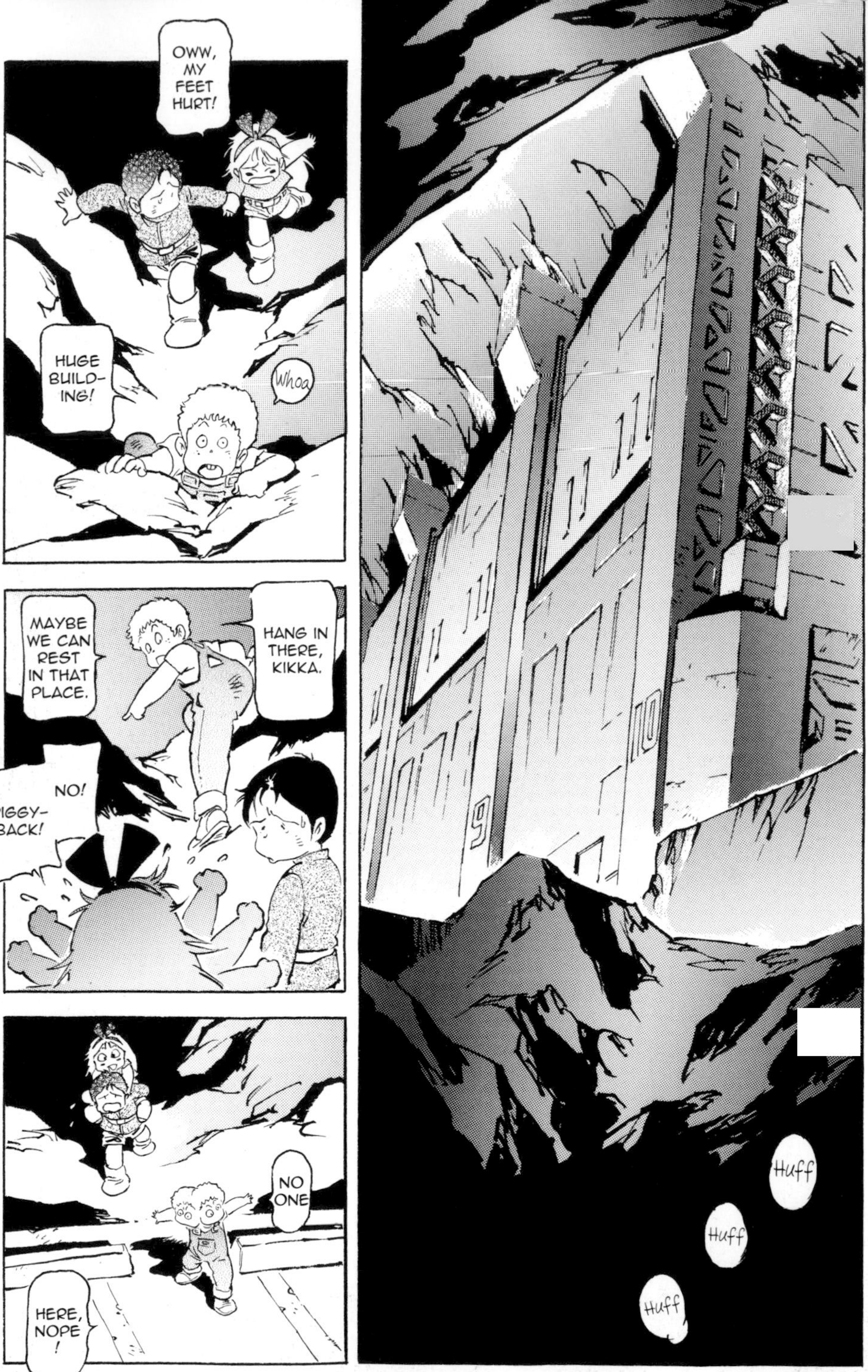
Huff
Huff
Huff
OWW, MY FEET HURT!
Whoa
HUGE BUILD-ING!
HANG IN THERE, KIKKA.
MAYBE WE CAN REST IN THAT PLACE.
NO! PIGGY-BACK!
NO ONE
HERE, NOPE!

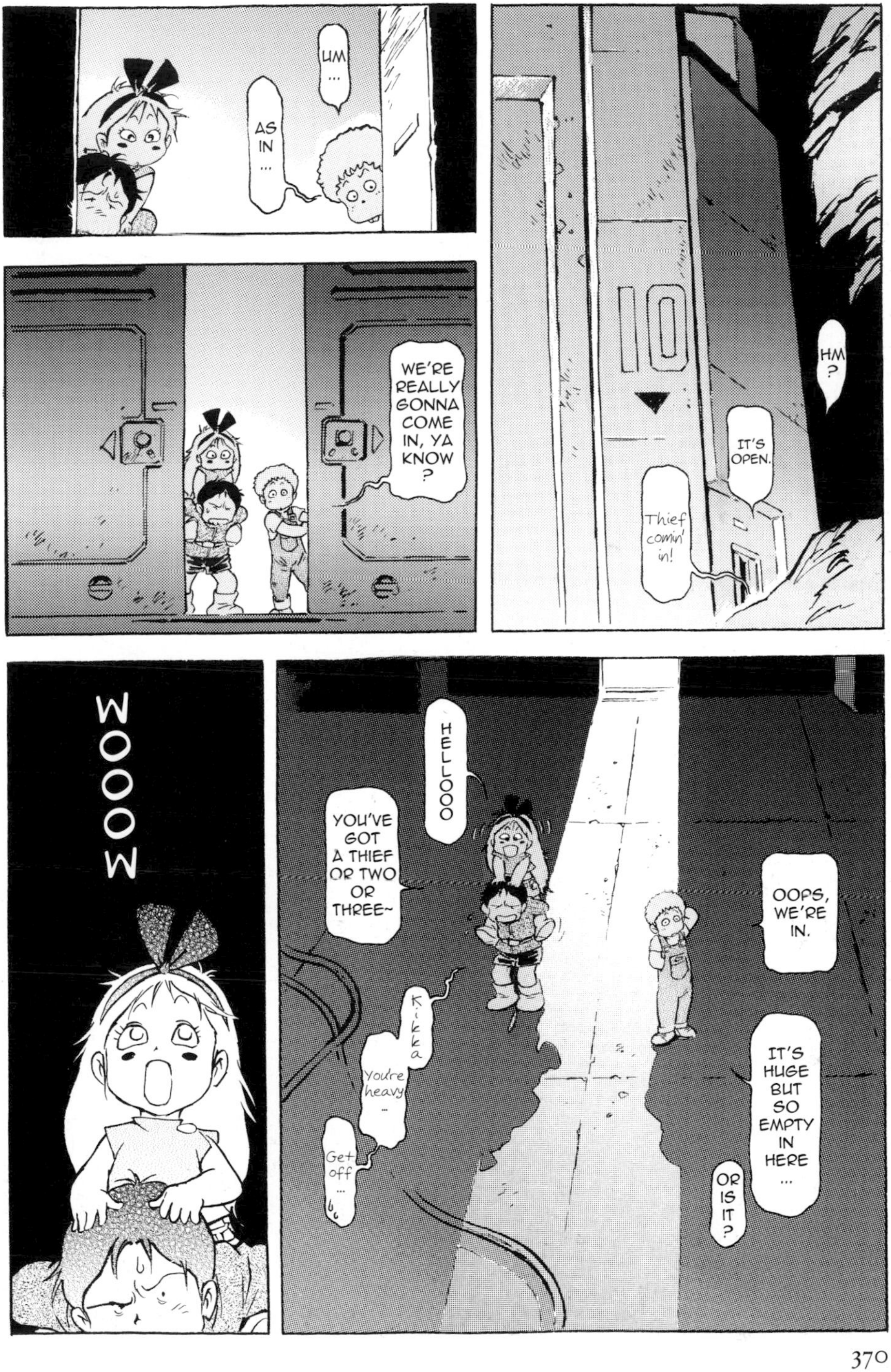
HM?
IT'S OPEN.
Thief comin' in!
UM...
AS IN...
WE'RE REALLY GONNA COME IN, YA KNOW?
HELLOOO
YOU'VE GOT A THIEF OR TWO OR THREE~
OOPS, WE'RE IN.
IT'S HUGE BUT SO EMPTY IN HERE...
OR IS IT?
Kikka
You're heavy...
Get off...
WOOOW

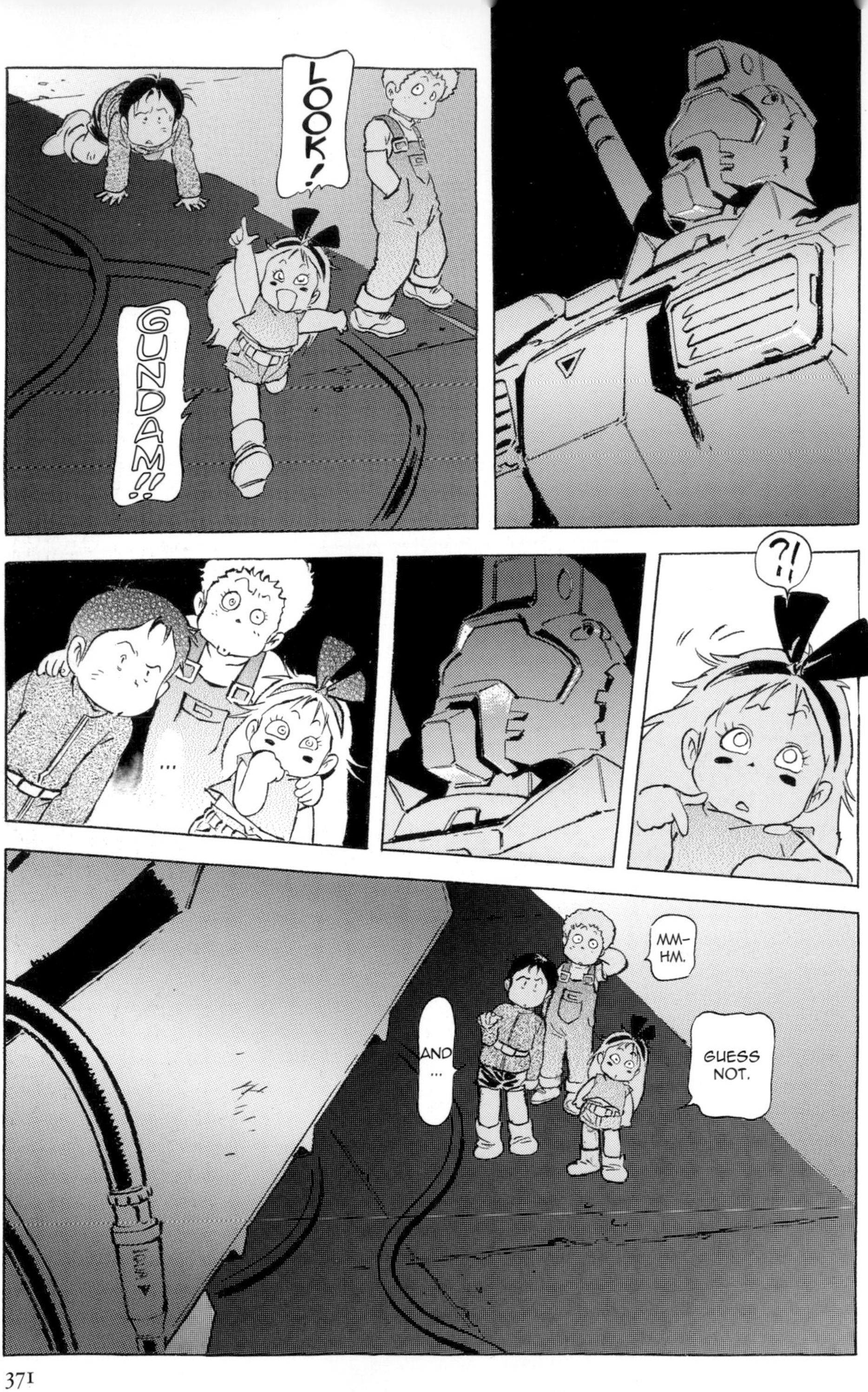
LOOK!
GUNDAM!!
?!
...
MM-HM.
GUESS NOT.
AND ...

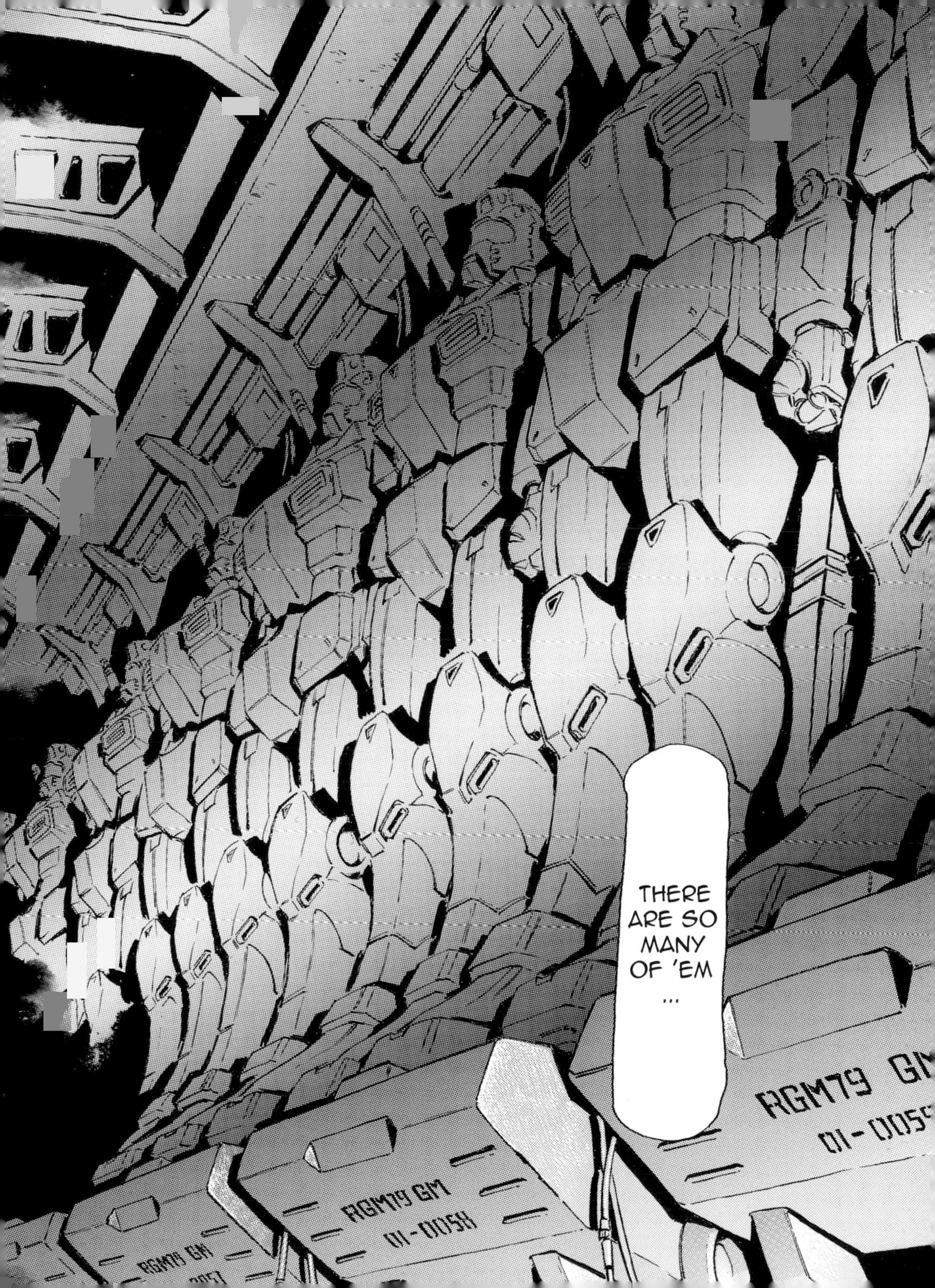
THERE ARE SO MANY OF 'EM ...
RGM79 GM
01-0058

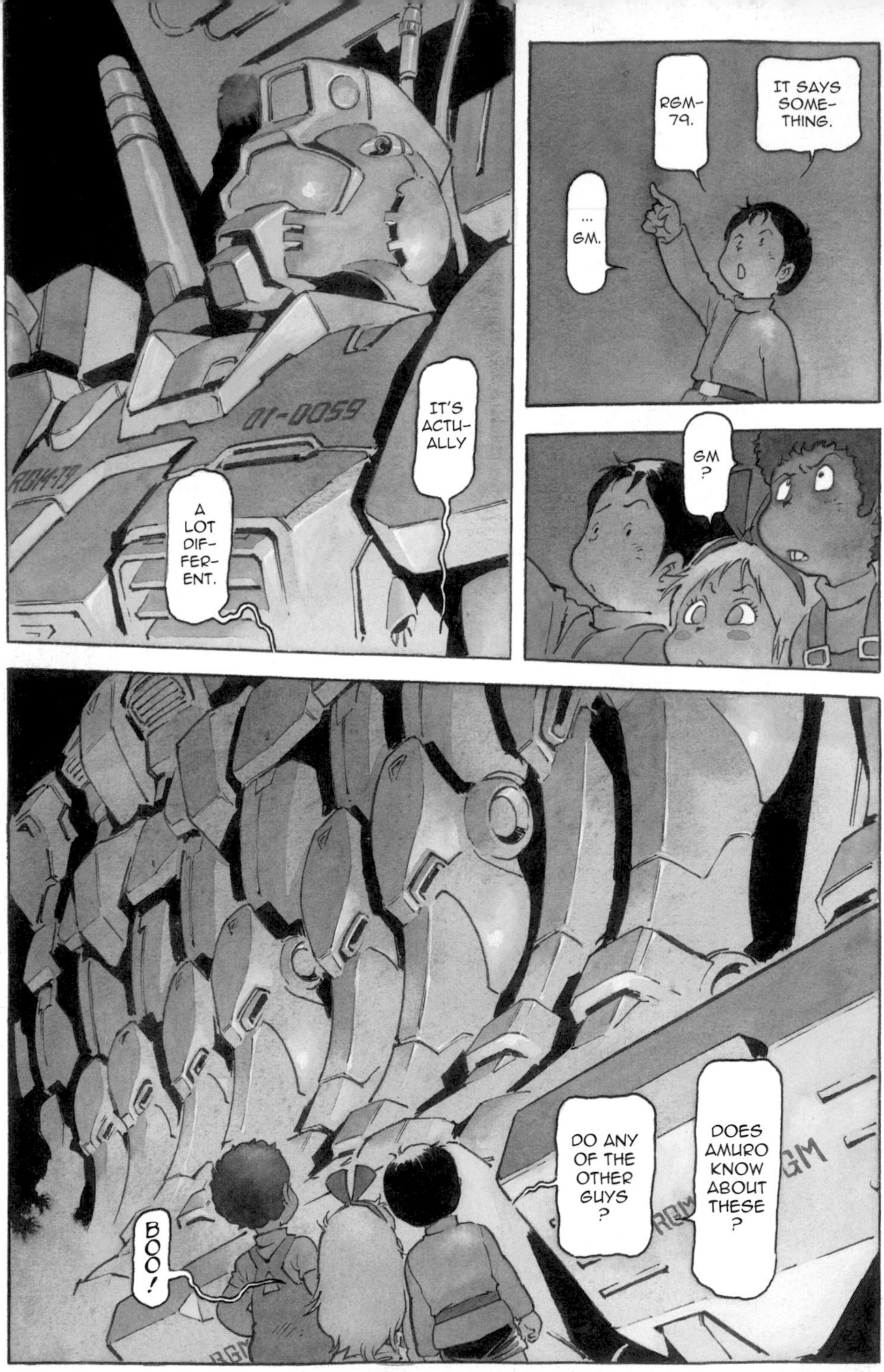
IT SAYS SOMETHING.
RGM-79.
... GM.
GM?
IT'S ACTUALLY
A LOT DIFFERENT.
01-0059
DOES AMURO KNOW ABOUT THESE?
DO ANY OF THE OTHER GUYS?
BOO!

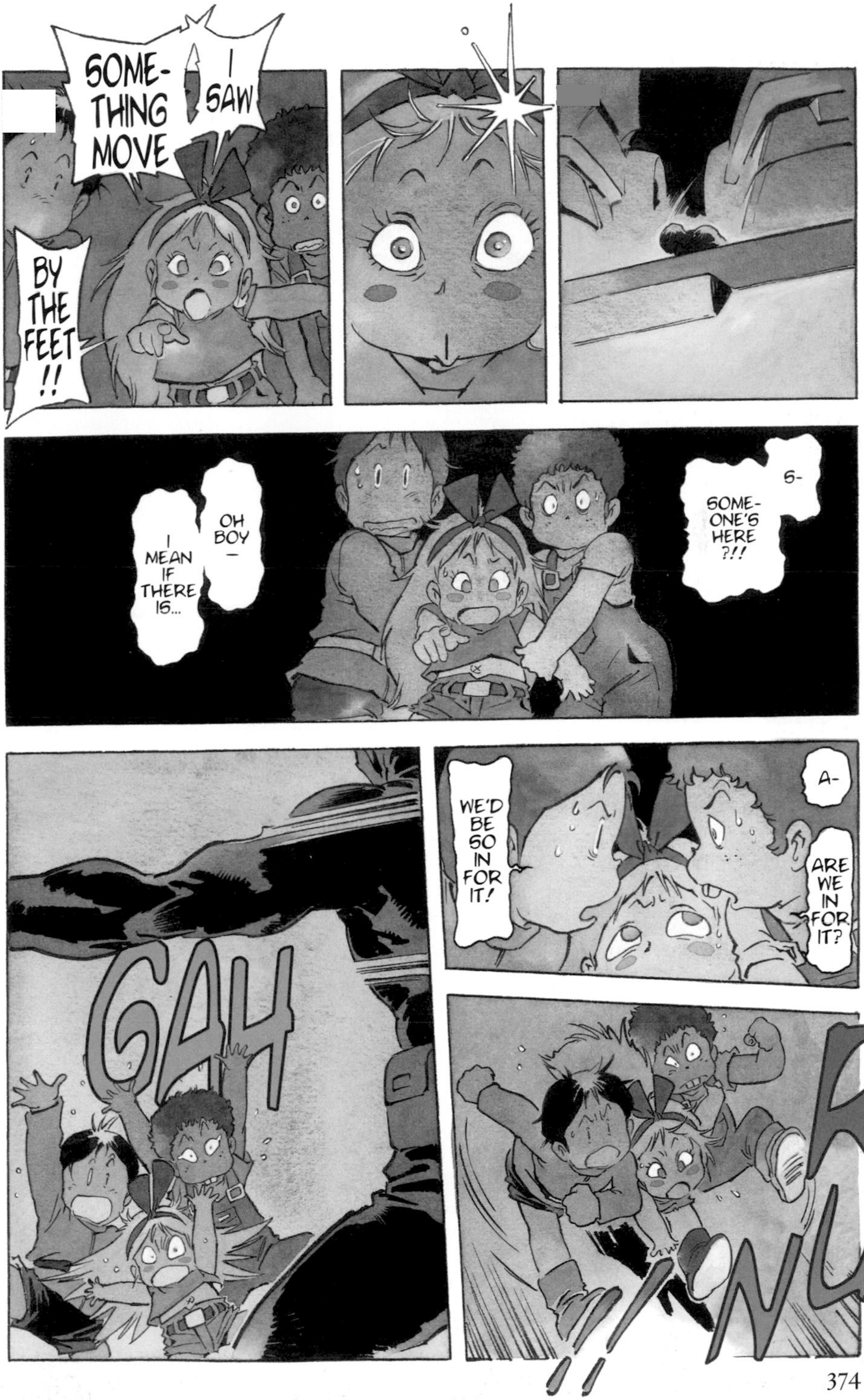
I SAW
SOME-THING MOVE
BY THE FEET!!
S-
SOME-ONE'S HERE?!!
OH BOY—
I MEAN IF THERE IS...
A-
ARE WE IN FOR IT?
WE'D BE SO IN FOR IT!
RUN
GAH

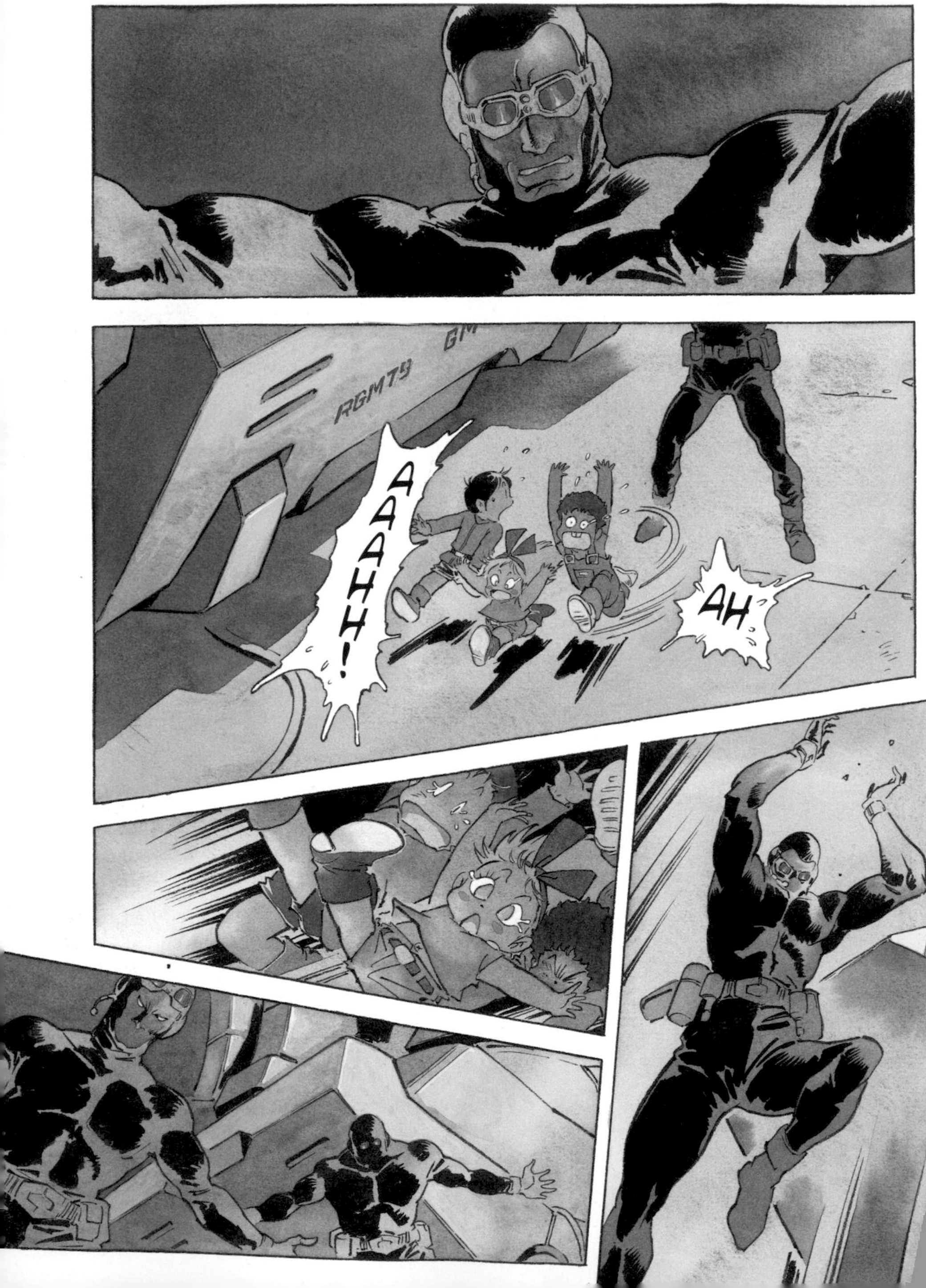
GM
RGM79
AH
AAAAHH!

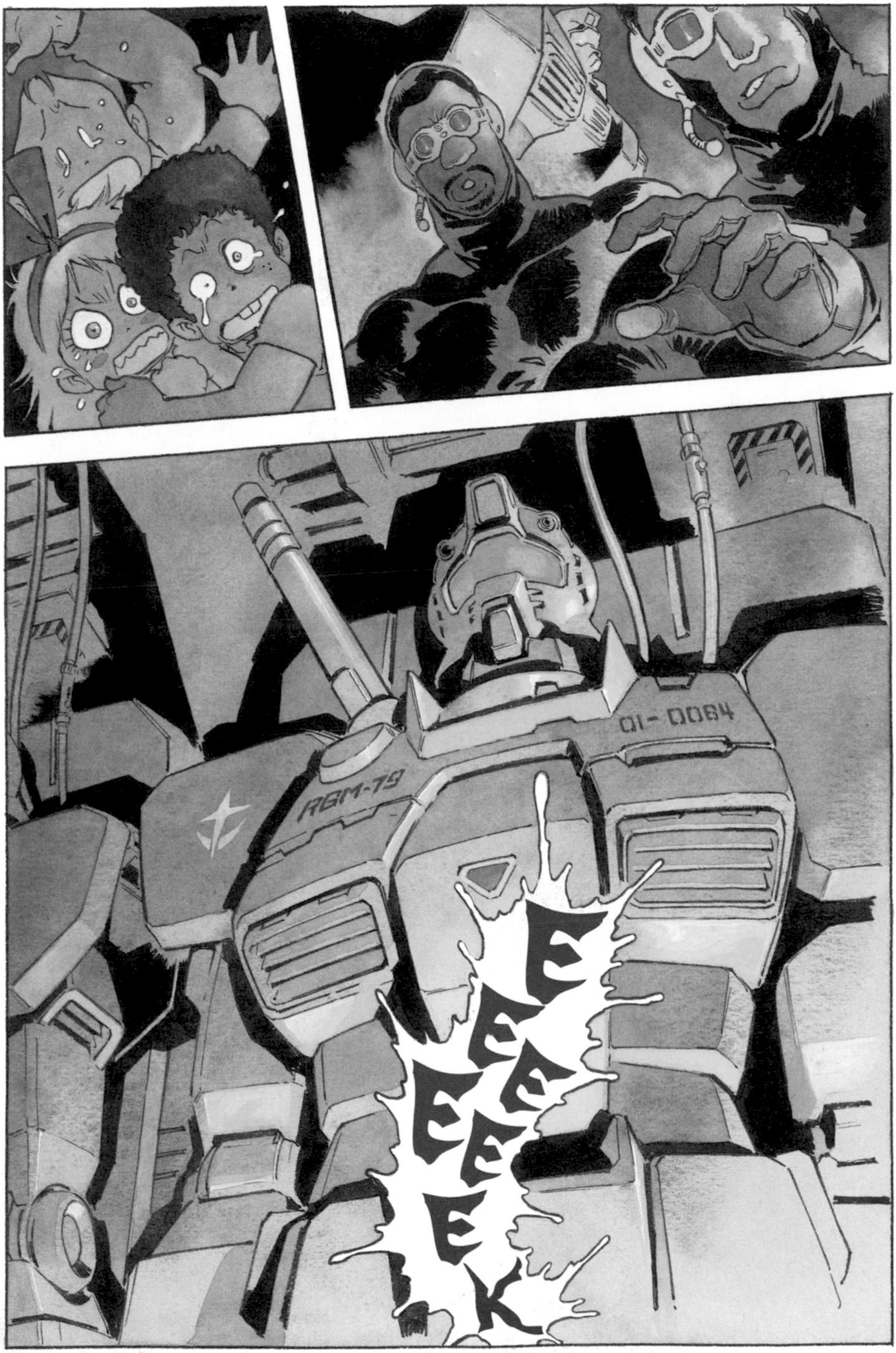
01-0064
RGM-79
EEEEEEK

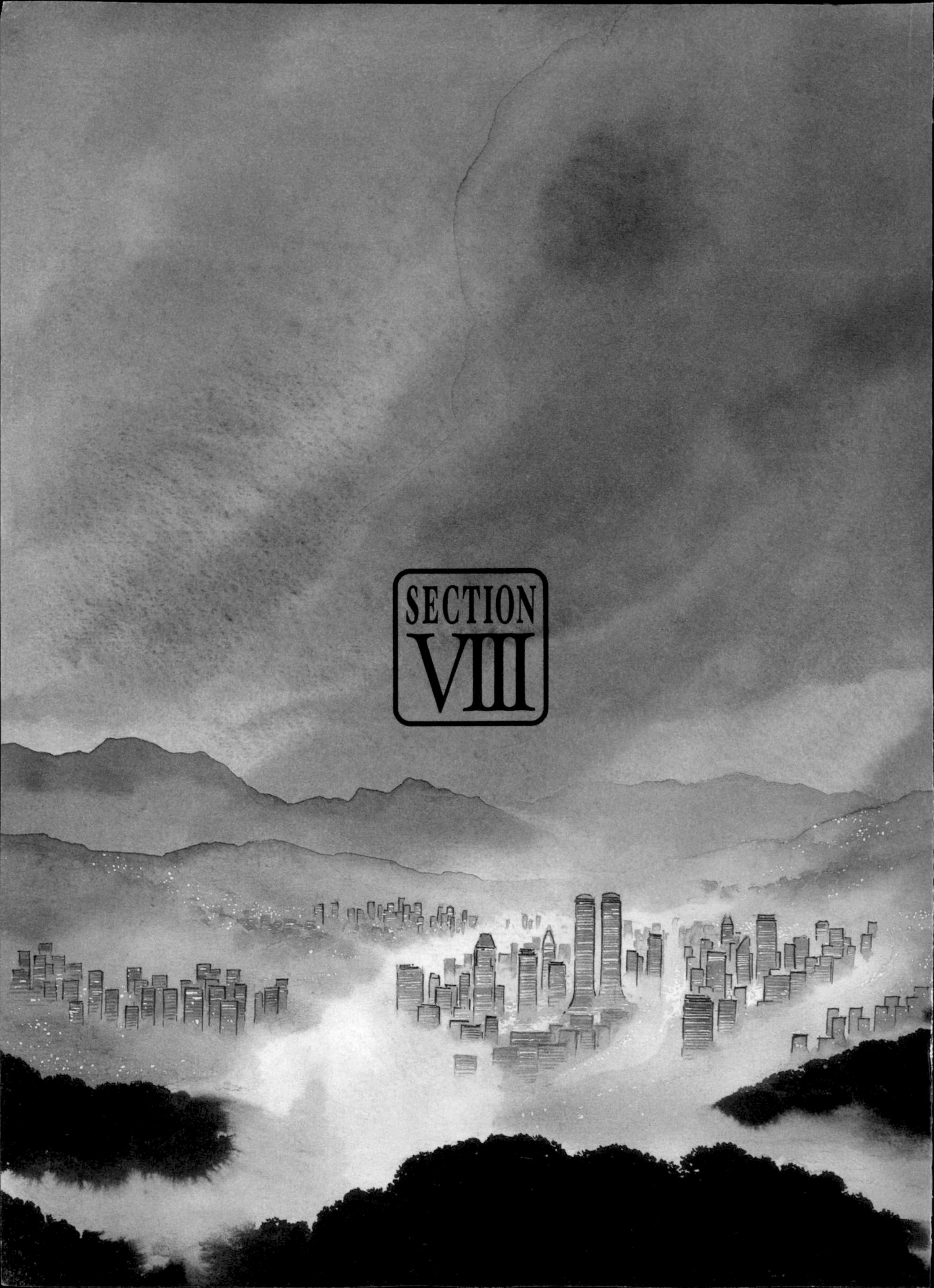
SECTION
VIII

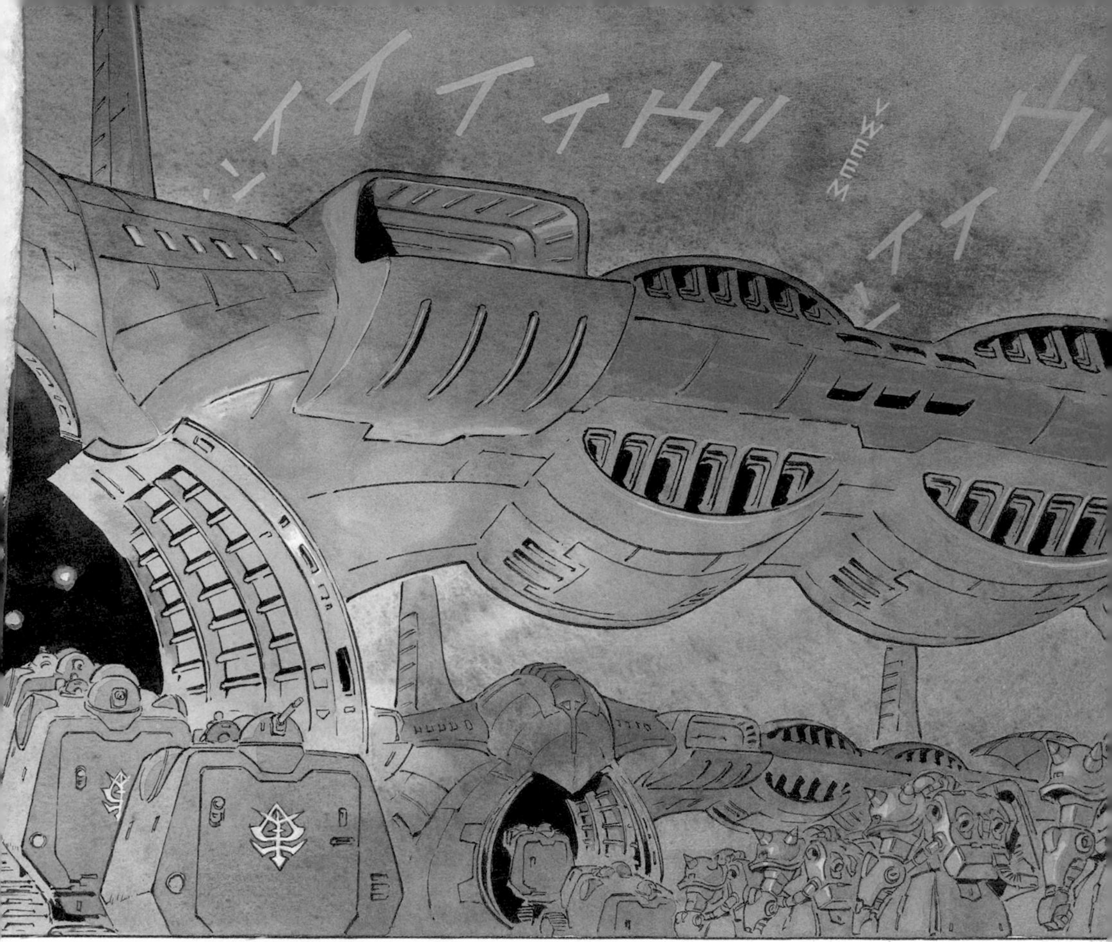

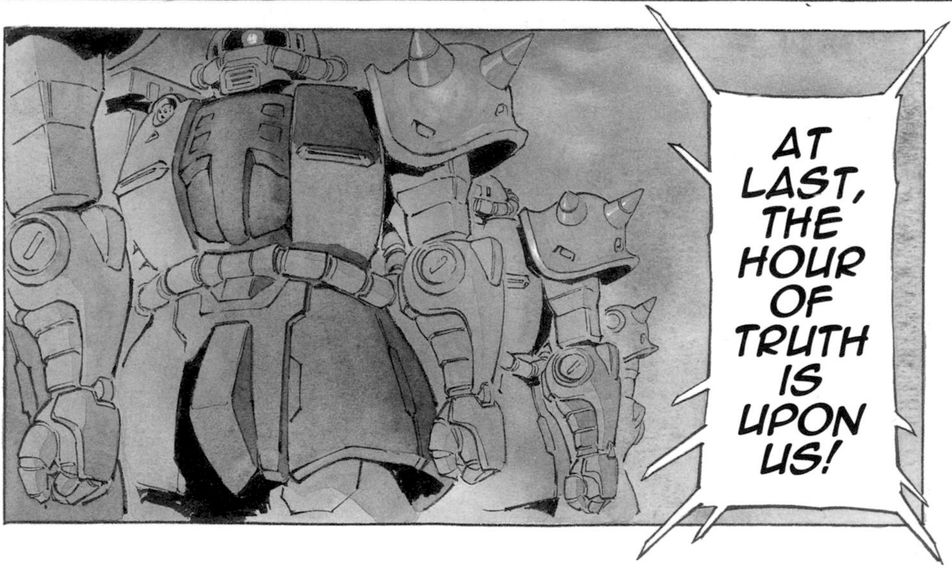
AT LAST, THE HOUR OF TRUTH IS UPON US!

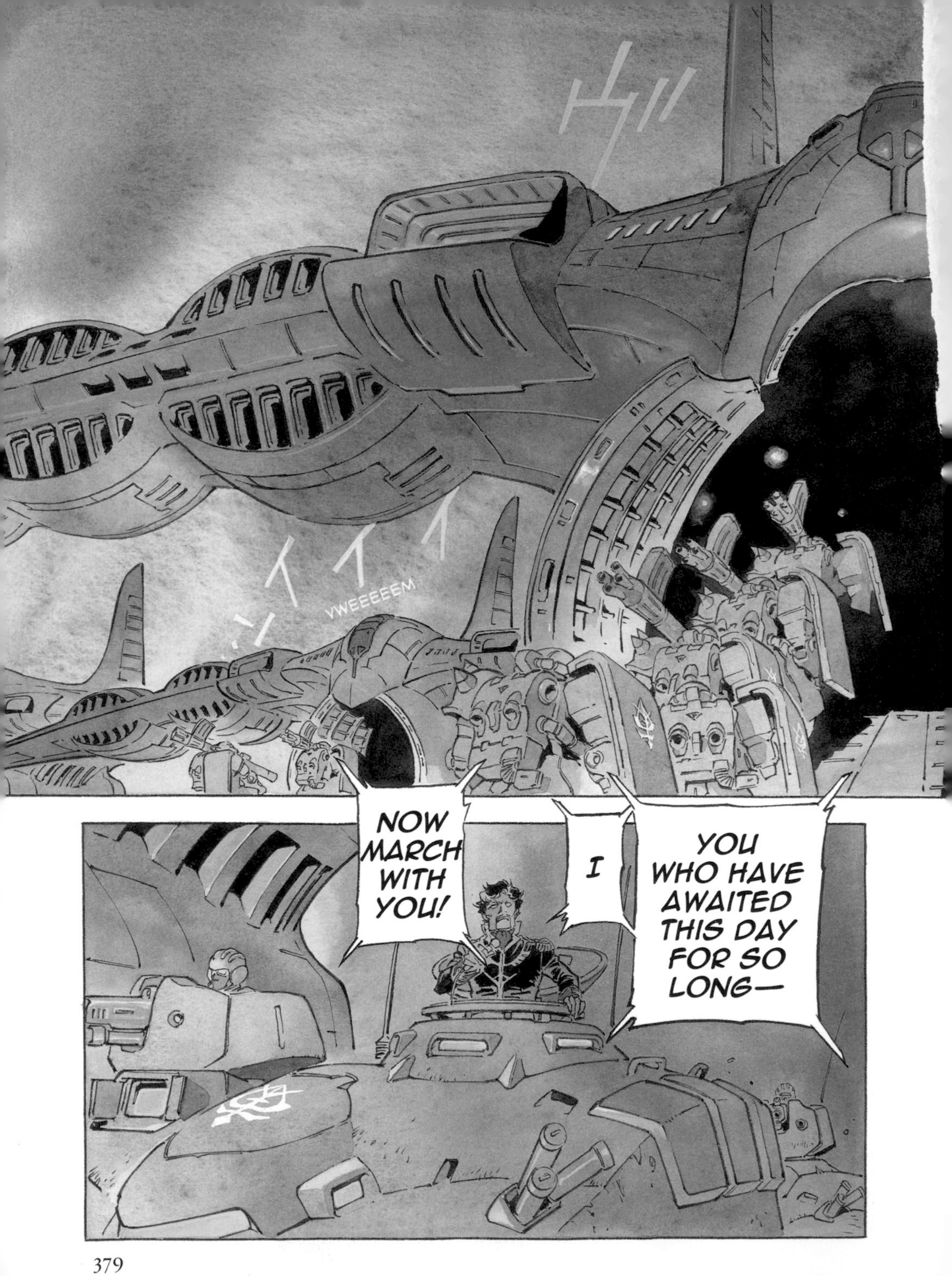
VWEEEEEM
YOU WHO HAVE AWAITED THIS DAY FOR SO LONG—
I
NOW MARCH WITH YOU!

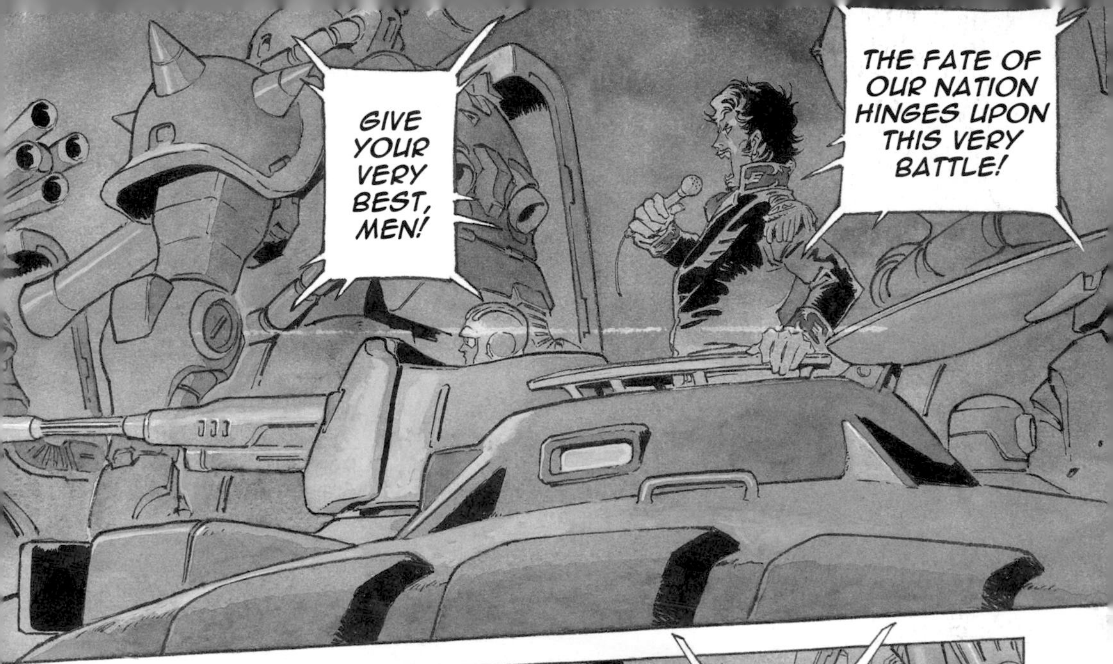
THE FATE OF OUR NATION HINGES UPON THIS VERY BATTLE!
GIVE YOUR VERY BEST, MEN!

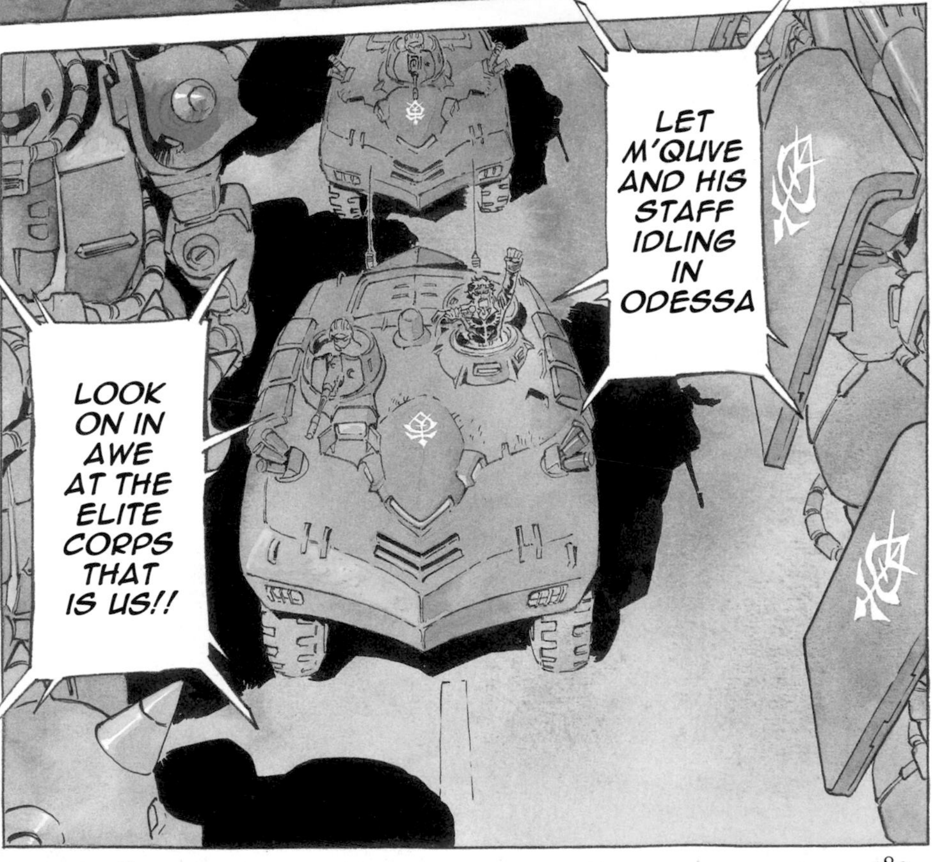
LET M'QUVE AND HIS STAFF IDLING IN ODESSA
LOOK ON IN AWE AT THE ELITE CORPS THAT IS US!!

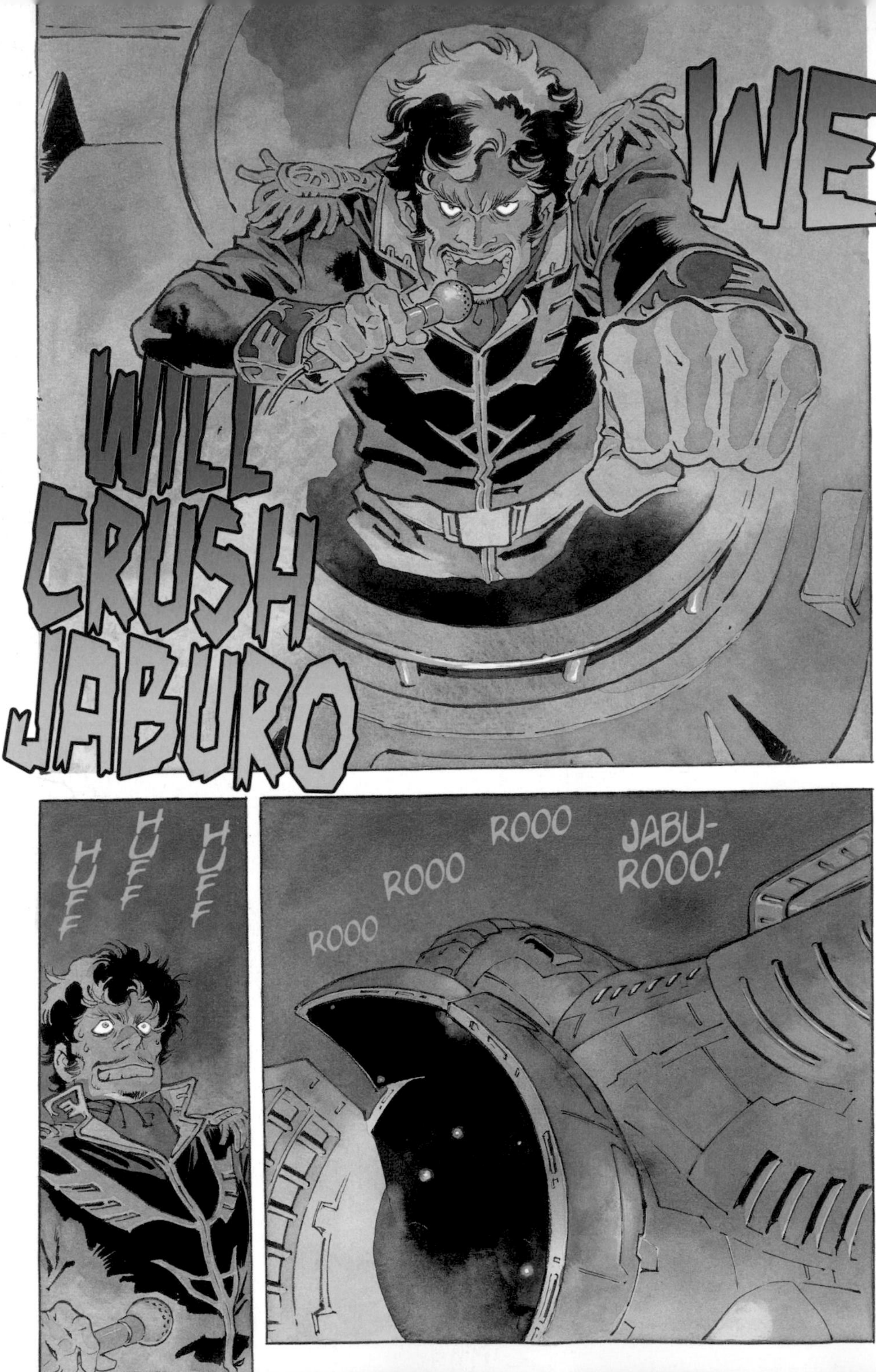
WE WILL CRUSH JABURO
JABU-ROOO!
ROOO
ROOO
ROOO
HUFF
HUFF
HUFF

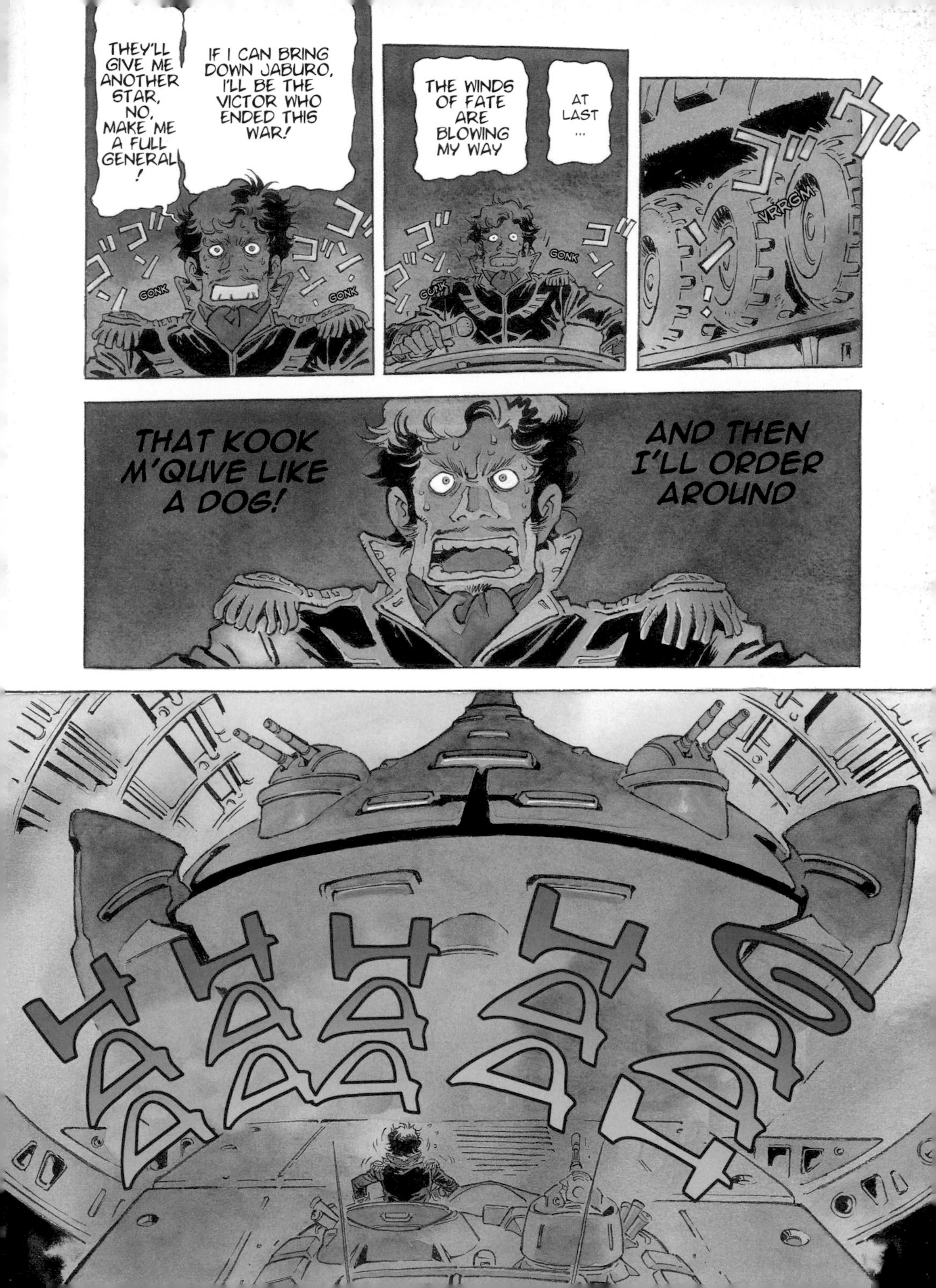
VRRGM
AT LAST ...
THE WINDS OF FATE ARE BLOWING MY WAY
GONK
GONK
IF I CAN BRING DOWN JABURO, I'LL BE THE VICTOR WHO ENDED THIS WAR!
THEY'LL GIVE ME ANOTHER STAR, NO, MAKE ME A FULL GENERAL!
GONK
GONK
AND THEN I'LL ORDER AROUND
THAT KOOK M'QUVE LIKE A DOG!

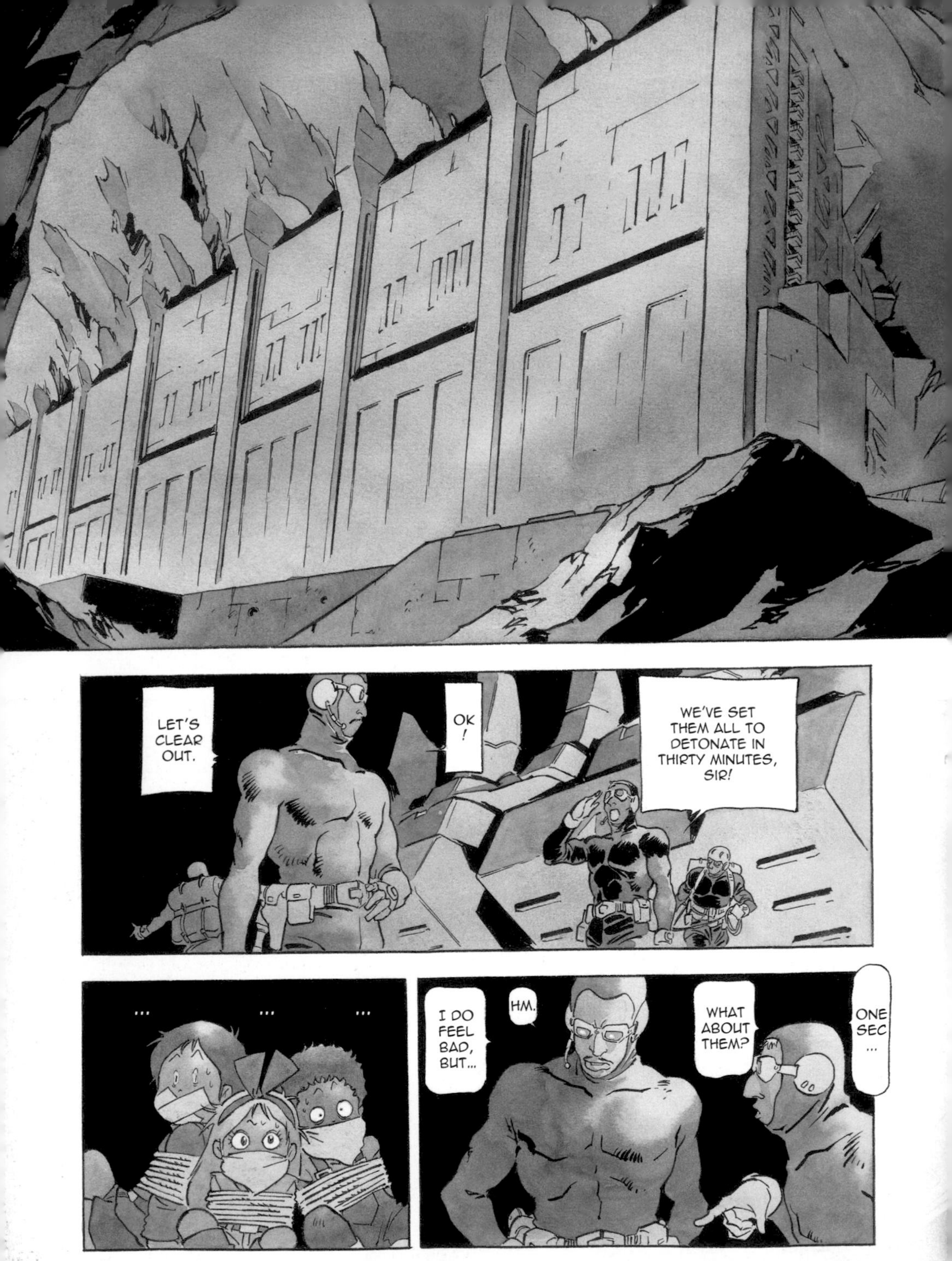
WE'VE SET THEM ALL TO DETONATE IN THIRTY MINUTES, SIR!
OK!
LET'S CLEAR OUT.
ONE SEC...
WHAT ABOUT THEM?
HM.
I DO FEEL BAD, BUT...
...
...
...

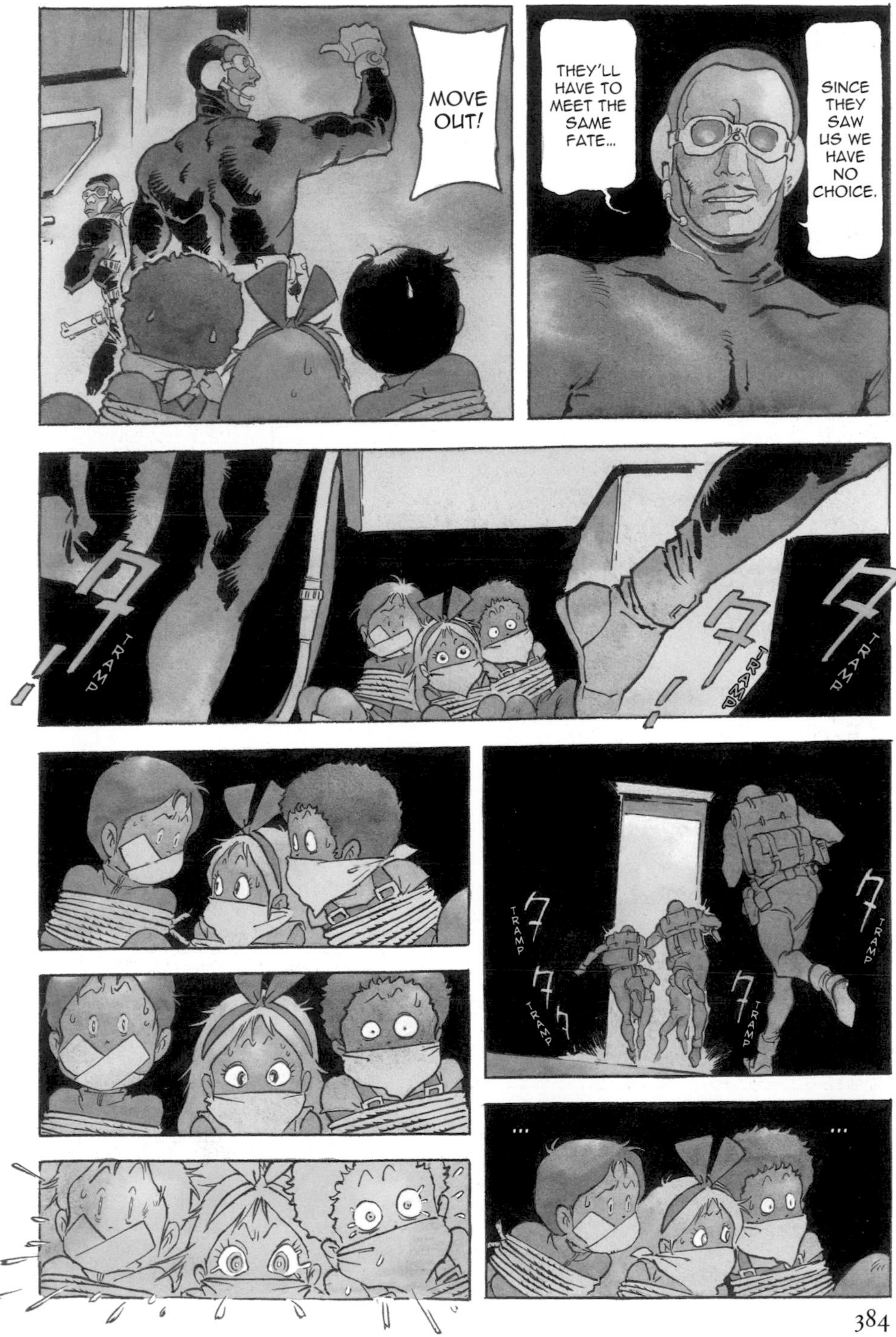
SINCE THEY SAW US WE HAVE NO CHOICE.
THEY'LL HAVE TO MEET THE SAME FATE...
MOVE OUT!
TRAMP
TRAMP
TRAMP
TRAMP
TRAMP
TRAMP
TRAMP
...
...

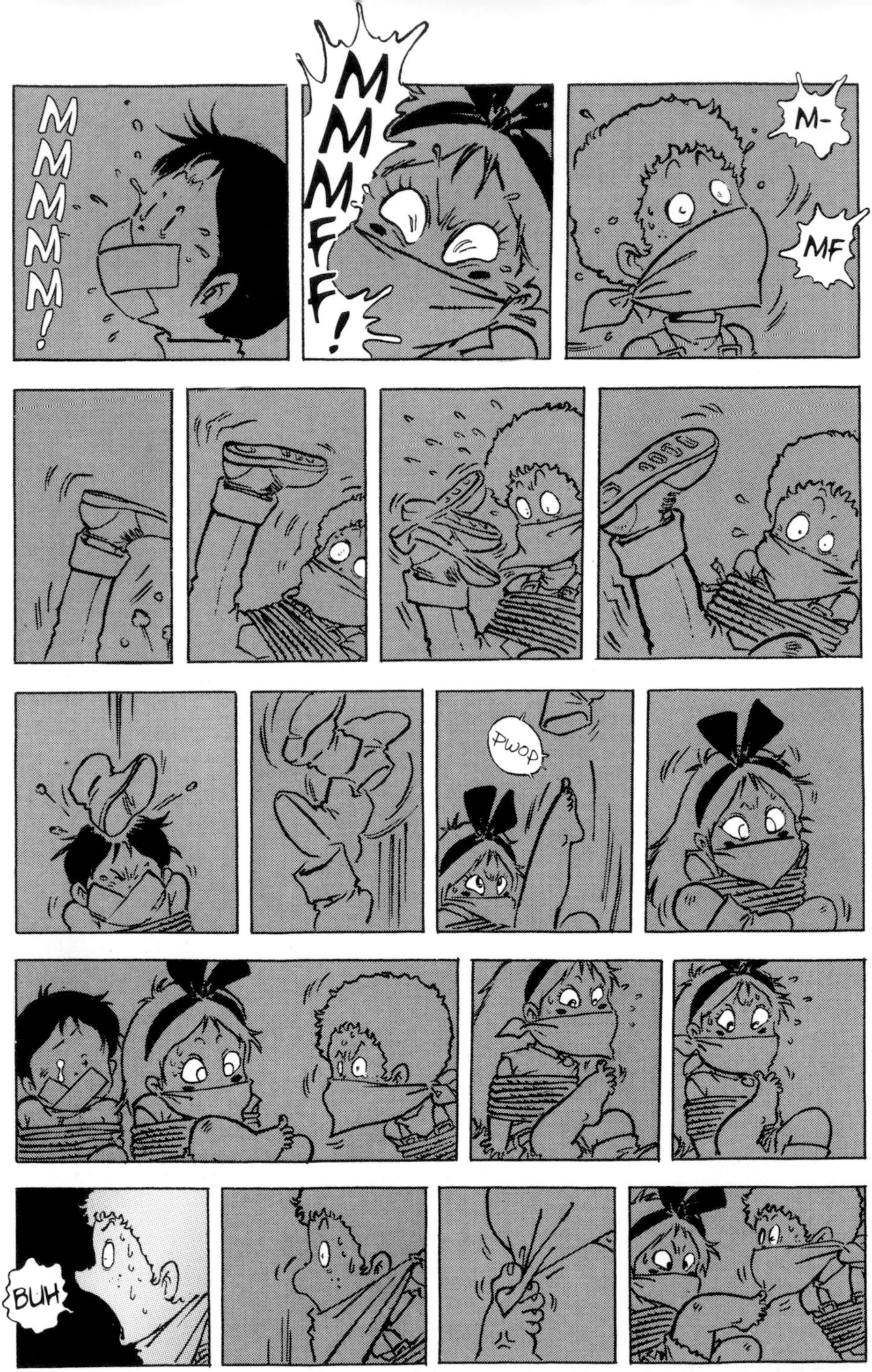
M-
MF
MMMFF!
MMMMMM!
PWOP
BUH

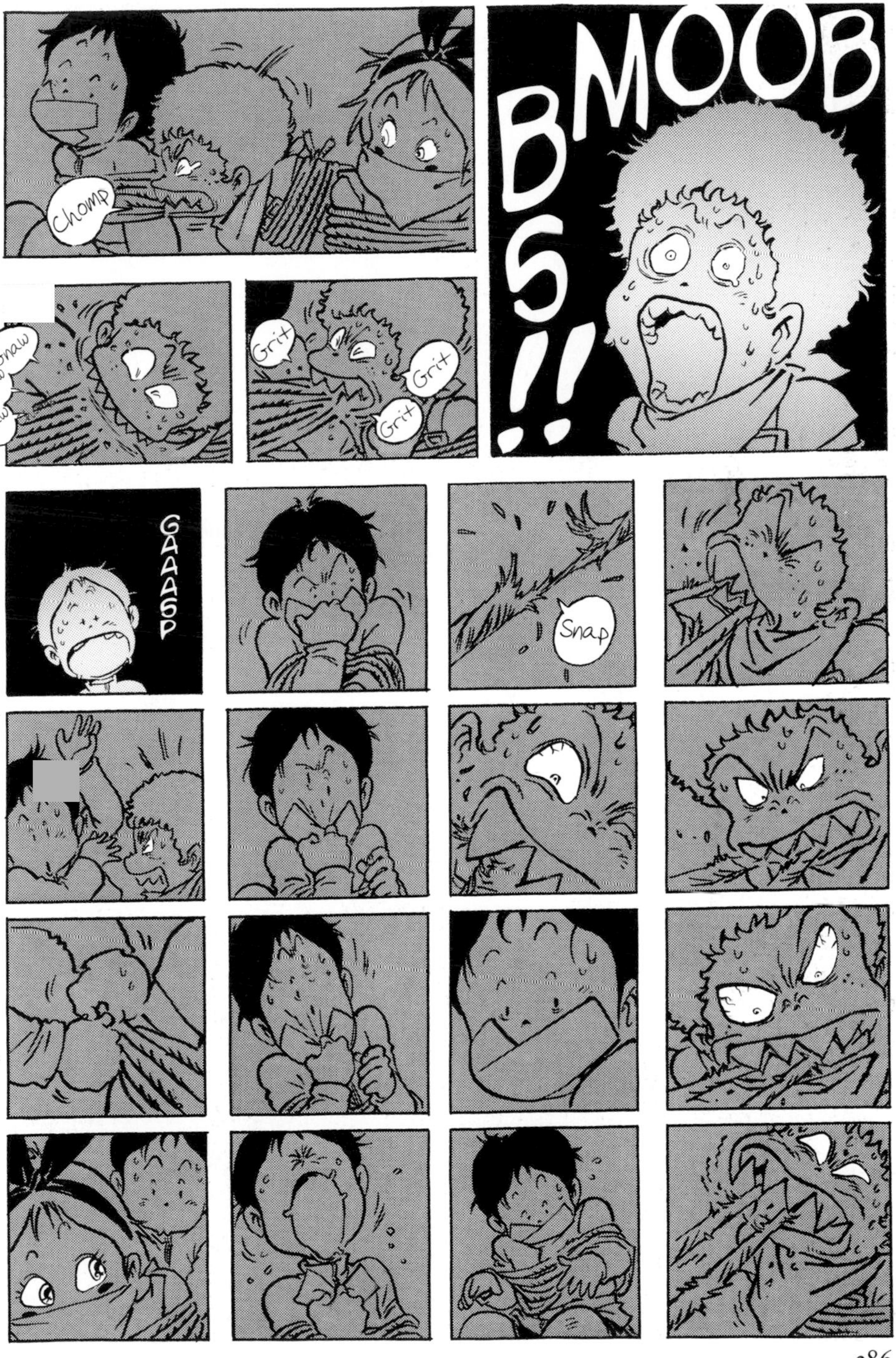
BMOOBS!!
Chomp
Grit
Grit
Grit
Gnaw
Gnaw
Gnaw
Snap
GAAASP

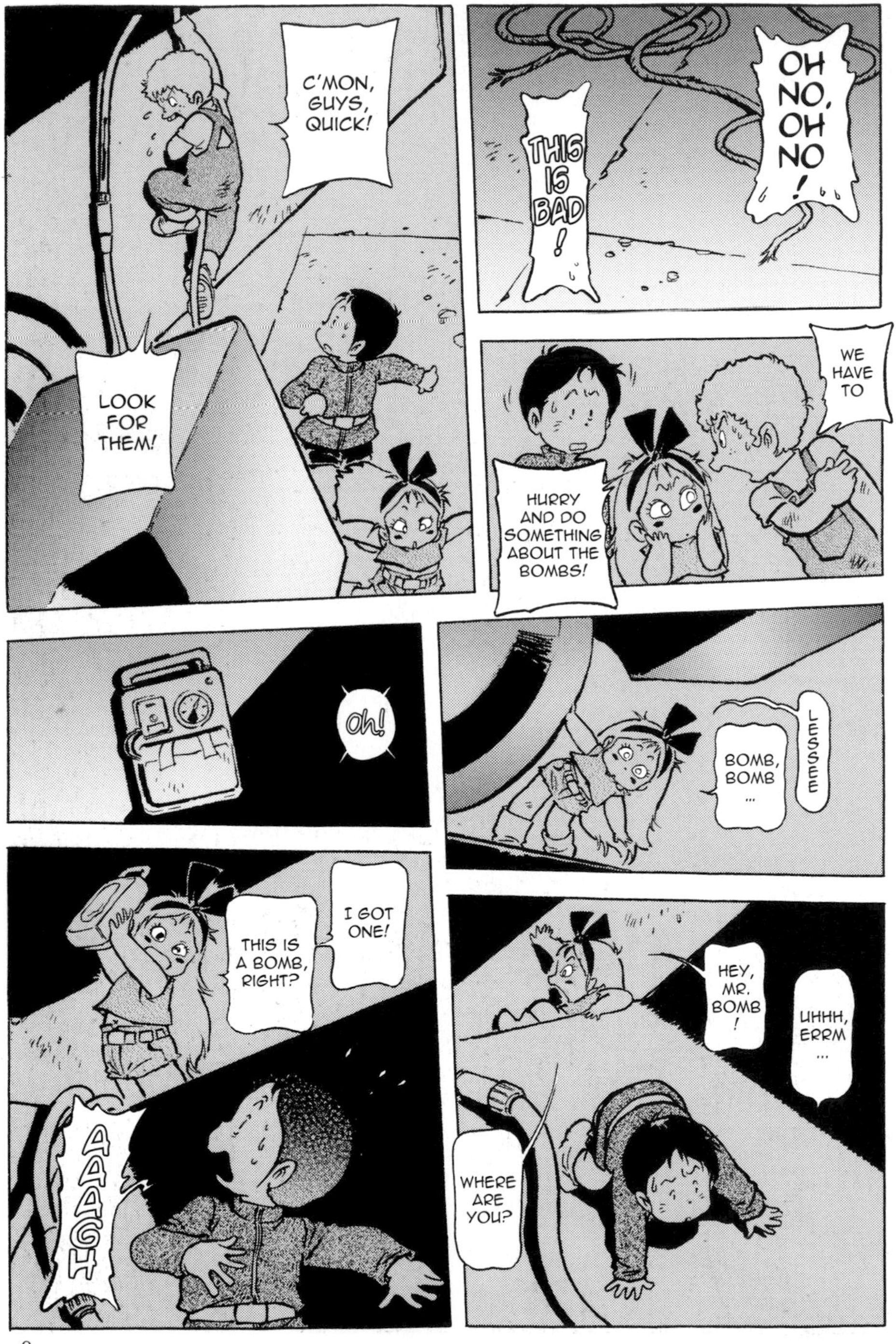
OH NO, OH NO!
THIS IS BAD!
WE HAVE TO
HURRY AND DO SOMETHING ABOUT THE BOMBS!
C'MON, GUYS, QUICK!
LOOK FOR THEM!
LESSEE
BOMB, BOMB ...
Oh!
HEY, MR. BOMB!
UHHH, ERRM ...
WHERE ARE YOU?
I GOT ONE!
THIS IS A BOMB, RIGHT?
AAAGH

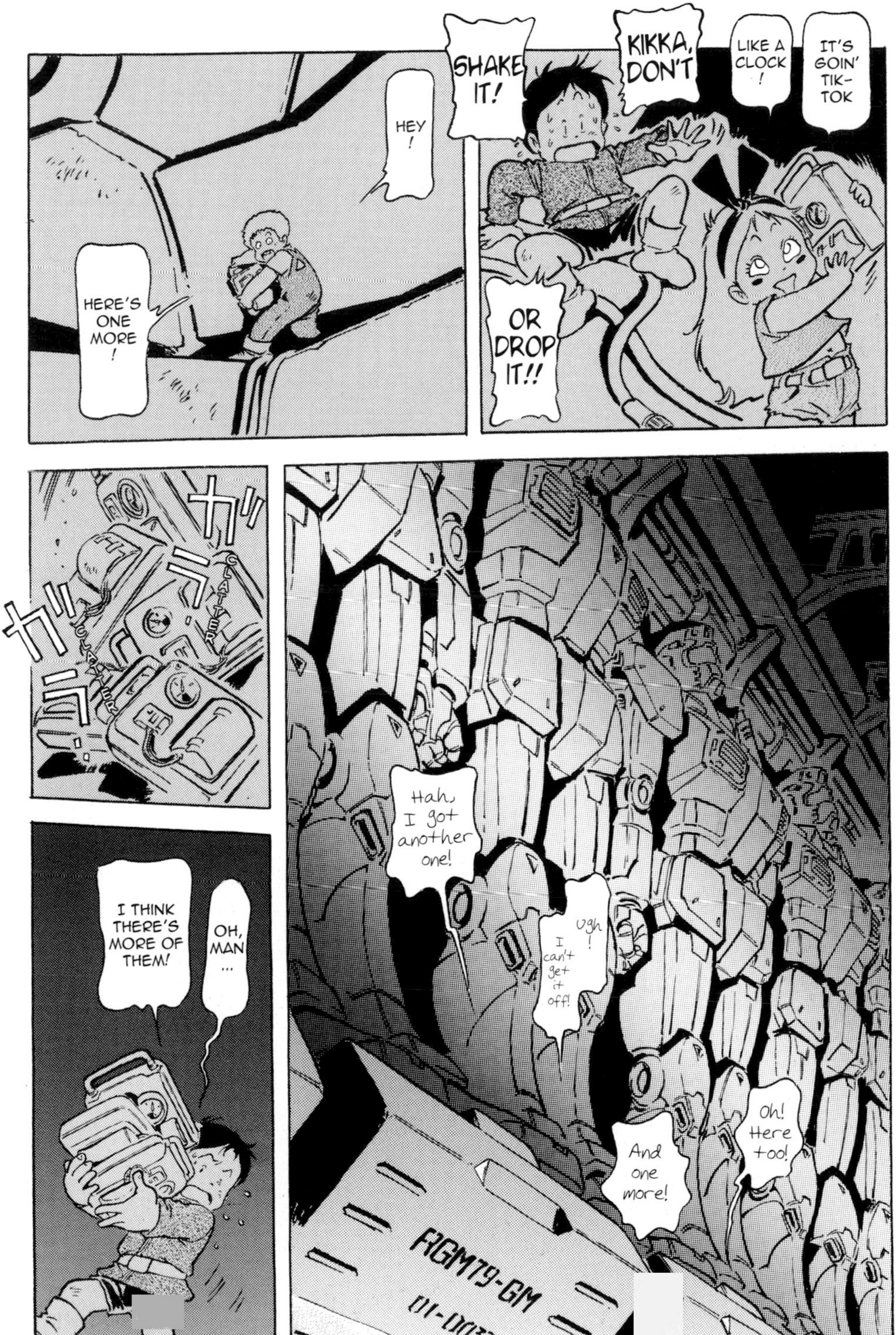
IT'S GOIN' TIK-TOK
LIKE A CLOCK!
KIKKA, DON'T
SHAKE IT!
OR DROP IT!!
HEY!
HERE'S ONE MORE!
Ugh! I can't get it off!
Hah, I got another one!
Oh! Here too!
And one more!
RGM79-GM
01-0032
CLATTER
CLATTER
OH, MAN...
I THINK THERE'S MORE OF THEM!

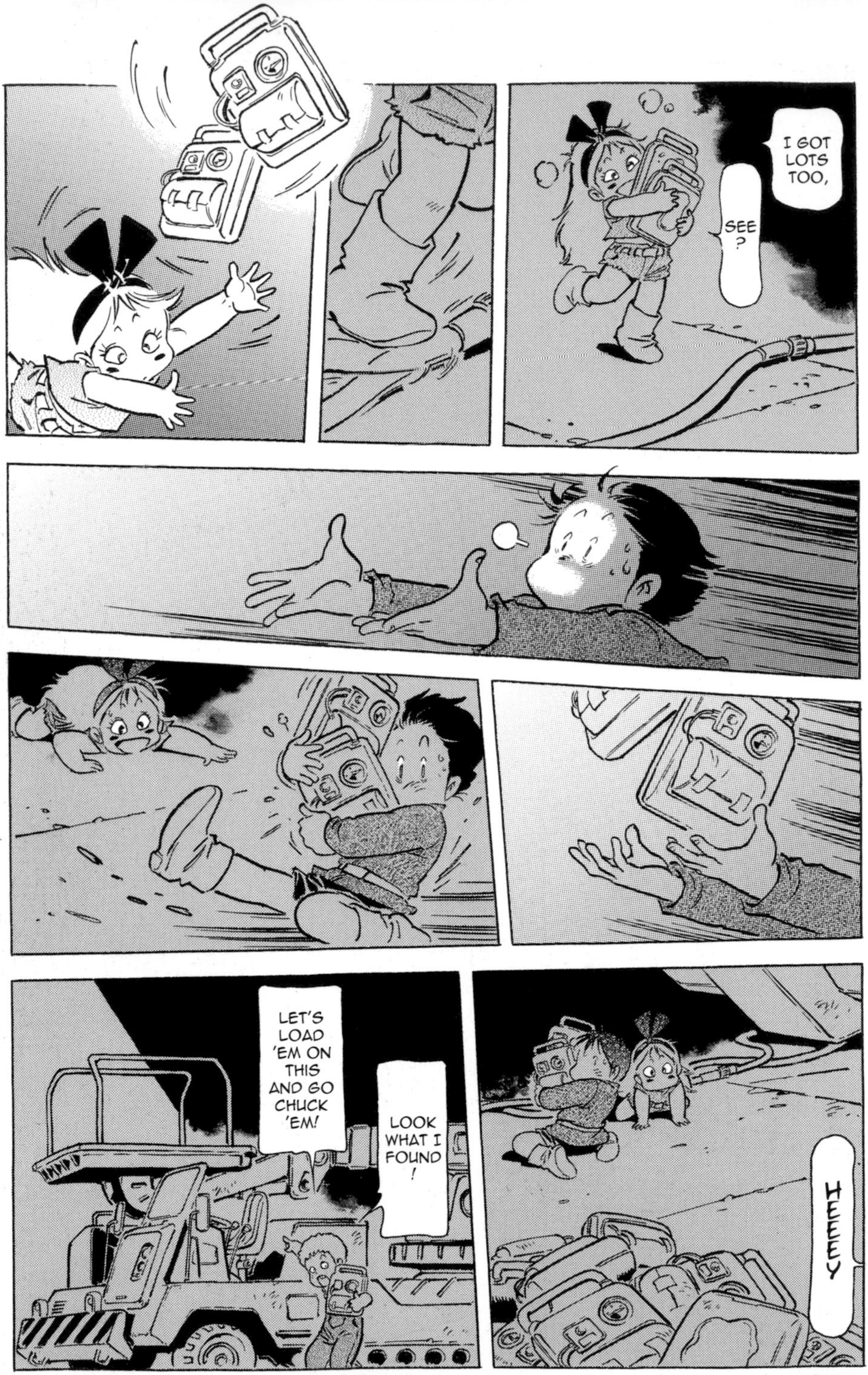
I GOT LOTS TOO,
SEE?
HEEEY
LOOK WHAT I FOUND!
LET'S LOAD 'EM ON THIS AND GO CHUCK 'EM!

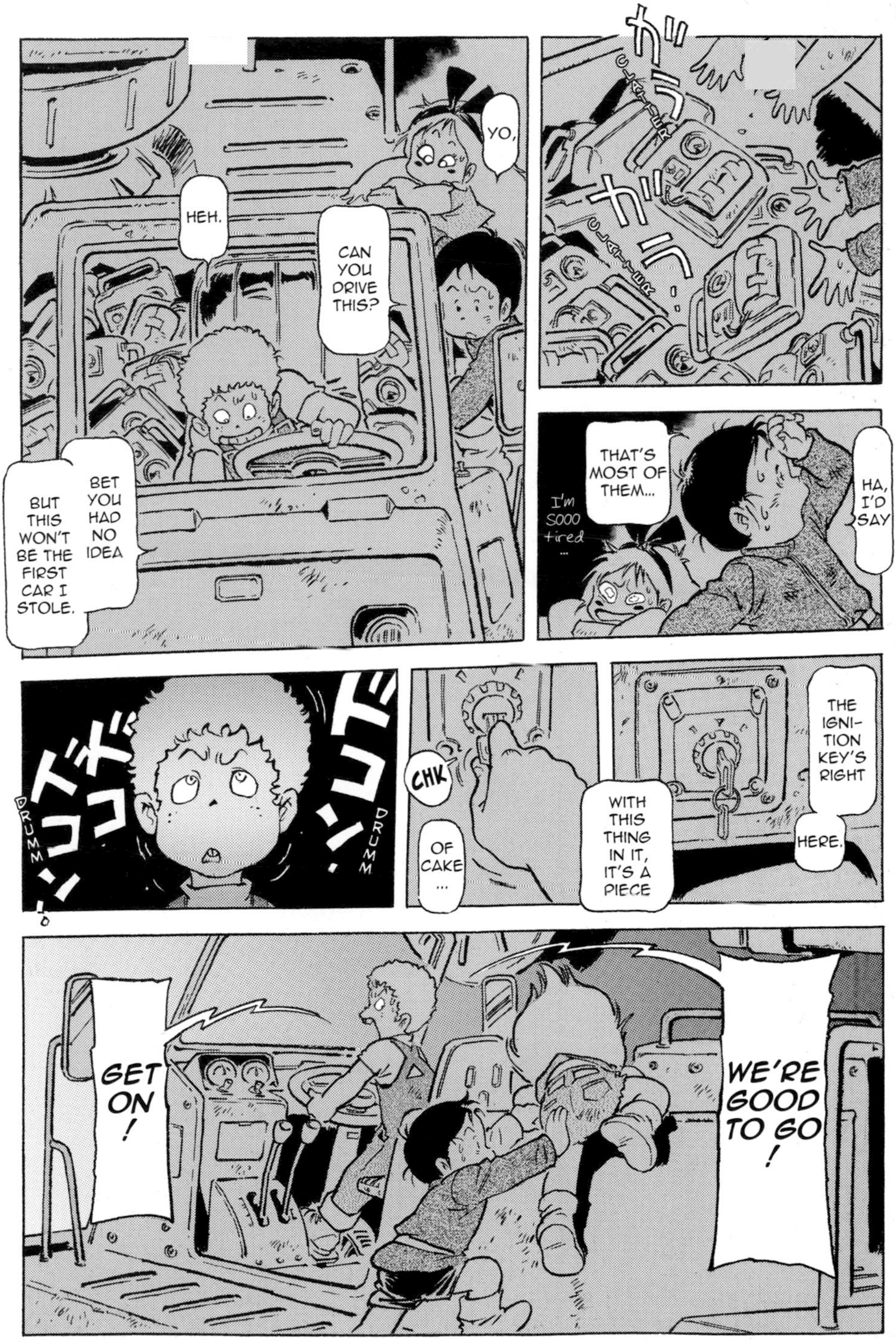
ガラ
CLATTER
ガラ
CLATTER
HA, I'D SAY
THAT'S MOST OF THEM...
I'm SOOO tired...
YO,
HEH.
CAN YOU DRIVE THIS?
BET YOU HAD NO IDEA
BUT THIS WON'T BE THE FIRST CAR I STOLE.
THE IGNITION KEY'S RIGHT
HERE.
WITH THIS THING IN IT, IT'S A PIECE
OF CAKE...
CHK
DRUMM
DRUMM
WE'RE GOOD TO GO!
GET ON!

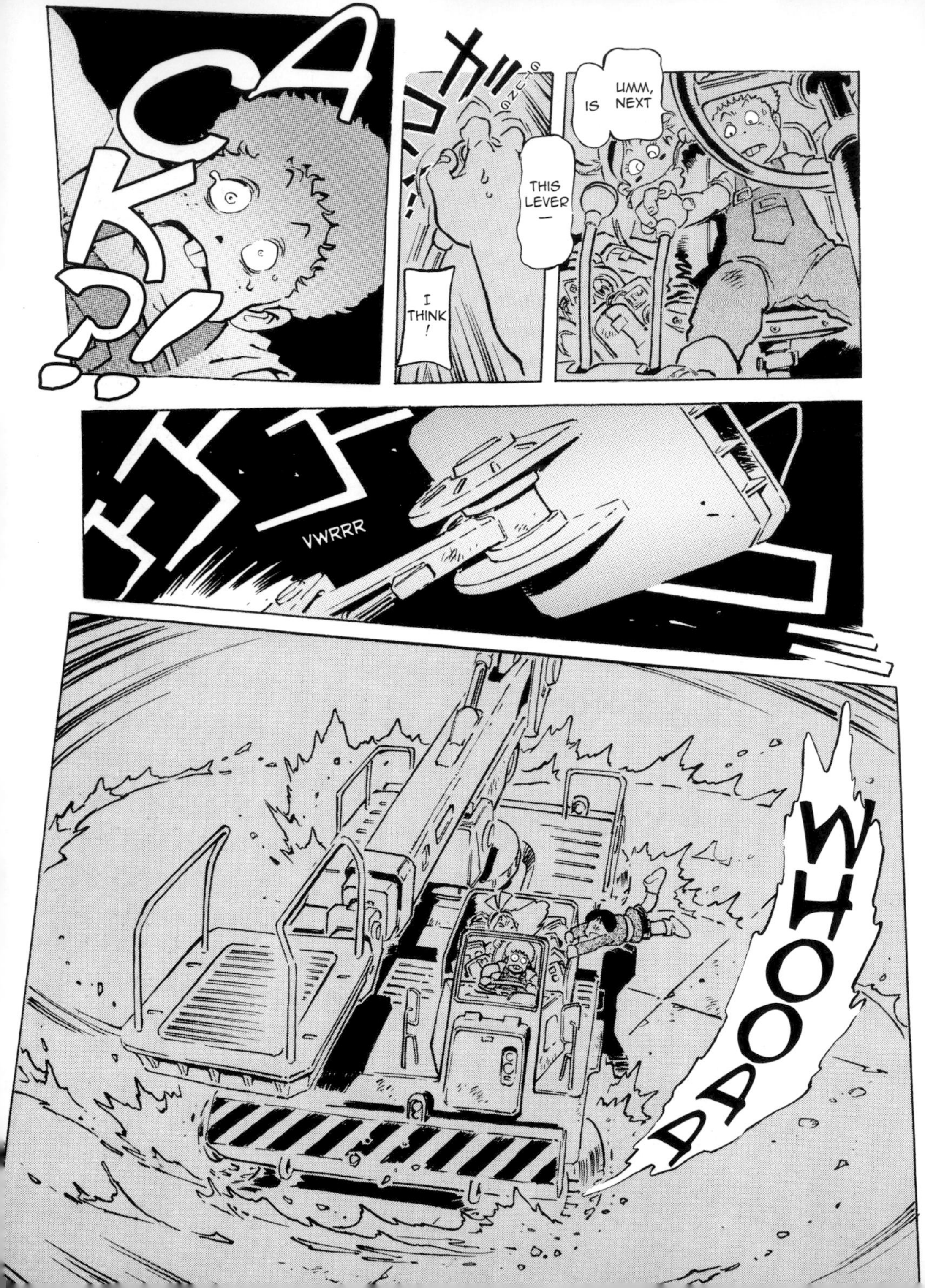
UMM, NEXT IS
THIS LEVER —
I THINK!
GZUNG
CAK?!
VWRRR
WHOOOAAA

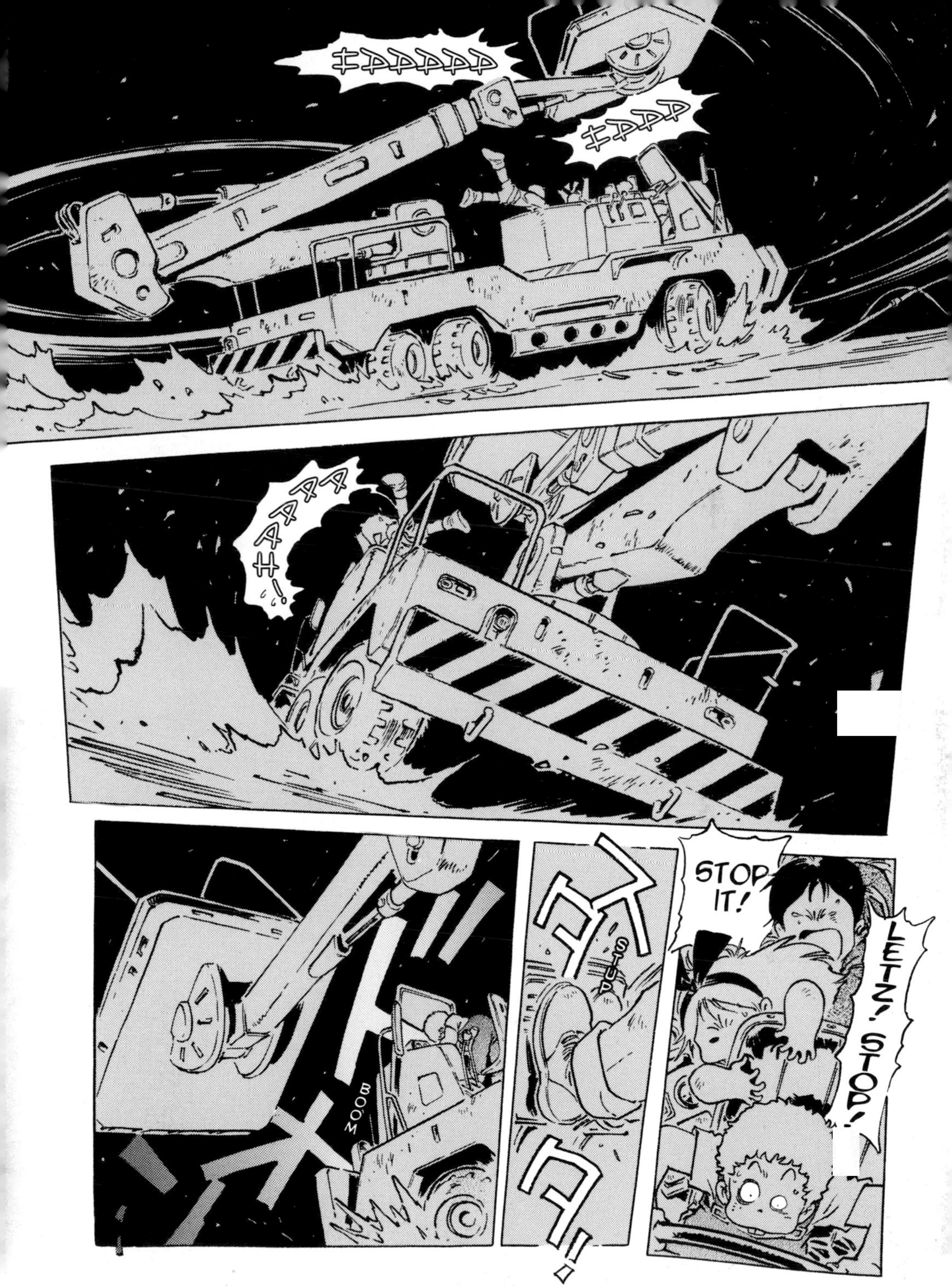
AAAAH!
STOP IT!
LETZ! STOP!
STUP
BOOM

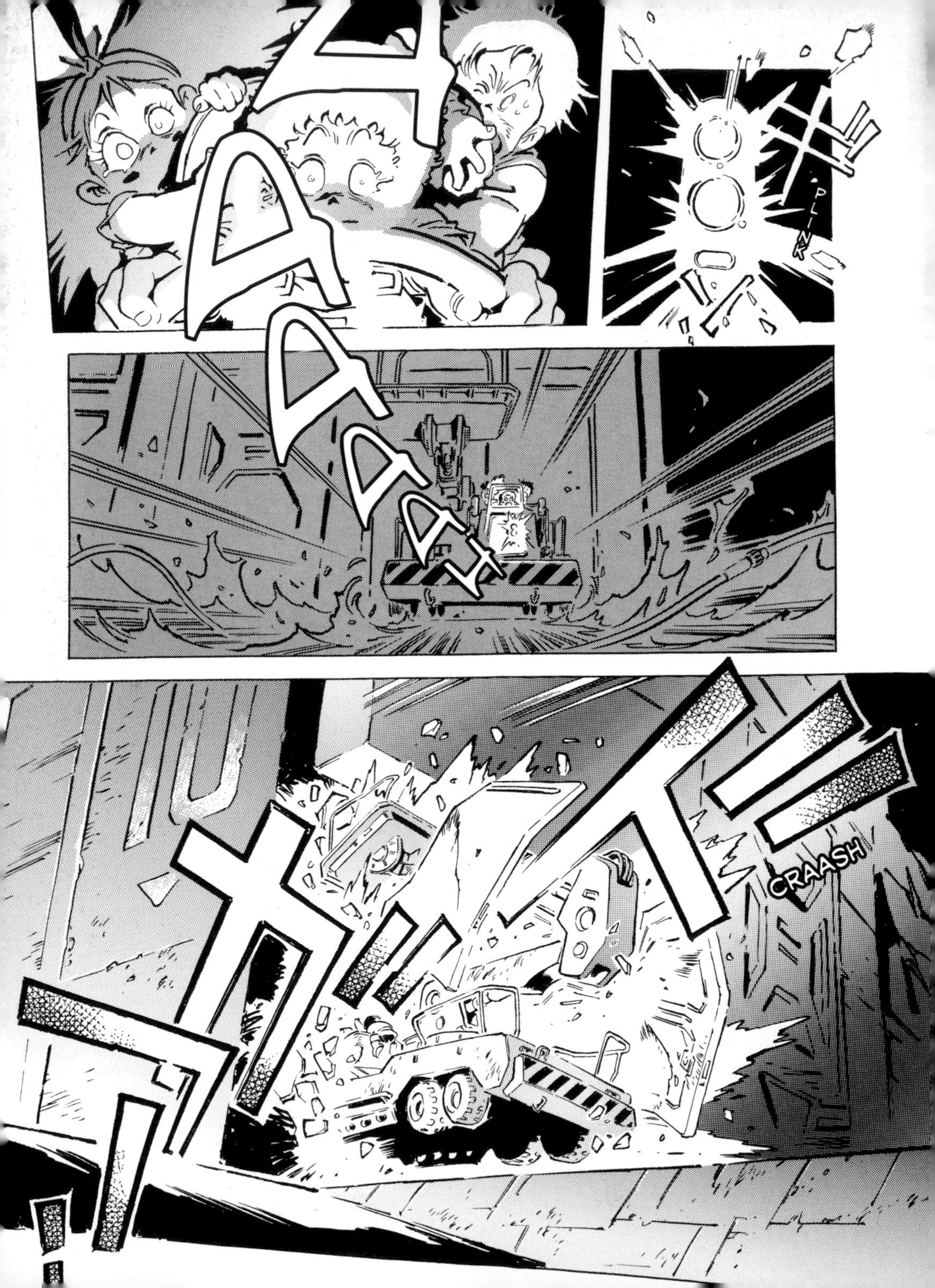
PLINK
AAAAAAH
CRAASH

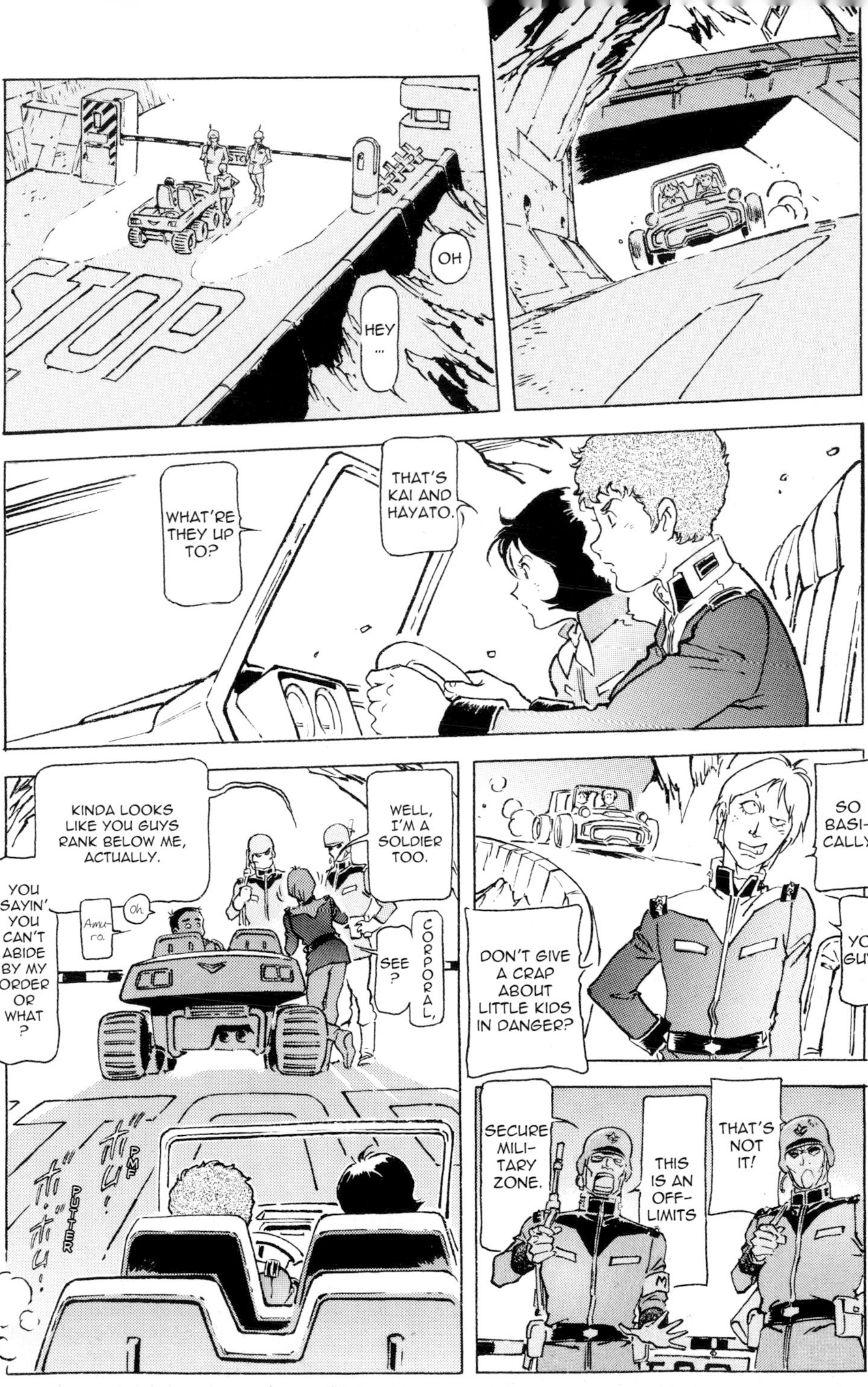
OH
HEY ...
THAT'S KAI AND HAYATO.
WHAT'RE THEY UP TO?
SO BASI-CALLY
YOU GUYS
DON'T GIVE A CRAP ABOUT LITTLE KIDS IN DANGER?
WELL, I'M A SOLDIER TOO.
CORPORAL, SEE?
KINDA LOOKS LIKE YOU GUYS RANK BELOW ME, ACTUALLY.
Oh.
Amu-ro.
YOU SAYIN' YOU CAN'T ABIDE BY MY ORDER OR WHAT?
THAT'S NOT IT!
THIS IS AN OFF-LIMITS
SECURE MILI-TARY ZONE.
PMF
PUTTER

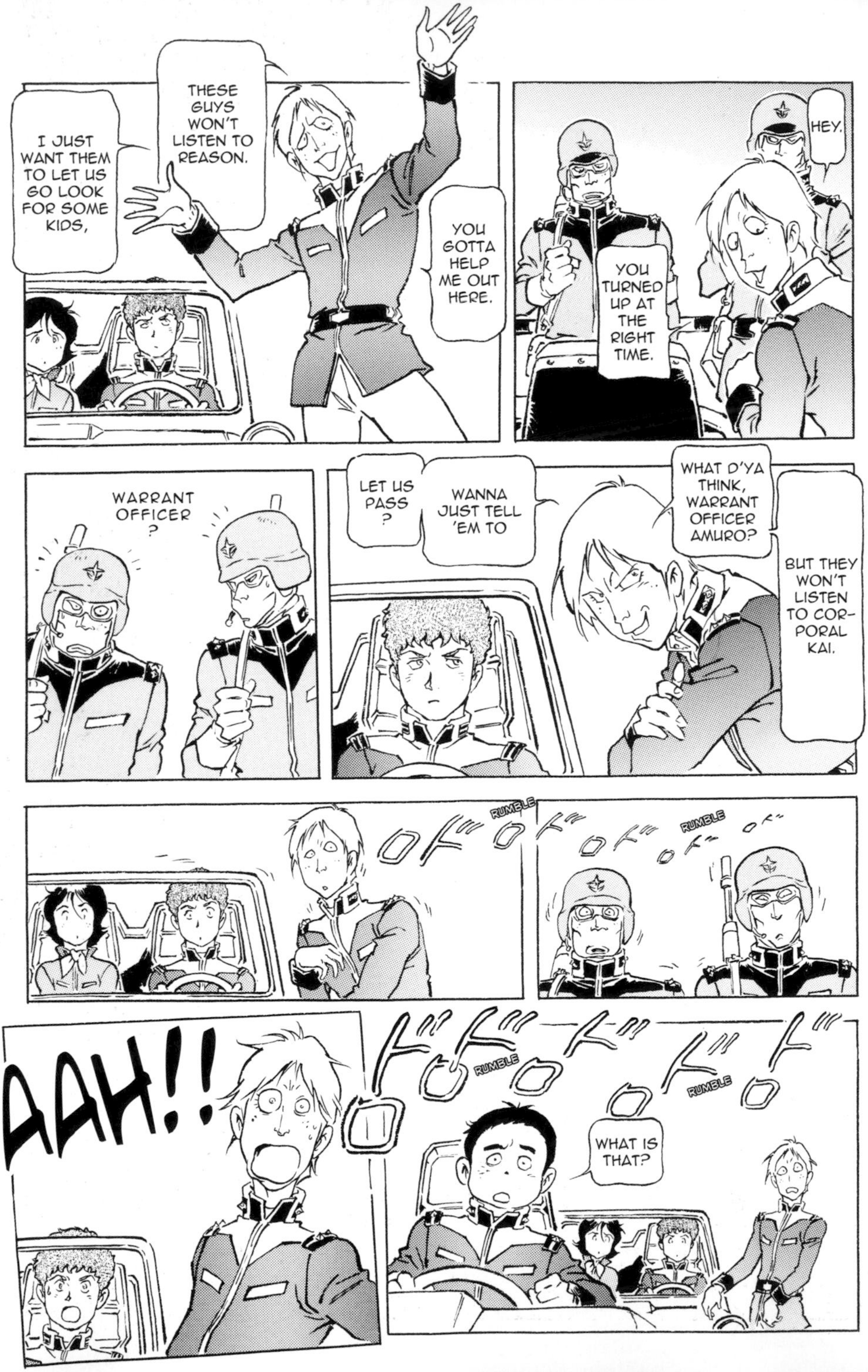
HEY.
YOU TURNED UP AT THE RIGHT TIME.
THESE GUYS WON'T LISTEN TO REASON.
I JUST WANT THEM TO LET US GO LOOK FOR SOME KIDS,
YOU GOTTA HELP ME OUT HERE.
BUT THEY WON'T LISTEN TO COR-PORAL KAI.
WHAT D'YA THINK, WARRANT OFFICER AMURO?
WANNA JUST TELL 'EM TO
LET US PASS?
WARRANT OFFICER?
RUMBLE
RUMBLE
RUMBLE
RUMBLE
WHAT IS THAT?
AAH!!

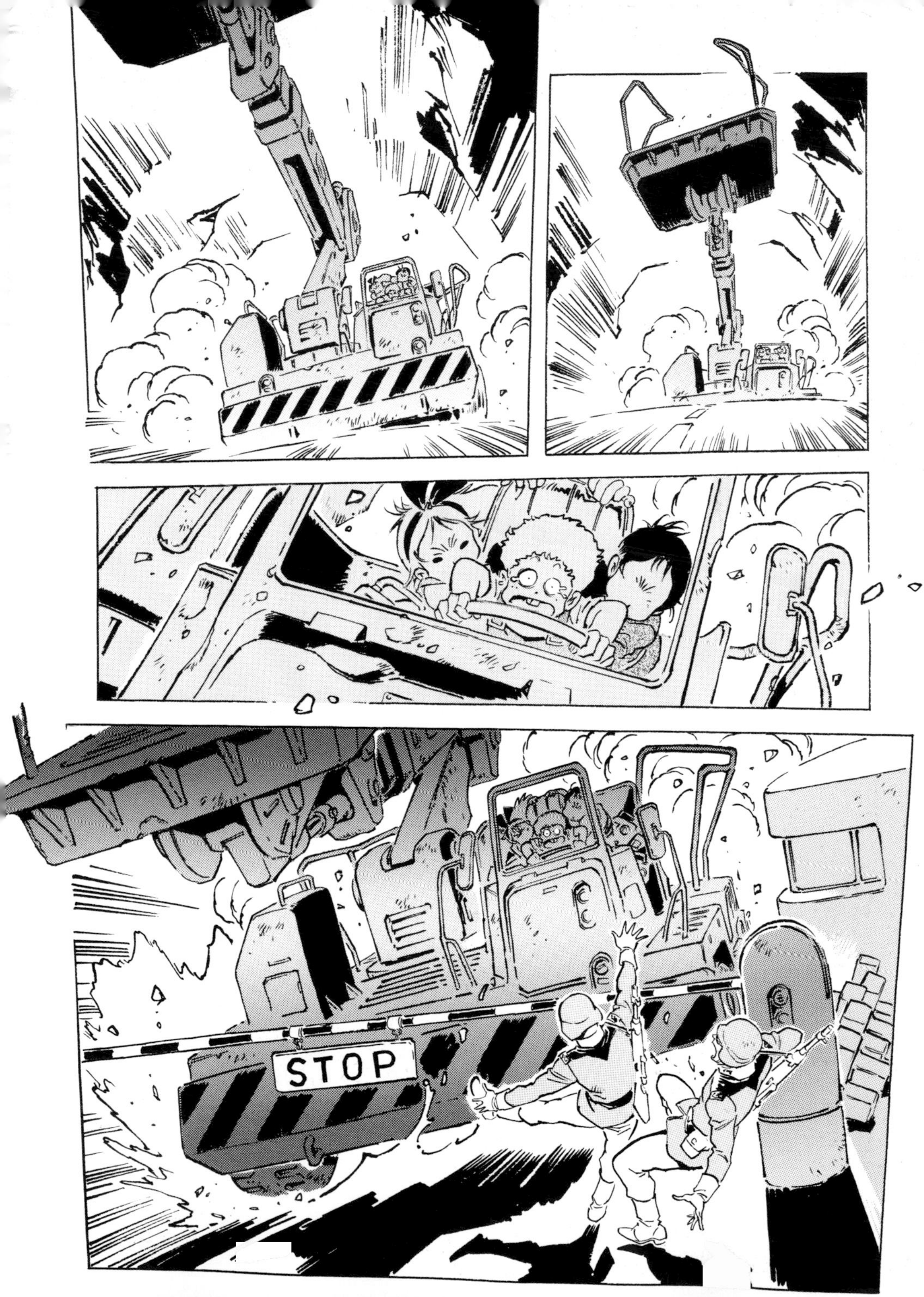
STOP

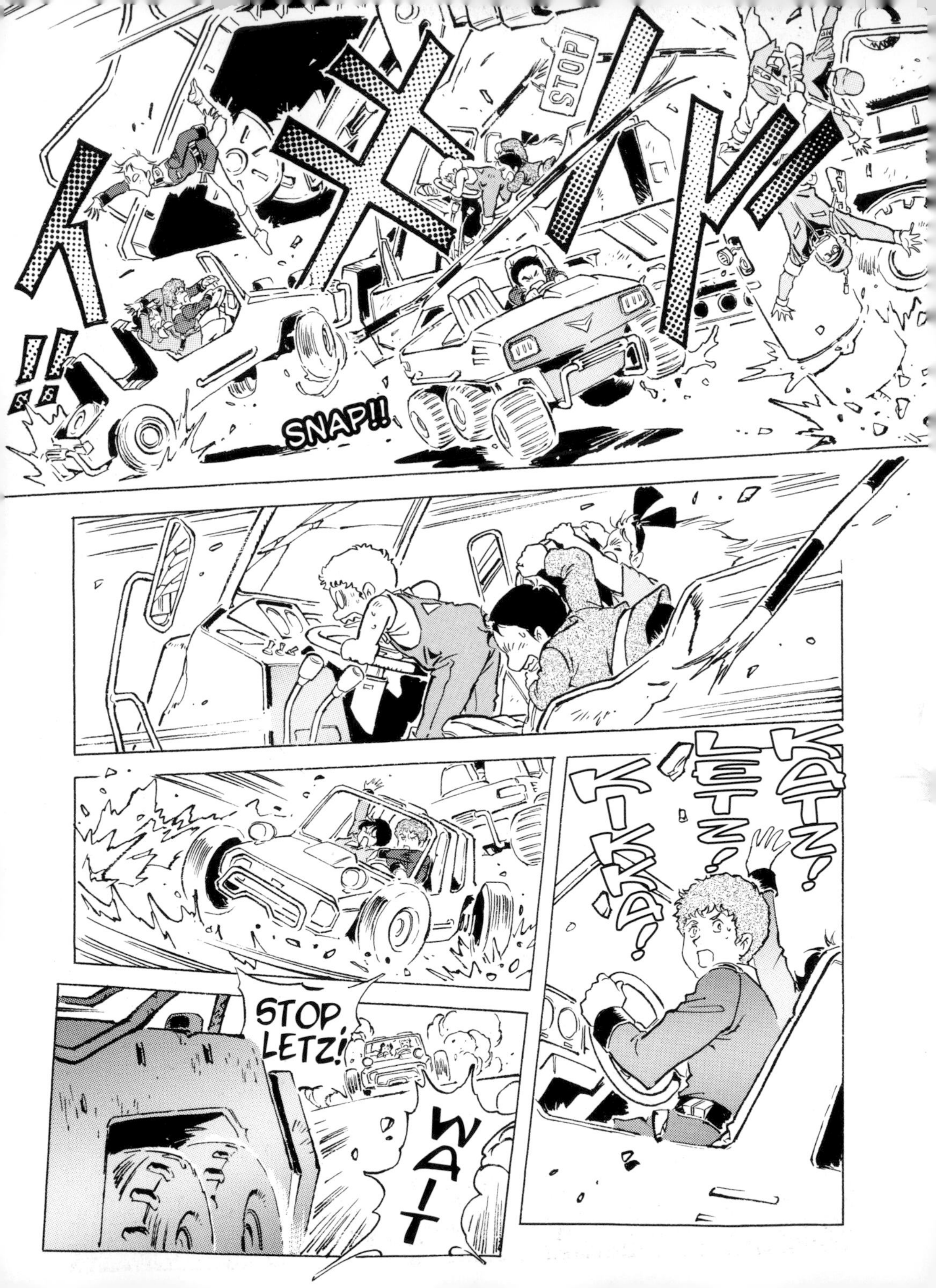
SNAP!!
KATZ!
LETZ!
KIKKA!
STOP LETZ!
WAIT

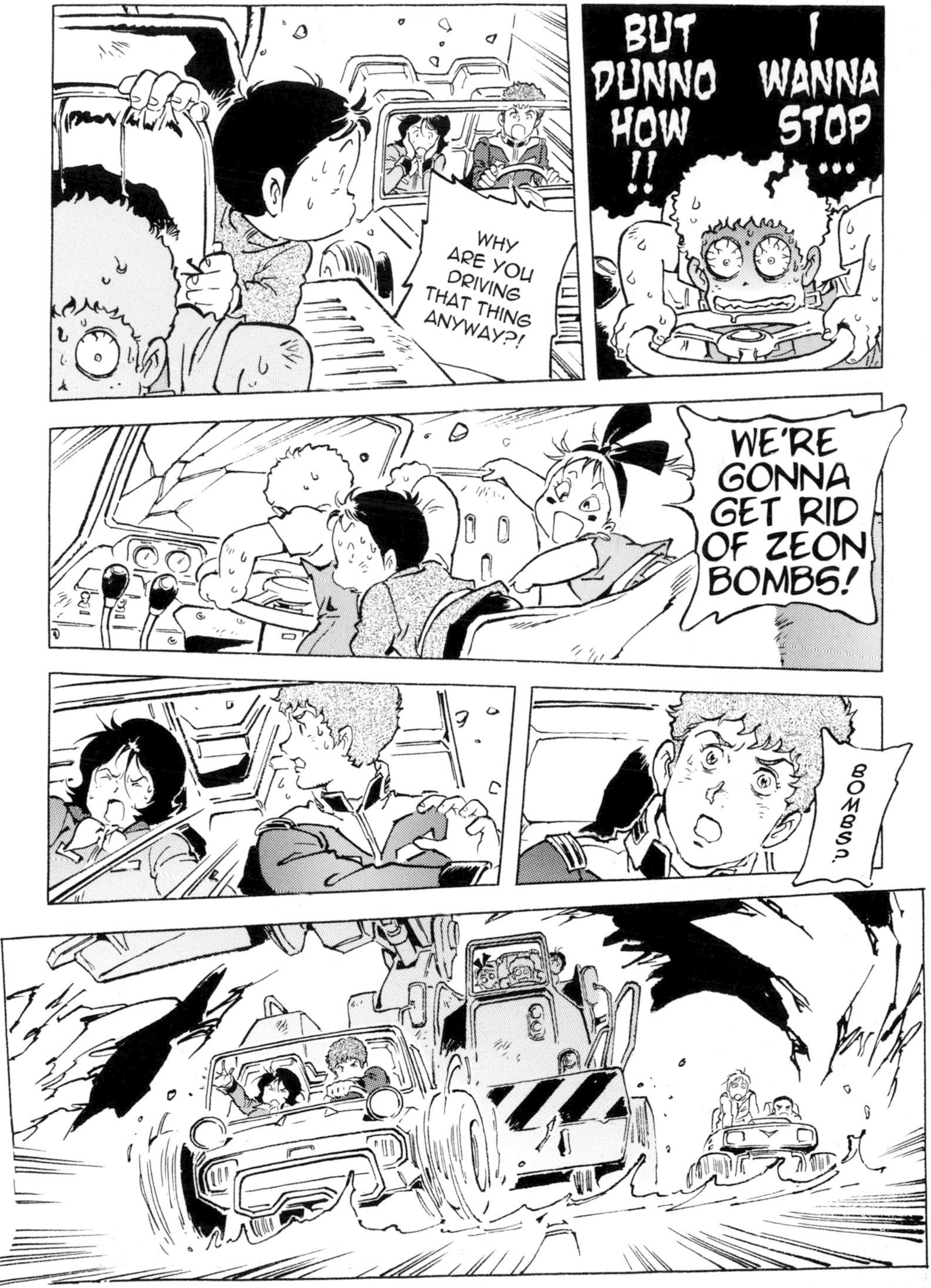
I WANNA STOP...
BUT DUNNO HOW!!
WHY ARE YOU DRIVING THAT THING ANYWAY?!
WE'RE GONNA GET RID OF ZEON BOMBS!
BOMBS?

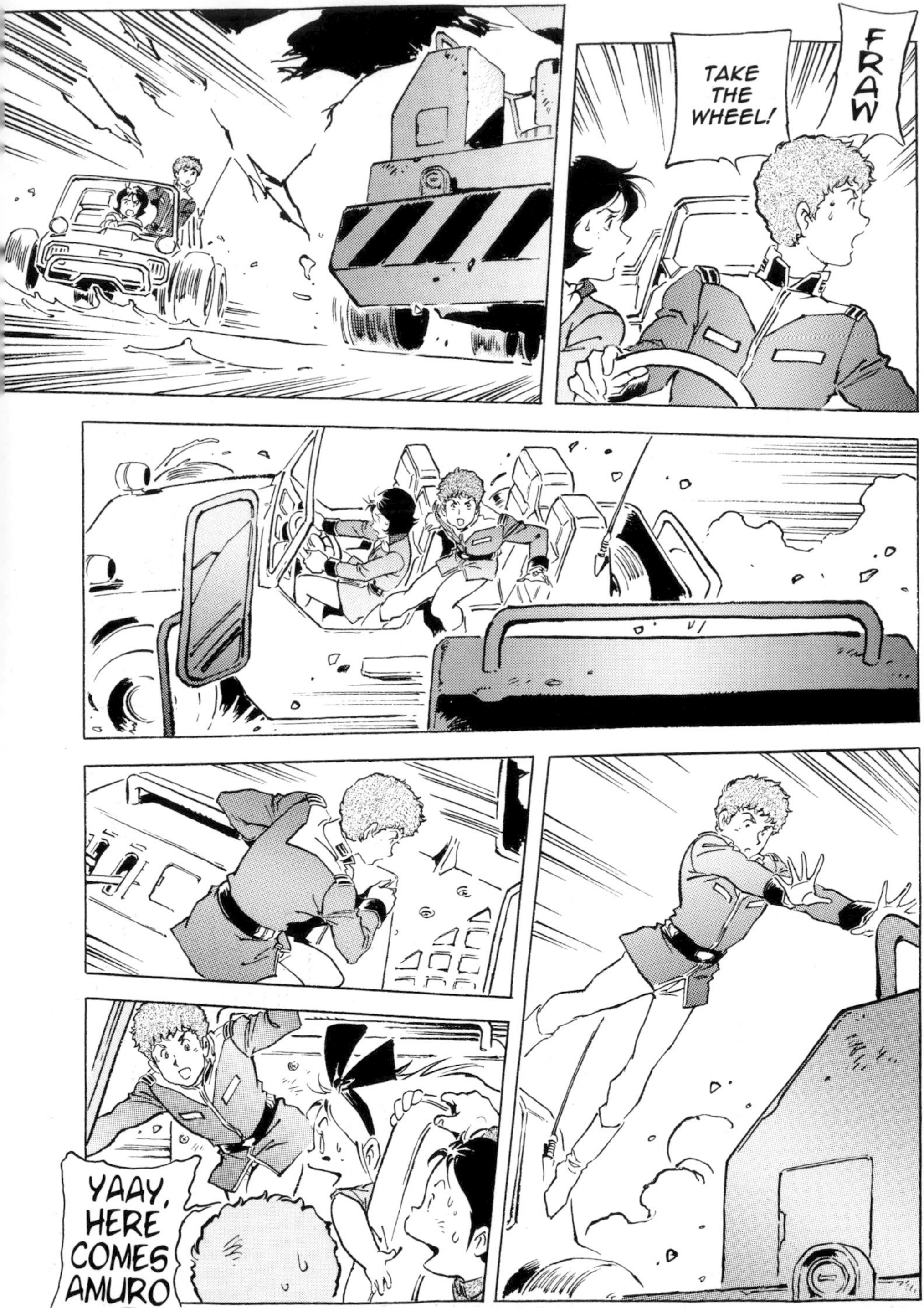
FRAW
TAKE THE WHEEL!
YAAY, HERE COMES AMURO

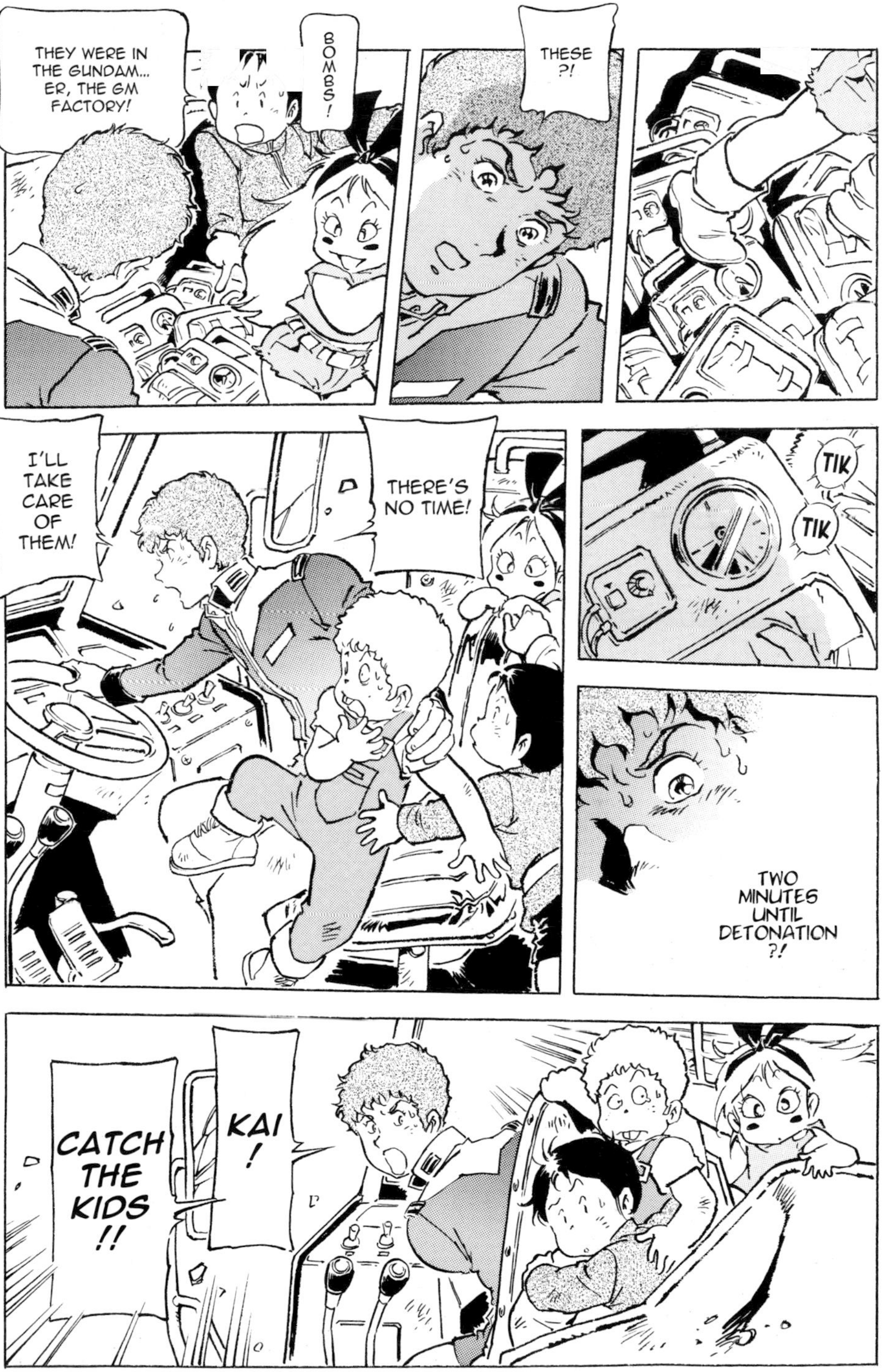
THESE ?!
BOMBS!
THEY WERE IN THE GUNDAM... ER, THE GM FACTORY!
TIK
TIK
TWO MINUTES UNTIL DETONATION ?!
THERE'S NO TIME!
I'LL TAKE CARE OF THEM!
KAI!
CATCH THE KIDS!!

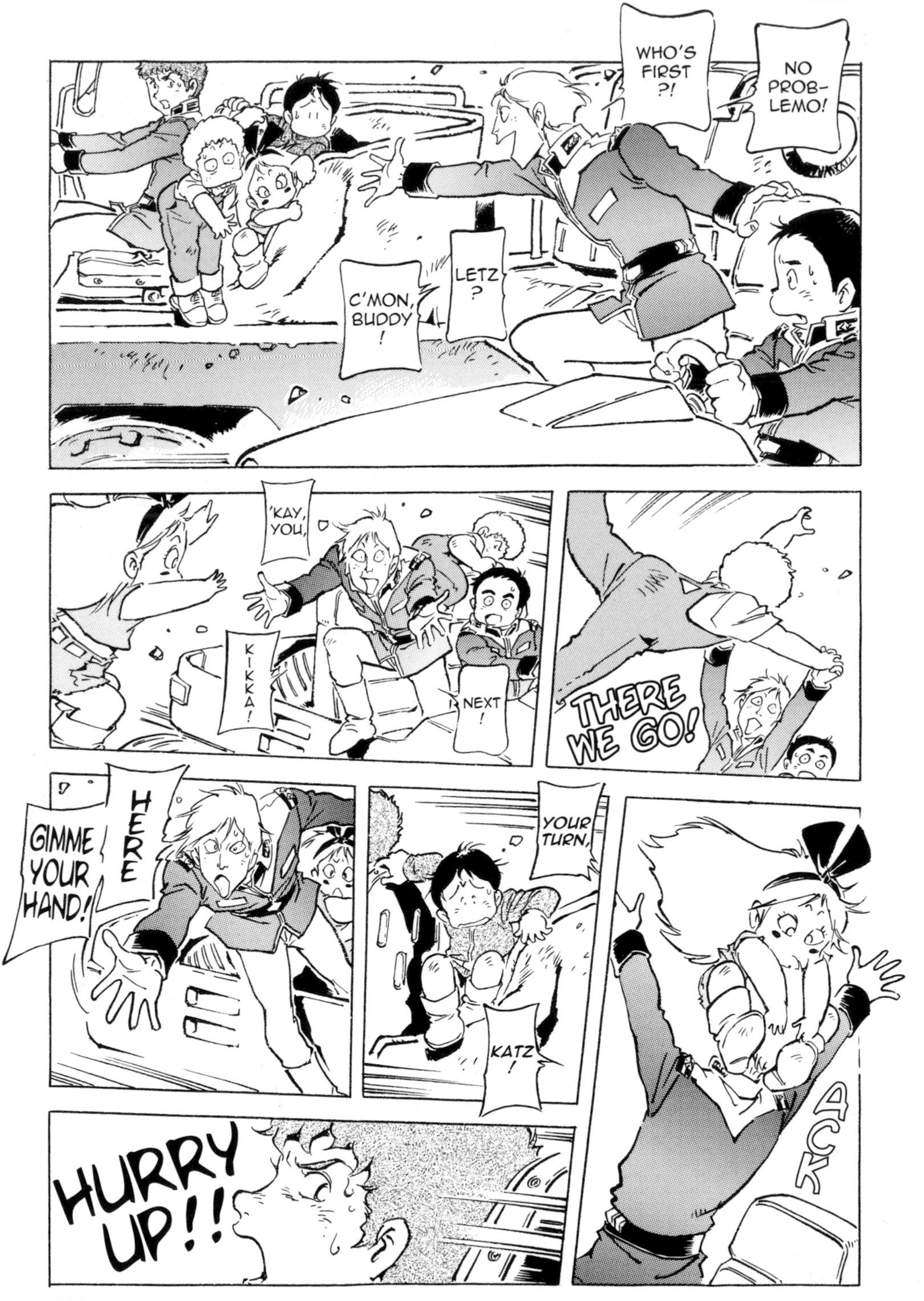
NO PROB-LEMO!
WHO'S FIRST ?!
LETZ ?
C'MON, BUDDY !
THERE WE GO!
'KAY, YOU,
KIKKA !
NEXT !
ACK
YOUR TURN,
KATZ !
HERE
GIMME YOUR HAND!
HURRY UP!!

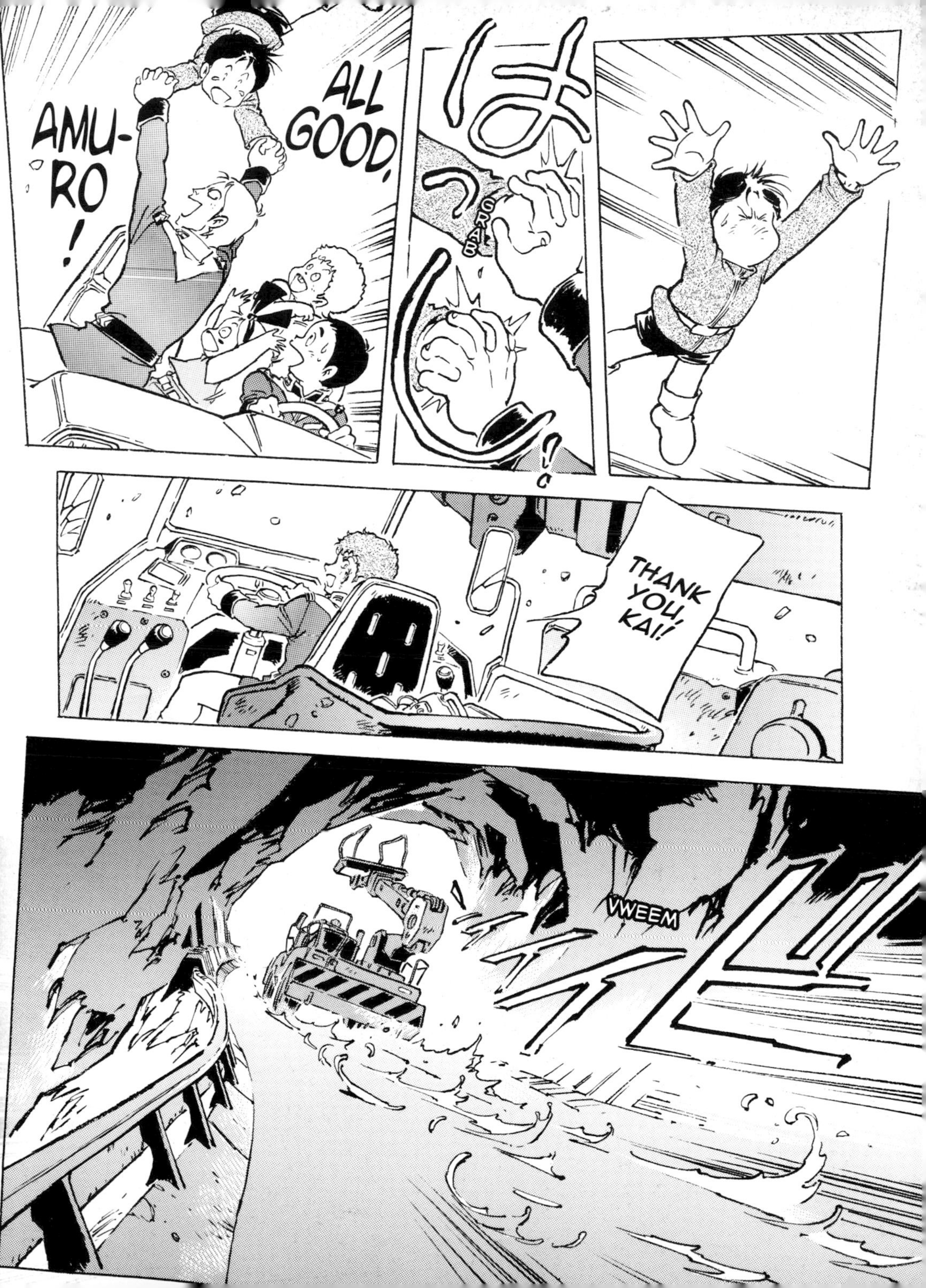
はっ
GRAB
!?
ALL GOOD,
AMU-RO!
THANK YOU, KAI!
VWEEM

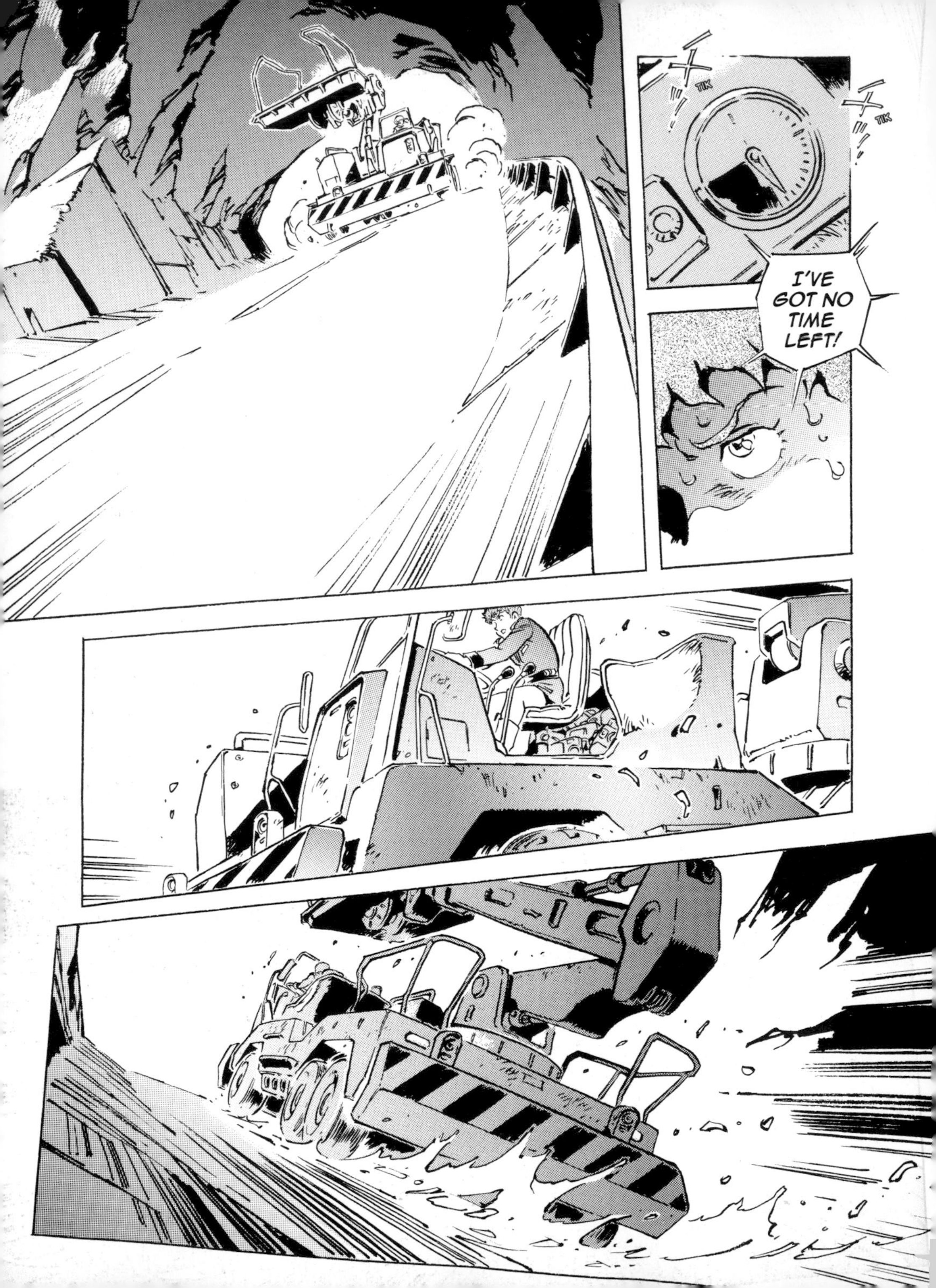
TIK
TIK
I'VE GOT NO TIME LEFT!

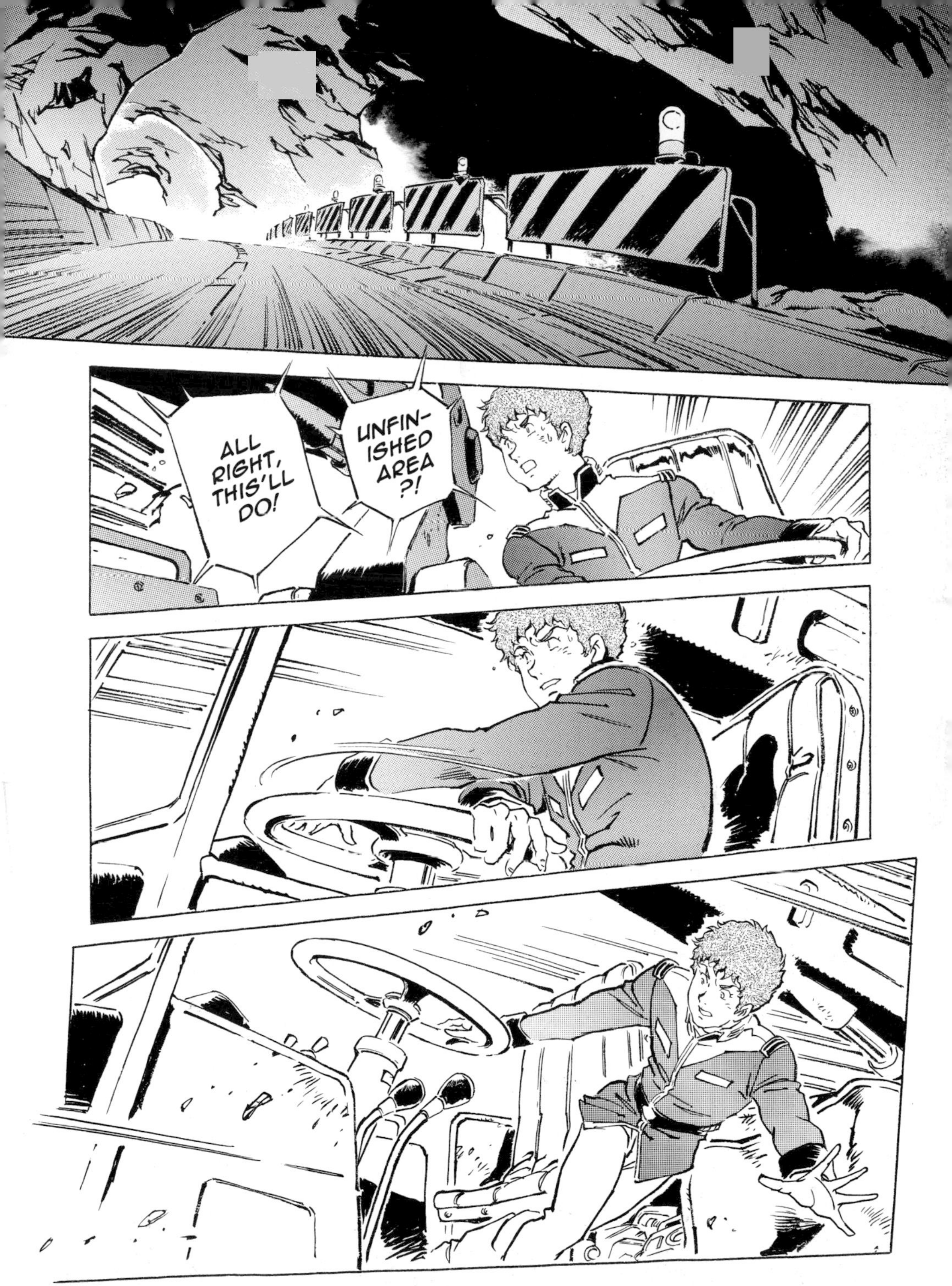
UNFIN-ISHED AREA ?!
ALL RIGHT, THIS'LL DO!

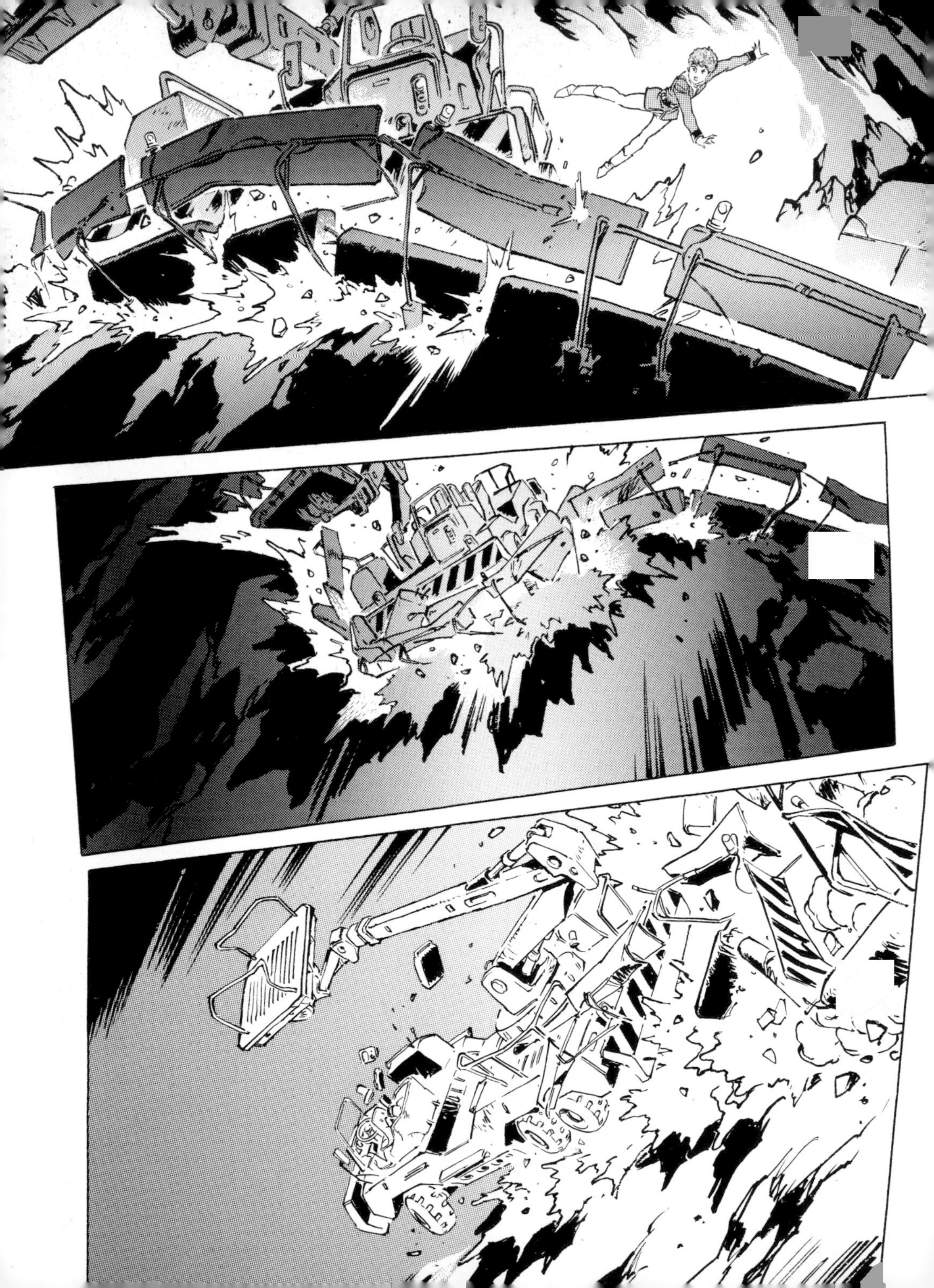

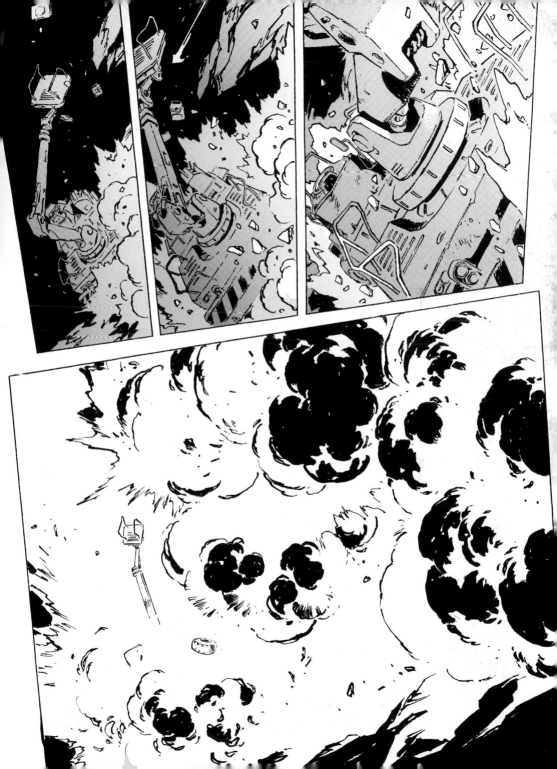

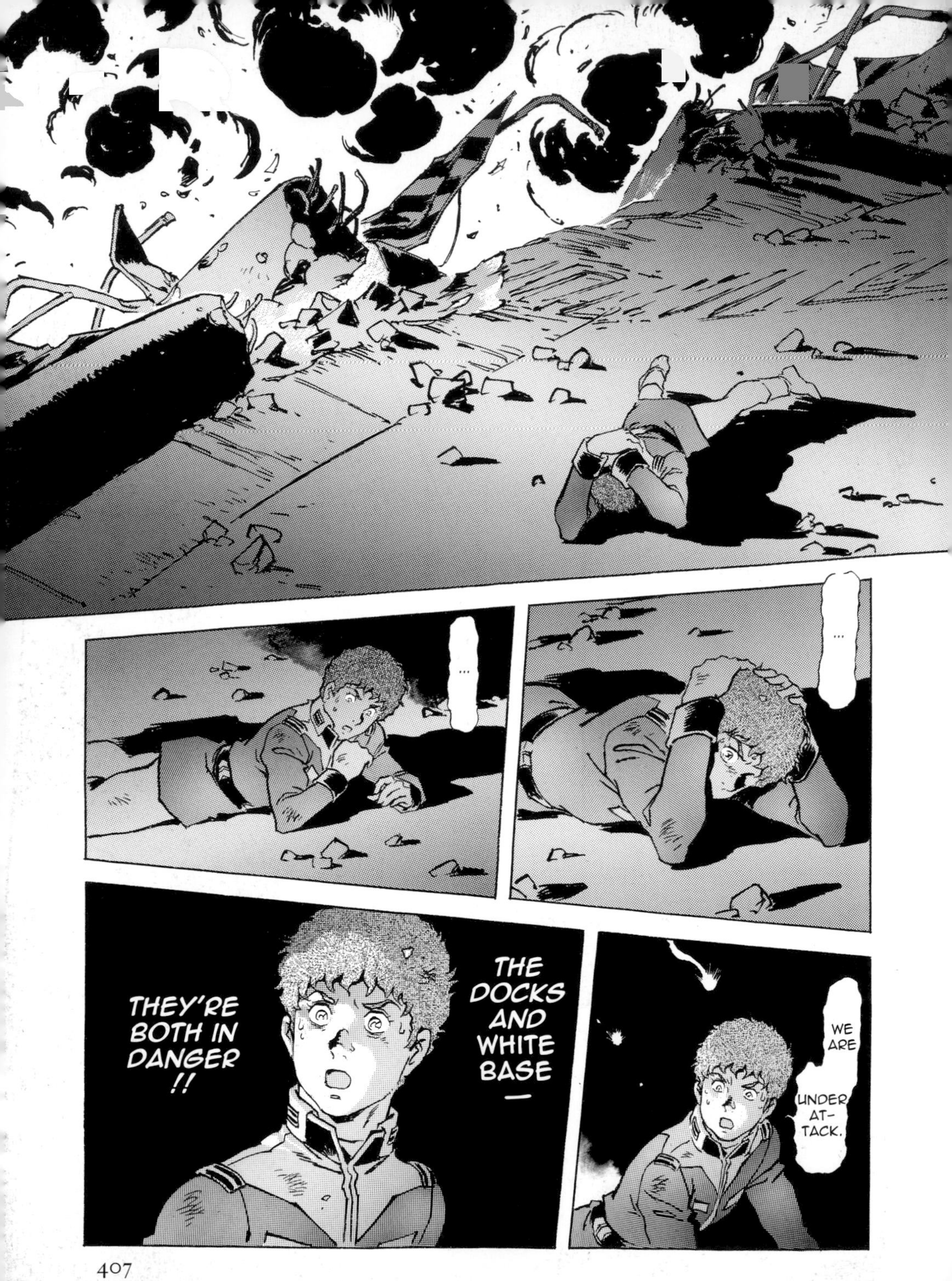
...
...
WE ARE UNDER AT-TACK.
THE DOCKS AND WHITE BASE —
THEY'RE BOTH IN DANGER !!

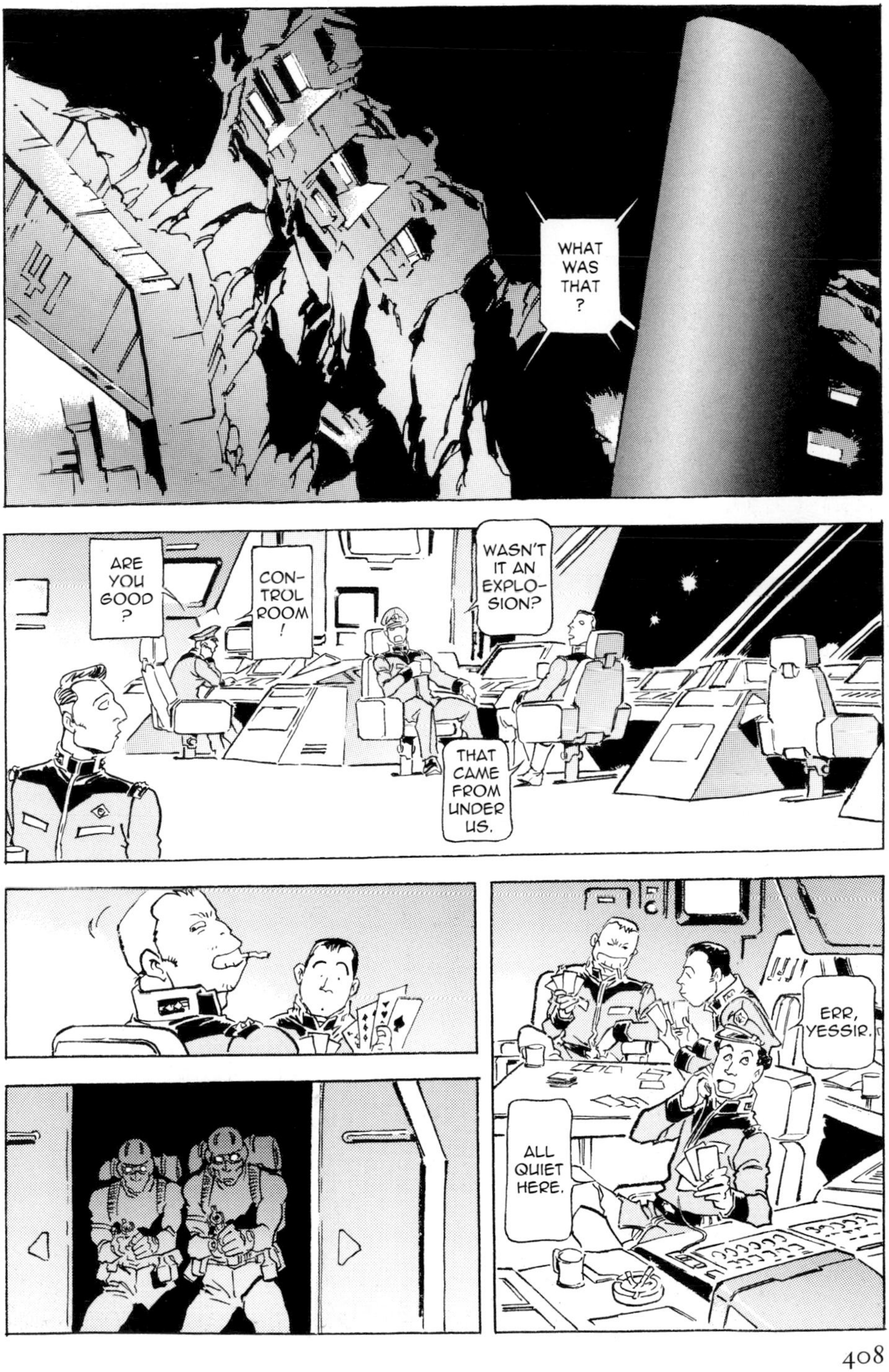
WHAT WAS THAT?
WASN'T IT AN EXPLOSION?
THAT CAME FROM UNDER US.
CONTROL ROOM!
ARE YOU GOOD?
ERR, YESSIR.
ALL QUIET HERE.

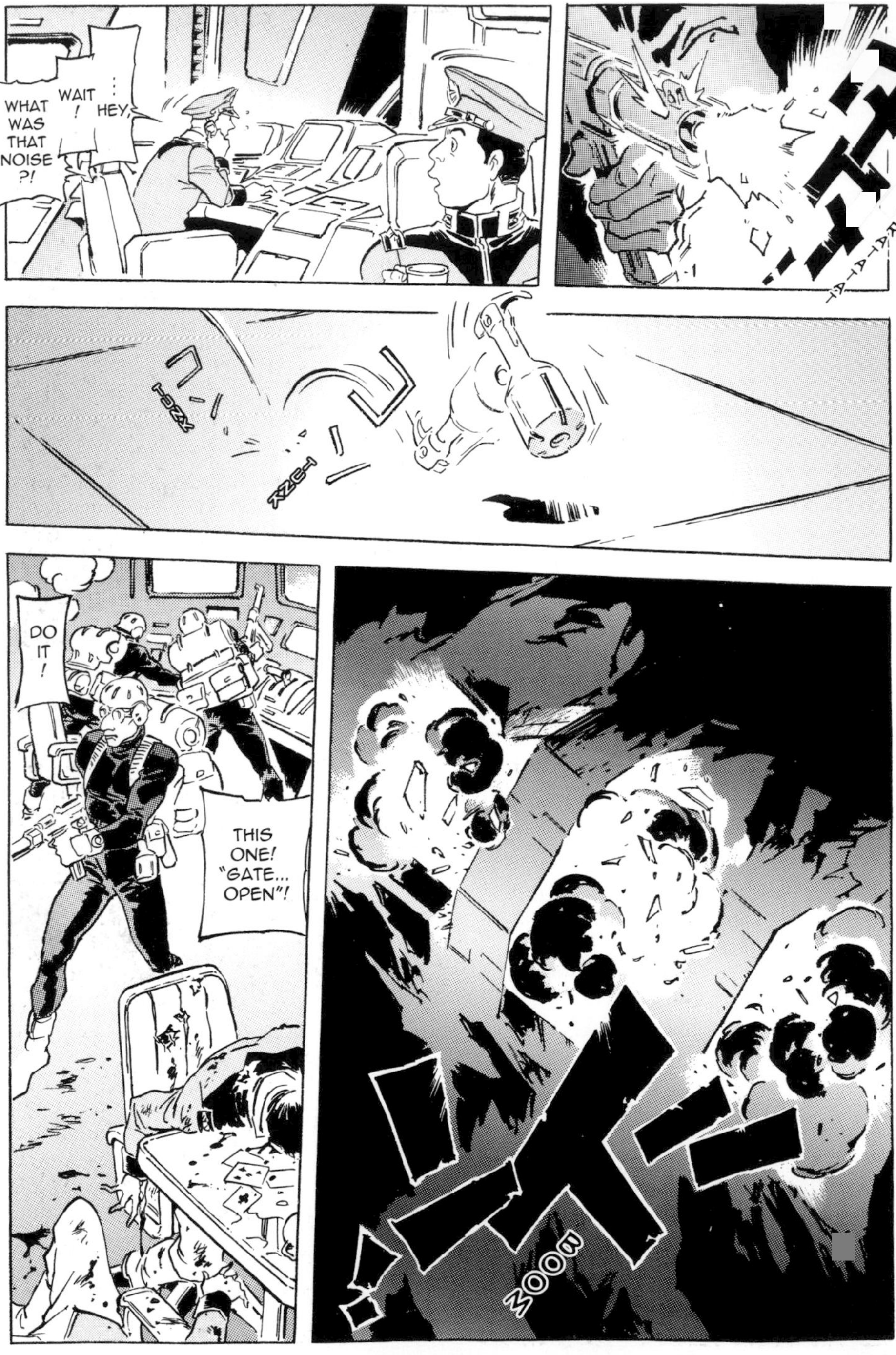
R-A-T-A-T-A-T
HEY, ...
WAIT!
WHAT WAS THAT NOISE?!
BOOM
DO IT!
THIS ONE! "GATE... OPEN"!

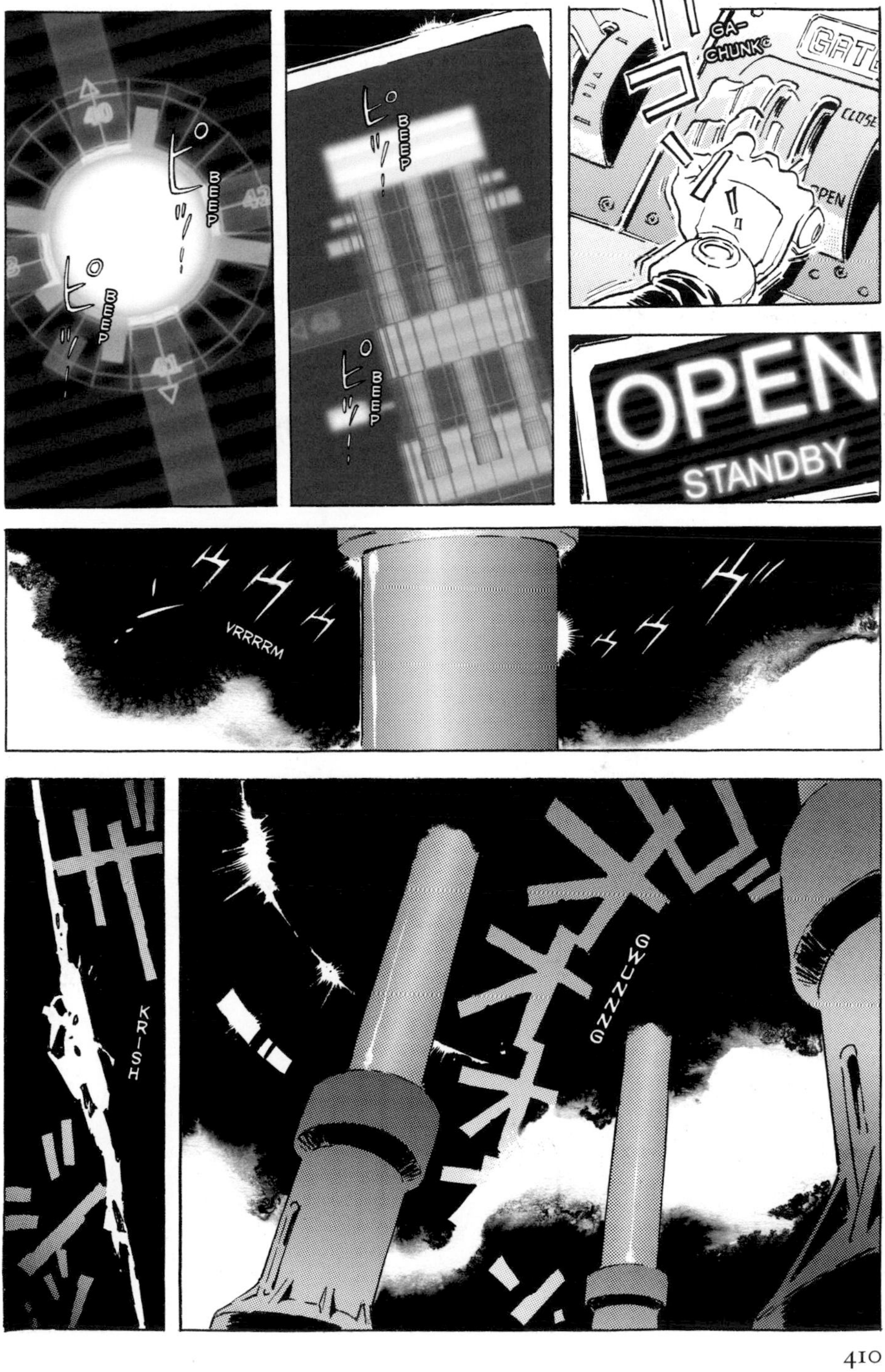
ガッ
GA-CHUNK
GATE
CLOSE
OPEN
OPEN
STANDBY
ピッ
BEEP
ピッ
BEEP
ピッ
BEEP
ピッ
BEEP
VRRRRM
GWUNNG
KRISH

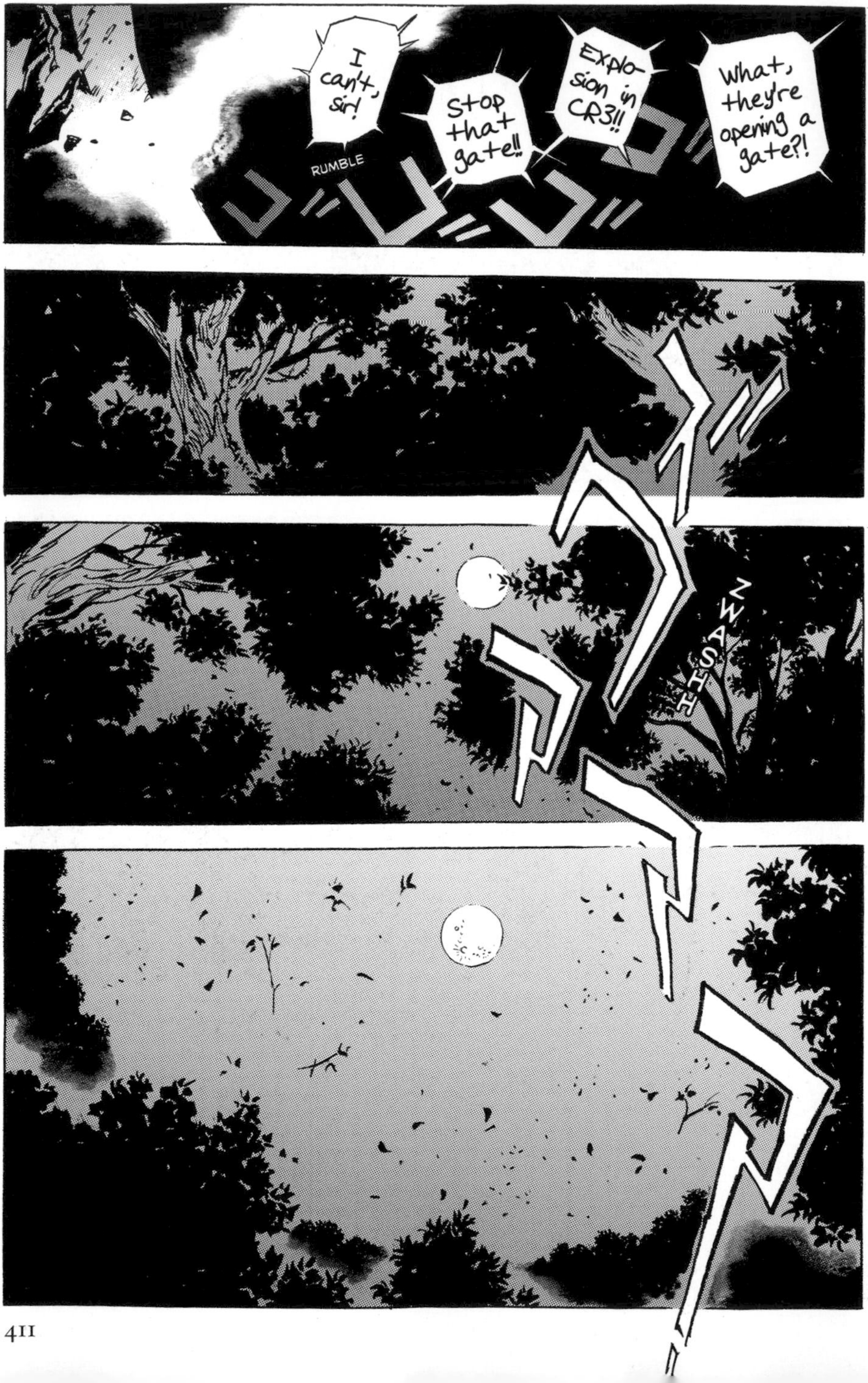
What, they're opening a gate?!
Explosion in CR3!!
Stop that gate!!
I can't, sir!
RUMBLE
ZWASHH

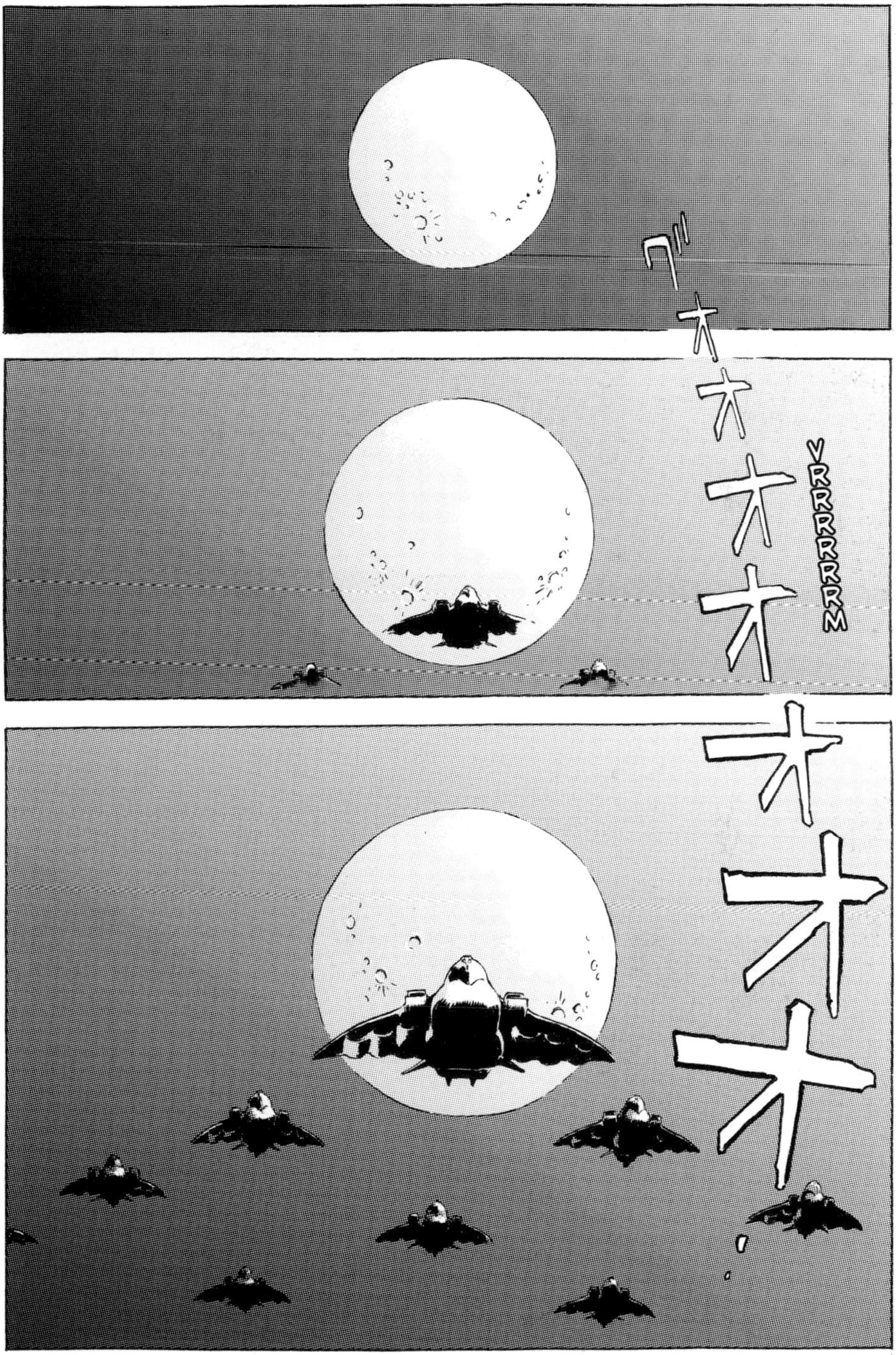
グォオオオオオオ
VRRRRRRM

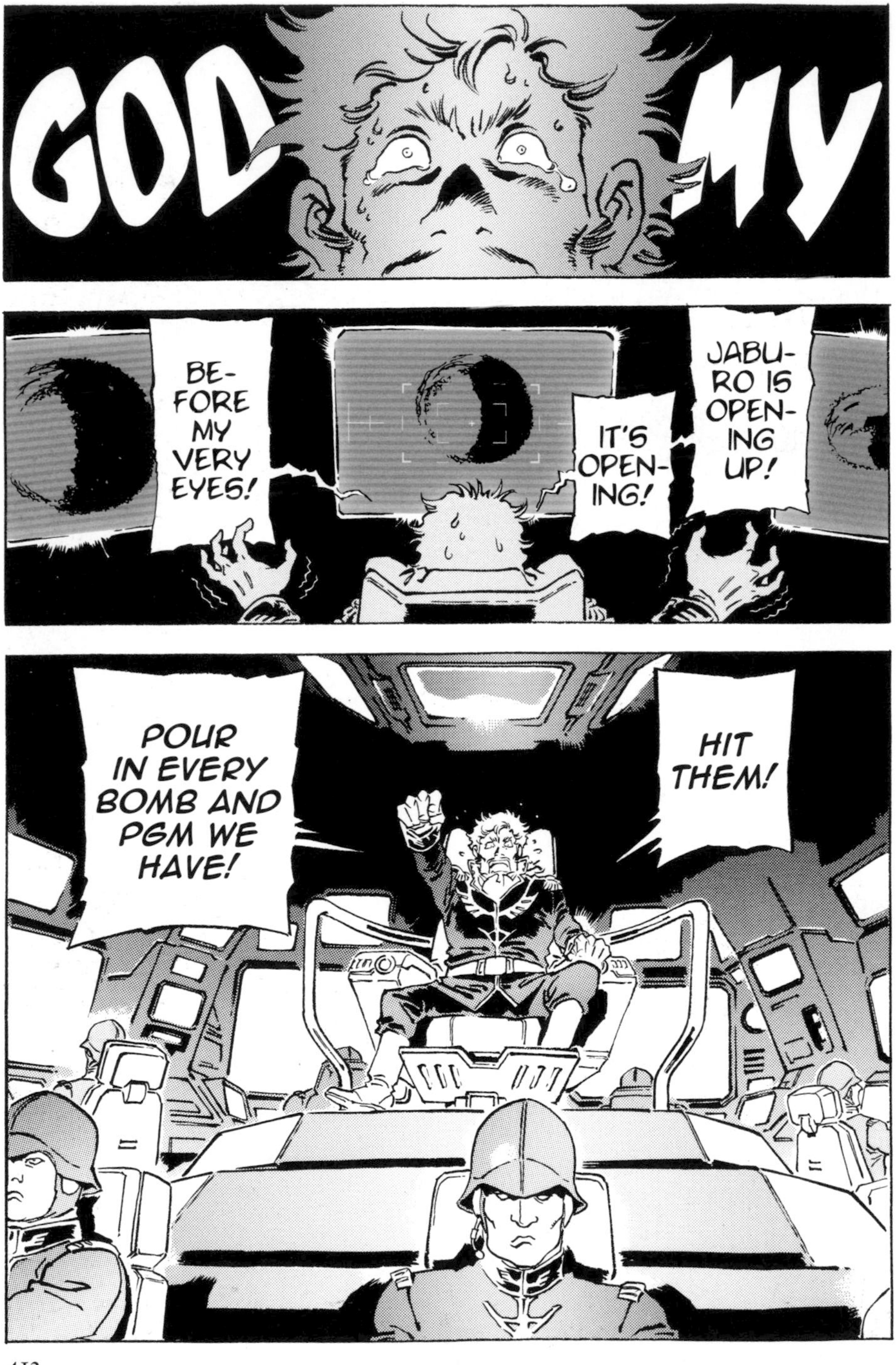
MY
GOD
JABURO IS OPENING UP!
IT'S OPENING!
BEFORE MY VERY EYES!
HIT THEM!
POUR IN EVERY BOMB AND PGM WE HAVE!

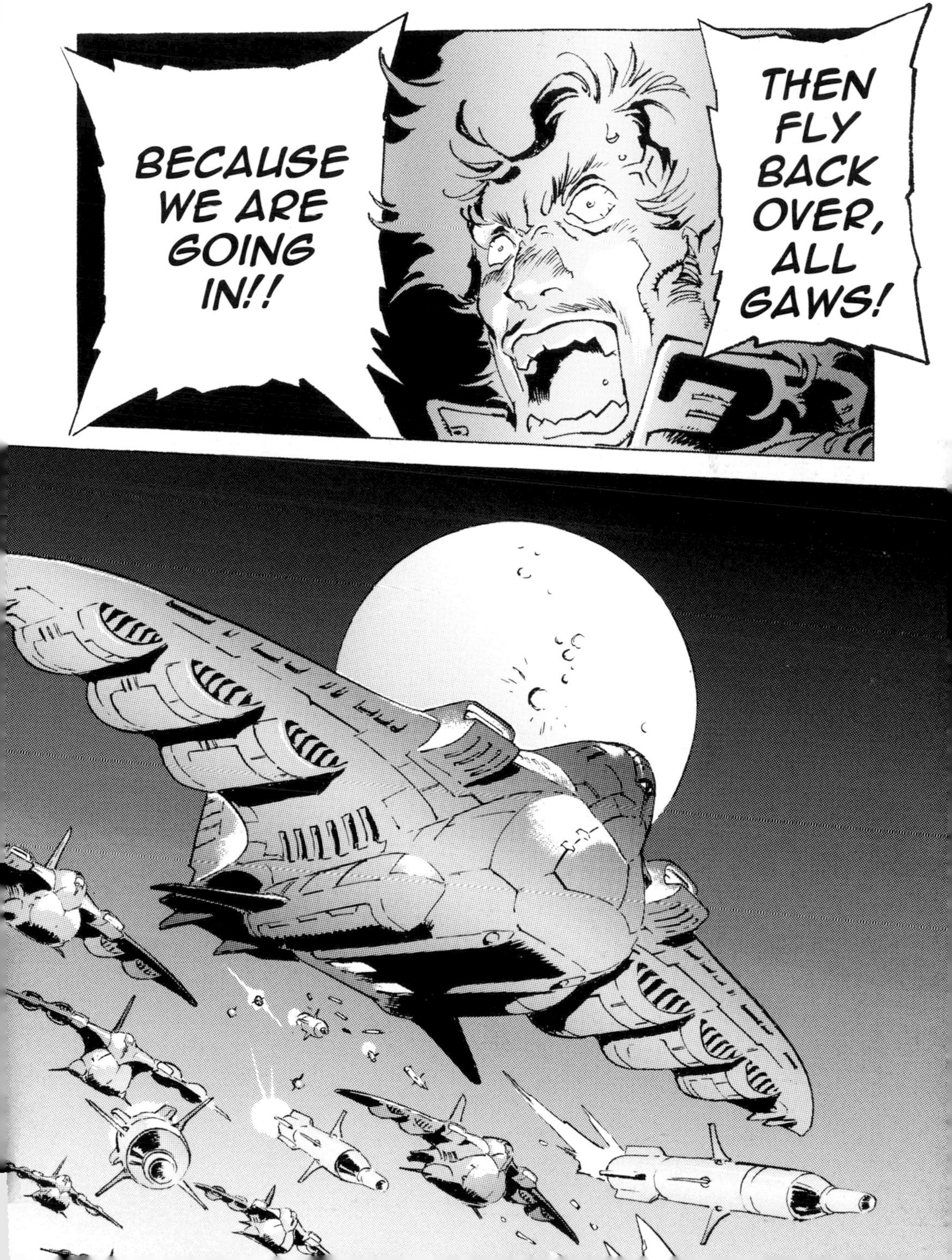
THEN FLY BACK OVER, ALL GAWS!
BECAUSE WE ARE GOING IN!!

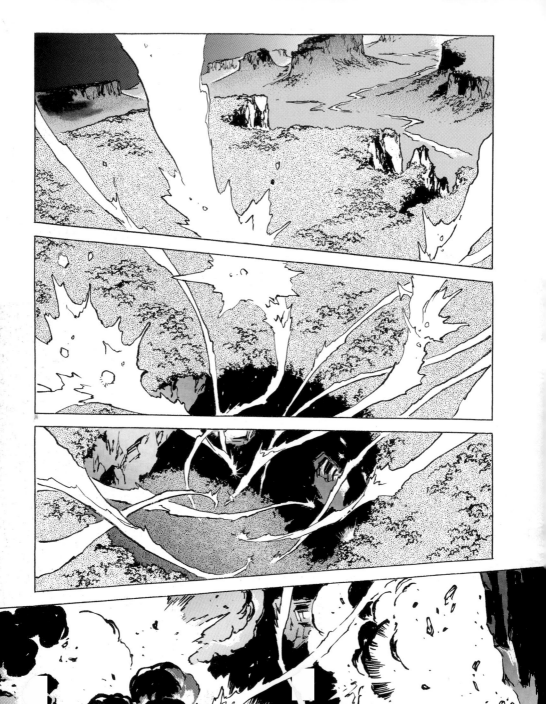

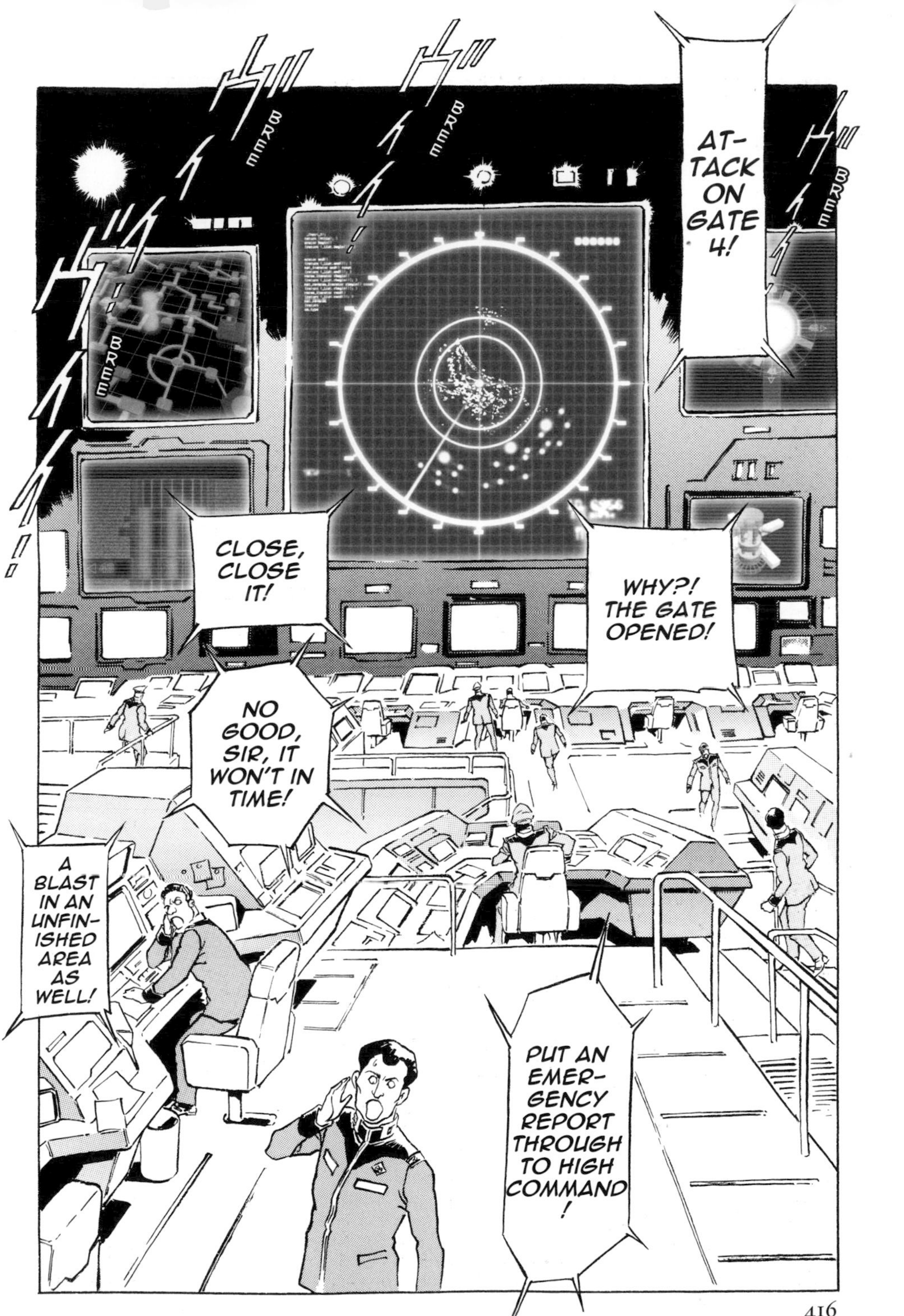

BREE
ATTACK ON GATE 4!
BREE
BREE
BREE
WHY?! THE GATE OPENED!
CLOSE, CLOSE IT!
NO GOOD, SIR, IT WON'T IN TIME!
PUT AN EMERGENCY REPORT THROUGH TO HIGH COMMAND!
A BLAST IN AN UNFINISHED AREA AS WELL!

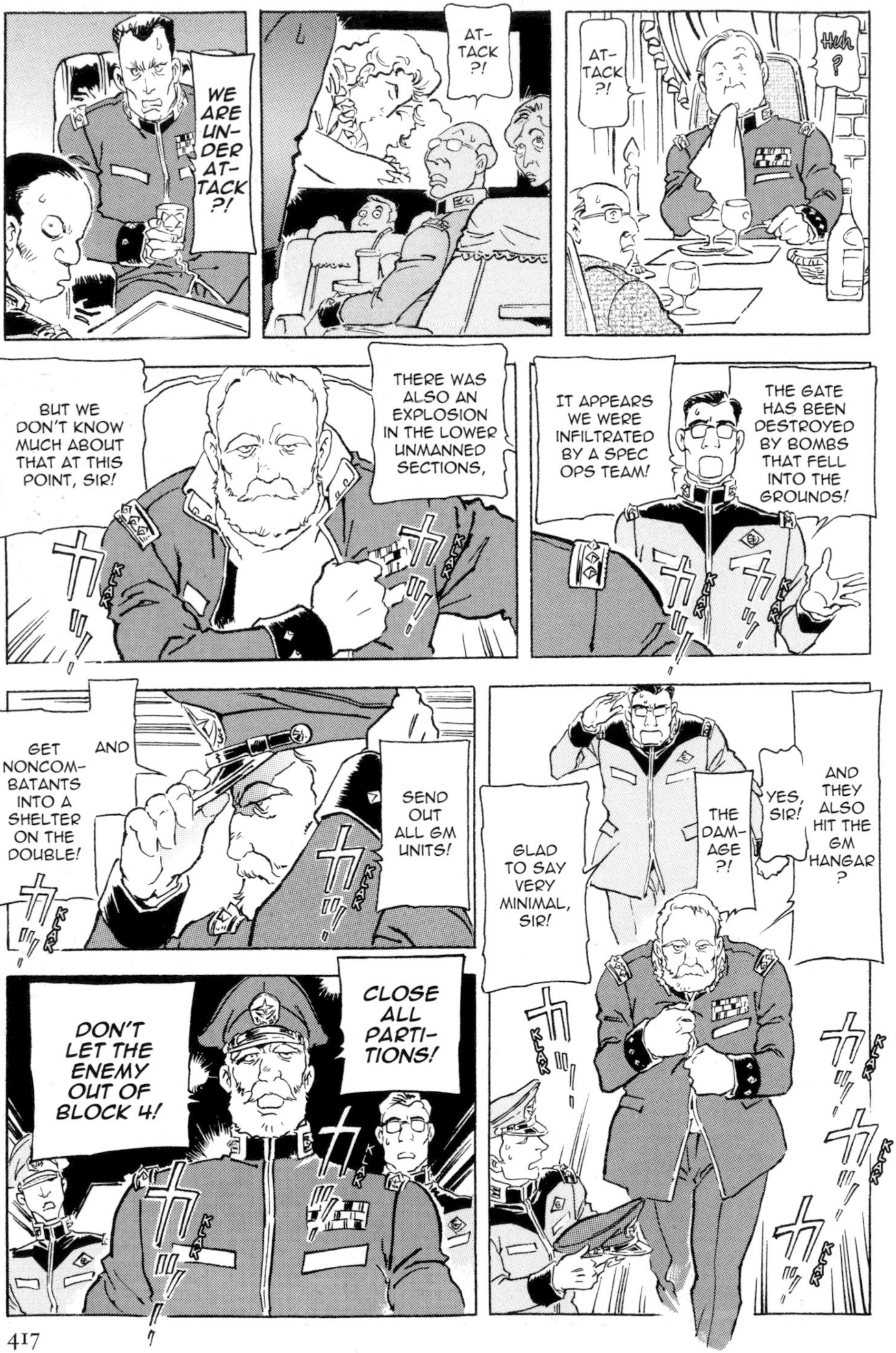
Huh?
AT-TACK?!
AT-TACK?!
WE ARE UNDER AT-TACK?!
THE GATE HAS BEEN DESTROYED BY BOMBS THAT FELL INTO THE GROUNDS!
IT APPEARS WE WERE INFILTRATED BY A SPEC OPS TEAM!
KLAK
KLAK
THERE WAS ALSO AN EXPLOSION IN THE LOWER UNMANNED SECTIONS,
BUT WE DON'T KNOW MUCH ABOUT THAT AT THIS POINT, SIR!
KLAK
KLAK
AND THEY ALSO HIT THE GM HANGAR?
YES, SIR!
THE DAM-AGE?!
GLAD TO SAY VERY MINIMAL, SIR!
KLAK
KLAK
KLAK
SEND OUT ALL GM UNITS!
AND
GET NONCOM-BATANTS INTO A SHELTER ON THE DOUBLE!
KLAK
KLAK
CLOSE ALL PARTI-TIONS!
DON'T LET THE ENEMY OUT OF BLOCK 4!
KLAK
KLAK

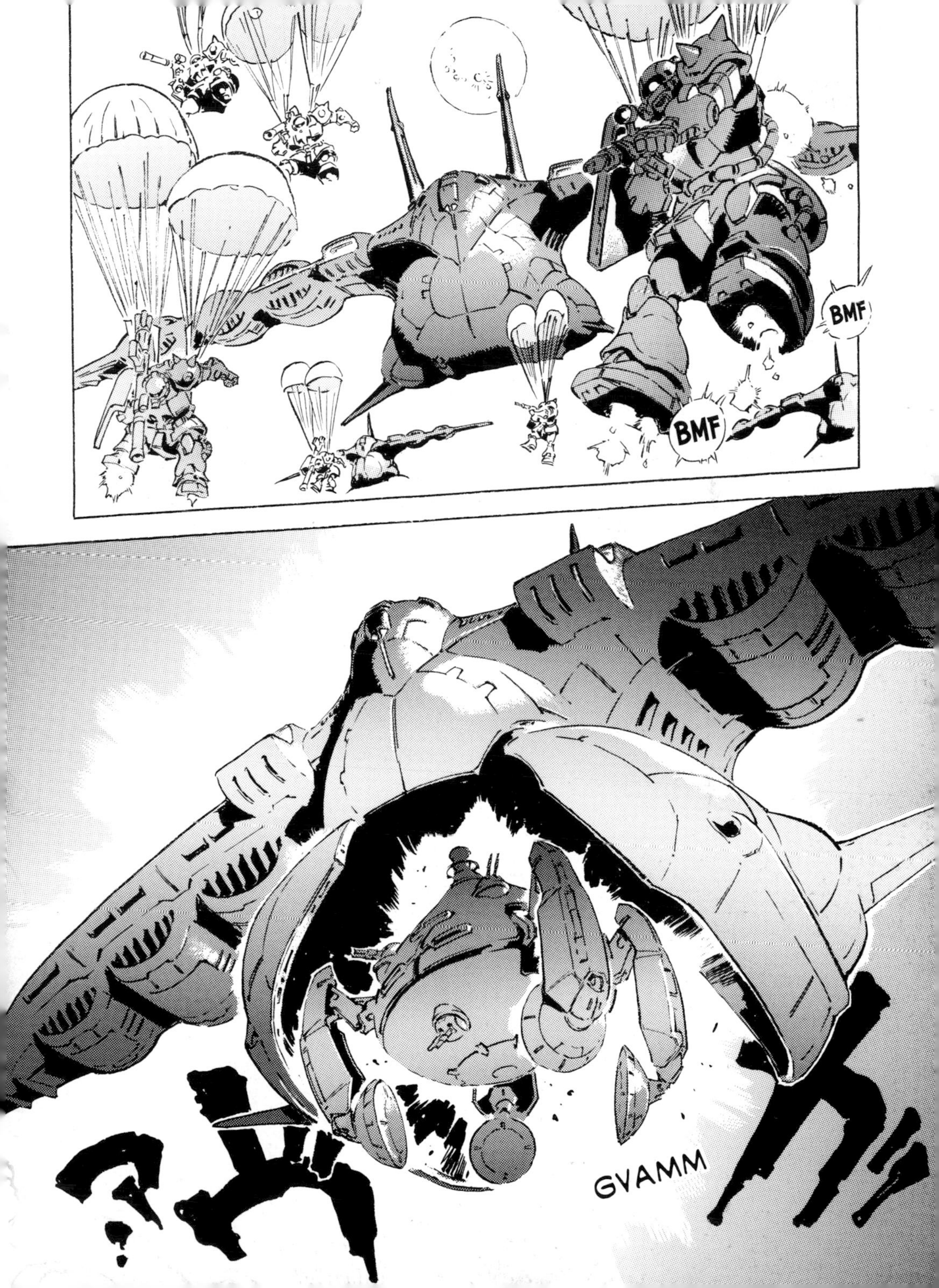
BMF
BMF
GVAMM

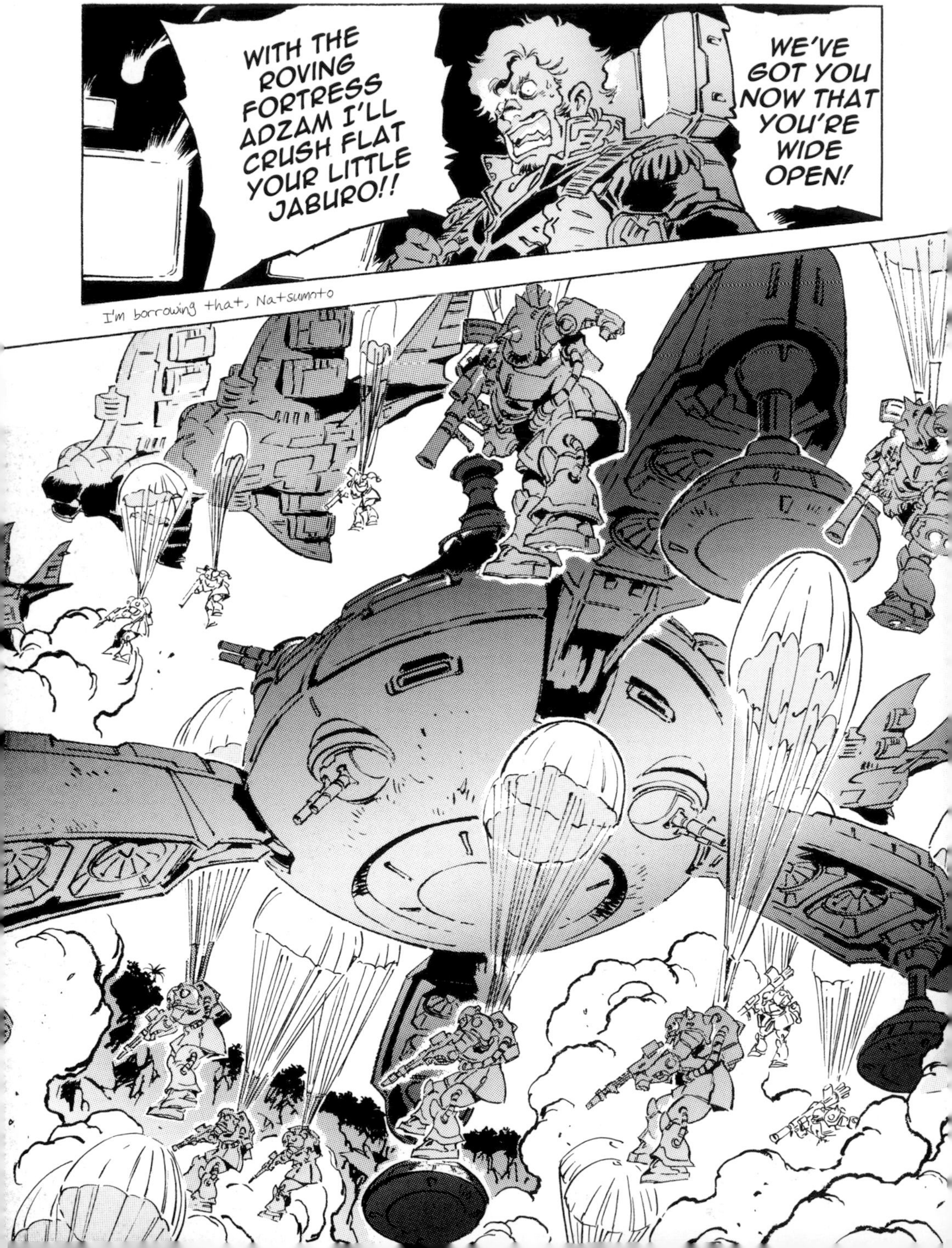
WE'VE GOT YOU NOW THAT YOU'RE WIDE OPEN!
WITH THE ROVING FORTRESS ADZAM I'LL CRUSH FLAT YOUR LITTLE JABURO!!
I'm borrowing that, Natsumoto

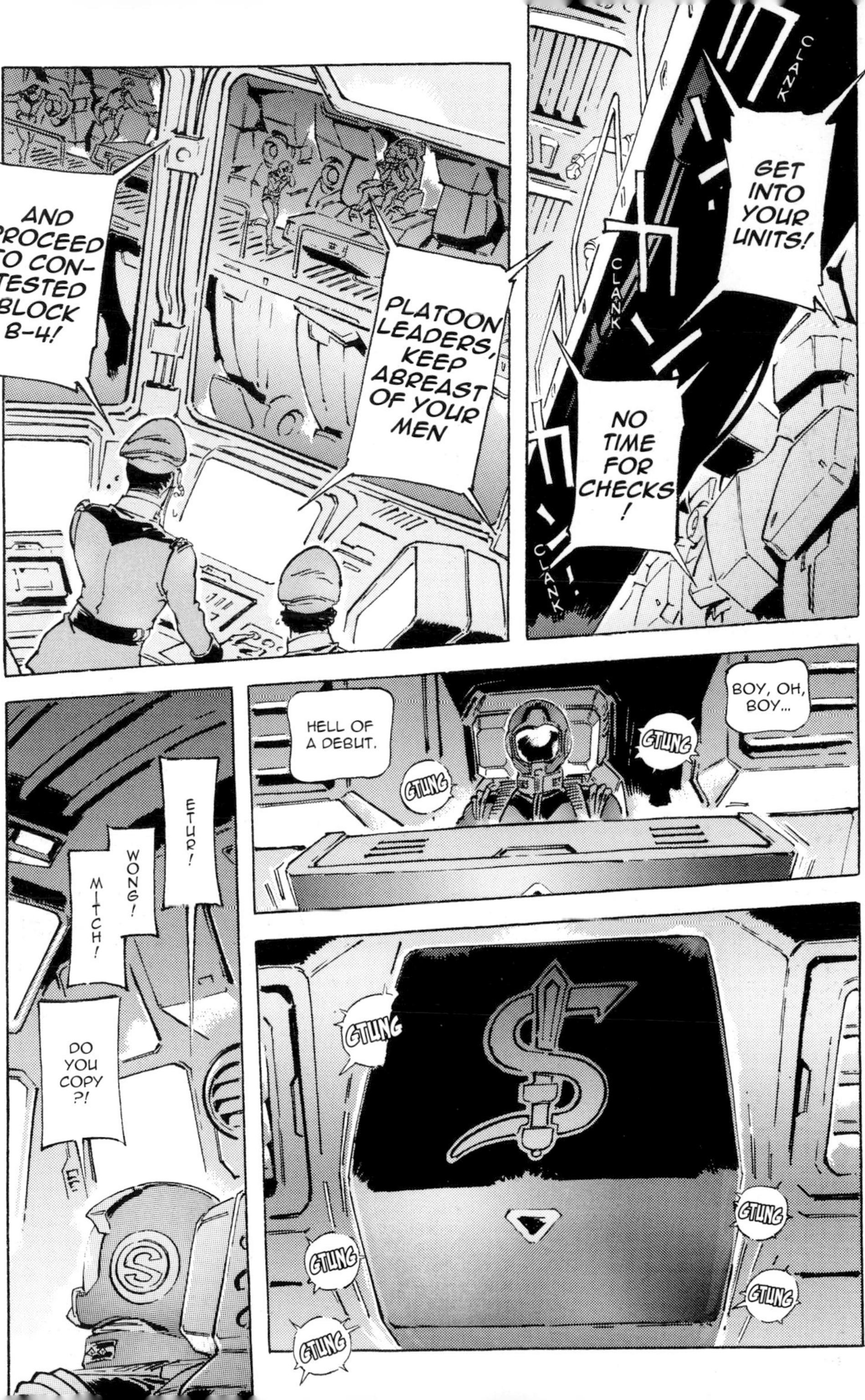
CLANK
GET INTO YOUR UNITS!
CLANK
NO TIME FOR CHECKS!
CLANK
PLATOON LEADERS, KEEP ABREAST OF YOUR MEN
AND PROCEED TO CON-TESTED BLOCK B-4!
BOY, OH, BOY...
GTUNG
HELL OF A DEBUT.
GTUNG
GTUNG
GTUNG
GTUNG
GTUNG
GTUNG
ETUR!
WONG!
MITCH!
DO YOU COPY?!

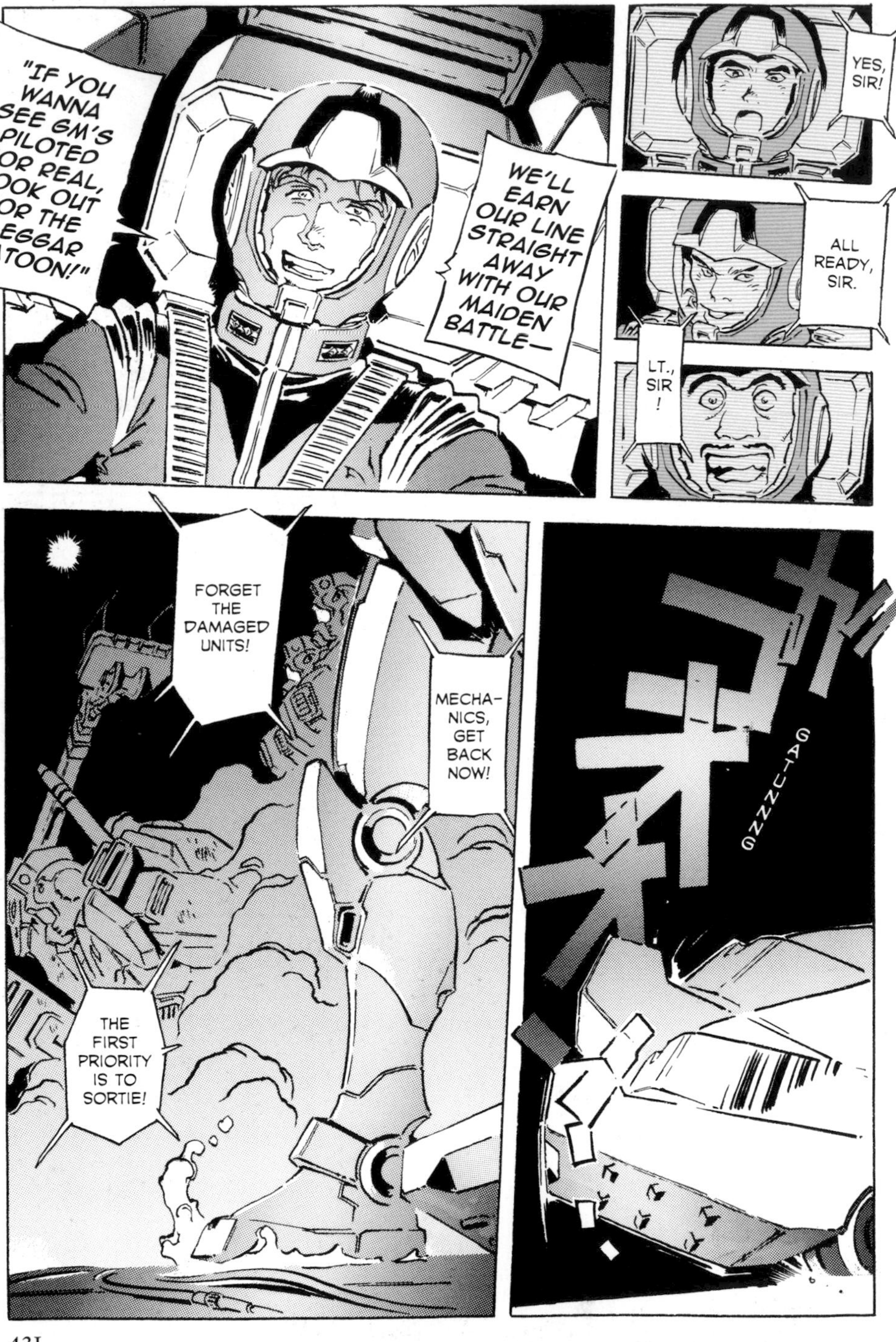
YES, SIR!
ALL READY, SIR.
LT., SIR!
WE'LL EARN OUR LINE STRAIGHT AWAY WITH OUR MAIDEN BATTLE—
"IF YOU WANNA SEE GM'S PILOTED FOR REAL, LOOK OUT FOR THE SLEGGAR PLATOON!"
GA-UNNNG
FORGET THE DAMAGED UNITS!
MECHANICS, GET BACK NOW!
THE FIRST PRIORITY IS TO SORTIE!

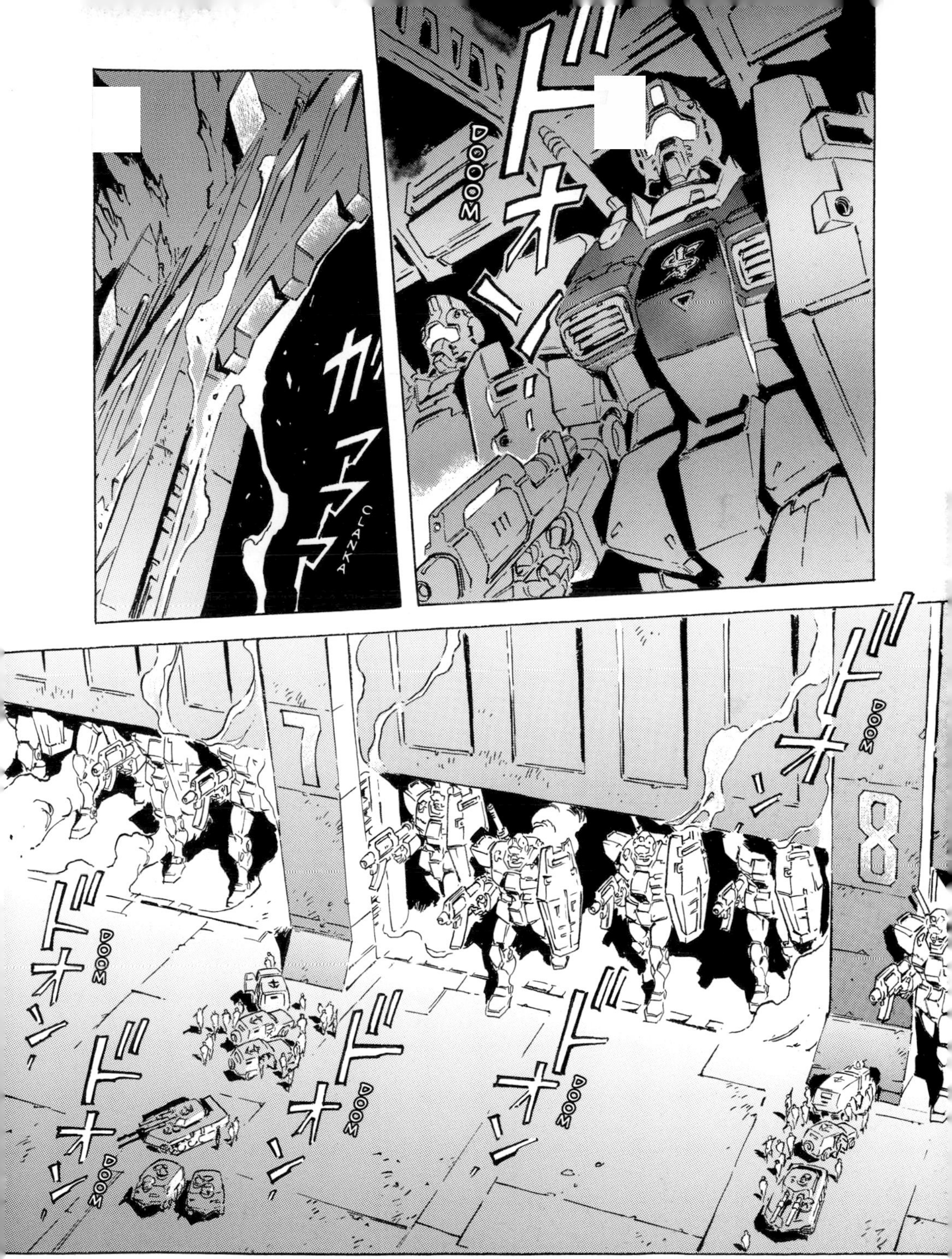
DOOOM
CLANKA
DOOM
DOOM
DOOM
DOOM
DOOM

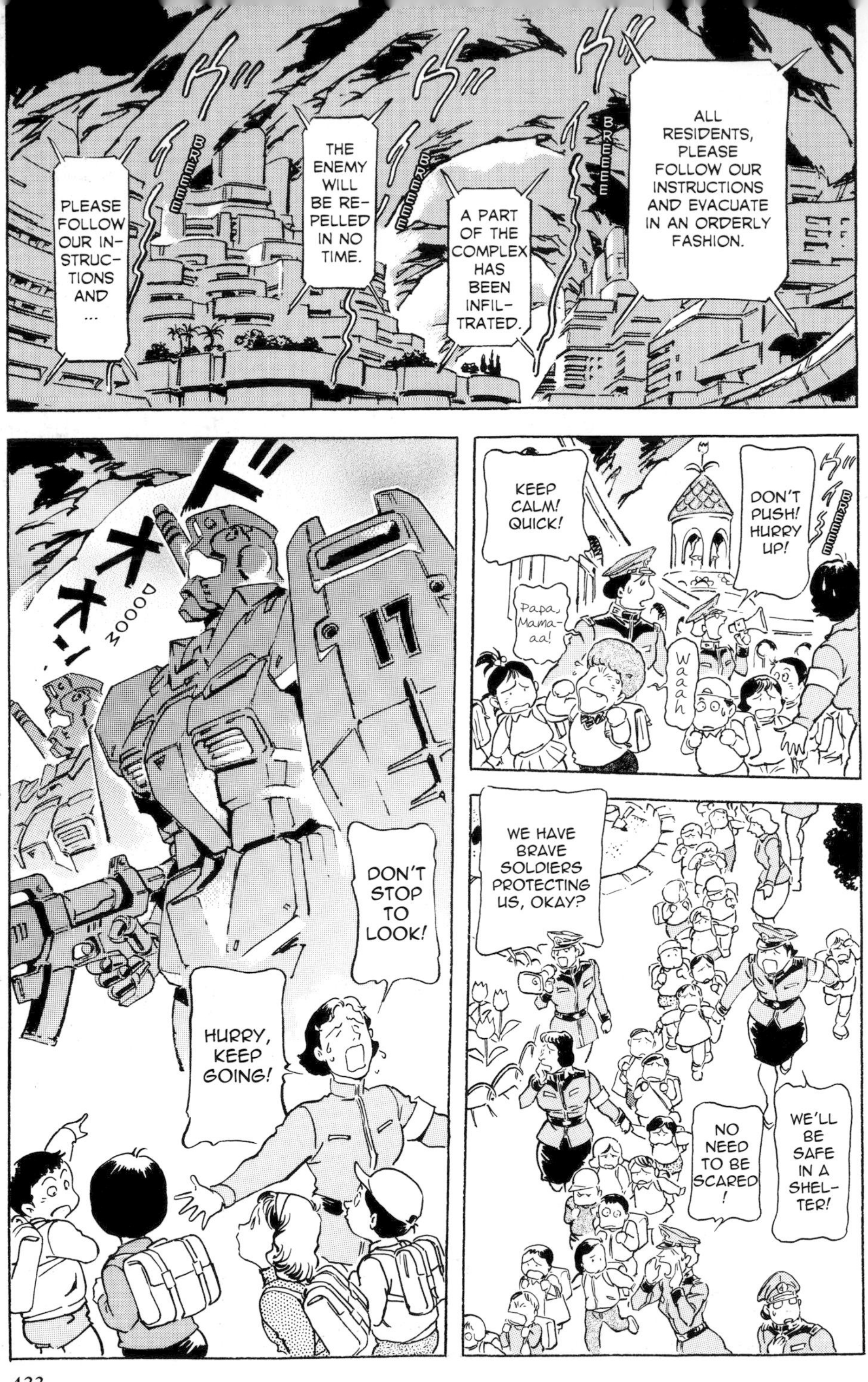
BREEEE
ALL RESIDENTS, PLEASE FOLLOW OUR INSTRUCTIONS AND EVACUATE IN AN ORDERLY FASHION.
A PART OF THE COMPLEX HAS BEEN INFIL-TRATED.
BREEEE
THE ENEMY WILL BE RE-PELLED IN NO TIME.
BREEEE
PLEASE FOLLOW OUR IN-STRUC-TIONS AND ...
BREEEE
DON'T PUSH! HURRY UP!
KEEP CALM! QUICK!
Papa, Mama-aa!
Waaah
WE HAVE BRAVE SOLDIERS PROTECTING US, OKAY?
WE'LL BE SAFE IN A SHEL-TER!
NO NEED TO BE SCARED!
DOOOM
DON'T STOP TO LOOK!
HURRY, KEEP GOING!

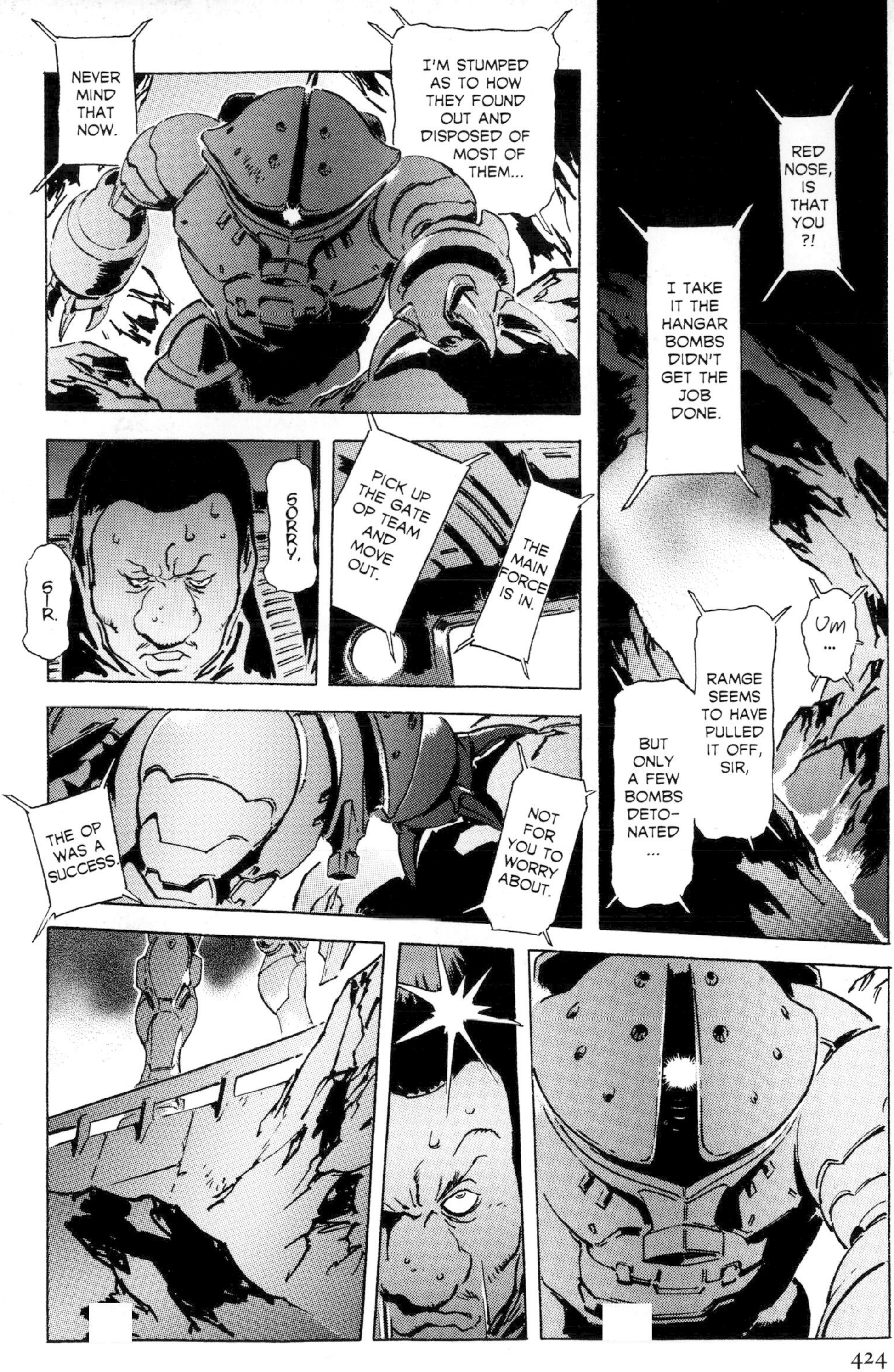
RED NOSE, IS THAT YOU?!
I TAKE IT THE HANGAR BOMBS DIDN'T GET THE JOB DONE.
UM...
RAMGE SEEMS TO HAVE PULLED IT OFF, SIR,
BUT ONLY A FEW BOMBS DETONATED...
I'M STUMPED AS TO HOW THEY FOUND OUT AND DISPOSED OF MOST OF THEM...
NEVER MIND THAT NOW.
THE MAIN FORCE IS IN.
PICK UP THE GATE OP TEAM AND MOVE OUT.
SORRY,
SIR.
NOT FOR YOU TO WORRY ABOUT.
THE OP WAS A SUCCESS.

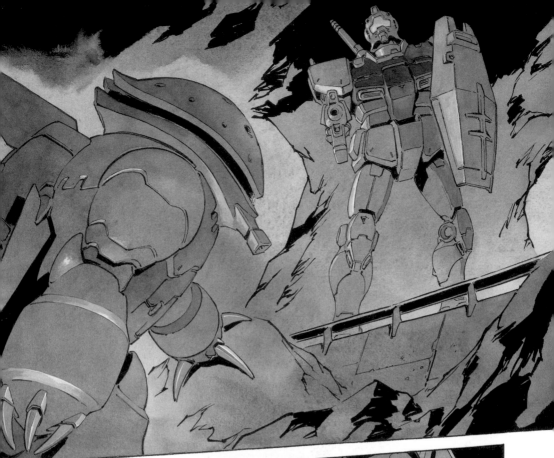

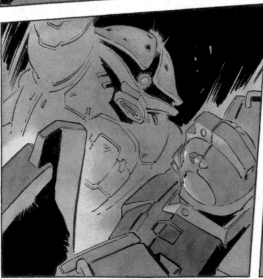

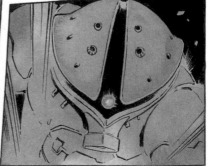

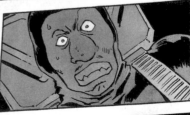

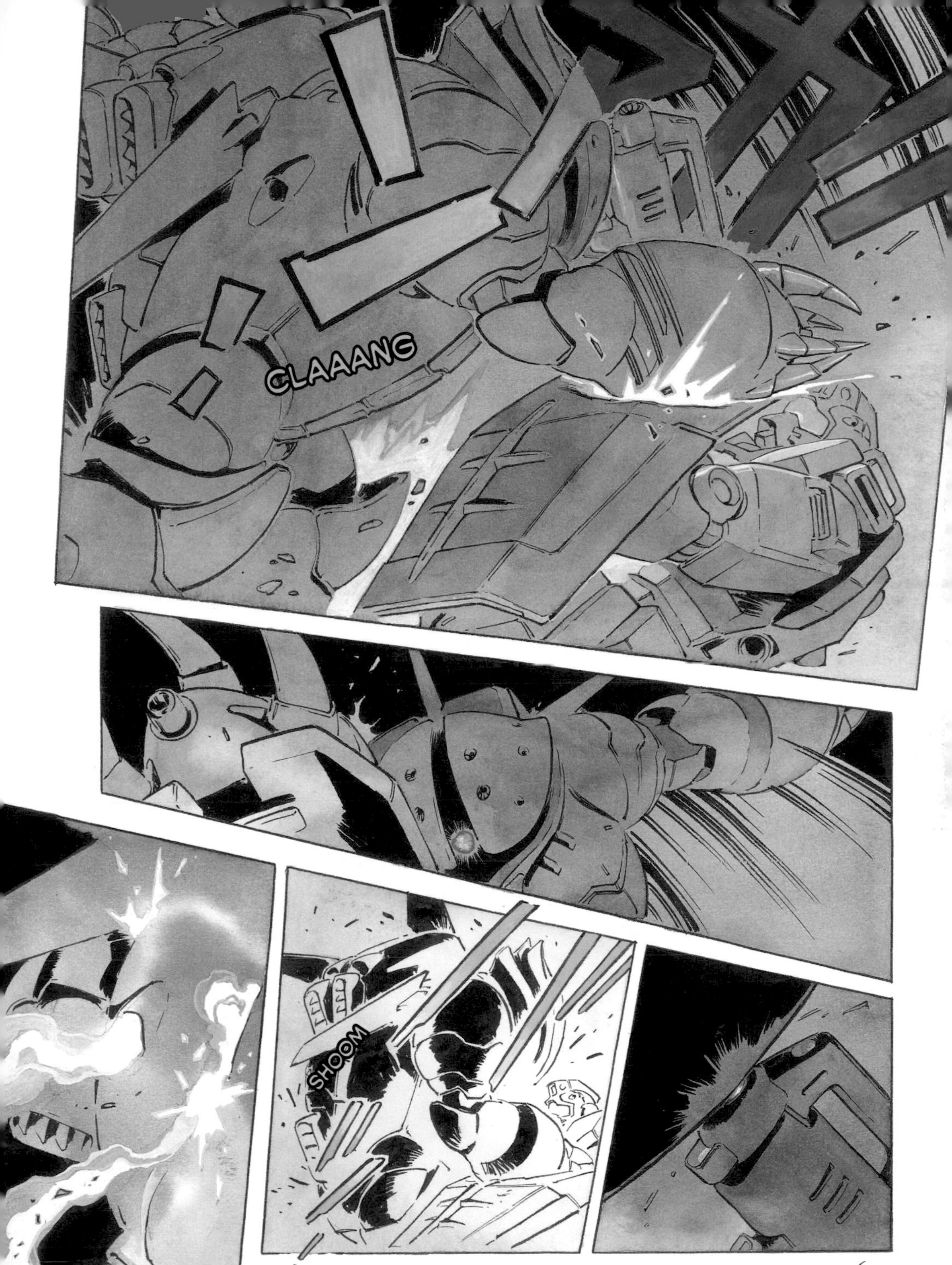
CLAAANG
SHOOM

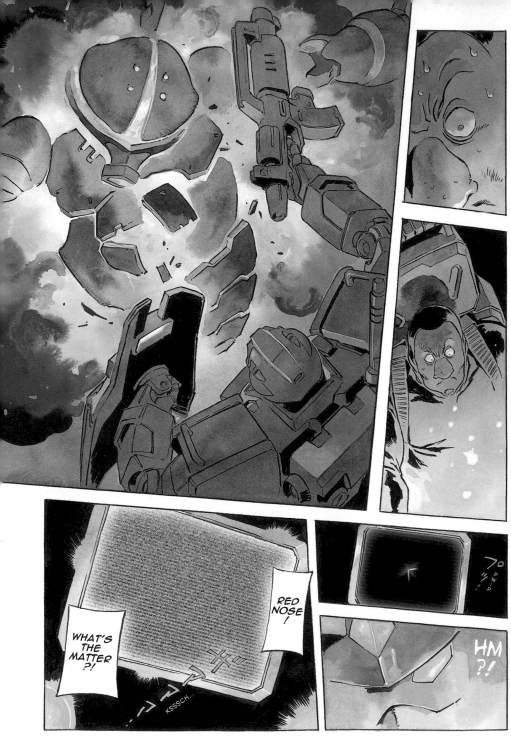

RED
NOSE
!

WHAT'S
THE
MATTER
?!

KSSSCH...

HM
?!

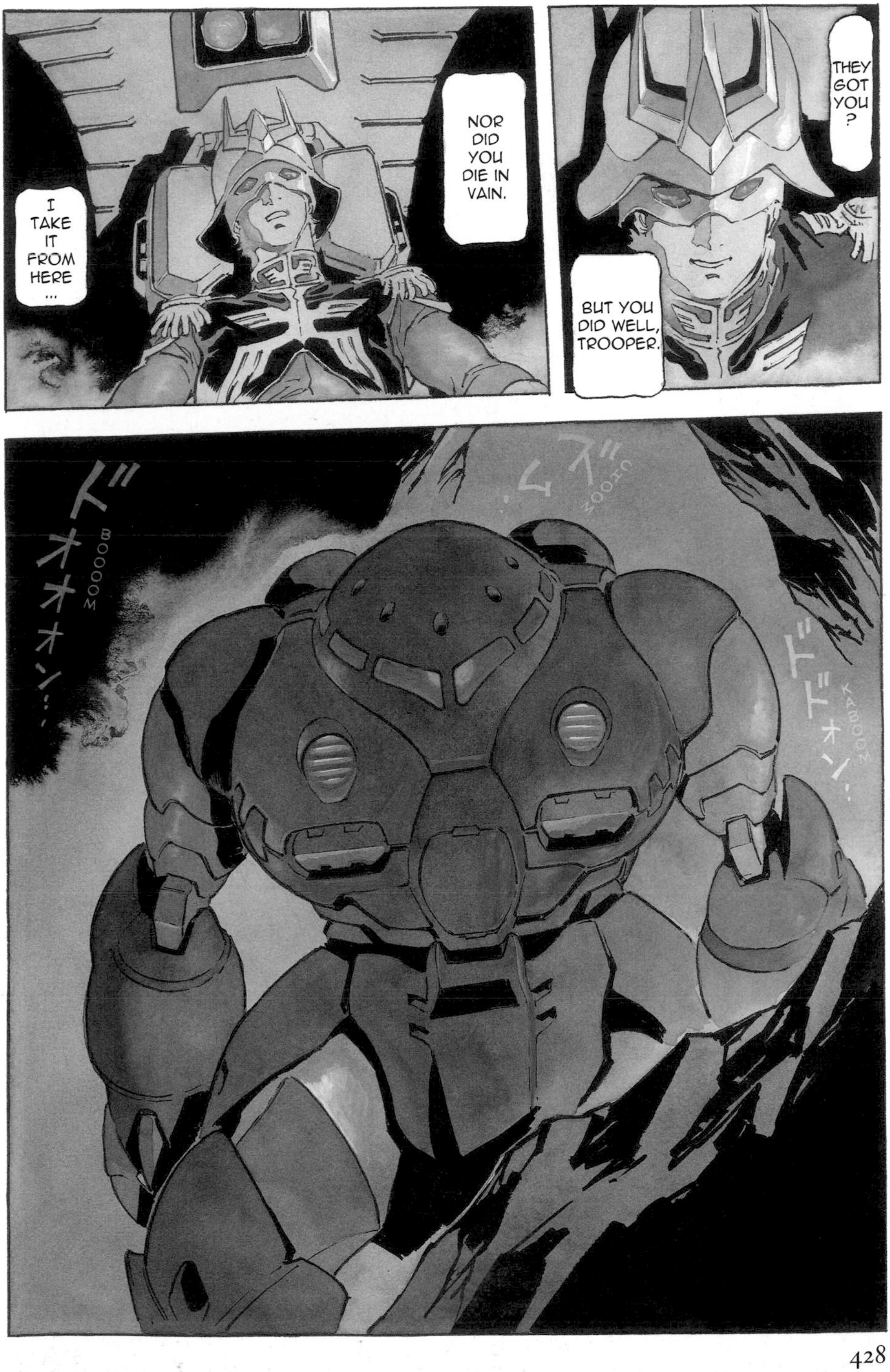
THEY GOT YOU?
BUT YOU DID WELL, TROOPER.
NOR DID YOU DIE IN VAIN.
I TAKE IT FROM HERE...
ズム.. CHOOM
ドドオン.. KABOOM
ドオオオン.. BOOOOM

SECTION IX

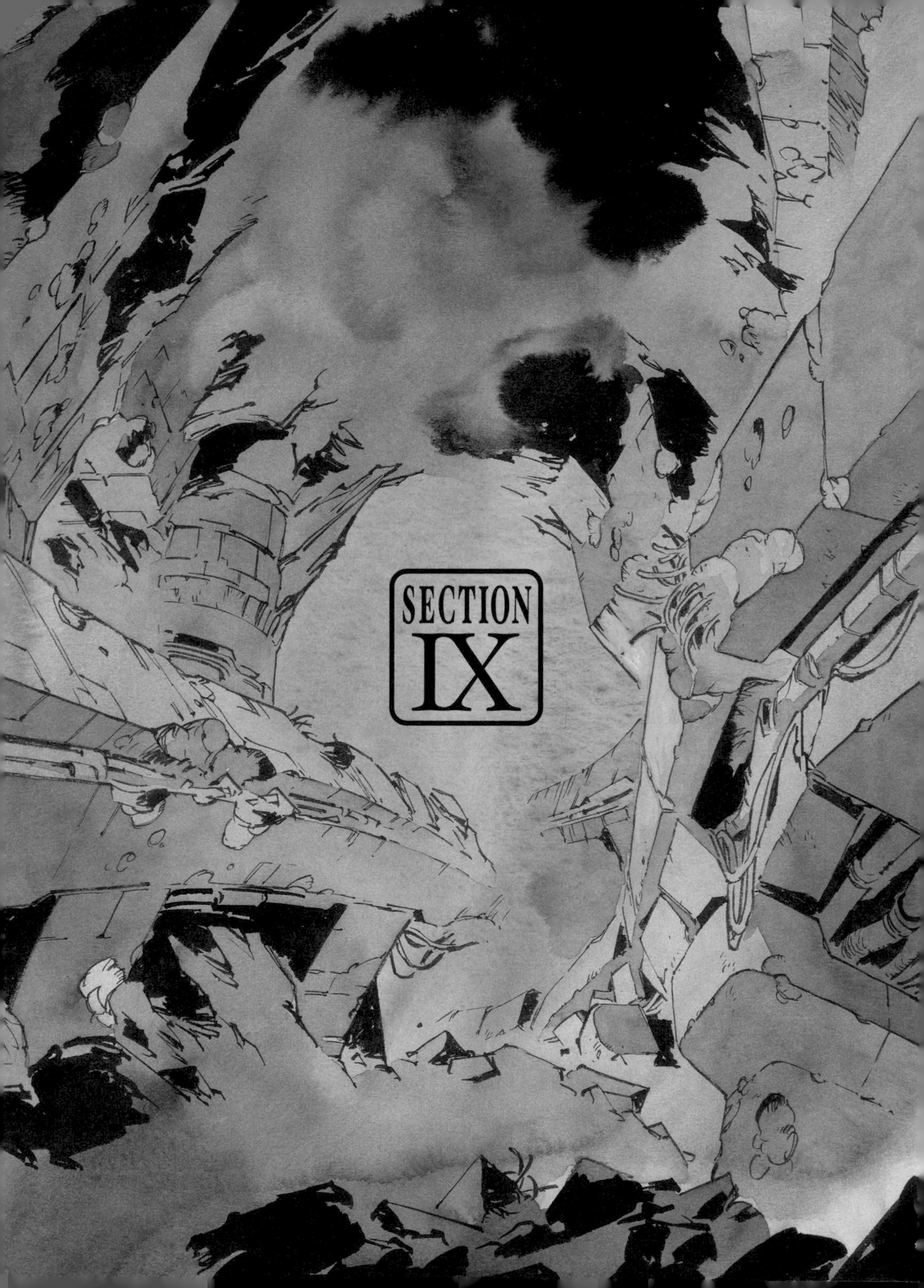

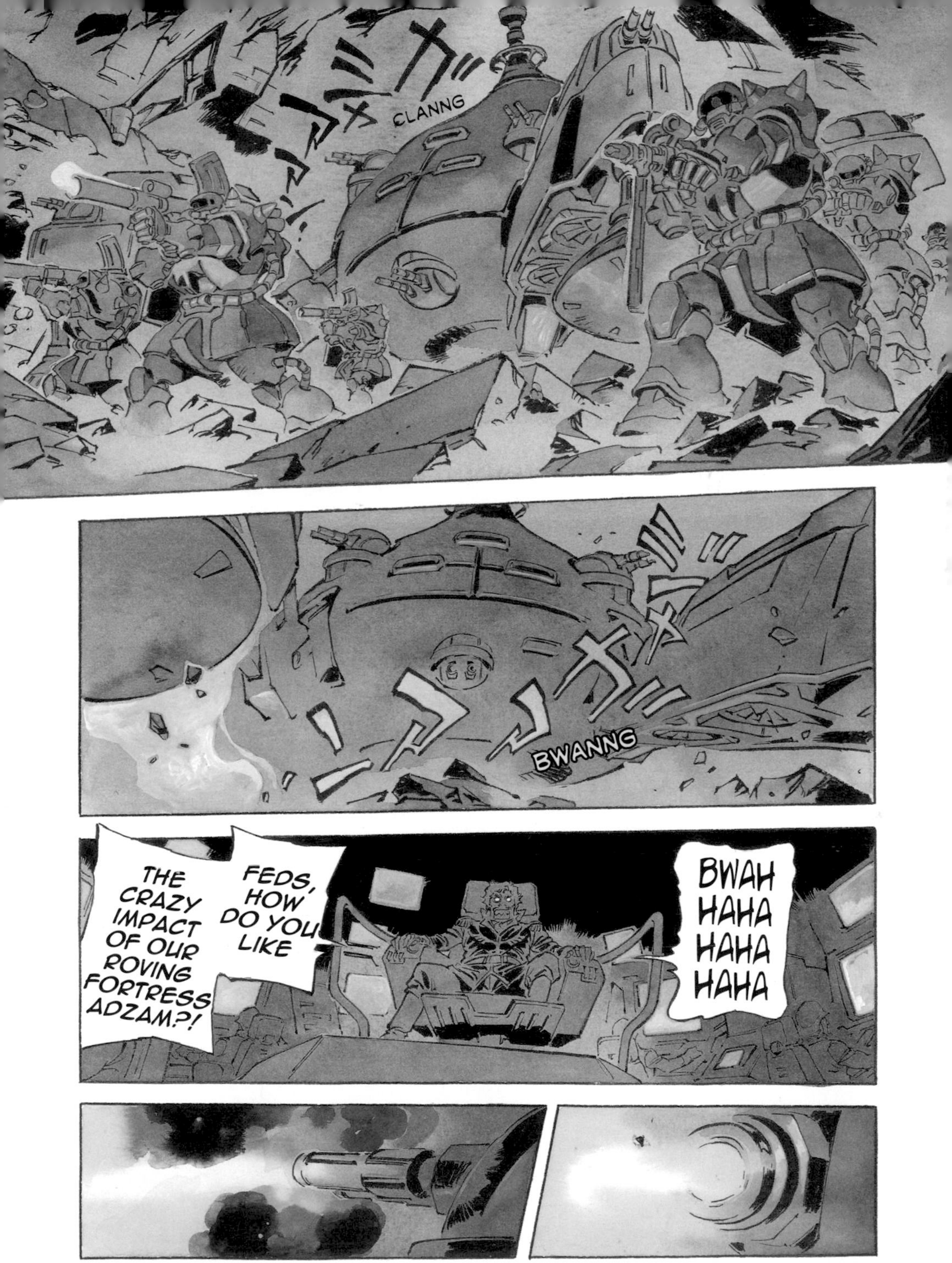
CLANNG
BWANNG
BWAH HAHA HAHA HAHA
FEDS, HOW DO YOU LIKE
THE CRAZY IMPACT OF OUR ROVING FORTRESS ADZAM?!

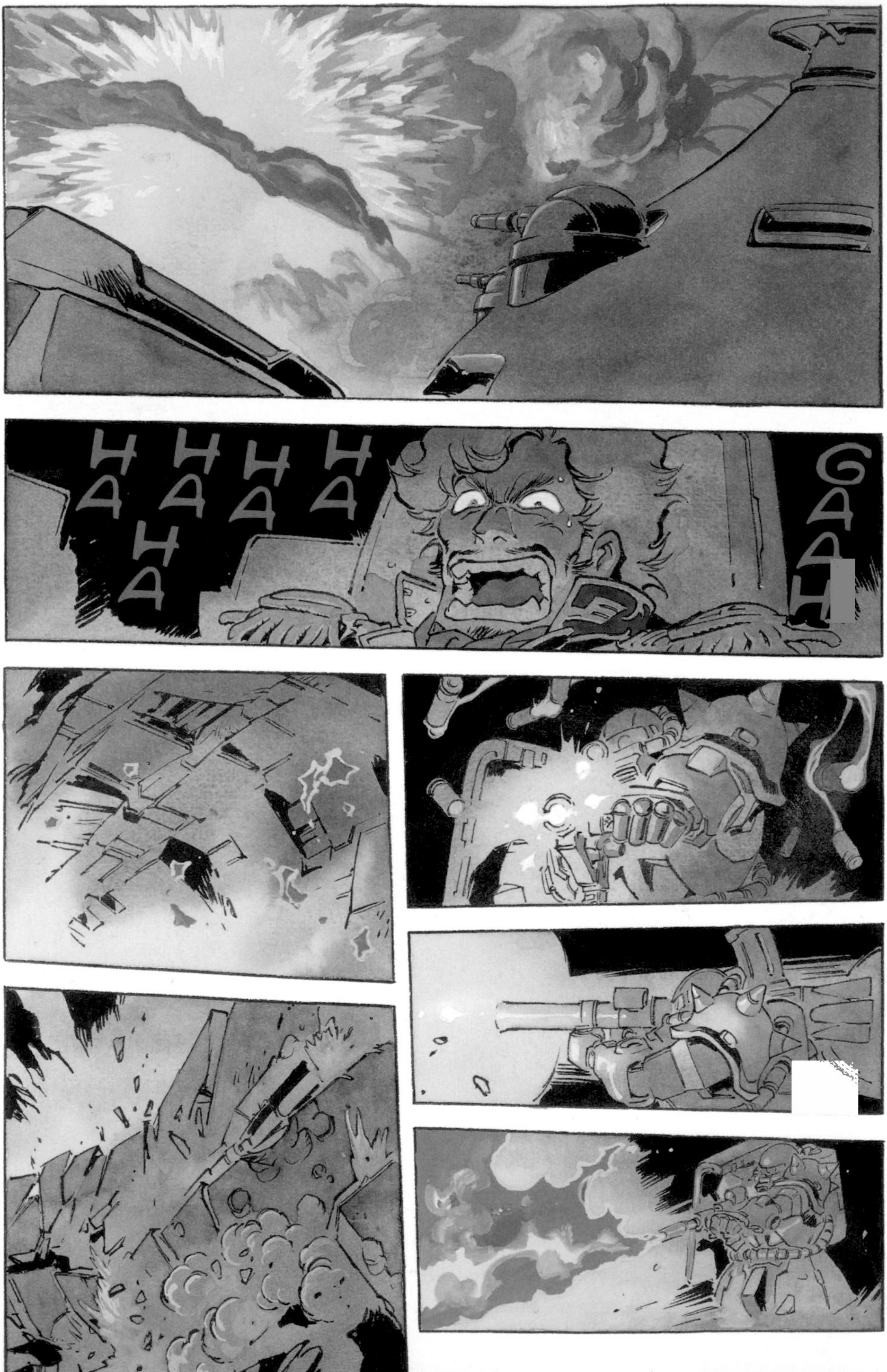
GAAH
HA
HA
HA
HA
HA

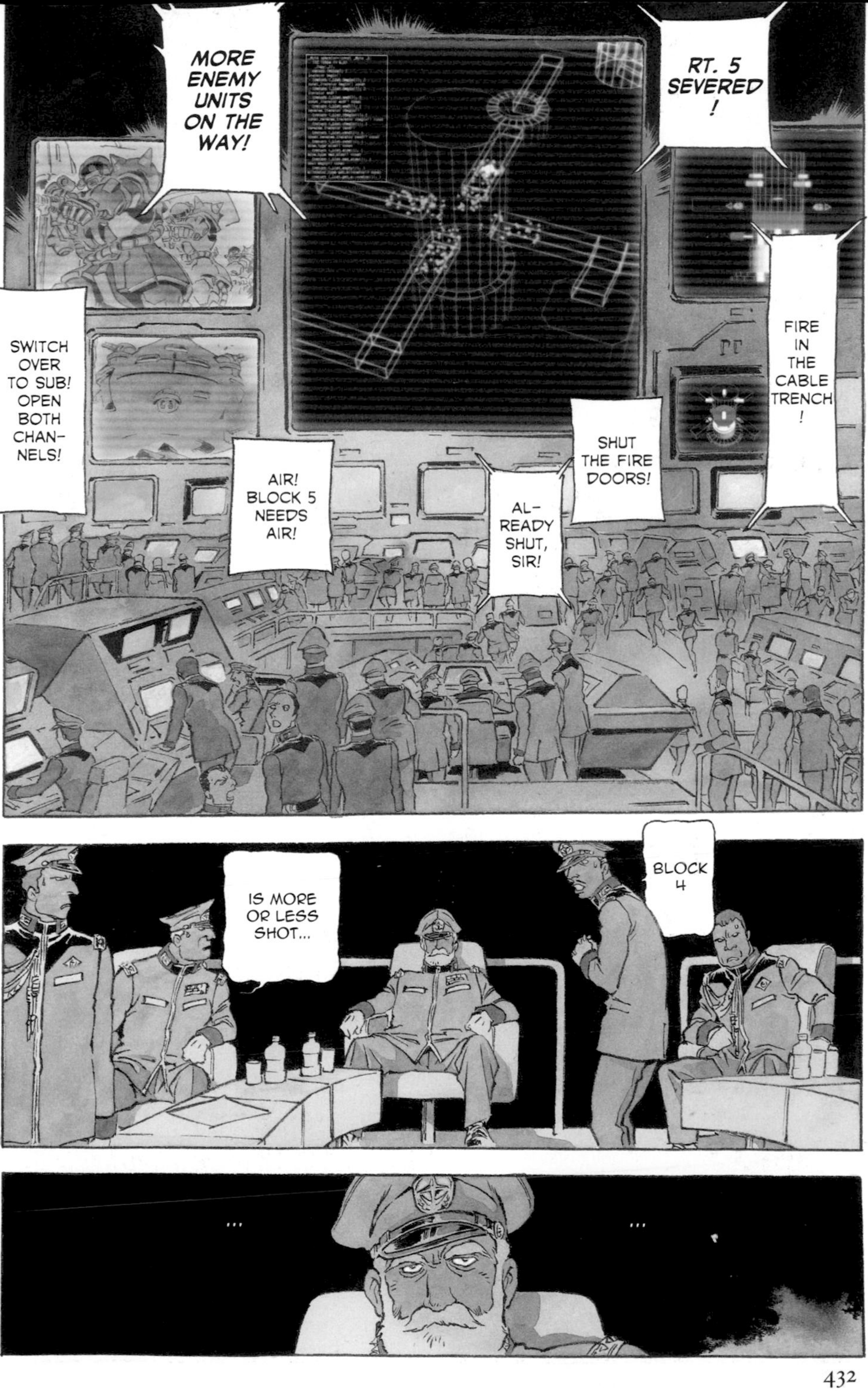
RT. 5 SEVERED!
MORE ENEMY UNITS ON THE WAY!
FIRE IN THE CABLE TRENCH!
SHUT THE FIRE DOORS!
ALREADY SHUT, SIR!
AIR! BLOCK 5 NEEDS AIR!
SWITCH OVER TO SUB! OPEN BOTH CHANNELS!
BLOCK 4
IS MORE OR LESS SHOT...
...
...

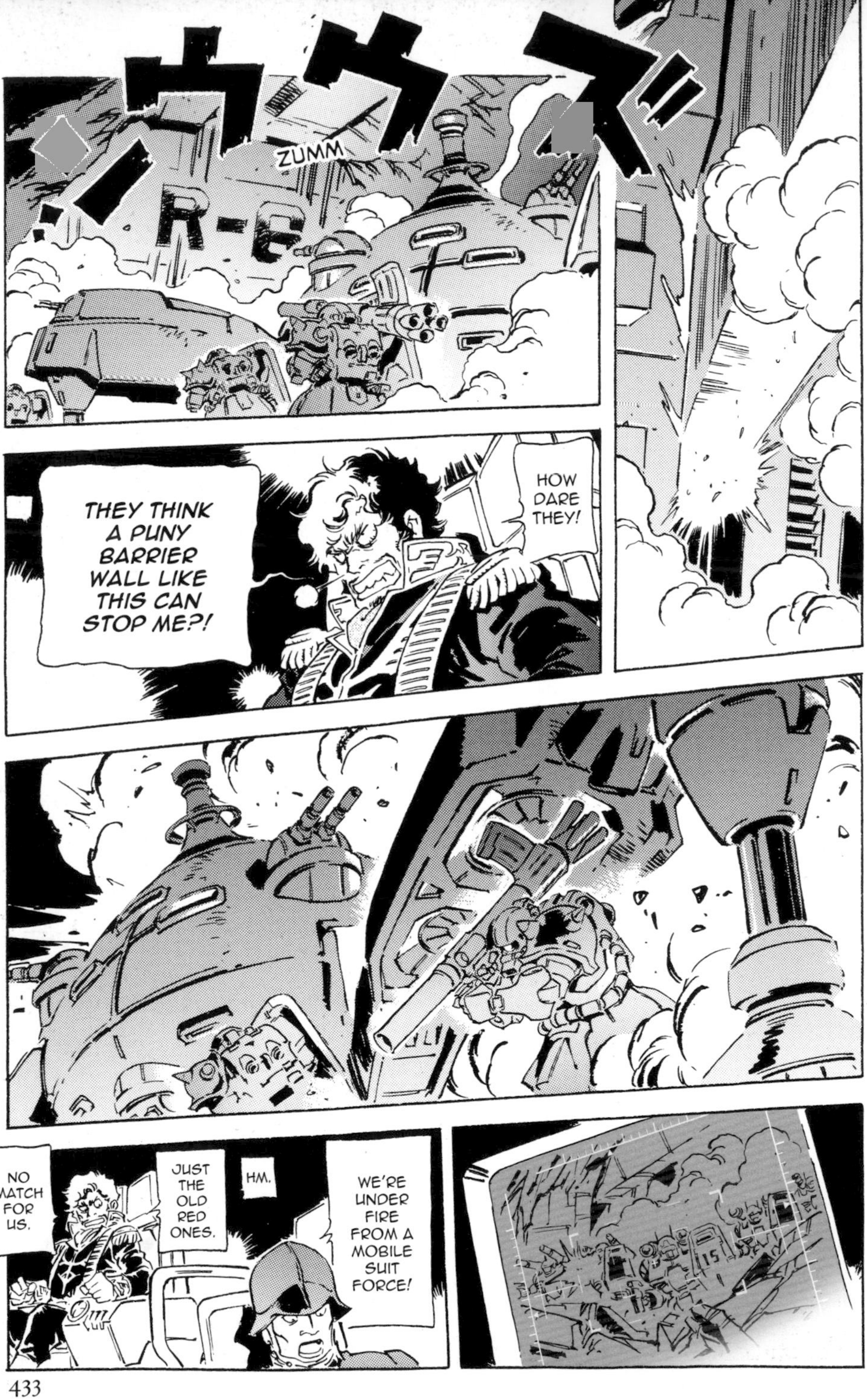
ZUMM
HOW DARE THEY!
THEY THINK A PUNY BARRIER WALL LIKE THIS CAN STOP ME?!
WE'RE UNDER FIRE FROM A MOBILE SUIT FORCE!
HM.
JUST THE OLD RED ONES.
NO MATCH FOR US.

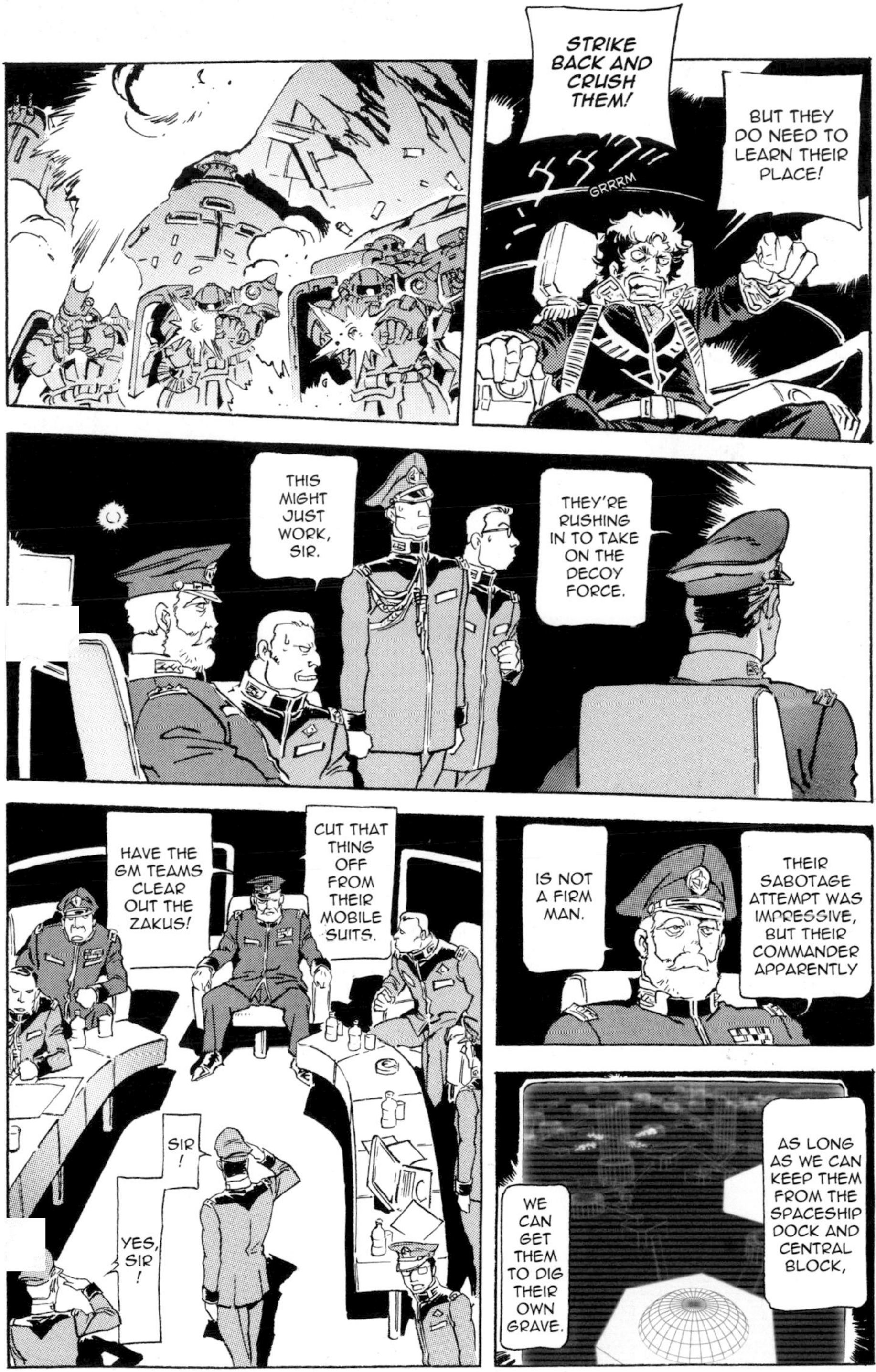

STRIKE BACK AND CRUSH THEM!
BUT THEY DO NEED TO LEARN THEIR PLACE!
GRRRM
THEY'RE RUSHING IN TO TAKE ON THE DECOY FORCE.
THIS MIGHT JUST WORK, SIR.
THEIR SABOTAGE ATTEMPT WAS IMPRESSIVE, BUT THEIR COMMANDER APPARENTLY
IS NOT A FIRM MAN.
AS LONG AS WE CAN KEEP THEM FROM THE SPACESHIP DOCK AND CENTRAL BLOCK,
WE CAN GET THEM TO DIG THEIR OWN GRAVE.
CUT THAT THING OFF FROM THEIR MOBILE SUITS.
HAVE THE GM TEAMS CLEAR OUT THE ZAKUS!
SIR!
YES, SIR!

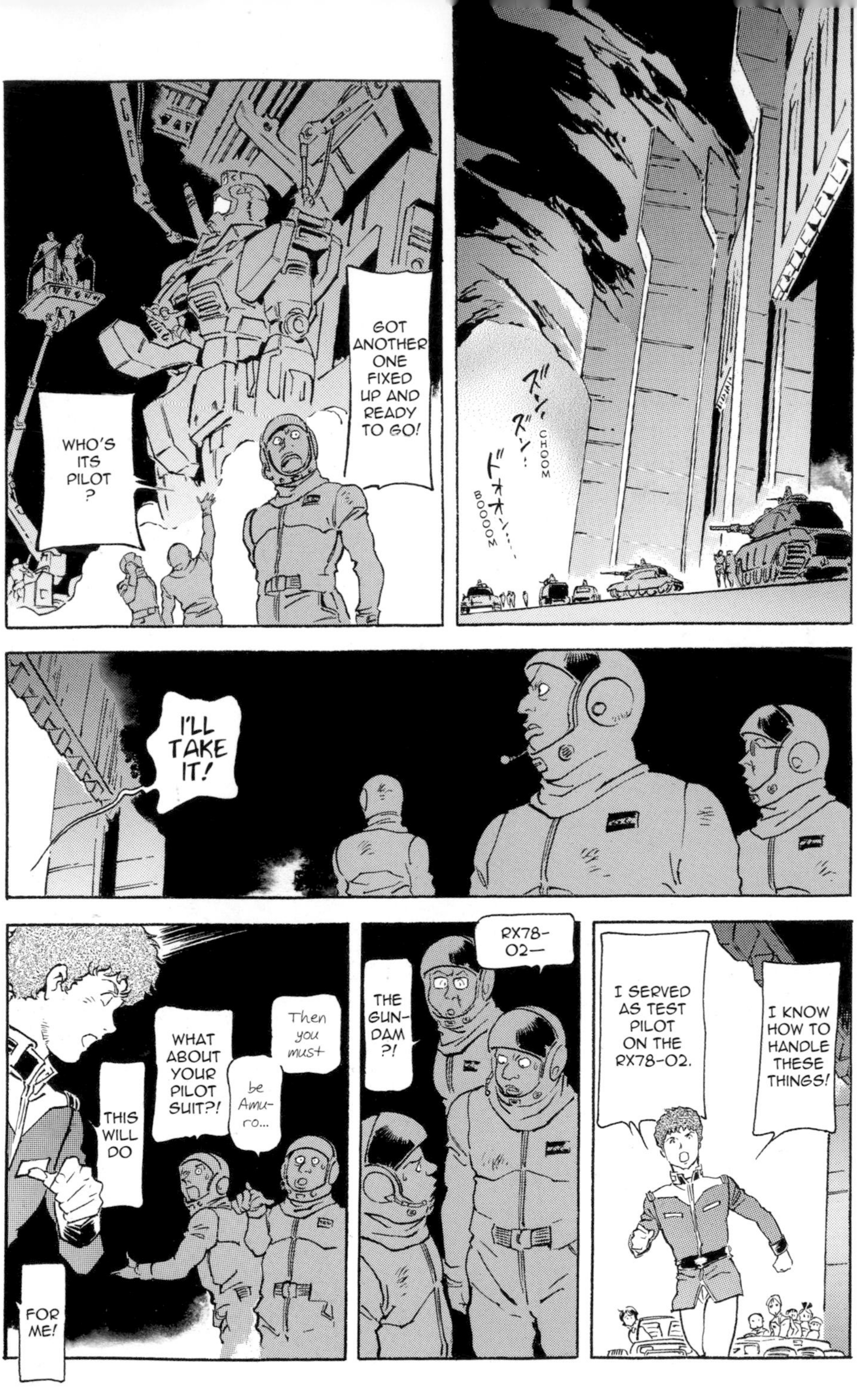
ズン、ズン…
CHOOM
ドオオン……
BOOOOM
GOT ANOTHER ONE FIXED UP AND READY TO GO!
WHO'S ITS PILOT?
I'LL TAKE IT!
I KNOW HOW TO HANDLE THESE THINGS!
I SERVED AS TEST PILOT ON THE RX78-02.
RX78-02—
THE GUNDAM?!
Then you must be Amuro...
WHAT ABOUT YOUR PILOT SUIT?!
THIS WILL DO
FOR ME!

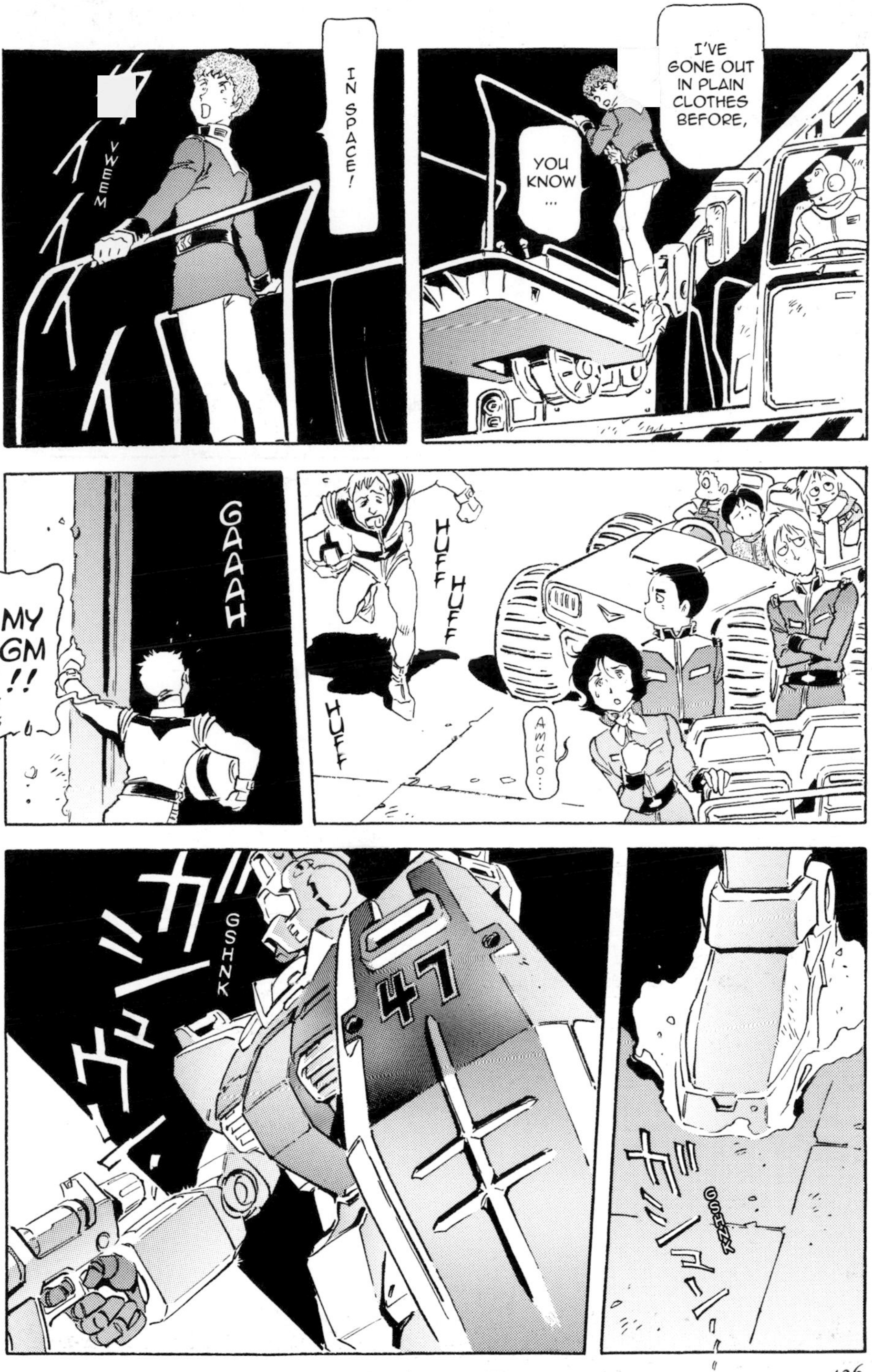
I'VE GONE OUT IN PLAIN CLOTHES BEFORE,
YOU KNOW ...
IN SPACE!
VWEEM
HUFF
HUFF
HUFF
HUFF
Amuro...
GAAAH
MY GM!!
GSHNK
GSHNK

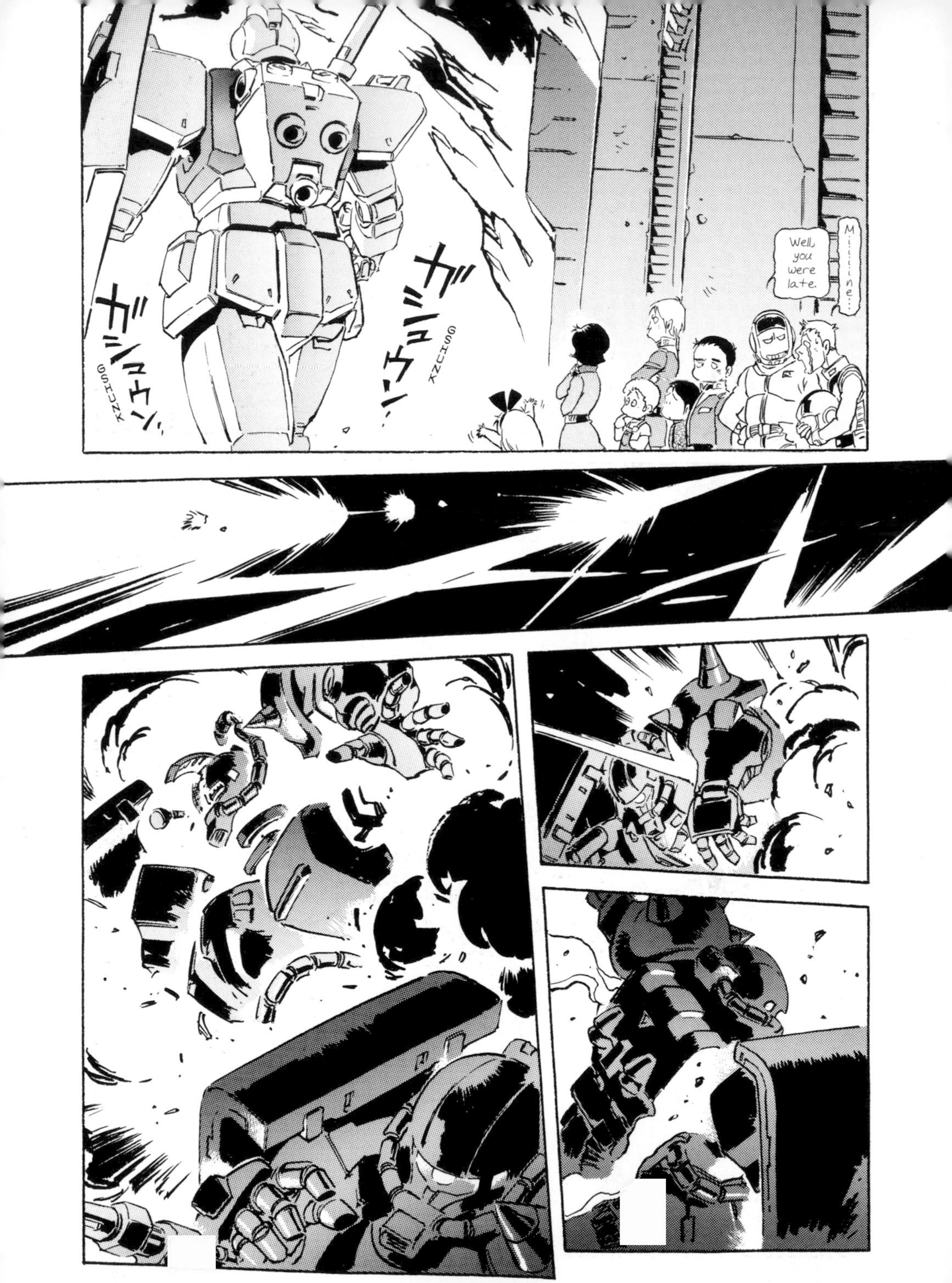
M...i...i...ne...
Well, you were late.
ガシュウン!
GSHUNK
ガシュウン!
GSHUNK

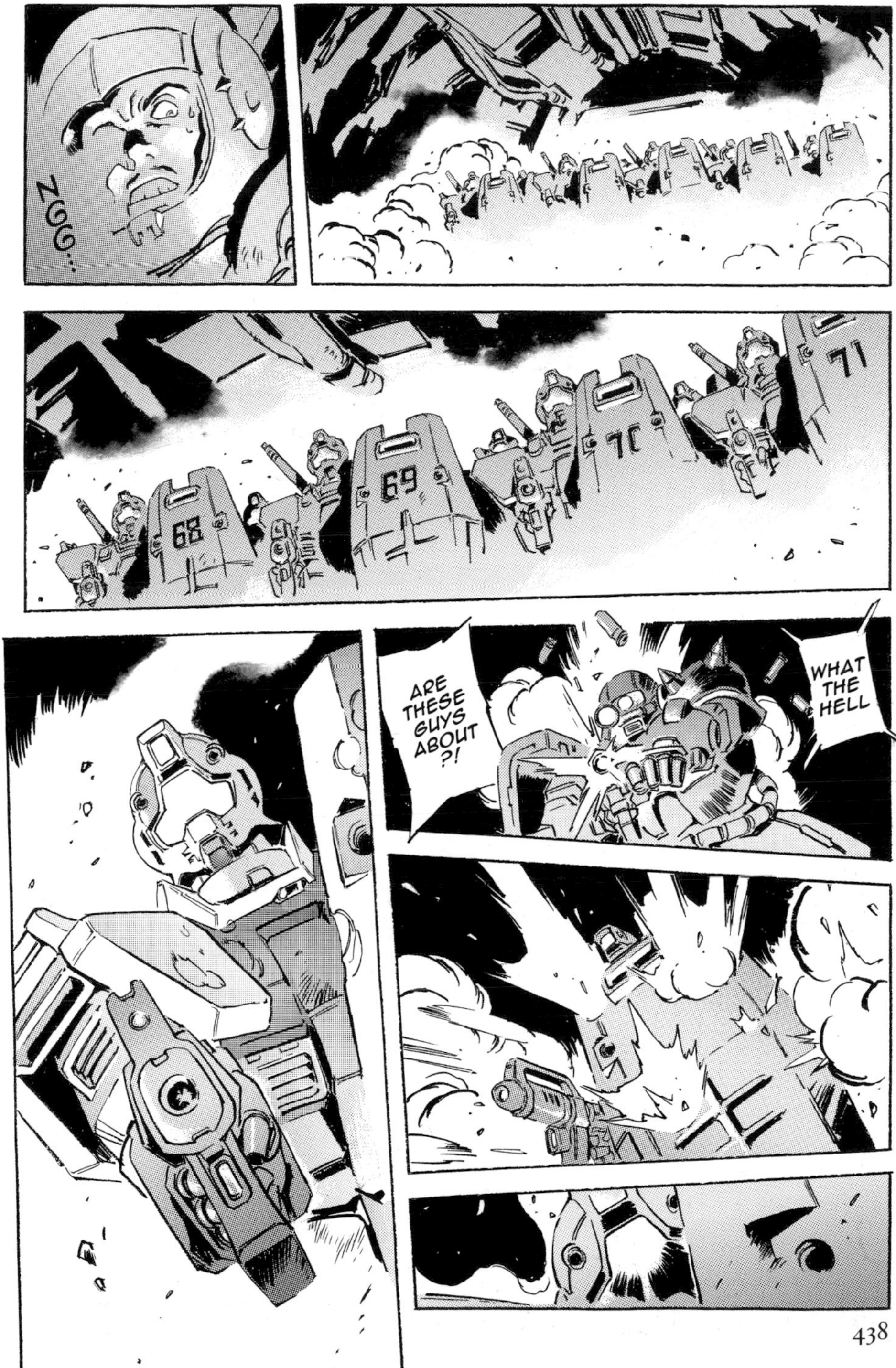
ZGG...
71
70
69
68
WHAT THE HELL
ARE THESE GUYS ABOUT ?!

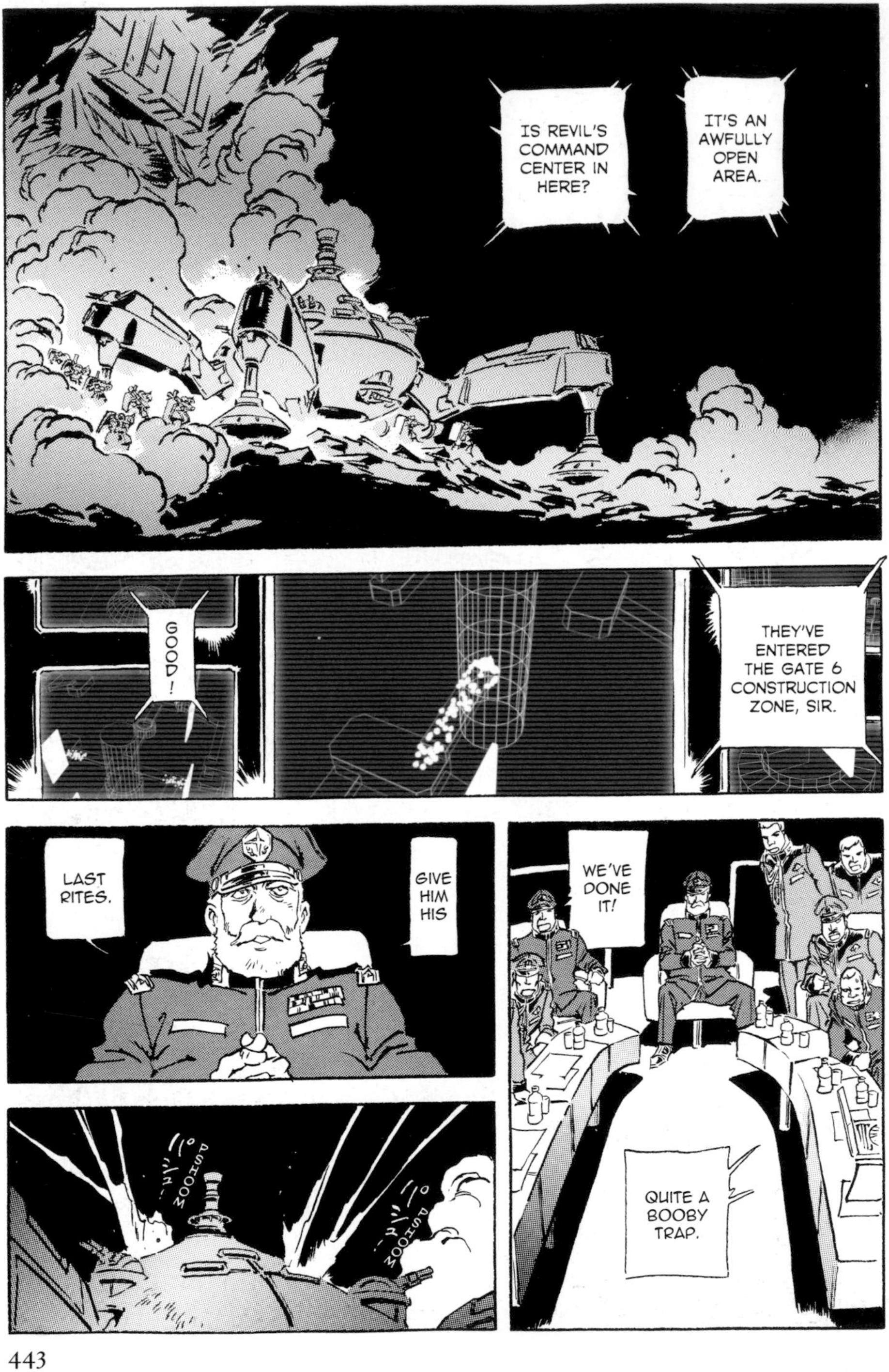
IT'S AN AWFULLY OPEN AREA.
IS REVIL'S COMMAND CENTER IN HERE?
THEY'VE ENTERED THE GATE 6 CONSTRUCTION ZONE, SIR.
GOOD!
WE'VE DONE IT!
QUITE A BOOBY TRAP.
GIVE HIM HIS
LAST RITES.
PSHOOM
パシュ…
PSHOOM
パシュ…

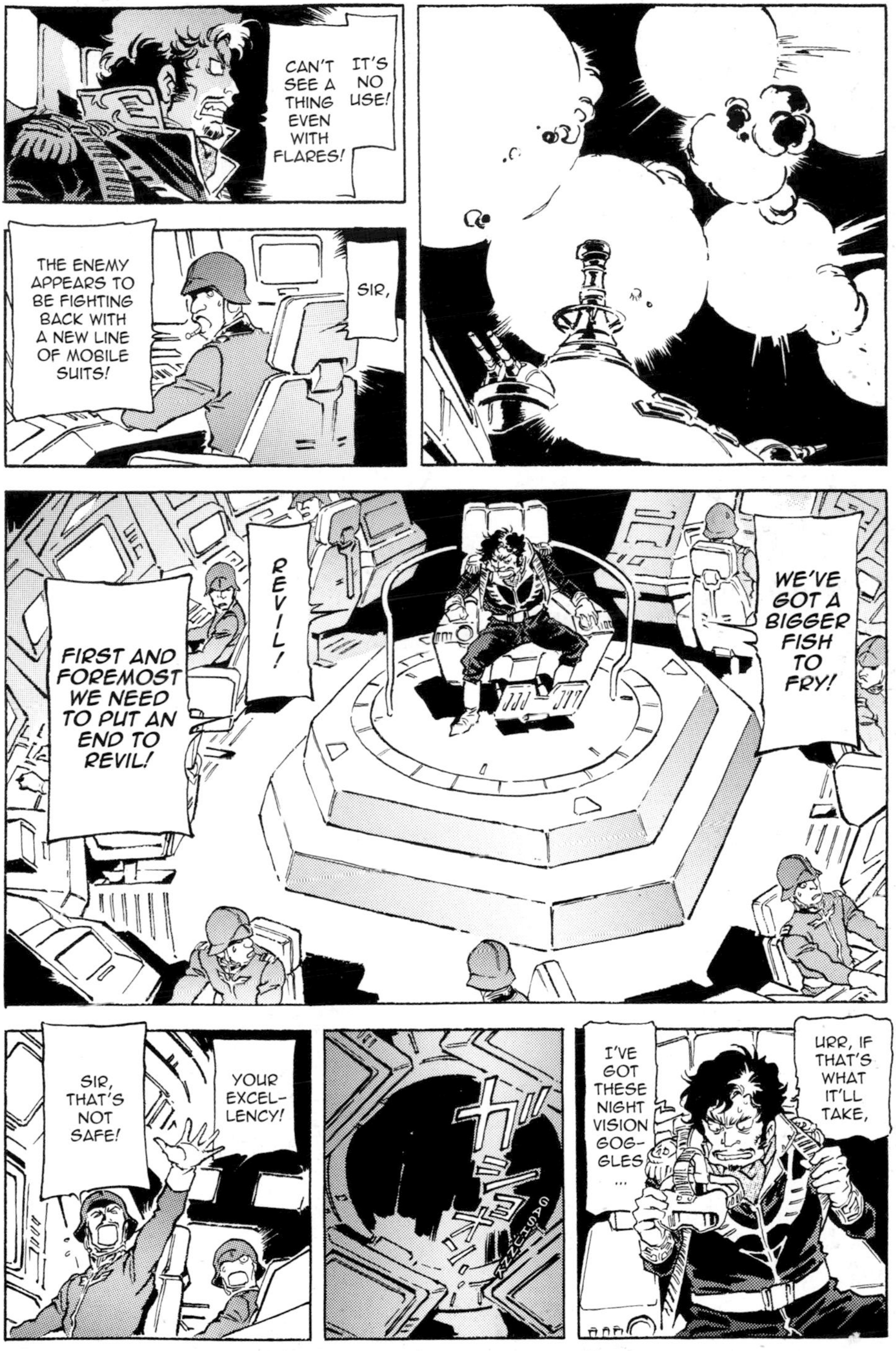
IT'S NO USE!
CAN'T SEE A THING EVEN WITH FLARES!
SIR,
THE ENEMY APPEARS TO BE FIGHTING BACK WITH A NEW LINE OF MOBILE SUITS!
WE'VE GOT A BIGGER FISH TO FRY!
REVIL!
FIRST AND FOREMOST WE NEED TO PUT AN END TO REVIL!
URR, IF THAT'S WHAT IT'LL TAKE,
I'VE GOT THESE NIGHT VISION GOGGLES...
YOUR EXCELLENCY!
SIR, THAT'S NOT SAFE!

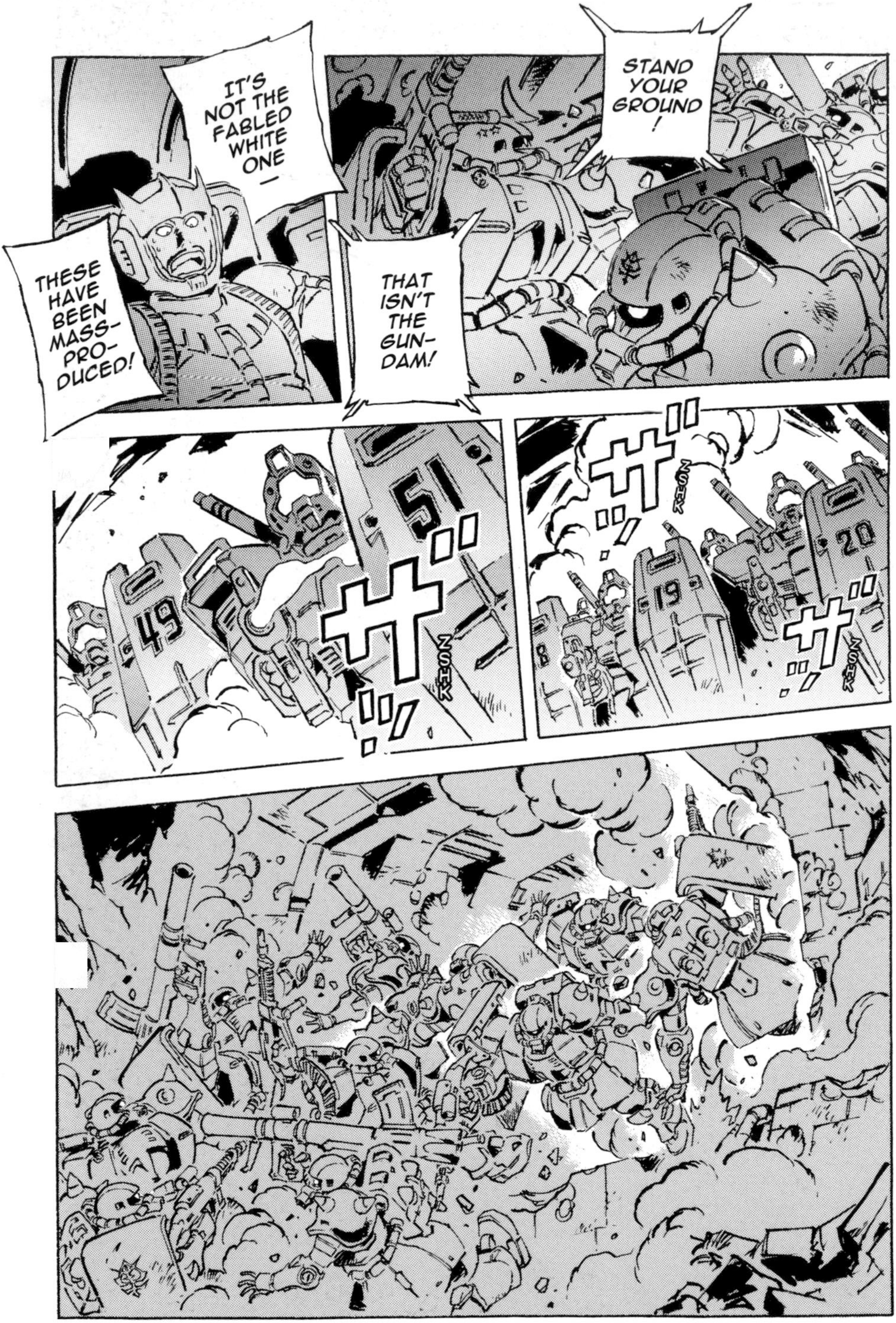
STAND YOUR GROUND!
THAT ISN'T THE GUNDAM!
IT'S NOT THE FABLED WHITE ONE—
THESE HAVE BEEN MASS-PRODUCED!
ザッ
ZSHK
ザッ
ZSHK
ザッ
ZSHK

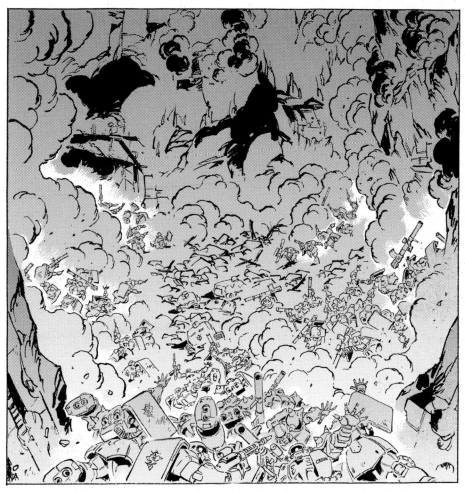

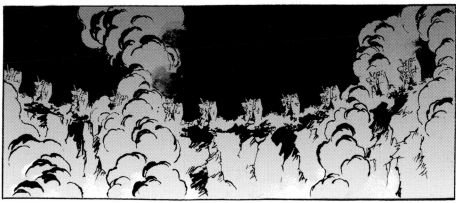

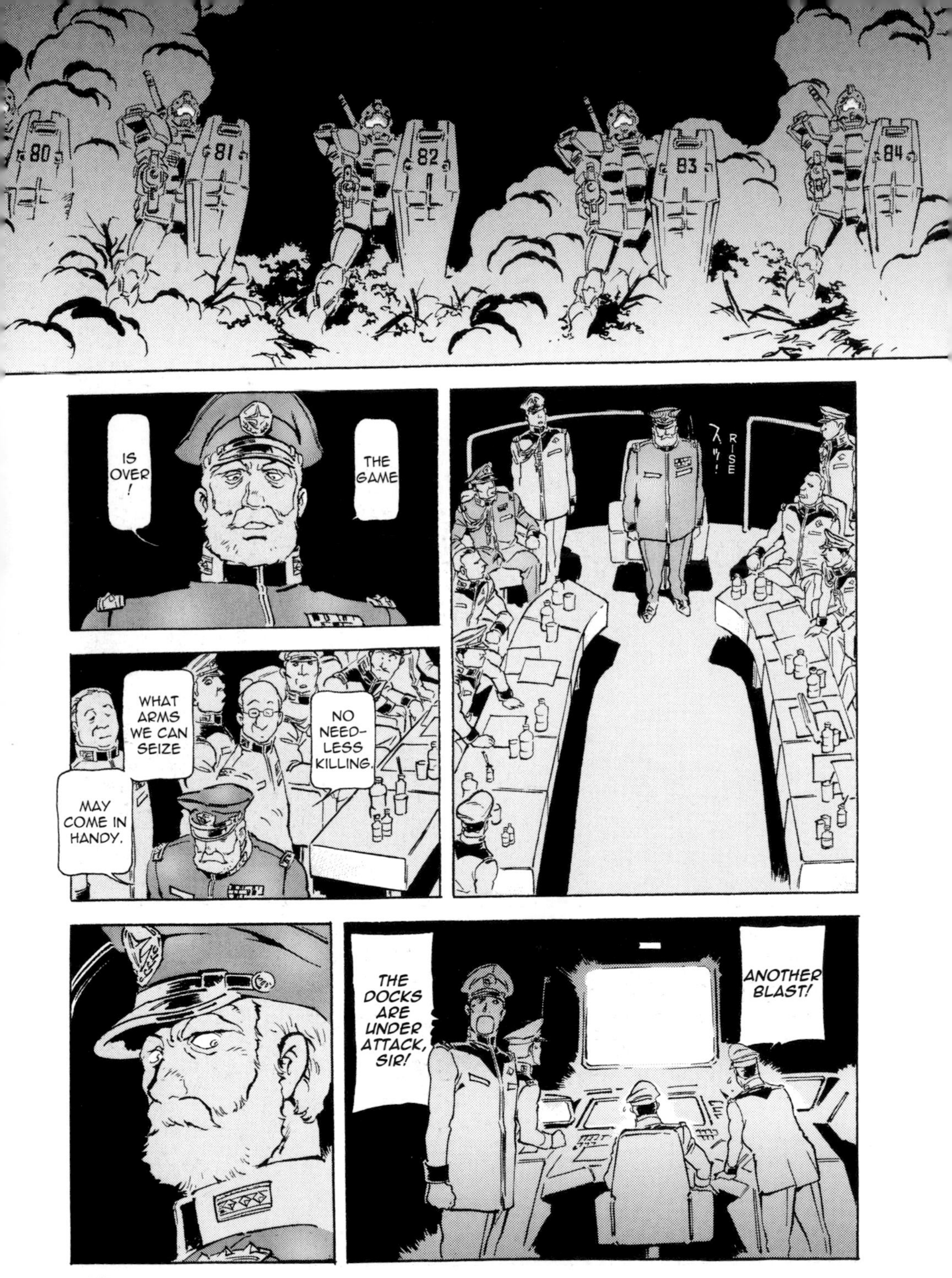
80
81
82
83
84
RISE
THE GAME
IS OVER!
NO NEEDLESS KILLING.
WHAT ARMS WE CAN SEIZE
MAY COME IN HANDY.
ANOTHER BLAST!
THE DOCKS ARE UNDER ATTACK, SIR!

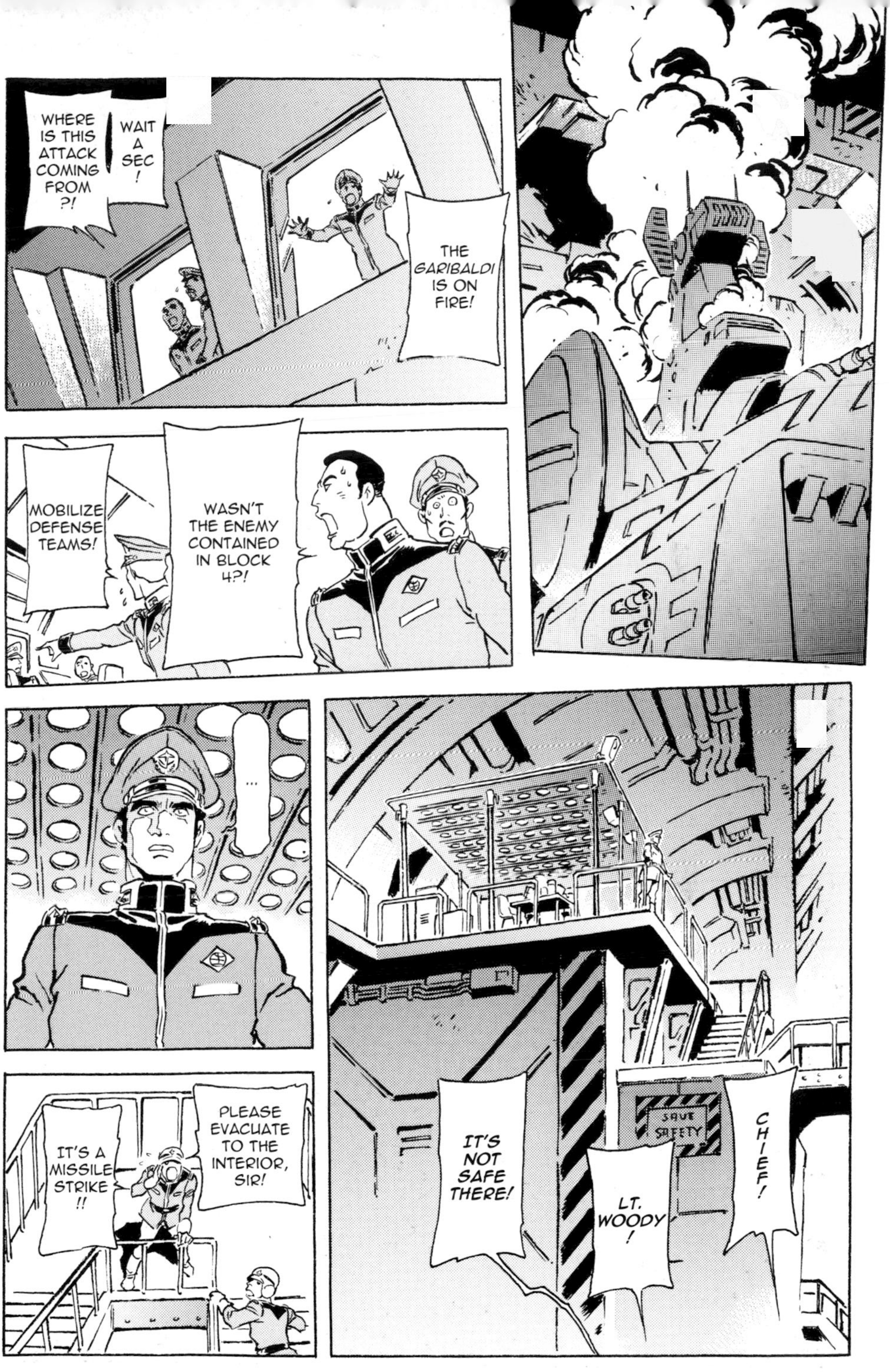
THE GARIBALDI IS ON FIRE!
WAIT A SEC!
WHERE IS THIS ATTACK COMING FROM?!
WASN'T THE ENEMY CONTAINED IN BLOCK 4?!
MOBILIZE DEFENSE TEAMS!
CHIEF!
LT. WOODY!
SAFETY
IT'S NOT SAFE THERE!
...
PLEASE EVACUATE TO THE INTERIOR, SIR!
IT'S A MISSILE STRIKE!!

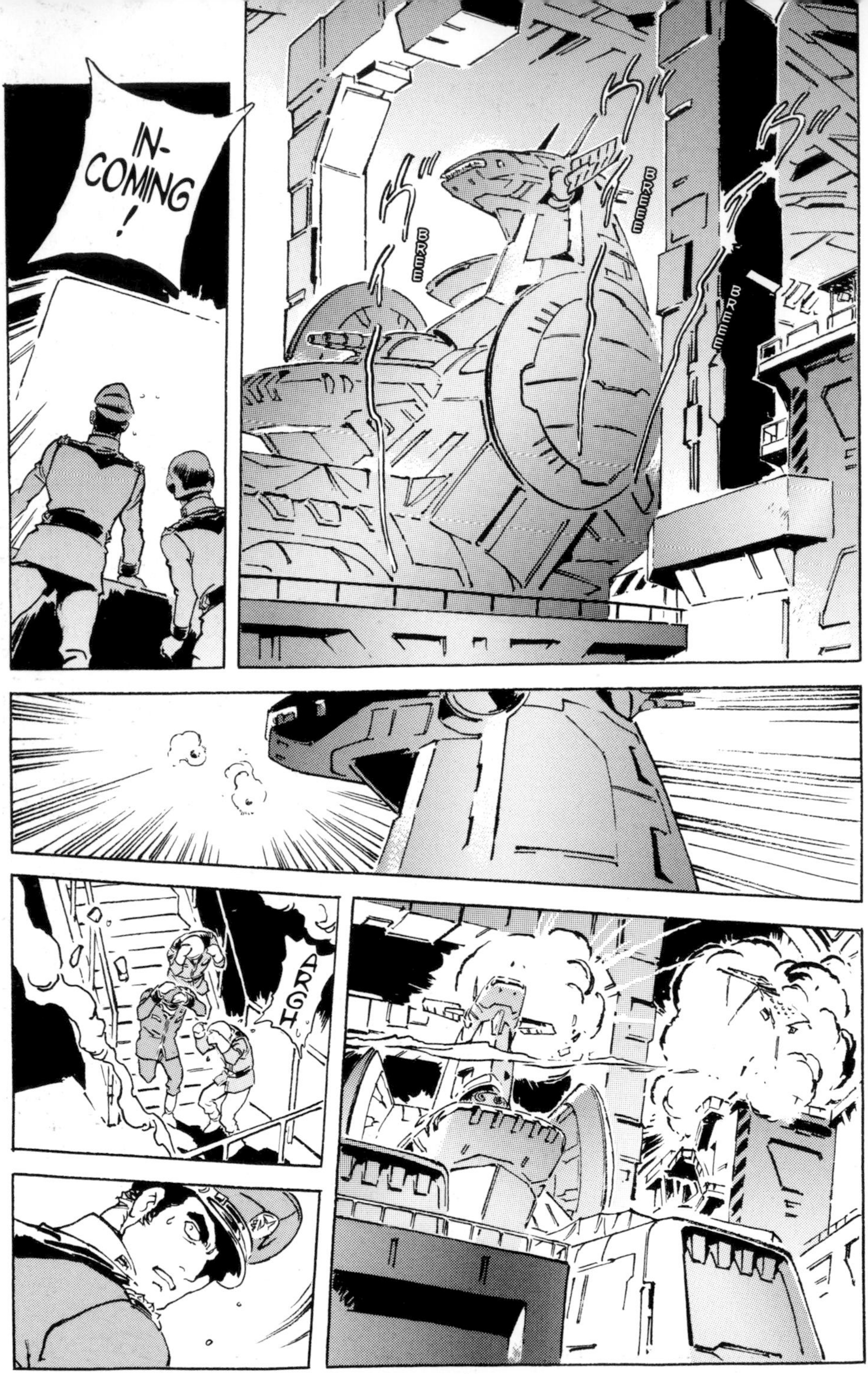
BREEEE
BREEE
BREE
IN-COMING!
ARGH

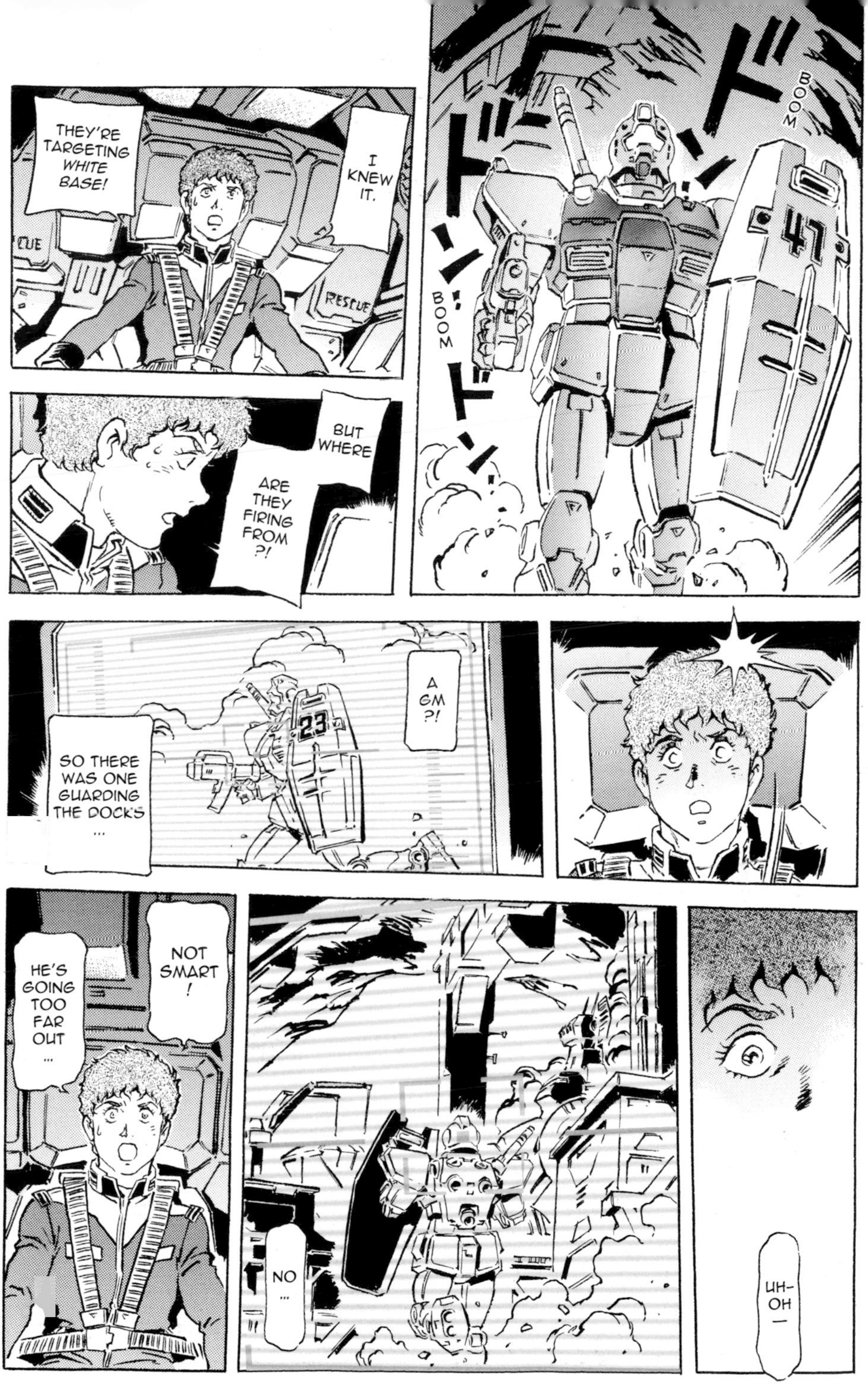
BOOM
BOOM
I KNEW IT.
THEY'RE TARGETING WHITE BASE!
BUT WHERE ARE THEY FIRING FROM?!
A GM?!
SO THERE WAS ONE GUARDING THE DOCKS...
UH-OH—
NO...
NOT SMART!
HE'S GOING TOO FAR OUT...

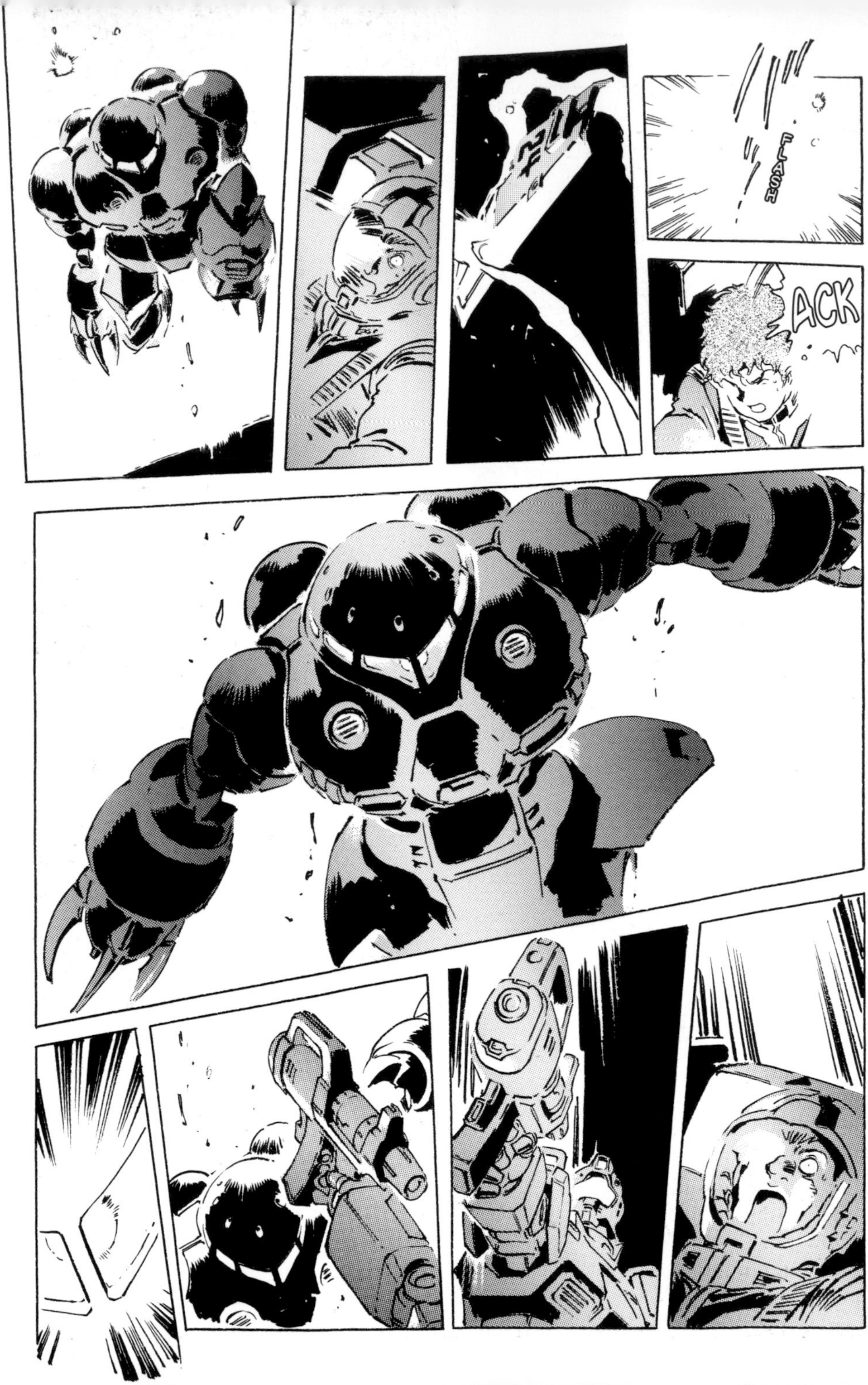
FLASH
ACK

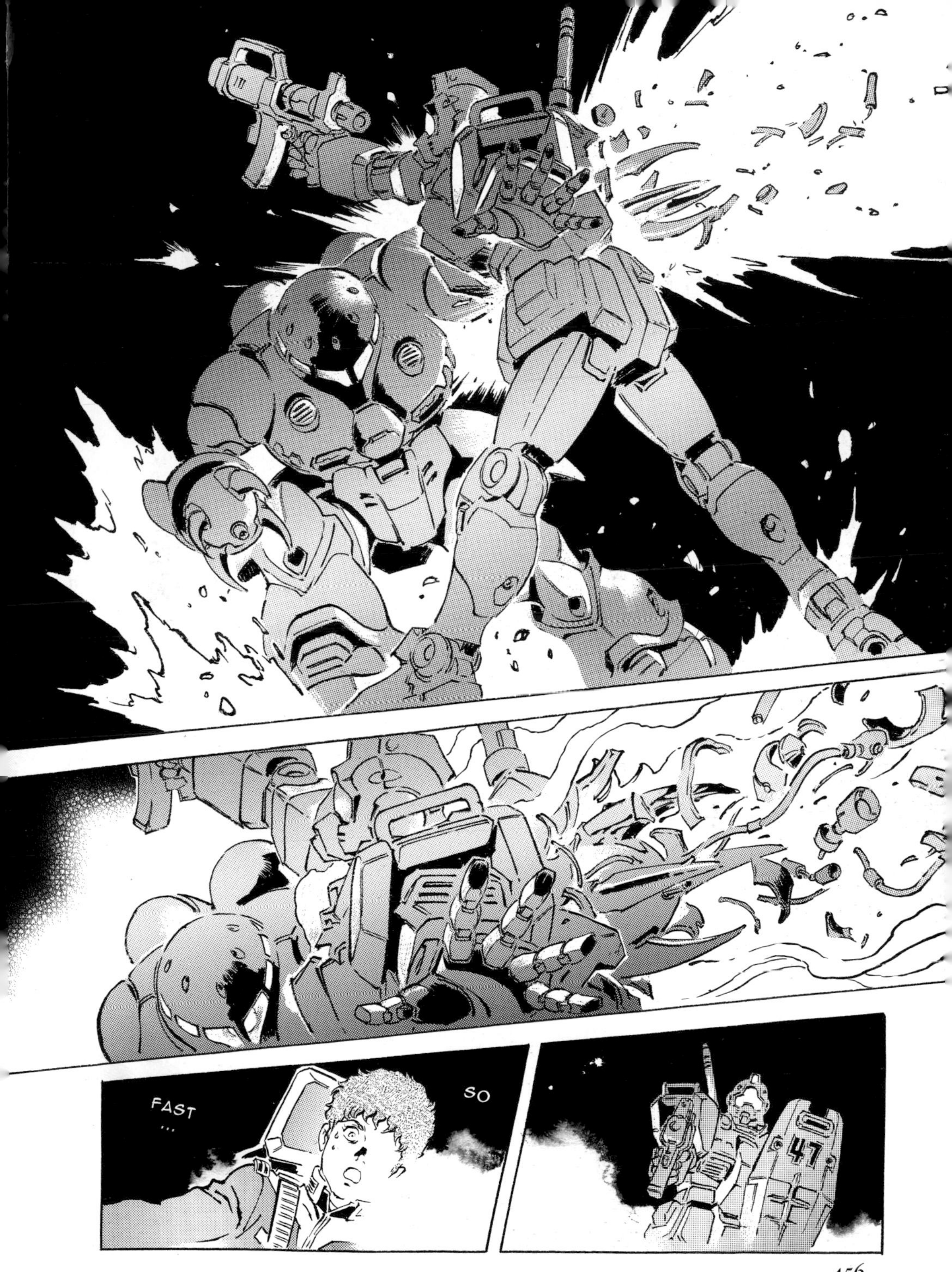
SO
FAST ...

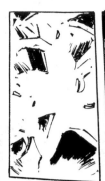
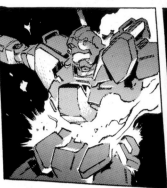
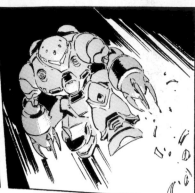
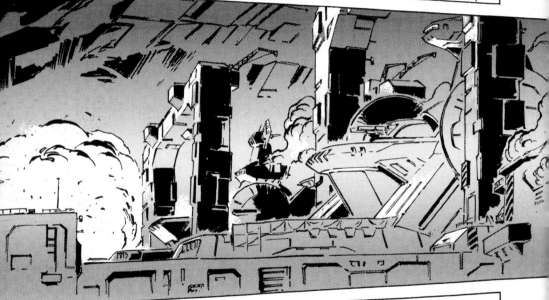
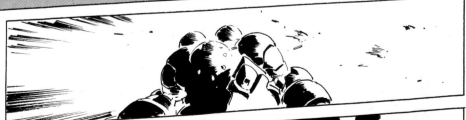
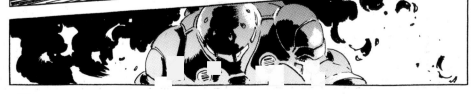

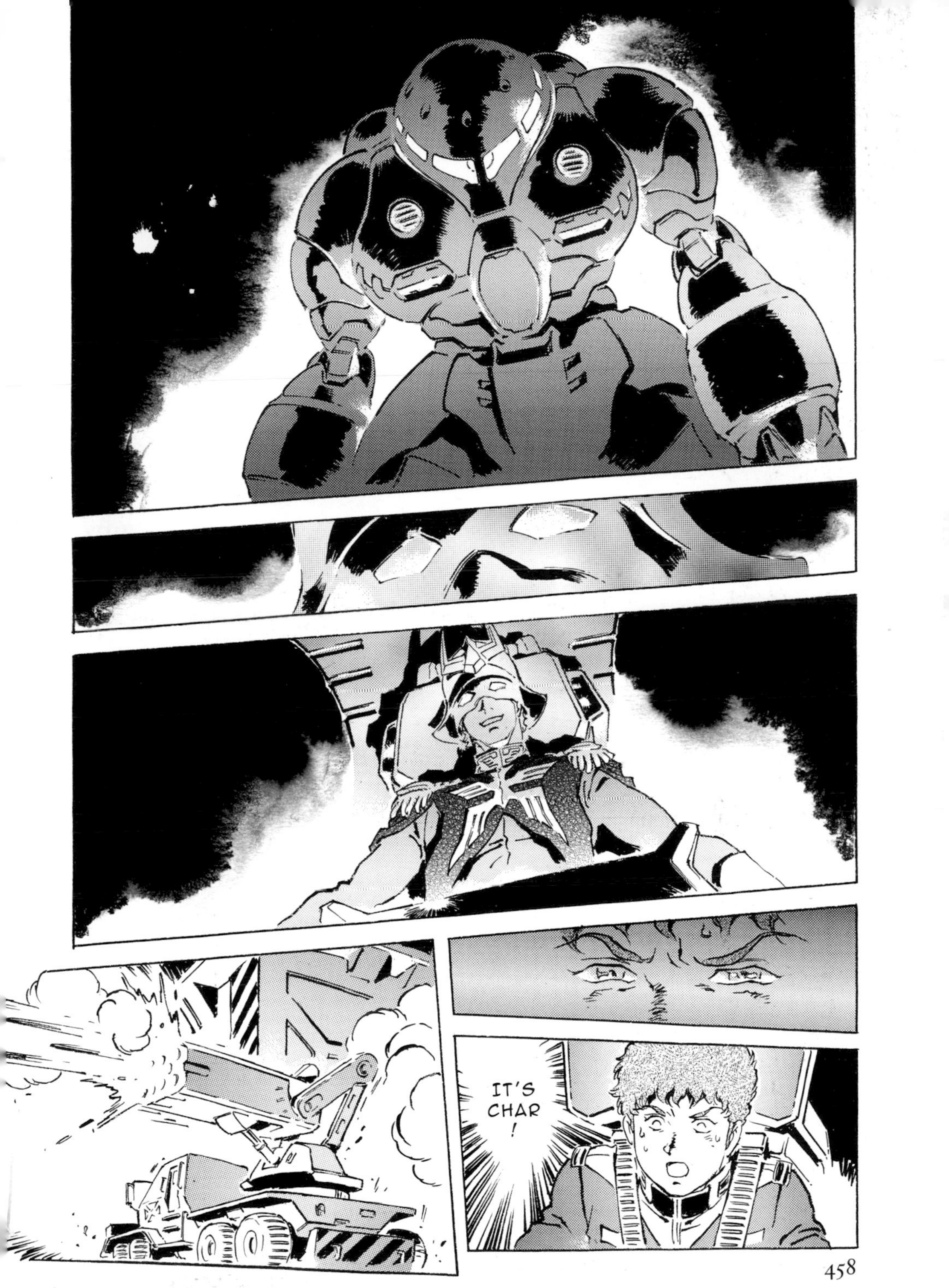
IT'S CHAR!

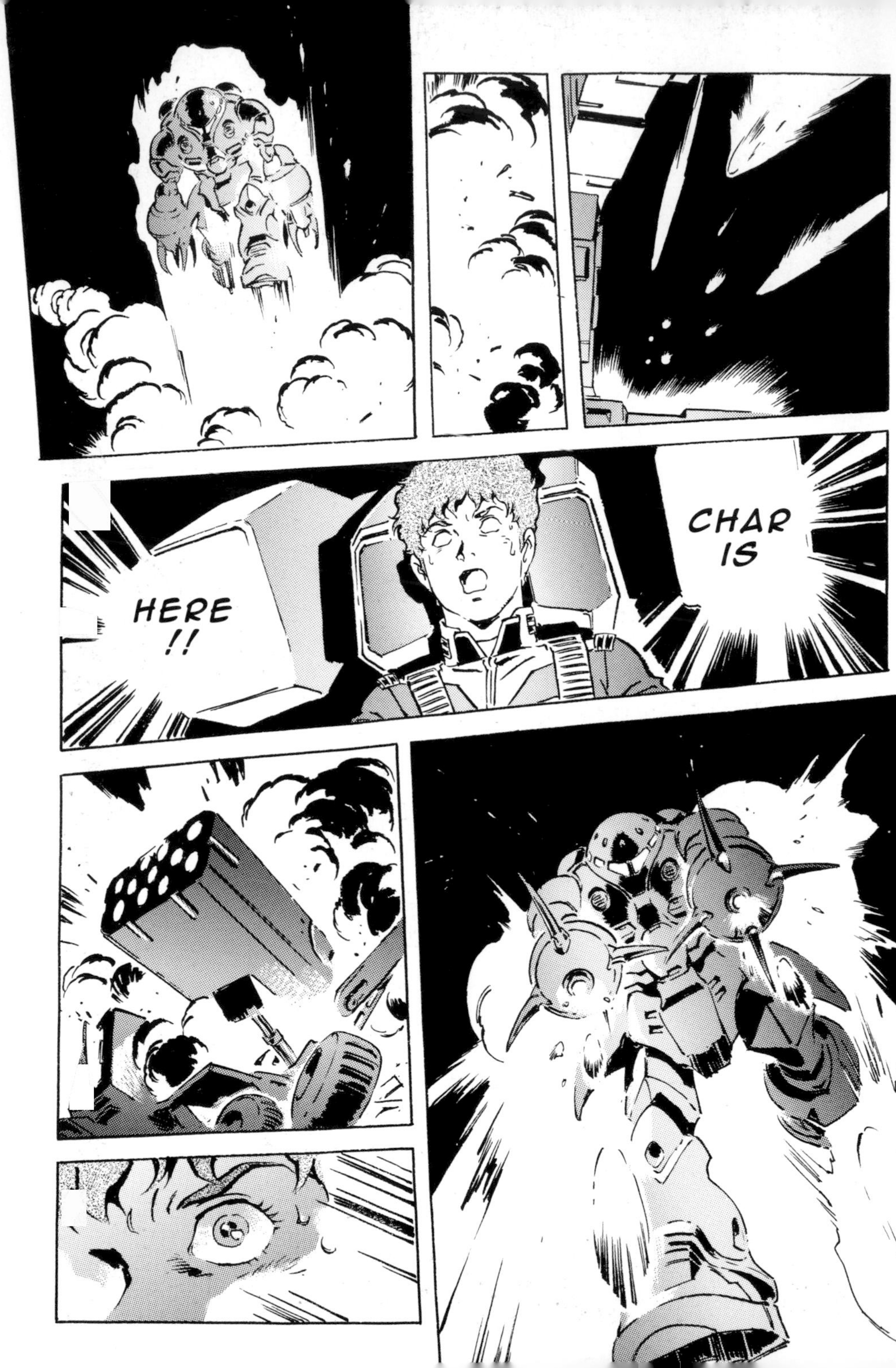
CHAR IS
HERE !!

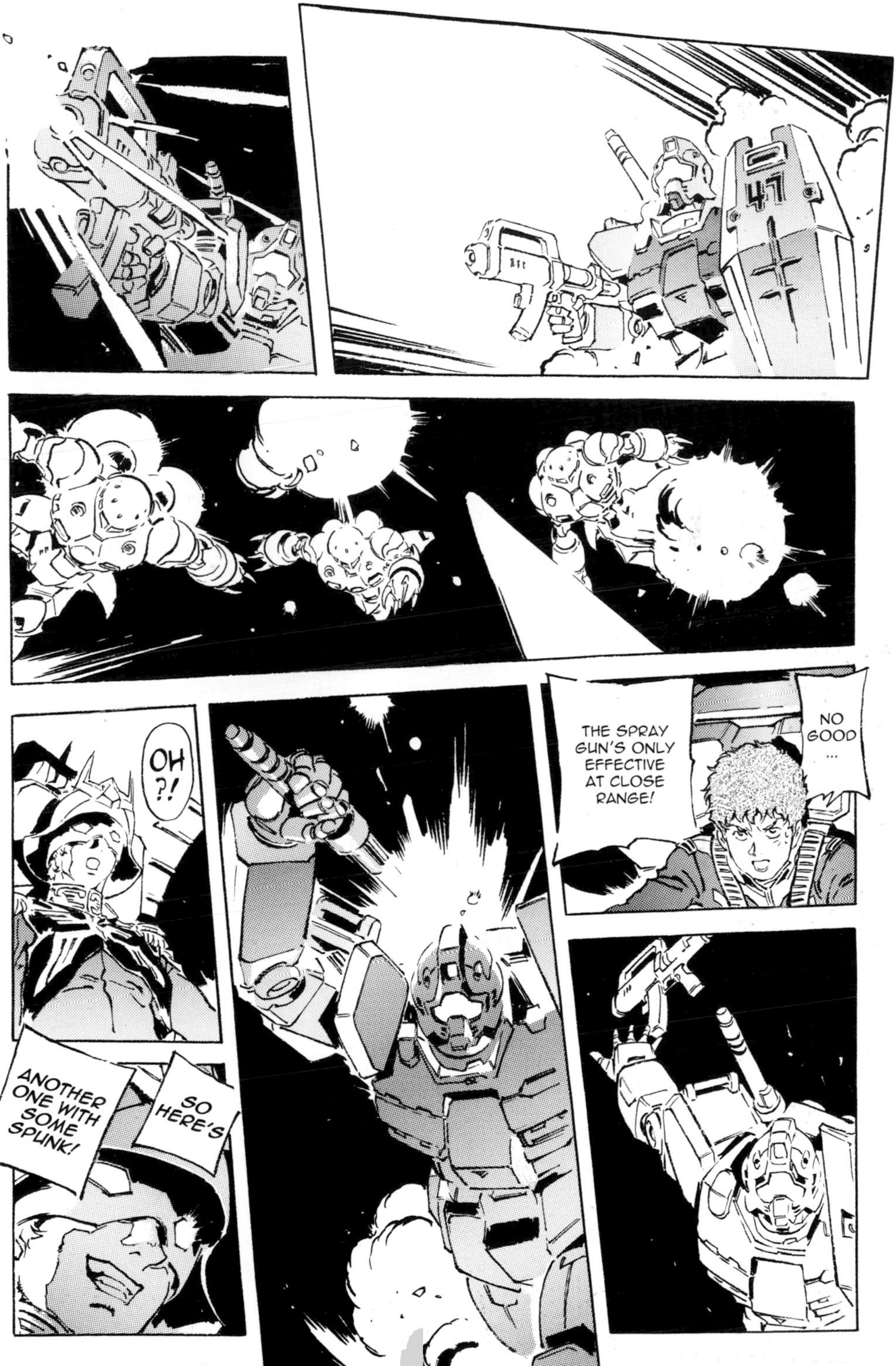
NO GOOD ...
THE SPRAY GUN'S ONLY EFFECTIVE AT CLOSE RANGE!
OH ?!
SO HERE'S
ANOTHER ONE WITH SOME SPUNK!

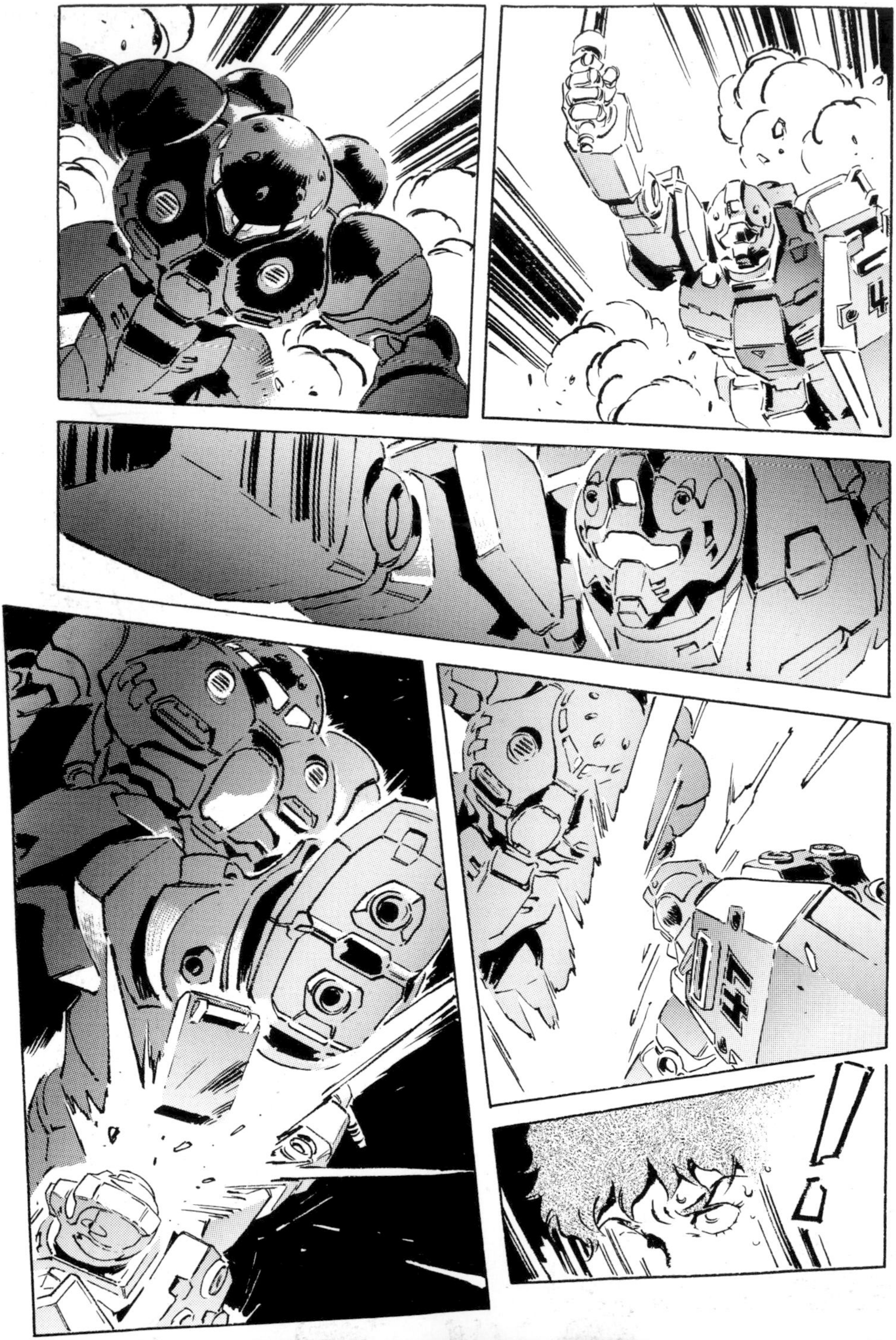
!

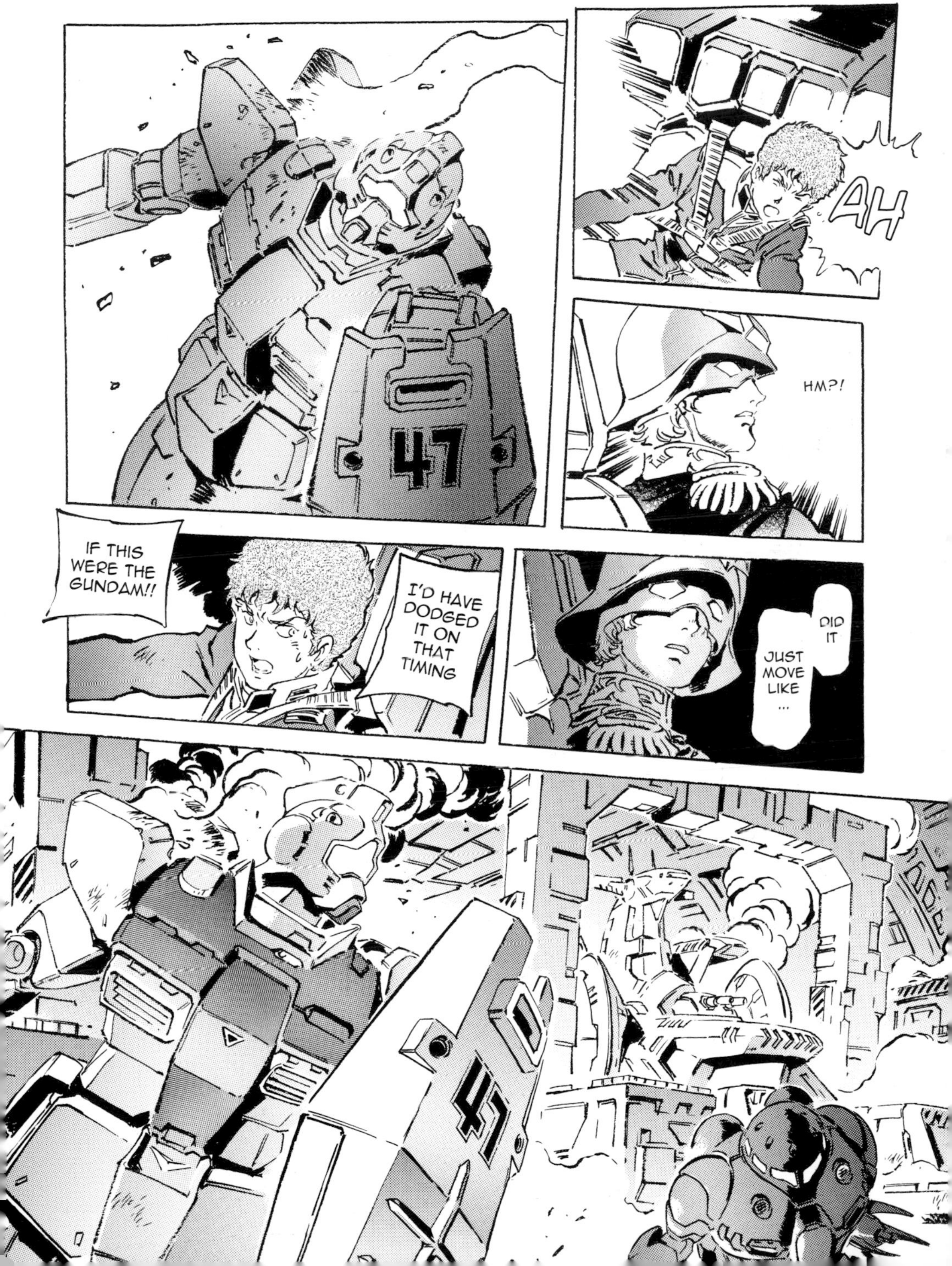
AH
HM?!
DID IT JUST MOVE LIKE ...
IF THIS WERE THE GUNDAM!!
I'D HAVE DODGED IT ON THAT TIMING

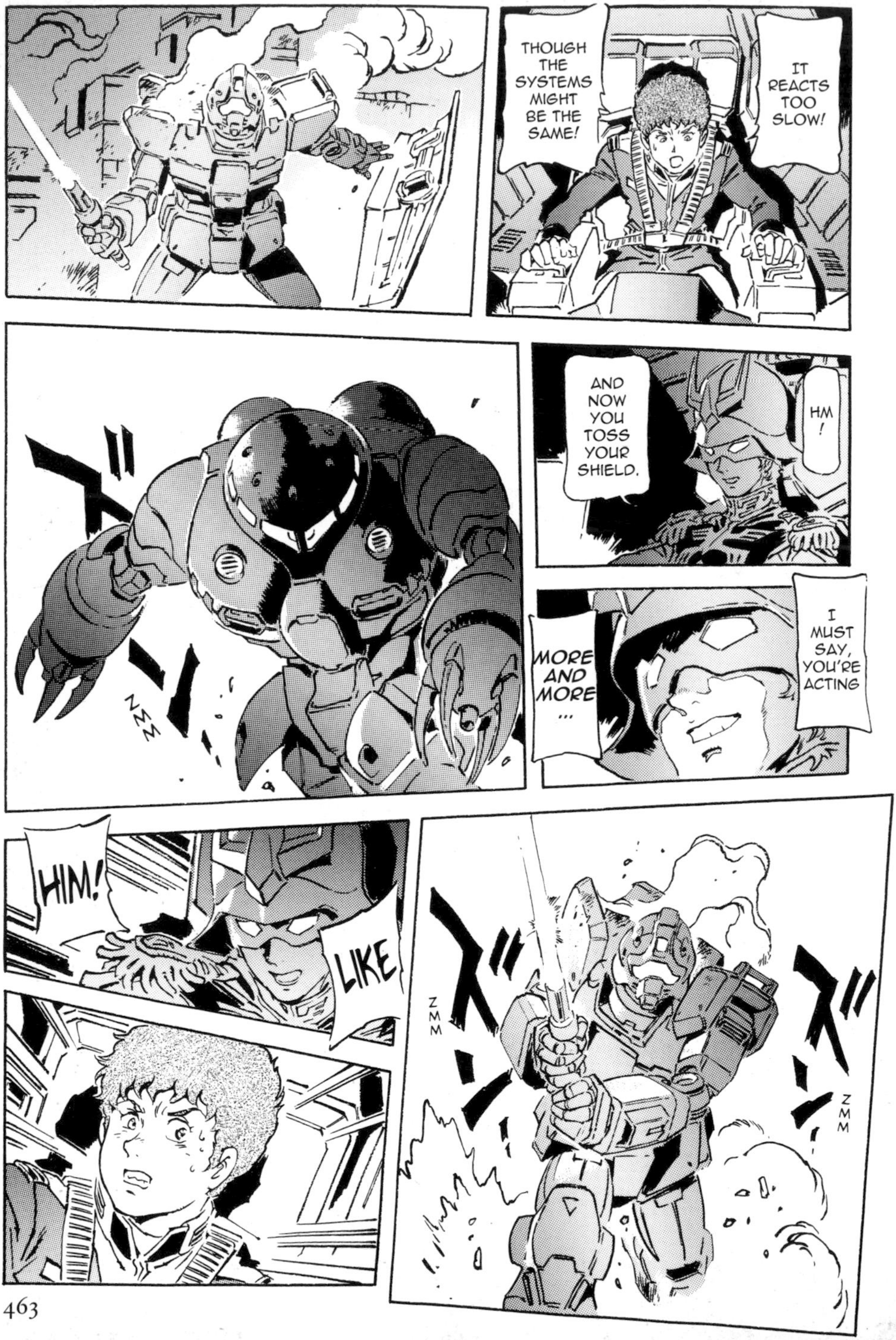
IT REACTS TOO SLOW!
THOUGH THE SYSTEMS MIGHT BE THE SAME!
HM!
AND NOW YOU TOSS YOUR SHIELD.
I MUST SAY, YOU'RE ACTING
MORE AND MORE ...
ZMM
ZMM
ZMM
LIKE
HIM!

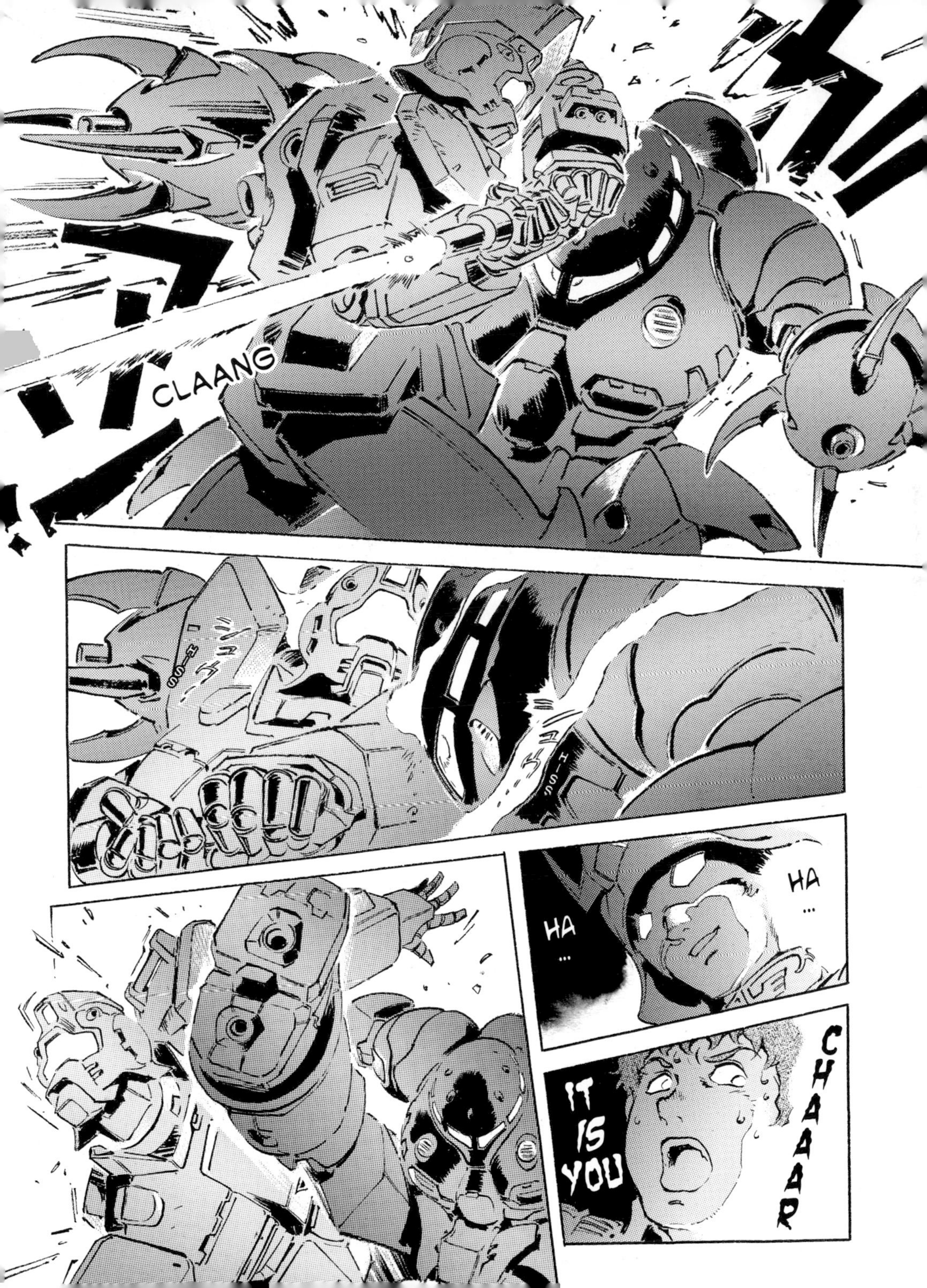
CLAANG
H-SS
H-SS
HA ...
HA ...
IT IS YOU
CHAAAAR

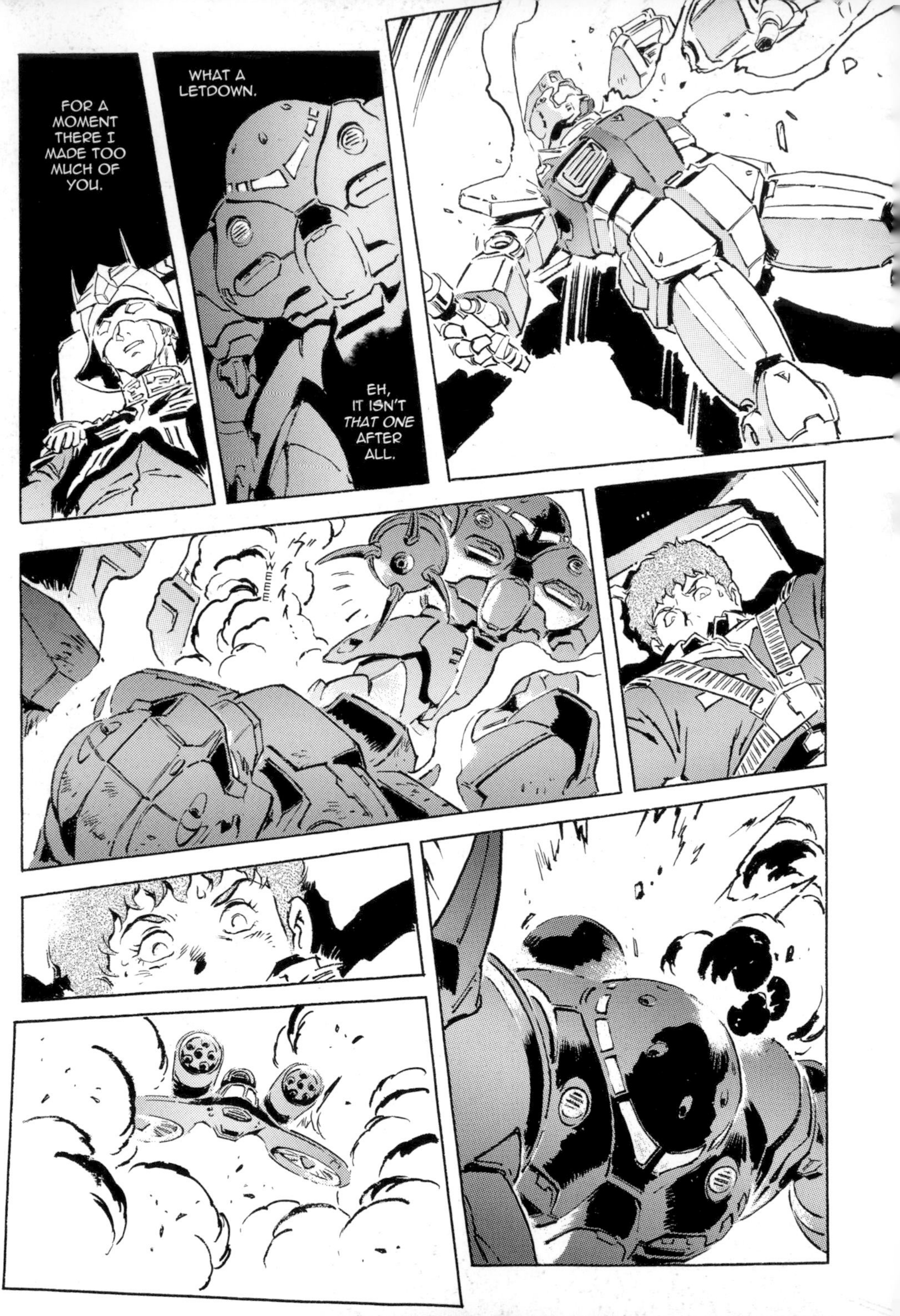
WHAT A LETDOWN.
EH, IT ISN'T *THAT ONE* AFTER ALL.
FOR A MOMENT THERE I MADE TOO MUCH OF YOU.
...
VWEEE

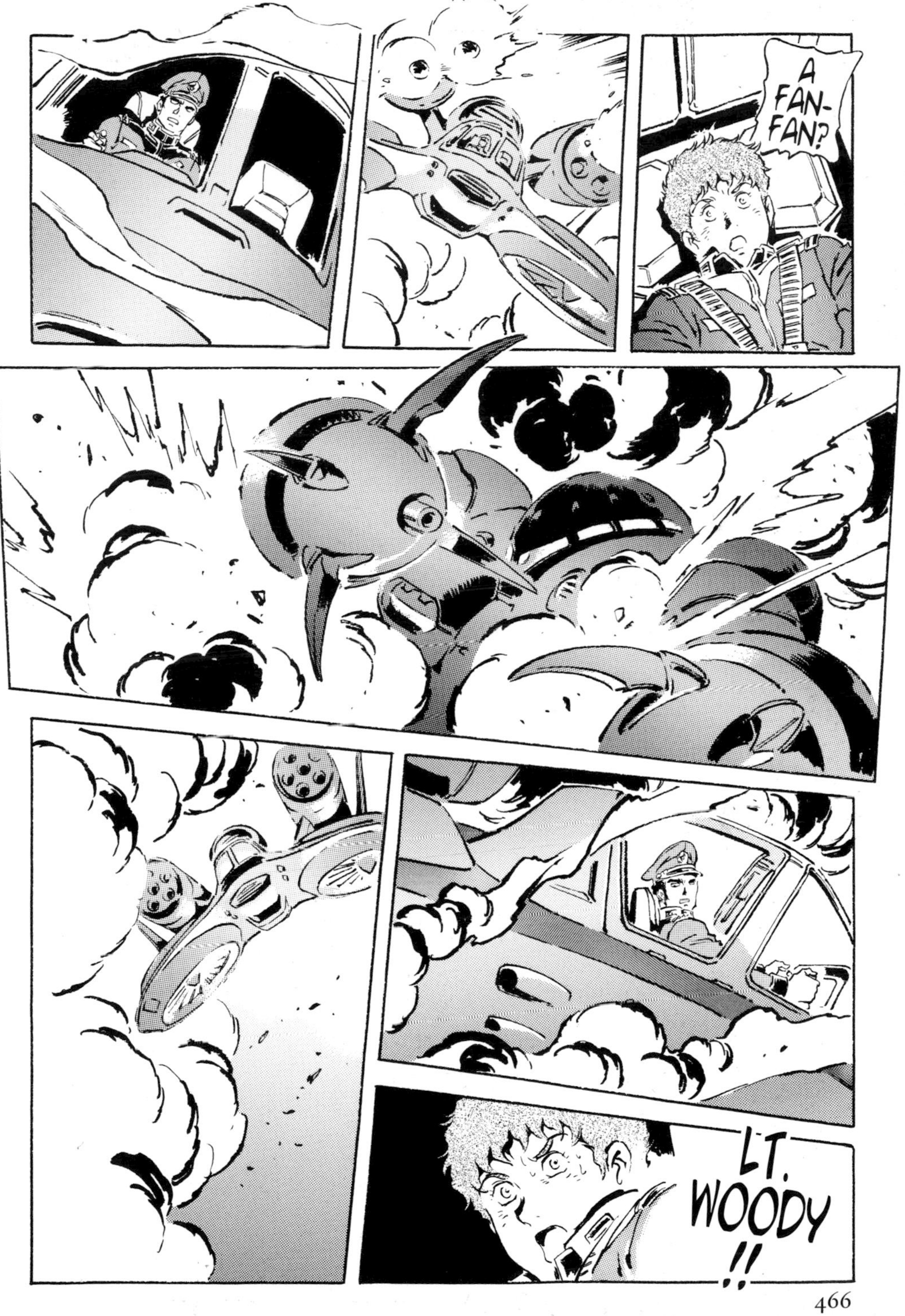
A FAN-FAN?
LT. WOODY!!

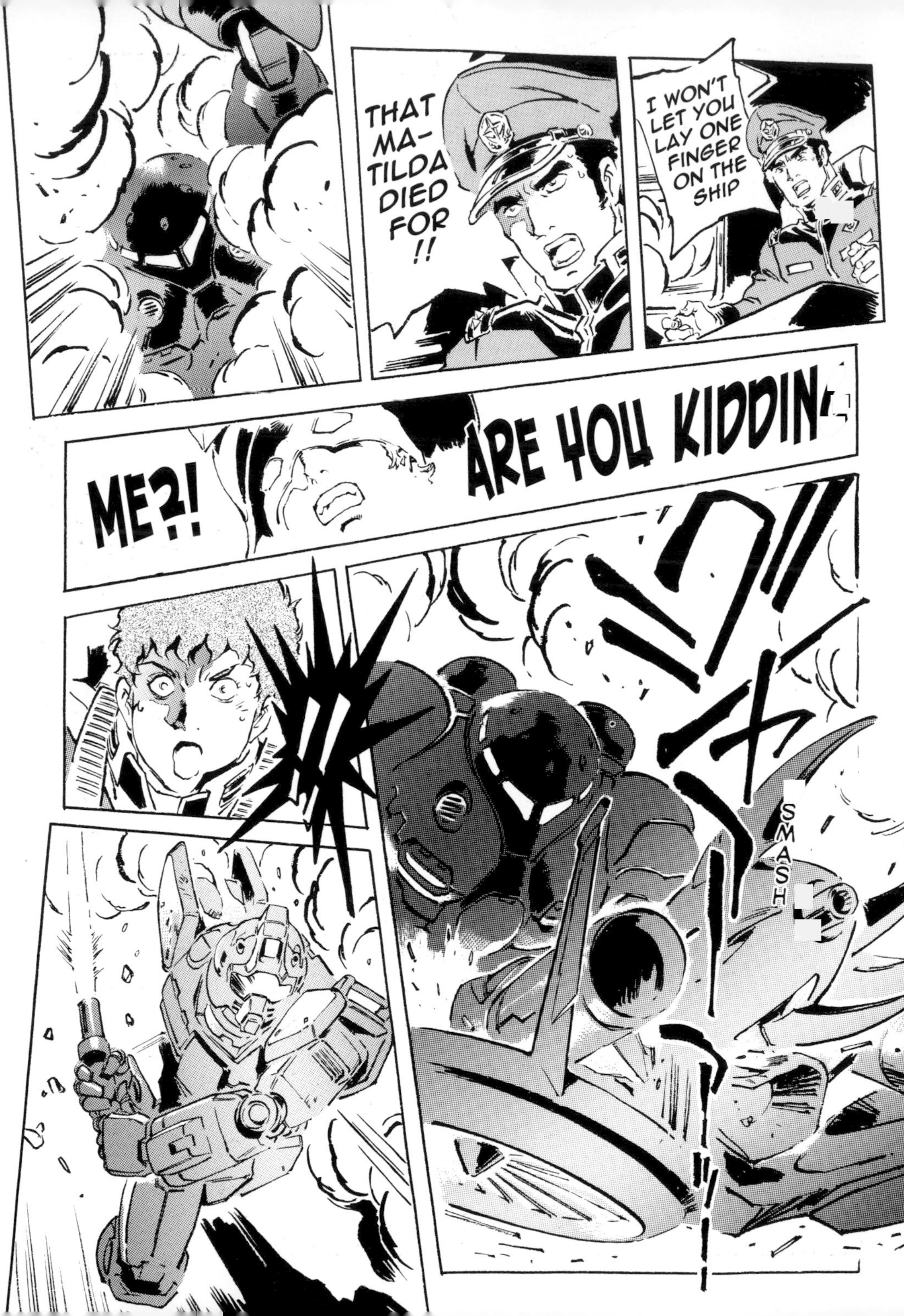
I WON'T LET YOU LAY ONE FINGER ON THE SHIP
THAT MA-TILDA DIED FOR!!
ARE YOU KIDDIN
ME?!
SMASH

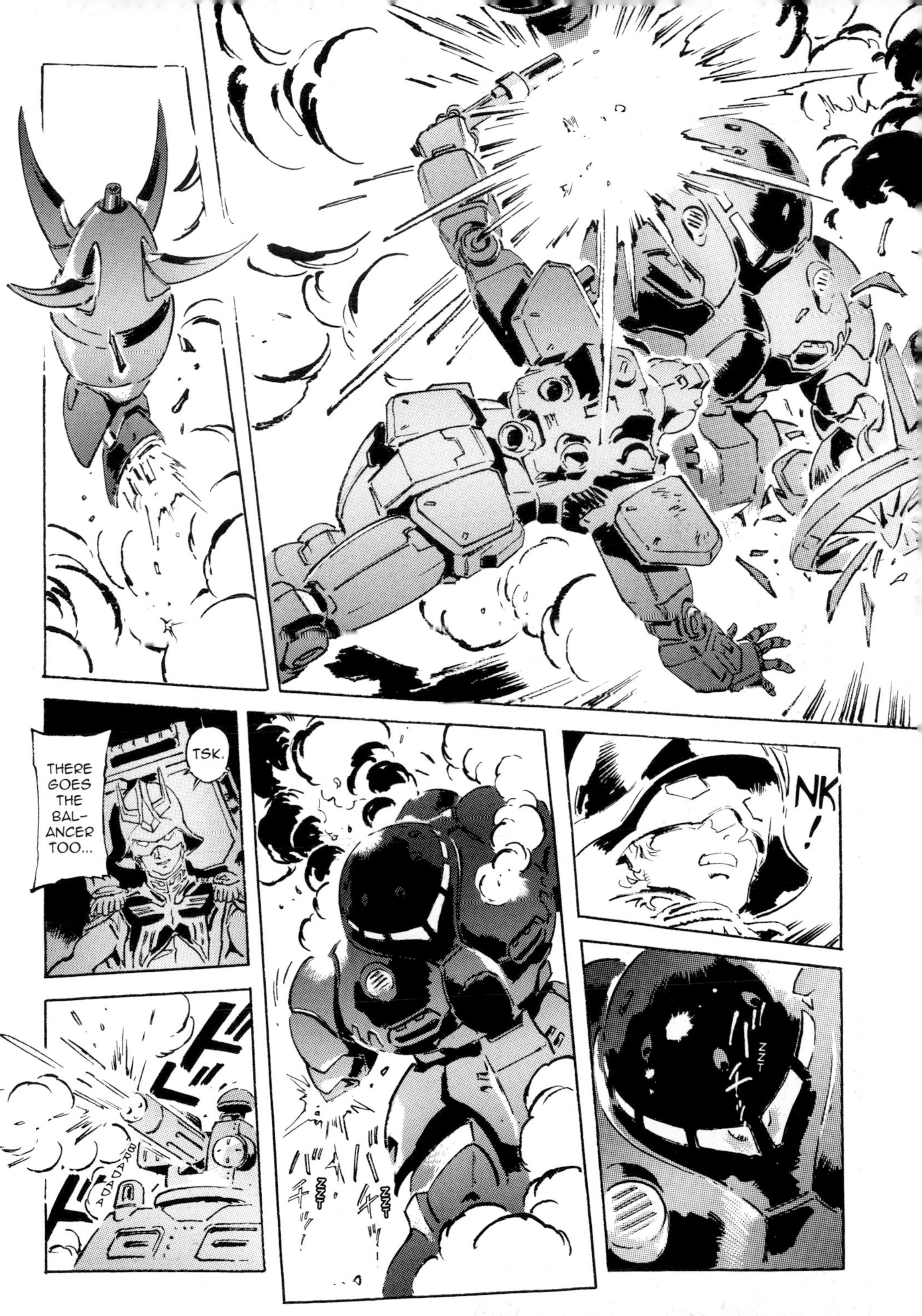
NK!
ZZT
ZZT
ZZT
TSK.
THERE GOES THE BAL-ANCER TOO...
BRADADA

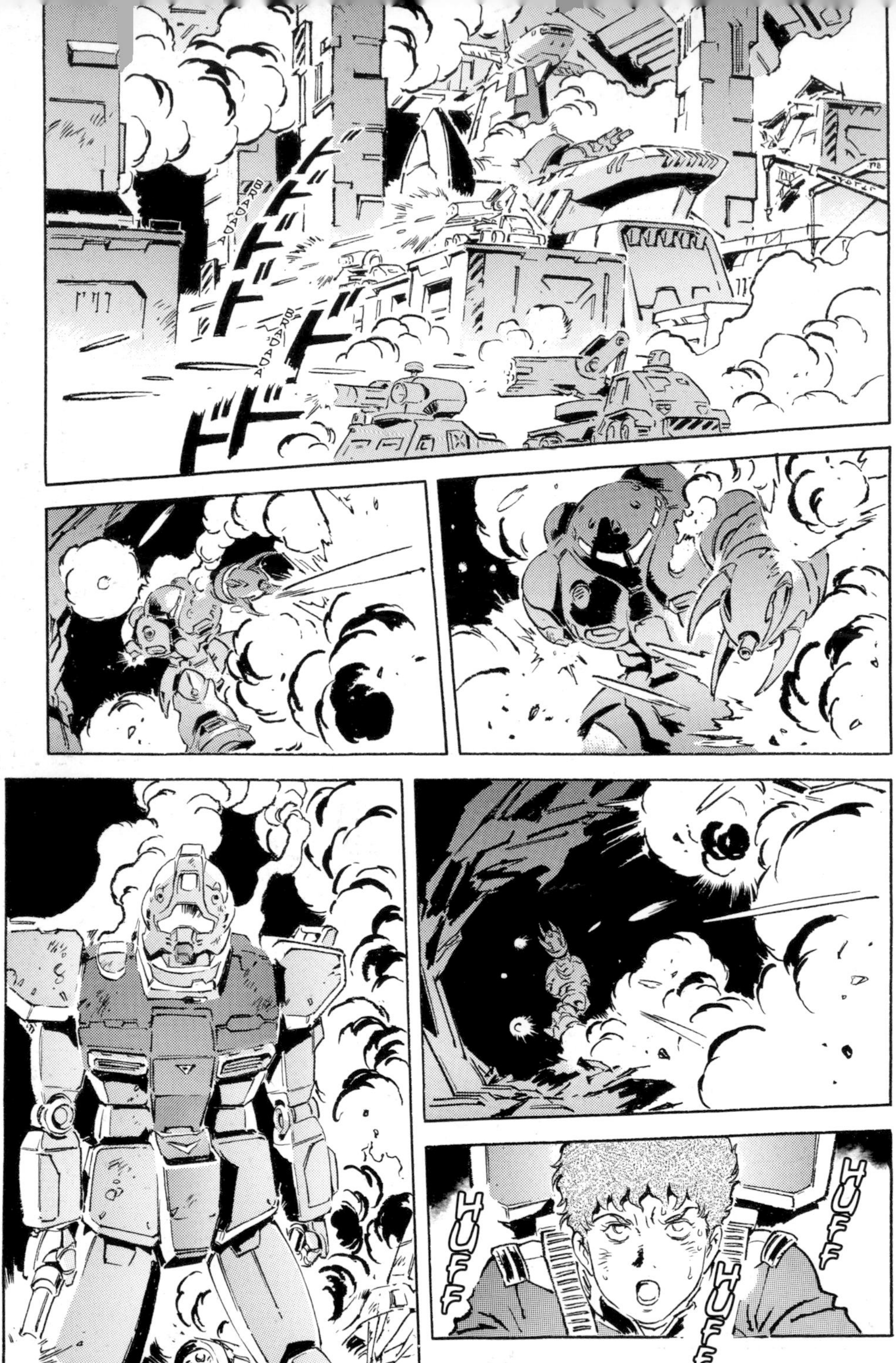

ドドドドドドド
BRADADA
BRADADADA
HUFF
HUFF
HUFF

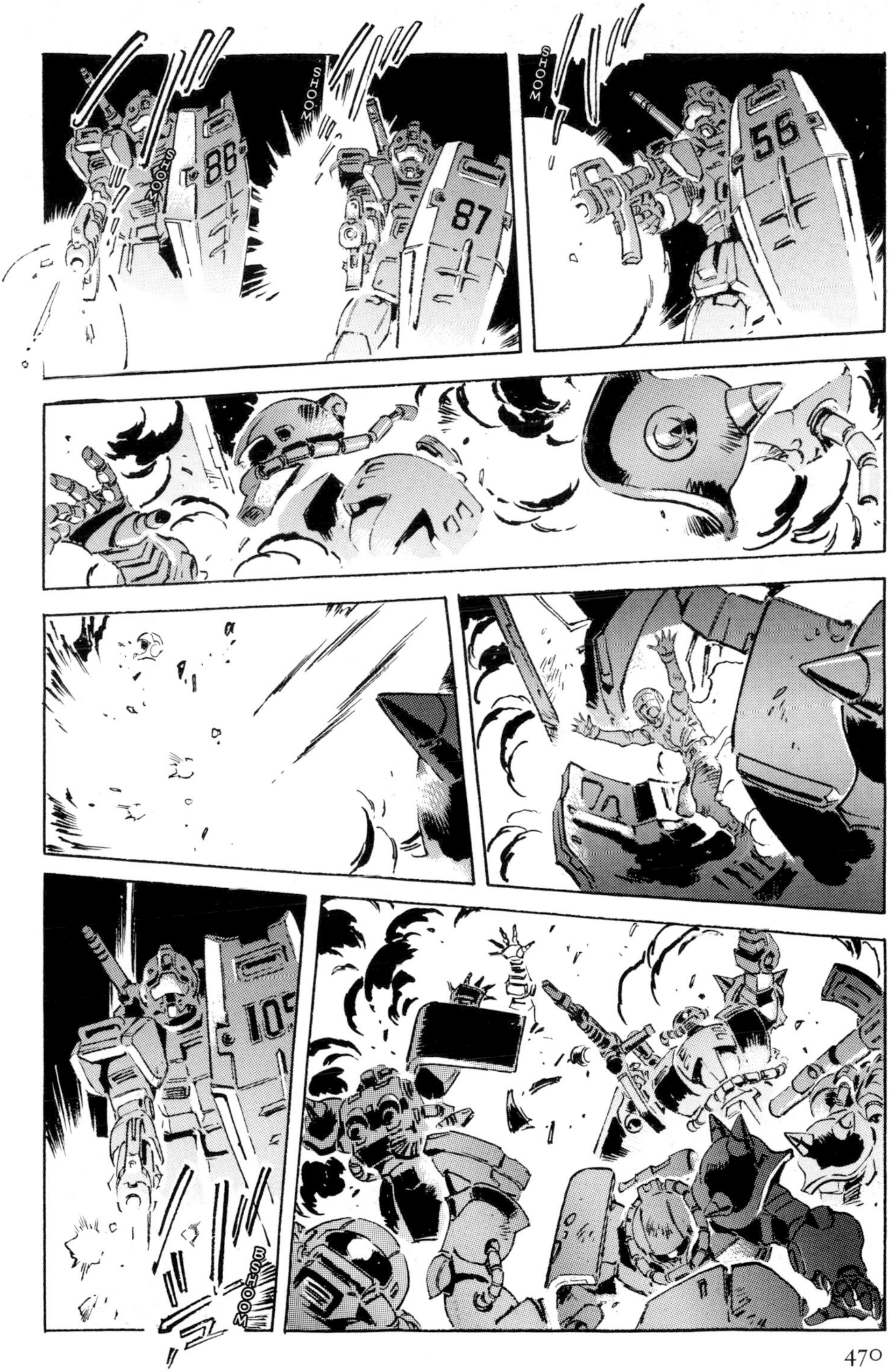
SHOOM
SHOOM
SHOOM
BSHOOM

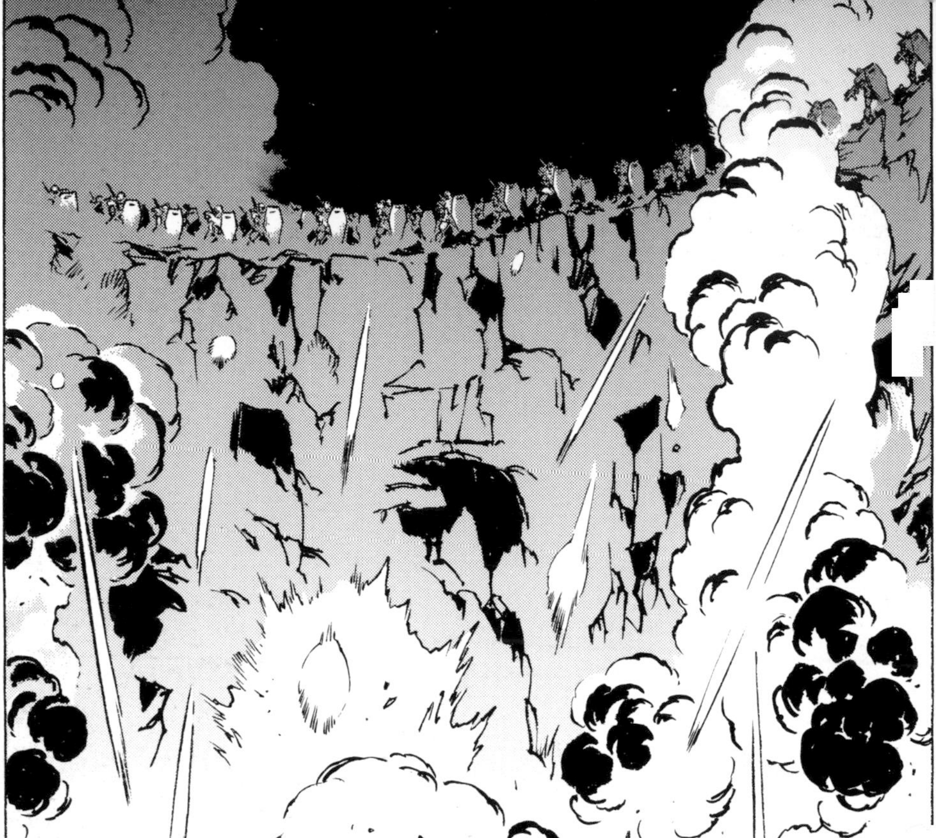

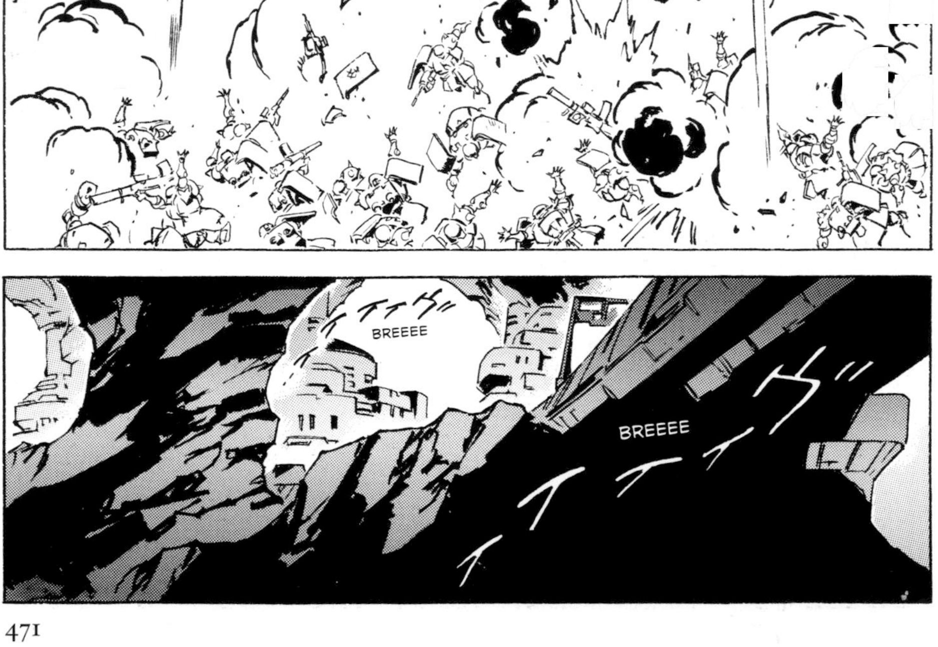
ィィィィヴ
BREEEE
ィィィヴ
BREEEE

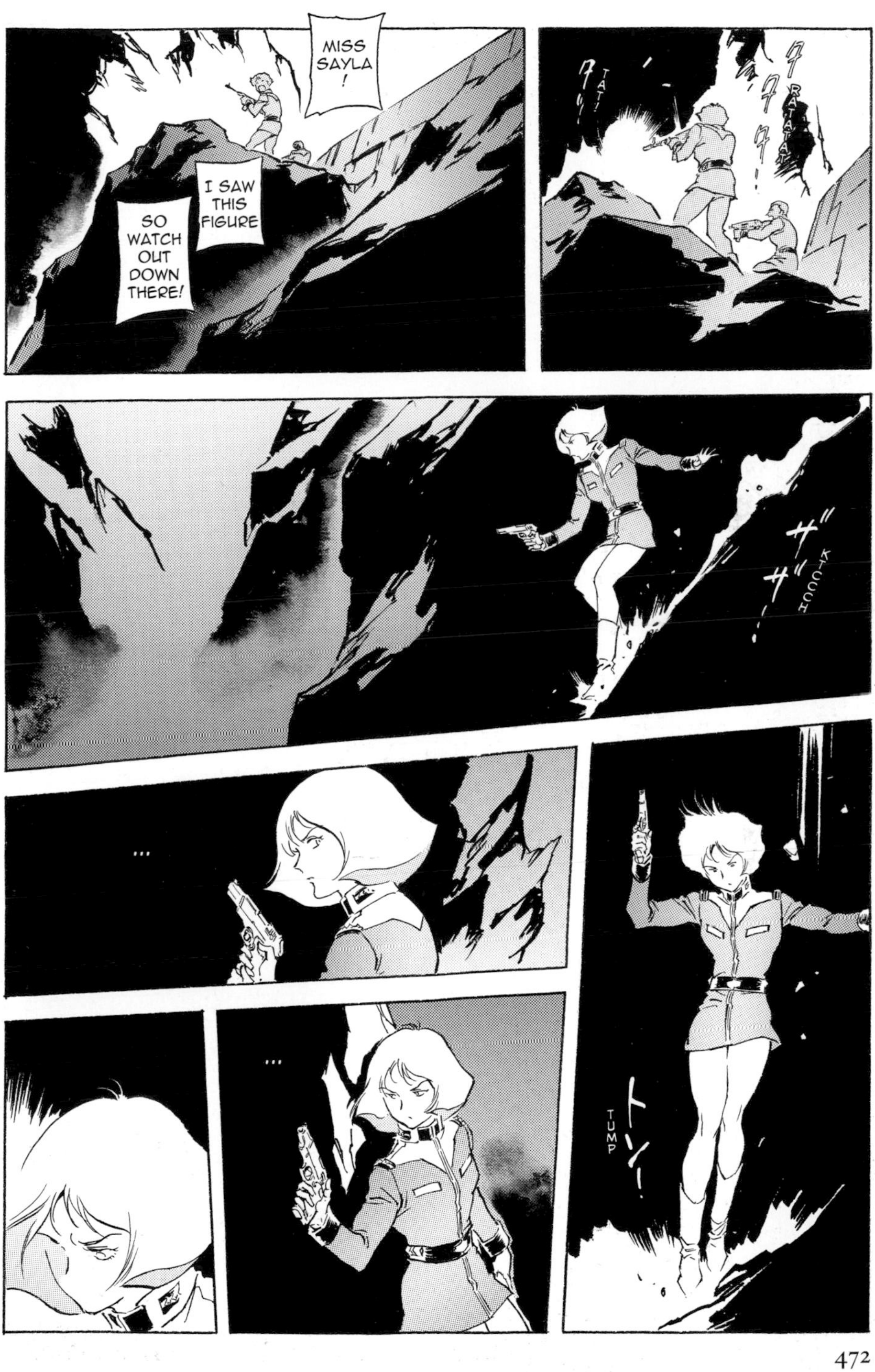
TATI!
RATATAT!
MISS SAYLA!
I SAW THIS FIGURE
SO WATCH OUT DOWN THERE!
KTCCCH
TUMP
...
...

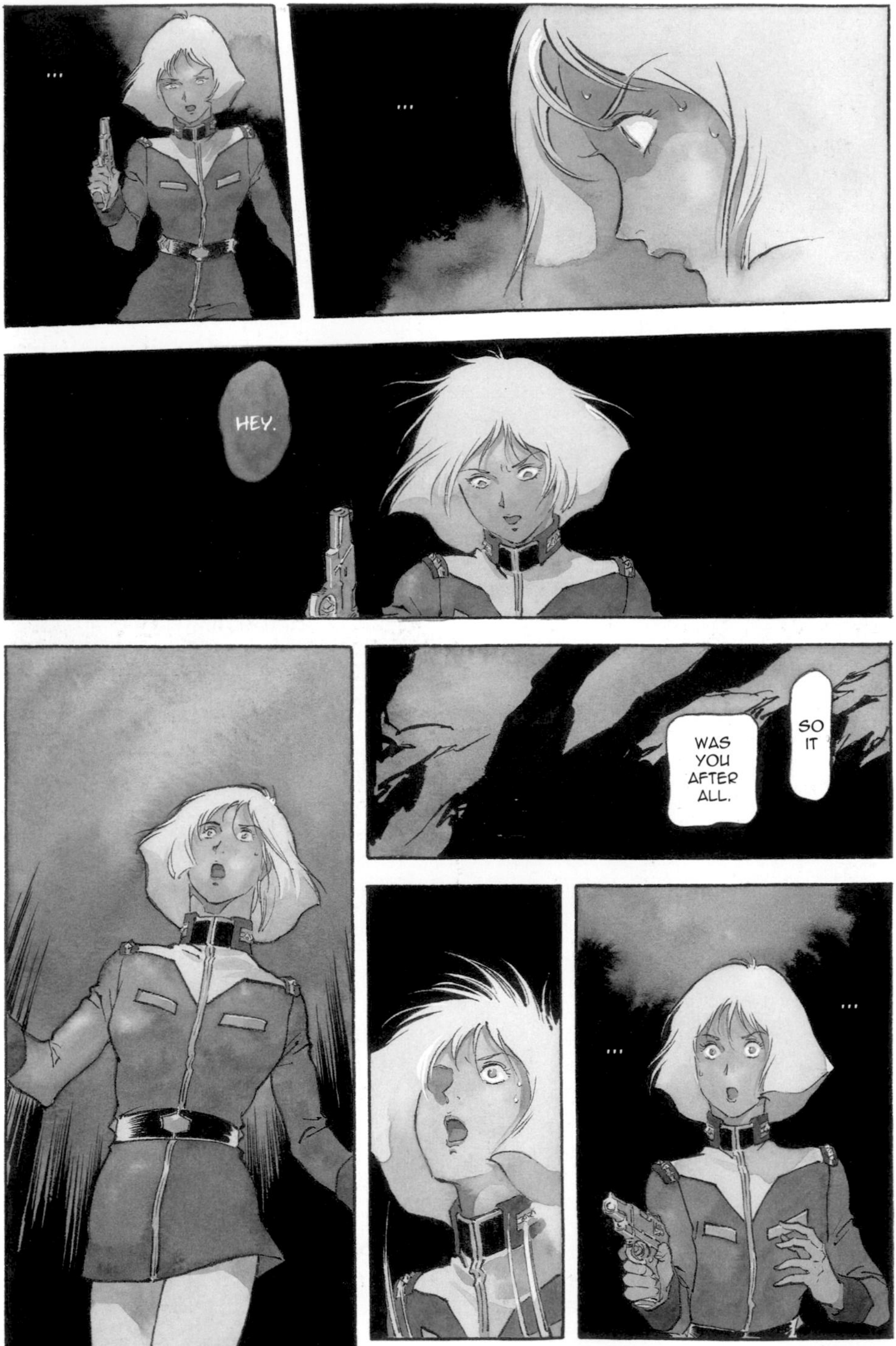
...
...
HEY.
SO IT
WAS YOU AFTER ALL.
...
...

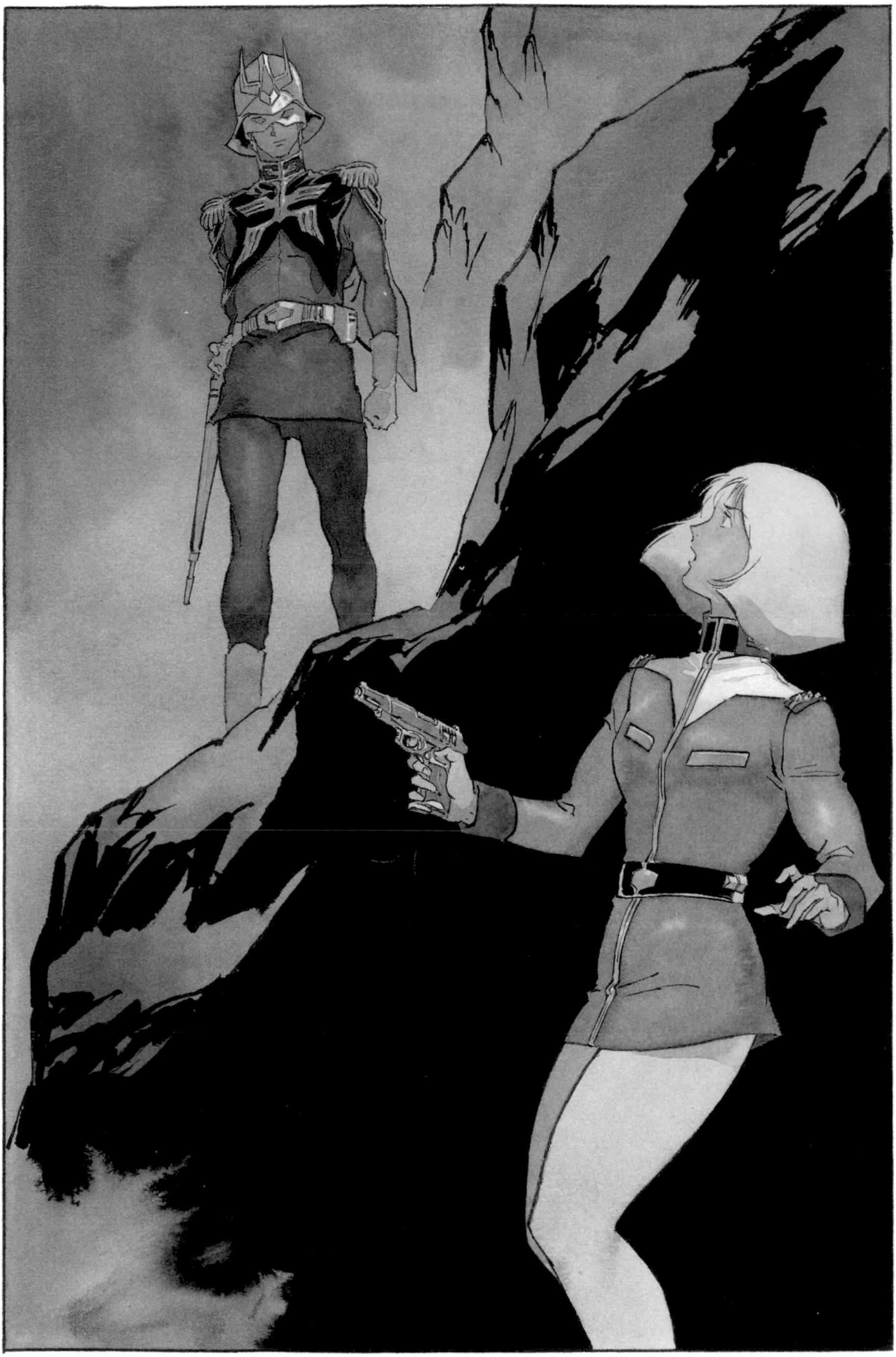

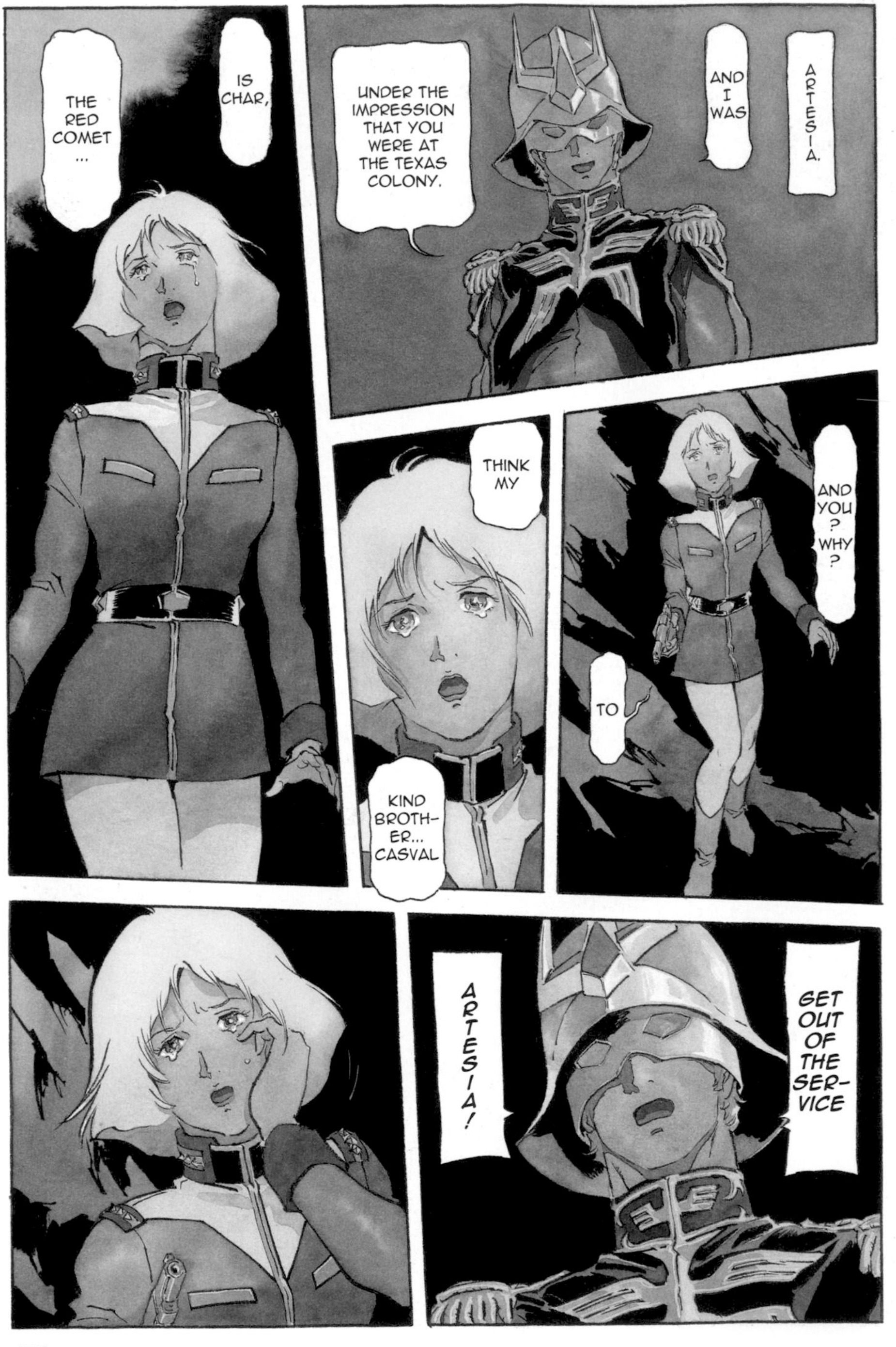
ARTESIA.
AND I WAS
UNDER THE IMPRESSION THAT YOU WERE AT THE TEXAS COLONY.
AND YOU? WHY?
TO
THINK MY
KIND BROTH-ER... CASVAL
IS CHAR,
THE RED COMET ...
GET OUT OF THE SER-VICE
ARTESIA!

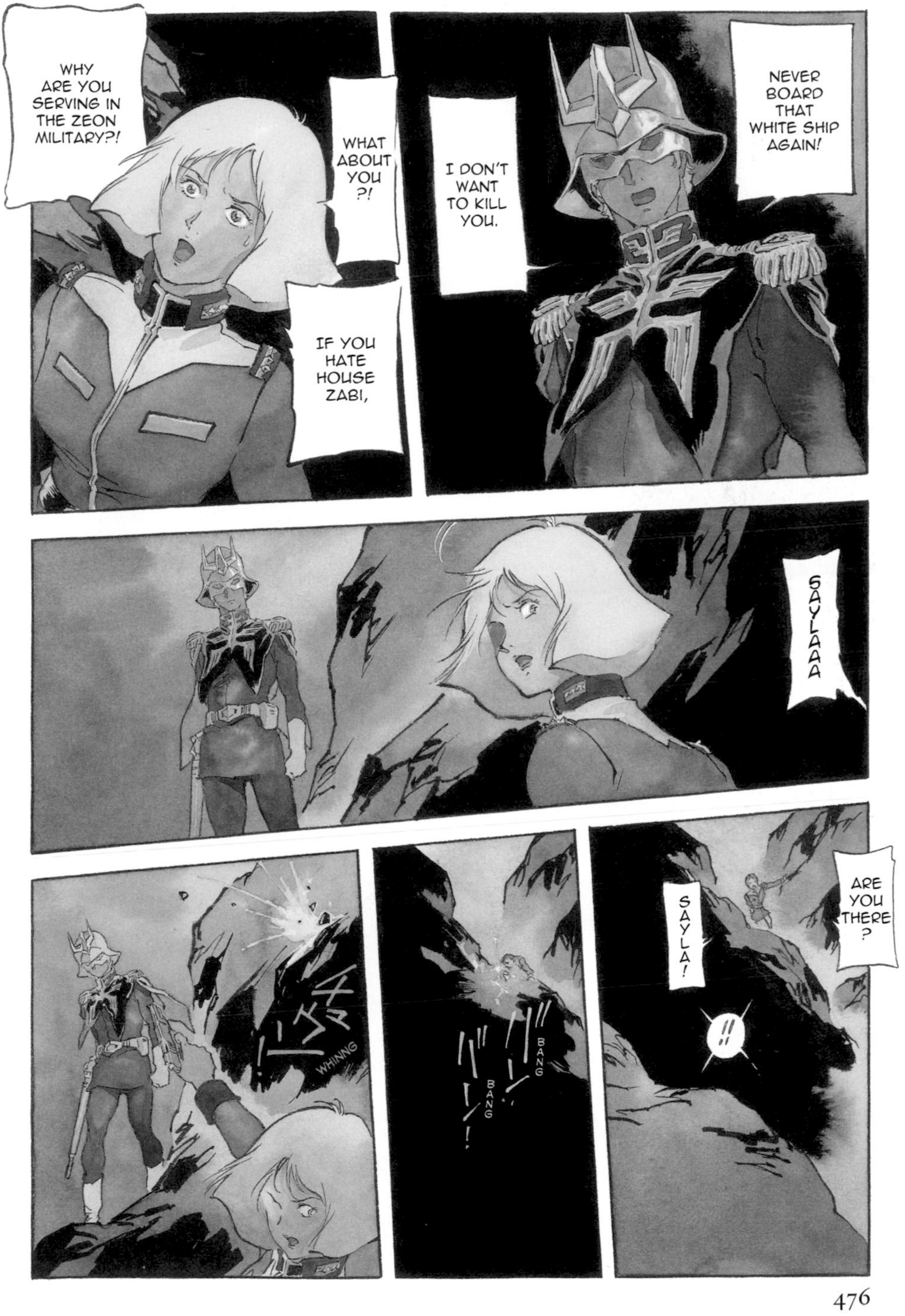
NEVER BOARD THAT WHITE SHIP AGAIN!
I DON'T WANT TO KILL YOU.
WHAT ABOUT YOU?!
IF YOU HATE HOUSE ZABI,
WHY ARE YOU SERVING IN THE ZEON MILITARY?!
SAYLAAA
ARE YOU THERE?
SAYLA!
!!
BANG
BANG
WHINING

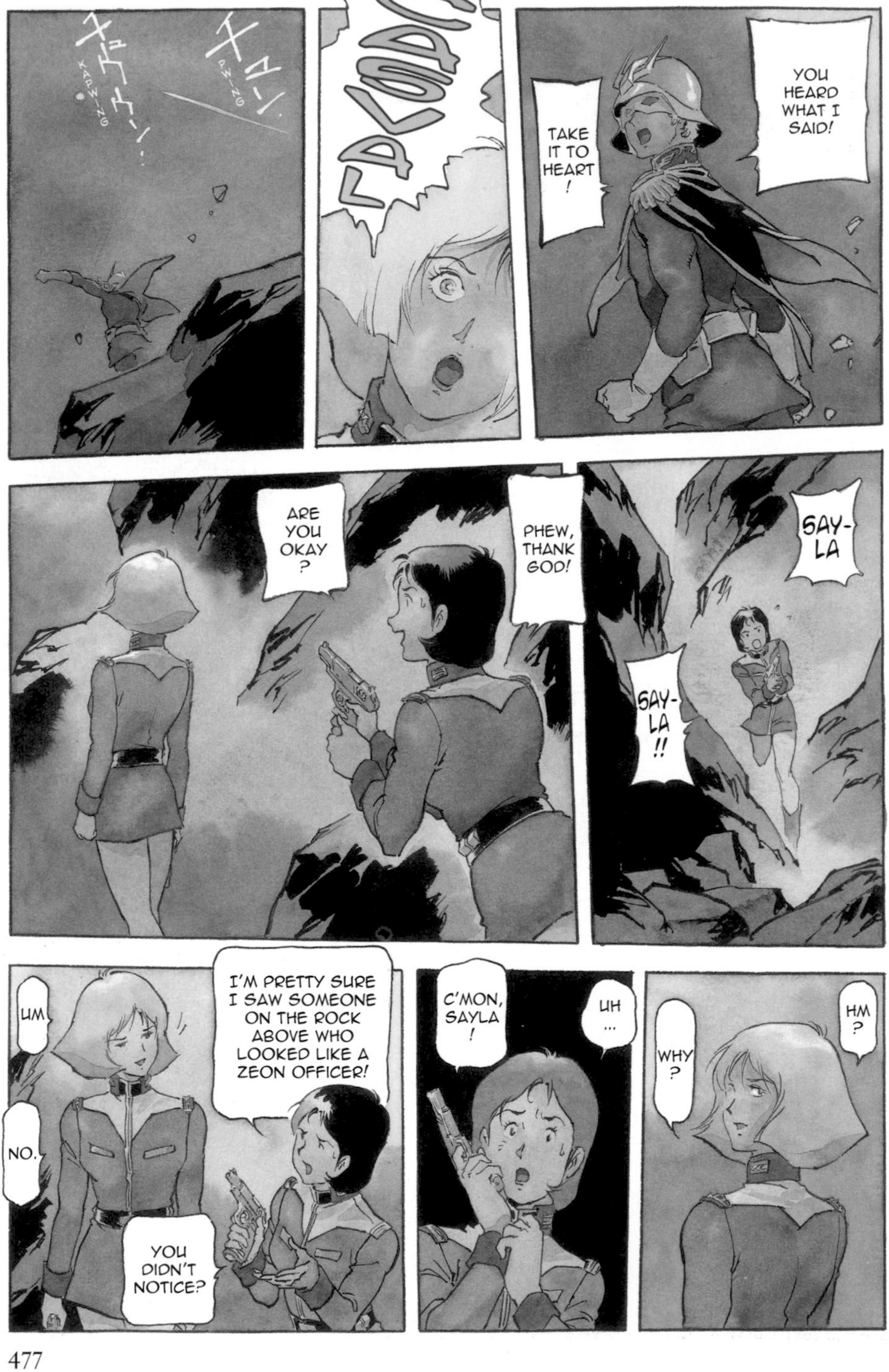
YOU HEARD WHAT I SAID!
TAKE IT TO HEART!
PWING
KAPWING
SAY-LA
SAY-LA!!
PHEW, THANK GOD!
ARE YOU OKAY?
HM?
WHY?
UH...
C'MON, SAYLA!
I'M PRETTY SURE I SAW SOMEONE ON THE ROCK ABOVE WHO LOOKED LIKE A ZEON OFFICER!
UM
NO.
YOU DIDN'T NOTICE?

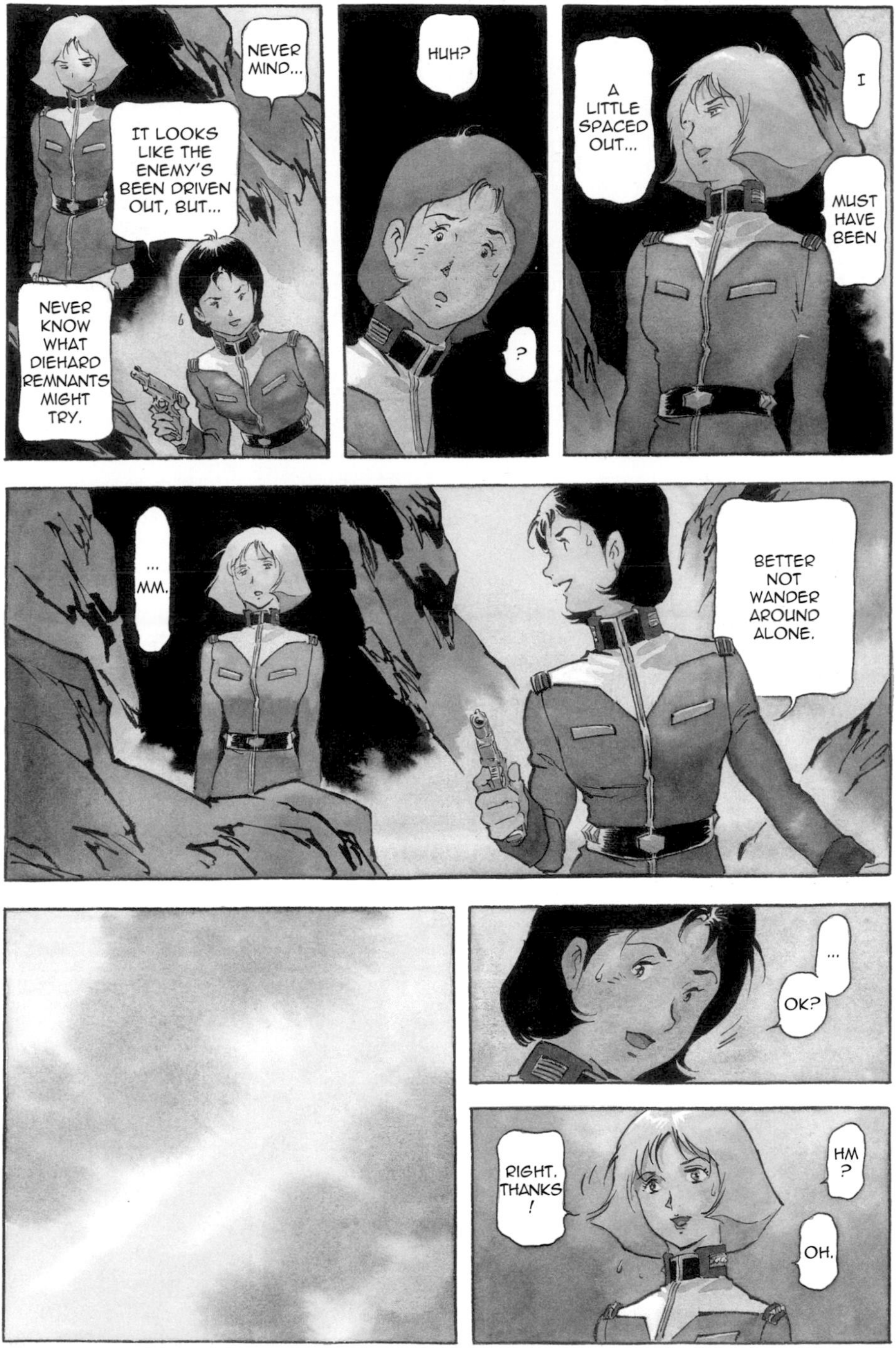

I
MUST HAVE BEEN
A LITTLE SPACED OUT...
HUH?
?
NEVER MIND...
IT LOOKS LIKE THE ENEMY'S BEEN DRIVEN OUT, BUT...
NEVER KNOW WHAT DIEHARD REMNANTS MIGHT TRY.
BETTER NOT WANDER AROUND ALONE.
... MM.
... OK?
HM ?
OH.
RIGHT. THANKS !

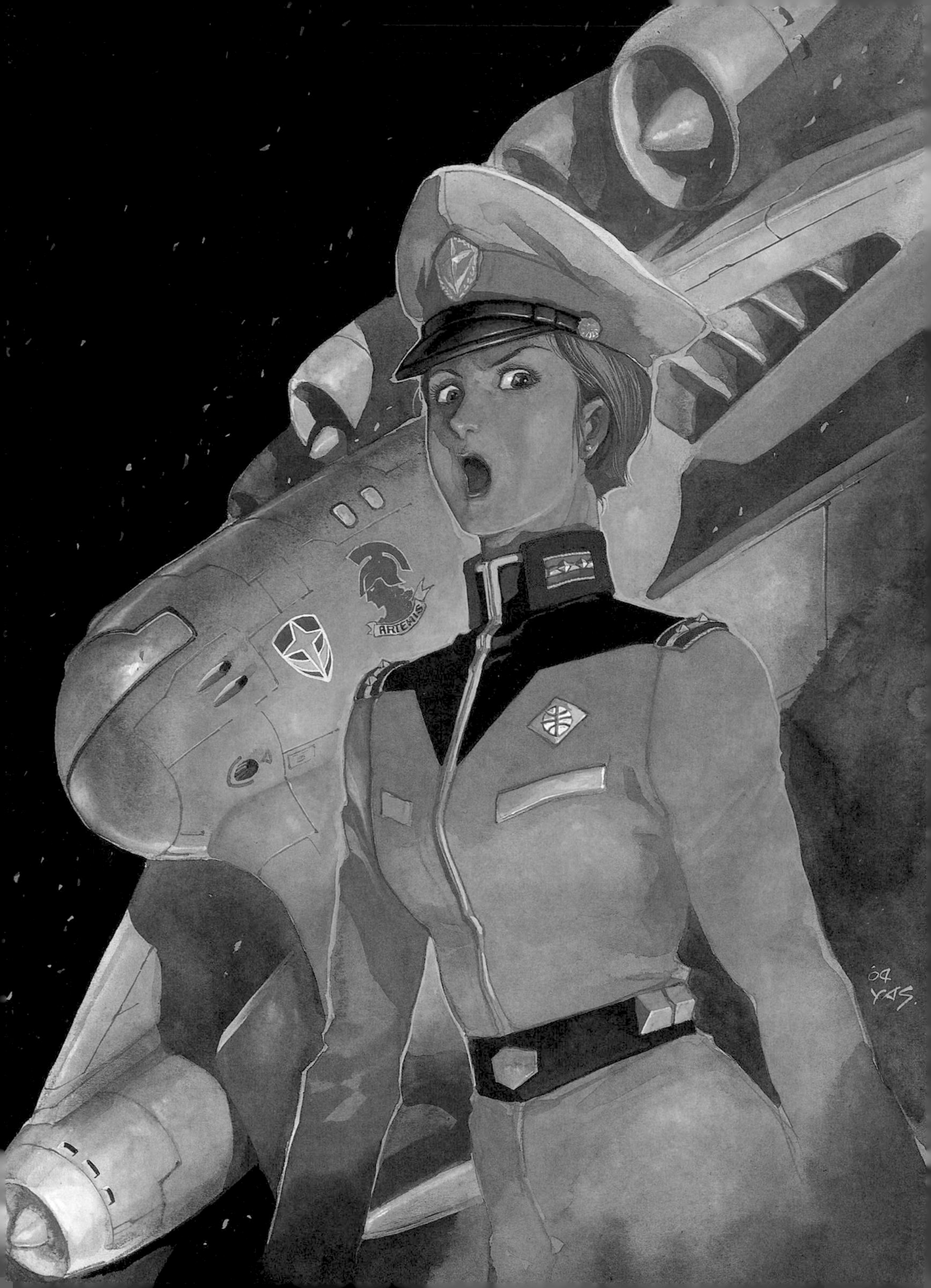
ARTEMIS
'04
YAS.

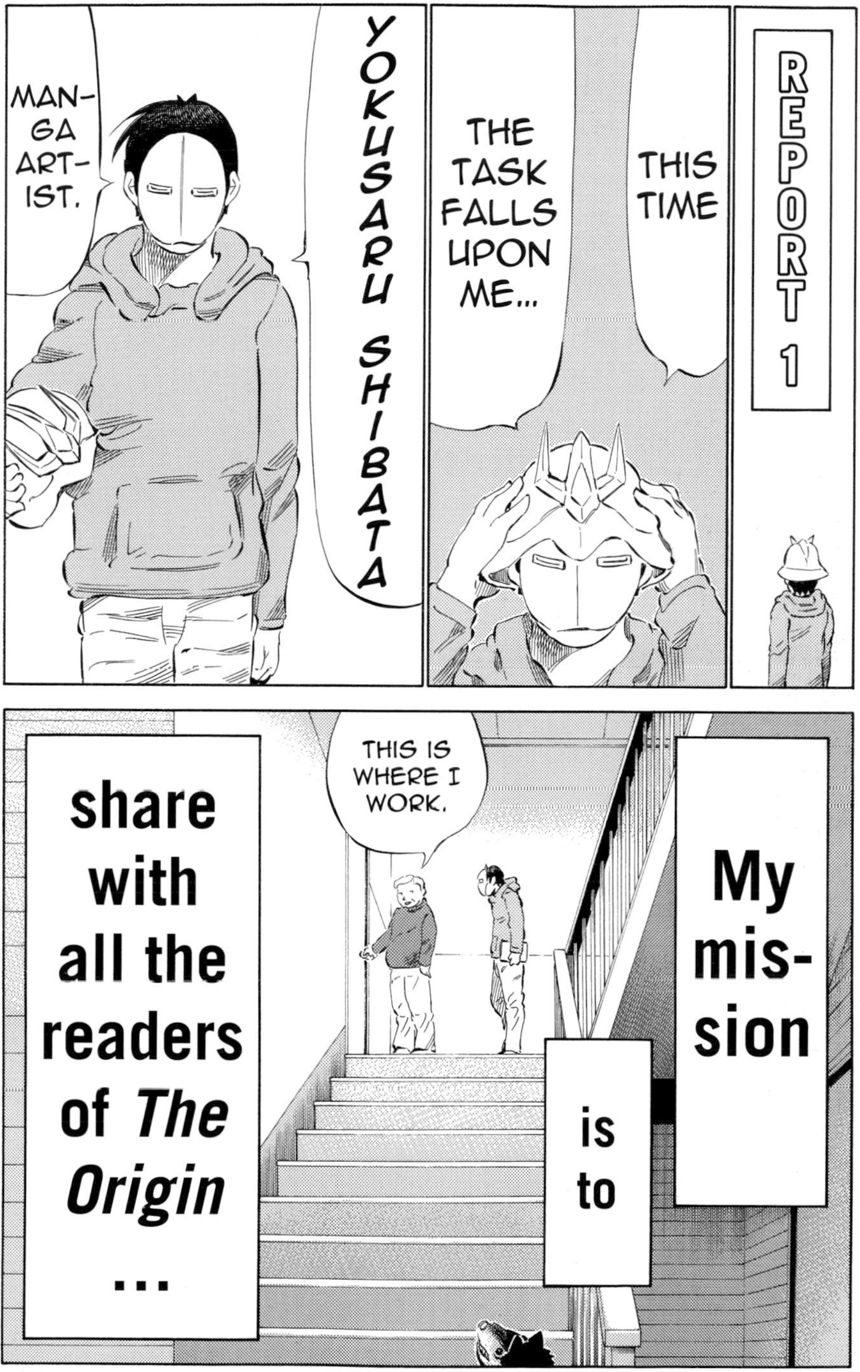
REPORT 1
THIS TIME
THE TASK FALLS UPON ME...
YOKUSARU SHIBATA
MAN-GA ART-IST.
My mis-sion
is to
THIS IS WHERE I WORK.
share with all the readers of *The Origin* ...

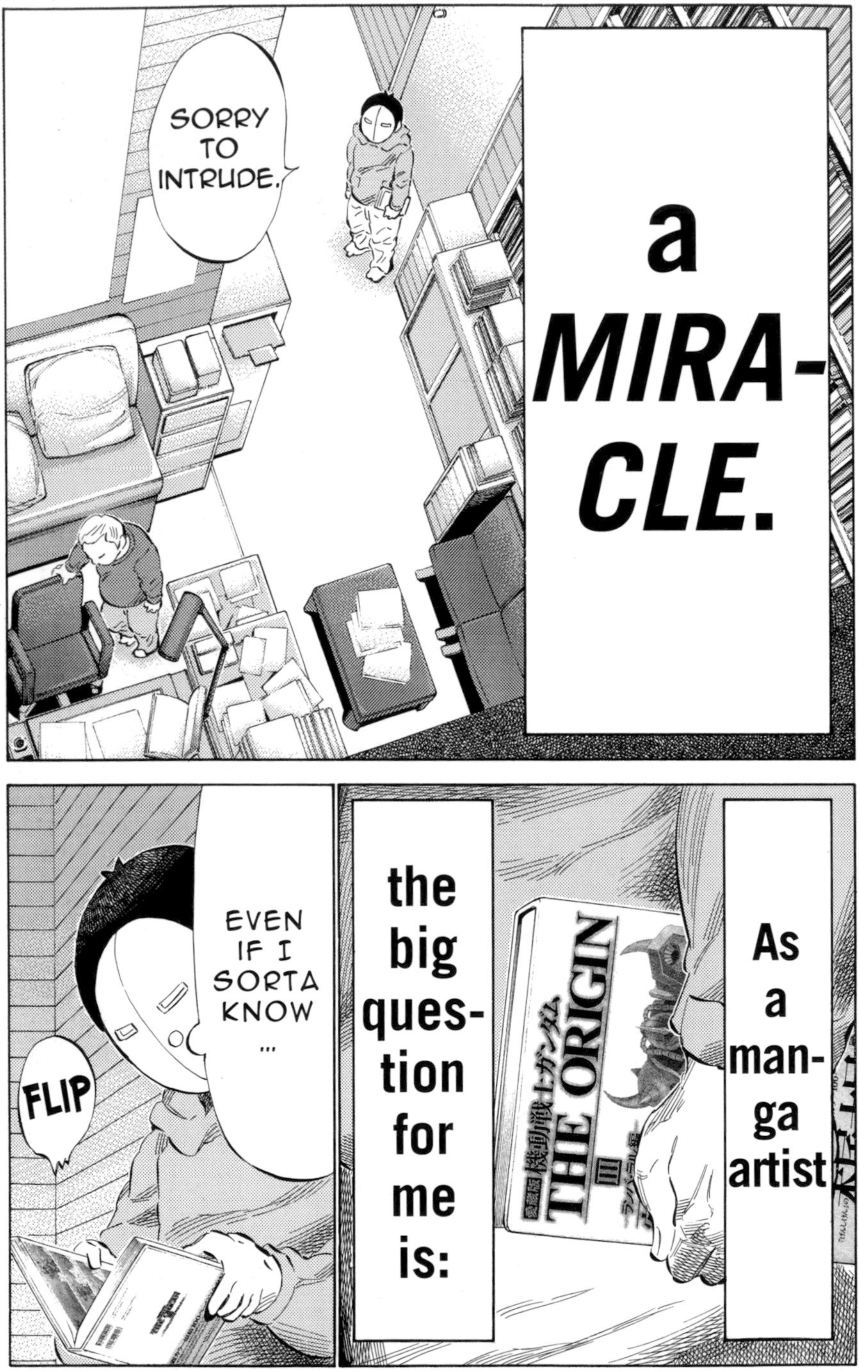
a MIRA-CLE.
SORRY TO INTRUDE.
As a manga artist
THE ORIGIN
the big question for me is:
EVEN IF I SORTA KNOW ...
FLIP

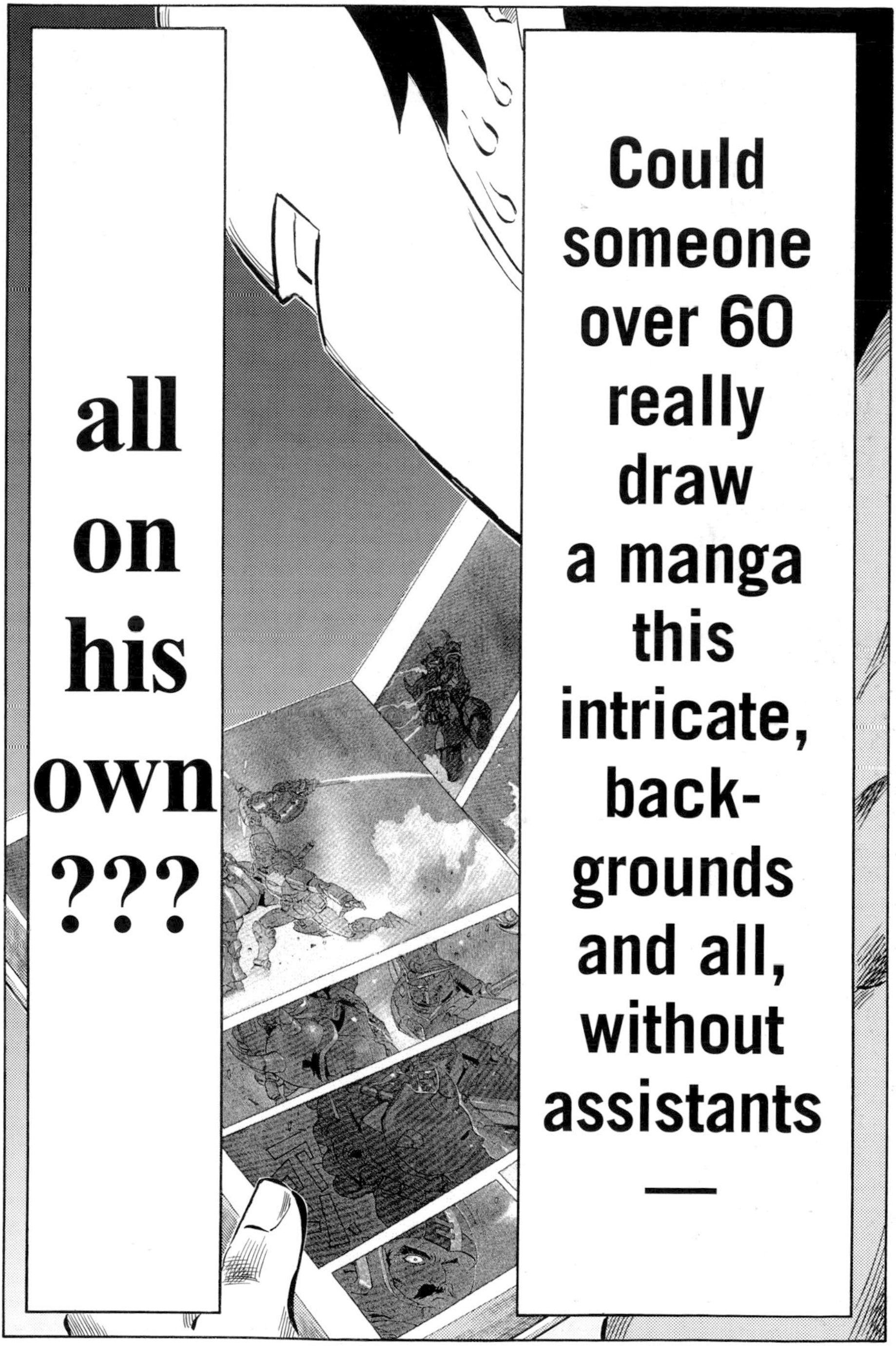
Could someone over 60 really draw a manga this intricate, back-grounds and all, without assistants —
all on his own???

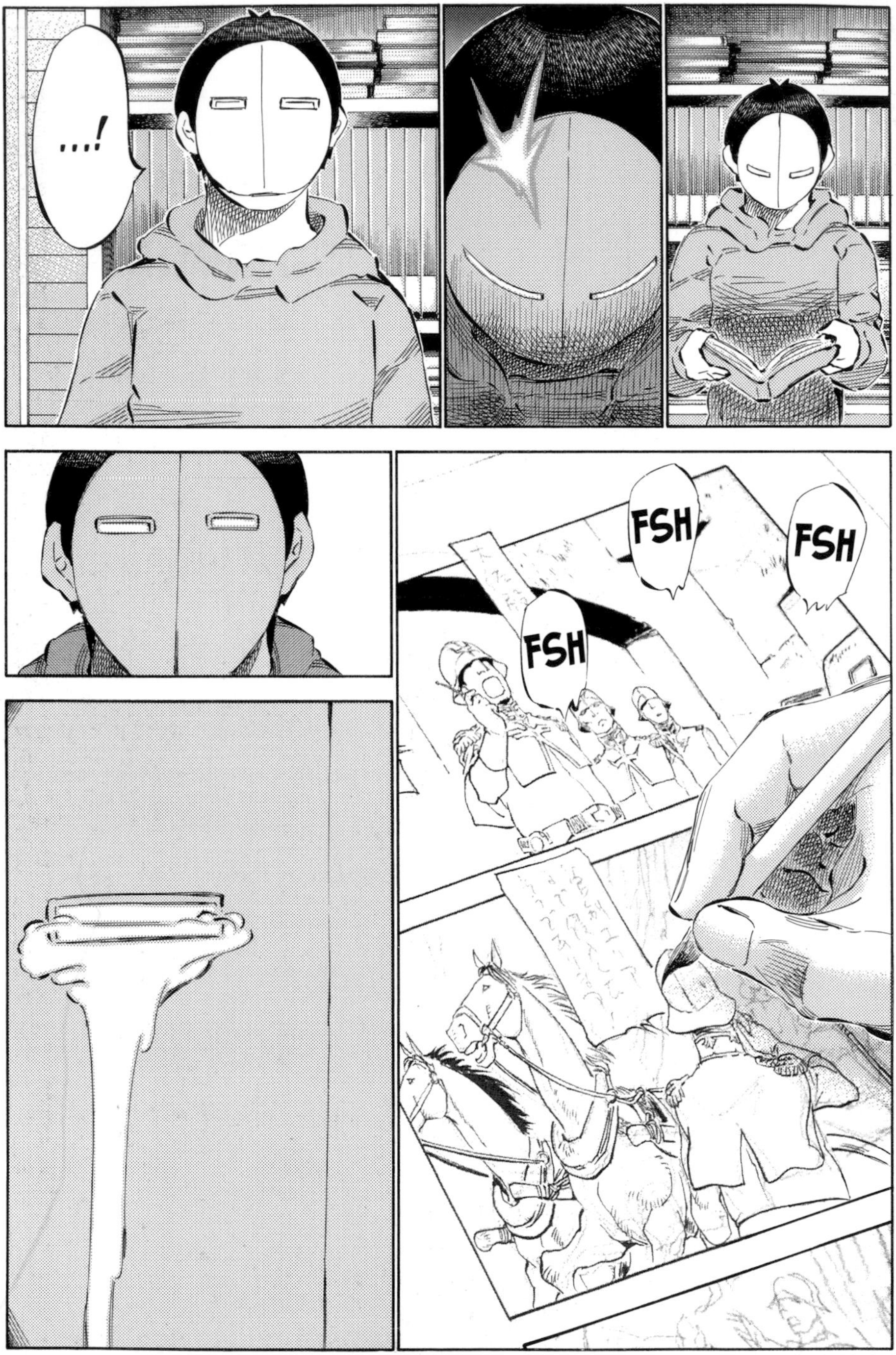
...!
FSH
FSH
FSH

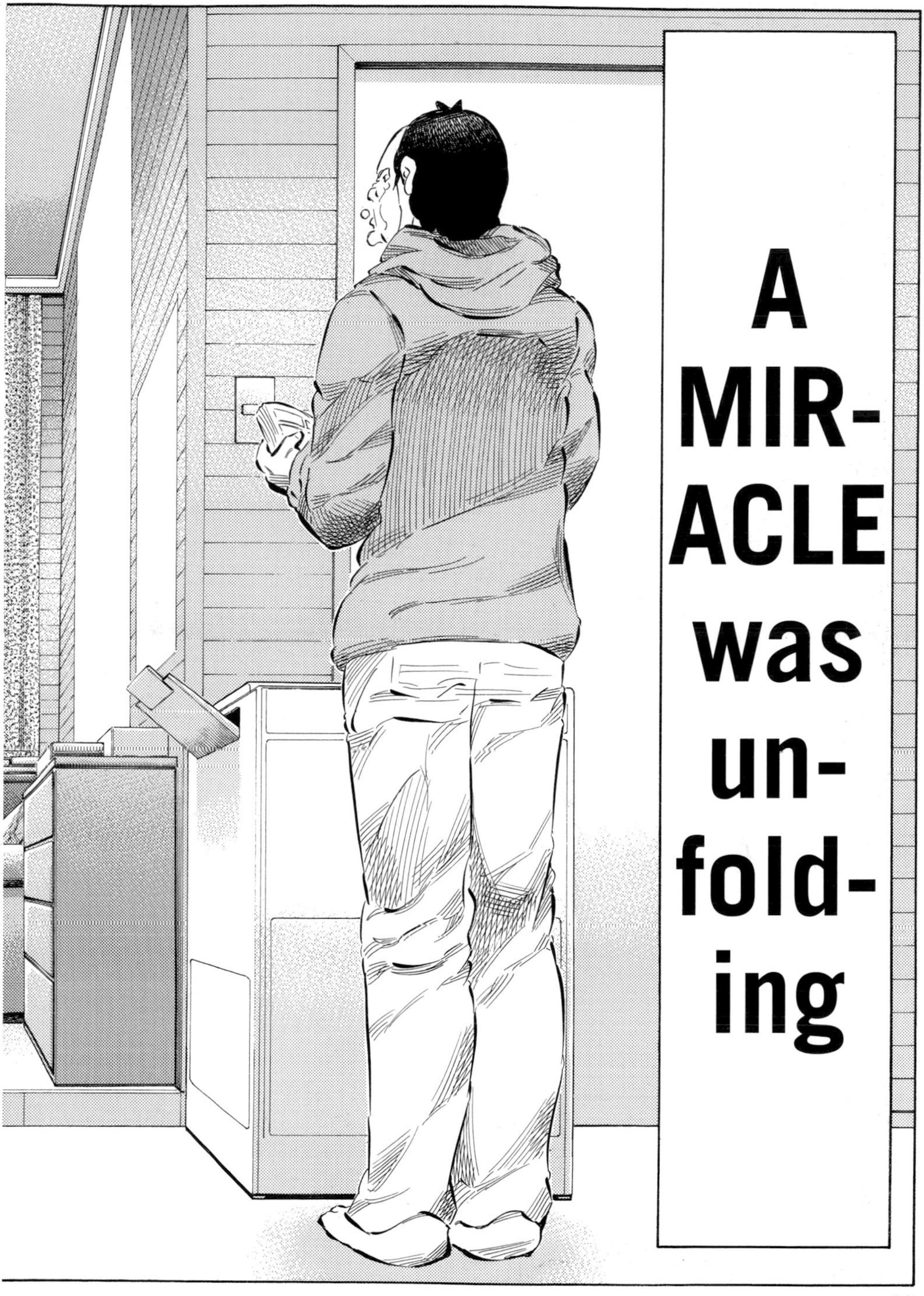
A MIR-ACLE was un-fold-ing

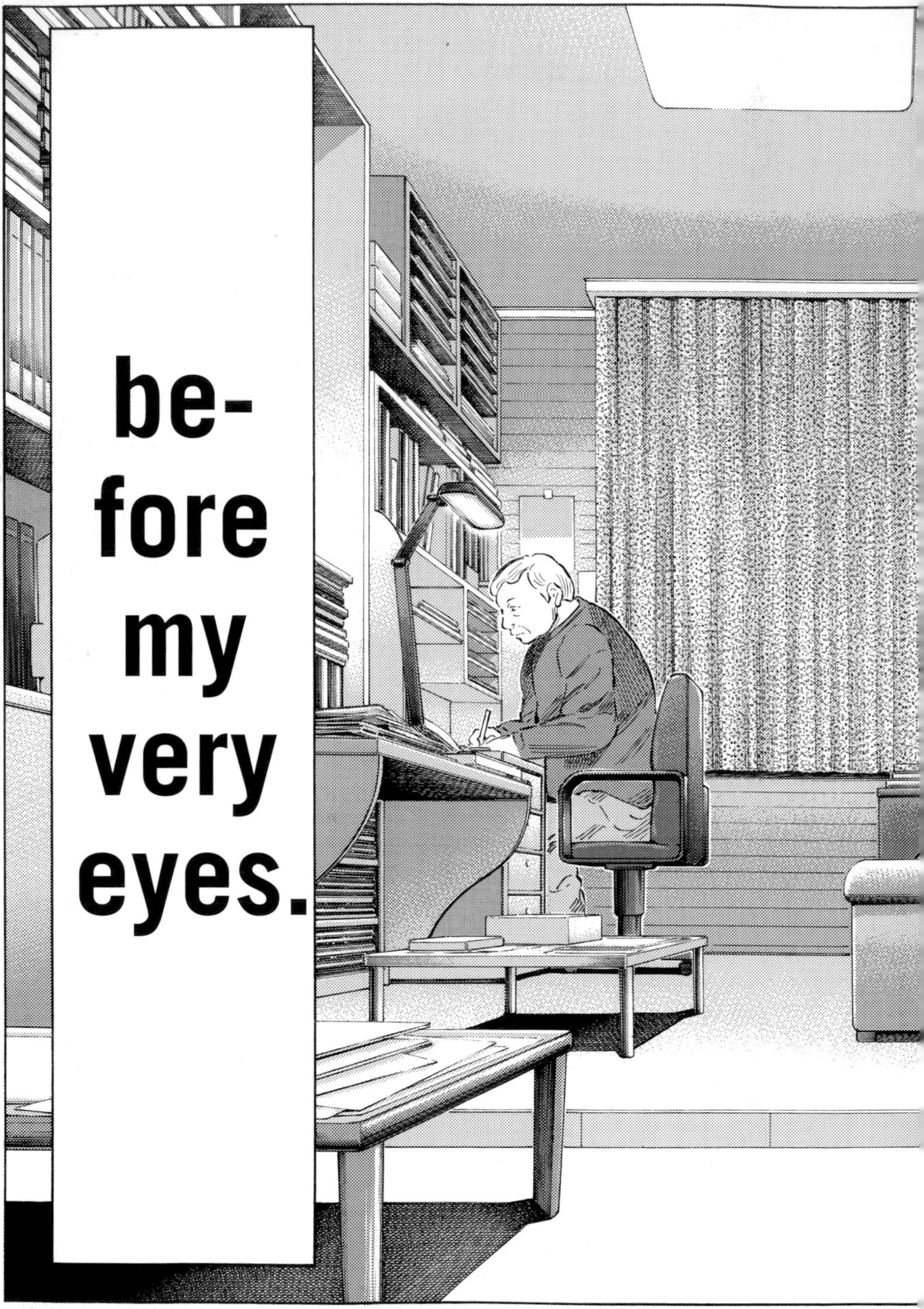
be-
fore
my
very
eyes.

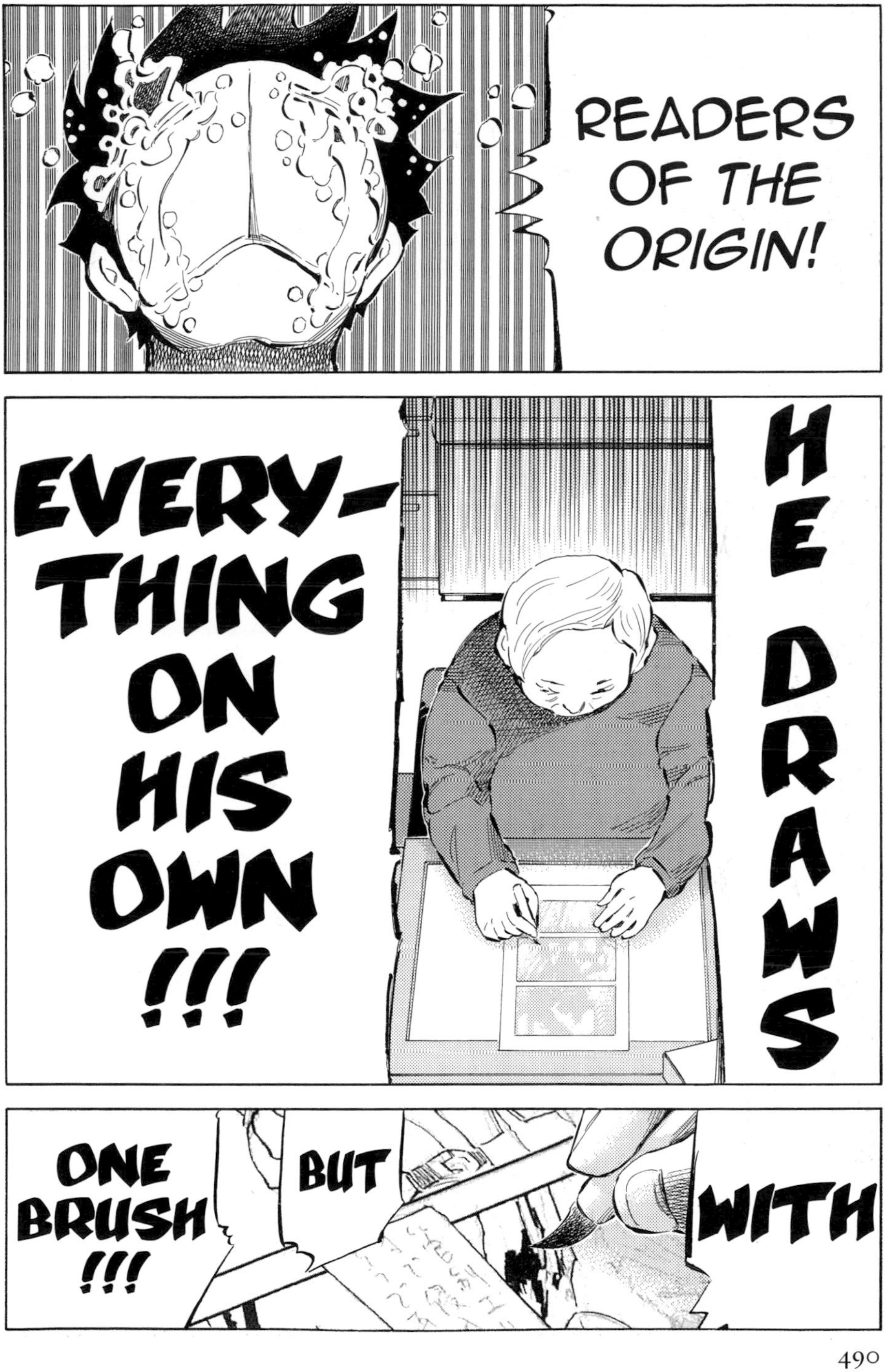
READERS OF THE ORIGIN!
HE DRAWS
EVERY-THING ON HIS OWN!!!
WITH
BUT
ONE BRUSH!!!

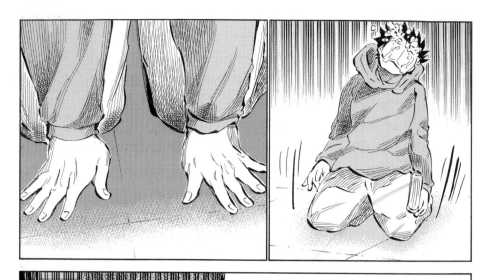

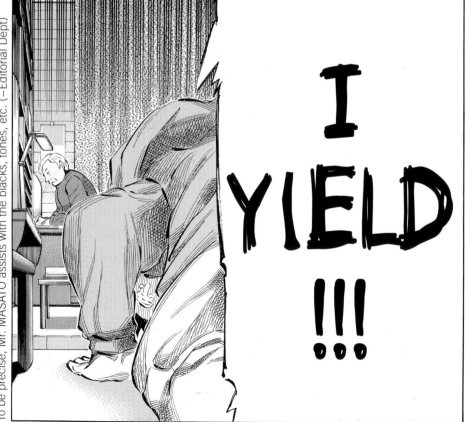

To be precise, Mr. MASATO assists with the blacks, tones, etc. (–Editorial Dept)

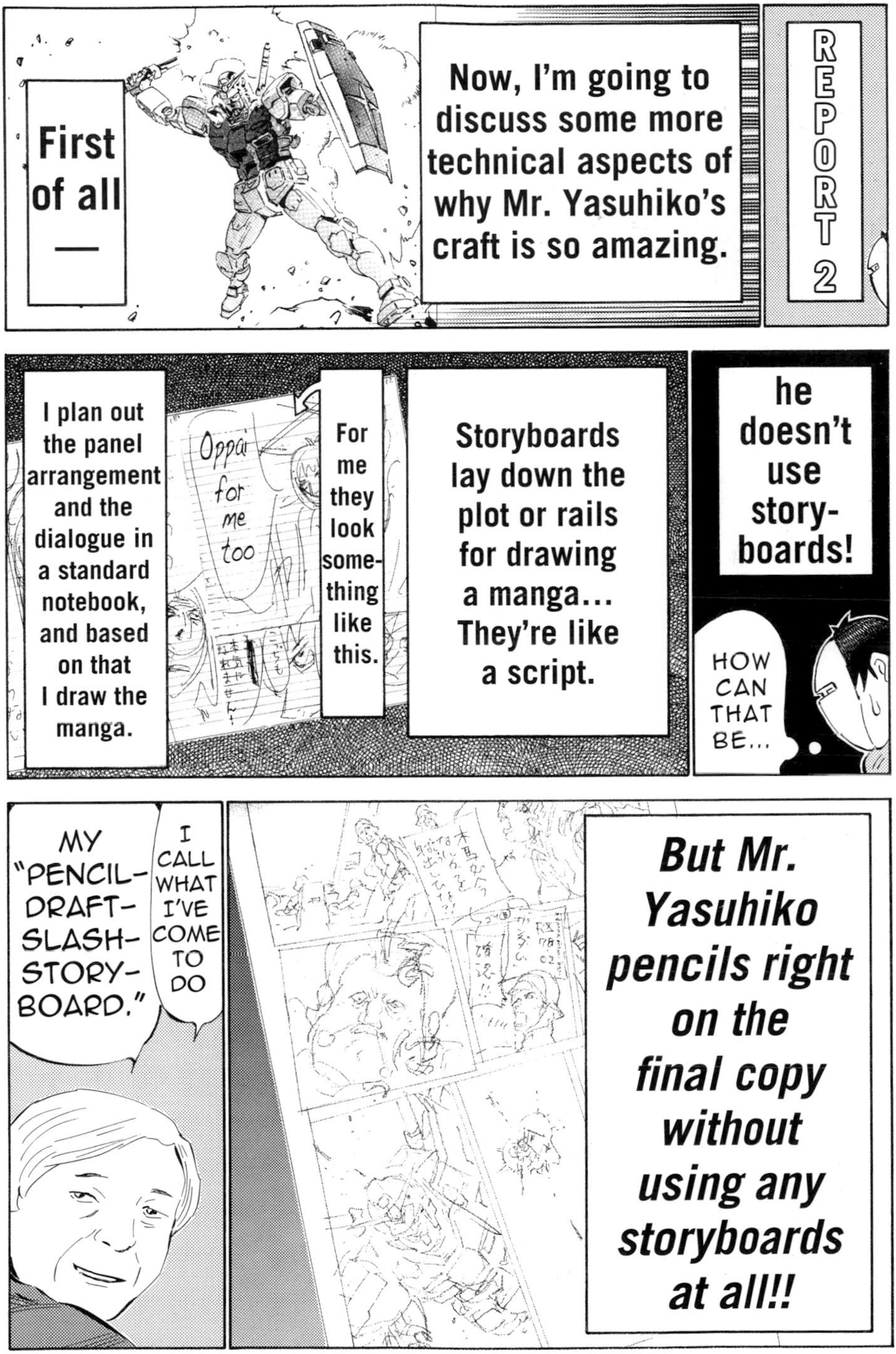
REPORT 2
Now, I'm going to discuss some more technical aspects of why Mr. Yasuhiko's craft is so amazing.
First of all —
he doesn't use story-boards!
HOW CAN THAT BE...
Storyboards lay down the plot or rails for drawing a manga... They're like a script.
For me they look some-thing like this.
Oppai for me too
I plan out the panel arrangement and the dialogue in a standard notebook, and based on that I draw the manga.
But Mr. Yasuhiko pencils right on the final copy without using any storyboards at all!!
I CALL WHAT I'VE COME TO DO
MY "PENCIL-DRAFT-SLASH-STORY-BOARD."

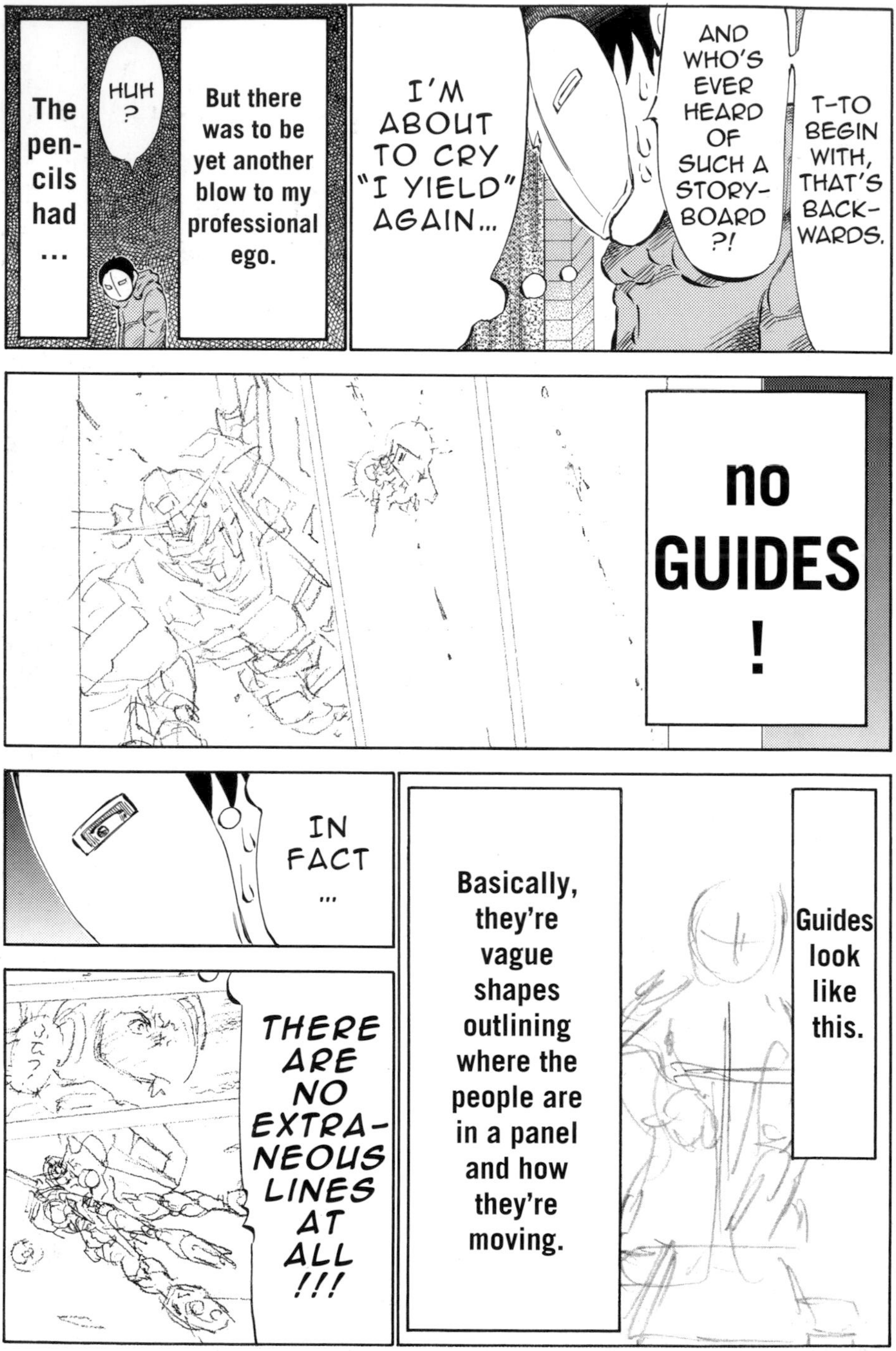
T-TO BEGIN WITH, THAT'S BACKWARDS.
AND WHO'S EVER HEARD OF SUCH A STORYBOARD ?!
I'M ABOUT TO CRY "I YIELD" AGAIN...
But there was to be yet another blow to my professional ego.
HUH ?
The pencils had ...
no GUIDES !
Guides look like this.
Basically, they're vague shapes outlining where the people are in a panel and how they're moving.
IN FACT ...
THERE ARE NO EXTRANEOUS LINES AT ALL !!!

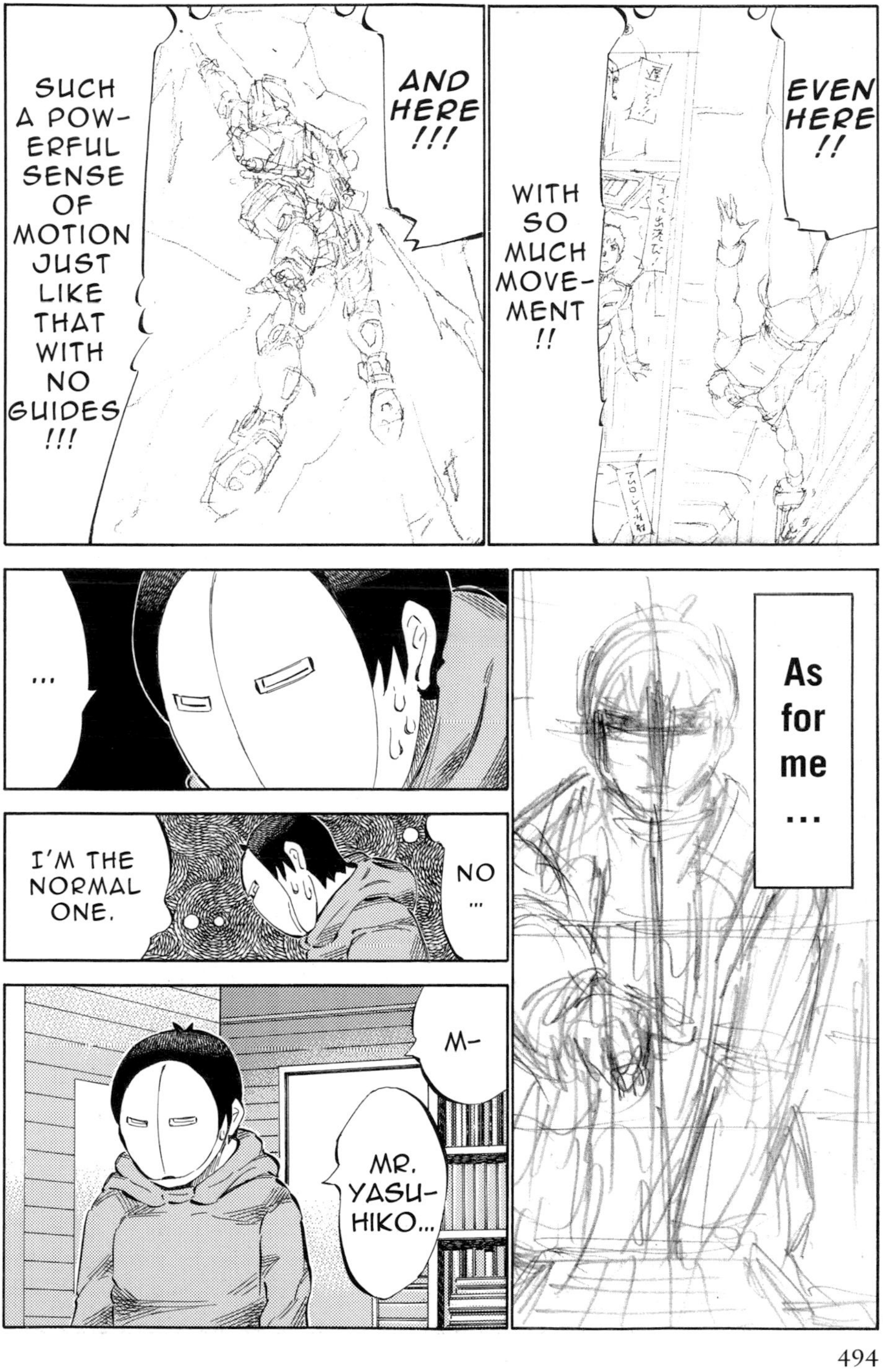
EVEN HERE!!
WITH SO MUCH MOVEMENT!!
AND HERE!!!
SUCH A POWERFUL SENSE OF MOTION JUST LIKE THAT WITH NO GUIDES!!!
As for me…
…
NO…
I'M THE NORMAL ONE.
M-
MR. YASUHIKO…

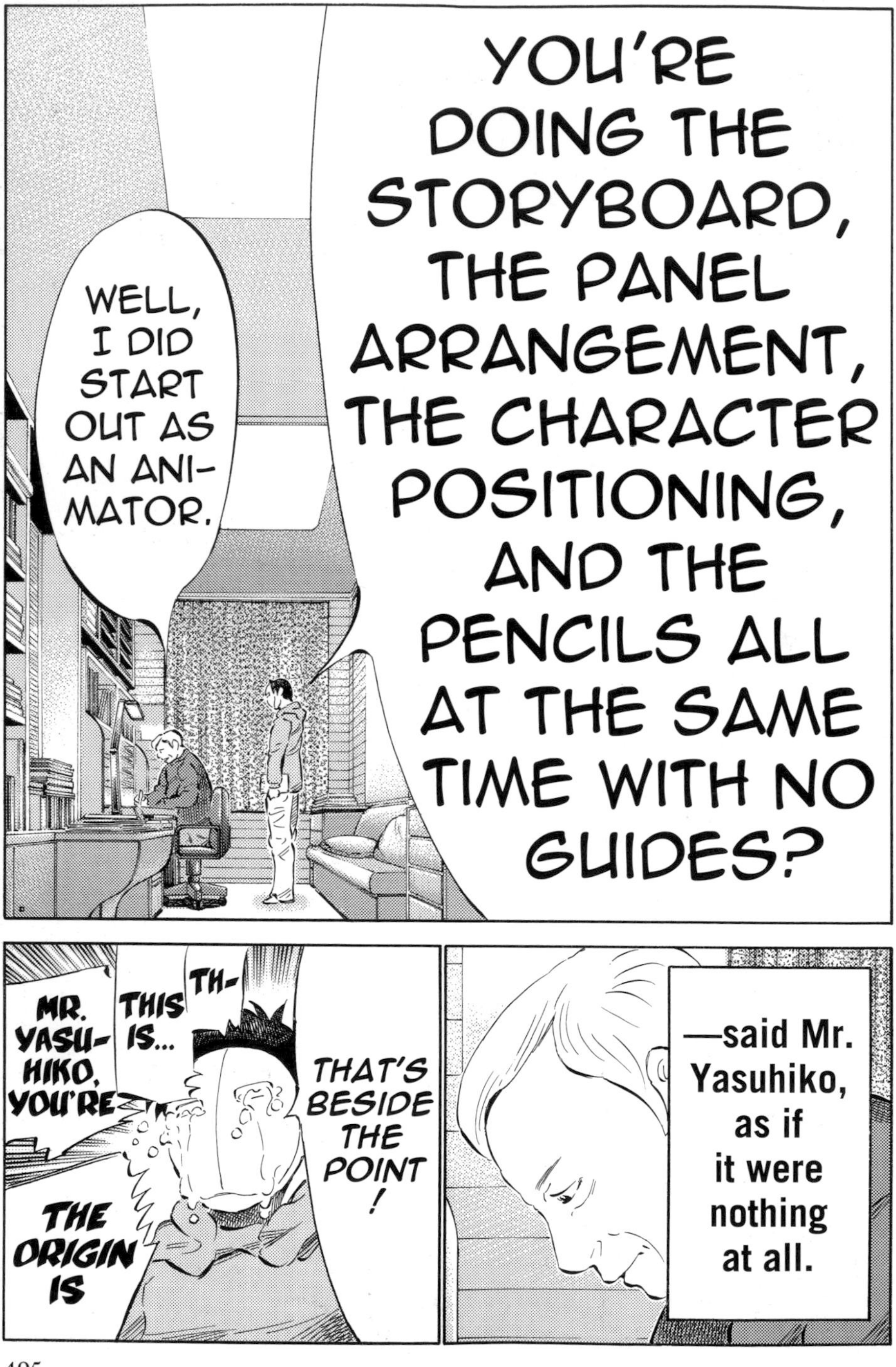
YOU'RE DOING THE STORYBOARD, THE PANEL ARRANGEMENT, THE CHARACTER POSITIONING, AND THE PENCILS ALL AT THE SAME TIME WITH NO GUIDES?
WELL, I DID START OUT AS AN ANI-MATOR.
—said Mr. Yasuhiko, as if it were nothing at all.
TH-
THIS IS...
THAT'S BESIDE THE POINT!
MR. YASU-HIKO, YOU'RE
THE ORIGIN IS

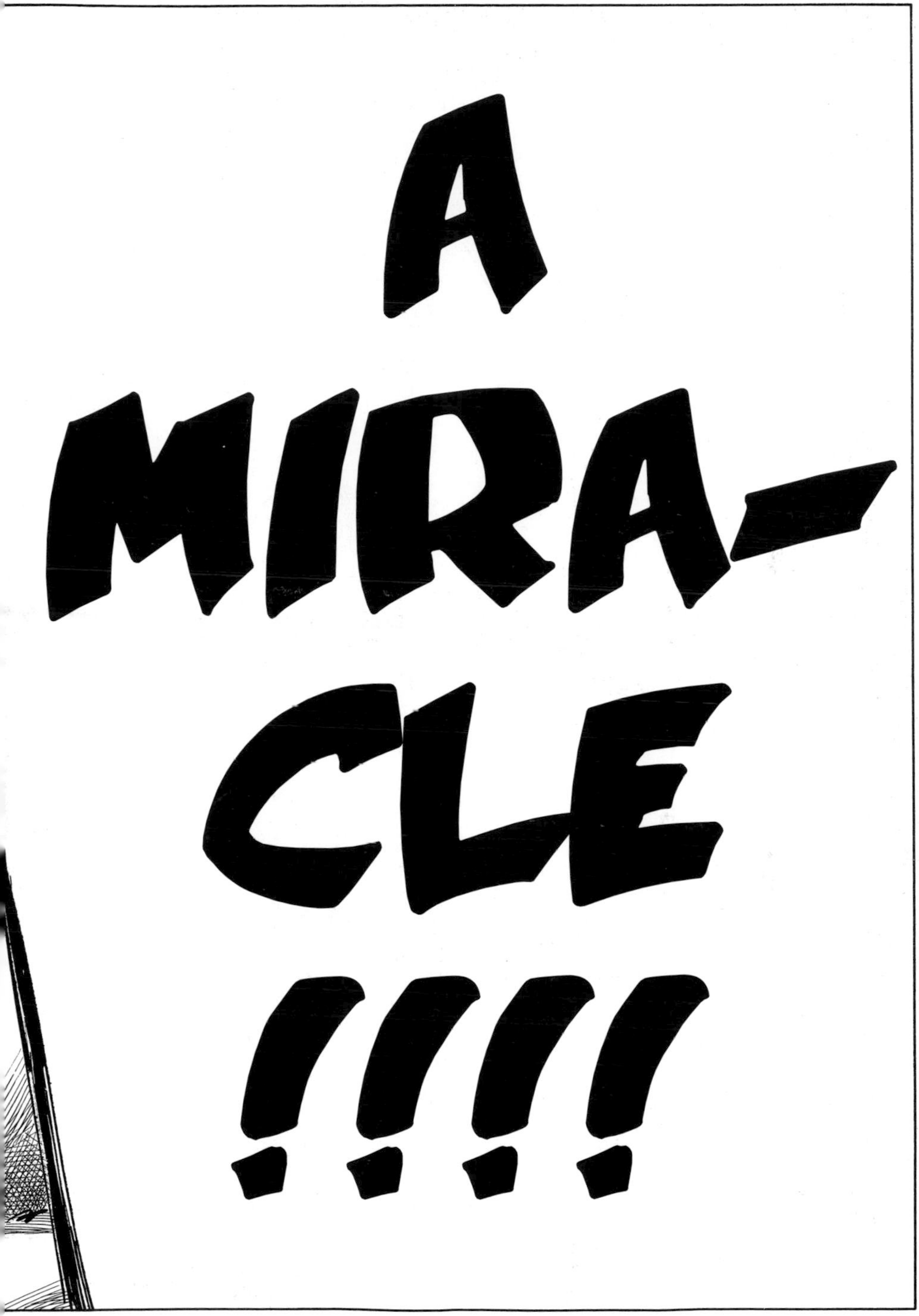
A MIRA-CLE!!!!

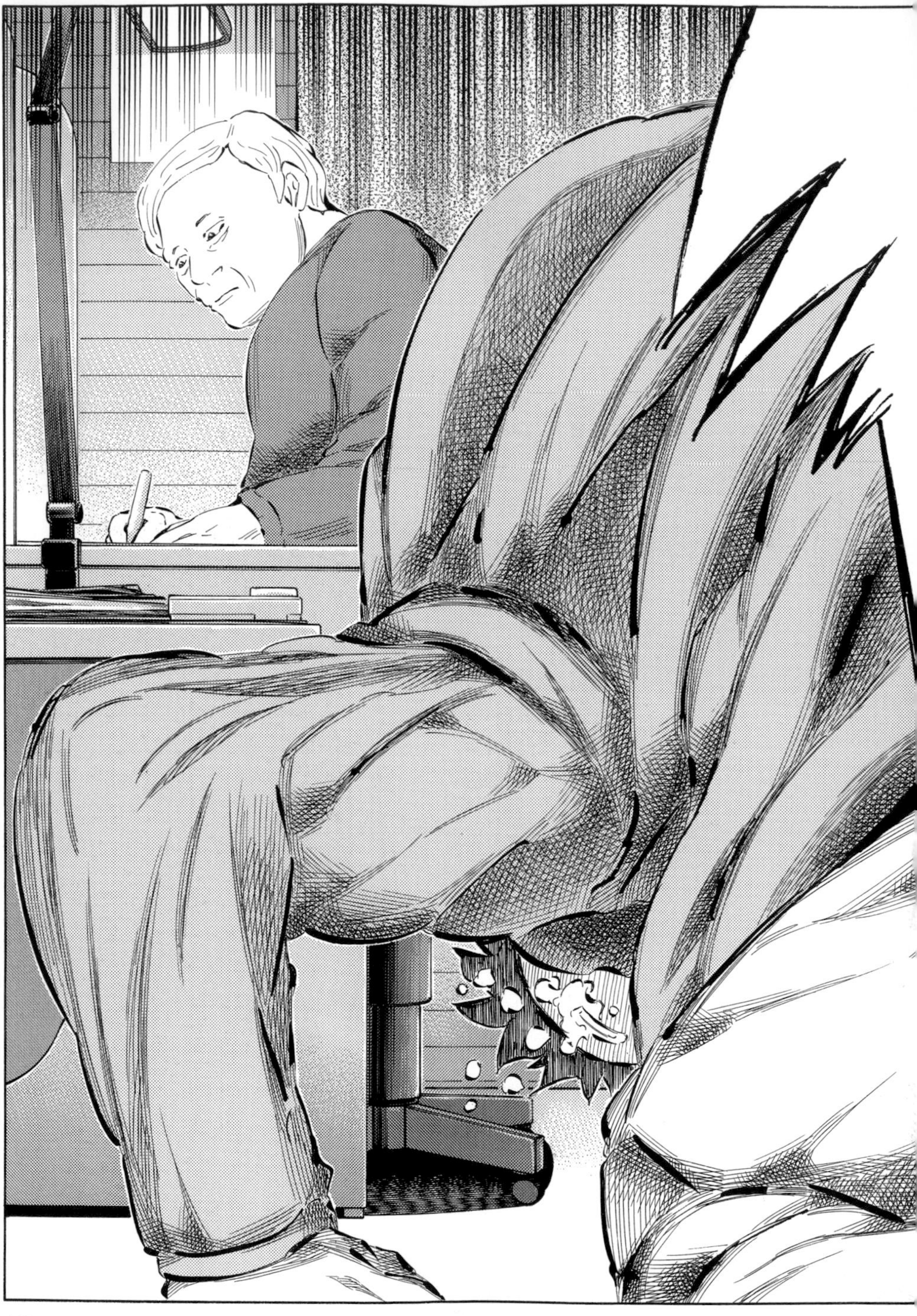

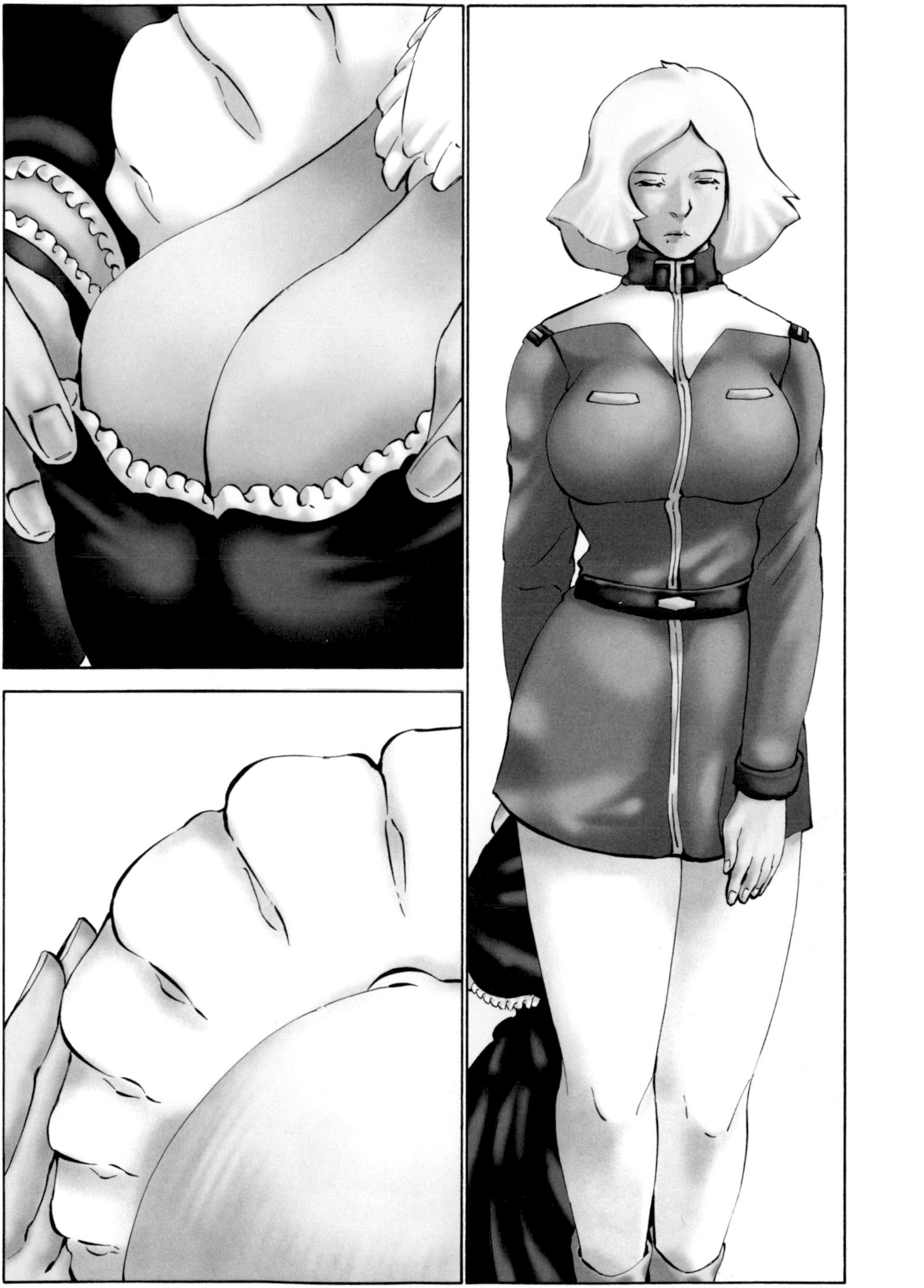

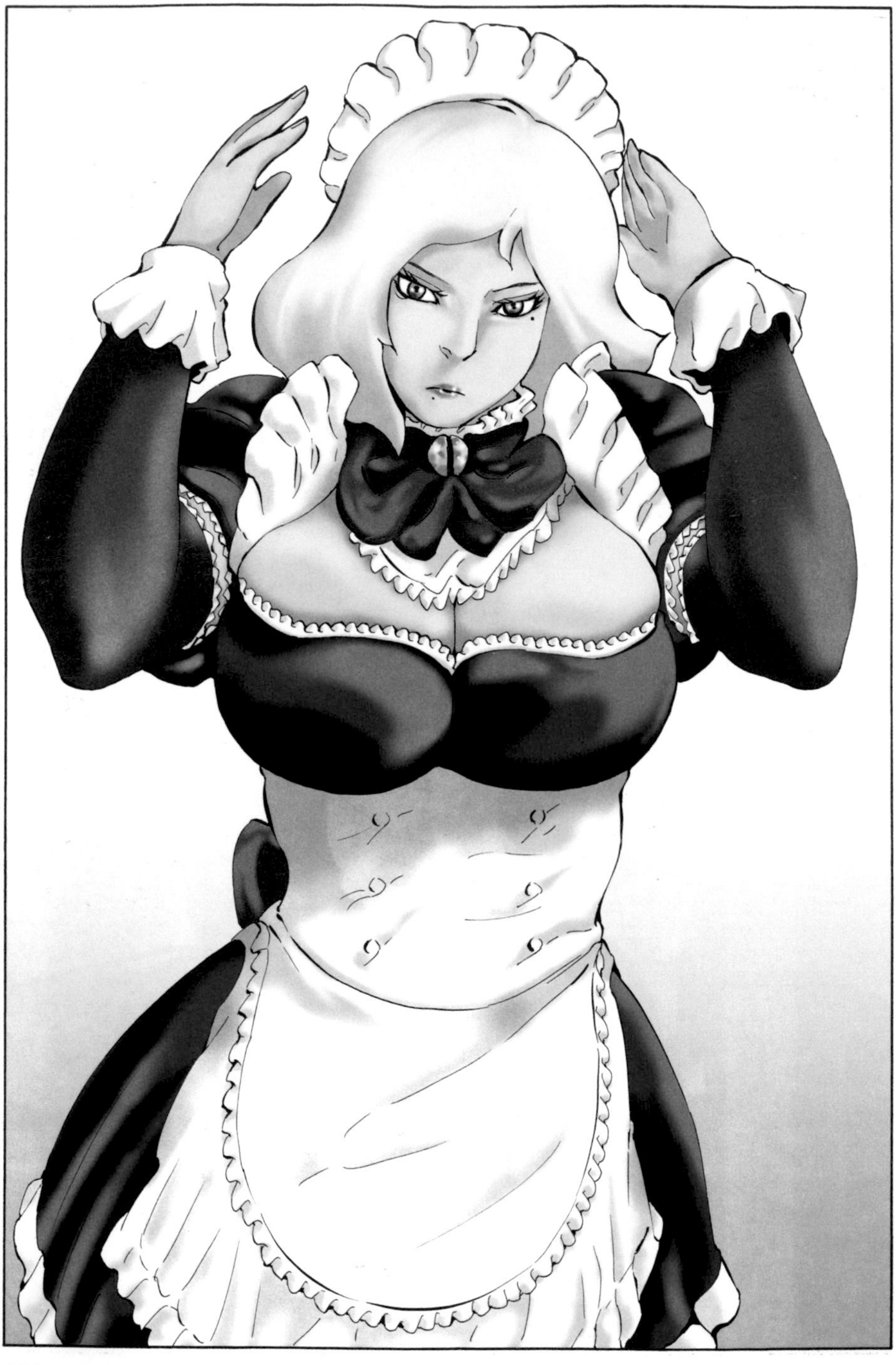

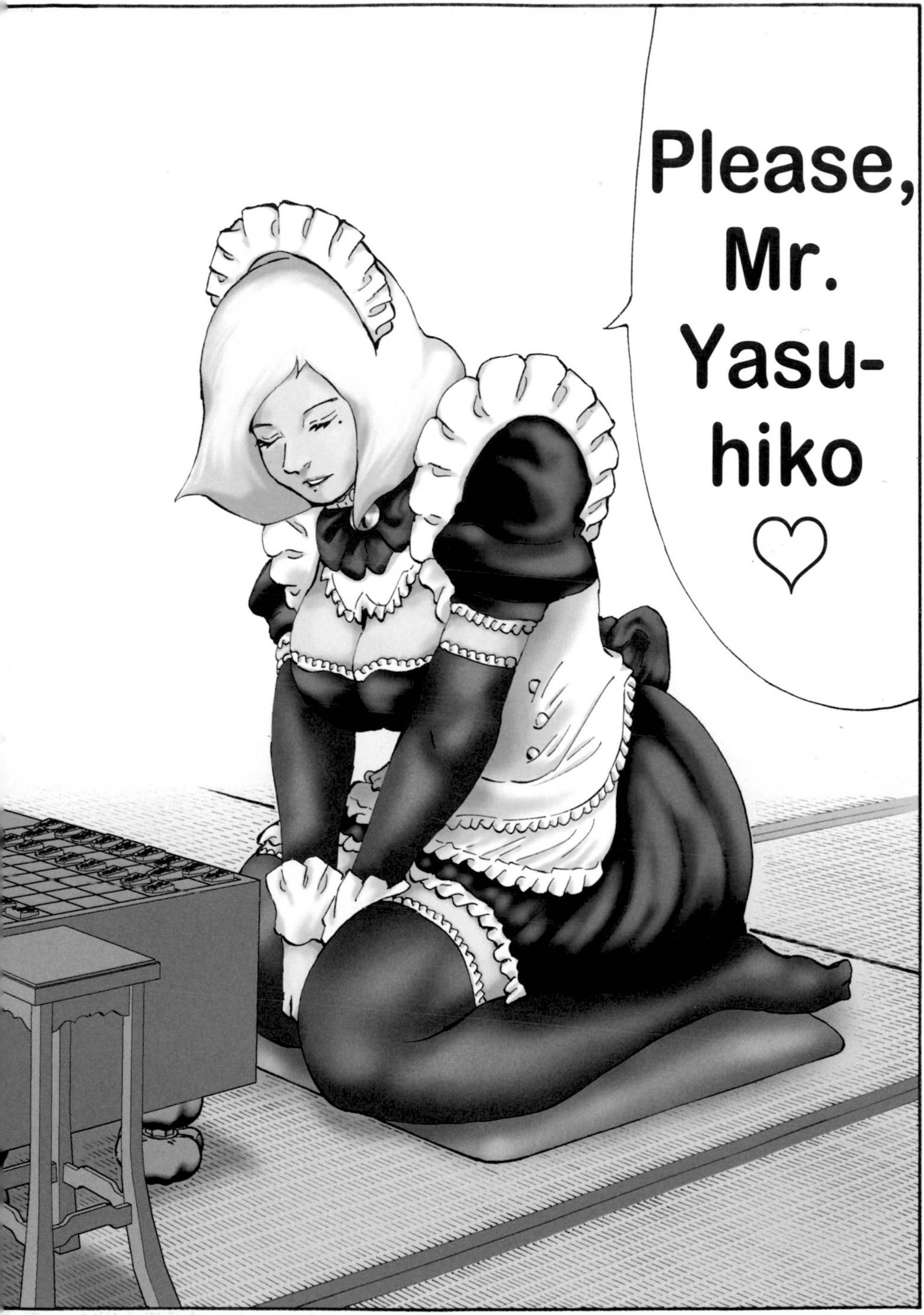
Please, Mr. Yasu-hiko ♡

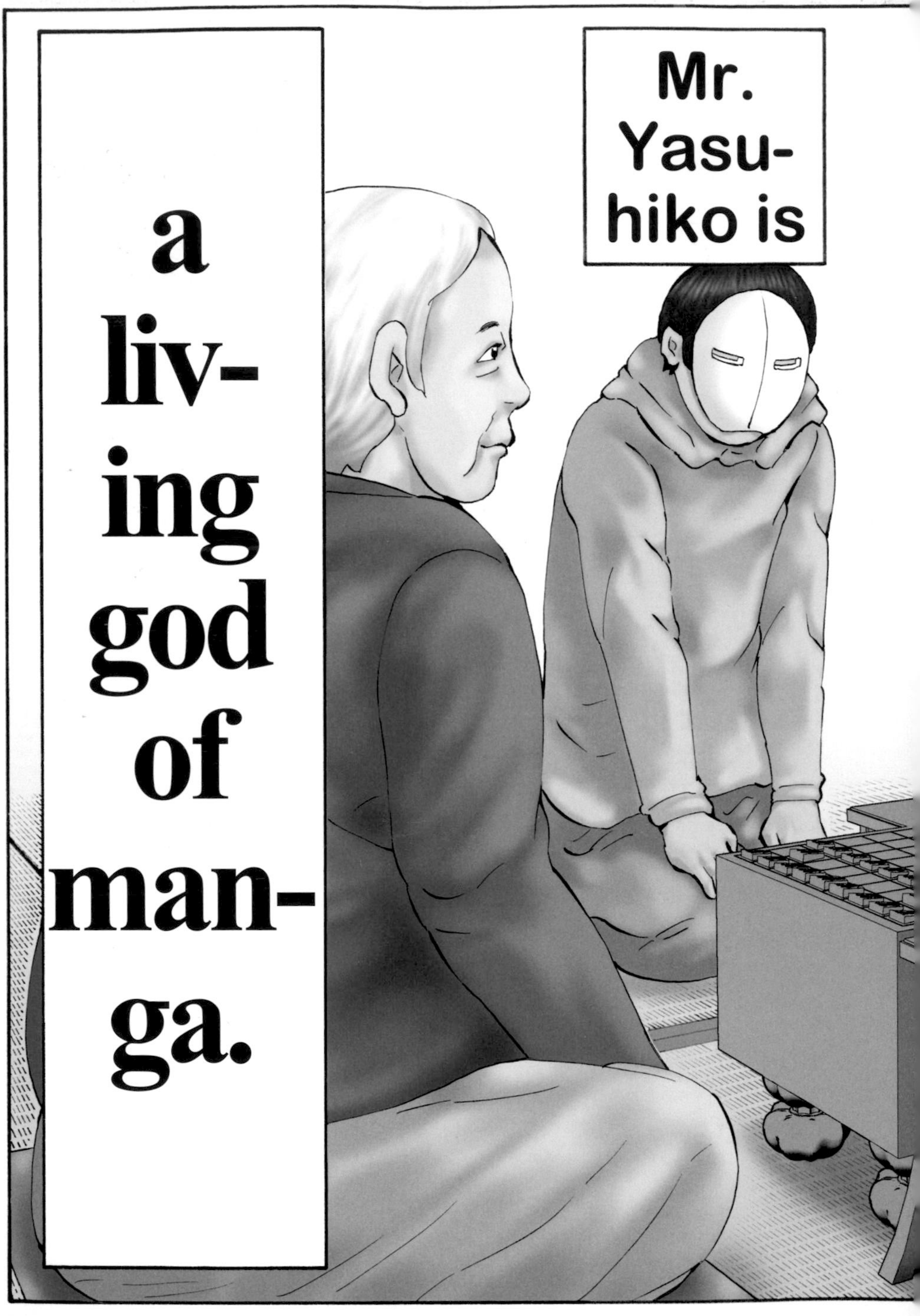
Mr. Yasu-hiko is
a liv-ing god of man-ga.

And for me, a country boy who wanted to be a manga artist, Mr. Yasuhiko became a pillar of inspiration and a source of pride! He is a treasure for all his readers, too, and a national treasure for Japan!

"Japan has Yoshikazu Yasuhiko!"

I'm thankful for the miracle of living in a time when I can read *Gundam: The Origin* as it comes out!!!

Yokusaru Shibata

Yokusaru-sensei... Really? (sweat drops) —Yasuhiko

Yokusaru Shibata
Born in 1972, he grew up in the town of Rubeshibe (now the city of Kitami). He made his debut in 1992 with *Tani Kamen* (Valley Mask) in *Young Animal* magazine. His series *Hachiwan Diver* (81 Diver) is running in *Weekly Young Jump* magazine as of 2008.

ESSAY

Thank you so much for giving me the chance to visit Mr. Yasuhiko at work!

After drawing manga basically non-stop for sixteen years, I think I have some degree of understanding of what "manga" is. So just let me say this right off the bat—a hundred manga artists working as one would have nothing on the colossus that is Yoshikazu Yasuhiko!

I grew up in a tiny town called Rubeshibe (now merged into the city of Kitami) in Hokkaido, and in middle school, I heard a rumor.

"The guy who drew *Gundam* is from the next town over."
"No way."

Lots of people work on any given anime, so a rumor about "the guy who drew *Gundam*" was pretty vague... But in fact, it was none other than the animation director of *Mobile Suit Gundam*, Mr. Yoshikazu Yasuhiko.

AIZOUBAN MOBILE SUIT GUNDAM THE ORIGIN vol. 4

Translation: Melissa Tanaka

Production: Grace Lu
Hiroko Mizuno
Anthony Quintessenza

Edited by KADOKAWA SHOTEN
First published in Japan in 2008 by KADOKAWA CORPORATION, Tokyo

English translation rights arranged with KADOKAWA CORPORATION,
through Tuttle-Mori Agency, Inc., Tokyo

Published by Vertical, Inc., New York

Originally published in Japanese as *Kidou Senshi Gundam THE ORIGIN*
volumes 7 and 8 in 2003, 2004 and re-issued in hardcover as *Aizouban Kidou Senshi Gundam
THE ORIGIN IV -Jaburo-* in 2008, by Kadokawa Shoten, Co., Ltd.

Kidou Senshi Gundam THE ORIGIN first serialized in *Gundam Ace,*
Kadokawa Shoten, Co., Ltd., 2001-2011

ISBN: 978-1-935654-98-8

Manufactured in the United States of America

First Edition

Vertical, Inc.
451 Park Avenue South
7th Floor
New York, NY 10016
www.vertical-inc.com